D1312358

CAREERS
2017
13th edition

trotman

05092516

Careers 2017

This thirteenth edition published in 2016 by Trotman Education, an imprint of Crimson Publishing Ltd, 19–21c Charles Street, Bath BA1 1HX.

© Trotman Education 2016

Contributors: Matthew Chorley, Laura Christopher, Victoria Daniel, Alexander Everill, Holly Ivins, Francesca Jaconelli, Emily Kendall, Elizabeth Mann, Meghann McKeague, Della Oliver, Lee Riley, Matt Russell, Sarah Skinner, Lucy Smith, Jessica Spencer, Charlotte Turner, Abigail Van-West and Libby Walden.

British Library Cataloguing in Publication Data
A catalogue record for this book is available from the British Library

ISBN: 978 1 90931 986 8

The information in this book was correct to the best of the publisher's belief at the time of going to press. However, if you would like to contact the publisher to report any recent changes please do so at the following address: enquiries@trotman.co.uk

European Union Referendum: This edition was compiled prior to the 23rd June 2016 referendum on the UK's membership of the European Union and the information was correct at the time of writing. At the time of going to press, the UK remains a constituent member of the Union, which allows the free movement of people, capital, goods and services across the 28 Member States. Formal proceedings for negotiating the terms of the UK's withdrawal from the Union can only commence when the UK government triggers Article 50 of the Lisbon Treaty and, at the time of going to press, information was not available regarding the projected timescale for this process. Until that time, the information provided on the European Union remains valid.

Typeset by IDSUK (Data Connection) Ltd
Printed and bound in Malta by Gutenberg Press Ltd

CONTENTS

WELCOME TO CAREERS 2017

When you first start looking at the options for your future career, it can seem like a daunting and complicated process. With a vast range of opportunities within the current job market and new options emerging all the time, how do you begin to search for something that would suit you?

Careers 2017 is here to help.

By breaking down the job sector and grouping similar professions into 'families', we aim to give a clear and concise description of the jobs that may be of interest to you, as well as suggesting similar but alternative options that you may not have thought of before.

We understand that everyone has different values, interests, qualifications and ambitions so the job profiles within *Careers 2017* list the key aspects of each job to help you find the right one for you. Each one of the hundreds of job profiles within this book contains information on entry requirements, typical activities and working conditions, future prospects, advantages and disadvantages, salary information and a short description on the type of person suited for this position.

By annually researching and updating the content *Careers 2017* aims to give you an easy to use and accurate guide to the UK job market, helping you to find answers to the following questions.

- Which career will suit me?
- What qualifications will I need?
- How much can I hope to earn?
- What are the future prospects with that career?

There is a sample job profile overleaf to help demonstrate how you can use this book effectively, and get as much from the information included as you can.

We hope that you enjoy using *Careers 2017* and wish you all the best with your future career!

The Trotman team.

An example job profile

All of the job profiles in *Careers 2017* are laid out in the same style with the same sections. This is an example job profile showing you what each section refers to and the information it contains.

Heading/job title

This refers to the title of the job you will find on the page. In some cases, when two jobs are very closely linked, you will have two job titles listed in the heading and the profile will contain information on both.

Qualifications and courses

This section looks in detail at the most common ways to enter a profession and the qualifications and courses you will need. If there are different qualifications available depending on whether you live in England, Scotland, Wales or Northern Ireland, these variations will be listed here too.

As qualifications and courses often change, we recommend that you use the **Further information** section to get more detailed advice on which qualifications you will need in order to enter your chosen career.

What the work involves

This is a quick overview of what the job is like and typical tasks associated with the role.

Type of person suited to this work

Within this category you will find lots of information to help you match your strengths, weaknesses, likes and dislikes to the individual job.

Sadly it is very common for someone to start a job not knowing what they will be expected to do. They might then be confronted with something they find either too hard or not enjoyable; this might mean leaving a job they studied a long time for. To make sure this doesn't happen to you, think carefully about the information provided here and whether it matches your skills, experience and personality. If you think it does, then you should also do some further research to get more detailed and comprehensive information.

TOURISM OFFICER
ENTRY LEVEL 6

Qualifications and courses

New entrants to this profession will typically hold an Honours degree. Relevant subjects include tourism management, hospitality management, public relations, business studies, and marketing. Entrants may also be sourced from a far wider range of academic backgrounds such as modern languages, journalism and media studies. Entry onto a degree course is usually with 2 A levels/3 H grades and 5 GCSEs/National 5s (A*–C/A–C) and courses typically take 3-4 years to complete.

Postgraduate study is not a requirement for entry, but may be valuable if your first degree is in an unrelated subject. Relevant subjects at postgraduate level include master's degrees in tourism, tourism management, or marketing. Entry onto a master's degree is usually with a 2.1 (or higher) Honours degree.

Relevant work experience will set you at a considerable advantage and will demonstrate a good level of commitment to the industry when looking to gain employment. Paid and voluntary placements can be available on a part-time or seasonal basis. Undertaking clerical or administration work at a tourist attraction or volunteering at cultural and heritage or recreational events will give you a great understanding of the sector.

What the work involves

Tourism officers work to stimulate economic growth in an area by developing visitor facilities and promoting tourism in the region. You may work for local governments, or more commonly for public or private tourism and management firms.

Your work is varied and could consist of developing and enhancing existing tourist attractions and venues and promoting them through marketing and advertising campaigns; researching local cultural and historical interest in order to plan new visitor facilities; assessing the social and economic impact of planned developments; and encouraging growth in the tourism job market through expansion and development.

Type of person suited to this work

A keen and demonstrable interest in the tourism industry is essential. You must care about creating great tourist services and facilities for families and individuals of all ages.

You will need excellent interpersonal skills, and the ability to liaise with community groups, developers and tourism industry stakeholders effectively.

Strong leadership and project planning skills are a must; as is the ability to manage both large- and small-scale tourist developments.

Working conditions

You will work a typical Monday to Friday week, 9am to 5pm. However extra or irregular hours may be expected in the run-up to attraction openings or in the planning of large-scale developments.

Work is mostly office based, but may involve regular travel to visit tourist sites or to meet with facility developers and event planners.

Future prospects

In terms of employment, tourism has been the fastest growing sector in the UK in recent years. It is expected to continue to grow quickly over the next 10 years.

There is scope for career development, and opportunities to progress into more senior or management roles do exist.

You may need to be geographically mobile and willing to relocate in order to take advantage of vacancies that need filling.

There is potential to move into other, similar areas of work such as area regeneration and economic development.

With enough experience you could look for work with private consultancy firms, or even work on a self-employed consultancy basis.

Opportunities for travel or work overseas may be available.

Advantages/disadvantages

There is great job satisfaction in knowing that you will play an active role in creating jobs and promoting economic development through the tourism industry.

You will regularly be meeting with lots of different people, providing a varied and interesting working environment.

Time spent away from home, possibly overseas, may be a requirement; this may be an attractive prospect to some or be off-putting to others.

Money guide

Salaries vary depending on employer and the location you are working in with top tourist destinations likely to offer the best rates of pay.

Entrants can expect salaries of between £15,000 and £19,000 per year.

With several years' experience, salaries can increase to up to £28,000 per year.

After five years, salaries for those in senior or managerial roles can reach up to £40,000 per year.

Related opportunities

- Community Education Officer p180
- Holiday Representative p368
- Theme Park Assistant/Manager p375
- Tour Guide/Manager p376

Further information

Institute of Travel and Tourism
www.itt.co.uk

Tourism Management Institute
www.tmi.org.uk

VisitBritain
www.visitbritain.org

VisitEngland
www.visitengland.com

VisitScotland
www.visitscotland.com

VisitWales
www.visitwales.com

377

LEISURE, SPORT AND TOURISM

Working conditions

This section explains where you can expect to be working, whether it's outside or inside, in an office or travelling around the country. It also tells you the typical working hours you can expect and whether you are likely to work at weekends, evenings and on shifts. This will give you a good idea of the day to day life you can expect on the job.

Entry level

This number corresponds to the *Careers 2017* level of qualification you need to start your career in a particular job. For more information about what the entry levels in *Careers 2017* mean, see the next page.

Future prospects

This section shows you where you could progress to within a certain career. This may be in terms of climbing the career ladder, or branching into new territory as a career sector develops and changes. Of course, no one can predict the future of any career sector completely but important changes to the economy, reductions and increases in the labour force as well as technological advances will have an impact upon how a sector develops. This information will give you a balanced view of what your future could be in any given career.

Advantages/disadvantages

It's important that, when choosing a career, you have a well-rounded and honest view of what the work will be like. This section gives you an idea of the most common good and bad points about a job so that you can decide if a job matches up to your expectations.

Money guide

For some people one of the most important things they'll consider before undertaking a new course, qualification or a career is 'how much can I expect to earn?'

To help you we have included:

- the most up-to-date information about pay scales

- where possible, what you can expect at entry, intermediate and senior levels

- any regional differences.

Related opportunities

This section lists jobs that are similar in style and the skills that they require to the job profile you are looking at. This is to give you lots of options to choose from if you haven't decided which career interests you the most.

You might not have considered or heard of some of these before, so it will help you to broaden out your ideas further.

Further information

Listed here are the websites of organisations that can help you continue your research into your chosen job areas.

Qualifications: what do the entry levels in *Careers 2017* mean?

You will see that every job profile in this book has an entry level number, ranging from 1 to 8, assigned to it. This refers to the lowest qualification level that you need to achieve in order to enter the profession.

The number shown indicates the level of qualification you are most likely to need:

- to enter the job and
- to enter the job and to train while working.

The qualifications grid

Opposite is a grid which shows what the levels in *Careers 2017* refer to in terms of qualifications that you can take in England, Wales, Northern Ireland and Scotland.

The information from three qualifications frameworks has been incorporated into this table: the Regulated Qualifications Framework (RCF), the Scottish Credit and Qualifications Framework (SCQF) and the Framework for Higher Education Qualifications (FHEQ).

Because the frameworks all have their own levels please be aware that this grid cannot accommodate subtle differences between the frameworks and you should refer directly to the websites below for more information.

The Regulated Qualifications Framework (RCF)

The RCF has now replaced the QCF (Qualifications and Credit Framework) and is the basis of the qualifications grid on the following page. The framework contains both academic and vocational qualifications offered in England, Wales and Northern Ireland from Entry level to Level 8.

The Framework for Higher Education Qualifications (FHEQ)

The FHEQ includes higher education qualifications from Certificates of Higher Education through to Doctoral degrees. It applies to qualifications offered in England, Wales and Northern Ireland and includes five levels, each indicated by a letter corresponding with the initial of the main qualification offered at that level.

The Scottish Credit and Qualifications Framework (SCQF)

The SCQF is a 12-level framework including vocational, occupational and academic qualifications offered in Scotland. It covers all levels including further and higher education, from Access through to Doctoral degrees.

Further information

Each framework is under continuous review, but information in this book was correct at the time of writing.

For further details and the most up-to-date information, refer to the following websites:

- RCF: www.ofqual.gov.uk
  www.wales.gov.uk; www.ccea.org.uk
- FHEQ: www.qaa.ac.uk/en/publications/Documents/
  Framework-Higher-Education-Qualifications-08.pdf
- SCQF: www.scqf.org.uk

Key

Qualifications that are available in England, Wales, Northern Ireland and Scotland.

Qualifications that are available in England, Wales and Northern Ireland.

Qualifications that are available in Scotland.

Careers 2017 level	Rough equivalent framework level	General and academic qualifications	Vocational and occupational qualifications
Entry level	RCF Entry Level Skills for Life at entry level SCQF Access Levels 1–3	**Entry Level Certificate National 1, 2, 3**	**National Progression Award (start at SCQF Level 2)**
1	RCF Level 1 SCQF Level 4	*GCSE grade D–G* *14–19 Foundation Diploma* *Skills for Life* *Key Skills Level 1* **Intermediate 1** **National 4**	NVQ/SVQ Level 1 *BTEC Introductory Certificate/* *Diploma* *Level 1 Certificate* *Cambridge Nationals* **National Progression Award**
2	RCF Level 3 SCQF Level 5	*GCSE grade A*–C* *14–19 Higher Diploma* *Skills for Life* *Key Skills Level 2* **Intermediate 2** **National 5**	NVQ/SVQ Level 2 *Level 2 Certificate/Diploma* *BTEC Diploma/Extended Certificate/* *Certificate* *Apprenticeship* *BTEC Nationals* *Cambridge Nationals* **National Progression Award**
3	RCF Level 3 SCQF Level 6	*A level* *Key Skills Level 3* *Advanced Extension Award* *Mathematics* *Extended Project* *International Baccalaureate* **Scottish Higher**	NVQ/SVQ Level 3 *A levels in applied subjects* *Level 3 Certificate/Diploma* *BTEC Extended Diploma/Diploma/* *Subsidiary Diploma/Certificate* *Advanced Apprenticeship (England)* *BTEC Nationals* *Cambridge Nationals* *City & Guilds Level 3* **Modern Apprenticeship (Scotland, Wales, Northern Ireland)** **Professional Development Award**
4	RCF Level 4 FHEQ Level C SCQF Level 7	Certificate of Higher Education *Key Skills Level 4* **Scottish Advanced Higher** **Higher National Certificate**	NVQ/SVQ Level 3 *Level 4 Certificate/Diploma* *BTEC Professional Diplomas,* *Certificates and Awards* *City & Guilds Licentiateship* **Professional Development Award**
5	RCF Level 5 FHEQ Level I SCQF Levels 8 and 9	Foundation degree Diploma of Higher Education *Diploma of Further Education* *Higher National Diploma*	NVQ/SVQ Level 4 Higher National Certificate/Diploma (HNC/HND) *BTEC Professional Diplomas/* *Certificates/Awards* *National Diploma in Professional* *Production Skills* *Level 5 Certificate/Diploma* *City & Guilds Full Technological* *Certificate (FTC)* **Professional Development Award**
6	RCF Level 6 FHEQ Level H SCQF Level 10	Bachelor's degree Graduate Diploma Graduate Certificate	*NVQs* *Level 6 Certificate/Diploma* *BTEC Advanced Professional* *Diplomas/Certificates/Awards* *City & Guilds Graduateship* **Professional Development Award**
7	RCF Level 7 FHEQ Level M SCQF Level 11	Master's degree Postgraduate Diploma (PgDip) Postgraduate Certificate (PgCert) Integrated Degree *Diploma in Translation*	NVQ/SVQ Level 5 *Level 7 Diploma/Fellowship* *Level 7 Advanced Professional* *Certificate* *BTEC Advanced Professional* *Diplomas/Certificates/Awards* *City & Guilds Membership* **Professional Development Award**
8	RCF Level 8 FHEQ Level D SCQF Level 12	Doctorate	Specialist awards and diplomas from professional bodies *City & Guilds Fellowship* **Professional Development Award**

Job families

The jobs in this book have been divided into job families to make it easy for you to go straight to the right section and find the job you are interested in. At the beginning of each job family section is an introduction to the career sector and a list of all the jobs that will appear in the section. You will also find information on other similar job families and where to find them in the book.

There are 20 job families in *Careers 2017* which are:

 Administration, Business, Office Work and Financial Services

Building and Construction

Catering and Hospitality

Computers and IT

Design, Arts and Crafts

Education and Training

Engineering, Manufacturing and Production

Environment, Animals and Plants

Healthcare

Languages, Information and Culture

Legal and Political Services

Leisure, Sport and Tourism

Marketing, Advertising, Media, Print and Publishing

Performing Arts

Personal and Other Services including Hair and Beauty

Retail, Sales and Customer Services

Science, Mathematics and Statistics

Security, Emergency and the Armed Forces

Social Work and Counselling Services

Transport and Logistics

What do the icons mean?

The icons used in this book are the same as those used in the CRCI (Connexions Resources Centre Index) and they will appear at the beginning of each section to make it easy and clear to see exactly which job families are being covered.

Administration, Business, Office Work and Financial Services

To work in this sector you often need to have a great head for numbers and be very good at managing your time effectively. The variety of jobs in this family is huge, so you could work in a large, busy office or you could work for yourself dealing with clients from a host of different professions. Many jobs require you to have an eye for detail as you could be compiling reports and advising organisations on how they could work more effectively or safely or organising other people's time and schedules. In all cases, you should be highly motivated and organised. If you enjoy this responsibility and like the idea of the challenge of keeping a business running like clockwork there are many jobs that would suit you in this sector.

For a full list of jobs in this section turn to page 1.

Building and Construction

The jobs in this sector are very varied; some require a high level of personal fitness, while for others a creative flair is essential. You may be interested in working on a construction site with a team of people and for this you would need to demonstrate excellent personal safety and be happy to work outside in all weathers. Alternatively, your interest may lie in buying and selling property or maybe working in an office is more your sort of thing. All the jobs in the sector require someone with a great eye for detail who is very good at working with others.

For a full list of jobs in this section turn to page 57.

Catering and Hospitality

Working in this sector, you will meet a wide variety of people and probably need to be a very strong team player. For some of the jobs, you need to be outgoing, confident and sociable and may end up working early mornings or late nights. For many jobs in this sector you need to be very meticulous when it comes to standards of cleanliness and tidiness. Workers in this sector thrive on providing an impeccable service and ensuring customers are completely satisfied and are given a wonderful experience whether that be in a restaurant, hotel or bar.

For a full list of jobs in this section turn to page 121.

Computers and IT

This sector is still fairly new and so it is expanding all the time, creating new jobs for a whole range of people. You may have a mathematical brain or a real creative ability – or a bit of both! Essentially, you must be passionate about computers to consider working in this sector. You could be working directly with clients and customers, helping them to rectify problems with their computers or you could be researching and developing the latest console for the games market. In all cases you need to keep right up to date with the latest technologies and IT developments as well as people's tastes, interests and hobbies to enjoy working in this sector.

For a full list of jobs in this section turn to page 137.

Design, Arts and Crafts

The idea of turning your arts and crafts hobby into a career may be one you like the thought of. Jobs in this sector can involve working in any medium, from textiles or jewellery to metalwork or children's toys. Some jobs may involve you researching current styles and trends and creating your own designs whereas others will involve working to a set brief set out by your customer to create a bespoke product. You may find yourself working for a company but many people in this industry are self-employed, working for a range of clients. This means you need to be very organised and have brilliant communication skills to ensure you can give your clients exactly what they want. People working in this industry are extremely passionate about their careers and have a real sense of perfectionism to produce a beautiful finished article.

For a full list of jobs in this section turn to page 157.

Education and Training

To work in this sector you need to be motivated and enthusiastic about other people's learning, whether it's adults or children. There are jobs suitable for people with all levels of qualification, but whatever your entry level you will need to be interested in keeping up to date on the latest developments in education and will enjoy working with other people. If you choose to teach, the range of subjects available is huge so whatever your interest – languages, art, sciences, cooking, sports – you can become a teacher in that field. Jobs in this sector require a multitude of skills including: creativity, imagination, numerical skills, good communication and organisational skills and, in some cases, having a lot of patience!

For a full list of jobs in this section turn to page 179.

Engineering, Manufacturing and Production

There are a number of highly-skilled jobs available in this job family and workers need to be creative and methodical, combining brilliant technical skill with spatial awareness. Engineers are very well qualified indeed so you should be willing to study hard for good qualifications. Jobs in this sector can take you into a range of different fields, from scientific research to car production to working out at sea; there's something for anyone who has an inquisitive mind and a high level of technical capability. Another attractive element of this industry is that you can work with an enormous variety of different materials. You may be interested in food production but equally your passion could lie in working with aircraft or marine manufacture. People in these professions share the ability to concentrate for long periods of time and work meticulously on a job to finish it to a

high standard. Some will also be highly trained with specialist equipment which may sometimes be hazardous to use so a high level of personal safety awareness is vital.

For a full list of jobs in this section turn to page 199.

Environment, Animals and Plants

Some people working in this sector spend a lot of their time outdoors. This means the jobs are perfect for those of you who don't want to spend every day behind a desk in an office, although this is not to say that you will not need to spend time writing reports and keeping a log of research findings or clients' information. Workers in this sector are passionate about animals or about caring for and maintaining the environment. You will sometimes work in unpredictable settings, especially if you are working outside or have close contact with animals. You should also have brilliant people skills especially if you find yourself responsible for the welfare of someone else's animal. You should be someone who is very observant and interested in the natural world, not just from a welfare point of view but also from an economic one; many jobs in this sector involve using the environment for financial gain but increasingly industry is interested in doing so responsibly.

For a full list of jobs in this section turn to page 237.

Healthcare

If you are keen to pursue a career in healthcare you must be compassionate and enjoy either caring for people or deciding what treatment they should receive. There is such a wide variety of jobs available in this sector simply because you can specialise in absolutely any aspect of human healthcare. Maybe you're interested in working with athletes or perhaps working with children interests you more. You could be part of the rehabilitation process after an illness or injury or find yourself working as a mental health nurse. Many jobs require a lot of training and you can expect to work in some highly pressurised and sometimes distressing situations. Workers in healthcare are extremely dedicated and enthusiastic about their careers, which rarely constitute a 9am–5pm job. You can expect every day to be different and you should relish the challenges working with people of all ages can bring.

For a full list of jobs in this section turn to page 269.

Languages, Information and Culture

If you are really interested in history or perhaps would like to use another language as part of your career, a job in this sector could be right for you. The jobs in this family are quite varied in terms of whether you would work with other people or by yourself. You could find yourself working in a range of different places, from museums to antiques fairs to conferences. Some of the jobs in this family are more unusual and are perfect for those of you who want a fascinating job that allows you to indulge in your passion for historic artefacts and artwork or languages and foreign countries. To excel in this sector you should have an inquisitive mind, be meticulous in your work and enjoy carrying out research. If you are keen to work with languages you should also be willing to travel in order to improve your language and your knowledge of the culture and history.

For a full list of jobs in this section turn to page 325.

Legal and Political Services

Are you interested in justice and fairness for all? Do you relish the opportunity to speak out for what's right and enjoy the challenge of persuading others that everyone needs an equal voice? Maybe you find the law a fascinating subject and you feel you would enjoy a challenging career where the rewards are a good salary and a real sense of achievement when your hard work pays off. If so, a job in this sector could be what you are looking for. Workers in this sector are fiercely passionate about their careers and have, more often than not, completed a lot of training and worked hard to establish themselves in this competitive field. You need to be driven and thrive on pressure and tight deadlines; this is a sector for someone who is ambitious and very talented at working tactfully with people.

For a full list of jobs in this section turn to page 341.

Leisure, Sport and Tourism

This sector relies on a motivated, upbeat and outgoing workforce for its success. You will need to show that you can work very well with other people, providing them with an excellent service when they want to enjoy themselves on holiday or if they are keen to improve their fitness and sporting ability. If you are keen to work with professional sports players or become one yourself you should be very aware of how to keep the body fit while avoiding injury. It's also important that you can keep a level head as you will often be responsible for other people's welfare. You should be warm and friendly but be able to maintain a high level of professionalism at the same time. You should also demonstrate you have patience and tact and be clued up on health and safety regulations.

For a full list of jobs in this section turn to page 361.

Marketing, Advertising, Media, Print and Publishing

Do you consider yourself to be a great communicator? Are you interested in working in an exciting and often fast-paced environment with passionate, driven and ambitious individuals? If so, a career in this industry could be right for you. People who work in this sector are exceptionally motivated and are willing to put in long hours often on low starting wages because of their love of the job. While you need to be good at preparing your work alone, people who work in this sector tend to be very good at working with others and build up strong professional relationships as part of their job. You should have a great sense of creativity and imagination and be good at putting your ideas on paper, but you will often also need strong business acumen as many of your decisions will be made from an economical point of view as well as a creative one.

For a full list of jobs in this section turn to page 381.

Performing Arts

This job family contains a wide range of exciting jobs for those of you who want to work in theatre, music, on screen or behind the scenes. People working in this sector do so because they are passionate, creative and love the arts. Jobs can be scarce, so you will need to demonstrate that you are willing to work very hard but the rewards of being part of a fantastic production can be huge. You won't necessarily be confined to working in one place as your job may take you on tour all over the world. There are also jobs available in this sector for those of you who are more technically minded – sound and lighting engineers also play a vital role in this industry as do people who have trained in fashion and textiles. Make-up artists also play an important part in theatre, television and music production.

For a full list of jobs in this section turn to page 415.

Personal and Other Services including Hair and Beauty

This is a very wide job family and covers everything from hairdressing and beauty to cleaning and wedding consulting. You can enter this career sector with a host of different skills and qualifications. What all of the jobs have in common is that they provide a particular service that a customer has asked for so you need to be good at listening to others and giving customers exactly what they want – people in this sector have a brilliant way with people. You should also demonstrate creativity and strong practical and technical skills as many of the jobs in this family require you to use specialist equipment, and have knowledge of health and safety.

For a full list of jobs in this section turn to page 441.

Retail, Sales and Customer Services

Jobs in this sector are suited to those of you who are very good at communicating with others and are interested in making your customers happy. Maybe you're interested in working with food and want to give your customers high quality, fresh produce. Your interest may lie in fashion retail and you could spend your time providing style advice. You should also be commercially minded and think about how your work relates to the success of the company you work for. Jobs in this sector also involve maintaining standards such as safety and quality to ensure guidelines are met, so a practical outlook can be useful.

For a full list of jobs in this section turn to page 461.

Science, Mathematics and Statistics

Do you have a very mathematical brain? Are you logical in how you approach tasks? Maybe you are fascinated by scientific advances and would like to be involved in future discoveries? People who work in this sector can spend long periods of time carrying out meticulous research. You may find yourself working for a variety of employers, from the health service to a cosmetics company or even a charity. You should be willing to work on your own but also be happy to present your findings in reports to others. People in this sector are very highly skilled individuals who have often been through a lot of training, and possess a questioning and inquisitive mind.

For a full list of jobs in this section turn to page 489.

Security, Emergency and the Armed Forces

Working in this sector may give you many incredible experiences and opportunities not open to most people. You need to be an excellent team player and in some instances you may find yourself in a potentially dangerous situation. Working in this sector you can expect to spend your day absolutely anywhere! Some roles involve a lot of office work whereas others can involve spending a lot of your time on the road, or even at sea. If you're looking for a job that will be exhilarating but are able to remain calm and professional under pressure this sector could offer you a lot of opportunities.

For a full list of jobs in this section turn to page 529.

Social Work and Counselling Services

People who work in this sector are dedicated to caring and talking through people's problems and anxieties to improve their general well-being and their future prospects in life. The work requires a lot of patience, an open mind and a friendly and approachable personality. You could be helping people who are distressed and need help and guidance but equally you may be helping people who want to move on to the next stage in their careers or educational choices. Either way, you should be someone who enjoys helping people change their lives for the better. If you are interested in working in this field you need to show that you are compassionate and very good at communicating with people from all walks of life and of all ages. You should also be someone who can maintain a strong sense of professionalism as you could be in a position of trust and you must be very respectful of your clients' privacy.

For a full list of jobs in this section turn to page 557.

Transport and Logistics

The jobs in this sector are immensely varied because of the wide range of transport and communication links that exist today to keep our lives running. You could need a high level of technical knowledge in this sector especially for jobs such as pilot or train driver. But you could also be great at keeping attention to detail and maintaining schedules if logistics is more where your interest lies. Jobs in transport and logistics require very efficient and practical people to ensure that our infrastructure continues to run smoothly and safely. You may need to cope well under pressure. As you will probably have contact with the general public you should be good with people, and have a calm, professional manner.

For a full list of jobs in this section turn to page 581.

Where to go for more help

Below is a brief explanation with some contact details of the main organisations that can help you find out more about the career you are interested in.

England

Speak to the careers adviser at your school or college. Alternatively there is a wide range of information on the National Careers Service website. You can also contact a trained careers adviser by phone, through their website with an email or by using the webchat service. The website also has moderated chatrooms and message boards.

Tel: 0800 100 900
Email: use the contact form on the National Careers Service website

https://nationalcareersservice.direct.gov.uk

Northern Ireland

If you want advice from a careers adviser you can attend one of the local careers offices throughout Northern Ireland. Here you will get information on all aspects of work, education and employment issues. Careers advisers visit schools regularly and you should speak to your careers teacher to arrange a careers interview. If you have left school you should contact your local JobCentre to make an appointment to speak to a careers adviser. The NI Government Careers Service website is also packed with information.

Tel: 0300 200 7820
Email: use the contact form on the NI Government Careers Service website

www.nidirect.gov.uk/careers

Scotland

Skills Development Scotland

Skills Development Scotland is available to both young people and adults looking for information about careers, education or employment options.

Tel: 0800 917 8000
Email: use the contact form on the Skills Development Scotland website

www.skillsdevelopmentscotland.co.uk
www.myworldofwork.co.uk

Wales

Careers Wales

Offering help to both young people and to adults, Careers Wales provides advice on any issues you have related to careers, work, education or training. The Careers Wales website offers a personalised career search with the option to create your own career profile, save your CV online, search and save career options and receive immediate advice from their online webchat service. Talk to your careers adviser in school or visit the website for more information.

Tel: 0800 028 4844
Email: use the contact form on the Careers Wales website

www.careerswales.com

England, Wales and Northern Ireland

learndirect

If you need advice on any aspect of your careers, training or educational options try contacting learndirect. learndirect has trained advisers who can discuss your options over the phone or you can attend one of the many learndirect centres available throughout England, Wales and Northern Ireland. Their help is available to anyone of any age, although it is mainly aimed at adults.

Tel: 0800 101 901

www.learndirect.com

Administration, Business, Office Work and Financial Services

To work in this sector you need to have a great head for numbers and be very good at managing your time effectively. Jobs in business and finance can be fast-paced and exciting and workers in all four of these areas are highly motivated and enjoy working in an office environment. The jobs featured in this section are listed below. For similar jobs to this job family please go to the section: *Legal and Political Services* on page 341.

- Accountant p2
- Accounting Technician and Accounts/Finance Clerk p4
- Actuary p5
- Auditor p8
- Bank Cashier/Customer Adviser p9
- Bank Manager p10
- Business Adviser p11
- Chartered/Company Secretary p12
- Civil Service Administrative Officer p13
- Civil Service Executive Officer p14
- Company Director p15
- Compliance Officer p16
- Credit Analyst p17
- Debt Collector p18
- Diplomatic Services Operational Officer p19

- Economist p20
- Education Officer p21
- Environmental Health Practitioner/Officer p22
- Equality and Diversity Officer p23
- Ergonomist p24
- Estates Officer p25
- Financial Adviser p26
- Health and Safety Adviser p27
- Human Resources/Personnel Officer p28
- Insurance Broker p29
- Insurance Risk Surveyor p32
- Insurance Underwriter p33
- Investment Analyst p34
- Investment Banker p35
- Legal Secretary p36
- Loss Adjuster p37
- Management Consultant p38
- Medical Receptionist p39
- Payroll Manager p40

- Pensions Administrator p41
- Pensions Adviser p42
- Personal Assistant p43
- Project Manager p44
- Quality Manager p45
- Receptionist p46
- Recruitment/Employment Agency Consultant p47
- Regeneration Manager/ Economic Development Officer p48
- Registrar of Births, Deaths, Marriages and Civil Partnerships p49
- Risk Manager p50
- Secretary p51
- Stock Market Trader p52
- Stockbroker p53
- Tax Adviser p54
- Telephonist p55
- Training and Development Officer p56

ACCOUNTANT

Qualifications and courses

In order to practise, accountants will need to hold a qualification from one of the recognised accountancy bodies: Association of Chartered Certified Accountants (ACCA), Institute of Chartered Accountants in England and Wales (ICAEW), Institute of Chartered Accountants of Scotland (ICAS), Chartered Accountants Ireland (CAI) or Association of International Accountants (AIA). The websites for each organisation contain full details of the qualifications they provide.

You can qualify for these training programmes with or without a relevant degree, though having one is advantageous (usually 2.2 Honours degree or higher) and most accountants follow a graduate route. If your degree is in accounting or a related subject you may be exempt from certain papers of the professional qualifications so it is worth checking course details to see if this is the case. Owing to an increase in global companies, graduates with language degrees are in high demand.

The minimum entry requirements for a degree vary depending on the institution; however, they are normally 2 A levels/3 H grades and 5 GCSEs/National 5s (A*–C/A–C) including Maths and English.

Without a degree, you can qualify for the professional courses by following a vocational route provided by the above recognised bodies. For this it is useful to have a minimum of 3 GCSEs/National 5s and 2 A levels/3 H grades, in 5 separate subjects including Maths and English, but there are still options even without these. Each body provides different options depending on the qualifications you already have.

To become a chartered management accountant, you are required to pass the Chartered Institute of Management Accountants (CIMA) Professional Qualification and complete a minimum of 3 years' relevant work experience. To become a chartered financial accountant you will need to study for the Chartered Institute of Public Finance and Accountancy (CIPFA) Professional Qualification. This is made up of 3 parts and will usually take up to 3 years to complete.

It is becoming increasingly more competitive to secure a training contract with an employer that is approved by the bodies listed above so it is useful to gain pre-entry work experience.

What the work involves

Accountancy involves providing a company or individual with trustworthy information about their financial records.

By analysing a company's or individual's finances, accountants identify ways to maximise profits. They provide professional advice on financial planning and development, tax returns, future costs and budgets.

You will keep detailed accounts, carry out internal audits and produce regular statements on whether the company's systems are efficient and cost effective.

There are 3 main areas of accounting and within each sector you can become either a certified or chartered accountant. Chartered accountants work to a globally recognised standard and are often sponsored by their employer to achieve this qualification.

Industrial and commercial

Employed directly by a company, you will provide them with a range of services.

You will help to plan the company's development by predicting costs, benefits and risks.

You may be expected to make business decisions along with other managers.

Private practice

You will work for a specialist accountancy firm that offers services to clients.

Smaller practices usually work for local businesses. However, accountancy firms can be huge and some companies provide services to multinational corporations.

Your clients can vary from small businesses that do not employ their own in-house management accountant to large companies or wealthy individuals.

Public sector

Working for public bodies such as the NHS, universities and local authorities, you will offer advice on tax, financial problems, raising money, financial IT systems and management consultancy.

Your role will be to help provide an efficient, quality service that is within the budgets set by the government.

You will play an important part in making sure that public money is spent properly.

Type of person suited to this work

As you will be giving presentations and working with people at all levels, you will need excellent written and verbal communication skills.

Much of your work will involve dealing with confidential reports and financial information so reliability, honesty and integrity are essential attributes.

Time management and organisational skills are key as you must be able to work under pressure and meet deadlines.

As you are required to study whilst working and remain up to date with developments in the field, it is important to be self-motivated and committed to your career.

Confidence working with numbers and an interest in how businesses work is essential.

You will need problem-solving and research skills and the ability to process and analyse complicated financial information, therefore a good eye for detail is essential.

Working conditions

You could work in an organisation of any size and will generally be office based, spending a lot of time using IT, sitting at a desk or meeting clients. Smart dress will be required.

Depending on your role, you might have the opportunity to travel both in this country and abroad to meet clients so a driving licence could be useful.

Although you will normally work office hours from Monday to Friday, you might need to work extra hours at busy times, especially during February to April (the end of the financial year).

Flexible working is possible (once you are qualified) and there is the opportunity to set up as an independent practitioner.

Future prospects

The growing importance of information technology is having a major impact on the accountancy sector. Access to faster communication systems means that more companies are becoming global, which in turn will have an impact on the numbers required within the accountancy sector.

It is recommended that you think carefully about the area within accountancy that you would like to focus on at an early stage of your career as this may enable you to specialise in that field.

There are lots of structured routes for progression and an accountant can often become a manager after just 2 years and a senior manager 3 years after that. The next level is partner and although this is very competitive in certain firms, it is possible to achieve this 8–15 years after qualifying.

In the long term you could choose to become self-employed, offering consultancy services to clients.

There is also the opportunity to progress to general management roles within business.

Industrial and commercial
There is a high demand for trainees, with opportunities throughout the country but as you would probably be working for a larger organisation you will probably be based in a city. Once you are qualified and experienced you could move into a highly paid senior management position, or you could choose to move to a larger multinational company for promotion.

Private practice
You could work for a small company, offering a personal service to local businesses and individuals or for a huge multinational firm. Job opportunities are good and there is high demand for qualified accountants.

After a time, you could set up your own private accounting practice or work independently by working on a freelance basis.

Public sector
The public sector covers a wide range of services, including education, healthcare and social services. Government changes mean that budgets are increasingly held at local level, opening up opportunities across the country.

If you do well, you can move into a high-level management position.

Advantages/disadvantages

Accountancy is a varied career and there are many opportunities both in this country and abroad.

You must be prepared to cope with a lot of responsibility, stress and pressure.

You will need to be committed and determined to manage training, studying and taking exams whilst you work.

Salaries in this field tend to be extremely high and progression can be quite rapid.

Money guide

During their training, graduates can earn up to £25,000 a year, depending on the stage they have reached in their training, the sector and the location.

Recently qualified graduates can earn £26,000 to £50,000.

With experience accountants can earn £40,000 to £100,000. Directors can earn £140,000 and more.

Salary will depend on location and size of the organisation. The highest salaries are within London and the south-east of England; the lowest are in Northern Ireland, Scotland and the north-east of England. Graduates usually receive higher salaries than school leavers during their training.

Related opportunities

- Accounting Technician and Accounts/Finance Clerk p4
- Actuary p5
- Auditor p8
- Financial Adviser p26
- Insurance Broker p29

Further information

Association of Chartered Certified Accountants
www.accaglobal.com/uk

Association of International Accountants
www.aiaworldwide.com

Chartered Accountants Ireland
www.charteredaccountants.ie

Institute of Chartered Accountants in England and Wales
www.icaew.com

Institute of Chartered Accountants of Scotland
www.icas.com

Institute of Financial Accountants
www.ifa.org.uk

ACCOUNTING TECHNICIAN AND ACCOUNTS/FINANCE CLERK

Qualifications and courses

There are no formal academic requirements to train to be an accounting technician although some GCSEs/National 5s (A*–C/A–C) would be an advantage, particularly English and Maths as they demonstrate a reasonable level of the essential literacy and numeracy skills. Other qualifications such as the Advanced Diploma in Business, Administration and Finance or A levels/H grades and BTEC Awards in subjects such as accounting, finance and business could also be useful.

You will need to train for a professional qualification with the Association of Accounting Technicians (AAT) or the Association of Chartered Certified Accountants (ACCA) to enter this profession. This is usually done on-the-job and studied part-time via distance learning. The AAT Accounting Qualification provides flexible training and is comprised of 3 levels: Level 2 (L5 in Scotland), Level 3 (L6 in Scotland) and Level 4 (L8 in Scotland). You might be exempt from some levels if you have relevant qualifications or experience. To become a technician you will also need to complete 1 year's work experience. This is usually done while studying for the qualification part-time. Once you have both the qualification and the experience you will be able to use the letters MAAT after your name.

Alternatively, the ACCA provides a Certified Accounting Technician (CAT) qualification. First you complete their 3 Foundations in Accountancy exams, followed by a year's practical experience, the Foundations in Professionalism module and 2 additional specialist exams.

What the work involves

Accounting technicians are responsible for financial issues including company expenditure, tax returns and payroll. Your work will include collecting and analysing information, controlling company budgets, keeping financial records and writing reports.

In a large firm, you will probably work as part of a team and support qualified accountants. In a smaller company, you might cover a wider range of tasks and be responsible for most of the finances.

Different financial sectors demand specialised knowledge and so, once you are qualified, you could choose to specialise in a specific financial area, for example insolvency or tax analysis.

Type of person suited to this work

You will need to be confident with numbers, and have the ability to gather, analyse and record information accurately when under pressure from deadlines. Good IT skills are also important, as most of the work is computer based.

Good verbal and written communication skills are essential, as you will often have to explain complicated financial issues to clients in a clear manner.

You must be willing and committed to further study in order to pass your technician exams. You will be expected to continue learning throughout your career, as it is important for accounting technicians to keep up to date with changes in financial law.

Working conditions

You will normally work standard office hours from Monday to Friday, however at busy times you might need to put in extra hours over evenings or weekends.

Most work will be office based, although you may also travel to meetings with clients within your working day so a driving licence could be useful.

Future prospects

Accounting technicians can progress to positions such as finance controllers, internal auditors, payroll managers, tax analysts and audit seniors. Many go on to become self-employed or become chartered accountants by studying for the qualifications of a chartered accountancy body. All of the chartered accountancy bodies offer fast-track routes for AAT and ACCA CAT qualified students.

Since the accounting technician qualifications are internationally recognised, it is also possible to work abroad.

Advantages/disadvantages

You will usually be working in a team environment, which means that you will build strong relationships.

The work can be slightly monotonous.

Money guide

As a trainee accounting technician you can expect to earn between £16,000 and £22,000 per year.

When fully qualified and with experience, earnings can be up to £32,000.

Salaries are geographically sensitive and tend to be higher in southern England, particularly in London.

Related opportunities

- Accountant p2
- Bank Cashier/Customer Adviser p9
- Pensions Administrator p41

Further information

Association of Accounting Technicians
www.aat.org.uk

Association of Chartered Certified Accountants
www.accaglobal.com/uk

ACTUARY

Qualifications and courses

To enter the actuarial profession you should first study for a degree in a numerate subject, such as actuarial science, maths or economics, and join the Institute and Faculty of Actuaries (IFoA, also known as The Actuarial Profession) as a student member. Most employers prefer candidates to have achieved a 2.1 Honours degree or higher, as well as at least a B in A level/H grade Maths.

If you do not have the entry requirements for the IFoA there is the option to take their Certificate in Financial Mathematics (CT1) exam which will enable you to become a member of the profession.

Once you have graduated, qualification as an actuary requires a further 3 to 6 years of studying for professional qualifications with the IFoA and on-the-job training. You should start looking to apply for graduate trainee positions in your final year of university, before October or November, as this is when most employers' deadlines will be and competition for places will be fierce.

While you train, you will study part time for the professional qualifications with the IFoA. There are 15 exams. It is possible to gain exemption from some exams, and therefore qualify faster, if you are a member of IFoA and have studied your degree at a university that holds exemption or accredited agreements or if you have a postgraduate qualification. If you did not, you may still be eligible for exemption from some exams depending on the subjects covered by your degree and your performance in them.

Pre-entry experience could also be useful. Some companies offer internships or work experience placements for students looking to become actuaries, and though this is not required to enter the profession, it may give you an edge when competing for graduate jobs. Talking with people already in the profession by approaching them at careers events or work shadowing can also be invaluable.

What the work involves

Actuaries evaluate, manage and calculate financial risks. Using statistics and knowledge of investments, law, business and economics, they make financial predictions to help design products such as insurance and pensions. They use their specialist economic and mathematical knowledge to assess situations in the financial world and relay reports and information to non-specialists.

As an actuary you would help set insurance premiums based on statistics, probability and risk. You would also use your knowledge to help companies make long-term financial decisions.

You might work in insurance, life assurance, pensions, investments or for the government.

Type of person suited to this work

You must be good with numbers and enjoy solving complicated mathematical problems. You should also be analytical, able to think logically, and be skilled at problem-solving.

You will need to have excellent communication skills as you must explain complicated financial issues in a clear and understandable way to clients.

Actuaries must pay close attention to detail and work to deadlines. You must keep up to date with new developments, such as the laws governing the industry. You will be expected to have excellent IT skills.

Working conditions

Most actuaries work within life assurance companies but numbers in general insurance are increasing rapidly. You will normally work standard office hours, 9am–5pm, during the week and most of your work will be office based. Jobs are available throughout the country but most are based in large cities, such as Edinburgh and London, and the south-east of England.

As a trainee you will have to study in your own time but once you are qualified you could work abroad and might be able to work part time.

Future prospects

As a fully qualified actuary you can specialise in a particular field, work in a consultancy, or you could travel as your qualifications will be recognised all over the world. Within larger companies there are opportunities for promotion to very senior positions.

Advantages/disadvantages

Training after university takes up to 6 years and involves studying while working full time.

Actuaries have good long-term career prospects and opportunities for promotion.

UK qualifications are recognised worldwide giving you the opportunities and option to work abroad.

Money guide

The actuarial profession is one of the highest paid.

Starting salaries for graduates are around £25,000–£36,000. Once you are qualified this rises to between £40,000 and £60,000.

Senior actuaries with 10–15 years' experience usually earn in excess of £60,000 with senior directors often earning £185,000 or more.

Salaries vary based on location and specialty and are likely to be higher in London and the south-east of England.

Related opportunities

- Financial Adviser p26
- Risk Manager p50
- Stockbroker p53

Further information

Association of Consulting Actuaries
www.aca.org.uk

Institute and Faculty of Actuaries
www.actuaries.org.uk

Institute
and Faculty
of Actuaries

INSTITUTE AND FACULTY OF ACTUARIES

Do you love maths? Love solving problems? Then consider a career as an actuary

What do actuaries do?

Actuaries are experts in risk management. They use their mathematical skills to help measure the probability and risk of future events. This information is useful to many industries, including healthcare, pensions, insurance, banking and investments, where a single decision can have a major financial impact. An actuarial career can be one of the most diverse, exciting and rewarding in the world.

Where do actuaries work?

Actuaries provide financial advice on the management of assets and liabilities – especially where long-term management and planning are key. Actuaries work in many areas, such as finance and investment, risk management, general and life insurance, pensions and healthcare. Every area of business is subject to risks, so there are no limitations to where an actuary can go; they can even be employed in the marketing and development of sophisticated financial products.

What is the salary like?

Salaries and benefit packages are excellent, even for those starting out in their career. In fact, it's one of the highest paid professions wherever you go in the world. Trainees earn from £33,000 a year and newly qualified actuaries earn £55,000. In later years, senior actuaries' salaries range from £70,000 to £200,000. So, despite the hard work, it is a very well rewarded job.

Who should become an actuary?

- A graduate with a 2:1 in a numerate subject
- Someone who loves logic and problem solving
- A good communicator
- Someone with excellent business acumen.

How do you become an actuary?

In your final year at university you need to consider applying for graduate schemes within actuarial employers. Once you secure a trainee position your employer will help you become a member of the IFoA so you can get started with actuarial exams. You can study at your own pace while working – many employers give you time off to study. In addition to passing the exams, you'll work with your employer to meet the practical work-based skills requirement.

Where can you find out more information?

If you want to find out more about becoming an actuary, visit the IFoA website at www.actuaries.org.uk/become-actuary.

Case Study

INSTITUTE AND FACULTY OF ACTUARIES

Name: John Small

Job Role: Actuarial Trainee,

Company: First Actuarial LLP

Location: Tonbridge, Kent

Course: Actuarial Science

University: University of Kent

I first heard of First Actuarial in my second year at the University of Kent, when I picked up a copy of the Directory of Actuarial Employers. In my third year, I went to a careers fair organised by the university and spoke to a guy called Tim (who I now sit next to!). He went through with me what they look for in a CV and covering letter.

I was fortunate enough to get invited to two interviews and was then offered the job during February. This gave me time to concentrate on my exams and enjoy my summer, knowing that I had a job lined up. There was obviously a bit of luck in this, but if you can put in the legwork during the winter of your final year of university it can definitely pay off.

Over the last three years I have gone back to the University of Kent for talks and careers fairs, hoping to recruit more graduates.

The biggest change I found when I started work was going from full-time study and part-time work, to full-time work and part-time study. When you start studying for the exams it can be nice having a day out of the office, doing something a bit different from your day-today work. However, it can get stressful nearer to the exam, when you're spending a lot of time both working and studying. An actuarial student needs to be able to work hard to pass the exams, but, as long as you are organised and set time aside to study, it will be very rewarding, and you can still have a life at the same time!

Working for a consultancy, communication is a key skill and can be a great asset. If you come into the profession from a mathematical background, there may not have been many opportunities to establish this skill and so any opportunities at university or elsewhere should be taken. I have never been a fan of presenting to people, but I took the opportunity at university to go into local schools and talk about university life, and I feel that this really helped me in my interview and has since helped me with my day-to-day work.

As you might expect, there are calculations to do. However, a lot of calculations are similar for different clients. Therefore, we have standard software and spreadsheets set up to do these more quickly.

A major part of what we do involves writing letters and reports. It's all well and good calculating the numbers, but we actually need to tell our clients what these numbers mean for them. To do this, we either use template documents or set them up from scratch. This can be a tricky skill at first, but it becomes easier with practice. An important skill is therefore being able to describe potentially complicated concepts in easy to understand language.

Overall, a consultant is giving advice. Initially, an actuarial student will have little practice of direct contact with clients, but as they become more senior, this becomes part of everyday work. This might involve emails and phone calls, or it might involve more face-to-face meetings.

AUDITOR

Qualifications and courses

To become either an external or internal auditor you will usually hold a degree in a numerical subject, such as maths or finance. The minimum requirements for a degree vary depending on the institution, however they are usually 2 A levels/3 H grades and 5 GCSEs/National 5s (A*–C/A–C), including Maths and English.

To become an external auditor, you must first qualify as a chartered accountant with one of the main accountancy bodies: the Association of Chartered Certified Accountants (ACCA), the Institute of Chartered Accountants in England and Wales (ICAEW), the Institute of Chartered Accountants of Scotland (ICAS), Chartered Accountants Ireland (CAI) or the Association of International Accountants (AIA). Most students enrolling on these courses are graduates, though there are vocational routes in as well. Graduates will usually study for a professional qualification while working.

The National Audit Office runs an ACA School Leaver Scheme which is a 5-year fast-track scheme for school leavers to qualify as a chartered accountant with the ICAEW. Applicants need to have 5 GCSEs/National 5s (A*–C/A–C) including English and Maths, and a minimum of 120 UCAS points across their top three grades at A level or equivalent.

If you are a member of the Chartered Institute of Public Finance and Accountancy (CIPFA), you can only carry out audits in the public sector. If you have qualified with the Chartered Institute of Management Accountants (CIMA), you can only conduct internal audits unless you take audit training with another accounting body.

Candidates keen to work in internal auditing do not have to be a qualified accountant and can come from a variety of academic backgrounds, though experience in business or finance can be an advantage. Entry is with either a degree or recommendation by an employer and candidates can strengthen their application by taking the Chartered Institute of Internal Auditors' (IIA) Certificate in Internal Audit and Business Risk (IACert).

What the work involves

Specialising in audit work means exploring all aspects of a business, talking to staff and ensuring that the paperwork and accounts give a true picture of the company's finances.

Internal auditors work for a company preparing their accounts for external auditors to check. They are also responsible for assessing other risks, not just finances. Most businesses and government departments must be externally audited by law, with a few exceptions.

As an external auditor you will create an independent report for a company, stating that the accounts are true and accurate and recommending possible improvements to the business.

Type of person suited to this work

You must be happy working with numbers and interpreting statistics and be a thorough and methodical person with the ability to work independently. As you will be using your skills and experience to solve financial problems you need to enjoy researching all aspects of a business.

It is important that you have excellent communication skills so that you can present your findings clearly. You should also be able to work effectively as part of a team and with the company you are auditing. You should be well organised, able to work under pressure, meet deadlines and have excellent IT skills.

Working conditions

Large companies have internal auditors who prepare their accounts for inspection. External auditors are based temporarily in the firms they are auditing, so they may have to travel and stay away from home. A driving licence can be useful.

You will work normal office hours but might have to work evenings and weekends.

Future prospects

There is an increasing demand for qualified auditors. As an internal auditor you could work for a business or government department, work for yourself or as a consultant.

External auditors are employed by accountancy firms, the National Audit Office (the Accounts Commission in Scotland) auditing central government departments, or the Audit Commission working with public sector organisations such as local authorities or the NHS.

Advantages/disadvantages

Accountancy training takes 3–6 years and involves studying in your own time.

There are opportunities to work abroad during a secondment.

Money guide

Trainees on the National Audit Office's ACA School Leaver Scheme earn £23,060 per year if based in London or £17,572 if based in Newcastle.

Graduates and part-qualified auditors can earn £18,000–£25,000 a year during training, which could rise to £30,000–£45,000 once you are qualified.

A senior auditor can earn £50,000–£90,000. Audit directors or head auditors could potentially earn up to £150,000.

Related opportunities

- Actuary p5
- Chartered/Company Secretary p12
- Financial Adviser p26

Further information

Association of Chartered Certified Accountants
www.accaglobal.com/uk

Chartered Institute of Internal Auditors
www.iia.org.uk

Chartered Institute of Management Accountants
www.cimaglobal.com

BANK CASHIER/CUSTOMER ADVISER

ENTRY LEVEL 1

Qualifications and courses

Different employers have different entry requirements for this profession. Some may ask for a minimum of 4 GCSEs/National 5s (A*–C/A–C) including English and Maths. Others may not ask for qualifications but require you to pass an entry test upon application. Once employed you will take part in your employer's in-house training scheme and learn on the job.

Other useful qualifications include City & Guilds Award in Customer Service (Levels 1, 2 and 3), City & Guilds Certificate/Diploma in Business and Administration (Levels 2 and 3), the *ifs* Level 3 Diploma in Financial Studies (DipFS), BTEC Nationals in Business or Personal and Business Finance, and the CCN Professional Bankers qualifications (Level 3).

Any customer service experience would be an advantage, as would cash handling experience and basic computer skills in any work environment. You can also enter this career by completing the Intermediate Level apprenticeship in Providing Financial Services.

Employees will normally be required to undergo Disclosure and Barring Service (DBS) background checks.

What the work involves

Bank cashiers/customer advisers work for banks and building societies, and are the first point of contact for customers with enquiries or complaints.

You may be working in a branch dealing with customers face to face, or you could be based in a contact centre liaising with them over the phone or by email.

You will be handling customers' accounts, including the paying in and withdrawing of money using computerised systems. You will also be expected to sell the company's products and services, which will involve working to set sales targets.

Type of person suited to this work

You will need excellent customer service skills so that you can process customers' requests efficiently, and also gain their trust in order to advise them on a range of financial products.

You must be confident working with figures and IT, and working to targets. As you will be handling money, you should be trustworthy and able to work accurately, paying close attention to detail.

Since you will be working as part of a team, a helpful and positive attitude coupled with the ability to use your own initiative is valuable.

Working conditions

In a branch you will probably work normal office hours, and Saturdays if the bank is open. Call centres usually offer a 24-hour service, so you should expect to work shifts that include nights and weekends.

Part-time and flexible working hours are commonly available.

You should be well presented, and will usually be required to wear a uniform.

Future prospects

Research suggests that there will be a growing demand for skilled people in all areas of customer service and relationship management, and opportunities are available to further your career.

A well established career pathway offers employees the potential to progress from customer service adviser to supervisor, or to specialise in an area such as mortgages or pensions or go into management. Some gain further professional qualifications in order to train as a financial adviser or bank manager. Some banks offer internal fast-track management programmes. You might be able to move into corporate or investment banking and there has also been growth in Islamic banking.

Advantages/disadvantages

Looking after customers and helping to solve their queries can be interesting and rewarding.

Banks offer well-structured training programmes on entry and you will have a clear route for career progression.

Due to the economic downturn, entry into this profession is more competitive than ever before.

Money guide

The starting salary for a trainee ranges between £12,000 and £17,000 a year. Apprentices can expect to earn between £11,000 and £15,000 once qualified.

With several years' experience and supervisory responsibilities you could be earning between £18,000 and £30,000 a year.

You may also receive bonuses for meeting sales targets and employers often offer packages that include cheaper mortgages, pensions, loans, shares and insurance.

Related opportunities

- Bank Manager p10
- Financial Adviser p26
- Pensions Adviser p42

Further information

ifs University College
www.ifslearning.ac.uk

Financial Skills Partnership
www.financialskillspartnership.org.uk

BANK MANAGER

Qualifications and courses

There are 3 main ways to become a bank manager. One is to join a bank or building society's graduate management scheme. These usually last 18–24 months and competition is high, so you will need at least a 2.2 Honours degree (some banks require a 2.1 Honours degree), ideally in business, finance, economics, management or marketing. If you wish to apply to an international bank a foreign language qualification could be advantageous. Degree courses will usually require at least 2 A levels/3 H grades and 5 GCSEs/National 5s (A*–C/A–C). Pre-entry work experience can also help you get on a graduate scheme.

Another way to become a bank manager is by internal promotion from a customer service role via an in-house management training programme. Many banks have fast-track programmes. You will obviously need good job performance to be eligible for this, including supervisory experience, a good track record in meeting sales targets and the right drive and commitment.

A third way is, once you have completed the Advanced Apprenticeship in Providing Financial Services, progressing onto the Level 4 Higher Apprenticeship in Banking which will enable you to learn the management and leadership skills necessary for a bank manager position.

Qualifications studied part-time from the Institute of Financial Services' School of Finance or the Chartered Banker Institute can also be useful.

Disclosure and Barring Service (DBS) checks and bankruptcy checks will normally be carried out.

What the work involves

Bank managers are responsible for running branches of retail, commercial or corporate banks. You will be accountable for staff recruitment, motivation and training, as well as meeting budget and sales targets for products and services.

You will be required to keep up to date with a range of financial products, and market your services to individuals and businesses.

Attending meetings and preparing reports on branch operations for both staff and head office will also be important tasks.

Type of person suited to this work

Bank managers work with people at all levels, so excellent verbal and written communications skills are essential.

You will be expected to deal with customers on a daily basis, as well as leading and motivating your team, both of which require confidence, organisation, negotiation skills, initiative and the ability to think on your feet.

You should be comfortable working with numbers as you will have to meet budget and sales targets, and calculate profits.

Working conditions

You will usually work normal office hours and occasional Saturdays, in keeping with the opening hours of your bank. If you manage a call centre, you will probably be required to work shifts in order to provide a 24-hour service to customers.

As well as working in an office, you will occasionally travel to visit clients at their business premises, so a driving licence could be useful.

Future prospects

Despite recent bank mergers and closures, branch management positions are still available. From branch manager you could progress to area and regional manager, and then into operations management or other areas such as risk or compliance. Sometimes you may be expected to relocate to other areas, usually within the UK. You may also move banks in order to progress.

More and more managers are completing technical qualifications for regulated financial products and services, such as digital banking, from organisations such as the *ifs* School of Finance, the Chartered Institute of Bankers in Scotland and the Chartered Insurance Institute.

London is one of the leading financial centres of the world and offers the best opportunities for pursuing a high-level career. There are also numerous roles located overseas.

Advantages/disadvantages

This challenging, fast-moving industry offers roles in various sectors such as telephone and internet banking.

Most towns have bank branches so there are opportunities to work throughout the UK.

You will need to meet challenging targets in an increasingly competitive market which is sensitive to changes in the national and global economy.

Money guide

Graduates on bank management training schemes can make £18,000 to £25,000 a year. With extra training and experience this can increase to £26,000–£40,000.

Senior staff, such as branch managers, can earn salaries of £40,000–£60,000. Regional and head office managers may make in excess of £70,000.

You may also receive bonuses for meeting targets with additional benefits usually including cheaper mortgages, pensions, loans and insurance.

Related opportunities

- Accountant p2
- Bank Cashier/Customer Adviser p9
- Financial Adviser p26
- Insurance Broker p29

Further information

ifs University College
www.ifslearning.ac.uk

Chartered Banker Institute
www.charteredbanker.com

BUSINESS ADVISER

Qualifications and courses

There are no specific entry qualifications but advisers must have a proven track record in business. Many advisers have prior experience running a business or working as a management consultant. Others have expertise in a key area of business, such as project management, marketing, human resources or finance.

Employers are generally more interested in your experience than your qualifications; however, you may want to start off with GCSEs/National 5s and A levels/H grades in applied business or business studies before gaining practical experience in the industry. Business-related degree courses and diplomas that include a year in the industry may also be helpful.

The Institute of Consulting and the Chartered Management Institute provide various entry-level qualifications for those wishing to start a career as a consultant or adviser, such as Level 5 in Professional Consulting, Level 5 in Business Support and Level 7 in Professional Consulting.

Further business support and mentoring qualifications are provided by the Small Firms Enterprise Development Initiative (SFEDI) and include the Level 3 Certificate in Enterprise Coaching and the Level 3 and 4 Award/ Certificate in Enterprise Mentoring.

You will be required to purchase professional indemnity insurance before becoming a business adviser.

What the work involves

Business advisers provide independent advice to an array of small- and medium-sized businesses or enterprises in order to improve their success.

You will provide advice on prospective business plans and recommend relevant specialist services and suppliers that could support the venture. You may run workshops and seminars that offer basic support and information for new or existing businesses.

You will need to be informed about numerous areas of business but you will often choose to specialise in a specific area, such as marketing and public relations (PR), accountancy and taxation or law.

Type of person suited to this work

You will need to have a good understanding of a variety of business environments and sizes. You must be able to use your knowledge to offer advice on current business issues, geographical trends and financial help available to support new or failing businesses.

You need to be logical and objective, yet approachable and enthusiastic. You will need the ability to manage a variety of projects whilst consistently meeting tight deadlines.

Working conditions

Hours tend to follow the national average of between 37 and 40 hours a week, working 9am–5.30pm, Monday to Friday.

Occasionally you might be required to attend weekend or evening events.

You will be mostly office based, with occasional visits to clients' premises, suppliers or networking events. If you became a self-employed consultant then you would have the opportunity to work from home.

Future prospects

You can take further training throughout your career to enhance your prospects, such as an Institute of Consulting Certificate or Diploma in Business or a postgraduate course in Business Coaching and Mentoring.

If you take an IC qualification you automatically become a member. After 2 years' experience, members can choose to be assessed for the Certified Business Adviser Award and after 3 years they can apply for the Certified Management Consultant (CMC) Award. These give you independent recognition for your skills and competence.

Advisers with a Diploma in Business or the CMC Award can join the National Register for Business Support Professionals.

Business advisers can progress first to team manager and then to senior management positions, or else specialise in a particular area of business. They can also go on to become a self-employed consultant.

Advantages/disadvantages

Employment as a business adviser enables you to work autonomously and use your initiative.

You will work on a variety of projects and have the opportunity to build relationships with a range of people.

It is necessary to have a wealth of business experience before you can become a business adviser.

It is important to gain recognised awards, such as those offered by the Institute of Consulting, in order to prove to clients that you are a certified adviser.

Money guide

Business advisers can expect a starting salary of £20,000 a year. After several years' experience, salaries increase to around £35,000.

Those in senior positions can expect £50,000 or more.

Self-employed freelancers charge a daily rate, which could be between £150 and £400 a day.

Related opportunities

- Company Director p15
- Management Consultant p38
- Project Manager p44

Further information

Chartered Management Institute
www.managers.org.uk

Institute of Consulting
www.iconsulting.org.uk

National Enterprise Network
www.nationalenterprisenetwork.org

CHARTERED/COMPANY SECRETARY

Qualifications and courses

While not required by law, the majority of companies will want someone with a degree, Foundation degree, HNC/HND or equivalent. At least 1 A level/2 H grades and 4 GCSEs/National 5s (A*–C/A–C) or equivalent are required for entry onto an HNC/HND course, while degree courses require 2 A levels/3 H grades and 5 GCSEs/National 5s (A*–C/A–C). This sector is open to all graduates but entrants with degrees in business, law, accountancy, politics or administration are preferred. A postgraduate degree is not necessary but could be useful.

Substantial relevant experience is essential to this role and it is possible to gain further qualifications if interested in becoming the secretary of a public company for which a registration with the Institute of Chartered Secretaries and Administrators (ICSA) is necessary. This is achieved by either completing the ICSA's Chartered Secretaries Qualifying Scheme (CSQS) or by undertaking an ICSA-approved postgraduate course.

The CSQS typically takes 1–3 years to complete and has 2 levels, each with 4 modules. Previous qualifications may lead to automatic exemption from some CSQS modules; you will need to consult the website for more details. When you complete CSQS you automatically become a graduate member of the ICSA. To become a full member at associate level you will need at least 3–6 years' further work experience, depending on whether or not you have a degree. You are eligible to become a Fellow of the institute when you reach a senior level and have 8 years' work experience.

What the work involves

This is a vital administrative and managerial role. You will have a high level of responsibility. You will be in a very senior position advising executives and directors on finance and company law.

You will be responsible for the legal reports all companies are required to keep, reporting to Companies House and other institutions such as the Stock Exchange.

You will be responsible for running board meetings and could be responsible for financial planning, accounts, wages, human resources and all administrative and IT systems.

Type of person suited to this work

You will need excellent communication skills to be able to work with people at all levels. You should be interested in business and have a thorough knowledge of how your organisation works. You will need to understand complicated legal and financial issues and be able to use your knowledge to solve problems, maximise efficiency and advise ways of improving and developing the company.

You should be highly organised, able to deal with several tasks at once and pay close attention to detail. You will analyse figures and accounts and work to strict legal guidelines. You must be confident giving presentations to high-level staff.

Working conditions

Most of your work will be office based, attending lots of meetings, including working at other sites and outside organisations, which could involve some travel and possibly going abroad.

You will normally work office hours but will have a heavy workload and a lot of responsibility; you will need commitment and dedication to work overtime and meet deadlines.

To be successful, a high level of personal and professional integrity is important.

Future prospects

The Companies Act 2008 means that private companies are no longer legally required to have a company or chartered secretary. Despite this change, businesses will still have to meet a range of legal requirements so most will continue to employ one.

An experienced company secretary will have opportunities to work in highly paid jobs in a range of organisations. Some move into senior management, some change to other sectors such as law and finance, and some go on to become a self-employed consultant or company formation agent. Further opportunities are within the public, voluntary and charity sectors, local and central government and educational institutions.

Advantages/disadvantages

This is a high-level career which is interesting, varied and challenging. You will use a wide range of skills and knowledge, prospects are good and earnings can be high. But you will have to take on a lot of responsibility and work long hours; you might have to prepare information for directors if the company is doing badly.

Money guide

Salaries vary depending on the job role, type of organisation and location.

A company secretarial assistant can earn between £30,000 and £50,000 per year. Senior company secretaries earn about £70,000.

Once fully qualified, a chartered secretary working in the private sector can achieve a salary of £100,000 to £150,000.

Experienced secretaries working for FTSE100 companies can earn up to £280,000.

Additionally, many company secretaries receive annual bonuses.

Related opportunities

- Accountant p2
- Barrister/Advocate p343
- Company Director p15

Further information

Companies House
www.companieshouse.gov.uk

Institute of Chartered Secretaries and Administrators
www.icsa.org.uk

Skills CFA
www.skillscfa.org

CIVIL SERVICE ADMINISTRATIVE OFFICER

ENTRY LEVEL 2

Qualifications and courses

Each department within the civil service organises its own recruitment and sets its own entry requirements so you will need to consult each job description carefully when applying. Some departments do not require specific qualifications and instead prefer applicants to take aptitude tests in areas such as teamwork, communication skills or numeracy. You should also expect to be assessed on skills, competencies, knowledge and behaviour that fit in with the values of the civil service. Generally, administrative officers will need at least 5 GCSEs/National 5s (A*–C/A–C), including Maths and English with many applicants having 2 or more A levels/H grades or a degree.

Previous experience of clerical work is helpful.

A Civil Service Fast Stream scheme is open to all graduates, which allows a more focused and rapid career progression from administrative to management level.

To work for the civil service you will need to be a British national, a Commonwealth citizen or a national of the member states within the European Economic Area.

What the work involves

Administrative officers will often be the 'face' of one of over 170 government departments or agencies, dealing with members of the public over the phone, via email, or in person. You may also be charged with reviewing and acting on recent cases, in accordance to the departmental rules and regulations.

You will often work alongside administrative assistants to research relevant information for your department, deal with paperwork (filing, photocopying, etc.), update information on the department's general records and process benefit payments.

Civil service administrative officers will work either for specific national government departments, such as planning or environmental, or within the central administrative, policy and support services. If you work in local government, you are more likely to work across a range of areas such as leisure, environment and public health.

There are also some opportunities in departments such as human resources, neighbourhood renewal, social justice and European and international relations.

Type of person suited to this work

You will need excellent organisational skills as you will be responsible for administering numerous important projects at a time. The ability to use your initiative, prioritise your workload, and work on your own are also essential.

A high level of accuracy and attention to detail is required in order to keep good records and produce clear correspondence.

Since you will be liaising with team members and the public daily, excellent verbal and written communication skills are vital. You will also need to have an understanding of some specialist terminology.

Working conditions

You will mainly be office-based, working normal office hours during the week, though some offices may operate a flexitime policy. Part-time, temporary work and job-sharing opportunities are widely available and you may be based in an office that is open to the public.

Future prospects

The civil service has a well established training programme and a clear promotion structure that is based on merit. You will have several weeks of in-depth training when you start your job and may get the chance to take nationally recognised work-based qualifications such as NVQs in Business and Administration, and Customer Service. You will have access to in-house training and development throughout your career.

Opportunities to progress from administrative assistant to administrative officer, then to executive officer and beyond become available as you gain experience and new qualifications.

Advantages/disadvantages

Public sector work offers good holidays, flexible working hours and excellent perks.

Even without advanced qualifications there are opportunities to progress into higher level jobs.

In the initial stages of employment and training, work can be repetitive.

Money guide

You will often progress to an administrative officer from the position of an administrative assistant who start with an annual salary of £11,000 to £13,000 per year.

Administrative officers can expect to start with a salary of around £14,000 a year, rising to £20,000 with experience.

Typical salaries for middle management roles can range from £22,000 to £40,000.

Graduates on the Civil Service Fast Stream scheme receive a starting salary between £25,000 and £27,000. Increases in pay are based upon performance and if you are promoted, which generally takes about 4–5 years, graduates may earn over £45,000.

Related opportunities

- Personal Assistant p43
- Project Manager p44
- Secretary p51

Further information

Civil Service Fast Stream
www.faststream.civilservice.gov.uk

Local Government Association
www.local.gov.uk

CIVIL SERVICE EXECUTIVE OFFICER

Qualifications and courses

Entrants may be recruited directly at executive level or can work their way up from the administrative grade. Entry requirements vary between the different departments and agencies so you should examine each job description carefully. Some departments require 2 A levels/3 H grades while others do not ask for formal qualifications but prefer to rely on performance in aptitude tests and interviews.

Prospective employees will be invited to attend an interview and may be required to complete a range of tests designed to highlight ability in numeracy, communication, interpersonal, decision-making and analytical skills. You will mainly be assessed on whether your natural values fall in line with those associated with the civil service.

Candidates who hold a 1st or 2nd class Honours degree can apply for the 4-year Civil Service Fast Stream scheme which allows a more focused and rapid career progression from administrative to management level. Applicants from all degree disciplines will be considered although some departments may prefer subjects relevant to their work. Competition for this scheme is fierce and you must pass a series of tests and interviews.

To work for the civil service you will need to be a British national, a Commonwealth citizen or a national of the member states within the European Economic Area.

What the work involves

There are over 170 different civil service departments and agencies you could be placed in, with each offering a different service and following different policies. A civil service executive officer helps to manage these departments in accordance with the government policies they adhere to.

Civil service executive officers will manage a small team of administrative officers and are expected to apply complex governmental policies and procedures to individual cases, enquiries or complaints, managing the expectations of and offering advice to the general public.

You will often have to prepare and present reports on specific projects and communicate regularly with senior managers.

Type of person suited to this work

You should have a neutral interest in governmental affairs, and enjoy providing a service to members of the public. You will need to understand government legislation and be able to explain it clearly to others.

Those wishing to become executive officers should have excellent management, leadership and communication skills, as much of the work requires liaising with your team and different departments.

Much of the information that you will be coming into contact with is of a confidential nature and so you must be appreciative of privacy rules.

Working conditions

Civil servants usually work between 35 and 37 hours a week, Monday to Friday, although hours may increase during busier periods. There are flexitime schemes in place for all government employees, which allow staff to work overtime to gain extra holiday time. The ability to work part-time and job shares are also widely available.

These positions are office based, but it is occasionally necessary for executive officers to visit members of the public or organisations.

Future prospects

The civil service is committed to training and you will learn both on the job from more experienced staff and also from in-house training courses. Your individual training needs will be identified and your skills will be developed.

There is also a clearly defined promotion structure which is based on merit. Executive officers may work their way up through junior to middle management and then on to more senior roles. When an employee joins the civil service through the Fast Stream entry plan, promotion is often awarded after 3–5 years.

If an executive officer has at least 2 years of experience and was not employed through the Fast Stream service, they are eligible to be nominated as an applicant to the In-service Fast Stream system.

Advantages/disadvantages

There are various promotion opportunities on offer, alongside rewarding salaries and the opportunity to help members of the public.

Limited budgets sometimes mean an increased workload when colleagues go on leave or progress to other positions and funds are not available for their replacement.

Money guide

Starting salaries are £21,000–£24,000, depending on which department you work within, rising to around £30,000 with experience.

Those on the Civil Service Fast Stream scheme will commence their career with a salary of £25,000 to £27,000. After 4–5 years' service, candidates should expect a salary of £45,000.

All employees of the civil service receive a variety of benefits, such as a pension scheme and discounts on sports and social facilities.

Related opportunities

- Civil Service Administrative Officer p13
- Diplomatic Services Operational Officer p19
- Project Manager p44
- Quality Manager p45

Further information

Civil Service Fast Stream
www.faststream.civilservice.gov.uk

COMPANY DIRECTOR

Qualifications and courses

There is no set route to becoming a company director but you will usually need experience at senior management level. You could enter the company at any level and then as you gain qualifications and work experience, you can progress up to management roles and eventually become company director. Alternatively, people who set up their own company may be appointed as director at the time their company is registered.

Entrants often have a degree, either in a business related subject or a specialist subject relevant to the company's business area. After completing a degree or Level 3 qualifications, candidates could start on a management trainee scheme.

The Institute of Directors (IoD) and the Chartered Management Institute (CMI) offer courses for the professional development of managers. The CMI offers both apprenticeships and higher level qualifications. The Certificate in Company Direction is one of the many courses available at the IoD.

What the work involves

As company director you will have responsibility for every aspect of your business and your skills as a leader will constantly be in high demand. You will be responsible for setting the company's aims and policies and ensuring that it achieves these as efficiently as possible.

You might own the company or head a board of directors. In a large company you will probably lead a team of managers who specialise in specific areas such as sales, finance or product development but you will have overall responsibility.

Type of person suited to this work

The ability to analyse problems, find solutions, make decisions and think through their long-term effects is vital. You will need excellent communication skills to motivate staff and help sell your ideas, products and services to your customers and investors.

You should be highly motivated and prepared to work long hours. You must be able to prioritise, work to deadlines, supervise others, take advice and respond to change.

An excellent knowledge and understanding of your business and its markets will be necessary to make your company successful.

Although you will probably be advised by a team of experienced and knowledgeable managers, you will make the final decision and must be prepared to take risks and accept consequences.

Working conditions

You will probably be office based but will attend a lot of meetings with customers, financial and legal advisers and staff. You should be prepared to work long hours and to travel in the UK and abroad.

Future prospects

Once you are at manager level, you can take professional courses to develop your skills and become a member of the IoD. IoD members may become qualified as Chartered Directors. There is the opportunity for progression to chief executive and then chair of an organisation. You could also become a part-time non-executive director for other organisations.

If you are successful, there is no limit to what you can achieve.

Advantages/disadvantages

You can get enormous rewards and satisfaction from seeing the company grow and succeed.

You could start your own business based on a personal interest or skill.

You will have huge responsibility and need to be dedicated, hard-working and able to cope with failure as well as success.

Money guide

Earnings will vary enormously depending on the size and success of the business though salaries tend to be higher in London.

Directors can earn anything between £50,000 and £1.5 million a year plus huge bonuses and share options.

Related opportunities

- Accountant p2
- Financial Adviser p26
- Management Consultant p38

Further information

Chartered Management Institute
www.managers.org.uk

Institute of Directors
www.iod.com

COMPLIANCE OFFICER

ENTRY LEVEL 5

Qualifications and courses

While there are no set qualifications for this profession, most employers prefer candidates with a relevant degree and a background in accountancy, auditing or law. Professional qualifications in investments, insurance or banking are also useful. Entry requirements for financial degree programmes vary but are usually a minimum of 2 A levels/3 H grades and 5 GCSEs/National 5s (A*–C/ A–C), including Maths and English.

There are a number of professional bodies that offer relevant qualifications, including the Chartered Insurance Institute's (CII) Award/Certificate/Diploma/Advanced Diploma in Financial Planning and the *ifs* School of Finance's Level 3 Certificate for Financial Advisers or Level 4 Diploma for Financial Advisers. Several compliance qualifications are also available through the International Compliance Association (ICA). These vary from short introductory courses to a BSc degree in Management with Compliance.

The Financial Conduct Authority (FCA) offers 6 graduate programmes. The main Graduate Development programme has an intake of 40 to 50 graduates per year and requires a 2.1 degree in any subject, 120 UCAS points and the unrestricted right to work in the UK.

Many employers offer in-house training programmes. Trainees will work under the supervision of an experienced colleague, whilst gaining qualifications through part-time study or via distance learning.

What the work involves

Compliance officers work for financial services organisations, and are responsible for aiding senior management in ensuring that their firm is complying with the rules set by the FCA.

Alongside this you will investigate complaints from clients that relate to possible breaches of these rules.

You will explore the ways in which business efficiency can be improved within the FCA rules through the monitoring of sales processes, checking of paperwork and telephone recordings.

Type of person suited to this work

You will need to have an enquiring, analytical mind, enjoy analysing information and be interested in the legal aspects of selling financial products.

It is important that you are an easily approachable person with good communication skills and excellent report writing skills.

The job may be quite demanding and so you should be able to work well under pressure and be capable of working on a variety of projects at one time, whilst remaining organised and informed.

Working conditions

Compliance officers are generally office based, with attendance at meetings being a regular occurrence. They might have to travel around the country, or even overseas for an international company.

Generally, a compliance officer will work in the region of 37 hours a week, 9am to 5pm, Monday to Friday. However, changes to FCA policy may mean that extra hours need to be worked in order to implement changes.

Future prospects

Competition for FCA training posts is high, however you will be entering one of the fastest growing areas in financial services. There are around 9,000 compliance officers in the UK and many other positions involved with compliance, which highlights that the future is alive with prospects.

There are financial services companies in almost every town but most jobs are concentrated in the major financial centres, such as London, Manchester, Birmingham, Norwich, Bristol, Edinburgh and Glasgow.

As you progress within this role you will have the opportunity to experience greater levels of responsibility and roles within management.

Advantages/disadvantages

There are chances for progression within this vocation and opportunities to work from home as a consultant.

You may feel under pressure at times and will often be asked to explain changes to the financial system in a clear and concise way.

Money guide

Income varies greatly between roles and operations, and depending on location. Some financial organisations provide a 'large town allowance' for employees whose roles will see them relocating to expensive areas.

Newly trained administrators or junior officers generally earn a starting salary of £15,000 to £20,000 per year. Qualified officers, or those enrolled on a Graduate Development Programme, can expect to earn in the region of £22,000 to £40,000 with the potential for a joining bonus in excess of £2,000 in addition to other bonuses and benefits.

With experience, compliance officers may earn up to £70,000 a year, with directors and heads of compliance earning in excess of £80,000 a year dependent on role.

Related opportunities

- Auditor p8
- Financial Adviser p26
- Risk Manager p50

Further information

ifs University College
www.ifslearning.ac.uk

Association of Professional Compliance Consultants
www.apcc.org.uk

Chartered Insurance Institute
www.cii.co.uk

International Compliance Association
www.int-comp.org

CREDIT ANALYST

Qualifications and courses

Credit analysts will usually have a degree (preferably a 2.1 Honours degree or higher) or HND and enter the profession through a graduate training scheme. Degree courses that include a high level of numerical content are often preferred, such as economics, finance, maths, accounting and statistics.

In order to be accepted onto one of the above degree courses, prospective students will need at least 5 GCSEs/National 5s (A*–C/A–C) and 2 A levels/3 H grades. However, most degree courses will ask for qualifications above this minimum suggestion.

Entry without a degree or HND is possible but generally larger companies will prioritise graduates in their selection process. Professional qualifications in areas such as accountancy will improve career prospects, as can experience in finance or insurance. Professional bodies that offer relevant qualifications include the *ifs* School of Finance, the Chartered Financial Analyst Institute (CFA) and the Chartered Institute of Credit Management (CICM).

Competition for places is fierce as enhanced regulations and the more risk-aware banking sector invest heavily within risk analysis. Therefore pre-entry commercial experience and a relevant postgraduate qualification, such as an MSc in Risk Management, may improve chances of employment.

Once in employment, credit analysts are expected to take part in continuing professional development (CPD), which will involve reading relevant journals and undertaking skills-related courses.

What the work involves

Credit analysts deal with both personal and business credit. They assess the individual circumstances of the application, using statistical and accounting criteria in order to decide the extent of the risk involved when lending.

Much of the work involves administration and figure work, due to a need for the analysis of given data and the writing of reports and presentations.

To thoroughly assess an application, an analyst must have an understanding of legal, compliance and business issues. For instance, a business application would be considered against economic growth and the country's financial stability.

Type of person suited to this work

You should have an interest in the financial sector and have a general and varied knowledge of the business world. Much of the work deals with statistics and so analysts need computer skills and the ability to work with spreadsheets and specialist statistical software packages.

You need to have good organisational and both verbal and written communication skills so that you can explain concepts to non-specialists.

Working conditions

Daily working hours are 9am–5pm, Monday to Friday. There may be times when you will be required to work extra hours. However, there are also opportunities for part-time working.

Generally, credit analysts are based in offices, with much of their work involving computer-based activities and the monitoring of the financial markets, with the occasional need to present changes in the market to senior staff.

Future prospects

This profession holds many avenues for promotion or progression into other areas of banking. Prospects may be improved by professional qualifications. Many of the larger commercial and investment banks have graduate or career training programmes. There may also be the option to undertake higher-level qualifications such as a master's degree.

Most opportunities are available in London, West Yorkshire, Cardiff and Scottish cities.

Advantages/disadvantages

There are many opportunities for promotion and progression within this career.

Salaries tend to be very rewarding.

Credit analysts must be able to handle high levels of pressure and responsibility as they often have to make difficult decisions about awarding or denying credit.

Money guide

Credit analysts usually receive a starting salary of £22,000 to £25,000 a year.

Average salary rises to £35,000 with experience and can increase to £60,000 per year.

Income varies by location, and the highest paid roles are generally located in London and the south-east of England.

A senior analyst or risk manager for a major corporation may earn up to £90,000.

Additional benefits could include monetary bonuses, subsidised mortgages, pensions and private healthcare.

Related opportunities

- Bank Manager p10
- Economist p20
- Insurance Broker p29

Further information

ifs **University College**
www.ifslearning.ac.uk

Chartered Financial Analyst Institute
www.cfainstitute.org

Financial Skills Partnership
www.financialskillspartnership.org.uk

DEBT COLLECTOR

Qualifications and courses

This role does not require specific qualifications as debt collectors normally train on the job. However, employers may look for GCSEs/National 5s (A*–C/A–C) in English and Maths.

Though it is not essential in this line of work, a degree with an element of credit management, such as business studies or finance, could be useful if you want to progress to management roles. For degree entry you will need at least 2 A levels/3 H grades and 5 GCSEs/National 5s (A*–C/A–C) or equivalent.

Prospective debt collectors could take credit management training courses to enhance their employability. The Chartered Institute of Credit Management (CICM) offers courses on debt collection, negotiation, the psychology of a debtor and legal actions as well as a Level 5 Diploma in Credit Management with potential for progression onto the final year of a BA degree. CILEx offers a Level 4 Diploma in Debt Recovery and Insolvency and the Credit Services Association (CSA) offers Awards/Certificates/Diplomas in Debt Collection. These courses include information on how to deal with abusive debtors and telephone collection techniques, and may offer exemptions from certain elements of study for students with good GCSEs/National 5s in Maths, English and IT.

What the work involves

Debt collectors are employed to recover assets for the organisation that is owed the money. The debtor is firstly contacted by letter or telephone, they then receive a personal visit should this not work, and are finally contacted by a solicitor if the matter remains unresolved.

The 5 areas of specialism include consumer debt collection, commercial debt collection, international collection, legal collection and debtor tracing.

Specific activities include helping debtors by arranging payment through instalments and becoming involved with debt collections that have entered the legal system.

Type of person suited to this work

The job of a debt collector can often be challenging and sometimes confrontational, so a person entering this profession needs to be resilient, determined and skilled in all forms of communication. Empathy with the debtor's situation is required at times and is often just as important as assertiveness and the ability to negotiate a suitable solution for both parties.

Debt collectors require commercial awareness and an understanding of consumer and credit law, should they be involved in legal collections. Knowledge of the financial and credit industries, and numeracy and IT skills, will also be of benefit.

Working conditions

Commercial debt collectors work from 9am to 5pm, Monday to Friday. It may sometimes be necessary to work extra hours, in this case in order to meet monthly collection targets.

In comparison, consumer debt collectors may work from 8am to 9pm, Monday to Saturday. However, these hours are usually part of a flexible shift system.

Most debt collectors will be office based and work in teams; in comparison field agents are often based at home and are self-employed, often visiting debtors' homes or places of work. For this reason, a driving licence will be useful.

Future prospects

You will be entering an ever-expanding profession that employs around 10,000 people, with employment opportunities existing throughout the UK.

Due to the UK being a capitalist, consumer society, overdue debt is a constant problem, with this allowing for good opportunities in the future of debt collecting.

Advantages/disadvantages

The job can often be confrontational and challenging, with consumer debt collectors sometimes working unsociable hours.

You may be working with clients who are quite emotional or aggressive which could create an uncomfortable working environment on occasion.

However, the salary is often rewarding and helping debtors arrange more manageable repayments can often be gratifying.

Money guide

The average starting wage for a debt collector is about £14,000 a year.

On advancing to a supervisory role, salaries can see increase to up to £27,000.

If debt collectors become self-employed and establish a successful business, they can earn in excess of £35,000 a year.

Debt collectors employed by a company can receive target-related bonuses or commission on top of basic salaries.

Related opportunities

- Bailiff/Enforcement Agent p342
- Debt Counsellor/Money Advice Caseworker p562
- Financial Adviser p26

Further information

Chartered Institute of Credit Management
www.cicm.com

Credit Management Training Ltd
www.cmtltd.co.uk

Credit Services Association
www.csa-uk.com

DIPLOMATIC SERVICES OPERATIONAL OFFICER

ENTRY LEVEL 6

Qualifications and courses

Operational posts within the Foreign and Commonwealth Office (FCO) are available to those with a minimum of a 2.2 Honours degree and candidates from all degree disciplines are considered. Entry onto a degree course usually requires a minimum of 2 A levels/3 H grades and 5 GCSEs/National 5s (A*–C/A–C). Entry with an HND only is not possible. Many entrants have a pre-entry postgraduate qualification, although this is not essential.

All applicants into the Diplomatic Services must be British citizens and meet the FCO's residency requirements. You must be prepared to be placed anywhere in the world, pass a medical, and a security vetting process which could take up to 9 months.

One way to enter the FCO is through the graduate Civil Service Fast Stream scheme as a Policy Entrant. The application process has various stages which involve aptitude tests, assessment centres and interviews and opens for applications in mid-September. Applicants to the scheme require an achieved or predicted minimum of a 2.2 Honours degree in any subject. Competition for places on the scheme is tough so it is worth being persistent and applying again if you are unsuccessful. Previous applications will not be taken into account.

For the European Fast Stream, which will prepare you to work for the EU, you will also need French or German at A level/H grade (A–C). If you want to apply for a diplomatic placement within the Government Economic Service (GES), you must have a minimum of a 2.1 Honours degree in an economics-based subject.

What the work involves

Candidates on the Civil Service Fast Stream for Diplomatic Service will spend their first 2 years working at the Foreign and Commonwealth Office in the UK. The role involves delivering policy and delivering services. You could spend your time dealing with security issues, working to improve human rights abroad or assisting British citizens who are overseas.

Candidates will then work abroad, in one of the 200+ British embassies, for a 3–4 year posting. You will promote British interests overseas, providing advice and support to ministers developing UK foreign policy in many areas including politics and commerce.

For school leavers interested in joining the FCO, there are opportunities to work as an administrative assistant (providing clerical support) or an executive assistant (drafting letters, handling accounts and invoices, and providing clerical support).

Type of person suited to this work

An interest in foreign policy and international issues is essential, as is a willingness to work abroad.

You will need to have excellent organisational and communication skills and be able to prioritise conflicting tasks and deadlines.

You will need to be highly literate and numeracy is important for posts where you will be handling accounts. Strong customer service and IT skills are also essential.

It would be an advantage to speak another language or have the ability to learn new languages.

Working conditions

You work in the UK for the first few years of your career and then have the opportunity to work in various different countries. Most new entrants will be based in the FCO's London office, though there are some positions in Milton Keynes.

Approximately two-thirds of your career will be spent abroad and overseas postings will often last 3–4 years.

You would generally work normal office hours (9am–5pm, Monday to Friday) but if you are working overseas these may vary according to the culture of the country.

Future prospects

Promotions are based on performance. Working in the Fast Stream Programme, you could reach senior management in as little as 4–5 years.

The British government is currently encouraging and promoting career opportunities for British citizens at European level.

Advantages/disadvantages

The government provides good benefit schemes and officers receive a range of allowances such as rent-free accommodation and travel expenses when posted abroad.

The regular hours in the UK allow for a good work–life balance.

You will have the opportunity to live in many different countries and cultures, although frequent relocation could be disruptive to family life.

Money guide

Administrative officers will start on £19,437 a year whereas an operational officer's starting salary will be around £22,000 per year.

Policy officers and graduates recruited from the Civil Service Fast Stream receive a starting salary of £25,000 to £27,000.

Salaries are often performance-related.

Related opportunities

- Civil Service Administrative Officer p13
- Civil Service Executive Officer p14
- Politician p358

Further information

Civil Service Fast Stream
www.faststream.civilservice.gov.uk

Foreign and Commonwealth Office
www.fco.gov.uk

ECONOMIST

Qualifications and courses

Candidates with a Foundation degree or HND only will not be able to enter this profession as a 2.1 Honours degree or higher, preferably in economics, is essential. A joint Honours degree in economics and another related subject, such as finance or maths, is also often acceptable, however you should ensure that the majority of your modules are in economics and that you study both microeconomics and macroeconomics. Many employers are also increasingly requiring candidates to hold a postgraduate economics qualification. A good Honours degree in a subject other than economics may be accepted if it is followed by a postgraduate economics degree.

Entry onto a degree course usually requires at least 2 A levels/3 H grades, including Maths and preferably Economics, and 5 GCSEs/National 5s (A*–C/A–C), including Maths and English. For entry onto a postgraduate degree you will need a 2.1 Honours degree.

If you meet the above criteria and have less than 3 years' professional experience, you can apply to the Government Economic Service's Fast Stream Economist programme. This is designed to develop your economic, managerial and communications skills to prepare you for early promotion to more senior jobs.

On top of academic achievement, knowledge of a foreign language may aid employment prospects (particularly for candidates who wish to work on secondment), as would relevant work experience. The Government Economic Service and the Bank of England offer work experience placements, internships, sandwich placements, gap year placements and vacation work placements for students and graduates.

What the work involves

Economists play a vital role in a country's financial stability, using their specialist knowledge to advise government and financial institutions and major businesses to help develop financial policy and strategy.

Economists research and analyse a variety of mathematical modelling techniques and data, with the information received being used to identify and predict economic changes. The work is diverse as research projects can cover a wide range of subjects – from the economic impact of major national events, to analysing company performance for fund managers and investors.

Many economists work alone, although much of their work will be through consultation with statisticians, civil servants and marketers.

Type of person suited to this work

Strong economic, business and financial understanding is essential as you will be required to analyse and apply economic theory to a variety of subjects. The work of an economist takes into account many factors and so it is also necessary for you to have an awareness of current affairs, politics and social welfare.

Much of the job centres on the research, analysis and prediction of market trends, so a good eye for detail and methodical nature is essential. Economists must be able to communicate their understanding of a situation in a clear and concise way as you will often be explaining complex economic procedure to non-economists.

Working conditions

Economists tend to work regular office hours, 9am–5.30pm, Monday to Friday. However, some related sectors could require extended hours due to the work topic being unpredictable. For those that work in the civil service and similar sectors, flexibility may be allowed in relation to hours worked, with part-time work and job sharing being an option.

Economists are mostly office based, with the occasional need to travel to meet clients or to be present at conferences and seminars, to which they may need to contribute.

Future prospects

This profession holds many exciting opportunities, such as the chance to progress to an economic adviser after 3–4 years, based on your ability and drive. Many economists choose to become self-employed or to work abroad with multinational companies after gaining experience and establishing a reputation.

Advantages/disadvantages

This job offers fantastic career prospects, with there being opportunities for progression in a short amount of time once training has been completed.

The salary is highly competitive, when compared with other professions, and the working hours are relatively average.

Tight deadlines, political pressure and the need to juggle different projects can make the job a demanding one.

Money guide

Economists will usually have a starting salary of £25,000–£35,000, rising to in excess of £40,000 with a few years' experience.

Those at senior level, with 10–15 years' experience, can achieve earnings of £50,000–£80,000 with earnings for the top economists in finance and consulting reaching up to £250,000.

Salaries vary greatly, with economists working in banking, consulting, industry and financial services sectors, and those working in London usually earning more.

Related opportunities

- Accountant p2
- Actuary p5
- Mathematician/Mathematics Research Scientist p515

Further information

Bank of England
www.bankofengland.co.uk

Government Economic Service
www.ges.gov.uk

Royal Economic Society
www.res.org.uk

EDUCATION OFFICER

Qualifications and courses

In the role of an education officer you should be educated to degree or HND level. The normal minimum entry requirements for degrees are 2 A levels/3 H grades and 5 GCSEs/National 5s (A*–C/A–C), and for Foundation degrees or HNC/Ds, 1 A level/2 H grades and 3 GCSEs/National 5s (A*–C/A–C).

Though applicants may apply for an education officer position with any degree subject, it would be advantageous to have a degree relevant to the area you are applying to. For example, to work as an education officer in a museum or gallery, useful degree/ HND subjects would include history, archaeology, anthropology, museum studies, cultural studies, history of art and education. For an environmental education officer position a degree/HND in a biological or environmental science, such as ecology, conservation or zoology, would be beneficial.

Qualifications and/or experience in teaching or community education, such as a PGCE or master's degree in education or education management, are useful and may be required. Relevant work experience is essential in order to secure a paid position.

Entry without a degree is possible but only if you have extensive voluntary experience. However, these positions are becoming increasingly difficult to find and career progression may be limited as graduate candidates would take precedence for higher-level roles.

What the work involves

Education officers will prepare educational materials and resources to highlight and raise awareness for a particular issue or promote a certain gallery, museum or organisation. It will be your responsibility to increase public awareness about new exhibitions and/or events, and to update the educational sections of your website.

You will be responsible for teaching a wide range of age groups and liaising with communities and companies on a variety of topics. You will construct and be expected to run educational campaigns, talks, workshops and activities in line with the ethos of your organisation.

Additionally, it will be your responsibility to collect and review public feedback on the initiatives that you organise and promote, using this information to ensure that the work that you do and the educational activities that you provide remain fresh, exciting and insightful.

Type of person suited to this work

You will need self-confidence and an ability to talk to people in a way that will interest and excite them. You must be bright, interesting, humorous, have lots of patience and a willingness to listen.

You will always be busy, so you will need good organisational skills, as well as excellent written and verbal communication skills. An understanding of IT and confidence in handling budgets will also be useful.

Working conditions

Your time will be spent in an office, lecture room or working within the community where you will represent your organisation. You might be expected to wear a uniform or protective clothing.

Depending on your organisation you might spend some of your time outdoors in all weathers, for example at a zoo or community farm. You might do some evening work, especially if you work with community groups.

Future prospects

Entry to this profession is very competitive and in the early stages of your career you are likely to discover that relevant voluntary or unpaid work experience will be very valuable to employers. Nevertheless, there is a steady increase in the number of educational jobs available in organisations.

Alongside traditional exhibits, learning through demonstrations, videos, talks and other presentations is being introduced by education officers as interactive experiences increase in popularity.

Advantages/disadvantages

This profession offers an opportunity to be involved in teaching without being in the classroom as well as learning effective marketing and events organisation.

You will help make a visit to your workplace a more memorable experience for everyone and create a positive public profile.

You will be juggling lots of different tasks at once which could be overwhelming.

Money guide

Starting salaries typically range from £17,000 to £20,000.

For senior level posts where officers have approximately 10 years' experience, salaries will rise to between £31,000 and £45,000.

For management positions within private organisations where you are responsible for developing policy and a multidisciplinary team, salaries can reach up to £50,000.

Related opportunities

- Arts Administrator/Manager p329
- Environmental Health Practitioner/Officer p22
- Learning Mentor p187
- Museum/Art Gallery Curator p337

Further information

GEM
www.gem.org.uk

Museums Association
www.museumsassociation.org

ENVIRONMENTAL HEALTH PRACTITIONER/OFFICER

Qualifications and courses

To become an environmental health practitioner you will need a BSc or MSc in Environmental Health, accredited by either the Chartered Institute of Environmental Health (CIEH) or the Royal Environmental Health Institute of Scotland (REHIS).

Entry to an undergraduate degree normally requires 2 A levels/3 H grades and 5 GCSEs/National 5s (A*–C/A–C) including English, Maths and a science. Appropriate GNVQ, BTEC or Foundation degrees may also be acceptable. Graduates who do not have an accredited undergraduate degree but one related to environmental health, such as a science, are able to enter an accredited MSc programme providing they have at least a 2nd class Honours degree.

After academic study, candidates need to complete a 9–12 month practical training course with the CIEH/REHIS. In England and Wales, this can be incorporated into an undergraduate degree through a sandwich year or completed after graduation. Candidates receive a Certificate of Registration from the Environmental Health Registration Board when they successfully complete the training requirements and professional exams.

In Scotland, the REHIS scheme consists of a 48-week placement with a local authority. Training may be undertaken during university holidays or after graduation. Successful completion of all the training requirements and professional exams leads to the REHIS Diploma in Environmental Health.

If you do not have a relevant degree, an alternative route to become an environmental health practitioner is to start work as an environmental health technician, study part time for a degree in Environmental Health and work your way up. For this you will need 5 GCSEs/National 5s (A*–C/A–C), or previous experience and qualifications in related work, such as health and safety.

A full UK driving licence is usually required for most positions.

What the work involves

Some environmental health practitioners are responsible for all aspects of environmental health in their local areas, while others specialise in either food safety, housing conditions, workplace health and safety, or environmental conditions.

Your tasks might include developing public health policies, carrying out inspections in premises such as restaurants and workplaces to identify any hazards and ensure that relevant laws are being followed and educating and advising the public and businesses.

You will also carry out investigations of accidents or outbreaks and contaminations.

Type of person suited to this work

You must be interested in finding ways of improving public health, and will need a scientific and logical approach to collect and assess evidence and use it to identify and solve problems. Excellent written and verbal communication skills are vital for explaining regulations clearly and simply to a wide range of people.

You have to be able to handle challenging situations, for example when confronting noisy neighbours. You must be able to enforce the law when necessary.

You need to be comfortable working both alone and as part of a team.

Working conditions

You will be office based, but spend a lot of time visiting homes and businesses in your local area. Some of the places you visit will be smelly, dirty or potentially dangerous and you will sometimes have to wear protective clothing.

You will probably work a normal working week Monday–Friday, but you will occasionally have to work evenings and at weekends.

Future prospects

After 5 years of professional experience you can apply to the CIEH for Chartered Environmental Health Practitioner status. In Scotland you can apply to the REHIS for Chartered Environmental Health Officer status with 3 years' professional experience, provided all continuing professional development (CPD) requirements are met.

In the public sector, with experience, you could progress to higher levels such as senior, principal or chief environmental officer. There are also promotion opportunities in the private sector. Self-employment and working abroad are also options.

Advantages/disadvantages

It can be challenging dealing with people who are angry or distressed, for example when enforcing regulations.

You will have the satisfaction of protecting the health and safety of people and improving their quality of life.

You may have to face some distressing sights.

Money guide

Starting salaries range from £25,000 to £35,000.

With experience, senior level salaries increase to £38,000–£60,000.

Environmental health practitioners working for private companies typically earn more than employees in the public sector.

Related opportunities

- Health and Safety Adviser p27
- Health Promotion/Education Specialist p288
- Trading Standards Officer p484

Further information

Chartered Institute of Environmental Health
www.cieh.org

Royal Environmental Health Institute of Scotland
www.rehis.com

EQUALITY AND DIVERSITY OFFICER

ENTRY LEVEL 5

Qualifications and courses

Most people enter this profession with a degree, HNC/HND or equivalent. While graduates in any subject can work in this field, degrees and HNCs/HNDs in education, law, business/management and human resources are useful.

Experience working in law, human resources, social work or teaching is very beneficial. Relevant experience can also be gained by getting involved in equality and diversity committees and societies at university, doing voluntary work or work shadowing. Many equal opportunities advisers are members of the Chartered Institute of Personnel and Development (CIPD). To work as an equality and diversity officer in schools you may have to train as a teacher first.

Relevant postgraduate courses include race relations or disability studies. These qualifications can be beneficial in acquiring a senior level position and for people whose first degree was not in a subject related to the field. There are part-time and full-time postgraduate courses in equality and diversity available at selected universities.

The CIPD offers short courses for further study, such as Discrimination and the Law and Managing Diversity.

What the work involves

Your role is to ensure that businesses and public organisations do not discriminate on the basis of disability, race, gender, sexuality, age or religion. You will make sure that services such as education and health are accessible to everyone.

Working for organisations such as civil service departments and agencies, local authorities, universities and educational institutions, unions and large businesses, you will promote positive images of all groups and promote diversity in all company literature.

You will advise on how to attract job applicants from all sections of the local community and ensure the company is following all the relevant legislation.

Type of person suited to this work

You should be committed to working for change, be persuasive and good at negotiating. At the same time you need to be a good listener, be sensitive and diplomatic in the way you deal with people and situations.

You will need excellent communication skills and should be confident in giving presentations, advising management and delivering training.

You will need to be able to understand all the relevant equal opportunities laws and regulations and be able to apply them to all policies and procedures within the company, offering advice on any new developments and how to implement them. For some jobs you might need specialist skills such as being able to speak another language.

Working conditions

Much of your time will be office based, working normal office hours. However, you will probably do quite a bit of evening and weekend work too, organising special events and working with community groups.

You may visit other businesses and organisations, so a driving licence may be useful.

Future prospects

Opportunities vary from employer to employer. Government departments, local authorities, universities, trade unions and large companies employ specialist equal opportunities advisers, and there may be more scope to develop your career within these types of companies by moving into management roles. In smaller companies the work is covered by the human resources department and you may need to move company to gain a promotion.

Employers will usually provide on-the-job training and you may be encouraged to work towards a relevant qualification such as a postgraduate degree or professional CIPD qualifications.

With significant experience you could work for yourself, offering a consultancy service to companies to ensure they are working within equal opportunities legislation. Some will go on to specialise in one particular area, such as disability, while others will continue to work across a range of areas.

Advantages/disadvantages

You will be working for a cause you feel passionately about and could be making a real difference to people.

The work can be stressful – you will be dealing with sensitive issues and may be working with people who do not share your beliefs or who have no desire to change.

Money guide

Starting salaries are between £18,000 and £28,000 per year.

With experience you can expect to earn between £25,000 and £50,000 per year.

Those in managerial roles within large companies can earn in excess of £50,000, with better salary potential if working for an employer in London.

Related opportunities

- Human Resources/Personnel Officer p28
- Training and Development Officer p56
- Welfare Benefits Adviser/Welfare Rights Caseworker p578

Further information

Equality & Human Rights Commission
www.equalityhumanrights.com

Equality Commission for Northern Ireland
www.equalityni.org

ERGONOMIST

Qualifications and courses

Entry to this profession requires an undergraduate degree in either Ergonomics or Human Factors that has been accredited by the Chartered Institute of Ergonomics & Human Factors (CIEHF) or a degree in a related subject, such as biology, engineering, design, medicine or psychology, followed by an accredited postgraduate course in Ergonomics. For entry onto an undergraduate degree programme in Ergonomics you will need at least 3 A levels/4 H grades, with useful subjects including maths, physics, biology and psychology.

Graduates of degree courses accredited by the CIEHF are then able to join the Institute as Graduate Members. This is a useful way to make professional contacts within the industry.

Entry onto degree courses and into the industry is very competitive, so an excellent academic record as well as recent, relevant work experience, paid or voluntary, is highly recommended. A relevant postgraduate qualification could help your employment prospects, even if you have a CIEHF-accredited undergraduate degree.

It is possible to begin a career in ergonomics with an HND in a relevant subject, providing you have 4 years' experience and can demonstrate significant knowledge in the key ergonomics areas, such as physiology or psychology. You will probably have to take a relevant course to support any job applications but this may not necessarily be a degree-level qualification.

The CIEHF encourages students and newly qualified ergonomists to take part in their Opening Doors work experience scheme. Many other organisations across the UK also offer schemes that are helpful to those entering the profession.

What the work involves

An ergonomist creates designs that aid society, such as a comfortable chair or a social environment that accounts for the disabled and the elderly.

People within this profession aim to improve the health, safety and efficiency of different equipment and systems.

Designs are informed by biomechanics, physiology, psychology, engineering, industrial design and IT. Ergonomists consult with other professionals including design/production engineers, health and safety practitioners, computer specialists and industrial physicians.

Type of person suited to this work

An interest in the human body and mind, and the ways in which designs can aid quality of life, is an important part of this profession. Ergonomists must be analytical, observant and able to conduct detailed research into the needs of society.

As the role involves creating high-quality designs and solutions, entrants need to have problem-solving skills, attention to detail and persistence.

Interaction with clients is frequent so good communication and negotiation skills are a must.

Working conditions

Those within the profession usually work normal office hours, 9am–5pm, Monday to Friday. However, overtime or weekend work may be required depending on the project and deadline.

Working environments are variable and involve a combination of office, laboratory and field work.

Ergonomists are often required to travel within the working day, with occasional overnight stays and trips abroad.

Future prospects

Developing a specific area of interest early in your career can be useful and can lead to opportunities within specialist consultancies.

Self-employment as a consultant is a common option for ergonomists and it is also possible to move into a research role with universities or organisations.

Those keen to progress within the industry are more likely to gain promotion by changing employer and so a willingness to be geographically mobile is helpful.

Advantages/disadvantages

Ergonomics is a fairly small professional community so there are opportunities to become actively involved with industry bodies and network with your colleagues.

As the technology and industry are constantly changing, ergonomists must be willing to continue learning and training throughout their careers.

The work can be stressful as you are required to meet the varying demands and deadlines of your clients.

Money guide

Graduates entering the profession can expect to earn between £20,000 and £25,000 a year.

After about 5 years' experience, ergonomists have an average salary of £25,000 to £40,000.

If you reach a senior level within the field, you can achieve a salary in excess of £60,000.

Salaries vary with the size of the company, geographical location and terms of employment.

Related opportunities

- Consumer Scientist p500
- Health and Safety Adviser p27
- Product Designer p173

Further information

Chartered Institute of Ergonomics & Human Factors
www.ergonomics.org.uk

Loughborough University
www.lboro.ac.uk

ESTATES OFFICER

Qualifications and courses

There are no set minimum entry requirements but it is still a good idea to get at least 5 GCSEs/National 5s (A*–C/A–C) and 2 A levels/H grades and an increasing number of applicants hold a relevant degree or HNC/HND qualification, often in surveying or a related subject.

You can work towards professional qualifications through the Royal Institution of Chartered Surveyors (RICS) or the Institute of Revenues, Rating and Valuation (IRRV). If you work in construction or estate management you can study remotely through the College of Estate Management.

There is also an Advanced Apprenticeship in Surveying that you can do.

Alternatively, another route in would be as a surveying technician. This would require an HND/HNC qualification, for which you will need a minimum of 1 A level/2 H grades or a BTEC National Diploma/Certificate plus 4 GCSEs/National 5s (A*–C/A–C).

What the work involves

Estates officers manage, refurbish and uphold land and property that belongs to private landlords, local authorities and organisations involved in land and property owning.

Specific activities include the management of an organisation's property portfolio, such as ensuring the amount of rent being paid is sufficient, dealing with tenancy agreements/applications, checking that properties are not being maltreated, and organising any necessary building repair or environmental work.

Letting, acquisitions and management are areas of specialism.

Type of person suited to this work

This job is suitable for someone who is able to communicate well in order to co-ordinate the work of colleagues, and has good negotiating skills when discussing tenancy agreements and the terms of a contract.

Organisation is of importance when overseeing a portfolio of properties for a client, with an appreciation for detail being paramount when examining a property, proposed legal documents or finances.

It is often necessary to be analytical when dealing with written and numerical information and the ability to write clear and concise reports and presentations is an important requirement of the job.

Working conditions

Working hours tend to be 9am–5pm, Monday to Friday.

As with many jobs, extra hours may need to be worked in order to attend committees or meet deadlines, although there are also opportunities for flexitime, job sharing and part-time work.

This job is mostly office based, although site visits to portfolio buildings may involve being outside in all weathers, a lot of walking, and the climbing of ladders.

Future prospects

Self-employment or employment with a commercial business may be the most sustainable career path for estate officers, due to local authorities privately contracting work to outside companies.

Health authorities, civil service departments, university estates departments, charities and the Office of Government Commerce also provide work opportunities.

Opportunity for promotion is more likely in larger estates businesses and departments, with progression leading to appointment as the head of a unit, a specialist area, or department.

Advantages/disadvantages

This position holds a fair amount of responsibility, with the use of leadership qualities and organisational skills on a regular basis increasing the chances of promotion.

Although mostly office based, estate officers often have to make visits to buildings within their remit, which may mean having to work outside in all types of weather.

Money guide

A junior estates officer can expect to earn £21,000 to £25,000 per year.

Through gaining experience and further qualifications, this amount may rise to £27,000–£35,000 per year.

For senior level posts, salaries can reach up to £50,000.

Salary can vary widely depending on qualification and responsibilities.

Related opportunities

- Chartered Surveyor p70
- Facilities Manager p85
- Health Service Manager p290

Further information

Chartered Institute of Housing
www.cih.org

Institute of Revenues Rating and Valuation
www.irrv.net

Royal Institution of Chartered Surveyors
www.rics.org

University College of Estate Management
www.ucem.ac.uk

FINANCIAL ADVISER

Qualifications and courses

There are no specific entry routes and qualification requirements depend on the employer, although it is common for employers to request a minimum of 2 A levels/3 H grades and 5 GCSEs/National 5s (A*–C/A–C), including English and Maths. In some cases, employers consider a background in customer or financial services and proven communication skills to be more important than formal academic qualifications but it is worth checking this with employers directly.

This area of work is open to graduates of all disciplines but graduates in finance, business management and accountancy may be at an advantage. Other useful qualifications include the Level 3 BTEC National Award in Personal and Business Finance, the Level 3 BTEC National Award in Business and the Level 3 BTEC Award in Providing Financial Advice. A pre-entry postgraduate qualification is not needed.

Whatever your academic background, to become a financial adviser you will be required to take one of a number of professional diplomas: the Diploma in Regulated Financial Planning from the Chartered Insurance Institute (CII), the Diploma in Investment Planning from the Chartered Banker Institute, the Level 4 Diploma for Financial Advisers from the *ifs* School of Finance, the Investment Advice Diploma from the Chartered Institute for Securities and Investment (CISI) or the SQA/RQF Level 4 Diploma in Professional Financial Advice.

Prior experience through part-time or vacation work could be helpful and apprenticeships in Providing Financial Services are available.

Some banks, building societies and financial advice firms have graduate training schemes and trainees will usually begin as tied advisers.

What the work involves

Financial advisers offer client consultations on a wide range of financial issues including mortgages, pensions and investments.

You will also be producing reports and annual summaries for clients to keep them up to date with their financial situation.

Tied advisers work for a financial institution, like a bank, advising clients on their services. Independent advisers sell products and services offered by a range of companies.

Type of person suited to this work

Good communications skills are essential in order to explain complex financial matters simply to your clients. You will need to enjoy working with numbers, and have the ability to analyse and understand technical financial information.

You should be honest and reliable. This will allow you to gain the trust of your clients and subsequently sell your products. You must be self-motivated and organised with good IT skills.

You will also need an understanding of the relevant financial laws and to keep up with changes in the industry.

Working conditions

You will usually work standard office hours but you should be prepared to work longer hours at busy times.

Tied advisers usually work some Saturdays. Independent advisers may have to work evenings and weekends to suit their clients.

You will be expected to dress formally, and to visit clients in their homes or offices so a driving licence would be useful. Jobs are available throughout the UK, but the majority are based within London and the south-east of England.

Future prospects

The demand for financial advisers is growing as people increasingly take charge of their own pensions and finances.

Financial advisers work in insurance companies, banks and other businesses, and there is also the option of being self-employed.

Promotion prospects are good, and there are opportunities to take additional qualifications and move into management jobs. You could also specialise in a particular area, perhaps training others or marketing products.

Advantages/disadvantages

Pay and prospects are good; you can specialise in specific financial areas, such as savings or pensions, or become self-employed.

The job comes with a high level of responsibility, and you will be under pressure to sell products and meet targets.

Money guide

Entry salaries at trainee adviser level vary from £22,000 to £30,000.

A typical salary for a qualified adviser is £30,000 to £45,000.

Senior level financial advisers can earn £60,000 to £70,000.

Bonuses or commission on mortgage or insurance products may also be offered and these can be uncapped.

Related opportunities

- Bank Manager p10
- Business Adviser p11
- Stockbroker p53

Further information

ifs University College
www.ifslearning.ac.uk

Chartered Banker Institute
www.charteredbanker.com

Chartered Insurance Institute
www.cii.co.uk

Financial Skills Partnership
www.financialskillspartnership.org.uk

Qualifications and courses

To enter this career you will need an industry-recognised professional qualification. These include a City & Guilds Level 3 NVQ in Occupational Health and Safety or a relevant course from either the National Examination Board in Occupational Safety and Health (NEBOSH) or British Safety Council. You can study either full time before looking for work or part time while gaining experience in a related field.

There is an increasing number of entrants who now have an undergraduate degree or HND. Though the subject is not specified by the industry, graduates in health studies, occupational safety, engineering or life science would be at an advantage. Entry to a degree is usually with 2 A levels/3 H grades and 5 GCSEs/National 5s (A*–C/A–C), or equivalent, and for an HND 1 A level/2 H grades and 3 GCSEs/National 5s are often required. There are also industry-related Postgraduate Diplomas and Master of Science courses available.

Experience of working at an operational level within risk assessment, construction, engineering, manufacturing or scientific work can be very valuable when applying for jobs in health and safety. Knowledge of computer applications for preparing and analysing statistics is also desirable, as is physical fitness.

What the work involves

You will help maintain a safe workplace by developing and implementing health and safety policies and procedures.

You will inspect premises and ways of working, according to your industry knowledge of health and safety legislation, ensuring all relevant regulations are followed correctly. You will be committed to maintaining a working knowledge of all Health and Safety Executive (HSE) legislation and review company policy accordingly.

The work involves investigating and reporting on accidents and giving specialist advice and training to staff on health and safety issues, such as fire regulations and dealing with dangerous chemicals. You may also be involved in carrying out risk assessments for companies, ensuring safe installation of new equipment and developing internal policies related to promoting workplace health and safety.

Type of person suited to this work

You must be investigative, diplomatic and able to visualise the big picture of how a company works and how it can improve.

You will need to understand technical and operational processes and be able to explain your findings and recommendations in a clear and straightforward way.

You should be thorough, methodical and able to understand and apply relevant regulations. You will also need good IT and administrative skills and need to be reasonably fit for working safely on large outdoor and industrial sites.

Working conditions

You will be office based but depending on where you work, may have to spend a lot of time visiting factories and building sites. This could mean having to wear protective clothing, working outdoors in all weathers and at heights or in hot, noisy conditions.

You will work normal office hours but may need to be on-call at other times in case of emergencies.

Future prospects

The government and European Union are producing more regulations to help companies ensure a safe working environment for staff. This means that opportunities are increasing as employers need help implementing and monitoring new legislation.

Additionally, you may be expected to engage in continuing professional development (CPD) and often be required to work towards new qualifications and accreditations, such as Chartered Membership of the Institute of Occupational Safety and Health (CMIOSH).

Many health and safety advisers work in engineering, construction and manufacturing; there are also opportunities to specialise or do consultancy work.

Advantages/disadvantages

The work can be varied and you will be instrumental in helping to save people's lives.

You will be dealing with important issues that affect people's safety and wellbeing, so there is a lot of responsibility.

The conditions you have to work in will sometimes be dangerous, dirty and noisy. You may also have to work in extreme weather.

Money guide

Those entering this occupation can earn a starting salary of £22,000 to £35,000 per year.

After several years' experience, salaries can increase to £50,000 per year or more whilst senior managers can earn in excess of £200,000.

Levels do vary according to sector. However, generally graduates and those with a postgraduate degree often earn more than non-graduates.

Benefits may include bonuses, a company car and medical insurance.

Related opportunities

- Human Resources/Personnel Officer p28
- Road Safety Officer p608
- Trading Standards Officer p484

Further information

British Safety Council
www.britsafe.org

Health and Safety Executive
www.hse.gov.uk

Institute of Occupational Safety and Health
www.iosh.co.uk

National Examination Board in Occupational Safety and Health
www.nebosh.org.uk

HUMAN RESOURCES/ PERSONNEL OFFICER

Qualifications and courses

Whilst there are no formal entry requirements for this career employers are likely to expect candidates to have a minimum of 5 GCSEs/National 5s (A*–C/A–C), including English and Maths, and some A levels/H grades. Most human resources officers, however, will have a degree or postgraduate qualification in a relevant subject, such as business studies, human resource management, management, social administration or psychology. Entry onto a degree course will require a minimum of 2 A levels/3 H grades and 5 GCSEs/National 5s (A*–C/A–C).

Some employers prefer candidates, on application, to have a professional HR qualification accredited by the Chartered Institute of Personnel and Development (CIPD), such as the Level 3, 5 or 7 Certificate in Human Resources Practice or the Level 3, 5 or 7 Award in Human Resources Management, whereas others will sponsor your studies part time whilst you work. Prior relevant work experience will improve your chances of securing a graduate job.

A common entry route is to start out in administration within an HR company/department and gain experience until a suitable internal vacancy arises. Alternatively, some companies offer a graduate training scheme. Usually you will need a minimum of a 2.2 Honours degree in any subject for these schemes, although degrees in human resources and business may be more relevant. Early application is advised as there will be a lot of competition.

What the work involves

Human resources officers are responsible for recruiting the right staff for jobs at all levels, developing company staff and recruitment policies and helping existing staff to get the appropriate training and development that they and the company need.

You will be charged with managing complaints and disciplinary procedure, administering and maintaining company payroll and staff records, devising and implementing personnel-related policies as well as advising on staff development.

There will be some involvement with negotiations between staff and trade unions on issues such as pay and conditions but this is dependent on the sector in which you are working. In large companies HR officers may specialise in one aspect of the role, whereas in smaller companies you would be expected to cover all aspects of the job.

Type of person suited to this work

You will work with people at all levels, including staff who could be angry or upset, so you will need excellent communication skills. You should be interested in people and be able to solve problems. You will need to help with negotiations between staff and managers over issues such as pay and conditions.

You may be involved with disciplinary procedures and redundancies which can be very stressful. In these situations you will need to be tactful and diplomatic.

You will have to understand and implement employment legislation, manage a budget, write clear and accurate reports, be organised and methodical and be able to work under pressure.

Working conditions

You will work standard office hours, 9am–5.30pm, Monday to Friday, although you might need to work extra hours during busy periods. You will visit the different locations and sites of your organisation so that people get to know and trust you, which could also involve being outdoors or in noisy, dirty places.

You must be able to work well with others as you will probably be working as part of a human resources team.

Future prospects

All types of businesses employ human resources staff but it's a popular and competitive career so work experience is vital. Many human resources personnel officers have a degree but you could work your way up from an administrative role.

You may get more responsibility in a small company but have better prospects in a larger one. You will need to take professional qualifications and could work abroad or become a self-employed consultant.

Advantages/disadvantages

This is a rewarding career if you are interested in people and helping them to develop their skills.

You can study for professional qualifications and gain promotion.

You will be involved in solving disputes between staff and the company, which can be stressful and you might have to make staff redundant.

Money guide

Salaries vary considerably between employers, sectors, office locations and job roles.

The average salary for a graduate-level human resources officer is between £18,000 and £25,000 a year.

The top human resources positions can be lucrative. Human resources managers earn on average between £25,000 and £50,000, and HR directors can receive salaries of up to £100,000.

Related opportunities

- Recruitment/Employment Agency Consultant p47
- School Administrator/Secretary p192
- Work-based Training Instructor p198

Further information

Chartered Institute of Personnel and Development
www.cipd.co.uk

Qualifications and courses

Although there are no formal entry requirements, most organisations prefer graduates with at least a 2.2 or, preferably, a 2.1 degree. Any subject area is accepted, though a degree in accounting, economics, maths, business or management would be advantageous. Larger companies offer specialised training schemes for graduates.

It is possible for non-graduates to gain entry-level positions in support or administration and progress to a broking career after gaining industry qualifications. For this you will need at least 2 A levels/H grades and GCSEs/National 5s (A*–C/A–C) in English and Maths.

Some previous work experience in customer service or finance, whilst not essential to a new entrant, will be looked upon favourably by employers. Many major insurance companies have summer internships and work experience schemes.

Apprenticeships at Levels 2 and 3 in Providing Financial Services are also available as an entry route with options to pursue financial advice, general insurance or long-term care insurance.

The Chartered Insurance Institute (CII), the Institute of Financial Services (*ifs*), and the British Insurance Brokers' Association (BIBA) run relevant courses for new entrants. Additional qualifications are offered by the *ifs*, which are particularly relevant for those seeking to work in financial planning. Recruiters generally look for entrants with no criminal record.

What the work involves

Insurance brokers act as an agent between clients and insurance companies. You will advise on the best policies to meet the client's needs and negotiate deals. You could advise individuals or business clients.

You will have to research policies from many different insurance providers, and you will need to be impartial to ensure your client receives the best deal. You will have to negotiate with these insurance companies to get policies at the best terms for your client.

As a broker you could work in a small company, dealing with a wide range of services, or specialise in a specific area such as household or risk insurance within a larger organisation. You will also collect premiums and process all of your accounts.

Type of person suited to this work

Brokers need excellent verbal and written communication skills to negotiate deals, sell policies and explain complicated financial issues to clients in simple terms. It is essential to be detail oriented and good with numbers.

You will also need to be personable and trustworthy in order to gain the confidence of your clients. Good negotiating skills are imperative if you want to secure the best deal for your client. You should be able to manage your time well as you will work on multiple projects at once.

Working conditions

Brokers could work in a high-street location, selling policies to the public, or in an office where customers call for quotes or claims updates.

Although you will work normal office hours you might need to work the occasional Saturday to meet the needs of your clients.

Smart dress is important as you must be presentable when meeting with clients.

Future prospects

With experience you might choose to move into a management role or become an account executive dealing with more complex claims and visiting clients on their own sites. You also have the option to train further and become a chartered broker.

Eligibility for chartered status requires at least 5 years' experience. CII qualifications are very well regarded and have become essential rather than optional to ensure recognised professional status.

Advantages/disadvantages

The insurance industry offers good career prospects.

Insurance qualifications gained in the UK are respected worldwide allowing you to work abroad.

The work can involve a lot of responsibility and stress as you will be dealing with huge sums of money.

As this is a commission-oriented job you may experience extra pressure to perform and earn.

Money guide

Non-graduate trainee insurance brokers can expect to earn approximately £16,000 a year.

Graduates on training schemes may earn between £22,000 and £26,000.

Over time and with experience you can progress to earning between £40,000 and £80,000 or more per year, not including potential bonuses and other benefits.

Your pay may vary based on where you live, with higher salaries normally in London. Your salary may also be performance-related.

Related opportunities

- Financial Adviser p26
- Insurance Risk Surveyor p32
- Insurance Underwriter p33
- Loss Adjuster p37

Further information

ifs University College
www.ifslearning.ac.uk

British Insurance Brokers' Association
www.biba.org.uk

Chartered Insurance Institute
www.cii.co.uk

Financial Skills Partnership
www.financialskillspartnership.org.uk

Organisation Profile

INSURANCE

Driverless cars, drones and hacks.

Insurance is about understanding and managing global risks. Everything has a risk attached to it, from data to footballers' legs, from supertankers to climate change. Every risk also has a price and a context – and that's where sector professionals play their part.

The CII is the world's largest professional body for insurance and financial planning, with more than 120,000 members in over 150 countries.

The variety of roles is wide – client-facing brokers and underwriters negotiate on risks to be insured; claims experts and loss adjusters deal with the aftermath of local and global events; back-office risk analysts and catastrophe modellers run complex programmes to understand the potential impact of events on people and businesses; there are also professionals in marketing, IT, HR and other business support areas.

You can join from school, college or university. Wherever you start, you can earn a very large salary and work anywhere in the world, since risk principles are global.

After school or college, you could take an Apprenticeship that includes a globally recognised CII professional qualification either in a local small business or in a huge corporation such as Aon, Lloyd's of London or Zurich. Find out more by visiting www.cii.co.uk/apprenticeships. Remember, an apprenticeship still offers a path to a degree – it just costs far less money than three or four years at university, and you get qualified at the same time.

If you are set on university, remember that it's your personality – your communication, negotiation, analytical and problem-solving skills – and not the subject you study that will get you a place on an internship and graduate scheme. That's why you find engineering, religious studies and fine art graduates working in risk, alongside those with degrees in business, finance and law.

Larger employers have well-established graduate schemes that offer two approaches – the rotational scheme to expose you to different business areas; and the specialist scheme which builds expertise in one business area from day one.

Don't overlook smaller companies though – they may only offer one or two graduate roles but they will allow you to grow within a business and gain an understanding of broader business operations.

Being a professional includes completing professional qualifications and, in most cases, your company will pay for you to study CII programmes. Available at three levels – Certificate, Diploma and Advanced Diploma – many graduate schemes will fast-track to the Advanced Diploma in Insurance, completion of which gives you the designatory letters ACII. These letters are globally recognised and valued by employers. Find out more about CII qualifications by visiting www.cii.co.uk/qualifications.

With the ACII and five years' experience under your belt, you can apply for Chartered status, the pinnacle of a profession. The more qualified you are, the more your earning power.

The CII's Discover Risk website www.discoverrisk.co.uk is an invaluable resource of jobs, case studies and employer information.

Networking is key to finding a job and developing a career. Our free Discover membership makes it easy for you to do this. Email discover@cii.co.uk to find out more.

Case Study

DISCOVERING RISK

Victoria Woor's story

Victoria works as an Account Handler at Willis Towers Watson, one of the world's largest brokers. Victoria works within the Fine Art, Jewellery and Specie division.

What do you do in a typical working day?

I correspond with clients, either to make amendments to their policy or to discuss renewal terms. I then correspond with the brokers in our London team, so they can visit the market to have these amendments agreed. I then complete the processing and administrative work for these policies and endorsements.

What do you enjoy most about your job?

I enjoy seeing the end-to-end process of a policy, from receiving the renewal application to binding cover and satisfying the client's needs. It is then that you receive a real sense of achievement.

What is the most challenging part of your role?

The most challenging part can be the demanding timeframes in which a policy document needs to be issued or cover needs to be confirmed so a policy does not lapse. Communication can also be a challenge as many of my clients are located outside the UK in different time zones.

What do you need to be successful in your role?

I need to be able to work well under pressure so that deadlines are met and my work remains of extremely high quality. I need to be able to work extremely well in a team, adapt to difficult situations and be comfortable with ambiguity. I need to be agile, use my initiative and be enthusiastic to enable self-development.

Have you taken any professional qualifications?

So far I have completed the CII Certificate in Insurance (Cert CII). I am now studying to gain my Diploma in Insurance (Dip CII). I have found that completing these professional qualifications has already greatly helped me develop my knowledge and expertise within my job role.

What have been your career highlights so far?

My main career highlight so far has been the recognition I received for gaining my Certificate in Insurance. This was a real sense of accomplishment.

Why did you choose a career in insurance?

I knew I wanted a job that was interactive, stimulating and rewarding. Insurance was a sector that I knew was diverse, and the range of different divisions fascinated me. I also knew that to work within insurance would require a strong sense of teamwork and determination, both of which for me were a necessity.

To find out more about other people working in the profession, email discover@cii.co.uk or visit www.discoverrisk.co.uk

INSURANCE RISK SURVEYOR

Qualifications and courses

This is not generally considered to be an entry-level position, although some large companies do run graduate trainee schemes. Normally you will need to have gained significant experience in the insurance industry, usually as an underwriter. Qualifications and experience in a related, specialised profession like building surveying will also be accepted.

A degree or HND is increasingly normal among those entering the profession, usually a 2.1 degree qualification. Any subject is accepted but degrees in science, risk management, insurance or business studies will be useful. If you want to specialise in engineering insurance you will need an engineering degree. Although requirements vary between universities and colleges, most degree courses will require at least 2 A levels/3 H grades and 5 GCSEs/National 5s (A*–C/A–C).

Non-graduates who complete a Higher Diploma in Business, Administration and Finance may be able to get a job as a technician, risk assistant or claims handler and work their way up while studying for professional qualifications such as the CII Diploma in Insurance.

All trainees are expected to qualify as a Chartered Insurance Institute (CII) Associate. The qualifications can be studied at Certificate (Cert CII), Diploma (Dip CII) and Advanced Diploma (ACII) level and many candidates will already be at this level through roles in underwriting.

What the work involves

You will provide insurance companies with relevant information about a site that may affect their decision to accept requests for insurance cover.

You will investigate sites that need to be insured and prepare reports detailing the risks and recommend ways underwriters can reduce these.

Your reports will enable underwriters to decide whether or not to accept these risks and what terms and conditions should go into their policies. You may specialise in one of 4 areas: engineering, fire and perils, burglary or liability.

Type of person suited to this work

You will come into contact with a diverse range of people and must be able to communicate complicated and technical information in a clear way. In order to obtain accurate information for your employer you should have excellent observational skills and be able to communicate well.

An investigative nature will help you survey a variety of risks and you will need to be able to pay close attention to detail and work efficiently under pressure when writing up your reports for insurance companies. Workloads can be heavy so you should be self-motivated and organised.

Good IT skills are essential.

Working conditions

Most of your time will be spent investigating a variety of sites which could include industrial plants, engineering plants, oil rigs and construction zones. These can be potentially dangerous and polluted and may require you to work at heights. You will need to wear business attire when in the office but change into protective gear when surveying the site.

You will most likely work Monday to Friday during normal office hours but might need to work evenings or weekends depending on the availability of sites to visit. Working from home will give you greater flexibility and is increasingly favoured over being office based.

Future prospects

Career prospects may be affected by the financial climate. However, insurance risks are a high priority for many companies and jobs are available.

You may choose to specialise in one area of risk such as business interruption or you may travel overseas to work for a global insurer dealing in international risks.

You could be promoted to corporate risk manager or head of department but this will mean a less hands-on role. Many surveyors also move out of insurance and into the public sector.

Advantages/disadvantages

You will always be developing and growing in knowledge as no two days will be alike. You also have the chance to meet new people and to travel the world.

Sometimes customers may prove difficult to work with. Visiting hazardous sites on a regular basis can be physically and emotionally demanding.

Money guide

Starting out, trainee insurance surveyors earn between £20,000 and £22,000 a year.

With experience and professional qualifications you can earn between £35,000 and £50,000.

Senior risk managers can earn up to £70,000 whilst specialists' salaries can reach £100,000.

Many employers also offer additional benefits such as medical insurance and a company car.

Related opportunities

- Building Surveyor p65
- Civil/Construction Engineer/Civil Engineering Technician p71
- Insurance Broker p29
- Insurance Underwriter p33

Further information

Chartered Insurance Institute
www.cii.co.uk

Lloyd's of London
www.lloyds.com

INSURANCE UNDERWRITER

Qualifications and courses

Many companies offer graduate training schemes that require a 2.1 degree for entry. All subjects will be accepted but degrees in business, statistics, law, accounting, financial services and economics are useful.

Non-graduates with A levels/H grades or equivalent qualifications, as well as GCSEs/National 5s (A*–C/A–C) in English and Maths, can join the industry in a support or assistant role while studying for the professional qualifications required to become an underwriter. It is also common for people to switch to underwriting from actuarial, risk management or claims management roles.

Although it is not essential, pre-entry work experience with an insurance company can be advantageous, especially when applying for graduate training schemes, as competition is fierce.

A Level 2 Apprenticeship and Level 3 Advanced Apprenticeship in Providing Financial Services are also available as entry routes with options to pursue general insurance.

The Chartered Insurance Institute (CII) offers certificates, diplomas and advanced diplomas in insurance for new entrants, and also offers the Level 3 Award in London Market Insurance as an established qualification for brokers working in London.

What the work involves

Underwriters decide whether applications for insurance cover should be accepted and under what terms. They assess the size of risks against the likelihood of claims in order to work out premiums for their prospective clients.

In all negotiations you should make a profit for your company and protect it from losses. You will often specialise in one type of insurance, either in general (home, pet, household, etc.), life, commercial, or reinsurance.

You will be expected to conduct in-depth research, study insurance proposals, interview specialists, analyse statistics and write up policies, often inserting additional conditions. You will be expected to keep detailed reports and records of policies you have written and the decisions made in relation to them.

Type of person suited to this work

Underwriting is a specialist job that requires an in-depth knowledge of risk in order to make predictions from applications. You will need excellent attention to detail, along with numeracy skills, in order to solve complex problems and prepare accurate and detailed reports.

You must be able to work well under pressure and make quick, difficult decisions. You should have a good sense of judgement and be trustworthy when handling confidential information.

Negotiation and communication skills are essential when arranging deals with brokers.

Working conditions

Underwriters' work is mainly office based and travel is rare although commercial underwriters will occasionally travel to meet clients. You will work Monday to Friday but might need to stay late at the office to meet deadlines. Most underwriters do have the option to work on flexitime which means you can shape your hours around what works best for you.

You will spend most of your time at a computer researching and writing up reports. You may need to investigate dangerous or distressing situations at times.

Future prospects

As you gain experience you will attract more difficult and complicated cases, enabling you to earn a promotion or switch companies more easily. Many underwriters choose to move into management or training roles or specialise in one type of insurance such as aviation.

You may wish to set up your own broking company, switch to reinsurance or train in sales and sell insurance packages which can prove to be a profitable option.

Advantages/disadvantages

Underwriters are constantly researching risks and are therefore learning new information every day which makes the job diverse and exciting. It also offers excellent benefits, such as share schemes and bonuses.

You may feel under pressure as you must make difficult decisions regarding risks often at short notice. Insurance can be a tough industry to work in during a recession.

Money guide

Starting in a support role with the intention of taking professional qualifications in order to progress to an underwriter position, you can expect to earn £15,000 to £30,000 per year.

Trainee underwriters on a graduate programme will earn around £25,000 a year.

Senior level salaries are generally between £30,000 and £65,000.

With the right experience, qualified underwriters could earn £100,000 or more per year.

Benefit packages can include discounted personal insurance and subsidised mortgages.

Related opportunities

- Actuary p5
- Insurance Broker p29
- Insurance Risk Surveyor p32

Further information

Chartered Insurance Institute
www.cii.co.uk

Financial Skills Partnership
www.financialskillspartnership.org.uk

International Underwriting Association of London
www.iua.co.uk

INVESTMENT ANALYST

Qualifications and courses

Entry to this profession is usually through a graduate programme. For this you will need at least a 2.1 degree in any discipline, though a qualification in a relevant subject such as economics, accountancy, maths or statistics may be advantageous. To qualify for a degree course most applicants will need at least 2 A levels/3 H grades and 5 GCSEs/National 5s (A*–C/A–C).

A relevant postgraduate qualification is desirable, though not essential. The internationally recognised Chartered Financial Analyst (CFA) qualification or a Master in Business Administration (MBA) are good options. Pre-entry work experience, such as summer internships, is beneficial; often as many as 60%–95% of interns will be offered full-time employment.

Should you choose not to study for a degree, another possible entry route is as a junior researcher or administrator, which allows for progression to a position as an analyst. Applicants should ensure that they have good A levels/H grades and relevant commercial experience.

A second language, particularly French, German or Japanese, can be useful.

What the work involves

The main job of an investment analyst is to inform other professionals, such as stockbrokers, traders and fund managers, about the best and worst investments for making a profit.

Sell-side analysts assess an individual company's financial output and report this to private investors and unit trust fund managers. Buy-side analysts research investment opportunities for pension funds, investment banks, and insurance and life assurance companies.

Activities include analysing the economic stability of various countries, predicting the movement of share prices and taking account of the economic implications of events, such as warfare or devolution.

You might work for an investment management company where you will collate information to advise in-house fund managers. Alternatively, you could work for stockbrokers and investment banks where you will be assisting portfolio managers and the employer's clients.

Type of person suited to this work

This job is suitable for someone who has an interest in current affairs and the impact these have on the financial markets. A certain amount of research is required in order to make informed, accurate decisions on possible financial opportunities.

You will be expected to present your findings and this requires tenacity and self-belief. The pressured environment, and constant need to be reliable, requires someone who can be resilient and trustworthy when calculating risks and forecasting trends.

In order to present findings in an effective way, employees need to be good communicators who have initiative and are numerically skilled.

Working conditions

This profession requires employees to work long hours, often starting work before 7am in preparation for the opening of the London Stock Exchange and closure of Far Eastern markets, and working until after 6pm. These hours could change, or even increase, for analysts who need to cover markets operating in different time zones.

A lot of time is also spent in front of computer screens, which can be tiring.

Future prospects

For graduates, there are annual recruitment opportunities with large companies, particularly in London, Manchester and Edinburgh. Application deadlines will usually occur in between October and January of your final year of your degree.

Opportunities for promotion are related to individual performance, with 3 years of service seeing an analyst progress to associate level and a further 2 to 3 years to the position of company vice-president. Should an individual or team appear to perform extremely well, competing companies will often headhunt successful employees. Relocation to another country or city may be required to progress.

Advantages/disadvantages

This is an extremely well paid job that allows for progression within a relatively short period of time.

Due to the fast moving stock market and the responsibility for vast sums of money, this job can often be highly pressured, yet rewarding.

Long days and intense work can lead to high stress levels.

Money guide

Entry level graduate positions typically pay between £18,000 and £30,000 a year, though salaries of up to £40,000 are possible in London.

With experience you could earn between £50,000 and £100,000 a year. Senior roles can pay in excess of £110,000 per year.

In addition to this, analysts will often receive substantial bonuses of up to 200%, low-rate mortgages, medical insurance, and life and pension cover.

Related opportunities

- Credit Analyst p17
- Economist p20
- Stockbroker p53

Further information

Association of Certified International Investment Analysts
www.aciia.org

Financial Conduct Authority
www.fca.org.uk

The Chartered Institute for Securities & Investment
www.cisi.org

Qualifications and courses

Entry without a degree is unlikely. Most entrants will hold an Honours degree (usually a minimum of a 2.1) in any subject, however a relevant academic field such as business management, law, economics or mathematics may put you at an advantage. Entry onto a degree is usually with 2 A levels/3 H grades and 5 GCSEs/National 5s (A*–C/A–C).

A common route into this profession is through an investment analyst graduate programme, progressing to associate investment banker through a combination of in-house training, experience, and good performance, typically after a period of 3 years. All new trainees are required by the regulator to complete Financial Conduct Authority exams and training. Some employers might also ask for further professional qualifications. Applicants to graduate programmes usually require at least a 2.1 Honours degree.

Postgraduate study is not a requirement for entry, however a Master in Business Administration (MBA) or another relevant postgraduate qualification can improve employment prospects, or facilitate career development. Entry onto postgraduate courses is usually with a good bachelor's degree.

Awareness of the different market sectors that clients operate in is highly valued, and experience gained from internships or through office or clerical work in a financial or investment banking environment will be regarded favourably; often as many as 60%–95% of interns will be offered full-time employment.

A second language will be advantageous, particularly when looking to work for an international firm.

What the work involves

Investment bankers lend their expertise to companies, institutions and the government, advising them on how to achieve their financial goals.

They are responsible for strategising and overseeing mergers, acquisitions and privatisation deals, and managing the investment of large sums of money for their clients.

Typical work involves assessing investment ideas on behalf of, or submitted by clients; predicting financial outcomes by way of simulated financial models. Depending on this analysis, it is then the investment banker's responsibility to negotiate and execute the deal, preparing the necessary documents and ensuring that all legislative regulations and obligations are being observed and met.

Type of person suited to this work

You will need to enjoy working with numbers and strong maths skills are paramount, as is the ability to analyse detailed and complex information.

The work involves responsibility for large sums of money, therefore confidence and the ability to work well under pressurised circumstances are essential.

Since work is often carried out in teams, good teamwork and communication skills are essential.

Working conditions

The working day can be long, often reaching 15 hours. 100 hour weeks are not unheard of, and weekend work is common.

Travel within the UK or overseas may be expected if you work for a large or international firm or institution.

There is a higher concentration of graduate opportunities in London and the south-east of England.

Work is typically carried out in teams of professionals from backgrounds such as legal and accountancy. Teams may specialise, focusing on specific types of investments or market sectors.

Future prospects

Most entrants will progress from a position as an investment analyst. These are training positions and can last up to 3 years.

Once employed as an investment banker good performance will help you establish yourself in the industry and could lead to being headhunted for better-paid positions.

London and New York are the main global financial centres, however there are others within Europe and further afield, therefore there are opportunities to work abroad.

Advantages/disadvantages

This is an extremely well paid job with potential for performance-based progression in a relatively short period of time.

Given that you will be dealing with large sums of money, the work can be highly pressurised and target driven.

Long working days, particularly around peak times in the financial calendar, mean that this can be a stressful career.

Money guide

The average starting salary for graduates is £35,000 to £40,000 a year. With experience, this can rise to £50,000 a year.

After progression to an investment banker role, pay is often performance based, however with a good deal of experience and based on strong performance, you could earn up to £150,000 a year, or more.

Related opportunities

- Economist p20
- Investment Analyst p34
- Stock Market Trader p52
- Stockbroker p53

Further information

British Bankers' Association
www.bba.org.uk

Financial Conduct Authority
www.fca.org.uk

The Chartered Institute for Securities & Investment
www.cisi.org

LEGAL SECRETARY

Qualifications and courses

There are no set entry qualifications to become a legal secretary and requirements will vary among employers, though many will require a minimum of GCSEs/National 5s (A*–C/A–C) in English and Maths. A degree/HND in secretarial studies, law, business with a language or government/public administration can increase your chances of employment.

You can take an NVQ at Levels 1–4 or City & Guilds qualification at Levels 2 and 3 in Business. City & Guilds diplomas are also available in keyboarding, text production skills and office procedures, as well as the OCR Certificate in Text Processing.

More specific legal secretarial courses are also available. A course in conveyancing, family law or wills, probate and administration could be useful or the Institute of Legal Secretaries and PAs offers the Legal Secretaries Diploma. Additionally, the Institute of Legal Executives provides the Level 2 Certificate and the Level 3 Diploma for Legal Secretaries and Pitman Training has various relevant diplomas and courses.

Relevant experience is valued more highly by some employers than qualifications. This can be gained through working as a clerical assistant, temping through agencies or undertaking voluntary work. Apprenticeships are also available.

Having another language such as French, Italian or Japanese may also give you an advantage.

What the work involves

Legal secretaries deal with the day-to-day tasks of the law firm.

You will provide administrative support and carry out tasks such as arranging meetings, making travel arrangements and updating filing systems.

You will also help lawyers, legal executives and paralegals with specialist tasks such as studying different parts of the law for cases and making notes at court, police stations and appointments with clients.

You will be responsible for typing legal documents and arranging statements and paperwork for court. Secretaries may also manage cases in fields such as debt recovery.

Type of person suited to this work

You will need to be very organised, have fast typing skills and a good grasp of spelling, grammar and punctuation.

You must also have a good eye for detail as you will be checking and handling confidential legal documents.

A legal secretary will have to be aware of different legal terminology and processes and possess excellent research skills.

You should be able to work to tight deadlines and be friendly, polite and helpful at all times.

Working conditions

You will work normal office hours (9am–5pm) and will spend a great deal of time using a computer as well as other office equipment.

You may also have to attend court to make notes, make visits to police stations, deliver legal documents and attend meetings, and at all times you will need to be well presented.

Future prospects

After 2 years' experience, it is possible to become an associate member of the Institute of Legal Secretaries and PAs.

You could progress to a role as senior secretary, personal assistant or office manager. There is a higher chance of promotion into a senior role within a bigger organisation.

With further training, you can become a legal executive, paralegal or licensed conveyancer.

Some secretaries go on to study for a law degree in order to become a solicitor or barrister.

Advantages/disadvantages

You will often be entrusted to work on your own, so you can be independent.

With further qualifications, there is the opportunity to progress into related legal careers.

The job can be repetitive, particularly as you will be mainly at your desk. Tight deadlines and a heavy workload can be very stressful.

Money guide

Salaries will depend on the location and size of the employer. Higher salaries are often available in London and other big cities.

A legal secretary in their first job can expect between £18,000 and £22,000.

With experience, this can rise to between £22,000 and £33,000.

Legal secretaries with extensive experience and qualifications working in top law firms can earn up to £40,000.

Related opportunities

- Bilingual Secretary p330
- Personal Assistant p43
- Receptionist p46

Further information

Chartered Institute of Legal Executives
www.cilex.org.uk

Institute of Legal Secretaries and PAs
www.institutelegalsecretaries.com

National Association of Licensed Paralegals
www.nationalparalegals.co.uk

Qualifications and courses

Loss adjustment is not normally an entry-level position although some larger companies do run graduate training programmes. Any degree subject may be accepted, although finance, business studies, construction or engineering are beneficial. Entry is usually with a 2.2 degree or higher.

Entry without a degree or HND is possible. Many candidates will start in the claims handling department of an insurance company and progress to loss adjusting. There are also some loss adjusting administrator/assistant positions, which could be an entry point. All entrants must have GCSEs/National 5s (A*–C/A–C) in English and Maths. Entry to this career is feasible through a Level 2 Apprenticeship or Level 3 Advanced Apprenticeship in Providing Financial Services, taking the General Insurance pathway.

Relevant practical experience is just as important as academic qualifications. You could start out as a claims technician and, with experience and qualifications gained on the job, such as the Chartered Insurance Institute (CII) Level 3 Certificate, Diploma and Advanced Diploma in Insurance, progress to a loss adjuster position. Organisations running trainee and graduate development schemes will always look at paid or unpaid industry-related vacation work or work experience placements favourably.

Most qualified loss adjusters will become associate members of the Chartered Institute of Loss Adjusters (CILA). To take the CILA exams, you will first need to be an ordinary member, have at least 5 years' work experience in the office of a member company and have a relevant professional qualification. To become an ordinary member of the CILA, you will need to be aged 21 or over and working for a company or an independent loss adjusting firm.

What the work involves

Loss adjusters are independent specialists who work for insurance companies, investigating and advising on large or complicated claims or where there is a dispute.

You will visit premises, check damage and inspect reports from other professionals such as the fire service or police force to assess whether loss resulting from an incident is covered by the insurance policy. On completing your research, you will recommend the size of payments and offer advice to both claimants and insurers.

You could be investigating numerous claims which can involve a lot of responsibility, dealing with huge sums of money and sometimes being drafted in following major incidents such as plane crashes.

Type of person suited to this work

You will need excellent communication skills for contact with distressed claimants in order to be sympathetic while maintaining a professional distance.

Part of your job will be resolving disputes between organisations and/or individuals, which will require you to be calm and focused in order to make impartial decisions based on evidence.

You could be dealing with a number of complex cases at once, so good time management and organisational skills are important.

Working conditions

You will usually work normal office hours, although you could be called to look at premises in the evening or at weekends in emergency cases.

The majority of work is office based but you will have to travel to sites within the local area or overseas to make assessments.

You may be asked to assess the potentially distressing aftermath of situations such as fires, robberies, and train crashes, in which case you must be emotionally prepared. You will be required to wear relevant safety equipment when on-site.

Future prospects

Loss adjustment is a highly competitive area of work but opportunities are increasing.

You could work in a large firm, which may allow you to focus on a particular area of interest and could create an excellent route of career progression into a management role.

Smaller insurance firms usually hire loss adjusters on a case-by-case basis, so there is the possibility to work on a freelance basis. With experience, you could set up your own firm.

Advantages/disadvantages

Loss adjusters who specialise in major risks can earn extremely high salaries.

Insurance is a major industry overseas, so this career offers plenty of international opportunities.

Money guide

The typical starting salary for a trainee loss adjuster can be anywhere between £15,000 and £30,000.

Typical salaries with 5 years' experience are £25,000 to £60,000.

With specialist skills or management duties and extensive experience this can increase to in excess of £80,000.

Additional benefits could include a pension scheme, bonuses, company car and medical insurance.

Related opportunities

- Accountant p2
- Actuary p5
- Financial Adviser p26

Further information

Chartered Institute of Loss Adjusters
www.cila.co.uk

Chartered Insurance Institute
www.cii.co.uk

Financial Skills Partnership
www.financialskillspartnership.org.uk

MANAGEMENT CONSULTANT

Qualifications and courses

Entry to this profession will generally require a minimum of a 2.1 Honours degree. Any subject can be accepted but having a degree in either business, management, maths, economics, finance, engineering and science or a related area can be an advantage. The typical minimum entry requirements for a degree are 2 A levels/3 H grades and 5 GCSEs/National 5s (A*–C/A–C).

A postgraduate qualification, such as a Master of Business Administration (MBA), can be an advantage; entry will usually require a good first degree and substantial work experience may also be required.

Mature entry may also be possible with relevant work experience that shows evidence of analytical business skills. Some entrants have an accountancy qualification with one of the main accountancy bodies. The Institute of Business Consulting (IBC)'s Certificate in Management Consulting Essentials is designed for people who want to move into consultancy from another area. You should have a degree and at least 2 years' business experience for this.

Pre-entry work experience is useful as competition is extremely intense. This can be acquired from part-time work, voluntary work or internships.

What the work involves

You will work with organisations and companies to help and advise them on developing and improving their efficiency, services, products or staffing.

This might involve observing and evaluating working practices, researching information, training staff or developing new ways of operating. You will need extensive knowledge of the sector you are working within.

Consultants can work for a private consultancy organisation, be members of a specialised team or be freelance/self-employed.

Type of person suited to this work

You must be dynamic, confident and self-motivated. You will need to be able to research information, talk to staff and develop a thorough knowledge of an organisation. You must be good at identifying problems and problem-solving. You may need to develop training programmes.

You will need excellent communication skills for writing reports, dealing with staff and presenting information.

You may have to review budgets and make savings, which may result in redundancies or spending cuts. Therefore you will need to have good financial skills, be able to justify your decisions and cope with any criticism.

Working conditions

A lot of your time will be spent travelling to different companies, so you will probably have to spend time away from home.

Working to deadlines can be stressful. The work can be pressured as you will have to take responsibility for high-level decisions which could have far-reaching consequences.

You could be self-employed, work for a private consultancy service or be part of a team of company improvement specialists.

Future prospects

While the financial crisis initially caused a fall in revenue in 2009–10, the UK consulting industry has rebounded and is expected to continue to grow over the next few years.

Graduates tend to start out as analysts before progressing to the full consultancy role. The next step is usually to manager or senior consultant, which can be achieved in as little as 3 years. From there consultants can go on to become partner or director of a firm. Going freelance is also possible.

Advantages/disadvantages

This is a rewarding, varied and interesting career with lots of opportunities.

Salaries can be high and you may be able to travel.

This job can be stressful and demanding, and hours can be long and unpredictable.

Money guide

If you are freelance or self-employed you will probably be paid per day and your earnings will depend on your success.

Entry level consultants may earn from £25,000 to £30,000.

With several years of experience, salaries can reach £75,000.

Senior consultants can earn much more and also receive commission and bonuses.

Related opportunities

- Equality and Diversity Officer p23
- Financial Adviser p26
- Human Resources/Personnel Officer p28

Further information

Chartered Management Institute
www.managers.org.uk

Institute of Consulting
www.iconsulting.org.uk

Management Consultancies Association
www.mca.org.uk

MEDICAL RECEPTIONIST

Qualifications and courses

There are no minimum entry requirements, although employers sometimes ask for 5 GCSEs/National 5s (A*–C/A–C), including English and Maths.

Other qualifications that may be useful include Diplomas in Business Administration or Society, Health and Development, the City & Guilds Level 2 Certificate in Medical Reception or the Edexcel Level 2 NVQ in Support Services in Health Care.

Work experience in administration or in customer service is helpful. Apprenticeships in Business and Administration are available for candidates aged between 16 and 24.

Medical receptionists will be trained on the job and may be encouraged to undertake further training. The Association of Medical Secretaries, Practice Managers, Administrators and Receptionists (AMSPAR) and the British Society of Medical Secretaries and Administrators (BSMSA) both offer several training courses, such as the Certificate in Health Service Administration and the Level 2 and Level 3 Certificates in Medical Administration.

What the work involves

Medical receptionists book appointments for patients, organise the appointment diaries, answer the telephone and take messages.

You will be responsible for greeting patients when they arrive, making sure they are in the right place, and answering their queries.

You will also carry out some general administrative work, such as preparing patients' notes and files, dealing with post and typing letters.

Type of person suited to this work

It is important that you are well presented, friendly and reassuring. You will be the first point of contact for patients, so you will need to make a good first impression.

Excellent communication skills are required as you will be interacting with patients and other medical staff all day, in person and on the telephone.

Most receptionists are required to have a good working knowledge of basic computer programs as the majority of work is computer based.

You will need to be well organised and efficient, as you might be dealing with several queries at once and will need to make sure they are all dealt with as quickly and accurately as possible.

As you will be helping sick, ill or distressed patients it is important to be sympathetic when dealing with their problems.

You will often be dealing with confidential information and so it is important that you are respectful and professional.

Working conditions

You will be working standard office hours, Monday to Friday. However you may work shifts including the weekends and evenings if your place of work offers extended opening hours.

You will spend most of your time in an office, sitting at a desk, and looking at a computer screen.

Future prospects

Medical receptionists are needed all over the UK, so there are good job prospects. Most are employed by the NHS but there are opportunities in the private sector.

Progression in this career is relatively easy. With some training you could become a medical secretary or move into a supervisory or managerial role.

Advantages/disadvantages

Helping people who are sick or distressed will bring great job satisfaction.

You will have to deal with patients who could be angry or distressed which could be upsetting.

This job will be great for you if you enjoy meeting new people.

Part-time work is widely available.

You will work in accordance with surgery hours which can sometimes mean finishing late with extended opening hours and weekend work.

Money guide

Starting salaries in the NHS, coming under band 2 of the Agenda for Change pay scale, are £15,100 to £17,800.

With experience this could increase to between £18,000 and £20,000.

Those in senior positions or with extra responsibilities might be paid up to £22,000.

London pay rates are likely to be above the national rates.

Related opportunities

- Hotel Receptionist p130
- Personal Assistant p43
- Secretary p51

Further information

Association of Medical Secretaries, Practice Managers, Administrators and Receptionists
www.amspar.com

Skills CFA
www.skillscfa.org

The British Society of Medical Secretaries and Administrators
www.bsmsa.org.uk

PAYROLL MANAGER

Qualifications and courses

You will not be required to have any specific qualifications to become a payroll clerk, supervisor or manager. However, employers prefer candidates with GCSEs/National 5s (A*–C/A–C) or equivalent, including English and Maths.

It is extremely unlikely that you will be able to go straight into a managerial role, as most employers will want at least 5 years' experience. Your skills, experience and industry knowledge are likely to be more relevant than any formal qualifications you may hold.

The Diploma in Business, Administration and Finance or the Levels 1–3 qualifications in Payroll from the International Association of Book-keepers (IAB) can both be useful for entry into this line of work.

Both intermediate and advanced apprenticeships are available in Payroll. Relevant experience in areas such as bookkeeping is welcome.

You will train on the job but there are also professional qualifications you can take while working, eg the Foundation degree in Payroll Management from the Chartered Institute of Payroll Professionals (CIPP).

What the work involves

Payroll managers are employed by organisations to arrange and manage employees' salaries. You will ensure that each member of staff receives the correct amount on the correct date. When doing this you will take into account laws regarding tax, national insurance, sick pay and maternity/paternity leave.

Your tasks will include keeping records of hours worked, calculating repayments for salary advances or student loans, calculating pay, pensions and tax deductions.

As you progress from payroll clerk to payroll supervisor and payroll manager you will gradually take on more responsibilities, such as managing and delegating tasks to a team of payroll clerks, and creating and documenting payroll policies.

Type of person suited to this work

As you will be in contact with many employees and work alongside other payroll staff, you must enjoy working with other people and be able to work in a team. You should be sensitive in your approach to discussing earnings with employees, and treat their information with confidentiality.

As you will be responsible for maintaining records and large amounts of information you must be organised and methodical in your work.

You will need strong numerical and IT skills as you will be working with figures and working on computerised systems. You should also be able to multi-task and work to tight deadlines.

Working conditions

From Monday to Friday you will work around 37 hours per week. You might have to work overtime, especially at the end of a financial year which can be a busy time.

You might have the option of working part-time or flexible hours and there may even be opportunities for job sharing.

You will be largely office based. You will have a desk from which you will answer the phone, send emails and make calculations. You may have to attend meetings at times.

Future prospects

You will enter this profession as a payroll clerk and after you have gained a few years' experience and qualifications you will be able to progress to payroll supervisor and payroll manager.

These roles will involve more responsibility and managerial tasks such as liaising with HM Revenue & Customs, organising training for other members of payroll staff and being involved in business strategy.

Advantages/disadvantages

You will build relationships with a variety of people as you will potentially be working with each employee within an organisation.

At times the administrative nature of your work may become repetitive and monotonous.

Money guide

As a payroll clerk your starting salary can be around £13,000 to £18,000 per year.

With experience you can progress to a supervisory position and earn between £22,000 and £25,000 a year.

The salary for a payroll manager is dependent on the size of the team and your responsibilities. Starting salaries are likely to be between £25,000 and £35,000 with some positions available in excess of £40,000.

Related opportunities

- Accounting Technician and Accounts/Finance Clerk p4
- Bank Cashier/Customer Adviser p9
- Pensions Administrator p41

Further information

Association of Accounting Technicians
www.aat.org.uk

Chartered Institute of Payroll Professionals
www.cipp.org.uk

International Association of Book-keepers
www.iab.org.uk

PENSIONS ADMINISTRATOR

Qualifications and courses

The entry requirements can vary widely but you will need a minimum of 4 GCSEs/National 5s (A*–C/A–C) including English and Maths.

It is highly likely that you will be expected to work towards a professional qualification as you work. The Pensions Management Institute (PMI) has numerous courses available, including an Award/Certificate in Pensions Essentials, a Certificate/Diploma in Pensions Administration and a Certificate in Pension Calculations (CPC). Advanced level apprenticeships in Providing Financial Services are available. Following this route can lead to a career as a pensions administrator, pensions team leader or pensions manager.

Previous experience in office work, an accounts role or a customer service role will be useful.

What the work involves

As a pensions administrator you will be responsible for the general management and maintenance of pension schemes and life insurance policies.

You will answer queries from customers by telephone or email and complete the necessary associated administration. This can include information on policies in general, tax relief entitlement, cash sums on retirement and options for benefit transfer.

You will undertake a variety of administrative tasks such as calculating pension forecasts, processing pension contributions and maintaining and updating accounts when, for example, someone retires. When a policy has to be paid out, in case of retirement or a death, you will organise all of the paperwork and arrange the payment of lump sums.

Type of person suited to this work

You should enjoy methodical, detailed work. You will need strong mathematical and IT skills in order to work out calculations and check databases for information.

As you will be dealing with the public a great deal you should be friendly and polite and be able to explain detailed policies in laymen's terms. You should have an interest in the financial sector and tax regulations and keep up to date with economic developments.

As you will be maintaining records and referring back to them frequently you must have excellent organisational skills. You must be able to multi-task and prioritise your workload.

Working conditions

You will work Monday to Friday, 35 hours a week. At times you may be required to work overtime at weekends or in the evenings. You are likely to be able to work part-time with flexible hours or job sharing.

You will be office based, which will have certain benefits depending on the organisation you work for.

You will have a mainly sedentary working lifestyle, sitting at a desk using computers and answering the telephone.

A good deal of on-the-job assessment and training is required throughout your career, for example pensions companies must assess staff involved in pension schemes owing to the Financial Conduct Authority (FCA) requirements.

Future prospects

With experience and further qualifications you may be promoted to team leader or a management position.

There may also be opportunities to move up to pension advice or consultancy where you will provide information and guidance regarding financial planning and employee benefits.

Advantages/disadvantages

Each day you will have to deal with a variety of different queries from customers.

Although you may have to deal with stressed and annoyed customers, generally the work will be fairly unstressful.

Some aspects of your work may be repetitive and will include sitting at a desk and in front of a screen for much of your working day.

Money guide

As a trainee pensions administrator you can earn from £15,000 to £18,000 per year.

For experienced pensions administrators, annual salaries are typically between £20,000 and £24,000.

In a senior role or as a team leader you can earn up to £30,000 per year.

Benefits packages may be available, including pension, insurance and bonuses based on personal or company performance.

Related opportunities

- Bank Cashier/Customer Adviser p9
- Insurance Broker p29
- Pensions Adviser p42

Further information

Chartered Insurance Institute
www.cii.co.uk

Pension Careers
www.pensioncareers.co.uk

Pensions Management Institute
www.pensions-pmi.org.uk

Qualifications and courses

Most pensions advisers have a degree. It may be possible to enter this line of work through a graduate training programme, for example with a large pension or insurance company. You will ideally need a degree or HND in economics, business and finance, mathematics or management. Entry to a degree will usually be with 2 A levels/3 H grades and 5 GCSEs/National 5s (A*–C/A–C).

Graduate training programmes are very competitive, so prior experience in a customer-facing, sales or financial role can be useful.

Alternatively, many people in this job role start out as pensions administrators and work their way up to adviser while earning professional qualifications. To become an administrator you will need at least 4 GCSEs/National 5s, including English and Maths. Some employers may require a minimum of A level qualifications or equivalent. Pensions can also be a second career for people with a background in financial services or working with the public. Many employers consider a strong financial or sales background and good people skills to be more important than formal qualifications.

All pensions advisers will need to take professional qualifications before they can give advice. The Chartered Insurance Institute (CII) and the Pensions Management Institute (PMI) provide qualifications, including the CII Certificate in Life and Pensions and the PMI Certificate in Pensions Calculation.

There are also apprenticeships in Providing Financial Services or in Advising on Financial Products which may be useful.

What the work involves

Pensions advisers help individuals and organisations to choose, create and manage a pension plan that is most suited to their needs.

You will work in-house, or as a consultant for businesses and other organisations, to set up and maintain pensions that will suit all employees while remaining within budget.

Knowledge of the markets and government policy will help inform your decisions, along with an understanding of your clients' assets, circumstances, and financial situation.

Type of person suited to this work

As you will be working closely with the public you should have excellent communication and interpersonal skills in order to explain complex policies in layman's terms and in a polite, friendly manner. You should have a genuine interest in answering consumers' financial queries.

You must have strong numerical skills in order to make accurate financial estimates and economic forecasts and IT skills to keep records of current policies and procedures.

You must have excellent organisational skills and pay attention to detail.

An interest in financial markets and products could be beneficial, along with excellent concentration and a long attention span.

Working conditions

You will work around 40 hours a week, Monday to Friday. You may have to be flexible with your hours to suit clients who need weekend or evening appointments.

You will be mainly office based but you might occasionally have to travel within the UK to meet with clients and organisations or to liaise with other financial advisers.

Future prospects

As the financial sector is constantly changing and adjusting its regulations, and you must be aware of new developments, you will be subject to training and continuing professional development (CPD).

You may be promoted to senior roles, progress to other advisory roles in financial areas in actuarial firms, with accountants or solicitors for example. You may also be able to become self-employed.

Advantages/disadvantages

Your work will be diverse as you will meet with different customers on a daily basis and tailor your advice to each new client.

Some aspects of your work might be stressful, particularly if you are on performance related pay.

Money guide

As a trainee adviser, you can expect to earn a starting salary somewhere in the region of £15,000 to £28,000 per year, rising as you advance and develop your skills and knowledge.

As you gain experience and qualifications, you can generally earn between £22,000 and £55,000 a year.

If you work in a senior role for a large firm you can earn in excess of £80,000.

Performance bonuses are often available and benefits may include low rate insurance and mortgages.

Related opportunities

- Accountant p2
- Actuary p5
- Financial Adviser p26

Further information

Pension Careers
www.pensioncareers.co.uk

Pensions Management Institute
www.pensions-pmi.org.uk

PERSONAL ASSISTANT

Qualifications and courses

There are no specific qualifications required but employers do want you to have a good standard of general education, including GCSEs/National 5s (A*–C/A–C) in English and Maths. A business-related BTEC or HND could help you find a position with greater responsibilities.

You may find it useful to have an NVQ Level 2 and/ or 3 in Business and Administration or a City & Guilds Certificate/Diploma in Business and Administration. Advanced apprenticeships are also available.

Some employers may expect a bachelor's degree or equivalent. Any subject is acceptable but business, administration, secretarial studies and management degrees may increase your chances.

Previous experience, usually about 2 years, in other administrative or clerical roles is vital. For this reason graduates are unlikely to enter directly into a PA position. Since junior level administrative roles are very competitive, registering with temp agencies could be the best way to gain initial experience.

To show your commitment to the career, it may be beneficial to take the Private and Executive Secretary's Diploma offered by London Chamber of Commerce and Industry (LCCI) International Qualifications or Pitman Training's Executive PA Diploma. These are also useful for developing desirable skills such as shorthand and audio typing. A foreign language can also be helpful.

What the work involves

Personal assistants ease the workload of senior managers and directors, allowing businesses to run more efficiently.

They are responsible for administrative and secretarial duties.

You will work on a one-to-one basis with your manager, often making decisions on their behalf and representing them at events.

It will be your job to organise efficient administrative systems, both paper and IT based. You will maintain diaries, take minutes, answer phone calls, greet visitors, write letters and arrange meetings and travel.

Type of person suited to this work

Excellent organisational skills are essential. The role involves juggling several things at once so you need to be adaptable, efficient and able to work to deadlines. You will have to follow instructions but also use your initiative and manage your own workload.

You will need a good knowledge of the company you work for and you may have to deal with budgets. Strong written and verbal communication skills are a must.

You should be discreet and reliable as you may be dealing with confidential information. Excellent IT skills are essential in this role.

Working conditions

You will work in an office and your hours will mainly be 9am–5pm but occasionally you may have to work overtime to meet deadlines.

As the role involves frequent contact with colleagues and clients, you will be expected to dress quite formally.

Future prospects

With experience, PAs can progress rapidly to senior roles with increased responsibility and the possibility of managing junior employees.

PAs gain insight into all aspects of a business and these skills can be transferred to roles in other sectors, such as human resources or public relations.

There are opportunities to work throughout the UK and, if you have language skills, abroad.

Experienced PAs can become self-employed as 'virtual assistants', working from home for a range of clients.

Advantages/disadvantages

The job can be varied and interesting with a lot of responsibility.

If you have a good working relationship with your manager then the role can be very rewarding.

As you work in a support role, it can be frustrating if your contribution is not recognised within the company.

Money guide

Salaries vary according to the size and type of company you work for and your level of responsibility.

Wages tend to be higher in London and south-east England.

A starting salary tends to be around £17,000 to £25,000 per year.

A senior personal assistant in a large company could achieve a salary of up to £50,000.

Related opportunities

- Human Resources/Personnel Officer p28
- Public Relations Officer p404
- Receptionist p46
- Secretary p51

Further information

Institute of Administrative Management
www.instam.org

London Chamber of Commerce and Industry
www.londonchamber.co.uk

Skills CFA
www.skillscfa.org

PROJECT MANAGER

Qualifications and courses

There are no formal academic requirements but all entrants will need extensive experience in business, management, engineering, construction, IT, science, or whichever sector they are hoping to work in. Many project managers start in a project support team or gain experience managing smaller projects as part of another job.

It is increasingly common, and in some cases a requirement, for entrants into the field to hold a foundation degree, degree or postgraduate qualification in a relevant area of study, such as project management, business management, IT or construction management. Entry onto degree courses requires at least 2 A levels/3 H grades and 5 GCSEs/National 5s (A*–C/A–C), or equivalent.

Knowledge of PRINCE2 and specialist software such as MS Project or Workbench could be an advantage, though not essential.

There are options to study while you are working by taking online or part-time courses. The Association for Project Management (APM), The Chartered Institute for IT (BCS) and the Project Management Institute (PMI) all offer a range of professional qualifications which are suitable for both entry-level and experienced project managers.

What the work involves

Many project managers specialise in a particular area, such as the managing of commercial business improvements.

As project manager, you will oversee all aspects of a project, from plans to budgets. In the course of a job, a project manager will liaise with the client, create a timescale, a budget plan that keeps to agreed standards, and choose a capable project team. Furthermore, you will report back to your line manager or senior manager and clients, updating them on the progress, scheduling, and difficulties of the project.

You will need to access specialist software for scheduling, risk analysis, costing and estimating.

Type of person suited to this work

The project manager is relied upon to co-ordinate the team's operations and solve any problems that may arise. Due to this, it is necessary for people thinking of entering this profession to enjoy teamwork and have strong people management, communication, and organisational skills. In order to solve any problems which may arise, a project manager must be logical and methodical, especially when under pressure.

In addition to this, the job of a project manager requires good computer skills and an ability to understand complex information and control budgets, whilst working on several other projects.

Working conditions

A certain amount of variation must be allowed for from these hours due to variety in projects. However, generally, hours range from 9am–5pm, Monday to Friday. Like many jobs, the meeting of deadlines may mean these hours are occasionally increased.

Managers are often office based, with the occasional need to visit sites or clients to check progression. Should a manager be working on a project abroad, it may be necessary to spend prolonged periods of time away from home.

Future prospects

By becoming a project manager you will be joining a growing industry. Upon entering the profession, most people will make up part of the project support team, progressing to team leader after the gaining of experience, which gradually leads to a position as project manager.

There are opportunities for promotion to senior management posts, although this may mean changing companies, with some managers setting up their own consultancy business. There are opportunities to work abroad.

Advantages/disadvantages

This job allows for variety due to there being many different projects to work on. Although this may cause the employee to feel pressured, the rewards of the completed project may be of greater benefit.

Salaries are very rewarding and the expansion of the industry indicates that this is fast becoming a thriving industry with long term employment prospects.

Money guide

The starting salary for people joining the profession in a support role ranges from around £25,000 to £30,000 a year.

Earnings for experienced project managers can be between £30,000 and £60,000.

Top salaries can reach in excess of £75,000.

Freelance project managers will be paid a daily rate.

There are often opportunities for bonuses when a deadline or objective has been met.

Related opportunities

- Business Analyst p138
- Construction Supervisor/Manager p76
- Risk Manager p50

Further information

Association for Project Management
www.apm.org.uk

Chartered Management Institute
www.managers.org.uk

Project Management Institute
www.pmi.org.uk

QUALITY MANAGER

Qualifications and courses

There are no set entry requirements although many entrants hold a degree or HND. The general entry requirements for a degree are 2 A levels/3 H grades and 5 GCSEs/National 5s (A*–C/A–C). HNDs usually require at least 1 A level/H grade and 4 GCSEs/National 5s. Depending on the industry that you want to move into, useful subjects may include business studies, engineering or physical, mathematical or applied sciences. Some areas require a technical background but others are open to all graduates. A pre-entry postgraduate qualification is not needed, although they are available.

You will need previous experience in quality control or management. Graduates can gain experience by trying to get a relevant summer job, arrange a work shadowing placement or seek out and talk to staff in supporting roles. You can also start in a technical job and progress to quality control.

Entry without a degree or HND is sometimes possible if an applicant has significant training and experience in a technician role, or is moving across from another vocational field involving quality or management. Having a relevant BTEC, HND, degree or professional qualification can boost your promotion prospects, so if you don't currently hold any higher qualifications it might be something to consider if you wish to progess. Providers of professional qualifications include the Chartered Quality Institute (CQI) and the Chartered Management Institute (CMI).

What the work involves

Quality managers are employed by an organisation to ensure that quality assurance aims are met in relation to products or services; this includes legal compliance levels and customer expectations.

Practices include monitoring and advising on existing systems in order to consistently improve current standards, and publishing data and reports that inform management.

Quality managers must ensure that the company they are working for is applying the required level of environmental and health and safety standards. Encouraging staff to adhere to new doctrines and legislation is fundamental.

Type of person suited to this work

This job is suited to someone who has an interest in securing and improving standards of quality. In order to do this, it is necessary to have good communication skills in order to influence and persuade others to follow set regulations and uphold required standards.

Problems may arise due to complicated legislation and staff lacking interest and so quality managers must be resilient and create ways in which models of quality can be easily understood and adhered to. An organisation's customers must be listened to and so quality managers must be adaptable and approachable.

Working conditions

Normal working hours apply when employed by the government or a bank, although a position in engineering, production or retail could involve shift work. Offices and laboratories are where most are based, although those with experience often become consultants to smaller firms once they have gained enough experience to be self-employed.

It may be necessary to travel to different clients during the working day, or even to stay overnight.

Future prospects

There are around 25,000 quality managers in the UK with employment opportunities in a wide range of industrial, commercial and public sector organisations. You can work for small companies or large multinational corporations.

Career development prospects are good. Experienced quality managers may be able to progress to senior management or director-level positions. It is possible to progress within the quality function or to go on to management jobs in other areas of the business. Some go on to become freelance consultants.

Advantages/disadvantages

Quality managers have high levels of responsibility and so the work they undertake can be both rewarding and respected.

Career progression or movement to self-employment is possible.

Quality legislation is constantly changing so entrants must be willing to remain up to date with developments in the field.

Money guide

Quality managers can expect a starting salary in the region of £20,000 to £25,000.

As you gain experience and progress to a senior role, you can achieve earnings of £25,000 to £50,000.

Salaries vary according to the sector you are working in, company size and geographical location.

Related opportunities

- Project Manager p44
- Quality Control Inspector p226
- Statistician p524

Further information

British Quality Foundation
www.bqf.org.uk

Chartered Management Institute
www.managers.org.uk

Chartered Quality Institute
www.thecqi.org

RECEPTIONIST

Qualifications and courses

There are no minimum entry requirements, although employers are likely to ask for 5 GCSEs/National 5s (A*–C/A–C), including English and Maths, or NVQs/SVQs at Levels 1 or 2.

IT skills such as word processing and previous office experience will be a distinct advantage. You can gain experience through temping for agencies. Foreign languages may also be useful if you're applying to an organisation that deals with international visitors and clients.

There are various relevant training options available that might give you an advantage. City & Guilds offer several courses such as the Level 2 Diploma in Reception Operation Services and the Level 3 Advanced Diploma in Reception and Front Office Services. There is also an NCFE Level 1 NVQ Certificate in Customer Service and a Level 2 Certificate in Customer Service Knowledge.

An intermediate level Apprenticeship in Business and Administration may be available for candidates aged 16–24 who are interested in becoming a receptionist.

Once entrants obtain a position, training will be provided on the job and many employers encourage further study.

What the work involves

You will be greeting visitors, signing them in and out of the building, checking they know where they are going and answering any queries.

Often based by the entrance, you will be the first point of contact for the organisation both for visitors and those phoning to make enquiries.

You will be responsible for answering the telephone, transferring calls and taking messages, as well as managing queries via email.

You may also manage incoming and outgoing post and handle cash transactions.

Type of person suited to this work

You will create the first impression of your organisation, so it is vital that you should be friendly, welcoming, outgoing and well presented.

Excellent communication skills are essential as you will be solving problems and queries for visitors and other members of staff.

You will need to be able to remain calm under pressure and balance a heavy workload, as the reception desk could get very busy at times.

Good organisation skills and efficiency are needed for dealing with visitors' queries swiftly and accurately.

Working conditions

Receptionists are based at a reception desk, with access to a phone and computer.

You will normally work standard office hours Monday to Friday, but this does depend on the opening hours of your place of work. You may need to work evenings and weekends.

How busy you are is entirely dependent on the size and nature of the organisation you work for.

There are usually opportunities to work part-time or on temporary contracts.

Future prospects

All types of organisations employ receptionists including law firms, banks, garages, leisure centres and veterinary practices. There are therefore good job prospects across the UK.

Reception work offers progression into other areas such as office or customer service work; you will develop a good range of transferable skills.

You may be able to progress to a managerial role or supervisory position after a few years' experience and further training.

Once within a company, you may also be able to sound out other opportunities, even if unrelated to your field.

Advantages/disadvantages

This is a great job if you enjoy meeting people and providing good customer service.

Some people you encounter may be rude or angry if they have a problem with the company you work for.

There are good opportunities to enter other professions such as office or secretarial work.

Money guide

Starting salaries are around £11,500 to £19,000.

Senior receptionists with extra responsibilities may earn £25,000 or more.

Temporary and part-time receptionists can earn up to £10 an hour.

Related opportunities

- Medical Receptionist p39
- Personal Assistant p43
- Secretary p51

Further information

London Chamber of Commerce and Industry
www.londonchamber.co.uk

Skills CFA
www.skillscfa.org

RECRUITMENT/EMPLOYMENT AGENCY CONSULTANT

Qualifications and courses

Employers are likely to ask for a minimum of 5 GCSEs/National 5s (A*–C/A–C), although many entrants are graduates. The general entry requirements for a degree are 2 A levels/3 H grades and 5 GCSEs/National 5s (A*–C/A–C). Graduate schemes are available and although most subjects are welcome, a degree in human resources, business or a subject related to the industry the agency recruits for may give you an edge.

While there are many entry-level and trainee vacancies available there is also a lot of competition for them, so prior experience in sales, human resources or another customer-oriented role will be an advantage.

Your skills and personality will often be more important than your academic qualifications. Good sales skills, an excellent telephone manner and a positive attitude are vital.

The Institute of Recruitment Professionals (IRP) delivers various levels of career development through apprenticeships, training and certification, on behalf of the Recruitment and Employment Confederation (REC). Additionally, the Chartered Institute of Personnel and Development (CIPD) also offers various courses to help you develop throughout your career.

What the work involves

As a recruitment consultant, it will be your job to match up candidates with jobs. Your clients will be both the companies you recruit for and the candidates you are recruiting.

You will help companies recruit the right staff for permanent and temporary jobs through advertising, networking, headhunting and referrals.

Your work will include carrying out a preliminary interview and background check and then helping suitable candidates to find work to suit their skills and experience.

You will assess people's skills to help them decide on the type of work they want, and may suggest further training, which could be available through your company. You will spend time making contacts with new companies to sell your agency's services.

Type of person suited to this work

You will be selling your agency's services so will need to be well presented with excellent sales ability.

You will probably be working on commission so should be able to remain calm when working to tight deadlines.

You will need to be persuasive as it is essential that employers continue to use your agency. You may need to be persistent if they do not respond after a first approach.

Working conditions

Office hours will often be long as you might have to speak to clients outside working hours.

You will be doing a lot of work on the phone and some agencies are internet based. You may need to visit employer premises, so a driving licence would be needed. You will probably work in a team and be expected to dress smartly.

Future prospects

Recruitment consultancy is a growing industry, and almost 100,000 people already work in recruitment. Opportunities depend on the economy and which sectors are hiring new staff.

You could work for a specialist agency, for example supplying medical staff, but may need experience within that sector first. Some people work as 'head hunters', actively searching out people for specific high-level jobs.

With good results you could be promoted to senior consultant and then branch manager. You may go on to start your own agency or you could move into a related area such as human resources.

Advantages/disadvantages

You will meet people at all levels and will get satisfaction from helping them find the right job or career.

You will develop transferable interpersonal skills and a better understanding of the recruitment process if you ever decide to change careers.

Working on commission can be stressful and clients and businesses can be demanding.

This is a very competitive career and your success will depend on your sales ability.

There are often targets to hit which need to be balanced alongside finding the right candidate for the role.

Money guide

Recruitment consultants often work on commission and receive bonuses for meeting sales targets. This means that you can earn considerably more than your basic salary if you perform well.

Trainees usually start on a basic salary between £15,000 and £20,000 per year, plus commission.

Managers with 10–15 years' experience can achieve over £40,000 basic salary (£60,000 after commission).

Wages are higher in London and the south-east of England.

Related opportunities

■ Human Resources/Personnel Officer p28
■ Marketing Manager/Director p395
■ Secretary p51

Further information

Chartered Institute of Personnel and Development
www.cipd.co.uk

Recruitment & Employment Confederation
www.rec.uk.com

REGENERATION MANAGER/ ECONOMIC DEVELOPMENT OFFICER

Qualifications and courses

Entry without a degree is possible with significant skills and experience, although many entrants to this profession are graduates. Useful subjects include regeneration, housing, planning and surveying, and economics. Entry for a degree requires at least 2 A levels/3 H grades plus 5 GCSEs/National 5s (A*–C/A–C), including English and Maths. BTECs, HNC/HND qualifications and postgraduate study may all be beneficial as well.

You should also gain relevant pre-entry work experience in areas such as housing, planning, urban design or surveying or do voluntary environmental work in order to improve career and employment prospects. Job placements within regeneration are not recommended for new graduates as several years' relevant experience may be required.

Knowledge of government regeneration policy and the main sources of funding may also strengthen applications. Voluntary placements are available with organisations such as Groundwork and the Prince's Regeneration Trust.

You may start out as an administrator, assistant or researcher in an economic development unit and work your way up.

What the work involves

Regeneration managers aim to improve the living standards within their community by developing local projects with the aim to increase job opportunities and stimulate economic growth. The extent of involvement ranges from the presentation of an idea, to ensuring that the project is completed on time and on budget, and the generation of financial support and planning permission.

You will also be charged with improving relations between local businesses and government, improving business networks, setting up training schemes for the unemployed, applying for national and European funding as well as promoting the local area to tourists and new employers.

Typical areas you would be expected to help develop would include residential areas where local industries have closed down, areas of low income and high unemployment, and areas with poor access to healthcare and education.

Specialist fields include economic development, planning, surveying and housing.

Type of person suited to this work

It is necessary to have an interest in the ways in which communities and living environments can be managed and improved.

As this profession involves a lot of negotiation with a variety of people, you will need good communication skills and should be able to influence people towards contributing in a positive way.

Regeneration managers often need to be strict with budgets and able to solve problems that may arise; both of which need a strong will and an ability to deliver results in a set amount of time.

Working conditions

Working hours are typical of those for an office job, with the number of hours worked usually being around 37 a week. However, on occasion, you will be expected to attend a residency meeting during the evening or at weekends.

Employment with local councils tends to be employee focused, with most offering part-time or job sharing contracts, alongside flexitime schemes.

Although mostly based in an office, you will need to travel to sites that are undergoing the regeneration process in order to meet with residents, clients and agencies.

Future prospects

The government is currently committed to improving community areas through regeneration schemes, making this a very positive vocation to get involved with.

Opportunities are available within local authorities and government agencies, regional development agencies and English Partnerships and the government's national regeneration agency. There are also employment possibilities with private consultancies, housing associations and property developers.

Advantages/disadvantages

Both the public and private sector are becoming involved in regeneration projects, with opportunities opening up in senior management roles for those with experience.

You get to implement and oversee development and growth in local areas which will hopefully provide young adults especially with opportunities otherwise denied to them.

This job may be extremely challenging when you have to convince people that regeneration is positive, especially when they have lived in a location for a certain number of years.

Money guide

Initially regeneration managers can expect to earn approximately £22,000 a year.

Salaries steadily increase to around £25,000 to £35,000 as you gain experience.

Those in senior management roles can achieve a salary of up to £50,000 a year, depending on their level of responsibility.

Related opportunities

- Building Conservation Officer p63
- Chartered Surveyor p70
- Project Manager p44

Further information

British Urban Regeneration Association
www.rudi.net/partners/bura

Homes and Communities Agency
www.homesandcommunities.co.uk

Local Government Association
www.local.gov.uk

Qualifications and courses

There are no set entry requirements for this career, although candidates with 3 GCSEs/National 5s (A*–C/A–C), including English and Maths, would be at an advantage. Whilst training in registration law and procedures is given on the job, experience of dealing with a wide range of people and public speaking might be useful when making your application.

In England and Wales training is organised by the General Register Office and candidates can take the Registrar General's Certificate of Competence in Registration Law and Practice. In Scotland, training is organised by the General Register Office for Scotland and candidates take the Certificate of Proficiency in the Law and Practice of Registration, eligibility for which requires at least 2 years' work experience. The Local Registration Services Association (LRSA) launched a new qualification in 2014 to bring together all local authorities under one unified set of standards and professional expectations.

Training in customer care and dealing with bereavement is also highly likely.

Applicants from certain professions are prohibited from becoming registrars, including doctors, midwives, ministers of religion, funeral directors and anyone working in the life assurance industry.

What the work involves

Registrars record all births, stillbirths, marriages, civil partnerships and deaths in their local area, making sure all details are accurate.

After a birth, you will interview parents, record the baby's name and date of birth and issue a birth certificate. After a death, you will interview relatives before providing a death certificate and informing the coroner or procurator fiscal if anything seems suspicious.

You will interview people planning to marry or enter a civil partnership to check that they are legally eligible to do so and you will conduct marriage and civil partnership ceremonies.

Type of person suited to this work

You will need to be a good listener and have the ability to communicate effectively with a wide range of people.

As you will often be dealing with people in difficult circumstances, discretion, tact and patience are essential attributes.

Confidence with public speaking is important for conducting marriages and civil partnerships.

Attention to detail, accuracy and the ability to work neatly are all vital when completing forms and ensuring that all legal requirements have been met.

You must be able to use your initiative and judgement to assess whether someone is withholding information.

Working conditions

You will be based in the registrar's office for your district and much of your day will be spent interviewing people by appointment.

You will work a 37 hour week which will often include Saturdays. You may also need to be on-call to work evenings, Sundays or bank holidays.

You will conduct ceremonies in various locations such as hotels, civic buildings and other public places so a driving licence is useful.

Future prospects

Vacancies within this field only arise occasionally.

In England and Wales the usual career path is from assistant registrar to deputy registrar, then to registrar and finally to superintendent. In Scotland there are only 2 grades: assistant registrar and registrar.

You will have opportunities for in-house training and you could move into other administration-based careers.

The increase in the number of civil ceremonies may present more opportunities for registrars to become celebrants, or those who are employed to conduct marriages and civil partnerships only. These jobs are often seasonal and part-time.

Advantages/disadvantages

The work is varied and no two days are the same.

You have the opportunity to meet many different people who will be at their happiest or saddest moments.

You will work some weekends and bank holidays and may be on-call at other times.

This is regarded as an important community position to hold so you are likely to be well respected.

Money guide

Assistant registrars usually start on around £16,000 to £17,000.

Registrars can expect to earn between £25,000 and £35,000.

A superintendent registrar could earn around £48,000.

Part-time celebrants earn a set fee for each ceremony they conduct.

Related opportunities

- Court Administrative Officer p347
- Legal Executive p353
- Magistrates' Court Legal Adviser/Sheriff's Clerk p355

Further information

General Register Office
www.gro.gov.uk

Local Government Careers
www.lgjobs.com

The Association of Registrars of Scotland
www.aros.org.uk

RISK MANAGER

Qualifications and courses

Entry without a degree is possible and entails following the career path from an administrative role to a risk assistant position and finally to a risk management role. Employers would require A level qualifications or equivalent for this route.

However, the majority of risk managers do have a degree. Some larger companies run graduate trainee schemes, which will usually require a 2.1 degree. Preferred degree subjects include risk management, economics, finance, management, building surveying, engineering, business studies or actuarial science, although graduates from other disciplines will be considered too. Graduates from risk management courses are particularly sought after. Entry to a degree will require a minimum of 2 A levels/3 H grades and 5 GCSEs/National 5s (A*–C/A–C). Prior work experience in insurance may also be required, which graduates can gain through summer placements.

If your first degree is not in a relevant subject, or as a way to strengthen your application, you can study for the Institute of Risk Management (IRM)'s Certificate in Risk Management in Financial Services or for a postgraduate degree. If you have not done so already, your employer will expect you to go on to qualify as an Associate of the Chartered Insurance Institute (ACII) by studying for their Advanced Diploma in Insurance.

What the work involves

Risk managers are responsible for assessing the viability and risks of a business or project within a business. They identify, analyse, control and monitor each risk for the safety of the business as well as develop coping strategies when issues arise or things go wrong.

Risks can be different in each organisation; financial companies are concerned with market risks and even the health service needs to identify risks to patients and staff.

You will be doing a variety of tasks including risk surveys, designing strategies to prevent risks, and presenting all of your findings to the head of the business. You will be charged with conducting policy audits, liaising with internal and external parties as well as making sure that the company complies with professional standards.

Type of person suited to this work

You will need to have in-depth knowledge of the organisation that you work for and excellent research skills to be able to identify potential risks.

Good problem-solving skills will be essential for creating strategies as will knowledge of regulations which are relevant to your company.

It is important to have excellent communication skills, both written and oral, as you will need to write up reports of your findings and present these back to your colleagues or clients. Being persuasive and tactful will help you convince people to support your view of how to deal with a potential risk.

Working conditions

You will be working around 37 hours a week, Monday to Friday, however a heavy workload might require longer hours.

Although the majority of your time will be spent in an office, you might need to visit sites which could be dangerous, or industrial locations such as engineering plants and building sites.

It would be helpful to have a driving licence and your own vehicle for travelling between sites.

Future prospects

There are jobs available across the UK, with risk managers being employed in both the private and public sector; employers may include banks, local authorities, engineering firms and the emergency services. There is currently a shortage of financial risk managers.

Promotions are possible from risk manager to chief risk officer; you might need to move around different companies though to gain enough experience. You can also go into self-employment as a consultant or trainer. There are promotional possibilities to senior positions through the gaining of experience, with opportunities increasing throughout the UK when specialising in a technical field or industry sector.

Advantages/disadvantages

This is an exciting and varied career as you can work in a range of sectors from financial to the emergency services.

There could be dire consequences if you make a mistake and neglect a risk.

There are opportunities to be self-employed as a consultant and to travel abroad.

Money guide

The typical starting salary for a risk assistant or technician position is £21,000 to £22,000.

With the opportunity to progress to risk analyst, after gaining 1 to 6 years' experience, salary potential increases to between £29,000 and £44,000.

At director level or as a highly experienced and specialised risk manager, it is possible to reach a salary in excess of £70,000.

Related opportunities

- Chartered Surveyor p70
- Insurance Broker p29
- Insurance Risk Surveyor p32

Further information

Association of Insurance and Risk Managers in Industry and Commerce
www.airmic.com

Institute of Risk Management
www.theirm.org

SECRETARY

Qualifications and courses

Required qualifications vary depending on the employer and sector and there are vacancies for all levels of candidates from school leavers to those with a postgraduate degree. As a minimum you should have some GCSEs/National 5s (A*–C/A–C), including English, and a GCSE in Business Studies could be helpful.

Vacancies aimed at graduates may involve more responsibility. Although there are no specific degree subjects required, degrees in business with languages, government and public administration, business, management, law, and secretarial studies would be particularly useful.

Excellent IT skills are a must in this job role, including a typing speed of at least 50 words per minute. Other specific skills that are sometimes sought include shorthand and minute taking, and audio transcription. A good way to gain these is by taking a secretarial course.

There are courses available for both school leavers and graduates. For example there are NVQs in Business and Administration at Levels 1–4 and also private colleges such as Pitman Training which offer diplomas in Secretarial Studies. Foundation degrees in Business and Finance, BTEC National Certificates and apprenticeships are also available.

However, relevant experience is often more highly valued than specific, formal qualifications, especially since competition for vacancies is high. Part-time jobs and temping for employment agencies are a good way to start and can sometimes lead to permanent positions.

A second language, particularly French, Italian or Japanese, is often useful if you wish to work for an international company or explore opportunities abroad.

What the work involves

Secretaries are responsible for giving clerical assistance to professionals in order to ensure the efficient running of an organisation. They are responsible for the coordination of office procedures and are often in charge of monitoring certain projects or junior staff.

The role and the responsibilities associated with it are entirely dependent on the size, sector and nature of the company you work for. Typically, most secretaries will be expected to type letters, emails and reports, set up and update filing systems, take care of diaries and travel arrangements as well as coordinate meetings and appointments.

Type of person suited to this work

You must be highly organised, efficient and able to multi-task.

You will need a good grasp of spelling, grammar and punctuation as well as a fast typing speed. It is important that you are IT literate, have a good attention to detail and are able to work to tight deadlines.

You should have excellent communication skills and be friendly, helpful and discreet, especially when dealing with confidential information.

The ability to work on your own, as well as part of a team, is also essential.

Numerical skills are an advantage as your role may include dealing with financial tasks.

Working conditions

Your working hours will typically be from 9am to 5pm, with longer hours during busy periods.

You will probably be located in an office, spending the majority of your day on the phone and working at a computer.

Future prospects

You could progress in a bigger company to a job with a more senior manager, or to a role as a personal assistant.

You could find a role in human resources, sales or marketing.

With experience, many secretaries are working as a virtual assistant from home.

Advantages/disadvantages

You can use your experience in a particular company or department to gain a promotion.

Part-time and temporary work is widely available in this line of work.

This job could be a practical way of using your skills and interests.

Tight deadlines and a heavy workload can make this job stressful. The work can often be repetitive.

Money guide

You can expect a starting salary of between £14,000 and £19,000 when working outside London, and £20,000 to £24,000 within London.

After significant experience, or with specialised responsibility, salaries could increase to between £28,000 and £33,000.

Roles in banking, law and finance are more highly paid than those in the media, charities and smaller companies. Working for FTSE100 companies can lead to higher salaries. Annual and performance-related bonuses are possible in some sectors.

Related opportunities

- Bilingual Secretary p330
- Personal Assistant p43
- Receptionist p46

Further information

Institute of Chartered Secretaries and Administrators
www.icsa.org.uk

Skills CFA
www.skillscfa.org

STOCK MARKET TRADER

Qualifications and courses

You will need at least a 2.1 degree or higher, preferably in subjects with a strong numerical focus such as actuarial science, economics, accountancy, maths or finance. Minimum requirements for degree courses are often at least 2 A levels/3 H grades and 5 GCSEs/National 5s (A*–C/A–C), including English and Maths.

You will also need a professional qualification that meets the Financial Conduct Authority (FCA)'s requirements and be registered with them as an 'approved person' before being allowed to trade.

Competition for positions is incredibly intense and the selection process is demanding, often involving psychometric tests. It is a good idea to try and gain an internship or financial work experience as networking is a large part of this industry. Alternatively, major investment banks offer graduate training schemes, which you will need to apply for by October/November the year before you plan to start.

Fluency in foreign languages is highly sought after within international companies and candidates will need to demonstrate strong skills in team-working, numeracy and communication skills as well as a decisive nature and ability to work under pressure.

Entry without a degree or HND is difficult, though possible if you work your way up through the administrative roles and make contacts.

What the work involves

Traders use their knowledge of the market to make the highest possible profit on behalf of investors by buying and selling shares, bonds and other assets.

There are three types: market traders operate on behalf of clients; sales traders highlight new financial ideas, but take direct orders from clients; and proprietary traders make investments for banks.

You will be dealing with large sums of money, so your decisions must be quick and well informed. You will need to build strong contacts in order to be successful in this business.

Type of person suited to this work

You should have enthusiasm for the financial sector and enjoy a working environment that is highly performance related.

Alongside this, you will need to be extremely confident and full of informed initiative, whilst having the ability to cope with the constant pressure of trading with large sums of money that belong to other people.

As well as demanding accuracy, skilled analysis and responsibility, the job also requires that you be forceful and competitive, an excellent verbal communicator and a team player.

Working conditions

Traders often need to begin work at 7am in order to be on top of overnight developments in foreign markets, ready for the 8am opening of the London Stock Exchange, often not finishing their working day until 5pm.

The highly pressurised trading arena involves the monitoring of markets on a screen and making deals over the phone. You have to be reactive to even the smallest of changes and so the work environment is very noisy as each trader is either on the phone or liaising with colleagues.

Future prospects

Competition for entry level and traineeship roles is fierce.

Once in the industry however, there are many opportunities for progression. With two years' experience and qualifications with either the Chartered Institute for Securities and Investment (CISI) or as a Chartered Financial Analyst (CFA), you can be promoted to an analyst or trader. After a further five years you will be put in charge of a team or gain the responsibility of a new trading desk. These positions often lead to associate, senior associate and director level.

International offices are common with investment banks, bringing an opportunity to work in foreign arenas.

Advantages/disadvantages

This is an exciting and rewarding job that changes on a daily basis due to the constant changes in the financial market.

The highly pressurised environment can be stressful and means the professional duration of a stock market trader is generally less than those in other professions.

Money guide

The starting salary for a trainee stock market trader is usually £26,000 to £32,000, plus a small signing-on bonus.

A typical, experienced trader will be earning £45,000 to in excess of £150,000 per year.

An associate with experience selling credits can expect a salary of around £140,000 per year in a top tier bank or around £230,000 if working in more lucrative markets. (These are figures for markets in London and other regions will sometimes pay far less than these top figures.)

In addition to these impressive salaries are large bonuses and other possible benefits including non-contributory pensions and mortgage subsidies.

Related opportunities

- Investment Analyst p34
- Risk Manager p50
- Stockbroker p53

Further information

Financial Conduct Authority
www.fca.org.uk

Financial Skills Partnership
www.financialskillspartnership.org.uk

London Stock Exchange
www.londonstockexchange.com

STOCKBROKER

Qualifications and courses

You will normally need at least a 2.1 degree. Any discipline will be considered but employers prefer degrees in economics, business studies, maths, physics, accountancy or law. Entry onto a degree programme normally requires 2 A levels/3 H grades and 5 GCSEs/ National 5s (A*–C/A–C).

Possession of a postgraduate qualification such as a Master of Business Administration (MBA) or a master's in subjects such as business or economics has become increasingly common.

Graduate trainee positions are available. The application process may include psychometric and aptitude testing or making a presentation to a group panel. Pre-entry experience, such as internships, placements and vacation work, will give you a distinct advantage as competition for entry is intense. Many employers will offer full-time jobs to their interns.

Entry without a degree or HND is difficult, though it may be possible for individuals with A levels/H grades and relevant experience to move into stockbroking from administrative or research roles.

In order to trade, all stockbrokers require a professional qualification that meets the Financial Conduct Authority (FCA)'s requirements and must be registered with it as an 'approved person'.

What the work involves

Stockbrokers work for individuals or companies investing their clients' money to make them a profit by buying and selling stocks, bonds and shares.

You will be managing investments, advising your clients on investing their money and trading on behalf of your clients, often dealing with huge amounts of money.

You will have to keep up to date with economic trends, interpret and analyse market information, and predict how a company's stocks and shares are likely to perform.

You will have to respond rapidly to changes in trends and stock market fluctuations.

Type of person suited to this work

To succeed as a stockbroker you must be confident, determined, competitive and outgoing.

You will have to predict trends in a constantly changing market and take risks with huge sums of money so must be decisive and able to remain calm under pressure. You will need to be personable, trustworthy and honest with a good reputation.

You will need excellent IT skills and will be expected to work long hours and to dress smartly.

Working conditions

You will be office based, acquiring much of your market information from computers and doing much of your work by telephone.

Hours are long: you will probably start early and finish late in order to accommodate international markets in different time zones. You will most likely work over the weekend as well. Much of your day will be spent in a very busy, tense and pressurised environment.

Future prospects

You could be working for a firm which specialises in this work or for other financial institutions such as banks or building societies. Your career will develop by taking on more responsibilities and more important clients.

Competition for jobs is intense so work experience is vital. Economic changes can happen fast so jobs are not always secure.

This is a high pressure job and many stockbrokers finish their careers in their 40s. You could move into other areas within finance such as fund management or become self-employed as a consultant.

Advantages/disadvantages

The hours are long and the work is very pressurised and stressful.

It is a very competitive job and you will need to be tough and determined to succeed.

The work can be very rewarding and is extremely well paid.

No two days will be the same, the market is in constant fluctuation and you will be required to respond accordingly. This gives a diverse and exciting environment to work in.

Money guide

In addition to their regular salary, stockbrokers receive bonuses on the trade they do and can earn substantially more.

As a basic salary, you could earn between £24,000 and £30,000 a year when you first start work and training after university.

With experience you could earn between £45,000 and £80,000. After many years of experience and depending on location, some stockbrokers can earn over £100,000, including bonuses.

Related opportunities

- Accountant p2
- Bank Manager p10
- Economist p20
- Stock Market Trader p52

Further information

Financial Conduct Authority
www.fca.org.uk

London Stock Exchange
www.londonstockexchange.com

TAX ADVISER

Qualifications and courses

There are no set entry routes, and entry without a degree is possible as an apprentice or trainee. However, entrants holding a degree in subjects such as accountancy and finance, law, economics or mathematics may enjoy better employment prospects. Entry onto a degree is usually with 2 A Levels/3 H Grades and 5 GCSEs/National 5s (A*–C/A–C).

Graduate entrants will typically look to gaining a professional qualification in taxation, often whilst employed as a tax trainee or technician. An Association of Taxation Technicians (ATT) qualification can be undertaken via distance learning, day or block release, or through evening or weekend courses. Once qualified, ATT certificate holders are eligible to take the Chartered Institute of Taxation (CIOT) Chartered Tax Advisers (CTA) examination.

Alternatively, graduates with professional chartered or certified qualifications in fields such as accountancy or law could transfer to this career, but would usually be required to sit the CTA examination.

Graduate training scheme opportunities are available, for which a 2.1 Honours degree in a relevant subject is the usual requirement. HM Revenue & Customs run a Tax Professional Graduate Programme and KPMG offer the Tax Graduate Programme, comprised of 9 months' technical training and a 3 year working contract.

ATT runs a Level 4 Higher Apprenticeship in Tax. Apprentices will work towards awards such as the Level 4 Diploma in Tax Practice and Level 4 Diploma in Tax, in addition to the standard ATT qualification. Availability of the apprenticeship may be limited on the basis of geographical location.

What the work involves

Tax advisers draw upon a combination of law, administration and accountancy knowledge in order to advise clients on the right amount of tax they need to pay. Clients could be large firms, small companies, or individuals.

Most advisers work in either corporate or personal tax.

Work will consist of meeting with clients to assess their financial situation before developing and implementing strategies to help them meet their tax obligations.

You will be required to stay informed about developments in tax and financial law, and must be able to explain these laws to your clients.

Type of person suited to this work

You will need to enjoy working with numbers. Strong maths skills are paramount, as is the ability to retain knowledge of financial and tax law and keep up to date with developments.

You must have strong analytical skills and be a competent researcher and problem solver.

Good communication skills are essential as you will frequently be in contact with clients whose needs will be varied.

Working conditions

You will typically work standard office hours, with possible extra hours at peak periods, such as the end of the tax year.

Work is mostly office based, but you will need to travel regularly in order to meet with clients. For this reason a valid driving licence will be helpful.

Work is available throughout the UK, however there is a higher concentration of graduate opportunities in London and the south-east of England.

Future prospects

Employment prospects are significantly improved on achieving CTA status with the CIOT and there are good opportunities for CTA qualified tax advisers.

With experience you could progress into a consultancy role. Additionally, if you are employed by a large firm, you could specialise in areas such as corporate finance or mergers and acquisitions.

Advantages/disadvantages

Prospects are favourable, with plenty of opportunities for CTA qualified advisers.

At times the work may feel pressurised, particularly towards the close of the tax year.

Money guide

Salaries for corporate and personal tax advisers often differ.

Entrant advisers who do not hold a degree can expect to earn between £18,000 and £25,000 a year in their first year of employment.

Graduate trainees can earn between £20,000 to £32,000 a year during their 2 years of training.

Chartered tax advisers with 2–4 years' experience can earn salaries of up to £55,000 a year.

Those who take on management or senior management responsibilities could stand to earn between £50,000 and £95,000 a year.

Directors can earn up to £140,000 per year.

Related opportunities

- Business Adviser p11
- Compliance Officer p16
- Financial Adviser p26

Further information

Association of Taxation Technicians
www.att.org.uk

Chartered Institute of Taxation
www.tax.org.uk

TELEPHONIST

Qualifications and courses

There are no formal entry requirements for this work, but 5 GCSEs/National 5s (A*–C/A–C), including English language and Maths, will be a distinct advantage. Many colleges offer relevant courses in customer service and telephone skills at Levels 1–3, including City & Guilds certificates and BTECs.

Basic computing skills or an IT qualification are useful, as is some basic experience in telesales or customer care. Temporary work is a good way to get experience and could lead to a permanent job offer. Apprenticeships are also available.

Being able to speak a foreign language may be an advantage depending on the organisation you're working for. Knowledge of alternative telephone systems, such as Type Talk, Meridian and Minicom, could also be helpful.

Most training is done on the job with a senior member of staff. Your employer may encourage you to study for NVQs such as Levels 1–4 in Customer Service, Levels 1 and 2 in Contact Centre Operations or Levels 2 and 3 in Contact Centre Professionals.

What the work involves

Telephonists work at a switchboard, answering calls, connecting callers to the right person and advising them on which department or person they need to speak to.

You will be responsible for a caller's first impression of your company.

Your job will include taking messages, testing phone lines and reporting faults. You may need to respond to out-of-office calls left on answering machines.

You might do other reception duties such as meeting and dealing with visitors, taking deliveries and other clerical work.

Type of person suited to this work

You will need a professional and friendly telephone manner, a clear and polite voice and good listening skills.

Excellent customer service is essential. You must be assertive with impatient and rude callers while at the same time remaining calm and understanding even when you are busy.

You should be someone who enjoys working with people in a team and who can work quickly and accurately.

It's also important to have a good understanding of how your organisation works in order to answer calls effectively.

Working conditions

Most of your work will be in an office or telephone room, probably with other people. You might be based at a reception desk.

Although you will probably work normal office hours, you might need to be at work to take calls before the company opens.

Some switchboards provide a 24-hour service which means working shifts including nights and weekends.

You will be wearing a headset and using computer databases and automated switchboards.

Part-time and flexible working hours are commonly available, particularly if you are working for the government, NHS, or for a school or other educational institution.

Future prospects

Most large or medium-sized companies need people to answer their phones and provide a reception service, so job opportunities are good.

You could work in finance, industry, schools, government, NHS, emergency services or transport companies and call centres.

You may lead a team of other telephonists or move into a job in telesales. You could become a senior telephonist receiving training in customer service skills and gaining administrative experience.

You could then move into a wide range of jobs working in business administration in offices or with the public.

Advantages/disadvantages

On a busy switchboard you will be working under pressure and could be working shifts.

Dealing with the public means staying polite and calm no matter what happens.

You will gain valuable customer service and administration skills to help you progress.

Money guide

As a trainee your starting salary is normally around £12,000 per year.

With more experience this can rise to between £15,000 and £19,000.

Earnings for a senior telephonist with experience and more responsibility, such as supervising other staff, may reach £21,000 or more.

Some employers offer an hourly rate of £7 to £9.

Related opportunities

- Court Administrative Officer p347
- Receptionist p46
- Secretary p51

Further information

Institute of Customer Service
www.instituteofcustomerservice.com

Skills CFA
www.skillscfa.org

TRAINING AND DEVELOPMENT OFFICER

Qualifications and courses

With relevant experience and skills entry is possible with or without a degree or HND, although having one can be an advantage. Useful subjects include human resources, psychology, IT and business. Entry onto degree courses usually requires a minimum of 2 A levels/3 H grades or equivalent and 5 GCSEs/National 5s (A*–C/A–C). Entry onto HND courses requires 1 A level/2 H grades and 4 GCSEs/National 5s.

Postgraduate qualifications are not necessary, although a master's or a diploma recognised by the Chartered Institute of Personnel and Development (CIPD) can improve your chances of success when applying for roles in the early stages of your career, or open up opportunities for advancement later on. When you sign up to a CIPD course you become a student member and when you finish you can upgrade to Associate Membership or Chartered Membership, depending on how senior your job role is.

Graduates can boost their application by gaining relevant work experience through summer placements, work shadowing or voluntary work. Getting involved in university societies that allow you to develop organisational, teamwork or leadership skills can also help.

New graduates are not always recruited directly into training roles, though some companies may have graduate schemes. Many will start out as an administration assistant and work their way up to training officer. Training manager positions require significant experience in an officer role. Entrants without a degree can also work their way up this way.

What the work involves

You will be responsible for making sure your company's staff have the skills and knowledge they need to make the business as efficient as possible.

Some of your work will involve looking at how to provide the best training at the lowest cost – from different options such as in-house, distance learning, IT packages or college courses. Some roles may involve a strong element of research and continuing professional development (CPD) in order to track developments in technology and operations in the field or industry that you are working in.

You will also deliver training yourself or organise other trainers to do this. You will have to write reports and make presentations assessing the value of training.

Type of person suited to this work

You should be interested in people and in helping them to develop and improve their skills. You will need to be able to pass on your knowledge and expertise in a lively, interesting way by designing imaginative and varied training that appeals to everyone.

You will need to be organised and able to plan ahead, meet deadlines and assess the effectiveness of training. To do this you will need excellent IT skills and an understanding of costs and budgets.

Working conditions

You will usually do normal office hours but may have to work longer at busy times or attend residential, evening or weekend events.

You will be based in an office, probably working as part of a team, but will spend a lot of your time out and about – delivering training, finding training venues, going to meetings and visiting staff in their work places.

Future prospects

Training managers come from a variety of backgrounds as they often become experts in their own field before moving into training people within the industry, but it is possible to start as a graduate trainee.

There are opportunities all over the country as all types of organisations have training managers. Developments in new technology and more on-the-job training have increased the need for staff training. More companies are using consultants to deliver training to their staff so opportunities to become a self-employed consultant are increasing. It is also possible to gain promotion or move into related areas.

Advantages/disadvantages

The work can be varied and you will have the satisfaction of passing on your expertise to help people learn and develop.

You may need to work hard to motivate staff who are having to do training they are not interested in or do not feel they need.

Money guide

Starting salaries at officer level are typically £22,000 to £30,000.

Experienced and qualified training managers can earn between £25,000 and £40,000. Senior training managers in large companies could earn £40,000 to £65,000.

Salaries will vary depending on experience, responsibility level, location and the size of the company. CIPD qualifications could also help you get a higher salary.

Related opportunities

- Further Education Lecturer p185
- Human Resources/Personnel Officer p28
- Work-based Training Instructor p198

Further information

Chartered Institute of Personnel and Development
www.cipd.co.uk

Building and Construction

Are you interested in working on a construction site with a team of people? Maybe your interest lies in buying and selling property and working in an office is more your sort of thing. All the jobs in the sector require someone with a great eye for detail, creative flair and someone who is very good at working with others. The jobs featured in this section are listed below. For similar jobs to the ones in this section why not have a look at *Engineering, Manufacturing and Production* on page 199.

ARCHITECT

Qualifications and courses

Professional architects must have chartered membership of the Royal Institute of British Architects (RIBA) and registration with the Architects Registration Board (ARB). The main route to qualification is through a RIBA/ARB-recognised degree. Minimum entry requirements are 3 A levels/H grades which should be drawn from academic fields of study. In addition you must have passed at least 5 GCSEs/National 5s including English, Maths and Physics or Chemistry. Equivalent qualifications such as a BTEC certificate/diploma may be accepted. Potential students may also be expected to present a portfolio at the interview stage.

Candidates without the usual entry requirements for a degree may be able to take a Foundation year at a school of architecture instead. Mature students with relevant experience may also be accepted.

Training as an architect takes 7 years. Candidates spend 3 years studying for an undergraduate degree in architecture (RIBA Part 1) and then undertake 12 months of supervised practical training in an architect's office or in some sector of the building industry. Then 2 years are spent studying for a diploma, further degree (BArch) or Master of Architecture (MArch) (RIBA Part 2). After completing a further 12-month work placement, trainees are then eligible to complete the RIBA Part 3 Examination in Professional Practice and Management.

If you have passed Part 1, you may be able to work as an architectural technician.

Alternatively, an office-based route for people with experience is also available whereby candidates are able to self-study for the RIBA Examination in Architecture while continuing to work full time.

What the work involves

Architects design new buildings, the spaces around them as well as any proposed changes to existing buildings.

Your work will include agreeing design briefs with clients, researching development sites, deciding which materials to use for particular buildings and drawing technical plans. You will also be responsible for testing new ideas, obtaining planning permission and inspecting building work while it is in progress.

You could specialise in a particular field such as building heritage and conservation, sustainable and environmental design, or project management.

Type of person suited to this work

You must be able to produce creative, detailed designs that meet the needs of your clients.

You will need excellent verbal communication skills for working with other professionals and for presenting your ideas to them and your clients. You also have to be organised and have good research and problem-solving skills.

As you will use computer-aided design (CAD) in your work, IT skills are also useful.

Working conditions

Although architects are based in offices, you will go out to visit construction sites and meet clients. You will need to pay attention to health and safety regulations when on-site. A driving licence may be necessary.

You are likely to work regular office hours, although you might have to do some work at weekends and during the evenings.

Future prospects

Generally, you would start work in a private architect's practice to gain wide experience of the work, but you may also work for other employers later on.

Self-employment is common for experienced architects.

Your career will be dependent on your experience, ability and competence. If you decide to remain in private work you could progress to associate level and possibly become a partner. Some of the larger architectural practices win international contracts so you could work on projects abroad.

You could continue to develop your knowledge by completing a postgraduate course in a subject related to architecture, such as civil engineering, town planning, and surveying, among others. These courses are offered by most schools of architecture.

Advantages/disadvantages

There may be problems to overcome when making design decisions, such as conflicting views to deal with.

There is personal satisfaction in dealing with these problems and creating designs for buildings that will influence the landscape for many years to come.

Money guide

Graduates who have completed Part 1 of their training can expect a starting salary of £15,000 to £20,000.

Upon completion of Part 2, salaries rise to £20,000–£26,000.

Once fully qualified as an architect, you can earn £26,000–£35,000 a year.

Those who reach senior level or become a partner in a firm can achieve a salary up to £80,000.

Related opportunities

- Architectural Technician p59
- Architectural Technologist p60
- Construction Supervisor/Manager p76

Further information

Architects Registration Board
www.arb.org.uk

Royal Incorporation of Architects in Scotland
www.rias.org.uk

Royal Institute of British Architects
www.architecture.com

ARCHITECTURAL TECHNICIAN

Qualifications and courses

The most common route into this career is to complete an HNC/HND in Architectural Design or Architectural Technology or alternatively, to gain a Foundation degree in Architectural Technology. HNC/HND courses usually require applicants to have acquired at least 1 A level/2 H grades (relevant subjects include Physics and Maths) as well as a GCSE/National 5 (A*–C/A–C) in your A level/H grade subject. You should also have another 3 or 4 GCSEs/National 5s (A*–C/A–C) including Maths, English and a science subject. Some candidates may be considered on the basis of relevant experience rather than qualifications.

You can also complete a degree but most employers will not expect applicants to be graduates. Candidates with at least 4 GCSEs/National 5s (A*–C/A–C) may seek apprenticeship training provided by employers in the workplace. Apprenticeship schemes tend to award candidates a qualification such as a BTEC/SQA or NVQ/SVQ.

To become a qualified architectural technician you will need to apply to become an Associate Member of the Chartered Institute of Architectural Technologists (CIAT). To pass the required Architectural Technician Professional and Occupational Performance (POP) Record, candidates must undertake 2 years of supervised work experience and be assessed against CIAT's professional standards.

What the work involves

This is essentially a support role; you will be providing assistance to the other members of the team including architects, architectural technologists, surveyors and engineers, enabling them to complete their work as efficiently as possible. You will be responsible for liaising between the construction and design teams, making sure everyone is up to date with the latest project developments.

You will gather and organise all of the technical information required throughout the project.

You will prepare drawings, plans and specifications using computer-aided design (CAD) software and also by hand.

Type of person suited to this work

You need good drawing skills, both hand and CAD. You will need an ability to visualise in three dimensions.

You must also be able to develop a scientific and technological knowledge of building materials. You will need to understand building regulations and techniques and be able to explain them to others.

You will need to be able to work well alone, as well as having good verbal communication skills for working with other professionals, such as architects, surveyors and engineers. Your organisational, research and problem-solving skills will need to be excellent.

Working conditions

Architectural technicians are based in offices, but you may visit sites to inspect work in progress so a driving licence might be useful.

You will need to be aware of health and safety regulations when on-site and will be expected to wear safety clothing. When working on-site you will be outdoors in all weathers and may need to climb ladders or scaffolding.

You are likely to work normal office hours (9am–5pm, Monday to Friday), although you might have to work late and at weekends on some projects.

Future prospects

An architectural technician may take further CIAT-accredited training to develop their skills and apply to work as an architectural technologist.

You could choose to work in private practice or alternatively within the public sector in an area such as local government, research, education or central government. You may need to change employers in order to progress.

There is also the possibility to work freelance or on short contracts.

Advantages/disadvantages

As you are the main point of contact between contractors and clients, you will be at the centre of any confrontations that arise.

If you work for a larger company you will have the opportunity to work on a range of projects which will keep your job interesting.

Money guide

Architectural technicians usually receive a starting salary of £15,000–£20,000.

With experience this could rise to between £30,000 and £45,000 a year.

Architectural technicians employed on a freelance/self-employed basis can expect to earn a higher hourly rate than those in full-time employment.

Earnings vary widely depending on location and the individual employer.

Related opportunities

- Architectural Technologist p60
- Surveying Technician p112
- Town Planner/Planning Technician p115

Further information

Chartered Institute of Architectural Technologists
www.ciat.org.uk

Chartered Institute of Building
www.ciob.org.uk

Construction Industry Training Board (CITB)
www.citb.co.uk

Qualifications and courses

The preferred route to becoming an architectural technologist is to complete a degree in Architectural Technology which has been accredited by the Chartered Institute of Architectural Technologists (CIAT). Admission to a degree course relies on candidates gaining at least 2 A levels/3 H grades and 5 GCSEs/National 5s (A*–C/ A–C). There are currently over 30 accredited degree programmes and they are listed on CIAT's website. Candidates who take an accredited degree benefit from exemptions when they study for their Professional and Occupational Performance (POP) Record which is a necessary requirement when becoming a chartered architectural technologist (MCIAT).

There is also the opportunity to gain entry to the field for candidates who choose to complete a degree in a related area of the industry such as architecture, architectural engineering, building services engineering, building/ construction, built environment studies, civil and structural engineering, computer-aided engineering or surveying.

Completion of an HNC/HND in Architectural Technology or a Foundation degree in Architectural Technology will enable you to become a qualified architectural technician. Once you have had more than 10 years' experience and after successful completion of CIAT's professional standards assessment you could become an architectural technologist. Those with a relevant HNC/HND may also opt to convert their qualification to a degree by completing a 1-year top-up course or alternatively, may be granted acceptance onto the second year of a degree course.

What the work involves

You will be responsible for ensuring that the architect's design is translated into a functioning building. You will be involved right from the start, helping to liaise with the client and the architect and advise them on any issues that might affect the build.

You will make sure that the more practical elements of the build run smoothly, by ensuring that the right materials are used and that all legal requirements and building regulations are met.

You will have a leading role within the construction team including developing project briefs, coordinating, negotiating contracts and providing guidance.

Type of person suited to this work

You need good drawing skills, both hand and computer-aided design (CAD). You will need an ability to visualise in three dimensions.

You must also be able to develop a scientific and technological knowledge of building materials. You will need to understand planning regulations and construction law, and be able to explain them to others.

You will need good communication skills for working with other professionals. Your organisational, management, research and problem-solving skills will need to be excellent.

Working conditions

Architectural technologists are based in offices, but you may need to visit sites to inspect work in progress so a driving licence could be useful.

You will generally be working weekdays 9am–5pm, but you might need to work extra hours to meet deadlines.

You will need to be aware of health and safety regulations when on-site and will wear safety clothing. On-site work can be cold and wet or hot and dusty, as you will be outdoors in all weathers.

Future prospects

Architectural technologists, with CIAT qualifications and experience, may set up their own practice or work in a partnership with other architectural technologists or architects.

It is also possible to progress within private firms to more senior positions or move to other companies which attract larger and possibly international contracts. Promotion is generally easier within larger firms but you may still need to change employers in order to progress.

Advantages/disadvantages

There may be problems to solve at any time during the architectural process, for example, issues with the supply of the right materials.

It is rewarding to make your contribution to the design and construction of buildings that will influence the landscape for many years to come.

Money guide

Generally salaries are higher in London and the south of England.

A junior technologist typically has a starting salary of £15,000–£23,000 a year.

After 3 years' experience you should be earning between £24,000 and £28,000 a year.

Once you are in a senior position and have been working for 10 years, you could achieve a salary of £30,000–£80,000.

Higher salaries are also possible for people who acquire extensive experience. Benefits such as company cars and pension schemes may also be offered by some practices.

Related opportunities

- Architect p58
- Architectural Technician p59
- Cartographer p68
- Town Planner/Planning Technician p115

Further information

Chartered Institute of Architectural Technologists
www.ciat.org.uk

Construction Industry Training Board (CITB)
www.citb.co.uk

Qualifications and courses

There is no specific entry route for this career although you will need a relevant degree in a subject such as land management, real estate management, property development and valuation, building surveying, or quantity surveying and commercial management, in order to gain entry to a company as a trainee.

You could study for a degree in property and valuation accredited by either the Royal Institution of Chartered Surveyors (RICS) or the College of Estate Management (CEM) and join a surveying firm or you could enter a different area, such as estate management, and train as a property consultant on the job. Entry to a degree is normally with a minimum of 2 A levels/3 H grades and 5 GCSEs/National 5s (A*–C/A–C).

Training is carried out on the job under the supervision of a senior consultant. The National Association of Valuers and Auctioneers (NAVA) offers property auction workshops to help develop trainees' skills. The National Federation of Property Professionals (NFoPP) offers a Level 3 Technical Award in Real Property Auctioneering which is made available through distance learning. Completion of this is necessary for membership of NAVA.

It is important to commit to a continuing professional development (CPD) programme to keep your skills and knowledge of property law and auctioning methods up to date.

What the work involves

You will be responsible for valuing property and land, from listed buildings to new builds, assessing the current market and organising the property or land to be auctioned off.

You will be meeting prospective clients, researching their property or land, attending the auction and getting the best price for the client.

You will need to make detailed reports of the property you value, and report back to your client. You might also have other duties such as advising clients how auctions work and of any other services your company offers.

Type of person suited to this work

You will need excellent communication skills to successfully run an auction, and be firm when settling a bid.

Being lively, outgoing and confident will help when you have to address a large crowd of people; a clear and authoritative voice will be beneficial.

You will need good observational skills for valuing land and property, with a good knowledge of the property market. You will need to keep up to date with current property laws.

Working conditions

You will typically work between 37 and 40 hours a week, Monday to Friday, with the possibility of working evenings and weekends, depending on when the auction is.

Jobs in the public sector may be based on flexitime. In the private sector, extra hours are regularly expected, particularly around deadlines or to meet a demand during a period of high interest.

You will spend a lot of time in an office, but you will be out and about on a daily basis, meeting clients and valuing properties. You will need to work in all weather conditions, and travel around regularly – a driving licence and vehicle will be very useful.

Future prospects

There are jobs available across the UK, with international auction houses being based in London. There is currently a need for property auctioneers due to the increase in popularity of property auctions, therefore job prospects are good.

You can progress into a senior auction role or managerial position. It may be possible to move into different areas of auctioning, such as livestock or antiques.

Advantages/disadvantages

Auctions are fast paced and lively events; this job offers an exciting day's work!

It could be frustrating when an auction does not go the way you planned and profit is not made.

You get great job satisfaction when you successfully auction off a property.

Money guide

The amount that you earn depends on which type of organisation you work for and where it is located. For example, an auction house may pay less than a private chartered surveyor company.

Starting salaries tend to be between £20,000 and £26,000 a year.

With experience, earnings can rise to £27,000–£35,000.

Chartered land and property valuers can earn in excess £40,000 a year.

Those who choose to work freelance may charge fees according to their experience and the type of contract undertaken.

Related opportunities

- Auctioneer p463
- Surveying Technician p112

Further information

National Federation of Property Professionals
www.nfopp.co.uk

Royal Institution of Chartered Surveyors
www.rics.org

University College of Estate Management
www.ucem.ac.uk

BRICKLAYER

Qualifications and courses

The main route to entering the field is to train via an apprenticeship, splitting your time between working on-site and training for a qualification at college. In England and Wales, the Construction Apprenticeship Scheme (CAS) allows you to study for NVQ Levels 2 and 3 whilst in Scotland a modern apprenticeship offers trainees the chance to gain an SVQ Level 2. Northern Ireland offers 4 different types of apprenticeships for people in different circumstances, each leading to a qualification in your chosen trade. Apprenticeships normally require candidates to have some GCSEs/National 5s (A*–E/A–E) in subjects such as English, Maths, a science and technology.

Many employers now require trainees to have a Construction Skills Certification Scheme (CSCS) card before working on-site, something that can only be achieved through a formal qualification, such as a BTEC Introductory Certificate and Diploma in Construction, BTEC Certificate and Diploma in Construction or a City & Guilds Certificate in Basic Skills (6081). Those without qualifications may work for an NVQ and a CSCS card via the CITB's On-Site Assessment and Training (OSAT) programme.

What the work involves

Bricklayers build and repair external and internal walls.

You will use a range of materials including bricks, stones and mortar as well as specialist tools to build walls that often include ornamental and decorative effects.

Jobs include building houses as well as office buildings, other public venues, shopping centres and stadiums. You will spend a lot of your time outside doing manual work.

Type of person suited to this work

As the work requires you to move around a lot and lift materials, you must be physically fit and able to work at height.

You need to be able to follow plans and work with accuracy and attention to detail, so that the walls you build are structurally perfect and create the right visual effect.

You also need to work in a team with other bricklayers and those in other construction trades and professions.

Working conditions

You will often be working outdoors and in all weather conditions. This can mean being cold and wet in the winter and hot and dusty in the summer.

To keep yourself and others safe you will need to observe health and safety regulations, which will include wearing protective clothing.

You are likely to work a normal working week, although weekend and evening work is common.

Future prospects

Construction is one of the largest industries in the UK. Recent surges in demand for new housing have led to an increase in demand for bricklayers, but following the severe job losses during the recession, there are not enough bricklayers to keep up with demand. With the current shortage of bricklayers, job prospects are promising, but the market is still volatile.

In the long term, you could progress to technical, supervisory and managerial roles or move into related areas such as estimating and construction management. Encouragingly, the number of managerial positions required by the industry has rapidly increased over the last five years. You can also become an instructor in a training school.

The construction industry has one of the highest percentages of self-employment and bricklayers are no exception. Many have set up their own businesses, often working on smaller, local contracts. You may also opt to specialise in different trades such as stonemasonry, restoration or conservation.

Advantages/disadvantages

The work can be physically demanding for some people.

This is a great career if you like being outdoors, doing practical and creative work.

As you develop your skills there are great opportunities for progression.

Money guide

Trainees and labourers can earn up to £15,000 a year until they become qualified, when they can earn anything between £16,000 and £23,000.

Experienced bricklayers and instructors can earn up to £30,000.

Overtime is often available and on some projects there are bonuses based on fast outputs which can lead to higher earnings. If you are self-employed you have more freedom to negotiate your rate of pay with your clients.

Related opportunities

- Building Technician p66
- Dry Stone Waller p79
- Stonemason p110

Further information

Construction Industry Training Board (CITB)
www.citb.co.uk

Federation of Master Builders
www.fmb.org.uk

Scottish Building Apprenticeship and Training Council
www.sbatc.co.uk

BUILDING CONSERVATION OFFICER

Qualifications and courses

Most entrants are graduates with a degree in a relevant subject such as building and construction, civil or structural engineering, surveying, architecture, or design. More specific courses in architectural heritage, conservation, building conservation, and management are offered by some universities. Many graduates will have an accredited or recognised postgraduate degree that meets the requirements of the Institute of Historic Building Conservation (IHBC). Membership of the IHBC is usually a requirement for jobs within this field.

Entry with an HND is possible, or alternatively you can enter as a planning technician after gaining considerable experience.

Training is usually provided on the job but employers do value candidates with demonstrable interest and experience within the field. Volunteering and work experience are particularly important if your degree is not directly relevant. The National Trust and the National Trust for Scotland have around 47,000 positions available for volunteers.

The Society for the Protection of Ancient Buildings (SPAB) also runs a lecture series each year aimed at professionals in the industry which is useful in providing network-building opportunities. Once on the job, it is important to undergo continuing professional development (CPD) every 2 years. The IHBC offers its members numerous courses and seminars to ensure officers continue to enhance their skills.

What the work involves

Building conservation officers protect and restore buildings of special historical or architectural interest, such as houses, churches, windmills, factories and lighthouses.

You will be involved in planning the development of listed buildings and sites, recommending buildings for conservation, writing reports on their condition, making schedules and estimates for work required and giving advice to architects, local authorities or planning committees on building conservation.

You might have to source suppliers or craftspeople who work with specialised or traditional building materials.

Type of person suited to this work

You will be working to restore historic buildings and sites so it is important that you are interested in history, architecture and construction. An understanding of historical architecture, building methods and techniques would be very useful.

You will need excellent communication skills as you will coordinate the many different aspects involved in the development of one site. You must have excellent verbal and written skills to give presentations to planning authorities or government agencies to persuade them to follow your advice.

Working conditions

Your work is occasionally office based but much takes place outdoors on-site. This can be dusty and dirty, working at

heights and confined spaces in adverse weather conditions. Protective clothing, including hard hats and safety boots, is necessary as you may be visiting buildings in poor repair.

Travel during the day with the occasional overnight stay may be necessary. Working as a consultant may involve travel all over the UK or visiting sites in remote areas so a car and driver's licence are useful. Working hours include regular extra hours but not weekends or shifts.

Future prospects

Positions as a historic building inspector or conservation officer can be found in local authorities, district and county councils. Within the private sector there may be opportunities for promotion, eg to senior conservation officer or managerial roles, but, due to the low turnover of staff, it may be necessary to relocate in order to achieve career progression. In small organisations, promotions may be limited.

There are many opportunities in national government organisations such as English Heritage and charities such as the National Trust, the Victorian Society or the Georgian Group.

As a qualified and experienced professional you can be self-employed. With substantial experience and industry contacts you can become involved in consultancy which focuses on advisory and design work. You may even opt to move into lecturing in universities.

Advantages/disadvantages

You will gain a great deal of satisfaction from working to ensure the survival of listed buildings.

Buildings are often in a poor state of repair and building sites may be hazardous.

Money guide

Starting salaries range from £18,000 to £26,000.

Experienced building conservation officers earn between £26,000 and £32,000.

Salaries at senior levels may rise to £40,000 or more after 10–15 years' experience.

Related opportunities

- Architect p58
- Architectural Technologist p60
- Building Surveyor p65

Further information

Institute of Historic Building Conservation
www.ihbc.org.uk

National Trust
www.nationaltrust.org.uk

National Trust for Scotland
www.nts.org.uk

Society for the Protection of Ancient Buildings
www.spab.org.uk

BUILDING SERVICES ENGINEER

Qualifications and courses

To enter this profession you will need a relevant degree in a subject such as building services engineering, mechanical engineering, maths or physics. Entry to a degree usually requires 2 A levels/3 H grades with Maths or a science and 5 GCSEs/National 5s (A*–C/A–C) including English and Maths. Gaining work experience during school holidays can be useful in enhancing future job applications and ensuring you secure important contacts.

Accredited HNDs or Foundation degrees in engineering or technology can be used to progress to full degree courses or trainee posts. Some apprenticeships may also be available through the modern apprenticeship scheme, SummitSkills.

As a trainee you will need to complete Initial Professional Development (IPD) to become a professional engineer. You can train for this through your employer. You can then work towards incorporated engineer (IEng) or chartered engineer (CEng) status by gaining membership of the Chartered Institution of Building Services Engineers (CIBSE). In order to do so, you will need a 1st in an accredited Master of Engineering (MEng) degree.

It is important that you commit to a continuing professional development (CPD) programme in order to keep your skills up to date.

What the work involves

Building services engineers are responsible for each aspect of energy-using building services such as lifts, lighting, heating, air conditioning, water supply, ventilation and electrical supply.

You will design and plan services that are efficient, cost effective, sustainable and in the interest of public safety. You will also be responsible for organising and supervising the installation and maintenance of these services, working with architects and clients to reduce the environmental impact.

Although the industry is becoming increasingly multidisciplinary, you will probably specialise in mechanical engineering, electrical engineering or public health.

Type of person suited to this work

You will need to be highly practical as well as having excellent problem-solving, communication and interpersonal skills. Teamworking skills are essential so that you can work with those involved in other aspects of each project's design and construction.

You should have an aptitude for design and technical drawing, model making and show proficiency working with computers and computer-aided design (CAD) software.

Working conditions

Your time will be divided between office-based work, such as planning, designing and estimating costs of projects, to spending time on-site, coordinating installation or managing existing systems.

You may work on sites such as airports, hospitals, industrial plants, domestic housing, leisure pools, hotels and cinemas; for this you might need specialist skills.

You will usually be expected to work more than the average office hours but not weekends or shifts. Some roles require on-call availability in case of emergencies. You may have to travel within a day but overnight stays are uncommon.

Future prospects

Opportunities in this field are numerous with demand for building services engineers usually exceeding supply.

Progression within the role is fairly scripted, with graduate engineers progressing to project engineers, associates, a director/partner and then a managing director. As a chartered engineer you may establish yourself as an independent consultant.

Your choice of specialism is important in determining your career development so it is important to decide early in order to gain as much practical experience as possible.

Training in design, installation or maintenance can increase your chances of progression as does training in new specialties such as intelligent buildings and organic lighting.

Advantages/disadvantages

The profession was traditionally separated into electrical and mechanical roles, but is now becoming increasingly multidisciplinary so your role may be more flexible and diverse.

This profession depends heavily on the economic climate of the construction industry, so you need to be aware of this as it will affect your chances of employment.

Money guide

Your starting salary could range from £20,000 to £28,000.

With experience this can rise to between £25,000 and £40,000.

At senior level it is possible to earn in excess of £55,000 and as a partner of a consultancy firm it is possible to earn upwards of £80,000 a year.

Salaries vary according to an engineer's experience rather than qualifications, therefore the more experience you gain, the higher your wage.

Related opportunities

- Architect p58
- Civil/Construction Engineer/Civil Engineering Technician p71
- Electrical Engineer p207

Further information

Chartered Institution of Building Services Engineers
www.cibse.org

Institution of Engineering and Technology
www.theiet.org

Qualifications and courses

You will be required to hold a relevant degree accredited by the Royal Institution of Chartered Surveyors (RICS) in a subject such as surveying, construction, civil or building engineering. The Chartered Institute of Building (CIOB), the Association of Building Engineers (ABE), and the British Institute of Facilities Management (BIFM) also offer professional qualifications. Completing a RICS-accredited degree course, however, will automatically qualify you to train as a chartered surveyor allowing you to carry out the Assessment of Professional Competence (APC), entitling you to RICS membership. The APC scheme allows you to train as you work and normally takes between 2 and 3 years.

Candidates with a non-accredited degree, or a degree in a non-vocational subject, can opt for a RICS-accredited postgraduate conversion course. It is also possible to enter the industry at technical surveyor level if you hold a relevant HNC/HND or Foundation degree. To reach the level of a building surveyor will require you to complete further qualifications whilst you work.

Alternatively, the Chartered Surveyors Training Trust (CSTT) offers work-based training for young people aged 16–24 in London and the south-east of England who would otherwise face barriers to accessing the profession. Applicants must have 4 GCSEs/National 5s (A*–C/A–C) or equivalent, preferably in English, Maths and a science.

Graduates who have completed a year in the industry as part of their degree maintain a distinct advantage when seeking work.

What the work involves

Building surveyors work on new building projects as well as making suggestions on how to improve or enhance existing structures.

You could work on residential and commercial building projects, and will advise on a number of areas including design, restoration, sustainability and repairs.

You may also be responsible for ensuring that buildings meet health, safety and access regulations.

Type of person suited to this work

Since the job involves explaining ideas and negotiating with industry professionals and clients, good communication skills are vital. You will produce detailed reports, so a good standard of written English is required.

You will need excellent time management skills and a head for figures to ensure that projects come in on time and within budget.

You will need a logical, analytical and practical approach to work, along with the ability to organise and manage a team. As much of the work involves computers and electronic equipment, you will need to have good IT skills.

Working conditions

Working hours are normally 9am–5pm, although longer hours and evening meetings with clients are not uncommon. Most surveyors divide their time equally between the office, external client meetings, site visits and surveys. These travel commitments mean it is helpful to have a driving licence and transport.

When on-site you will need to stick to health and safety regulations and be prepared for all types of weather.

You may occasionally be called to give evidence in court proceedings concerning a breach of building regulations.

Future prospects

Although the industry was affected by the recent financial crisis, the demand for building surveyors is on the rise alongside a possible shortfall in graduates.

You could work for a variety of employers including surveying practices, construction companies, government departments, and mortgage and property companies, both in the UK and abroad. Freelance and consultancy work are also a possibility. Gaining chartered status opens up further opportunities for career progression.

With experience, you could become a partner in a company or establish your own firm. You could also specialise in one area such as advising on the restoration and improvement of historic or architecturally valuable buildings.

Advantages/disadvantages

Surveying provides a varied career as each day is different and there is a range of areas to work in.

Many surveyors are self-employed and enjoy the flexibility of working freelance.

Money guide

Graduate surveyors can expect a salary of £18,500–£22,000. Those with chartered status are more likely to start on a higher salary, as are those working in London.

Experienced surveyors can earn between £23,000 and £38,000 whilst senior chartered surveyors can earn in excess of £60,000.

Being a partner in a firm could offer you a six-figure salary.

Benefits, such as a company car, mobile phone and pension scheme, are also available.

Related opportunities

- Civil/Construction Engineer/Civil Engineering Technician p71
- Quantity Surveyor p102
- Rural Property/Practice Surveyor p105

Further information

Chartered Institute of Building
www.ciob.org.uk

Royal Institution of Chartered Surveyors
www.rics.org

BUILDING TECHNICIAN

Qualifications and courses

Building technicians normally need to train to NVQ/SVQ Levels 3 or 4. It is possible to train as a building technician with an employer, as a construction apprentice. Apprenticeship schemes require a minimum of 4 GCSEs/National 5s (A*–C/A–C), including either Maths, a science, Design and Technology, or equivalent vocational qualification. Most apprentices start between the ages of 16 and 18, though entry is possible after this. In order to carry out an apprenticeship, you will need to find an employer who will sponsor your training.

The Construction Industry Training Board (CITB) offers apprenticeships through the bConstructive scheme for those interested in beginning a career in construction and who have already found an employer to sponsor their training. These typically require 2 to 4 years to complete, with the potential to gain a Level 4 qualification in your desired field.

HNDs in building studies or similar subjects can be studied over 2 years full time. Applicants should ideally have a science A level/H grade. Introductory courses to a career at technician level include BTEC Level 3 diploma/extended diploma or Scottish Group Award in Construction.

Many companies offer training schemes, day-release study (for HNC and Chartered Institute of Building exams), time spent on building sites, in-house training courses, and the CITB Technician Training Scheme.

Once qualified as a building technician, there are lots of opportunities to further your training whilst you work. You may for example, train for your NVQ Level 3 in Construction Site Supervision or NVQ Level 4 in Construction Site Management.

What the work involves

Building technicians support the work of construction professionals including surveyors and construction managers. They play an integral role in organising the construction of buildings by acting as a link between senior management and on-site labourers.

Your work will vary depending on your employer but might include planning work schedules, drawing up plans and estimating project costs and time scales. Knowledge of computer-aided design software (CAD) is necessary as technicians often have to make changes to plans and blueprints.

A building technician is also responsible for the negotiating and buying of materials, ensuring they are of good quality and are cost-effective. Another of your jobs will be to prepare sites prior to the commencement of a building project and later, to supervise staff whilst the work is being carried out. Monitoring building sites in terms of health and safety will be also be a high priority for you.

Type of person suited to this work

Organisational skills are essential as you ensure each construction job is completed accurately and efficiently.

Mathematical and IT skills are important for calculating costs, taking measurements and using CAD.

You must have an understanding of the technical aspects of construction. You must be dependable and will need strong communication skills for working with suppliers, site teams and other professionals.

Working conditions

When on site you will need to wear a safety helmet, overalls and boots at all times.

You are likely to work regular hours, but you may also have to start early, finish late or work at weekends on occasion as well as spend time away from home for various projects.

Future prospects

There is a steady supply of vacancies and a shortage of qualified applicants, particularly in London and Scotland.

Building technicians work for employers such as contractors, construction companies, property developers, surveyors' practices as well as within the public sector. You may also have the opportunity to work abroad.

There are vast opportunities for extending your responsibilities once employed. With experience and further qualifications, you may be promoted to a higher position such as building/construction manager. You may also choose to specialise in an area of expertise such as buying, drafting or estimating.

Advantages/disadvantages

It can be stressful having to work to deadlines.

Construction sites are dirty and dusty and some of your tasks may be dangerous.

Your work will be varied and interesting and you will be an integral part of the team producing all sorts of different buildings.

Money guide

Entry level salaries are typically £18,000–£22,000.

The average salary for an experienced building technician is £25,000 per year.

Senior building technicians can earn in excess of £30,000.

Related opportunities

- Architectural Technologist p60
- Construction Supervisor/Manager p76
- Surveying Technician p112

Further information

Chartered Association of Building Engineers
www.cbuilde.com

Chartered Institute of Building
www.ciob.org.uk

Construction Industry Training Board (CITB)
www.citb.co.uk

Qualifications and courses

Although there are no formal entry requirements, GCSEs/National 5s in Maths, English and technology will be helpful for calculations, measurements and theory. Most employers will require some on-site experience so you may choose to shadow a professional or begin your career as a labourer. Your employer may then offer you training in carpentry.

Alternatively, another route into the industry involves attending college in order to gain a qualification. City & Guilds offer Certificates in Basic Construction Skills such as Carpentry and Joinery (6217-02) and Woodworking (6217-05) for young learners under the age of 16. By doing one of these, your chances of securing full-time work will be increased. Once employed, you can work towards NVQs/SVQs in Carpentry, both on the job and at college.

Three-year Apprenticeships in Construction Building are available for school leavers. Diplomas and NVQs can be studied without an apprenticeship, or alongside practical work, by attending a training centre or college.

NVQs in Wood Occupations are available, such as the Diploma in Site Carpentry (Levels 2 and 3) and the Certificate in Shopfitting Site Work (Levels 2 and 3).

The Construction Awards Alliance (CAA) runs a Foundation Certificate in Building Craft Occupations. Young Apprenticeships for 14–16 year olds may be available through the Construction Industry Training Board (CITB).

What the work involves

Carpenters/joiners make, put in place or repair the wooden parts of buildings. You may be hired to make and install floorboards, skirting boards, cupboards, partitions, windows or doors. Other tasks may include fitting large wooden structures within the building trade, such as floor and roof joists or staircases.

You will work with different types of wood and use specialist hand tools such as hammers, chisels and planes, as well as power tools like jigsaws and sanders. You will work either in a workshop or on-site with other building professionals.

Type of person suited to this work

You must have good practical skills and enjoy working with your hands and different tools.

You will be expected to follow plans and work carefully with attention to detail so that the structures you make fit into place correctly. As you will need to take measurements and calculate angles and dimensions, you will have to be good at maths and be accurate.

You should be physically fit in order to move around and lift materials. You must also be able to work in a team with other carpenters and those from the other construction trades.

Working conditions

You may work in a workshop or on construction sites, or divide your time between the two.

This can be heavy, dangerous and dusty work. You will need to keep to health and safety regulations, which may include wearing protective gear such as safety goggles and a mask. You are likely to work a normal working week, usually with an early start, although weekend work may also be required.

Future prospects

Across the UK there are around 240,000 carpenters/joiners, but employers are finding it difficult to recruit well-qualified and experienced workers. Many qualified carpenters are self-employed or work as sub-contractors.

With experience, you could move into a related occupation like shopfitting, kitchen fitting or furniture making, or you may progress to technical, supervisory or managerial level. You may opt to specialise in one particular area, for example, in restoring old buildings or creating props. Alternatively, you might even consider instructing trainee carpenters in a college.

Advantages/disadvantages

Work can be seasonal: working fewer hours in the winter or having jobs cancelled is common.

You will develop a lot of new skills and you can specialise in certain areas such as listed buildings.

You get a sense of achievement when you see your woodwork in a building.

Money guide

Trainees start on a salary of around £15,000 a year.

Qualified carpenters can earn anything in the range of £18,000–£25,000 per year.

Experienced joiners may earn around £26,000–£30,000 a year.

Very skilled and experienced joiners could earn £40,000 or more per year.

The Building and Allied Trades Joint Industrial Council (BATJIC) agrees minimum wages annually.

Overtime is often available and on some projects you will receive bonuses based on output which can increase your earnings.

Self-employed carpenters will negotiate their own rates of pay.

Related opportunities

- Building Technician p66
- Construction Operative p74
- Window Fitter p119

Further information

British Woodworking Federation
www.bwf.org.uk

Institute of Carpenters
www.instituteofcarpenters.com

CARTOGRAPHER

Qualifications and courses

The usual entry requirement for a cartographer is a relevant degree. Useful degree subjects include geography, geographical information systems, urban/land studies, surveying and mapping sciences. GCSEs/National 5s in English and Maths are generally needed for entry to these degrees and 2 A levels/3 H grades, including a science, Maths or Geography, would also be expected. Employers are increasingly seeking graduates with degrees in geographical information systems given the upturn in demand for digital map-making.

It may also be useful to hold a postgraduate qualification in a relevant subject, for example cartography, geographical information systems or remote sensing, if you are interested in more specialised areas.

Once employed, you will receive on-the-job training in relevant software and techniques. Government departments that employ cartographers have their own training schemes. It is also possible to work towards an NVQ/SVQ at Levels 3 and 4 in Spatial Data Management.

The Royal Air Force and Ordnance Survey may have opportunities for school leavers to study for a Certificate/Diploma or HNC/HND in Cartography by day release while training on the job.

The minimum entry requirements for a cartographic technician are 3 GCSEs/National 5s (A*–C/A–C), including Maths, English and occasionally a science. In practice, most entrants have A levels/H grades and some enter with a National Certificate/Diploma or HNC/HND in a relevant area.

Entry into the field is highly competitive, therefore by becoming a member of the Society of Cartographers and the British Cartographic Society, you will be able to secure important contacts and remain on top of current developments.

What the work involves

Cartography involves collecting, evaluating and displaying information gained from a variety of sources, including satellite technology, to create or update maps and navigation charts. This is achieved by using artistic, scientific, and technological methods.

Due to advances in information technology, geographical information systems and digital mapping techniques are now frequently used in this sector. You will use a range of sophisticated technology in all aspects of your work.

Type of person suited to this work

You will need to have strong IT, scientific and mathematical skills and an interest in geography.

Due to the nature of the work, it is essential that you have good spatial awareness, colour vision and an eye for layout and design. One sheet of a map can take months to produce, so you must be patient and dedicated to your work. A high level of accuracy and attention to detail is needed so that the map provides the best possible information for the user.

You must be willing to keep up with developments in the field and experiment with new ways of producing maps.

Working conditions

You are likely to work normal office hours at a workstation where you will have access to a computer.

At a senior level you will have more opportunity to meet and interact with colleagues and clients.

Part of your job will involve travelling around the UK to carry out surveys.

Future prospects

Most work is available in government departments, such as Ordnance Survey, the Hydrographic Office and the Meteorological Office. You could also work for local authorities, universities, councils, commercial map publishers, oil companies and motoring organisations.

With experience, you could become a freelance cartographer, provide consultancy services or work within higher education as a tutor.

Willingness to be geographically mobile can improve your chances of career progression.

If you are interested in living abroad, there are opportunities to work in cartography all over the world.

Advantages/disadvantages

Producing a map that looks good, is user friendly and likely to be used by many people is a very satisfying and rewarding experience.

As you near project deadlines, there is a higher level of pressure and you may be required to work late.

The work is varied and combines a variety of subject areas, from design to geography to maths.

Money guide

Starting salaries are usually between £18,000 and £22,000.

With experience, your earnings could increase to between £20,000 and £30,000.

It is possible for senior cartographers to earn up to £47,000.

Earnings vary depending on the size of the company and whether you work in the public or private sector.

Related opportunities

- Geographer p507
- Land/Geomatic Surveyor p94
- Town Planner/Planning Technician p115

Further information

Association for Geographic Information
www.agi.org.uk

British Cartographic Society
www.cartography.org.uk

The Survey Association
www.tsa-uk.org.uk

CEILING FIXER

Qualifications and courses

No specific qualifications are required, although GCSEs/ National 5s or a BTEC in Construction and the Built Environment may be helpful. Useful GCSE/National 5 subjects include Maths, Design and Technology, a science and English.

You could approach companies directly in order to seek work as a trainee. You will be trained on the job whilst working towards qualifications. This may also involve going to a college or training centre on day or block release. Prior construction experience, for example as a labourer or tradesperson, may support you in your search for work.

Alternatively, you could develop your skills by completing an NVQ/SVQ in Interior Systems (Construction) Ceiling Fixing (Levels 1–3). The Construction Specialist Apprenticeship may also be available for those aged 16–24 who are looking to become a ceiling fixer.

You can also train by carrying out one of the Construction Industry Training Board (CITB)'s bConstructive Apprenticeships which involves both studying and on-site experience. CITB apprenticeships take between 2 and 4 years to complete.

Many employers require you to have the CSCS card issued by the Construction Skills Certification Scheme as proof of your competence working on-site. This can only be granted if you hold a valid qualification or have on-site experience.

What the work involves

As a ceiling fixer you will fit suspended ceilings into new and existing commercial or public buildings.

Your work will involve fitting a ceiling grid in place and inserting tiles by using tools such as metal cutters and screwdrivers. The ceiling is fitted to the concrete floor of the room above and may hide wiring and air conditioning systems.

As the job requires you to work at heights and on construction sites, your safety training must be up to date.

Type of person suited to this work

You will need to be comfortable working at heights and you must be physically fit to do the necessary climbing, carrying and bending.

You need to be thorough and accurate. An understanding of technical plans is essential and you must be able to follow instructions but also use your initiative. Numeracy skills are important to measure materials and calculate weights. As you will work alongside other ceiling fixers, electricians, heating and ventilating fitters, painters and decorators you need to be a good team player.

Working conditions

You will need to travel to various construction sites so a driving licence will be useful. The sites you work on will mainly be indoors and you will most likely work from a ladder in confined spaces.

You will need to take safety precautions for yourself and your colleagues and you will be expected to wear protective clothing such as a hard hat, boots and overalls. You are likely to work Monday to Friday, normal office hours, although overtime may be available at the weekends.

This could be dusty work which might be difficult if you suffer from some allergies.

Future prospects

Demand for qualified ceiling fixers in the construction industry is expected to increase over the next few years, with job opportunities likely to be available once trained.

You will most likely start out as a tradesperson. With experience, you may progress to a supervisory or managerial position, or perhaps run your own company. You could also become a subcontractor.

Advantages/disadvantages

Working at heights and in confined spaces may be stressful for some people.

It is satisfying to see the transformation that takes place when you have worked on fitting a ceiling.

You will have the opportunity to work on a variety of projects in different types of buildings.

Money guide

Trainees can earn up to £13,000 a year.

Once qualified as a ceiling fixer, you can expect to earn anything between £16,000 and £22,000.

Highly skilled and experienced workers within the role can earn in excess of £27,000.

Those who do contract/temporary work may receive a higher hourly/daily rate than those in full-time employment.

There are often opportunities to increase your earnings through shift allowances, working overtime and receiving performance-related bonuses.

Related opportunities

- Construction Operative p74
- Plasterer p99
- Roofer p104

Further information

Construction Industry Training Board (CITB)
www.citb.co.uk

Finishes & Interiors Sector
www.thefis.org

CHARTERED SURVEYOR

Qualifications and courses

You must become a member of the Royal Institution of Chartered Surveyors (RICS). For this you must complete an RICS-accredited degree course or a postgraduate conversion course. Degree entry requires 5 GCSEs/National 5s (A*–C/A–C) and 3 A levels/4 H grades, or the relevant BTEC/SQA national awards. After completing an RICS-accredited course you must gain practical experience and undertake training before you will be fully qualified.

If you do not have the appropriate A levels or GCSEs you can take HNC/HND courses or Foundation degrees which can then be supplemented by an RICS-accredited degree course.

You can also train on the job as part of the Chartered Surveyors Training Trust scheme. This is available to those aged 16–24 who have 4 GCSEs/National 5s (A*–C/A–C) or equivalent. This programme involves a 2-year apprenticeship which will grant you Associate membership of the RICS. You then have the option to study for an accredited degree and take the RICS Assessment of Professional Competence to become a chartered surveyor.

You will be required to undertake continuing professional development (CPD) to keep up to date with surveying trends and skills.

What the work involves

As a chartered surveyor you will offer professional advice within the field of surveying in which you choose to specialise. This can be in building, construction, planning, the environment or quantity surveying. You will also spend time negotiating and explaining design/construction issues to clients.

You will have a variety of tasks to do such as examining plans, designs and project briefs, taking measurements, recording and analysing data and interpreting it through charts, maps or diagrams.

You may oversee entire construction projects, where you will ensure that specifications are met, calculate supplies needed and advise clients on the purchase, sale or development of property or land.

Type of person suited to this work

You should have an interest in construction, architecture, landscape and the environment.

As you are required to liaise with construction workers and clients, you must have excellent communication, negotiation and problem-solving skills and the ability to delegate tasks.

You need to be highly organised, methodical in your work and have a keen eye for detail as you may be coordinating several complex projects at the same time.

Working conditions

You will probably work 9am to 5pm, Monday to Friday. You may have to work longer hours to meet deadlines. Part-time work is available.

You will primarily be based in an office but you will also spend a considerable amount of time on-site.

Depending on your field of specialisation, you might have to work in various weather conditions and wear protective clothing when on-site.

You may have to travel for your work, both abroad and within the UK. For this reason a driving licence is strongly recommended.

Future prospects

There are good prospects for people training as chartered surveyors as the current demand for them exceeds supply.

You may follow a formal promotion structure to gain senior management roles.

You could choose to become self-employed or to join a private practice.

As a qualified chartered surveyor and member of the RICS you will have to take part in Continuing Professional Development (CPD). For this you must accumulate 60 hours of CPD every 3 years.

Advantages/disadvantages

Employers may provide benefits such as a company car, mobile phone, bonuses and pension scheme.

There is significant competition for graduates wishing to gain entry to some areas of chartered surveying.

Money guide

As a graduate, your starting salary may range from £18,500 to £30,000 a year.

The RICS estimates that those with chartered status have the potential to earn 15% more than those without.

Within 5 years of qualifying and achieving chartered status, you can expect to earn up to £48,000.

Senior chartered surveyors can earn up to £60,000 whilst partners and directors have the potential to earn six figure salaries.

Geographical location does have an effect on how much chartered surveyors can earn with the highest wages typically found in London.

Depending on the type of project you are working on, very generous bonuses may be available.

Related opportunities

- Land/Geomatic Surveyor p94
- Surveying Technician p112
- Town Planner/Planning Technician p115

Further information

Chartered Association of Building Engineers
www.cbuilde.com

Chartered Surveyors Training Trust
www.cstt.org.uk

Royal Institution of Chartered Surveyors
www.rics.org

BUILDING AND CONSTRUCTION

Qualifications and courses

Entrants to civil engineering are usually graduates, although there are opportunities to progress from a craft or technical level.

The main route to becoming an engineer is a degree in the relevant branch of engineering or a closely related subject. It is recommended that you study a civil engineering course which is accredited by the Institution of Civil Engineers (ICE). The normal minimum entry requirements for an engineering degree are 3 A levels/5 H grades including Maths and a science, usually Physics or Chemistry. Equivalent qualifications such as BTEC/ SQA Level 3 Certificates or Diplomas may be accepted.

Candidates who do not have the relevant A levels or equivalent may gain entry to an engineering degree by taking a 1-year Foundation course. Foundation courses are offered by universities and are sometimes taught at local partner colleges.

Once you have gained your degree you may then join a company's graduate scheme whereby you train alongside and with the support of a professional mentor for 1 to 2 years.

It is possible, however, to enter engineering after taking GCSEs/National 5s and progress to technician or professional level by studying part time for an HNC/ HND or NVQ/SVQ Levels 4 or 5. You will need GCSEs/ National 5s (A*–C/A–C) in English, Maths and a science. There are also BTEC and SQA Level 3 Certificates or Diplomas which will give you the relevant qualifications and can be studied at any age.

Alternatively, some engineering technicians gain entry to the career by firstly working through an engineering apprenticeship scheme. To gain a place you may need 4 GCSEs/National 5s with grades (A*–C/A–C) in subjects including Maths, a science or Design and Technology, or equivalent qualifications. The availability of apprenticeship schemes depends on the job market of your local area and on the skills required by your local employers.

Professional engineers can work towards becoming chartered or incorporated members of one of the engineering professional bodies, such as ICE or the Chartered Institution of Building Services Engineers (CIBSE). The usual requirement for chartered status is an accredited MEng degree or equivalent. For incorporated status, a 3-year accredited BEng or BSc degree or an HND or equivalent, plus an additional period of learning, is required.

Undertaking a summer work experience placement or choosing a degree course with a year in industry can be useful ways to develop contacts within engineering and extend your knowledge.

What the work involves

Civil engineer (consulting)
You will be designing and developing plans for construction projects such as roads, tunnels, bridges, railways, reservoirs, pipelines and major buildings.

Your work could span many areas including waste management, coastal development and geotechnical engineering.

Your job will involve communicating with clients and once you have gained significant experience, you can run projects as a project manager.

Civil engineer (contracting)
You will take the consulting civil engineer's designs and make them into a reality at ground level, overseeing and managing the construction project.

This will include recruiting a team, sourcing materials, managing budgets and ensuring that the project is completed on time.

Contractors will sometimes create a design and build a team themselves. The roles of consultants and contractors are therefore not always entirely different from one another.

Civil engineering technician
You will be responsible for providing technical support to the civil engineer, which may include producing costing and timing estimates for a project and helping with recruitment.

The role will also include aspects of land and quantity surveying, as well as the production of design drawings.

Projects in which you are involved will fall under the categories of structural, transportation, environmental and maritime.

Type of person suited to this work

Regardless of the area you decide to work in, you will need to enjoy finding creative but workable solutions to problems.

You will need to be confident when using computers to produce designs, work out budgets and undertake research.

You should also be good at maths and science so that you can make accurate calculations and understand the different building materials available to you.

You must be able to think three-dimensionally so that you can visualise and design different buildings and structures.

Written and verbal communication skills are important as you will have to write reports, explain your designs to clients and other professionals and supervise construction staff. You will work as part of a team so you must be able to communicate and cooperate with people at all levels.

An understanding of environmental building issues, such as the use of energy efficient materials and land protection, is of increasing importance.

Working conditions

Working hours are typically longer than the average working week and can include early morning and evening work on-site.

Weekend or shift work is rare for civil engineers, although civil engineering technicians can be required to remain on 24-hour call for some projects.

Your work will involve being both indoors and out on-site. When working on-site you will need to stick to health and safety regulations and be aware of your own and colleagues' safety. You will have to wear safety clothing including a helmet.

You could spend time in dangerous places or in difficult environments, for example you may have to work at height, up ladders or on scaffolding.

When you are in your office, you will be based at a workstation where you will use a computer with specialised software and possibly a drawing board. You will attend meetings and speak to clients on the phone or in person.

It is also likely that you will have to work away from home occasionally, both within the UK and abroad, but the extent of this will depend on the size of the company you work for and the type of contracts they attract.

Future prospects

Job prospects for civil engineers tend to remain steady, and are promising. Around 100,000 professional civil engineers work in the UK for a range of employers including health trusts, local authorities, central government and energy suppliers (including water, gas, nuclear and electricity companies), contractors, consultancies and transport networks.

Work is available on a variety of projects including the building of new schools, hospitals and the upgrading of public transport networks.

Many UK civil engineering companies also operate globally, increasing the opportunities to work overseas. The range and size of opportunities open to you will depend on the size of the company you work for and the types of contracts won.

Civil engineering technicians can undertake job-related training and study for more qualifications to become a civil engineer.

There is scope to undertake further study and specialise in areas such as environmental engineering, coastal and marine engineering, geotechnics or tunnelling.

With experience, you can progress into management or possibly associate/partnership positions within UK or international companies. Within the public sector, there are opportunities for management and chief engineer jobs. Another career option is to become self-employed or to provide training or consultancy services.

Advantages/disadvantages

You will play an important part in the design and construction of buildings and structures throughout the world so you are likely to be well respected.

Seeing a project come to completion can be very satisfying.

Having an engineering background and qualifications opens up opportunities to enter other non-engineering careers at senior levels.

There is the opportunity to become self-employed or work overseas.

Work is varied, each day is different and you will be meeting and dealing with a wide range of people.

The pace of work varies quite extensively as you will alternate between a heavy workload and quieter periods.

There is a high level of responsibility in this field so the work can be demanding and occasionally stressful.

Money guide

Civil/Construction engineer

Starting salaries for civil engineers, either contracting or consulting, are around £24,000.

With more experience, engineers can earn anything between £25,000 and £40,000 a year.

Qualifying as a member or fellow of the Institution of Civil Engineers (ICE) can see salaries for civil engineers rise to between £50,000 to in excess of £100,000 per year.

Civil engineering technician

Civil engineering technicians start on about £14,000–£20,000.

With experience, earnings increase to £21,000–£35,000 a year.

As a senior technician you can earn salaries of up to £40,000 and if you train as a civil engineer your earning potential will increase as above.

Earnings are likely to be considerably higher in London and they vary depending on the size of the company.

Many employers offer additional benefits including a pension scheme, life insurance, a healthcare package and possibly a company car.

Related opportunities

- Architect p58
- Building Surveyor p65
- Insurance Risk Surveyor p32
- Town Planner/Planning Technician p115

Further information

Engineering Council UK
www.engc.org.uk

Institution of Civil Engineers
www.ice.org.uk

WISE
www.wisecampaign.org.uk

CONCRETER

Qualifications and courses

There are no formal qualifications required in order to become a concreter. After you have completed school you may choose to seek employment within the industry. Training is usually available on the job.

An increasing number of employers require their employees to hold a Construction Skills Certification Scheme (CSCS) card to show proof of their competence working on-site. This can only be gained by having completed, or being in the process of completing, a vocational qualification and health and safety test.

Apprenticeships are a common route into the construction field. It would be useful to have GCSEs/National 5s (A*–E/A–E) including Maths, Design and Technology and English. You may be required to complete a test in order to secure your apprenticeship.

As a trainee, you can work towards NVQs in Trowel Occupations (Levels 1 and 2), Erection of Precast Concrete (Level 2) and Specialist Concrete Occupations such as Concrete Repair, Sprayed Concrete or Concrete Drilling (Level 2).

Alternatively, Foundation Construction Awards in Trowel Occupations are available if obtaining experience in the workplace for NVQs is a challenge. Colleges offer these awards alongside an apprenticeship.

What the work involves

Your job will include initially levelling and compacting the ground to prepare it for concreting and then the construction of drives and pathways, floor slabs, foundations, columns and beams.

You will be working as part of a construction team, working with other specialists on building projects.

You will take early-morning deliveries of concrete, dig foundation trenches, mix, lay and level the concrete on the prepared ground, vibrate it to remove air trappings, and wrap it in polythene sheeting in order to cure it.

As well as laying fresh concrete you may also be required to reinforce existing concrete structures, repair cracks that have been caused by moving ground and create different styles and effects within the setting concrete for aesthetic purposes.

Type of person suited to this work

You should have a careful, methodical approach to your work and have good hand skills.

Maths skills are important as you will be calculating quantities for materials.

You should enjoy working outdoors, as part of a team or on your own. Being fit and active is essential as you will be required to work long and at times hard hours.

You need to be aware of health and safety requirements when working on-site.

Working conditions

Your work will be site based, largely undertaking manual labour in dirty or dusty surroundings.

You will work 37 hours a week, including some early mornings and late nights.

You could work on a building site, motorway, private driveway or the interiors of large buildings.

Protective clothing is needed, as the work is messy and at times, potentially dangerous.

You will use traditional hand tools such as shovels as well as machinery such as cement mixers.

Future prospects

You can move into specialised areas of work such as concrete spraying or concrete repair. It is also possible to progress to a managerial or supervisory role.

After gaining experience, many concreters choose to become self-employed. You could start your own company or work on a labour-only basis for a contractor.

You can work for building and engineering contractors, local authorities and public organisations. Job opportunities are also available abroad, as well as throughout the UK.

Advantages/disadvantages

You have the opportunity to earn good money if you work hard.

There is an increased risk of injury on construction sites. The cement in concrete can cause burning or inflammation and you should avoid contact with the skin.

The work is physically draining, as it involves a great deal of practical work and, at times, heavy lifting.

Money guide

As a trainee you can expect to earn around £12,500.

With experience this can rise to £20,000–£25,000.

Concrete sprayers with a lot of experience can earn up to £30,000.

Salaries can be boosted by bonuses and overtime.

You may earn more if you set up your own contracting firm.

Related opportunities

- Bricklayer p62
- Construction Operative p74
- Plasterer p99

Further information

Chartered Institute of Building
www.ciob.org.uk

The Concrete Centre
www.concretecentre.com

Women on the Tools
www.womenonthetools.org.uk

CONSTRUCTION OPERATIVE

Qualifications and courses

Your training will take place mainly on the job by experienced labourers/construction operatives and tradespeople. Employers may ask for a number of GCSEs/National 5s in subjects such as English, Maths and Technology or equivalent qualifications. Once employed, there may be opportunities to study for NVQs/SVQs (Levels 1 and 2) in Construction and Civil Engineering or in Specialised Plant and Machinery Operations.

Many employers require you to hold a CSCS card issued by the Construction Skills Certification Scheme as proof of your competence working on site. A health and safety test and evidence of a vocational qualification is usually necessary in order to qualify for one of these.

City & Guilds offer Certificates in Basic Construction Skills (6217) for young learners under the age of 16 and an Award/Certificate/Diploma in Basic Construction Skills for 14–19 year olds. BTEC Certificates and Diplomas are available in Construction as well as a Foundation Certificate in Building and Craft Occupations.

You can also train to be a construction operative via a 2-year Construction Civil Engineering Apprenticeship scheme and choose to complete an extra year for a Level 3 Construction Diploma.

If you are a full-time student doing a construction-related course you can qualify for a programme-led apprenticeship (PLA) and gain experience up to NVQ Level 2.

What the work involves

Construction operatives support the work of other construction workers by doing various practical tasks.

Your work might include digging trenches, moving building materials and tools, putting up signs and safety barriers, helping to lay drains, and paving roads.

You will also mix and lay cement as well as operate construction equipment and vehicles.

Type of person suited to this work

As the work requires you to lift heavy materials and be on the move a lot you must be physically fit. You must also not mind working at great heights or depths.

You need to be able to follow and carry out instructions and work well in a team with other labourers and professionals.

It is essential to be hands on, flexible and trustworthy.

Working conditions

You will be working both indoors and outdoors in all weather conditions.

The work is often dusty and dirty and may be difficult for people suffering from allergies.

You will need to pay attention to both your own and your colleagues' health and safety. You will be expected to follow procedures for each type of work you do, including the wearing of protective clothing.

You may work a normal week, although evening and weekend work may also be available, and you might need to start early or finish late for some projects as well as work away from home at times.

Future prospects

Building projects, new builds and renovations cannot happen without construction operatives so they are in strong demand when business is doing well.

You could work for contractors or local authorities.

You may progress to a specialist craft career such as carpentry or bricklaying or advance to a supervisory role. You also have the option of becoming self-employed or finding work abroad.

Advantages/disadvantages

The work can sometimes be physically demanding.

You have the opportunity to learn a wide range of skills and work on a different project every day.

Your role on-site is important as you pave the way for tradespeople to complete their tasks.

Money guide

As a trainee starting out you can expect a salary of up to £15,500 per year.

As a qualified construction operative you could earn £16,000–£21,000.

Depending on the project they are working on, skilled operatives or operatives in a leadership or supervisory role may receive up to £24,000 a year.

Overtime is often available for those who wish to increase their earnings.

On some projects there are bonuses based on outputs which can lead to higher earnings.

Related opportunities

- Bricklayer p62
- Building Technician p66
- Mastic Asphalter p95

Further information

Construction Industry Training Board (CITB)
www.citb.co.uk

Federation of Master Builders
www.fmb.org.uk

Women on the Tools
www.womenonthetools.org.uk

CONSTRUCTION PLANT OPERATOR

Qualifications and courses

There are no set academic entry requirements, although GCSEs/National 5s or equivalent in English, Maths and a science or technology are useful, alongside any equivalent vocational qualifications. It is also possible to take NVQs/SVQs in Specialised Plant and Machinery Operations (Levels 1 and 2) and Foundation, Intermediate and Advanced certificates in Maintenance of Construction Plant.

The minimum age to operate plant and equipment is 18 but 17-year-olds may work under supervision while they are training.

Construction civil engineering apprenticeships may be available for those over the age of 16 who wish to train as a construction plant operator. Another option is to train as an apprentice in Crane Operation or Plant Operations with the National Construction College. This route involves practical training and studying for the NVQ Diploma and Certificate in Plant Operations (Level 2).

The Construction Plant Competence Scheme (CPCS) card is required in order to operate most categories of plant, including cranes. New applicants must pass a health and safety test and technical test for a red CPCS card which allows trainees to work on-site. After working 300 hours and completing an NVQ/SVQ you can obtain a blue card.

What the work involves

Construction plant operators operate and maintain different forms of plant (machinery) used for tasks such as moving soil and building materials, flattening the earth and preparing concrete.

You may operate bulldozers, excavators, diggers, cranes and fork-lift trucks.

In larger organisations you may specialise in operating one type of plant. For example, crane operators control the machine to load and unload materials, working in conjunction with a signaller on the ground.

Type of person suited to this work

As you will often handle large and complex machines, you need to be good with your hands and have keen safety awareness. You will also need good mechanical knowledge.

You need to stay focused and communicate with your workmates so that you can operate safely. If you are working on cranes, you need to be comfortable working at heights, be alert and be a skilled driver.

Working conditions

You will work outdoors and on a variety of sites. Expect to get hot, dusty and dirty in the summer and cold, muddy and wet in the winter. You will have to stick to health and safety regulations and wear a protective helmet and boots.

You are likely to work a normal working week from Monday to Friday but you may also work extra hours at weekends. Some construction firms operate longer hours during the summer months and shorter during the winter. You might have to travel away from home on some contracts.

A driving licence (often a large goods vehicle category C licence) is essential for crane operators.

Future prospects

Work is available across the UK with crane-hire companies, manufacturers, local authorities and construction companies. For operators specialising in engineering work there is a high concentration of jobs available in the Midlands and in the north of England.

With experience, you may progress to using a wider range of plant and you may supervise or train plant operators or work as a safety inspector. You may also choose to specialise in operating one type of plant.

With experience and financial backing, it may be possible to start your own construction plant operation or hire business.

Advantages/disadvantages

Working on construction sites can be noisy, dusty and dirty although you will have safety equipment/clothing such as ear protectors. Working at heights may be demanding for some people.

It is a skilled and varied career where you are responsible for some impressive machinery. It can be satisfying to be able to control the machinery efficiently and safely.

Money guide

Trainee construction plant operators typically have a starting salary of £13,000.

As you gain qualifications, your earnings can increase to £15,000–£19,000 a year.

Very experienced plant operators or those with specialist skills can achieve £20,000–£26,000.

It is possible to increase your earnings through bonuses and working overtime.

Related opportunities

- Construction Operative p74
- Demolition Operative p78
- Highways Maintenance/Road Worker p91

Further information

Chartered Association of Building Engineers
www.cbuilde.com

Construction Industry Training Board (CITB)
www.citb.co.uk

CONSTRUCTION SUPERVISOR/ MANAGER

Qualifications and courses

The normal entry qualification required to be a construction manager is a degree, HND or Foundation degree. Relevant subjects include construction project management, building services engineering and building technology. For entry to a degree, 5 GCSEs/National 5s (A*–C/A–C) including Maths and a science and 2 A levels/3 H grades are normally required. You could seek financial sponsorship from an employer whilst you complete your studies and then go on to work for them after you graduate.

If you chose a degree unrelated to the construction industry, you may still be able to enter the field by completing a Graduate Diploma Programme offered by the Chartered Institute of Building (CIOB).

Alternatively, it may be possible to work your way up from technician level, as an estimator or as a site supervisor. The NVQ/SVQ in Construction Site Supervision (Level 3) and Construction Site Management (Level 4) are open to anyone with experience in building site supervision and management. Technicians can also study part time towards an HNC or degree.

The Chartered Institute of Building (CIOB) offers qualifications at Levels 3 and 4 in Site Management and Site Supervisory Studies which could improve your career prospects.

Recently qualified graduates are likely to continue training on programmes designed for professional and managerial staff. The CIOB runs a professional development programme (PDP) leading to chartered membership of the Institute.

What the work involves

Construction supervisors/managers run both new build and maintenance construction sites. Your duties will include planning the build, preparing the site, arranging deliveries, and checking quality and cost of building materials and equipment.

You will also have the responsibility for overseeing the construction project, hiring and managing staff, making sure everyone is safe on-site, and solving problems when they arise.

You will need to report directly to whoever is paying for the work to be done and keep them updated on progress.

Type of person suited to this work

You have to be able to plan ahead and have good management and problem-solving skills so that projects run smoothly. Numeracy skills are important in order to budget your projects.

You need to be a good communicator, energetic, hard working and diplomatic in order to motivate and manage your staff effectively. You must be able to develop an in-depth knowledge and understanding of all aspects of the construction business. You will use computer software packages to plan workflow, so IT skills are also useful.

Organisational skills are essential and you should be prepared to take responsibility for anything that happens on your site.

Working conditions

You will be based on construction sites and are likely to work from a portable office. You will work outdoors in all weathers.

You may work a normal working week, but you may also have to start early, finish late or work at weekends on some projects. As some companies win contracts all over the UK, you might have to work away from home.

Future prospects

With growth in the construction industry projected at a steady 2.9% per year until 2019, a rise in activity across all sectors indicates that there are increasingly good opportunities for construction supervisors on a wide range of builds, including multi-million pound projects as well as opportunities abroad.

You may work for contractors, construction companies, project management companies, surveyors' practices, public services, utility companies or retailers.

With experience, you may be promoted to work as a contract manager on bigger and more prestigious projects. You could go into teaching the trade or work as a health and safety inspector.

Advantages/disadvantages

There is a great deal of satisfaction to be obtained from knowing that you have the ability to begin with an empty piece of land and leave a finished construction behind.

When there is a tight deadline to meet and a problem arises, the work can be stressful – particularly as many projects are on large but tightly planned budgets.

Money guide

Trainee construction managers usually have an annual salary of around £20,000.

Once you have gained experience as a manager, your earnings can rise to in excess of £50,000.

For senior managers, a salary of more than £60,000 is possible.

Earnings vary depending on geographical location and your particular employer.

Related opportunities

- Architectural Technician p59
- Building Surveyor p65
- Civil/Construction Engineer/Civil Engineering Technician p71

Further information

Chartered Institute of Building
www.ciob.org.uk

Construction Industry Training Board (CITB)
www.citb.co.uk

DAMP PROOFER

Qualifications and courses

There are no set academic requirements. However GCSEs/National 5s in English and Maths (A*–E/A–E) are an advantage as you will need to calculate quantities, form estimates and maintain written records.

Currently, there are no colleges that provide apprenticeships specifically for those wishing to go into the field of damp proofing. Some private companies, involved in Investors in People, may consider apprenticeships however.

On-the-job training is provided by experienced damp proofers. Damp-proof installer companies may also provide courses on safety awareness.

Technicians can take short courses at the British Wood Preserving and Damp Proofing Association. You can study for the Level 2 NVQ in Insulation and Building Treatments, a course developed by the CITB. Courses accredited by the CITB are recognised throughout the industry.

In order to work on a building site, you must also hold a Construction Skills Certification Scheme (CSCS) card which acts as proof of your competency. Completing a vocational qualification before or whilst you train will qualify you for one of these.

What the work involves

You will provide guidance and solutions to people in residential or commercial properties who experience damp problems.

As a damp proofer, you inspect and assess properties using moisture meters to aid you in your discovery of a client's damp problems. Drawing on your knowledge and experience within the industry, you will provide your clients with recommendations as to how to eradicate their damp issues and suggest a suitable price at which to do so.

You also may need to install damp-proof courses to buildings. This is a horizontal layer of water-repellent/proof material that prevents moisture rising from the ground up the walls. This involves drilling holes in walls to inject mortar or creams/gels at varying pressures.

Type of person suited to this work

As you will be working on buildings or engineering projects, you should have an interest in construction and architecture. You should also be in good health and have an understanding of health and safety protocol.

You should have good problem-solving skills and relish new challenges. You should be able to work in a team and cooperate with colleagues and customers. You will need good written and communication skills to give and follow instructions and guidelines.

You need to have a keen eye for detail and have good practical skills to operate drills and specialist machinery such as moisture meters to check damp levels. You should also be willing to travel.

Working conditions

You will usually work 38 hours a week, Monday to Friday. You may have to work overtime and this could include evenings and weekends. These hours will vary depending on where you are working, who you are working for and even the weather.

You will have to do a lot of travelling to each new site. A driving licence and car would be useful.

Your work will be largely outdoors, so can be affected by the weather.

Future prospects

You can find job opportunities with the 1,500 damp proofing contractors across the UK. You can also find employment in related fields such as timber treatment, waterproofing and pest control.

With experience you will be eligible for promotion to remedial treatment surveyor or supervisory posts. The Wood Protection Association (WPA) runs its own training courses for surveyors and technicians and with an NVQ/SVQ Level 2 in Insulation and Remedial Maintenance you can apply for occupational assessment under the CSCS.

You may become self-employed.

Advantages/disadvantages

As a damp proofer you will have plenty of opportunities to travel around the UK and abroad.

Bonus payments are extremely common within this field of work.

You may have to work in uncomfortable weather conditions and antisocial working hours.

The work is very physical and demanding and a lot of your time will be taken up travelling between different work sites and projects.

Money guide

Starting salary can range between £12,000 and £15,000 a year.

With experience, this can rise to £25,000 a year.

With specialised skills and training you can earn in excess of £35,000.

Related opportunities

- Building Technician p66
- Concreter p73
- Thermal Insulation Engineer p114

Further information

Institute of Specialist Surveyors and Engineers
www.isse.org.uk

The Damp Proofing Association
www.dampproofingassociation.com

Wood Protection Association
www.wood-protection.org

DEMOLITION OPERATIVE

Qualifications and courses

No formal qualifications are required to be a demolition operative. However GCSEs/National 5s (A*–E/A–E) in Maths, science subjects and English or a background in general construction may be useful for calculations, measurements and theory. The BTEC Diplomas (Levels 1–3) in Construction and the Built Environment may also be relevant for this job.

You can enter via the CITB Apprenticeship in Demolition Plant Operation, if you are under 16, but you need to be at least 18 to work as a demolition operative. There is also a specialist apprenticeship for people who work in demolition but do not handle machinery.

Most training is done on the job, with special attention given to health and safety – including accident prevention, manual handling, noise control and fire control/prevention. You can study for the NVQ Level 2 in Demolition and Demolition Plant. Other NVQs are available for specialist work such as the Level 2 in Removal of Hazardous and Non-Hazardous Waste.

You will need a Certificate of Competence of Demolition Operatives (CCDO) card to prove you are qualified to carry out the job safely. To qualify for one of these, you are normally required to have completed or signed up for a vocational qualification.

What the work involves

Demolition operatives demolish or dismantle buildings and structures. The job can be highly dangerous if the right precautions are not taken so you will be responsible for assessing structures and planning for the safest and most efficient way to demolish them.

You will clear and prepare sites, put up fencing and scaffolding, strip out fittings, and remove, sort and grade reusable materials.

You will use a variety of tools such as chisels, crowbars and axes for hand demolition of brick and stone and you may also use specialised machinery including pneumatic drills, steel girders, chainsaws and even explosives for bigger jobs.

Type of person suited to this work

As you will be involved in the construction industry you should have an interest in building, construction and the environment.

You should have a high level of fitness as your work will be quite physical a lot of the time, involving lifting and carrying, and you should be able to work at heights. You will also need good manual skills to operate equipment and tools and an aptitude for more delicate tasks such as hand demolition.

You should have a strong eye for detail and be able to follow health and safety instructions rigorously.

You should be willing to work as part of a team and be conscious of your safety and that of those around you.

Working conditions

You will normally work 39 hours per week. This will frequently include weekends and overtime.

As you will be working on construction sites you should be willing to work outdoors in dirty, dusty, noisy conditions in all weathers. This will also involve lifting, bending and working at heights.

You will need to wear protective equipment including helmets, boots, gloves and goggles which will be provided by the employer. You may also be required to wear breathing equipment for some jobs.

Future prospects

There are opportunities for demolition operatives on many building and development projects throughout the UK. You can find employment in specialist companies which may be based nationally but many companies are based in urban and traditionally industrial areas of the UK.

If you work hard and commit yourself to the job, there are fantastic opportunities for progression and personal achievement.

Advantages/disadvantages

Although it is unusual to be self-employed in this profession, with experience you can set up your own contracting business.

At times your work can be strenuous and potentially hazardous if you do not follow safety procedures.

Money guide

Demolition operatives have nationally recommended minimum rates of pay.

The starting salary for a trainee is around £13,000 a year.

Once qualified as a demolition operative, your salary will rise to anything between £17,000 and £21,000.

As an experienced senior operative you can earn up to around £25,000.

You may earn significantly more with overtime or for carrying out specialist responsibilities such as operating plant machinery or handling explosives.

Related opportunities

- Construction Operative p74
- Quarry Worker p228
- Scaffolder p106

Further information

Construction Industry Training Board (CITB)
www.citb.co.uk

National Federation of Demolition Contractors
www.demolition-nfdc.com

DRY STONE WALLER

Qualifications and courses

No specific qualifications are necessarily required in order to become a dry stone waller. You can train with an experienced professional or do a land-based training course that includes dry stone walling.

The Dry Stone Walling Association of Great Britain (DSWA) runs a Craftsman Certification scheme at 3 levels (Initial, Intermediate and Advanced), which is open to anyone, including complete beginners. Completion of these usually leads to the DSWA Master Craftsman Certification. These qualifications are available through some colleges and across the DSWA branch network, including Scotland and Wales. These branches also offer short courses and practice days aimed at improving the skills of beginners and are usually led by a DSWA instructor over a period of one weekend.

Alternatively, you may choose to go down the apprenticeship route. A number of colleges across England offer Lantra Certificates in Dry Stone Walling (Levels 1 and 2) as part of a more general Diploma in Environmental Conservation. You will need sponsorship from an employer in order to complete this.

What the work involves

Dry stone walls are built as boundaries in rural landscapes, and sometimes in gardens and parks. Unlike other walls, they are built without the use of mortar or cement.

As a dry stone waller, you will build new walls and maintain and rebuild existing walls, using the existing or newly quarried stone.

You will prepare foundations, set up a frame and lay stones, as well as strip out any existing wall or stones. You will need to be able to use tools such as hammers, sledgehammers, pickaxes and tape measures.

Type of person suited to this work

You need to be thorough, methodical and good with your hands.

Being physically fit is essential as you will be lifting and carrying heavy stones. You will also need endurance and self-motivation as you will most likely be self-employed.

An eye for design is useful for creating decorative effects. You may also need to work in a team with other dry stone wallers.

You will need to respect the plants, animals and insects that live within, on or around the walls and other parts of your working area so having an interest in conservation and the environment is useful. You should also be aware of health and safety regulations.

Working conditions

Your work will be physically demanding and take place outdoors in most weather conditions. The work may also be dusty and dirty.

You will need to wear protective gear such as boots, strong gloves and safety goggles.

Your working hours are likely to vary according to daylight hours and when the work is available. You may need to work weekends.

Future prospects

Dry stone walling is prospering due to the increased interest in conserving walls and the growth in artistic landscape projects. Given that dry stone walls are composed of natural materials, they are highly valued in a society increasingly concerned about its environment.

As a highly important feature of the British landscape, there is a demand for the maintenance, repair and creation of dry stone walls in farms, parks and gardens. Work is available in all rural areas of the UK for skilled members of the profession.

Employment is possible with organisations such as National Parks and The National Trust – although most experienced dry stone wallers are self-employed.

You can begin by working for an experienced dry stone waller and gain the necessary skills before working for yourself.

Many experienced wallers travel around the UK to complete projects. A few wallers combine this work with traditional bricklaying projects.

Advantages/disadvantages

The work can be physically demanding.

It is rewarding to use craft skills to build dry stone walls that are not only functional, but also enhance the landscape and become part of our heritage.

You also have the chance to be creative when producing decorative effects.

Money guide

For dry stone wallers new to the profession, earning up to £14,500 is possible.

Very skilled dry stone wallers with a lot of experience and contacts are able to earn up to £21,000, however earnings vary widely across the UK.

Related opportunities

- Blacksmith p202
- Construction Operative p74
- Stonemason p110
- Thatcher p113

Further information

Dry Stone Walling Association of Great Britain
www.dswa.org.uk

Lantra
www.lantra.co.uk

ELECTRICIAN

Qualifications and courses

An industry-recognised Level 3 NVQ qualification and a technical certificate are required in order to become a qualified electrician. Examples of these Level 3 qualifications include: a City & Guilds/EAL-approved Level 3 NVQ or Diploma in either Electrotechnical Services (Electrical Maintenance) (2356), Installing Electrotechnical Systems & Equipment (Buildings, Structures and the Environment) (2357) or Electrical Installations (Buildings and Structures) (2365).

The most common route to training as an electrician is by undertaking an electrotechnical advanced apprenticeship. This route will involve working towards a Level 3 NVQ Diploma in the workplace whilst studying for a technical certificate one day a week at college. You will be required to secure employment prior to signing up for the apprenticeship and typical entry requirements include 3 GCSEs/National 5s (A*–C/A–C) including English, Maths and a science. You must be 16 or over.

The City & Guilds Certificate in the Requirements for Electrical Installations (2382) helps to ensure that those practising in the electrical industry are up to date with the latest safety regulations.

Those experienced in areas such as electronics may qualify for entry to a training course. Colleges and private organisations offer their own courses but candidates must show practical work ability. Other qualifications include the City & Guilds NVQ in Engineering Maintenance (1788) and the BTEC Certificates/Diplomas in Engineering.

Entry to the profession is quite competitive and you must pass a colour vision and selection test.

What the work involves

Electricians install and inspect the wiring systems in all kinds of buildings (residential and commercial) and mechanical equipment.

You will follow detailed diagrams and plans when checking and installing new systems. Once installed you will test them to make sure they are safe.

You may work on quite complex wiring systems, ranging from security circuits and computer networks to traffic lights and other street lighting.

Type of person suited to this work

You must have the practical skills to be able to use tools such as pliers, screwdrivers and drills as well as the ability to follow wiring diagrams and work within strict safety regulations. Knowledge of maths and physics is beneficial.

You will need to be physically fit as the work involves bending, stretching, kneeling and generally being active. It can also involve working at heights, so you must be comfortable with this.

You may work alone or in a team but either way you will be talking to customers and explaining electrical problems, so good communication skills are an asset.

Working conditions

You may work a normal working week from Monday to Friday, but most electricians work 37–40 hours including evenings and weekends to accommodate the needs of their customers.

Electricians work in a variety of locations from people's homes to offices or building sites. You will almost certainly need a driving licence. The work can be dusty and dirty.

You will need to keep to health and safety regulations otherwise working with electricity can be exceedingly dangerous.

Future prospects

Employment prospects for new trainees are good as demand remains consistent.

Work is extremely varied and available in all kinds of environments including in housing associations, general building companies and public services such as local authorities and health trusts.

Most large employers have a formal progression structure, therefore, as you gain more experience, opportunities for supervisory and managerial responsibilities will become available and you may even move into consultancy work or training. Owning your own company and working abroad are also possible.

Advantages/disadvantages

You are providing a vital service and it is particularly rewarding to solve problems for people.

Many electricians are self-employed so you could have increased control over your work–life balance.

You may be required to work long hours and sometimes in physically difficult circumstances.

Money guide

The Joint Industry Board (JIB) for the Electrical Contracting Industry sets salary rates for apprentices and qualified electricians.

Trainee electricians may begin on around £8,000.

Once qualified, salaries rise to between £19,000 and £22,000.

Earnings increase with experience and those who specialise in a certain area can make £23,000–£30,000 a year.

Overtime and bonuses are also possible.

Related opportunities

- Bricklayer p62
- Carpenter/Joiner p67
- Plumber p100

Further information

Scottish Electrical Charitable Training Trust
www.sectt.org.uk

Organisation Profile

NICEIC

About NICEIC

NICEIC is the UK's leading voluntary regulatory body for the electrical contracting industry. It has been assessing the electrical competence of electricians for sixty years and currently maintains a roll of over 27,000 registered contractors.

Choosing an NICEIC registered electrician is a householder's best way to ensure a safe job. Electricians registered with NICEIC are assessed on a regular basis to ensure high standards, and their work is checked against the IEE Wiring Regulations BS 7671 as well as other standards.

Why choose an NICEIC registered electrician?

NICEIC operates an independent complaints procedure governing the technical standards of its Approved Contractor and Domestic Installer Schemes. If the work of a registered contractor is found to be below the accepted technical standard, NICEIC can require the contractor to correct the work at no additional cost to the customer.

Approved contractors undergo a rigorous assessment process, covering a representative sample of their work, their premises, documentation, equipment and the competence of their key supervisory staff. They are then re-assessed on a regular basis to ensure continued compliance.

Once registered with the NICEIC, contractors can access a range of support services, including technical advice, industry-recognised training, online certification and contractor insurance.

NICEIC regularly promotes the importance of employing an approved contractor to homeowners. Aside from the assurance of safety and competence of work, additional benefits to the consumer include guaranteed compliance with building regulations, a platinum promise which guarantees the standard of the work carried out, and access to an independent complaints procedure, should a problem arise.

Looking after the industry

NICEIC is committed to improving standards within the industry.

NICEIC believe apprenticeships make industries more effective, productive and competitive by addressing the skills gap directly; they are the proven way to train the workforce of the future. The NICEIC Apprentice Competition recognises the talents of electrical apprentices and acknowledge all the good they do.

NICEIC is also committed to improving opportunities for women in the electrical contracting industry. Women are severely under-represented in most trade professions, with less than one in every thousand electricians a female – despite there now being a valid business case to employ more women. In response to this, NICEIC launched its Jobs for the Girls campaign. Through its extensive media coverage, the campaign has raised awareness of the opportunities available to women in the industry. It also garnered the support of a cross-party band of MPs and NICEIC was invited to Westminster to host a parliamentary reception about the campaign. You can find out more at www.jobsforthegirls.com.

For more information or to find a qualified electrician in your area, visit www.niceic.com.

Case study

ELECTRICIAN

Steven Bastien, NICEIC Approved Contractor

When I was younger, during the weekends I would accompany my electrician uncle on his jobs in London, to earn extra pocket money. I was about 14 and I found it interesting working in different types of buildings and areas. The excitement and adventure of going to different places and meeting different people made it enjoyable.

Until the age of 16 I continued working with my uncle at weekends. I learnt how to install new electrical installations and rewire properties. At first, the jobs I did were mainly manual, moving furniture, lifting up carpets and floorboards, etc. Sometimes I would get the opportunity to chase out walls to bury cables. I also had to pack away the tools at the end of the day, and make sure none were missing!

As time went on, I realised I really enjoyed electrical work. It made me feel important and valued. I felt good about myself. I felt I was doing something that was a skilled trade … so becoming an electrician was a straightforward choice. I was advised by my careers adviser and teachers what subjects would be best to study; these subjects were science, maths, English, history and geography.

After leaving school, I studied at college for two years, taking relevant City & Guilds qualifications. I studied very hard to make sure I would pass – which I did with a distinction and passes. I then applied to electrical companies for an electrical apprenticeship. I was successful and offered a five-year JIB Apprenticeship. It was here I gained a vast amount of experience in the electrical field, working in offices, schools, factories and shops. I carried on at college where I continued my studies to gain more qualifications in Electrical Installations.

Three years later I became a Qualified Electrician. I then decided to become even more adventurous by becoming self-employed. This gave me the opportunity to work on major building projects throughout the UK. I worked in a variety of places, such as Fleet Street where I worked for different newspapers. I even worked on a building that had a helicopter pad on top of it. That was quite exciting! I also worked on the first tower block of Canary Wharf. I worked on Tower Bridge, the NEC in Birmingham, the first Toyota Car Factory in the UK, and many more.

I then started working for local authorities, carrying out maintenance work as well as emergency callouts. Callouts give you a good feeling as you have helped someone in need.

Recently, I formed my own company – Facelift Electrical Services Ltd – and successfully became an NICEIC Domestic Installer. I then become an NICEIC Approved Contractor, which involved taking more qualifications.

I can now say to any young person who would like to become an electrician, that it's a very enjoyable and satisfying career. It's great when you see the beginning of the project and see it through to the end. It's great to know you were part of that project being completed.

For further information visit www.niceic.com or call 0870 013 0382

Qualifications and courses

No formal qualifications are required to become an estate agent. It is useful for entrants to have 5 GCSEs/National 5s (A*–C/A–C). Most entrants start as a trainee negotiator and undertake an NVQ in the Sale of Residential Property (Level 2). A degree, Foundation degree or HND in subjects such as property management, urban and land studies or civil and structural engineering, may increase your chances of employment in a competitive industry or a background in sales, customer service or administration could be advantageous.

Training is mostly carried out on the job. It may involve studying for Technical Awards offered by the National Federation of Property Professionals (NFoPP), such as the Sale of Residential Property, Residential Letting and Property Management and Commercial Property Agency. NFoPP also offer Certificates in these subjects which are intended for those with around 3 years' experience. Both the Technical Awards and the Certificates may be studied by distance learning or part-time at a college. Further training may qualify you to become an energy assessor or surveyor.

School leavers looking to become an estate agent administrator can enrol on the Intermediate Level Apprenticeship in Property Services and those who want to become an estate agent could consider the Advanced Apprenticeship.

As an estate agent, you will be required to hold a valid driving licence.

What the work involves

Estate agents are responsible for selling or letting residential or commercial properties on behalf of their clients.

Properties are valued based upon factors such as their condition, location, comparison to other properties and the current housing market.

Estate agents market a property, show prospective buyers around and negotiate prices to ensure the best deal for their client.

During the selling process you will have to liaise with banks, surveyors, mortgage brokers and solicitors.

Type of person suited to this work

You will need excellent speaking and listening skills so that you can recommend suitable properties to potential buyers. You also have to be good at negotiating so that you can help buyers and sellers to agree prices for properties.

You must be confident dealing with people and prepared to work hard to achieve sales.

As you will be dealing with the figures when valuing properties or negotiating prices, you will need numeracy skills and an interest in keeping up to date with what is happening in the housing and property markets.

Working conditions

Some of your time will be spent in the branch office, and the rest of the time you will be visiting properties, so a driving licence is needed.

Estate agency branches are often modern and open plan with up-to-date equipment. You will spend a lot of your time working at a computer and speaking to your customers on the phone.

This can be very stressful work as you will have sales targets to reach and your earnings will depend on your selling ability. You are likely to need to work at the weekends and evenings (with some time off during the week instead).

Future prospects

Estate agents are located throughout the UK but there tend to be fewer opportunities in a poor housing market and within rural areas. Positions are not always advertised, therefore you may need to make general enquiries.

With experience and qualifications, there are opportunities for promotion, especially in larger companies. You may move from trainee to negotiator, then to senior negotiator and on to branch manager. If you have established a substantial client base, you may opt to become self-employed or to carry out freelance work. You could set up your own agency or become a partner in a firm.

Advantages/disadvantages

The work can be stressful if you are finding it hard to meet sales targets, especially if you are working on a commission-only basis in a slowing housing market.

When the property market is booming, or for those who are very skilled in sales, the financial rewards can be high.

Money guide

Estate agents' earnings are usually a combination of a basic salary plus commission based upon their sales figures. Some estate agents work for commission only.

Starting salaries for new entrants are between £12,000 and £20,000.

With experience you can expect to earn between £20,000 and £35,000 a year.

Those employed at a managerial level can achieve up to £60,000.

Related opportunities

- Auction Property Consultant p61
- Planning and Development Surveyor p98
- Property Valuer p101

Further information

National Association of Estate Agents
www.naea.co.uk

FABRICATOR

Qualifications and courses

Whilst there are no specific entry qualifications to becoming a fabricator, GCSEs/National 5s (A*–E/A–E) in English and Maths are useful. A science and Design and Technology are also beneficial as you must have an understanding of calculations, measurements and theory.

Many trainees develop their profession through an apprenticeship scheme. The Level 3 Advanced Apprenticeship in Metal Processing will give you a broad understanding of the metal industry as well as the opportunity to develop and make a range of metal products, including structural steelwork. Construction apprentices learn practical skills under the supervision of skilled fabricators, as well as taking courses at a college or training centre. These relevant courses include NVQs/SVQs such as Level 1 in Construction and Civil Engineering Services, Fabrication and Welding Engineering (Levels 2 and 3), Carpentry and Joinery (Levels 2 and 3), and Level 4 in Construction Site Management.

A Construction Skills Certification Scheme (CSCS) card is needed to work on a building site as it acts as proof of your competence within the field. In order to qualify for one of these, you must have completed or be registered with a scheme that offers you an industry recognised qualification. CSCS cards are granted in accordance with your qualifications and experience.

What the work involves

Fabricators manufacture, assemble and install structural frames of buildings.

You will extend and adapt existing buildings or work on manufacturing the entire framework for new ones. This may include houses, public buildings, swimming pools, airport terminal buildings and caravans.

Your work will be influenced by architectural demands and advances. The need for thermal performance, speed and versatility in architecture means that traditional forms of construction such as concrete, steel and glass are being replaced with new, more efficient materials. You will probably work with a diverse range of materials such as aluminium, PVC foam, timber, natural stone and fibreglass.

Type of person suited to this work

As a fabricator you should have an interest in machinery and the construction industry.

You will be working on-site or in a manufacturing plant; as this may include physical labour you should be fit and have good manual skills.

You should also enjoy working in a team and have excellent knowledge and awareness of health and safety practices. You should be organised and know how to plan ahead.

Working conditions

You will typically work 39 hours per week, Monday to Friday. This may vary depending on the project you are working on.

You may also be required to do shifts and overtime or work evenings and weekends.

You may work in a variety of locations; outdoors, indoors and at heights. Weather conditions may make this work uncomfortable or delay work.

As a fabricator you might have to operate machinery such as mobile cranes.

Future prospects

As you gain experience you will have the opportunity to specialise in a certain area of fabrication. This could be as an aluminium fabricator (curtain walls, windows and frames), a conservatory fabricator (working with timber, aluminium or PVC to erect conservatories), or a window fabricator (working with frame makers and door makers building off-site manufactured rooms that can be assembled on-site).

As you accumulate experience you can progress to a higher level position such as a supervisor or you may also choose to become self-employed. There are also fantastic opportunities to take your skills abroad.

Advantages/disadvantages

New and exciting developments and improvements in materials and technology mean that your work is likely to include scope for diversity and creativity.

Your work at times may be very physically demanding.

Money guide

The wages of fabricators are normally paid according to the nationally recommended industry rates. Earnings of trainees are graded to a nationally agreed minimum rate.

Your starting salary may be around £18,000 a year.

With experience your earnings could increase to up to £25,000 per year.

Highly experienced fabricators and those in supervisory roles may earn up to £35,000 a year.

Wages will increase in the event of overtime and shift allowances.

Related opportunities

- Building Technician p66
- Carpenter/Joiner p67
- Ceiling Fixer p69

Further information

Construction Industry Training Board (CITB)
www.citb.co.uk

National Association of Shopfitters
www.shopfitters.org

FACILITIES MANAGER

Qualifications and courses

You can become a facilities manager by completing a degree in any discipline although many entrants are graduates of property or land-based subjects such as building management or surveying. Others gain experience in relevant fields such as construction, building services engineering or hospitality in order to acquire the necessary skills to become a facilities manager. Postgraduate diplomas and master's degrees in facilities management, although not a prerequisite, can be particularly useful in aiding career progression, especially if you want to gain chartered status later on in life.

Alternatively, you can take vocational courses in facilities management. These include appropriate NVQs/SVQs or professional qualifications from the British Institute of Facilities Management (BIFM). You can also study for a Foundation degree (developed by Asset Skills), or an HND in Facilities Management. Entry into the field with these qualifications will usually be at a lower level however.

Work experience is recommended and employers will seek candidates with good experience. For graduates, year-long placements are invaluable.

What the work involves

Facilities managers are responsible for the management and administration of premises, including offices, schools and commercial properties. You will provide a safe and efficient work environment for staff by implementing procedures to improve facilities, reduce costs and increase productivity.

Your day-to-day work will depend on the type of organisation you work for, but will include a broad spectrum of tasks such as coordinating and managing central services, organising mail receipt and despatch, arranging contractors for security or supervising cleaning and catering.

You must be able to respond to all problems that arise unexpectedly, and react to them appropriately and efficiently.

Type of person suited to this work

As you will be coordinating many different aspects of an organisation, or many organisations in one location, you need to be highly organised. You should be able to meet deadlines and have strong problem-solving skills.

You will lead a team so you should have excellent negotiation skills and strong written and verbal communication ability. As you will be working with a variety of different people you should have good customer service skills.

You should also be aware of environmental issues affecting premises and how budgets are planned and controlled.

Working conditions

Your hours will vary depending on the organisation you work for but on average you will work from 9am to 5pm. You will mainly be office based, but you will move around a lot to inspect and supervise various projects throughout the location you work in.

You may have a permanent contract or work on a fixed-term contract. At times you may be required to be available at any time in the event of emergencies.

Future prospects

You may begin as an assistant in a particular support field such as IT, HR, finance, purchasing or health and safety and then progress to functional manager, senior manager and director positions.

You can work as a facilities manager in-house or join a facilities management provider or consultancy. This will provide a variety of projects and responsibilities but will not have the same level of stability.

It is recommended that you seek opportunities in different organisations to secure promotion.

Advantages/disadvantages

Prospects for career development can be excellent. If you are hardworking, flexible, and efficient, have commercial acumen and the ability to juggle tight budgets you can progress to higher level management jobs.

You may find it difficult to move from an in-house role to a position with a service provider as there is a perceived difference in outlook and experience.

Money guide

A starting salary for an entry-level assistant role may range from £20,000 to £27,000 per year.

An experienced facilities manager can earn between £27,000 and £45,000 a year.

Senior and regional facilities managers can earn in excess of £60,000.

Directors of operations can earn £70,000 or more.

Wages are typically higher in the south-east of England and in London. Financial bonuses may also be available.

Related opportunities

- Building Services Engineer p64
- Health and Safety Adviser p27
- Quality Manager p45

Further information

British Institute of Facilities Management
www.bifm.org.uk

Chartered Management Institute
www.managers.org.uk

FLOOR LAYER/FINISHER

Qualifications and courses

No specific qualifications are required, although a common route of entry is through an apprenticeship scheme where GCSEs/National 5s (A*–E/A–E) in Maths, Design and Technology, a science and English might be a requirement.

As an apprentice you will be trained on the job while working towards vocational qualifications. You may go to a college or training centre on day or block release. The Construction Industry Training Board (CITB) offers an apprenticeship scheme in Floor Covering, which will provide you with a Level 2 Construction Diploma in Floor Covering and a Level 2 NVQ Diploma in Flooring Occupations.

Alternatively, fast-track short courses are available from independent providers like the Flooring Industry Training Association as well as NVQs/SVQs in Floor Covering at Levels 1–3. These awards allow you to specialise in impervious coverings, textile carpeting or wood block flooring. You may also be able to acquire some of the necessary skills to become a floor layer by completing a BTEC Level 2 or 3 Certificate or Diploma in Construction.

Many employers on construction sites require workers to have a Construction Skills Certification Scheme (CSCS) card. This demonstrates that the holder has health and safety training. In order to be granted one of these, you must have completed or be registered with a scheme that awards you an industry recognised qualification.

Once employed, you may be required to hold a valid driving licence in order to commute between projects.

What the work involves

Floor layers fit various rooms and buildings with many different types of flooring, such as vinyl, wood, carpet, tiles, rubber or plastic. You will often work with materials chosen by the client but on occasion may be asked to make recommendations on the best material to use for the particular type of floor.

You will use various tools to prepare the surface, cut the flooring material to size and lay the floor.

You will work from technical plans and diagrams in order to lay and fit each floor correctly.

Type of person suited to this work

To do this work you will need accurate numerical skills in order to calculate the exact amount of flooring material you will need for each job.

You should be physically fit as you will spend a lot of time lifting and carrying materials, or working on your hands and knees.

You may work alone for some smaller jobs, but you must also be able to work in a team with other construction professionals for larger jobs. Good planning skills are helpful when organising your workload, and you should be happy meeting and talking to lots of different people.

Working conditions

You will usually work normal Monday to Friday office hours, but you may also need to work through the night or over weekends on some contracts, so that you can lay floors without disrupting the work of shops and businesses.

Most of your work will be spent indoors in a variety of locations including people's homes, hospitals, offices and construction sites, some of which will be dirty and dusty. This is mobile work, so a driving licence is useful.

Some contracts may involve absence from home overnight or for longer periods of time.

Future prospects

Employment for floor finishers is expected to remain relatively steady given the variety of industries readily employing the small number of people within the profession.

Once you have qualified, work will be available within small or large flooring companies or contractors across the UK. You could work across numerous industries including construction, retail trade and manufacturing.

You may choose to specialise in using one type of flooring material such as tiles or laminates.

With experience, you can progress to supervisory or managerial posts. Alternatively, you could set up your own business as a self-employed floor layer.

Advantages/disadvantages

An attractive and well-laid floor can transform a room. The ability to use your skills and a range of materials to create this effect can give you great job satisfaction.

You will spend a lot of time travelling to and from jobs, and may need to spend time away from home on big flooring projects.

Money guide

The salary of a trainee ranges from £12,000 to £16,000 per year.

As a fully qualified floor layer you could earn £20,000 to £25,000.

Highly skilled, experienced floor layers can earn salaries of up to £30,000 a year.

Many floor layers are self-employed and earnings will depend on the ability to win contracts.

Related opportunities

- Carpenter/Joiner p67
- Plasterer p99
- Roofer p104

Further information

Construction Industry Training Board (CITB)
www.citb.co.uk

Flooring Industry Training Association
www.fita.co.uk

Case Study

THE FLOORING TRADE

Here's Matthew Blackbourn's story

On the job training has formed a key part of 30-year-old Matthew's journey into the flooring trade, fitting carpets and other floor coverings in domestic homes. He firmly believes that ensuring you begin your working life with a reputable, established company is vital. Matthew has supplemented the experience he has gained on site with training courses through the Flooring Industry Training Association (FITA), after which he applied to become a 'Masterfitter' in carpet via the National Institute of Carpet & Floorlayers (NICF). Although he has a passion for installation and gets a true buzz from a job well done, Matthew hopes to grow more into the management side. However, his positive experience of training has also led him to have ambitions to become an instructor and give something back.

For Matthew the future in flooring is bright and full of opportunity.

What the job entails

'Working for a small business in the domestic market means that the range of tasks involved are enormous. I generally find myself fitting floors during the day, and enjoy the diversity of products and skills I have to employ. I also like working with the public, and when we are busy I tend to help out with measures in the evenings. More recently, I have started to get involved with pricing and ordering stock, etc.

'The commercial sector is, of course, slightly different, with work typically taking place in offices, hospitals and schools. Generally being on a bigger scale, some of the contracts involve materials worth many thousands of pounds. Main contractors are often working to tight timescales and floor layers have to enjoy working in a team in what is often essentially a construction environment. As well as a craft and a skill, floor laying is becoming increasingly technical, and finding the solution to meet the needs of a client (many working on fast-track projects) are some of the demands and challenges of the "on site" role.

What you need to succeed

'Flexibility, good communication, as well as an obvious natural tendency towards good practical skills, are all qualities required to succeed in the flooring industry. The ability to use your own initiative, as well as to work in a team, is often an advantage.

'Practical site experience will always be required, but formal qualifications, such as an Level 2 NVQ Diploma in Floorcovering Occupations, are recognised qualifications that can currently be gained through a number of routes, including a modern apprenticeship. This can be supplemented with short training courses through organisations such as FITA as both an introduction as well as a career building strategy.'

For further information or advice contact:
The Contract Flooring Association (CFA)
Telephone: 0115 941 1126

The Flooring Industry Training Association (FITA)
Telephone: 0115 950 6836

The National Institute of Carpet & Floorlayers (NICF)
Telephone: 0115 958 3077

GAS SERVICE TECHNICIAN

Qualifications and courses

At least 4 GCSEs/National 5s (A*–C/A–C) including English, Maths and sometimes science or technology subjects are normally required to enter this career. Practical subjects such as metalwork and woodwork are also useful.

Apprenticeships/Skillseekers are available for people aged 16–24. An Advanced Level Apprenticeship in the gas industry is a good route for those who wish to become a gas service engineer. Apprentices work towards the NVQ/SVQ in Domestic Natural Gas Installation and Maintenance and Emergency Services Operations (Levels 2 and 3) awarded by City & Guilds (6034). You will normally need to be employed by a company willing to sponsor you prior to signing up to an apprenticeship. Gas service companies also run their own apprenticeship schemes.

Trainees must gain registration with the Gas Safe Register. To become registered, you will need to work towards the above City & Guilds NVQ/SVQ or complete equivalent in-house training with a company. Technicians with qualifications or training other than the NVQ/SVQ must complete Accredited Certification Scheme (ACS) assessments.

Gas service technicians have to demonstrate their gas safety competence on a 5-year cycle by successfully completing nationally agreed ACS assessments.

A valid driving licence is essential to allow travel between clients' premises.

What the work involves

Your job will be to install, maintain, repair and test gas appliances such as fires, cookers, heating systems, shower units and industrial equipment. You will carry out scheduled maintenance checks on systems and equipment.

You could work in private homes or on business premises.

You may also have to give customers quotes for costs and timescales, sell additional company services and deal with complaints.

As a trained professional, you will be required to give advice on the safety and efficiency of gas systems and equipment.

Type of person suited to this work

You will need excellent practical and problem-solving skills as you will be required to investigate and fix faults.

Gas appliances are potentially dangerous so you should be very thorough, reliable and aware of safety practices.

As you will be visiting clients' homes, you should be personable and presentable.

Working conditions

Working hours are generally 8am to 5pm, Monday to Friday. However, if your employer offers 24-hour emergency cover, you may have to undertake shift work.

Although most of your work will take place in customers' homes or business premises, you will also need to work on many different construction sites. You will need to wear protective clothing, such as a hard hat, goggles and gloves.

You will be required to travel to jobs in a van which stores your parts and equipment.

Future prospects

Job prospects for gas service technicians are favourable given the national shortage of trained personnel. There are opportunities for work throughout the UK.

You can work for national or private companies. From a position within a larger company you can apply for training posts at local colleges or within private organisations.

Once you have gained enough experience, you could progress into gas engineering, a supervisory/management role or become self-employed. Your employer may even sponsor you to study further qualifications.

You could also choose to specialise in a specific area such as energy efficiency, oil-fired equipment or environmental technologies.

Advantages/disadvantages

If your employer offers 24-hour emergency cover, you may have to work some unsocial hours.

The job can be strenuous and can involve working at heights or in confined spaces.

There is a high demand for gas service technicians and career progression opportunities are good.

Successfully repairing a potentially dangerous gas leak can be a rewarding experience.

Money guide

During your apprenticeship, you can expect your salary to start from between £12,000 and £15,000 per year.

Salaries for qualified gas service technicians range from £25,000 up to £30,000.

Those who become self-employed and manage their own company and employees can achieve in excess of £40,000.

It is also possible to increase your earnings through overtime and shift work.

Related opportunities

- Gas Network Engineer p214
- Heating and Ventilation Engineer p90
- Plumber p100

Further information

Energy & Utility Skills
www.euskills.co.uk

Gas Safe Register
www.gassaferegister.co.uk

GLAZIER

Qualifications and courses

GCSEs/National 5s (A*–C/A–C) or relevant vocational qualifications can improve your chances of getting work in the industry. Maths, English and technology-based subjects are useful for the areas of the job that involve measurements and calculations and for theoretical training.

You can train and gain vocational qualifications while you work by completing an apprenticeship. You will be taught practical skills by an experienced professional and may spend time off-site at a college or training centre. Apprenticeships in the Glass Industry are available at both Intermediate and Advanced Levels and last for 2 to 3 years. You are likely to work towards NVQs in glass-related subjects. These include Glazing Installation and Maintenance, Automotive Glazing, and Fenestration Installation and Surveying at both Levels 2 and 3. You will have to complete an aptitude test and have a selection interview prior to acceptance onto an apprenticeship.

Glass Training Limited (GTL) also provides flexible learning schemes that offer candidates in full-time employment the opportunity to gain an NVQ/SVQ through a distance learning programme.

To work as a glazier you need to have a Construction Skills Certification Scheme (CSCS) card or be registered with an affiliated scheme. This scheme requires an NVQ Level 2 and the completion of a health and safety test.

What the work involves

Glaziers use specialist cutting and fixing tools to cut glass to the correct size and fit it into place.

You might fit glass into houses, shop fronts, office blocks or roofs.

You might be working on new buildings or replacing existing or broken glass.

You will use your knowledge to choose a suitable type of glass for each job.

Type of person suited to this work

You should be able to follow technical drawings accurately and have a good eye for detail when measuring the materials for a job.

As you will be using different hand tools a practical ability will be necessary. You will also need to be physically fit so that you can carry glass and be comfortable working at heights (sometimes extreme heights).

You may work alone for some jobs, such as in people's homes, but you must also be able to work and communicate with other glaziers, especially when working on large jobs with big, heavy panes of glass.

Working conditions

You will work indoors and outdoors in many different locations. A driving licence may be useful.

You will need to work safely and be aware of your own, the public's and your colleagues' safety when carrying, cutting and fixing glass.

You may work normal working hours during the week, but you may also need to work at weekends and during evenings, possibly offering emergency cover for households and businesses when replacing broken glass.

Future prospects

Work is available with glazing and construction companies throughout the UK and the demand for trained glaziers is high.

The range of jobs in glazing work is also increasing to include specialist areas, for example automotive glass repair and replacement.

After gaining sufficient experience, you may progress to technical or supervisory levels, or you could decide to start your own glazing business. The majority of glaziers are self-employed.

Advantages/disadvantages

Working at extreme heights may be demanding for some.

You will get to work in a variety of locations on a wide range of projects.

Cutting tools and glass can be dangerous, so you will have to be aware of health and safety regulations.

You could be called out at all hours for emergency jobs but the rates of pay for this type of work will be higher.

Money guide

Newly qualified glaziers earn between £13,000 and £17,000.

Well qualified glaziers with a few years' experience can earn up to £20,000.

Those who are highly skilled, with experience and extra responsibilities such as emergency call-outs, might achieve anything from £23,000 to £35,000.

Shift allowances and the opportunity to work overtime can supplement your income.

Related opportunities

- Building Technician p66
- Ceiling Fixer p69
- Window Fitter p119

Further information

Glass and Glazing Federation
www.ggf.org.uk

Glass Qualifications Authority
www.gqaqualifications.com

Proskills UK
www.proskills.co.uk

HEATING AND VENTILATION ENGINEER

Qualifications and courses

To become a heating and ventilation engineer, you will need to work towards an NVQ Diploma in Heating and Ventilation (Level 2 or 3). Most entrants to the profession study for these qualifications during an apprenticeship or Skillseekers scheme. Apprenticeships in Heating and Ventilation are available at Intermediate and Advanced Level with 5 GCSEs/National 5s (A*–C/A–C) including Maths, English and a science subject required for entry. You will also need to pass a colour vision test and selection test.

Apprenticeships/Skillseekers involve being trained by and working alongside a professional engineer whilst also attending college on day or block release. You may therefore be required to secure employment prior to signing up. NVQs/SVQs cover industrial, commercial, ductwork installation, service and maintenance of components. It usually takes 2 to 4 years to become fully qualified.

Other options for training include a City & Guilds Certificate in Heating and Ventilation (Domestic Systems Installation) (6128) if you seek to become a domestic fitter and the Oil Firing Technical Association (OFTEC)'s training scheme for those who wish to work with oil-fired equipment.

It is also possible to achieve higher level qualifications including NVQ Level 4, Foundation or master's degree which can lead to professional membership of the Chartered Institution of Building Services Engineers (CIBSE).

What the work involves

Heating and ventilation engineers install equipment such as pipework and boilers for systems including central heating, hot and cold water services, and gas supplies in industrial and commercial buildings.

Your work will include cutting, bending and joining pipes that will need to withstand high pressures, so welding is an important part of the work.

When you have installed a system, you will test it to make sure that everything is working properly.

Type of person suited to this work

You must be a practical person so that you can use the equipment for the job. Understanding and following diagrams is an essential part of the work, so you need a logical, mechanically minded approach to your work. You will also need to be good at maths for making calculations.

It can be physically demanding work, as you will be bending, kneeling and working in tight spaces. You also need a head for heights and a safety-conscious attitude, because you will often be working from ladders and scaffolding.

Teamwork and communication skills are also important when you are installing large systems.

Working conditions

A lot of your time will be spent indoors, but you will also need a driving licence to travel between various construction sites, where you will need to wear safety protective clothing.

You may work a normal working week, but there may be times when you will work weekends and evenings to avoid disruption to clients or if you provide emergency cover. You may also be expected to work away from home.

Future prospects

There is currently a shortage of skilled heating and ventilation engineers with around 56,000 currently working in the UK.

Once you are qualified, work will be available with specialist heating and ventilation companies, or organisations such as the NHS or local authorities. With the government targeting greater energy efficiency, you may also opt to complete training that will allow you to install and maintain renewable energy technologies, eg solar powered heating systems. Some qualified fitters become self-employed, joining up with other engineers to offer sub-contracting services.

There are good prospects for advancement to supervisory roles and it is possible for you to become a heating and ventilation technician. If you take additional qualifications and higher education, progression to professional engineering level is also possible. There are also opportunities to work overseas.

Advantages/disadvantages

Working in cramped and awkward spaces can be uncomfortable.

Transforming a building from an empty shell into a warm, comfortable environment can be rewarding.

Career progression opportunities are excellent and there is demand across the country for work in this area.

Money guide

As an apprentice your starting salary could be between £10,500 and £15,000.

A newly qualified engineer could expect to earn up to £22,000.

With experience, you could achieve £23,000–£32,000.

Working overtime and receiving bonuses could increase your pay.

Related opportunities

- Gas Network Engineer p214
- Gas Service Technician p88
- Thermal Insulation Engineer p114

Further information

Building Engineering Services Association
www.thebesa.com

Building Engineering Services Training
www.best-ltd.co.uk

HIGHWAYS MAINTENANCE/ROAD WORKER

Qualifications and courses

There are no formal entry requirements for this work but GCSEs/National 5s in Maths, English and Design and Technology may be helpful. Personal skills and physical fitness are usually more important than qualifications. Employers may also want you to have some on-site experience, for example, as a construction labourer.

Your training will mainly be given on the job by experienced road workers. After you have secured employment, you may be able to study at a local college on day or block release to progress. You could work towards an NVQ Level 2 Certificate in Construction and Civil Engineering, an NVQ Level 2 Certificate/Diploma in Highways Maintenance, an NVQ Level 2 Diploma in Roadbuilding or a City & Guilds Level 2 Award in Winter Maintenance Operations. Your NVQ may cover areas such as excavation, re-surfacing, drainage, kerb laying and pavement construction.

Alternatively, you may opt to gain relevant skills prior to accepting full-time work by completing a City & Guilds (6217) Basic Construction Skills course or a BTEC Level 2 in Construction.

To become a fully qualified site operative, you need to register with the Street Works Qualifications Register (SWQR) by studying for either a City & Guilds Certificate in Streetworks Excavation and Reinstatement, an SQA national award in Excavation and Reinstatement or a Street Works Excavation and Reinstatement qualification awarded by CABWI.

If working with plant machinery, you will need to be 18 or over. A driving licence will also be required and an LGV licence may be needed for some jobs.

What the work involves

Road workers' tasks include building new roads, re-routing or widening existing roads, and repairing potholes and cracks in roads.

You will also have other duties such as putting up warning signs and barriers, controlling the movement of traffic near the work site, laying kerbstones and pavements, and gritting roads in the winter.

You will work with numerous building materials including concrete, tarmac and paving slabs. You will use a range of tools and equipment in your work, including specialised, heavy machinery such as diggers and rollers.

Type of person suited to this work

You must have a good standard of fitness, as the work involves a lot of hard, physical work and requires you to lift and carry heavy materials.

Practical ability with tools such as picks and shovels is useful, as is experience of operating equipment such as cement mixers, diggers and rolling machines.

As much of your work will be undertaken as part of a team of road workers and supervisors, it is important that you can get along with colleagues at all levels.

Working conditions

You are likely to work a normal 37 hour working week, although you may also work weekends and evenings to avoid disrupting traffic.

You will need to be aware of the danger of traffic and mindful of health and safety for yourself and your colleagues. On-site, you will wear protective clothing such as a safety helmet, fluorescent jacket and boots.

Future prospects

Road workers may work for local authorities or, as work is increasingly contracted out, for specialist road-building or civil engineering companies.

Work is available across the UK. Some work is short term or seasonal. You could become self-employed and work on a contract basis.

As you develop and gain experience and qualifications, you may go on to lead a small team or become a supervisor.

Advantages/disadvantages

You will be helping to maintain and improve the safety of the roads in your local area which can be personally rewarding.

You will be carrying out physically demanding work outdoors during all weathers so you can expect to get hot in the summer and cold in the winter.

Money guide

Trainee road workers have a starting salary of £12,000–£15,000.

As you gain experience, you could earn between £17,000 and £20,000.

Road workers with additional responsibilities, such as supervisory duties, can achieve a salary of £24,000.

Those who operate plant machinery may receive additional payments and you can increase your earnings with overtime and shift work.

Related opportunities

- Bricklayer p62
- Concreter p73
- Construction Operative p74

Further information

Construction Industry Training Board (CITB)
www.citb.co.uk

Street Works Qualification Register
www.swqr.org.uk

HOUSING OFFICER

Qualifications and courses

It is possible to enter at an administrative level with GCSEs/National 5s (A*–C/A–C) and work your way up to housing officer. Personal qualities and pre-entry experience in housing or customer service is highly valued and, at times, more sought after by employers than qualifications.

Larger housing associations are, however, more likely to recruit graduates, therefore you may choose to study a degree or postgraduate qualification in a relevant subject such as housing, social policy, town planning or urban studies. You will need 2 or 3 A levels/H grades to be accepted. Those with an unrelated degree can complete the Chartered Institute of Housing (CIH) Level 4 Certificate in Access to Housing before progressing to the postgraduate diploma or master's degree in housing.

Housing officers whose degrees do not include a work placement will be expected to gain industry experience before they become a member of the CIH. Voluntary work in local authority housing departments, experience in a customer service role or as a member of a tenants' committee could all be useful when seeking employment.

The CIH also offers courses which can be studied part time and through distance learning; these include the Certificate in Housing Practice (Levels 2–4).

What the work involves

You will manage and maintain rented housing, usually for a housing association or local authority. Tasks include assessing housing needs in an area and making policies to provide for them, allocating housing to applicants and planning property maintenance and repair.

You will also need to set rent rates, deal with tenants who are behind with their payments, resolve neighbourhood disputes and answer tenants' enquiries.

You will find yourself working with a variety of different people, ranging from vulnerable members of the community to those in challenging economic situations.

Type of person suited to this work

As most of your work will involve talking and listening to people, you will need excellent communication and negotiation skills. You should have an interest in working with diverse social groups and be sensitive to the needs of tenants and colleagues.

Maths and numeracy skills are useful for dealing with rental payments, maintenance and repair costs, and budgets.

It is important to keep up with developments in a range of housing and tenant welfare issues, be flexible and have the ability to solve problems as and when they arise. You will also need to be capable of working both independently and as part of a team.

Working conditions

Many housing officers are based in an office but regularly travel to make property inspections, visit tenants or attend meetings. As some of your work will involve travelling, a driving licence and your own vehicle is often required. Although you will normally work standard office hours, you might have to do some weekend work or unsocial hours.

You should be prepared to deal with rude and aggressive tenants.

Future prospects

Social housing is currently a growth area, with organisations taking on a number of new trainees as well as experienced staff.

Most housing officers work for local authorities and housing associations but you may also work for voluntary organisations, property companies, private landlords and housing trusts. You can work in various other sectors such as finance, IT, PR or law and with different groups of people, eg the homeless or elderly, students or people with disabilities.

With experience, you may specialise in one area, for example, homelessness assessment, special needs housing, urban renewal or tenant support. Alternatively, you may become a team leader or housing manager. Housing managers are particularly in demand in London and the south-east of England.

Housing associations have a strong tradition of developing the talent of their staff so there are great opportunities for progression.

Advantages/disadvantages

You will be responsible for resolving complicated issues, such as misuse of property, and disputes between residents.

Helping people find a home can be personally rewarding.

Money guide

Salaries for those in housing assistant/customer service positions are between £15,000 and £21,000.

Housing officers usually have a starting salary of £21,000 to £29,000.

Those who become housing managers can expect to earn £30,000 to £43,000.

At senior manager level, you can achieve earnings in excess of £50,000.

Related opportunities

- Residential Support Worker p572
- Social Worker p573
- Welfare Benefits Adviser/Welfare Rights Caseworker p578

Further information

Chartered Institute of Housing
www.cih.org

Scottish Federation of Housing Associations
www.sfha.co.uk

LAMINATOR

Qualifications and courses

No formal qualifications are normally required, however some GCSEs/National 5s in subjects such as Maths or design might be useful as you must have an understanding of design technology and calculations. Other relevant qualifications include a BTEC Diploma Level 2 in either Manufacturing and Product Design, Engineering or Construction and the Built Environment.

Some employers will take on school-leavers as technician apprentices. Apprenticeships require 4 GCSE/National 5s (A*–C/A–C) including Maths, a science or technology. A GCSE/National 5 in Manufacturing or Engineering may also be appropriate for this entry route. Apprentices are usually aged between 16 and 24.

As an apprentice, on-the-job training is provided by experienced professionals. You will also undertake further training at college through courses that focus on the safety requirements of your job, for example First Aid and health and safety. You can train for an NVQ Level 2 in Polymer Processing Operations or Performing Engineering Operations, an NVQ Level 3 in Polymer Processing and Related Operations or BTEC Level 3 Certificates/Diplomas in Polymer Processing and Materials Technology. If the training does not include NVQ Level 3, a workplace assessment will be carried out to check competence at this level.

Companies also tend to use a series of short course programmes with a specialist training provider to gradually build up the skills and knowledge required of a laminator.

Once technician status has been achieved it is possible to combine studying with further experience to gain an HND in Manufacturing Engineering (Metallurgy and Materials), Polymer Science or Polymer Technology.

With 4 years' experience, relevant NVQs/SVQs or a BTEC certificate/diploma, you could apply for membership of the Institute of Materials, Minerals and Mining.

What the work involves

Laminators work with polymer composite materials to make a variety of products such as hockey sticks, snowboards, canoes, car bodies, yachts and aircraft cabin interiors.

You will follow a brief for the design of a product, taking into consideration any requirements regarding strength, colour and finish. You will then choose the appropriate material to be pressed, sprayed or poured into a mould, prior to it being shaped into the final product.

You will work with traditional materials such as wood laminates, fibre glass and resin, and new products such as Kevlar.

Type of person suited to this work

You should have a keen interest in design and technology, engineering and materials science.

You should like practical work and have practical skills to handle tools and use specialist machinery. You need to be reasonably fit and have good vision for monitoring quality and noticing detail.

You should have initiative, follow a brief and work to a deadline. You should also be interested in, and keep up to date with, technological advancements in laminate materials. You should like to work in a team.

Working conditions

Your working hours will depend heavily on the project you are working on. Typically they can range from 37 to 40 hours but will vary according to the rate of your work and deadlines.

You will usually work in an environmentally controlled building. This means that the temperature is controlled and maintained to help resin harden quickly. Air is changed frequently to remove dust and the strong smell of resin.

You will be required to wear full protective clothing.

Future prospects

You may be employed by an engineering consultancy that undertakes installation projects for companies.

With experience and training there are opportunities to be promoted to roles such as technician and senior technician, or to move into design, research or development work for specialist composite laminate manufacturers.

Advantages/disadvantages

You may have the opportunity to work on products that are on the cutting edge of design such as speedboats, Formula 1 racing cars and craft for the military.

Your working environment will frequently be dusty and involve the use of strong industrial chemicals which may be hazardous if handled incorrectly.

Money guide

A salary for an apprentice laminator starts at around £10,000 per year.

With further experience and qualifications this may increase to £25,000 per year.

A senior laminator can earn up to £30,000 per year.

Related opportunities

- Carpenter/Joiner p67
- Marine Craftsperson p218
- Polymer Technologist p225

Further information

British Plastics Federation
www.bpf.co.uk

Institute of Materials, Minerals and Mining
www.iom3.org

LAND/GEOMATIC SURVEYOR

Qualifications and courses

Most entrants have completed a Royal Institution of Chartered Surveyors (RICS) accredited degree in subjects like surveying and mapping science, geomatics or geographic information systems as well as a period of supervised instruction. If you wish to specialise in a particular area, such as hydroinformatics or environmental management, or if you are a graduate with a non-accredited degree, a postgraduate qualification may be required.

It may be possible to enter the industry at a lower level, for example, as a digital mapping assistant or as a computer-aided design (CAD) technician, with an HND or Foundation degree in a related area such as applied science, civil engineering or land/estate surveying.

Alternatively, apprenticeships for school or college leavers in land/geomatics surveying are also available. You will begin as an assistant surveyor and progress through a combination of training on the job and studying for an NVQ. GCSEs/National 5s (A*–C/A–C) in English, Maths and IT are usually required.

Once qualified, many surveyors work towards achieving chartered status and undertake further courses and assessment through bodies such as the Chartered Institution of Civil Engineering Surveyors (ICES) and the Royal Institution of Chartered Surveyors (RICS). This usually takes between 4 and 5 years. Regardless of your position, it is advisable to become a student member of RICS or ICES in order to keep up to date with developments in the industry and to support you in your continuing professional development.

What the work involves

Land/geomatic surveyors collect and analyse information to map the land and/or sea, which is then used when planning construction and civil engineering projects.

You will use satellite images, GPS, digital mapping and other equipment to produce surveys that record features such as contours, materials below the Earth's surface and man-made objects.

You will use technical software such as computer-aided design (CAD) to record and present the data you have gathered. You will also have to interpret data from maps and plans and explain it to clients.

Type of person suited to this work

You will be working with clients and other professionals on a daily basis, so excellent verbal and written communication skills will be needed to present and explain complex information.

As much of the work involves using technical equipment and producing maps, plans and reports using specialist computer software, you will need to have very strong analytical and IT skills with specific knowledge of geographical information systems (GIS) and AutoCAD.

Working conditions

Working hours are usually 9am to 5pm, but you may need to work unsocial hours to ensure projects are finished on time. Weekend or shift work may also be needed for certain projects.

As you will often work away from home, you will be paid more for overseas work and most contracts are on a short-term basis, although multinational companies offer good long-term opportunities.

Self-employment is an option, but finding work is not always easy so most surveyors choose to work in salaried employment.

Future prospects

As a result of the changing nature of mapping and spatial data management, there continues to be a current shortage of land/geomatic surveyors.

Most graduates start as a junior surveyor, from which there is a natural progression to surveyor and then on to a team management position. You could undertake further study and gain a qualification as a chartered surveyor as this can enhance opportunities for progression and improve pay. Ease of progress will depend on professional qualifications and the size of your employing organisation. Geographic mobility can also be helpful to career development.

Alternatively, you may decide to specialise in different areas such as offshore engineering and exploration or cartography and it is also possible to move between the public and private sectors.

Advantages/disadvantages

You will have the opportunity to travel throughout the UK and overseas.

You could be playing a key role in land and environmental development.

A considerable amount of time is spent outdoors so be prepared to get cold, wet and muddy.

Money guide

For newly qualified land surveyors, salaries may be between £20,000 and £25,000.

With chartered status, your salary could be between £25,000 and £45,000.

At a senior level, either as a manager or a partner, salaries can reach £70,000.

Related opportunities

- Planning and Development Surveyor p98
- Rural Property/Practice Surveyor p105
- Town Planner/Planning Technician p115

Further information

Chartered Institution of Civil Engineering Surveyors
www.cices.org

Chartered Institution of Water and Environmental Management
www.ciwem.org

MASTIC ASPHALTER

Qualifications and courses

To train in this field, it is useful to have some GCSEs/National 5s (A*–E/A–E) in English, Maths, Design and Technology. Alternatively, vocational qualifications such as the BTEC Level 1 or 2 Certificate/Award/Diploma in Construction, the Foundation, Intermediate and Advanced Levels in Construction Awards and the Scottish Progression Award/Skills for Work Award in Building Crafts may prove useful for introducing you to the basics of the industry.

Most entrants into the field complete an apprenticeship programme in Mastic Asphalting accredited by the Construction Industry Training Board (CITB) or organised through the bConstructive apprenticeship scheme. These usually take 2 to 4 years to complete and apprentices typically study an NVQ Diploma Level 2 or 3 in Mastic Asphalting (Construction). You may be required to complete an aptitude test prior to your acceptance. Training typically involves a combination of block or day-release training at an approved college or training centre, alongside on-the-job training from an experienced professional.

Additionally, if you decide to specialise in roofing, it would be useful to undergo examinations offered by the Institute of Roofing.

Mastic asphalters employed on construction sites require a Construction Skills Certification Scheme (CSCS) card. This demonstrates that the holder has health and safety training, as well as aiming for competence in a particular occupation. You will need to have or be working towards an NVQ or equivalent in order to be granted a CSCS card.

What the work involves

You will work with material called mastic asphalt, a mixture of limestone and bitumen which turns to liquid when heated. You will inspect a site, clean it, lay out membranes and guides and then spread hot liquid asphalt onto the area. It will cool into a protective waterproof surface.

You will work on surfaces such as dams, landfills, riverbank protection, car parks, bus stations, pathways and the roofs of buildings.

You will use various specialised tools such as boilers, mixers and cylinders in order to prepare surfaces and apply the asphalt.

Type of person suited to this work

You need to have good practical skills to be able to spread and form the mastic asphalt. Maths skills will be useful too, for calculating quantities of materials.

It is important to be able to understand plans, follow instructions and work well in a team.

As it is an active job you must be physically fit, and you must be happy climbing and working at heights. Agility is essential and you should be able to work quickly but accurately.

Working conditions

You will mainly work outdoors, although some of the work may be under cover. You will travel regularly between sites. You will need to wear protective gear such as a safety helmet, gloves and boots.

If you suffer from claustrophobia, vertigo or breathing problems, this work might be difficult for you.

You are likely to work a normal working week, although you might need to work evenings and weekends as well.

Future prospects

Most opportunities are with specialist mastic asphalt contractors. Self-employment is also common if you are skilled.

You can work your way up to become a supervisor, manager or trainer in large companies. Alternatively, you could set up your own contracting business.

You may need to move between employers for promotion.

Advantages/disadvantages

Working at heights on roofs, or in cramped conditions when working in tanks or underground spaces, can be demanding for some people. There is the possibility of fumes and accidental burns in this line of work.

You will develop a range of skills and work on a variety of surfaces.

Money guide

The average wage for a trainee starting in this line of work is £10,000 per year.

Once qualified, your wage may rise to around £16,000 a year.

With experience, your salary could reach £31,000.

Overtime is often available, and on some projects there are bonuses based on outputs, which can lead to higher earnings. Travelling expenses will be reimbursed.

Related opportunities

- Floor Layer/Finisher p86
- Roofer p104
- Thatcher p113

Further information

Construction Industry Training Board (CITB)
www.citb.co.uk

Mastic Asphalt Council
www.masticasphaltcouncil.co.uk

NAVAL ARCHITECT

Qualifications and courses

In order to become a naval architect, you will need to gain a degree in a relevant subject such as naval architecture, ship science or ocean, offshore or marine engineering, ideally one accredited by the Royal Institution of Naval Architects (RINA). Newcastle University, University of Southampton, University of Strathclyde and University College London are the main institutions offering a degree specific to naval architecture, which may increase your chances. Typical entry requirements for a degree course include 2 A levels/3 H grades, including Physics and Maths, and 5 GCSEs/National 5s (A*–C/A–C). A postgraduate qualification may also be useful, particularly when later seeking chartered status.

If you have work-based qualifications, eg a BTEC, HND or HNC from time as a technician, you can transfer to an engineering degree. Alternatively, you may be able to join a marine engineering apprenticeship after school through the Royal Navy or local ship builders.

As a graduate, you will carry out a RINA-accredited training scheme within the workplace where you will be trained by experienced professionals in areas including design, engineering practice and management services. Alternatively, the Ministry of Defence offers a Defence Engineering and Science Group Graduate Scheme, although it is competitive.

With 2 years' work experience and the relevant qualifications, full membership of RINA and registration as a chartered (CEng) or incorporated (IEng) engineer are possible.

What the work involves

As a naval architect you will be responsible for the design, construction and repair of marine vessels and offshore structures, including merchant ships, submarines and offshore drilling platforms. You will have to coordinate a team of engineers working on a project.

You will ensure that the structure you are working on is safe and seaworthy, within budget and to the designated specifications.

Your work will depend on the specialism you choose, but you could prepare architectural designs, work with computer or 3D models, source materials or evaluate the safety of the design.

Type of person suited to this work

As you will be working with others and as part of a team you will need to have good written and verbal communication skills.

You will be coordinating various aspects of a project such as budget, location and facilities, so you must be organised and efficient in your work. You must also be able to lead a team and work to a deadline.

Strong IT and numeracy skills and a keen eye for detail are also necessary.

Working conditions

You will work average office hours, 5 days a week. However you might have to work extra hours to meet deadlines.

You may be office based while working on design work, or visiting construction sites, docks and shipyards within the UK or overseas. Your surroundings may be noisy and dirty. If you are working onboard a craft you may encounter fumes, heat and noise and you will have to work in all weather conditions. You may have to wear protective clothing.

Future prospects

As a naval architect you can become self-employed, work for a company or as a design consultant. Given the small size of shipyards in the UK, there are limited openings for naval architects to work on the construction of new ships but you could find work in the design and production of small crafts and yachts or in maintenance and repair.

You can move up from technical roles to general management and on to senior roles. With chartered status, you can specialise in particular areas such as design, research or consultancy. Alternatively, you could work as a ship surveyor, assessing the safety of ship and marine structures. You may even opt to instruct at universities.

Organisations such as RINA provide continuing professional development (CPD) courses which cover areas such as new technologies, management systems and communication.

Advantages/disadvantages

There are lots of opportunities to work abroad for a ship surveying company, or you may work on a large scale project abroad.

Competition for jobs as a naval architect is high.

Some aspects of the work may involve working in difficult and physically demanding conditions.

Money guide

Your starting salary as a graduate can range from £22,000 to £28,000 per year.

With experience this can increase to £35,000–£55,000.

You could earn in excess of £65,000 if you are highly experienced and working for a large organisation.

Your income will vary when undertaking freelance or contract work.

Related opportunities

- Aerospace Engineer p200
- Marine Engineer p219
- Merchant Navy Engineering Officer p599

Further information

Defence Engineering and Science Group
www.gov.uk/defence-engineering-and-science-group

Royal Institution of Naval Architects
www.rina.org.uk

WISE
www.wisecampaign.org.uk

Qualifications and courses

It is useful to have some GCSEs/National 5s (A*–E/A–E) in subjects such as Maths, Design and Technology and English. Numeracy skills are particularly important as calculating area and quantities will be a large part of your job.

Vocational qualifications, such as the City & Guilds Level 1 Certificate/Award in Basic Construction Skills may also offer you opportunities to grasp the basic skills required by the industry. Working as a decorator's labourer may also allow you to do this.

A common route of entry is a construction apprenticeship which leads to an NVQ/SVQ Level 3. As an apprentice, most of your training is carried out on the job whilst taking day or block-release at college in order to obtain qualifications such as an NVQ/SVQ Diploma in Decorative Finishing – Painting and Decorating (Construction) (Level 2 and 3) and CITB Diplomas in Decorative Finishing and Industrial Painting Occupations (Construction) (Level 2 and 3). You could also apply for a Construction Building apprenticeship through the bConstructive apprenticeship scheme.

Those interested in heritage work can also train in graining, marbling and gilding, by completing the NVQ Level 3 in Heritage Skills (Construction).

A Construction Skills Certification Scheme (CSCS) card is mandatory in order to work on-site. You will need to have a relevant NVQ qualification and pass a health and safety test. A trainee card is available for those working towards a qualification.

A driving licence is also necessary in order to transport materials and equipment.

What the work involves

Painters and decorators improve the interior and exterior of people's homes and other buildings. On occasion, they may also be required to paint larger structures such as bridges.

Your work will include preparing surfaces by making sure they are clean and smooth, applying primers, undercoats and topcoats of paint and putting up wall coverings such as wallpaper.

You will use a range of tools including brushes, rollers and spraying equipment.

Type of person suited to this work

You need to be good with your hands, and particularly skilful when using fine decoration techniques. You will also need an eye for colour and design and an interest in décor.

You need to be friendly, personable and able to work well in a team. You will need to be fit and active as you will have to climb ladders and carry tools. You should not mind working at heights.

You must be able to measure accurately so that you can work out how much paint and other material you will need.

Working conditions

Most of the work is indoors, but some is outdoors. You will regularly work on ladders or on scaffolding. You might have to wear a mask to prevent you from breathing in paint fumes.

You are likely to work a normal working week, although weekend work and overtime is common. You may need a driving licence.

Future prospects

The building and construction industry is the largest employer in the UK and whilst there may be a shortage of skilled painters and decorators, the demand for people in this profession largely depends on the state of the economy.

You can work for painting and decorating companies or building contractors, local authorities or the NHS. Painting and decorating companies may offer a range of work or may specialise in work such as domestic, commercial, new build or industrial.

After gaining experience, it is possible to progress to a supervisory role or transfer into related areas such as estimating or contract management, particularly in the larger organisations. With further training, you may opt to specialise in restoration or even instruct on a college course as a lecturer or craft teacher.

A popular option is to become self-employed and work on a sub-contract basis. Alternatively, you could take your skills abroad.

Advantages/disadvantages

Working at extreme heights may be difficult for some people.

It can be rewarding to see the improved look of a newly painted building or structure and you have the opportunity to be creative.

Money guide

New entrants/trainees can expect to earn between £14,500 and £17,000 per year.

NVQ Level 2 or 3 qualified painters and decorators can earn between £17,500 and £23,000.

Decorators with specialist skills and supervisory duties can earn £23,000 or more.

Overtime is often available, and on some projects there are bonuses based on outputs. Those who are self-employed set their own rates of pay.

Related opportunities

- Construction Operative p74
- Plasterer p99
- Wall/Floor Tiler p116

Further information

Painting & Decorating Association
www.paintingdecoratingassociation.co.uk

PLANNING AND DEVELOPMENT SURVEYOR

Qualifications and courses

In order to enter this profession, you will need a Royal Institution of Chartered Surveyors (RICS) accredited degree in a relevant subject such as surveying, estate management, economics or land and property development. Entry requirements for most degree courses are a minimum of 3 A levels/H grades and 5 GSCEs/National 5s (A*–C/A–C), or the relevant BTEC/SQA National Awards (or equivalent).

For graduates without an accredited degree or with a non-property related degree, a postgraduate conversion qualification approved by RICS is essential. Some large surveying firms may support you in your conversion training through a distance learning graduate traineeship or alternatively, you may complete this full time prior to employment.

Those with a relevant HND/HNC or NVQ/SVQ, plus significant work experience, may be able to enter the field as a surveying technician. With further training, you could qualify as a planning and development surveyor.

Once employed you will continue to update your skills by working towards chartered status. In order to do so, you will be required to complete the Assessment of Professional Competence with the RICS or register with the Chartered Institute of Building's (CIOB) Faculty of Architecture and Surveying. Subject to a minimum of 2 years' experience and your performance in an interview, you will gain chartered status.

What the work involves

Planning and development surveyors develop and manage new building or refurbishment projects. You will create proposals and oversee projects from conception through to completion.

You will be responsible for recruiting team members for each project, as well as liaising with external industry professionals throughout.

You will also give valuations on properties and developments, advise clients on financing options for their building plans, and prepare their applications for planning permission.

Type of person suited to this work

As you will be managing team members, briefing other professionals and dealing with clients, well-developed communication and negotiation skills are required.

Good numeracy skills, coupled with scientific aptitude, are essential to successfully write proposals and manage financial details within a project. An understanding of legal matters within the building and construction industries is helpful, as is an interest in architecture, history or preserving the natural landscape.

Working conditions

You may have to work longer than the standard 35 hour week, but weekend and shift work is unusual.

Work exists in a variety of areas including local authorities, construction firms, property developers and building conservation.

Although there is some day to day travelling involved, overnight stays are uncommon.

Most jobs are found in cities where there is a high level of commercial activity. You could work for public sector or private companies, which range in size from very small practices up to large multinational firms. Work in the public sector is becoming increasingly flexible, with part-time work and career breaks available.

Future prospects

As a graduate trainee you can progress to surveyor, to senior surveyor, and up to associate or partner with several years' experience. If you progress to become an equity partner you will earn a high salary and also get a cut of the company's profits.

If you work in the public sector, you could enhance your career prospects with a Royal Town Planning Institute (RTPI) qualification, or develop a more specialised career in one area of surveying. Specialist knowledge in regeneration, conservation or land management is particularly useful in a society where sustainable development is growing in importance.

You may also consider transferring to other areas of surveying, eg waste management, arts and antiques or telecommunications. You could even take your skills abroad, eg to assist disaster-relief projects.

Advantages/disadvantages

Work is varied and you have the opportunity to travel within the UK and overseas.

Although you might need to work extra hours, weekend work is rare.

You will have a lot of responsibility which can be stressful at times.

Money guide

New graduates will earn £20,000–£24,000.

Experienced chartered surveyors can achieve a salary of £25,000–£42,000.

Those in senior positions can earn in excess of £50,000.

Related opportunities

- Land/Geomatic Surveyor p94
- Rural Property/Practice Surveyor p105
- Town Planner/Planning Technician p115

Further information

Chartered Institute of Building
www.ciob.org.uk

Chartered Institution of Civil Engineering Surveyors
www.cices.org

Royal Institution of Chartered Surveyors
www.rics.org

PLASTERER

Qualifications and courses

A common route of entry into the plastering industry is to serve an apprenticeship. In order to be eligible for the Construction Apprenticeship Scheme (CAS) you will need some GCSEs/National 5s in English, Maths, and Design and Technology and an employer to sponsor your training.

Apprenticeship schemes are available at both Intermediate and Advanced Levels and offer a structured training programme leading to an NVQ/SVQ Level 3. Trainees will follow routes in solid plastering, fibrous plastering or dry lining. Programmes are validated by the Construction Industry Training Board (CITB) and last 2–4 years in England and Wales, and 4 years in Scotland. Most training is done on the job whilst attending college to obtain qualifications such as NVQs/SVQs in Plastering (Levels 1–3) or the City & Guilds Certificate in Basic Construction Skills – Plastering (6217-04). Further options available through City & Guilds include the Foundation/Intermediate Construction Awards. If you wish to specialise in the repair and conservation of historic buildings, you could also take an NVQ Level 3 in Heritage Skills (Construction).

Construction Skills Certification Scheme (CSCS) cards are required by plasterers employed on construction sites as proof of your competency on-site. You will need to have gained or be working towards a formal qualification, eg an NVQ, in order to qualify for one of these.

What the work involves

There are three types of plastering that you could do: solid, fibrous or dry lining. Solid plastering involves the application of plaster or cement to internal and external walls, ceilings and floors.

Fibrous plastering involves making ornamental plaster work, such as the kind you see on decorative ceilings.

Dry lining involves the use of plasterboard to construct walls or partitions and then skimming over the joins with plaster making them ready for decoration.

Type of person suited to this work

To be able to use your tools skilfully, you need to be good with your hands. An ability to use basic maths for calculating the amounts of materials you will need for a job is also helpful.

You will need to be able to work in a team with other plasterers, and with those in other construction trades.

You should be physically fit, as the work is very active. It can also be dusty when working with the plaster powder; this may be difficult if you suffer from certain allergies. You will be climbing ladders and possibly scaffolding, so you must be fine with heights.

Working conditions

Solid/dry lining

Most of the work for solid plasterers and those doing dry lining work is indoors, although you might have to work outdoors if working on exteriors. You will work from ladders and scaffolding.

Fibrous

Most fibrous plasterers work in workshops, although you may also install your work on-site.

All plastering requires an understanding and appreciation of health and safety regulations, which includes wearing protective gear. You may work a normal working week, although you might need to start early or finish late, and weekend work may also be available.

Future prospects

The building industry is cyclical therefore during a recession, there may be less of a demand for plasterers. Shortages of qualified plasterers do exist however, particularly in the domestic market and as a fibrous plasterer.

Besides being employed by specialist plastering firms and building contractors, you can also work in the cultural heritage or public sectors, conserving and restoring historic buildings. Due to its rapid expansion, many plasterers are also moving into the related area of dry lining. Opportunities to diversify and move into tiling, estimating or site management are also possible.

After you have gained sufficient experience, you could progress to technical, supervisory or managerial roles or alternatively, you may opt to become self-employed. You may even be able to seek contract work overseas.

Advantages/disadvantages

Working at heights may be difficult for some people.

You will be able to work in a variety of locations and those in fibrous plaster work have opportunities to be creative.

Money guide

As a trainee you could earn around £14,000–£17,000.

Once qualified, salaries can rise to £17,500–£25,000. High earning plasterers could earn upwards of £35,000.

Overtime, shift allowances and performance-based bonuses can increase earnings. Self-employed plasterers negotiate their own rates.

Related opportunities

- Building Technician p66
- Mastic Asphalter p95
- Wall/Floor Tiler p116

Further information

Construction Industry Training Board (CITB)
www.citb.co.uk

Finishes & Interiors Sector
www.thefis.org

Scottish Building Apprenticeship and Training Council
www.sbatc.co.uk

PLUMBER

Qualifications and courses

To grasp some of the basic practical skills, you might first complete a course relevant to the industry such as the City & Guilds Level 1 Certificate in Introduction to Plumbing Skills (2000-14), the City & Guilds Level 2 Diploma in Access to Building Services Engineering (2000-02) or the City and Guilds Diploma Level 2 in Plumbing Studies (6035-02). These courses could be used as the first step towards a higher level qualification or as support when seeking employment.

A very common route of entry into plumbing is through an apprenticeship, lasting 2 to 3 years. This would involve a combination of learning on the job from experienced professionals whilst studying at a college for a qualification, eg an NVQ. In order to become a qualified plumber you will need to complete an industry-recognised qualification at Level 2 or 3, something you can do whilst taking part in an apprenticeship. Typical qualifications include City & Guilds NVQ Diploma in either Plumbing and Heating or Installing and Maintaining Domestic Heating Systems, the Excellence, Achievement & Learning Limited (EAL)'s Level 2 Diploma in Plumbing and Heating and Level 3 Diploma in Domestic Plumbing and Heating. Entrants for apprenticeships or training schemes need to pass a selection test and have their colour vision tested.

Once you have passed recognised qualifications and gained practical experience, it is possible to become a member of the Chartered Institute of Plumbing and Heating Engineering (CIPHE).

Gas Safe registration and possession of a Gas Safe ID card is a legal requirement for anyone installing or repairing gas fittings or appliances.

What the work involves

Plumbers install, maintain and repair plumbing, heating and water systems in various locations including people's homes and public buildings. You will also be responsible for routine check-ups on appliances such as boilers.

You will use a range of hand and power tools, such as wrenches, cutters and welding equipment.

When you have completed a job, you will need to test the system to make sure that everything is working properly.

Type of person suited to this work

Good practical skills are essential. You must be careful, accurate and follow instructions to ensure that systems work properly and safely. Analytical and problem-solving skills are also important.

You might be bending, kneeling and squeezing into tight spaces so it would help if you were physically fit. You need to be comfortable working at heights.

You need to be a team player but also willing to work alone. You should keep a good appearance and have excellent communication skills when dealing directly with customers.

Working conditions

You will work both indoors and outdoors, possibly within confined spaces and at heights. Travelling will be required for jobs so it would be useful to have a driving licence and your own vehicle.

You may work a normal working week but, if your organisation offers a 24/7 call-out service, you need to be available at all times of the day or night, any day of the week.

Future prospects

Work is available across the UK, though the job market is more competitive in London.

As a plumber, you can use your skills in a variety of areas, including heating and ventilation, refrigeration, air-conditioning, gas servicing, kitchen and bathroom fitting. With additional training, you could move into gas central heating installation and repair. You may also opt to install and maintain renewable energy technologies, solar water heating systems and ground source heat pumps given the increasing importance placed on sustainable systems.

You can progress to supervisory, training or managerial positions or move into estimating or contract management. Self-employment is also available, with lots of plumbers opting to set up their own businesses.

Advantages/disadvantages

You could be called out any time of day to deal with plumbing emergencies, which can be difficult for those with family commitments.

Being able to solve a difficult problem and make a customer happy can be very rewarding.

Money guide

Trainee plumbers typically start on £10,000 per year.

Newly qualified plumbers' earnings increase to £18,000–£22,000.

Experienced plumbers can expect £22,000–£35,000.

Earnings for self-employed plumbers can be much higher as they negotiate their own rates of pay.

Overtime is often available and those who attend emergency call-outs can receive higher pay for working unsociable hours.

Related opportunities

- Gas Network Engineer p214
- Heating and Ventilation Engineer p90
- Refrigeration and Air Conditioning Engineer/Technician p103

Further information

Chartered Institute of Plumbing and Heating Engineering
www.ciphe.org.uk

SummitSkills
www.summitskills.org.uk

PROPERTY VALUER

Qualifications and courses

Although entry requirements vary depending on employer, in order to become a property valuer you would normally hold a degree or professional qualification accredited by the Royal Institution of Chartered Surveyors (RICS) in a relevant subject such as residential surveying and valuation, building surveying, law or real estate management.

If you hold an HND or HNC you could enter the profession as a surveying technician and after further training and experience, you could progress from associate level to chartered status.

Once employed within the industry, you should work towards gaining chartered membership of a professional body such as the RICS or the Institute of Revenues Rating and Valuation (IRRV). Graduates of an RICS-accredited degree are required to complete the Assessment of Professional Competence (APC) in order to do so. Subject to 2 years' postgraduate work experience and your performance in an interview with a panel of assessors, you can gain chartered status.

Those who have not studied a degree in a relevant subject can take an RICS-accredited postgraduate degree or diploma course in an auctioneering/valuation subject. You may have to combine these courses with work experience and further professional qualifications.

It is important that you update your skills throughout your career. The IRRV offers qualifications and training that cover the valuation, legal and taxation aspects of your job, ensuring continuing professional development.

Given the nature of your work, it is likely that you will require a driving licence.

What the work involves

As a property valuer you will assess the value of property (buildings, land or personal items) for a client and advise them on how the property may be sold, loaned, taxed, acquired by a company or made part of a compensation claim. Local authorities also use these valuations to help set council tax and rating levels.

You will assess new commercial and industrial property and reassess existing property that has been altered.

You will provide reports on your valuations which may be important if property becomes part of legal negotiations or insurance claims. You may have to run live auctions where you will sell items that you have valued or you may pass them to a specialist.

Type of person suited to this work

You should have a keen interest in property valuation, law and taxation. You must have strong numerical skills to make accurate calculations, such as working out taxes or analysing accounts. As you may be hired by a company on a freelance basis, you will also need to be organised and able to use your initiative.

You need to have excellent written and verbal communication skills in order to communicate with clients, employers and government bodies.

Working conditions

You will work about 35–40 hours per week, Monday to Friday. You may have to work weekends depending on the project or your employer.

You will mainly be office based but will frequently have to visit and inspect properties or meet clients. As you might need to travel locally, a driving licence is recommended.

Future prospects

There are many opportunities in the UK. You could work in an estate agency valuing property that is being sold, rented or mortgaged. You may find work in the Valuation Office Agency assessing property for local authorities and government departments.

Valuers are also required by HM Revenue & Customs (HMRC) where you will value property and land that must be taxed when it is sold or bought.

Once you have gained sufficient experience, you could become a project manager, company partner or work as a freelance consultant.

Advantages/disadvantages

The job tends to be diverse and interesting as you will usually combine your role as a valuer with other areas such as estate management, surveying and even auctioning.

Property and land valuations may become part of compensation claims which involve a lengthy legal process.

Occasionally, property viewings and auctions will take place in the evenings and at weekends.

Money guide

Your starting salary may be £20,000–£26,000. With experience, earnings can increase to between £27,000 and £35,000.

A property valuer with chartered status can earn in excess of £40,000 a year.

Freelance property valuers negotiate their own wage.

Related opportunities

- Auction Property Consultant p61
- Insurance Risk Surveyor p32

Further information

Institute of Revenues Rating and Valuation
www.irrv.net

National Association of Valuers and Auctioneers
www.nava.org.uk

Royal Institution of Chartered Surveyors
www.rics.org

101

QUANTITY SURVEYOR

Qualifications and courses

This career requires a degree or professional qualification accredited by the Royal Institution of Chartered Surveyors (RICS). If, however, you hold a non-accredited degree, or you opt to study a subject other than quantity surveying, you will be required to complete a 1-year postgraduate conversion course that is recognised by the RICS. Other first degree subjects which may be relevant include geography, maths, urban and land studies, economics, construction, civil and structural engineering. Entry to a degree will require a minimum of 2 A levels/3 H Grades and 5 GCSEs/National 5s (A*–C/A–C).

An HND in a related subject is also valued by employers and may gain you employment as a surveying technician. You can then progress to quantity surveyor level by studying, either part time or via distance learning, for RICS-recognised qualifications.

Once you are in employment, you should work towards gaining membership of the RICS or the Chartered Institute of Building's (CIOB) Faculty for Architecture and Surveying in order to become a fully qualified chartered surveyor. To gain chartered status, you must complete a 2-year training programme called the Assessment of Professional Competence (APC). Subject to you having gained a RICS-accredited degree, 2 years' work experience and your performance in an interview with assessors, you will gain chartered status.

What the work involves

Quantity surveyors are responsible for calculating costs, issuing contracts, keeping projects to time and within budget, managing subcontractors and arranging payments for work.

You will need a good understanding of building regulations to ensure that projects meet the required standards of quality and safety.

You could work on a wide variety of projects from residential developments to hospitals or sports stadiums.

Type of person suited to this work

You must have a high level of numeracy as you will be responsible for all the financial details of projects. Good negotiation skills are also important, as you must agree contracts and prices with workers and contractors.

Excellent verbal and written communication skills are vital for leading and motivating the on-site team, liaising with clients and subcontractors, and producing accurate and detailed progress reports.

Finally, a good understanding of business and legal matters in relation to the building and construction industry is needed, since you will be responsible for ensuring that all projects meet current regulations and standards.

Working conditions

Working hours are slightly longer than average and will include early starts, late evenings and weekend work.

You will usually be office based, although it is not uncommon for the office to be in the form of a temporary hut on-site. Travel to client meetings and other projects is also expected.

Self-employment is possible, and many companies use freelance quantity surveyors on projects. There is also the opportunity to travel overseas.

Future prospects

Your opportunities are likely to lie within local authority or government departments, private practices, building contractors, property companies or commercial organisations both in the UK and abroad.

With experience, you can undertake a more comprehensive project management role and have the satisfaction of taking a job through from conception to completion. You may opt to specialise in certain areas such as value engineering, risk assessment, capital allowances or supply chain management or, alternatively, you could become self-employed.

There is usually a natural progression from quantity surveying to commercial management. Gaining chartered status will aid you in your bid for career progression.

Advantages/disadvantages

Working on numerous projects and with a range of people makes the job varied.

There are good opportunities for career progression and specialisation.

Hours are longer than average, with occasional weekend work.

Money guide

Starting salaries for quantity surveyors can range from £20,000 to £30,000, rising to £30,000–£45,000 a year with experience.

Senior surveyors can earn £45,000 to £65,000 or more and partners in private firms can expect considerably more.

With chartered status, extra responsibilities or further qualifications, your earnings can significantly increase.

Benefits include shift and site allowances, pension schemes, healthcare packages and a company car.

Related opportunities

- Civil/Construction Engineer/Civil Engineering Technician p71
- Insurance Risk Surveyor p32
- Town Planner/Planning Technician p115

Further information

Construction Industry Training Board (CITB)
www.citb.co.uk

Royal Institution of Chartered Surveyors
www.rics.org

Qualifications and courses

The most common form of entry into the refrigeration and air conditioning industry is by undertaking an apprenticeship. In order to be considered, you are likely to need 4 GCSEs/National 5s (A*–C/A–C) in English, Maths, Physics and Design and Technology.

Apprenticeships offer candidates the opportunity to gain the appropriate NVQs/SVQs required of a qualified refrigeration and air conditioning engineer/technician. As an apprentice, you will work towards either an NVQ in Servicing and Maintaining Refrigeration Systems (Level 2 and 3), an NVQ in Refrigeration/Air Conditioning Equipment Engineering Technology (Level 2 or 3) or, in Scotland, an SVQ in Install, Commission and Maintain Refrigeration Systems (Level 2 or 3). Alongside gaining an industry recognised qualification, you will also be educated in the necessary health and safety procedures.

Apprenticeships are open to people aged 16 or over and take 2 to 4 years. A combination of on-the-job training from experienced professionals and day or block release formal instruction at a college takes place. There are limited places available to candidates over 25.

Further qualifications such as HNCs/HNDs in Refrigeration and Air Conditioning and Foundation degrees in Building Services Engineering are also available. Alternatively, if you wish to specialise in fluorinated gas (F gases) or ozone depleting substances (ODS), you could complete the City & Guilds Level 2 Award in F-gas and ODS Regulations (2079). You may also apply to be a member of the Institute of Refrigeration which offers a variety of continuing professional development (CPD) workshops as you progress throughout your career.

What the work involves

Your work as a refrigeration and air conditioning engineer will involve the design, installation and repair of refrigeration equipment and air conditioning systems. You will be called out to undertake repairs and maintenance, estimate costs of construction and installation projects, inspect existing equipment, and give advice on adjustments and improvements.

Refrigeration and air conditioning engineers aim to create and maintain comfortable working/living environments in offices and homes that are both energy-efficient and safe.

Your work in commercial buildings and factories will be to provide refrigeration systems that keep food at the correct, safe temperature.

Type of person suited to this work

It is important that you like hands-on work and have a practical approach to problem-solving.

You should be interested in the building services industry and keep up to date with relevant developments in legislation and technology.

Written and spoken communication skills are important as you will be in contact with clients and planning projects. You should also have an aptitude for maths and physics and have strong technical skills.

Working conditions

You will normally work around 37 hours a week and how this is spread over a week may vary. However you might have to work longer hours during the summer which is peak time for refrigeration engineers.

You will be office based to plan visits to sites and organise jobs, but you will also visit various locations such as offices, shopping centres or factories. This will be to complete practical jobs such as maintenance, repair and installation.

You may also work in refrigeration transport, on specially adapted vehicles such as trucks, aircraft and fishing vessels or in vehicle workshops. On certain visits you might have to wear protective clothing or equipment.

Future prospects

As you gain experience in the field you will find opportunities for progression to supervisory and managerial roles.

To improve your skills you may take further qualifications such the NVQ in Building Services Engineering (Level 3 and 4) or in other refrigeration and air conditioning specific topics. Such courses act as a stepping stone to membership of the Chartered Institution of Building Services Engineers (CIBSE).

You can add further experience with further qualifications and work towards becoming an incorporated or chartered engineer. Alternatively, you may opt to become self-employed or move into teaching.

Advantages/disadvantages

There are opportunities to work abroad as UK qualifications are internationally respected.

You may also be required to do overtime work and to be on call overnight and at weekends.

Money guide

Trainees can earn around £11,000 to £19,000 a year, depending on the stage.

Starting salaries once you have qualified are around £20,000 to £25,000 a year.

This can increase to between £26,000 and £35,000 with experience, supervisory responsibilities and qualifications.

There are also opportunities for bonuses and overtime pay.

Related opportunities

- Civil/Construction Engineer/Civil Engineering Technician p71
- Electrical Engineer p207
- Electrician p80

Further information

Institute of Refrigeration
www.ior.org.uk

ROOFER

Qualifications and courses

In order to train as a roofer it may be useful to have some GCSEs/National 5s (A*–E/A–E) in relevant subjects such as Maths, English, craft, Design and Technology or a vocational qualification, eg a BTEC Certificate/Diploma in Construction and the Built Environment or a City & Guilds Certificate in Basic Construction Skills (6218). Introductory vocational qualifications are available at some schools and colleges and act as a foundation for further training or preparation for first employment.

One means of entry into the roofing industry is to find work post-secondary school as an entry-level roofing labourer. This way you will gain both valuable on-site experience and opportunities for further training in roofing techniques.

Alternatively, you could enter the profession through an apprenticeship programme with a building or roofing company. The CITB bConstructive scheme offers a range of general and more specialised construction apprenticeships. Most of the training is carried out on the job and you will earn a wage whilst attending a college or training centre to obtain qualifications such as NVQs/SVQs in Roofing Occupations and Mastic Asphalting.

You will need a Construction Skills Certification Scheme (CSCS) card in order to work on-site. The purpose of this card is to demonstrate that the holder has health and safety training and maintains professional competency. You will normally have to have completed, or be in the process of completing, an industry recognised qualification as proof of your capability.

You could later gain membership of the Institute of Roofing (IOR) which offers numerous continuing professional development (CPD) schemes that update your skills.

What the work involves

Roofers remove old roofs and replace them, fit new roofs and repair existing ones. You will have a choice of roofing materials to work with, such as tile, slate, felt, thatch and sheet. You could specialise in flat or pitched (sloping) roofs or work on both.

When working on flat roofs you will need to spread a waterproof bitumen layer. On all types of roofs your work will involve measuring and cutting materials, layering them on the roof and using mortar or cement to seal it.

You could also carry out lead work or liquid applied roofing.

Type of person suited to this work

You need to have good practical skills and be physically fit, so that you can climb ladders and scaffolding and carry roofing materials. You must be comfortable working at heights.

It is important to be able to understand plans and follow instructions. You should be a team player with good communication skills when dealing with customers.

It will also be useful to be interested in building construction and to enjoy being outdoors.

Working conditions

You will work outdoors on roofs in various locations from people's homes to historic cathedrals and construction sites. The work can be dusty and dirty.

As you will be working up ladders, on scaffolding or on the roof itself, you will need to pay close attention to all health and safety procedures, which includes wearing protective gear such as a safety helmet and boots.

You are likely to work a normal working week, although extra work may be available at weekends.

Future prospects

There is a good demand for qualified roofers across the UK at the moment. Work is available within roofing companies, contractors, roofing material suppliers, local authorities and other public organisations.

You can decide to specialise in using one type of roofing material, such as slate, or you can train to become skilled in several types.

You may work your way up to technical, supervisory and managerial levels. After you have gained enough experience, you could start your own roofing company or seek contract work abroad.

Advantages/disadvantages

Working at heights may be difficult for some people.

You could get to work on some impressive projects such as fitting the roof on a new football stadium. It is satisfying to produce a lasting structure that is functional and looks good.

You will gain an understanding of other construction work, such as joinery.

Money guide

Trainee salaries are about £13,500–£15,000 a year.

As a qualified roofer you can earn £16,000–£24,000.

With experience, your salary can increase to £31,000.

Self-employed roofers negotiate their own rates.

Overtime and bonuses are often available.

Related opportunities

- Construction Operative p74
- Scaffolder p106
- Thatcher p113

Further information

Construction Industry Training Board (CITB)
www.citb.co.uk

Institute of Roofing
www.instituteofroofing.org

Qualifications and courses

This sector normally requires a Royal Institution of Chartered Surveyors (RICS) accredited degree in a related subject such as agriculture, forestry, estate, land or property management and surveying. Most degree courses require 5 GCSEs/National 5s (A*–C/A–C), 2 A levels/3 H grades or relevant BTEC Diplomas/Certificates (or equivalent).

If your first degree was in an unrelated or unaccredited subject, a postgraduate conversion course offered by the College of Estate Management (CEM) can be studied via distance learning. It is also possible to take a degree or postgraduate course at a college recommended by the Central Association of Agricultural Valuers (CAAV).

If you have a relevant HND or Foundation degree then you can qualify for Associate/RICS status. However, you will usually have to top up your qualifications to degree level in order to become a fully chartered surveyor.

Once qualified, you will need to complete the Assessment of Professional Competence (APC) during your first 2 years of employment, in order to gain chartered status.

Competition for training places in the industry is fierce and pre-entry work experience may increase your chances of employment. By completing work experience during your undergraduate year, not only are you developing your confidence in dealing with members of the rural community, but you are also enhancing your career prospects. Relevant work experience placements may include a working farm or estate agent.

It is highly recommended that you also gain a valid UK driving licence.

What the work involves

Rural property/practice surveyors manage properties in the countryside such as farms and estates. You will give professional and technical advice to rural landowners on how to develop their assets – land and property – as well as providing business and resource management and consultancy for land, construction and property industries.

Giving advice on the buying and selling of properties, on farming grants and subsidies and how national and EU law affects clients' businesses is a typical example of work involved.

However, jobs do vary between those who work for corporations who deal with several clients and those who manage estates. You can also choose to specialise in specific areas, such as auctioneering or environmental sustainability, but this can limit employability to an extent.

Type of person suited to this work

Excellent communication skills are needed as you will need to negotiate and liaise with people of all ages and backgrounds.

You must have an analytical mind and a clear, concise writing style in order to explain detailed statistical information.

A good understanding of rural issues, including knowledge of crops, is essential in order to assess a client's economic viability with accuracy. Problem-solving and forward-planning skills are also essential to keep on top of a heavy workload.

Working conditions

The average working week can reach over 40 hours and early morning and weekend work is common as you need to adapt around clients as well as rural events such as harvests.

You will mostly work outdoors, regardless of the weather. If you are office based, it will usually be in rural market towns or villages. You should be prepared to drive and travel regularly as work will often cover a large geographical area.

Future prospects

Your career path is narrowed but progression can occur very quickly. In larger companies, there may be the opportunity to specialise in areas such as pure agriculture or renewable energy use. By contrast, a smaller company could give you a greater range of projects which will build broader experience but with fewer opportunities for specialising.

With 10–15 years of experience, you could become a partner in a firm.

Advantages/disadvantages

You will be based in peaceful rural locations.

You will be instrumental in developing the future of the countryside and rural industries.

Hours can be long and you should expect to regularly work early mornings and weekends.

Money guide

Average earnings for new graduates are £20,000–£25,000.

With experience, this can increase to between £26,000 and £40,000.

A senior chartered surveyor can receive a salary in excess of £45,000.

Additional benefits such as bonuses, a company car or health insurance are sometimes offered and subsidised accommodation may be available for surveyors managing a farm or estate.

Related opportunities

- Auction Property Consultant p61
- Building Surveyor p65
- Civil/Construction Engineer/Civil Engineering Technician p71

Further information

Agricultural Development and Advisory Service
www.adas.co.uk

Department for Environment, Food and Rural Affairs
www.defra.gov.uk

Royal Agricultural College
www.rac.ac.uk

SCAFFOLDER

Qualifications and courses

There are no set entry requirements but some GCSEs/ National 5s (A*–E/A–E) in subjects such as English, Maths, a science and Technology or a vocational qualification, such as the BTEC Introductory Certificate or Diploma in Construction (Level 1) are useful.

In order to become a scaffolder, you will normally be trained on the job whilst studying for industry recognised qualifications part-time at a college or training centre. Employers often expect some on-site experience so it may be useful to develop your skills by working first as a labourer.

The Construction Industry Scaffolders Record Scheme (CISRS) operates a systematic card system at all levels, ie labourer, trainee, scaffolder and advanced scaffolder, and is the recognised qualification for scaffolding. The CISRS card system ensures that operatives are properly trained and sufficiently experienced to work safely and competently. After on and off-site training and an NVQ Level 2 in Accessing Operations and Rigging, you can apply for a Scaffolder card. This will allow you to carry out basic scaffolding tasks as part of a scaffolding gang.

For the Advanced CISRS Card, scaffolders must have a Scaffolder Card, 12 months' subsequent experience and complete the 10-day Advanced Scaffolding course provided by CISRS and the NVQ Diploma in Accessing Operations and Rigging (Construction) (Level 3).

What the work involves

Scaffolders put up scaffolding so that new constructions, or the maintenance of existing buildings and structures, can take place. You will put together metal tubes, fittings and wooden or metal platforms to create the scaffolding.

You will use tools such as swivel spanners and spirit levels in your work.

You may also put up spectator stands, stages and rigging for outdoor concerts and events.

Type of person suited to this work

Safety is the main priority in scaffolding. You need to ensure that it is safe for the people who will be working on it, passers-by, workmates and yourself. For this reason, you have to be able to keep your concentration, have good practical skills, be well organised and be able to follow instructions and take measurements accurately.

You must be physically fit so that you can lift and carry equipment up and down ladders and, of course, you must be happy working at heights.

You also need to be able to work as part of a team of scaffolders.

Working conditions

You will be working mainly outdoors in most weather conditions, often at great heights.

You will need to wear protective equipment such as a hard hat, boots and a safety harness.

You may work a normal working week from Monday to Friday, although you might need to start work early or finish late. Extra hours at weekends may also be available.

Future prospects

There is currently a good demand for scaffolders across the UK. There are lots of opportunities within specialist scaffolding firms and building contractors as well as in oil and power companies, particularly in the east of England and Greater London.

You may progress from basic to advanced scaffolder, and then on to supervisory and managerial positions where you might move into estimation or construction management. The CISRS offers supervisors/managers training in health and safety, risk assessment, design and resource management. If you possess computer-aided design skills, progression to project design and management is possible.

With experience you may set up your own business or take up contract work overseas.

Advantages/disadvantages

This job can be physically challenging and working at heights can be demanding for some people.

You will get to work in a variety of locations and you might have the chance to put up scaffolding for major sports and music events or for film sets.

Money guide

Starting as an apprentice or trainee, you can earn up to £14,000 per year.

Once qualified as a scaffolder, salaries range from £17,000 up to £27,000 depending on experience.

Self-employed or contract scaffolders can often negotiate higher rates of pay.

Overtime is frequently available and on some projects there are performance-related bonuses which can lead to higher earnings.

Related opportunities

- Building Technician p66
- Construction Operative p74
- Roofer p104

Further information

Construction Industry Training Board (CITB)
www.citb.co.uk

National Access and Scaffolding Confederation
www.nasc.org.uk

SHOPFITTER

Qualifications and courses

No formal academic qualifications are required but some employers might expect entrants to have GCSEs/National 5s (A*–E/A–E) in English, Maths and a science. GCSEs/National 5s in Art, Design and Technology might also be useful. The BTEC Certificate and Diploma in Construction (Levels 1 and 2) and the City & Guilds Diploma in Shopfitting Joinery (Levels 2 and 3) (6706) are also relevant.

In order to become a shopfitter, you could begin as a trainee in a relevant area of the industry such as a shopfitting joiner, wood machinist or metal fabricator.

Alternatively, you could serve an apprenticeship with a shopfitting company. As an apprentice, you will experience a combination of work-based training from professional shopfitters and a series of day or block release at a college studying for qualifications. NVQs/SVQs in Shopfitting (Levels 2–4) or an NVQ Diploma in Wood Occupations (Levels 1–3) which will include training, on-site work, bench work and site management are typically studied as part of an apprenticeship.

With experience you can apply for membership of the National Association of Shopfitters (NAS) for further training in areas such as contract law, estimation and site management, provided by the Shopfitting Independent Training Forum (SITF).

Many employers require you to have the CSCS card issued by the Construction Skills Certification Scheme as proof of your competence and a skills card distributed by the Shopfitting and Interior Contracting Competency Scheme (SICCS) specific to shopfitters. In order to obtain these, you will have to have completed or be in the process of completing an industry recognised qualification.

What the work involves

As a shopfitter you will create and install the interiors and exteriors of commercial buildings such as shops, banks, offices, restaurants and hotels. You may be working from designs made by an architect or designer, or you might have to research and prepare your own design drawings.

You will prepare, assemble and finish joinery and metalwork according to the design, before bringing each part together and assembling them on-site.

You will probably specialise in a particular area. These include a metal fabricator, cutting and shaping metal components; a wood machinist, using specialist machinery to cut precise parts for joiners.

Type of person suited to this work

As you will be working in a workshop or on-site you should have a keen interest in practical work and have good hand skills. You should also be interested in design and construction.

You should have an eye for detail and a high level of concentration, but you will also need a certain level of fitness as you will be required to work long and at times, hard hours.

As you will be taking measurements and making calculations frequently you should have good spatial awareness and an aptitude for maths.

Working conditions

You will work around 40 hours per week, with overtime often required, in a variety of locations. You may have to travel to work on-site and this may involve working away from home at times.

You may have to work irregular hours, overnight or at weekends to accommodate clients – work may need to be done during the night when premises are closed.

On-site work may be dusty, dirty and noisy and usually involves physical work such as lifting and bending.

Future prospects

Once you are qualified and have built up experience, you could progress to a supervisory or managerial role, ensuring your team's work meets the necessary standards. Experienced shopfitters may be able to apply to become masters of their trade through the Institute of Carpenters.

It is possible to establish your own shopfitting business.

Alternatively, the skills that you develop as a shopfitter could be utilised in various other building trades.

Advantages/disadvantages

Shopfitting is a diverse profession as your work will change according to the project that you are working on as well as the materials you will work with.

You will meet and work with many other professionals involved in construction such as engineers, architects, electricians and plumbers.

The job is physically demanding and you may be required to work long or unsocial hours.

Money guide

Your starting salary may be around £13,500 to £16,000.

With experience and qualifications, earnings can rise to between £17,000 and £22,000.

As a shopfitter with supervisory duties you may earn around £30,000 per year.

Related opportunities

- Builders' Merchant/Assistant p465
- Carpenter/Joiner p67
- Furniture Manufacturing Operative p213

Further information

Construction Industry Training Board (CITB)
www.citb.co.uk

Institute of Carpenters
www.instituteofcarpenters.com

National Association of Shopfitters
www.shopfitters.org

SITE MANAGER/CLERK OF WORKS

Qualifications and courses

There are no set qualifications to become a site manager/clerk of works. Experience in a relevant industry, however, is necessary, perhaps at craft or technician level in construction or civil engineering. It is not normally a profession that you can enter when you first leave school.

As well as experience, you may need certain construction and civil engineering qualifications. You may decide to seek employment at trainee level and work your way up after completing some introductory courses. These might include a City & Guilds Award/Certificate/Diploma in Basic Construction Skills (Level 1), NVQs Level 2 or 3, a BTEC/SQA Level 2 or 3, a BTEC Higher National Diploma (HND) or Higher National Certificate (HNC) or a Foundation or Honours degree. Graduates may be taken on by companies as apprentices where they will learn on the job.

Once in employment, you can gain NVQs in Site Inspection (Levels 3 and 4) which will cover areas such as health and safety, inspecting property, planning, monitoring and maintenance of projects in construction.

As you accumulate qualifications you can achieve different levels of membership with the Institute of Clerks of Works and Construction Inspectorate (ICWCI). Although this membership is not essential, it is increasingly sought after by employers and beneficial to your career progression. To enter each level of membership you will need to have a relevant qualification, a report of your professional history, a professional practice interview and a materials identification test.

You may be required to obtain a Construction Skills Certification Scheme (CSCS) card as proof of your competency working on-site. Subject to your qualifications, your membership with ICWCI and an examination, you will be eligible for a CSCS card.

What the work involves

As a site manager/clerk of works you will be responsible for supervising all the on-site aspects of a construction contract.

You must ensure that good standards are maintained and that work is carried out efficiently and on time.

You will inspect and monitor materials, procedures and work so that the client is guaranteed quality and value for money. You will also act as a superintendent, advising contractors about aspects of work and solving problems as they arise.

Type of person suited to this work

You should have an interest in construction and should enjoy working outdoors and in all weather conditions. You will need to be physically fit and have a head for heights.

You need to be responsible, organised and honest as you may be in control of projects involving large teams of workers and a variety of materials. You will need a keen eye for detail and to be thorough and vigilant in maintaining quality standards of work and materials.

You should have excellent communication skills, be able to lead a team and to establish appropriate working relationships with contractors' staff.

Working conditions

You will usually work around 40 hours a week, Monday to Friday. However you will frequently have to work at the weekend and during the evening depending on deadlines.

You will be based in a site office which will usually be a temporary structure. You will have to spend much of your time outdoors in all weather conditions.

You may have to climb ladders and scaffolding or, in tunnel construction, work underground. When you are inspecting a site you might have to wear protective clothing such as a hard hat and work boots.

Future prospects

There is currently a shortage of site managers in the UK.

As an experienced clerk of works you must undertake continuing professional development. This is so that you can keep up to date with advances in areas such as new materials, practices, law and regulations, and health and safety issues.

Clerks of works can move up to roles in site management or other management roles in the construction industry.

You may have the opportunity to specialise in your chosen field or become self-employed. You may even take your work abroad.

Advantages/disadvantages

You can choose to specialise in particular areas such as building, civil engineering or mechanical and electrical installations.

On-site inspection may be dusty, dirty and noisy.

Money guide

The starting salary for a clerk of works can be between £21,000 and £40,000 a year.

With experience, your salary can be in excess of £50,000 depending on the contract undertaken.

Related opportunities

- Building Surveyor p65
- Civil/Construction Engineer/Civil Engineering Technician p71
- Construction Supervisor/Manager p76

Further information

Chartered Institute of Building
www.ciob.org.uk

Institute of Clerks of Works
www.icwgb.org

STEEPLEJACK

Qualifications and courses

There are no formal entry qualifications for this job but you will find it useful to have GCSEs/National 5s (A*–E/A–E) in Maths, English, a science and Technology. Pre-entry experience within the construction industry, as a labourer or tradesperson, may be advantageous.

Young entrants can train on the job with an employer or as an apprentice within an approved apprenticeship scheme. The CITB bConstructive programme provides opportunities for apprenticeships. Entrants may be required to take aptitude tests in maths and problem-solving and will be assessed in literacy and their ability to work at heights. Apprentices are sponsored by an employer and spend 6 months out of a 2-year period at the residential National Construction College. College-based training begins in January each year.

Candidates will work towards NVQs/SVQs Levels 2 or 3 in Accessing Operations and Rigging – Steeplejacking and various other CITB-accredited courses such as Health and Safety, First Aid, Mobile Towers, Fire Fighting, Safe Use of Ladders and Industrial Rope Access.

Many employers require you to have the CSCS card issued by the Construction Skills Certification Scheme as proof of your competence working on-site. You will need to have completed or be working towards an industry recognised qualification in order to be granted one.

In order to remain up to date with current issues within the industry, you may find it useful to gain membership with the Association of Technical Lightning and Access Specialists (ATLAS).

What the work involves

Steeplejacks work on high structures including power station chimneys, cooling towers, oil refineries, factories and church spires. Your work on these structures will involve climbing to high places with your tools to complete routine maintenance, repairs or renovation projects.

You will plan each job carefully. To ensure a safe and accessible working environment you will put in ladders, specialist scaffolding or industrial rope access (abseiling), work platforms (cradles) and bosun's seat (harness) and fall-arrest devices.

You will be working on both historic buildings and modern constructions, in urban and rural areas.

Type of person suited to this work

You should be organised as you will have to make sure in advance that you have the right safety equipment and tools to complete the job. The ability to work well as part of a team is also important.

You must be comfortable working at heights or in confined spaces, have a good sense of balance and be physically fit. Good coordination and practical skills are required to use the tools of the trade.

You should enjoy working outdoors in all weather conditions and you must be very conscious of, and committed to, health and safety procedures.

Working conditions

Though you will typically work a 40-hour week, shifts can vary and you might have to work during the evenings and weekends.

Your work will be physically demanding as it will involve rigging, climbing, carrying ladders and tools and working with your hands. You will need to wear protective clothing and headgear. You may have to work on industrial chimneys which can be extremely dusty, requiring respiratory equipment.

A driving licence is useful as you may have to travel.

Future prospects

As a steeplejack you will probably work for construction firms that specialise in steeplejacking. These tend to be based in the major UK cities such as London, Manchester, Nottingham, Bristol, Cardiff, Edinburgh and Glasgow, and tend to seek local employees.

With experience you will be eligible for promotion to a role as a supervisor or manager within a firm. With significant experience you can become self-employed, although this is not particularly common.

There are, however, increasing opportunities to work abroad.

Advantages/disadvantages

There are currently between 800 and 1,000 steeplejacks in the UK. As a qualified steeplejack you may find work easily and there are plenty of opportunities in this area.

Your work may be hampered by weather conditions, for example, high winds may prevent access to structures and delay completion of projects.

Money guide

Trainee steeplejacks can earn between £15,000 and £17,000 a year.

Once qualified, your salary may increase to £21,000.

With experience, advanced skills and extra responsibilities, senior engineers can earn in excess of £25,000 a year.

Your wage can significantly increase with overtime and shift allowances.

Related opportunities

- Bricklayer p62
- Scaffolder p106
- Stonemason p110

Further information

Association of Technical Lightning and Access Specialists
www.atlas.org.uk

Construction Industry Training Board (CITB)
www.citb.co.uk

STONEMASON

Qualifications and courses

There are no formal entry requirements to train as a stonemason but an interest in art and design is desirable and it may also be useful to have GCSEs/National 5s (A*–C/A–C) in English, Maths, Design and Technology in order to calculate areas and volumes. Pre-entry on-site experience, as a labourer for example, is highly valued by potential employers and may offer you a route in for subsequent stonemasonry training.

Another common form of entry is via an apprenticeship with a building or stonemasonry firm. Training is provided on the job by experienced professionals and combined with part-time attendance at college or training centre in order for you to gain relevant NVQs/SVQs, for example, in Stonemasonry Levels 2 and 3. Candidates will have to complete an aptitude assessment and may have to secure employment prior to acceptance.

As an apprentice you may work towards relevant qualifications in stonemasonry offered by the Construction Awards Alliance (CAA). NVQ Diplomas in Heritage Skills (Construction) – Mason (Level 3) or the City & Guilds Diploma in Masonry (Levels 1–3) (6715) are available. Courses cover estimating, planning and setting out projects, as well as understanding product information and tools.

You might opt to complete a relevant course full-time at college but you may find that future employers do value on-site experience.

Many employers on construction sites require workers to have a Construction Skills Certification Scheme (CSCS) card as proof of one's competence working on-site. A driving licence may also be useful, particularly for fixer masons, who will be required to travel between jobs.

What the work involves

Stonemasons carve, shape and arrange stone to create buildings, sculptures and structures.

While the work is manual and strenuous it is also highly creative. You may work on new buildings but could also work on restoring and repairing old buildings.

Type of person suited to this work

It is useful to be interested in architecture and history, as much of the work involves restoring old buildings. Different types of stonemason include:

Banker mason

As a banker mason you will cut, shape and carve stone for building designs. You will need to be good with your hands and accurate. You also need artistic skills for producing decorative finishes.

Fixer mason

As a fixer mason you would assemble and fix stones into place. You must be physically fit so that you can lift the stones, although you will use special equipment to lift the heaviest ones. You must not mind working at heights.

Monumental mason

In this sector, you will carve stone to make things such as plaques and headstones. You may be working closely with the funeral industry, so you need to be sensitive to people's requirements and have a good eye for design.

Working conditions

Banker masons and monumental masons mainly work in a workshop, while fixer masons work on-site in all weather conditions, often at heights.

All masonry work can be dusty, noisy and unsuitable for people who have allergies. You will need to follow health and safety procedures and wear protective clothing.

You will normally work a 39-hour week but overtime may be required when nearing a project deadline.

Future prospects

There is good demand for stonemasons in the UK given the shortage of traditional craft skills.

You can choose to work for stonemasonry firms and larger building contractors. If you work for a small stonemasonry company you are likely to have to do both banking and fixing work. There are fewer opportunities in small, family-run businesses however.

With experience, you may wish to specialise in restoration work or new buildings or to take on supervisory roles. You may even opt to instruct at a college or to become self-employed.

Advantages/disadvantages

The physical nature of the job, including working at heights, may be strenuous for some people.

You may have the opportunity to work on impressive restoration projects, for example in cathedrals or stately homes.

It can make you proud to produce work on a building that will be admired for many years.

Money guide

Starting salaries can range between £15,000 and £18,000 a year.

With experience, your salary could rise to between £20,000 and £30,000.

Overtime and bonuses are often available. Self-employed stonemasons negotiate their own rates.

Related opportunities

- Bricklayer p62
- Building Technician p66
- Dry Stone Waller p79

Further information

National Heritage Training Group
www.the-nhtg.org.uk

Stone Federation Great Britain
www.stonefed.org.uk

Qualifications and courses

Entrants normally have gained an accredited degree and/or postgraduate qualification in structural or civil engineering. Those who have studied another engineering subject or a highly numerate science degree may be able to enter the profession but their career progression may be slower and increasingly limited. In order to be accepted onto a degree course in engineering, you will normally be required to have achieved 2 A levels/3 H grades and 5 GCSEs/National 5s (A*–C/A–C). This should include Maths and any science subject, although Physics is at times specifically requested by certain universities.

It is possible to enter this career after studying for an HNC/HND or Foundation degree in Engineering. You will have to enter at technician level (TIStructE) and work your way up to engineer status by training on the job and gaining further qualifications. The Initial Professional Development (IPD) scheme lays out the skills you need to prove your ability as an engineer and work towards incorporated or chartered status. This takes 3 to 4 years before being completed with an exam and interview, the Professional Review Interview (PRI). Success will allow you to become a professional Chartered Structural Engineer (MIStructE) or Incorporated Structural Engineer (AMIStructE).

Graduate structural engineers are advised to pursue membership with the Institution of Structural Engineers (IStructE) and the Engineering Council as this can greatly improve your employability, salary and progression into senior or specialised roles.

You may opt to study for a master's prior to securing employment in order to work towards chartered status immediately, or alternatively, your employer may sponsor your studying whilst you work at associate level, for example, through a graduate training scheme.

What the work involves

Structural engineers design structures that are able to withstand the high pressure they are placed under.

You will work with architects on the design and construction of a variety of structures including bridges, tunnels, domestic houses, offices or sports stadia.

Among other tasks you will calculate the loads and stresses of a structure, analyse potential problems and test digital models to examine how they will endure influences such as wind, gravity and earth tremors. You will investigate soil conditions, visit construction sites, and undertake projects that involve demolition or repair of a structure.

Type of person suited to this work

You will need to be good at technical drawing and have 3D concept skills. You must have a keen eye for detail and accomplish your work efficiently and with the utmost accuracy.

You should have an aptitude for problem-solving and analytical thinking. You should also have strong skills in maths, physics and IT.

You must be able to work in a team as well as being able to work with other professionals from across the construction industry.

Working conditions

You will work a total of approximately 40 hours a week, Monday to Friday. You might have to work at the weekend.

You will work both in an office and on-site. This can be in all weather conditions and you will have to wear protective clothing such as a hard hat.

You will frequently have to travel from site to site and a driving licence may be useful for this.

Future prospects

The Construction Skills Network anticipates good demand for workers in this field between 2016 and 2019, particularly in Scotland, Wales and the East of England.

Many employers provide training schemes for new structural engineers which allow you to work towards achieving professional status.

You may work in an engineering consultancy or construction company and later, specialise in a specific type of work, such as concrete buildings or refurbishment.

With chartered status you could become self-employed or move into research or lecturing. You could also find contract work abroad or go on to become a Fellow of the IStructE, a recognition of excellence in structural engineering.

Advantages/disadvantages

You should be prepared to work in all weather conditions.

Travel within a working day is common and you may be required to work away from home sometimes.

This is an important job with high levels of responsibility so you are likely to be well respected.

Money guide

Graduate trainees have a starting salary of £22,000–£32,000.

With experience, you could earn £24,000–£40,000.

A senior employee with chartered status could receive up to £50,000.

Related opportunities

- Architect p58
- Quantity Surveyor p102
- Surveying Technician p112

Further information

Association for Consultancy and Engineering
www.acenet.co.uk

Construction Industry Training Board (CITB)
www.citb.co.uk

Institution of Structural Engineers
www.istructe.org

SURVEYING TECHNICIAN

Qualifications and courses

There are a number of routes of entry into this profession, one being completing a relevant course at college to gain the basic skills required by the job. Introductory courses that are suitable include the Level 3 Diploma in Construction and the Built Environment or Civil Engineering for Technicians. These courses provide candidates with a useful foundation of knowledge which they can draw upon when training for more advanced qualifications such as a BTEC HNC/HND in Construction or a Foundation degree in Surveying, Construction or Civil Engineering.

Alternatively, the Chartered Surveyors Training Trust (CSTT) offers work-based training for young people aged 16–24 living in England. Applicants must have a minimum of 4 GCSEs/National 5s (A*–C/A–C) or equivalent. CSTT apprentices train for 2 years and, upon completion, have the option to study for a Royal Institution of Chartered Surveyors (RICS) accredited degree.

Another route for school leavers is to apply for the Advanced Level Apprenticeship in Surveying. Apprentices will typically work towards gaining an industry-recognised qualification, for example, an NVQ/SVQ Level 4 in either Quantity Surveying Practice, Valuation, Spatial Data Management or Town Planning.

Once you have acquired the relevant qualifications and at least 12 months' industry experience (2 years' with a vocational qualification such as a HND/NVQ/SVQ), you can work towards becoming an Associate Member of the RICS (AssocRICS). In order to do so, you will need to complete a 6–12-month period of assessment involving a summary of experience, an evaluation of continuing professional development (CPD) over a period of 12 months, a 2,000-word case study of a recent project and an ethics test.

Once you have qualified as a surveying technician, further training is possible in the form of NVQs. This may lead you to specialise in a particular area of surveying.

What the work involves

Surveying technicians work alongside chartered surveyors, providing hands-on support across the full range of surveying specialisms including building, land, rural and commercial.

You will be expected to carry out a range of administrative tasks associated with each project, such as putting together contracts and writing reports.

You will also be using complex computer programs and technical equipment both on-site and in the office in order to create reports and survey drawings, and to assess various aspects of each project.

Type of person suited to this work

You will be working closely with other professionals and clients at all levels, so the ability to communicate both orally and in writing is vital.

Because you will be dealing with very specific technical issues in each project, you will need to have an accurate and methodical approach to work, good numerical skills and the ability to multi-task.

You will need a good level of IT skills, and confidence in using the wide range of sophisticated equipment required for the job. Knowledge of business, law and health and safety-related regulations is also desirable.

Working conditions

Working hours usually follow those of a normal office job, but you will occasionally be called to work early mornings, evenings and at weekends during busy times or for certain site visits.

Most of the work is office based, but you will also spend time working on-site. This means you must be prepared for all weathers and wear appropriate safety equipment at all times.

You could work with a variety of contractors, ranging from central or local government to smaller surveying companies or even financial businesses and auction houses.

You will be carrying out a lot of complex technical tasks which require excellent concentration and can be quite tiring.

Future prospects

You could progress to become a consultant, a partner in a firm or even move into related sectors such as town planning or chartered surveying with the right qualifications. Self-employment is also an option.

Advantages/disadvantages

Job satisfaction is likely to be high as you will provide invaluable support on a number of important projects.

There is the opportunity to become self-employed or work overseas.

Earning potential is not as high as in some other roles in surveying and hours can be long and unpredictable at busy times.

Money guide

Salaries start from £18,000 to £22,000 per year.

With experience, you can earn up to £30,000 and more.

Salaries are generally higher in London.

Related opportunities

- Civil/Construction Engineer/Civil Engineering Technician p71
- Construction Supervisor/Manager p76
- Quantity Surveyor p102

Further information

Chartered Association of Building Engineers
www.cbuilde.com

Chartered Surveyors Training Trust
www.cstt.org.uk

Royal Institution of Chartered Surveyors
www.rics.org

Qualifications and courses

There are no set entry requirements for this profession, however it may help to have GCSEs/National 5s (A*–E/A–E) in English, Maths and IT. The BTEC Diploma/Certificate in Construction and the Built Environment offered by some schools and colleges may also be relevant to the skills of a thatcher.

There are no formal apprenticeship schemes for thatching, therefore it is recommended that you contact experienced senior thatchers or thatching companies to try and secure a training or apprentice role. In order to make the necessary contacts within the industry, you may find it useful to seek the help of the National Society of Master Thatchers, the National Council of Master Thatchers Associations or the Thatch Advice Centre. The National Society of Master Thatchers in particular offers a membership scheme, training courses and advice on technical issues, that could help you develop your career, ensure your skills are up to date and ultimately, enhance your career progression.

Those aged 16–18 can apply for entry onto the Young Heritage Apprentices programme where they will experience training in a variety of heritage crafts and trades before being given the opportunity to specialise in fields such as roofing and thatching and landcrafts. Apprentices work towards gaining a Level 2 NVQ in their desired specialism.

An NVQ in Roofing Occupations (Thatching) at Level 2 or 3 familiarises candidates with health and safety procedures and equips candidates with the skills and specialist knowledge necessary to prepare and construct roofs and thatching materials.

The Traditional Building Skills Bursary Scheme seeks to address skill shortages in traditional crafts by offering bursaries and work experience placements for eligible applicants.

What the work involves

Thatching is the covering of roofs with plant stems such as water reed, combed wheat reed and long straw. Your tasks will include thatching new roofs and repairing or re-thatching existing thatched roofs.

Your work will involve using many different tools, including mallets, hooks, needles, knives and shears.

As thatchers work outside all year round, your hours will differ depending on the season.

Type of person suited to this work

You need to have good practical skills to use the specialised equipment and to develop an expertise in the craft. You must be physically fit so that you can climb ladders and scaffolding whilst carrying thatching materials. You will need to be comfortable working at heights.

It is important to be able to measure roofs accurately in order to calculate the required amount of thatching material so strong numerical skills are required.

Working conditions

You will work outdoors on roofs in rural locations in most weather conditions. The work can be dusty, which can be difficult if you suffer from certain allergies.

It is important that you follow health and safety procedures closely when working on roofs.

Your working hours are likely to vary according to when the work is available. This can be seasonal work, meaning you will be busiest during the spring and summer months when the weather is best.

Future prospects

There are approximately 500 thatcher businesses in the UK and, as about half of all thatched buildings need to be re-roofed every 15–20 years, there is a steady demand for thatching work. Conservation regulations do not allow owners of thatched properties to replace their roofs with any other material, therefore the number of thatched buildings requiring repair/replacement remains reasonably stable.

There is fierce competition for training vacancies and some thatchers have another job to supplement their income. Not all areas of the UK have thatched buildings so you may find you will need to relocate to an area where the skills are more in demand, ie in rural areas.

Your work opportunities are likely to be on a self-employed basis. It can take a number of years to become highly skilled.

Advantages/disadvantages

It is rewarding to practise an ancient craft and create thatched roofs that are both functional and decorative.

The job involves being active and working outdoors.

Working at heights may be demanding for some people and potentially dangerous.

You may need a second job to supplement your earnings.

Money guide

The starting salary for a qualified thatcher ranges between £13,000 and £18,000.

With experience, you could earn up to £25,000 a year.

Self-employed thatchers who have established a good reputation with their clients can achieve around £35,000.

Related opportunities

- Roofer p104
- Stonemason p110

Further information

Lantra
www.lantra.co.uk

National Heritage Training Group
www.the-nhtg.org.uk

Thatching Advisory Services
www.thatchingadvisoryservices.co.uk

THERMAL INSULATION ENGINEER

Qualifications and courses

There are no formal entry requirements for this profession though a possible route of entry is through a 3-year Thermal Insulation Engineering Apprenticeship programme with the Thermal Insulation Contractors Association (TICA) accredited by Edexcel and the Scottish Qualification Association (SQA). You will have to pass an entry test assessing your ability to work at heights and a medical screening, after which you will undertake on-the-job training by experienced professionals and a period of off-the-job instruction at college.

Apprentices will work towards an NVQ/SVQ Level 2 in Thermal Insulation Engineering, complete a Level 2 Certificate in Thermal Insulation and a course in Employment Rights and Responsibilities.

Once employed, you may opt to complete short training courses offered by the Asbestos Control and Abatement Division (ACAD) of TICA if you are an engineer working closely with asbestos.

Many employers on construction sites require workers to have a Construction Skills Certification Scheme (CSCS) card and a CCNSG Safety Passport. This demonstrates that the holder has health and safety training and is competent working on-site. You will need to have gained or be working towards completing an NVQ in order to be granted a CSCS card. If you are working without qualifications, the On-site Assessment Workshop or Experienced Worker Practical Assessment schemes will help you gain the qualifications required.

What the work involves

You will use various types of insulation to either prevent heat loss or keep heat out within different types of products and equipment, such as boilers, pipework, refrigeration or air conditioning. The types of insulation you will use will be dependent on the actual project but could involve silicate or foam.

You will measure, cut and shape insulating materials to fit around pipes, boilers and duct work. Once the item is insulated, you will cover it using sheet metal or another cladding material.

You will assess clients' needs and advise them on the best plan to solve their insulation problem.

Type of person suited to this work

You may be exposed to some potentially dangerous materials, so you must follow health and safety regulations carefully.

You should be able to understand instructions, have a practical approach to your work and enjoy using manual skills, particularly for cutting and fitting materials. Mathematical skills are useful for measuring and working out quantities.

Much of the work involves strenuous lifting, balancing and climbing up scaffolding, so you will have to be physically fit, as well as able to work within confined spaces and at height.

The ability to work in a team and get on with other people will be important as you will often work alongside other professionals from the construction and engineering industries.

Working conditions

You could be working indoors or outside at heights, in places that are cramped or difficult to access.

You may be exposed to harmful substances and be working in dusty and dirty environments, so you will wear protective clothing, like goggles and sometimes a face mask.

You will normally work a standard 38-hour week, but overtime and evening or weekend work might be required. Travelling around the country to visit different sites and projects may be necessary.

Future prospects

There is currently a growth in the demand for qualified thermal insulation engineers given the increasing focus on environmental conservation.

After training and experience, you could find a job within building, building service engineering or specialised energy conservation companies or you could move into areas such as heating and ventilation engineering or refrigeration.

Within the larger companies it might be possible to progress into technical, supervisory or managerial posts such as a site safety officer or contracts manager.

Advantages/disadvantages

You will be working alongside people from different industries. Opportunities are good and overseas work may be possible.

You will need many different skills to complete one job.

You may need to work away from home which could be difficult if you have family commitments.

Money guide

Apprentices usually earn £10,000–£16,000 a year, depending on the stage of training.

With qualifications this rises to £17,000–£24,000.

Senior thermal insulation engineers can earn up to £30,000.

Contract work is common and allowances could be made for working away from home.

Related opportunities

- Damp Proofer p77
- Gas Network Engineer p214
- Heating and Ventilation Engineer p90

Further information

Construction Industry Training Board (CITB)
www.citb.co.uk

Thermal Insulation Contractors Association
www.tica-acad.co.uk

TOWN PLANNER/PLANNING TECHNICIAN

Qualifications and courses

Town planner

You will need to have a Royal Town Planning Institute (RTPI) accredited qualification such as a degree or a postgraduate qualification. For degree entry you will need at least 2 A levels/3 H grades. For entry to a postgraduate course, a degree in a related subject such as geography, architecture or urban studies is required. To ensure chartered status, it is recommended that your qualifications be completed on a combined level of study, meaning both spatial planning and a specialist area of planning are covered.

Chartered (MRTPI) membership of the RTPI is available after graduation from an accredited qualification, 2 years' relevant work experience and completion of an Assessment of Professional Competence (APC).

Continuing professional development (CPD) forms an essential part of advancement in your career. You will be expected to undertake relevant courses and maintain an annual professional development plan.

Town planning technician

There are no set qualifications, but at least 4 GCSEs/National 5s (A*–C/A–C) including English and Maths, are usually required. Many entrants also have A levels/H grades, Foundation degrees or other relevant qualifications, such as a Scottish Group Award (SGA) in Construction, a HND in Planning or a graphic design or IT qualification. You may also find having relevant work experience, preferably in a planning office, advantageous when seeking employment.

Planning technicians are trained on the job by experienced professionals whilst studying part-time or via distance learning for an NVQ/SVQ in Town Planning Support (Level 3–4).

Technical Membership (TechRTPI) of the Royal Town Planning Institute (RTPI) requires a recognised qualification at NVQ Level 3 or higher and 2 years' work experience.

What the work involves

Town planner

You will manage and develop urban or rural areas to best serve the population. When deciding how to use the land you will take into account commercial, social, environmental and heritage needs.

Town planning technician

You will support the work of town planners.

You will carry out surveys, map areas, record information, analyse and present reports and provide advice on planning permission.

Type of person suited to this work

You will need excellent communication skills as you will need to explain your ideas clearly and produce comprehensive written reports.

You must be organised with good research, problem-solving and analytical skills to investigate the potential effects of different proposals for land use.

Specialist skills required include competency in graphic design, desktop publishing and familiarity with computer-aided design (CAD), geographical information systems (GIS) and cartography.

Working conditions

Regular office hours are likely, although you may sometimes need to attend meetings in the evening.

Most town planners are based in offices but often go out on site visits. A driving licence might be necessary.

Future prospects

There is a huge demand for more qualified planners in the UK and overseas.

Most employers are local authorities and planning consultancies, but opportunities also exist within central government, construction companies and environmental organisations.

With experience and chartered status, you may be promoted to senior or county planning officer or you could specialise in areas such as urban design or conservation. Alternatively, you could move into related careers such as recreation management, market research or property development.

Advantages/disadvantages

It is satisfying to deal with public problems and to improve the environment in which people live and work.

It can be frustrating to compromise on planning initiatives.

Dealing with angry or upset members of the public can be difficult.

Money guide

Newly graduated town planners could earn between £15,000 and £28,000. This will be more if you are a registered member of the Royal Town Planning Institute (RTPI).

With experience, salaries can range between £29,000 and £45,000.

Chief planning officers, heads of department and company directors can earn between £55,000 and £100,000.

Technicians can start on £16,000 a year and earn up to £28,000 with experience and supervisory experience.

Related opportunities

- Land/Geomatic Surveyor p94
- Planning and Development Surveyor p98
- Quantity Surveyor p102

Further information

Royal Town Planning Institute
www.rtpi.org.uk

115

WALL/FLOOR TILER

Qualifications and courses

A common route of entry into this industry is to complete an apprenticeship with a building or tiling firm. There are no specific qualifications required, although GCSEs/National 5s (A*–E/A–E) in subjects like Maths, technology or English may be required by some employers and are helpful when dealing with calculations, measurements and theory. Similar subjects or equivalent vocational qualifications such as the BTEC Introductory Certificate/Diploma in Construction may also be useful in introducing candidates to the basic skills required in the industry.

An apprenticeship is a possible route into this career, where you will receive on-the-job training and work towards industry-recognised qualifications. These qualifications include an NVQ/SVQ in Wall and Floor Tiling at Levels 2 and 3. Apprenticeships are available to those aged 16–24 and may involve a skills learning exercise prior to your acceptance. You will have to secure employment prior to starting an apprenticeship and employers often value people with some on-site experience. You might first, therefore, gain experience as a labourer before applying for a formal training scheme.

It is becoming increasingly necessary to have a Construction Skills Certification Scheme (CSCS) card to work in construction as proof of your competency. You must have gained or be working towards an NVQ in order to be granted one.

What the work involves

You will fit tiles in various locations, from bathrooms and kitchens to hospitals and swimming pools. You may work with many kinds of tile including ceramic, stone, glass, terracotta, granite, marble and mosaic.

First you will set out (known as marking) an area by calculating the amount of tile and adhesive needed. You will then use bench-mounted or hand tools to cut the tiles to the correct size and shape.

You will level the surface with plaster, cement or sand, fix the tiles in the correct position and then fill in the gaps with grout.

Type of person suited to this work

Maths skills are essential as you will need to measure and calculate how much material you will need. You must work carefully and accurately. It is important to match colours and patterns, so a flair for design is useful.

You need to be physically fit for carrying the materials and for working on your hands and knees.

You need to be able to work on your own initiative as well as in a team. You should be presentable and pleasant when dealing with customers.

Working conditions

You will work mainly indoors in a variety of locations, ranging from a client's home to offices, factories and construction sites. A driving licence might be useful.

You may work a normal working week, but you may also need to work evenings or weekends so that you can tile walls and floors without disrupting businesses.

As you will use special cutting tools and adhesives you will need to be aware of health and safety procedures.

Future prospects

Work is available with specialist tiling companies and building contractors, or you may choose to become self-employed, providing services to individuals or sub-contracting for organisations. Demand for tilers very much depends on the current state of the economy.

It is possible to specialise in one type of tiling, for example flooring tiles, mosaic work or bathrooms.

With experience and further training, you may be able to progress into technical, supervisory or managerial positions. You could even move into college instruction.

Advantages/disadvantages

You will be on your hands and knees, sometimes working in dusty, dirty or cramped conditions.

The work is varied and you can achieve spectacular results using coloured and textured tiles to decorate walls and floors.

Money guide

Wall and floor tilers typically earn a starting salary of £14,000.

With qualifications and experience this can increase to £17,000–£23,000 per year.

Tilers with supervisory duties, or those with training responsibilities, can earn between £25,000 and £30,000.

Overtime is often available, and on some projects there are bonuses based on outputs, which can lead to higher earnings.

Related opportunities

- Building Technician p66
- Construction Operative p74
- Floor Layer/Finisher p86

Further information

Construction Industry Training Board (CITB)
www.citb.co.uk

Construction Skills Certification Scheme (CSCS)
www.cscs.uk.com

The Tile Association
www.tiles.org.uk

Qualifications and courses

There are no formal academic qualifications required to become a wastewater treatment plant operator. Some companies, however, do seek employees with a minimum of 4 GCSEs/National 5s (A*–E/A–E) in Maths, English and a science or technology subject. The BTEC Diploma in Engineering or Environmental and Land-based Studies may also be relevant for this type of work.

The most common form of entry into the industry is by a water industry apprenticeship. The minimum age for apprentices is generally 18 and applicants will normally be required to pass a medical examination prior to acceptance. Previous work experience on a building site or within plant maintenance may be advantageous, not only in introducing you to the basics of the industry but in your bid to secure an employer to sponsor your training.

As an apprentice, you will combine on-the-job training from experienced professionals with a series of day or block release instruction at a college or training centre where you will work towards achieving an industry-recognised qualification. Courses include the NVQ/SVQ Level 2 in Operating a Process Plant (Water/Waste Water/Sludge), the Level 2 Certificate or Diploma for Water Sector Competent Operator (Water/Waste Water/Sludge), or the Level 2 Diploma in Water Engineering (Waste Water Operations).

To further your career, you may also choose to pursue an HNC/HND or degree which will qualify you for more senior roles.

In order to work as an operator, employers may require you to register with an appropriate safety passport scheme, eg the Energy and Utilities Skills Register (EUSR).

What the work involves

Water treatment plant operators monitor wastewater as it goes through various treatment processes which remove harmful substances. They ensure that treated water is returned to the water cycle and that waste is removed and destroyed as appropriate.

You will be responsible for the operation and maintenance of the plant, ensuring that septic tanks, filters and screens are disinfected, checking water samples, and adding treatment micro-organisms and chemicals to the water when necessary.

You will conduct tests on samples, take readings from monitors and adjust treatment equipment as necessary. You will work with a team composed of a supervisor, senior technicians, engineers and a manager.

Type of person suited to this work

You need to have a passion for the environment, science and technology. You also need to be happy to work with new technology which you will use on a daily basis.

You must be able to communicate effectively and work well in a team. You will have to follow health and safety regulations. It is important that you are fit and active as you may be doing practical, strenuous work at times, such as cleaning and maintenance.

You must be organised and methodical as you will be testing samples to ensure that harmful substances are removed from the water cycle.

Working conditions

You will work approximately 37 hours a week. Overtime may be possible but part-time work is rare. You will probably have to work shifts as water treatment plants operate 24 hours a day. You may have to join a call-out rota to cover nights and weekends.

You will be based indoors in control rooms but some of your work will involve being outside in all weather conditions. You may also have to carry out work at heights or in confined spaces.

Protective clothing is provided. This may include a breathing apparatus, and should be worn to prevent contact with harmful substances.

Future prospects

After gaining experience, you could progress to a role as a supervisor and from there, on to roles as an inspector, a superintendent or a plant manager. You may also choose to move into a related area such as treatment plant design.

You can also take a Higher National Certificate, Diploma or degree which will allow you to move to higher positions.

Advantages/disadvantages

You may find opportunities to increase wages by taking extra shifts, going on stand-by and doing overtime.

Your working environment in the plant may be smelly and wet.

You may sometimes be called into work if there is an emergency situation.

Money guide

Starting salaries are between £14,500 and £18,000 per year.

With qualifications you can earn up to £25,000.

Experienced operators and leaders can earn between £25,000 and £32,000.

Overtime and extensive shift work can greatly increase salary.

Related opportunities

- Brewery Worker p203
- Energy Engineer p209
- Water/Sewerage Network Operative p118

Further information

Energy & Utility Skills
www.euskills.co.uk

Energy & Utility Skills Register
www.eusr.co.uk

Water UK
www.water.org.uk

Watertrain
www.watertrain.co.uk

WATER/SEWERAGE NETWORK OPERATIVE

Qualifications and courses

There are no formal academic requirements needed to become a water/sewerage network operative but a number of GCSEs/National 5s (A*–C/A–C) including Maths, English, a science or technology may be useful in supporting your search for employment as is a history of relevant work experience, in site maintenance for example. Equivalent vocational qualifications such as the BTEC Diploma in Engineering may also be relevant to this line of work.

The most common route of entry is via an apprenticeship. Entrants combine on-the-job training from experienced professionals with a series of day or block release instruction at a training centre or college where you will work towards industry recognised qualifications. The Certification and Assessment Board for the Water Industry (CABWI) offers a range of relevant awards, including Level 2 Diplomas in Distribution Control and Operating Process Plant (Water) and Level 3 Diplomas in Leakage Control, Controlling Process Operations and Network Construction Operations.

An alternative route to an apprenticeship is work experience in a related area, such as road working, construction or plant machine operation.

Registration with an appropriate safety passport scheme, such as the Energy & Utilities Skills Register (EUSR), may be required by some employers for you to be able to work on-site. The passport acts as proof of competency to work on the water network.

A driving licence may be useful for some roles.

What the work involves

Water/sewerage network operatives lay, maintain and repair the pipework that carries drinking water, waste water and sewage.

Your tasks might include digging trenches in roads and relaying them afterwards, putting up barriers and warning signs, laying pipes, repairing leaks, clearing blockages and installing water meters.

You will use a range of tools such as welding equipment to join pipes together and machinery such as mechanical diggers.

Type of person suited to this work

You must have good practical skills and be mechanically minded so that you can use tools, equipment and machinery effectively. You must be able to follow health and safety regulations as working on-site can be dangerous. You will have to follow plans and instructions accurately, so that systems are installed correctly and safely.

You must be fit and active for bending, kneeling and carrying materials and equipment.

You will have to deal with complaints from the public, who might be upset that their water services are disrupted. You must also be able to work in a team with other water/sewerage network operatives. You may need a driving licence.

Working conditions

You will work outdoors in all weather conditions. The work can be dusty, dirty and wet, as well as smelly.

You will need to follow strict health, safety and hygiene regulations, which may include wearing a breathing apparatus, a safety helmet, boots and gloves.

You may work normal working hours or shifts, but the particular hours you work will vary according to the needs of the job and the hours of daylight available. You may be on-call 24/7 in case of the need for emergency repairs.

Future prospects

There is currently a strong demand for water/sewerage network operatives because the privatised water companies, who manage water supply and sewerage disposal, are investing money in developing their systems. The industry currently maintains an ongoing system of construction, operation and maintenance of water and waste water infrastructure, thus there is a steady supply of jobs available.

You can find work with water companies and construction firms across the UK. After gaining experience, you could progress to a role as a team leader or in senior management and with further training, as an engineering technician or incorporated/chartered water engineer.

You could move into related areas such as water distribution inspection work.

Advantages/disadvantages

The work can be physically demanding and it can get smelly if you are working on sewerage systems.

Helping to provide people with an essential service can be rewarding.

Money guide

Apprentices earn around £12,000 a year.

Once qualified, this can rise to between £17,000 and £25,000.

Your salary can rise with overtime and shift allowances.

Related opportunities

- Construction Operative p74
- Gas Network Engineer p214
- Plumber p100

Further information

Energy & Utility Skills
www.euskills.co.uk

Energy & Utility Skills Register
www.eusr.co.uk

Water UK
www.water.org.uk

WINDOW FITTER

Qualifications and courses

There are no formal entry requirements but you might find employers value candidates with some GCSEs/National 5s in subjects such as English, technology and, particularly, Maths, as calculations and measuring are important aspects of your job. Equivalent qualifications, such as a BTEC Certificate/Diploma in Construction, may introduce you to some of the basic skills required in the industry.

Previous experience within related areas of the field, in carpentry or joinery for example, may be helpful if you decide to seek entry-level employment as a fitter's 'mate' or labourer.

The most common route of entry, however, is via an apprenticeship with a glazing company. An apprenticeship will typically involve a combination of on-the-job training from experienced professionals and a series of day or block release instruction at a college or training centre in order for you to work towards industry recognised qualifications. Applicants normally need GCSEs/National 5s (A*–E/A–E), or an equivalent qualification and may be required to pass an aptitude test prior to entry.

Whilst you train, you will have the opportunity to work towards gaining vocational qualifications such as NVQ/SVQ Diplomas in either Fenestration Installation (Levels 2–3) or Fire Resistant Glazing (Levels 2–3). Your training will cover areas such as the removal and fitting of window frames, health and safety, customer relations and relevant paperwork.

The Glass Qualifications Authority offers many NVQs related to the manufacture and installation of glass and other products.

Many employers require their staff to hold a Construction Skills Certification Scheme (CSCS) card as proof of one's competency working on-site. You normally have to be working towards or have gained an NVQ in order to be granted one.

A driving licence may also be required in order for you to travel between clients.

What the work involves

Window fitters install windows in new and existing buildings.

You will use hand and power tools to take out any old windows and fit new ones. You will work with materials such as glass, plastic and wood.

Once you have fixed a new window into the allocated space, you will need to give it a weatherproof seal. Your job may also involve fitting doors, conservatories and weatherboarding.

Type of person suited to this work

You will need good practical hand skills for using tools and you will need to be physically fit as you will be lifting and carrying windows. Maths skills are essential in order to make accurate calculations and fit frames properly.

You should be safety conscious and comfortable working on ladders.

You may work on your own for some jobs, but you will often work with one other window fitter, or in a small team so you must be able to work with others. You should also be able to get on with customers because you will spend a lot of time on their premises.

Working conditions

You will work indoors and outdoors in a variety of locations, and you will be working in most weather conditions. A driving licence may be useful.

You will need to pay attention to health and safety, especially when working with glass, and be happy clearing up after your work has finished.

You are likely to work normal working hours during the week, but overtime may be available at weekends.

Future prospects

Work is available throughout the UK. There is an increasing demand for double-glazed windows and for conservatories so job prospects are good.

You may find opportunities for work within large national firms or smaller local companies and you could go on to specialise in fire-proof glazing or film application (applying film to glass for privacy). There are also openings within the sales and marketing sides of the industry.

After gaining sufficient experience, you may progress to team leader or supervisory positions or move into window surveying or estimating. You may even opt to become self-employed and run your own window-fitting business.

Advantages/disadvantages

Lifting and carrying windows and working at heights is physically demanding.

It is satisfying to make customers happy by improving the appearance, value and function of their buildings by installing and repairing windows.

Money guide

As a trainee, you can expect a salary of £14,000.

Once qualified, your salary will increase to between £16,000 and £25,000 a year, depending on your experience.

Overtime and shift allowances may increase your earnings. Self-employed fitters negotiate their own rates.

Related opportunities

- Carpenter/Joiner p67
- Ceiling Fixer p69
- Glazier p89

Further information

Glass and Glazing Federation
www.ggf.org.uk

Proskills UK
www.proskills.co.uk

Catering and Hospitality

Working in this sector, you will meet a wide variety of people and probably need to be a very strong team player. Workers in the sector thrive on providing an impeccable service and ensuring customers are completely satisfied and are given a wonderful experience whether that is in a restaurant, hotel or bar. The jobs featured in this section are listed below. For similar jobs to the ones in this section why not have a look at *Leisure, Sport and Tourism* starting on page 361 and *Retail, Sales and Customer Services* from page 461.

- Bar Manager/Licensee/ Publican p122
- Catering/Restaurant Manager/Maître d'Hôtel p123
- Cellar Technician p124
- Chef/Sous Chef p125
- Concierge p126
- Food Safety Officer p127
- Hotel Manager p128
- Hotel Porter p129
- Hotel Receptionist p130
- Hotel/Accommodation Room Attendant p131
- Housekeeper/ Accommodation Manager p132
- Kitchen Assistant/Supervisor p133
- Waiting Staff p134

BAR MANAGER/LICENSEE/ PUBLICAN

Qualifications and courses

There are no formal entry requirements, although a degree or HND in subjects such as business and hospitality or hospitality management may help you progress faster.

There are several possible entry routes. You could start as a bar person and train on the job to progress to a supervisory or management position. Alternatively, school leavers may be able to enter through an Apprenticeship in Hospitality and Catering (Food and Beverage Services).

Some larger companies have graduate training schemes. You would enter as an assistant manager and train on the job before taking the licensing exams. There are no specific degree subjects required but you must have previous customer service experience in a pub, bar or food establishment, preferably at supervisory level.

To be a bar manager/publican you will need a personal licence, for which you will need to be at least 18 years old and have an accredited licensing qualification from the British Institute of Innkeepers Awarding Body (BIIAB). In England and Wales this means passing the Level 2 Award for Personal Licence Holders. In Scotland it's the Scottish Certificate for Personal Licence Holders. You will also need an in-date Disclosure and Barring Service (DBS) check.

What the work involves

Your duties will include the recruitment, training and management of staff. You will also deal with the accounts, stock replenishment, maintaining links with suppliers, and business development.

You will need to keep up to date with any changes to licensing laws and other legal requirements such as health and safety or fire safety regulations, and ensure that your customers and staff adhere to them.

In addition, you will demonstrate a high level of customer service to ensure client satisfaction.

Type of person suited to this work

It is essential to have excellent communication skills and to enjoy meeting and speaking to people of all ages. A confident, professional attitude is needed to deal with customer or supplier problems.

Being physically fit and able to stay on your feet all day is helpful. You should be practical, flexible and good at multi-tasking.

Good numeracy skills are expected as you will be managing cash on a daily basis. You should keep up to date with legal requirements, and ensure that those that affect you are enforced within your establishment.

Working conditions

Although pubs, clubs and bars can remain open for 24 hours a day, most only extend their hours at weekends or for special events.

You will work long hours in an environment which can be busy, noisy and hot. You will be required to stand for lengthy periods and lift and carry heavy items such as barrels.

You may have to deal with demanding or difficult customers who are intoxicated. Changes to smoking legislation have resulted in the expectation of the provision of outside facilities, where problems are more likely to occur.

Future prospects

The number of pubs has been gradually decreasing for some time now. With up to 29 pubs closing each week, the availability of publican jobs has seen a decline. However, the growing influence of organisations such as the Campaign for Real Ale (CAMRA), and recent changes to duty on alcohol could provide the industry with a much needed boost. There has been a reported boost in the number of managerial roles available in the sector already.

Bar manager jobs at other types of establishments, such as bars, hotels, high street chains, restaurants and clubs, are still available but may have been affected by the industry only having had slight growth in recent years. Managers could progress to larger or different types of establishments, become area managers for a chain, open their own premises or move into a different area of hospitality.

Advantages/disadvantages

The hours will be long and irregular which might affect your personal life.

You will have to deal with drunk customers, who may be difficult or aggressive, on a fairly regular basis.

The working atmosphere is informal and enjoyable.

You may have the opportunity to live on the pub premises which can reduce your living expenses.

Money guide

Assistant managers can expect a starting salary in the region of £16,000 to £21,000 per year. Once you reach manager or licensee level, you could earn £25,000 to £35,000.

Those who work in a very successful or large establishment, or become area managers for a pub company, can achieve earnings of up to £50,000.

Earnings vary according to the type, size and location of the premises you work in. Benefits can include pension schemes, health insurance and cheap or free accommodation.

Related opportunities

- Brewery Worker p203
- Hotel Manager p128
- Waiting Staff p134

Further information

British Beer and Pub Association
www.beerandpub.com

Wine & Spirit Education Trust
www.wsetglobal.com

CATERING/RESTAURANT MANAGER/ MAÎTRE D'HÔTEL

ENTRY LEVEL 1

Qualifications and courses

There are no formal entry requirements for this profession. School leavers could start as a kitchen assistant, waiter/waitress or chef and gradually progress to management level. Studying for relevant qualifications, such as NVQs and diplomas in hospitality and catering, could help you progress.

Many hotel and restaurant chains offer training schemes. It may be possible to join a scheme with A levels/H grades or equivalent but the usual requirement is a degree or HNC/HND in a relevant subject, such as hospitality management, hospitality and catering, hotel management or international hospitality management. The minimum requirements for degree entry are usually 5 GCSEs/ National 5s (A*–C/A–C) and 2 A levels or 3 H grades.

Relevant work experience is important, for example through part-time or seasonal work or an Apprenticeship in Hospitality.

What the work involves

You will manage, train and employ staff in a kitchen or restaurant. A maître d'hôtel is specifically responsible for running a hotel restaurant.

Part of your work will involve planning menus, checking stocks of food and drink and ordering fresh supplies when needed. You will be expected to handle paperwork, manage budgets and organise staff rotas.

You will be responsible for the health and safety of both your staff and customers.

Type of person suited to this work

You will be dealing with kitchen staff, suppliers and other business professionals so you must be confident and have excellent communication skills. It is essential to provide good customer service at all times.

As you will be involved in an industry centred on preparing food for the public, you will be required to follow and keep up to date with health and safety laws. You will also need an interest in service delivery and food.

Good management skills, including an understanding of the different roles undertaken by your staff, are essential. Exceptional organisational abilities and good numeracy skills are also important.

Working conditions

Much of your time will be spent in your kitchen or restaurant, which can get very hot and busy. Expect to be on your feet for long periods of time.

You might wear a uniform or protective clothing and regularly work unsocial hours. It is important to follow high standards of food safety and hygiene.

It is possible to work as a catering manager in the armed forces, in which case you might find yourself working in challenging environments, anywhere in the world, in a variety of climates.

Future prospects

Some restaurant/catering managers move on to running their own businesses, either a restaurant or private contract catering company. Managers of single restaurants may progress to area manager for a particular chain.

There are opportunities to work abroad, possibly within the same company. Some managers may also move into hotel or leisure management.

Advantages/disadvantages

You will be working in a fun and lively atmosphere and you might have the chance to organise the catering for special events such as weddings or parties.

This can be a very busy job where you will be doing several tasks at the same time.

Hours are long and will include weekend or evening work.

Money guide

Salaries vary significantly depending on the type of establishment you work in. The highest salaries are in London and the south west of England.

As the manager of a casual dining restaurant, you could earn between £18,000 and £30,000 a year.

In a fine dining establishment, your salary could be between £22,000 and £40,000.

Senior managers could make up to £70,000 a year.

Related opportunities

- Events and Exhibition Organiser p391
- Food Safety Officer p127
- Kitchen Assistant/Supervisor p133

Further information

Hospitality Guild
www.hospitalityguild.co.uk

Institute of Hospitality
www.instituteofhospitality.org

People 1st
www.people1st.co.uk

CELLAR TECHNICIAN

Qualifications and courses

There are no required qualifications to become a trainee cellar technician, although some employers prefer you to have GCSEs/National 5s (A*–C/A–C) in Maths, a science or technology subjects, or a BTEC, NVQ or City & Guilds qualification in engineering.

Experience working in a bar is useful and many cellar technicians work their way up from bar staff level. Cask Marque offers a 1-day course in Cellar Management Training for those already employed in the sector. Experience in engineering or electrical work is also an advantage.

Employers provide training that covers areas such as health and safety, customer care, refrigeration, checking systems and working with equipment. They may also expect you to study for a British Institute of Innkeeping Awarding Body (BIIAB) Level 2 Technical Certificate in Cellar Service, Installation and Maintenance (NCCSIM) with an association or institution such as the Brewing, Food & Beverage Suppliers Association (BFBi). This involves classroom and on-the-job training while candidates study for 5 units.

Once you have acquired the BIIAB certificate, you could take other qualifications such as an NVQ/SVQ Level 2 or 3 in Drinks Dispense Systems or Cellar Service.

What the work involves

You will set up and maintain the systems that keep alcoholic and soft drinks at a consistent quality in pubs, hotels and other sites.

Visiting a range of locations, you will install equipment such as high-pressure gas systems, and check that they are compatible with existing water, electricity supply or drainage systems.

You will undertake regular maintenance checks to make sure that everything works properly, train the staff in how to operate it and deal with any problems.

Type of person suited to this work

You will need good practical skills and the confidence to work and operate different systems quickly and efficiently.

As you will be handling heavy equipment, a good level of physical fitness is helpful.

Good communication skills are useful, as is a confidence in your ability to do the job well.

As you will be providing a service on behalf of your company for lots of different licensed premises you will need to have excellent customer care skills.

Working conditions

You will spend lots of time driving from site to site.

Some of your work will be attending emergency call-outs which could include evenings and weekends. The extended pub opening hours might mean this includes 24-hour call-out duties.

You will work in dark, cramped conditions using specialist tools and equipment such as electrical testing devices.

Future prospects

There is a steady demand for experienced cellar technicians.

The main employers are breweries, drink-dispensing equipment manufacturers and soft drinks manufacturers.

Many applicants come from the licensed trade who have watched the job and become interested. It is therefore useful to have pub experience or relevant qualifications before applying.

With experience you can apply for senior/managerial posts or move into other areas of the licensed or food and drink sector such as sales.

Advantages/disadvantages

This job combines meeting and training people with lots of practical work.

You might have to travel long distances to reach customers.

You might work in uncomfortable conditions, for example when fitting a new dispensing system in a cellar.

Money guide

Starting salaries for cellar technicians range from £15,000 to £18,000 per year.

With experience, earnings can increase to around £20,000 to £30,000.

The highest salary for a cellar technician is about £35,000.

You may be paid overtime for emergency call-out duties or for working evenings/weekends.

Related opportunities

- Bar Manager/Licensee/Publican p122
- Brewery Worker p203
- Plumber p100

Further information

Brewing, Food & Beverage Industry Suppliers Association
www.bfbi.org.uk

British Soft Drinks Association
www.britishsoftdrinks.com

People 1st
www.people1st.co.uk

CHEF/SOUS CHEF

Qualifications and courses

Academic qualifications are not essential to enter this profession as a trainee (commis) chef, although some employers prefer you to have a good general standard of education and possibly qualifications in hospitality or catering. Most training is on the job and you will be taught by an experienced chef whilst you work in the kitchen. It is possible to work your way up to chef level with enough experience.

There are a number of qualifications available that could give you an advantage, for example GCSEs in Hospitality and Catering, a City & Guilds Diploma in Professional Cookery (Levels 1–3) or an NVQ Diploma in Professional Cookery (Levels 2 and 3). Further qualifications are also available, including degrees, Foundation degrees and HNC/HNDs in Professional Culinary Arts and Culinary Arts Management.

Intermediate and advanced apprenticeships may be available.

Many employers will require you to have health and safety and/or food hygiene certificates so it would be useful to study for these while training as a chef.

What the work involves

Chefs and sous chefs cook for restaurants, cafés, bars, cruise ships and catering firms. Some also work for specialist food companies, helping to create new products. You will coordinate kitchen activities and supervise the preparation of food by your team of kitchen staff.

Commis chefs are trainee chefs. Sous chefs are second-in-command of the kitchen. They will be required to recruit and train kitchen staff.

Planning new menus and dishes, checking stocks of food and drink and dealing with suppliers are also included in the sous chef role.

Type of person suited to this work

Kitchens can be hot and hectic environments, therefore you need to be able to remain calm under pressure.

Good teamwork, communication and multi-tasking skills are important to ensure the smooth running of the operation. As you are responsible for the health and safety of your team, you must also be vigilant at all times.

You should have excellent cooking skills, be very creative and have a passion for food. This role would suit someone who is keen to try out new things and set trends. Good numeracy skills are also required to manage budgets and stock levels.

Working conditions

Most of your work will be in a kitchen which will be hot, busy and noisy. You will be required to use equipment that can be dangerous if not used correctly.

As you will be preparing food, you will need to wear protective clothing and pay attention to health and hygiene.

Hours are typically 40 per week in a shift pattern and include evenings and weekends. Part-time work can be found.

Future prospects

There is currently a shortage of qualified chefs in many areas of the UK.

Starting as a commis chef you will help in different sections of the kitchen. With experience you can progress to sous chef, where you act as deputy to the chef and manage your own section, and then to head chef.

Gaining significant experience may allow you to open your own business or even become a lecturer.

Advantages/disadvantages

Preparing high-quality food that your customers enjoy is very rewarding.

You will have the opportunity to combine creativity with practical skills.

You will work long, unsocial hours when you will be on your feet in a hot and busy environment.

Money guide

Salaries vary significantly depending upon the size, reputation and location of the restaurant, with the highest salaries in London and the south-east of England.

A commis chef may earn around £13,000 per year.

Section chefs (chef de partie) earn £16,000 to £25,000 per year.

Sous chefs usually earn between £22,000 and £30,000 per year.

A head or executive chef could earn anything from £30,000 to in excess of £50,000, depending on their skills and the style of hotel or restaurant.

Related opportunities

- Catering/Restaurant Manager/Maître d'Hôtel p123
- Food Safety Officer p127
- Kitchen Assistant/Supervisor p133

Further information

Institute of Hospitality
www.instituteofhospitality.org

People 1st
www.people1st.co.uk

CONCIERGE

Qualifications and courses

There are no required academic qualifications for this profession, however useful qualifications may include the BTEC Award in Principles of Customer Service in Hospitality, Leisure, Travel and Tourism (Level 2) or an NVQ/SVQ in either Hospitality and Catering (Level 2) or Multi-skilled Hospitality Service (Level 2). The ability to speak a foreign language would also be very beneficial.

You will usually start in a front-of-house role, such as a porter, bellboy or receptionist, and progress to the role of concierge with experience. You could train in-house or through an Apprenticeship in Hospitality.

You will learn and train as you work. This may include gaining knowledge of the establishment's policies and techniques in waiting and room service. It is also important that you have good knowledge of the local area.

Previous work experience in reception is recommended, particularly when applying to 4 or 5 star hotels.

What the work involves

Concierges work as part of the front-of-house team in a hotel, apartment block or corporate organisation. You will be responsible for greeting guests, assisting with their baggage, answering questions, giving advice or directions and generally making them feel as comfortable as possible.

If you work in a hotel you must keep up to date with events and functions in the hotel and you may be asked to book tickets or organise travel for guests.

You may manage a team of other concierges, reception or door staff. Some organisations may require you to undertake extra services such as shopping and pet walking/sitting.

Type of person suited to this work

As you will be the first point of contact for guests and visitors to the establishment, you should look presentable, enjoy meeting new people and thrive in a busy environment.

You must be polite, friendly, helpful and informative at all times. You should have an interest in the catering and hospitality industry.

You need to have a practical approach to problem-solving and be able to remain calm. As you will be entrusted with important errands and messages, you must be responsible, reliable and trustworthy.

You should also have a certain level of strength and fitness to carry bags and work long shifts.

Working conditions

On average, you will work 40 hours a week. This will mainly be shifts of 12 hours and will include working at night, early mornings and weekends.

You may have a desk or an office where you will use the telephone or computer but you will spend the majority of your time on your feet in the reception area, meeting and helping guests or running errands within the establishment or around the local area. You may be required to lift heavy bags.

Your employer will usually provide you with a uniform.

Future prospects

The hospitality industry has had only very small growth in recent years, which could affect the number of positions available. Despite this, the British Hospitality Association (BHA) reports a favourable contrast between unemployment figures and job creation in the hospitality industry.

Establishments may have formal progression routes that could involve moving up from a position as a porter to deputy head concierge, head concierge and then up again to front office management positions.

You could transfer to another discipline within hospitality or even set up your own business.

There are international opportunities within certain establishments so you may be able to live abroad.

Advantages/disadvantages

You will have the opportunity to meet a variety of new people from different countries each day.

You will be responsible for a wide variety of guests or visitors and their requirements.

You may have to work long and unsociable hours.

Money guide

Your starting salary as a concierge can be around £12,000 per year. As you gain experience you can earn up to £20,000.

If you reach the position of head concierge in a 4 or 5 star establishment, you could achieve £25,000 or more.

Salaries can be boosted by tips, although if you are required to live in the hotel your salary may be reduced to cover accommodation and food costs.

Related opportunities

- Customer Services Assistant/Manager p468
- Personal Assistant p43
- Receptionist p46

Further information

British Hospitality Association
www.bha.org.uk

Hospitality Guild
www.hospitalityguild.co.uk

Institute of Hospitality
www.instituteofhospitality.org

People 1st
www.people1st.co.uk

FOOD SAFETY OFFICER

ENTRY LEVEL 6

Qualifications and courses

In England, Wales and Northern Ireland most entrants train as an environmental health officer before they specialise in a career path such as food safety officer.

An undergraduate or postgraduate degree in environmental health/science which has been accredited by the Chartered Institute of Environmental Health (CIEH) in England, Wales and Northern Ireland, or the Royal Environmental Health Institute of Scotland (REHIS) in Scotland is the most common gateway to a career in environment health, and then food safety.

Entry to a degree normally requires 2 A levels/3 H grades including a science subject, plus 5 GCSEs/National 5s (A*–C/A–C) including English, Maths and a science. Entry to a Master of Science (MSc) requires a degree in a relevant science or technology subject.

Before qualifying as an environmental health officer, graduates must complete an Experiential Learning Portfolio (ELP) by undergoing a period of work-based learning through a placement with an approved organisation and by passing professional exams.

CIEH also offers a wide range of food safety qualifications at Levels 1–4 which may be useful. These awards cover food safety issues within catering, manufacturing and retail.

Food safety officers in Scotland must meet the requirements of the Scottish Food Safety Officers' Registration Board. Candidates for the Higher Certificates in Food Premises Inspection and Food Standards Inspection must have a minimum of an HND in Food Science or Food Technology. Candidates undertake 6 months' structured practical training with a local authority and complete written assessments.

What the work involves

You will advise those working in catering/food premises by providing information on the safe presentation, preparation and storage of food for public consumption.

Your role will be to investigate outbreaks of food-related illnesses and implement hazard warnings in places such as butchers, retailers and restaurants.

You will enforce accurate food labelling. You will also advise schools and businesses on food regulations as well as nutritional awareness.

Type of person suited to this work

You need excellent communication skills as you will be advising and educating people on food safety and nutrition. You should be able to explain technical information in a simple and clear way. You must also be tactful when investigating food poisoning and other hazardous issues.

It's important to be analytical and methodical in your work. Good attention to detail is essential. You need to be able to juggle many different jobs at once and be a confident decision maker.

Working conditions

Although you will be office based, most of your time will involve travelling to businesses, following up complaints and giving advice. A driving licence is essential.

The places you investigate may be smelly and unpleasant at times. You will need to wear protective clothing such as masks, hair protection and boots. You will work normal office hours, but some evenings and weekends may be required.

Future prospects

You may be employed by a local authority or by a food company.

Outside of Scotland, most food safety officers begin as environmental health officers and specialise later. In Scotland, inspection and food hygiene is undertaken by registered food safety officers.

With experience you can progress to senior positions within food safety or return to other areas of environmental health. You could also set up your own consultancy.

Advantages/disadvantages

This job offers flexibility (with opportunities available for part-time work or job shares) and variety (as you will be visiting a range of different premises).

You have a chance to make a difference to public health.

Investigations can occasionally be stressful if you have to enforce regulations or close down a business.

You will sometimes have to visit dirty or unpleasant establishments.

Money guide

Starting salaries for environmental technicians are usually £17,500 to £22,000 per year.

Fully qualified officers can earn from £25,000 to £35,000. Food safety officers employed at a senior or managerial level can achieve up to £45,000.

Those employed by private companies earn more than workers in the public sector.

Related opportunities

- Environmental Health Practitioner/Officer p22
- Health and Safety Adviser p27
- Meat Hygiene Inspector p474

Further information

Chartered Institute of Environmental Health
www.cieh.org

Royal Environmental Health Institute of Scotland
www.rehis.com

HOTEL MANAGER

Qualifications and courses

No specific academic qualifications are required as it is possible to enter the industry at a lower level and work your way up. However it is possible to enter as a management trainee if you have a relevant degree or HNC/HND qualification. Relevant subjects include hotel and hospitality management, business with languages, and travel, tourism or leisure studies.

Knowledge of a foreign language could be useful. If you are entering as a graduate you should have some prior work experience as well as your degree. Experience in a hotel is desirable; however other customer-oriented work such as bartending or retail work would also be considered highly relevant.

School leavers could apply for an Advanced Apprenticeship in Hospitality Catering, which involves on-the-job training and the opportunity to study for relevant NVQs.

Existing employees, graduates or those with previous hotel experience may be eligible for one of the fast-track training schemes offered by some of the larger hotel companies.

The Institute of Hospitality provides a range of qualifications for those pursuing a management or leadership role within the hospitality industry.

What the work involves

You will manage the services and staff of your hotel, ensuring that it is a successful business and gains new customers to make a profit.

You will be responsible for checking that the buildings and grounds of your hotel meet health and safety regulations and other professional standards.

Your work could involve promoting and developing the hotel to increase numbers of customers. You could work in all types of hotel, from a small private one up to large national or international chains.

Type of person suited to this work

As you will manage budgets and cash flow, you will need a good level of numeracy and the confidence to handle large amounts of money. Communication skills are very important as you will be organising staff and dealing with guests. You will be working in a sociable and busy environment, so you will need to enjoy meeting lots of different people.

You should be well organised and able to meet targets. Strong customer service and good business skills are essential, as is flexibility, as you will be working long and unsocial hours.

An interest in local tourism may also be useful.

Working conditions

This work involves working long hours that include evenings and weekends. You might spend some of your evenings living-in so you can be on-site in case of emergencies. You are also likely to work shifts.

Some members of the public can be rude and aggressive so you will need to maintain a calm professional manner at all times.

You will need to have a smart appearance and you might have to wear a uniform.

Future prospects

The workforce in the hotel industry is often young and there is a high staff turnover. Depending on the size of the hotel and job performance, graduate trainees could progress from assistant managerial roles to deputy or head of department roles within 2 years, and then to general manager within a further 5 or 6 years.

With experience, you could work overseas, open your own hotel or progress from hotel management into other areas of a company such as human resources, finance and IT.

Advantages/disadvantages

There are opportunities to travel and work overseas.

You can progress to be a manager of a large hotel relatively quickly.

As you are responsible for the welfare and happiness of the guests, there will be a lot of pressure and demands.

Money guide

Salaries will depend on the size, reputation and location of the hotel in which you work.

Assistant or trainee managers can earn £19,000 per year.

Managers of small hotels or deputy managers of large hotels could earn £21,000 to £40,000.

Senior and general managers can earn in excess of £60,000 and salaries for those employed in large, global hotels can be considerably higher.

Benefits can include pension schemes, healthcare, live-in accommodation and discounts on staying in other hotels. If the manager is required to live at the hotel, the salary could be reduced to cover accommodation and food costs.

Related opportunities

- Bar Manager/Licensee/Publican p122
- Holiday Representative p368
- Housekeeper/Accommodation Manager p132

Further information

British Hospitality Association
www.bha.org.uk

Hospitality Guild
www.hospitalityguild.co.uk

Institute of Hospitality
www.instituteofhospitality.org

Springboard UK
www.springboard.uk.net

HOTEL PORTER

Qualifications and courses

There are no minimum entry requirements for this job but some employers prefer individuals with a good general education. Good English and maths and basic IT skills are preferred and previous experience in a customer service field may also be required.

You may be able to enter this profession through an Apprenticeship in Hospitality and Catering. Professional qualifications, such as the City & Guilds Level 2 Award in Introduction to Employment in the Hospitality Industry, may be an advantage.

Many hotels will provide training to new staff, whether or not they have previous experience. This is usually gained over a period of several weeks or longer, under the supervision of a more experienced member of staff. As you are required to lift and carry luggage, some of the training may be concerned with health and safety and risk assessment for manual handling.

What the work involves

As a porter, you will greet hotel guests and offer directions in and around the hotel premises, answer the phone, take reservations, arrange transport and deal with general enquiries.

You will also be responsible for moving guests' luggage to and from rooms.

If you work as a night porter, you will look after the security and safety of the hotel site.

As a head porter in a large hotel, you will be responsible for a team of porters that will include night, conference and kitchen porters.

Type of person suited to this work

This is primarily a customer-facing role and you will need excellent customer service skills, a smart appearance and extensive knowledge of the local area.

Strong communication skills and the ability to work as part of a team are highly sought after and, as you may be asked to undertake duties at short notice, you will need a flexible, punctual and enthusiastic attitude.

You must be fit and active as you will do a lot of lifting and carrying.

Being responsible for the security of the hotel site and guests' belongings means that you must be honest, reliable and aware of security issues.

Working conditions

The work can be physically demanding as you will spend a lot of time on your feet and lifting luggage. You will primarily be based inside the hotel but you may be required to greet guests outside in all weather conditions.

You may work shifts or standard hours. If you work as a night porter your working hours may affect your personal life. If you live in the hotel you might be on-call.

You might have to wear a uniform which should be provided by your employer.

Future prospects

You can work in hotels all over the country and possibly abroad. Part-time and seasonal work is also available.

Smaller hotels tend to employ one porter so you would need to move to larger hotels if you want to progress. For this reason, willingness to be geographically mobile could be helpful.

In larger companies, you could work towards a job as a head porter or a reception-based role.

Advantages/disadvantages

In some hotels you would be required to live on-site.

If you find a seasonal position this job can fit around educational commitments but some hotels prefer to employ mature individuals.

You will have the opportunity to meet and help many different people so your work will be rewarding and interesting.

Money guide

Salary levels vary according to the type of hotel you work for and geographical location.

Starting salaries are around £12,000 per year.

As you gain experience, your annual earnings can increase to about £16,000.

Head porters in large hotels can earn in excess of £18,000.

Shift allowances, overtime work and tips from guests can all increase your earnings. Salaries may be reduced if the porter is living in the hotel. Benefits can include staff meals and free or discounted use of hotel facilities.

Related opportunities

- Concierge p126
- Hotel/Accommodation Room Attendant p131
- Receptionist p46

Further information

Hospitality Guild
www.hospitalityguild.co.uk

Institute of Hospitality
www.instituteofhospitality.org

People 1st
www.people1st.co.uk

Qualifications and courses

There are no minimum entry requirements, although employers may ask for GCSEs/National 5s (A*–C/A–C), including English and Maths. They will usually also want to see evidence of communication skills so having some office or customer service work experience would be helpful for this career.

The Intermediate Apprenticeship in Hospitality would also be useful for those seeking a reception role and candidates keen to progress to head of reception could take the Advanced Apprenticeship.

There are various qualifications available that might help your employment prospects and give you more insight into the industry. These include the City & Guilds Level 1 NVQ Certificate in Hospitality Services (7131-04), the Level 2 NVQ Diploma in Front of House Reception (7132-01) and the Level 3 Award in Hospitality Supervision and Leadership Principles (7108-12).

Further training is usually provided by the employer and new entrants often work under the supervision of more experienced reception staff.

What the work involves

You will be responsible for welcoming guests to the hotel, checking them in and out, managing any requests and allocating them a room. You will also prepare guests' bills, take payments and handle foreign exchange. You will answer the telephone, take messages and bookings and inform guests about the local area.

Hotel receptionists work closely with other members of staff to ensure the smooth running of the hotel. In a large hotel you might work within a team of receptionists whereas in a small hotel you may work alone and have extra duties including housekeeping and waitressing.

Type of person suited to this work

You should be a friendly, welcoming and well-presented person as you will be the first point of contact for hotel guests.

Good communication skills are essential as you will be interacting with all types of people and a polite telephone manner will be necessary when making calls and taking messages.

You will be very busy at times but will have to stay calm and polite even under pressure, making sure that each guest gets the service they expect.

It would be helpful to be knowledgeable about the local area and the hotel. Being able to speak a foreign language would also be desirable, as you might have foreign guests staying at the hotel or you may want to work overseas.

Working conditions

Hotels are open 24/7 so you will probably do shift work to ensure the reception desk is manned at all times. There are opportunities to work part time or seasonally.

You will work behind the reception desk the majority of the time, where you will have access to a computer and a telephone. You might be provided with a uniform.

Future prospects

The tourism industry has had only slight growth in recent years and job opportunities may be affected. While vacancies are available throughout the UK, the majority of hotels are in the south-east of England, Scotland and the west country.

As a hotel receptionist you could progress to being a supervisor or manager of a team of receptionists, or move to a different area of the hotel industry, such as event organisation.

Your transferable skills would enable you to work as a receptionist in other sectors.

Advantages/disadvantages

You will be responsible for dealing with complaints and disturbances which could be stressful or frustrating.

This is a varied and active role which will suit those who like to keep busy and meet new people.

You could have the opportunity to work in hotels overseas.

Money guide

Your salary may depend on the location and size of the hotel you work for.

Starting salaries range from £12,000 to £14,500 per year.

Senior receptionists or those in supervisory roles can achieve £15,000 to £18,000. As front desk manager, you can expect to earn up to £23,000 a year.

Additional benefits may include meals and accommodation. Overtime pay and allowances for working unsociable hours may be available.

Related opportunities

- Personal Assistant p43
- Secretary p51
- Travel Agent p379

Further information

Hospitality Guild
www.hospitalityguild.co.uk

Institute of Hospitality
www.instituteofhospitality.org

People 1st
www.people1st.co.uk

HOTEL/ACCOMMODATION ROOM ATTENDANT

Qualifications and courses

There are no minimum entry requirements for this job. Employers are more concerned with hiring people who are honest, reliable and hardworking. Some relevant cleaning experience could be useful but is not essential.

The intermediate level Apprenticeship in Hospitality could provide a route into this line of work.

While not required, there are pre-entry qualifications available that could be helpful. City & Guilds run an Entry Level Award and a Level 1 Certificate in Introduction to the Hospitality Industry (7107). Edexcel offer a Diploma in Hospitality and there is an NVQ/SVQ Level 2 in Hospitality and Catering also available.

Once you find a position as a room attendant you will receive on-the-job training, usually under the supervision of a more experienced member of staff. This could include aspects such as safe lifting methods and furniture and carpet cleaning.

What the work involves

You will clean, tidy and prepare guest rooms to a high standard. This could include cleaning bathroom and toilet areas and other parts of the hotel.

Work involves stocking up levels of supplies as they are used and keeping records of any items of lost property left in rooms.

Using a trolley or cart, you will move supplies of linen, towels and other items around the hotel. You will also check for maintenance problems or damage to hotel property.

Type of person suited to this work

As much of the work involves cleaning areas of the site and moving supplies around, you will need a good level of physical fitness.

You must be well organised, enthusiastic and able to work quickly to get all your tasks completed on time. In order to keep up standards of cleanliness, you need a good eye for detail.

A polite and friendly manner when liaising with guests is essential. As you will be cleaning areas around guests' personal belongings, it is important to respect their privacy.

Working conditions

This is physical work so expect to be on your feet for much of the time, using cleaning equipment and pushing a cart from room to room.

You will be working with cleaning fluids and other cleaning equipment on a daily basis which could affect those with skin problems.

You will probably work shifts and may need to work early mornings, late at night and at weekends.

Future prospects

You could work in a hotel, bed and breakfast or leisure facility. Larger employers provide staff with good training and development support.

You may have opportunities to work abroad for an international hotel or in a resort.

With experience, you could go on to work as an accommodation manager or housekeeper and have responsibility for other staff.

Advantages/disadvantages

Some employers allow you to live on-site and will provide your meals.

There are opportunities to gain seasonal/holiday work and this type of job is available on a part-time basis.

The work is quite physically demanding and involves bending, stretching and some heavy lifting.

During busy periods when many guests are staying at the hotel, you will have to work efficiently to meet tight deadlines.

Money guide

Earnings vary according to employer and location.

Many room attendants receive an hourly rate which can start at National Minimum Wage. For those earning an annual salary, £11,000–£15,000 is likely.

Guests often leave tips for room attendants. Overtime work or shift allowances could also increase earnings.

Related opportunities

- Cleaner p448
- Hotel Manager p128
- Hotel Porter p129

Further information

Institute of Hospitality
www.instituteofhospitality.org

People 1st
www.people1st.co.uk

HOUSEKEEPER/ACCOMMODATION MANAGER

Qualifications and courses

It is possible to enter this career without academic qualifications by working your way up from a room attendant position. Employers will want to see evidence that you are organised and have good customer service skills.

Any professional qualifications you have gained while working at a lower level can also help you achieve promotion to manager. You can study for qualifications through the Institute of Hospitality. There are also various City & Guilds awards and NVQs available such as the Level 1 Award in Introduction to Employment in the Hospitality Industry (7040) and the Level 2 Award in Principles of Customer Service in Hospitality, Leisure, Travel and Tourism (4421).

HNCs/HNDs, Foundation degrees or degrees in subjects such as hospitality or hotel management can be useful. Large hotels sometimes run management training schemes, for which you will need a degree.

Previous work experience, perhaps from part-time or holiday work, is preferred for entry, as is supervisory experience. Intermediate or Advanced Apprenticeships in Hospitality can also be a good entry route.

What the work involves

You will be in charge of a team of cleaners and will ensure that all rooms on your premises are clean, tidy and hospitable.

You may work in hotels, conference centres, private households, hospitals, care homes and university halls of residence.

You will manage a housekeeping budget, recruit and train staff, and organise work rotas and duties.

On a day-to-day basis you will inspect rooms, take care of repairs, and ensure linens, soaps, towels and other necessities are always in stock.

You will also be responsible for sorting out lost property and filing maintenance reports.

Type of person suited to this work

As you will be in charge of a team, good organisational, delegation and management skills are essential, as is the ability to motivate and encourage staff. You should be capable of managing budgets and solving problems.

Strong verbal communication skills are important as you will interact with both customers and staff.

Working conditions

Although you will have an office, you will be on your feet for the majority of the time.

Some establishments will require you to live on-site and you might have to work shifts or unsocial hours.

Future prospects

There is scope to develop a career in management in this area but you have to work your way from junior or deputy housekeeper to senior housekeeper.

In larger hotels, you could progress to a role in head office, in areas such as human resources or training. There are also opportunities in facilities management.

International companies could provide the opportunity to work overseas.

With enough experience, you could go on to own and run your own cleaning service company or even your own hotel.

Advantages/disadvantages

Larger hotel and leisure companies often provide staff with leisure and restaurant discounts.

You will be responsible for generating customer satisfaction which can be very rewarding.

Depending on the size and location of the establishment, the work may be seasonal.

Money guide

Salaries vary significantly depending on the size, reputation and location of the establishment.

A graduate trainee accommodation manager will start on £16,000 to £25,000 per year.

Senior housekeepers can expect to earn £22,000 to £40,000 or more.

If accommodation is provided, salaries might be reduced to cover rent and living expenses. Benefits can include pensions and free or discounted accommodation or meals.

Related opportunities

- Cleaner p448
- Hotel Porter p129
- Hotel/Accommodation Room Attendant p131

Further information

Hospitality Guild
www.hospitalityguild.co.uk

Institute of Hospitality
www.instituteofhospitality.org

People 1st
www.people1st.co.uk

Springboard UK
www.springboard.uk.net

Qualifications and courses

Kitchen assistant

There are no minimum qualifications but a good general secondary education and previous catering or kitchen experience are helpful. Most employers provide on-the-job training.

Qualifications such as a GCSE/National 5 in Food Technology, the City & Guilds Level 1 Certificate in Food Preparation and Cooking (8065-01) and City & Guilds Level 2 Food & Beverage Service (8066-02) are useful. In Scotland the SQA National Qualification in Health and Food Technology is available. There may also be apprenticeships in hospitality and catering available in your area.

Kitchen supervisor

To become a supervisor you will ideally have health and safety or food hygiene qualifications and previous experience working in a kitchen, possibly as a kitchen assistant or commis chef. Management experience also helps.

Sometimes employers will ask for Level 2 qualifications, such as the City & Guilds Diploma in Professional Cookery (7100), an NVQ in Kitchen Services or even the City & Guilds level 3 Diploma in Hospitality Supervision and Leadership. HNC/HND and degree qualifications in hospitality will also increase your chances of getting a job.

What the work involves

Kitchen assistant

You will keep the kitchen clean, wash up equipment, peel and chop fruits, vegetables and meat and check on stock levels. You will also prepare quick, simple dishes.

Kitchen supervisor

Kitchen supervisors are experienced, trained chefs who oversee the running of a kitchen and hire, train and manage all kitchen staff.

You will plan menus, order ingredients, oversee food preparation, presentation and quality control and contact suppliers to place orders and negotiate prices.

Type of person suited to this work

Kitchen assistants need to be on time for work, able to follow directions and to work efficiently at a fast pace.

As a supervisor you need to be assertive, patient and composed as you will have to delegate tasks, resolve disputes, negotiate prices, keep records and stay in control of a team.

Both roles will require employees to have good teamwork, communication and multi-tasking skills and to adhere to and impose strict health and safety procedures and hygiene standards.

Working conditions

Most kitchen assistants work part time on a shift system including split shifts and overtime. Supervisors generally work a 40-hour week. All kitchen staff should be prepared to work holidays and weekends.

Kitchens can be noisy, hot and cramped places to work. You will need to wear protective clothing to ensure food is not contaminated.

While both kitchen assistants and supervisors will spend most of their time standing and lifting heavy items, supervisors will also have a small office in which they organise their paperwork.

Future prospects

Kitchen workers are constantly in demand. You may work in a wide range of settings from restaurants, bars and hotels to hospitals, schools or the armed forces.

Kitchen assistant

You may progress to an assistant chef position or move into food service or bar work.

Kitchen supervisor

You may be promoted to general manager. You may also choose to set up your own independent restaurant or catering company.

Advantages/disadvantages

Working with a team in a fast-paced kitchen can be fun and exciting.

You may need to work long shifts at unsocial times.

The work can be stressful and physically demanding.

Money guide

Kitchen assistant

Salaries start at £11,500 to £12,500 per year which can increase to £15,000 with experience.

Kitchen supervisor

Kitchen supervisors can earn £16,000 to £35,000 with salaries varying depending on the type, size and geographical location of an establishment.

Related opportunities

- Catering/Restaurant Manager/Maître d'Hôtel p123
- Chef/Sous Chef p125
- Waiting Staff p134

Further information

Hospitality Guild
www.hospitalityguild.co.uk

Institute of Hospitality
www.instituteofhospitality.org

Qualifications and courses

Waiter/waitress

No minimum qualifications are required, however communication and numeracy skills are important and some previous experience is often preferred. School leavers could apply for an Intermediate Apprenticeship in Hospitality and Catering.

While looking for work you could study for qualifications such as an NVQ/SVQ Level 2 Diploma in Hospitality and Catering or the City & Guilds Level 1 and 2 Certificate/Diploma in Professional Food and Beverage Service (7103). These are not essential but could give you an advantage.

High profile restaurants, those with Michelin stars for example, may require staff with experience in fine dining and silver service. The Academy of Food and Wine Service provides short courses such as the Licence to Work in Banqueting Service.

Butler

Qualifications in general hospitality and catering are not required but are well regarded. These may include an NVQ Level 2 in Food and Beverage Service or Level 3 in Hospitality Supervision and Leadership. The City & Guilds Level 3 Diploma for Butlers (7105-02) would also be a useful qualification.

Significant hospitality experience is essential. This could be from working as a housekeeper, footman or under-butler, or you could transfer from a hotel or catering background.

Some large institutions such as hotel chains provide formal training and there are private butler training schools, although these are expensive. You will probably need a driving licence and a second language may be useful.

Sommelier

There are no minimum qualifications required, however relevant experience working in a bar or restaurant is desirable and fluency in a foreign language, especially French, is useful.

The Wine & Spirit Education Trust (WSET) offers qualifications in wines, spirits and wine service ranging from Level 1 Awards up to a Level 5 Honours Diploma. Employers may require you to have completed some of these courses.

The Academy of Food and Wine Service offers specialist training sessions in this sector, including the one-day Licence to Work in Wine Service course.

School leavers have the option of entering through an Apprenticeship in Hospitality and Catering (Drinks Service Route).

What the work involves

Waiter/waitress

You will take food orders from customers and provide meals through table or counter service. You will supply accurate bills for meals and take payment from customers. Before and during your shift you will probably have to keep the eating area clean and prepare tables for customers.

Butler

You will work in a private household where you will be responsible for arranging travel and security, providing and serving food and welcoming visitors. You will usually work within a wealthy household, including those of celebrities or royalty.

Sommelier

You will be responsible for the provision of wines or other alcoholic beverages such as spirits. You will be expected to attend tastings and to design a wine list or cocktail menu. It is important to understand how beverages complement food in order to aid customer selection. You will need to serve beverages correctly at the expected temperature.

Type of person suited to this work

Waiter/waitress

As you will be working with the public, you should possess a polite attitude, a neat appearance and good customer service skills. You may have to explain parts of the menu to customers so an interest in food and drink is useful.

You will need a good memory and communication skills to take food orders correctly from customers and pass them on to kitchen staff. You should be happy to work as part of a team.

The ability to work with numbers and deal with cash is important. You must work to a high standard of health and hygiene at all times.

Butler

In addition to the above skills, you should be impeccably presented, honest and reliable. Your employers will expect you to be dedicated, loyal and discreet as you will be responsible for their day-to-day security, their home and their personal affairs.

Sommelier

It is essential that you are enthusiastic about wines and have an interest in food. You should understand tasting notes, have a good palate and demonstrate a thorough knowledge of wines and beverages from all over the world.

Working conditions

Waiter/waitress

This role involves shift work and you will have to work unsocial hours including evenings and weekends. It is essential to have lots of energy as you will be on your feet most of the time, carrying heavy plates and dishes.

Most waiting staff serve a number of tables at once and have to remember different customer requests. It is important to have the ability to remain calm in the face of customer complaints.

You will be required to wear a uniform and may be exposed to a hot, noisy kitchen environment. You will be expected to work to a high standard of cleanliness at all times.

Butler

You will probably work within luxurious surroundings in the UK or abroad and will normally live-in and have your own quarters.

You may be required to care for the home whilst your employer is away and you may also escort them overseas.

Sommelier

You will probably wear a uniform and work shifts, including weekends and evenings, until the early hours of the morning.

You will spend most of your time front of house and should be energetic and have high hygiene standards.

You may have the opportunity to travel domestically and internationally to attend tastings.

Future prospects

Waiter/waitress

The hospitality industry in the UK has had only slight growth in the past few years so vacancies may be affected, particularly at entry level. Opportunities to work abroad are available.

If you do not already have them you may be encouraged to take Level 2 or 3 qualifications, such as the City & Guilds Level 3 Certificate in Food and Beverage Service Supervision. You may also receive training in food safety and food hygiene.

Once you gain experience, you could become junior or head waiter. Larger employers such as hotel chains increasingly provide formal training and support for staff and may allow inter-departmental movements, such as to stock control or purchasing. You could also move into more specialist posts like sommelier.

Butler

The popularity of _Downton Abbey_ has caused the demand for butlers to more than double in the past few years and the International Guild of Professional Butlers estimates that there are now a few million members of the profession in the world today. English butlers are particularly in vogue among foreign employers, for example in the United Arab Emirates.

Although, historically, this has been a largely male profession, positions for women are on the rise.

You are more likely to get a job if you are willing to be flexible and take on other responsibilities, such as those of a personal assistant or providing some childcare services. Many catering firms have butler services and there is demand from contract caterers, hotels and financial institutions.

Many of the jobs are overseas and the most successful butlers are willing to be geographically mobile.

Sommelier

There are opportunities to work in a variety of outlets in the UK and abroad. Traditionally a man's profession, an increasing number of women are now becoming sommeliers.

With experience it is possible to progress to a higher managerial position in the hospitality industry, start your own business in the wine sector or become a wine taster or manager for an importer or manufacturer. Qualifications from the Court of Master Sommeliers or the Institute of Masters of Wine may increase promotion prospects.

Advantages/disadvantages

Waiter/waitress

Catering staff are often provided with uniforms, free meals and accommodation.

The role can be physically draining.

Butler

Your job could include lots of travelling and the opportunity to live in the luxurious homes of the rich and famous.

This job can affect your personal life as it is difficult to be off-duty.

Sommelier

You may have the opportunity to travel within the UK and abroad.

Working long and unsociable hours can affect your personal life.

Money guide

Waiter/waitress

Salaries will depend on the location, size and reputation of your employer.

Salaries start at £12,000 to £16,000 for full-time work.

With experience and extra responsibilities you can earn £17,000–£20,000 per year.

Your income can be supplemented by tips from customers. Benefits include free meals while on duty.

Butler

Your salary will depend on your experience and your employer.

Starting salaries are between £15,000 and £20,000.

This will increase as you gain experience and the most successful butlers working in the private sector can receive £25,000 to £50,000 or more.

You may also be provided with free accommodation or a car.

Sommelier

Salaries will depend on the location, size and reputation of the organisation you work for.

A trainee can expect around £13,000 per year.

Salaries increase to £30,000 as you gain experience.

A head sommelier could earn £45,000 or more.

Benefits may include tips, bonuses, free meals and accommodation.

Related opportunities

- Concierge p126
- Cruise Ship Steward/Purser p589
- Housekeeper/Accommodation Manager p132
- Kitchen Assistant/Supervisor p133

Further information

Institute of Hospitality
www.instituteofhospitality.org

Springboard UK
www.springboard.uk.net

Wine & Spirit Education Trust
www.wsetglobal.com

Computers and IT

This sector is still fairly new and so it is expanding all the time, creating new jobs for a whole range of people. You may have a mathematical brain or a real creative ability – or a bit of both! Essentially, you must be passionate about computers to consider working in this sector. You need to keep right up to date with the latest technologies and IT developments as well as people's tastes, interests and hobbies to enjoy working in this industry. The jobs featured in this section are listed below. For similar jobs to the ones found in this section have a look at *Administration, Business, Office Work and Financial Services* on page 1 and *Retail, Sales and Customer Services* starting on page 461.

BUSINESS ANALYST

Qualifications and courses

Most entrants have a degree, Foundation degree or HNC/HND in a relevant subject, such as software engineering, business studies, IT or computer science. Entry for degrees usually requires 2 A levels/3 H grades and 5 GCSEs/National 5s (A*–C/A–C). For Foundation degrees or HNCs/HNDs, 1 A level/2 H grades and 3 GCSEs/National 5s (A*–C/A–C) are necessary. Maths might be a required subject. Degree courses usually last 3 to 4 years or 4 to 5 years for sandwich courses. Although not essential, a postgraduate qualification may be advantageous.

BTEC Level 3 qualifications in an IT or business-related subject could also be helpful. The Chartered Institute for IT (BCS) offers business analysis certifications at various levels. There are also specialist training centres, such as Business Analyst Solutions, that provide short courses in a variety of business analysis certifications as well.

A sponsored degree in Information Technology Management for Business (ITMB) accredited by the Tech Partnership is available. This is focused on learning through project work in teams with external mentors from sponsoring organisations such as BT, John Lewis, IBM, Deloitte, Citibank and Asda. The opportunities to network with industry professionals could be invaluable when pursuing a graduate career.

There may be relevant apprenticeships available as a funded route and these can lead on to a full Honours degree in addition to vocational, technical and Key Skills qualifications and work experience.

Business analysts are required to undertake continuing professional development (CPD) in order to keep up to date with industry developments.

What the work involves

You will be responsible for inspecting businesses, to see if there are any improvements to be made or current problems that can be solved using information technology. Your aim is to generate higher efficiency and profits for the company.

You will work with managers in order to learn more about the organisation structure and the technology it uses. You will map out a new business plan and train staff on how to implement it.

You will ensure that project deadlines and budgets are met on time.

Type of person suited to this work

Your understanding of how businesses work is the key to being a successful business analyst – you will be aware of the need to balance costs with solutions.

You will also need to be a good negotiator, able to influence managers who may not understand how the new solutions or products you are suggesting can benefit their businesses.

Excellent communication skills are crucial because you will need to put across your ideas in meetings and in written reports. You will also need a strong knowledge of what is

available in the technology market and how it works in order to develop project briefs.

Working conditions

You will work standard office hours, although work in the evenings and at weekends will be necessary when projects are near to completion. You will spend a lot of time working with other members of the project team.

It is likely that your job will also involve travelling to meet clients at all stages of the project.

Future prospects

There are vacancies in all areas of business including finance and retail. Employers also include specialist management consultancies, software houses and computer companies.

There is a growing market for business analysts with the right combination of skills and talents. Analysts with e-commerce technology skills and experience are in particular demand, due to the continued growth of internet use in business.

Progression is possible into senior analyst jobs and on to project management or consultancy work.

Advantages/disadvantages

You can get a real sense of satisfaction from producing successful solutions that transform a business.

There often has to be a trade-off between the solution you would like to recommend and the limitations set by your client's budget.

Entry to this profession can be quite competitive.

You will have the opportunity to meet a range of people and gain exposure to various business sectors.

Money guide

Starting salaries can range from £17,000 to £25,000.

Earnings rise to £30,000–£50,000 with experience.

Senior business analysts can make £50,000–£70,000 per year.

Salaries vary greatly depending on location and are highest in London. Additional benefits may include profit sharing, performance-related pay and a company car.

Related opportunities

- Software Developer/Programmer p150
- Systems Analyst p152
- Technical Sales Engineer p153

Further information

BCS, The Chartered Institute for IT
www.bcs.org

IT Management for Business degree
www.thetechpartnership.com/techfuture/degrees

The Tech Partnership
www.thetechpartnership.com

Qualifications and courses

Many employers will ask for a minimum of a degree and although entry into the industry is possible with a HND, many developers are graduates. A portfolio of game projects or designs is also beneficial although this is largely dependent on the kind of job you apply for; depending on either artistic or programming requirements. Relevant industry experience is a must and many people work initially as a tester of quality assurance in a games studio. The Chartered Institute for IT (BCS) offers the Professional Certification in Software Testing at Foundation, Intermediate, Practitioner or Higher level for quality assurance testers which may also help your application.

Useful degree subjects include computer games technology, computer arts or computer animation. The computer games industry is constantly developing, and as games grow closer to traditional cinema, developers may value knowledge of cinematography or a flair for storytelling. At least 2 A levels/3 H grades are required for entry to related degrees. A relevant postgraduate qualification may also prove advantageous in this increasingly competitive industry.

A funded route that may be on offer in your area is the Higher Apprenticeship in IT. This can lead on to a full Honours degree in addition to vocational, technical and Key Skills qualifications as well as much valued work experience. Apprenticeships in Quality Assurance and Games Production are also available. Training programmes are on offer for graduate entrants from any discipline.

What the work involves

Employers are specialised companies producing games for computers or games consoles such as Wii U, Xbox One or PS4.

Using storyboards and flowcharts, you will present your ideas for a new computer game to a panel for acceptance or rejection.

If it is accepted you will manage all aspects of the playing experience, from scripts to programming and from animation to sound effects and music.

You will work with a team of specialists, such as programmers and graphic artists, to produce a prototype. Once a computer games playtester has picked out any flaws and if the panel think it is a winner, it will go into full development by your team.

Type of person suited to this work

To be a top-class computer games designer you will need creativity and an ability to see how ideas fit together. You will also have a passion for and knowledge of the computer games market.

Your ideas need to be technically viable and cost effective, so you will need a broad understanding of computers and games consoles, multimedia and the internet.

You will need to be a team player to work with specialists such as graphic designers to make sure that their part of the project fits in with the final version of the game.

Working conditions

You will be mainly based in an office or studio working with other members of the games project team.

Although you will work Monday to Friday, you might need to work overtime in the evenings and at weekends to meet deadlines.

Future prospects

The revival of the Prototype Fund has encouraged growth in the UK video games industry and also created funding opportunities for training development talent in games and other creative industries through the Skills Investment Fund.

It is a popular career choice so entry is competitive. You will need talent and project/people management skills in order to be promoted from junior to designer and then to lead designer.

There may be opportunities to work abroad. Progression is possible into management or consultancy work.

Advantages/disadvantages

Games designers say it is enjoyable creating entertainment for a living, and there is the opportunity to be creative.

It is a young, vibrant business and the rewards can be high.

It can be tough when a game does not sell or receives poor reviews.

It is stressful producing a game for a timed release such as the Christmas market.

Money guide

£18,000 to £25,000 per year is the usual starting/training salary for designers with prior industry experience. For senior or lead designers this can then rise to between £30,000 and £50,000 with several years' experience.

Those in management or leadership roles can go on to earn up to, or in excess of, £70,000.

Additional benefits usually include profit sharing and performance-related pay or a bonus.

Related opportunities

- Interactive Media Designer p146
- Online/Web Content Manager p149
- Software Developer/Programmer p150

Further information

BCS, The Chartered Institute for IT
www.bcs.org

Learning and Performance Institute
www.learningandperformanceinstitute.com

COMPUTER GAMES TESTER

Qualifications and courses

There are no formal entry requirements for a career in computer games testing. Knowledge of, and keen passion for, computer games and the gaming industry is of most value when looking for work in this field.

The Chartered Institute for IT (BCS) offers a Certified Tester qualification at Foundation level, in collaboration with the International Software Testing Qualifications Board (ISTQB) for those involved or looking to get involved in software testing. There are also certificates at Intermediate and Higher level. No prior experience is required in order to undertake the Foundation level certificate. Candidates for the Intermediate level certificates will already hold 18 months' industry experience in a software testing role, and those for the Higher between 5 and 7 years'.

Knowledge of programming will be beneficial to a career in computer games testing. This could be gained through a bachelor's degree route, undertaking a degree in a relevant subject such as computer games development, computer games technology, computer science or 3D animation. Entry onto a degree is usually with 2 A Levels/3 H Grades and 5 GCSEs/National 5s (A*–C/A–C) and courses typically take 3–4 years to complete.

Alternatively, funded apprenticeship routes may be available, depending on geographical location. The Tech Partnership offers Tech Industry Gold apprenticeship and degree apprenticeship schemes in software development at Intermediate, Advanced and Higher levels (Levels 2–6). Apprenticeships take between 12 months and 2 years to complete, combining on-the-job experience with formal learning at a college or university (training provider). Entry to higher and degree apprenticeships is usually with 2 A Levels/3 H Grades and 5 GCSEs/National 5s (A*–C/A–C).

Demonstrable passion for the gaming industry will be beneficial when looking for employment. Undertaking independent projects in games design or development, building a portfolio of storyboarded game designs, maintaining industry knowledge through magazines and other news outlets and submitting your own articles and reviews to blogs or user-generated media outlets will be regarded favourably when applying for jobs.

What the work involves

Computer games testing is a form of quality assurance (QA) work. As a computer games tester you will undergo intensive playtesting of computer, console and mobile games in order to ensure that gameplay runs smoothly and to discover any programming faults and inconsistencies in the software before it goes into distribution.

You will be expected to present your findings as a detailed bug report and liaise with games design and development teams, advising on how to address and correct the faults that your testing has brought to light.

As the first user of a computer game, you may also be consulted to provide feedback on elements of design such as user interface, sound and accessibility.

Type of person suited to this work

You will need outstanding analytical and problem-solving skills and the determination to be able to thoroughly playtest very small fragments of gameplay.

You will need passion for and skill at playing computer games as well as a creative approach to testing.

You will need to be a good written and spoken communicator, able to convey details of faults in games software to developers.

Working conditions

Work is mostly office based and hours can be unsocial, requiring regular work during evenings and weekends and through public holidays.

Overtime may be a regular requirement, particularly at busy periods prior to a game's release.

Future prospects

Career progression may require you to move through a number of temporary positions at different developers, gaining employment through agencies and working on a relatively large number of projects before securing a long-term contract as an in-house games QA tester.

Nevertheless, clear lines for career development have been established and computer games testers may undertake work with a view to advancing a career in software QA, moving into testing lead roles then on to testing department management or direction. Alternatively, testers may look for progression into computer games design or development.

Advantages/disadvantages

There can be great job satisfaction in seeing the release of a computer game that you have worked on.

Job security may be missing in the early stages of a career in computer games testing.

Money guide

Entrants can expect to earn between £12,000 and £20,000 a year.

With experience you could progress to a testing lead role, earning between £25,000 and £30,000 a year.

Progression to more senior roles, such as games developer, can increase yearly earnings to between £30,000 and £50,000 a year.

Related opportunities

- Computer Games Designer p139
- Software Developer/Programmer p150

Further information

BCS, The Chartered Institute for IT
www.bcs.org

Creative Skillset
www.creativeskillset.org

COMPUTER HARDWARE ENGINEER

Qualifications and courses

Whilst it is possible to start at basic technical support level and work your way up, the majority of employers look for prospective employees to have a degree when recruiting for this position. The normal minimum entry requirements for degrees are 2 A levels/3 H grades and 5 GCSEs/National 5s (A*–C/A–C). Useful degree subjects include computer systems engineering or electronic engineering and for technical degrees A levels/H grades in Maths, technology or a science subject may be required.

You may choose to enter this career through an Apprenticeship in IT and Telecoms Professionals. Getting a City & Guilds Level 2 Diploma in Consumer Electrical and Electronic Product Servicing (2359) or equivalent could help get you a job as a technician. You could then look to build your qualifications while working.

Training programmes are on offer for graduate entrants from any discipline. Engineers must ensure their technical knowledge is always up to date by completing continuing professional development (CPD) courses. Once qualified, computer hardware engineers register with the Engineering Council as an incorporated engineer (IEng) or chartered engineer (CEng). Registration can aid career advancement and CPD, as it can expose you to networking, training and job opportunities.

What the work involves

You will be responsible for developing, installing and repairing computer hardware – the computer itself rather than the applications or software.

You will be designing computer components, including microchips and circuit boards, and testing these systems.

When repairing a fault or upgrading a machine you will open up the computer and use tools to install upgrades or replace faulty parts.

You may specialise in installing new computer systems and training the people who use them.

Type of person suited to this work

You will need both technical skills and practical ability. Building your own computer system and repairing friends' machines is something you will probably already be doing in your spare time.

You should be a good problem solver. You will need to be able to identify what is wrong and put it right within a strict deadline, especially as your customer may be losing money while you do the repair.

It is important to be inquisitive and adaptable as you will need to absorb new information quickly in order to carry out many repairs.

You should pay close attention to detail and be thorough and accurate in your work. Often working on your own, you will also need to be reliable and able to work unsupervised.

Working conditions

You might be based in a workshop or in an office, but many engineers travel to individual customers' premises or homes.

Computer hardware engineers are employed by computer manufacturers, computer service firms and by a range of large organisations such as banks, hospitals and universities.

You will work a 37 to 40 hour week, but as businesses generally need major work to be done in the evenings and at weekends, you will have to work shifts or be on a call-out rota.

Future prospects

The IT industry is constantly expanding and is therefore a stable area of work as computers require regular repair and upgrading to improve performance and/or capacity.

Promotion could be to team leader or supervisor and then on to senior engineer. Self-employment as a freelance/consultant engineer is possible.

Advantages/disadvantages

It is rewarding to get a computer up and running again.

Your customer may have a service agreement requiring you to put the problem right in a fixed period of time, which can be stressful.

Money guide

When you begin work as a computer hardware technician you can expect your starting/trainee salary to be around £18,000 per year.

This could then increase once you have experience to between £25,000 and £40,000.

Salaries can rise to between £40,000 and £50,000 at senior level.

Related opportunities

- Computer Support Technician/Helpdesk Adviser p142
- Software Developer/Programmer p150
- Software Engineer p151

Further information

The Tech Partnership
www.thetechpartnership.com

Tomorrow's Engineers
www.tomorrowsengineers.org.uk

COMPUTERS AND IT

COMPUTER SUPPORT TECHNICIAN/ HELPDESK ADVISER

Qualifications and courses

It is possible for school leavers to enter this profession via an Intermediate Apprenticeship for IT, Software, Web and Telecoms Professionals. Those with limited IT experience can also obtain qualifications in customer service and support from the Help Desk Institute (HDI). However, some employers may prefer you to have relevant qualifications, such as a BTEC Level 3 in IT, or a HNC/HND or degree in computing or a related subject. Applicants for degree programmes usually require at least 2 A levels/3 H grades or equivalent qualifications.

For computer support technicians, the Computer Technology Industry Association (CompTIA) provides the A+ Certification and the Service Desk Institute (SDI) also offers qualifications suitable for both entry level and experienced IT support workers.

Other acceptable entry qualifications include the City & Guilds Levels 1–4 Certificate/Diploma in ICT Professional Competence (4520), accredited by the Chartered Institute for IT (BCS). Levels 2–4 are the latest components for the IT, Software and Telecoms Apprenticeship Framework. BTECs are also available. There is also the OCR iPRO Certificate and Diploma in ICT Systems Support, and the Chartered Institute for IT offers various courses.

Microsoft, Linux, Unix, Oracle and Cisco offer certification courses in their own products, such as the Microsoft Certified Solutions Associate (MCSA) and the Microsoft Certified Solutions Expert (MCSE). These qualifications are the most broadly accepted technical certifications.

What the work involves

Computer helpdesk advisers answer telephone calls or emails from computer users who are having technical problems and will advise the customer on how to correct the fault.

A computer support technician will also try to solve customers' technical problems by phone or email, and will also go to the user's workstation to fix the problem if it is more complex. You might also install new systems and upgrades and train staff in their use.

Type of person suited to this work

You will need to be both technical and practical to resolve hardware or software problems.

You will also need to be a good communicator and be able to explain technical language to inexperienced users.

You need to cope well with stress and deadlines. You will be under pressure to get the problem sorted quickly so that staff can get back to work. A keenness to stay up to date is vital – you will be expected to be the expert.

Working conditions

You will probably be based in an office with a technical workshop attached.

You may have to work shifts to cover your employer's hours of operation, which may be 24/7, or to install or repair equipment outside office hours.

Computer helpdesk advisers are mostly employed by computer hardware and software manufacturers or internet service providers, who offer support to their customers. The main employers of computer support technicians are large organisations such as banks, retail chains and hospitals.

The employers of computer support technicians may have several sites you need to travel between, sometimes in different parts of the UK.

Future prospects

The number of technical support positions has reduced, due to the shift in IT companies offering remotely managed services and the recession. Similarly, employers sometimes source helpdesks outside the UK to reduce costs.

However, with experience and a good working reputation, promotion for a computer support technician could be to team leader, network manager/administrator or on to network development. You could also become self-employed. For a computer helpdesk adviser, promotion to supervisory and management work is possible.

Advantages/disadvantages

It is a rewarding experience to help people and solve problems.

The job can be stressful because customers might be angry and frustrated.

Money guide

Starting salaries can range from £16,000 to £23,000.

With experience this can rise to between £26,000 and £35,000 and those in managerial or supervisory roles can earn £30,000 to in excess of £40,000 a year.

Related opportunities

- Computer Hardware Engineer p141
- Network Manager p148
- Technical Sales Engineer p153

Further information

BCS, The Chartered Institute for IT
www.bcs.org

Learning and Performance Institute
www.learningandperformanceinstitute.com

The Tech Partnership
www.thetechpartnership.com

Qualifications and courses

Entrants to this work normally have a degree, Foundation degree or HNC/HND in a relevant subject, such as computer science, software engineering, operational research, e-commerce, technology or maths. The normal minimum entry requirements for degrees are 2 A levels/3 H grades and 5 GCSEs/National 5s (A*–C/A–C). For Foundation degrees or HNCs/HNDs you will need 1 A level/2 H grades and 3 GCSEs/National 5s (A*–C/A–C). For technical degrees, an A level/H grades in Maths or a science may be required. Other qualifications may be acceptable, such as BTEC Level 3 qualifications and NVQs/SVQs.

Entry without a degree may be possible if you have significant programming experience and knowledge. A funded route for school leavers is the Advanced Apprenticeship for IT, Software, Web and Telecoms Professionals. Entrants will receive practical and technical training in database administration and have the opportunity to work towards relevant qualifications.

Once employed, database managers may also take courses in particular operating systems/packages offered by the manufacturers.

Industry bodies also provide professional development awards. These include the e-skills UK Professional Programme, the BCS Certificate, Diploma and Professional Graduate Diploma, and the IMIS programmes.

Software development companies also offer database certification programmes, including the Microsoft Certified Database Administrator, the Oracle PL/SQL Developer, the Sybase Adaptive Enterprise Server, and the IBM Certified Database Administrator.

Database administrators also need to know structured query language (SQL) and database management systems (DBMS).

What the work involves

Your job is to ensure that databases are accurate, accessible and secure. A database will be used if a huge amount of information needs to be stored with the capacity to search and access specific parts of the data. For example, a hospital uses a database to manage information about its patients.

To keep the data secure you will back up the content regularly, train users and issue them with passwords.

You may also be responsible for setting up and testing a new database.

Type of person suited to this work

Databases function to provide people with the information they require to do their jobs, so you will need effective communication skills.

You should be a good negotiator. To train users to input or access a new or modified database you will need to be able to convince them that these changes will benefit them.

To set up or develop a database you will need to be very technical with a high level of programming knowledge. You will also need to be a good listener, able to find out what the database users want including the new design they wish to achieve.

Working conditions

The main employers of database administrators are large organisations, such as banks and retailers. You could also work for a specialist IT firm providing a complete database service to customers.

You will be based mainly in your own office although in some cases the work can be carried out at home or in a place of your choice using laptops and broadband wireless technology.

Your employer may have several sites you need to travel between, sometimes in different parts of the UK.

You may have to be on-call to deal with problems outside your normal working hours.

Future prospects

This is a growth area because increasing numbers of businesses are developing databases for their websites to allow customers to look at information about their goods online and then go on to buy them.

With experience, you could specialise in network development or move into consultancy work.

Advantages/disadvantages

If you are methodical and analytical you will enjoy the complex job of creating a new database.

It can be frustrating when database users cause problems by not keeping their information up to date or by leaving out vital parts.

The job can be flexible as there are often opportunities for freelance and part-time work, self-employment and working from home.

Money guide

Starting salaries for graduates in this field can be up to £25,000. As you gain experience, your earnings will increase up to £35,000 a year.

Those employed at a senior level can earn in excess of £45,000 per year.

Related opportunities

- IT Trainer p147
- Network Manager p148
- Software Developer/Programmer p150

Further information

BCS, The Chartered Institute for IT
www.bcs.org

The Tech Partnership
www.thetechpartnership.com

Qualifications and courses

Employers usually look for a higher education qualification, such as a Foundation degree, HND or degree. Relevant subjects include graphic design, IT, computer science, educational technology or multimedia design. Graduates can, however, be sourced from other academic backgrounds such as teaching or education. Entry onto a degree is usually with 2 A levels/3 H grades and 5 GCSEs/National 5s (A*–C/A–C).

Access to this career may be gained through an apprenticeship scheme, taking a software design or interactive media design route. Apprenticeships last between 12 months and 4 years and combine work with a structured training programme. College-based learning can be undertaken via day or block-release. The Tech Partnership has developed the accredited Tech Industry Gold apprenticeship in collaboration with a number of technology industry-leading recruiters such as IBM, BT and Visa.

Newly developed degree apprenticeships are being made available through the Tech Partnership. These apprenticeships will award you with a bachelor's degree on completion, and can facilitate entry to a variety of technology industry sectors.

Experience and qualifications in programming languages such as HTML5 and JavaScript may be useful. Training providers such as Media Training offer certificated courses in programming languages, some of which are approved by software developers. Some knowledge of Sharable Content Object Reference Model (SCORM) principles will be useful when looking for employment.

What the work involves

As an e-learning designer, you will be responsible for the design and development of innovative and engaging online training, course templates and content, widely known as virtual learning environments (VLEs).

Design work will incorporate mixed media such as text, graphics, video, animation and audio. Using a working knowledge of instructional design and development software tools and methodologies, you will storyline VLEs based on a client or end user's training requirements.

You will oversee the planning, coordination and execution of a VLE brief, and will be involved in the testing and integrating phases in addition to assisting with installation at the organisation's or client's site.

Type of person suited to this work

You will need outstanding creative vision and the ability to work dynamically with a variety of media in order to create engaging learning programmes.

Work will involve collaborating with a client or organisation to create a design brief based on end user training requirements and existing software or hardware limitations, therefore good problem-solving and communication skills will be essential.

Strong project management skills are a must, as you will be responsible for seeing your design briefs executed from conception, through development, to testing and installation.

Working conditions

You will typically work 35 to 40 hours a week, Monday to Friday. Extra hours may be necessary during busy periods such as when deadlines are near.

Your work will typically be office-based, however you may need to travel in order to attend meetings with clients or development teams.

Future prospects

This is a new and rapidly developing industry. You could work in-house for educational institutions such as universities, colleges or libraries; designing, implementing, testing and installing VLEs, then carrying out maintenance and administration as part of an IT support team.

Alternatively you could move into external consultancy, working for a private design firm or, with experience, self-employment, selling your design skills to other organisations.

There is scope for skills diversification into other, similar roles such as educational software design or interactive media design.

Advantages/disadvantages

You will have the opportunity to carry out design work in a growing industry, using cutting-edge technology and media.

There is a great sense of satisfaction on completing a project and seeing VLEs that you have designed being used by learners.

You may have to make trade-offs between design features and limitations in budget.

Money guide

Software or web developer apprentices undertaking Tech Industry Gold apprenticeships can earn a training salary from £18,000 and up a year.

Graduate entrants can expect a starting salary of between £19,000 and £25,000 a year.

With some experience salaries could increase to between £25,000 and £35,000 a year.

With several years' experience, after taking on team leadership or department management responsibilities, salaries can be in excess of £50,000 a year.

Related opportunities

- Interactive Media Designer p146
- Online/Web Content Manager p149
- Software Developer/Programmer p150

Further information

Advanced Distributed Learning
www.adlnet.gov

The Tech Partnership
www.thetechpartnership.com

Qualifications and courses

Most entrants will hold an Honours degree in a relevant subject such as IT, cyber security, network engineering or forensic computing, however candidates can be from a wide range of STEM backgrounds. Entry onto a degree is usually with 2 A levels/3 H grades and 5 GCSEs/National 5s (A*–C/A–C).

Graduate entry may be possible through a graduate scheme or programme, and may be available to graduates from any academic field. While postgraduate study is not an essential requirement, entrants may find their prospects improved after achieving an MSc in subjects such as cyber security or information security. Relevant MSc degrees are available from universities throughout the UK.

Entry without a degree is possible, but is becoming less common. You could hold a position in IT support such as helpdesk adviser or be employed as a database administrator before entering this profession. For support roles, the BTEC Level 3 in IT, and the City & Guilds Levels 1–4 Certificate/Diploma in ICT Professional Competence (4520), accredited by the Chartered Institute for IT (BCS), may be useful qualifications to hold. A funded route for school leavers is the Advanced Apprenticeship for IT, Software, Web and Telecoms Professionals. Entrants will receive practical and technical training in database administration and have the opportunity to work towards relevant qualifications. With several years' experience, this could facilitate progression to a role in information security.

As some roles, such as those in healthcare, government or law enforcement, will give you access to sensitive information, you may need security clearance and may be expected to undergo screening by the Disclosure and Barring Service (DBS).

What the work involves

You will assist in the planning, management and execution of vulnerability and risk assessment projects across an organisation's IT systems. This involves documenting weaknesses and recommending procedures to mitigate risks to the security of information or data, and investigating issues and breaches in security that may occur.

As part of your role you'll be responsible for keeping informed of new risks and developing IT security solutions, which you will analyse and potentially integrate into the digital framework of the organisation or client you work for.

You will develop a keen knowledge of best practice, industry standards and legislation in regard to storing, using and securing digital information, and will be the first point of contact when colleagues are making use of the organisation's digital resources.

Type of person suited to this work

You will need strong attention to detail with the analytical ability to spot trends in data and react swiftly and appropriately.

Strong problem-solving skills are a must, with the ability to pair the right technical solution with incidents such as security breaches.

You will have excellent research skills and should enjoy learning about new developments in IT and information security.

Working conditions

You will typically be working 35-40 hours per week, however extra hours may be necessary during periods of implementation, or when investigating breaches in security.

You may be employed on a call-out rota basis, working shifts across a 7-day week. Work is mostly office based, but you may need to travel in order to meet with clients. For this reason a valid driving licence will be helpful.

Depending on the sector you work in, you may be subject to non-disclosure agreements (NDAs), limiting what you can say about your role and your responsibilities to others.

Future prospects

You could work for large organisations such as betting agencies, government and military departments, or healthcare, educational and financial institutions.

Most roles are based in London and the south-east of England, however opportunities are available throughout the UK.

With experience you could move into a self-employed or consultancy role.

Advantages/disadvantages

This is a particularly well paid career path, with good opportunities for progression.

There may be trade-offs between the solutions you would like to recommend and the limitations set by an organisation's budget.

Money guide

Salaries vary depending on the size and type of organisation, geographical location and the industry sector you are working in.

Graduates entering the industry could expect a salary of between £20,000 and £28,000 a year. With some experience this could increase up to £35,000 a year.

In more senior roles, with five years or more of experience, you can expect to earn between £40,000 to £60,000 per year.

Related opportunities

- Business Analyst p138
- Database Administrator p143

Further information

BCS, The Chartered Institute for IT
www.bcs.org

The Tech Partnership
www.thetechpartnership.com

145

INTERACTIVE MEDIA DESIGNER

Qualifications and courses

Entrants often have a Foundation degree, Diploma, HNC/HND, or degree in interactive media design or an art and design-related subject such as graphic or multimedia design. The normal minimum entry requirements for degrees are 2 A levels/3 H grades and 5 GCSEs/National 5s (A*–C/A–C). For Foundation degrees or HNCs/HNDs you usually need 1 A level/2 H grades and 3 GCSEs/National 5s (A*–C/A–C). For entry onto a technical degree course, an A level/H grade in Maths or a science may be required.

Entry without a degree, Foundation degree or HNC/HND is possible for those with IT skills and creative talent. The BTEC Level 3 qualifications in Interactive Media could be beneficial. Other useful qualifications include NVQs/SVQs at Levels 3 and 4 in Communication and Technology, the A level in Applied Art and Design, and the BTEC Level 3 qualifications in subjects such as E-Business, and IT Practitioners (Software Development).

There is an Advanced Apprenticeship for IT, Software, Web and Telecoms Professionals to gain qualifications and practical training. Additionally, Creative Process runs a Level 3 and 4 Digital Apprenticeship scheme in the south of England for those aged 16 or over who do not already hold a degree.

All entrants should try to get as much experience in the field as possible and it is essential that you compile a portfolio with relevant samples of your interactive media work, produced either at home or during a work placement.

The Chartered Institute for IT (BCS) and the Institute for the Management of Information Systems (IMIS) also offer qualifications which may be useful.

What the work involves

Interactive media designers will usually work as part of a product development team. They use a mix of visuals, sounds, animation, text and effects to produce multimedia and communication tools such as apps and content for phones and tablets and interactive websites.

You will work with a team to develop a brief, finding out what your client wants and determining how to find the best solution. You will create simulations along the way to show the client your ideas.

Your role will also involve planning, coordinating and overseeing the whole project as well as testing, integrating and, if needed, installing at the customer's site.

Type of person suited to this work

Your creative skills need to be outstanding for this job. Every project will be different and you will need the vision to be able to think about what a client wants to achieve and then develop ideas to produce a solution.

You need to be good at working in a team and motivating others to meet tight deadlines. You must be organised, have a keen eye for detail and possess good drawing skills.

You should have excellent presentation and communication skills, as you might need to bid against other designers to win contracts for new projects.

Working conditions

Employers include specialist multimedia consultancies, internet service providers, e-learning specialists, mobile phone companies, software houses and hardware manufacturers.

You will spend time at your workstation, working in an office or studio, but you will also be working with your project team and meeting customers and may also have the opportunity to work from home.

You may have to travel regularly to clients, to meet and present your solutions to them.

Although you will work normal hours from Monday to Friday, you may need to work overtime when a deadline is approaching.

Future prospects

Interactive media is an incredibly fast growing industry with various platforms to work on. Competition for jobs is very high with applicants outnumbering the number of places. In spite of this, skilled media designers are constantly in demand at the moment with over 50,000 people currently working in the interactive media sector and the mobile app industry experiencing a high rate of growth.

Once experienced, you could become self-employed, or work on a contract or consultancy basis.

Advantages/disadvantages

This is a young, vibrant industry where you will be using cutting-edge technology.

Seeing people use apps and websites that you have created is very rewarding.

The fast pace of development in this field means that you will have to continue learning to remain up to date.

Money guide

Starting salaries are usually between £15,500 and £22,000.

Experienced interactive media designers can expect an average salary of £31,800.

Those who are highly experienced could earn in excess of £45,000.

Related opportunities

- Online/Web Content Manager p149
- Software Developer/Programmer p150
- Software Engineer p151

Further information

British Interactive Media Association
www.bima.co.uk

The Tech Partnership
www.thetechpartnership.com

Qualifications and courses

To work as an IT trainer you need to first gain the relevant skills and experience in IT. There are no set qualifications required, but it might be advantageous to have a degree, Foundation degree or HNC/HND in a relevant subject, such as computer science, e-business/commerce or software engineering. The normal minimum entry requirements for degrees are 2 A levels/3 H grades and 5 GCSEs/National 5s (A*–C/A–C). For Foundation degrees or HNC/HNDs you need 1 A level/2 H grades and 3 GCSEs/National 5s (A*–C/A–C). You could enter this job without a degree if you have got significant experience and training in IT.

An IT Management for Business (ITMB) degree, accredited and developed by the Tech Partnership in collaboration with over 90 employers representing a broad range of industry sectors, is beneficial for those seeking entry via a degree route. Additionally, there are qualifications in specific desktop applications and technical areas, such as the Microsoft Certified Trainer (MCT), Technology Specialist (MCTS), Systems Engineer (MCSE), and Systems Developer (MCSD) certifications.

The Institute of IT Training is the certification awarding body for a range of courses in e-learning training skills offered by the Training Foundation. Through the Institute of IT Training you can qualify as Certified Training Practitioner.

Once you have qualified, it is advisable that you join the Chartered Institute for IT (BCS), giving you the opportunity to interact with others in the industry and pursue courses to continue your professional development and knowledge in what is a continually evolving industry.

What the work involves

IT trainers give people user skills, for example in applications such as Word, Excel or desktop-publishing packages. You may also train people in advanced computer skills such as programming languages.

Planning courses, preparing learning materials and setting up the computers ready for a session will be part of your typical day. You will give presentations and network some materials. You will demonstrate the software being taught and assist students with any problems.

Evaluating clients' existing knowledge and developing future learning materials as required will also be part of your job.

Type of person suited to this work

The constant release of new IT products guarantees a future for trainers but only if you are keen to stay up to date. For example, social media courses are becoming increasingly popular and relevant qualifications may broaden your job opportunities. City & Guilds and BTEC offer a Level 3 qualification in Social Media for Business.

You will need lots of self-discipline to do research and prepare learning materials. As e-learning and virtual classroom technology expand, more students are being taught over the internet. Therefore, you will need to be up to date with e-learning tools, technologies and processes.

This job is about helping others to learn. Whether you train face to face or by virtual technology, you will need strong interpersonal and communication skills. Students can be sensitive to criticism and need to be motivated and encouraged.

Working conditions

Employers such as hardware and software manufacturers, IT consultancies, training organisations and colleges employ IT trainers. There is a strong demand for trainers, especially in the south-east of England.

You may be based in a training centre or you may travel to clients' premises to train their staff on-site.

Although your hours will usually be scheduled Monday to Friday, you will need to spend time preparing learning materials and working some evenings and weekends to fit in with students' timetables.

Future prospects

This is not considered to be an entry-level post. Most trainers have gained experience in other areas of computing first.

Experienced IT trainers can move into self-employment as consultants. Promotion into supervisory or management roles may be possible.

Advantages/disadvantages

It can be personally rewarding when you succeed in making a student understand a difficult subject.

This job can be affected if the economy is depressed as training is often the first thing businesses cut back on in difficult times.

Money guide

Graduate IT trainers usually earn around £18,000–£20,000. Experienced trainers can earn between £21,000 and £32,000 a year. Those with management responsibilities can earn £45,000 to £60,000.

Salaries can be higher for trainers in specialised or technical areas of work. For example, experienced legal IT trainers earn over £40,000 per year on average.

Freelance or self-employed trainers might charge a daily rate of £250 to £450.

Related opportunities

- Business Analyst p138
- Secondary School Teacher p194
- Work-based Training Instructor p198

Further information

BCS, The Chartered Institute for IT
www.bcs.org

Learning and Performance Institute
www.learningandperformanceinstitute.com

The Tech Partnership
www.thetechpartnership.com

Qualifications and courses

To become a network manager you will need experience within the sector, for example as a network engineer or in more general IT management and work your way up. Entry at this lower level is usually by means of a degree, Foundation degree or HNC/HND in a relevant subject, for example control and network computing, software engineering, artificial intelligence or computer science. The normal minimum entry requirements for degrees are 2 A levels /3 H grades and 5 GCSEs/National 5s (A*–C/A–C), and for Foundation degrees or HNC/HNDs, 1 A level/2 H grades and 4 GCSEs/National 5s (A*–C/A–C). For entry onto a technical degree, an A level/H grade in Maths or a science may be required.

Other useful qualifications include the City & Guilds Level 4 Diploma in ICT Systems and Principles for IT Professionals (7630), the Institute for the Management of Information Systems Foundation Diploma and the Network/Telecoms Manager Higher Apprenticeship.

Training programmes on offer to graduates from any discipline include the Graduate Professional Development Award. This offers training and accreditation to IT professionals in work.

Many accredited courses are offered by various professional bodies. For example, Cisco offers the Cisco Certified Network Associate (CCNA), Certified Network Professional (CCNP), and Certified Internetwork Expert (CCIE) qualifications, whilst Microsoft offers the Certified Systems Engineer (MCSE) and Certified Systems Administrator (MCSA) qualifications.

You may also need to train in specialist areas such as wireless networking or satellite communications. For example, Cisco offers the CCNA Wireless or CCNP Wireless qualifications and the Lever Technology Group offer many different courses, including Understanding Satellite Communications Systems and the Certified Wireless Network Administrator (CWNA) certification.

What the work involves

You will design, set up and maintain a network of computers and any linked equipment such as printers. This could be in just one building or extend across different sites around the UK or perhaps the world. It will be your responsibility to solve the network users' problems.

Managing access to and the security of your network, you will put in place and monitor firewalls, password systems and antivirus software.

In large organisations you could manage a team of IT technicians and carry out duties such as training staff, organising work rotas and allocating staff duties.

Type of person suited to this work

You need to have excellent communication skills in order to explain technical issues clearly and simply to computer users who need to get back onto the network.

Technical ability and determination are needed for this job. You might develop and write software programs for your network and need to be logical to work out how to sort out any problems.

Network solutions are developing very quickly so you will need to be prepared to carry on learning to keep up your expert status.

Working conditions

You will work standard office hours, though longer hours can be required when installing systems or on-call.

You will use a computer to manage the system. You may need to work in the same room as a noisy mainframe server.

You may have to move around your company's site to attend meetings, train staff and resolve problems.

Future prospects

Most organisations use networks to enable their staff to work together, communicate and share resources from their own workstations. Employers include industry, retailers, schools and universities, hospitals, local and central government and financial companies. You could work within an organisation as a network manager, or as part of an external IT agency and work in many different companies.

Promotion could be into the job of senior network manager and then project manager. A talented network manager could also move into freelance or network design consultancy work. Other possibilities include lecturing or training.

Advantages/disadvantages

You will feel valued because communication and the sharing of information are central to the effective running of any organisation.

This job can be stressful as problems will need to be solved quickly so that users can go back to work.

Money guide

Starting salaries are usually about £24,000–£27,000 per year. Salaries in the public sector may be slightly lower.

With experience you could earn from £30,000 to £50,000.

Senior network managers can earn in excess of £70,000.

Additional benefits may include profit sharing or performance-related pay.

Related opportunities

- Computer Hardware Engineer p141
- Computer Support Technician/Helpdesk Adviser p142
- Database Administrator p143

Further information

BCS, The Chartered Institute for IT
www.bcs.org

The Tech Partnership
www.thetechpartnership.com

Qualifications and courses

There is no fixed entry route into this industry. You may wish to pursue a degree, Foundation degree or HNC/HND in a relevant subject, such as e-systems design/technology, graphic design, computer science, e-business/commerce, journalism, publishing, media and communications, or marketing. The normal minimum entry requirements for degrees are 2 A levels/3 H grades and 5 GCSEs/National 5s (A*–C/A–C). For Foundation degrees or HNCs/HNDs you will be expected to have 1 A level/2 H grades and 3 GCSEs/National 5s (A*–C/A–C). Postgraduate degrees may help your application.

Experience in writing is essential and can be achieved in voluntary work or writing a personal online blog. Training will be provided on the job but any experience that you have working with HTML, web content management systems (WordPress, Drupal, Convio, Kintera, etc) or particular programs (eg Adobe Creative Suite), packages or operating systems, search engine optimisation (SEO), web analytics and social media platforms may prove advantageous. A portfolio of previously developed or published content may also help.

Vacation work or voluntary placements within the sector would also provide useful experience and enable you to develop industry contacts.

A funded route that may be on offer for school leavers is the Advanced IT Application Specialist Apprenticeship. Entrants will gain practical training and relevant qualifications which will help them to secure a suitable role within this industry.

What the work involves

You might work in or supervise a team of staff who design, programme and maintain the various pages that make up an internet site. This may include the company's various social media platforms.

You might write or develop content or develop a content management program for authorised staff to contribute material. You may also have to copy-edit and proofread content. Search Engine Optimisation (SEO) techniques could be beneficial here.

Content is typically required to fit within a marketing strategy and marketing ability is one of the most consistently required skills in relevant job advertisements.

Many jobs combine management with writing and web design. In a small company, you might be the programmer, designer and master/manager of the site.

Type of person suited to this work

You must have good attention to detail and be able to carefully check your work. You will need to set up secure data entry checking systems and regularly test them for faults. You must be able to respond quickly and calmly when faults occur, such as the wrong prices being matched to the wrong products on a shopping site, and be able to work efficiently to fix them.

It will be your responsibility to create your own website or maintain one from the group of sites you work with. Creativity is important, as is accuracy; you need to make sure the site is easy to use.

Excellent management and communication skills are vital as you may be required to lead a project team at senior level.

Working conditions

You will mainly be office based, using a computer to manage the website. You may have to move around your company's premises to train, meet with managers and discuss website improvements.

You could work for web-based retailers, travel companies, the multimedia industry, local and central government and financial companies.

You will work a 37–40 hour week, normally Monday to Friday, but if you are working to maintain and support a 24/7 site you will work shifts as part of a team to cover all hours.

Future prospects

Websites are big business, with growing numbers of organisations using them to share information, market themselves, sell goods or services and advertise jobs.

After gaining experience, you could progress to project management level. A talented web content manager could move into freelance or website development consultancy work.

Advantages/disadvantages

This is an expanding market with high rewards on offer if you are creative and have technical skills.

As you are responsible for your company's website, the work will sometimes involve high levels of pressure.

The skills that you will develop in this role are transferable and could open up opportunities to work for a variety of companies.

Money guide

The starting salary for a web content manager would usually be in the region of £24,000.

Those with experience in the field could expect to earn £25,000–£35,000 a year.

Senior web managers with additional responsibilities could achieve £40,000–£50,000.

Related opportunities

- Database Administrator p143
- Network Manager p148
- Software Developer/Programmer p150

Further information

British Interactive Media Association
www.bima.co.uk

Society for Editors and Proofreaders
www.sfep.org.uk

COMPUTERS AND IT

COMPUTERS AND IT

Qualifications and courses

Entry is usually by means of a degree, Foundation degree or HNC/HND in a relevant subject, for example programming, software engineering or computer science, or a degree with modules in computer graphics or HTML and Java programming. The normal minimum entry requirements for degrees are 2 A levels/3 H grades and 5 GCSEs/National 5s (A*–C/A–C), and for Foundation degrees or HNC/HNDs 1 A level/2 H grades and 3 GCSEs/National 5s (A*–C/A–C) are typically required. For entry onto a technical degree, an A level/H grade in Maths or a science may be required. You could also complete a postgraduate degree and specialise in a specific branch of IT or computer science, such as artificial intelligence.

Entry with a degree in an unrelated subject area is possible; larger employers recruit graduates from all disciplines. However as the industry is competitive it may be beneficial to take a conversion course or postgraduate course in a computing subject.

Entry without a degree, Foundation degree or HNC/HND is unusual unless you have substantial experience in programming work and experience of designing or programming websites using new media. A strong portfolio will be required.

Further study is available, from in-house training to professional qualifications. These include the BCS Professional Certification, Diploma and Professional Graduate Diploma in IT and the Institute for the Management of Information Systems (IMIS) Foundation Diploma, Diploma and Higher Diploma.

A Software Development for Business (BSc) degree is accredited by the Tech Partnership. The syllabus is led by industry employers and offers students the opportunity to learn both technical programming and development skills in conjunction with project management and communication.

Software companies also offer training courses, which include the Microsoft Certified Solution Developer (MCSD) and Certified Applications Developer (MCAD) certifications, the Sun Microsystems Java Certified Programmer (SCJP) and Developer (SCJD) certifications, and the Oracle PL/SQL Developer (databases) certification.

What the work involves

You will be designing, developing and testing computer software for your clients to improve their business's productivity and efficiency.

You may also improve existing software by analysing and fixing any problems.

Your clients could be companies from the finance, insurance, retail or building industries.

You will work closely with a team of other programmers and designers to develop a detailed specification for the software and present this back to your client.

You will write the programming code for the new software from scratch or adapt an existing code.

You will then be responsible for testing and maintaining the software, and making sure your client is happy with the new system.

Type of person suited to this work

You will need to have excellent IT skills, with an in-depth knowledge of up-to-date packages and software coding techniques.

You must be a good communicator, as you will be working with other IT professionals and members of staff.

Being logical and having a knack for problem-solving will be vital in this work, as you will need to come up with new programming codes and restore existing ones.

Working conditions

Most software developers/programmers work normal office hours. If there is a deadline to meet you might work overtime or at the weekend.

Software developers/programmers are employed by a variety of industries; these include retail, finance, engineering and government bodies.

You will be based in an office, but you might need to travel around the country when meeting clients.

Future prospects

You can progress into senior or management roles, or work as a contracted IT consultant.

Some software developers/programmers become self-employed or become trainers.

Advantages/disadvantages

You will need to keep up to date with new and developing IT techniques; this could prove difficult if you wanted a career break.

There are great opportunities for promotion, leading to senior management roles and consultancy.

Money guide

Starting salaries may be around £22,000–£26,000.

This can increase to £28,000–£45,000 once you have gained several years' experience.

Senior and management roles can pay over £50,000.

Related opportunities

- Interactive Media Designer p146
- Online/Web Content Manager p149
- Website Designer p155

Further information

British Interactive Media Association
www.bima.co.uk

The Tech Partnership
www.thetechpartnership.com

Qualifications and courses

The usual entry qualification is a degree or a master's in a relevant subject, for example software engineering, computer science, or electronic engineering. The normal minimum entry requirements for degrees are 2 A levels/3 H grades and 5 GCSEs/National 5s (A*–C/A–C). Required subjects usually include Maths and Physics. IT conversion courses are available for those without a computing degree.

Pre-entry experience is advantageous in this competitive industry. There are sandwich degrees containing 1-year work placements, and voluntary work and internships are also possible.

Should you have no formal qualifications, there may be the opportunity of an apprenticeship in IT.

In the past, engineers just designed software to meet a business's needs, but you now generally need to know how to perform a computer programmer's work as well. Most companies offer employees ongoing training, but you will need experience using different programming languages, real-time operating systems (RTOS), embedded systems, microcontrollers, device drivers, microprocessors or system-on-chip technology etc.

Companies such as Apple, Oracle and Microsoft offer appealing certifications in their own products. For example, Microsoft offers the Microsoft Certified Solutions Developer (MCSD) and Certified Solutions Expert (MCSE). Experience in business, management and finance may also prove advantageous.

Software engineering is a constantly evolving profession and you must ensure you keep up to date by completing continuing professional development (CPD) courses available from institutes such as the Chartered Institute for IT (BCS).

What the work involves

Software engineers test and evaluate software that helps computers to run effectively. You will then debug faulty software and constantly research new technologies to find the best solutions.

You may also develop new software such as computer games, operating systems and business applications.

As well as providing technical support to businesses and organisations, you may also build new computer systems for them from scratch.

You will work with computer codes and will usually specialise in either systems or applications.

Type of person suited to this work

You will need technical, practical and creative ability. It will be useful if you have a personal interest in writing your own programs or have built your own computer system.

You should be an excellent problem solver. You will need to be able to anticipate problems and work out ways to prevent them.

You must be patient and methodical to be able to produce accurate work when your deadline is close and your tests are not going well.

Your teamwork and communication skills should be strong as you will be working with a project team. At higher levels you will be giving presentations or lectures.

Working conditions

You may be based in a laboratory, a research and development unit, or a workshop.

At project management level you may travel nationally and internationally to meetings and conferences.

You will work a 37 to 40 hour week but you will need to be flexible and put in extra hours at key times.

Future prospects

Talented software engineers are increasingly in demand, and so job prospects are good in many sectors, including academia, government research, computer manufacturing, software development and electronics and telecommunications.

You will have more opportunities if you are both creative and technical.

You will start work as a junior member of a project team. With experience you could move into lecturing or project management. You might also choose to become an IT consultant or work as a contractor.

Advantages/disadvantages

Your team's work could make the headlines. New products and cutting-edge research, such as the building of world-class supercomputers, are of international interest.

Solutions to problems do not happen quickly. It can be really frustrating to retest hundreds of times and still not get the result you are looking for.

Money guide

The starting salary for a graduate software engineer typically starts at £18,000.

On average, software engineers earn between £35,000 and £50,000 per year.

Senior software engineers and those with managerial responsibilities usually earn £45,000 to in excess of £70,000 a year.

Related opportunities

- Computer Hardware Engineer p141
- Interactive Media Designer p146
- Software Developer/Programmer p150

Further information

Institution of Analysts and Programmers (IAP)
www.iap.org.uk

The Tech Partnership
www.thetechpartnership.com

SYSTEMS ANALYST

Qualifications and courses

A degree, Foundation degree or HNC/HND is usually required. Useful degree subjects include computer science, information technology and e-systems design and technology. Minimum entry requirements for these degrees are usually 2 A levels/3 H grades (including Maths) and 5 GCSEs/National 5s. Work experience is important to enter this profession, so taking a course with a placement year could prove advantageous. Entry to the profession is open to those with unrelated degrees but a postgraduate conversion course in IT may be needed. A sponsored degree in Information Technology Management for Business (ITMB) from the Tech Partnership is available. This is focused on learning through project work in teams with external mentors from sponsoring organisations.

Alternatively, entrants can gain industry experience through a Higher Apprenticeship for IT, Software, Web and Telecoms Professionals which combines practical training with a professional qualification. For entry onto a Higher Apprenticeship you will need qualifications such as A levels/H grades or a Level 3 NVQ. As part of your apprenticeship you may study an NVQ in Communication Technology for Practitioners and Professionals (Levels 1–4), the City & Guilds Level 4 Diploma in ICT Systems and Principles for IT Professionals (7630) or the BTEC Level 3 qualifications in IT.

You will be expected to have a working knowledge of programming skills and analysis methods. Industry bodies such as the Chartered Institute for IT (BCS), the Tech Partnership, and the Institute for the Management of Information Systems (IMIS) offer relevant development courses that can be completed whilst working. Certifications are also available from program vendors such as Microsoft, IBM and Oracle.

What the work involves

You will prepare a brief of what your client wants a computer system to do and then translate this brief into recommendations for IT solutions.

To determine the system needed you will use performance monitoring or sizing tools. You will then design, cost and recommend suitable hardware/software solutions.

If purpose-built software is needed, you may write it or brief a programmer on your team. You will go on to install and test the configuration you have developed.

Type of person suited to this work

An excellent all-round knowledge of IT, including hardware and software, is vital. You will also have to keep up to date with new IT products as you will be expected to be the technical expert.

Your teamwork and communication skills will need to be good as you will be working with business clients and colleagues such as business analysts and programmers to produce the best value system as a team.

To make systems that work well and enhance profitability and efficiency for your customer, you will also need to be a problem solver who understands how businesses work.

Working conditions

Employers include software and systems houses, IT consultants as well as organisations in sectors such as commerce, finance and banking, retail and health.

You will be mainly based in an office, working with other members of the project team. You will have to travel to clients at all stages of the project and may be away for several days when installing and testing the new system.

Although your hours will be usually Monday to Friday, you will need to work some evenings and weekends to meet deadlines.

Future prospects

You could move from this broad-based job either to specialise in offering IT solutions for business, or into a technical area such as software or website development.

Progression is possible into a senior analyst role, project management or consultancy work. The speed of advancement depends upon the size and type of organisation you work for. You could also become an independent consultant.

Advantages/disadvantages

It is rewarding to combine hardware and software to create a unique solution designed for your customer.

You will have the opportunity to meet a range of people and work on a variety of IT projects.

Trying to work to strict deadlines and a tight budget can involve high levels of pressure.

You have full responsibility for meeting your clients' needs which could be stressful.

Money guide

Graduates usually receive a starting salary of £20,000–£27,000.

Experienced systems analysts can expect to earn £30,000 to £45,000.

Senior analysts can earn up to £60,000 a year.

Salaries tend to be higher in London, the south-east of England and the Midlands.

Related opportunities

- Database Administrator p143
- Network Manager p148
- Software Developer/Programmer p150

Further information

BCS, The Chartered Institute for IT
www.bcs.org

Learning and Performance Institute
www.learningandperformanceinstitute.com

The Tech Partnership
www.thetechpartnership.com

TECHNICAL SALES ENGINEER

Qualifications and courses

You will usually need a degree, Foundation degree or HNC/HND in a computer-related subject to enter this job. The normal minimum entry requirements for degrees are 2 A levels/3 H grades and 5 GCSEs/National 5s (A*–C/A–C), and for Foundation degrees or HNC/HNDs, 1 A level/2 H grades and 4 GCSEs/National 5s (A*–C/A–C). Maths and Physics are often required subjects for entry.

A funded route that may be on offer in your area is the IT and Telecoms Professionals Apprenticeship.

Experience in sales is extremely useful. If you have a sales or telesales background and want formal IT training you can pursue a BTEC Level 3 qualification in IT Practitioners.

An IT Management for Business (ITMB) BSc integrates a BSc Honours degree with learning, teaching and assessment aspects and is a solid entry route for those looking to become qualified to a degree level. The course has been designed in collaboration with over 90 industry employers, such as Ford, Asda, HSBC and Deloitte, and is accredited by the Tech Partnership.

Initial training is usually intense as you will need to gain a thorough technical knowledge of your employer's products and their preferred communication style.

The IT industry is constantly developing and it is essential you keep up to date with new technologies. Professional qualifications may prove useful and can be obtained from the various professional bodies, such as the Chartered Institute for IT (BCS). IT companies such as Microsoft also offer sales workshops.

What the work involves

You will talk to customers interested in your product, finding out what they are looking for, answering technical questions and explaining how the product works.

You will then present what the client requires to an in-house technical team and work on adapting the product to suit the client.

Presentation of the finished product to your client is an important part of making the sale.

Type of person suited to this work

It is essential to be personable and persuasive. You will also need good oral and written communication skills as you will be dealing with customers as well as writing up reports and proposals.

You must be able to clearly explain technical jargon to customers who may have no technical knowledge. Equally, you will need to understand all the technical specifications of your products as some of your customers will be experts.

It is a competitive market so you will need to be good at selling, negotiating and building customer loyalty. You will also need to be up to date with all the products out there so that you know the competition.

Working conditions

Employers include large IT companies producing and retailing products such as mobile phones, computer hardware and software. Large specialist IT retailers also employ technical sales staff.

You might be based in an office, dealing with customers by phone or email, or in a retail outlet selling directly.

If you specialise in selling to retail chains or organisations, you will spend a lot of time driving and in meetings. A driving licence will be useful.

Your hours will depend on your customers. Your employer may operate a shift system to deal with queries and sales from early until late, 7 days a week.

Future prospects

The demand for new IT products continues to grow but new competitors are always entering the market. Strong areas of demand include secure wireless broadband and mobile working.

You might be able to gain promotion to a supervisory or sales management role, or work as an IT consultant, a lecturer or contractor.

Advantages/disadvantages

If you close a deal at a good price or sell extras such as a service contract, you could be paid a bonus.

Selling can be very stressful, with high sales targets to achieve.

It can be frustrating if you spend a lot of time with a customer without it resulting in a purchase.

Money guide

Starting salaries are usually £19,000–£30,000 per year.

As you gain experience you could earn £30,000 to £45,000 a year.

Senior managers can earn £50,000 to in excess of £70,000.

Additional benefits may include profit sharing, performance-related pay, mobile phone, laptop and a car.

Related opportunities

- Business Analyst p138
- Computer Support Technician/Helpdesk Adviser p142
- IT Trainer p147

Further information

BCS, The Chartered Institute for IT
www.bcs.org

Institute of Sales & Marketing Management
www.ismm.co.uk

The Tech Partnership
www.thetechpartnership.com

TELECOMMUNICATIONS TECHNICIAN

Qualifications and courses

You can enter this profession as an apprentice, where you will be supervised by a qualified telecommunications technician. Apprenticeships usually last for 2 years, giving you practical work experience as well as the opportunity to work towards a relevant professional qualification such as an NVQ/SVQ Level 2 or 3.

There are no formal entry requirements for an Intermediate IT, Software, Web & Telecoms Professionals Apprenticeship, however most employers will require you to hold 5 GCSEs/National 5s (A*–C/A–C), including English and Maths. There are Intermediate (Level 2), Advanced (Level 3), and Higher (Level 4) Apprenticeships available. The Tech Partnership offers a Tech Industry Gold accredited apprenticeship scheme for IT Technicians that might also be valuable to entrants to the field.

HNCs/HNDs, undergraduate or postgraduate degrees are available in subjects such as telecommunications, communications engineering, electrical engineering, data communications and digital communications. The normal minimum entry requirements for a degree are 2 A levels/H grades, including Maths, Electronics or a physical science, and 5 GCSEs/National 5s (A*–C/A–C). HNCs/HNDs and Foundation degrees typically require 1 A level/H grade and 4 GCSEs/National 5s (A*–C/A–C), including English and Maths.

There are also various vocational qualifications available, including the City & Guilds Level 2 Award in Communications Cabling (3667-02) and Level 3 Certificate in Designing and Planning Communications Networks (3667-03), the Level 3 Diploma in ICT Professional Competence (4520-03) and the NVQ Level 3 in Engineering Maintenance (Communication Electronics) (1788-39).

Depending on the company you work for, continuing in-service training may be available. This can be combined with specific manufacturers' courses and vendor qualifications such as the networking qualifications offered by Cisco and Microsoft.

What the work involves

Telecommunications technicians install, test and repair networking and communications technology and systems across a range of applications, including mobile phones, telephones, satellite and radio networks and aerials.

Your day to day tasks will vary but you may be assembling, installing and testing telecommunications equipment; laying copper and fibre optic wire in the street or other sites; setting up or repairing networks.

You may also be involved in designing or consulting on plans for telecommunications systems.

Type of person suited to this work

You should be interested in maths, IT, electronics and communications.

As you will be working in a team and explaining technical terms to customers you should have good communication and customer service skills. You should also have good writing skills to write up reports and produce statistics.

As you may be installing systems and laying wires which may involve heavy lifting and carrying, digging or using ladders, you should be fit and have a good head for heights.

Working conditions

You will work between 9am and 5pm, Monday to Friday. You may be required to work shifts which may include evenings, weekends or to be available on-call. Overtime may be necessary to complete projects or meet deadlines.

You may be based in a factory workshop or in a control centre from where you will travel to complete projects. These may be in homes, offices or outdoors and a driving licence may be required.

Future prospects

To progress as a telecommunications technician you can apply to become a professionally recognised engineering technician (EngTech) or ICT technician (ICTTech) with an industry body, which include the Engineering Council and the Institution of Engineering and Technology (IET). You need to possess at least a Level 3 BTEC, NVQ or equivalent qualification.

With experience and qualifications you may be promoted to senior technician or supervisor. With further experience, qualifications and skills you can apply for incorporated and chartered engineer status.

You can become self-employed, or work on a contract basis. There are also numerous opportunities to work abroad.

Advantages/disadvantages

You may be in a diverse working environment as new and exciting developments in technology are occurring rapidly.

You may have to work outdoors in uncomfortable weather conditions.

Money guide

Your starting salary will be around £18,000 a year.

With experience and qualifications you can earn up to £25,000.

The most experienced technicians can earn in excess of £30,000.

Earnings can increase with shift allowances and overtime.

Related opportunities

- Computer Hardware Engineer p141
- Electrical Engineer p207
- Network Manager p148

Further information

Institute of Telecommunications Professionals
www.theitp.org

Institution of Engineering and Technology
www.theiet.org

WEBSITE DESIGNER

Qualifications and courses

There are no specific qualifications needed to become a web designer, although most designers have experience in other design fields or have taken training in web design. Most employers will expect you to have some experience and to have a related qualification such as a Foundation degree, computer-related Honours degree or HND that covers internet technology, graphic or interactive design. To gain entry to a degree you will need 2 A levels/3 H grades and 5 GCSEs/National 5s, whilst Foundation degrees or HNDs require 1 A level/2 H grades and 4 GCSEs/National 5s (A*–C/A–C) or equivalent qualifications.

A good working knowledge of HTML is essential. It could be useful to have experience working with Dreamweaver, Photoshop, Flash and Fireworks, CSS, Javascript and .Net. Professionally accredited training courses and online tutorials are also available from a number of recognised institutions such as the Chartered Institute for IT (BCS).

On-the-job training is common, but you will also need to keep updated with the latest developments in the field.

You could also study for qualifications such as the BTEC Interactive Use of Media Levels 1–3, OCR ITQ Levels 1–3, OCR Creative iMedia Levels 1–3 and City & Guilds ICT Systems and Principles (7540) Level 2 (Award) and Level 3 (Diploma).

The Certified Internet Web Professional (CIW) also offers industry certifications you could work towards, such as the CIW Site Development Associate and CIW Web Design Specialist courses. The courses are completed on a home study basis and typically require 160 hours of self-directed study. Examination and certification can also be purchased.

What the work involves

Web designers build new or improve existing websites. You will be responsible for dealing with the visual image of the website but you will not necessarily be involved with coding the website or making it function.

You will need to ensure your websites are designed to be accessible through different, evolving platforms, such as PCs, Macs, mobile phones, tablets, and digital television.

You will meet with clients and discuss what they want their website to look like and who it is aimed at. You will then have to use their requirements to create the design.

Type of person suited to this work

You will need excellent communication skills, as you have to understand the requirements of your client and create a design from their instructions.

You will need a great deal of creativity, to make the site as attractive as possible, but it is also essential to have a good understanding of consumer needs, in order to make the design comprehensible and functional.

Good time management is necessary, as you will be working to very strict deadlines.

Working conditions

You will usually work 37 to 40 hours a week, Monday to Friday, although you will sometimes have to work extra hours to meet a deadline, or when problems occur with a website.

Most of your time will be spent indoors in an office, or at home on your own computer if you are self-employed. When meeting clients, it may sometimes be necessary to travel.

Future prospects

You could work for web design companies, in the IT departments of large public and private organisations, or as a freelance designer.

Working for a company could give you the opportunity to work your way up into a design team management post, or expand your skills to become a web content manager. Once you have gained enough experience, you could set up your own web design business.

Working in the visual media environment, many website designers develop and maintain a professional portfolio. This is useful when applying for courses, new jobs, or if you are moving into self-employment or starting your own business.

Advantages/disadvantages

If you enjoy being creative, web designing will give you the opportunity to express your passion on a daily basis.

You will also feel a sense of achievement when you are able to see your finished piece being put to use.

Your clients could be relying on you to create a website that will generate them more business, which could mean a lot of pressure to do an excellent job.

You will have to work to strict deadlines and this could mean working extra hours.

Money guide

Starting salaries begin at around £18,000 to £24,000 a year.

Experienced designers can earn between £24,000 and £40,000 per year.

Senior designers and those with specialist skills can earn in excess of £40,000.

Related opportunities

- Business Analyst p138
- Interactive Media Designer p146
- Online/Web Content Manager p149
- Website Developer p156

Further information

BCS, The Chartered Institute for IT
www.bcs.org

British Interactive Media Association
www.bima.co.uk

UK Web Design Association
www.ukwda.org

Qualifications and courses

Many who are just starting out in this career now have either a Foundation degree, BTEC, HNC/HND award or degree in web development or web design, multimedia design, digital media development, computer programming or a related subject.

Alternatively, there are various vocational qualifications you could complete, such as the BTEC Level 3 qualifications in Art and Design (Multimedia), Computer Studies or IT. Applicants typically need 4 GCSEs/National 5s (A*–C/A–C) for entry. Alternatively, NVQs/SVQs are available in IT practitioner subjects, including website development, and there are HNCs/HNDs in various IT and design-related subjects. Entry to these courses typically requires at least 1 A level/2 H grades and 4 GCSEs/National 5s (A*–C/A–C).

It is possible to become a web developer without qualifications, but employers will want evidence of your experience and employability. You should therefore keep a portfolio of your work. Developing and designing sites for local community groups or voluntary agencies could be a useful way to get your portfolio started.

It is important to be familiar with a number of areas, including the various computing languages, common operating systems and servers, databases and web programming, networking and security, graphics, animation and web design software. Training courses are available from national bodies and program vendors such as Microsoft and Oracle.

You should also have an understanding of the World Wide Web Consortium (W3C) standards for website accessibility.

Due to the evolving nature of the IT industry generally, you should try to keep up to date with industry developments, and continuing professional development (CPD), through courses run by larger companies or membership of The Chartered Institute for IT, is advised.

What the work involves

As a web developer, you will be in charge of working with a client, learning what they require from their website and then programming the website to make sure it functions as it should.

You will often work alongside a web designer to work on the site's appearance.

You will have to make sure that the site can be smoothly integrated into the client's existing network and also find and fix any 'bugs' before the site goes 'live'.

Type of person suited to this work

Excellent web and database programming skills are essential. These should coincide with good problem-solving skills.

You will need to be committed to working to deadlines and to keeping up to date with developments in the latest technology.

It is also very important to have good communication skills, as you will be working with clients and listening to their requirements, before ensuring that their website functions in the way they desire.

Working conditions

Normal working hours are 37 to 40 hours a week, Monday to Friday. Near to deadlines some evening and weekend work may be necessary. As this is an industry with a large proportion of workers who are self-employed, working hours can be also be very flexible.

Work is mostly office based. If you work for a company, this will usually mean working on one site, but self-employed web developers will often have to work from home or from the client's premises.

Future prospects

The internet and e-commerce are constantly expanding and consequently, you could find opportunities in a range of industries.

Once you have gained enough experience, you could specialise in a particular area, such as e-commerce.

You could also progress to more senior roles, such as project leader or lead programmer. Alternatively you could work for yourself and run your own company.

Advantages/disadvantages

It is extremely satisfying to see your finished website up and running.

You need to make sure you are up to date with new design trends and software, which could be challenging.

You will also face a lot of pressure from clients, who wish to see their website completed to a deadline and to a high standard.

Money guide

Salaries start at between £19,000 and £25,000 a year.

With experience this can rise to between £25,000 and £35,000.

Lead developers could earn £35,000 to £50,000 a year.

Related opportunities

- Interactive Media Designer p146
- Software Developer/Programmer p150
- Website Designer p155

Further information

BCS, The Chartered Institute for IT
www.bcs.org

The Tech Partnership
www.thetechpartnership.com

World Wide Web Consortium (W3C)
www.w3.org

Design, Arts and Crafts

The idea of turning your arts and crafts hobby into a career may be one you like the thought of. Jobs in this sector can involve working in any medium, from textiles to jewellery to metalwork or children's toys. You may find yourself working for a company but many people in this industry are self-employed working for a range of clients. This means you need to be very organised and have brilliant communication skills to ensure you can give your clients exactly what they want. The jobs featuring in this section are listed below. For similar jobs to these have a look at these sections: *Marketing, Advertising, Media, Print and Publishing* on page 381 and *Performing Arts* starting on page 415.

ANIMATOR

Qualifications and courses

Entry requirements vary, however you will usually need an HND, Foundation degree or degree in animation, art and design, media production (animation) or a related area for an entry level position. Since animation is a highly competitive industry, a relevant postgraduate qualification in a subject such as directing animation, digital animation or games design and development will almost certainly be an asset.

A portfolio of relevant work demonstrated by a show reel is essential. Some people study a Foundation course in art and design before starting their degree in order to develop a portfolio. 5 GCSEs/National 5s (A*–C/A–C) are usually required for this. Unpaid work experience as a general or animation assistant is also a good way to build up relevant skills, as is applying for a residency.

The usual entry position for animators is studio runner. There are no entry requirements for this position, so candidates without a degree/HND who are particularly talented may still be able to break in, but in practice most runners are graduates. Progression could then be to a junior role such as assistant animator, storyboard artist, inbetweener or digital painter.

Entering animation competitions, submitting short films and ideas to broadcasters or visiting festivals are all good ways to show enthusiasm, develop your reputation and increase your chances of finding work. Building a network of contacts can help you get started and find work in the future.

What the work involves

Animators produce images that appear to come to life on the screen, for use by TV companies, games developers, on websites and in films and adverts.

There are 4 specialisms: traditional (2D drawn), 2D computer generated, 3D computer generated and stop frame or stop motion. In all of these styles you will work to create a continuous story.

Type of person suited to this work

You will need strong creative flair and imagination to develop new ideas for animated stories and characters.

You must have excellent computer skills; a knowledge of software such as Flash, Maya and After Effects is essential. However modelling and life drawing are still important.

You must be patient, have a keen eye for detail and be able to work in a team as well as under pressure. Problem-solving skills are also necessary in a job where you might need to adapt to technical challenges.

Working conditions

Your working environment will depend on the type of animation you do. In some jobs, you will work with tools to hand-create images or forms in different materials and you could be on your feet (using your hands) all day: bending, lifting and shaping models.

On the other hand, many new animation jobs involve work with specialist computer-aided design (CAD) packages at a computer console; this can be done individually or as part of a team.

Most of your work will be done during normal office hours except when projects have tight deadlines!

Future prospects

This is a highly competitive field. Although there are still some opportunities for traditional drawing-based animators, the main area of growth is in computer generation.

The UK is good for stop motion and children's animation opportunities and the video games industry is also doing very well, however you may have to move abroad for opportunities in other types of animation. Within the UK the best places for opportunities are London, Bristol, Cardiff, Dundee and Manchester.

Once in the industry, contracts are usually short term, but it is possible to move from working as a key animator to an animation director role. At senior levels, you would have more creative input and be less directly involved with the technical side. With experience, you could set up as a freelance animator or start your own company.

Advantages/disadvantages

This type of work can be highly satisfying, providing opportunities to develop your own creative ideas and style. Animation is rising in popularity amongst the public with many animated films being highly successful at the box office.

In more commercial jobs, you would need to produce work under pressure to meet a client's requirements.

Money guide

The Broadcasting, Entertainment, Cinematograph and Theatre Union (BECTU) sets minimum wage guidelines. In the computer games industry bonuses at the end of a project are common.

A new animator can expect a starting salary between £12,000 and £20,000 per year.

An experienced animator could earn up between £23,000 and £30,0000 and senior animators can expect a salary in excess of £36,000.

Contact BECTU for details of current freelance remuneration.

Related opportunities

- Cartoonist p159
- Fine Artist/Sculptor p162
- Graphic Designer p165

Further information

Broadcasting, Entertainment, Cinematograph and Theatre Union
www.bectu.org.uk

Creative Skillset
www.creativeskillset.org

CARTOONIST

DESIGN, ARTS AND CRAFTS

Qualifications and courses

A strong portfolio and relevant experience are usually more important than formal qualifications. However, most entrants have an HNC/HND or degree in an art and design subject, such as graphic design, illustration or fine art. A minimum of 1 A level/H grade in an art and design subject, a relevant BTEC award or a BTEC Diploma in Foundation Studies (Art and Design) are usually needed for entry to an HND/HNC.

In England, Wales and Northern Ireland, many students preparing for a degree also take the art Foundation course. In Scotland the first year of an art and design degree equates to the Foundation year. 5 GCSEs/National 5s (A*–C/A–C) and a relevant A level/H grade are usually required for entry to both the Foundation course and the degree.

Sometimes well-established cartoonists run workshops for both adults and young people. These may be at the Cartoon Museum in London, at conventions or privately. The Cartoonists' Club of Great Britain and the Professional Cartoonists' Organisation (PCO) also run training events and competitions which are useful in establishing and developing skills at any stage in a cartoonist's career and keeping up to date with the industry.

Cartoonists are required to convey a message with humour, and are increasingly required to have websites that show examples of their work so a qualification in IT could be very useful. It is also useful to be informed on copyright and ownership legislation.

What the work involves

You will plan and draw original cartoons and captions. These can be single images, whole cartoon strips or entire books. You will promote and market your work, for example by sending out samples to newspapers and advertising through the internet.

Cartoonists create images for greetings cards, adverts, book illustrations, magazines, newspapers and websites.

A small number of cartoonists are employed to run regular cartoon features in newspapers or other media whereas others maintain a web comic of their work.

Type of person suited to this work

Creativity and an excellent sense of humour are essential. You should have a wild imagination and be up to date with current trends. Cartoon ideas often draw on situational humour or arise in quick response to headline news.

Even if you use a software art package, good drawing skills and a developed, individual style are very important. You may have to work to deadlines so need to be well organised, with good business management skills. Self-motivation is important.

As you will be sending out examples of your work to potential employers, you will need to be able to deal with rejection and have the confidence to persevere.

With commissioned work you will need to be able to stick to a design brief and show awareness of the target market as well as incorporating your unique flair.

Working conditions

Most professional cartoonists work on a freelance basis, either in a studio or from home. This can be isolating as many work alone. Much of your time will be spent at a drawing board or a computer where you will either sit or stand using the materials required.

If you are self-employed you will have the freedom to set your own working hours. You might need to attend meetings with clients or potential employers, which could involve travelling long distances and working longer hours.

Future prospects

With a good reputation and popular style or cartoon character, you could be employed by publishers, advertising agencies, television studios, newspapers, magazines or theme parks. With experience you could run workshops in schools, libraries and museums.

You could also specialise in one form of cartoon such as political satire or comic strips, or move into other areas such as illustration or graphic design.

Advantages/disadvantages

As cartoonists are usually paid for individual pieces of work they have little job security, especially at the start of their careers.

You would have the satisfaction of creating original work and seeing it in print.

If you are working from home, set-up costs are relatively low.

Money guide

Salaries vary greatly due to the freelance nature of the industry and cartoonists are usually paid for each piece of commissioned work. A skilled, established cartoonist may charge £300 per picture.

As a guide, new cartoonists with regular work could earn up to £15,000 per year. Established, well-known cartoonists whose work is in demand could earn up to £50,000.

It is possible to earn higher levels of pay by doing commercial work for greetings cards and adverts. Cartoonists creating work to illustrate books can earn royalties from sales.

Related opportunities

- Animator p158
- Fine Artist/Sculptor p162
- Graphic Designer p165

Further information

Arts Council England
www.artscouncil.org.uk

Creative and Cultural Skills
www.ccskills.org.uk

The Cartoon Art Trust
www.cartoonmuseum.org

DESIGN, ARTS AND CRAFTS

Qualifications and courses

Entry without qualifications may be possible, however most people have a Foundation degree, degree or postgraduate diploma in a relevant subject, such as art, costume design, fashion, theatre design or performing arts (production). Entrants commonly begin their career as a wardrobe assistant or costume maker and progress to designer as they develop experience and build contacts.

Useful training courses include the City & Guilds Level 2 and 3 qualifications in Design and Craft – Fashion (Theatre Costume) (7716-42 and 7716-71), the Royal Academy of Dramatic Art (RADA)'s 2-year vocational course in Theatre Costume, and various awards from the National Open College Network (NOCN).

Work experience is invaluable as it helps you to build up a portfolio or 'showreel' of your design work. As well as contacting theatres and film and TV companies, you could become involved in student productions or amateur theatre, or possibly undertake a work placement as part of your degree. There are also Apprenticeships in Costume and Wardrobe available.

Joining the Society of British Theatre Designers or the Costume Society might facilitate networking and lead to work experience opportunities.

What the work involves

You will design, buy or hire the clothes and accessories worn by casts in films, plays and TV shows.

You will read scripts, research the period and setting of a production and come up with original sketches to best represent the director's vision. You will then decide which fabrics and materials to use. You could also be involved with making costumes or overseeing costume production.

You will be responsible for organising fittings and ensuring that costumes are delivered on time, are comfortable and within budget. Depending on the size of the production, you may also manage a team of costume professionals.

Type of person suited to this work

Creativity and originality are essential. Having the skills to draw designs by hand and to use specialist computer-aided design (CAD) software when required is also important.

You should have a meticulous eye for detail and demonstrate a passion for costume history, fashion and the arts. It is important to be a good communicator and to work well in a team.

You must be organised to ensure that projects are carried out on time, within budget and as requested. As deadlines can be tight, you need the ability to work well under pressure.

Working conditions

Hours are long and irregular, including evenings and weekends. It is possible to work for production companies but most costume designers are freelancers who travel around the UK and sometimes overseas.

You will normally work in a studio using drawing tables, computers, cutting tables and sewing machines.

It is likely that you will be standing for long periods of time and you may do some heavy lifting.

Future prospects

Costume designer vacancies are rarely advertised and most work is centred in major cities such as London and Manchester. It is essential for costume designers to have a strong portfolio and to build up good contacts.

If you work for a large organisation such as the BBC you could progress to head of department or to head of wardrobe for a theatre company.

Advantages/disadvantages

It is rewarding to see your original work on the stage or screen, providing enjoyment for viewers.

You might be able to work flexible hours but they could also be unsocial.

You will often be required to work to tight deadlines which could be stressful.

Money guide

Industry salaries vary depending on the type of employer and geographical location. Earnings in film and TV are generally higher than in theatre.

The starting salary for a costume designer is typically £18,000 per year rising to in excess of £28,000 with experience.

Senior designers can earn £35,000 or more.

The Broadcasting, Entertainment, Cinematograph and Theatre Union (BECTU) website lists guidance on the rates charged for freelance work dependent on the budget and seniority involved.

Related opportunities

- Fashion Designer/Milliner p161
- Tailor/Dressmaker p231
- Visual Merchandiser p177

Further information

Broadcasting, Entertainment, Cinematograph and Theatre Union
www.bectu.org.uk

Costume Society
www.costumesociety.org.uk

Society of British Theatre Designers
www.theatredesign.org.uk

Qualifications and courses

Entrants to this profession usually have a degree, Foundation degree or HNC/HND in a relevant subject such as fashion, textiles or millinery. City & Guilds and the National Open College Network provide other general design courses whereas a postgraduate degree may help those who wish to specialise in a particular area or whose first degree was in an unrelated subject.

Candidates without a degree or graduates from non-related subjects can sometimes enter this industry but they must have relevant work experience and be able to demonstrate expertise and interest in fashion.

All entrants are strongly advised to pursue work experience, either voluntary or paid, to build up their portfolio of designs, technical drawings and garments. Placements show commitment to the profession and provide opportunities to make industry contacts. Some graduates choose to gain international experience with European or American designers before looking to break into the UK market.

New designers are normally selected based on their portfolio and an interview. Your portfolio should include technical drawings, mood boards and designs. Some interviews may require evidence of actual garments you have made. Networking is also a very important tool when trying to find work, so it is important during your education to make as many contacts with people in the industry as possible.

What the work involves

Using your design sense and knowledge of textiles and other materials you will develop clothing, shoes and accessories. A milliner specialises in creating headwear.

You could work in haute couture, ready-to-wear or high street fashion. Most designers work two seasons ahead, and you will liaise with industry buyers and forecasters analysing trends in fabrics, colours and shapes.

As well as creating initial designs by hand and with computer-aided design (CAD), you may also oversee the manufacture of these items.

Type of person suited to this work

It is essential to have the creativity and the imagination to develop original designs as well as the foresight to read future fashion trends.

Having the skills to draw designs by hand and to use specialist CAD software is also important, as are technical skills, such as pattern cutting, and a good eye for design, colour and detail. These abilities should be balanced with good business sense and the competence to see a project through.

You will also need excellent communication, negotiation and organisational skills to ensure that projects are carried out on time, within budget and as requested.

Working conditions

You will usually work alone or in a small team in a studio. The environment can be dusty and you will be using specialist equipment such as cutting tools and sewing machines.

Hours could be irregular including overtime in the run-up to shows when changes to designs might need to be made at the last minute.

You will also spend some of your time visiting textile producers and clients at their premises which could be overseas.

Future prospects

There are roughly 12,000 fashion designers in employment in the UK and most work in and around the fashion hub of London.

Career progression depends upon the individual's talent and reputation. You will most likely start as a design assistant and progress to a role as a designer. With experience, it is possible to become a senior or head designer or work in an area such as style consultancy or fashion journalism. There are fewer opportunities for promotion in millinery owing to the smaller size of the industry.

The UK fashion industry has an excellent international reputation, offering the chance to work overseas if desired.

Advantages/disadvantages

Seeing your original ideas in the public eye is satisfying.

You will have the opportunity to travel and meet interesting people of different nationalities.

Working to tight deadlines in the lead-up to shows can be stressful.

Money guide

Salaries vary according to the company type and location.

Newly qualified designers can expect to earn £16,000 to £22,000 per year.

After 3 to 4 years of experience, you could have a salary of £25,000 to £40,000. Senior designers can earn in excess of £60,000.

Your salary will be determined by your success and the most famous designers have very high incomes. Rates for freelance designers vary widely and if they have an agent, that agent will generally take up to 30% of earnings.

Related opportunities

- Illustrator/Technical Illustrator p166
- Interior Designer p167
- Visual Merchandiser p177

Further information

British Fashion Council
www.britishfashioncouncil.co.uk

Design Council
www.designcouncil.org.uk

Qualifications and courses

There are no specific entry requirements, artistic talent being the most important attribute. However, the majority of artists choose to pursue formal qualifications to increase their chance of success. A degree or HNC/HND in fine art, art and design or a related subject would be useful. Postgraduate qualifications in fine art are also available. Sculptors usually have a fine art degree with a specialisation in sculpture. Entry requirements for degree courses vary. Some institutions require A levels/H grades in relevant subjects, some want the student to have completed a Foundation degree and others accept students solely on the strength of their portfolio.

Artists without a degree often take short courses, including evening or weekend classes, one-week intensive classes, certificates and diplomas. Entrants who undertake voluntary work experience or community projects, or work shadowing in the creative industries, can improve their employment prospects.

It is up to artists and sculptors to create their own opportunities for showcasing their work through self-promotion. Gallery owners and curators are always looking for new artists but you can also display your work online through your own website or established ones, through social media or by collaborating with other artists and collectives. Networking is important and having an agent may be useful.

What the work involves

Fine artists work with various media such as oil paints and charcoal to create 2D pieces of various sizes. Sculptors create 3D pieces and use materials like clay, stone and metal.

You will be responsible for promoting your work to sponsors, galleries and other organisations by networking or issuing publicity material.

You might organise solo or joint exhibitions in a variety of venues to showcase your work. Some residencies are available in institutions such as schools and prisons.

Type of person suited to this work

You will be creating original works of art so need strong artistic and technical skills, well-developed powers of observation and a vivid imagination.

Self-belief and motivation are important as it takes perseverance to turn an original idea into a finished piece. Sculptors will also require a high level of manual dexterity.

Many artists are self-employed, necessitating good business sense and organisational skills. Strong communication skills will help you to negotiate exhibitions with galleries and network with contacts in the art world.

Working conditions

You will work in a studio, on location or teach workshops at a residency. Much of your time will be spent alone and you will set your own hours.

Many artistic materials are dusty, oily or may stain and, even wearing overalls, you can expect to get dirty. You might have to work with solvents and other chemicals.

Sculptors will work with dangerous tools such as knives, chisels and welding equipment.

Future prospects

This job demands confidence and persistence as few artists and sculptors earn their living from art alone. You could earn additional income by working in related areas such as arts education, community development and in art galleries.

A developing artist should join networks to make contacts. It is possible to sell your work through a number of galleries, shops, workshop co-operatives, studios and the internet. You could progress from showcasing your work in a group exhibition to securing a solo exhibition. You could eventually have your own studio, secure an agent and have your work displayed in national and international art fairs.

Advantages/disadvantages

The job is fulfilling as you will have the pleasure of seeing customers enjoy and appreciate your art.

It can be an isolated way of life and you may not always receive recognition for your work.

Money guide

Artists' earnings vary depending on their talent, experience and reputation.

While it is possible to earn a regular income from your work, many artists have another job to provide a more stable source of income.

The Artists Information Company have an artist's fees toolkit on their website which provides guidance on the rates artists should charge for their work.

New artists displaying at degree shows should expect no more than £1,000 for a BA-level piece of work or £2,000 for MA work.

Related opportunities

- Cartoonist p159
- Graphic Designer p165
- Illustrator/Technical Illustrator p166

Further information

a-n The Artists Information Company
www.a-n.co.uk

Arts Council England
www.artscouncil.org.uk

Arts Council of Northern Ireland
www.artscouncil-ni.org

Arts Council of Wales
www.artswales.org.uk

Creative Scotland
www.creativescotland.com

GEMMOLOGIST

Qualifications and courses

Some people enter this profession with relevant experience in areas such as cutting or retailing gems, dealing, mining or auctioneering, however there are no set entry requirements. Some entrants are graduates of relevant subjects such as art, craft, earth sciences, geology, science (physics in particular) and technology. Other useful qualifications include a degree in a geoscience subject, such as geology, geophysics or geochemistry, and an HND in Gemmology is available from Birmingham City University.

Entrants are most likely to train on the job and study for qualifications on a part-time basis. The Gemmological Association (GEM-A) offers qualifications which combine theoretical and practical work. These generally take 3 months to a year to complete and can be taken on-site in London, through online distance learning (ODL) or via a combination of the two. Jewellery courses and qualifications are available in many institutions throughout the UK.

What the work involves

Gemmologists work with diamonds, gems, precious stones and other ornamental materials. You will identify such materials and examine their quality. This may involve assessing or grading the cut of the stone, or identifying flaws or imitations (stones that are made of synthetic or artificial materials).

You are likely to work for a jewellery house where you will be involved in making valuations for customers and clients, and buying and selling stones.

You may also be employed by an insurance company where you will make appraisals for those who wish to insure their jewellery.

Type of person suited to this work

It is important that you have an interest in rocks, gems and crystals, design, the earth sciences and geology. You should also have a keen eye for detail as you will have to look for the slightest qualities to make valuations and identify stones.

As your work will mainly be hands-on you should be good with your hands and have good eyesight and memory.

You should be trustworthy and happy to work in high-security environments.

Working conditions

Your working hours will depend on the type of organisation that you work for. If working for a retail jeweller, you might work around 40 hours a week, including weekends.

You could work in an office, laboratory, workshop or studio. If you become involved in mining or travelling to gem markets you might have to work in remote and uncomfortable conditions.

You will use specialist equipment such as lenses, refractometers, spectroscopes and microscopes to examine gemstones. Owing to the nature of your work, you will have to adhere to strict security protocol, including locked doors, barred windows, armed guards, CCTV surveillance and alarm systems.

Future prospects

After you have finished your training and gained qualifications and experience, you may move up to senior management positions.

You may find opportunities in wholesale organisations, retail operations such as jewellery houses, and insurance companies. There may be opportunities to work abroad.

With significant experience and good contacts you may become self-employed, work as a consultant or jewel sourcer.

Some gemmologists, after years of experience, decide to combine their market knowledge with a more creative output by setting up their own business as a jewellery maker or designer.

Advantages/disadvantages

As a self-employed gemmologist your work may involve travel to mines, markets and international gem-selling centres such as Africa, Russia, Australia, Thailand, Brazil or Madagascar.

As you may be working with valuable materials you might have to work in restricted, high security environments.

Money guide

Starting salaries for gemmologists are around £14,000 per year.

As an experienced gemmologist you can earn between £25,000 and £35,000 a year.

Salaries for senior gemmologists can be in excess of £50,000.

Self-employed gemmologists' salaries vary.

Related opportunities

- Gold/Silversmith/Engraver p164
- Jeweller p472
- Materials Scientist p514

Further information

GEM-A The Gemmological Association of Great Britain
www.gem-a.com

Jewellery and Allied Industries Training Council
www.jaitc.org.uk

DESIGN, ARTS AND CRAFTS

Qualifications and courses

No formal qualifications are required but it may be usual to have an artistic background or art and design qualification. GCSEs/National 5s in Art and Design or Design and Technology are useful.

Many different qualifications in design crafts and art and design are available. Entrants could take BTECs, Foundation degrees or NVQ/SVQ courses in art and design or 3D design.

For the creative side of engraving, there are degrees and master's degrees in metalwork, jewellery making, goldsmithing and silversmithing. Entry for a degree usually requires a portfolio of work, an art and design Foundation course and/or a relevant BTEC National Diploma. Whilst a candidate's creative ability and potential, as displayed in their portfolio, are valued highly, degree courses usually also require a minimum entry requirement of 2 A levels/3 H grades and 5 GCSEs/National 5s.

The National Association of Goldsmiths (NAG) has created many distance learning courses which would be very useful. The course fees are lower for NAG members.

Some employers offer training positions, working with an experienced goldsmith, silversmith or engraver. Alternatively, the Goldsmiths' Company offers official apprenticeships which combine practical training with study towards professional qualifications, for those aged 16–21. Apprenticeships last up to 5 years.

A portfolio of work will be useful as evidence of your work and skill level.

What the work involves

Gold/silversmiths create large and small items such as boxes, figures, picture frames and clocks in gold and silver. You will also be expected to undertake repair work on existing items.

Engravers will create and insert or engrave images, words or patterns onto stone, glass, metal or wood. You will be required to work with your hands and use specialist equipment.

You may create objects commissioned by jewellers or individual clients, or develop your own craft pieces to sell through galleries and craft shops.

Type of person suited to this work

This job demands dexterity and conscientiousness. A technical and creative approach is useful to help you plan a piece and decide on the amount of material needed.

An artistic flair is essential in this type of work, as is the ability to see a project through from start to finish. You will need considerable patience to undertake delicate and sometimes repetitive work with specialist materials and equipment.

If you run your own business you will need a confident and determined approach in order to promote yourself and your products. Financial and business skills are also needed.

Working conditions

You will probably work in a workshop or studio – either with other craftspeople or on your own. You may work in a shop and have meetings with customers to discuss pieces of work.

You will use specialist tools for heating, cutting, bending and shaping the metals, tools which can be dangerous if used incorrectly. You will therefore need to wear eye, face, hand and possibly ear protection for some jobs.

Future prospects

Most gold/silversmith employers are based in London, Birmingham, Sheffield, Glasgow and Edinburgh. Entry level and apprenticeship positions are very competitive.

Once in the profession you may progress to become a workshop supervisor, international buyer or manager, or become self-employed.

For engravers, promotion to senior engraver, supervisor or manager may be possible within larger companies.

Engravers may also become self-employed.

Advantages/disadvantages

This type of work provides the intense satisfaction of creating attractive and lasting objects.

Working with expensive materials such as glass and metal can be challenging, time-consuming and allows little room for mistakes.

Money guide

It is quite common for a gold/silversmith or engraver in the early stages of their career to supplement their income with another job.

Apprentices progressing through their apprenticeship and gaining experience could earn between £18,500 and £20,000 per year.

Salaries for qualified goldsmiths are between £20,000 and £25,000 and with extensive experience this could potentially increase to between £40,000 and £50,000 a year.

The salary for engravers starts at around £11,500 and could climb to £30,000 or more for experienced, self-employed engravers.

Earnings for those who are self-employed will vary depending upon their sales and reputation.

Related opportunities

- Gemmologist p163
- Jewellery Designer p168
- Model Maker p170

Further information

Crafts Council
www.craftscouncil.org.uk

Institute of Professional Goldsmiths
www.ipgoldsmiths.com

National Association of Jewellers
www.naj.co.uk

GRAPHIC DESIGNER

Qualifications and courses

The majority of entrants have a degree in a visual arts subject such as graphic design, fine art, illustration or 3D design. Entry without a higher education qualification is possible if you have an exceptional portfolio but progression is difficult without formal training. The minimum requirements for a degree are usually 2 A levels/3 H grades, including an art-related subject, and 5 GCSEs/National 5s. It is also recommended to complete a Foundation diploma or BTEC National in art and design, as entry to an undergraduate art degree without these qualifications is rare.

School leavers have the option to apply for an apprenticeship in design and train to become a graphic design assistant or junior graphic designer.

Competition within this industry is strong so pre-entry experience, for example from work experience placements or internships, is essential. Work experience will also allow you to build up a portfolio of your design work which is essential for interviews, and networking with graphic designers during a placement could help you to secure employment in the future. Creating a website to showcase your work is also advised.

D&AD publish information about, and host training events and awards for designers with a particular emphasis on design and media for advertising.

A working knowledge of computer design software such as QuarkXPress, FreeHand, Illustrator or Photoshop is beneficial.

What the work involves

Graphic designers produce original images and designs for use in published or other materials such as leaflets, brochures, websites, logos and stationery. Most work is now done on computer, although manual techniques are occasionally used.

You will need a thorough understanding of clients' needs in order to develop appropriate designs for specific projects.

You will be responsible for producing time and budget schedules and ensuring that they are adhered to.

Type of person suited to this work

It is essential to have a strong creative flair, the imagination to develop original designs and a good eye for layout. Having the skills to draw designs by hand and to use industry-specific graphics or multimedia software packages is also important.

You need good communication skills and the confidence to present ideas to colleagues and clients. It is likely that you will work in a fast-paced environment with tight deadlines so you need to be able to multi-task and work well under pressure.

Organisational skills are essential to ensure that projects are carried out on time, within budget and as requested.

Working conditions

Most of your work will take place at a computer and drawing board within a studio. However, you may undertake external research in order to gain inspiration for a project and you will also be required to attend client meetings to present your ideas.

The majority of graphic designers work 37 hours a week, Monday to Friday. You will be expected to work overtime in order to meet deadlines. Part-time work is available and many experienced designers become freelancers.

Future prospects

In the UK there are about 18,000 businesses in this sector, with about 34% of its workforce in London and the south-east of England. The diversity of graphic design qualifications available has resulted in increased competition for positions.

There is the possibility to work for a range of clients in an agency or in-house for a large organisation such as a bank. Junior designers in larger organisations can progress to senior level and eventually a director role.

In smaller companies, many designers will decide to become self-employed within 5 to 10 years in order to progress and diversify their workload.

With experience there are many freelance opportunities.

Advantages/disadvantages

Creating original work and seeing your ideas being used in the public eye is satisfying.

Competition is becoming increasingly fierce as the number of available qualifications in this field rises.

Money guide

Earnings vary according to the type and size of employer and geographical location. Salaries tend to be higher within in-house design teams than in design agencies.

A junior designer can expect to earn £14,000–£19,000 at the start of their career.

As you gain experience in the field, your salary could increase to £18,000–£35,000.

Senior graphic designers can earn £32,000–£55,000 and creative directors can make in excess of £60,000 per year.

Freelance designers could be paid hourly or daily, which could range from £200 to £300 a day.

Related opportunities

- Advertising Art Director p383
- Animator p158
- Illustrator/Technical Illustrator p166

Further information

D&AD
www.dandad.org

Design Council
www.designcouncil.org.uk

Qualifications and courses

While a higher education qualification is not needed for this profession, most professional illustrators have an HNC/HND, Foundation degree or a degree in art and design related subjects. A postgraduate qualification but may also be useful, particularly for illustrators who are also interested in teaching or those who do not have a design-related first degree.

A strong portfolio is essential, and an excellent portfolio can be a substitute for academic qualifications.
The ability to produce work in multimedia format is increasingly sought after.

Technical illustrators are required to demonstrate a good knowledge of science and/or technology depending on your desired specialisation.

The Association of Illustrators (AOI) offers practical advice to illustrators and runs training seminars on business and computer related subjects.

What the work involves

You will create original illustrations for published material such as books, magazines and greetings cards. You may also create images for TV and the internet.

You will work with specialist design software, pen and ink and other media to develop strong designs. Your work will include attending client meetings, agreeing payments and contracts, and working to fulfil specific clients' requirements.

Technical illustrators design accurate graphics or illustrations to accompany and clarify often complex technical information in product and systems manuals, training materials, presentations and technical websites.

Type of person suited to this work

You will need strong design skills, a creative flair and imagination for illustration work. You should also be able to work well with computer design software. You will require a good knowledge of legal issues in order to protect your copyright and licence rights.

Technical illustration necessitates high attention to detail and strong technical drawing skills to plan and create accurate images.

Sharing ideas and working around another person's vision or 'brief' demands good communication skills. As many illustrators/technical illustrators work on a self-employed basis, you will need the confidence to promote your services as well as good business and financial sense.

Working conditions

You are likely to work in a shared studio or at your own premises. Technical illustrators occasionally work in offices, and some illustrators are employed in publishing or design houses, but freelancing is becoming increasingly more common.

You will probably use paints and adhesives which may cause respiratory problems or skin allergies for susceptible people.

Future prospects

The internet and email have made it easier for illustrators to promote themselves and find work, and it is now possible to gain work from clients based overseas.

More illustrators are now using agents to find work for them. Agents used to mostly take on clients who were already established in the field but more of them are now taking on new talent.

Some people choose to specialise in competitive areas such as medical, botanical or technical illustration.

To subsidise their income, some illustrators also teach, lecture or work in other related areas. A small number write and illustrate their own books. Others supplement their salary by selling illustrations, prints and paintings through galleries.

Advantages/disadvantages

This type of work provides the satisfaction of seeing your work in print and often in the public domain.

Working on a freelance, job-by-job basis can be an insecure way to make a living. Generally, illustrators have a second job to support them during quiet periods.

Money guide

Salaries vary according to employers and individual projects. Projects can range from one image to a series of illustrations. The NUJ Freelance Fees Guide website has guidelines on freelance fees for various types of projects.

Income for employed new entrants is around £14,000 to £19,000 per year.

Experienced illustrators could earn £20,000–£30,000.

With experience the best known can earn in excess of £40,000 per year.

Starting salaries for technical illustrators tend to be around £20,000–£25,000. With experience this can increase up to £40,000.

Related opportunities

- Cartoonist p159
- Graphic Designer p165
- Medical Illustrator p169

Further information

Association of Illustrators
www.theaoi.com

Institute of Scientific and Technical Communicators
www.istc.org.uk

INTERIOR DESIGNER

Qualifications and courses

The preferred route is to take a degree or HND/HNC in interior design, interior architecture or spatial design. Other related subjects are also acceptable. 2 relevant A levels/3 H grades and 5 GCSEs/National 5s (A*–C/A–C) are usually required for degree entry, or 1 A level/H grade and 4 GCSEs/National 5s for HNC/HNDs. Many applicants also complete a Foundation Diploma in Art and Design before applying for higher education.

Entrance in the absence of formal qualifications may still be possible for an applicant with relevant experience, enthusiasm and an exceptional portfolio.

Regardless of qualifications held, prior voluntary or part-time work experience is usually imperative to securing full-time employment. Placements will enable you to become familiar with computer design software and build up your portfolio of design work. The British Institute of Interior Design, the Chartered Society of Designers and the Directory of Design Consultants provide contact details for interior designers which may be useful when looking for work placements. Competition is fierce so networking and sending speculative applications are recommended. Traineeships are unusual and many designers take other jobs before starting in design.

What the work involves

Interior designers create specific, coordinated styles for homes, commercial spaces and other buildings.

You will be required to assess spaces, produce detailed designs, be familiar with computer-aided design (CAD) software, and choose suitable materials for the project which may include upholstery, wallpaper, furniture and decorative objects.

You will need to get a good understanding of the client's needs and negotiate fees with them. You will provide supervision to ensure that the project is completed accurately and in accordance with the budget and schedule.

Type of person suited to this work

It is essential to have a strong creative flair and the imagination to develop original designs. Having the skills to draw designs by hand and use specialist CAD software is also very important.

You will be required to keep up to date with changes in design and architecture, and to understand building regulations. You also need good business sense and the competency to see a project through.

You should have good communication, negotiation and organisational skills to ensure that projects are carried out on time, within budget and as requested.

Working conditions

The main employers in this sector are design and architectural firms. However, many designers are self-employed and part-time work is possible.

Client meetings often occur in the evenings and at weekends. You could be working on several contracts at the same time and tight deadlines can result in overtime.

Your work will be divided between meeting clients in their own premises and working in your studio or other work space. Smart dress is expected and protective clothing may be required on-site.

Future prospects

There is a growing demand for good interior designers but the sector is intensely competitive.

Although many interior designers work for design and architectural companies, some are freelance and many choose to start up their own design companies, either immediately after graduation or once they have gained experience.

There is no established career structure; however it is possible to progress to a partner role in a consultancy.

Working for a smaller company can lead to more responsibility than a larger consultancy. The UK industry has an excellent international reputation so you could work overseas.

Advantages/disadvantages

Creating original work and seeing your ideas being used in a practical or decorative way is satisfying.

Working as a freelance designer can result in greater flexibility.

Meeting deadlines and budgets can be stressful.

Money guide

A junior/trainee interior designer would usually start on £18,000–£23,000.

Those with experience can expect to earn £24,000–£40,000 a year.

Senior designers can achieve £45,000 and up. Directors may earn up to £75,000.

Freelance designers set their own rate based upon their reputation and experience.

Related opportunities

- Illustrator/Technical Illustrator p166
- Model Maker p170
- Visual Merchandiser p177

Further information

British Institute of Interior Design
www.biid.org.uk

Chartered Society of Designers
www.csd.org.uk

Design Council
www.designcouncil.org.uk

JEWELLERY DESIGNER

Qualifications and courses

Most jewellery companies ask entrants to the industry to hold a degree in jewellery design, although it is still possible to enter this career through skill alone.

GCSEs/National 5s and A levels/H grades in Art and Design or Design and Technology may help you to gain entry to this profession or to higher level courses as they demonstrate both creativity and commitment. Other useful qualifications include HNDs, Foundation degrees or degrees in art and design or more specific subjects like goldsmithing, silversmithing and jewellery design.

Typically, qualifications are not as important as craft skills. Work placements can help you to accumulate experience of the jewellery industry and build up a network of contacts which will help you to develop skills and find buyers and sellers for your work.

The Holts Academy runs apprenticeships in jewellery manufacture at Levels 2 & 3. There is also the Holts Academy Employability Bootcamp, designed to equip attendees with industry related skills that will help them gain employment for an apprenticeship or go on to further education in jewellery manufacture and design.

It is common for designers to take other jobs in related areas first in order to build experience. It may be possible to move across from another relevant subject such as fashion design, textile design, fine art or applied arts if you build up a suitable portfolio.

What the work involves

Jewellery designers are involved in each aspect of the production of decorative pieces of jewellery of various types, including the selection of materials such as gold, silver, precious metals and stones.

You will research the design and the function of a piece; its symbolism, the materials used, the cost, the potential buyer and even current trends.

You will prepare detailed drawings which you or a craftworker will create using traditional crafting methods or using high-tech machinery. A design may be for a one-off piece or part of a range of pieces. You will undertake tasks such as stone cutting and setting, model-making, mounting, engraving, enamelling, welding, chain-making, cleaning and polishing.

Type of person suited to this work

You should have a strong interest in art, design, fashion and craftwork. As your sales may be influenced by the current design marketplace, you should keep up to date with jewellery fashion and design trends.

Reputation is increasingly important for developing and sustaining a successful career. You should be skilled at marketing and self-promotion and willing to visit trade fairs, enter competitions and write articles for trade magazines to establish your brand.

You must have a keen eye for detail and patience as you will be working with small scales and intricate and delicate designs.

You will need to be organised and self-motivated as you will probably be working on a variety of projects at the same time. You should also be able to visualise 2D designs as 3D objects.

Working conditions

If you are employed by a company you will usually work 35–40 hours a week, Monday to Friday, including late nights or weekend work when deadlines are approaching.

You can also work on a freelance basis which will involve working on commission and producing designs specifically tailored to the client's requirements.

You may work in a studio which can be bright and airy or in a large workshop, which may be noisy and dusty. You must wear protective clothing.

Future prospects

Salaried positions for graduates are limited and you will probably need to start as a freelancer or run your own business. This could involve selling your designs to manufacturers or making the items and selling them yourself through galleries, shops or online. You should also attend trade fairs and exhibitions.

Specialising in creating products for a particular market is important. In order to keep up to date with trends and techniques you should also be willing to continuously research and retrain, either through postgraduate or specialist short courses.

Advantages/disadvantages

You may be able to work from your own designs and see your creations become popular pieces.

As a self-employed jewellery designer you may find that without the right support system in areas such as promotion, marketing and sales it can be difficult to become established.

Money guide

As a graduate in an employed position your salary can start at around £16,000 per year.

This can increase to between £20,000 and £50,000 or more with experience.

Your salary will depend greatly on factors such as whether or not you are self-employed, experienced and have enough success to gain a reputation within the industry.

Related opportunities

- Fashion Designer/Milliner p161
- Gold/Silversmith/Engraver p164
- Product Designer p173

Further information

Crafts Council
www.craftscouncil.org.uk

Qualifications and courses

Entry into this profession is not possible without a relevant degree or HND. Desirable degree subjects include medical illustration, clinical photography, and photography with typical entry requirements being 2 A levels/3 H grades, often including Biology and Photography, and 5 GCSEs/National 5s.

Medical illustrators usually enter the profession as trainees and learn on the job while working towards a medical illustration qualification. Students on a recognised course of study or training are entitled to become a student member of the Institute of Medical Illustrators (IMI).

A voluntary national register for medical illustrators was formed in 2010 by the Committee for the Accreditation of Medical Illustration Practitioners (CAMIP). The register was formed with the aim of regulation and maintaining high standards in the profession.

You will need to have a good portfolio of work to help you stand out in a specialised field. Pre-entry work experience in a placement, project, or in a caring capacity would be useful. It may lead to freelancing opportunities for medical books.

What the work involves

Medical illustrators create annotated or labelled images to provide visual information to professionals and trainees working in medical care, research and education.

You may also work as a medical photographer or video producer (digital technician), or combine all these functions in one role.

You will have to record images of patients and develop graphics for health/medical publications such as information leaflets and websites. You could work in wards, operating theatres, pathology labs, mortuaries and clinical exam centres.

Type of person suited to this work

Good visual sense and attention to detail is very important. You should have excellent technical skills to work with equipment such as videos and cameras, and will have to work creatively yet accurately with computer design packages.

As you will have to record images of patients, a sensitive, tactful and ethical approach is necessary. You should also have a knowledge of physiology and anatomy.

Also required is the ability to communicate with all sorts of people, some of whom could be very ill. You must be able to cope with upsetting situations and sights, for example, if visiting someone who is terminally ill.

Working conditions

You may be based within a group of hospitals and other centres and have to travel regularly between these. During the day you will visit theatres, wards, training centres and mortuaries – all of which could involve distressing sights and intense odours. You may have to be on-call at night to photograph emergency operations.

Using a computer and software design packages, you will work within an office or studio to prepare and produce images and visual information. You may also have to record laboratory results.

Future prospects

This is a small and specialised profession, with great competition for jobs. There is, however, great opportunity to train and further specialise in niche fields.

Gaining a range of technical skills and experience rather than specialising in one area could open more opportunities.

After training, it is possible to progress within one organisation to head of department or you could go on to provide freelance services for medical establishments or medical and scientific publications.

Advantages/disadvantages

This job gives the satisfaction of providing valuable visual information to help medical professionals and their patients.

You may have the opportunity to freelance, which offers flexibility.

You will work with sick and sometimes distressed patients and may have to deal with upsetting sights. You may also have to be on call at night in order to photograph emergency operations.

Money guide

The Agenda for Change (AfC) NHS pay structure means medical illustrators start on Band 5, earning between £21,692 and £28,180 a year.

With experience, senior medical illustrators progress to Band 6, earning between £26,041 and £34,876.

When in charge of a team you progress to Band 7, which pays from £31,072 a year.

Medical illustrators in large university teaching hospitals could be employed on a number of pay scales covering technicians, medical laboratory officers, or sterile services technicians. Check with the university teaching hospitals for more details. Freelance work in photography or illustration for medical books can supplement income.

Related opportunities

- Fine Artist/Sculptor p162
- Graphic Designer p165
- Photographer p399

Further information

Association of Illustrators
www.theaoi.com

Health and Care Professions Council
www.hpc-uk.org

Institute of Medical Illustrators
www.imi.org.uk

Qualifications and courses

There are no formal entry requirements to this industry, however, the ability to work with your hands and use specialist tools is very important. It is important to note that most entrants complete a model-making course and have a strong portfolio of work.

With an increasing emphasis on computer-aided design, there are a wide variety of courses available to help improve knowledge and skills including a City & Guilds Level 2 Certificate in Engineering (2850), ABC Level 3 Award in Visual Art (Exploratory Model Making), Foundation degrees in 3D design and degrees in design modelling. Entry requirements vary but most institutions will expect some GCSEs/National 5s in subjects such as Maths, Design and Technology, and Physics. For entry onto a degree course, you will need at least 2 A levels/3 H grades and 5 GCSEs/National 5s in relevant subjects.

Entry via an Engineering Manufacture (Craft and Technician) Apprenticeship may be possible in your area, which would combine the practical work experience of a job with the study of a professional qualification. You will need to be employed to qualify for an apprenticeship and work experience in areas such as engineering, electronics, carpentry or furniture making may help with finding work.

Professional bodies such as the Design Council and D&AD provide various opportunities for continuing professional development. The New Bloods scheme in particular includes awards, exhibitions, workshops and intense training courses in order to get under-24s noticed by the industry. The Institution of Engineering Designers operates a membership scheme with events and classes which are useful to share ideas and network.

What the work involves

Working with materials such as fibreglass, resin, wood and rubber you will create 3D images or models.

You will construct detailed and accurate models of buildings, prototypes of items, engineering products and figures for museums and TV or film companies.

You will work with clients to develop their ideas into a convincing and practical model, deciding which materials to use. You will plan the model using technical drawings or computer software.

Type of person suited to this work

You will need a strong creative flair to visualise and develop models. Producing detailed models out of fragile materials demands tremendous patience and good technical skills. You should have a logical approach in order to plan and create accurate work.

The tasks will demand great attention to detail and good eyesight. A feel for, and interest in, design will enable you to create well-planned models.

You will also need a basic knowledge of maths and the ability to understand technical drawings. The capacity to work effectively with computer design packages is increasingly important in this area of work.

Working conditions

Most model makers work within London and the south-east of England. There is still a demand for traditional model makers but often this is combined with computer-aided design (CAD).

Most model makers work standard office hours, but evening and weekend work may be required to meet deadlines.

Your work will be carried out in a studio, where you will wear protective clothing to suit the materials and tools you are using. Sometimes you may be based in an office, planning models with specialist design software.

You may need to travel around the UK or overseas to meet clients and assemble or install models for them.

Future prospects

The majority of model makers are self-employed and move from project to project as required in sectors such as architecture, film and TV and engineering. Often this type of business is set up after developing a strong portfolio, gaining a good reputation and undertaking courses on running a small business.

The industry recognises a need for model makers to think beyond the craft and to take responsibility for elements of project management, media production, architectural design and interpretation, and exhibition design. Experience and development in these areas could be beneficial in progressing a career in model making.

Advantages/disadvantages

This job can provide the satisfaction of developing original work.

You will need to create highly detailed work to fairly limited deadlines, which can be stressful.

Some of the materials you work with may produce unpleasant or dangerous fumes.

Money guide

Starting salaries are around £19,000 per year.

With experience this rises to between £23,000 and £30,000.

Freelancers negotiate a set fee for each project.

Related opportunities

- Fine Artist/Sculptor p162
- Graphic Designer p165
- Toymaker/Designer p176

Further information

Creative and Cultural Skills
www.ccskills.org.uk

D&AD
www.dandad.org

Design Council
www.designcouncil.org.uk

Qualifications and courses

There are no set qualifications for this type of work; however you will require the specialist skills to make/ repair your particular type (family) of instruments.

BTEC awards in Music Technology are available and courses in musical instrument making are available up to degree level from specific colleges and universities, such as London Metropolitan University. Entry requirements for these courses vary, but it will be necessary to have relevant GCSEs/National 5s and A levels/H grades for some courses. Others will accept you without these if you have relevant practical experience. For full details of course providers visit the National Association of Musical Instrument Repairers website.

When you begin employment you may receive on the job training from an experienced instrument maker/repairer and develop skills through part-time, specialist courses.

What the work involves

You will make, repair and service musical instruments such as pianos, flutes and violins but normally will specialise within one family of instruments.

The work will include building new instruments and working with specialised equipment and materials, replacing worn-down or broken parts and checking for the cause of specific faults by undertaking assessments. This could range from fine tuning to significant maintenance work.

You will work with customers, dealing with repair requests or commissions for new instruments.

Type of person suited to this work

A passion for music and a practical understanding of how musical instruments function is essential. They are complex objects so you will need a good eye for detail, excellent hearing and a patient approach.

Strong technical skills will enable you to design, create or repair instruments. You will need to be dexterous and confident in working with your hands and in using materials such as wood and glue.

You need to have excellent communication and interpersonal skills in order to deal with customers, particularly if you are self-employed.

Working conditions

This is a specialised area of work, but you could work for educational music departments, major orchestras, opera houses and theatres, rehearsal studios, retailers, and individual musicians.

You will work with a range of specialised tools in the workshop of a specialist company or from home if self-employed.

You will normally work a 40-hour week, Monday to Friday, however if you are self-employed you will often have to adapt your working hours to meet demand and clients' timetables.

With larger instruments, such as pianos, organs or timpani, you will need to visit private homes and other locations (such as concert halls, theatres or music studios) to do repairs on-site.

It would be useful to have a driving licence and your own transport.

You need to have strong manual handling skill. This job may be difficult for people with skin or respiratory conditions owing to some of the specialist materials used.

Future prospects

Specialising in a specific area such as classical guitars or making unusual instruments from commissions can enhance your reputation and build a strong client base in niche markets.

You may also be able to sell instruments to enhance your income as you will have ready access to the market.

A lot of people are self-employed and some music shops will publicise local repairers, instrument makers and tuners, rather than employing their own.

Advantages/disadvantages

Many musical instrument repairers/makers are freelance and work on a project-by-project basis, which can create some job insecurity.

This career has excellent fringe benefits as you could work for some of the best musical talents in the UK.

Money guide

In some parts of the country there is not sufficient work for full-time employment so most musical instrument makers and repairers are self-employed. Earnings will depend on your location, the local music scene and your specialism.

Work permitting, you could earn around £15,000–£20,000 per year once trained.

The most experienced people can earn up to £30,000 a year.

Related opportunities

- Art Therapist p274
- Musician p429
- Private Music Teacher p191

Further information

British Violin Making Association
www.bvma.org.uk

Crafts Council
www.craftscouncil.org.uk

Institute of Musical Instrument Technology
www.imit.org.uk

National Association of Musical Instrument Repairers
www.namir.org.uk

DESIGN, ARTS AND CRAFTS

PICTURE FRAMER

Qualifications and courses

There are no formal educational requirements, though you should have a good standard of general education and gaining relevant qualifications will help you to learn the specific skills and techniques that the job requires. Courses are available from local colleges and education services. These could be residential, weekend or part-time courses and they might last from 8 weeks up to a year.

An interest and experience in woodwork, metalwork or textiles would be useful. GCSEs/National 5s, A levels/H grades, certificates, diplomas, NVQs, Foundation degrees or degrees can also be an advantage; relevant subjects include art and design, creative arts and contemporary crafts.

Training is usually done on the job alongside an experienced professional. In order to work with high-value items, framers need to be trained to conservation standards.

Picture framers are able to work towards the Guild Commended Framer (GCF) qualification from the Fine Art Trade Guild, which involves both practical and written assessments. This qualification sets an internationally recognised standard for picture framers.

What the work involves

You will plan and create attractive and protective surrounds or frames for prints, paintings, photographs and 3D objects. Working with specialist equipment and materials you will create strong, high-quality frames.

Helping customers choose the most suitable style and size of frame will be part of your job and you will advise them on the most practical and appropriate method of framing and glazing the artwork.

If you work on a self-employed basis you will need to promote your services to potential customers.

Type of person suited to this work

Creativity is essential in order to design the frame. You will also need good customer service skills. Technical skills and the ability to work safely with potentially dangerous equipment are highly important.

Paying attention to detail and taking a pride in your work will ensure that you produce high-quality frames. You will need to be able to work under pressure as short deadlines can be a part of this job. You should also be commercially aware. If self-employed, you will require business, financial and marketing skills to be successful.

Working conditions

You could work in a shop or workshop. When working in the shop you will have to deal with customers who can sometimes be rude or confrontational if dissatisfied. Workshops can be noisy and busy.

Picture framers generally work 40 hours a week, with weekend work often needed and overtime during busy periods. Many picture framers work on a part-time basis.

Picture framers work with potentially dangerous equipment such as specialist cutting machinery so you will need to be aware of health and safety requirements and wear protective clothing.

Future prospects

Success depends upon the skills and reputation of the individual.

Many picture framers set up their own studios or shops where they also sell works of art and artists' materials. Others work solely in framing and are employed in larger workshops, mass-producing framed prints and mirrors. There is the possibility of promotion to a supervisory or managerial role in bigger companies.

Some picture framers take additional training so that they can teach part time. In addition to the Guild Commended Framer (GCF) award, the Fine Art Trade Guild also offers an Advanced GCF award in specialist areas such as textile framing, mount design and function, and conservation framing for skilled and experienced picture framers who wish to develop their skills and teaching accreditation further.

Advantages/disadvantages

This job provides the satisfaction of creating enduring and high quality items.

If you are employed in a gallery or museum, you will have the opportunity to work with famous and valuable pieces of art.

The nature of the work requires you to be precise, careful and patient.

Money guide

The starting salary for a trainee picture framer is between £13,500 and £16,000.

With experience, your earnings could rise to between £17,000 and £20,000 or more.

Specialists who work with high value artwork in a gallery or museum could earn in excess £25,000.

Earnings for self-employed framers vary depending on location, expertise and the success of their business.

Related opportunities

- Conservator/Restorer p331
- Gold/Silversmith/Engraver p164
- Model Maker p170

Further information

Fine Art Trade Guild
www.fineart.co.uk

Institute of Conservation
www.icon.org.uk

PRODUCT DESIGNER

Qualifications and courses

Entry without a HNC/HND, Foundation degree or degree in product design, industrial design or a related subject is unlikely. Design courses can be centred on the art or engineering sides of product design. Students should check which universities offer modules in areas they would like to specialise in. Those choosing the art-based route sometimes take a 1-year Foundation course in art and design before their degree. A portfolio of design work is essential to prove creative skill, knowledge and the ability to work to a brief.

Entry requirements for degree programmes are usually a portfolio and 2 A levels/3 H grades and 5 GCSEs/National 5s (A*–C/A–C). For an HND you need 1 A level/H grade in an art and design subject and 3 GCSEs/National 5s. A BTEC qualification in art and design or 3D design could also be useful.

A postgraduate qualification enables you to specialise in a specific area and may provide an advantage when working with certain European clients.

Previous experience through industrial placements, freelance work or design competitions is invaluable. This sector is very competitive so you should make contacts during work placements or by joining the Chartered Society of Designers. Employers will look for a strong portfolio which showcases your design work.

What the work involves

Product designers (sometimes called industrial designers) create new products and improve the design, functionality or cost efficiency of existing products. These could be day-to-day products like tables or specialist ones like medical equipment.

You will decide upon a design brief with your client and carry out research into similar products and consumer behaviour. You will use both traditional drawing techniques and specialist computer software to develop appropriate designs.

You will select materials, produce prototypes and ensure that the project is completed on time and to budget.

Type of person suited to this work

This job requires both creativity and technical expertise. You should have a good eye for design as well as technical drawing and IT skills. It is important to understand how different materials and production methods function.

You need good communication skills and an understanding of clients' needs and consumer behaviour.

Problem-solving and organisational skills are essential to ensure projects are completed on time and within budget.

Working conditions

Product designers work in manufacturing firms and design companies which produce material for a variety of sectors. Employment is available all over the UK but most design consultancies are based in London and the south-east of England.

The majority of product designers work 37 hours a week, Monday to Friday. You will be expected to work extra hours in order to meet deadlines. Part-time and freelance work is quite common.

Most of your work will take place in a bright, clean studio or office. However, you will undertake some experiments and material testing in lab conditions, using specialist tools and equipment. You might also have to visit production factories which may be dusty and noisy.

Future prospects

There is strong competition for entry level jobs but there is significant demand for experienced product designers with a high level of technical expertise, particularly in niche areas.

Experienced designers may have the opportunity to work abroad or freelance. You could progress to a senior or managerial level.

Advantages/disadvantages

You will have the opportunity to use your imagination and technical skills.

Creating original work that is used by the public is satisfying.

Competition for entry level jobs is fierce.

Working to tight budgets and project deadlines can be stressful.

Money guide

Earnings vary according to the geographical location, type and size of employer.

Starting salaries for junior designers are around £19,000–£25,000.

Those with experience typically earn £30,000–£40,000 per year.

Very experienced and senior product designers can make in excess of £50,000.

Contract or freelance designers set their own rates depending upon their reputation and client contacts.

Related opportunities

- Manufacturing/Production Engineer p217
- Toolmaker p234
- Toymaker/Designer p176

Further information

Chartered Society of Designers
www.csd.org.uk

SIGNWRITER/ SIGNMAKER

Qualifications and courses

There are no formal educational requirements for either role, but GCSEs/National 5s in art or relevant vocational qualifications can be useful. You can specialise in signwriting after completing a BTEC or HNC/HND in Graphic Design.

Training is usually done on the job, especially in the case of signwriting. Many employers offer apprenticeships for people aged between 16 and 24 for signmaking which can combine employment with the study of a relevant professional qualification. Applicants normally require 4 GCSEs/National 5s (A*–E/A–E), including Maths, English Language, a science and an art and design subject, or other evidence of aptitude.

It is possible to take a full- or part-time course in signwriting and signmaking, such as the NVQ Level 2 or 3 in Signmaking. There are specialist courses available, such as gold leaf gilding, that can improve your skills and job prospects.

Due to having to work on site, as a signmaker you will need to gain a Constructions Skills Certification Scheme (CSCS) card as a Sign Installer – Illuminated/ Non-Illuminated. This card acts as a passport to work and is proof of an NVQ and having passed a health and safety test. The Prefabricated Access Suppliers' and Manufacturers' Association (PASMA) or the International Powered Access Federation (IPAF) provide accreditation for working at heights.

What the work involves

You will design, plan and produce signs with graphic images, lettering and logos to publicise companies, attract customers and draw attention to specific locations.

You will work closely with customers to develop appropriate, appealing designs that match their requirements.

You could work with any number of different materials and methods; from plastics to glass to sketching as well as computer-aided design (CAD).

You will produce signs for shop fronts, roadsides, hospitals, vehicles and even boats!

Type of person suited to this work

As you will be creating signs to interest or warn people, you will need strong graphic design skills. A creative flair and drawing skills are also important.

You will need an understanding of the materials you work with and good manual skills.

You must be methodical and have strong attention to detail. Technical skills will allow you to work with a range of equipment. IT skills and an ability to use programs such as Omega are becoming increasingly important.

Good written and verbal communication skills, along with excellent people skills, will help you to meet client requirements accurately and avoid expensive errors.

Working conditions

You could work within a studio or manufacturing site, which can get messy and noisy.

You might attend meetings with customers and make site visits. Much of your time will be spent drafting signs at a computer using special software.

You may work with large or small-scale specialist equipment, with printing inks and chemical finishes, which can affect people with skin or respiratory conditions.

Future prospects

You could work in the more commercial side of signwriting, within a specialist company on the design or manufacturing side, or you could work within the more creative, hand-crafted side of the industry.

Some signwriters go into set or prop design for theatre, film or TV programmes.

With experience, you could start your own business – perhaps specialising in pub or restaurant signs.

Despite being a declining industry, signmaking is still a fairly competitive area; the demand from a range of organisations for high-quality signs means that there are opportunities throughout the country.

Advantages/disadvantages

This kind of work can provide opportunities to be creative and to use your imagination to help customers, for example when designing a company logo.

You might need to travel frequently to a range of locations in order to take measurements or photographs. There is the option of working abroad.

Money guide

Signmakers can earn between £16,000 and £19,000 per year.

Signwriters are usually self-employed and their earnings vary depending on demand and their own level of success in the market. Salaries usually range from £18,000 to £24,000 a year.

Related opportunities

- Cartoonist p159
- Fine Artist/Sculptor p162
- Graphic Designer p165

Further information

British Sign and Graphics Association
www.bsga.co.uk

Creative and Cultural Skills
www.ccskills.org.uk

Faversham House Group
www.favershamhouse.com

Qualifications and courses

It is possible to enter the industry without any formal qualifications as a designer's assistant or prop maker in the theatre or as a runner or art department trainee in film and TV and then work your way up. The key skills of creativity, vision and design are essential.

Most people, however, have a HND, degree or postgraduate diploma. Specialist courses include theatre design, performing arts (production) and design for film and television, but other art and design related subjects such as architecture, interior design and fine art can be useful too. For a degree you should have 2 A levels/3 H grades or a HNC/HND in a relevant subject, 5 GCSEs/ National 5s (A*–C/A–C) and a good portfolio. For an HNC/ HND you are normally required to have 1 A level/H grade.

A design qualification is useful as it enables you to further build your portfolio which will be essential when securing employment. You also must demonstrate a passion and commitment to stage and set design.

It is helpful to obtain experience before entering this highly competitive profession as it highlights commitment and helps you build contacts as well as skills. Experience can be achieved by means of an unpaid placement, freelance work and involvement in student productions, amateur theatre, independent films or design competitions. There are also apprenticeship schemes available.

What the work involves

Stage/set designers are responsible for the visual elements of a theatre (stage designer), TV or film production (set designer) including sets, locations and possibly props and costumes.

From background research, you will be required to create original ideas which accurately reflect the relevant style and historical period of the piece.

Working closely with the production team, you will oversee the development and installation of the sets and ensure that everything is delivered on time and within budget.

Type of person suited to this work

It is essential to have a strong creative flair and a good eye for design. Having the skills to use specialist computer-aided design (CAD) software, to draw designs by hand and to create scale models when required is also very important.

You should be detail orientated and demonstrate a passion for history, culture and the performing arts. These abilities should be balanced with good communication skills to aid leadership and self-promotion.

Organisational skills are important to ensure that projects are carried out on time, within budget and as requested. As deadlines can be tight, you should also have the ability to work well under pressure.

Working conditions

Some designers work directly for a production company, however most entrants to the field can expect a primarily freelance career. Working hours are long and unsociable and you will be expected to work supplementary hours in order to meet deadlines.

Your work will be divided between being in a studio designing and building models of the sets, and then supervising in their creation on-set. Normally this happens behind the scenes in theatres, television studios or purpose-built warehouses.

You will work on large pieces, which necessitates the use of ladders and scaffolding.

Future prospects

Stage designers work for theatres and opera houses and may have the opportunity to oversee a travelling production. There is fierce competition for entry-level positions.

Set designers can work for the BBC or one of the 1,500 production firms in the country.

Part-time work is difficult to find and although there are many freelancers in the industry, work can be sporadic.

Advantages/disadvantages

The creation of original work and seeing your ideas being used in the public eye and in high profile productions is satisfying. Working as a freelancer can also result in greater flexibility.

Competition for entry-level jobs is fierce and a strong portfolio and good networking skills are important.

Meeting tight deadlines can result in high stress levels.

Money guide

Most designers work freelance as very few companies have resident designers now. Earnings will be dependent on individual ability, location and the contract size.

The Independent Theatre Council recommends a design fee of £2,450 in 2016/17 and a weekly fee for set building and other duties to be £480.

Contact the Broadcasting, Entertainment, Cinematograph and Theatre Union (BECTU) for information on minimum pay guidelines.

Related opportunities

- Costume Designer p160
- Interior Designer p167
- TV, Film and Radio Production Assistant/Runner p414

Further information

Broadcasting, Entertainment, Cinematograph and Theatre Union
www.bectu.org.uk

Design Council
www.designcouncil.org.uk

Society of British Theatre Designers
www.theatredesign.org.uk

DESIGN, ARTS AND CRAFTS

Qualifications and courses

There are no formal entry requirements but many entrants have a background in art and design. An HND or degree can be an advantage and relevant subjects include art and design, product design, graphic design or 3D design. Qualifications in child behaviour and psychology may also be useful. Higher education institutions sometimes have links with toy manufacturers which can provide a useful first step into the industry.

Minimum entry requirements for a degree are usually 2 A levels/3 H grades or equivalent, 5 GCSEs/National 5s (A*–C/A–C) and a portfolio of work. In England, Wales and Northern Ireland many students take a 1-year Foundation course as preparation for entry to an art and design degree. In Scotland, the first year of a 4-year degree equates to the Foundation year.

Alternatively, those who do not wish to pursue a degree could take the Edexcel BTEC Level 3 Award/Certificate/ Diploma in Design Crafts or the BTEC Higher National in 3D design (Levels 4 and 5).

Product design experience is useful. Toymakers involved in market research with children may need to undergo a Disclosure and Barring Service (DBS) check. You will also have to be aware of toy safety regulations as well as legislation, for example in relation to toy guns.

What the work involves

You will design, plan, test and create toys for babies, children and, possibly, adults.

As a traditional toymaker, you could make toys by hand, such as doll houses and rocking horses. If you work for a large manufacturer you will develop new products based on original ideas and sketches.

You will spend time promoting your work and design services to clients and customers. Your work could be sold in shops or at craft and toy fairs.

Type of person suited to this work

You will need creative flair to develop original ideas and a genuine interest in how individuals respond to toys. Practical design skills and an active imagination will help you create long-lasting and functional toys.

If creating objects by hand, you will need good manual skills and an understanding of the materials you work with. Knowledge of 3D design is fast becoming essential.

If self-employed, you will also need good business and financial skills and the confidence to promote your work.

Working conditions

Most toymakers/designers spend a lot of time in a workshop, planning and developing their products.

If employed as a toy designer by a manufacturer, you may work purely with computer design software and create, rather than construct, your designs.

You could work on a self-employed basis, making and designing toys. A small number of toymakers also restore antique toys.

Future prospects

There are limited opportunities in established companies for toymakers and designers. Mass production of toys normally takes place overseas and UK-based businesses tend to be small with fewer than 5 employees.

Toy design in the UK, however, is still strong and there is a growing market in toys with 'green' designs that are ethically created from renewable materials.

Some toymakers/designers own shops where they sell their own handmade toys and a growing number sell their products at craft fairs, on the internet or by mail order.

Within larger companies it may be possible to progress from junior to senior design roles. You can also move into development, buying and marketing.

'Techno toys' as well as sporting events can help to provide interest and growth in the toy industry.

Advantages/disadvantages

Creating fun, attractive toys to be enjoyed by children and adults alike is a rewarding career.

It is satisfying to see your original designs come to life as a finished product.

Competition is high and vacancies for toy designers are limited at manufacturing companies.

Those who become self-employed can expect it to take time and hard work to establish a business.

Money guide

Starting salaries for toy designers working for toy manufacturers range from £10,000 to £15,000 per year.

Those with experience who work in a large company can expect £23,000–£35,000.

The most successful designers of popular toys can achieve in excess of £45,000.

Traditional toymakers are usually self-employed and salaries will depend on the success of the business.

Related opportunities

- Animator p158
- Carpenter/Joiner p67
- Picture Framer p172

Further information

British Toymakers Guild
www.toymakersguild.co.uk

Crafts Council
www.craftscouncil.org.uk

Design Council
www.designcouncil.org.uk

Qualifications and courses

You could start as an in-store sales assistant and work your way up to trainee visual merchandiser. If you want to start out as a visual merchandiser, there are no formal entry requirements but many employers will look for relevant qualifications in design or retail.

Many different courses are available at Level 5 in display or design, marketing or retail. Degree courses in visual merchandising usually require 2 A levels/H grades and 5 GCSEs/National 5s (A*–C/A–C) or equivalent. Foundation degrees typically require 1 A level/H grade and 4 GCSEs/National 5s (A*–C/A–C) or equivalent.

Other relevant qualifications include the Fashion Retail Academy (FRA)'s full time or fast track Visual Merchandising (Level 4) course and the distance learning Certificate in Display and Visual Merchandising from the British Display Society. ABC also offers a Level 3 Diploma in Retail Skills (Visual Merchandising).

The Intermediate Level Apprenticeship in Retail involves training for the visual merchandiser role and you can progress to the level of visual merchandiser supervisor by taking the Advanced Apprenticeship. Apprenticeships combine practical work experience with the opportunity to study for a relevant, professional qualification. Applicants for an apprenticeship often require a minimum of 1 A level/H grade or strong GCSEs/National 5s, typically within a design-related subject.

A portfolio of art and design work is usually required by employers. Experience in display and the retail/exhibition sector can also be helpful.

What the work involves

Using your technical design skills, you will plan and design eye-catching window or shop front displays for shops, businesses and other organisations. You will work closely with clients to make sure that your designs meet their requirements.

Once you have identified materials and props for a window display, you will design an arrangement to create a striking theme or effect.

You might also provide advice to other shop branches or organisations on successful display design.

Type of person suited to this work

It is important to have strong creative ability, as well as excellent technical drawing and computer-aided design (CAD) skills. You need to have excellent communication skills to be able to balance your vision with that of your client and work with a wide range of people.

Certain roles will require you to keep up with new trends and products in fashion and culture. You must also be numerate, as one of your responsibilities will be to manage project budgets. A good level of fitness is also needed as assembling displays can be tiring.

Working conditions

Normally, you will be working indoors with different hand tools, materials, fabrics and the products to be displayed in the window or display. The work can often be pressured due to strict deadlines. You might have to work late especially in the build up to holiday seasons such as Christmas.

The job can involve a great deal of manual work. You will do lots of lifting and be on your feet for long periods, which can be very tiring. A driving licence would be useful as you will have to travel to meet suppliers and visit exhibitions and different company stores.

Future prospects

There are a range of opportunities, for example working for specialist display consultancy firms, large retailers, museums and other visitor attractions.

You will probably start as a junior and progress to a more senior position as supervisor, head designer, merchandiser and possibly department manager.

If you work for a multinational company, the opportunity may arise to work abroad. You could also go on to teach or lecture in design-related subjects. With experience, some display designers set up their own businesses or provide consultancy support to other organisations.

Advantages/disadvantages

This type of work can involve high levels of pressure due to tight deadlines.

You will have the satisfaction of seeing people enjoying your displays and giving you positive feedback.

You could have the opportunity to work with special effects like animatronics.

Money guide

Starting salaries are usually in the range of £12,000 to £18,000.

Once you have gained experience, your salary could rise to £20,000 to £27,000.

Visual merchandising managers or designers can earn £25,000 to £55,000.

At director level you could earn £45,000 to in excess of £60,000.

Related opportunities

- Interior Designer p167
- Model Maker p170
- Retail Buyer p477

Further information

British Display Society
www.britishdisplaysociety.co.uk

Design Council
www.designcouncil.org.uk

Education and Training

To work in this sector you need to be motivated and enthusiastic about other people's learning, whether it is adults or children. If you chose to teach, the range of subjects available is huge so whatever your interest – languages, art, sciences, cooking, sports – you can become a teacher in that field. Jobs in this sector require a multitude of skills including: creativity, imagination, numerical skills, good communication and organisational skills and, in some cases, having a lot of patience! The jobs featured in this section are listed below. For similar jobs to the ones in this sector turn to *Social Work and Counselling Services* on page 557.

Qualifications and courses

You can gain entry to this profession with a degree, a diploma or an HND/Foundation degree. A qualification in a relevant subject such as community education, sociology, social sciences, educational studies or youth work may improve your chances of employment. Some undergraduate and postgraduate courses offer part-time or distance learning options which will enable you to work/volunteer alongside your studies and some employers will offer formal support for students.

Employers usually seek candidates who have combined their qualification with paid or voluntary community experience. Some entrants come from a teaching background, while others have experience in the youth and community sector. Information and advice about voluntary work is available from YouthNet, the Workers' Educational Association (WEA) and local volunteer centres. Paid vacancies could arise from voluntary placements.

If you have no qualifications but you have accumulated significant experience then it may be possible for you to secure a post in the voluntary sector. However, it is likely that you will be required to have academic qualifications to reach a senior level. Some postgraduate courses will accept candidates with extensive experience as a substitute for qualifications and others offer the opportunity for those already employed to obtain a postgraduate qualification whilst working, both of which significantly improve your career prospects.

Depending on whether you specialise within certain demographics, or work with certain organisations, you could need Disclosure and Barring Service (DBS) clearance.

What the work involves

Community education officers provide all members of the community with information on, and access to, educational and developmental programmes. You may work in areas of social deprivation or high unemployment, or with certain disadvantaged groups such as ethnic minorities or the homeless.

You will identify the needs and interests of the community, and sensitively and creatively organise a variety of suitable activities and courses to improve learning, career and personal development opportunities.

You will plan projects and outreach programmes, liaise with community and local authority groups, and recruit and train staff. At a senior level your job will involve developing policies and negotiating funding.

Type of person suited to this work

You should have a genuine interest in helping people and charitable work. As you will be liaising with communities, government departments and voluntary bodies, you must be able to communicate with a variety of different people, in both casual and formal situations, whilst maintaining a professional approach.

You should be a good listener and have a practical, optimistic approach to problem-solving.

You will need to show initiative and be able to work as part of a team. Patience is essential as many projects are long-term developments rather than quick-fix solutions.

Working conditions

Many posts are short-term contracts because their existence is heavily dependent on funding. This can be difficult as projects often require long-term support. There is plenty of opportunity for part-time work and flexible hours but these may involve working during the evening and at weekends.

You will have an office based in a community centre, a local authority or a college, from which you will travel to the surrounding region. A driving licence is useful.

Future prospects

Once you have secured a post you will receive formal training consisting of short courses that will develop skills or examine new issues such as health development.

You may find that postgraduate programmes in community studies and education are beneficial to your progress. NVQs and diplomas in relevant subjects such as youth and community work will boost your opportunities for progression.

Willingness to be geographically mobile will greatly enhance your career prospects.

Advantages/disadvantages

Providing communities with the educational opportunities they require for personal or career growth can be highly rewarding.

You will have the opportunity to work with a variety of people from different backgrounds.

Limited funding may prevent you from providing the courses and programmes that you wish to which can be frustrating.

Money guide

Starting salaries are usually between £23,000 and £28,000.

Those employed at a senior level can earn £26,000 to £30,000 or more.

Salaries in the voluntary sector are usually lower than in the public sector.

Related opportunities

- Social Worker p573
- Volunteer Manager p577
- Youth and Community Worker p579

Further information

Workers' Educational Association
www.wea.org.uk

EDUCATION AND TRAINING

Qualifications and courses

The usual entry route for a dance teacher is to study for a degree, HND or Foundation degree in a dance-related subject.

If you want to teach dance in a state school you will need to reach Qualified Teacher Status (QTS). This can be achieved by doing a Postgraduate Certificate in Education (PGCE) after your degree or, alternatively, some undergraduate degrees in dance subjects incorporate study for QTS.

Those who wish to become a dance teacher in the private sector can take vocational qualifications available at certain dance and performing arts institutions. The Royal Academy of Dance (RAD) offers diplomas, bachelor's degrees and master's degrees which provide students with RAD Registered Teacher Status (RTS). The Imperial Society of Teachers of Dancing (ISTD) also has teaching qualifications at both initial and advanced level. These schools are both accredited by the Council for Dance Education and Training (CDET), as are some courses taught at colleges and professional schools. The list of all accredited schools is on CDET's website.

Once you have qualified you could apply for the CDET Recognised Awards scheme, which will help demonstrate a commitment to safe and professional standards of teaching.

As well as having qualifications, you will need to maintain a high standard of personal performance. Many who have forged successful careers as performers opt to go into private dance teaching later on in their career.

Joining the National Dance Teachers Association (NDTA) will ensure you remain up to date with new training, developments and teaching resources.

What the work involves

You will plan dance lessons for pupils that adhere to a syllabus or curriculum set out by a school. In the private sector you will train and prepare pupils for dance exams.

You will help your pupils to develop their fitness and agility, ensuring that they do so safely without causing injury to themselves or others.

You will choreograph dance routines, as well as choosing music and costumes.

Type of person suited to this work

You need to have a high level of fitness and be able to demonstrate complicated dance moves and positions to your pupils.

You should also be very enthusiastic about music and the performing arts in general and possess good rhythm and balance.

As a teacher of any subject it is imperative that your communication skills are impeccable but for dance teachers this is especially important because you need to ensure that everyone in your class is dancing safely.

Creativity and self-discipline are very important traits to possess as well.

Working conditions

If you are employed in the state school sector you will be working during the school day but it is likely that you will also run classes after school in the early evening. This is certainly true of the private sector.

If you are a freelance teacher you can expect to travel as you will work at a variety of different venues; from schools and colleges to theatres and community centres.

Future prospects

As a dance teacher you can progress to becoming self-employed and even to running your own dance school.

There are also other performing arts sectors you could branch into such as choreography.

For experienced dance teachers there is the possibility to move into community work as a dance therapist.

Advantages/disadvantages

The job is very active so you will stay fit and healthy.

Your work will often be fun as it is a very creative and expressive art form.

You may injure yourself from constantly dancing and this could jeopardise how much you can work.

Preparing for a big performance can be stressful, especially if you are working with children who can be unpredictable!

Money guide

Earnings vary according to what sector you work in and location.

Newly qualified teachers in state schools start on a salary of around £22,244, or £27,819 in London.

As state teachers gain experience and increased responsibilities, they can earn up to £32,831, or £37,862 if they are working in London.

Earnings for dance teachers in the private sector depend upon the size, type and reputation of the dance school.

Self-employed dance teachers charge an hourly rate which can range from £12 to £50. These fees have to cover the cost of hiring a venue.

Related opportunities

- Choreographer p419
- Dancer p422
- Primary School Teacher p190

Further information

Council for Dance Education and Training
www.cdet.org.uk

Imperial Society of Teachers of Dancing
www.istd.org

National Dance Teachers Association
www.ndta.org.uk

EDUCATION AND TRAINING

EDUCATION AND TRAINING

Qualifications and courses

It is best to check with the nursery you want to work for about the qualifications they require, as each nursery may differ. However, recent government proposals are demanding that all childcare professionals have sufficient professional qualifications in order to better deal with the increasing number of children any one member of staff is responsible for at any one time.

To become a nursery nurse, you must hold a full and relevant Level 3 qualification. For example, a Level 3 Diploma in Children and Young People's Workforce or the recently introduced Level 3 Diploma for the Early Years Workforce (Early Years Educator). Full and relevant qualifications have been structured to meet particular legislative standards set out by the Government.

It may be useful to start out as a nursery assistant while working towards these qualifications. At least 4 GCSEs/National 5s may be required for some of the qualifications, and certainly ones in English and Maths.

In Scotland, registration of nursery workers has been introduced. Early years practitioners with qualifications such as SVQ Level 3 in Social Services (Children and Young People) at SCQF Level 7 can register to work with the Scottish Social Services Council (SSSC).

To be an Early Years Specialist, you will need at least an NVQ Level 4 in Early Years Care and Education or a Diploma in Early Childhood Studies. In order to progress, you may opt to complete higher qualifications such as a BTEC HNC/HND in Advanced Studies in Early Years or a Foundation degree or degree in early childhood studies during your career.

All applicants must pass a Disclosure and Barring Service (DBS) check to work with children.

What the work involves

Within a nursery or private home, early years specialists/ nursery nurses look after young children, from newborn babies up to the age of 8, ensuring they are safe and comfortable.

Much of your work will involve feeding, changing, dressing and bathing babies, and helping older children to develop in areas such as language, art, practical skills and music.

You will plan the day to include play, exercise, meals and rest, to keep children healthy and mentally stimulated.

Type of person suited to this work

It is essential to enjoy caring for young people and to be outgoing, with a friendly manner towards children and adults alike. You also need to be patient and tolerant to deal with different types of behaviour.

Planning activities needs imagination, and it is helpful to be good at art, practical tasks and singing.

You will need to be flexible, enjoy working in a team and be comfortable working with many different types of people from all cultures and backgrounds.

You will also need excellent diplomacy and communication skills as you will need to discuss the children's development and progress, and any other issues, with their parents or carers.

Working conditions

The majority of nursery nurses work 40 hours a week, however hours can vary depending on parents' requirements.

Most of your work will be indoors in a nursery, school, hospital or private home. You may 'live in' if you are a nanny in a private home.

The work involves playing with children, bending and lifting so you need to be physically fit.

Future prospects

Nursery nurses work in nurseries, schools and hospitals, and as nannies in private homes. You can start to train straight from school or after gaining experience in other types of work.

With the large rise in working mothers, there is high demand for qualified childcare staff throughout the UK.

Promotion prospects are limited. After gaining experience and further specialist qualifications you could become a nursery manager or you could take further training to enter paediatric nursing or primary school teaching. Sometimes, there are opportunities to travel, particularly in private work.

Advantages/disadvantages

The work is varied and rewarding.

You will have the opportunity to work with a wide variety of children, all at different stages of development, which makes for an exceptionally diverse work environment.

The hours can be long, particularly in nanny work, and you might have to work shifts and weekends.

Money guide

As a nursery nurse, expect to start on around £10,000– £14,000.

With experience earnings can increase to £15,000–£22,000.

Salaries can rise to between £18,000 and £35,000 for a nursery management post.

Related opportunities

- Childminder p559
- Children's Nurse p276
- Teaching Assistant/Learning Support Assistant p197

Further information

CACHE
www.cache.org.uk

Care Inspectorate
www.careinspectorate.com

Qualifications and courses

Registered inspectors in England and Wales, and inspectors in Scotland, must be qualified as teachers and have 5 years' experience working in education.

Qualified Teacher Status (QTS) is gained through Initial Teacher Training (ITT). The two main routes are a first degree followed by a Postgraduate Certificate in Education (PGCE), or a first degree (BEd/BA/BSc) leading to QTS.

Registered inspectors also need to have completed 3 years' experience in a leadership or a managerial role. Many inspectors are ex-head teachers or childcare managers. An understanding and up-to-date knowledge of the curriculum and the latest developments within the education sector is vital.

Training for inspectors is provided by the Office for Standards in Education (Ofsted) in England, Estyn or the Care and Social Services Inspectorate in Wales (CSSIW), HM Inspectorate of Education in Scotland, and the Department of Education for Northern Ireland. This includes, in England, additional courses which continue into the first year of employment.

In Wales, candidates undertake a 3-day course on which they are taught and assessed on the Common Inspection Framework. You can then undertake a further 2 days' training in a chosen specialism.

You will need a current and up-to-date Disclosure and Barring Service (DBS) check in order to work alongside children and vulnerable adults. Access to transport is also recommended.

All inspectors, throughout the UK, will be expected to keep their knowledge up to date through a series of continuing professional development (CPD) courses.

What the work involves

You will use your extensive experience gained from working in schools, colleges, nurseries or youth service settings to conduct inspections.

You might inspect early years learning, or focus on secondary education and preparation-for-work organisations. Inspections cover special schools and out-of-school learning units.

Inspectors look at the quality of teaching, curriculum, standard of leadership and pupils' achievement levels. During the visit you will contribute to the inspection report, which is then made publicly available on the internet.

Type of person suited to this work

You must be knowledgeable about the types of organisations you will be inspecting. You should be observant and possess a high level of integrity. Strong analytical skills are essential. You will be gathering evidence and interviewing a variety of people so you need to be an effective communicator and be able to make appropriate and fair judgements.

It's important to work to a high standard but also to work quickly and to deadlines. Good IT and report writing skills are also important.

Working conditions

You will visit organisations across the country and will need to spend long periods of time away from home.

Most of the work takes place in classrooms or offices where you will speak to head teachers, pupils, parents, governors and the other professionals linked to the organisation.

Future prospects

You could be working for Ofsted, Tribal Inspections, Serco Education and Children's Services or the Centre for British Teachers Education Trust. These organisations have offices in London, Bristol and Manchester although most inspectors work from home.

Inspectors working for Ofsted are called HMIs (Her Majesty's Inspectors). AIs (Additional Inspectors) work for organisations under contract to Ofsted such as CfBT in the north of England and Tribal in the south of England. AIs can apply to be HMIs. Early years inspectors can be promoted to adult and senior children's services. There is also the chance to be promoted to managerial level in all groups.

Advantages/disadvantages

This job offers you the chance to use your experience to make sure that the right quality of provision is in place in an institution.

You have the chance to travel around the country.

It's challenging when you need to give an 'inadequate' judgement to an institution.

Money guide

Early years inspectors are usually employed by private organisations; salaries vary but as a guide starting salaries are between £24,000 and £27,000 a year.

HMIs earn around £64,800 per year for full-time employment, pro rata for part-time work. Some roles may offer an annual £5,000 contribution to CPD and improvement work.

AIs can earn £300–£500 per day and have expenses paid.

Related opportunities

- Education Officer p21
- Secondary School Teacher p194
- Work-based Training Instructor p198

Further information

Care and Social Services Inspectorate in Wales (CSSIW)
http://cssiw.org.uk

Department of Education, Northern Ireland
www.deni.gov.uk

Education Scotland
www.educationscotland.gov.uk/inspectionandreview

Ofsted
www.ofsted.gov.uk

EDUCATION AND TRAINING

Qualifications and courses

There are a number of routes into this profession though candidates generally have relevant work experience in areas such as special education, teaching, counselling or youth work.

Employers often expect you to have, or be studying for, a qualification in social work. Qualifications in education welfare, teaching or youth and community work may also help you gain entry to this profession. Degree courses usually require a minimum of 2 A levels/3 H grades and 5 GCSEs/National 5s (A*–C/A–C) or equivalent including English and Maths.

The Open University Faculty of Health and Social Care runs social work programmes ranging from introductory courses to degree and postgraduate degree qualifications.

Those without a professional qualification who have extensive experience working with children/young people and their families may be accepted into assistant level positions but they will usually be expected to have at least A levels/H grades or equivalent. You could work towards an NVQ in Learning, Development and Support Services for Children, Young People and Those who Care for Them (Levels 3 and 4) whilst you work.

Regardless of qualification level, all candidates are advised to gain as much experience as possible by seeking opportunities through Community Service Volunteers (CSV). Experience in caring for people or advising/counselling work and skills in communication, IT and teamwork would also be valuable. You will need Disclosure and Barring Service (DBS) clearance to work with children.

Once employed, you will work closely with more senior colleagues, receiving ongoing training and professional development throughout your career.

What the work involves

You will work with young people who are not attending school, and their families, to support them back into education.

It will be your responsibility to issue education supervision orders, school attendance orders and truancy schemes. You may have to prosecute parents of children who continue to play truant despite your efforts to help the children return to school.

You will help families get all the benefits they are entitled to, such as free school meals, clothing or transport. As a link between families and schools, you will try to improve existing relationships – writing reports, attending meetings and case conferences.

Type of person suited to this work

As there can be many reasons for poor attendance at school, such as fear of bullying, caring responsibilities at home or difficulty in coping with school work, it is important to be open minded and impartial. You will also need to be strong enough to prosecute a family if it becomes necessary.

You must enjoy working with young people and have a strong conviction as to the value of education as you may have to spend time convincing parents who do not share your views.

You will also have to keep up to date with legislation and you must be able to work on your own and as part of a team.

Working conditions

You will have an office base, but most of your time will be spent visiting young people and their families at home or looking for young people in the local area, so a driving licence is useful.

You may go to other agencies' offices to attend meetings and case conferences.

Families may view your interventions as interfering rather than assisting; you must always consider your safety.

Future prospects

There are about 4,500 education welfare officers in England, Wales and Northern Ireland. In Scotland, they are called attendance officers.

There is a promotion structure within local authorities and you can become a senior education welfare officer, team leader or manager.

There is the opportunity to become a specialist, for example dealing only with primary school pupils.

With further training, you can do similar work in care and social services.

Advantages/disadvantages

You will have the satisfaction of helping people – sometimes quite profoundly.

You may have to work in the evenings to meet parents when they are available.

Some people may be abusive and you could find yourself in stressful situations.

Money guide

Wages vary depending on your geographical area and the local authority you work for.

You should expect a starting salary of around £22,000 per year.

With experience, this could rise to over £30,000.

Those with relevant qualifications are likely to receive higher salaries.

Related opportunities

- Careers Adviser p558
- Social Worker p573
- Youth and Community Worker p579

Further information

Health and Care Professions Council
www.hpc-uk.org

Northern Ireland Social Care Council
www.niscc.info

Qualifications and courses

New entrants need a relevant degree, Foundation degree or HND in the subject they wish to teach or can apply with a significant amount of work experience and a qualification at Level 3 in their chosen subject. You will need to register with the Institute for Learning (IfL) in order to practise as a lecturer.

In England and Wales you will need to hold, or be working towards either the Level 3 Award in Education and Training, the Level 4 Certificate in Education and Training or the Level 5 Diploma in Education and Training. You may also study the Level 5 Diploma with a specialist pathway such as Teaching English (Literacy), Teaching Mathematics (Numeracy) and Teaching Disabled Learners. Consult individual FE providers for the level of qualification expected.

Due to the widening use of information technology in education many colleges, universities and training centres are likely to assess your skills in ICT, as well as English and maths. You may need a minimum of a Level 2 qualification in these areas in order to be accepted onto a teaching course.

Relevant classroom experience gained through voluntary work shadowing will help you come to an understanding of the skills required of a further education lecturer as well as improving your chances of securing employment.

Within 5 years of starting to teach, all new lecturers must pass a process of Professional Formation monitored by the IfL. Evidence of your teaching qualification together with proof of your continuing professional development (CPD) will lead to confirmation of Qualified Teacher Learning and Skills (QTLS) or Associate Teacher Learning and Skills (ATLS) status.

What the work involves

You will teach students aged 16 and over on vocational or academic courses at a further education college.

Your work will involve planning and preparing lessons, setting assignments and marking pupils' work. You will also undertake administrative tasks and keep records of students' progress.

As well as teaching your main subject, you will arrange work placements, visit students to assess their progress, act as a student mentor and meet colleagues to develop courses.

Type of person suited to this work

Lecturers need to be interested in teaching people of all ages. You must be comfortable talking to large groups of students.

You need extensive knowledge of your subject and the ability to explain things to students at a level that they will understand.

You should be creative to devise lectures, activities and materials which will interest your students. Planning and organisation skills are essential.

Working conditions

Further education lecturers mostly teach in classrooms, labs or workshops. If you teach a practical subject you may work outdoors. Occasionally you might take students on field trips.

When you are not teaching, you will be researching, writing papers and marking students' work. Consequently, you will have to work some evenings and weekends.

Depending on the institution you are employed by, you will usually work during term-time and have school holidays off.

Future prospects

Further education lecturers could progress to more senior roles such as senior lecturer, curriculum manager, head of department or divisional manager. However, tight college budgets have led to a reduction in the number of management positions. For this reason, you will need a willingness to be geographically mobile if you are keen to gain a promotion.

You could move into other areas of education, for example, you could take further training to become a higher education lecturer.

You could also progress to a non-teaching position in college management.

Advantages/disadvantages

You are able to teach in a less formal environment than a school.

Witnessing students' progression is rewarding.

You will be required to spend a lot of time planning lessons and marking work, which may interfere with your personal life.

Money guide

Salaries are dependent on your experience and expertise, and the size and status of your college.

Starting salaries for full-time, qualified lecturers start from around £23,000 and could rise to around £36,000 depending on experience.

Salaries are typically higher in London.

Leadership and management jobs can have salaries of over £80,000.

Related opportunities

- Primary School Teacher p190
- Secondary School Teacher p194
- Work-based Training Instructor p198

Further information

Society for Education and Training
https://set.et-foundation.co.uk

The Education & Training Foundation
www.et-foundation.co.uk

University and College Union
www.ucu.org.uk

HIGHER EDUCATION LECTURER

Qualifications and courses

Entry is with a 2.1 or higher bachelor's degree, typically relating to the subject or research interest you wish to pursue. Entry onto a degree is usually with 2 A levels/3 H grades and 5 GCSEs/National 5s (A*–C/A–C). Most higher education (HE) lecturers will have undertaken postgraduate study at master's level. For those whose undergraduate study is unrelated to the field they wish to teach, conversion master's degrees may be available in the subject you wish to move to.

All higher education lecturers will have been or be working towards a PhD. Full-time doctoral study typically takes up to 3 years, during which you will undertake highly specialised and largely self-directed study in a research area of your choosing. Professional PhDs are available and may be of benefit to those pursuing careers in vocational lectureship in subjects such as engineering.

Additionally, you will need demonstrable experience in or aptitude for teaching. Postgraduate master's or PhD students may be able to gain experience as a teaching assistant at the academic institution they are studying at. You may also be required to hold or study for a Postgraduate Certificate in Teaching in Higher Education or Academic Practice, or a Postgraduate Diploma in Learning and Teaching in Higher Education (HE).

In addition to academic qualifications, HE lecturers undertaking teaching and research in vocational fields must also hold several years' industry experience in their chosen field. This can be of equal weighting or even be substituted for PhD study when applying for a vocational HE lectureship.

What the work involves

Working at universities and other educational institutions, higher education lecturers undertake teaching and research within a specialised academic or vocational field. You will make use of lectures, seminars, laboratory work and field trips to teach students aged 18 and over at undergraduate and postgraduate level.

You will design new teaching units and course components for taught courses and will assess students' work through a variety of means such as timed examinations, written assessments and project work, providing feedback and guidance.

In addition to teaching responsibilities, you will also undertake research in highly specialised subject areas related to the field that you teach. This can be funded through the institution you work for or through interested sponsors, for which you will submit applications and research proposals.

Type of person suited to this work

You will need expert knowledge of, and a passion for, the subject or field you wish to research and teach.

Since you will be spending a lot of time teaching, sometimes to audiences of hundreds of students, you will need fantastic communication and presentation delivery skills.

You will need outstanding research skills and a strong aptitude for self-directed study in order to pursue research interests throughout your career.

The ability to motivate is a must, as you will be guiding students through complex material and may encounter pupils who have lost sight of, or are struggling with, their own studies or research interests.

Working conditions

Hours will be split between office-based work and time spent teaching in classrooms, lecture theatres and labs etc.

Hours can be long with evening work being a regular requirement.

Part-time contracts and flexible hours are becoming increasingly more available in HE lecturing.

Future prospects

Depending on your field of study your research could open up prospects for periods of overseas travel.

Opportunities to engage with the academic community at national and international levels are available. You may be invited to present your research at conferences or as a guest lecturer at other universities and HE institutions. Additionally, there may be opportunities to take on additional responsibilities such as management of a department's pastoral care, or even department headship.

Advantages/disadvantages

You are able to teach in an environment that is less formal than a school.

Seeing students excel in their work provides great job satisfaction. Equally, pursuing your own research interests can be just as rewarding.

Your teaching responsibilities may occasionally conflict with your freedom to pursue your own research interests.

Money guide

The University and College Union (UCU) negotiates the salaries and rates of pay for higher education professionals annually.

Higher education lecturers can expect salaries of between £33,000 and £43,000 a year, or more.

Senior or principal HE lecturers can earn £39,000–£58,000 a year.

Related opportunities

- Further Education Lecturer p185
- Teacher of English to Speakers of Other Languages p196

Further information

The Higher Education Academy
www.heacademy.ac.uk

University and College Union
www.ucu.org.uk

Qualifications and courses

Whilst there are no formal entry requirements for this career, nearly all entrants have a degree, HND or equivalent vocational qualification with relevant degree subjects including social sciences, early childhood studies, psychology and any of the National Curriculum subjects. Typical entry requirements for a degree subject include 2 A levels/3 H grades and 5 GCSEs/National 5s.

The NVQ Level 3 in Learning, Development and Support Services for Children and Young People is the minimum requirement for many local authorities, but not all. The NVQ/SVQ Level 4 is normally required to become a learning mentor coordinator.

Experience of working with young people is normally required, and time spent volunteering in a related area such as social work, counselling or teaching may improve your chances of securing employment within a somewhat competitive industry. Some universities offer the opportunity to participate in mentoring schemes.

The majority of newly appointed learning mentors will participate in a standardised induction programme aimed at support staff in education. You will also receive specific mentor training, usually from the area learning mentor coordinator. It is also common for newly appointed mentors to keep a portfolio of evidence detailing their work.

All candidates are required to undergo a Disclosure and Barring Service (DBS) check in order to practise as a learning mentor.

What the work involves

Your work will be complementary to teachers and other school support staff as you support students while they are learning to overcome obstacles and meet their learning objectives.

Working on a one-to-one basis, you will listen to your mentee's difficulties and offer various solutions, covering a range of topics from bullying to abuse to gifted and talented students.

You will help everybody you work with to succeed in and enjoy their learning experience.

Type of person suited to this work

To be a good learning mentor, you will need to have experience of the subject you mentor, along with an understanding of different styles of studying.

You should enjoy helping and listening to people and have good communication skills. You should be patient and willing to listen.

The best mentors are those who can be a critical friend, know the benefits of learning and can explain them to the people they work with.

You should be able to handle emotional stress, be adaptable, non-judgemental and encouraging.

Working conditions

You can work on a part- or full-time basis with people at school, home or sometimes at a college, university or training centre.

You might be employed on a term-time only basis or all year round. Some of your work might involve weekends and evenings.

You will meet in a quiet, confidential area where you will examine workbooks and essays, talk over any issues and offer help.

Future prospects

There are opportunities to progress to management roles or even to head of year at some schools.

You may choose to study further and become a teacher, youth worker or social worker.

You could also specialise in various areas including working with refugee families or children with behavioural disorders.

As the profession is still developing, current learning mentor coordinators have often come from other professions such as careers advisory roles or social work but it is possible to progress from a learning mentor to coordinator through experience and further training.

Advantages/disadvantages

This job involves a variety of roles – friend, confidence builder and motivator.

Results have shown how important this job can be in helping learners to succeed.

You will be working with students without being a teacher.

Money guide

Within schools, salaries for newly appointed mentors range between £14,500 and £18,000 per year.

With experience, you can expect this to increase to between £18,000 and £25,000.

A salary of £32,000 is possible with managerial responsibilities.

The salary can vary a lot between different employers. The professional status of the role is in contention, as some employers recognise the expertise as similar to a new teacher or social worker (and this is reflected in the salary offered) whereas other employers only view the position in a supporting capacity.

Related opportunities

- Careers Adviser p558
- Learning Disabilities Nurse p296
- Special Educational Needs Teacher p195
- Youth and Community Worker p579

Further information

Mentoring and Befriending Foundation
www.mandbf.org

Skills for Care and Development
www.skillsforcareanddevelopment.org.uk

EDUCATION AND TRAINING

187

Qualifications and courses

It is necessary to have between 2 and 4 years' occupational experience, and often a Level 3 vocational qualification in the subject or work area to be assessed. For this reason it is not possible for school or college leavers to enter this profession straight away.

It is also necessary to have an assessor qualification. You may study for a Level 3 Award in either Assessing Competence in the Work Environment or Assessing Vocationally Related Achievement, or a Level 3 Certificate in Assessing Vocational Achievement. Each of these will include a knowledge and understanding unit (Level 3 Award in Understanding Principles and Practices of Assessment) and a practical application unit. The qualification you choose to complete will depend on the environment in which you wish to assess, ie in the workplace, in a college or both. You can also choose to study on the City & Guilds Training Assessment Quality Assurance (TAQA) e-learning programme.

Qualified assessors can carry out further training to work as an NVQ/SVQ verifier, a post that ensures assessment methods meet quality standards. A number of Level 4 Awards and Certificates are available for both internal and external verifiers.

Once you begin your training you can join the Institute of Assessors and Internal Verifiers (IAV) as an Associate member. After gaining 12 months' experience you can apply for Licentiate membership and you will be added to the IAV's National Register. After 5 years you can apply for Fellowship.

The work involves a great deal of travelling between test centres and places of employment so a driving licence is essential.

What the work involves

NVQ/SVQ assessors work alongside trainees to ascertain their current knowledge and formulate a plan for their development.

You will offer feedback on their progress as they gain experience and take their NVQ/SVQ qualifications.

You will observe how trainees perform different tasks and measure their achievements against the standards for the qualification. You will also read through each trainee's portfolio of evidence, checking that tasks are undertaken.

Type of person suited to this work

It is essential to demonstrate an interest in other people and a commitment to helping them to progress. You will need to motivate and encourage all kinds of individuals – some of whom will not have enjoyed school and find training difficult.

Excellent communication skills are important for the amount of speaking, questioning, listening and reporting that is involved.

You should be organised and able to interpret the different standards in ways that are helpful to those who are learning. You should also have an interest in the area you are assessing.

Working conditions

You will have access to an office where you will use a computer to update learner records and check portfolios. You will also spend lots of time travelling to meet employers and trainees at their places of work.

Depending on your specialist area you could have very early starts (for example assessing bakers at work) or late finishes (assessing car finishers working nights).

It is necessary to keep up to date with the changes and developments in your occupational area.

It is possible to work freelance.

Future prospects

The government is currently focussed on encouraging learning through work-based qualifications and school/ college leavers now have more opportunities to pursue apprenticeships, national traineeships or Skillseekers.

Therefore, there is currently a national shortage of skilled professionals in this area, and there will be increasing need for NVQ/SVQ assessors in the future.

It is possible to expand your role by becoming an internal or external verifier. With experience, it is also possible to move into further education teaching or training.

Advantages/disadvantages

This work involves being at the centre of improving the skills levels of the workforce. You will spend lots of your time meeting, speaking to and getting to know other people.

Depending on your specialist area, you might have to work unsociable hours in order to assess candidates in their workplace.

It can be challenging to motivate and encourage candidates who do not enjoy learning towards a qualification.

Money guide

Average starting salaries are between £18,000 and £24,000.

With experience and responsibilities, this can reach £30,000 a year.

Related opportunities

- Education and Childcare Inspector p183
- Further Education Lecturer p185
- Training and Development Officer p56

Further information

Chartered Institute of Personnel and Development
www.cipd.co.uk

The Education & Training Foundation
www.et-foundation.co.uk

The Institute of Assessors and Internal Verifiers
www.iavltd.co.uk

Qualifications and courses

Most people enter this career as a play assistant for which you will need an NVQ Level 3 in Childcare. There are apprenticeships available in health and social care and children's care which may also be useful when entering this career. Apprenticeships offer entrants the chance to combine practical work experience with study towards a professional qualification, such as the Council for Awards in Care, Health and Education (CACHE) Certificate in Playwork and NCFE Certificate in Playwork, both at Level 2, and the CACHE Certificate and Diploma in Childcare and Education.

You might still be able to work as a playworker without the qualifications, under the supervision of a senior playworker. You would also have to demonstrate some commitment to attaining the qualifications in future.

To become a registered hospital play specialist, you must be aged 20 or over and have a Foundation degree in a hospital play specialism, approved by the Hospital Play Staff Education Trust (HPSET). To be accepted onto the Foundation degree course applicants must have an appropriate Level 3 qualification in a subject such as childcare, nursery nursing, teaching or social work, and at least 2 years' experience working in a related field. GCSEs/National 5s (A*–C/A–C) in English and Maths and a pre-organised hospital placement will also be required.

The 2-year Foundation degree course is delivered by means of formal teaching and practical experience with a mentor. Once this is completed you can apply for a licence to practise from the HPSET. You will have to re-register with the HPSET every 2 years thereafter. In order to do so, you will need to show evidence of your continuing professional development (CPD).

What the work involves

Play workers and hospital play specialists are responsible for ensuring that children between the ages of 5 and 15 play in a safe environment.

You will encourage children and young people to learn through play by giving them the freedom to explore and get to know themselves.

Hospital play specialists use play to entertain children and help them to deal with their experiences in hospital. This includes using play to prepare them for treatments and diverting their attention from unpleasant procedures. You may work with severely disabled children.

Type of person suited to this work

Imagination and creativity are needed to do this job well. It is essential that you like being with children of all ages, understand what they like to do and recognise how they change as they develop.

You should be positive and patient with lots of energy and stamina. As the safety of the children will be your responsibility, you will need high levels of concentration and an awareness of any health and safety issues in the surrounding environment.

A hospital play specialist needs to be sympathetic to the needs and issues of each child, have some understanding of medical conditions, and must be able to cope with distressing situations.

Working conditions

You will normally work in the early evening, at weekends and in school holidays, as many jobs are seasonal and most are part time.

Hospital play specialists work in children's hospitals, children's wards and outpatient clinics. You may take children on trips or visit them in their homes, so you might need a driving licence.

Future prospects

This area of work is rising in importance and is part of the National Childcare Strategy, which recognises the significance of giving young people opportunities to improve their lives through education, sport and leisure.

There is currently an increase in the number of hospital play specialist posts available nationally. Most opportunities are with NHS hospitals but you could also work in hospices or community paediatric teams.

With at least 2 years' experience, it is possible to move into senior or managerial roles.

Advantages/disadvantages

Helping children who are ill to enjoy themselves can be extremely rewarding.

You will receive immediate feedback from the children which will help you develop and adapt to different situations quickly.

Hospital play specialists may have to deal with distressing situations and face challenging children.

Money guide

Starting salaries for hospital play assistants range from £13,000 to £18,000.

For specialists, salaries can increase to between £19,000 and £22,000.

As a senior manager, it is possible to achieve salaries up to £28,000.

Hospital play staff working for the NHS will earn a salary between Band 4 and Band 6 of the Agenda for Change pay system.

Related opportunities

- Childminder p559
- Teaching Assistant/Learning Support Assistant p197
- Youth and Community Worker p579

Further information

CACHE
www.cache.org.uk

National Association of Health Play Specialists
www.nahps.org.uk

Qualifications and courses

You can enter this career with a Bachelor of Education (BEd) degree or a BA/BSc degree with Qualified Teacher Status (QTS).

If you have obtained an Honours degree in an unrelated degree subject, you could complete a Professional Graduate Certificate in Education (ProfGCE) or a Postgraduate Certificate in Education (PGCE). In Scotland you can complete a Professional Graduate Diploma in Education (PGDE). Whilst these courses are open to all graduates, those with a degree in a National Curriculum subject will be at an advantage given the competitive nature of entry into these courses.

Alternatively, you could gain qualifications whilst working. In England and Wales, if you have a degree, it is possible to apply for School Direct, school-centred initial teacher training (SCITT) or Teach First programmes where students are employed by a school and earn a salary while they train. Competition for the limited places available on employment-based schemes is high so entrants are advised to gain as much classroom experience as possible.

All entrants are required to have GCSEs/National 5s (A*–C/A–C) in English, Maths and a science subject and a history of relevant experience. Prior to your acceptance, you must also pass numeracy and literacy skills tests and obtain clearance from the Disclosure and Barring Service (DBS). Knowledge of a foreign language is important given its compulsory inclusion in the National Curriculum.

As a newly qualified teacher (NQT) you will undertake a 1-year probationary period where you will be continually monitored and supported. You will undergo continuing professional development (CPD) throughout your career in order to remain on top of new developments in the curriculum.

What the work involves

You will teach young children the key subjects of English, maths and science as well as IT, history, religious education, geography, art, languages and physical education.

Primary schools admit pupils aged 5–11 and have children of a wide range of abilities in the same class.

In a state school, you will teach children reading, writing and numeracy following the frameworks outlined in the National Curriculum. Private schools can set their own teaching guidelines.

You will prepare resources for structured play and social development work as well as conducting individual assessments on the students in your care.

Type of person suited to this work

You should be assertive and able to uphold discipline within the class. It is also important to be able to encourage and motivate your students – no matter how small their achievements are.

Planning activities requires creativity. You need to have excellent organisational skills and be able to communicate with children, parents and colleagues.

Working conditions

The majority of primary school teachers work over 50 hours a week with 12–13 weeks' holiday per year when the school closes. Preparation for lessons and marking is often completed during holiday time, as well as in the evenings and at weekends during term-time. Extra responsibilities include parents' evenings, after-school activities and school inspections.

You will be based in a classroom and will have a great deal of freedom over your teaching timetable for the day. It is also possible to gain part-time supply work.

Future prospects

You could become a coordinator of your subject or work with teachers in nearby schools as an advanced skills teacher (in England and Wales) or a chartered teacher (in Scotland).

The National College for Leadership of Schools and Children's Services provides programmes which offer greater salaries and responsibilities to gifted teachers.

Progression to deputy headteacher/headteacher can be achieved in 10 years.

Other options include jobs in local or national government, such as an Ofsted inspector. Some teachers offer private tutoring or prepare educational texts.

Advantages/disadvantages

Being responsible for your students' educational development can be very rewarding.

The job is demanding as you will have to carry out many duties, such as marking and preparing lessons, and you will be required to complete this work in the evening and at weekends.

Money guide

The main pay scale for qualified teachers in England and Wales ranges from £21,804 to £32,831 a year. This increases to between £27,819 and £37,862 in Inner London.

Teachers on the main pay scale move up to the next point each year if their performance has been satisfactory. Those who take on additional responsibilities can earn up to £37,871.

Advanced skills teachers have a salary of £38,598–£58,677 and those in senior roles can earn considerably more.

Related opportunities

■ Secondary School Teacher p194
■ Teaching Assistant/Learning Support Assistant p197

Further information

Department for Education
www.gov.uk/dfe

Qualifications and courses

For private music teachers there are no set qualifications, however most do have a degree. It is also useful to study for further teaching and performance and theory qualifications. The most important qualification, however, is excellent musical competence and knowledge of your instrument, usually at a grade 7/8 from an Associated Board on a first instrument and grade 6 on a second.

Private music teachers can join the Incorporated Society of Musicians (ISM) Music Directory which lists available teachers and their credentials. The ISM awards Approved Private Teacher status to those members who have obtained a clean Disclosure and Barring Service (DBS) check, a good reference from a current pupil or their parent/guardian and actively adhere to the ISM Code of Practice for Private Music Teachers.

There is also a wide range of courses available for music teachers. Rockschool offers a music educator course and a Diploma and Licentiate in Music Teaching (Levels 4 and 6). The Associated Board of the Royal Schools of Music (ABRSM) also offers introductory and continuing professional development (CPD) courses at various levels. You could even work towards a postgraduate qualification in instrumental teaching.

For private music teachers who want to work in state schools, Qualified Teacher Status (QTS) could improve your chances of securing employment. QTS can be achieved through a first degree followed by a Postgraduate Certificate in Education (PGCE) or a Professional Graduate Diploma in Education (PGDE) in Scotland or a Bachelor of Education (BEd) degree that includes QTS.

Practical experience and a demonstrable passion for music will not only enhance your applications but help you to establish a client base. Take every opportunity to raise your profile through giving local performances, networking with local musicians and gaining membership with professional bodies such as the Musicians' Union (MU), as clients are usually secured through personal recommendation and advertising.

What the work involves

Private music teachers provide vocal, instrumental and theoretical music training for a range of people and ages. You will work at a variety of different levels.

Your teaching may take place in a classroom, in either a primary or secondary school, in a community setting, at your pupil's home or in your own home. You will be expected to plan lessons, organise groups such as orchestras, and you might have to prepare students for external exams.

You may be hired by a particular local authority music service, schools, a music centre or be self-employed and many private music teachers work in a combination of these settings and roles.

Type of person suited to this work

You should be patient, have a caring attitude towards others and an interest in drawing out and developing an individual's potential in learning about music.

Excellent communication skills are important, as are firmness and commitment, imagination and creativity. You have to be well organised, flexible and able to change plans and the sequence of lessons to accommodate unexpected events.

It is important to be comfortable in maintaining discipline and be confident when speaking to large groups of young people and also to other professionals.

Working conditions

Music teachers work indoors in all kinds of settings within public and private sector schools and learning centres, and in their own or pupils' homes as tutors.

Work in schools will usually be between 8.45am and 3.45pm, with some evening and weekend work required for tuition, rehearsals and concerts.

It is likely that you will work evenings and weekends, and part-time work is common. You should expect to carry out some travelling and you may be expected to lift and carry heavy musical instruments.

Future prospects

Many private teachers combine their teaching work with composing, performing or directing choirs/orchestras, and career breaks are common. If you can play the piano and have excellent sight reading, you could accompany students at examinations and recitals.

Advantages/disadvantages

Teaching is a rewarding profession in which you can witness a student's progression.

You will be kept very busy with preparation, classes, assessing your students, communicating with examining bodies, meetings and ordering materials.

Money guide

For private teachers the Musicians' Union recommends a rate of £30 an hour.

For teachers visiting schools pay varies between £25 and £35 an hour, depending on reputation, location and qualifications.

After considerable experience, at least 10–15 years, private music teachers can expect to earn £40 or more per hour.

Related opportunities

- Dance Teacher p181
- Primary School Teacher p190
- Secondary School Teacher p194
- Teaching Assistant/Learning Support Assistant p197

Further information

Incorporated Society of Musicians
www.ism.org

Musicians' Union
www.musiciansunion.org.uk

Rockschool Ltd
www.rslawards.com

Qualifications and courses

There are no formal entry requirements but many employers value 5 GCSEs/National 5s (A*–C/A–C) or equivalent and a good standard of maths and English. Adult entry is common and many candidates have several years of office experience.

You will need keyboard and word-processing skills. Other IT skills such as an ability to maintain databases, spreadsheets and to manage accounts computer packages is useful, as is knowledge of shorthand. Training is mostly on the job however, and some schools will require you to undergo external instruction via courses and workshops.

If you do not have sufficient office experience, you might consider starting out as a clerical assistant in a school before working your way up to a post with more responsibility.

Once employed, you may be encouraged to work towards work-based qualifications such as the Institute of Administrative Management (IAM)'s National Level 3 Certificate in Educational Administration at the School of Educational Administration & Management (SEAM). This course can be undertaken in 1 year by distance learning and it covers topics such as government policies, education and the law, and business management.

In addition, an NVQ/SVQ in Business and Administration (Levels 1–4) is available, and City & Guilds offer an Award/Certificate/Diploma in Support Work in Schools (Levels 2 and 3).

You will need to gain clearance from the Disclosure and Barring Service (DBS) in order to work alongside children.

What the work involves

School administrators/secretaries are responsible for greeting visitors and answering telephone calls.

You will develop administrative systems (both paper and IT based) to keep information organised and easily accessible.

In some schools you might also collect money for lunch and school trips and you could be in charge of the medical room.

Type of person suited to this work

You will be highly organised and efficient with excellent written and verbal communication skills. You should be confident dealing with people at all levels, including teachers, students and their guardians. You might need to work with people who are ill, angry or upset.

You should have an excellent telephone manner and possess keyboard skills and knowledge of IT packages and information systems.

You must be responsible, flexible, and able to prioritise your workload and use your initiative. You should also be able to work calmly under pressure, meet deadlines and handle confidential information discreetly.

Working conditions

You will usually be office based, doing normal school hours (8.30am–4pm). You will use a range of office equipment, including computers, photocopiers, telephones and fax machines.

School offices are open to visitors and pupils and can be very busy. On a reception desk you will be responsible for greeting visitors and showing them to their meeting room or contacting colleagues. Business dress is often required.

Many school secretaries work part time and do not work at all during the school holidays.

Future prospects

In the UK there are about 55,000 administrators employed in nursery, primary and secondary schools. There are job opportunities in all areas of the country, although entry can be competitive as the working hours and holidays are appealing.

Much of the work is part time and there are not many opportunities for promotion. However, you could work your way up to become a school business manager/bursar or move into secretarial work outside the education sector.

Advantages/disadvantages

The working hours, holiday allowances and opportunities for part-time work make this job ideal for someone with family commitments.

You will learn key, transferable skills that could be used in many other jobs and sectors.

The work can be routine and repetitive.

Money guide

In a state school, you would usually receive a starting salary of £15,000–£19,000.

With experience in the role, or if you take on additional responsibilities, your earnings could increase to £22,000.

Salaries in large secondary schools and private schools may be higher.

Related opportunities

- Arts Administrator/Manager p329
- Personal Assistant p43
- Receptionist p46
- School Business Manager/Bursar p193

Further information

School of Educational Administration & Management
www.admin.org.uk

Qualifications and courses

Most entrants have experience in a related field and many hold a degree or professional qualification in a business or finance-related subject. Management experience in the education, accounting or personnel sectors would be useful. Those seeking entry to this career may find it an advantage to study for the NVQ/SVQ in Business and Administration (Levels 1–4) or the NVQ/SVQ in Management and Team Leading (Levels 2–5).

You could start out as a school administrator or secretary and work your way up to school bursar/ business manager.

Alternatively, for those already employed as a school business manager, the National College for School Leadership offers a professional development programme. The Certificate of School Business Management (CSBM) is an entry-level qualification aimed at newly appointed bursars or those in school administration posts, and the Diploma of School Business Management (DSBM) is intended for experienced bursars/business managers. An Advanced Diploma of School Business Management (ADSBM) is also available, as is a School Business Director Programme aimed at managers seeking to reach the highest levels of the profession. Each qualification consists of an 8–15 month period of short courses and distance learning, eventually leading also to Institute of Administrative Management qualifications and membership.

The Independent Schools' Bursars Association also offers induction courses for new bursars working in independent schools and a series of professional development seminars.

With experience, the appropriate qualification and membership of the National Association of School Business Management (NASBM), you may consider the MSc in Educational Leadership (School Business Management).

What the work involves

You will be responsible for the financial and strategic planning, human resources and environmental issues of a school or college.

The term 'bursar' is common in independent schools; in the state sector you might be called a school business manager or finance manager.

Your role will involve organising staff pay and recruitment, as well as managing contracts with maintenance companies. You will have to keep all the school premises' insurance documents up to date. In independent schools, you will also set fees and distribute bursaries, scholarships and awards.

Type of person suited to this work

You will need a polite yet firm approach and excellent communication skills as you will deal with the head teacher and senior staff, other professionals (auditors, company managers, etc) as well as parents and students.

You should have a head for figures and be happy using computers and financial software. You need to be very organised in order to oversee all of your responsibilities.

Working conditions

Usually you will work in an office sitting at a desk. You will have access to a computer and spend lots of time talking to people – both in or outside of your organisation.

You will attend lots of meetings with the head teacher and other professional staff – sometimes staying late to give reports to your school's governing body.

You may also need to work during the evenings and school holidays.

Future prospects

Most bursars progress to the role after working in a private financial organisation or as an accountant. Some bursars work their way up within a school, possibly from a secretarial role.

With experience, bursars can move to larger organisations or return to the private sector. You could also work in British schools overseas.

Posts are advertised in local and national publications such as the *Times Educational Supplement*. Jobs are also posted on the National Association of School Business Management (NASBM)'s website.

Advantages/disadvantages

The role is varied and allows you use your initiative.

You will have the opportunity to work with people of all ages and backgrounds.

You are usually required to work during the school holidays.

There is a high level of responsibility involved in this job so your work may occasionally be stressful.

Money guide

Salaries for bursars vary greatly depending on the size, type and location of the institution you work in.

The average starting salary in a state school or college ranges from £16,000 to £25,000.

As you gain experience, you could expect to earn between £30,000 and £50,000.

Salaries are higher in the independent sector and it is possible to achieve up to £90,000.

Related opportunities

- Accountant p2
- Accounting Technician and Accounts/Finance Clerk p4
- Financial Adviser p26

Further information

Independent Schools' Bursars Association
www.theisba.org.uk

National Association of School Business Management
www.nasbm.co.uk

EDUCATION AND TRAINING

193

Qualifications and courses

To enter this profession you will need to hold either a Bachelor of Education (BEd) degree, a BA/BSc degree with Qualified Teacher Status (QTS) or, if you wish to teach in Scotland, a teaching qualification (TQ). Alternatively, you can complete an undergraduate degree followed by a Postgraduate Certificate in Education (PGCE) or a Professional Graduate Diploma in Education (PGDE) if you live in Scotland. You should study for a degree related to the subject you wish to teach.

Employment-based routes are also available for those who want to work in a school whilst they qualify. The school-centred initial teacher training (SCITT) is a 1-year course open to graduates who hold a degree in the subject they wish to teach. Alternatively, the School Direct programme involves training graduates in a classroom environment with the expectation that candidates will go on to work in that same school once qualified. Teach First offers a 2-year Leadership Development Programme in which graduates study for a PGCE whilst training on the job.

All entrants must have GCSEs/National 5s (A*–C/A–C) in English and Maths and Disclosure and Barring Service (DBS) clearance. Literacy and numeracy skills tests must also be passed prior to acceptance. Relevant work experience will improve your chances of securing entry onto a programme.

As a newly qualified teacher (NQT), you will serve a 1-year probationary period of assessment, monitoring and support until QTS is confirmed.

What the work involves

You will be a specialist in 1 or 2 subjects and teach students aged 11–19.

You will also take on the role of form tutor and be responsible for encouraging personal development and good behaviour.

In state schools, you will follow the National Curriculum. Private and independent schools are free to set their own educational standards.

Type of person suited to this work

You must be patient, caring and have excellent communication skills in order to relate to and teach your pupils. You should also be assertive and able to maintain discipline with large groups of young people.

You must be imaginative and creative to design lessons which capture your students' attention.

It is important that you are highly organised as this job involves a lot of marking and lesson planning.

Working conditions

You will be based in a classroom and will teach classes from about 9am until 4pm. However, you will have to come in early, stay late and work from home in order to carry out preparation for lessons and finish marking pupils' work.

Schools are usually open for 39 weeks of the year but teachers often carry out preparatory work during the holidays.

Teachers sometimes go on school trips or visit students on work placements. Modern foreign language and PE teachers should be prepared to go on school trips overseas.

Future prospects

There are currently shortages teachers of science, maths, modern foreign languages, design and technology (food and textiles or resistant materials) and computing with IT in secondary education and many universities offer attractive bursaries in order to encourage graduates to train in these areas.

As you gain experience, you could move into a role as a Key Stage coordinator, a head of a department or year group, or work with teachers as an advanced skills teacher. You could also go into teacher training, ';y work or become a school inspector. The National College for School Leadership provides opportunities for gifted teachers to develop skills and improve their leadership.

You should undertake continuing professional development (CPD) throughout your career so as to remain on top of any curriculum changes. Curriculum changes are occurring both in GCSEs and A levels. The replacement of ICT with a new computing curriculum means teachers need to be increasingly confident in elements of computer science.

Advantages/disadvantages

Helping your students to learn and progress can be very rewarding.

The holiday allowance is very generous.

Pupils can sometimes be difficult and disruptive.

You will have to work from home in order to finish marking and preparing lessons.

Money guide

Qualified teachers in England and Wales earn £22,244–£32,831. London wages are higher.

With additional responsibilities, you can earn £35,218–£37,871.

Advanced skills teachers typically earn £38,598–£58,677 and those in senior roles can earn considerably more.

Related opportunities

- Education and Childcare Inspector p183
- Primary School Teacher p190
- Teaching Assistant/Learning Support Assistant p197
- Work-based Training Instructor p198

Further information

Department for Education
www.gov.uk/dfe

General Teaching Council for Scotland
www.gtcs.org.uk

Qualifications and courses

It is generally necessary to have teaching experience in a mainstream school before you can work as a teacher for pupils with special educational needs. In England and Wales you must have Qualified Teacher Status (QTS) and in Scotland you should have a teaching qualification (TQ). In order to obtain these you should have a Postgraduate Certificate in Education (PGCE) or a Postgraduate Diploma in Education (PGDE), a Bachelor of Education (BEd), or a BA or BSc with QTS. Employment-based training programmes such as SCITT or Teach First are also available.

It may be possible to secure work first as a special needs teaching assistant before working your way up to the position of a special educational needs teacher, although this is rare.

The Training and Development Agency for Schools provides courses that cover ways of teaching different subjects, such as maths and science, to children with special educational needs. It also offers courses which raise awareness of special educational needs (SEN) teaching methods and practices.

Postgraduate qualifications are available in subjects such as special educational needs, specific learning difficulties (dyslexia), and visual impairment. You can study part time or by distance learning.

You must have relevant qualifications if you are teaching children with visual, hearing or multi-sensory impairments. Qualified teachers of hearing impaired pupils are required to have a Stage 1 qualification in sign language, or equivalent, from the Council for the Advancement of Communication with Deaf People (CACDP). Qualified teachers of visually impaired pupils must be proficient in Braille.

You will be required to gain clearance from the Disclosure and Barring Service (DBS) in order to work with children and vulnerable adults.

What the work involves

Teachers for special educational needs help children with disabilities, learning difficulties or emotional or behavioural problems to achieve their best. You might also work with exceptionally gifted children.

Working with educational psychologists, social workers, other teachers and learning support workers, you will assess each child's individual needs and draw up an Individual Education Plan (IEP).

In each of these teaching jobs, you will accompany students on visits and trips, help them understand the world around them, and teach life skills to give them greater independence.

Type of person suited to this work

You must be patient and determined in order to deal with challenging behaviour and solve communication problems with pupils. You should be observant and must be able to recognise and praise efforts and achievements, however small.

You need to be kind and have excellent communication skills as well as a commitment to drawing out and developing individuals' potential in learning. You have to be well organised, flexible and able to change plans and the sequence of lessons to accommodate unexpected events.

Working conditions

There are opportunities all over the UK. You may be based in one school or work in teams covering a number of institutions. Part-time work is possible if you are registered with your local authority. Freelance or self-employment is less common.

You will work 39 weeks a year in school. Hours are usually 9am to 4pm, Monday to Friday. Additional hours will be required to create lesson plans and attend meetings.

Future prospects

There are over 150,000 SEN teachers in the UK. Most work in mainstream schools, whilst others work in special schools like hospital schools, pupil referral units, youth custody centres and community homes. There is a shortage of skilled candidates.

SEN teachers working in a mainstream school may have the opportunity to be promoted to special education needs co-ordinator. You could also progress to a role as a special needs assessor in a local education authority.

Advantages/disadvantages

Helping children with disabilities, learning difficulties or emotional or behavioural problems and knowing that you helped them to progress is extremely rewarding.

You will be kept very busy with duties including preparation, classes, marking and assessing, analysing coursework, communicating with examining bodies, meetings and ordering materials, which can be stressful.

Money guide

Salaries are based on the teaching pay scale and range from £22,244 to £32,831. An additional allowance ranging from £2,001 to £4,034 for teachers working in the SEN field is allocated.

Once you reach the top of the main salary scale you can apply to be assessed for the upper salary scale which ranges from £35,218–£37,871.

Salaries in central London are higher.

Related opportunities

- Education and Childcare Inspector p183
- Further Education Lecturer p185
- Work-based Training Instructor p198

Further information

National Association for Special Educational Needs
www.nasen.org.uk

EDUCATION AND TRAINING

Qualifications and courses

It is becoming increasingly necessary to have a degree to enter this occupation, especially in England. Useful degree subjects include English, linguistics, modern foreign languages and education.

In addition, you will need the Level 5 Certificate in Teaching English to Speakers of Other Languages from either Cambridge ESOL (CELTA) or from Trinity College London (CertTESOL). These are the most commonly recognised qualifications and allow you to teach English as a foreign language worldwide. Certificates are also available from the same organisations for those wishing to specialise in the teaching of English to children or young learners (aged 4–18).

Higher-level courses are also available for people with an initial language qualification (such as CELTA or CertTESOL) and at least 2 years' Teaching English as a Foreign Language (TEFL) or Teaching English to Speakers of Other Languages (TESOL) experience. Cambridge ESOL offers the Level 7 Diploma in Teaching English to Speakers of Other Languages (DELTA) and Trinity College London provides the Level 7 Licentiate Diploma in Teaching English to Speakers of Other Languages (DipTESOL). These courses are aimed at people seeking career progression.

You will generally need to be aged 18 or over in order to gain entry onto a course with good A levels/H grades and an excellent standard of English. Pre-entry experience gained through overseas voluntary work or home tutoring is also desirable. Employers tend to favour accredited courses that encompass both theory and teaching practice in classrooms.

Experienced teachers with a degree and/or TESOL qualification can also study for a master's in TESOL.

Candidates who wish to teach in a state school must have Qualified Teacher Status (QTS) which can be obtained from studying for a BA/BSc with QTS or a Postgraduate Certificate in Education (PGCE) or a Postgraduate Diploma in Education (PGDE) in Scotland.

What the work involves

You may be based in the UK or overseas and will teach English to students who are not native speakers. The term TESOL is only used when the students are in the UK. Teaching English as a Foreign Language (TEFL) is used if you are teaching students abroad.

You will teach pupils of all ages who want to learn to speak English for educational, cultural or business reasons.

You will want to demonstrate your passion for the English language as well as inspiring and encouraging your students.

Type of person suited to this work

It is essential that you have an excellent grasp of the English language. You should be patient and have an interest in developing individuals' learning potential. Good communication skills are important, as is commitment and imagination.

You have to be well organised and flexible. You must be able to recognise and praise efforts and achievements.

You should be comfortable in maintaining discipline and be confident when speaking to large groups.

Working conditions

If you teach English as a foreign language, you may work in this country or abroad, teaching in community and learning centres or commercial and industrial settings.

Hours vary according to the employer, however evening and weekend work is common.

Future prospects

There is always a need for English language teachers to cope with the high demand of people who wish to learn English. However, competition is fierce for full-time positions.

Most English language teachers are employed overseas on temporary contracts during the academic year. They may return to the UK to teach during the summer.

It is possible to progress to become a course director or course co-ordinator. With experience, you could get involved in teacher training or set up your own private language school.

Advantages/disadvantages

This is a very busy and demanding job as you will have to deal with preparation, teaching, marking and different examining bodies.

Teaching is a rewarding profession in which you can witness a student's progression and know that you played a major role in helping them master the English language.

Money guide

Teaching English in a UK commercial language school, you can expect a starting salary of £14,000–£25,000.

Experienced teachers or those in a senior role can earn £25,000–£38,000.

Those who work on a part-time or seasonal basis usually receive an hourly or weekly rate.

If you work outside the UK, your salary is likely to be much lower.

Incentives offered by overseas language schools may include flights and accommodation.

Related opportunities

- Education and Childcare Inspector p183
- Further Education Lecturer p185
- Teaching Assistant/Learning Support Assistant p197

Further information

Cambridge ESOL
www.cambridgeenglish.org

Qualifications and courses

There are no specific academic requirements for entry to this career as local education authorities set their own requirements, however employers typically expect candidates to have GCSEs/National 5s (A*–C/A–C) in English and Maths. You need to be at least 18 years old to apply and must obtain clearance from the Disclosure and Barring Service (DBS). Previous relevant experience or qualifications, for example in nursing, childcare or youthwork, is an advantage when seeking employment as competition for posts is fairly strong.

The Council for Awards in Care, Health and Education (CACHE), NCFE and Edexcel (BTEC) offer the Level 2 Award/Certificate/Diploma in Support Work in Schools which may be useful for those new or not yet employed in a teaching assistant role. The Apprenticeship in Supporting Teaching and Learning in Schools is available to school leavers at both Intermediate and Advanced level and leads to NVQs at Levels 2 or 3.

Once employed, you will be trained on the job and local authorities in England and Wales may encourage you to study for professional qualifications while you work. Upon entry you can study for the NVQ in Supporting Teaching and Learning in Schools (Levels 2 and 3) or the SVQ in Supporting Teaching and Learning in Schools (Classroom Assistants) (Levels 2 and 3). Another option is the City & Guilds (5329) vocational Certificate in Supporting Teaching and Learning in Schools (Levels 2 and 3).

Experienced teaching assistants in England can work towards Higher Level Teaching Assistant (HLTA) status. Alternatively, you may opt to gain a Foundation degree. These two qualifications will not only enable you to take on extra responsibilities, but they can significantly improve your career prospects and salary.

What the work involves

Teaching/classroom assistants help pupils to learn by supporting the teacher and, sometimes, by describing the work in a more visual way or reading questions aloud.

You may be required to plan and deliver parts of a lesson for the main teacher, working together to make the best use of time and resources.

Some teaching/classroom assistants will offer one-to-one support to students with learning difficulties or disabilities.

Type of person suited to this work

In this work, you need to like children to help them make the most of their time in school.

You will need lots of patience and possess the ability to stay calm, as all pupils have their off-days when they are noisy or upset.

Sometimes, you will work with students who need extra help so you should have an interest in young people who have special needs.

Working conditions

Many learning support assistants work in mainstream schools, but some are employed in independent schools, in residential institutions for students with special needs or specialist colleges.

You will normally work between 8.30am and 4.30pm, although you might have to attend meetings after this and sometimes at weekends.

Future prospects

Recent changes to teachers' workload have involved freeing them from some administrative tasks so they have more classroom time. This has increased the need for teaching assistants working across the UK although competition for posts is strong.

You can progress to become a Higher Level Teaching Assistant (HLTA), which involves increased responsibility.

Experienced teaching assistants often train to become teachers themselves and there are Initial Teacher Training courses especially for teaching assistants.

Special needs learning assistants may specialise in helping young people with a particular disability.

Advantages/disadvantages

This can be a very rewarding job as you will witness students' educational development and growth.

You might help students take steps towards independent living.

You will be very busy and will have limited time to hold meetings with colleagues.

Money guide

Wages are set by local education authorities so the rates can vary across regions.

The starting salary for a teaching assistant ranges from £13,000 to £18,000.

Experienced HLTAs can achieve £16,000–£25,000 per year depending on the level of seniority.

Related opportunities

- Childminder p559
- Play Worker/Hospital Play Specialist p189
- Primary School Teacher p190

Further information

CACHE
www.cache.org.uk

Department for Education
www.gov.uk/dfe

EDUCATION AND TRAINING

Qualifications and courses

Whilst there are no set entry requirements, training instructors must maintain a high level of knowledge and experience of the skill which is being taught and therefore many have completed academic or vocational qualifications relevant to that skill. Although there is no minimum age limit, it is likely that you will not have developed the sufficient level of knowledge and experience required to become an effective instructor until the age of 21.

Many who have secured work as a work-based training instructor have worked their way up from other positions in the same organisation, eg in a customer services team or as a supervisor on a production line.

Others train specifically for a career in work-based training. In order to secure employment in a training consultancy, you will typically be required to hold a recognised training qualification. NVQs/SVQs in Learning and Development (Levels 3–5) are available. The Chartered Institute of Personnel and Development (CIPD) also offers a host of qualifications at Foundation, Intermediate and Advanced Levels that aim to prepare candidates for a career in training and development. You would normally start by completing a CIPD Level 3 Certificate or Diploma in Learning and Development (L&D) which is equivalent to an NVQ/SVQ Level 3. Upon completion, you can apply for Associate Membership of the CIPD and work your way up to higher qualifications appropriate for those seeking training manager positions.

Postgraduate qualifications are also available in subjects such as education and training management, training and development, mentoring and coaching. These can usually be studied part time or by distance learning. Entry requirements are a degree or equivalent professional qualification.

Training practitioners can also work towards gaining NVQ assessor qualifications. Entry requirements are at least 2 years of occupational experience in the subject or work area to be assessed.

Associate teachers at further education colleges or organisations funded by the government need a Certificate in Teaching in the Lifelong Learning Sector. Full teachers need to take a 1-year course to obtain the Diploma in Teaching in the Lifelong Learning Sector.

What the work involves

You will work alongside employees, in their workplace or in a training centre, and teach them new skills or develop existing skills.

You will liaise closely with the employer's training or human resources manager in order to ascertain the type of training needed.

It is likely that you will specialise in an area such as IT, management, personal development, customer service or craft.

Type of person suited to this work

It is essential to demonstrate a real interest in helping people to learn and progress.

You must be patient, organised and up to date with the latest developments in your occupational area. Good IT skills will also be helpful.

Excellent communication skills are important for the large amount of speaking, questioning, listening and reporting that are involved.

Working conditions

You will work in an office where you will use a computer to prepare lessons and update learner records. However, you will also spend lots of time travelling to meet employers and learners at their workplaces.

You will work normal office hours, Monday to Friday.

Future prospects

New media and different ways of working mean that there is a continual need to help businesses and industry develop the right people to carry out new work tasks.

All companies today are expected to develop their workforces and the government is currently encouraging learning through work-based qualifications. Additionally, school/college leavers now have a wider range of opportunities to pursue such as apprenticeships.

Promotion to a training manager or consultant post is possible with experience and further qualifications such as NVQs at Levels 4 and 5.

Advantages/disadvantages

This work involves being at the centre of improving the skills levels of the workforce.

You constantly have the opportunity to learn new things.

It can be challenging to motivate trainees who do not have an interest in studying towards a qualification.

Money guide

Salaries vary depending on the type and size of employer and location. Salaries increase if you teach a specialised skill in high demand.

Starting salaries for training assistants are £15,000–£20,000.

Training officers can earn £20,000–£30,000 a year.

Senior officers can achieve up to £35,000 a year.

Related opportunities

- Further Education Lecturer p185
- Human Resources/Personnel Officer p28
- Training and Development Officer p56

Further information

Chartered Institute of Personnel and Development
www.cipd.co.uk

Engineering, Manufacturing and Production

There are a number of highly skilled jobs available in this job family and workers need to be creative and methodical and combine brilliant technical skill with spatial awareness. You may be interested in food production but equally your passion could lie in working with aircraft or marine manufacture. People in these professions share the ability to concentrate for long periods of time and work meticulously on a job to finish it to a high standard. Some will also be highly trained with specialist equipment which may sometimes be hazardous to use so a high level of personal safety awareness is vital. The jobs featured in this section are listed below.

Qualifications and courses

Most entrants are graduates of an aeronautical/aerospace engineering degree although employers may accept those who have gained a bachelor's in other relevant disciplines, such as electrical, mechanical or manufacturing engineering, computer software, physics or maths.

A Bachelor of Engineering degree (BEng) lasts 3 years whilst a Master of Engineering degree (MEng) lasts 4. You will need at least 2 A levels/H grades, including Maths and Physics, and 5 GCSEs/National 5s (A*–C/A–C) in order to ensure entry onto a degree course. Completing a postgraduate qualification is advantageous, as well as being particularly useful to those whose first degree was in a different subject.

Many companies offer graduate training schemes and some are accredited by professional bodies such as the Royal Aeronautical Society. Your scheme may offer you a placement overseas and the chance to work towards an engineering licence accredited by the Civil Aviation Authority (CAA). Employers often value graduates with prior work experience, therefore completing a voluntary work placement or sandwich placement as part of your degree may improve your employability.

It is possible to enter the industry at a lower level by training as a craft or technician straight from school but you will have to complete further qualifications in order to become an engineer. Apprenticeship schemes offered by airline operators, manufacturers or with a service engineering company usually require good GCSE/National 5s in English, Maths and Physics. A HNC/HND in Aeronautical or Aerospace Engineering, Avionics, or Air Transport Engineering may improve your chances of employment at technician level.

To enhance opportunities for progression, you may decide to work towards incorporated or chartered status further on in your career whilst undergoing a series of continuing professional development (CPD) courses.

What the work involves

Aerospace engineers research, design and manufacture space vehicles, satellites, missiles and aircraft. You can specialise in mechanical, electrical or electronics engineering, and within these areas you can focus on airframes, hydraulics, materials and structures, or engines.

Your work might involve research, design and manufacture, or experimenting with new materials.

You may also undertake flight test programmes, and maintain and improve fleets of aircraft all over the world.

Type of person suited to this work

You should have a logical mind and be good at problem-solving. You should also be good at maths, and be able to produce good drawings and diagrams, as well as being able to interpret them well.

Your oral and written communication skills should be good as you will need to communicate ideas effectively. Teamworking skills are essential but you must also be able to take on responsibility and work independently.

You will be expected to keep up to date with new technology and developments in the industry, and for some roles you will need to have normal colour vision.

Working conditions

It is usual to work 37–40 hours a week, but this depends a lot on project deadlines and what is currently taking place: hours can be longer.

Work usually takes place in clean quiet laboratories, but visits to production areas are essential and these areas are usually dirty and noisy.

Visits to airfields also take place, where you might be required to inspect and test the functions of the aircraft.

Future prospects

There are good opportunities for promotion in aerospace engineering with the industry maintaining a strong record of investing in its workforce. The skills you will acquire will make you suitable for higher positions even in other branches of engineering, and many move into consultancy, management or research roles as their career progresses.

Some aerospace engineers work independently as consultants, and others find work abroad for foreign governments or aircraft construction companies. With chartered status, your earnings and responsibilities will increase.

Advantages/disadvantages

You may have to work long hours, evenings and weekends. Stress levels can also be high if you are trying to meet deadlines.

The starting salary is relatively high, and you can work your way up to a good wage with time and experience.

Money guide

Starting salaries for graduates tend to range from £20,000 to £28,000 per year.

Depending on your professional status, your earnings will increase to £28,000–£40,000.

Senior engineers might earn £45,000 to in excess of £65,000.

Related opportunities

- Electrical Engineer p207
- Marine Engineer p219
- Mechanical Engineer p221

Further information

Institution of Engineering and Technology
www.theiet.org

Royal Aeronautical Society
www.aerosociety.com

ASSEMBLER

Qualifications and courses

There are no formal entry requirements for this line of work. However, GCSEs/National 5s in English, Maths, Design and Technology or equivalent vocational qualifications in engineering/manufacturing are valued by employers.

The most common route of entry is via an apprenticeship where you will undertake a combination of on-the-job training from experienced professionals and a series of day or block release instruction at a college or training centre in order to work for industry recognised qualifications. NVQs/SVQs in Performing Manufacturing Operations (Levels 1 and 2), Performing Engineering Operations (Levels 1 and 2) and Electrical Assembly/ Installation (Levels 2 and 3) are available.

As a new recruit you will learn about the company's health and safety policies, welfare and conditions of employment whilst being trained under the supervision of a more experienced colleague in the use of appropriate tools and machinery and the ability to read assembly diagrams. You may also acquire the skills necessary to inspect the quality of finished products and, in the event that new working methods are introduced, you will receive further training.

In order to secure a trainee position within the industry, you may have to undertake an entry test and an interview that will assess your reading and writing skills and your practical aptitude, eg your ability to work quickly and accurately with your hands. Normal colour vision is a requirement for work involving electrical and electronic assembly.

What the work involves

You will work on an assembly line within a factory or workshop, or at a bench. You could work on products within sectors as diverse as: engineering, furniture production, soft furnishings, domestic electrical equipment, vehicles or electrical circuit boards.

Assembly line

You will assemble products or components as they arrive at your work area. Sometimes they may not stop, but keep moving along a belt or route in the factory. As the line needs to keep going at a set speed, you will be required to work at the same pace as everyone else.

Bench

Using hand tools, and in some cases simple machinery, you will carry out specific assembly tasks or create a finished product.

Type of person suited to this work

You will need to have practical skills and enjoy making or repairing items. In order to construct your product or components, you will have to follow diagrams and instructions and be able to work quickly and precisely.

You need good interpersonal skills and a solid work ethic.

Whilst carrying out repetitive tasks, you must be able to concentrate and maintain a fast pace of work for long periods of time.

Working conditions

Assembly line

You can expect to be in a large factory – in some sectors this could be noisy, dirty and busy and in others, such as the electronics industry, it would be clean and dust-free.

Some assembly lines require 24/7 production; if so, you will normally work a shift pattern.

Bench

You will be sitting or standing using the tools and machinery positioned around you. If you need to use a soldering iron for assembly it can be hot work and may cause fumes. You can also work part time.

Future prospects

The largest employers of assemblers are the electrical, electronic and information technology industries.

As machines are increasingly replacing some of the assembly work that used to be done by people, jobs are reducing. However, there is still demand for assemblers to work on the assembling of products that are too intricate to be done by machine, or on small batches of goods.

With experience, you may be able to progress into a team leader or supervisory role or within other areas of manufacturing such as quality control. You could also go on to train as an engineering craft worker.

Advantages/disadvantages

Your surroundings may be dirty and noisy.

Due to advances in technology, the need for workers will continue to drop.

Part-time work is also available, which is attractive to people with families wanting to supplement their income.

Money guide

Starting salaries for assemblers are between £12,500 and £15,000.

With experience, salaries can range from £15,000 to £20,000.

Very skilled and experienced assemblers in certain parts of the industry, such as automotive assembly, or those with supervisory responsibilities can earn in excess of £20,000 a year.

Related opportunities

- Food Processing Operative p212
- Mechanical Engineer p221
- Welder p236

Further information

Institution of Engineering and Technology
www.theiet.org

Proskills UK
www.proskills.co.uk

Semta
www.semta.org.uk

BLACKSMITH

Qualifications and courses

One route of entry is via an apprenticeship. As an apprentice you will typically experience a combination of on-the-job training from professionals and a series of day or block release at a college or training centre in order to work towards industry recognised qualifications, such as an NVQ/SVQ in Fabrication and Welding. There are no specific academic qualifications required for entry, however you will need to approach individual employers in order to see if they are willing to take you on as an apprentice. Availability is not always guaranteed and will depend on your local jobs market.

Alternatively, you may opt to complete a full-time college course with a focus on either traditional blacksmithing skills or design. Courses such as a BTEC Level 3 in Blacksmithing and Metalworking may require specific GCSEs/National 5s and forge-work experience. HNDs and degrees in creative aspects of blacksmithing are also available. To gain entry, you will need 2 A levels/3 H grades and 5 GCSEs/National 5s (A*–C/A–C), an understanding of design and a portfolio of artwork.

Herefordshire and Ludlow College offers a degree in Artist Blacksmithing and diplomas in Blacksmithing and Metalwork as well as a Level 2 Farriery Access course. As contacts are so important in securing work, it may be beneficial to join the British Artist Blacksmiths Association (BABA) in order to attend relevant courses and meet new people. Awards distributed by the Worshipful Company of Blacksmiths are also available.

What the work involves

You will shape and join metals such as steel, iron, copper and bronze to produce decorative pieces, such as gates and furniture or functional objects for use by companies, such as fire escapes and security screens. You may also restore antique ironwork.

You may create specially commissioned pieces such as a stairway for a building project or specialise in an area such as agricultural engineering or security.

If you specialise in artistic work, you are likely to be self-employed. Your job will therefore include all of the administrative tasks needed to run a business, alongside the general work as a blacksmith. You will have to actively promote your services in order to gain customers and this may involve attending craft shows and fairs.

Type of person suited to this work

Much of your time will be spent on your feet using different hand tools, often near to the forge which will be very hot. You will need to be very responsible, as the tools and materials that you will be working with can be dangerous.

Having a creative flair will help you to use your materials imaginatively and you will need an understanding of the way products function and how different metal properties will affect the end product.

Working conditions

You will work with various metals and use different hand and bench tools and a forge. This will result in conditions that can be noisy, dirty and sometimes cramped. You will spend much of the time on your feet and you will wear protective clothing such as gloves, ear protectors and goggles.

You could work in rural areas or in mines, docks and with engineering companies. Artist blacksmiths are less restricted geographically and can be based within both larger cities and rural communities.

Future prospects

The demand for industrial blacksmiths working in mining sites, docks and engineering is decreasing but, due to an increased interest in decorative metalwork, the skills of artistic blacksmiths are often in demand for commission work.

Working under commission is unreliable and so many blacksmiths are forced to accept other types of work in order to earn a living wage.

Most blacksmiths are self-employed but there are still opportunities for work within small, usually family-run businesses, though positions are very limited in number. With experience, you might progress into supervisory or managerial posts or you may opt to work for a museum or heritage centre.

Entry into trainee positions is competitive and you may need to relocate in order to find one. Future success will rely on your ability to build a reputation.

Advantages/disadvantages

Much of the work is done alone and can be isolating.

The work is tiring, but when you have created what a customer requires it can be satisfying too.

If you are involved in a creative project such as a commissioned sculpture, it can be very rewarding.

Money guide

Starting salaries generally range from £12,000 to £16,000 a year.

Once training has been completed you could earn in excess of £25,000.

Earnings tend to vary as most blacksmiths, being self-employed, are free to negotiate their own rates.

Related opportunities

- Bricklayer p62
- Farrier p249
- Sheet Metal Worker p230

Further information

British Artist Blacksmiths Association
www.baba.org.uk

British Farriers and Blacksmiths Association
www.forgemagazine.co.uk

Worshipful Company of Blacksmiths
www.blacksmithscompany.org

BREWERY WORKER

Qualifications and courses

There are no set entry requirements for this career. GCSEs/National 5s in English, Maths and a science may be useful though, particularly when seeking work. Employers often value those with qualifications when promoting workers to supervisory and management positions. Sometimes it is possible to enter the industry in a related area such as in a manufacturing, processing or packaging operations environment, whilst later progressing to the role of brewery worker.

Alternatively, there may be an apprenticeship available in your area in food manufacturing which leads to this career. Apprenticeships typically involve a combination of on-the-job training and assessments from experienced professionals covering all stages of the beer-making process, with a series of day or block release instruction at a college or training centre in order to gain industry recognised qualifications. NVQs/SVQs Levels 1–3 in Food Manufacture are usually the qualifications trainee brewery workers work towards achieving. It may be helpful to complete the NVQ Level 3 in Food Manufacture if you wish to progress to a supervisory post.

Brewing Research International (BRI) offers the opportunity to progress into the more technical side of the industry, although this requires you to be educated to degree level. The Institute of Brewing and Distilling also offers courses, such as the General Certificate, Fundamentals or Diplomas in Brewing, Distilling and Packaging.

What the work involves

You will make and package beer, stout and lager for a variety of outlets including shops and pubs.

You could be involved in the whole beer making process or just certain stages.

You will work as part of a team supervised by a technical brewer. Your jobs will include weighing and mixing ingredients, monitoring quality, labelling and packing the product and loading the beer ready for dispatch.

Type of person suited to this work

You will need to enjoy working in a team, and be aware of the health and safety regulations to keep yourself and others safe at work.

The work is quite physically demanding; you will be lifting and operating heavy machinery so will need to be fit and healthy.

Good numeracy skills will be helpful when measuring out ingredients and checking the amount of products produced.

Working conditions

Most large breweries have a shift system in place for their workers. You will usually work around 40 hours a week, and can work overtime if necessary.

You will be working with machinery and fermenting ingredients, therefore overalls, gloves and goggles may be worn to limit contamination and to keep you safe.

You will have to work through all weather conditions, loading products and unloading raw materials.

Future prospects

Due to the increasing usage of machinery and automated processes in the mass production of beer and the decline in the number of large breweries in the UK, there are fewer industry vacancies available to brewery workers.

However, there has been a significant rise in micro-breweries producing craft beer in the last few years which has created more jobs, due to a large change in consumer behaviour. With 1,424 micro-breweries in operation in the UK, you may find yourself working for a more specialised employer, in a supervisory or management role, or opening your own once you have specialist training and gained technical brewing status.

Advantages/disadvantages

Due to the decline in multinational brewing companies across the UK, it can be difficult to find work and many smaller micro-breweries are family run, employing very few staff with limited promotional opportunities.

Working in a brewery can be smelly, hot and physically demanding; this may be stressful or tiring at times. However, working in a team of other brewery workers creates a lively and fun atmosphere.

Making beer, stout and lager is a satisfying job role as you know you are creating beverages that people enjoy drinking.

Money guide

The amount you earn does depend on the location and size of the brewery you work for.

Average starting salaries can be up to £15,000, with this rising to £20,000 or more with a few years' experience.

Senior brewery workers or those in supervisory roles may earn in excess of £29,000.

Those working within a shift system may get a shift allowance.

Related opportunities

- Cellar Technician p124
- Craft Technical Brewer p206
- Food Processing Operative p212

Further information

Campaign for Real Ale (CAMRA)
www.camra.org.uk

Campden Brewing Research International
www.campdenbri.co.uk/brewing-services.php

Institute of Brewing and Distilling
www.ibd.org.uk

Qualifications and courses

One route of entry into this industry is to begin as a trainee technician, developing your skills via an Advanced Apprenticeship in Engineering Manufacture (Craft and Technician). The Engineering Construction Industry Training Board (ECITB) offers a 3-year apprenticeship for design and draught technicians.

As an apprentice, you will typically experience a combination of on-the-job training from skilled professionals and a period of day or block release instruction at a college or training centre. You are likely to work for industry-recognised qualifications; the actual subjects you study will depend on your employer's business. They may include an NVQ Level 1 and 2 in Performing Engineering Operations, an NVQ Level 2 and 3 in Engineering Technical Support, a City & Guilds Certificate or BTEC Certificates/Diplomas. Applicants for an apprenticeship will require 4 GCSEs/National 5s (A*–C/A–C) or equivalent including Maths and science or technology.

Alternatively, you may opt to study relevant pre-entry qualifications at college, such as the City & Guilds Awards and Certificates in Computer-Aided Design and Manufacturing (Levels 1–3), the City & Guilds Award in Computer-Aided Design and Parametric Modelling (Levels 1–3), the BTEC Certificate/Diploma in Engineering (Levels 2–3) or the BTEC Level 3 Certificate/Diploma in Mechanical, Manufacturing or Civil Engineering.

Upon completion of your training, CAD draughtspeople are encouraged to seek engineering technician (EngTech) registration with the Engineering Council UK in order to improve your career prospects. As technology changes, you should update your skills throughout your career through a series of continuing professional development (CPD). Employers may offer you the chance to gain further qualifications such as HNCs/HNDs or training in your company's specific software.

What the work involves

You will produce the drawings and instructions that will enable others to create structures, equipment or components.

Using a computer-aided design (CAD) workstation you will draw up technical drawings for components or sections of a structure, or for different products.

Depending on the specialism of the company you work for, you may design part of a structure as large as a factory or bridge, or a component as small as an electronic circuit.

Type of person suited to this work

You should be patient, accurate and have a good understanding of different production processes.

You need to be organised and methodical in your work and able to work to tight deadlines.

Good IT, technical drawing and numerical skills are essential.

You will need to be able to solve design problems in a creative way and you should be comfortable communicating your work to others.

Working conditions

Most of your work will be done sitting in front of your computer or drawing board in an office or design area.

You will work normal office hours but you might need to work overtime when deadlines are close.

Sometimes you will visit the shop floor or factory area where the product you are designing is being made and conditions could be noisy, hot and dirty. However, your own workspace will be quiet as a lot of concentration is required.

Future prospects

All construction and manufacturing companies across the UK need trained draughtspeople which means they are in constant demand, however, your job prospects may also depend on the economic state and the fluctuating nature of the construction and manufacturing industries.

You may work within fields including aeronautical, civil, electrical, mechanical and marine engineering companies, central and local government and public utilities.

You can progress to senior, supervisory and team-leader work and with further qualifications you could become an architect or a chartered engineer. There are also opportunities to work abroad or work freelance.

Advantages/disadvantages

As much of your work involves using your drawing board or computer, your eyes could get tired and strained.

If you want to progress, you can move to supervisor level within your own company or elsewhere.

With experience, it may be possible to work on a freelance basis, being contracted by smaller companies who do not employ their own draughtsperson.

Money guide

Starting salaries typically range from £15,000 to £20,000.

With experience, you can expect to earn £22,000–£35,000.

High earners employed at a senior level can make £40,000 or more per year.

Related opportunities

- Architectural Technician p59
- Architectural Technologist p60
- Graphic Designer p165

Further information

Chartered Institute of Architectural Technologists
www.ciat.org.uk

Tomorrow's Engineers
www.tomorrowsengineers.org.uk

Qualifications and courses

Ideally you should gain an Institution of Chemical Engineers (IChemE) accredited degree or postgraduate qualification in chemical, biochemical or process engineering. Other relevant degree subjects such as chemistry, polymer science, environmental or nuclear engineering may be considered, but an accredited postgraduate qualification, such as an MSc in Process Engineering, will significantly improve your chances of both employment and chartered status further on in your career.

HNDs in similar subjects are also considered although you may have to start your career as a technician and work up to the position of chemical engineer as you gain further qualifications. You will need a minimum of 3 A levels/H grades and 5 GCSEs/National 5s (A*–C/A–C), including English, Maths and a science, in order to gain a place on an engineering or related degree/HND course.

Entry without a degree or HND is uncommon, although you may be able to secure an Apprenticeship in Engineering, which could lead to a role as an engineering technician, providing you with the opportunity to study for a relevant degree.

Many companies offer graduates internal training programmes, some of which are IChemE certified. These Accredited Company Training Schemes (ACTS) ensure graduates become competent professional engineers whilst covering the requirements of chartered status. Employers are placing increasing value on candidates with appropriate work experience, thus, carrying out voluntary work may enhance your employability.

Chemical engineers need to commit to a programme of continuing professional development (CPD) to make sure their skills are kept up to date throughout their career.

What the work involves

You will devise low-cost, safe and environmentally friendly methods that will transform raw materials into products such as fuel, pharmaceuticals, plastics and toiletries.

You might research ways to improve the future of our planet which could include discovering renewable energy sources or producing replacement human organs.

You might work in manufacturing and help to design and construct plants for mass production of products. You will then oversee the running of the plant and the quality of its products.

Type of person suited to this work

You will need to have good oral and written communication skills in order to brief colleagues and compile extensive reports from research you have undertaken. Project management skills are also very important.

An analytical mind and the ability to problem-solve are helpful when designing and testing products or equipment in the plant itself.

You will also need to be creative in order to come up with cost-effective products and solutions to problems.

An aptitude and interest in chemistry are also recommended, as is a good understanding of engineering and maths.

Working conditions

Working hours are normally standard office hours from Monday to Friday, although you might have to work overtime on occasion (including evenings and weekends), particularly if you are developing a new product.

You will usually work in a plant, laboratory or research establishment so conditions can vary from peaceful, sterile labs to noisier factory floors.

You might need to wear appropriate safety equipment for certain aspects of the job.

Future prospects

Jobs are available across the UK in a range of industries, from pharmaceuticals to oil and gas.

Opportunities for progression and promotion are good; you could obtain a position in senior management or a project leader role.

Chemical engineers are encouraged to achieve chartered or incorporated status.

Advantages/disadvantages

You will continue to learn new skills and gain qualifications throughout your career.

You will have the opportunity to work in a range of industries and possibly abroad.

Some of the conditions that you work in could be distracting or challenging.

Money guide

Salaries are likely to vary according to the sector, size and location of the industry in which you work, however a typical graduate starting salary is around £28,000–£29,500.

Experienced engineers can expect to earn £53,000 a year or more.

Senior chemical engineers with chartered status can make between £60,000 and £70,000 per year.

Related opportunities

- Environmental Engineer p211
- Manufacturing/Production Engineer p217
- Mechanical Engineer p221

Further information

British Chemical Engineering Contractors Association
www.bceca.org.uk

Institution of Chemical Engineers
www.icheme.org

Semta
www.semta.org.uk

ENGINEERING, MANUFACTURING AND PRODUCTION

Qualifications and courses

Trainee technical brewers are usually required to have a degree or postgraduate qualification. Heriot-Watt University offers a specialist degree in brewing and distilling through their International Centre for Brewing and Distilling (ICBD) but other subjects such as food studies, chemical and mechanical engineering and biology will also provide you with some of the relevant skills required in the industry. Entry requirements for a degree are typically 2 A levels/H grades and 5 GCSEs/National 5s. Those whose first degree is not related to the field of brewing may benefit from completing a postgraduate qualification in brewing science or biotechnology.

Alternatively, you could begin you career as a brewery worker or production assistant before progressing to technical brewing roles by gaining further qualifications as you train. Usually a number of GCSEs/National 5s are needed to be accepted onto an Apprenticeship in Food Manufacturing.

After completion of your degree, graduate training schemes may be offered by some of the larger brewery companies but competition is fierce. You may find pre-entry experience, eg work placements or shadowing opportunities in a brewing environment, advantageous as employers often look for candidates who can demonstrate a familiarity with technical language, teamwork skills, management experience and a logical approach.

Once employed, you are likely to undergo a series of continuing professional development (CPD) programmes in order to update your skills and qualifications. The Institute of Brewing and Distilling offers a range of courses for general brewing and specialist subjects; these include a general certificate in brewing, distilling and packaging, a diploma in brewing modules and master brewing modules.

What the work involves

You will be overseeing the whole brewing process, managing the brewery workers and monitoring the condition of the brewing equipment.

Technical brewers are responsible for checking the quality of raw materials and testing the product regularly for texture, taste and appearance.

In a large brewery you may specialise in a certain area of brewing, such as fermentation, packaging or quality control, whereas in a small brewery you are likely to be involved with all aspects of the brewing process.

You will be responsible for developing new brewing methods, and designing and developing new beers, stouts and lagers.

Type of person suited to this work

You will need to be scientific, with an enquiring mind and a particular interest in biochemistry. Both a practical ability and an interest in engineering are also useful.

Leadership and interpersonal skills are needed as you will be managing a team of brewers. Good communication skills are

also needed as you will be responsible for writing reports, keeping records and presenting new brewery methods to your colleagues.

Working conditions

As brewing is a continuous process, you will work shifts including nights and weekends. Usually you will work no more that 40 hours a week.

Some technical brewers will need to be on their feet all day, checking the brewing process, in hot and noisy conditions.

Some time will be spent in an office organising paperwork and making reports on production, stock quality and budgets.

Future prospects

The number of large breweries in the UK is in decline and the increased use of machinery and automated processes means that competition for positions will be high. The majority of available industry jobs are concentrated around the east of England, the London area, Glasgow and Aberdeen.

With experience you can progress to managerial roles and senior brewer positions in a large brewery, such as a head brewer or technical director where you will lead a team of specialist staff. Alternatively, you could move into related areas such as research and development, quality control, distribution, sales or personnel.

The number of UK micro-breweries and market demand for craft beer have risen dramatically in the last few years and diversified the opportunities available for craft technical brewers. You could work within a very small, specialised team or open your own micro-brewery.

Advantages/disadvantages

This is an interesting and diverse role, which can lead to good promotions and self-employment.

Working night shifts in a hot and smelly environment may be tiring and stressful.

Money guide

Starting salaries are generally between £15,000 and £25,000 per year.

With experience this is likely to increase to £25,000–£33,000.

Senior brewers may earn in excess of £40,000.

Related opportunities

- Biotechnologist p495
- Brewery Worker p203
- Cellar Technician p124

Further information

Campaign for Real Ale (CAMRA)
www.camra.org.uk

Campden Brewing Research International
www.campdenbri.co.uk/brewing-services.php

Institute of Brewing and Distilling
www.ibd.org.uk

Qualifications and courses

You will need a degree or postgraduate qualification in a subject such as electrical or electronic engineering, mechanical engineering, applied physics or computer science. For degree entry you will need at least 2 A levels/H grades and 5 GCSEs/National 5s (A*–C/A–C) including Maths and a science. Relevant HNDs or Foundation degrees, in Electrical, Mechanical or Building Services Engineering for example, may also be considered, although employers often place value on those who have studied at degree level. Some universities may offer those diplomates with relevant work experience the opportunity to accelerate into the final year of a degree programme.

Alternatively, you could enter the field at a lower level by first training as an electrical engineering technician and working your way up by gaining experience and higher qualifications. Advanced Apprenticeships in Engineering Manufacture (Craft and Technician) or the Higher Level Apprenticeship in Engineering Manufacture (Senior Technician) are available. You will need good GCSEs/National 5s (A*–C/A–C) in English, Maths, a science or technology in order to be considered. You will need to study for a degree, however, if you wish to become a professional electrical engineer.

Many companies offer graduates training schemes post-university. Programmes vary according to the size of the company but typically involve a series of on-the-job training and structured continuing professional development (CPD). Undertaking work experience or a vacation placement will benefit your application as employers often like to see evidence of a candidate's enthusiasm, ability to work in a team and commercial awareness.

Those with a bachelor's degree in engineering (BEng) or equivalent can apply for incorporated engineer (IEng) status via the Engineering Council and those who have studied to master's level can gain chartered engineer (CEng) status further on in their career.

What the work involves

Electrical engineers research, design and develop a range of electrical equipment. You will be making, testing and servicing all types of electrical equipment and machinery, and as such you will be involved in projects from conception to completion.

You will usually work on projects with a team of professionals, including contractors and engineers from other industries.

You will also be liaising with clients and contractors about the development of each project, which will involve preparing reports and giving presentations.

Type of person suited to this work

You should have excellent mathematical ability and a very analytical mind in order to successfully design and develop complicated new electrical systems. A logical approach to problem-solving is also beneficial.

You will need good communication skills, both oral and written, for working alongside team members and clients. This will involve explaining and talking through projects, as well as compiling written reports and leading presentations.

You must have normal colour vision and natural manual dexterity.

Working conditions

Although electrical engineers usually work within the normal working week, you may find that you need to work additional or unsocial hours in order to solve problems and meet project deadlines.

Your time will be divided between office-based and on-site work. You can expect to travel on a daily basis so a driving licence is useful.

Conditions on-site can often be dirty, cramped and potentially hazardous so you should be prepared to get your hands dirty and wear safety equipment.

Future prospects

There are no set pathways of career progression for electrical engineers and many decide to stay in a purely engineering role for the duration of their working life.

Alternatively, there are possibilities to move into project management, become a consultant or take on a more managerial role within a company.

Advantages/disadvantages

Your work will be undertaken at a variety of indoor and outdoor locations so you will not be confined to an office environment.

You will play an instrumental role in developing new and increasingly safe electrical equipment for a variety of important functions.

Hours can be long and unpredictable, especially when nearing completion of a project.

Money guide

The starting salary for a graduate electrical engineer can range from £20,000 to £25,000.

Experienced or incorporated engineers are likely to earn £25,000–£40,000 a year, with chartered engineers usually receiving a salary of £40,000–£60,000 or more.

Some companies offer excellent benefit packages and bonus schemes in addition to a basic wage.

Related opportunities

- Civil/Construction Engineer/Civil Engineering Technician p71
- Mechanical Engineer p221
- Telecommunications Engineer p232

Further information

Institution of Engineering and Technology
www.theiet.org

Qualifications and courses

The most common route of entry into a career as an electricity distribution worker is via an apprenticeship, for example the Advanced Apprenticeship in Engineering Manufacture (Craft and Technician) may be available. Although there are no set qualifications required to gain access to a training scheme, most employers seek a minimum of 4 GCSEs/National 5s (A*–C/A–C) including English, Maths and a related subject such as a science, Design and Technology or Engineering.

Apprenticeships are open to those aged 16–24 and typically take 4 years in which to become fully qualified. You are likely to undertake a combination of on-the-job practical training from experienced professionals and college-based instruction where you will work towards achieving industry-recognised qualifications, such as a City & Guilds NVQ in Electrical Power Engineering (Levels 2 and 3) with options in overhead lines or underground cables or the BTEC Level 3 Certificate/Diploma in Electrical/Electronic Engineering. Short courses in areas such as high voltage safety are also possible options to further your career.

On completion of your training, you could work towards becoming a registered engineering technician (EngTech) with the Engineering Council, which will improve your earning potential and career prospects. Appropriate qualifications, 3 years' experience, membership of the Institution of Mechanical Engineers (IMechE) or the Institution of Engineering and Technology (IET) and a professional review are required.

As proof of your competency working on-site, your employer may need you to be registered in an appropriate safety passport scheme.

What the work involves

Electricity distribution workers are responsible for installing, checking and maintaining all machinery and equipment that supplies electricity to commercial and residential properties. You will be working on a variety of projects from small-scale domestic problems to regional electrical concerns.

You will be working on the overhead lines, masts and underground cables that run from power stations and connect all the electricity networks together.

You could work as a cable jointer who mainly works on the underground cables, an overhead line worker or an electrical fitter who installs, tests and repairs equipment in the regional electricity substations.

Type of person suited to this work

You will need to be practical and good with your hands as you will be using a variety of tools and undertaking fiddly tasks. You must have normal colour vision and pay meticulous attention to detail.

You should be reasonably fit with a head for heights, as some jobs may require lifting and carrying heavy equipment or working high above the ground.

Since you will be working with live electricity, you must be aware of your own safety and that of others around you. You may need to wear protective equipment at times.

Working conditions

Although you will usually work an average of 37 hours a week, these may involve shift patterns including evenings and weekends. You should also expect to work overtime on occasion in order to complete projects on time.

The work can be physically demanding as you will be bending and carrying large cables and equipment. You may work outdoors in damp and muddy trenches and you can expect to be carrying out tasks in cramped conditions sometimes.

Future prospects

As an electricity distribution worker, you will have various options available as you progress in your career. You may go on to become a supervisor or manager and be responsible for a team of workers. Alternatively, you could move into another related job within the industry.

Your career prospects could be improved by studying for additional qualifications as you work, such as an NVQ Level 4 in Electrical Engineering, or even a relevant degree.

Advantages/disadvantages

You will be on-site for the majority of your time so you will not be confined to an office environment.

Possibilities for career progression or diversification are good.

Conditions can be unpleasant owing to extreme weather or space constraints.

You may have to work irregular/unsocial hours.

Money guide

Apprentices typically earn around £15,000 per year, depending on the stage of their training.

You can expect your salary to increase to between £23,000 and £35,000 a year, or more, depending on your qualifications and experience.

Related opportunities

- Electrical Engineer p207
- Electrician p80
- Gas Network Engineer p214

Further information

Engineering Council UK
www.engc.org.uk

Institution of Engineering and Technology
www.theiet.org

ENERGY ENGINEER

Qualifications and courses

This career is open to graduates of a relevant accredited engineering degree, such as environmental, petroleum, electrical, mechanical or chemical engineering as well as other science-related subjects such as chemistry, physics or earth science. Due to an increase in profile and application of renewable and sustainable energy solutions, a number of specialist degrees have become increasingly available, such as energy engineering, sustainable energy and climate science.

Entry requirements for engineering or related degrees are a minimum of 2 A levels/3 H grades and 5 GCSEs/National 5s (A*–C/A–C) including English, Maths and a science. Alternative entry qualifications may include relevant BTEC Diplomas or Access courses.

For those with non-accredited degrees, you will need to complete a postgraduate conversion course in renewable energy engineering, sustainable energy systems or energy futures, in order to upgrade your qualifications. A postgraduate course in engineering may be beneficial to all candidates however, as this will enhance your career prospects and support your pathway to gaining chartered status.

Graduate training programmes are available to those post-university. Most entrants for schemes within the larger oil companies will have gained a 2.1 in their degree subject, but postgraduate qualifications are generally preferred. Experience is also valued by employers so work placements may be worthwhile in a somewhat competitive jobs market.

Becoming a member of relevant organisations will also ensure you remain up to date with the latest developments in the industry, allow you to make essential contacts and inform you of new training courses. To improve your prospects further, you could work towards gaining chartered status via the Institution of Engineering and Technology (IET).

What the work involves

You will be involved with the extraction of oil and gas and the production of energy from renewable or sustainable sources, such as wind power, solar power or biofuels.

You will have to calculate how much oil or gas a well will produce and decide how to extract as much as possible and also oversee the drilling operations on an offshore rig.

You could also have to research new ways of generating energy, whilst developing ways of improving existing processes.

Type of person suited to this work

Excellent communication and interpersonal skills are needed for teamwork and to build strong relationships with other professionals and clients.

You should have a high level of numeracy and good IT skills, as well as scientific understanding of related fields such as geology and chemistry.

You will need to have excellent planning, organisational and problem-solving skills to successfully run a project.

Working conditions

If you become involved with power plant or drilling operations, you could work on a 7-day shift system, which would include nights and weekends, whereas working in design, research and development will mean working more standard office hours.

The work is both mentally and physically demanding and conditions on-site are often noisy, wet, cold and inhospitable.

Some jobs may involve international travel and long stays away from home.

Future prospects

The renewable energy industry is rapidly expanding, due to an increased interest in environmental issues, the rise in demand for oil and gas and the pressure on businesses to reduce their carbon footprint.

Renewable and sustainable energy has become a government priority and so job prospects for energy engineers are very good with growth areas including corporate social responsibility (CSR), teaching roles and positions in research and development.

You could be employed in the oil and gas industry, energy production companies or you could move into the education field by teaching or conducting university research.

With experience, you could move into planning, policy development, or freelance consultancy.

Advantages/disadvantages

Oil drilling in particular operates in some of the most dangerous and hostile areas of the world, so your safety could be threatened on a daily basis.

It will be rewarding to know that you have helped to minimise environmental damage.

You will have to be prepared to spend some time away from home.

Money guide

Salaries for graduates typically range from £20,000 to £30,000, with the larger earnings coming from the big oil companies.

Those with experience or in senior management roles could earn between £35,000 and £80,000.

Related opportunities

- Civil/Construction Engineer/Civil Engineering Technician p71
- Environmental Engineer p211
- Mechanical Engineer p221

Further information

Engineering Council UK
www.engc.org.uk

Rigzone
www.rigzone.com

Qualifications and courses

The most common route of entry into this career is via an Advanced Apprenticeship in Engineering Manufacture (Craft and Technician). Most employers require candidates to have 5 GCSEs/National 5s (A*–C/A–C) in subjects including, English, Maths, a science and either technology or Engineering. Employers value candidates who have shown demonstrable interest within the engineering field, by either completing work experience in the sector, carrying out a 14–19 Young Apprenticeship in Engineering or Manufacturing or completing the Intermediate Level Apprenticeship in Engineering Manufacture.

As part of the selection process, you may be required to complete basic literacy, numeracy, communication skills and spatial awareness tests and an interview prior to being accepted.

As an apprentice, you will undertake several months of training away from the workplace to develop specialist skills. You will then spend 2–3 years working for a company whilst also attending college and studying towards relevant professional qualifications. There are several possible pathways leading to careers in different areas of the field, such as fabrication and welding, electronics, aerospace or marine engineering, therefore the qualifications you study will be vital in determining your chosen pathway. These qualifications could include the BTEC Level 2 Certificate/Diploma in Engineering, the NVQ/SVQ in Mechanical Manufacturing Engineering (Levels 2–3), the BTEC Level 3 Certificate/Diploma in Mechanical Engineering or Manufacturing Engineering or the City & Guilds Certificate/Diploma in Engineering. More specialist qualifications such as an NVQ/SVQ in either Engineering Woodworking, Pattern and Model Making, Marine Engineering or Toolmaking (all Level 3) may be encouraged by your employer.

What the work involves

Engineering machinists make engineered parts from various materials, such as metals or heavy and lightweight plastics. You could make parts for a variety of products, from domestic appliances and machines to wind turbines and aeroplane engines.

You will be using a range of machinery, including grinding and cutting machines, drills and presses. Increasingly, computer numerically controlled (CNC) machinery is being used which combines some of the manufacturing processes.

You will need to interpret complicated engineering drawings in order to assess which materials, tools and machines to use to produce each part.

Type of person suited to this work

You will need to have good eyesight, excellent coordination and sound practical ability in order to operate machinery safely and accurately.

Good mathematical skills and the ability to read complicated engineering drawings and interpret them into a 3D part are essential.

You should have strong communication skills as you will mainly be working in a team environment. A good level of physical fitness is also beneficial as the job involves lifting heavy materials and standing or bending over machinery for the majority of the day.

Working conditions

Working hours are usually around 38 hours a week, Monday to Friday, although you will usually start early in the morning and finish early in the afternoon.

Some larger companies operate 24-hour production and would require you to work shifts including evenings and weekends. Conditions in factories and workshops are usually fairly pleasant, although it can be noisy at times.

As you are operating machinery, you will need to wear appropriate safety equipment at all times.

Future prospects

Job prospects are good as there is currently a shortage of skilled machinists in the engineering sector. There are jobs available for machinists throughout Britain, although the majority are found in larger cities and within general mechanical engineering companies. You could work in mechanical engineering, automotive or aerospace industries or within shipbuilding.

With experience, you could be promoted to team leader or supervisor and if you gain further qualifications you could move into engineering technician roles such as design.

Advantages/disadvantages

Jobs are available throughout the UK and there is little travelling involved so you will rarely be absent from home.

It is a physically demanding role, with large amounts of time spent standing or bending over machinery and lifting heavy materials and equipment.

You may have to work unsocial hours owing to early starts or unpredictable shift patterns.

Money guide

Starting salaries for trainees are usually between £12,000 and £15,000.

With experience, your earnings can rise to £16,000–£25,000.

Those employed in a senior position with supervisory responsibilities can achieve up to £30,000 a year.

Related opportunities

- Motor Vehicle Technician p222
- Sheet Metal Worker p230
- Toolmaker p234

Further information

Semta
www.semta.org.uk

ENVIRONMENTAL ENGINEER

Qualifications and courses

Most employers require candidates to have a good degree, usually a 2.1 minimum, or postgraduate qualification in a relevant subject such as civil or environmental engineering. You will need at least 2 A levels/H grades and 5 GCSEs/National 5s (A*–C/A–C), including Maths and Physics, for degree entry. You may be considered if you have studied another engineering subject, or something related such as physics, applied physics or maths but the field is highly competitive and you may have to supplement your degree with a postgraduate qualification. Candidates are encouraged to complete a master's degree as this will be beneficial further on in your career when seeking chartered status.

Alternatively, it may be possible to enter the field with an HND in a relevant subject such as general engineering, civil engineering, environmental engineering, applied physics or computing and IT. As some employers prefer graduates, supplementing your HND with work experience is highly recommended.

Some companies offer a sponsorship scheme for candidates who have completed their A levels/H grades. This sponsorship consists of financial support to the candidate throughout their degree programme and the offer of an apprenticeship upon graduation.

Many employers offer graduates opportunities to enter structured graduate development programmes once in employment. With the training and supervision of senior mentors, graduates will work towards becoming professional engineers of either incorporated (IEng) or chartered (CEng) status or becoming specialists in their individual fields.

What the work involves

Environmental engineers work on projects concerning waste management, land reclamation and pollution control, and liaise with a variety of clients from local authorities to private property developers.

You will visit and assess numerous sites in relation to their environmental impact, and will explain your findings to clients via presentations and reports.

You may also communicate the environmental issues of a project or site to the general public, green groups and regulatory authorities.

Type of person suited to this work

You should have excellent mathematical ability and a very analytical mind in order to successfully carry out complicated procedures and calculations to assess sites and projects. A swift and logical approach to problem-solving is also needed when dealing with often unforeseen environmental complications.

Good oral and written communication skills are essential for working alongside team members and clients.

Negotiation skills are also helpful as you might need to reach compromises over projects with local government officials, residents or clients.

Working conditions

You will usually work 35–40 hours from Monday to Friday, although additional or unsocial hours are not uncommon should problems occur or if deadlines need to be met on a project.

Your time will be divided between office-based and on-site work, so you can expect to travel on a daily basis. A driving licence is essential.

You will work in all weather conditions on-site, so should be prepared to get cold and muddy. You will also have to adhere to site safety regulations and wear relevant protective clothing.

Future prospects

As environmental concerns become an increasingly important aspect of construction projects across the globe, there are good prospects and opportunities within this field for career progression.

With experience, you could move into consultancy and set up your own firm. Alternatively, you could specialise in an area such as treatment of industrial waste, or provision of drinking water in developing countries.

You could work in a small company, or in much larger multinational firms. There are also numerous opportunities to work on projects abroad.

Advantages/disadvantages

You will be responsible for minimising the environmental impact of building projects and protecting the wellbeing of the natural surroundings, which will be rewarding.

Working on potentially controversial developments could lead to confrontations with local residents or clients.

There are excellent opportunities to work overseas, or set up your own company.

Money guide

The starting salary for an environmental engineer can range from £17,000 to £25,000.

With a few years' experience, you can expect to earn anything up to £55,000 a year.

Senior environmental engineers with chartered or incorporated status could earn £90,000.

Related opportunities

- Environmental Health Practitioner/Officer p22
- Marine Engineer p219
- Mechanical Engineer p221

Further information

Chartered Institution of Water and Environmental Management
www.ciwem.org

Engineering Council UK
www.engc.org.uk

Society for the Environment
www.socenv.org.uk

FOOD PROCESSING OPERATIVE

Qualifications and courses

There are no set qualifications required for this profession though some employers may ask for basic levels of literacy and numeracy and, depending on the shift patterns and machinery involved, some employers will require employees to be at least 18 years of age.

A common route of entry into the industry is via an Apprenticeship in Food Manufacture. Apprenticeships are structured training schemes that typically combine on-the-job training with a series of day or block release instruction at a college or training centre where you will work towards gaining industry-recognised qualifications. Depending on the area of the sector in which you work, your employer may encourage you to work towards awards such as an NVQ/SVQ in Food and Drink Manufacturing Operations (Levels 1–4), an NVQ/SVQ in Chemical, Pharmaceutical and Petrochemical Manufacture (Levels 1–4) or a BTEC Level 3 Certificate/Diploma in Food Science and Manufacturing Technology. Practical skills as well as general health and safety with food will be taught.

With time, you can work towards progressing to a management role or supervisory position. In order to do this, you might need GCSEs/National 5s (A*–C/A–C) in English, Maths, a science or Food Technology in order to be considered later on in your career. At an operative level, you can choose to move to different areas of food production, such as baking, freezing or brewing.

What the work involves

Food processing operatives can be involved in one of many areas of food processing. These include freezing, canning, baking, drying, cooking, chilling, pasteurising or a combination of several of these processes.

Since much of the work above is carried out by machines, you may be involved in operating the machinery and you might also be expected to carry out basic maintenance on it.

You might be involved in the production of the food, for example placing different components of foodstuffs in containers. Packaging and labelling are other tasks that you might be required to carry out.

Type of person suited to this work

It is helpful if you have an interest in food and food processing.

You should be good at working in a team, and be able to respond quickly to problems that may arise. You need to be able to stay alert and perceptive at all times, even if tasks are mundane or boring. A good ability to concentrate and observe what is going on around you will really help with this.

Good literacy and numeracy skills are also essential, and you will need to be able to follow instructions easily, both written and spoken. A thorough understanding of health and safety requirements is also an advantage.

Working conditions

You will be working in a factory environment most of the time. This will involve standing in a production line, as well as bending and lifting. Temperature in the factory varies according to the processes taking place.

You will almost certainly be required to wear protective clothing, such as overalls and hats, and a high level of personal hygiene is essential.

You can expect to work 37 to 40 hours a week, usually on a shift system which may include weekends. Overtime is often available.

Future prospects

The food and drink manufacturing industry is extremely large, employing more than 500,000 workers in over 30,000 companies. The sector is currently set to expand, thus there are good job prospects for food processing operatives.

Many industries are now shifting to automated processes, higher value products and niche markets, such as organic food production and processing, therefore, if you hold qualifications or specific technical skills, you will maintain a distinct advantage.

Progression within the food and drink industry is relatively common and, if committed, you stand a good chance of moving up in your company or moving on to others. You can progress to supervisory and management positions quite quickly and opportunities for work within quality control roles are common. Most managers in this sector started out as a food processing operative or something similar.

Advantages/disadvantages

The working environment may not always be pleasant: it can be very hot or very cold. Work may be mundane at times, and the salary is not very high.

There are usually plenty of jobs available in this sector, and prospects for promotion are good. If you work your way up jobs become more interesting and better paid.

Money guide

Salaries typically start at £12,000 per year.

This can rise to £16,000 as you gain experience.

Supervisors and managers can earn up to £20,000.

Related opportunities

- Brewery Worker p203
- Food Safety Officer p127
- Meat Process Worker p220

Further information

Food and Drink Federation
www.fdf.org.uk

Improve Ltd
www.improveltd.co.uk

Scottish Food and Drink Federation
www.sfdf.org.uk

Qualifications and courses

Most employers do not require furniture manufacturing operatives to hold any specific academic or vocational qualifications, but a number of GCSEs/National 5s (A*–C/A–C) may be valued and could support you in your search for employment. You may need to pass an eyesight and colour vision test in order to be considered for work.

The most common route of entry into this industry is via an Apprenticeship in Wood Making or Making and Installing Furniture. As an apprentice, you will typically experience a combination of on-the-job training from professionals in a furniture manufacturing or other relevant company, and a series of day or block release instruction at a college or training centre where you will work towards gaining industry-recognised qualifications.

Awards such as the City & Guilds Level 1–3 qualifications in Furniture and Furnishings (5782), or an NVQ/SVQ Level 1 in Supporting the Production of Furniture and Furnishings, a Level 2 in Making and Installing Furniture, a Level 3 in either Making and Repairing Hand-Crafted Furniture and Furnishings or Making and Installing Production Furniture, and a SQA HNC in Furniture Construction and Design may also be available.

What the work involves

Furniture manufacturers construct pieces of furniture; they may either use machinery, or construct furniture by hand.

This involves cutting and shaping individual parts of each piece, then assembling them to make a finished item. You may then have to smooth and finish items, getting them ready for sale.

You will usually then be asked to add handles and hinges, and sometimes to upholster the furniture too.

Type of person suited to this work

You must be practical and good with your hands.

You should also have excellent eyesight and full colour vision. Hand-to-eye coordination is a must.

Some jobs will also require artistic ability. You must be accurate, careful, and above all patient.

Your physical strength should be reasonably good, as you will need to lift and carry things.

You must be able to take orders, and work under supervision. It is also important to be able to work in a team.

Tasks may become repetitive, but you need to be able to stay focused at all times.

Working conditions

You will be working in a factory, so the environment may be noisy. Most jobs require you to stand in a production line all day, and the air may be dusty and smell strongly of the products used to treat finished furniture.

Protective clothing is usually worn, including ear protectors and face masks for many jobs. Many jobs involve standing for long periods, lifting heavy weights, and bending.

It is normal to work a 39 hour week. Shift work might be required and overtime is common during seasonal peaks or when the factory has a delivery deadline.

Future prospects

The furniture manufacturing industry currently employs around 115,000 workers within 8,116 businesses, alongside a further 15,000 related companies offering opportunities for operatives to work across the UK. You may have to relocate to areas where companies are more concentrated, for example in the major UK cities, the Midlands, the north-west of England, Edinburgh and Aberdeen.

With the increased mechanisation and use of technology, employees with good IT skills who can operate specialist machinery and understand complex systems, are rapidly replacing the need for those workers with physical strength.

Promotion is a possibility, and many manufacturers move into more senior roles within companies, managing projects and gaining responsibility. Others choose to specialise in specific areas of furniture manufacture, for example furniture restoration, craft cabinet making or even furniture design.

More furniture manufacturers are now choosing to teach their craft or set up their own business by becoming self-employed.

Advantages/disadvantages

If you are interested in your craft and willing to put a little time in, a career in furniture manufacture can really grow, and so can your salary.

This job can be satisfying if you enjoy building and making things and are good at DIY.

Working on constructing the same item over and over again can get repetitive.

Money guide

Most operatives start on a salary of around £12,000 per year.

With experience, this might increase to £15,000.

If you become highly skilled, you can expect to earn in excess of £25,000.

Related opportunities

- Carpenter/Joiner p67
- Ergonomist p24
- Shopfitter p107

Further information

Association of Master Upholsterers and Soft Furnishers
www.upholsterers.co.uk

British Furniture Manufacturers
www.bfm.org.uk

British Woodworking Federation
www.bwf.org.uk

ENGINEERING, MANUFACTURING AND PRODUCTION

Qualifications and courses

The most common route of entry into a career as a gas network engineer is via an apprenticeship. There are no formal qualifications required for traineeships but a good standard of education would be expected. For entry you will need a minimum of 4 GCSEs/National 5s (A*–C/A–C), in Maths, a science, English and a practical technical subject such as Engineering or Design and Technology.

Once employed in a company as an apprentice, you will experience a combination of on-the-job training from professional engineers and a series of day or block release instruction at a college or training centre where you will work towards achieving industry-recognised qualifications. NVQs in Gas Network Operations (Mains Laying, Service Laying or Craft) (Levels 1–3) and an NVQ Level 3 in Gas Emergency Service Operations are some of the qualifications available to study. These awards are often undertaken on a progressive basis, meaning the more experience and skills which you develop, the more equipped you are to gain the higher level qualifications.

After completing an NVQ Level 3, it is possible to apply for a HND/degree or higher level NVQs. Graduate engineering and management training schemes are also available. It is also possible to undertake a 3-year National Grid Advanced Apprenticeship.

Employers will consider it necessary for you to have a safety passport from an appropriate industry scheme, with Energy and Utility Skills for example, in order to demonstrate your competency working on-site.

What the work involves

Gas is transported from its supply points (called beaches) to domestic and industrial customers by a network of pipes and meters that will be your responsibility to fit and maintain.

To gain access to pipework you will probably need to dig a hole in a road, garden or pavement. This can be a physically demanding job. You will be using digging and excavating tools and pipe-laying equipment.

You will be responsible for the safety of yourself and others when carrying out work. This will include putting up warning signs, barriers and traffic control if needed. You may have to deal with emergency gas leaks.

Type of person suited to this work

You will normally work in a small team, so you should enjoy working with and be able to get on with people. You will be meeting new customers each day, so being polite and courteous are also important characteristics.

An ability to follow instructions and an understanding of technical language and drawings are essential as these will be used to tell you what you need to do on a daily basis.

When the job is complete, you will have to ensure the finished surface is safe and as good as it was when you started, so you should be tidy and efficient.

Working conditions

You will be working in a team outdoors in all weathers. You will normally work 37–40 hours a week; overtime and weekend work will be expected on a rota basis.

You will be using equipment which can be physically demanding and you will get dirty. As this can be dangerous work you will wear protective clothing such as high-visibility and fireproof clothing, steel toe-capped boots and head gear.

Future prospects

The National Grid coordinates and monitors the gas distribution network in the UK. There are 4 gas distribution companies: National Grid Distribution, Wales and West Utilities, Northern Gas Networks and Scotia Gas Networks (operating in the south of England as Southern Gas and in Scotland as Scotland Gas Networks).

There is currently a high demand for gas network engineers due to both an extensive 30-year pipeline replacement programme and an ageing workforce, particularly in the north of England. You could find work in one of the regional gas distribution companies, for a utility contractor or a construction company building new developments.

With experience and training, you could progress from craftsperson status to a technician, team-leader or management position where you would be responsible for managing a number of teams.

Advantages/disadvantages

You will be working outside in all weathers.

You may have to deal with complaints from angry customers about holes in their road.

Giving the public a gas supply for their homes and businesses can be rewarding.

Money guide

Whilst training, workers can earn £11,000–£15,000 per year.

Salaries for experienced engineers and team leaders range from £25,000 to £32,000 per year.

Related opportunities

- Construction Operative p74
- Construction Plant Operator p75
- Water/Sewerage Network Operative p118

Further information

Energy & Utility Skills
www.euskills.co.uk

Energy & Utility Skills Register
www.eusr.co.uk

Northern Gas Networks
www.northerngasnetworks.co.uk

Scotland Gas Networks
www.sgn.co.uk

Qualifications and courses

This career is open to all graduates with a degree in engineering, and specific degree qualifications in subjects such as agricultural engineering, environmental engineering, electrical engineering, ergonomics, off-road vehicle design or mechanical engineering may improve your chances. HNDs in similar subjects are also considered for entry level, technician, positions and some employers may be willing to support further study to take you to degree level. You will need a minimum of 2 A levels/3 H grades and 5 GCSEs/National 5s (A*–C/A–C) including English, Maths and a science, for degree entry.

Your degree or HND must be accredited by the Institution of Agricultural Engineers (IAgrE), or a similar licensed body of the Engineering Council, if you would like to progress to incorporated (IEng) or chartered (CEng) engineer status. Those with an accredited bachelor's degree or HND are eligible for IEng status and those who have studied to master's level can pursue CEng status. These qualifications will significantly enhance your career prospects and earning potential.

For those looking to work as a technician, the Intermediate or Advanced Apprenticeship in Land-based Engineering may be available. However, if you wish to become a fully qualified engineer, you will need to study for a degree.

Some larger organisations may offer graduate training schemes post-university. When seeking employment as a graduate, you will be at a distinct advantage if you have had some pre-entry experience within the field as employers often look for candidates who can show evidence of teamwork, an ability to record and analyse data and an understanding of equipment. Some university courses may include a year of paid, practical work experience.

What the work involves

Land-based engineers design, develop, test and modify agricultural and horticultural equipment in order to ensure that these industries stay up to date.

You will need to carry out extensive research into the needs of those using the equipment you are producing, as well as assessing and limiting the environmental impact of your projects.

You will also be required to compile reports, present your findings and offer expert advice to colleagues, clients and other professionals.

Type of person suited to this work

You will need great ingenuity in order to find solutions to problems or design new equipment to aid agricultural and horticultural processes.

Excellent communication skills are required to understand the needs of your clients and translate them into designs and instructions for your team.

Good IT skills, problem-solving abilities and a flexible approach to work are also essential in order to cope with the various demands of differing projects.

Working conditions

You will usually work a normal working week, although occasional overtime may be necessary to meet project deadlines.

Although you will be office based for the majority of the time, there will be some on-site and field work so that you can assess projects and carry out tests on equipment.

You may find that you have to work outdoors in unpredictable weather or cold, wet and muddy conditions. You will also need to wear relevant safety equipment whilst on-site.

Future prospects

There are opportunities for land-based engineers to work all over the world, undertaking a variety of projects from food production in the UK, dealing with natural disasters and war, to creating effective water supplies in areas of the developing world. There is currently a national shortage of professional engineers; therefore, job prospects are good.

Larger firms offer greater scope for career progression and you could soon be managing your own projects. You could specialise in design or testing and development, where it is also possible to become self-employed. Alternatively, you could move into sales and marketing or even research and teaching. Smaller firms offer less opportunity for progression, so you might have to move to another company to develop in your field.

Advantages/disadvantages

Each day will present new problems and challenges so the work will always be interesting and stimulating.

You will be working with a variety of people from many professional sectors and areas of the community.

On average, you will earn less than engineers in other industries.

Money guide

Starting salaries are usually between £20,000 and £25,000.

Once you have gained 10–15 years' experience, you could expect earnings in the range of £25,000–£30,000.

Chartered land-based engineers can earn £40,000 to in excess of £60,000.

Related opportunities

- Agricultural Scientist p239
- Environmental Engineer p211
- Land/Geomatic Surveyor p94

Further information

British Agricultural and Garden Machinery Association
www.bagma.com

Engineering Council UK
www.engc.org.uk

215

LOCKSMITH

ENGINEERING, MANUFACTURING AND PRODUCTION

Qualifications and courses

There are no specific educational requirements but most applicants will be expected to hold GCSEs/National 5s (A*–C/A–C) in English, Maths and preferably a practical subject such as craft or technology.

Locksmithing apprenticeships have recently become available for study for those aged 16 years and over. These courses are run by either the Master Locksmiths Association (MLA) or the Skills Funding Agency (SFA). Applicants must first secure employment for an apprenticeship, and will then begin to combine on-the-job training under professionals at their place of work with day or block release instruction at a college or training centre, working towards industry-recognised qualifications. Apprentices are required to hold good GCSEs/National 5s (A*–C/A–C) in English and Maths. Applicants without these will be required to study for the Functional Skills qualifications in these subjects as additional learning units. The 'Find a Locksmith' database on the MLA's website is a useful resource when looking for employment for an apprenticeship.

Alternatively, the MLA, the recognised authoritative body for locksmithing, offers a General Locksmithing Course at their training centre in Northamptonshire. As part of this course, candidates will study industry-recognised qualifications such as the City & Guilds Award in Basic Locksmithing. To apply for training you must be a member of the British Locksmiths Institute (BLI). Individuals over the age of 16 can apply for student membership without any prior experience. Advanced Student membership is for those who have 12 months' practical training in locksmithing and have passed the entry exam.

An NVQ in Providing Security, Emergency and Alarm Systems (Levels 2 and 3) and City & Guilds vocational courses in security and alarm systems are also available.

What the work involves

You will sell, install and fix the locks of houses, cars and businesses for your customers.

You will use specialist machinery to cut replacement keys for locks.

Advising on, repairing and installing security and closed-circuit television (CCTV) systems may be part of your job.

Type of person suited to this work

As a locksmith you will have to be calm and patient – reassuring your customers, who may be distressed, whilst providing a prompt and reliable service. Good communication skills are important in this job.

Your customers and employer will also expect you to be totally trustworthy and honest.

To do this job you will have to enjoy using your hands, different tools and equipment. You should enjoy practical tasks and be able to offer solutions to security problems. Carpentry or general engineering skills are also helpful.

Working conditions

Employers include independent small locksmiths, larger national companies offering a 24-hour call-out emergency service, specialist security companies, DIY hardware stores and shoe repairers that offer a key-cutting service.

If you work in a shop you will probably have a 40-hour, Monday–Saturday week. Self-employment is possible.

If you or your employer offers a 24-hour call-out service, you could be working at all times of the day or night.

You will mainly operate from a van that holds your tools so a driving licence is essential.

Future prospects

Progression for locksmiths is mainly achieved by becoming self-employed and building up a profitable business.

It is also possible to progress into more specialist areas of work such as safe engineering, installing CCTV and electronic access systems, or security and safety consultation.

Advantages/disadvantages

This can be a varied job as your work and location will change with each customer.

You will have the opportunity to meet many people and have the satisfaction of helping them.

Working unsocial hours/during the night can affect your personal life.

Call-outs to replace locks after burglaries can be distressing.

Money guide

Trainee locksmiths can expect a starting salary of around £13,000.

Qualified locksmiths' salaries can increase to between £16,000 and £24,000.

With experience, you could earn in excess of £30,000.

You will usually receive bonuses or higher rates for emergency call-outs.

Self-employed locksmiths establish their own rates based upon their company's success and reputation. Successful business owners can earn £30,000 or more.

Earnings can vary with geographical location.

Related opportunities

- Carpenter/Joiner p67
- Glazier p89
- Shoe Repairer p481

Further information

Master Locksmiths Association
www.locksmiths.co.uk

Skills for Security
www.skillsforsecurity.org.uk

Qualifications and courses

The most common entry route is with a relevant degree in an engineering subject. For degree entry, you will need 2 A levels/3 H grades (including Maths and Physics) and 5 GCSEs/National 5s (A*–C/A–C). It is becoming increasingly common for candidates to obtain a master's degree as this will be benefit you when seeking chartered engineering (CEng) status further on in your career. HNDs in similar subjects are also considered by employers, but you will have to undertake further study towards degree level qualifications whilst working.

It is recommended that your degree be accredited by the Engineering Council as this will make the process of gaining incorporated (IEng) or chartered (CEng) engineering status quicker. The most direct way to reach incorporated engineer (IEng) status is through obtaining a relevant degree, but it can also be achieved through a HNC or Foundation degree in Engineering or an appropriate NVQ Level 4 or SVQ Level 4 qualification. A postgraduate qualification or an MEng is required in order to become a chartered engineer.

You may be able to secure a graduate training scheme or in-house training programme, post-university. These offer recently qualified engineers the opportunity to gain experience within several departments of a company whilst working towards professional engineering status. When seeking work, academic qualifications are not always considered essential, but you must be able to show good problem-solving and project management skills, leadership, an ability to work to deadlines and have an awareness of health and safety issues in the workplace. Work experience within the manufacturing industry will improve your chances of gaining employment.

What the work involves

Manufacturing engineers design, implement and maintain manufacturing processes. You will be consulting with other professionals, such as design engineers, in order to produce high quality products efficiently and with minimum cost.

You could work in a variety of industries, including food and drink, fashion, and pharmaceuticals. You could work widely across a project, from design and research to after-sales care. Therefore, you will be using a variety of manufacturing equipment and computer systems on a daily basis.

Type of person suited to this work

You should be able to work as part of a team, as you will be liaising with other professionals on a daily basis to discuss product ideas and manufacturing solutions.

You should be good at analysing and solving problems in order to understand and stay ahead of potential manufacturing issues. The ability to prioritise your workload is also beneficial. Strong numerical skills are essential.

Working conditions

You will usually work 37 hours a week, but this often includes evening and weekend work. Extra or unsocial hours can be expected when a new production process is being tested, or if the company you are working for operates a shift system.

You will divide your time between office-based work, meetings and time spent on the shop floor or in the factory. When on the shop floor, you might have to wear safety equipment or protective clothing.

Future prospects

It is encouraged that you join your relevant professional body, dependent on your specialism, once you have qualified. These include the Institution of Mechanical Engineers (IMechE) and the Institution of Chemical Engineers (IChemE). This also lets you keep your training up to date through the continuing professional development (CPD) courses many of them run. You could work in a variety of manufacturing sectors, building diverse experience that will help you move across industries and sectors within manufacturing, taking up managerial or marketing roles.

Alternatively, you could specialise in a certain area (such as pharmaceuticals or clothing) and move into production management or consultancy; here you would draw upon your knowledge and experience to motivate and advise others.

There are also numerous short-term contracts available for manufacturing engineers, which would allow you to become self-employed.

Advantages/disadvantages

Manufacturing engineers enjoy one of the most creative roles in the engineering sector, with great input into product design and final function.

If you work in a large company, there may be opportunities to travel.

You may work evenings and weekends on a regular basis.

Money guide

The average graduate starting salaries, on completion of initial training, range from £22,000 to £28,000.

With 5–10 years' experience, you could earn up to £40,000.

Senior manufacturing engineers can expect to earn £40,000–£60,000.

Progressing into a consultancy role will allow you to set your own rates on an hourly or daily basis.

Related opportunities

- Electrical Engineer p207
- Mechanical Engineer p221
- Textile Operative p233

Further information

Institution of Engineering and Technology
www.theiet.org

Institution of Mechanical Engineers
www.imeche.org

Semta
www.semta.org.uk

MARINE CRAFTSPERSON

Qualifications and courses

Many employers ask for GCSEs/National 5s (A*–C/A–C) in English, Maths, a science and another related subject, such as Engineering or Design and Technology. Sometimes employers will ask for further qualifications, or even require candidates to complete an aptitude test.

The most common route of entry into a career as a marine craftsperson is via an apprenticeship within a firm of shipbuilders, repairers or boat builders. As an apprentice, you will undertake a combination of on-the-job training from experienced marine craftspeople with a series of day or block release classroom-based instruction, which most employers will be willing to fund. Training usually begins with health and safety regulations and an induction course, followed by basic skills including selecting materials, interpreting drawings and how to use relevant tools, before practising and furthering your abilities by working towards industry-recognised qualifications.

Possible boat-building courses that may be available to you include a Level 3 NVQ in either Engineering Maintenance or Marine Engineering Operations, and the City & Guilds Levels 2–3 Certificate/Diploma in Marine Construction, Systems Engineering and Maintenance (2463). You could also take a specialist degree in Leisure Boat Design and Construction.

Alternatively, you could develop your skills by studying general engineering college courses full time. Some colleges situated in coastal, boatbuilding areas may run introductory courses in marine crafts. BTEC Certificates/Diplomas in Mechanical, Electrical or Electronic Engineering are available, as are higher-level qualifications, such as HNCs/HNDs in Marine Engineering. Experience working in other related craft industries, such as welding, plumbing or joinery, may also support you in your search for employment.

What the work involves

A marine craftsperson takes part in the building and repair of many different kinds of ships and boats.

Repairers and shipbuilders work with big vessels such as ferries, dredgers, tugs, submarines, tankers and warships. Boat builders work with smaller boats, such as wooden dinghies, sailing boats, narrow boats and powerboats.

Both crafts require you to work from a design to create the ship or boat. This has usually been created on a computer, and you work at marking and cutting out shapes, welding, and cutting and bending steel and other materials.

Type of person suited to this work

You should be a good teamworker, and a good communicator.

A practical, logical and problem-solving mindset is essential, as you will not only be required to interpret drawings and plans but will also need to solve problems on the job quickly and intelligently.

You should also be good with numbers, and have good eyesight and good physical fitness.

Working conditions

Marine craftspeople tend to work a normal 37-hour week, but overtime is usually available. Some urgent repair jobs may take place overnight and during weekends, but this is relatively rare.

Working at heights is normal, and you will probably spend the majority of your time indoors.

Future prospects

Opportunities for boatbuilding and repair work are more likely to be found in coastal areas, therefore you may have to relocate in order to secure employment. Work in shipyards, building larger vessels, is found in Scotland, Northern Ireland and the north of England.

As you gain experience, it may be possible to progress to a position such as supervisor or inspector. You could also work towards becoming workshop manager.

Another option is to use your experience to become self-employed in areas such as boat building and repair.

Some people choose to gain further qualifications and become a marine engineering technician, move into marine design or specialise in equipment sales and support. You may even opt to transfer your skills into the wider engineering or construction industries.

Advantages/disadvantages

If you have an interest in practical work and building things, and in ships and maritime matters, then this job can be really enjoyable. It can be really satisfying to create something you are passionate about.

The dirty working conditions might not sit well with everybody, so if you want to work in a clean and tidy environment your skills may be better suited elsewhere.

Money guide

Starting salaries range from around £18,000 to £24,000 per year.

As a senior craftsperson you could earn more than £25,000 a year.

Related opportunities

- Civil/Construction Engineer/Civil Engineering Technician p71
- Marine Engineer p219
- Merchant Navy Engineering Officer p599

Further information

British Marine Federation
www.britishmarine.co.uk

Semta
www.semta.org.uk

The Institute of Marine Engineering, Science and Technology
www.imarest.org

Qualifications and courses

Entry to this career is usually with a degree or a BTEC HNC/HND in a relevant subject such as marine engineering, naval architecture, marine technology or offshore engineering. Entry to a degree course usually requires at least 2 A levels/3 H grades, including Maths, English and a science subject, and 5 GCSEs/National 5s (A*–C/A–C). Entry requirements for an HND course are usually 1 A level/Higher or a BTEC Level 3 Certificate/ Diploma in a relevant subject.

When seeking employment, you may be able to secure a graduate apprenticeship scheme post-university, provided by some companies, where you will receive training on the job. The Royal Navy also accepts applications for engineering officers from candidates in their final year of university. Upon completion of your service, you could then move into the commercial marine engineering industry.

Alternatively, you could enter the industry at a lower level by undertaking an apprenticeship as a marine engineering technician and then later working your way up to marine engineer by undertaking additional training and qualifications on the job.

The Merchant Navy Training Board (MNTB) also offers routes into engineer officer training, primarily through a Foundation degree in marine engineering. Entrants require a minimum of 48 UCAS points and at least four GCSEs/ National 5s (A*–C/A–C) in English, Maths and Physics. They must be in good health and will be required to pass a statutory medical exam prior to being employed at sea. You must also seek sponsorship from a shipping company or training provider prior to acceptance. Trainees will spend alternate periods at college and at sea, whilst working towards industry-recognised qualifications and professional maritime certificates. MNTB routes provide opportunities for progression through the ranks, eventually reaching chief engineer level.

To update your skills, improve your career prospects and ensure a salary increase, you may wish to work towards securing incorporated (IEng) or chartered engineer (CEng) status.

What the work involves

Marine engineers design, construct and maintain ships' seafaring equipment, as well as developing and preserving offshore systems.

You could work in a shipbuilding company, on-board ships and submarines, in marine surveying, in an oil company or in the leisure industry.

You will work across a range of engineering disciplines, including electrical, construction and mechanical. You will work closely with naval officers, architects, other professionals and team members.

Type of person suited to this work

You will need excellent communication skills, both oral and written, in order to manage and lead your team as well as liaise with other professionals and clients.

Excellent maths and IT skills are essential, as is an ability to solve problems under pressure. Prioritising your workload through careful planning and project management is also very important.

You should be good at working within a team, especially as you might have to live and work with colleagues in confined areas when undertaking projects on boats or submarines.

Working conditions

You could work anywhere from an office to a boatyard, or even on a submarine, and many jobs involve a combination of office-based and on-site work.

If you are working on projects on a ship or offshore installations, living accommodation can be tight and you will probably need to spend time away from home.

The job involves climbing and lifting equipment so you will need to be physically fit.

Future prospects

Prospects are good for marine engineers. You could work for a variety of companies, from small shipping businesses, to leisure cruise liners, through to joining the Royal or Merchant Navy.

When you have gained skills and experience, you could go on to specialise in project management, marine research, or even consultancy work.

There are plenty of opportunities to work abroad.

Advantages/disadvantages

There are a huge variety of employment options available to you, from conservation projects to defence systems.

You will work in numerous diverse areas, and with many different people, so the work will always be interesting.

You may be working in cramped, uncomfortable conditions for long periods of time. This includes living and working with colleagues 24 hours a day on certain projects.

Money guide

As a graduate marine engineer, you could expect to earn £24,000–£26,000.

Experienced marine engineers can expect a salary of between £28,000 and £50,000 a year, depending on experience.

Related opportunities

- Electrical Engineer p207
- Marine Craftsperson p218
- Mechanical Engineer p221

Further information

Engineering Council UK
www.engc.org.uk

Merchant Navy Training Board
www.mntb.org.uk

The Institute of Marine Engineering, Science and Technology
www.imarest.org

Qualifications and courses

Whilst there are no formal entry qualifications needed to work as a meat processor, some employers value GCSEs/National 5s in English and Maths, particularly when considering candidates for supervisory, inspection or technical levels.

One route of entry into the industry as a meat process worker is via an apprenticeship. The most relevant apprenticeships available include the Improve Proficiency Apprenticeship in Food and Drink (Meat and Poultry Industry Skills) and the Improve Proficiency Apprenticeship in Food and Drink (Food Manufacturing Excellence).

As an apprentice you will typically experience a combination of on-the-job training for professional meat process workers with a series of day or block release instruction at a college or training centre where you will work towards gaining industry-recognised qualifications. The courses that may be available to you include the NVQs/SVQs in Meat and Poultry Processing or Food Manufacturing Excellence (Levels 2–3) and then on to an NVQ/SVQ Level 4 in Meat Processing Management or Food Safety Management. The Meat Training Council (MTC) also offers a number of further education courses, such as the Intermediate Certificate in Meat and Poultry. Your training will cover health and safety procedures, food hygiene and quality assurance. Alternatively, you could opt to complete courses such as these full time at college before seeking employment.

To work at an abattoir or meat processing plant you must be aged 18 or over, and hold a Certificate of Competence in the Protection of Animals at Time of Killing. A driving licence may be required, particularly in operating forklift trucks.

To enhance your contacts and ensure you remain up to date with any industry developments, you may opt to register with the Worshipful Company of Butchers Guild.

What the work involves

Meat process workers do everything from herding animals, to slaughtering, to cutting up carcasses, to packaging and grading meat and ensuring it is free from contamination and ready to sell to the public. A meat process worker could specialise in either of the following roles.

Abattoir operative

You will slaughter animals for food.

After the animals have been humanely killed, you will separate the edible meat from the waste.

Meat manufacturing operative

You will manufacture meat products.

You may also weigh, wrap and label the meat.

Type of person suited to this work

This can be distressing work, so you should be prepared to cope with blood and mess.

As you will have to do lots of lifting and operating machinery, you will need to be physically fit.

You should have a responsible attitude as you may use dangerous knives and machinery. You also need to be aware of your personal cleanliness as you are part of a food production process.

Working conditions

Refrigerated areas are cold and all areas need frequent cleaning and so may be wet. You will be expected to wear protective clothing, including footwear and hairnets.

You will normally do a 40-hour week, usually from 7.30am to 3.30pm although shift and part-time work are possible.

Future prospects

Abattoir operative

With experience you could apply for senior positions or look to move to related areas such as butchery, retail or food marketing. Other options are jobs in quality control, health and safety consultancy or self-employment.

Meat manufacturing operative

With experience you could apply for supervisory, quality control and management jobs or move into related areas of work such as retail butchery.

With the right experience, qualifications and training you may be able to progress into work on the meat inspection teams employed by the Meat Hygiene Service (MHS) – part of the Food Standards Agency.

Advantages/disadvantages

This can be cold, smelly and dirty work. The job can be repetitive and monotonous.

You will be part of a team and often there is a good working atmosphere.

Money guide

Abattoir operative

Salaries start at around £10,500 per year (although apprentices may receive less). For senior roles, salaries range from £14,000 to £22,000 a year.

Meat manufacturing operative

The starting salary is usually around £12,500–£14,000 per year. Experienced meat manufacturing operatives can expect a salary of between £15,000 and £20,000.

Related opportunities

- Butcher p466
- Kitchen Assistant/Supervisor p133
- Meat Hygiene Inspector p474

Further information

Department for Environment, Food and Rural Affairs
www.defra.gov.uk

Food Standards Agency
www.food.gov.uk

Meat Training Council
www.foodtraining.org.uk/mtc

Qualifications and courses

Most employers require candidates to have completed a degree in a relevant subject such as mechanical, nuclear, aeronautical, civil or computer-aided engineering. For entry on to a degree course you will need at least 2 A levels/3 H grades, including Maths and Physics, and 5 GCSEs/National 5s (A*–C/A–C). An accredited Foundation degree or BTEC HNC/HND can also provide a path into the industry with further training later. Some employers place as much emphasis on general communication skills and commercial awareness as they do on a candidate's degree class, but if you wish to seek chartered status (CEng) later on in your career, a postgraduate qualification or a Master of Engineering (MEng) is recommended.

Some employers recruit graduates only, therefore you may struggle securing employment as a diplomate. However, diplomates are considered for technician level posts which are entered via an apprenticeship. To apply for an apprenticeship you will need GCSEs/National 5s (A*–C/A–C) in English, Maths and a science. You will work towards an NVQ in Performing Engineering Operations, Mechanical Manufacturing Engineering or Technical Services (Levels 1–3). In order to progress however you will need to take a top-up course to convert to degree level.

Some companies may offer graduate training schemes for newly qualified engineers. If you aim for incorporated (IEng) or chartered (CEng) status, it is important that your training scheme be accredited by the Institution of Mechanical Engineers (IMechE). A mentor will monitor the early stages of your development while you undertake a structured programme of training. With appropriate experience and the necessary qualifications, you will gain professional status, significantly improving your prospects and salary as a result.

What the work involves

Mechanical engineers design, develop and maintain the moveable parts of all equipment, ranging from those in small household appliances up to large machinery.

You will probably work on a project from start to finish, so will be involved with all aspects from design and development through to manufacture.

You could work in a number of industries, including manufacturing, sport, medicine or transport.

You will also have to manage budgets, resources and people on each project.

Type of person suited to this work

You will need an exceptionally high level of scientific knowledge and technical ability in order to design mechanisms and solve practical problems as they occur in the development process.

Good communication skills, both oral and written, are essential for dealing with colleagues, other professionals and clients on a daily basis. You will also be required to produce detailed reports and presentations.

Excellent organisational skills and the ability to work under pressure are a must, as are good IT skills including knowledge of computer-aided design (CAD).

Working conditions

You will usually be required to work longer hours than those of the average working week, but evening or weekend work is rare.

You will be based mainly in an office although you will also spend a good amount of time on site, whether in a factory, workshop, hospital or other building. Despite this travel, overnight absence from home is uncommon.

You will need to wear a smart suit while in the office, but appropriate safety equipment when on-site.

Future prospects

Job opportunities for mechanical engineers are found throughout the UK, particularly in cities. There are also excellent opportunities for working abroad.

With experience, you will be able to qualify for chartered engineer (CEng) status. You could become self-employed and undertake freelance work which will give you greater flexibility over your work–life balance. Alternatively, you could go on to increasingly senior engineering posts, or even set up your own consultancy.

Some engineers choose to move into a more business-orientated role within their company such as sales.

Advantages/disadvantages

It is exciting to be at the forefront of creating new products and finding solutions to mechanical problems across numerous industries. You will be working on a variety of projects and meeting a range of people, so the work is rarely boring.

There are excellent opportunities for career development, including the option of working overseas.

You may have to work long hours to meet project deadlines.

Money guide

Starting salaries can range from £20,000 to £28,000 and, with experience, could increase to between £25,000 and £50,000.

Engineers with chartered status/10–15 years' experience can earn up to or in excess of £60,000.

Related opportunities

- Clinical/Biomedical Engineer p278
- Electrical Engineer p207
- Marine Engineer p219

Further information

Engineering Council UK
www.engc.org.uk

Institution of Mechanical Engineers
www.imeche.org

ENGINEERING, MANUFACTURING AND PRODUCTION

Qualifications and courses

Although you do not need any formal qualifications to begin training as a motor vehicle technician, most employers, particularly larger companies, value those candidates with 4 GCSEs/National 5s (A*–C/A–C) in English, Maths and a science.

There are several ways to enter the industry at a trainee level. A common route is via an Intermediate or Advanced Apprenticeship in Vehicle Maintenance and Repair. This scheme involves learning on the job while gaining qualifications at college.

Another option is to study full-time at college for relevant qualifications. Many training centres have links with local employers which could be a route into work experience or employment. City & Guilds provide the NVQ in Automotive Maintenance and Repair, Body and Paint, Vehicle Fitting and Roadside Assistance (4101) (Levels 1–3). IMI Awards offer VCQs/NVQs such as the Level 2 in Maintenance and Repair Competence specialising in either Light Vehicle, Heavy Vehicle or Motorcycle repair. Those who wish to pursue higher qualifications could take the BTEC Level 3 Certificate/Diploma in Vehicle Technology, the BTEC Higher National Certificate/Diploma in Automotive Engineering (Levels 4 and 5) or the City & Guilds Level 4 Certificate in Advanced Automotive Diagnostic Techniques.

To enable career progression, you may later opt to complete a qualification that allows you to specialise in a particular area, such as in MOT testing, air-conditioning or LPG conversions.

You are likely to require a driving licence for the type of vehicle you work with. You also need good colour vision.

What the work involves

Motor vehicle technicians are responsible for the maintenance and repair of all vehicles, including cars, motorbikes, lorries and coaches.

You will need to carry out routine jobs, such as servicing a vehicle, and identify technical problems, advising customers which repairs are necessary and the costs involved.

You will work on a variety of different mechanical and electrical systems and use a range of tools and equipment.

Type of person suited to this work

You need an excellent technical and mechanical knowledge of most motor vehicles and you will be expected to build on this knowledge throughout your career to ensure that you are familiar with technological changes.

Strong communication skills are required for advising customers and you must be able to work well within a team.

Full colour vision, a good level of fitness and the ability to think quickly and work methodically are all essential. You will also need good IT skills in order to understand and fix the computerised equipment in vehicles.

Working conditions

You will usually work 40 hours a week, just above the national average. Most of your work will involve regular hours but occasionally, depending on your employer, you may be expected to work shifts, weekends and overtime.

If you specialise in repairing broken-down vehicles, you might have to travel to their location at any time of the day or night.

You will usually work in a garage, which can be noisy, and cold in winter. You will need to wear overalls and use other safety equipment to protect you while you work.

Future prospects

Being a motor vehicle technician provides good career opportunities as there is currently a shortage of skilled technicians across the UK. The variety of work available is good with opportunities possible in garages, freight transport, construction, vehicle hire or breakdown companies, car dealerships as well as in local authorities.

Within a larger organisation, you could progress to a senior or supervisory level as a technician, or alternatively move into a management or training role. You could also specialise in a specific type or make of vehicle.

There is also the option of setting up your own repair business, although the initial costs of hiring and equipping premises can be high.

Advantages/disadvantages

There is demand for technicians throughout the UK so you should be able to find a job in the location of your choice.

The hours are fairly regular and it is unlikely that your work will involve absences from home.

You may have to work in cold or cramped conditions which can be unpleasant.

Money guide

Trainee motor vehicle technicians have a starting salary of around £10,500.

Once qualified, you could expect £15,000–£20,000.

Those with extensive experience in the industry can achieve in excess of £25,000.

Garage owners and self-employed technicians can earn considerably more.

Related opportunities

- Electrician p80
- Highways Maintenance/Road Worker p91
- Sheet Metal Worker p230

Further information

The Institute of the Motor Industry
www.theimi.org.uk

NUCLEAR ENGINEER

Qualifications and courses

Candidates seeking to become a nuclear engineer require a degree in mechanical, electrical or chemical engineering but you could still enter with a related degree subject such as maths, physics or science. Some universities offer specialist degrees in nuclear engineering and the Nuclear Industry Association (NIA) provides further information on these courses. For degree entry you will need at least 2 A levels/3 H grades, including Maths and a science subject, and 5 GCSEs/National 5s (A*–C/A–C). A postgraduate qualification, although not a requirement, may give you an advantage when looking for work and will make the process of seeking chartered engineer (CEng) status easier.

The nucleargraduates scheme is available to graduates from a variety of academic fields. Successful applicants engage in a 2-year programme in their chosen discipline (engineering, science or commercial) structured around three 8-month secondments at sponsor firms, typically based in the UK.

You can also enter the industry with an HND in a relevant subject such as General Engineering, Civil Engineering, Maths or Physics. Entry requirements are usually 1 A level/2 H grades or a BTEC National Certificate in a relevant subject.

When you are seeking employment, some companies offer opportunities for apprenticeships or training schemes which combine study at degree or postgraduate level with work-based learning. The Nuclear Technology Education Consortium (NTEC) offers professional development courses which your employer may encourage you to undertake. Entry requirements are usually a minimum of a 2.2 degree in a relevant subject.

Once experience has been gained, nuclear engineers with a Master of Engineering (MEng) can apply for chartered engineer (CEng) status with the Engineering Council and those with a bachelor's degree are eligible for incorporated engineer (IEng) status. Professional membership with the institutional body relevant to your role will significantly improve your career prospects and earnings.

What the work involves

Nuclear engineers work mainly in the large-scale production of nuclear energy, although they can be involved in smaller industrial or medical projects.

Alternatively, you could work in developing effective nuclear waste management systems.

You might lecture and train other people on the subject of nuclear power.

Type of person suited to this work

You will need excellent communication skills, both oral and written, in order to manage and lead your team, and liaise with other professionals and clients. The ability to work effectively as part of a team is also important.

You should possess an analytical mind and a logical approach to problem-solving. Excellent maths and IT skills are also essential.

As you will be working with nuclear hazards, you must be able to take responsibility for your own safety and that of your colleagues.

Working conditions

You will usually work a normal 37-hour week, although you may be required to work additional hours as project deadlines approach. If you work in a nuclear power station, your hours will usually adhere to a 7-day shift system.

The majority of the work will be indoors in a power plant, laboratory, office or factory.

You may have to work in hot, cramped conditions and you will have to wear protective clothing in certain situations. As you will be working with radioactive substances, you will also need regular medical check-ups.

Future prospects

Prospects are good for nuclear engineers. More than 63,000 people are currently employed in the UK's civil nuclear sector and it is thought that the nuclear new build programme in the UK could generate up to 40,000 new jobs, at its peak, for workers in the industry.

With continued study and increased experience, you can move into more senior positions within any company or discipline.

Advantages/disadvantages

Nuclear power is a growing industry so employment opportunities will increase accordingly.

You have the opportunity to work freelance after building significant experience so you can achieve a suitable work–life balance.

You will be working in an environmentally controversial industry which could potentially upset your friends and family.

Money guide

Graduate nuclear engineers typically have a starting salary of £20,000–£25,000.

With increased experience, earnings rise to between £30,000 and £50,000.

Senior engineers with chartered status could achieve £55,000 or more.

Some companies offer excellent benefit packages and bonus schemes.

Related opportunities

- Aerospace Engineer p200
- Chemical Engineer p205
- Mechanical Engineer p221

Further information

Nuclear Industry Association
www.niauk.org

Semta
www.semta.org.uk

ENGINEERING, MANUFACTURING AND PRODUCTION

Qualifications and courses

There are no formal entry requirements in order to become a paper manufacturer, but having some GCSEs/National 5s (A*–E/A–E) in English, Maths and a science will be useful.

You can usually enter the field straight from school, working your way up whilst training on the job as an apprentice. Apprenticeships typically involve a combination of on-the-job training and formal instruction at a college or training centre where you will work towards industry-recognised qualifications.

Courses that may be available include an NVQ in Combined Working Practices (Levels 2–3), Performing Manufacturing Operations (Levels 1–2), Fibreboard Operations (Levels 2–3) or a Certificate in Paper Technology (Levels 2–3). There are also short courses and workshops in paper technology offered by the Confederation of Paper Industries (CPI). Your employer will also offer you additional training in health and safety, the operation of machinery and possibly, in forklift truck driving.

To become a technologist, you will need a BTEC HNC/HND in Applied Science (Chemistry) or a relevant degree in a science or engineering discipline. You will gain experience and training within different departments once employed and you may be offered the opportunity to study at postgraduate level, for example in paper science or packaging technology.

To improve your prospects, membership with the Paper Industry Technical Association (PITA) is advised.

What the work involves

Paper manufacturers/technologists work with the equipment and systems that turn wood pulp and other materials into many different kinds of paper.

As a manufacturer, you might be operating the machine that breaks down the raw materials, managing what is going on inside, checking consistency, adjusting the controls or managing the steam system that dries the paper, or overseeing the packaging process.

As a technologist, you would design and test the equipment used in the manufacturing process. You may trial new products, ensure the quality and safety of materials, write technical reports or supervise the work of manufacturers.

Type of person suited to this work

You need to be good with your hands, and good at team-working and communication with others.

Being able to act on your own initiative is important, and you should have an accurate and methodical mindset.

Following plans and diagrams is a big part of the job, so you should be confident in this, and the ability to work with chemicals is also important.

A lot of the work will involve using computerised machinery. You must be capable of adapting to new equipment and learning to use it safely and accurately.

Working conditions

This kind of work usually takes place in shifts. You could be working daytimes, evenings, nights or weekends depending on your company, and it may well be a combination of them all.

It is normal for you to work 38 to 40 hours a week. Overtime is usually available and often encouraged.

You will be working on the factory floor most of the time or in the control room. This is so that you can monitor the processes being carried out by the machines you are looking after.

It will sometimes be necessary to work outdoors in order to load and unload delivery wagons.

Future prospects

As a manufacturer or technologist, you could find work within the paper mills and paper recovery plants based in Scotland and the north-west, south-west and south-east and Yorkshire areas of England.

With experience you can apply for positions at technician and supervisor level, which can turn into engineering roles. As a technologist, it may be possible to move into research posts in universities or with companies overseas.

You could also move around in the industry, changing to a career such as management or sales.

Advantages/disadvantages

Opportunities to progress are good in this job, and even if you come straight from school and work on the factory floor, you could move up to sales or management relatively quickly.

The work may be a little mundane to start with.

Conditions inside the factory can be noisy, hot and humid.

Money guide

A paper manufacturer can start on a salary of £13,000–£17,000 and with experience, this can increase to between £18,000 and £25,000.

Starting salaries for paper technologists are between £17,000 and £20,000, with £25,000 or more being possible after experience.

Related opportunities

- Chemical Engineer p205
- Manufacturing/Production Engineer p217
- Textile Operative p233

Further information

Confederation of Paper Industries
www.paper.org.uk

Paper Industry Technical Association
www.pita.org.uk

Proskills UK
www.proskills.co.uk

Qualifications and courses

Most entrants to this profession have a degree in a related subject such as polymer science, materials engineering, materials technology or materials science. For entry onto a degree course you will need at least 2 A levels/3 H grades in subjects including Chemistry, Maths or Physics and 5 GCSEs/National 5s (A*–C/A–C). A 1-year Foundation degree may be available for those who wish to take a relevant degree but do not have the required scientific subjects. Several universities provide their students with first-hand experience of polymer processing equipment and small-scale production.

A postgraduate qualification, in materials engineering or polymer technology for instance, is recommended to those candidates whose first degree was in a broad engineering or science subject.

It may be possible to gain entry into this profession with an HNC/HND in polymer technology or manufacturing engineering. Given the variety of skills required of a polymer technologist, entrants with relevant experience are welcomed.

Some companies offer training programmes in engineering that combine study at degree or diploma level with structured work-based learning. Entrants are paid in terms of how much time is spent in the workplace and this could offer an effective way of securing employment once qualified.

The British Plastics Federation (BPF) provides professional development for those within the industry, offering both short courses and the master's level Materials for Industry (MfI) programme.

What the work involves

Polymer technologists use polymer materials, such as plastics, rubber, adhesives, resins and fibres, to manufacture products. You will utilise these materials to make a wide range of products including toys, casings for mobile phones, medical devices, tyres, wetsuits and hoses.

You might also use composite polymer materials when manufacturing car bodies or aircraft wings instead of traditional materials such as metal.

You will be responsible for developing the moulds used to form materials during manufacture. This is a job that requires specialist skills as a minor flaw could ruin an entire batch of products.

Type of person suited to this work

You should have a strong interest in materials science, chemicals, engineering and design technology. A good understanding of manufacturing processes and construction methods is also important.

Familiarity with computer-aided design and developed IT skills would be beneficial.

Analytical and numeracy skills are required for analysing projects or problems that arise.

You must be able to communicate effectively with people as you will be working within, and possibly leading, a team.

You should be able to take initiative, use your creativity and find a solution when you are confronted with a problem.

Working conditions

You will work between 35 and 40 hours per week, Monday to Friday. It may be necessary for you to work additional hours to meet deadlines. Overtime and weekends will increase your pay accordingly.

Your time may be divided between the office, the laboratory and the factory. As you will be required to travel, it would be useful to have a driving licence.

You will be expected to wear protective clothing in some of your working environments.

Future prospects

Polymer science is a growing industry with a shortage of qualified staff. As new uses are found for plastic, rubber and composite materials, the industry will continue to develop. There are many opportunities for promotion within the field.

You could work for a variety of companies including manufacturers of medical equipment, toy companies and aerospace engineering firms. Smaller businesses tend to specialise in the manufacturing of electrical switches and light fittings, whilst the larger companies produce goods such as food packaging and fragile components.

Alternatively, you could choose to specialise in a specific area such as vehicle manufacturing, aviation or medical equipment.

Advantages/disadvantages

You may have the opportunity to travel locally and abroad as part of your work.

The factory or laboratory conditions that you work in may sometimes be noisy and messy.

Money guide

Starting salaries are around £14,000.

With experience, you can expect to earn £20,000–£25,000.

Those at senior level or who work as a specialist technologist can achieve £35,000 or more.

Related opportunities

- Aerospace Engineer p200
- Chemical Engineer p205
- Manufacturing/Production Engineer p217
- Materials Scientist p514

Further information

British Plastics Federation
www.bpf.co.uk

Institute of Materials, Minerals and Mining
www.iom3.org

Qualifications and courses

Most entrants have prior experience in a relevant industry. For example, you might have started your career in a production role and then progressed to the level of quality control inspector. Employers usually seek applicants with 4 GCSEs/National 5s (A*–C/A–C) including Maths, English and a science subject or equivalent vocational qualifications in engineering or food science.

As a quality control inspector you could specialise in a particular sector such as aerospace or pharmaceuticals. For this you may require A levels/H grades, a BTEC/SQA National qualification, an HNC/HND or a degree in science, technology or quality management.

Engineering apprenticeships may offer an alternative route of entry for a career as a quality control inspector. Intermediate Apprenticeships in Improving Operational Performance or the Intermediate, Advanced and Higher Apprenticeships in Food and Drink are available. You will experience a combination of on-the-job training from professionals and formal instruction at a college or training centre where you will work towards industry-recognised qualifications in quality control or management. Awards available include an NVQ in Food Manufacture (Levels 1–3), a Diploma in Engineering Inspection and Quality Control, and a Chartered Quality Institute (CQI) Certificate/Diploma in Quality or Quality Management (Levels 3–5).

To enhance your career prospects, it is recommended that inspectors gain membership with the CQI. By doing so, you can apply for Chartered Quality Professional (CQP) status and significantly increase your earning potential.

What the work involves

Quality control inspectors work in a variety of industries such as engineering, food, pharmaceuticals and clothing, where manufacturing procedures must be monitored to ensure that products meet specified standards.

You will test products as they go through each stage of production by observing, measuring and weighing samples, and comparing results with specified requirements. You will also work to ensure that quality and safety standards are maintained by checking and testing materials sourced from external suppliers.

You will write reports on the tests that you carry out and help to come up with solutions to any problems or inconsistencies that arise.

Type of person suited to this work

As you will be regularly inspecting products and manufacturing processes, you must be highly organised and methodical with a keen eye for detail.

You should be responsible, thorough and able to solve problems efficiently.

You will have an aptitude for communicating with others and for advising and persuading people to improve standards.

Good written communication skills are required for writing up reports on testing methods and results.

You should have an interest in the science and technology of the industry that you are monitoring.

You also need a keen awareness of health and safety procedures.

Working conditions

You will work 35–40 hours a week and this will often include shift work, weekends and nights.

You could be based in a laboratory or an office. You will also frequently visit factories or warehouses to monitor production processes or meet with staff. These locations may be clean and bright or noisy and dirty. Protective clothing is often required.

Future prospects

Though quality control is an important part of company competitiveness, sophisticated equipment that can identify faults in products means that there are usually fewer jobs available. With greater emphasis on workers taking responsibility for the quality of their output, inspection activities are less in demand.

However, there are opportunities to work in many different sectors such as cosmetics, textiles and electrical goods.

When you have some experience you may progress to become a team leader, supervisor or quality manager. You could also move into technical sales or production management.

Advantages/disadvantages

There may be opportunities to travel and work abroad as a quality control inspector.

You could become self-employed.

Due to developments in technology, companies are increasingly using advanced equipment to monitor quality standards.

Money guide

Average salaries begin at £12,500–£15,000.

Qualified inspectors with experience can earn £18,000–£25,000 a year.

With responsibility, you can earn up to £30,000.

Freelance inspectors who specialise in high-technology disciplines can earn £40,000–£60,000.

Related opportunities

- Laboratory Technician p512
- Quality Manager p45
- Trading Standards Officer p484

Further information

Chartered Quality Institute
www.thecqi.org

Semta
www.semta.org.uk

QUARRY MANAGER

Qualifications and courses

You will need a degree or HND in a relevant subject such as minerals engineering, environmental sciences, geology or mining engineering, although candidates with degrees unrelated to engineering or mining are sometimes considered. You will typically need at least 2 A levels/3 H grades in sciences and 5 GCSEs/National 5s (A*–C/A–C) in order to gain entry onto a degree course. Postgraduate qualifications, although not essential, are available in quarry management and may enhance your career prospects. You could also take a year-long industrial placement with a large organisation as part of your degree which will support you post-university, in your search for employment.

Graduate management schemes with large organisations are available and employers often seek candidates with a degree in quarry engineering, IT or business. Trainees gain experience within a variety of company departments before deciding on which function to work in permanently. You may be offered support when studying for further management qualifications. Work experience on a quarry site would be very useful as employers often seek candidates who can show evidence of an ability to communicate effectively, have knowledge of health and safety and a strong level of technical understanding.

The Mineral Products Qualifications Council (MPQC) offers many useful qualifications in risk assessment, supervising safety in quarries, quarry safety inspections and understanding quarries regulations. Entrants will typically acquire professional accreditation with the Institute of Quarrying or the Institute of Materials, Minerals and Mining.

What the work involves

Quarrying involves opencast mining to extract minerals and other materials to manufacture goods such as chemicals. Your job will involve managing staff in the office and quarries.

On-site you will inspect the quality of the minerals and other products mined as well as ensuring production is on schedule and checking equipment.

In the office you will manage the sales department, look after the budget, produce performance reports and plan changes to the production system when different materials are needed.

Type of person suited to this work

You will need to have good communication skills as you will be liaising with a wide range of people. You must also have a good technical knowledge of the production system in quarries. You should be business minded with excellent management skills.

You will need to be aware of health and safety legislation as well as government regulations and ensure that these are followed on-site. It is important to have a good understanding of technical drawings and plans.

Working conditions

You will be on-call in case of emergency. You will typically spend 2 days on-site and 3 days based in an office.

You must wear protective clothing such as helmets and ear protectors when on-site and be prepared to work in all weathers.

Future prospects

The variety of different areas within the quarrying sector means that there is a great deal of work available to quarry managers within a strong industry that offers workers a well-established career route and a comparatively low level of job competition.

After gaining experience, it might be possible to progress into a managerial role in area operations but you may have to relocate in order to increase your level of responsibility. The type of quarry you specialise in, eg hard rock quarrying or sand and gravel, will impact your career progression and the skills which you will need to develop.

It would be helpful to become a member of the Institute of Quarrying. It has a professional development system which ranges from student to fellowship levels. Career prospects can be improved by further qualifications in management and quarry legislation. It will be necessary to take jobs at different quarries to improve career progression, unless you work for a big company. However, personal development generally remains in the hands of the individual.

Advantages/disadvantages

You will have a high level of responsibility.

You will spend time working outdoors. Long hours, including work at weekends, are common in this industry.

Working conditions on sites are dirty, dangerous and noisy, with sites often based in rural areas.

Money guide

A new assistant quarry manager can earn £23,000.

A typical starting salary for a quarry manager is £30,000–£50,000.

A unit manager who is in charge of a number of quarries or a big quarry can earn in excess of £50,000.

Salaries will depend upon the location of the site and the employer. Benefits such as private healthcare and bonuses may be offered.

Related opportunities

- Construction Operative p74
- Demolition Operative p78
- Quarry Worker p228

Further information

Institute of Materials, Minerals and Mining
www.iom3.org

Institute of Quarrying
www.quarrying.org

Proskills UK
www.proskills.co.uk

QUARRY WORKER

Qualifications and courses

This job does not have any formal educational requirements. Some employers do, however, generally seek candidates who hold at least 5 GCSEs/National 5s (A*–C/A–C) in relevant subjects such as English, Maths, a science and technology. The Diploma in Engineering or Construction and the Built Environment could be useful when seeking employment, as is any experience of construction, mining or mobile plant machinery operation.

Apprenticeships in Extractive and Mineral Processing Operations may offer a route of entry into the industry. Construction companies and quarrying firms offer school-leavers both on-the-job training and the opportunity to study for work-based qualifications accredited by the Mineral Products Qualifications Council (MPQC). Courses you may work towards include a Level 3 Certificate/Diploma in the Extractive and Minerals Processing Industries, an NVQ Certificate in Processing Operations for the Extractive and Minerals Processing Industries or an NVQ Diploma in Complex Processing Operations for the Extractive and Minerals Processing Industries. Short courses in risk assessment and hazards, safety passports, quarry regulations and competency schemes are also available.

Once on the job, you could also work towards an NVQ in either Specialised Plant and Machinery Operations (Levels 1–2) or Level 2 in Drilling Operations. An NVQ Level 3 in Blasting Operations or equivalent is needed to work with explosives. If you wish to progress into managerial jobs, a bachelor's degree will normally be required.

A LGV licence would be helpful, but some vehicles can be driven on a full category B driving licence.

What the work involves

There are many types of quarry worker. A machine operator controls heavy equipment whilst a plant and process operator is focused on the screening plant.

Shotfirers are responsible for explosives and drillers are responsible for creating holes for explosives and investigation.

Truck drivers, maintenance workers and laboratory technicians are also needed to undertake quality control and investigate samples from the site.

Type of person suited to this work

You need to be strong, fit and active to do this job.

You must also follow safety regulations at all times owing to the dangers that could arise when using heavy machinery.

You need to be able to work well with others as teamwork is a big part of this job.

An interest in mechanical work is also crucial. Quarry workers should enjoy working outdoors and be prepared to do so in all weathers.

Working conditions

You will often work in shifts, which will include early mornings and late nights. Floodlights will be switched on during these periods.

You should be prepared to travel for long periods of time to reach sites, as they are predominantly located in rural areas.

Working conditions are often dirty, noisy, muddy and dangerous. Protective clothing such as helmets and ear protectors must be worn at all times. Work will often include a lot of carrying and climbing.

Future prospects

Over 2,000 active quarries and mines exist in the UK. Although each local authority will have a quarry, the majority of them are located in the East Midlands and south-west of England.

After gaining experience and the necessary further qualifications, you may be able to progress into a role as a supervisor, manager, laboratory or quality control technician or health and safety inspector.

Drivers, mechanics and fitters can undergo training to become drillers or shotfirers.

Advantages/disadvantages

You could use powerful machines such as drills and excavators or explosives.

You will work outdoors. Working conditions are muddy, noisy and dangerous.

Travel times to work can be fairly long as sites are often located in remote, rural areas.

Money guide

Salaries will depend upon the location of the site and the employer. They can also be boosted by extra payments from overtime, bonuses and shift work.

The starting salary for a trainee operator is about £15,000.

After gaining experience, this could rise to between £16,000 and £22,000.

Supervisors can to earn up to £25,000 per year.

Related opportunities

- Construction Operative p74
- Demolition Operative p78
- Quarry Manager p227

Further information

Institute of Materials, Minerals and Mining
www.iom3.org

Institute of Quarrying
www.quarrying.org

Proskills UK
www.proskills.co.uk

RAILWAY FITTER/ ELECTRICIAN

Qualifications and courses

The typical entry route into this profession is through an Apprenticeship/Skillseekers scheme or a training scheme with one of the major rail engineering firms, such as Network Rail. The Advanced Apprenticeship in Rail Traction and Rolling Stock Engineering is available. Entry requirements are usually 3–5 GCSEs/National 5s (A*–C/A–C) including English, Maths, a science and technology. It would be very beneficial if you have experience working as a mechanical fitter, electrician or craftsperson in another industry.

The selection process for employment involves a medical exam that aims to test candidates' physical fitness, eyesight and hearing. An aptitude test may also be set in order to assess your existing skills and knowledge.

As an apprentice, you will first be trained in basic engineering craft skills before experiencing a combination of on-the-job practice alongside professional fitters and technicians and a series of day or block release instruction at a college or training centre where you will work towards gaining industry recognised qualifications. Relevant qualifications include the NVQ Level 2 in Rail Transport Operations and the NVQ in Railway Engineering (Traction and Rolling Stock) (Levels 2 and 3). These awards cover areas such as safe working, maintaining equipment, testing systems and preventative maintenance.

An ability to drive and access to personal transport is often required, as is a track safety card. Your employer will put you through a Personal Track Safety (PTS) course in order to gain one of these.

What the work involves

A mechanical fitter will maintain and service the traction and rolling stock, plant, machinery and passenger coaches.

You could also repair station equipment such as customer lifts and hoisting equipment.

An electrical fitter will work alongside mechanical fitters and other engineers, specialising in the electrical side of the maintenance and servicing work on the traction and rolling stock, plant machinery and passenger coaches.

A multi-skilled fitter will possess the skills held by both mechanical and electrical specialists so they will be able to work in all aspects of railway maintenance.

Type of person suited to this work

You should enjoy working with your hands, diagnosing faults and working out solutions. You will be comfortable using different hand tools and equipment and enjoy working in a team alongside other fitters.

Physical fitness is important as you will be on your feet, working at your bench or directly within the various railway stock.

You should be happy to follow verbal and written instructions, be able to read and understand technical drawings and diagrams and have a responsible attitude to health and safety.

Working conditions

Much of your work will take place within heated workshops or depots. Sometimes you will have to visit jobs which are outdoors, for example near railway sidings or within a station. On these occasions it might be cold and dark.

As many of the work places are in remote areas, it is often essential to have your own transport.

You will have to wear protective clothing and be prepared to work in cramped places, engaging in lots of bending and lifting.

You will have a 37-hour working week with shifts that cover early, late, evening and weekend hours. You might also need to be on-call for emergencies that occur outside your working hours.

Future prospects

The rail industry is one of the largest industries in the passenger transport sector and is continuing to expand, therefore the demand for new recruits is increasing.

Well-developed promotional and in-service training programmes exist which help fitters to progress to supervisor, technician, team leader and management levels.

Many specialist maintenance companies carry out work for operating companies and engineering companies, making new traction units and carriages.

Advantages/disadvantages

Owing to the range of jobs within the railway industry, it is possible to move sideways into other related job areas.

Working on the railway tracks is hazardous so you must be aware of health and safety procedures.

Money guide

Trainees will usually earn £18,000–£22,000 per year.

Those with experience and relevant qualifications can achieve a salary of up to £30,000 a year.

Further benefits include increased pay for working overtime and free or discounted rail travel.

Related opportunities

- Mechanical Engineer p221
- Rail Signalling Technician p604
- Rail Track Maintenance Operative p605

Further information

Engineering Council UK
www.engc.org.uk

GoSkills
www.goskills.com

Network Rail
www.networkrail.co.uk

ENGINEERING, MANUFACTURING AND PRODUCTION

229

Qualifications and courses

Entry into a career as a sheet metal worker is usually via a training scheme. The Apprenticeship in Engineering Manufacture (Craft and Technician) is available at Advanced Level. To qualify for an apprenticeship, you will need to have at least 5 GCSEs/National 5s (A*–E/A–E) in subjects including Maths, English and a science. Vocational awards in engineering drawing, metalwork or other practical subjects may also be considered by employers.

The Engineering Construction Industry Training Board (ECITB) offers an Advanced Apprenticeship in Engineering Construction with an option to specialise in pathways such as Plating. ECITB apprenticeship schemes typically take 3 to 4 years to complete. Successful applicants combine on-the-job training from professionals at their place of work with day or block release for college- or training centre-based learning. Applicants opting into the Plating pathway will study for competence- and knowledge-based qualifications such as the Level 3 Diploma in Fabricating Engineering Construction Steel Structures – Plating, the BTEC Level 3 Diploma in Mechanical Engineering and the BTEC Level 3 Diploma in Operations and Maintenance.

Other relevant courses for sheet metal workers include an NVQ in Fabrication and Welding Engineering (Levels 2 and 3) and the BTEC Level 3 National in Manufacturing Engineering. The Welding Institute (TWI) also offers qualifications for those who wish to specialise in welding techniques.

You will be required to hold a Client Contractor National Safety Group (CCNSG) Safety Passport in order to work on-site.

What the work involves

Sheet metal workers produce parts for a number of important items ranging from vehicles and aeroplanes, through to electrical equipment and common domestic appliances.

You will be using complex engineering drawings as a guide for marking out and cutting each piece.

You will also be operating a variety of machines including hand-powered tools, cutting and pressing devices and computer numerically controlled (CNC) devices.

Type of person suited to this work

You should have good communication skills and be able to build strong relationships with colleagues as you will be working within a team.

Good numerical skills and the ability to interpret complicated technical drawings are essential for making accurate calculations and creating precise parts. You should also have good IT and technical skills as computer-operated machinery is increasingly being used in this role.

You need a fairly high level of fitness as you will be expected to lift large items and operate heavy machinery. Good eyesight and excellent practical skills are also required in order to use tools and equipment safely.

Working conditions

You will usually work a 37–39 hour week but shift work and overtime is common. If you are producing bespoke items for a customer to a tight deadline, you may be required to work overnight on occasion.

Work is usually undertaken in a factory or workshop. You will spend the majority of your time at a bench so you will be bending over for most of the day. The work also involves lifting and spending hours on your feet.

You will be required to wear appropriate safety clothing at all times.

Future prospects

Prospects are good for sheet metal workers.

Once your initial training is completed, you could work towards qualifying as an engineering technician.

Alternatively, you could become a supervisor/manager of an engineering workshop which would increase your responsibility and salary.

Owing to demand, opportunities are available on small and large projects both in the UK and overseas.

Advantages/disadvantages

You will work with a variety of materials and tools, enabling you to build specialist understanding and knowledge quickly.

With overtime, it is likely that you will work considerably longer than the average working week.

Money guide

Starting salaries for trainees within this sector are usually in the region of £18,000.

As you gain experience you can expect to earn between £18,000 and £24,000.

Workers with supervisory responsibilities or those who are highly skilled in using computer-controlled equipment can achieve in excess of £25,000.

Shift allowances and overtime can increase earnings.

Related opportunities

- Assembler p201
- Blacksmith p202
- Welder p236

Further information

Engineering Construction Industry Training Board
www.ecitb.org.uk

Semta
www.semta.org.uk

TAILOR/ DRESSMAKER

ENTRY LEVEL 2

Qualifications and courses

If you wish to become a tailor or dressmaker, you can seek employment or a trainee scheme as a school-leaver. A history of work experience is not required as you will be provided with on-the-job training from more experienced colleagues or a master tailor, however a demonstrable aptitude for design, sewing and art is usually highly valued by employers. GCSEs/National 5s (A*–C/A–C) in English, Maths, Textiles or Art will also be valuable in securing entry-level employment.

To increase your employability, you may opt to gain some of the skills required in the industry by completing a course such as the City & Guilds Levels 1–3 Award/Certificate/Diploma in Fashion Design (7160), the ABC Awards in Fashion and Textiles, the BTEC Certificate/Diploma in Art and Design (Levels 2–3) and the BTEC Higher National in Fashion and Textiles (Levels 4–5). These courses are available on a full or part-time basis or via distance learning.

If you are specifically looking to train as a prestigious Savile Row tailor, you could join the Bespoke Tailoring Apprenticeship programme run by Newham College in partnership with Savile Row Bespoke. This scheme teaches all the skills and knowledge you need to become a top tailor, including pattern cutting, garment construction and sewing by both machine and hand. The intensive programme could lead to an NVQ Level 3 in Bespoke Cutting and Tailoring. The number of opportunities is limited so competition for places is very strong.

Once you are qualified, you could continue developing your skills by working towards higher level qualifications such as an HNC, Foundation degree or degree in fashion or textile design. These qualifications would allow you to move into other sectors of the industry. Alternatively, it may be useful to complete an ABC Level 4 Diploma in Business for Creative Practitioners if you aim to become self-employed.

What the work involves

Tailors and dressmakers design and make made-to-measure, bespoke items of clothing. They may also be called upon to alter, repair or duplicate certain existing pieces.

Tailors usually make structured items such as suits, jackets and coats. Dressmakers can make a range of clothing, from day dresses and casual trousers to ball gowns and wedding dresses.

You will be working with numerous materials including silk, linen, cotton and polyester and you will also use equipment such as sewing machines, scissors, tape-measures and pins.

Type of person suited to this work

Since you will be dealing with a range of people, including clients and suppliers, you will need to have excellent interpersonal and verbal communication skills.

Understanding how different cuts, styles and colours flatter various shapes and figures is important for customer satisfaction, as is maintaining a smart/fashionable appearance.

You must be creative and innovative to produce fashion designs.

Working conditions

You can expect to work 37–40 hours a week. Weekend work is common as that is when most of your clients will be available for meetings and fittings. You could be situated in a workshop, small factory or work from home if you are self-employed.

A reasonable level of physical fitness and flexibility is required, as you will be bending and kneeling when measuring customers and fitting clothes. You may also need to lift and carry heavy rolls of fabric.

A lot of the work is very detailed so you will need a high level of accuracy and good eyesight.

Future prospects

You could work for a small or large company and create high fashion or more classic pieces. You can also opt to be self-employed.

In larger companies, you may be promoted to a supervisory position and there may also be the opportunity to diversify into pattern cutting or design.

There are opportunities to travel and work overseas, especially if you are involved in fashion and haute couture tailoring or dressmaking.

Advantages/disadvantages

You will be undertaking very creative work with lots of scope to use your talent and imagination on a daily basis.

Fashion is a fast-paced, interesting and potentially lucrative industry to be working in.

Making clothes requires many hours of concentration and patience.

Money guide

The average starting salary for both tailors and dressmakers ranges from £10,500 to £13,500.

With experience, your salary could rise to £14,000–£18,000.

Senior tailors or dressmakers, especially those located on Savile Row or who work in high fashion, could earn up to £40,000.

Self-employed tailors establish their own rates based upon their experience and reputation.

Related opportunities

- Costume Designer p160
- Fashion Designer/Milliner p161
- Textile Operative p233

Further information

ABC Awards
www.abcawards.co.uk

Newham College of Further Education
www.newham.ac.uk

ENGINEERING, MANUFACTURING AND PRODUCTION

231

Qualifications and courses

Most employers require an accredited degree in a relevant subject such as telecommunications, electronic engineering, computer science, information technology, physics or maths. You will need at least 2 A levels/3 H grades, including Maths and a science, and 5 GCSEs/National 5s (A*–C/A–C) to be accepted onto a degree course.

It is possible to enter this sector with an HND in a relevant engineering subject but you will only be able to work at technician level. You could complete a top-up course to convert it into a degree or you may be able to supplement your on-the-job experience with further qualifications at degree level.

Many employers also look for candidates who have a postgraduate qualification such as a Master of Science (MSc). Those with master's level qualifications and extensive industry experience are eligible to apply for chartered engineer (CEng) status through the Institution of Engineering and Technology (IET) which could improve long-term career prospects. Alternatively, you could gain Incorporated Engineer (IEng) status with a bachelor's degree.

A doctorate could help you to enter the industry at a more senior level or specialise in a particular area.

Post-university, you could seek an IET-accredited graduate training scheme offered by some companies, although competition is fierce and many employers value candidates with evidence of a technical ability, a good understanding of networks, teamwork skills, an ability to adapt and a commercial awareness. Gaining relevant work experience is a useful way to develop these skills and build contacts within the industry.

What the work involves

Telecommunications engineers are responsible for designing, testing and overseeing the installation of all telecommunications equipment and facilities.

You could work across a variety of engineering fields, including electronics and construction, providing technical guidance and offering solutions to other professionals and clients.

You will be responsible for the management of telecommunications projects which includes planning budgets, recruiting a team and implementing on-site safety. You will also produce written reports and verbal presentations in order to keep both your team and your clients up to date on how each project is progressing.

Type of person suited to this work

Good communication skills are essential for managing and briefing your team, as well as negotiating with clients and explaining complex technical information to them in a clear and simple manner.

You should have an analytical mind and be excellent at problem-solving. The ability to work efficiently under pressure and organise your workload effectively is also essential.

Working conditions

You will usually work a normal week of about 37 hours, Monday to Friday. Occasionally additional hours may be required, particularly as you progress to more senior positions.

Your working hours may be fairly flexible and you will not always be office based as the industry is seeking to promote working from home and part-time opportunities.

You will sometimes work on-site, checking and overseeing the installation of telecommunications equipment. In these instances, you may find yourself working outdoors or in cramped conditions. You will usually be required to wear appropriate safety equipment as well.

Future prospects

As the telecommunications industry is continually expanding, particularly due to customer demand for wireless services, job prospects for engineers in this sector are good.

Working in this fast-paced industry will require you to undertake further training throughout your career in order to stay up to date with new products, techniques and developments. Pursuing incorporated (IEng) or chartered (CEng) engineering status will significantly improve your prospects and earnings.

As you gain experience, you could move into senior or management positions. Alternatively, you could become a specialist in a particular sector, start your own company or move into training or consultancy.

Advantages/disadvantages

Hours are generally regular and there are increasing opportunities to work from home or undertake part-time hours.

In such a rapidly changing industry, you will be learning continually throughout your career.

You will have to spend time on-site which may involve working in cold, muddy conditions, at heights, or in cramped and uncomfortable surroundings.

Money guide

Starting salaries are typically £22,000–£28,000.

Once qualified, you could earn £35,000–£45,000.

At senior level and with chartered status, you could earn in excess of £60,000.

Related opportunities

- Civil/Construction Engineer/Civil Engineering Technician p71
- Electrical Engineer p207
- Electrician p80

Further information

Institution of Engineering and Technology
www.theiet.org

TEXTILE OPERATIVE

Qualifications and courses

There are no specific entry requirements as training usually takes place once employed under the supervision and mentoring of experienced professionals. The best way to get a position would be to apply directly to textile manufacturers.

Employers may, however, value candidates who have trained in some of the skills required in the role. Courses that may improve your employability include a GCSE/National 5 in Art and Design (including a textiles module), Edexcel BTEC Introductory Certificate/Diploma in Art, Design and Media, and Edexcel BTEC Level 1 Certificate in Art and Design. The Textile Centre of Excellence also offers a Technical Certificate in Textiles that provides a flexible, distance learning programme.

Alternatively, apprenticeships with textile manufacturers may also be available. These training schemes combine on-the-job training with college instruction, offering you the chance to work towards gaining relevant work-based qualifications such as the NVQ Level 2 Award in Manufacturing Sewn Products and the Level 3 Award in either Manufacturing Textile Products or Apparel Manufacturing Technology. As an apprentice, you will cover areas such as health and safety, the industry history, understanding materials, manufacturing techniques, the use of machinery and quality standards.

The Textile Institute (TI) also offers a range of globally recognised qualifications for professional development for those already working in the sector from licentiate to fellow level. ABC Awards offers a variety of courses in sewing, manufacturing and textiles, as do City & Guilds at Levels 1–3.

What the work involves

Textile operatives manufacture carpets, prepare the yarns of fibres to be woven or knitted (which may involve carding and combing or chemical processing), spin yarn on a machine or even make fabric on a loom.

You will carry out basic maintenance on your machinery, make sure you have a supply of raw materials and keep your work area clean and tidy in accordance with health and safety regulations.

You may also work on finishing processes such as dyeing or waterproofing fabrics.

Type of person suited to this work

You will need to be practical in order to operate the machinery skilfully and responsibly. In keeping with this, you should have good concentration as you will be doing repetitive tasks for long periods of time.

Manual dexterity and good spatial awareness, coupled with excellent eyesight and, usually, full colour vision, are also requirements for carrying out tasks such as spinning or weaving textiles.

A reasonable level of personal fitness, an understanding of, and adherence to, workplace health and safety rules, and enjoyment of working in a team are also relevant attributes.

Working conditions

Although you will work an average 37 to 40 hours a week, you will usually be doing shift work which is likely to involve early mornings or late evenings. Overtime and part-time work are also available.

You will usually work in a textile factory, which should be light and well ventilated, although the machines can be noisy and you will have to wear relevant safety equipment at all times.

It can be physically tiring, as you will spend the majority of your time standing over your machine or walking between the various pieces of equipment you are using.

Future prospects

Transfer of textile production abroad, along with the increased use of machinery, means that there are potentially fewer textile operative jobs. However, as the textile industry has a prominently mature workforce, retirements from the industry mean jobs will continue to be available. To improve your chances of employment, you should be skilled in as many aspects of textile production as possible.

If you gain experience in using a variety of machines and performing a range of tasks, you will find your prospects improve accordingly.

You could also choose to move into quality control or sales once you have gained a full knowledge of the textile industry.

Advantages/disadvantages

You will be putting your practical skills to good use creating a range of textiles for various purposes.

The work can become monotonous.

Hours can involve unsocial shift work in the early morning or evening.

Money guide

Starting salaries range from £12,500 to £15,000.

With a supervisory role and experience, you could earn up to £20,000 per year.

If you work shifts, or undertake overtime, earnings could be higher. Piecework payments (awarded for high production volume) can also boost earnings.

Related opportunities

- Costume Designer p160
- Fashion Designer/Milliner p161
- Tailor/Dressmaker p231

Further information

Society of Dyers and Colourists
www.sdc.org.uk

Textile Institute
www.textileinstitute.org

ENGINEERING, MANUFACTURING AND PRODUCTION

Qualifications and courses

One route of entry into a career as a toolmaker is via an apprenticeship. You will need at least 5 GCSEs/ National 5s (A*–C/A–C) or equivalent, in relevant subjects including Maths, English, a science, Engineering, and Design and Technology in order to be considered.

Most people start on the Advanced Apprenticeship in Engineering scheme on completion of school or college either as an apprentice machinist or multi-skilled apprentice. You will typically experience a combination of on-the-job training from your employer and formal instruction in a college environment. Here you will also work towards gaining industry-recognised qualifications such as an NVQ Level 2 in Performing Engineering Operations, or Mechanical Manufacturing Engineering (Levels 2–3) or Level 3 in Engineering Toolmaking. Qualifications such as these will instruct you in turning, milling, grinding and drilling and your employer may also train you in the use of CNC machines.

Many companies aim to train multi-skilled craftspeople rather than specialists. Apprentices may learn fabrication skills (welding and metalwork), computer-aided design (CAD) or computer-aided manufacturing (CAM). Only exceptional trainees are encouraged to focus completely on toolmaking.

Alternatively, you may opt to gain some of the skills required of the profession full-time at college. Courses available include a BTEC Certificate/Diploma in Engineering (Levels 1–3), a City & Guilds Levels 1–3 Certificate/Diploma in Engineering (2850) and an EAL Certificate/Diploma in Engineering (Levels 2–3).

What the work involves

Toolmakers make specialist tools and devices that are used to cut, shape, mould and form various materials for use in the production of all items; ranging from domestic appliances to aeroplanes. You will work with a range of materials, including metals and plastics.

You will also be using complex engineering drawings as a guide to marking out and cutting each piece.

You will be operating a variety of machinery including drills, grinding and milling machines, cutting and pressing devices and, increasingly, computer numerically controlled (CNC) equipment.

Type of person suited to this work

Good hand-to-eye coordination and a keen eye for detail will be beneficial, both when operating machinery and to check the quality of the tools produced. You will be making extremely precise devices, so it is essential to be able to spot any faults or errors before the tools are despatched to customers.

Good numerical skills and the ability to interpret complicated technical drawings are essential, both for making accurate calculations and creating precise parts.

Finally, you should have good IT skills as computer-operated machinery is increasingly used in this role.

Working conditions

You will usually work 39 hours a week, Monday to Friday. Although some larger companies operate shift patterns so evening and weekend work may be necessary.

Work is usually undertaken in a tool room within a factory or workshop. This means that you will be working in a fairly quiet environment, away from the main factory machinery.

You will normally stand for the duration of your working day, which can be tiring. You will be required to wear appropriate safety equipment at all times.

Future prospects

You will find your chances of securing work are enhanced if you have CNC machine skills as there is currently an increase in the number of computer-controlled machinery and precision casting techniques being used within the industry. The number of toolmakers in the industry has fallen due to this growth as workers struggle to deal with the introduction of new equipment and processes.

After gaining experience, you could move into a supervisory role within a company. This would involve overseeing production within a tool room or workshop. This could then lead into a senior or management position.

You could also undertake further qualifications in order to work towards employment as an engineering technician. This could then lead to you undertaking a degree course in order to become an engineer of some kind.

Advantages/disadvantages

You will be making tools which are vital for the construction of important equipment; these range from aeroplanes to washing machines.

You will be using both your practical skills and your mental abilities daily.

The work can be physically exhausting, as you will spend the majority of your day on your feet.

Money guide

Starting salaries range from £15,000 to £17,000 a year.

With experience, this can rise to £18,000–£24,000.

Highly skilled toolmakers, who are fully trained in using computer-controlled equipment, can earn £25,000–£30,000.

Related opportunities

- Motor Vehicle Technician p222
- Sheet Metal Worker p230
- Welder p236

Further information

Engineering Council UK
www.engc.org.uk

Semta
www.semta.org.uk

Qualifications and courses

Vehicle maintenance patrollers are qualified vehicle technicians, and as such must hold an NVQ Level 2 or 3 in Motor Vehicle Maintenance and Repair (or similar) along with having a minimum of 3 years of relevant experience in motor vehicle repair.

You will need a clean driving licence, and will have to pass a driving assessment, aptitude test and medical exam. For some positions, a LGV licence may be required. Most employers will expect you to have at least 4 GCSEs/National 5s (A*–C/A–C), including English, Maths and a science.

Some of the larger organisations such as vehicle breakdown companies, dealerships and garages offer apprenticeship programmes that allow new entrants to train on the job and learn skills such as customer service techniques, road safety and use of communications equipment, alongside building their technical knowledge. Employers may also support you in your study of relevant industry recognised qualifications such as NVQs in Roadside Assistance and Recovery (Levels 2–3), City & Guilds Level 4 Certificate in Advanced Automotive Diagnostic Techniques (4121) or the IMI Awards Level 4 Diploma in Automotive Master Technician.

Your career prospects and earnings will be significantly enhanced if you work towards Institute of the Motor Industry's Automotive Technician Accreditation (ATA). You would be required to complete a number of practical and theory exams in order to gain status as a Roadside Assistance Diagnostic Technician or Roadside Assistant Master Technician.

What the work involves

Vehicle maintenance patrollers travel to motorists who have broken down in order to diagnose the problem with the vehicle and fix it if possible. If repair is not possible, you will need to tow the vehicle to the nearest garage.

You will be responding to urgent calls from a central control centre, and may need to reassure worried or shaken motorists.

You will be driving a van or truck, and operating a range of electronic equipment alongside general tools and car parts.

Type of person suited to this work

You will need excellent communication skills in order to explain to motorists what is wrong with their vehicle and what can be done to fix it. You may be required to reassure people who are distressed or upset following an accident.

The ability to think quickly when assessing vehicles at the roadside is necessary.

You should be good with your hands as you will be operating various tools and machines and undertaking repairs within the small space of an engine.

Working conditions

An average working week comprises around 39 hours, usually worked on a shift system including evening, night and weekend work. You may also be required to remain on standby on occasion.

Since the majority of work is undertaken on the road, a driving licence is essential. Depending on the vehicle you drive, you may also need an additional HGV or LGV licence. You will be working on the roadside in all conditions, including hazardous weather such as snow and fog, so must wear relevant safety equipment at all times.

Future prospects

Vehicle maintenance patrollers enjoy a variety of employment options. You could work for a large, well known national organisation such as the Royal Automobile Club (RAC) or the Automobile Association (AA), or for a smaller garage providing a localised breakdown service.

With experience you may progress to a supervisory role in a larger organisation, in which you will oversee and develop the performance of a number of breakdown engineers across a region.

In larger organisations, you could also move into a managerial or senior administrative position.

Advantages/disadvantages

You will be providing a valuable and appreciated service to people every day.

There is great job satisfaction in being able to repair a vehicle at the roadside and send a happy customer on their way.

You will spend long periods of time on your own, which can get boring and lonely.

Money guide

The starting salary for a qualified vehicle breakdown engineer is around £20,000 to £30,000 per year.

With experience, you could expect to earn £35,000.

For senior roles within a large company, salaries can rise to £40,000.

The specialist skills you acquire, such as the ability to use lifting equipment to move a stranded vehicle, are likely to increase your pay. Shift work and overtime can also affect your earnings.

Related opportunities

- Assembler p201
- Highways Maintenance/Road Worker p91
- Motor Vehicle Technician p222

Further information

Royal Automobile Club
www.rac-careers.com

The Automobile Association
www.theaa.com

The Institute of Vehicle Recovery
www.theivrgroup.com

ENGINEERING, MANUFACTURING AND PRODUCTION

235

WELDER

Qualifications and courses

One route of entry into a career as a professional welder is via an Apprenticeship or Advanced Apprenticeship in Engineering. Most employers expect you to have least 5 GCSEs/National 5s (A*–C/A–C) or equivalent, including Maths, English and a science subject. You may have to pass a competency test prior to entry.

As an apprentice, you will experience a combination of on-the-job training from experienced professionals and a series of day or block release instruction at a college or training centre where you will work towards gaining industry-recognised qualifications. Relevant courses include NVQs in Performing Engineering Operations (Levels 1–2) and in Fabrication and Welding Engineering (Levels 2–3). Your training will cover areas such as how to read technical drawings, how to select materials and tools whilst also teaching you the relevant welding methods required of your specific job role.

Alternatively, you may opt to take related qualifications full-time at college in order to gain knowledge prior to entering the industry. Relevant qualifications include the ABC Certificate in Fabrication and Welding Practice (Levels 1–3), the BTEC Level 3 Diploma in either Manufacturing Engineering (Fabrication & Welding) or Mechanical Engineering, the City & Guilds Level 1–3 Award in Welding Skills/Advanced Welding Skills (3268), the City & Guilds Level 1–3 Certificate/Diploma in Engineering (2850), the Welder Approval Certificate and the EAL Award in Welding.

To enhance your career prospects and future earnings, you may decide to seek membership with The Welding Institute (TWI) which offers professional welders the chance to apply for chartered (CEng) or incorporated (IEng) engineering status or registration as an Engineering Technician (EngTech).

What the work involves

Welders work with metals and heavy-duty plastics, which they join together using heat to form plates, pipes and other items.

You could use a number of welding techniques that are classed as either manual, semi-automatic or fully mechanised. You will most likely specialise in one of these areas as opposed to working across all three.

You may have to work from technical drawings, using them as a guide by which to weld components together.

Type of person suited to this work

You will need good hand-to-eye coordination, coupled with manual dexterity, to successfully operate your tools and machinery.

You should be willing to work responsibly within strict health and safety guidelines, and to look out for the safety of others in your team. This will prove especially important when you work unsupervised.

Working conditions

Hours are usually 37 a week, often operating on a shift pattern, and opportunities for overtime are common.

You could find yourself working in almost any location, from standard factory or workshop roles to on-site jobs which could be outdoors or even under the sea. This means you might have to work in confined spaces which can be uncomfortable.

You will also need to wear safety equipment, including protective goggles to shield your eyes from UV light and sparks, and also fire-resistant aprons and gloves.

Future prospects

There are excellent employment opportunities for welders throughout the UK due to a shortage of skilled welders, although the majority of jobs are found in the more industrial areas.

There is a great variety of industries in which you could work, including civil engineering, agricultural engineering, shipbuilding and vehicle maintenance and repair. As your skills are transferable, you will find it easy to move between different fields of work as well as overseas.

As you gain experience within a company, you could move into a supervisory role such as a foreman/forewoman or a fabrication workshop manager. Alternatively, you could undertake further qualifications in order to specialise in a particular area of welding, move into inspection and quality control or work towards a career as an engineer.

Contract work and self-employment are also common.

Advantages/disadvantages

Practical work, where you can see the result of your efforts, is extremely rewarding.

Career prospects are good, with opportunities throughout the UK.

You will be operating machinery that is potentially dangerous.

Money guide

Starting salaries are usually between £16,000 and £18,000.

Experienced welders can expect to earn in the region of £20,000–£33,000 a year.

If you are working as a specialist welder you could earn up to or in excess of £40,000 a year.

Related opportunities

- Blacksmith p202
- Civil/Construction Engineer/Civil Engineering Technician p71
- Sheet Metal Worker p230

Further information

Engineering Construction Industry Training Board
www.ecitb.org.uk

The Welding Institute
www.twi-global.com

Environment, Animals and Plants

Jobs in this sector are perfect for those of you who do not want to spend every day behind a desk in an office, although this is not to say that you will not need to spend time writing reports and keeping a log of research findings or clients' information. Workers in this sector are passionate about animals or about caring for and

maintaining the environment. You should also have brilliant people skills especially if you find yourself responsible for the welfare of someone else's animal. You should be someone who is very observant and interested in the natural world, not just from a welfare point of view but also from an economic one; many jobs in this sector involve using the environment for financial gain but increasingly industry is interested in doing so responsibly.

The jobs featured in this section are listed below. For similar jobs to the ones in this section turn to *Leisure, Sport and Tourism* starting on page 361.

Qualifications and courses

The entry requirements vary depending on the specific role you wish to apply for. Some employers will expect you to have A levels in subjects such as a science, technology or Engineering, or equivalent qualifications such as the BTEC Level 3 in Agriculture or City & Guilds Levels 2-3 Awards in Agriculture (0073). At least 2 years' relevant work experience would also be beneficial. Extra qualifications that may be useful include the City & Guilds Level 4 Award/Certificate in Work-based Agricultural Management (Livestock or Crop Production) or City & Guilds Level 4 Diploma in Work-based Agricultural Business Management (0097).

For other roles you will be required to hold a degree or equivalent professional qualification. Subjects which may be beneficial for this career include environmental health, engineering and science. For degree entry you usually need a minimum of 2 A levels/3 H grades and 5 GCSEs/National 5s (A*–C/A–C) including Maths and English.

Once you have secured employment, training is provided on the job, usually over a 2-year period in which you accompany experienced inspectors during onsite visits and attend short courses.

Relevant professional qualifications include the NVQ in Occupational Health and Safety (Levels 3–5) and the BGAS-CSWIP Agricultural & Environmental Inspector course offered by TWI Training.

To work in a specialist sector, such as the Sea Fisheries Inspectorate, you may need relevant industry qualifications such as a degree in marine sciences, oceanography or fisheries studies. A competency certificate or naval qualification to act as an officer on a merchant ship or a mate of a fishing vessel would also be necessary.

What the work involves

You will be responsible for monitoring standards within agriculture and ensuring that regulations are followed. You are likely to be employed as one of the following:

Health and Safety Executive (HSE) inspector
You will be concerned with occupational health and safety and required to visit premises to check machinery, investigate accidents, write reports and at times give evidence in court cases.

Department for Environment, Food and Rural Affairs (DEFRA) inspector
You will enforce UK and EU legislation. This will involve collecting and analysing data, issuing certificates and planning for the prevention and control of animal and poultry disease.

Food assurance scheme inspector
You will check that agricultural practice meets the Assured Food Standards. You will also inspect the health and living conditions of livestock.

Type of person suited to this work

You must have knowledge and experience of agriculture and be able to carry out the inspections with impartiality, consistency and sound judgement. You need up-to-date knowledge of relevant laws.

Much of your job will involve monitoring others so observational and problem-solving skills are essential.

You will also need good written and spoken communication skills, as well as confidence using IT.

Working conditions

Normal working hours will be 9am to 5pm, Monday to Friday, although extra hours will sometimes be necessary.

You will have an office base but at least half your time will be spent visiting workplaces. You will therefore travel often and overnight stays may sometimes be required.

The job can involve a great deal of pressure as it will be your responsibility to ensure that legal requirements are followed effectively within agriculture. Your actions could determine the health and welfare of both people and livestock.

Future prospects

Once you have several years' experience, you could progress to a senior position or work as a consultant in occupational health.

With enough experience and training, you could move into education, becoming a lecturer in occupational health and safety.

Alternatively, you could work in public health or conservation.

Advantages/disadvantages

The job involves inspecting others and pointing out violations of the law so you may encounter confrontation.

It will be rewarding to know that you have ensured that livestock are treated correctly and people are working in a safe environment.

Money guide

Trainee inspectors could expect a starting salary between £23,000 and £26,000.

As you gain experience, your salary may increase to upwards of £30,000.

Those working in a specialist area could achieve up to £50,000.

Related opportunities

- Countryside Ranger p245
- Farm Manager p247
- Farm Worker p248

Further information

Assured Food Standards
www.redtractor.org.uk

Department for Environment, Food and Rural Affairs
www.defra.gov.uk

Health and Safety Executive
www.hse.gov.uk

Qualifications and courses

To enter this profession you will need a degree in a subject such as agriculture, biological science, horticulture, soil science or animal nutrition. Entry requirements for a degree are typically a minimum of 2 A levels/3 H grades, including Maths and Chemistry or another science, as well as 5 GCSEs/National 5s (A*–C/A–C) including English, Maths and a science. Equivalent qualifications may also be accepted.

It can be useful to have a postgraduate qualification in a specialist area, for example, a master's degree in animal production, soil science, poultry science or seed and crop technology.

It will also be valuable to have some work experience on a farm or in horticulture. Voluntary/unpaid opportunities are advertised online through charities such as World Wide Opportunities on Organic Farms (WWOOF). Useful qualifications include a City & Guilds Levels 2-3 Certificate/Diploma in Agriculture (0073) and BTEC Level 3 in Agriculture.

Those with an accredited master's degree and at least 4 years of work experience may be eligible to become a chartered scientist (CSci), a qualification which provides international recognition of your experience and expertise within your field.

What the work involves

Agricultural scientists carry out research to improve current farming techniques in crop production and the breeding and managing of livestock.

Using biology, biochemistry or chemistry, you will become a specialist in an area such as the study of soil, viruses, fungi, pests or genetics.

You will conduct tests, analyse the information and write reports. You could also teach farmers and companies that sell seeds or chemicals about your findings.

Type of person suited to this work

You must have an aptitude and a passion for science and the environment, especially biology and chemistry.

You will need strong communication skills as you will liaise with farmers and other growers to find out about their agricultural problems. You should be innovative and have strong research skills as you will spend much of your time in a laboratory or in the field, developing new solutions.

It is important to be patient, methodical and organised as progress in some research projects can take a very long time.

Working conditions

You will work 35–39 hours a week. It may be necessary to work early mornings, late evenings and weekends.

You will be based in either an office or a laboratory. Shift work could be needed when conducting experiments in the laboratory.

This job may be unsuitable for those with hay fever, dust allergies or animal allergies. A driving licence would be helpful as you might have to travel to farms or greenhouses.

Future prospects

Opportunities for general research are declining, although they are rising in some fields like genetic engineering. There is strong competition for jobs.

Vacancies are available with local and national government bodies, research organisations, and manufacturers of animal feed, fertilisers and chemicals.

After gaining experience, you could become a lecturer in a university, school or college. You may be able to move into sales-related work for production companies.

Advantages/disadvantages

This job is perfect for those with a passion for plants and wildlife.

Conducting scientific research and practical work can be interesting and varied.

Job opportunities are falling in some areas.

It can take a long time to see any progress in some research projects.

Money guide

Salaries will depend on your location and employer.

Certain private companies and the majority of public organisations have a structured pay scale.

The starting salary for an agricultural scientist is £17,000–£22,000.

With experience, earnings can increase to in excess of £30,000 per year.

Those in a senior role, including those with chartered status, could earn up to £50,000 a year.

Related opportunities

- Botanist p496
- Chemist p497
- Ecologist p502

Further information

Biotechnology and Biological Sciences Research Council
www.bbsrc.ac.uk

Department for Environment, Food and Rural Affairs
www.defra.gov.uk

Lantra
www.lantra.co.uk

Royal Society of Biology
www.rsb.org.uk

World Wide Opportunities on Organic Farms UK
www.wwoof.org.uk

ENVIRONMENT, ANIMALS AND PLANTS

AGRONOMIST

Qualifications and courses

Most entry-level candidates to this industry have a degree in a relevant subject, such as agriculture, ecology or biosciences. Typical entry requirements to a degree course are a minimum of 2 A levels/3 H grades, including at least one science, and 5 GCSEs/National 5s, including Maths, English and a science. Work experience on a farm is very useful in giving you an insight into the industry you will be working closely with. Those candidates who wish to specialise in a particular area of agronomy typically take a postgraduate qualification, such as a master's degree in soil science or seed and crop technology.

Other relevant qualifications include the FACTS Certificates, the BASIS Advanced Certificate or BASIS Diploma in Agronomy, and the Graduate Diploma in Agronomy with Environmental Management. The BTEC Level 1 in Land Based Studies (Agriculture) or BTEC in Agriculture (Levels 2–3) may also be helpful. On-the-job training is provided and a driving licence is often needed.

Alternatively, you can enter the profession in other ways, including as a field trials officer. As part of your career progression you can, with experience and training, become a senior field trials officer, progressing to the role of agronomy assistant and eventually rising to become a fully fledged agronomist.

Entry with only a Foundation degree/HND is limited, but does allow you enter as a technician or field trials officer, which can be an excellent way of gaining experience in the industry.

What the work involves

As an agronomist you will develop and implement production systems for the maximum economical production of high quality crops without harming the environment.

You will become an expert in areas such as irrigation, drainage, plant breeding, soil classification and soil fertility.

You will study any factors which could affect the crop, including the weather and water supply. You will carry out experiments, examine the results and then complete reports.

As a field trials officer you will need to organise different trials, either in the field or laboratory. You will be expected to write research proposals, record trial results accurately, developing experiments and ensuring government legislation is correctly followed. Other duties in support of the agronomist will also be expected.

Type of person suited to this work

You need to be good at problem-solving and have excellent research skills. You should be comfortable working on your own and as part of a team.

You must have strong analytical and communication skills in order to turn your research into practical solutions and explain them to farmers or businesses. It is important that you are methodical, practical and patient as it may take a long time to conduct successful experiments.

Working conditions

You will spend a lot of time working outdoors. You will also carry out experiments and tests in laboratories and write up reports in an office.

Hours are generally between 9am and 5pm, Monday to Friday, although you might have to work extra hours to complete some experiments.

Travelling to different locations such as farms can be necessary for some agronomists. Protective clothing is needed as you will probably work with hazardous equipment. This job may not be suitable for those with pollen or dust allergies. Good colour vision may be needed for certain jobs.

Future prospects

Job prospects are good. There is a lack of young people in the profession and companies are recruiting. Agronomists that specialise in certain fields, such as genetic engineering, are also desired.

A lot of agronomists work for the government, research organisations and agricultural development organisations as well as businesses that produce seeds, chemicals or food products.

After gaining experience, it is possible to become self-employed and work as a consultant. Lecturing in universities is another option. You could also progress to a role such as a manager in a research agency or a project supervisor.

Advantages/disadvantages

You will have the opportunity to work outdoors.

This role combines scientific research with practical work, making for a diverse work environment. Conducting successful experiments can take a long time and requires patience.

Money guide

The starting salary for an agronomist, and similar roles including a field trials officer, is between £18,000 and £20,000.

After gaining experience, salaries are around £28,000. If you progress to a senior role, you can expect a salary of up to £40,000.

Benefits, such as a pension scheme and company car, are sometimes included.

Related opportunities

- Botanist p496
- Chemist p497
- Ecologist p502

Further information

British Agrochemical Standards Inspection Scheme (BASIS)
www.basis-reg.co.uk

Department for Environment, Food and Rural Affairs
www.defra.gov.uk

Lantra
www.lantra.co.uk

Royal Society of Biology
www.rsb.org.uk

Qualifications and courses

There are several ways to qualify as an animal physiotherapist. The most typical is for a candidate to undertake a degree in human physiotherapy followed by a 2-year Postgraduate Diploma or Master of Science (MSc) in Veterinary Physiotherapy at either the Royal Veterinary College (RVC) or University of the West of England. You will need the highest level A levels/H grades in Maths and a science for entry onto an undergraduate degree course and entry onto a postgraduate course requires a suitable first degree, in equine sciences for example, of at least a 2.1 standard; however veterinary nurses with 4 years' experience are also considered. Upon completion, you can then become a member of the Association of Chartered Physiotherapists in Animal Therapy (ACPAT).

Alternatively, you can train for 2 years with a fully qualified member of ACPAT and complete the ACPAT education course or complete an animal physiotherapy course, such as the Certificate in Animal Physiotherapy offered by the National Association of Veterinary Physiotherapists (NAVP).

The College of Animal Physiotherapy also offers a Diploma in Animal Physiotherapy. This course lasts 1 to 2 years, part time. If you successfully complete this course you will be accepted into the International Association of Animal Therapists (IAAT).

Canine and Equine Physiotherapy Training (CEPT) offers an Advanced Certificate in Veterinary Physiotherapy. This course lasts 2 years, part time, and entry requires a good working knowledge of animal care and a relevant higher or further education qualification.

What the work involves

Animals suffer from joint and muscular pain in the same way that humans do. As a result, animal physiotherapy has become a regular part of animal care.

You would be used by many domestic pet owners and even more so by horse owners.

Techniques you will use may include soft tissue mobilisation, ultrasound (including long-wave), neuromuscular stimulation, joint mobilisation, magnetic field therapy, hydrotherapy and massage.

Type of person suited to this work

You must love animals and want to help in their recovery process. Whilst you will spend a vast majority of your time working closely with animals, this job does also involve working alongside veterinarians and owners so you will have to be able to communicate clearly with people too!

Working with animals can be messy and smelly, so you must be prepared to get dirty. You should expect the work to be occasionally distressing, especially if the animal is injured or dies.

You will need to have good dexterity and be physically fit. You should have experience of working with animals and the ability to match treatments with problems.

Working conditions

You will be working in clinics, clients' homes, farmyards and/or stables. You could be indoors or outside in all weathers.

A driving licence is essential for some posts and you will normally wear protective clothing. This job will probably involve some heavy lifting and you will need to be physically fit.

Some assignments will involve evening and weekend work, especially if you visit your clients and animals in their own homes. As most animal physiotherapists are self-employed, working hours must be flexible to suit the client.

Good business skills are essential if self-employed.

Future prospects

This profession is extremely competitive and employs very small numbers. Work experience will improve your chances of employment.

Some of the larger animal welfare charities and veterinary surgeries employ animal physiotherapists; however most are self-employed running their own practices. To be successful you will need to build up a client list and have good business skills. There is not a structured career path in place.

With experience you could work as a lecturer or consultant.

Advantages/disadvantages

You will be working with animals, perhaps helping them to have a better quality of life. Some aspects of the job may be messy and smelly.

There is the opportunity for self-employment.

Some heavy lifting will be required.

Money guide

Many working in this area are self-employed; average fees are around £20 to £70 for each consultation.

The average starting salary is about £18,500 per year; this can increase to around £20,000–£25,000 with experience.

As a senior animal physiotherapist or consultant you could earn up to £65,000 a year.

Related opportunities

- Pet Behaviour Counsellor p261
- Physiotherapist p312
- Veterinary Surgeon p266

Further information

Association of Chartered Physiotherapists in Animal Therapy
www.acpat.org

National Association of Veterinary Physiotherapists
www.navp.co.uk

The College of Animal Physiotherapy
www.tcap.co.uk

ENVIRONMENT, ANIMALS AND PLANTS

241

Qualifications and courses

There are no formal entry requirements to become an animal welfare officer but experience of working with animals is, unsurprisingly, expected. Opportunities for voluntary work are available on the Do-it website and through the RSPCA and the SSPCA. The City & Guilds Award/Certificate/Diploma in Work-Based Animal Care (Levels 1–3) may also be advantageous.

To be recruited by the RSPCA and SSPCA you will need a full UK driving licence and 5 GCSEs/National 5s (A*–C/A–C). A pre-entry NVQ/SVQ Level 3 in Animal Care or Level 4 in Animal Care and Management is also desirable. Physical fitness is also highly important; you must be able to swim 50m fully clothed and pass a medical examination.

Once employed by the RSPCA as a welfare officer you must complete their training course, comprised of 26 units spread across a series of learning modules, with a view towards becoming an inspector. This course must be completed within 3 years. Successful trainees become probationer inspectors for 6 months before confirmation as a full inspector.

The SSPCA training course lasts 6 months. After 2 years an intermediate examination is taken, and after 3 years you are required to sit the SVQ Level 3 in Animal Welfare.

Offers of employment are subject to passing the Disclosure and Barring Service (DBS) check.

What the work involves

You will work for an animal protection organisation or local authority offering a 24/7 service. You will undertake rescue work, visit and advise pet and animal owners, investigate cases of abuse and, when abuse is found, complete legal procedures.

You will be on-call to collect stray and injured animals or animals at risk from dangerous situations.

You will promote animal welfare in your area and you may be responsible for caring for any animals taken in by the organisation you work for.

Type of person suited to this work

You will find yourself in situations that could be potentially dangerous so you will have to be aware of your own, the public's and the animal's health and safety. Some work will be distressing, especially if the animal is in pain or has been mistreated.

Although you will often work on your own, you may well work within a team, especially in rescue situations.

Strong interpersonal skills are one of the RSPCA's key requirements and you must be able to handle confrontational situations in a calm and assertive manner. Accurate report writing ability is also important.

Working conditions

Each day will be different; you could be in a factory, private house, animal establishment or outdoors up to your waist in water.

You will spend a lot of time travelling around the local area in a van so a driving licence is essential. You will probably have to work shifts including evenings and weekends.

Animals can bite and kick, especially when they are distressed, so you will have to use your skills to make sure they remain safe and that you do not put yourself at risk. You will not be able to do this work if you suffer from animal or dust-related allergies.

Future prospects

You could work for a number of animal charities such as the RSPCA, SSPCA or the Blue Cross, or for a local authority. Within the RSPCA you can be promoted from animal welfare officer to inspector, with increased responsibility for animal cruelty cases. Further progression to chief inspector or superintendent level is possible.

You may be able to work overseas, providing support to local people in disastrous events, such as earthquakes, or informing local people about animal welfare.

You can also move into other related jobs as a local authority dog and animal warden, or kennel and cattery work.

Advantages/disadvantages

You will have the satisfaction of rescuing animals that are being abused and improving their quality of life.

There will be opportunities to work with a range of wild animals, farm animals and pets.

Some people will be abusive and you may encounter dangerous situations.

Money guide

Starting salaries for a trainee animal welfare officer are around £17,500. Once qualified, you will earn about £21,000.

After several years' experience, you could earn up to £29,000.

In the RSPCA, the starting salary for a trainee inspector is £19,284. On completion of the required training units, salaries can rise to between £24,00 and £27,000.

In the SSPCA, a probationary inspector earns £19,293 and a qualified inspector's salary begins at £22,792 along with a housing allowance.

Related opportunities

- Dog Trainer/Handler p246
- Veterinary Nurse p265

Further information

Royal Society for the Prevention of Cruelty to Animals
www.rspca.org.uk

Scottish Society for the Prevention of Cruelty to Animals
www.scottishspca.org

Qualifications and courses

There are no set academic requirements for this job but some employers do prefer people to have some GCSEs/National 5s. Entry is through a combination of work experience, on-the-job training and qualifications.

There are NVQs/SVQs available in Tree Work (Arboriculture) (Levels 1–2) which include workplace assessments. The BTEC qualifications in Forestry and Arboriculture (Levels 2–3), the ABC Level 2 Certificate in Arboriculture and the Royal Forestry Society (RFS) Level 2 Certificate in Arboriculture are also valuable qualifications for entrants to the field.

The National Proficiency Training Council (NPTC) also offers various short part-time and full-time courses at colleges of further education. Qualifications include the NPTC Level 2 Awards in Chainsaw Maintenance and Cross Cutting and Felling and Processing Small Trees up to 380mm, and the Level 3 Awards in Felling and Processing Trees over 380mm, Aerial Cutting of Trees with a Chainsaw Using Free-fall Techniques, Aerial Tree Pruning, Assisted Fell Operations and Preparing, Agreeing Emergency Treework Operations, and Installation and Maintenance of Structural Tree Supports. These could be completed pre-entry or on-the-job.

The Royal Horticultural Society also offers short courses leading to Arboricultural Association certificates and Lantra-accredited apprenticeships.

A Competency Certificate from the National Proficiency Training Council or Scottish Skills Testing Service is needed to work on your own or with machinery.

The National Trust can help in organising work experience placements. The Woodland Trust and the British Trust for Conservation Volunteers also provide volunteer opportunities.

What the work involves

You will carry out all kinds of work on the trees, shrubs and hedgerows in private and public gardens, parks, roadsides and on paths.

You will be responsible for planting new trees and shrubs, taking direction from a landscaper or garden designer.

Using chainsaws, hand tools, ladders and other specialised climbing equipment, you will use your knowledge of trees to make them safe, help them grow or increase the light available for other species.

Type of person suited to this work

You must have practical skills and be happy using potentially dangerous machinery and tools. You will also have to be interested in trees and the problems that can occur with them and be good with your hands.

This job is physically demanding and will include lifting, cutting and climbing so you will need to be strong and agile and good with heights. You will need to observe health and safety rules and be happy working in a team or on your own.

You will need excellent communication skills to deal with customers and explain what work needs to be done.

Working conditions

You will be outdoors in all weathers, hanging from ropes and using dangerous tools like a chainsaw.

If you suffer from pollen and dust allergies or vertigo, this work will be difficult for you.

You will have to wear protective clothing and be very safety conscious.

Future prospects

Demand for experienced workers has risen due to greater public interest and concern for the environment. Opportunities are available with the National Trust, contractors, landowners or private employers.

With further qualifications you could enter senior or managerial positions, but this might involve moving to larger organisations.

With experience you could set up your own business.

Advantages/disadvantages

The work can be hazardous so you must obey safety regulations.

You will be outside working in all weathers.

You could do very long hours in the summer and shorter hours in the winter, which may affect your earnings.

Money guide

Salaries will depend on whether you are working for a contractor or are self-employed, however you will probably earn more in the south-east of England.

The starting salary for a junior arboricultural worker is around £15,000–£21,000.

With experience, salaries can rise to between £22,000 and £30,000.

Salaries for managerial roles can range from £25,000 to £30,000.

Self-employed workers can earn more but it depends on how much they work and the region they are working in.

Related opportunities

- Countryside Ranger p245
- Gardener/Garden Designer p253
- Horticultural Worker/Manager p256

Further information

Institute of Chartered Foresters
www.charteredforesters.org

Lantra
www.lantra.co.uk

Royal Forestry Society
www.rfs.org.uk

ENVIRONMENT, ANIMALS AND PLANTS

ENVIRONMENT, ANIMALS AND PLANTS

Qualifications and courses

Whilst most entrants have completed a degree, it is still possible to enter this profession with a HND, Foundation degree or A levels/H grades. Degree programmes require applicants to have achieved at least 2 A levels/3 H grades and 5 GCSEs/National 5s (A*–C/A–C).

A postgraduate qualification may be beneficial as this field is becoming increasingly competitive. Subjects such as environmental science, biological sciences (such as zoology), environmental conservation, countryside management and earth sciences (such as geography) would all be relevant.

Voluntary and unpaid experience is extremely favourably regarded in this industry. Most, if not all, entrants demonstrate their commitment and enthusiasm for this line of work by way of completing up to 6 months' relevant work experience. Charities such as the National Trust, the Wildlife Trusts and the Royal Society for the Protection of Birds (RSPB) will aid in searching for and securing relevant experience and placements.

An alternative route into this industry is to start as a ranger or warden, gather experience and then apply for a countryside officer post. There are apprenticeships available, such as the Environmental Conservation Apprenticeship, and groups such as the Countryside Management Association or the National Trust offer a range of short courses and events – ranging from ecology and habitat management to the identification of fungi – to help you gain expertise and develop your career.

What the work involves

Countryside officers/managers preserve and protect important wildlife areas, including nature reserves and sites of special scientific interest. You will achieve this through methods such as raising awareness of the issues that affect the natural environment, monitoring species to see which require protection, and gathering evidence of pollution.

You will advise authorities and communities on the effect that developments will have on the natural environment. Managers are responsible for the hiring, training and supervising of staff. You will also be in charge of the way budgets are spent.

Type of person suited to this work

In order to pursue this career you must have an interest in, and a passion for, environmental conservation.

You should have strong observational skills. You will also need to be physically fit. You should be capable of conducting research, have strong communication and negotiation skills, both in person and on paper, and the ability to speak in public.

You might have to be involved in enforcing environmental laws and so you will have to be able to remain calm and logical.

Working conditions

You will spend some of your time in an office environment and the rest working outdoors.

Working hours will vary depending on the season, but the average is about 40 hours a week. This is not a 9am to 5pm job; working weekends, evenings and bank holidays is common.

You might be required to travel between sites and so a driving licence may be useful. As an officer you may be provided with protective clothing.

Future prospects

Officers may progress into a managerial position, for example countryside manager or senior officer. In order to gain this kind of promotion you will need to gather qualifications and experience. However, promotion opportunities can be hard to come by.

You could look for work with charities and organisations such as the RSPB or the National Trust, where a clearer and more structured path for career progress may be available.

You may also be able to specialise in a specific area of conservation such as rivers, coasts or access and recreation for the general public. Each of these could increase your employment potential.

Advantages/disadvantages

You will have to work outside in all weathers.

This job has many elements to it and so every day will be different.

You will have to enforce environmental legislation which might place you in heated situations.

Money guide

The average starting salary for a countryside officer is between £18,000 and £24,000 a year.

With many years' experience, this can increase to between £20,000 and £30,000 a year.

Those in a managerial role can earn in excess of £30,000 a year.

It is possible to earn more in the private sector or as a consultant.

Related opportunities

- Countryside Ranger p245
- Landscape Architect/Designer p258
- Landscaper/Landscape Manager p259

Further information

The Conservation Volunteers (TCV)
www.tcv.org.uk

The Countryside Management Association
www.countrysidemanagement.org.uk

Qualifications and courses

Relevant courses include the NVQ/SVQ in Environmental Conservation (Levels 2–3), BTEC Level 2 Certificate/ Extended Certificate/Diploma in Countryside and Environment, and BTEC Level 3 in Environmental Conservation and Countryside Management. BTEC/ SQA Higher National Certificates and Diplomas in Environmental Conservation and Countryside and Environmental Management are also available. You will require 1 A level/H grade and relevant work experience to gain entry to these. The Environmental Conservation Apprenticeship is also available.

Relevant degrees include countryside management, conservation and environment, and environmental studies. You will require at least 2 A levels/3 H grades, and 5 GCSEs/National 5s (A*–C/A–C). Postgraduate qualifications are also available.

Most training is done on the job. Courses for professional development are provided by Lantra National Training Organisation.

A driving licence is essential. Employers prefer applicants aged 21 or over. This can be a very competitive area to enter so unpaid experience can be vital. Most entrants have completed at least 6 months of voluntary work, which may be possible at the Wildlife Trust, the National Trust and Groundwork.

Membership of relevant professional bodies such as the Countryside Management Association may enhance job prospects.

Once employed it will be necessary to further your knowledge by completing short courses with organisations such as The Conservation Volunteers (TCV) and the Field Studies Council (FSC). Subjects include coppicing, species identification and habitat management.

What the work involves

By patrolling the countryside throughout the year you will monitor the success and progress of the plants/animals and the integrity of the fencing and buildings in your care. You will also perform practical tasks such as tree planting and pond management, as well as plan and create habitats for animals and plants.

You will manage exhibitions and resource centres, take part in community projects, give talks, lead guided walks and be responsible for the safety and enjoyment of any visitors, answer their queries and help them get the most from their visit.

You will keep a record of any work that is carried out, along with inspections, accidents and incidents.

Type of person suited to this work

You will need to enjoy being outdoors and have a strong interest in wildlife and the countryside.

To ensure the future of your area you will need to provide information to the public which could include talking to

potential funding organisations or local politicians. You will therefore have to be confident speaking in public and have excellent written and spoken communication skills. You might have to write reports and sometimes undertake research.

To find work you might have to start with some voluntary or community-based work, so it is important that you are keen and willing.

Working conditions

Most of your work will be outdoors, driving or walking around your area. You will be working in all weathers and despite protective clothing you will be, at times, cold and wet or hot and dusty. This is physically demanding work and is likely to involve walking over difficult terrain.

You are likely to work longer hours during the spring and summer, especially if there are animals or plants that require protection.

This work can be difficult if you suffer from pollen or dust allergies.

Future prospects

Once employed within the industry it is likely that you will need to move from employer to employer in order to progress.

After gaining experience, it is possible to enter lecturing, consultancy or research work. You could also progress to the role of officer or a more managerial position, which would be more office based. You might choose to move to leisure management, agriculture or horticulture work.

Advantages/disadvantages

You will spend a lot of time in the open air combining your interest in the countryside with work!

You could be working in remote areas.

Many jobs are offered on temporary contracts or on a seasonal basis.

Money guide

Initial salaries are from around £18,000 per year.

With experience this can rise to in excess of £25,000 a year.

The most senior countryside rangers can earn up to £30,000 per year.

Related opportunities

- Countryside Manager/Officer p244
- Farm Manager p247
- Gamekeeper p252

Further information

Lantra
www.lantra.co.uk

Natural England
www.naturalengland.org.uk

The Conservation Volunteers (TCV)
www.tcv.org.uk

ENVIRONMENT, ANIMALS AND PLANTS

DOG TRAINER/ HANDLER

Qualifications and courses

Dog handler

Dog handling is usually a second career. Employers such as the UK Border Agency, the police, the army and the fire service expect you to start in mainstream work in the service before applying. For example, the police force requires you to have at least 3 years of police work experience. The security industry requires you to have a Security Industry Authority (SIA) licence.

The National Search and Rescue Dog Association (NSARDA) requires at least 6 months' experience as a full-time member of a lowlands rescue team (12 months' for mountain rescue). You could also volunteer as a 'dogsbody', where you act as the victim being searched for and, after 4–6 months of experience, you could move into dog support/navigation work, complete first aid, radio and equipment training, and then apply for dog handling training.

You could start as an apprentice and work towards a Diploma in Work-Based Animal Care. There is also an ASET Level 2 National Award for General Purpose Security Dog Handlers, and a HABC or BTEC Level 2 Certificate in Providing Security Services, which include training with guard dog options.

Dog trainer

After working as a handler you can then apply to become a trainer. Some organisations, such as the police, require 3 GCSEs/National 5s (A*–C/A–C), including English and Maths. Voluntary work is recommended.

Foundation degrees and degrees are available in animal behaviour and training and animal studies. Typical entry requirements for a degree course include 2 A levels/3 H grades and 5 GCSEs/National 5s. It is also recommended that as a dog trainer you join a professional body through which you can pursue your continuing professional development (CPD).

What the work involves

Dog handler

Working as a team, you will search buildings, vehicles and open spaces for such things as people, illegal drugs, firearms or evidence. You may protect property including private property or military establishments.

You might attend large-scale disturbances to control crowds or search for casualties at disaster scenes.

Dog trainer

You could support security staff, the police force or animal charities such as the Guide Dogs for the Blind. Your work will be divided between training the dogs and their human carers.

You might run one-to-one and group classes on obedience training for dogs.

Type of person suited to this work

You may need to house and care for your dog from puppyhood right to the time it retires 7–10 years later. You will require a stable home environment.

Most police dog work involves attending incidents, so you will need to be able to stay calm in an emergency. You will need to be patient, self-confident, alert and observant.

Much of your time will be spent on your feet and may involve running, so a high level of fitness is required.

Dog trainer

You will need to be patient, firm and a good teacher. You will need to have a good imagination to make classes fun and also be physically fit.

Working conditions

If you work with domestic owners you will probably be self-employed and work from a community setting like a village hall.

Dogs are used in dangerous situations and so you will be at risk of injury.

Future prospects

The main employers are the police, armed forces and customs and excise. Some other organisations employ a few dog handlers, for example the fire service, security companies and search and rescue services.

This job is fiercely competitive as many handlers stay in the job for life.

However, there are potentially opportunities to work as a dog handler for a private security firm.

There is also the option of self-employment or lecturing on dog training courses.

Advantages/disadvantages

There is the possibility of self-employment.

You may at some point be bitten or scratched.

You will form a strong bond with your dog. It is really rewarding when the dog you have trained catches a criminal, or finds dangerous drugs or explosives.

Money guide

On average dog handlers earn between £15,000 and £25,000 a year depending on experience. Extra allowances are paid when the dog lives with and is cared for by you.

Domestic dog trainers earn £13,500–£15,000 a year. Police dog trainers make about £21,000 which can rise to £30,000 or more with experience. If you are self-employed your earnings will depend on your success.

Related opportunities

- Pet Behaviour Counsellor p261
- Police Officer p543
- Racehorse Trainer p262

Further information

Association of Pet Dog Trainers
www.apdt.co.uk

Police Recruitment
http://recruit.college.police.uk

FARM MANAGER

Qualifications and courses

There are no formal entry requirements but most people who enter this area have a HND, degree or other higher level qualification.

Courses are available in agriculture, agricultural science, land and property management, and agricultural engineering. A levels/H grades or their equivalent, often including a science subject will be required. Postgraduate courses are also available which will require a relevant degree or HNC/HND and experience.

Previous experience of farm work is as important as qualifications, and most degree-level courses include sandwich placements for this purpose. Organisations such as Velcourt, Sentry Farms, MDS and the JSR Farming group also offer graduate training schemes. A driving licence is essential.

It is possible to enter with an NVQ/SVQ Level 3 in either Agriculture Crop Production or Livestock Production, and/or a Level 4 in either Agriculture (Livestock Management) or Agricultural and Commercial Horticulture (Crop Management).

Apprenticeships are also available through organisations such as Co-operative Farms.

What the work involves

You will be responsible for the overall running of a farm. This includes making the decisions about which crops to grow or livestock to raise. You will supervise the work of your staff, keep up to date with farming developments and oversee the financial side of the business whilst satisfying the regulations set by the Department for Environment, Food and Rural Affairs (DEFRA).

You will have to communicate with government officials, farming suppliers and feed merchants and your customers who could be major supermarkets or small local shops. You will keep farm records up to date such as the budget and where crops and livestock are sold to and bought from.

In recent years smaller farms have started offering more activities and products to increase income. Farm managers can now be expected to run accommodation and camping sites, offer field sports, fishing and other rural activities.

Type of person suited to this work

You should have a passion for science, the environment and business, combined with a strong understanding of farming and a desire to learn.

You will also need an appreciation of health and safety and the ability to recruit, develop and retain your staff, as well as run the business of the farm.

You should be capable of motivating staff, be computer literate and work well when under pressure.

Working conditions

Farm managers tend to work long hours, with early morning starts as the norm. Particular times of year are exceptionally busy, such as harvest or lambing season.

Managers will spend a lot of their time doing accounts and making sure the farm is operating profitably, but may also need to participate in general farm work. On smaller farms this may be a regular occurrence. The outdoors work will involve heavy lifting and will be dirty and smelly.

Future prospects

Competition for jobs is intense and career progression is likely to involve moving between farms and from one part of the country to another.

With substantial experience and qualifications it is possible to progress into other related areas of agriculture such as plant breeding, crop protection, plant trials or genetics. These opportunities are available within private companies or academic/research organisations.

Training or research opportunities are also possible, as well as consultancy or civil servant work with DEFRA. There could be the chance to work abroad.

Advantages/disadvantages

You will spend a lot of time in the open air caring for living and growing things. You will get to combine business acumen and an understanding of nature.

At some times of the year your social life may be restricted.

Your future can depend on factors outside of your control such as bird flu or foot and mouth disease.

Money guide

There is a set minimum wage, decided upon each year by the Agricultural Wages Boards for England and Wales, Scotland and Northern Ireland.

Assistant or trainee farm managers earn between £20,000 and £22,000.

Salaries for farm managers range from £23,000 to £35,000, depending on the type of farming you work in (ie crop, dairy or livestock).

Managers of large farms, with at least 10 years of experience, may earn over £50,000.

Senior consultants or advisers can earn up to £70,000 a year.

Some jobs include rent-free accommodation and a vehicle.

Related opportunities

- Farm Worker p248
- Fish Farmer p250
- Parks Officer p260

Further information

Department for Environment, Food and Rural Affairs
www.defra.gov.uk

Lantra
www.lantra.co.uk

National Federation of Young Farmers' Clubs
www.nfyfc.org.uk

FARM WORKER

 ENTRY LEVEL 1

ENVIRONMENT, ANIMALS AND PLANTS

Qualifications and courses

There are no set entry requirements but many employers will expect you to have some form of work experience. An Advanced Apprenticeship in Agriculture is available for formal training. GCSEs/National 5s in English, Maths and a science may also be useful for gaining promotion and higher pay.

Candidates may choose to specialise in either livestock or crop agriculture.

Livestock
Lantra offers a variety of livestock courses including Herdsman Foot Trimming, Sheep (lambing) and Dairy (calf-rearing). You can train while on the job and work towards an NVQ in Livestock Production (Levels 1–3) or a Diploma in Animal Care.

You may choose to do an HNC in Poultry Production at the Scottish Agricultural College. Poultry husbandry courses are also available at many other colleges.

Crops
The Royal Agricultural College offers degrees in crops, sustainable soil management and agricultural science. You could also take a National Proficiency Tests Council accredited course in Tractor Driving or Pesticide Use.

Many employers will allow you to train on the job and undertake qualifications such as the NVQ in Agriculture, Mixed Farming and Crop Production (Levels 1–3), the BTEC in Agriculture (Levels 2–3) or the City & Guilds Diploma in Agriculture (Levels 2–3).

What the work involves

Livestock
You will work on farms or estates caring for livestock. You will need to feed and handle the animals, clean their living spaces, and prepare them for transport. You may need to milk cows and shear sheep.

You will tend to ill livestock, give them proper medication and help out with birthing procedures. You may be required to keep track of animals' breeding cycle and care for the animals through pregnancy and the birthing process.

Crops
You will work on arable farms, ploughing, planting, sowing, fertilising, spraying and harvesting a variety of crops. You will either handpick crops or use machinery.

You could work with crops such as wheat, barley and oats, non-food crops such as linseed and flax, or energy crops used for heat and power generation. You will also be responsible for general maintenance and upkeep of the farm.

Type of person suited to this work

You should be practical and have a passion for the outdoors and environmental issues. You should be strong, active and adaptable and prepared to work very long hours.

A good knowledge of plant and/or animal care is important. You may need to work out weights and other calculations so good numeracy skills are also useful. You also need to be able to follow instructions and work with care and caution.

Working conditions

Farm work is seasonal so you will be busier at certain times of the year, when you may need to work 16 hour days.

You will normally work 40 hours a week, including evenings, early mornings and weekends. You will work in all weathers and will often be expected to live on or near the farm.

The work on livestock farms can be dirty so you will need to wear protective clothing and footwear.

People with allergies such as hay fever may also find the work difficult.

Future prospects

You could be promoted to supervisory roles or train further and become farm manager. Most farms are small so you might need to move farms in order to be promoted. There are also opportunities to work overseas.

Livestock farms are mostly found in western parts of the UK. A rise in farmers' markets means that demand for meats is high and interest in organic foods has left ample opportunity.

Crop farms are mostly found in eastern parts of the UK. You could specialise in non-food crops such as pharmaceuticals, oils or materials such as hemp.

Advantages/disadvantages

Working on a farm, especially during busy seasons, can be exhausting and dirty.

It is an amazing experience to tend to and watch an animal give birth and rewarding to reap an abundant harvest.

Money guide

Starting salaries for farm workers are around £13,000.

This can rise to between £14,000 and £25,000 or more with 2 to 5 years' experience.

Many employers will provide free or low-rent accommodation. Overtime pay is also common.

Related opportunities

- Farm Manager p247
- Fish Farmer p250
- Gamekeeper p252

Further information

Department for Environment, Food and Rural Affairs
www.defra.gov.uk

Lantra
www.lantra.co.uk

National Federation of Young Farmers' Clubs
www.nfyfc.org.uk

Qualifications and courses

To train as a farrier you must be at least 16 years old and will need to take an advanced apprenticeship with a training farrier approved by the Farriers Registration Council (FRC). Only 80 to 100 apprenticeships are offered each year and they cost approximately £12,000 if you are not eligible for grant aid funding.

To be accepted for the advanced apprenticeship, you will need a minimum of 4 GCSEs/National 5s (A*–C/A–C), including Maths and English Language, or an NVQ Level 2 and the Level 2 Key/Functional Skills of Communication and Application of Number, or a BTEC Diploma and the Key/Functional Skills. As part of the entry requirements you will also have to pass a medical examination and complete a practical forging test. City & Guilds offer preparatory courses and certificates.

The apprenticeship takes 4 years and 2 months. The course combines on-the-job training with periods at a college. At the end you will also be awarded a NVQ Level 3 in Farriery and the Diploma of the Worshipful Company of Farriers. To work as a farrier you must register with the FRC. A driving licence is required.

For those who cannot satisfy the academic and/or practical entry requirements, an Access to Farriery Course is available at colleges such as Warwickshire, Chichester and Herefordshire & Ludlow.

A Foundation degree in Farriery at Myerscough College is also available for those who are already qualified and working. It is also possible to learn farriery with the Royal Horse Artillery whilst serving with the army.

What the work involves

Farriers shoe, trim and care for the feet of horses.

As well as the skills of removing and fitting new shoes, you will have to keep up to date with new practices and know about horse anatomy and illnesses that can affect horses' feet.

You would often work in partnership with vets to treat leg and joint problems.

Type of person suited to this work

You should enjoy being around horses and have the right temperament to handle them. You will need to get on with your customers and deliver high-quality care to them and their horses.

You will have to enjoy being outdoors working in all weathers, often in a muddy environment.

This work is both practical and physical, so you will need to be strong to do manual work using lots of hand tools and have good metalworking skills.

Working conditions

Weekend work is common and emergency cover can be needed at any time.

Your days will involve driving to each customer, working with the horses and returning to your forge to prepare shoes and collect materials. In the summer months your hours will be long, especially when more people are riding their horses. This can be hot, tiring work, especially if fitting shoes to a difficult horse.

You could work from a blacksmith's forge or travel to farms and stables and work out of a mobile workshop.

Future prospects

Riding is a very popular activity and there are stables all around the country.

There are about 2,890 registered farriers who are mostly self-employed. There is high competition for each apprenticeship. Larger riding schools, stables and horse breeders can offer permanent jobs. You could progress to become a senior farrier, 1 of only 300 current farrier trainers or into a managerial role.

Some farriers supplement their earnings by undertaking blacksmithing whilst they build up their farriery client list.

Advantages/disadvantages

This is a great job if you want to work with horses without riding.

Using your hands is a satisfying skill to have.

The work is physically demanding and can result in back injuries.

Money guide

Apprentices who start work aged between 16 and 17 are not entitled to the full national minimum wage until they are 19. Those who start aged between 18 and 25 will be paid a percentage of the national minimum wage for the first 12 months of their apprenticeship. This is typically in the region of £6,000–£7,000.

Once qualified, you can earn upwards of £16,000, depending on your success and the number of customers you have.

The average salary for an experienced farrier is £30,000 or more per year.

Related opportunities

- Farm Manager p247
- Pet Behaviour Counsellor p261
- Racehorse Trainer p262

Further information

Farriers Registration Council
www.farrier-reg.gov.uk

Worshipful Company of Farriers
www.wcf.org.uk

ENVIRONMENT, ANIMALS AND PLANTS

FISH FARMER

Qualifications and courses

Applicants do not necessarily need formal educational qualifications but most employers require GCSEs/National 5s (A*–C/A–C). The BTEC Level 2 Certificate in Fish Husbandry is available to those with 4 GCSEs/National 5s (A*–C/A–C). Students can then progress to the BTEC Level 3 Certificate in Fish Management. SQA also offer a National Progression Award (NPA) in Aquaculture (Levels 4–5).

Training can be done on the job with attendance at short courses. Entrants may study via distance learning for the Certificate or Diploma in Fisheries Management offered by the Institute of Fisheries Management (IFM).

In Scotland you may be able to enter through a Level 3 Modern Apprenticeship.

Those who would like to begin their career as a manager or assistant manager may require a degree in a relevant subject such as aquaculture and fishery management, biology or marine and freshwater biology.

Once you are employed in this sector, you may be expected to take industry recognised qualifications in emergency first aid, food hygiene and sea survival. A full driving licence is also required and you must be able to swim.

What the work involves

As a fish farmer you will raise fish from small (juvenile) fry until they reach saleable size. The most common fish to raise are salmon and trout. You will feed them, check and treat for disease, clean tanks and protect them from predators. The final stage of the process is to net the catch, harvest and pack them for market.

Some farms specialise in producing the breeding stock – the tiny fish that other farmers bring to saleable size – known as fingerlings. Some shellfish farms in coastal locations also produce oysters, scallops and mussels.

Type of person suited to this work

You must be a practical person, willing to get wet and dirty. You need a good knowledge of fish which you will develop throughout your career. Much of this work is scientific in approach, so you should have good observational skills to be able to identify anything that might affect the quality and success of the fish in your care.

You should be patient, hard working and able to persevere in challenging situations. This work is difficult and long-term security is not guaranteed.

Entrants to this profession must be comfortable working within a team and independently.

If you become a manager you will also require good business and administrative skills.

Working conditions

Working with fish is the same as any animal-based work, which means they need care and attention 24/7. You are likely to work on a rota basis with 2 days off every week. You will work very long hours including early mornings, late evenings and weekends.

Fish farms are usually isolated, and you will be outdoors in damp, cold conditions having to cope with all types of weather.

Some of the work will be unpleasant and will involve the sight of blood.

Future prospects

Fish farming is becoming quite important due to the problems with sea fish stocks. In the UK, there are around 1,100 fish farms employing 7,500 people, most of whom are based in Scotland.

Just as with other farming enterprises, fish farms are vulnerable to price fluctuations, so gauging industry trends can be difficult.

With experience you may move into a research-related role involving scientific and technical work. You could also start up your own fish farm or work abroad.

Advantages/disadvantages

You will spend a lot of time in the open air.

You will have the satisfaction of producing an in-demand product.

There are only limited areas of the UK where the work is available.

Having to work unsociable hours could interfere with your personal life.

Money guide

Fish farm workers can expect a starting salary in the region of £13,000–£18,000.

As you gain experience, you could expect to earn up to £21,000.

Experienced managers of a fish farm can achieve up to £45,000, whilst regional managers can earn even more.

Related opportunities

- Countryside Ranger p245
- Farm Manager p247
- Skipper/Deckhand p264

Further information

British Trout Association
www.britishtrout.co.uk

Institute of Fisheries Management
www.ifm.org.uk

Qualifications and courses

Forest worker

There are no formal entry requirements but at least 2 GCSEs/National 5s (A*–C/A–C) or a forestry qualification would be an advantage. Relevant qualifications include the City & Guilds Levels 2–3 Certificate in Forestry and Arboriculture (0077), the City & Guilds Levels 2–3 Diploma in Work-based Trees and Timber (0083), the BTEC Level 3 Extended Diploma in Forestry and Arboriculture or Countryside Management, the Diploma in Environmental Land Based Studies, the NPTC Diploma in Work-based Trees and Timber (Levels 2–3), the ABC Certificate in Practical Environmental and Conservation Skills (Levels 1–3), and the Lantra Awards Level 2 Certificate in Land-based Activities.

Alternatively, an Apprenticeship in Trees and Timber is available at Intermediate and Advanced Level.

The National Proficiency Tests Council (NPTC) and Lantra award certificates of competence in skills such as operating chainsaws and carrying out chemical spraying. A full driving licence is also required.

Forest officer

Entry is with a Foundation degree, HND, degree or postgraduate qualification in forestry, land management, horticulture or environmental science. For entry to a degree a minimum of 2 A levels/3 H grades, normally including Maths or a science, and 5 GCSEs/National 5s are required. At least 1 A level/H grade and 3 GCSEs/National 5s are required for entry to an HND or Foundation degree. It may be useful to gain some experience before applying for a course.

The Forestry Commission runs a 2-year graduate development programme for those who hold a 2.1 Honours degree. Entrants are considered from a wide range of academic fields. Natural Resources Wales continues the work carried out by the Forestry Commission Wales, and offers a number of work experience and placement opportunities.

What the work involves

Forest worker

Work includes planting and felling trees, managing weeds, maintaining fencing and carrying out tree surgery. In addition, you will use tools, drive vehicles and repair any broken fences.

Forest officer

You will plan and manage the annual programme of your forest. This includes organising the clearing of areas, planting and felling trees, and overseeing general maintenance.

Type of person suited to this work

Forest worker

It is important that you can follow instructions and safety procedures as the work is dangerous. You should enjoy being outdoors.

Forest officer

You must be organised as you will plan jobs months in advance. You need both technical skills and theoretical knowledge of forests and wildlife.

Working conditions

Forest worker

You will probably work a standard Monday to Friday week with overtime and weekend work during the busier summer months. You will have to be aware of health and safety legislation as this can be dangerous work, using potentially hazardous tools.

Forest officer

Much of your time will be spent outdoors but you will also work indoors planning duties for your staff. You are likely to do a lot of travelling whilst you check the different areas under your responsibility. A driving licence would be helpful as many of these places are isolated.

Future prospects

The range of employers includes the Forestry Commission, private landowners and estates, local authorities and large companies.

Career progression is likely to involve relocating as promotion is rare unless you work for a large company. Many contracts are seasonal or short term, so you need to have a flexible approach to employment opportunities. Consequently, around 50% of forest workers are self-employed.

With significant experience, self-employment as a consultant or trainer is possible.

Advantages/disadvantages

It is a perfect job if you love the outdoors.

As with all land-based careers, you are often at the mercy of the weather.

Money guide

Forest worker

You are likely to earn around £12,000 per year when starting out in this career.

With experience, salaries increase to between £18,000 and £21,000 and a supervisor could earn up to £27,000.

Forest officer

Starting salaries for this role are usually between £19,000 and £30,000.

An experienced forest officer could achieve in excess of £35,000.

Forest workers and officers employed by private estates may have accommodation provided.

Related opportunities

- Countryside Ranger p245
- Gardener/Garden Designer p253
- Rural Property/Practice Surveyor p105

Further information

Forestry Commission
www.forestry.gov.uk

Institute of Chartered Foresters
www.charteredforesters.org

Qualifications and courses

No formal qualifications are needed for this role, however, 3 GCSEs/National 5s (A*–C/A–C) may be an advantage. Relevant GCSE/National 5 subjects include Design and Technology, Mechanics, Geography, Environmental or Rural Studies, and Business Studies.

Voluntary or relevant work experience is very useful for gaining insight into the industry and valuable experience can be found, for instance, working as part of a beating team. Relevant apprenticeships may be available through Skillseekers for those aged between 16 and 24.

Whilst training is usually done on the job, there are some courses available to applicants who wish to progress. Such courses include the City & Guilds Level 1 Award in Land-based Studies (0361), the Level 2 Certificate in Countryside and Environment Management (0076), and the Level 3 Certificate in Countryside Management (also 0076). They also offer the Diploma in Work-based Game and Wildlife Management at Levels 2–3 (0069).

Other courses include NVQs/SVQs in Gamekeeping and Wildlife Management (Levels 2–3), the BTEC in Gamekeeping and Countryside Management (Levels 2–3), and the HNC in Gamekeeping with Wildlife Management, for which candidates would need practical experience and/or the Extended Diploma in Gamekeeping.

Foundation degrees are available in countryside and environment (gamekeeping) at several colleges if you wished to specialise your learning. These generally require a Level 3 qualification or 2 or more A levels/H grades for entry.

If you intend to deal with specific animals, such as deer, then further qualifications may prove helpful. For example, the British Deer Society offers deer management courses. You may also have to operate chainsaws or use pesticides and will be required by law to gain certificates in competence from the National Proficiency Tests Council (NPTC).

What the work involves

As a gamekeeper you will work on a large country estate, where shooting for sport is part of the estate business. You will also play an important role in managing the land.

You will be responsible for providing birds and other animals such as deer or hares for the clients to shoot, or possibly fish to catch. This is achieved by raising game birds and releasing them into the wild once they are mature enough, and protecting game from its natural predators such as magpies and rats.

You will also have to patrol the land at night to help protect game from poachers.

Planting and protecting crops, clearing the land, and keeping rivers clean may also be necessary.

Type of person suited to this work

You must have an unsentimental approach to wildlife as this job involves the killing of animals for sport.

To enable the clients to get the most from their day, you will need to be a good communicator and be able to offer advice about gun usage and how to hit targets successfully.

Physical fitness and stamina are essential. You must be alert and possess excellent practical skills. You must be happy to work on your own for long periods of time.

Working conditions

You will be outdoors in all weathers and seasons. Your hours will be flexible and will involve weekend working and late or early starts. You will spend long periods of time on your own, doing lots of walking to check the estate and the progress of the game.

You will be handling and using guns, traps and poisons so will have to be confident using them and very aware of your own safety and that of others.

This work will be difficult for those who suffer from allergies to animals, pollen or dust.

Future prospects

Most of this work is within remote parts of the country or on large country estates.

There is strong competition for jobs, so it is best to take a few training courses before applying.

With further skills in shoot or land management you can be promoted to head of estate; with experience and dedication you can advance from trainee to head keeper quickly.

Advantages/disadvantages

This job combines outdoor physical work with lots of practical skills.

You will spend a lot of time alone.

You might be provided with a house.

Money guide

Starting salaries for new entrants are around £12,000 per year.

With experience you may earn in excess of £20,000 a year.

A vehicle and accommodation are often provided for free or at a reduced cost.

Related opportunities

- Countryside Ranger p245
- Farm Manager p247
- Farrier p249

Further information

British Association for Shooting and Conservation
www.basc.org.uk

Game and Wildlife Conservation Trust
www.gwct.org.uk

National Gamekeepers' Organisation
www.nationalgamekeepers.org.uk

Qualifications and courses

Gardener

There are no set requirements for entry to this career, however some GCSEs/National 5s (A*–C/A–C) may be sought by some employers. Some specialist courses are available to those who wish to progress and these include the City & Guilds Level 2 Certificate in Gardening (0082) and Levels 1–3 Award/Certificate/Diploma in Work-Based Horticulture (0065). The Royal Horticultural Society (RHS) also runs the Advanced National Certificate in Horticulture and the Kew Royal Botanical Gardens offers a Diploma in Horticulture.

Apprenticeships in Horticulture are also available with various organisations, such as B&Q, the National Trust and Royal Parks, Capel Manor College, and Kew Gardens.

Garden designer

Although there are no formal requirements for this job, a design-orientated qualification is a definite advantage.

Many garden design courses are offered at land-based colleges and some art colleges. Courses include the Edexcel Diploma in Environmental and Land-based Studies (Levels 1–3), the BTEC Level 3 in Horticulture, the BTEC HNC in Horticulture (Garden Design), and the BTEC HND in Landscape and Garden Design, Horticulture and Plantsmanship, and Horticulture. NVQs/SVQs in Horticulture (Levels 1–4) are also available.

Foundation degrees in garden/landscape design and management, and degrees and postgraduate degrees in garden design and related subjects, are also available, as is a BA Honours Degree in Garden Design, run by Falmouth University College of Arts in collaboration with Duchy College in Cornwall.

The Institute of Gardening also offers a Diploma in Horticulture which can be studied at home.

Courses in computer aided design may also be beneficial. A driving licence will also be necessary.

What the work involves

Gardener

Gardeners work in a wide range of settings, from large gardens such as those in stately homes and National Trust properties, to small urban parks and private gardens.

Garden designer

You will advise clients on how to improve the look and planting of their garden. You will present your ideas as a series of plans, and supervise a landscape contractor to turn your design into reality.

Type of person suited to this work

Gardeners need to be physically fit and confident in using hand tools. You must also be creative and be able to picture how a piece of bare or neglected ground can be transformed into something beautiful.

As a garden designer, drawing and IT skills will be useful, as will an extensive knowledge of plants and the environments they need.

Good business and maths skills are necessary in order to keep to your clients' budgets. You will also have to keep to deadlines.

Working conditions

Gardeners mostly work outdoors. There will be a lot of physical work, lifting large pots and bags of peat, and digging and clearing beds.

Garden designers will spend most of their time in a studio designing and researching garden plans. You will spend some time outdoors overseeing practical tasks.

Future prospects

Gardener

Many gardeners are self-employed, offering services to both the public and private sectors. If you work for a local authority, with experience you could move on to supervisor or manager jobs, especially if you gain further qualifications. Gardeners can also train to be garden designers.

Garden designer

Half of all designers work in private practice. Some specialise in certain types of design such as planting, landscaping, etc. Some designers choose to be self-employed, offering services to private home owners.

Advantages/disadvantages

Designers can mix creative, practical and outdoor work.

Your work will depend on the weather.

You may work in beautiful places (or create them if you are a designer).

Money guide

Gardener

Gardeners working for a local authority start at around £12,000–£18,000 per year. Salaries for head gardeners can be in excess of £25,000. Senior managers with demanding grounds maintenance responsibilities can earn £30,000 or more a year. If self-employed, you will agree an hourly rate with your customer.

Garden designer

As a guide, starting salaries are around £15,000 per year. Depending on the level of experience, designers can earn £25,000–£40,000 or more. If self-employed, you will agree an hourly rate with your customer or give a project-specific price.

Related opportunities

- Groundsperson/Greenkeeper p255
- Horticultural Worker/Manager p256
- Landscape Architect/Designer p258

Further information

Grow
www.growcareers.info

Royal Horticultural Society
www.rhs.org.uk

Society of Garden Designers
www.sgd.org.uk

ENVIRONMENT, ANIMALS AND PLANTS

253

Qualifications and courses

Groom/stable hand

You must be at least 16 years of age and ideally you should have experience working with horses. Useful courses include the NPTC NVQ in Horse Care (Levels 1–3), the City & Guilds Certificate and Diploma in Horse Care and Management (Levels 2–3), the BTEC Level 2 in Horse Care, the BTEC Level 3 in Horse Management, and the BTEC Level 4 HNC and Level 5 HND in Equine Management. The Association of British Riding Schools (ABRS) offers the Grooms Certificate and Grooms Diploma, and the British Horse Society (BHS) have exams in Horse Knowledge Care and Riding at stages 1 to 4.

The British Racing School in Newmarket and the Northern Racing College in Doncaster offer a 9-week residential course, during which you could complete the Level 1 Diploma in Work Based Racehorse Care and Riding. Upon completion you can take another 9-week course and gain the Level 2 Diploma in Work Based Racehorse Care before undertaking the 18-month Advanced Apprenticeship Level 3 Diploma.

Stud hand

There are no formal entry requirements. Some knowledge of stable work and horse care is expected. The National Stud in Newmarket offers a free apprenticeship for school leavers. This involves 10 weeks of training at a residential centre and the opportunity for a 10-month placement. Those over the age of 18 with experience working with horses can apply for the free Diploma in Stud Practice and Management with the National Stud. Students spend 5 months undertaking practical training, attending lectures and workshops, and completing projects and exams.

What the work involves

Groom/stable hand

You will be responsible for the health and welfare of the horses in your care. You will groom, feed, muck out and tack up the horses. You could be based within a riding school, competition or livery yard, racing stable or veterinary hospital.

Stud hand

This is a specialised area of work as you will be working with stallions, brood mares and young stock. You will use your understanding and knowledge of breeding lines to help owners breed a foal that meets their requirements.

Type of person suited to this work

You must be comfortable and competent riding and working with horses. Good observation skills and patience are essential when caring for animals.

You need strong communication and teamworking skills to work with your colleagues, the horse owners and stable visitors.

You should be a practical person, physically fit and willing to work in messy conditions.

Working conditions

You will spend most of your time outdoors lifting heavy bags of feed, hay and bedding. You will carry tack, clean up the yard or ride. In the summer the work can be hot, dusty and smelly. In the winter it is cold, wet and muddy.

You will wear protective clothing and, as this work can be dangerous, you must be aware of your own and others' safety. Horses can kick and bite.

You can expect to work 24/7, including some holidays and weekends, especially if you live-in.

A driving licence is useful.

Future prospects

Groom/stable hand

With experience it is possible to specialise. Competition grooms (show-jumping, dressage and eventing) are in demand. Gaining your HGV driving licence can increase opportunities. Most grooms progress to more successful yards that compete internationally or keep more expensive and higher quality horses.

Stud hand

Interest in breeding quality British horses and ponies has increased due to European competition. Stud work is therefore rising in importance and those with skills are in demand.

With experience it is possible to progress to a position in stud management. Additionally, there are also opportunities to work abroad.

Advantages/disadvantages

This is the perfect job for a horse lover.

The pay is relatively low for such a demanding job.

Injury risks are high in all horse activities and this could affect your long-term career security.

Money guide

Unqualified grooms usually have a starting salary of around £10,000.

Once qualified, salaries rise to £12,000 a year.

With experience, you could earn £16,000 a year.

A head groom or stud manager could achieve up to £20,000.

Free or subsidised accommodation is commonly available for those living on the premises.

Related opportunities

- Farm Manager p247
- Farrier p249
- Racehorse Trainer p262

Further information

British Horse Society
www.bhs.org.uk

GROUNDSPERSON/ GREENKEEPER

ENTRY LEVEL 1

Qualifications and courses

There are no set entry qualifications for this role and training generally takes place on the job. The Apprenticeship in Horticulture is available at Intermediate and Advanced Levels.

Relevant qualifications offered by City & Guilds are the Levels 1–3 Award/Certificate/Diploma in Work-Based Horticulture (0065), the Level 2 Extended Certificate in Sports and Amenity Turf Maintenance (0078-32), and the Levels 2–3 Diploma in Horticulture (0078-02 and 0078-03). Other courses include the BTEC Level 2 Certificate/ Extended Certificate/Diploma in Horticulture, the BTEC Level 3 Certificate/Diploma in Horticulture, and the BTEC Level 4 HNC and Level 5 HND in Horticulture (Sports Turf Management).

Degrees and Foundation degrees in sports turf and golf course management are available. Entry requirements are 2 A levels/3 H grades and 5 GCSEs/National 5s (A*–C/A–C) including English and Maths.

The Institute of Groundsmanship (IOG) offers short courses in areas such as generic sports turf management, basic lawn care and synthetic surfaces.

The British and International Golf Greenkeepers Association (BIGGA) also have a range of qualifications, including the Master Greenkeeper Certificate for those with experience and expertise.

What the work involves

Your main role will be to prepare and maintain the grounds used for different sports. Although you might work on synthetic surfaces for games like hockey, most of the time you will be working with grass. You will cut, treat, weed and prepare the surface before each game, match or event.

You will be responsible for outlining the playing areas with tape or marking compound, ensuring that they adhere to the regulations of the appropriate governing body.

You will put up posts, nets and other equipment where needed.

Type of person suited to this work

You need specialist horticultural knowledge, combined with an understanding of the different sports and what the competitors of each sport need.

You should be good with your hands and have a working knowledge of machinery maintenance.

You will require lots of stamina and physical fitness to do a variety of jobs.

Working conditions

You will have to work flexible hours including evenings and weekends.

The role involves a lot of physical labour such as carrying heavy items and bending. This work may be unsuitable for those who suffer from hay fever or allergies to chemicals.

You will spend a lot of your time working outdoors, although you will probably be in a workshop when repairing and maintaining the equipment. You will need to wear protective clothing.

Future prospects

The range of potential places for you to work is increasing. You could work in a professional sports club, local authority education or sports and leisure department, hotel, university or college.

With additional qualifications and experience you could apply for promotion to team leader or supervisor, head groundsperson and then area manager. Bigger companies offer greater promotion opportunities.

It is possible to progress into a position in leisure management or estate management.

Advantages/disadvantages

This job provides the satisfaction of knowing that your work will be seen by thousands of people.

Sports fans will have the opportunity to work in a sector that they are passionate about.

You will spend most of your time working outside in all weather conditions.

Money guide

The IOG publishes its recommended basic salary payment guide annually.

A junior groundsperson, aged between 16 and 17, can earn between £12,265 and £14,769 a year. After training this can increase to up to £21,299.

An experienced and skilled groundsperson/greenkeeper could receive between £21,681 and £26,585.

A head groundsperson could achieve £28,338–£37,021 and progression to grounds management could result in a salary of up to £48,061.

Staff responsible for major sporting venues may have the highest earning potential.

Employers may also offer on-site accommodation or bonuses for overtime.

Related opportunities

- Countryside Ranger p245
- Gardener/Garden Designer p253
- Horticultural Worker/Manager p256

Further information

British and International Golf Greenkeepers Association
www.bigga.org.uk

Institute of Groundsmanship
www.iog.org

ENVIRONMENT, ANIMALS AND PLANTS

255

Qualifications and courses

There are no formal entry requirements for horticultural work, but some employers will prioritise candidates who have GCSEs/National 5s (A*–C/A–C), including a science, a BTEC Levels 2–3 in Horticulture, or the City & Guilds Levels 2–3 Certificate/Diploma in Horticulture (0078). Certificates of competence from the City & Guilds may also be required if your job involves dangerous tasks such as operating chainsaws or pesticide use. Work experience may also prove helpful.

There are a number of useful vocational qualifications that can enhance your skill set, such as the NVQ/SVQ in Horticulture (Levels 1–4) or a qualification in horticulture/practical horticulture from the Royal Horticultural Society (Levels 1–3). There are also Foundation degrees and degrees in horticulture available.

A Kew Diploma from the Royal Botanical Gardens can be obtained after 3 years. They also offer a 3-year Kew Apprenticeship and the International Diploma in Botanic Garden Management. Both the Royal Botanical Gardens and the Royal Horticultural Society, amongst others, offer work placements with accreditation.

What the work involves

You will undertake a variety of horticulturally related tasks and have a number of different responsibilities such as mowing lawns and tidying flowerbeds. You will also need to maintain equipment and tools and look after plants by checking for disease, feeding, watering, pruning and spraying them. To produce new stock, you will plant out cuttings and seedlings. You will also pot-up and pack plants for selling and shipping.

You may also be asked to strategically place plants in order to create naturalistic settings if employed by a botanical garden.

As a manager you will supervise, train and recruit staff and look after the day-to-day running of the organisation. You will decide which plants to grow, manage the budgets, ensure deliveries are despatched on time and develop a business plan for now and in the future.

Type of person suited to this work

Much of your day will involve carrying, bending and working with the plants, so you will need to be physically fit.

You will be outdoors for much of the time working in all weathers, doing dirty work.

These jobs could be difficult if you suffer from pollen or dust allergies.

Working conditions

You will normally work a 40-hour week and could be based at a garden centre, plant nursery, in a park or public garden. You will often have to work weekends and late evenings.

Work could be seasonal with more hours required at certain times of the year. You will spend much of your time outdoors, in all weathers.

Future prospects

There is a constant demand for workers, especially for those with experience.

Horticultural jobs are available within major plant producers, national parks, public gardens and local and national garden shops/nurseries.

After gaining experience and qualifications you could progress to a role as supervisor or manager, freelance work or start up your own shop. There is the opportunity to undertake training to help career development. The British Agrochemical Standards Inspection Scheme (BASIS) offers a number of courses on a range of technical subjects including fertilisers, pesticides and cultivation.

Advantages/disadvantages

There is a good mix of practical and managerial work.

These jobs combine lots of skills and can be very rewarding.

This is an expanding market with lots of opportunities.

Money guide

Salaries for horticultural workers are between £12,000 and £19,000 per year.

Horticultural managers can earn a starting salary of between £18,000 and £22,000 a year.

Salaries for senior managerial roles are around £40,000 per year.

Related opportunities

- Arboricultural Worker/Tree Surgeon p243
- Gardener/Garden Designer p253
- Groundsperson/Greenkeeper p255

Further information

British Agrochemical Standards Inspection Scheme (BASIS)
www.basis-reg.co.uk

Grow
www.growcareers.info

Institute of Horticulture
www.horticulture.org.uk

KENNEL WORKER

Qualifications and courses

There are no formal educational requirements although some employers will favour candidates with GCSEs/National 5s (A*–C/A–C) in English and/or Maths. As this is a practical vocation, paid or unpaid experience working with animals will vastly improve your chance of employability – most local organisations, as well as the RSPCA and Dogs Trust, require volunteers.

The Guide Dogs for the Blind Association can provide work experience for applicants aged over 18 and also offer the Dog Care Technician Training Programme for candidates who have 5 GCSEs/National 5s (A*–C/A–C) and 2 A levels/H grades. Hearing Dogs for the Deaf also recruit volunteer puppy socialisers from people who have experience of looking after young dogs and have an approved home.

Other relevant qualifications include the NVQs/SVQs Levels 1–3 and the BTEC Level 2 Certificate/Extended Certificate/Diploma in Animal Care, and the City & Guilds Levels 2–3 Certificate/Diploma in Animal Care (0074). There is also the BTEC Level 3 Certificate/Subsidiary Diploma/Diploma/Extended Diploma in Animal Management. The Animal Care College also offers training programmes which may prove helpful.

There are several apprenticeship/Skillseekers schemes for those aged between 16 and 24, such as the Apprenticeship in Animal Care. Training takes place on the job and is given by the manager or an experienced staff member and you are given the opportunity to combine practical work experience with study for a professional qualification.

What the work involves

There are lots of types of kennels including boarding, pet sanctuary, breeding and quarantine kennels for animals brought from overseas.

Administrative skills may be useful as you might need to answer the phones, take payments and keep records when medicine is administered or if any behavioural problems are displayed. As well as cleaning the kennels, you will feed, exercise and check on the general health of the dogs and cats.

In a pet sanctuary you might be required to show prospective owners around and answer any questions they have on animal care.

Type of person suited to this work

You will need to enjoy spending time outdoors and not mind getting dirty. Some of the animals you will be working with might have behavioural problems or nervous dispositions and so you will need to be calm and patient. A good knowledge of small pet care is vital.

You will require a good level of fitness as you will spend a large part of the day being active.

You should have strong communication skills and the ability to work well alone or as part of a team.

Working conditions

This is physically demanding work involving walking dogs and cleaning the kennels. You may work shifts and your hours will probably include evenings, weekends and public holidays.

Many animals will be frightened and confused so they could be aggressive; you will therefore have to be aware of not only your own, but the safety of those around you.

You will spend a lot of time outdoors in all weathers and the work can be smelly, dirty and noisy.

Future prospects

There are approximately 3,500 kennels in the UK, although the number of jobs available does not tend to fluctuate much. However, you could work for national charitable organisations such as the RSPCA, Guide Dogs for the Blind Association or a private breeder.

The army and police recruit service and civilian kennel staff, and it may be possible to use your experience to enter associated professions, such as dog trainer, RSPCA or SSPCA inspector or veterinary nurse.

In larger kennels there may be the opportunity to progress to the position of supervisor or manager.

Advantages/disadvantages

This is not a 9am–5pm job and the unsocial hours may affect your social or family life.

There is the possibility of being attacked by an animal.

It can be rewarding to help nervous animals become more friendly over time due to your care.

Many kennels may ask you to only work part time or seasonally.

Money guide

Pay will depend on the nature of your employer.

If you are working for a private kennels £12,000–£16,000 is likely. For animal charities and larger organisations you may get more. The RSPCA offers a minimum of £10,500 to its kennel workers (known as Animal Care Assistants).

You may be provided with accommodation and extra pay could be offered for overtime.

Related opportunities

- Dog Trainer/Handler p246
- Veterinary Nurse p265
- Zookeeper p268

Further information

Animal Care College
www.animalcarecollege.co.uk

Guide Dogs for the Blind Association
www.guidedogs.org.uk

Lantra
www.lantra.co.uk

Royal Society for the Prevention of Cruelty to Animals
www.rspca.org.uk

Qualifications and courses

You will need a bachelor's degree in landscape architecture that has been accredited by the Landscape Institute (LI) or, if not, a relevant first degree followed by a LI-accredited postgraduate qualification will qualify you for this profession. In order to gain entry to a degree course you will usually need at least 2 A levels/3 H grades and 5 GCSEs/National 5s (A*–C/A–C), or a diploma in an environmental or land-based subject. In order to gain entry to a postgraduate course you will usually need to complete an Honours degree in a relevant subject. It is not possible to gain accreditation with only a HND or Foundation degree.

Entrants who have completed an LI-accredited course can work towards chartered membership of the LI through the Professional Practice Examination.

Courses are also available at land-based colleges of further education, which offer a range of BTEC qualifications in relevant subjects.

Practical experience in a landscape-related field is very useful when applying to postgraduate courses.

The profession welcomes mature applicants.

What the work involves

You will design or develop a new or existing outside space. You will then make a plan, saying what plantings should be included, and calculate the cost. You will then see the project through to completion by supervising the work on-site.

Although you will understand garden design, you will also have to understand civil engineering, horticulture and planning law.

You could work on projects aimed to regenerate towns and cities and developments to combat climate change.

Type of person suited to this work

You will have to enjoy being outdoors and want to make a difference to the environment. You will need to be happy in the open in both the summer and the winter and be prepared to spend time away from home on some jobs.

You will have to be creative and have excellent design and drawing skills that may require computer-aided design (CAD).

You will be interested in making, building and constructing hard landscaping but will appreciate and understand the impact that different plants can have.

You should be physically strong and able to use machinery and hand tools. You must be creative, artistic and have strong computer skills. You should have solid communication and negotiation skills.

Working conditions

Landscape architects spend a lot of time in the design studio sitting at a computer and drawing board or attending meetings on-site at clients' premises.

You could spend about a quarter of your time at the project site, supervising operations. Some of your time will also be spent on the phone dealing with contractors and suppliers.

Site work will involve being outdoors in all weather. Average hours are about 37 per week, Monday to Friday. You may spend some time away from home.

Future prospects

Due to the impact of home improvement programmes, designing and developing gardens is now a popular and growing business. However, it can be a competitive area so many choose self-employment.

Organisations who recruit landscape staff include local authorities, botanical gardens, large private estates, the National Trust, English Heritage, building contractors and landscape design houses.

If you choose to become self-employed your success will depend upon finding customers, the quality of your work and how quickly you can build your reputation.

Advantages/disadvantages

There is a good mix of practical hands-on work with planning, design and meeting people.

You will get satisfaction from knowing your work will have an impact on future generations.

You could get wet, cold, hot and dusty.

You will not be able to do this work if you suffer from pollen or dust allergies.

Money guide

Starting salaries for a graduate landscape architect are around £20,000 per year.

This can increase to between £23,000 and £28,000 with three to five years' experience.

Once qualified as a chartered landscape architect, salaries could range from £25,000 to in excess of £45,000 a year.

If you work in private practice these figures could increase substantially, especially if you become partner.

Related opportunities

- Architect p58
- Landscaper/Landscape Manager p259
- Town Planner/Planning Technician p115

Further information

Be a Landscape Architect
www.bealandscapearchitect.com

Grow
www.growcareers.info

Landscape Design Trust
www.landscapedesigntrust.org

Landscape Institute
www.landscapeinstitute.org

Qualifications and courses

Landscaper

There are no required qualifications but relevant GCSEs/ National 5s, the National Proficiency Tests Council (NPTC) Certificates, the RHS Certificates/Diplomas in Horticulture (Levels 1–3), and the BTEC in Horticulture (Levels 1–5) are useful.

A driving licence is often required.

Landscape manager

Although there are no set qualifications this is still an extremely competitive industry. A HNC/HND, degree or postgraduate qualification in a relevant subject, such as garden design, would prove valuable. An NVQ Level 4 in Amenity Horticulture Management or a Level 3 Diploma in Work-Based Environmental Conservation may also be useful.

The Landscape Institute (LI) has accredited some degree courses, the completion of which can then offer you a pathway to chartership. Many employers may expect you to already be or working towards being a chartered member of the LI. While undertaking the pathway you will be mentored by a fully qualified professional member of the LI for 2 years before completing an oral exam.

Experience with computer-based design applications is also advisable.

For both positions it is possible to obtain a ROLO card. This entitles you to membership of the Register of Land Based Operatives. To qualify for this you will need a Level 2 or 3 Work Based Diploma (a new NVQ course), and accredited health and safety training. More information is available on the British Association of Landscape Industries (BALI) website.

What the work involves

Landscaper

You will do the practical work of turning a landscape architect's plan into reality.

You will operate machinery, carry out planting schemes, put up fences, create ponds, lay paths, construct decking and make terraces.

Landscape manager

You will use your specialist knowledge to advise others on the development and maintenance of a wide range of landscapes such as historic gardens, motorway verges and public parks. You will decide where to place features like footpaths and play areas, oversee the people contracted to carry out work, complete reports and manage budgets.

Type of person suited to this work

You must enjoy working outdoors and want to make a difference to the environment. You will be interested in making, building and constructing hard landscaping but will also appreciate and understand the impact that different plants can have.

Landscaper

You will need to be physically strong in order to use machinery and hand tools, be fit and enjoy the physical demands of this manual profession.

Landscape manager

An understanding of the laws surrounding the environment and the countryside is essential.

Working conditions

Landscaper

You will be outdoors in all weathers creating the design and working on landscape maintenance. There is a lot of physical labour involved such as heavy lifting, operating machinery and digging. You will need to wear protective clothing.

Landscape manager

You will work in an office for a lot of your time, but you will also go out for meetings to check and supervise work on-site. On average you will work 37 hours a week, though overtime may be required. You may need to spend time away from home.

Future prospects

Landscape staff work for local authorities, botanical gardens, large private estates, the National Trust, English Heritage, building contractors and landscape design houses.

Landscape managers in government can follow a structured career path; in other organisations you may find yourself moving companies in order to progress.

Self-employment is also an option.

Advantages/disadvantages

You will get satisfaction from knowing your work will have an impact on future generations.

You could get wet, cold, hot and dusty.

You will not be able to do this work if you suffer from pollen or dust allergies.

Money guide

Landscaper

Starting salaries are around £16,000–£20,000 per year increasing to £22,000–£30,000 for those with experience.

Landscape manager

Starting salaries are around £20,000 rising to between £24,000 and £38,500 with experience.

Related opportunities

- Gardener/Garden Designer p253
- Groundsperson/Greenkeeper p255
- Landscape Architect/Designer p258

Further information

British Association of Landscape Industries (BALI)
www.bali.org.uk

Landscape Institute
www.landscapeinstitute.org

Qualifications and courses

No formal qualifications are required for this work although 5 GCSEs/National 5s (A*–E/A–E) may be helpful. The Advanced Apprenticeship in Horticulture provides a good route to training as a parks officer.

Many people begin their career as gardeners/ horticulturists. NVQs/SVQs in Amenity Horticulture (Levels 1–2) are available and are useful qualifications to take at the early stages of your career. City & Guilds also offer several relevant courses such as the Level 1 Award in Practical Horticulture Skills (7573), the Levels 1–3 Award/Certificate/Diploma in Work-Based Horticulture (0065), and the Levels 2–3 Certificate/Diploma in Horticulture (0078).

Other training options include the BTEC qualifications in Horticulture or Countryside Management (Levels 2–3), the BTEC Level 4 HNC in Horticulture and the BTEC Level 5 HND in Horticulture. Due to job competition a Foundation or Honours degree in horticulture, landscape design, landscape management or a related subject may be required. The minimum requirements for entry on to a Foundation degree or HND are normally 1 A level/2 H grades and 4 GCSEs/National 5s (A*–C/A–C); for a degree course the minimum requirements are normally 2 A levels/3 H grades and 5 GCSEs/National 5s (A*–C/ A–C), usually including English and Maths, or equivalent.

The Royal Horticultural Society (RHS) also provides courses from entry to degree level, such as the Level 1 Award in Practical Horticulture, the Diploma in the Principles and Practices of Horticulture (Levels 2–3) and the Master of Horticulture (RHS) Award.

What the work involves

You will supervise the gardeners and horticulturists who maintain and look after local parks, sports and recreation centres, gardens and public places. As well as planning new planting schemes you will organise staffing rotas and annual work programmes. You will be responsible for the recruitment and monitoring of your team, as well as budget control.

You will have to liaise with your employer (normally your local government) and other department colleagues.

Type of person suited to this work

To do this work you must be organised, able to plan ahead and capable of managing people. You will need technical and practical horticultural skills, an understanding of budgets and you should be an effective negotiator.

You must have a good understanding of plants and how to present outside spaces so they look good throughout the year.

To do this job you will need to be physically fit and passionate about your work.

Working conditions

You will normally work Monday to Friday but at busier times, particularly in the spring and summer, you may do extra hours.

You will be provided with protective clothing and you will have to ensure that health and safety rules are followed by your teams. This work might be unsuitable if you suffer from asthma, pollen allergies or some skin conditions.

A small part of your job will involve working in an office at a computer where you will spend time ordering plants and materials.

Future prospects

Most parks officers are employed by a local or county council. A small number work for companies who win park management contracts. Some jobs have been hit by cutbacks from the recession, and cutbacks are still occurring across the country. This may affect the number of jobs available.

It is likely that you will start your career as a gardener or horticulturist and then progress to a parks officer role once you have gained sufficient experience.

You may also move into department or divisional management within local/county authorities.

Advantages/disadvantages

This is a mixture of indoor and outdoor work, using a variety of skills.

You will use your experience and knowledge to make a difference in your local community.

You might have to wait for opportunities to become available or be willing to relocate to progress in this career.

Money guide

Your earnings depend on the size and location of your local authority employer, and the number of staff and sites that you are responsible for.

Starting salaries are usually around £17,000.

Experienced parks officers could earn up to £27,000.

Those employed in a senior role could achieve between £30,000 and £37,000.

Related opportunities

- Countryside Ranger p245
- Groundsperson/Greenkeeper p255
- Horticultural Worker/Manager p256

Further information

Chartered Institute for the Management of Sport and Physical Activity
www.cimspa.co.uk

Convention of Scottish Local Authorities
www.cosla.gov.uk

Local Government Careers
www.lgjobs.com

Qualifications and courses

There is no specific route into this career but a degree is required to either join the Association of Pet Behaviour Counsellors (APBC) or to be registered as a Certified Clinical Animal Behaviourist by the Association for the Study of Animal Behaviour (ASAB). Candidates are advised to take a degree in one of the following subjects: biological science, behavioural science, animal behaviour or equine science. ASAB and APBC provide lists of approved courses.

Typical entry requirements for an appropriate Honours degree are 2 A levels/3 H grades (which should include Biology and/or another science subject) and 5 GCSEs/ National 5s (A*–C/A–C).

Those who are already employed within the animal care industry, for example as an animal welfare officer, may be able to progress into a role in pet behaviour counselling. Short training courses and diplomas are available from the Canine & Feline Behaviour Association (CFBA) and VetNet's Courses in Animal & Veterinary Education (CAVE).

It is essential that all entrants to this profession have practical experience working with animals. Opportunities to volunteer with animals in your local area are available on the Do-it website and through the RSPCA, SSPCA and the Blue Cross.

What the work involves

Pet behaviour counsellors advise owners whose pets have developed inappropriate and dangerous behaviour.

Although working with all domestic animals, you will probably focus on dogs, cats and horses. Typical problems include aggressive behaviour, soiling or destructiveness. You will also aid owners in achieving general control over their pets.

You could be connected to a veterinary practice, work in kennels, catteries and welfare societies or be freelance.

Type of person suited to this work

You will need a strong interest in animals, their care and welfare. As this job also involves working with the owner, you will have to be able to communicate with people too! You need to be tactful but also assertive.

Working with animals can be messy and smelly work, so you must be prepared to get dirty. You will also need to have lots of patience and the ability to remain calm.

You should be good at science, especially biology, and have a certain degree of business acumen along with the ability to keep records and accounts.

Working conditions

This work takes place in clinics and often in clients' homes so a driving licence would be beneficial. You could be indoors or outside in all weathers.

Some jobs will involve evening and weekend work, especially if you visit your clients and animals in their own homes. Most pet behaviour counsellors are self-employed and set their own hours.

The work can be dusty, dirty and physically demanding, so you will need to be fit and active. This profession is unsuitable for those with animal allergies.

Future prospects

Although demand across the canine and equine areas has increased due to television programmes and press coverage, there are still very limited career opportunities for this job.

Some of the larger animal welfare charities are starting to employ staff with these skills but most pet behaviour counsellors are self-employed and running their own practices.

Few people are able to work full time, so expect to supplement your earnings by teaching, lecturing and writing papers on animal behaviour.

Advantages/disadvantages

You will have the satisfaction of working with animals and improving their quality of life.

Some owners may be resistant to changing the way they deal with their pets which could be challenging.

This job offers the opportunity for self-employment but it can be difficult to establish a client list.

Money guide

Most pet behaviour counsellors are self-employed and charge fees of £85–£250 per consultation, depending on their experience and the size of the business.

Newly qualified pet behaviour counsellors can expect to earn around £15,000 per year.

With experience, you could achieve £25,000–£35,000.

Few people make a full-time living from this industry. Many supplement their income by lecturing or writing articles.

Related opportunities

- Animal Physiotherapist p241
- Animal Welfare Officer p242
- Dog Trainer/Handler p246
- Veterinary Surgeon p266

Further information

Association for the Study of Animal Behaviour
www.asab.org

Association of Pet Behaviour Counsellors
www.apbc.org.uk

ENVIRONMENT, ANIMALS AND PLANTS

Qualifications and courses

Racehorse trainers need to be licensed with the British Horseracing Authority with one of the 3 types of licence: a Combined Licence (which permits the training of horses for both flat and jump races), a Jump Only Licence and a Flat Only Licence.

All candidates for a trainer's licence must have the RQF Level 3 Diploma in Work Based Racehorse Care and Management and they need to attend 3 week-long courses in Racehorse Management, Business Skills for Racehorse Trainers and Staff Management.

The British Horseracing Authority also requires all applicants to have at least 5 years' experience working in training establishments which should include at least 2 years in a senior position, such as assistant trainer in a racing yard. Those who have been a successful jockey will often become a racehorse trainer later in their career.

What the work involves

Trainers usually own or lease their stables and train horses for owners as well as owning horses themselves. Most trainers start as a jockey or assistant trainer and progress to running their own yard.

You will have to prepare the horses for races by increasing their stamina, technique and fitness. In order to do this you will have to create training regimes.

To be successful you will work closely with everyone in your team including other professionals such as vets and farriers.

Type of person suited to this work

You should have a strong interest in horse racing, a flair for business and an inherent talent for training horses. You will need the ability to communicate well and be a strong leader and manager of people.

This role is ideal for people who love caring for horses, have the right temperament to work with them and plenty of patience.

You will need to enjoy working outside in all weathers as this is where most of your duties will take place. You should be a practical person who is willing to get their hands dirty. You will require a certain level of physical fitness.

You need to be able to foster and build strong relationships with clients, particularly if self-employed. Creating and developing a good reputation is essential in order to get new business, and how you interact and present yourself to clients will be an important facet of that, as well as your skill as a trainer.

Working conditions

Much of your work will take place outdoors. In the summer months it may be hot, smelly and dusty, whereas in winter it could be cold, wet and muddy. You will also spend some time in an office environment.

When riding you will wear a hard hat and a body protector. Horses can be unpredictable and so there is a certain level of risk involved.

The hours are long and include weekends. There will also be some travel involved if you are required to attend race meetings. A driving licence would be useful.

Future prospects

There are around 600 licensed trainers in the UK.

Before you are granted a licence, you need several years' experience as an assistant trainer. Your success will then depend on attracting and retaining the owners of good quality horses, and lots of luck! You will need to build up a strong client base in order to progress.

Managing your own successful yard may enable you to employ staff to complete some of the more mundane tasks.

Advantages/disadvantages

This can be an extremely lucrative profession if you are successful.

Injury risks are high in all animal-related careers. This could affect your long-term career security.

Looking after horses is not a 9am to 5pm job and the hours may affect your social or family life.

Money guide

As you are likely to be self-employed, your earnings will depend on the size, success and reputation of your yard. Most yards are usually fairly small or modest in size, but large trainers can be responsible for up to 150–200 horses.

You will establish your own fees and these will be influenced by a variety of factors including costs and the market rates.

As a guide, a trainer can earn anything from £15,000 per year to over £50,000 if they are very experienced and have a good record of winning.

Related opportunities

- Farm Manager p247
- Farrier p249
- Groom/Stable Hand/Stud Hand p254

Further information

Association of British Riding Schools
www.abrs-info.org

British Horse Society
www.bhs.org.uk

British Racing School
www.brs.org.uk

RECYCLING OFFICER

Qualifications and courses

A degree is not essential for entry to this career, and a demonstrable interest in and knowledge of environmental concerns and recycling and waste reduction principles may be of equal or higher value to employers in this industry.

One entry route is through a Level 3 Advanced Apprenticeship in Sustainable Resource Management, accredited by the Chartered Institution of Wastes Management. Apprentices will work towards competence and knowledge qualifications such as a Level 3 Diploma for Sustainable Recycling Activities (Supervisory) and Level 3 Certificate in Principles of Sustainable Resource Management. Apprenticeships take between 12 months and 2 years to complete, combining on-the-job experience with formal learning at a college or university (known as a 'training provider').

A bachelor's degree or HND may be beneficial when looking for work, or could improve progression prospects later in your career. Relevant degree subjects include environmental science, biology, earth sciences, and materials science. Entry onto a degree is usually with 2 A levels/3 H grades and 5 GCSEs/National 5s (A*–C/A–C) and courses typically take 3–4 years to complete.

Access to other undergraduate qualifications accredited by the CIWM may be possible, such as a HNC or Foundation degree in Wastes Management or HNC in Sustainable Resource Management.

A postgraduate degree is not a requirement for entry to a career as a recycling officer, but may be helpful. There are CIWM-accredited postgraduate qualifications such as an MSc in Environmental Technology or Waste and Resource Management, or Postgraduate Certificate (PGCert) in Energy and Fuels From Waste.

What the work involves

Recycling officers typically work for local authorities and councils, or contractors and environmental agencies. They are responsible for developing waste management and reduction policies such as recycling initiatives and recyclable waste collection services.

Work involves elements of administration such as monitoring use of recycling facilities in a district or locality and monitoring waste management and recycling budgets. Additionally, you may be responsible for outreach and media initiatives, planning campaigns and organising volunteers.

Type of person suited to this work

A keen awareness of recycling, sustainability and environmental issues is a must.

Excellent communication and presentation skills will be useful as work will involve teaching others about recycling and sustainability through campaigns.

You'll need to have outstanding organisation and project management skills in order to oversee campaigns and coordinate colleagues.

Working conditions

You will typically work 9am to 5pm, Monday to Friday. Extra hours at evenings or weekends may be a requirement when implementing new initiatives or attending meetings.

Flexitime is commonly available for roles in local or national government.

You will split your time between office-based work, carrying out administration and working on initiatives and schemes; and field work, travelling to waste management sites or presenting at schools or community events.

Future prospects

This is a young and energetic industry and development is rapid as public concern over the environment and sustainable living grows.

Routes for career progression are developing and strengthening. You could begin your career in voluntary or internship work as a campaigner or office administrator, and progress through roles such as campaign manager for a local authority or environmental agency, to more senior roles in local government.

Opportunities for self-employment are rare as most work is carried out by local authorities and environmental agencies. It is possible, however, to move towards freelance consultancy work, particularly as some aspects of waste management have been privatised.

Advantages/disadvantages

This job has plenty of different elements to it, from inspecting recycling sites to giving presentations to schools, so no two days will be the same.

You may be called to work outside in all weathers.

You may have to present to audiences who aren't as enthusiastic as you are about environmental issues.

Money guide

Apprentices on the Sustainable Resource Management apprenticeship can earn an average salary of £12,600 a year.

Starting salaries are usually between £19,000 and £28,000 a year.

In management roles you could earn up to £45,000 a year.

Progression to senior roles for a local authority could see you earning between £40,000 and £60,000 a year.

Related opportunities

- Environmental Engineer p211
- Environmental Scientist p504

Further information

Chartered Institution of Wastes Management
www.ciwm.co.uk

Energy & Utility Skills
www.euskills.co.uk

Qualifications and courses

There are no formal academic requirements to become a deckhand but you must be at least 16 years old. School leavers have the option to apply for the Apprenticeship in Sea Fishing. Alternatively, Seafish offer the Introduction to Commercial Fishing course and also run a Sea Fishing Apprenticeship programme in collaboration with the Maritime Skills Alliance. In England, apprenticeships are delivered through organisations such as the Whitby and District Fishing Industry Training School and, in Scotland, through the NAFC Marine Centre and North East Scotland College.

New entrants must take the Marine Coastguard Agency (MCA) approved basic safety training course. This programme consists of 4 days of training in sea survival, first aid, fire fighting and basic health and safety.

To become a skipper, you must have at least 2 years' experience working as a deckhand. Those who wish to be a limited area skipper (working around the UK coastline) must be over the age of 20 and have Seafish's Deck Officer (Fishing Vessel) Class 2 certificate. To work as an unlimited area skipper (fishing beyond UK coastal waters) you need to be at least 21 years old and study for Seafish's Deck Officer (Fishing Vessel) Class 1 certificate.

For those who wish to develop further skills and knowledge, Seafish offer various short courses on topics such as basic seamanship, net repair, navigation, engineering and stability awareness.

What the work involves

Deckhands are crew members on sea-going fishing vessels. You will spend anything from a few days to several weeks at sea. You will drop the nets, wind them in, sort the catch and then box it up. If your vessel has the facilities on board, you might help to process fish by gutting and filleting. You might keep watch, steer the ship and use winching gear. Duties may also include vessel maintenance and cooking.

Skippers are in charge of fishing vessels. Their role includes overseeing health and safety, navigation, paperwork and crew management. They also manage the business arrangements to ensure that fishing trips return a profit.

You may also choose to work with holiday companies who run independent boat charters, sea safari or wildlife trips for tourists.

Type of person suited to this work

This work is suited to someone with practical skills and a high level of physical fitness. You should be able to cope with challenging conditions while remaining positive and focused.

A deckhand needs teamwork skills and the ability to follow instructions. Skippers should be comfortable managing and leading a team of people and able to take control of situations.

Due to the physicality of the industry, you should be physically fit and comfortable with working manually for long periods of time.

Working conditions

This is a very tough outdoor job. You will work in cold, wet and rainy conditions during the winter and hot weather during the summer.

Fishing is the most dangerous industry in the UK, with big machinery and rough seas producing a combination of risks which must be treated with great caution.

You will have to work long hours at sea, often for substantial periods away from home, and conditions below deck may be basic and cramped. There could also be some heavy lifting and carrying.

Future prospects

The career progression route is from deckhand to ship's mate and then skipper with most jobs being located around the coasts of Scotland and the south-west and east of England.

Many jobs are within family-owned businesses which have been in existence for generations, making it difficult to find work. Some are seasonal, meaning long-term security can be difficult.

Advantages/disadvantages

This job is ideal for those who love working outdoors.

You will have the opportunity to develop strong relationships with the other crew members.

Your social and family life may be difficult as you could be away at sea for extended periods of time.

Jobs are limited to certain locations in the UK.

Money guide

Earnings from fishing can vary extensively as you are often paid a share of the total value of the catch. For this reason, pay depends upon the type of boat you work on, the amount of fish caught and the weather conditions.

New entrants can expect to receive around £10,000 per year as a starting salary. With experience, earnings can rise to £26,000.

Depending on the size and value of the catches, skippers can earn between £10,000 and £25,000 a year.

Skippers who work for large companies could achieve up to £65,000.

Related opportunities

- Coastguard Watch Assistant/Officer p534
- Fish Farmer p250
- Merchant Navy Deck Officer/Rating p598

Further information

Maritime and Coastguard Agency
www.gov.uk/mca

Scottish Fishermen's Federation
www.sff.co.uk

Seafish
www.seafish.org

VETERINARY NURSE

Qualifications and courses

You usually enter this profession through work-based training. For those aged 16–24, the Apprenticeship in Veterinary Nursing is available at Advanced Level.

Alternatively, you can study for the Level 3 Diploma in Veterinary Nursing from the Royal College of Veterinary Surgeons (RCVS). This can be completed on a full-time basis or alongside work in a veterinary practice. Qualifying takes 2–3 years and involves practical training and college-based learning.

Entry requirements for the RCVS scheme are 5 GCSEs/National 5s (A*–C/A–C) including English, Maths and 2 science subjects. Trainees must be at least 16 years old and there is strong competition for places. For those without these qualifications, an alternative route may be through the ABC Level 2 Certificate for Animal Nursing Assistants, the City & Guilds Level 2 Diploma for Veterinary Care Assistants (0048), the CQ Level 2 Diploma in Veterinary Nursing, or the BTEC Level 3 Certificate in Animal Management.

You could also complete an RCVS-approved veterinary nursing degree or Foundation degree. Entry requirements are 2 A levels/3 H grades, ideally in Biology and Chemistry, and 5 GCSEs/National 5s (A*–C/A–C).

Work experience with a veterinary practice or an animal charity would be helpful in supporting any job or course application.

What the work involves

Veterinary nurses assist vets in their work by helping to treat animals suffering from disease and injury. Most nurses also undertake the day-to-day care of animals recovering from treatment within veterinary hospitals.

As well as carrying out simple procedures, such as changing dressings and nail trimming, you will also examine blood and urine samples, give injections, prepare and help in the theatre and sterilise the instruments after use. You might also work in reception, giving an initial assessment of animals, ordering drugs and arranging future appointments.

Type of person suited to this work

You will have to be passionate about animals and want to help them. You need the capacity to learn scientific information about different diseases and treatments.

Although lots of animals recover, some of this work will be distressing. This means you will have to work in a practical and unsentimental way.

As you will work closely with animal owners, you will also need to have excellent communication skills to explain what is happening to their pet.

You may need administrative and IT skills to carry out duties on reception.

Working conditions

Depending on the type of practice you are employed by, your role may involve working with small animals, horses, farm animals, or even zoo animals.

Most of your work will take place indoors, possibly in a treatment room, operating theatre or on the reception desk. If you work with large animals, you may have to travel to visit farms or zoos.

Working with animals can be noisy and dirty. This job would be unsuitable for those with animal allergies or a fear of blood. You will usually be provided with a uniform and you will be expected to wear protective clothing during some procedures.

Future prospects

You could be employed by zoos, wildlife centres, animal welfare centres, veterinary hospitals and charities such as the People's Dispensary for Sick Animals (PDSA).

With experience, you could progress to become a supervisor, practice manager or head nurse, or move into related areas such as research.

You could also lecture, specialise in an area such as animal behaviour or become a representative for a veterinary drugs company.

Advantages/disadvantages

Helping sick animals is very rewarding.

The role is interesting, with lots of variety and the chance to meet many people and animals.

You will deal with illness and death which can be stressful and upsetting.

You may have to work irregular hours which will affect your social life.

Money guide

You can expect a starting salary of around £12,000.

Once qualified and as you gain experience, your earnings can increase to between £14,000 and £22,000.

Senior nurses or supervisors can achieve up to £26,000 depending on the size and type of the practice they work for.

Related opportunities

- Dog Trainer/Handler p246
- Veterinary Surgeon p266
- Zookeeper p268

Further information

British Veterinary Nursing Association
www.bvna.org.uk

People's Dispensary for Sick Animals (PDSA)
www.pdsa.org.uk

ENVIRONMENT, ANIMALS AND PLANTS

Qualifications and courses

In order to practise as a vet, all candidates are required to have a degree in veterinary science/veterinary medicine and register with the Royal College of Veterinary Surgeons (RCVS). Degrees approved by the RCVS are currently available at 7 institutions in the UK. Normal minimum entry requirements for a degree are 3 A levels/4 H grades including Biology and 1 or 2 from Chemistry, Physics or Maths. Depending upon the individual university, you will be expected to have either 2 A grades and a B or 3 A grades (or equivalent). A good range of GCSEs/National 5s (A*–C/A–C) is required. For the University of Cambridge, an additional admissions test, the BioMedical Admissions Test (BMAT), will need to be sat.

Degree courses usually last 5 years but courses may include an optional additional year in which students gain an Honours degree in a related science subject. All courses include the 38 weeks of practical experience required by the RCVS.

All universities expect applicants to demonstrate their passion for animals and commitment to a career as a veterinary surgeon by undertaking relevant work experience. Candidates could work on farms, in stables, kennels or vets and opportunities to volunteer with animals are available on the Do-it website or through the RSPCA, SSPCA and the Blue Cross.

What the work involves

Vets treat animals that are suffering because of disease or injury. They administer vaccinations, prescribe drugs and deliver newborn animals. They also advise owners on caring for their animals. You might carry out surgical operations and be involved in the inspection of livestock and meat.

You could work in local practices and become a specialist carrying out complex surgery on a certain part of the anatomy or become an expert on a particular animal.

Type of person suited to this work

You must have the capacity to learn large amounts of complex scientific information and apply this in a practical way to treat animals.

Some of your work will be sad or distressing, so you will have to work in a practical and unsentimental way. You must have good communication skills to talk to the owners.

Working with large animals is physically demanding so you will need to be in good health. This job will not suit those who dislike the sight of blood or suffer from animal allergies.

Working conditions

Your working conditions will depend on the type of practice that employs you. In veterinary practices for small animals, you will spend a lot of time in the surgery. Working with farm livestock and horses, you will travel to visit your patients.

Some of this work will be unpleasant or smelly and involve travelling long distances. A driving licence is required.

Your job may be dangerous as animals can be unpredictable. You will work long hours and be on call to cover emergencies 24/7.

Future prospects

With a strong record of work experience, there are still jobs and practices to join upon graduation, although it is not as easy as it was owing to an increased intake of veterinary science students by RCVS-accredited institutions.

As a graduate, you will normally join an established practice. With experience, you could progress to become a partner (effectively part-owner) of a practice.

There are around 20,000 registered vets in the UK. The majority of these work in private practice. Some vets work for the government or for firms researching and producing animal pharmaceuticals.

Advantages/disadvantages

The training is long and very competitive to enter. In this career you will never stop learning – more experience will make you a better vet.

It can be a very stressful but rewarding job, with lots of responsibility.

You will have to deal with the death of some of the animals you treat, including times when you put them down.

Money guide

Salaries vary according to experience, specialisations, and the size, type and location of the practice you work in.

Newly qualified vets have a starting salary of £21,000–£33,000.

As you gain experience, your earnings can range from £40,000 to £44,000.

A senior vet with many years experience can earn between £50,000 and £70,000 a year.

Employers may include accommodation and a company car within your benefits package.

Related opportunities

- Farm Manager p247
- Hospital Doctor p294
- Veterinary Nurse p265

Further information

British Veterinary Association
www.bva.co.uk

People's Dispensary for Sick Animals (PDSA)
www.pdsa.org.uk

Royal College of Veterinary Surgeons
www.rcvs.org.uk

Qualifications and courses

Fisheries officers generally enter with a degree/HND in subjects such as marine sciences, environmental sciences, and land management. Gaining a relevant postgraduate qualification may help candidates. If you do not possess these qualifications you could build up relevant work experience as a water bailiff.

In England and Wales, there are no set requirements for those wishing to become a water bailiff. In Scotland, you have to pass a training module set by the Institute of Fisheries Management and in Northern Ireland, you need at least 5 GCSEs/National 5s at C grade or above, including English and Maths.

Basic practical fishery experience is essential as competition is fierce. Many people work unpaid for angling clubs or undertake voluntary work on fishing boats. The Environment Agency (EA) also offers a summer placement programme.

The Scottish Institute of Fisheries Management (IFM) offers a course in Fisheries Management. You can choose between a 1-year certificate or 2-year diploma, covering all aspects of working with fish and pond life. You can also follow an NVQ in Fisheries Management if you choose to do so.

This is a popular second career, and if you want to get into the field then any experience you can gain in gamekeeping, security work, police work or farm work will be advantageous. Medical examinations usually need to be passed.

What the work involves

Water bailiffs work outdoors, maintaining lakes or rivers and everything that lives in them, for the purpose of legitimate recreational use.

You will confront 2 main problems in your work: breaches of the law and ecological problems.

You will basically be a gamekeeper for water. Water bailiffs have the same powers of search and arrest as police officers. You would mostly be looking out for poachers and lawbreakers, and you will be granted a warrant by the Environment Agency.

Type of person suited to this work

Ideally, you should be a friendly yet firm person, able to deal with members of the public effectively and politely, sometimes in difficult disciplinary situations.

An interest in the environment and working outdoors is really useful, as is knowledge of waterways. You need to be aware of the main environmental threats, understand the basics of how ecosystems maintain themselves and know about fish diseases and biology.

You also need to know about fishery law, not only in the UK (although this is most useful), but also at European level. Be aware that it may even be different at local level, for example if you live in Scotland.

Working conditions

You will spend the majority of your time outside, patrolling areas either in a car, by boat or on foot.

You will usually work between 37 and 39 hours per week, which will involve night shifts and weekends. Part-time or seasonal work is also available.

The work is physical and tiring. You may have to pursue offenders across rough terrain on foot, and could find yourself wading through cold rivers and ponds. For this reason, you will probably spend your days in waterproofs, wellies and even lifejackets.

Future prospects

The public sector provides well-defined career paths, although you may choose to move into private consultancy. The Centre for Environment, Fisheries and Aquaculture Science, and Marine Scotland are possible public organisations to work for, but it is likely you will end up with the Environment Agency in some capacity.

Once you are working for the Environment Agency, many possibilities arise. You will have the opportunity to become a team leader within the agency, and this may lead to promotion and managerial opportunities.

Another option would be to move into related areas of work, such as fish farming or gamekeeping. Once you have a little experience in the area it will be possible to choose what interests you most, and in which direction you want your career to progress.

Advantages/disadvantages

This can be a really satisfying and exciting job, and if you enjoy being outside, you will probably thoroughly enjoy the job.

It can be lonely, and conditions can be hard if you are not naturally a country person.

You need to be prepared for all weather conditions, and work can be cold, wet, and tiring.

Money guide

Starting salaries range from £20,000 to £25,000 per year.

With 10 to 15 years' experience you can expect to be earning up to £35,000.

Those in the most senior positions earn in excess of £40,000 per year.

Related opportunities

- Countryside Ranger p245
- Fish Farmer p250
- Gamekeeper p252

Further information

Environment Agency
www.gov.uk/government/organisations/environment-agency

Institute of Fisheries Management
www.ifm.org.uk

ENVIRONMENT, ANIMALS AND PLANTS

Qualifications and courses

No specific qualifications are required for entry although GCSEs/National 5s (A*–C/A–C), especially in English and science subjects, will be useful. It is, however, becoming increasingly necessary to gain higher level qualifications as this is a very competitive area.

Foundation degrees or Honours degrees in subjects like zoology are also available, for instance Sparsholt College in Hampshire offers a Foundation degree in Animal Management and Applied Science lasting 2 years. Typical entry requirements for a degree course are 2 A levels/3 H grades, including a science, and 5 GCSEs/National 5s (A*–C/A–C).

General animal care and management courses are available and include the NVQ in Animal Care (Levels 1–3), the ABC Award and Diploma in Work-based Animal Care (Levels 1–3), the City & Guilds Level 2 Certificate in Animal Care, the City & Guilds Level 3 Certificate in Animal Care, the Advanced National Certificate in the Management of Zoo Animals, and the Advanced National Level 3 Diploma in Animal Management. Alternatively, there are the BTEC qualifications in Animal Management (Levels 2–3), and the BTEC Level 4 HNC and Level 5 HND in Animal Management.

Experience, proven interest and interaction with animals is incredibly important, sometimes favoured over qualifications, but often a requirement of application. Volunteering at a zoo or animal sanctuary would be beneficial, but these programmes are very popular and you may be placed on a waiting list. Apprenticeships may be available if you are aged 16–24.

What the work involves

You could work in a zoo, safari, wildlife or birdlife park or aquarium where you will care for animals (ranging from mammals to birds, reptiles to amphibians, fish to invertebrates etc) and their surroundings.

You will provide food, water and fresh bedding for the animals in your care. You will clean out enclosures and check the animals for signs of injury or disease, keeping records of feeding, health and behaviour and informing veterinary staff if there are any issues.

Many zoos stress the importance of conservation and education and some of your work may involve leading tours and giving presentations to visitors.

Type of person suited to this work

You need to be passionate about the care and well-being of animals in your care. This requires patience, observation and the desire to handle and be around animals.

Most of this work is done outdoors and can be physically demanding so a fit, active person who is not afraid of physical work would be well suited to the job.

Some animals you will work with could be dangerous, so you will have to respect them and be aware of your own and others' safety.

Working conditions

Animals require 24/7 care so you will be expected to work 5–6 days a week. This is normally organised on a shift system which includes early mornings, late evenings, weekends and bank holidays, especially during busy periods.

Your work will be physically demanding and often dirty. A uniform will be provided. If you suffer from allergies, this work will be difficult for you.

Work could be seasonal as some centres close for part of the year.

Future prospects

There are over 350 zoos and wildlife parks throughout the UK, although the number of stand-alone zoos, rather than those as part of a larger complex, is significantly lower. Jobs can be hard to find and competition for employment will be high so be prepared to move for work or promotion.

You may choose to specialise and work with one species. You could also be promoted to senior keeper or head keeper.

You may also choose to move into related work such as becoming an RSPCA inspector.

Advantages/disadvantages

This can be difficult work to enter and progress in and the financial rewards can be small.

You will be working with some unusual or exotic animals, with some opportunity to specialise.

A variety of tasks with lots of different animals can keep the job interesting.

The role of zoos as centres of breeding and supporting conservation has increased recently, so you could undertake important work.

Money guide

Pay will depend on your location and type of zoo or animal park. Many jobs include free or subsidised accommodation.

Trainees can start at about £11,000–£13,000 per year.

With experience, this can rise to £17,000.

Senior keepers earn around £17,000–£24,000 a year.

Related opportunities

- Animal Welfare Officer p242
- Dog Trainer/Handler p246
- Veterinary Surgeon p266

Further information

Association of British and Irish Wild Animal Keepers
www.abwak.co.uk

British and Irish Association of Zoos and Aquariums
www.biaza.org.uk

Healthcare

If you are keen to pursue a career in healthcare you must be compassionate and enjoy either caring for people or deciding what treatment they should receive. There is such a wide variety of jobs available in this sector simply because you can specialise in absolutely any aspect of human healthcare. Many jobs require a lot of training and you can expect to work in some highly pressurised and sometimes distressing situations. Workers in healthcare are extremely dedicated and enthusiastic about their careers, which rarely constitute a 9am–5pm job. The jobs featured in this section are listed below. For similar jobs to the ones in this section turn to *Science, Mathematics and Statistics* on page 489 and *Social Work and Counselling Services* on page 557.

ACUPUNCTURIST

Qualifications and courses

Careers in acupuncture are open to all graduates and diplomates although a degree or HND in a related subject such as life or medical sciences may increase your chances of employment.

Degrees are not compulsory though and experience and determination is just as important. Previous experience of advice work or counselling may enable entry into the profession.

Acupuncture is currently only regulated by voluntary agreement but the British Acupuncture Council (BAcC) works with the British Acupuncture Accreditation Board (BAAB) to offer training courses. The courses generally take 2–3 years to complete full time. Entry onto one of the courses requires at least 2 or 3 A levels/H grades, science subjects preferred, and 5 GCSEs/National 5s. The British Medical Acupuncture Society (BMAS) also offers a Certificate of Basic Competence (COBC) and a Diploma in Medical Acupuncture (DipMedAc).

These accredited training courses lead to professional membership of the BAcC which offers protection and public liability insurance. You are also required to register with your local authority.

Courses vary, but generally cover topics such as anatomy and physiology, techniques and acupuncture points, ethical issues, clinical experience, and advice on setting up a practice.

Some courses are even available at postgraduate and doctorate levels.

What the work involves

Acupuncturists work from ancient Chinese holistic guidelines. They treat medical illnesses and imbalances by inserting very fine needles into identified pressure points on the human body.

You will need to talk to patients about their problems, taking plenty of notes, in order to explore their lifestyle and emotional state, and then assess all of these factors to determine a suitable treatment.

In addition you may carry out procedures such as burning herbs on needles, and passing small electric currents through them.

Type of person suited to this work

You must be very personable, with excellent communication skills in order to elicit trust and personal information from your patients, as well as being able to explain the techniques you are using to them.

You will need an analytical mind in order to understand each patient's problem and formulate a beneficial course of treatment. Being comfortable with close and physical contact is also important when examining and treating your patients.

As you will probably be running your own business, you will need excellent business acumen in order to successfully take on aspects such as marketing, accounting, and administrative tasks.

Working conditions

Hours vary and tend to fit around the needs of clients. This usually involves evening and weekend work.

You could work from your own rented treatment room, from home, in your patients' homes, or in hospices, health clinics and addiction treatment centres. As you may work across a number of locations, a driving licence is useful.

You will usually be working on your feet, standing and bending a lot. Conditions have to be clean and sterile, and there are strict health and safety guidelines to adhere to.

Future prospects

Most acupuncturists are self-employed, although a few find work at medical centres or centres which specialise in complementary medicine.

If you are self-employed, the success of your career depends on your reputation and marketing skills. If you build up a strong client base there are plenty of opportunities for expansion and even setting up your own health clinic.

Many practising acupuncturists choose to teach their subject, or carry out research and write articles for books and magazines.

Advantages/disadvantages

This can be a really rewarding career, especially if you like being with people and enjoy helping them.

You may hear distressing stories and have insight into some upsetting personal lives, so you need to be able to leave work at work.

Money guide

Earnings in acupuncture depend a lot on your situation, marketing ability, experience and how many patients you treat. As a newly qualified acupuncturist starting up your own practice, you will probably earn around £12,000 per year.

Once you have started to build up clients and gain experience, you can expect to earn up to £25,000 a year.

If you grow your business into a large established practice, your earnings can rise to in excess of £65,000 a year.

Per session, acupuncturists charge around £40, although this can rise to up to £90 in London.

Related opportunities

- Chiropractor p277
- Counsellor p561
- Homeopath p293

Further information

British Acupuncture Accreditation Board
www.baab.co.uk

British Acupuncture Council
www.acupuncture.org.uk

The Acupuncture Society
www.acupuncturesociety.org.uk

Qualifications and courses

You must hold a degree in adult nursing which has been approved by the Nursing and Midwifery Council (NMC). Minimum entry requirements for a degree are usually 2–3 A levels/H grades, ideally including a science-based subject, and 5 GCSEs/National 5s (A*–C/A–C) including English, maths and a science subject. All applicants must obtain clearance from the Disclosure and Barring Service (DBS) before commencing their training.

If you do not have the required GCSEs/A levels, some universities will accept other qualifications, such as the BTEC Level 3 qualifications in Health and Social Care (Health Sciences), or an Access to Higher Education Diploma in a science or health-related subject. Check your desired university for their specific entry requirements.

Graduates with a degree in a health-related subject such as human biology, life and medical sciences or biomedical science, may be eligible to enter the nursing profession by taking an accelerated 2-year programme which leads to a Master of Science (MSc) or Postgraduate Diploma.

Pre-entry experience is not essential, but relevant experience as a care worker or in some other work with people is good preparation.

You are eligible to register as a nurse with the NMC once you have completed an approved nursing degree. Nurses are expected to engage in continuing professional development (CPD) throughout their career to keep their skills and knowledge up to date.

What the work involves

Adult nurses assess the needs of each patient in order to plan a care programme for them. You will work alongside doctors and other medical practitioners to observe how patients progress on treatment plans and modify them as necessary. You will also give patients practical care such as administering medicines and injections, changing dressings and checking blood pressure.

You could work in a variety of positions, such as a community nurse, occupational nurse or healthcare assistant.

Type of person suited to this work

You will be working with patients from all parts of the community who will have a wide range of problems, so it is essential to remain non-judgemental and sympathetic. A clear understanding of confidentiality is essential.

You will need excellent communication skills in order to interact with patients, explain care plans and illnesses, and calm those who are angry or distressed.

You will also need to be very practical with good manual dexterity for undertaking precision jobs such as taking blood.

Working conditions

You will usually work 37.5 hours per week but overtime is available for those who want it. If you are working in a hospital, these hours will include night and weekend shifts.

You could work in a number of locations including hospitals, GP surgeries, prisons, hospices and in patients' homes. If you are required to travel around in the local community, a driving licence is useful.

Adult nurses in hospitals work in specific wards, such as intensive care or accident and emergency.

Future prospects

Despite student numbers increasing, there is still a shortage of trained adult nurses. Since 2010 around 4,000 senior nursing jobs have been cut, but employment prospects generally remain good.

The majority of job opportunities lie within the NHS, although other employers include private hospitals, the armed forces, hospices and nursing homes, and the prison service.

With experience and additional qualifications, you could specialise in a subject of interest such as neurology or cardiology, and go on to become a nurse consultant.

UK nursing qualifications are recognised across the globe so there are opportunities to work abroad.

Advantages/disadvantages

Helping a wide range of people to get better or become more independent is both rewarding and enjoyable.

There are opportunities to work flexible hours or part time. Career breaks are common and the NHS runs specialist courses to get nurses who have had a break back up to speed quickly.

You may have to deal with distressed, angry or violent patients.

Money guide

Nurses' salaries follow a rising scale divided into 9 bands. As a fully qualified nurse you could start in band 5, which pays between £21,909 and £28,462. Those who take on a senior position with additional responsibilities can advance towards band 6, which pays between £26,302 and £35,225.

If you specialise in a particular area and undertake the training to become a nurse consultant, you could advance towards band 7, which pays £31,383–£41,373, or band 8, which pays £40,028–£82,434.

Related opportunities

- Hospital Doctor p294
- Learning Disabilities Nurse p296
- Mental Health Nurse p299

Further information

NHS Careers
www.healthcareers.nhs.uk

Nursing and Midwifery Council
www.nmc.org.uk

Royal College of Nursing
www.rcn.org.uk

HEALTHCARE

271

ANAESTHETIST

Qualifications and courses

Candidates must first train as a hospital doctor by completing a medical degree which is approved by the General Medical Council (GMC). Entry requirements for medical school are very high A level/H grade results including relevant subjects such as the sciences and Maths. You may also be asked to take the UK Clinical Aptitude Test (UKCAT) when you apply for your degree.

After completing a medical degree, candidates undergo 7 years of specialist postgraduate training. Stage 1 involves a 2-year Foundation Programme of general training. This acts as the bridge between medical school and specialist training. The second stage is 3 years of core training in acute care and candidates then move on to the final stage: higher specialty training in anaesthesia, intensive care medicine and pain management.

After successfully completing the higher specialty stage, trainees receive a Certificate of Completion of Training (CCT) and become eligible to join the GMC Specialist Register.

Anaesthetists must engage in continuing professional development (CPD) throughout their career to ensure that their skills and knowledge are up to date. The Royal College of Anaesthetists provides information on available training.

What the work involves

Anaesthetists are qualified hospital doctors who have undergone further training in anaesthesia. You will prepare and administer drugs to make patients unconscious and pain free during surgery. You will monitor patients during the procedure and bring them back to consciousness afterwards. You will also give local anaesthesia to specific areas of the body.

In addition, you will give pain relief after surgery to seriously ill patients or during procedures such as childbirth. Anaesthetists also work in intensive care, resuscitation and pain management.

Type of person suited to this work

Anaesthetists need excellent communication skills: you must be reassuring and a good listener in order to gain patients' trust and explain procedures to them. You should work well in a team and be able to give and follow instructions.

You must be able to stay calm in an emergency and make decisions under pressure. You will need the confidence and skill to use complicated equipment and administer powerful drugs safely and accurately. You should have a strong sense of the responsibility involved in this job.

You will need to be prepared to undergo a long programme of education and training in order to gain the in-depth knowledge and skills necessary to become an anaesthetist.

Working conditions

Anaesthetists work in operating theatres, wards, clinics and accident and emergency departments within hospitals.

You will work shifts as part of an on-call rota, which includes working at nights, weekends and on bank holidays.

You will handle potentially dangerous drugs and equipment.

Future prospects

There are opportunities throughout the UK, mainly within the NHS but also in private hospitals and clinics.

Promotion to consultant posts is very competitive. Anaesthetists may work in sub-specialities such as paediatrics, obstetrics, cardiac surgery, resuscitation or intensive care.

Once fully qualified you will probably be expected to teach and examine students and trainees and to carry out research.

Advantages/disadvantages

Being responsible for the safety of patients in your care and dealing with emergency situations makes this a very demanding job.

It is rewarding to be able to help patients through surgery and other medical procedures by providing pain relief.

Money guide

For entrants at Junior Hospital Trainee level, the basic starting salaries are £27,000 for Foundation Year 1 and £30,000 for Year 2.

Doctors undertaking specialist training can earn a salary of between £37,000 and £48,000.

There is increased earning potential for doctors in training who work for longer than the typical 40-hour week, or those who work outside of the hours of 7am to 7pm.

On completion of training, speciality doctors can expect to earn a basic salary of between £37,547 and £70,018.

Consultant anaesthetists working in the NHS can earn between £76,001 and £102,465.

Related opportunities

- Doctor (GP) p287
- Hospital Doctor p294
- Pathologist p307

Further information

British Medical Association
www.bma.org.uk

The Association of Anaesthetists of Great Britain and Ireland
www.aagbi.org

The Royal College of Anaesthetists
www.rcoa.ac.uk

AROMATHERAPIST

Qualifications and courses

There are no formal academic requirements for aromatherapists. Professional training courses are the standard method of entry and you usually have to be at least 18 years old to enrol.

The General Regulatory Council for Complementary Therapies (GRCCT) has devised National Occupational Standards (NOS) for aromatherapy. If you wish to operate as a professional aromatherapist, you must ensure that you choose a course which meets the NOS. Courses which conform to the standards are offered at diploma, Foundation degree or degree level. Short courses are only advised for those with a personal (rather than professional) interest in aromatherapy. The Aromatherapy Council provides information on choosing a course. Prior experience in a related profession, such as massage, will help your application.

Most courses include modules on anatomy, physiology, pathology, therapeutic relationships and the theory and practice of aromatherapy. You will also consider the practicalities of being a professional aromatherapist, covering topics such as legal and ethical issues and business studies.

Once qualified, you can improve your career prospects by registering with the Complementary & Natural Healthcare Council (CNHC).

What the work involves

Aromatherapists use essential oils to improve the health and wellbeing of clients.

You will be required to look into the medical history of all your clients, discussing their lifestyle, diet, exercise, allergies and stress levels. Using the information gathered, you will decide on blends and mixes of oils appropriate for the needs of the client.

You will administer oils to the skin by massage, provide instructions for aftercare and maintain records of each of your clients.

Type of person suited to this work

You must be very personable with excellent communication skills in order to explain the techniques you are using and elicit trust and personal information from your patients. Being comfortable with close and physical contact is also important when examining and treating your patients.

You need an analytical mind in order to understand each patient's problem and formulate a beneficial course of treatment.

There is a lot to remember in aromatherapy so it requires a calm and intelligent person to be familiar with all the oils and administer them carefully.

As you will probably be self-employed, you need excellent business acumen to undertake marketing, accounting and administrative tasks.

Working conditions

Aromatherapists tend to run their own businesses so working conditions vary. You could rent a treatment room in a health clinic, gym or leisure centre, work from home or travel to patients' homes to provide treatment. Hours depend on individual schedules and the needs and demands of clients. You should expect to work evenings and weekends. Part-time hours are a possibility.

Rooms and workspaces must be clean and quiet, and most aromatherapists tend to wear white clothes.

You will be bending, stretching and spending most of the day on your feet.

Future prospects

Success in aromatherapy depends on effective business skills. If you build a strong client base and market your services well, your practice will grow into a successful business.

You could train in another relevant therapy such as homeopathy, reflexology or counselling, which could attract more clients.

If you like the idea of working abroad, you could take your skills overseas. You must ensure that the country you choose recognises your qualifications.

Advantages/disadvantages

This can be a really rewarding career, especially if you are sociable and enjoy helping people.

The working hours may be anti-social.

Money guide

Most aromatherapists are self-employed and charge a fee of between £25 and £70 per hourly session.

Income will depend upon your experience, reputation and the number of clients you treat.

During the process of building up your practice, earnings can be quite low – possibly ranging from £2,000 to £10,000 a year. Many aromatherapists have another job to supplement their income.

With experience and an established business, you could achieve between £15,000 and £30,000.

Related opportunities

- Acupuncturist p270
- Beauty Therapist p443
- Homeopath p293

Further information

Complementary and Natural Healthcare Council
www.cnhc.org.uk

General Regulatory Council for Complementary Therapies
www.grcct.org

Institute for Complementary and Natural Medicine
www.icnm.org.uk

HEALTHCARE

Qualifications and courses

To work as an art therapist you must complete a postgraduate qualification that has been approved by the British Association of Art Therapists (BAAT). It is also possible to specialise in music or drama therapy and for these roles you would need to complete a course by their specific approved association.

Although arts-based first degrees are preferred for entry to postgraduate courses, other subjects such as psychology, education and nursing may all be acceptable. To apply for a master's you will need a strong portfolio, and at least a year's experience in working in health, education or social care. Substantial clinical work experience or a relevant HND may also be considered for entry.

A master's degree course lasts 2 years full-time, or 4 years part-time. Many areas are covered, including psychodynamics, psychopathology of art, contemporary art therapy and practice skills.

You will have to have therapy yourself as part of training, and will also be expected to spend 120 days on clinical placement during the course.

Once you have qualified, you need to register with the Health & Care Professions Council (HCPC).

What the work involves

Therapists use a range of mediums of art to help clients who may have difficulty in expressing themselves through words.

You may work closely with people suffering from mental health problems, emotional problems, or those with drug and alcohol addiction, helping them to recover. People with speech and language difficulties also benefit from art therapy.

You will create a safe environment where patients feel free to express themselves and their feelings and move on positively.

Type of person suited to this work

If you want to work with people with emotional and psychological difficulties, you need to be a calm, caring, understanding and trustworthy person. You will need a lot of patience, excellent communication skills, and a very sensitive nature.

These skills need to be combined with strong artistic ability: you have to be a creative thinker prepared to take on the responsibility of helping clients who may be in a great deal of emotional pain. An interest in all forms of art is also essential.

If you plan on starting your own business, you will need good marketing and accounting skills.

Working conditions

Conditions depend on who you choose to work for. If being employed by the NHS appeals to you, you are likely to work 37.5 hours per week, with weekends free. If you work in private practice, your hours will vary and will probably include evenings and weekends.

As a therapist, you will probably have to travel around to give therapy, so a driving licence is really useful. You could work in hospitals, prisons, clinics and community centres.

Surroundings for therapy must always be warm, light and comfortable, so you can expect this to be your working environment.

Future prospects

There tend to be few advertised vacancies for art therapists. If you work for yourself, you can grow and expand your business by building up a solid client base and making good contacts.

If you choose to work for the NHS, you could be promoted to management positions; becoming a specialist, head of profession, or consultant.

You might decide to specialise within a particular area, such as mental health or palliative care. Alternatively, you could combine art therapy with another complementary treatment such as psychotherapy.

Advantages/disadvantages

If you have both a love of art and a desire to help people this will prove a very rewarding career.

Opportunities for progression are good, and experiences can be enriching and very fulfilling; there will never be a boring day at work.

You will have to deal with people who are in pain or mentally unstable, which can be extremely upsetting.

Money guide

As an entry level allied health professional working for the NHS you will be paid at Band 6 of the NHS Agenda for Change, earning between £26,302 and £35,225.

With experience you could reach Band 7, earning between £31,383 and £41,373.

If you set up your own practice your initial salary will probably be less.

As you gain experience this figure can rise to about £40,000 a year.

If you get into a principal, management or supervisory role, you can earn between £40,028 and £48,034 a year.

Related opportunities

- Clinical/Health Psychologist p560
- Counsellor p561
- Learning Disabilities Nurse p296

Further information

British Association of Art Therapists
www.baat.org

Health and Care Professions Council
www.hpc-uk.org

NHS Careers
www.healthcareers.nhs.uk

Qualifications and courses

The professional qualification for audiologists is a 4-year degree in audiology. The typical entry requirements for a degree course are 2 A levels/3 H grades, including at least one science subject, Maths or Psychology. You will spend the first 2 years of the course at university. During year 3, you will work in a placement in an audiology setting. The final year will be spent back at university learning about more advanced aspects of audiology.

It is also possible to enter this profession with a degree in another appropriate subject if you complete a Master of Science (MSc) in Audiology. Most people who follow this route work towards registering as audiological scientists.

The NHS Practitioner Training Programme (PTP) is also available. You will train as a healthcare science practitioner by completing a full-time (usually 3-year) accredited, integrated Bachelor of Science (BSc) degree in healthcare science at university. The NHS Scientist Training Programme (STP), specialising in neurosensory sciences, is available to those already with a relevant degree awarded at 2.1 classification.

If you want to practise as an audiological scientist or clinical scientist in audiology you will need to undertake a Higher Training Scheme (run by the British Academy of Audiology (BAA)). This involves on-the-job training and clinical supervision.

You will be expected to engage in continuing professional development (CPD) and to conduct ongoing research.

No pre-entry experience is required for audiology but experience working with young and elderly people is an advantage.

What the work involves

Audiologists examine patients to identify and assess hearing and balance disorders. You will usually work in one of four main areas: paediatrics, adult assessment and rehabilitation, special needs groups, and research and development.

As an audiologist, you will use specialist equipment to test patients and assess their problems and needs.

You will also fit hearing aids and give treatment and advice to patients on how to improve and manage their conditions.

Type of person suited to this work

As an audiologist you will need to speak clearly and be easily understood by people who are lip reading. You should also be flexible and able to work as part of a team.

You will need to be a caring person with excellent communication skills to deal sensitively with patients of all ages and backgrounds, listening to them and explaining the tests and procedures you are doing.

You will need to be practical to operate specialist equipment and take a logical, scientific approach to your work and be able to assess patients' needs and conditions correctly, keep accurate records and provide solutions and practical help.

Working conditions

Most audiologists work as part of a hospital team but you could also be based in a clinic or visit patients in their homes or in care homes or schools.

You could also be involved in teaching and research work in a university.

You will probably work Monday to Friday but could have to be on-call and cover shifts including nights, weekends and bank holidays.

Self-employment or freelance work, part-time hours and career breaks are all possible.

Future prospects

Audiology is a rapidly developing area of healthcare, there is a shortage of qualified staff so job prospects are good, although there are now more students training. There are opportunities within the NHS throughout the UK. There are also jobs available in research and in private hospitals.

You could specialise in one area such as paediatrics or adult rehabilitation.

Within the NHS you could progress to higher grades, where you will have more responsibility including managing and training others.

Advantages/disadvantages

You may need to deal with people suffering from an illness or disorder, such as those with dementia, and this can be emotionally draining at times.

It is fulfilling to know that you are using your skills to improve people's hearing and balance, providing them with a better quality of life.

Money guide

The NHS sets rates for audiologists. There are extra payments available, for example, if you work in London.

Trainees start on NHS band 5 and salaries range from £21,909 to £28,462 per year. Once qualified and registered as an audiological scientist you can reach NHS band 7 and earn between £31,383 and £41,373.

Senior posts have a salary range of £40,028 to £99,437 at bands 8 and 9.

Related opportunities

- Occupational Therapist p301
- Physiotherapist p312
- Speech and Language Therapist p320

Further information

British Academy of Audiology
www.baaudiology.org

British Society of Audiology
www.thebsa.org.uk

NHS Careers
www.healthcareers.nhs.uk

HEALTHCARE

CHILDREN'S NURSE

Qualifications and courses

All children's nurses must hold a degree in child nursing which has been approved by the Nursing and Midwifery Council (NMC). Minimum entry requirements for degree courses are usually 2 A levels/3H grades, ideally including a science-based subject, and 5 GCSEs/National 5s (A*–C/A–C) including English, Maths and a science subject. All applicants must obtain clearance from the Disclosure and Barring Service (DBS) before commencing their training.

If you do not have the required A levels/H grades or GCSEs/National 5s, some universities will accept other qualifications, such as the various BTEC Level 3 qualifications in Health and Social Care (Health Sciences) or an Access to Higher Education Diploma in a science or health-related subject.

Graduates with a degree in a health-related subject such as human biology, life and medical sciences or biomedical science, may be eligible to enter the nursing profession by taking an accelerated 2-year programme which leads to a Master of Science (MSc) or Postgraduate Diploma.

You are eligible to register as a nurse with the NMC once you have completed an approved nursing degree. Nurses are expected to engage in continuing professional development (CPD) throughout their career to keep their skills and knowledge up to date.

What the work involves

Children's nurses work specifically with babies and young people up to the age of 18. You will also work closely with the parents and families of your patients, providing support, education and advice on treatment and care plans.

You will take medical histories from children and their families, devise a care plan for them with the help of other medical professionals and record their treatment procedures and outcomes in detailed records. You will also have to carry out procedures such as checking blood pressure, taking temperatures, dressing wounds and taking blood samples.

Type of person suited to this work

You will need to be a very warm, approachable person in order to gain the trust of young patients and their families. At the same time, you must be highly professional and authoritative to deal with difficult children and situations.

You should be patient when teaching others, as you will need to demonstrate treatment techniques to both your patients and their parents or carers. You will also need to motivate them to continue treatment at home.

You must be observant, capable of making decisions and able to respond quickly to changes in children's health.

Working conditions

On average, you will work 37.5 hours per week and this will usually include early morning, evening, night and weekend work as part of a shift-based rota. Part-time and flexible hours are often available.

You could work on paediatric wards within NHS hospitals, specialist hospitals, hospices and GP surgeries. You may also work throughout the local community, visiting patients at home, in care homes or at school.

You will usually be required to wear a uniform and suitable sterile clothing, such as gloves and an apron, for certain procedures.

Future prospects

As you gain experience, you can undertake further training and specialise in a particular area such as neurological or cardiovascular conditions in children. You could eventually become a nurse consultant.

Alternatively, you could apply for team leadership roles such as staff nurse or sister. You could also move into general NHS management.

Advantages/disadvantages

Working with children, helping them to get better, managing their treatment and easing their suffering is extremely rewarding.

There are plenty of opportunities to work part time in order to fit your job around your family commitments.

It can be upsetting to deal with distressed or very ill children.

Money guide

A newly qualified nurse working for the NHS can expect a starting salary of £21,909, rising to £28,462 with experience.

Those who take on the additional responsibilities of a senior or team management position can achieve £26,302–£41,373.

If you specialise in a particular area and undertake the training to become a nurse consultant, you could earn up to £68,484.

Related opportunities

- Adult Nurse p271
- Learning Disabilities Nurse p296
- Speech and Language Therapist p320

Further information

NHS Careers
www.healthcareers.nhs.uk

Nursing and Midwifery Council
www.nmc.org.uk

Royal College of Nursing
www.rcn.org.uk

Qualifications and courses

Entrants must complete a degree course that has been accredited by the General Chiropractic Council (GCC). There are currently 3 institutions in the UK offering the GCC-recognised Master of Chiropractic (MChiro), which takes 4–5 years to complete. Upon graduation, candidates are eligible to register with the GCC, which is a legal requirement for anyone wishing to practise as a chiropractor.

You must be at least 18 years old to start training. Minimum entry requirements are 3 A levels/H grades or equivalent qualifications, including Biology and another science subject. For candidates who do not meet these requirements, year-long preliminary chiropractic courses are available as an entry route to the full degree.

More mature applicants looking to move into chiropractic as a second career are considered for degree courses without the usual entry qualifications, providing they have relevant experience or knowledge of science.

You must undergo a Disclosure and Barring Service (DBS) check prior to training as you will be working with children and vulnerable adults.

Registered chiropractors must undertake continuing professional development (CPD) throughout their career.

What the work involves

Chiropractors work with joints, bones and muscles, using their hands and other physical tools, as opposed to drugs, in order to treat patients. Techniques include massage, movement and applying ice or heat to troublesome areas.

You could treat a variety of ailments including back and neck problems, joint stiffness, postural and muscular complaints, headaches and sports injuries.

You will also need to carry out full patient examinations, listen to their concerns and complaints, and record detailed notes of each consultation.

Type of person suited to this work

You should have exceptional communication skills as you will need to listen to patients carefully in order to understand their complaint and to explain the techniques you are using to treat it.

You will need to be professional and approachable in order to inspire confidence and trust in your patients.

Good organisation and commercial awareness are essential if you are to run your own business.

Working conditions

Working hours are usually 9am–5pm, Monday to Friday, although some flexibility may be required to suit the needs of clients. Many clinics and practitioners are increasingly offering early morning, evening and weekend appointments.

Most chiropractors work either in a specialist clinic, a doctor's surgery, at home or at the homes of their clients. This means you could be working alongside other chiropractors/ healthcare professionals or alone.

It is a physically demanding job so you will have to ensure that your own fitness levels remain high in order to avoid work-related injuries.

Future prospects

The chiropractic profession continues to grow and develop. However, there are also many graduates competing for clients.

Most chiropractors are self-employed or work in private practice. A few are employed by the NHS.

Numerous options are open to you as you gain experience. You could choose to specialise in a specific area, such as children or sports injuries, you could set up your own practice or you could teach.

Advantages/disadvantages

Each day you will meet new people and relieve their physical aches and ailments which gives great job satisfaction.

Being self-employed can be extremely stressful as you are responsible for your own business administration and your earnings are dependent on the number of clients you attract.

Money guide

Most chiropractors are self-employed so their earnings depend upon the size, location and reputation of their practice, as well as how many clients they have.

Newly qualified chiropractors can expect a starting salary of £20,000 per year.

With experience, your earnings could rise to between £30,000 and £50,000 a year.

Once you are in a senior position within your own practice, you could achieve up to £80,000 a year.

Related opportunities

- Massage Therapist p297
- Osteopath p305
- Physiotherapist p312

Further information

British Chiropractic Association
www.chiropractic-uk.co.uk

General Chiropractic Council
www.gcc-uk.org

HEALTHCARE

HEALTHCARE

Qualifications and courses

You will need either a 1st or 2.1 degree in a subject such as mechanical, electronic or electrical engineering or biomedical science/engineering. You should choose a degree which is accredited by the Institution of Engineering and Technology (IET) or the Institution of Mechanical Engineers (IMechE). For degree entry you will need at least 3 A levels/4 H grades, including Maths and Physics.

Mature students without relevant qualifications may be considered if they have significant work experience in this area or complete an Access to Higher Education course.

Those who wish to work in the public sector can apply for the graduate NHS Scientist Training Programme (STP) which is offered in conjunction with the Institute of Physics and Engineering in Medicine (IPEM). Training takes 3 to 4 years and involves both work-based learning and studying for a master's degree in your chosen specialism.

You will need to commit to a programme of continuing professional development (CPD) throughout your career.

What the work involves

Clinical engineers design and maintain medical equipment such as scanners, x-ray machines, pacemakers, heart rate and blood pressure monitors, equipment for surgery and instruments used in medical research.

All kinds of engineers, from physicists to computer scientists, work on many different parts of the process.

You would test equipment and collaborate with hospital staff, installing equipment and teaching them how to use it.

Type of person suited to this work

If you are looking to go into this field, you need to have a natural interest in both electronic and mechanical engineering, and in health and medical issues. You must also be skilled in engineering and have in-depth knowledge of your subject.

You should be good at problem-solving and willing to keep up to date with developments in science, medicine and engineering.

You need organisational skills to effectively prioritise and plan your workload, and the ability to work within a budget.

Communication and teamwork skills are also essential.

Working conditions

You could work in a hospital or laboratory, depending on the nature of the work.

Those working in hospitals might have to work shifts and are often on standby for call-outs. Laboratory hours tend to be more fixed.

The usual working hours for clinical engineers are Monday to Friday and you would normally be working 37.5 hours a week.

Future prospects

There are good opportunities for progression and promotion for clinical and biomedical engineers.

With the right experience, you can move into management and senior management jobs, and if you work for the NHS you could be promoted to consultant level.

For those who do not wish to work for the NHS, other opportunities may be available in the private sector. For example, you could be employed by a medical equipment manufacturer.

Advantages/disadvantages

This career requires very skilled and well-educated professionals, and building up this knowledge, studying for your degree and putting it into practice can be a really rewarding experience.

You will be doing a worthwhile job as you will help many people by building and maintaining medical equipment.

The role can be stressful at times and involve high levels of pressure.

Working in a hospital environment will not suit everyone.

Money guide

In the NHS, entry-level engineers earn between £21,909 and £28,462 as healthcare science practitioners.

Trainee clinical scientists can earn between £26,302 and £35,225, and qualified clinical scientists can earn between £31,383 and £41,373.

Those with experience and further qualifications, such as Higher Specialist Scientific Training, can achieve up to £99,437.

Salaries in the private sector are comparable to those in the NHS and may be higher.

Related opportunities

■ Biotechnologist p495
■ Clinical Scientist p499
■ Medical Physicist p298

Further information

Association of Clinical Scientists
www.assclinsci.org

NHS Clinical Scientists Recruitment
www.nhsclinicalscientists.info

Qualifications and courses

To enter this profession, you will need either a 1st or 2.1 degree in a relevant subject such as biochemistry, biomedical sciences, physics, engineering or another science subject related to these disciplines. A 2.2 degree or alternative Higher Education qualification will suffice if followed up with a relevant postgraduate degree. For degree entry you will need 3 A levels/4 H grades, including Maths and a science subject (preferably Physics), and 5 GCSEs/National 5s including English Language, Maths, and two sciences.

Following your degree, you will have to complete the NHS Healthcare Scientist Training Programme (STP). The STP is a workplace-based salaried learning programme, which results in accreditation in 1 of 9 themed pathways, including critical care science. Applications for a place on the STP are incredibly competitive, so relevant work experience and voluntary work can greatly enhance your chances. Contact hospitals and try and get a role involving patient contact. Contact your course provider for more directed guidance on what to aim for.

Once qualified, you could become a member of the Society of Critical Care Technologies (SCCT) which is the governing body for critical care technologists, where you would have access to opportunities to develop your professional career.

You might also decide to study further and gain a PhD or join the NHS Higher Specialist Scientific Training programme (HSST).

What the work involves

Critical care technologists support other medical staff caring for critically ill patients by maintaining and operating life-support equipment in intensive care units.

You will work with equipment such as ventilators, brain monitors, blood filtration machines, electrocardiograms (ECGs) and infusion devices. Your job will involve setting up this equipment, taking readings, checking the equipment is working correctly, repairing it and ordering more supplies.

You will use diagnostic techniques to help the medical team assess a patient's needs and condition. You will also be required to keep detailed reports of all your work for patients' records.

Type of person suited to this work

You should have an interest in electronics, science and medicine, with a willingness to keep your skills and knowledge up to date.

You must be a practical person with good technical skills and the ability to work accurately and precisely when under pressure. Good problem-solving and decision-making skills are essential. You should have a responsible attitude to your work as patients' lives will depend on you.

You will need compassion and excellent communication skills to work with patients and their relatives at a time of intense stress, and to be able to explain things simply and clearly.

Working conditions

Critical care technologists work as part of a team in the intensive care unit of a hospital using specialist equipment and machinery.

You will need to follow strict health and safety regulations to ensure that infections and diseases are safely contained.

You will normally work shifts which include nights, weekends and bank holidays.

Future prospects

The requirement for a degree is a recent one and as such, competition for jobs may change in the near future. Job prospects are currently good though as there is a shortage of qualified applicants.

You could specialise in a particular area such as cardiology or respiratory units.

Many critical care technologists are involved in research and teaching, as well as in practice.

Advantages/disadvantages

Working under pressure in emergency situations will be emotionally and physically demanding.

It is extremely rewarding to help patients recover from illnesses.

You will have a varied working day which will involve using your technical skills and having contact with patients.

Money guide

The NHS sets pay rates for critical care technologists.

The current starting salary for someone on the STP is around £25,000 plus a location allowance where valid.

A qualified critical care technologist would move into the NHS wage Band 6 and could earn up to £35,225 with the potential to move up to Band 7 as a manager and earn up to £41,373.

If you work in London, you may receive an additional allowance and wages may be higher in the private sector.

Working overtime or being on-call can increase your earnings.

Related opportunities

- Audiologist p275
- Operating Department Practitioner p302
- Sterile Services Technician p322

Further information

NHS Careers
www.healthcareers.nhs.uk

Skills for Health
www.skillsforhealth.org.uk

Society of Critical Care Technologists
www.criticalcaretech.org.uk

HEALTHCARE

279

Qualifications and courses

To practice as a dental hygienist you will need to register with the General Dental Council (GDC) and have completed a GDC-approved course. This can be either a 2-year full-time Diploma in Dental Hygiene and Therapy, a Foundation degree in Oral Health Science, or a 3-year full-time BSc degree in Oral Health Science (Hygiene and Therapy) or Dental Hygiene and Dental Therapy. Minimum entry requirements for these courses are 2 A levels/3 H grades and 5 GCSEs/National 5s (A*–C/A–C), including English, Maths and a science-related subject, and an interview is typically arranged before an offer to study is made. Relevant work experience may also be advantageous.

Some institutions also accept a GDC-recognised qualification in dental nursing as long as it is accompanied by other qualifications such as an A level or AS in Biology or Human Biology (A–D). Equivalent qualifications may also be considered, such as an advanced GNVQ, BTEC, Access to HE Diploma or Advanced Diploma, all of which must be in a science-related subject.

Prior to their place at the dental school being confirmed, all potential students are required to pass a medical test and undergo screening for blood-borne viruses, such as hepatitis B and C, and HIV.

As you will work with children and vulnerable adults you will also need a Disclosure and Barring Service (DBS) check prior to training.

What the work involves

Dental hygienists are predominantly concerned with oral hygiene and help prevent tooth decay and gum disease in their patients whilst working closely with and under the instruction of dentists.

Your work will include scaling and polishing teeth, putting in temporary fillings, taking impressions and X-rays, and applying protective coatings to teeth to prevent decay. You will require sufficient bi-manual dexterity to simultaneously treat patients with the necessary equipment whilst using a dental mirror.

You will be using a range of instruments, including scraping devices and drills. You will instruct patients on the appropriate way to floss and brush as well as advise them on their diet.

Type of person suited to this work

You will need to have excellent communication skills and be warm and reassuring as you treat patients of all ages, advising them on oral care.

You will need to combine good scientific knowledge with a personable approach to your work in order to motivate patients and convince them to stick to dental routines. A genuine desire to help people is essential.

You will need good eyesight and precise manual skills so that you can carry out detailed dental work with delicate instruments. An ability to stay focussed for long periods of time is also important.

Working conditions

You will usually work a 37-hour week from Monday to Friday, although occasional evening and Saturday morning work may be required according to practice opening hours. Part-time work is also available.

If you work for a community dental service you may travel to see patients in various locations such as schools and residential homes. You may also work out of a mobile clinic.

Surgeries are clean and well-lit. You will need to wear a white coat, surgical gloves, a face mask and eye protection for various procedures.

Future prospects

There is not the shortage in the industry that there was a few years ago, but demand is still strong and job prospects are good.

Despite the majority of hygienists working in dental surgeries, you could also work for a community dental service, in a hospital or for the Defence Dental Agency (DDA), providing dental treatment for the British armed forces around the world.

You may be promoted to practice manager or go on to become an orthodontic therapist.

You could also become self-employed and work across several practices, undertaking part-time hours in each or teach a dental hygiene training course.

Advantages/disadvantages

You will meet all kinds of people, which can create a diverse and interesting working day.

It is satisfying to see a patient's condition improve based on your advice.

You may come across anxious patients who are difficult to calm down.

Money guide

Dental hygienists usually start in the NHS wage band 5 which means a starting salary of between £21,909 and £28,462 per year.

Moving up to band 6 could mean earnings between £26,302 and £35,225.

If you work in private practice, have considerable experience and a good reputation, you could earn up to £48,000 per year.

Related opportunities

- Dental Therapist p283
- Dentist p284
- Orthodontist p304

Further information

British Dental Association
www.bda.org

British Society of Dental Hygiene & Therapy
www.bsdht.org.uk

General Dental Council
www.gdc-uk.org

NHS Careers
www.healthcareers.nhs.uk

DENTAL NURSE

Qualifications and courses

Typically there are no academic entry requirements to work as a trainee dental nurse but in order to progress you will need to study a recognised qualification in dental nursing before becoming a dental nurse. These qualifications need to be approved by the General Dental Council (GDC) and many of these courses require GCSEs/National 5s (A*–C/A–C) in English, Maths and a science subject for entry.

Qualifications recognised by the GDC are the Certificate of Higher Education in Dental Nursing, City & Guilds Level 3 Diploma in Dental Nursing (5234), SQA Level 3 in Dental Nursing, National Examining Board for Dental Nurses (NEBDN) National Certificate or a Certificate of Proficiency in Dental Nursing from a recognised dental hospital.

Alternatively, you could complete an Advanced Apprenticeship, which will allow you to register with the GDC. The apprenticeship lasts 18 months and you will study for either a RQF Level 3 Diploma in Dental Nursing, NEBDN National Diploma in Dental Nursing, NVQ Level 3 in Dental Nursing, or Level 3 VRQ in Dental Nursing.

You will also need to be registered with the GDC in order to work.

The armed forces also offer several routes into dental nursing.

What the work involves

Dental nurses assist dentists in all aspects of clinical work and patient treatment.

You will be expected to prepare the surgery each day and for each patient, ensuring that all instruments are to hand and sterilised ready for use. You will also assist in dental procedures by holding suction devices in the patient's mouth, ensuring that they are comfortable throughout their treatment, and giving patients pre- and post-operative advice.

You may also take responsibility for the day-to-day running of the surgery, including maintaining stock and ordering equipment, and undertaking some administrative duties.

Type of person suited to this work

You should have excellent interpersonal skills as you will be dealing with patients on a daily basis, many of whom may be anxious about forthcoming treatment and in need of kindness and reassurance.

Good eyesight and manual dexterity are helpful when aiding in procedures, as is a calm approach to tasks and the ability to react quickly and calmly to unforeseen situations. As you will be working closely with a dentist and other colleagues, you will need to enjoy being part of a team environment.

Good time management and organisational skills are necessary in order to fulfil the range of duties you will be expected to undertake.

Working conditions

You will usually work from 8am to 5.30pm, Monday to Friday, and some evening or weekend work may be required. Part-time work is often available. If you work in a hospital, you may be asked to remain on-call over weekends and provide emergency cover at any time of day or night.

Dental nurses are also employed by the Salaried Primary Care Dental Service (SPCDS) to work in local communities, assisting with patient care in various locations such as mobile clinics, schools and residential homes.

You will have to wear a uniform, and relevant safety equipment such as surgical gloves and a face mask.

Future prospects

Once qualified, you could continue your studies in order to gain further qualifications that will allow you to take on additional responsibilities such as sedation of patients and radiography.

Another option is to train to become a specialist orthodontic dental nurse, or a dental hygienist.

Some dental nurses also move into teaching roles and train student nurses.

Advantages/disadvantages

You will be working in pleasant, clean environments helping to treat patients and maintain a high standard of dental care across the UK.

Hours are usually standard and regular, with the opportunity to work part time for a better work–life balance.

Money guide

Entry level dental nurses start in NHS band 3 and so can earn from £16,800 to £19,655.

With more experience this could rise to £22,458.

Specialists and team leaders could earn up to £28,462.

A dental nurse manager is under band 6 which goes up to £35,225.

These figures are based on the NHS's Agenda for Change pay rates. The exact rate of pay could depend on your location and employer. Private dental nurses may earn more.

Related opportunities

- Adult Nurse p271
- Dental Hygienist p280
- Dentist p284

Further information

British Association of Dental Nurses
www.badn.org.uk

General Dental Council
www.gdc-uk.org

HEALTHCARE

DENTAL TECHNICIAN

Qualifications and courses

Before working as a dental technician you will have to pass a qualification recognised by the General Dental Council (GDC) and then register with them. Relevant qualifications include the BTEC Level 3 Extended Diploma/Subsidiary Diploma, Foundation degree and degree in dental technology.

Entry requirements for the BTEC Level 3 Extended Diploma/Subsidiary Diploma are at least 4 GCSEs/National 5s (A*–C/A–C), including English, Maths and a science. For a Foundation degree in dental technology, you will need an A level/H grade and 4 GCSEs/National 5s (A*–C/A–C). Typical entry requirements for a degree course are 2 A levels/3 H grades, including a science such as Biology or Human Biology, and 5 GCSEs/National 5s (A*–C/A–C) including English, Maths and Chemistry or Dual Award Science.

You can work as a trainee in a laboratory or hospital whilst you study to obtain a relevant qualification that will enable you to register as a practising dental technician.

The armed forces also recruit dental technicians, but you will need to be fully qualified at the time of applying, and be under 33 years of age.

It is important to commit to a programme of continuing professional development (CPD) to keep your skills up to date.

What the work involves

Dental technicians can work within 3 different areas: prosthodontic technicians specialise in designing and making dentures and implants; conservation technicians specialise in crown and bridge work; orthodontic technicians produce braces. Some technicians may specialise in one discipline whilst others may work in all three.

You will follow detailed prescriptions, written by a doctor or dentist, in order to create individual, patient-specific appliances.

You will use a variety of materials for crafting each device, including gold, steel, porcelain and plastic. You will also use numerous technical instruments in order to accurately carve, mould or wire each accessory.

If you train as a healthcare scientist in reconstructive science via the NHS Scientist Training Programme (STP) or complete a Diploma or Master of Science (MSc) in Maxillofacial Technology you can also become a maxillofacial technician and help reconstruct the faces of patients damaged by accident or disease.

Type of person suited to this work

You will be producing extremely delicate, precise devices so you will need excellent manual dexterity, good eyesight and full colour vision. It also helps to have some artistic ability so that you can make items such as false teeth and crowns look as natural and aesthetically pleasing as possible.

You will need to be able to concentrate on a task for lengthy periods of time, and maintain a high level of accuracy throughout.

You should also be comfortable understanding and interpreting complex technical instructions in order to create them as 3D devices.

Working conditions

You should expect to work around 40 hours per week. Hours usually fall on weekdays but if you work in a hospital dental unit you might have to work evenings and weekends to cover emergency clinics.

Dental technicians usually work for commercial laboratories that produce equipment for a number of different practitioners in an area. These range in size from smaller businesses to large companies.

You will be working in a laboratory, either within a hospital, dental practice, or independent commercial facility.

You will be expected to wear protective clothing and safety equipment when undertaking certain tasks.

Future prospects

Alternative employers include hospital dental units, the Royal Army Dental Corps (RADC), the Royal Air Force, and the Royal Navy. There is also the option to be self-employed, although this is relatively uncommon.

Within larger companies, prospects for promotion are good.

Advantages/disadvantages

You will have job satisfaction in knowing you are producing high quality dental devices to improve a patient's dental health or appearance.

It is not a very sociable job. Although you will be working in a laboratory with other professionals, you will be responsible for your own projects and have no patient contact.

Money guide

Dental technicians for the NHS start in the NHS wage band 5, earning between £21,909 and £28,462.

With experience you could gain a position as a dental technician specialist increasing your salary to between £26,302 and £35,225.

Dental lab managers could earn between £40,028 and £68,484.

These figures are based on the NHS's Agenda for Change pay rates. Private dental technicians may earn more.

Related opportunities

- Dental Hygienist p280
- Dental Nurse p281
- Dental Therapist p283

Further information

British Institute of Dental and Surgical Technologists
www.bidst.org

General Dental Council
www.gdc-uk.org

DENTAL THERAPIST

Qualifications and courses

You will need to register with the General Dental Council (GDC) prior to working as a dental therapist. To do this, you will need either a Diploma in Dental Therapy (often combined with a Diploma in Dental Hygiene) or a GDC-approved degree in Oral Health Sciences or Dental Hygiene and Dental Therapy. Minimum entry requirements for these courses are 2 A levels/3 H grades and 5 GCSEs/National 5s (A*–C/A–C), including English, Maths and Biology. Degree courses typically take 3–4 years of full-time study to complete. Some schools may accept a GDC-recognised qualification in dental nursing in place of A levels.

In addition to all of the training applied to a dental hygienist you will also need clinical skills training in how to do fillings and extract deciduous (milk) teeth. As a student you can join the British Association of Dental Therapists (BADT) which can give you access to relevant job adverts as well as help you network.

Qualified dental hygienists and dental nurses can also become therapists either by completing a conversion course or studying a professional progression course such as the Dental Development programme in Science and Dental Therapy at the University of Portsmouth.

Qualified therapists need to complete 150 hours of professional development activity every 5 years in order to remain registered with the GDC.

You will need a Disclosure and Barring Service (DBS) check prior to training.

What the work involves

Dental therapists, or oral health practitioners, perform both clinical and educational dental tasks.

You will not only perform a hygienist's role such as scaling and polishing teeth, but you will also remove plaque from the root surface of the teeth and carry out fillings and nerve treatments on both adult and deciduous teeth.

You will educate patients on proper diet and ways to brush and floss their teeth. You could also need to administer a supervised local anaesthetic.

Type of person suited to this work

As you will treat everyone from children to the elderly you will need to be adaptable, good-natured and encouraging. Your patients must feel comfortable with you and trust you.

You need to be a clear and motivational communicator in order to educate patients on proper dental care.

It is essential to have both a solid understanding of biology as well as a sincere interest in the wellbeing of your patients. You will need endurance, the ability to focus for long periods of time and a precise hand for carrying out detailed procedures.

Working conditions

You will work in a clean and bright environment. Your hours will be standard Monday to Friday but you might need to work the occasional Saturday morning or evening surgery, depending on the opening hours of your dental practice. It might be possible to work freelance or on a part-time basis.

You might need to travel to schools or residential homes to visit patients if you are employed by a community dental service. This may include working from a mobile clinic.

For most procedures you will need to wear protective gloves, a facemask and uniform.

Future prospects

Good job opportunities exist for dental therapists throughout the UK. You may be employed by a general practice (private or NHS), a dental school, a cosmetic surgery, a Salaried Primary Care Dental Service or with a Primary Care Trust.

You could be promoted to a dental practice manager or become a researcher or lecturer. With further training you could also specialise in health promotion.

You might choose to set up your own dental practice.

Advantages/disadvantages

It is rewarding to see a patient satisfied at the end of their treatment.

Your work will be varied as each patient's case will be unique.

The job can be demanding as you must deal with the public all day and you might find it difficult to win a patient's trust.

Money guide

The starting salary for a therapist in the NHS is between £21,909 and £28,462 a year. As a specialist you may earn up to £35,225 a year.

Advanced therapists may earn up to £41,373 a year.

Your salary may increase based on your employer and where you live. If you are self-employed you will be able to negotiate your fees. These figures are based on the NHS's Agenda for Change pay rates.

Related opportunities

- Dental Hygienist p280
- Dental Nurse p281
- Dentist p284

Further information

British Association of Dental Therapists
www.badt.org.uk

General Dental Council
www.gdc-uk.org

NHS Careers
www.healthcareers.nhs.uk

HEALTHCARE

283

Qualifications and courses

To become a dentist, you need to complete a degree at one of the institutions approved by the General Dental Council (GDC). The standard programme lasts 5 years. You will need at least 3 good A levels/H grades, including Chemistry and Biology, and 5 GCSEs/National 5s (A*–C/A–C). Though not essential, work experience may be advantageous as competition for degree places is fierce. Some universities also require candidates to complete the UK Clinical Aptitude Test (UKCAT) or the Graduate Medical School Admissions Test (GAMSAT).

If you have good A level/H grade results, but not in the required subjects, you can apply for a 6-year programme that includes an initial 30-week Foundation course that will get you up to speed in chemistry, physics and biology.

If you already have a degree in another subject it is possible to take an accelerated degree lasting only 4 years. To qualify you will need a 2.1 classified degree, and have relevant qualifications (usually high quality A levels/H grades) in Biology and Chemistry.

Once you have completed your degree you will have 1 or 2 years of vocational training and will also need to commit to a programme of continuing professional development (CPD) to remain registered with the General

Dental Council.

What the work involves

Dentists are trained to recognise, diagnose and treat all problems that affect the teeth, gums and mouth.

You will examine teeth and carry out appropriate treatments, such as fitting or replacing fillings, scraping away plaque, polishing and removing teeth, as well as educating patients about good oral habits in order to prevent disease or decay.

You will also need to keep detailed dental records for each patient, alongside managing your staff and, if you are a practice manager, looking after the practice budget.

Type of person suited to this work

You will need to have excellent communication skills in order to inspire your team and build good relationships with your patients, who will represent all ages and backgrounds.

You should also be compassionate and sympathetic, as you will encounter patients who are nervous or anxious about their treatment and you will need to be able to soothe and reassure them.

You will need good eyesight, concentration and manual dexterity to successfully carry out complicated and delicate procedures. If you intend to run your own practice, you will also need good business acumen.

Working conditions

If you work in a dental surgery, you should have regular Monday to Friday hours, and may even enjoy some flexibility within this framework. Dentists who work in hospitals will usually work longer hours, including weekends, and will have to adhere to an on-call rota.

You could work across the community, travelling to provide treatment in locations such as schools and retirement homes.

You will need to wear protective, hygienic clothing such as a white coat and surgical gloves when dealing with patients.

Future prospects

Most dentists are self-employed, working in general practice across the UK. Some work for the NHS, and some take on a mixture of private and NHS patients. You could also work for the armed forces.

A recent surge in dental graduates has increased competition in this sector. There is still demand for graduates across the UK, but this is mostly within the NHS which is viewed by some as a less lucrative career move than private practice.

You could undertake further training to specialise in a field such as orthodontics, maxillofacial surgery or dental public health, which is a relatively new and expanding specialty with a shortage of consultants.

Advantages/disadvantages

The majority of dentists are self-employed and work in the private sector, so you have a good amount of control over the hours you work and the patients you see.

There are excellent opportunities for rapid career progression or further training if you want to specialise in a specific area.

You will mainly be undertaking routine check-ups and very standard procedures, so work can feel monotonous at times.

Money guide

Salaries for recently graduated, trainee dentists in general practice start at around £30,000 to £40,000 per year. If you start your career in the NHS your training salary will be in the region of £30,732.

Experienced dentists in general practice can earn between £50,000 and £110,000. Salaries can be even higher if you run your own surgery.

If you reach consultant level working for the NHS, your salary could exceed £100,000.

Related opportunities

- Dental Hygienist p280
- Dental Therapist p283
- Orthodontist p304

Further information

British Dental Association
www.bda.org

General Dental Council
www.gdc-uk.org

NHS Careers
www.healthcareers.nhs.uk

DIETITIAN

Qualifications and courses

To become a dietitian, an approved degree or postgraduate qualification in dietetics or human nutrition and dietetics is required. You must then register with the Health & Care Professions Council (HCPC) in order to practise. You will need 2 A levels/3 H grades, including Chemistry and another science, and 5 GCSEs/National 5s (A*–C/A–C), including English and Maths, for entry to a degree in dietetics. Entry requirements for a postgraduate diploma are typically an Honours degree in a science subject with an acceptable level of biochemistry and human physiology, along with a good command of spoken and written English.

The approved degree is usually a full-time course that lasts 3 or 4 years, while the postgraduate diploma takes 2 years. Both routes include practical training in a hospital or community setting.

Some institutions expect applicants to have undertaken some work experience with a dietetic department or related hospital setting before applying for a place.

Mature applicants can complete an Access course in science to be accepted onto a degree programme. If you don't have an approved degree or postgraduate diploma, entry is only available at assistant level.

Dietitians are regulated by the HCPC and are required to continue their professional development (CPD).

What the work involves

Dietitians use their scientific knowledge of food to provide advice and information about diet and nutrition. Dietitians might work in industry developing food products and even in the media.

You will give advice to a broad range of people, such as hospital patients, caterers, sports professionals and the general public.

You will help people improve their health and prevent disease by making changes in their diet.

Type of person suited to this work

You will need expert knowledge of the science of food and nutrition, and how this relates to the body.

You must have excellent communication skills to be able to give practical information and advice to a range of people, from school children to food manufacturers. You will need to be caring, supportive and non-judgemental, and able to understand the needs and issues of individuals, especially if you are working with sick people.

You should have good motivational skills so that people can follow your advice and make the changes that you recommend.

Working conditions

You could work in a range of locations such as hospitals, laboratories, offices and sports centres.

You are likely to work a standard working week from Monday to Friday, although in hospitals you may be called in to work at weekends and on bank holidays.

In most jobs you will be working directly with people who can be ill, distressed or reluctant to take your advice.

Future prospects

The British Dietetic Association has over 5,000 members and the profession is growing around the world. There are opportunities across the UK and abroad, but competition for jobs is fierce.

Most dietitians work in the NHS, but there are also many opportunities in areas such as sports nutrition, the food and pharmaceutical industries, scientific research, education and journalism. You could become self-employed working as a consultant or see private clients.

In the NHS, you could go on to specialise in areas such as cancer care, or with particular groups such as children or the elderly. You could also move into management.

Advantages/disadvantages

People might be unable or unwilling to take on your advice, which can be frustrating.

It is rewarding to see improvements in people when they put into practice the information and advice you have given them.

Money guide

NHS dietitians start work on the NHS wage band 5 and earn between £21,909 and £28,462 per year.

Specialist dietitians work in band 6 and earn from £26,302 to £35,225.

Salaries for senior grade dietitians working in band 7 can be between £31,383 and £41,373.

There are higher grades for chief members of staff, or for work outside the NHS, although salaries are not necessarily higher in private work.

You may earn more if you work in London or the south-east of England. In addition, salary premiums are offered where there are recruitment issues or for specialist positions.

Related opportunities

- Food Scientist/Technologist p505
- Health Promotion/Education Specialist p288
- Health Visitor p291

Further information

British Dietetic Association
www.bda.uk.com

NHS Careers
www.healthcareers.nhs.uk

Skills for Health
www.skillsforhealth.org.uk

HEALTHCARE

285

HEALTHCARE

Qualifications and courses

You must be registered with the General Optical Council (GOC). To qualify, you must complete an appropriate training course, pass the Professional Qualifying Examinations of the Association of British Dispensing Opticians (ABDO), and undergo a pre-registration year working under the supervision of a qualified optician.

The GOC has approved 3 routes into the profession: a 3-year day release training course in optical management combined with suitable employment; a 3-year distance learning course, combined with suitable employment; a 2-year full time diploma course or Foundation degree in ophthalmic dispensing, followed by one year of supervised salaried employment.

Typical entry requirements for a degree or Foundation degree are 2 A levels/3 H grades, normally including relevant science subjects, and 5 GCSEs/National 5s (A*–C/A–C), including English, Maths and a science. For a diploma, you will need at least 5 GCSEs/National 5s (A*–C/A–C), including English, Maths and a science.

You could also start as a trainee with a qualified optometrist and work part time towards qualifications. High street companies such as Specsavers and Boots also offer training programmes and certain colleges offer a 3-year day-release programme for those in suitable employment.

Relevant pre-entry experience is also desirable as many individuals who enter the profession already have experience as an optical assistant or other relevant professions, or in company positions such as receptionists or sales assistants.

What the work involves

Dispensing opticians use prescriptions from optometrists to supply and fit glasses.

The work you will do includes measuring the patient's face to ensure the glasses will fit and advising on lenses and frame styles to suit them and their prescription. You will check that the finished glasses meet the original specifications and supply them to the patient. You will also do repairs.

Some dispensing opticians take further training to supply and fit contact lenses.

Type of person suited to this work

Interpreting prescriptions requires specific scientific expertise.

You will be advising and listening to customers of many different ages and backgrounds, and working as part of a team with other professionals, so you will need excellent communication skills. It will be your responsibility to take measurements and repair glasses so manual skills are necessary.

You will need to be interested in fashion, as well as have strong commercial awareness and product knowledge.

You will need to be business minded if you choose to set up your own practice.

Working conditions

Most dispensing opticians work in high-street opticians. Financial and management challenges may arise if you are self-employed.

You may work 35–40 hours a week from Monday to Saturday (with some time off during the week instead).

You may have to work on Sundays and bank holidays or in shifts, including weekends, in big chains.

Registration with the GOC will allow you to work in other countries.

Future prospects

With experience you may specialise, for example in supplying and fitting contact lenses or low vision aids. You could also train new entrants.

You may also be promoted into a management position within a high-street optical chain.

With experience, some opticians choose to run their own practices, however, increasing numbers of dispensing opticians are choosing to work for established franchises rather than run an independent practice. This is due to the growing threat from big high street chains as well as online alternatives.

Advantages/disadvantages

It can be stressful having to meet sales targets in some opticians.

If you enjoy combining scientific knowledge with working with the public, this job could be good for you.

Money guide

Salary levels vary enormously and are usually higher for opticians with management responsibility.

Starting salaries are around £18,000 per year.

Salaries for specialist and managerial roles range from £25,000 to in excess of £35,000 a year.

Related opportunities

- Optometrist p303
- Pharmacist p308
- Sales/Retail Assistant p480

Further information

Association of British Dispensing Opticians
www.abdo.org.uk

General Optical Council
www.optical.org

NHS Careers
www.healthcareers.nhs.uk

Qualifications and courses

To become a General Practitioner (GP) you must first complete a degree in medicine that is recognised by the General Medical Council (GMC). The standard programme lasts 5 years and you will require at least 3 good A levels/H grades, including Chemistry and Biology, for entry. Some medical schools also require applicants to sit the UK Clinical Aptitude Test (UKCAT) or BioMedical Admissions Test (BMAT), which not only test academic ability but behavioural characteristics. It is now common, and expected, for applicants to have some work experience in healthcare, for example, as a care assistant in a nursing home or hospital.

If you do not have science A levels, some universities offer a 6-year programme that includes an initial 'pre-medical' year that will get you up to speed. If you already have a 2.1 degree in another subject, some medical schools offer an accelerated degree in medicine lasting only 4 years.

Once you have a degree in medicine, you will need to complete a 2-year foundation programme with specialist training in general practice before you can qualify as a GP. At the end of the foundation programme you would choose to train in general practice. This second stage of specialist training takes around 3 years to complete and will include at least 12 months working as a GP registrar in the NHS.

What the work involves

General practitioners (GPs) diagnose various health problems, physical or emotional, within their local community.

You will be talking to and examining patients in order to find out what is wrong with them, and then deciding on how to treat them. This could include giving them advice, prescribing medicine or referring patients to a specialist doctor.

You may occasionally have to perform minor surgery such as removing moles or warts. You are responsible for educating your patients about how to live a healthy lifestyle and prevent illness.

Type of person suited to this work

You will need to have excellent communication skills in order to gain the trust of your patients and build good relationships with them. You should be able to put them at their ease quickly whilst maintaining a professional attitude.

You must have excellent scientific and medical knowledge in order to assess problems quickly and reach a suitable diagnosis, all within the time limit of a 10 minute appointment.

You should have an enquiring mind as you will need to continually update your knowledge and learn about new techniques and medicines in order to keep up to date in this fast moving discipline.

Working conditions

You will usually work normal hours from Monday to Friday, although increasingly surgeries are offering evening and weekend appointments which you might have to cover on a rota basis. You may also have to spend some time on-call, visiting patients at home at any hour of the day or night.

GPs are practice based in small or large surgeries within cities, towns and rural areas. GPs have to adhere to time and budget constraints, which can make the work stressful and demanding.

Future prospects

The healthcare system is changing and the NHS will need more GPs in the future. Therefore, the number of training places is increasing and job prospects are promising.

As a general practitioner you will be able to work anywhere in the UK, in a larger practice with healthcare professionals from a number of disciplines, or a smaller surgery.

You could undertake work for the NHS, enjoy the freedom of self-employment, or opt for a combination of the two.

Advantages/disadvantages

The training period prior to qualifying as a GP is, on average, 10 years.

As a full-time GP 52-hour weeks, which could include evening and weekends as well as out-of-hours emergency work, are not uncommon.

Dealing with patients with varying complaints each day can be stressful, but helping them to recover is rewarding.

The work is varied and you will meet lots of different people on a daily basis.

Money guide

For a doctor in training, the basic salary is £27,000, rising to £30,000 in the second year of training. In the first year of specialist training, you can expect a salary of between £37,000 and £48,000.

You may get overtime pay for working more than 40 hours a week or outside the hours of 7am to 7pm. This could be as much as 50% of the basic salary.

As a fully-qualified GP your earnings could be between £55,965 and £84,543 a year.

Independent GPs are self-employed and have an NHS contract. As such they can earn more than salaried GPs, depending on the specialism, the services provided and the practice.

Related opportunities

- Hospital Doctor p294
- Pharmacist p308
- Surgeon p323

Further information

British Medical Association
www.bma.org.uk

General Medical Council
www.gmc-uk.org

Royal College of General Practitioners
www.rcgp.org.uk

HEALTHCARE

Qualifications and courses

Entrants to this profession need a degree in a relevant subject such as health studies or public health. Subjects such as psychology, social science or education can also be useful. Entry requirements for degrees are usually a minimum of 2 A levels/3 H grades and 5 GCSEs/National 5s (A*–C/A–C) or alternative qualifications such as a BTEC in health and social care. More senior posts generally require a Postgraduate Diploma or Master of Science (MSc) in health promotion. If you have a nursing diploma or a related Foundation degree, there is the option to take a top-up degree course in health promotion.

It may be possible to train on the job for recognised qualifications. The Open University offers a certificate in Health Promotion. Some colleges run a Health Studies Access course for candidates without the necessary entry requirements. The Royal Society for Public Health (RSPH) also offers the Level 1 Award in Health Awareness and the Level 2 Award in Understanding Health Improvement.

It is possible to enter the profession through related fields though it is advisable to undertake relevant voluntary work or short courses in areas such as stopping smoking and working with patient groups in order to demonstrate your commitment to the profession.

The Public Health Register maintains a voluntary register for specialists in this field, and recommends degree and postgraduate courses to its members.

What the work involves

Health promotion/education specialists aim to promote and improve public health in line with national recommendations. This could be done by running training courses and workshops, public health campaigns such as screening and immunisation, and producing publicity materials.

You could work with organisations such as schools or directly with individuals, groups or communities.

Your work might include advising individuals on how to make lifestyle changes, such as taking more exercise or giving up smoking, encouraging organisations like workplaces, schools and hospitals to improve diets and promote health or developing partnerships with communities to improve public health. Your role might also involve liaising with the press and compiling features to encourage healthy living.

Type of person suited to this work

You must be able to encourage individuals and communities to change their lifestyles. It is important to have excellent communication and negotiation skills as a large part of your job will involve dealing with people from all age groups and all walks of life.

You will need to be creative to find different ways of persuading people and organisations to make changes. Good research and writing skills are also necessary in order to put together clear reports.

You will need to be supportive and non-judgemental and able to relate to the needs of a wide range of people, communities and cultures. You must have good organisational skills to run and manage projects.

Working conditions

You could work in many different places such as health centres, local authority buildings, hospitals, workplaces and fitness centres.

You are likely to have a normal working week, Monday to Friday. Some employers offer flexible working schemes.

Travel within a working day is common as you will need to attend meetings, for example at local schools or community groups.

Future prospects

This is a very competitive industry and you will probably need to do work experience.

Most health promotion/education specialists work for the NHS, health promotion agencies, local authorities or in social and community settings.

You can progress to management roles or go into research and lecturing in health promotion.

Advantages/disadvantages

Changing people's habits can be difficult and take a long time.

Working to tight deadlines and targets can be very stressful.

Seeing improvements in public health when people put into practice the information and advice you have provided is very rewarding. You will have the opportunity to work with many different people.

Money guide

Salary levels are largely dependent on which health sector you work in and which health authority you work for.

In the NHS, the Agenda for Change salary bands states health promoters should start on NHS wage band 5, earning between £21,909 and £28,462.

More experienced and senior staff could progress to band 7, earning between £31,383 and £41,373.

Related opportunities

- Dietitian p285
- Health and Safety Adviser p27
- Youth and Community Worker p579

Further information

Faculty of Public Health
www.fph.org.uk

NHS Careers
www.healthcareers.nhs.uk

Qualifications and courses

Most employers require candidates to have at least 5 GCSEs/National 5s (A*–C/A–C), including English and Maths. Other relevant qualifications include the NVQ Level 1 or 2 in Business and Administration and the BTEC qualifications in Business (Levels 1–2). Previous administrative experience would also be advantageous.

Training is mostly done on the job, however you may also be offered the chance to formally study for professional qualifications such as the NVQ Level 2 in Support Services in Healthcare or the Level 3 in Business Administration. The Institute of Health Record and Information Management (IHRIM) offers several courses in healthcare administration including the Certificate in Health Records Management. If you have 12 months' experience, the Foundation degree in Health Informatics is available through the University of Central Lancashire.

Apprenticeships might enable you to enter this role for candidates aged 16–24.

As you will be working with children and vulnerable adults, you will need to pass a Disclosure and Barring Service (DBS) check.

What the work involves

Health administrators and records clerks are responsible for preparing and maintaining records of patients' medical notes, including details about the medicines they take and any other care needs.

You will be collating, organising and archiving relevant notes and documents in each patient's file, and also ensuring that they are easily accessible for other healthcare professionals.

You will be working with both paper documents and electronic records, which will include using equipment such as computers, photocopiers and scanners. You will also undertake other administrative duties, such as making and rearranging patients' appointments, sorting incoming correspondence and covering reception from time to time.

Type of person suited to this work

You will be working within a team of healthcare professionals as well as dealing with patient enquiries, so you should be personable and have excellent communication skills.

You will need good numeracy and IT skills. As you will be dealing with a variety of tasks each day, you will also need good organisational skills and the ability to prioritise your workload.

You will be working with confidential information so you must be discreet.

Working conditions

You could work in an office, a reception area, filing room, medical records library or a hospital ward. You will usually work a 37-hour week from Monday to Friday, although occasionally some jobs require employees to work shifts. Part-time opportunities are common.

As you will be moving and transporting large, heavy piles of paper files around the hospital or practice, you will need to be reasonably strong and fit.

The majority of the work is office based, although you might need to courier documents to various departments within your building. You will be expected to look fairly smart, although a business suit is unnecessary.

Future prospects

Although the NHS is the biggest employer of administrative staff, there are also opportunities in private hospitals and voluntary organisations.

Increasingly, the NHS is providing a structured career path for their administrators. With the correct training and experience there are positions within every NHS pay band. For example, you could progress towards a supervisory or managerial role within your department, become head of communications, or support a specialist area such as neurology or gastroenterology. You could also transfer to other similar departments, such as the clinical informatics or the information management staff, where there are a variety of more specialist roles.

Repercussions from the recession are still affecting the NHS and job opportunities may be harder to come by.

Advantages/disadvantages

You will be providing an essential service to both patients and other healthcare professionals by ensuring the smooth running of behind-the-scenes operations.

You can expect to have a heavy workload at times.

Hours are regular and there is plenty of opportunity for part-time work which fits in around family commitments.

Money guide

The salary for a health records clerk usually starts at between £15,251 and £17,978.

As you gain experience this should rise to between £16,800 and £19,655, whilst team leaders can earn up to £22,458.

If you move into a more senior supervisory or management position, you can expect to earn up to £28,462.

Salaries do vary according to your employer, where you work in the UK and the additional benefits on offer, such as a pension scheme.

Related opportunities

- Adult Nurse p271
- Health Visitor p291
- Pharmacy Technician p310

Further information

Institute of Health Records and Information Management
www.ihrim.co.uk

HEALTHCARE

Qualifications and courses

A typical way to enter into health service management is by starting out as an administrator and working you way up to a management role. For entry-level positions 5 GCSEs/National 5s (A*–C/A–C) or, more commonly, 2 A levels/3H grades are needed.

Once you are in an administrative post you can study for relevant management training courses, such as those offered by the Institute of Healthcare Management (IHM). The Association of Medical Secretaries, Practice Managers, Administrators and Receptionists (AMSPAR) offers a Level 5 Certificate/Diploma in Primary Care and Health Management in association with City & Guilds.

One of the most direct routes into health service management is through the NHS Graduate Management Training Scheme. The programme covers 4 specialisms: finance management, general management, HR management and informatics. Entry is with a 2.2 degree in any subject or equivalent qualifications that are health or management-related, including the NVQ Level 5 in Management and the Diploma in Management Studies (DMS). The recruitment process for this two-year graduate scheme is fiercely competitive and involves a variety of aptitude tests and rounds of interviews.

The private sector also has graduate management schemes. To apply for a position with BUPA and BMI Healthcare you will need a 2.1 in any degree or equivalent.

What the work involves

You will help run GP surgeries, hospitals and other health centres, either working for the NHS or within the private sector.

Your job will be varied; you might be controlling finances, managing staff, producing reports on performance, overseeing buildings and buying equipment.

There are specific areas that managers can work in, such as clinical, financial, human resources, IT and facilities. You could also be a practice manager who runs GP surgeries.

Type of person suited to this work

Strong leadership skills and a likable personality will be essential for managing your team. Good communication skills are important as you will be interacting with a variety of people including professionals and patients.

You should be comfortable making important decisions, be logical in your approach to problems and have good negotiation skills.

You must have excellent written communication skills to produce detailed reports and you should be comfortable working with figures, as you may be responsible for budgets and resources.

Working conditions

You will work standard office hours, Monday to Friday, but you could be on-call for emergencies or required to work weekends.

Most of your time will be spent in an office within hospitals, GP surgeries or health centres.

As a manager, you will be expected to dress smartly.

It is useful to have a driving licence as you might travel between sites or to attend meetings.

Future prospects

The NHS Graduate Management Training Scheme is fiercely competitive and changes in the NHS structure mean that job numbers fluctuate due to the constant possibility of cutbacks.

There is a structured career path if you are employed by the NHS and promotion is gained by moving into different departments and areas of management.

The NHS Gateway to Leadership is available for managers with substantial experience. This fast-track programme enables you to become a chief executive within 5 years. In private healthcare there are stages of promotion which can also be followed.

With experience you may choose to take your managerial skills into another industry or become a consultant.

Advantages/disadvantages

You will be in a very responsible position which could be daunting and stressful.

You will gain valuable management skills which are transferable to many other industries.

Meeting and helping lots of different people provides a strong sense of job satisfaction.

Money guide

On the NHS pay scale, Agenda for Change, graduates on the NHS training scheme have a starting salary of about £23,000.

Once qualified, you are placed on either NHS wage band 6, earning between £26,302 and £35,225 or band 7, between £31,383 and £41,373.

Those in the most senior positions will be on band 9, earning between £78,629 and £99,437.

Salaries in the private sector could be higher.

Related opportunities

- Accountant p2
- Archivist/Records Manager p328
- Human Resources/Personnel Officer p28

Further information

Institute of Healthcare Management
www.ihm.org.uk

NHS Careers
www.healthcareers.nhs.uk

NHS Graduate Management Training Scheme
www.nhsgraduates.co.uk

HEALTH VISITOR

Qualifications and courses

All health visitors must be registered nurses or midwives, but there is no minimum length of pre-entry experience required. To become a nurse or midwife, you must complete a degree in nursing or midwifery that is recognised by the Nursing and Midwifery Council. Generally, you will need 2 A levels/3 H grades and 5 GCSEs/National 5s (A*–C/A–C) to apply for a 3- or 4-year degree course.

Pre-entry experience may be useful and should be relevant to the work of a health visitor and demonstrate a desire and commitment to working in the community. More specialised experience, such as working with children, obstetrics or midwifery would also be advantageous.

Once you have completed your training as a nurse, you will need to complete the Specialist Community Public Health Nursing Health Visiting (SCPHN/HV) programme. This qualification usually consists of 45 weeks of study that must be completed within a 156-week period; part-time study should be completed within 208 weeks.

You will be required to undergo a series of pre-employment checks including occupational health and Disclosure and Barring Service (DBS).

What the work involves

Health visitors work with people of all ages, backgrounds and cultures in various settings such as residential homes, schools, GP surgeries and village halls.

You will provide advice on issues ranging from problems in children's sleep or feeding patterns, to postnatal depression, bereavement or relationship problems and your primary patients will be parents with babies and young children. Whilst you will provide care for all young families, extra time may be spent helping those with extra needs.

You will also be involved in organising community events designed to promote health and wellbeing.

Type of person suited to this work

You will be working closely with patients so you will need excellent communication skills.

You must be trustworthy, understanding, reassuring and professional in order to inspire confidence in your patients, mainly parents, and allow them to share their problems and concerns with you openly. You should also be able to motivate them to make important lifestyle changes on occasion.

You must be able to prioritise a heavy workload, and maintain discretion when dealing with confidential information.

Working conditions

You will usually work a 37-hour week from Monday to Friday, and flexible hours or part-time work are often available.

You will work in a variety of locations, including schools, GP surgeries, health centres and residential homes. Because this will require a good deal of travelling within the local area, a driving licence is usually required.

You will encounter patients who are extremely difficult or distressed at times, which can be upsetting.

Future prospects

All health visitors work for the NHS, and they can be based in larger areas such as cities and towns, or work across villages and rural communities.

The government is working to increase the number of jobs available in this sector: Over the last 4 years alone 4,000 extra roles have been created, and the structures in place for further training and progression have also been developed.

Career progression could take the form of managing a team of health visitors, moving into a role as a consultant nurse, specialising in a particular area of nursing, education or research, or even taking up a position in general management within the NHS.

Advantages/disadvantages

You will be offering healthcare advice and treatment across the community, including to those who may otherwise not be able to reach a doctor or hospital very easily such as the elderly.

There are opportunities to work part time or on a job share basis, which would allow you to work around other commitments.

You may have to deal with difficult, potentially threatening patients, which can be frightening and upsetting.

Money guide

Qualified health visitors working for, or under contract with, the NHS can earn between £26,302 and £35,225.

Progressing into a team management role will increase your earning potential to up to £41,373.

Extra allowance can be made for added duties, location and experience.

Related opportunities

- Adult Nurse p271
- Children's Nurse p276
- Midwife p300
- Occupational Therapist p301
- Paramedic p306

Further information

Nursing and Midwifery Council
www.nmc.org.uk

Royal College of Nursing
www.rcn.org.uk

HEALTHCARE

Qualifications and courses

There are no fixed entry qualifications for this job, however previous experience caring for people, either through paid or voluntary work, may be expected by some employers.

All entrants to this profession will be required to pass a medical test and obtain clearance from the Disclosure and Barring Service (DBS).

The Apprenticeship in Health and Social Care offers an ideal route into this career for school leavers and is available at both Intermediate and Advanced Levels. This gives candidates the opportunity to combine practical work experience with the study towards a relevant professional qualification. These courses could include a BTEC in Health and Social Care (Levels 2–3), an A level/H grade in Health and Social Care, NVQs/SVQs such as the Level 3 Health and Social Care, and RQF qualifications in Healthcare Support Services or Clinical Healthcare Support (Levels 2–3). Entry for an apprenticeship usually requires 4 GCSEs/National 5s (A*–C/A–C) or a BTEC Level 1 Certificate/Diploma.

Once you secure employment as a healthcare assistant, you will receive on-the-job training covering topics including hygiene, health and safety, personal care and communication skills. You could go on to take a Foundation degree or degree in a subject such as nursing, mental health or applied health and social care.

What the work involves

Healthcare assistants help people who find it difficult to look after themselves with everyday tasks. Your clients could be children, elderly people or people with disabilities living in residential care or in their own homes.

You will help them to bathe, dress and use the toilet or commode, as well as assisting them with eating, washing, ironing, cleaning and shopping.

Part of your time will be spent talking to your clients, helping them to write letters, budget their money or pay bills.

Type of person suited to this work

Healthcare assistants need to be cheerful, outgoing and friendly, as their clients may be lonely or depressed.

As the job involves working with people who need individual support, you will have to work out what help they need and provide it in a sympathetic and tactful way.

You must be trustworthy, discreet and able to keep clients' confidential information private, as you will handle money, and write and read personal/business letters.

The job usually includes domestic work so you need to be happy and skilled at doing housework and laundry.

Working conditions

Many healthcare assistants work in residential homes and day-healthcare centres, but more people are being cared for in their own homes.

As the main employers are health authorities, social services, private homes and voluntary agencies, most of your work will be looking after clients from the time they wake up to the time they go to bed, with the chance to supervise on hospital appointments or outings. You might have to live in for some jobs.

You will usually work on a shift system which will include early mornings, evenings, weekends and bank holidays.

You need to be physically fit and capable of heavy lifting as you may need to help people who are unable to move around themselves.

You will be expected to be very careful about health and safety issues, such as fire and hot water.

Future prospects

There are over a million healthcare assistants in the UK and demand is increasing as the NHS evolves due to cutback in other roles. The Cavendish Report (2013) makes several recommendations as to how healthcare assistants can receive training and their role in the NHS.

Promotion depends on qualifications and experience. With experience in healthcare work, you could train for related jobs such as social work or nursing.

Advantages/disadvantages

It can be satisfying to help people in need.

Working on public holidays, such as Christmas Day, can interfere with your personal life.

Some jobs can be messy and unpleasant.

Money guide

Salaries start between £15,251 and £17,978 a year.

With experience and relevant qualifications, you can expect to earn approximately £19,655 a year.

Allowances for working shifts and unsocial hours can increase your income.

Related opportunities

- Adult Nurse p271
- Childminder p559
- Social Worker p573

Further information

NHS Careers
www.healthcareers.nhs.uk

Skills for Health
www.skillsforhealth.org.uk

HEALTHCARE

HOMEOPATH

Qualifications and courses

Although it is not compulsory to hold a qualification, most patients would not feel comfortable seeing you if you are not registered with one of the UK regulatory bodies, the best known of which is the Society of Homeopaths (SOH).

In order to register, you will need to complete an accredited degree or licentiate diploma in homeopathy from a private college. Entry requirements for these courses are usually 2 A levels/3 H grades and 5 GCSEs/National 5s (A*–C/A–C). Degree courses can be taken full time over 3 years or part time over 4. Most private colleges may require 2 A levels/H grades, including a science subject, but your life and work experience and your interest in homeopathy are usually more valued.

Qualified healthcare professionals can undertake shorter accredited courses in homeopathy at various universities, each of which is regulated by the British Homeopathic Association (BHA).

What the work involves

Homeopaths use highly diluted doses of natural remedies to treat patients for a variety of ailments, ranging from simple headaches to complicated emotional issues, addiction and disease.

You will need to take into account not only patients' physical symptoms, but also their psychological and emotional state, as well as their lifestyle.

You will be working with a variety of patients of all ages, backgrounds and cultures. You could undertake general cases, or specialise in areas such as fertility and drug addiction.

Type of person suited to this work

You will need excellent communication and listening skills in order to quickly build a rapport with patients and encourage them to discuss their problems and concerns honestly.

As you will need to build your own practice and find clients from scratch, you must have good business acumen, confidence and motivation.

You should also be well organised and methodical, as you will need to undertake your own administration and keep detailed, informative patient notes.

You will be in charge of storing confidential information about patients and should be professional in your approach to each client.

Working conditions

You will be self-employed and reliant on your clients, so will find that you mainly work in the evenings and at weekends (especially when newly qualified) in order to fit around their lifestyles.

You could work in a clinic with other healthcare professionals, in an alternative therapy centre, in your own home, or you could travel to see patients in their homes.

Patient appointments can take anywhere between 45 minutes and an hour and a half. The work is therefore mentally and emotionally draining as it requires long periods of concentrated work and, because of this, most homeopaths only work part time.

Future prospects

Alternative therapy has increased in popularity in recent years. This means that there are more people willing to explore it as a means of treatment, but also that there are an increasing number of practising homeopaths. Competition for clients, especially in the early years, can be fierce.

The majority of homeopaths are self-employed, although there are opportunities in independent surgeries, outreach clinics, private hospitals and in one of the four homeopathic NHS hospitals in the UK: Bristol, Glasgow, Liverpool and Royal London.

With experience you could use your knowledge to teach in a university or college, or write related books and articles.

Advantages/disadvantages

Spending time talking to patients about their concerns and alleviating their ailments is extremely rewarding.

If you are self-employed, overheads such as renting clinic space and buying remedies and other equipment will eat into your earnings.

You must be commercially aware in order to successfully market your business, and be prepared to do your own complicated tax forms.

Money guide

Most homeopaths charge their patients directly by appointment. They usually charge between £40 and £100 per session, with higher fees being found in London and the south-east of England.

A newly qualified homeopath who is just starting to build a reputation and attract clients could earn £6,000 a year.

For top earning homeopaths with lots of experience, salaries can rise to £30,000.

Related opportunities

- Aromatherapist p273
- Chiropractor p277
- Osteopath p305

Further information

Alliance of Registered Homeopaths
www.a-r-h.org

British Homeopathic Association
www.britishhomeopathic.org

Society of Homeopaths
www.homeopathy-soh.org

HEALTHCARE

293

Qualifications and courses

To become a hospital doctor, all entrants need to hold a degree in medicine which has been accredited by the General Medical Council (GMC). Courses normally last 5 years and entry requirements are usually at least 3 very high A levels/H grades including Chemistry and Biology, and good GCSEs/National 5s (A*–C/A–C), including English, Maths and a science. Competition for places on medical degrees is very high and undertaking relevant pre-entry work experience as a care assistant, for example, may benefit your application. You may also be asked to take the UK Clinical Aptitude Test (UKCAT) to substantiate your suitability for a career in medicine.

For those without the relevant A levels or equivalent, some universities offer a 6-year medical degree, in which the first year is a preliminary course in chemistry, physics and biology lasting 30 weeks.

Graduates of a science-related subject (minimum 2.1) can apply for a 4-year, fast-track medical degree programme. Some universities will consider applications from non-science graduates.

Upon completion of your degree in medicine, you will need to complete 2 further stages of vocational training to qualify as a senior doctor or consultant in your chosen field. The first stage is the 2-year Foundation Programme which forms the bridge between medical school and specialist/general practice training. The second stage is higher speciality training in an area of medicine which particularly interests you and the length of time this takes depends upon the area you choose. Candidates apply for higher speciality training via the ST3 recruitment process.

What the work involves

Hospital doctors work in either NHS or private establishments, diagnosing illnesses, treating patients and monitoring their care.

You may treat patients yourself or, having assessed them, refer them to their general practitioner (GP) or another healthcare professional. You will work in one of over 60 specialisms which include cardiology, general medicine, paediatrics, orthopaedics and psychiatry.

You will also be required to carry out surgical operations within your specialism, for example fitting a pacemaker if you are in cardiology. You may be responsible for teaching medical students.

Type of person suited to this work

You must have excellent communication skills as you will be dealing with patients and healthcare professionals on a daily basis.

When handling patients, you should be empathetic, non-judgemental, professional and calm.

You should be good at working under pressure, making sensible, but sometimes difficult, decisions and solving problems.

Working conditions

Generally you can expect to work longer hours than in most other professions, although new guidelines prohibit junior doctors from working more than a 48-hour week. You will usually work on a shift pattern of days and nights which will sometimes involve being on-call.

You will work in a consulting room, on the wards and in operating theatres. Conditions are usually quiet and clean, although things can get very fast paced during times of emergency.

You will also be required to attend numerous meetings and conferences across the UK, Europe and perhaps worldwide.

Future prospects

Junior doctors can choose to specialise in an area such as gastroenterology or geriatric medicine. Once they have completed a training programme in their specialism and passed the necessary exams, they will become a consultant.

Increasingly, senior level hospital doctors undertake managerial responsibilities, alongside teaching and mentoring work with students or junior doctors.

Advantages/disadvantages

You will be responsible for helping patients get better and making them comfortable throughout their illness which is very rewarding.

Hours can be long and unpredictable so it can be difficult to get a satisfactory work–life balance.

Constant developments in medicine and medical technology mean that you will be continually learning and developing throughout your career.

Money guide

As a junior hospital trainee, the basic salary starts at £27,000 and rises in the second year of foundation training to £30,000.

A doctor in specialist training has a starting salary of between £37,000 and £48,000. Trainee doctors also receive extra pay for working more than 40 hours a week or outside of the normal working hours, 7am to 7pm, Monday to Friday.

Specialist doctors can earn £37,547 to £70,018, while consultants can earn a basic salary between £76,001 and £102,465.

Doctors in the private sector can earn more.

Related opportunities

- Children's Nurse p276
- Doctor (GP) p287
- Surgeon p323

Further information

British Medical Association
www.bma.org.uk

Joint Royal Colleges of Physicians Training Board - ST3 Recruitment
www.st3recruitment.org.uk

NHS Careers
www.healthcareers.nhs.uk

HEALTHCARE

HOSPITAL PORTER

Qualifications and courses

There are no formal entry requirements for this job, but applicants must be literate and have good all-round communication skills as well as good physical fitness.

There is no set minimum age, but most applicants are at least 18 years old, and there are good opportunities for mature entrants.

You will undergo a short induction once you start and then training is generally on the job. However, in order to strengthen your application or even once you have started work, you work towards several formal qualifications such as an NVQ Level 2 in Support Services in Health Care, the Level 3 Diploma in Healthcare Support Services or a BTEC in Health and Social Care (Health Sciences) (Level 2–3).

Previous experience of volunteer hospital work, or previous work with the public in a caring role, can be useful to your job application and a health and safety qualification may also be beneficial. Alternatively, Apprenticeships in Health and Social Care are available and will prepare you to be a hospital porter and other related roles.

Candidates usually have to pass a medical examination, and may be required to take a physical fitness test. A driving licence may be required so that you can work at a range of different sites.

What the work involves

Hospital porters transport patients, equipment and other items to where they need to go within the hospital.

One of your main tasks will be to move frail and ill patients between departments and wards, while keeping them safe and comfortable.

You will transport patients using wheelchairs and trolleys.

You may also have a variety of other tasks such as delivering mail and moving medical equipment and supplies.

Type of person suited to this work

Hospital porters need to be responsible and reliable with a positive attitude to make sure that people and equipment are transported to the correct part of the hospital on time.

You should be able to follow instructions and work well as part of a team.

Patients may be distressed or in pain so you must be caring and sympathetic and be able to reassure them and keep them comfortable. You must be able to cope with sickness and death.

Physical fitness is important, because you will walk long distances during your shift and you will have to lift and move patients and equipment.

Working conditions

You will work with patients and other staff, mainly indoors, although you might need to travel to other hospital sites to make deliveries.

You will need to pay attention to health and safety when lifting and handling people and equipment.

Porters usually wear a uniform and often need to work shifts, which includes working nights, weekends and bank holidays.

You may assist with hospital security which could involve working on reception.

Future prospects

Most jobs are within NHS hospitals, although there are also posts within private hospitals.

There are opportunities throughout the country but they can be competitive in some areas.

With experience you could become a supervisor and then take management qualifications for promotion to head porter or porter manager.

You could also do further training to move into related careers, such as healthcare assistant or ambulance work.

Advantages/disadvantages

The work can be physically demanding and stressful at times.

You will meet a variety of people and the job is active and busy.

It is satisfying to play a vital role within a hospital; without porters a hospital would not be able to function.

Money guide

The NHS sets national pay rates for hospital porters, with salaries in private hospitals being similar to those of the NHS.

Earnings start at upwards of £15,251 per year.

In time, this could increase to up to £17,978, or £19,655 with team management duties.

There are additional payments for overtime.

Related opportunities

- Hotel Porter p129
- Paramedic p306
- Sterile Services Technician p322

Further information

NHS Careers
www.healthcareers.nhs.uk

Skills for Health
www.skillsforhealth.org.uk

HEALTHCARE

HEALTHCARE

Qualifications and courses

Learning disabilities nurses must hold a degree in nursing which has been approved by the Nursing and Midwifery Council (NMC). Minimum entry requirements for degree courses are usually 2 A levels/3H grades, ideally including a science-based subject, and 5 GCSEs/National 5s (A*–C/A–C), including English, Maths and a science subject. All applicants must obtain clearance from the Disclosure and Barring Service (DBS) before commencing their training.

If you do not have the required GCSEs/National 5s or A levels/H grades, some universities will accept other qualifications, such as a BTEC in Health and Social Care (Levels 2–3) or the Access to Higher Education Diploma in a science or health-related subject.

Graduates with a degree in a health-related subject such as human biology, life and medical sciences or biomedical science, may be eligible to enter the nursing profession by taking an accelerated 2-year programme which leads to a Master of Science (MSc) or postgraduate diploma.

For this branch of nursing, you will usually be required to have relevant experience working with people with learning disabilities. Opportunities to volunteer may be available through the Charity Choice website.

Postgraduate courses are also available in topics such as mental health practice, cognitive behaviour therapy, forensic mental health practice, and acute and psychiatric intensive care settings.

What the work involves

Learning disabilities nurses work with people with learning disabilities in order to teach them new skills and support them in becoming as independent as possible.

You will be assessing patients and devising suitable care plans for them, as well as supporting their families or carers by helping them implement development strategies and arranging for them to take a break from their responsibilities when necessary.

You will work in a range of locations, including patients' homes, care homes and schools.

Type of person suited to this work

You will need excellent communication skills in order to develop a good relationship with patients and colleagues alike. To successfully help people to learn new skills, you must be a patient teacher.

You should be compassionate and empathetic in understanding your patients' feelings and frustrations, whilst maintaining a professional attitude so that you can distance yourself from your work at the end of the day.

You will need both physical and mental stamina to support your patients fully.

Working conditions

You will usually work 37 hours a week including evening, night and weekend work. Part-time work and flexible hours are frequently available.

As you will be working in the community, you will spend time travelling to and from patients' homes, schools, clinics and residential homes. A driving licence would be useful.

You may also accompany and support clients as they undertake everyday tasks such as going to the shops or the gym, booking a holiday, travelling on public transport or even going to work.

Future prospects

Most learning disabilities nurses are employed by the NHS, although there are also opportunities in the private sector and with local authority healthcare teams. The government's Strengthening the Commitment review of learning disability nurses makes many recommendations on career choices and developing new roles to fill skill gaps.

You may undertake further training that could allow you to specialise in an area that particularly interests you, such as education or cognitive disability.

You could go on to become a team leader, supervisor, or even a nurse consultant. Alternatively, you could move into research or teaching.

Advantages/disadvantages

You will be providing a life-enhancing service for a number of people in your local community.

There are good opportunities for career development or diversification, as well as the option of flexible working hours to suit your lifestyle and family commitments.

You may encounter difficult or abusive patients which can be distressing and unpleasant.

Money guide

A newly qualified nurse can expect a starting salary of between £21,909 and £28,462.

As a nurse specialist, your earnings can increase to between £26,302 and £35,225.

Those who take on a senior or management position with additional responsibilities can achieve £31,383–£41,373.

If you undertake the training to become a nurse consultant, you could earn between £40,028 and £68,484.

Related opportunities

- Adult Nurse p271
- Children's Nurse p276
- Health Visitor p291

Further information

NHS Careers
www.healthcareers.nhs.uk

Nursing and Midwifery Council
www.nmc.org.uk

Qualifications and courses

There are no set requirements to enter this profession, but many professional bodies recommend you take an in-depth course of at least 6 months full time or 12 months part time. You will need at least 5 GCSEs/National 5s to enrol on a course. The course you choose will need to be recognised by the General Council for Massage Therapy, and include beauty therapy, Swedish massage, holistic massage, and anatomy and physiology. Awarding bodies include the International Therapy Examination Council (ITEC) and Vocational Training Charitable Trust (VTCT). Once you start training you will cover not only massage itself but also first aid, health and safety, employment law, and assessing clients.

Relevant qualifications include the NVQ Level 3 in Beauty Therapy (Massage), the VTCT Level 3 Certificate/Diploma in Body Massage, Swedish Massage or Remedial Massage, the ITEC Level 3 Diploma in Massage, the ITEC Certificate in Anatomy and Physiology, and the City & Guilds Levels 2–3 Awards/Certificates in Complementary Therapies (7607).

You could begin on the path to massage by following an Apprenticeship in Beauty Therapy. If you already have experience of work in health and beauty, you can enter this field as a second career; many people choose to do this.

Once you are fully qualified you can choose to become a member of a professional body and register with the Complementary and Natural Healthcare Council. The Council regulates complementary therapists and manages complaints.

To specialise in a particular form of massage, such as baby and infant massage or sports massage, you will need to enrol on additional, specialist training courses.

What the work involves

A massage therapist uses massage as a therapy to relieve clients of pain or stress. Some practitioners specialise in specific areas of the body, whilst others work on the entire body. Many practitioners are self-employed and either work from home or run their own salons.

As a massage therapist, you are trained in techniques and movements that have proven therapeutic effects and aid the healing process.

Type of person suited to this work

You will need to be good with people and have a reassuring friendly manner.

You will need to be able to explain what you are doing clearly, and have to be able to respond to your client effectively and calmly. You should be very comfortable with close physical contact, and have good manual dexterity.

You should have excellent concentration skills, as the work demands great physical and mental energy. You will also need good organisational skills, as you may well end up running your own business. This will also require confidence and good business acumen.

Working conditions

If you work in a beauty clinic or spa, you will usually do a 40-hour week, whilst self-employed massage therapists can opt for fewer hours. Either way, you will have to work around your clients' lifestyles, which means working evenings and weekends.

You could work in hospitals, beauty salons, health spas, care homes, leisure centres, and clients' homes. You could also work from home, or even set up your own clinic.

Treatment rooms should be (and usually are) clean, warm and peaceful. You may often play calming music or use aromatherapy oils to add to the experience.

Future prospects

Once you have gained some experience you could set up your own practice, provided you have the business sense to do so.

Physiotherapy, sports or alternative medicine clinics are the biggest employers of massage therapists. You might also decide that you would like to learn about a similar profession such as reflexology or aromatherapy so that you can offer your clients a wider range of services.

You could even teach massage, if you are prepared to study for a teaching qualification.

Advantages/disadvantages

If you like working with and helping people you should really enjoy this work.

It is a good opportunity to use your skills, and you can really see the results.

The work can be tiring, and you need to be physically fit to do a good job and enjoy it properly.

Money guide

Many massage therapists are self-employed and charge by session or hourly rate. This could be between £25 and £60 an hour, depending on location.

A skilled therapist who has built a large, dependable client base could earn between £20,000 and £40,000. This could be supplemented through the sale of beauty products.

Related opportunities

- Acupuncturist p270
- Aromatherapist p273
- Physiotherapist p312

Further information

CIBTAC
www.cibtac.com

Complementary and Natural Healthcare Council
www.cnhc.org.uk

General Council for Massage Therapy
www.gcmt.org.uk

International Therapy Examination Council
www.itecworld.co.uk

HEALTHCARE

Qualifications and courses

Candidates will need a 1st or 2.1 degree in a subject such as physics, medical physics, physical science or electrical engineering. Entry to a relevant degree course requires at least 2 A levels/3 H grades, usually including Physics and Maths, plus 5 GCSEs/National 5s (A*–C/A–C), including English and Maths. A postgraduate qualification or industrial experience may also be useful to enter this career.

Candidates go into the profession as trainees and the competitive NHS Healthcare Scientist Training Programme (STP) is the specified entry route. Your application will be strengthened with work experience in a hospital medical physics department, which should also help you decide on a specialist area. The training programme lasts 3 years and you will study for a Master of Science (MSc) in Medical Physics. If you already have an MSc qualification, you need only to complete a 15-month training period based in a hospital.

Advanced trainee medical physicists undertake 2 years of training in a specialist field. You can then apply for an Academy for Healthcare Science Certificate of Attainment or Certificate of Equivalence. On completion, candidates are eligible for registration with the Health & Care Professions Council (HCPC) to work in unsupervised situations and in the NHS and apply for Membership of the Institute of Physics and Engineering in Medicine (IPEM), which is the professional body for this area of clinical science.

What the work involves

Medical physicists use their expert knowledge of physics to diagnose, prevent and treat disease.

You will be using specialist equipment and techniques to investigate patients' illnesses, this includes X-rays, radiography, ultrasounds, MRI machines, radiotherapy, and laser therapy.

You may be designing, developing and maintaining equipment, and advising medical staff on its use or planning the correct treatment for a patient using specific equipment. Your role may also involve patient contact, explaining procedures and results.

Type of person suited to this work

Medical physicists need to have expert skills in physical sciences and the ability to use their skills to solve problems and improve the diagnosis and treatment of disease.

You should have excellent research skills, be able to work accurately and be willing to take responsibility for decisions which will have a direct effect on patients.

You will need good communication skills to explain complex procedures clearly to patients, and to work as part of a team. You must also be prepared to keep up with the latest developments and continue to learn new skills.

Working conditions

Most medical physicists work in hospitals and laboratories and some have contact with patients on wards or in clinics.

You will need to work safely with equipment and chemicals in the laboratory, some of which can be hazardous.

You will normally work from Monday to Friday, but work outside normal hours and travel to conferences will sometimes be necessary.

Future prospects

The number of medical physicists is increasing, although trainee posts are competitive and you might have to relocate for some specialist roles.

Most jobs are in the larger NHS hospitals throughout the UK. There are also some opportunities in the nuclear energy industry, medical equipment industry, private hospitals and medical research institutes.

Within the NHS there is a recognised career path and you could even reach consultant level. Employment in the private sector is less structured.

There are plenty of opportunities for continuing professional development (CPD) which will improve your career prospects. IPEM also offers formal development courses in skills such as management, and once these have been completed you will have the opportunity to become a chartered scientist (CSci).

Advantages/disadvantages

Some of the work could be routine at times.

You will be playing an important role in the overall healthcare of the patients, as you will be contributing to the diagnosis and treatment of their diseases.

Money guide

In the NHS trainees could expect a starting salary of around £25,000.

Medical physicists working for the NHS usually start on the NHS wage band 6 of the Agenda for Change pay structure, earning between £26,302 and £35,225.

Team leaders could advance to band 7, £31,383 to £41,373. A healthcare consultant could earn up to £68,484 on band 8.

Salaries will differ if you work for private companies outside the NHS.

Related opportunities

- Physicist p522
- Radiographer p318
- Radiologist p319

Further information

Institute of Physics and Engineering in Medicine
www.ipem.ac.uk

NHS Careers
www.healthcareers.nhs.uk

Skills for Health
www.skillsforhealth.org.uk

HEALTHCARE

Qualifications and courses

All mental health nurses must hold a degree in mental health nursing which has been approved by the Nursing and Midwifery Council (NMC). Minimum entry requirements for degree courses are usually 2 A levels/3 H grades, ideally including a science-based subject, and 5 GCSEs/National 5s (A*–C/A–C) including English, Maths and a science subject. All applicants must obtain clearance from the Disclosure and Barring Service (DBS) before commencing their training.

If you do not have the required GCSEs/National 5s or A levels/H grades, some universities will accept other qualifications, such as the BTEC qualifications in Health and Social Care (Levels 2–3) or an Access to Higher Education Diploma in a science or health-related subject.

Graduates with a degree in a health-related subject such as human biology, life and medical sciences or biomedical science, may be eligible to enter the nursing profession by taking an accelerated 2-year programme which leads to a Master of Science (MSc) or Postgraduate Diploma. Part-time programmes are also provided by some universities and normally last for 5 or 6 years.

For this branch of nursing, it would be useful to have relevant experience working with people who use mental health services.

Once qualified, the NMC requires you to keep yourself up to date with health care issues and practice through continuing professional development (CPD).

What the work involves

Mental health nurses care for people with mental health problems both in hospitals and within the wider community. They help patients come to terms with their problems and overcome their limitations by listening to them as they discuss their illness and anxieties.

You will also work with a patient's friends and family where possible to create a stable and proactive network around the individual and also to provide support to those closest to him/her.

You could encounter patients with problems including stress-related conditions, eating disorders, drug and alcohol dependency, and personality disorders.

Type of person suited to this work

You will need excellent communication skills in order to develop a good relationship with patients, their families and other healthcare professionals.

You must be extremely observant so that you can spot any minor changes in a patient's condition and manage them before they trigger undesirable results.

You should be non-judgemental and empathetic in order to understand your patients' feelings and frustrations. In a difficult situation, you must be able to remain calm and assertive.

Working conditions

You will usually work 37 hours a week, including evenings and weekends.

You could work in a hospital, in the community, or undertake a mixture of both.

If you work across the community, you will travel to a variety of places including patients' homes, hostels, day centres and drug dependency units. A driving licence may be required.

Future prospects

Most mental health nurses are employed by the NHS, although there are also opportunities in the private sector and in local social services teams. Changes to legislation and funding mean new roles are being established, such as basing mental health nurses in police stations.

You may undertake further training to specialise in an area that particularly interests you, such as drug abuse.

You could go on to become a team leader, supervisor or nurse consultant, or you may progress to a general management position within the NHS. Alternatively, you could move into research or teaching.

Advantages/disadvantages

Providing a life-enhancing service for a number of people in your local community is highly rewarding.

After gaining a few years' experience, you should have the option of flexible working hours that will suit your lifestyle and personal commitments.

You may encounter difficult or abusive patients which can be distressing and unpleasant.

Money guide

A newly qualified nurse can expect a starting salary of £21,909 on Band 5 of the NHS Agenda for Change.

As you gain experience and specialise in mental health nursing, your earnings can increase up to upwards of £26,302 on Band 6.

Those who take on a senior position with team management responsibilities can achieve between £31,383 and £41,373.

If you undertake the training to become a nurse consultant, you could earn up to £68,484.

Related opportunities

- Health Visitor p291
- Learning Disabilities Nurse p296
- Occupational Therapist p301

Further information

NHS Careers
www.healthcareers.nhs.uk

Royal College of Nursing
www.rcn.org.uk

HEALTHCARE

Qualifications and courses

All midwives must hold a degree in midwifery which has been approved by the Nursing and Midwifery Council (NMC). Entry requirements for degree courses depend upon the individual university but you will usually need 2 A levels/3 H grades, ideally including a science-based subject, and 5 GCSEs/National 5s (A*–C/A–C), including English, Maths and a science subject. Relevant pre-entry experience is a distinct advantage. A degree in midwifery lasts 3 years when studied on a full-time basis and all applicants must obtain clearance from the Disclosure and Barring Service (DBS) before commencing their training.

If you do not have the required GCSEs/National 5s or A levels/H grades, some universities will accept other qualifications, such as a BTEC in Health and Social Care (Levels 2–3) or an Access to Higher Education Diploma in a science or health-related subject.

Those who have already qualified as an adult nurse and are currently registered with the NMC have the option of taking a shorter 18-month course to become a midwife.

You are eligible to register as a midwife with the NMC once you have completed an approved midwifery degree. Midwives are expected to engage in continuing professional development (CPD) throughout their career to keep their skills and knowledge up to date.

What the work involves

Midwives help and support women and their partners from early pregnancy, through the antenatal period, during the labour and birth, and also for up to a month after the baby has been born.

You will be responsible for monitoring your patient throughout her pregnancy, providing advice and support on issues including nutrition, methods of childbirth and breastfeeding.

You will deliver babies or assist in the birthing process. You will also be responsible for identifying high risk pregnancies and arranging specialist care and provisions where necessary.

Type of person suited to this work

You must be an excellent communicator as it is essential to form a good relationship with patients, their partners and other healthcare professionals. You need to be friendly and caring in order to gain the trust and confidence of the women under your guidance.

As childbirth is strenuous, messy and unpredictable, you should be able to stay calm under pressure, think on your feet and have good mental and physical stamina.

You need careful attention to detail when carrying out your work and completing patient notes.

Working conditions

You will usually work 37 hours a week and these will include evening, night and weekend work. You may also be on-call at times. Part-time work and flexible hours are frequently available.

You could be based in the maternity unit of a hospital or in a birth centre. Midwives are also increasingly affiliated with GP surgeries and other health centres.

You will probably spend time travelling from your place of work to your patients' homes so a driving licence would be helpful.

Future prospects

The effects of the recession are affecting the number of midwife jobs and cuts are expected to continue as the NHS is restructured. Midwifery 2020, a government evaluation of the sector, notes a change of working patterns from full-time to part-time.

In the NHS, midwives can progress to a senior level as a team leader or midwife consultant. You could take further training which would allow you to specialise in an area that particularly interests you, or to move into a related profession such as neonatal nursing.

Other opportunities include undertaking research, or training and teaching student midwives.

Advantages/disadvantages

Supporting women and families through pregnancy and childbirth is both rewarding and fulfilling.

This job can be distressing as you will have to deal with complications in pregnancy and labour.

Money guide

The starting salary for a newly qualified midwife is between £21,909 and £28,462.

As you gain experience, you can expect to earn up to £35,225.

Those in a senior position, such as a midwife team manager, typically earn £31,383 to £41,373.

If you specialise or become a midwife consultant, you could earn up to £68,484.

Salaries are usually higher in London and allowances for on-call duties can increase earnings.

Related opportunities

- Adult Nurse p271
- Children's Nurse p276
- Occupational Therapist p301

Further information

Nursing and Midwifery Council
www.nmc.org.uk

Royal College of Midwives
www.rcm.org.uk

Qualifications and courses

To become an occupational therapist, you will need a degree or postgraduate diploma in occupational therapy that has been approved by the Health and Care Professions Council (HCPC).

For degree entry, you will normally need at least 2 A levels/3 H grades including a science, preferably Biology, Human Biology or Psychology, and 5 GCSEs/National 5s (A*–C/A–C). The Advanced Diploma in Society, Health and Development may also be relevant. A degree in occupational therapy normally takes 3 years, however there is an accelerated 2-year diploma programme available to graduates from other degree disciplines who have experience in health or social care.

In-service courses are available for those employed as occupational therapy support workers or technical instructors. Courses are studied part time and lead to professional qualification as an occupational therapist.

Before you can register with the HCPC, you must undergo a Disclosure and Barring Service (DBS) background check.

To remain registered with the HCPC, occupational therapists must carry out continuing professional development (CPD) throughout the course of their career. You can do this by joining the British Association of Occupational Therapists (BAOT).

What the work involves

Occupational therapists help people overcome physical, psychological or social problems arising from illness or disability.

You could see patients with problems stemming from conditions such as multiple sclerosis or Parkinson's, those with physical and mental disabilities or issues, and those who are affected by drug and alcohol use.

You will help patients with everyday tasks such as washing, cooking and even going to work. Your care will focus on what patients can achieve, rather than on their disabilities. Your job will also include writing treatment plans, giving advice on practical issues such as disability equipment, teaching coping strategies and using activities to stimulate your patients.

Type of person suited to this work

You must have excellent interpersonal skills as you will need to inspire trust and confidence in patients with a range of problems, including some who are difficult, anxious or unpredictable. You will need to be patient, caring, and sensitive to your patients' needs, concerns and expectations.

You should have both mental and physical stamina as you will need to provide hands-on support to patients as well as coping with their emotional issues.

You should be a natural problem-solver with a flexible and creative approach to your work. The ability to motivate your patients and other professionals is also essential.

Working conditions

Most occupational therapists work a normal working week from Monday to Friday, although you might have to work evenings and weekends to provide a 24-hour community service.

You could work in a variety of locations, such as hospitals, a patient's home, residential homes, prisons and workplaces, so a driving licence would be useful.

Future prospects

Demand for occupational therapists is high, but you may still find that there is competition for jobs in certain areas.

You could be employed by the NHS, private hospitals, local authorities, charities or voluntary agencies. There are also opportunities to work abroad.

With experience, you could move into a more clinical position, take up a research post or set up your own practice. Alternatively you could progress to a managerial role within the NHS or opt to teach within your field.

Advantages/disadvantages

It is very rewarding to be able to help people to overcome difficulties and achieve their goals.

You could specialise in a variety of areas such as rehabilitation, learning disabilities or paediatrics.

The work can be emotionally and mentally demanding.

Money guide

Starting salaries for newly qualified occupational therapists begin at £21,909.

Salaries for specialists can reach between £26,302 and £35,225 per year.

In a more senior role that includes supervisory and managerial responsibilities or consultancy your earnings could rise to £41,373.

Related opportunities

- Health Visitor p291
- Learning Disabilities Nurse p296
- Mental Health Nurse p299

Further information

British Association of Occupational Therapists and College of Occupational Therapists
www.cot.co.uk

NHS Careers
www.healthcareers.nhs.uk

HEALTHCARE

Qualifications and courses

Entry into this profession requires a Diploma of Higher Education (DipHE) in Operating Department Practice approved by the Health and Care Professions Council (HCPC). Courses are available throughout the UK and generally last 2 or 3 years with normal minimum entry requirements being 5 GCSEs/National 5s (A*–C/A–C) preferably in English, Maths and/or a science-based subject or equivalent, but some institutions might require A levels/H grades. Access courses may be taken prior to Diploma programmes.

The minimum age for entry into this line of work is 18, and mature candidates are very common as many have experience of other types of hospital work, for example as a healthcare assistant, and apply to become operating department practitioners later.

A small number of universities also offer an undergraduate degree in Operating Department Practice, with entry requirements typically including 2 A levels/3 H grades and 5 GCSEs/National 5s (A*–C/A–C). Again, pre-entry work experience may be necessary for a successful application.

Once qualified, you will need to undergo a medical test, an occupational health screening and Disclosure and Barring Service (DBS) check. You can then be accepted on to the state register and be a member of the College of Operating Department Practitioners (CODP).

What the work involves

Operating department practitioners work alongside surgeons, anaesthetists and other staff before, during and after operations.

Before surgery you will help calm a patient's anxiety, plan treatment, sterilise equipment and bring the patient to the operating theatre. During surgery you will monitor effects of the anaesthetic, pass tools to surgeons, take care of surgical wounds and dispose of soiled dressings.

After surgery you will bring patients to the recovery unit, monitor their wellbeing, provide pain relief and evaluate care.

It will be your responsibility to anticipate the needs of your colleagues and respond effectively.

Type of person suited to this work

You will need the scientific knowledge and practical skills to prepare specialist equipment and drugs. You will be helping with operations so you cannot be squeamish.

You must pay close attention when monitoring patients because their lives depend on it. You need to be able to react quickly and accurately if the patient experiences any complications.

Excellent communication skills are essential and you will need to be caring and sensitive.

Working conditions

You will mainly work in operating theatres and recovery rooms in hospitals. However, operating department practitioners are increasingly being recognised for their skills in other critical areas.

You will need to follow hygiene procedures closely, wear a sterile gown and gloves during operations and be able to stand for long periods.

You will usually work shifts which may include working at nights, at weekends and on bank holidays. You might also have stand-by or on-call duties.

Future prospects

Demand for qualified operating department practitioners remains high, both within the NHS and the private health sector.

Most employment is available with the NHS throughout the UK. There are also opportunities in private hospitals.

You could progress into higher grade posts which involve more responsibility for managing and training others. It is possible to become a senior operating department practitioner or run your own theatre.

There are also opportunities to enter research or teaching.

Advantages/disadvantages

The work can be stressful at times and you will see some unpleasant things.

It is rewarding to be part of a team improving people's health and saving lives.

You could work in a range of areas, such as resuscitation, intensive care or day surgery.

Money guide

Salary figures for NHS staff are outlined in the organisation's Agenda for Change.

Rates of pay for qualified operating department practitioners are between £21,909 and £28,462.

With experience you can earn higher level salaries of up to £35,225.

It is possible for theatre practitioners with leadership responsibilities to earn up to £41,373.

Related opportunities

- Critical Care Technologist p279
- Paramedic p306
- Sterile Services Technician p322

Further information

NHS Careers
www.healthcareers.nhs.uk

Skills for Health
www.skillsforhealth.org.uk

HEALTHCARE

Qualifications and courses

In order to become an optometrist, you must obtain a degree that has been accredited by the General Optical Council (GOC). Degrees accredited by the GOC are offered at several universities and entry requirements may vary according to the institution. For entry onto a degree course, students are normally expected to have 2 A levels/3 H grades, including at least 2 from Biology, Maths, Physics and Chemistry, and 5 GCSEs/National 5s (A*–C/A–C), including English, Maths and Physics or Double Award Science.

Graduates with a 2.2 degree or higher and a valid Certificate of Clinical Competency, which is awarded on graduation and valid for 2 years, must then follow a pre-registration year of supervised clinical experience. Successful completion of this year of work-based training and completion of the final assessment examination from the College of Optometrists will enable you to register as an optometrist with the GOC.

If you did not achieve a 2.2 at undergraduate level, or if your Certificate of Clinical Competency has expired, you will need to complete the GOC's Optometry Progression Scheme before progressing onto the pre-registration year.

To remain registered with the GOC, continuing education and training (CET) is mandatory.

There are many advanced courses that allow qualified optometrists to specialise in other areas, such as paediatric vision, vision therapy and sports vision. Postgraduate qualifications are also available.

What the work involves

Optometrists examine the eyes of their patients for disease or abnormalities and carry out vision tests.

Your work will include shining a light on the retina, and using reading charts and other instruments to diagnose the needs of the patient.

You will determine prescriptions and may also supply and fit glasses or contact lenses. You will look out for signs of diabetes and eye diseases and refer patients to surgeons when needed.

Type of person suited to this work

Examining eyes and diagnosing problems requires a high level of scientific knowledge and a high attention to detail. Fitting contact lenses and handling instruments require good technical skills.

You need to have excellent communication and listening skills to deal with patients of all ages and backgrounds. You will need to put patients at ease and explain procedures simply and clearly to them.

You should have good interpersonal skill as you will have to work as part of a team with other professionals.

Working conditions

Optometrists work in high-street opticians and hospitals, in examination rooms which usually have no natural light and often have to be quite dark.

You will undertake 10 to 20 half-an-hour eye examinations per day.

You will probably have a normal working week from Monday to Friday, but may need to work on Saturdays as well.

Future prospects

Job prospects are good but vary throughout the UK.

You may work for a chain of opticians, an independent practice or a hospital. You could also do related work with lens manufacturers.

With experience you may specialise, for example, in children's vision, low vision or contact lenses. You could choose to run your own practice. There are also opportunities to move into research and university teaching.

Advantages/disadvantages

The work can be routine and repetitive at times.

If you enjoy combining scientific knowledge with working with the public, this job could be good for you.

Working closely with patients can be demanding.

Money guide

In private practices, trainees may earn between £17,000 and £21,000 during their one year pre-registration period. NHS trainees on the Agenda for Change pay scheme will earn at NHS wage band 4 (£19,217) at the same stage of training.

Once qualified, starting salaries in the private sector begin at around £28,000 and can increase to £60,000 a year or more with many years' experience.

In the NHS salaries begin at £26,302, rising to up to £35,225.

With specialist training, NHS optometrists can earn up to £41,373.

Consultants can progress to NHS wage band 8, with an income of up to £82,434.

Related opportunities

- Dentist p284
- Dispensing Optician p286
- Hospital Doctor p294

Further information

College of Optometrists
www.college-optometrists.org

General Optical Council
www.optical.org

HEALTHCARE

303

Qualifications and courses

All orthodontists must first qualify as a dentist. The standard degree programme lasts 5 years and you will need at least 3 good A levels/H grades, including Chemistry and Biology. GCSE/National 5s results may also be taken into account, and at least 8 passes (A*–C/A–C) are required for consideration. You may be asked to take the UK Clinical Aptitude Test (UKCAT) as part of your university application and pre-entry interviews are common.

If you have good A level/H grade results, but not in the required subjects for entrance onto the degree course, you can apply for a 6-year degree programme that includes an initial 30-week course that aims to get students up to speed with the sciences.

Owing to the competitiveness of dentistry degrees, students are sometimes choosing to do an initial degree before their dental degree or embarking on extensive work experience before applying to a course.

Once you have qualified as a dentist, you will need to gain 2 years of clinical experience before being able to apply for a postgraduate Master of Science (MSc) in Orthodontic Dentistry. Orthodontic training combines academic study with hands-on training in a hospital, and lasts 3 years full time. You will then sit the Membership in Orthodontics (MOrth) exam to qualify as an orthodontist.

If you are looking to progress to become a hospital consultant, you will need to undertake a further 2 years' training and pass the Intercollegiate Specialty Fellowship Examination.

What the work involves

Orthodontists examine and treat dental problems. These problems may be an aesthetic correction or a more serious dental issue, such as jaw realignment.

Treatment will usually involve correcting irregularities or abnormalities in terms of teeth growth or jaw position. Through treatment, you will be responsible for improving the patient's quality of life.

The most common procedures for an orthodontist are usually the fitting and maintaining of braces, and the extraction of teeth. You may occasionally have to carry out jaw surgery. You will also need to examine the mouths and teeth of your patients, take X-rays and impressions, and keep detailed medical records of their treatment. Owing to the further education, an orthodontist's remit extends beyond that of a dentist.

Type of person suited to this work

You will need to have excellent communication skills in order to gain the trust of your patients and build good relationships with them.

You will be working with and possibly managing other professionals, so you should also enjoy working in a team environment and motivating those around you.

Good eyesight and manual dexterity are essential for undertaking fiddly tasks such as fitting and tightening braces or performing

jaw surgery. The ability to maintain your concentration during occasionally lengthy procedures is also important.

Working conditions

If you work in private practice you can generally expect to do normal office hours, although some orthodontists choose to work evenings and weekends to suit their patients' lifestyles.

Those working in hospitals must be more flexible, occasionally undertaking emergency shifts and being on-call.

You will need to wear protective clothing, along with surgical gloves and a mask when working on patients in order to maintain high levels of hygiene and safety.

Future prospects

There is a constant demand for orthodontists in both the private and public sector, so career prospects are good.

Jobs can be found across the UK in both large cities and smaller towns. You could work in the NHS or as a self-employed professional.

There are opportunities to specialise in certain areas of orthodontics, such as adult cosmetic dentistry or children's corrective orthodontics.

Advantages/disadvantages

Many orthodontists are self-employed and work in the private sector. This provides more control over working hours and salary.

Orthodontic treatment for one patient can often last a few years; you get to build up a relationship with your patients. This can also make the process of improving their health and their smile all the more rewarding.

Despite the costs of education, it is a reliable source of income.

It can be a demanding and stressful job, with the need to work unorthodox hours at times.

Money guide

Generally, salaries start at around £28,000 to £30,000.

Working in a specialist private practice, you could earn anything from £40,000 to £90,000.

If you run your own practice you could earn in excess of £150,000.

Related opportunities

- Dental Hygienist p280
- Dentist p284
- Surgeon p323

Further information

British Dental Association
www.bda.org

British Orthodontic Society
www.bos.org.uk

NHS Careers
www.healthcareers.nhs.uk

Qualifications and courses

All osteopaths must be registered with the General Osteopathic Council (GOsC) before they are legally allowed to practise. In order to register, you must hold a qualification in osteopathy from one of the 11 osteopathic educational institutions currently providing courses recognised by the GOsC.

Most recognised courses are at bachelor or master's degree level. Each course takes 4 years when studied full time, and 5 years on a part-time basis. For entry onto these courses, most of the universities require a minimum of 2 A levels/3 H grades, with Chemistry or Biology preferred, and 5 GCSEs/National 5s (A*–C/A–C). If you do not have a science degree or appropriate A levels, you may still be considered but will have to take an intensive science course before beginning to train.

Though not essential, it may be advantageous to gain pre-entry experience by shadowing a practising osteopath or by working in a caring role.

Many people train in osteopathy as a second career. If you have relevant experience in healthcare or hold medical-related qualifications prior to commencing your degree, you may be exempt from parts of the course. Short courses are available for fully qualified healthcare professionals.

As part of your registration with the GOsC you will also have to pass a Disclosure and Barring Service (DBS) check and, once qualified, the GOsC requires you to complete 30 hours of relevant learning each year as part of the continuing professional development (CPD) scheme.

What the work involves

Osteopathy is considered a complementary medicine. It does not use surgery or drugs. Osteopaths usually work on the patient's musculoskeletal system. You may use medical techniques such as X-rays, as well as physical exams, observation, and talking with your patient to understand their ailment.

You will then use hands-on treatment such as massage, joint mobilisation and deep pressure to help the treat the problem. You may also advise on aspects of their lifestyle or diet to help remedy the problem.

Type of person suited to this work

You will need a highly developed sense of touch and strong observational skills in order to identify points of slight weakness or pain in your patients. Logic and problem-solving abilities will also help you diagnose correctly and treat the problem creatively where necessary.

Excellent communication skills are also essential to develop a good relationship with patients and in order to explain their treatment to them.

The work can be very physical, so you should also have a good level of fitness.

Working conditions

You could practise in a variety of locations including leisure centres, therapy centres, private clinics, hospitals and even your own home. You will probably have a treatment room in which to see patients.

Most professionals offer evening and weekend appointments as well as those during the day, as these tend to be more convenient for patients.

Future prospects

As awareness of osteopathy grows, there is increasing demand for qualified and registered professionals, so career opportunities are correspondingly positive.

Most osteopaths are self-employed, and usually start out by working as an associate in a practice to establish a reputation and solid client base. After a few years, many then go on to set up their own practice or become involved in the training of future osteopaths.

You could also choose to specialise in an area of particular interest to you, such as treating sports injuries or problems resulting from childbirth.

Advantages/disadvantages

As an osteopath, you will encounter a variety of complaints and challenges on a daily basis, which can be both refreshing and intellectually stimulating.

You provide an alternative to medicine and surgery for patients.

If you are self-employed, income might not be quite so predictable as for other medical professions, which can cause stress.

The work can be physically demanding.

Money guide

As the majority of osteopaths are self-employed and work varying hours, it is difficult to predict an exact level of earnings at any stage. Generally, most charge between £35 and £50 for a 30–40 minute session.

Newly qualified osteopaths in a practice can expect to earn around £18,000 in their first couple of years.

With experience, you could see this increase to around £45,000.

If you run your own practice or work in a well-established one, your salary could rise to £70,000 per year.

Related opportunities

- Acupuncturist p270
- Chiropractor p277
- Physiotherapist p312

Further information

British School of Osteopathy
www.bso.ac.uk

General Osteopathic Council
www.osteopathy.org.uk

The Institute of Osteopathy
www.osteopathy.org

Qualifications and courses

There are three approved routes you can follow. You could apply to an ambulance service trust for a role as a student paramedic, and they will put you through an approved course. Training takes between 2 and 5 years to complete and you will need at least 5 GCSEs/National 5s (A*–C/ A–C), including English and Maths, in order to apply.

Alternatively you could take an approved degree course in paramedic science which can take from 2 to 4 years to complete. Entry requirements are usually 2 A levels/3 H grades and 5 GCSEs/National 5s (A*–C/A–C), including English and Maths or a science subject.

As a third option, some ambulance service trusts are approved by the Health and Care Professions Council (HCPC) and provide training for the Institute of Healthcare Development (IHCD) Paramedic Award, leading to registration. You will need to possess a current IHCD Technician Certificate/BTEC Certificate to apply.

Useful pre-entry experience includes completing first aid certificates and voluntary experience, both of which are available with organisations such as St John Ambulance, St Andrew's Ambulance Association and British Red Cross. You could also volunteer as a community 'first responder' with a local ambulance service and gain experience in life-saving techniques.

A full clean driving licence, that allows you to drive larger vehicles and carry passengers, is essential. You will also need to pass a Disclosure and Barring Service (DBS) check, fitness test, and medical assessment before working and if you are employed with the NHS, you will need to be registered with the HCPC.

What the work involves

Typically working as one part of a two-person ambulance crew, as a paramedic you will often be the first healthcare professional to arrive at the scene of an accident or emergency.

You will be responsible for assessing the condition of a patient and administering immediate treatment.

You will stabilise patients using a variety of methods, including oxygen, drugs, and minor operations like tracheostomies. You will also ensure notes are made to brief hospital staff.

Some paramedics will work independently, using means of transport such as a motorbike or emergency response car.

Type of person suited to this work

You must have good communication skills and a caring disposition to successfully soothe and comfort patients. You should be mature, responsible and non-judgemental so that you can relate to people from a wide range of ages, backgrounds and cultures.

You must be able to keep calm in a crisis, as you will be making life and death decisions on a fairly regular basis.

A good level of physical fitness is required for lifting and carrying both patients and equipment. Mental stamina is also essential for coping with occasionally horrific and frightening circumstances.

Working conditions

You will work 37.5 hours a week on rotational shifts. This means you will work nights, weekends and on public holidays regularly. Part-time work is commonly available.

You will either work for a local ambulance service or be based at a hospital, but you will travel to a range of locations in response to emergency calls. You should be prepared to undertake treatment of patients in unfamiliar and potentially dangerous situations.

Because you will be responsible for full or shared driving responsibilities of your vehicle, you need a full, clean driving licence.

Future prospects

Career prospects for paramedics are good. Once you have completed your training and gained 3–5 years' experience you could be promoted to a team leader.

Further promotion can take you into management posts within the ambulance service, although you will need to supplement your work experience with further relevant qualifications to achieve this level.

You could also move into related careers such as nursing or occupational therapy.

Advantages/disadvantages

Providing rapid response in emergency situations means that you really will be responsible for saving lives on a weekly basis.

You could find yourself confronted with very difficult patients; those who are frightened, angry or under the influence of drugs and alcohol may be violent and hostile to treatment.

You will have to work unsocial hours fairly regularly.

Money guide

Salaries for student paramedics vary depending on the ambulance trust you train with.

Once qualified, salaries range from £21,909 to £28,462.

As a team leader or senior paramedic you could earn up to £35,225.

Related opportunities

- Adult Nurse p271
- Hospital Doctor p294
- Midwife p300
- Occupational Therapist p301

Further information

College of Paramedics
www.collegeofparamedics.co.uk

NHS Careers
www.healthcareers.nhs.uk

NHS Confederation
www.nhsconfed.org

HEALTHCARE

discover
r11sk
.co.uk

Do you have an ENQUIRING mind?

Have you got an enquiring mind?

Do you ask more questions than you can answer?

Want to know more?

Careers in podiatry

Opportunities in the world of Podiatry

www.careersinpodiatry.com

The Society of
Chiropodists an
Podiatrists

Institute
and Faculty
of Actuaries

Actuarial careers equal
unbeatable opportunities

You do the maths

If you're studying maths, or a related subject, an actuarial career could really add up for you.

You'll use your numerical skills to work out the risk of an event taking place and calculate what the impact of that would be for the business you're working for.

- How will long term weather patterns affect the price of grain?
- Will falling property prices in China impact on UK interest rates?
- Can the motor industry adapt to a call for driverless cars?

An actuarial career provides opportunities in every industry and is as challenging as it is rewarding. If you're ready to reach the heights of success, get in touch to find out how.

THE POWER TO SUPPORT YOU
ALL THE WAY

Considering a career in flooring?

A job within the flooring industry is a trade to be proud of and often very lucrative. Whether it be fitting floors in residential or commercial environments, the opportunities for individuals with good practical skills and an eye for detail are endless.

Whilst school leavers should, wherever possible, gain their skills from formal programmes like apprenticeships, they can also choose to supplement this through organisations such as FITA, the Flooring Industry Training Association, www.fita.co.uk, who offer practical training courses to suit all levels of experience, from real beginners just getting started in the industry to upskilling courses aimed towards the more seasoned professional.

The Contract Flooring Association (CFA) and the National Institute of Carpet and Floorlayers (NICF) offer guidance on all aspects of floor fitting to companies and individuals. For more information on the world of flooring from the leading trade associations representing the commercial and domestic markets visit their websites at www.cfa.org.uk and www.nicfltd.org.uk.

Whatever path you choose, from laying that perfect floor to estimating, planning and even self-employment, with experience and skills the future is bright in flooring!

For further information or advice contact:

The Contract Flooring Association (CFA)
Telephone: 0115 941 1126

The Flooring Industry Training Association (FITA)
Telephone: 0115 950 6836

The National Institute of Carpet & Floorlayers (NICF)
Telephone: 0115 958 3077

CONTRACT FLOORING ASSOCIATION
cfa
'QUALITY BY ASSOCIATION'

fita
THE FLOORING INDUSTRY TRAINING ASSOCIATION

n i c f
national institute of carpet & floorlayers

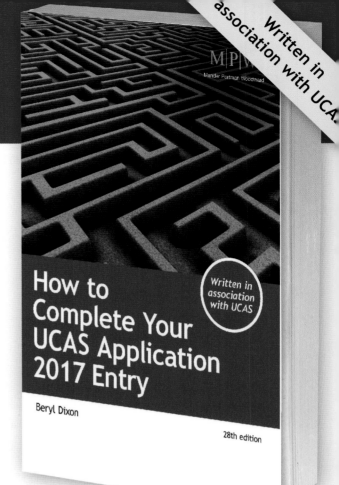
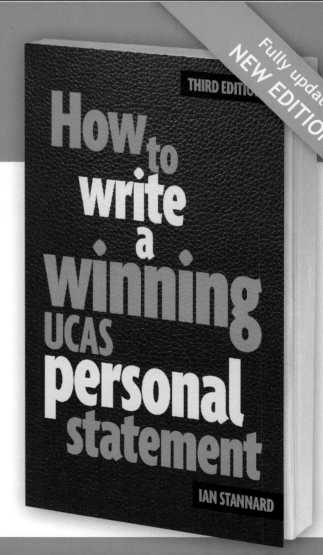

PATHOLOGIST

Qualifications and courses

Before becoming a pathologist, candidates must be qualified as a hospital doctor by completing a General Medical Council (GMC) approved medical degree. Entry requirements for medical school include very high A level/H grade results, including subjects such as science and Maths. Competition for places on medical degrees is tough and it is strongly advised that you have undertaken relevant pre-entry work experience.

After studying for a medical degree, graduates will take the 2-year foundation programme of general training which acts as the bridge between medical school and specialist training. Candidates then progress to 5–6 years of specialty training in a particular area of pathology, such as histopathology or chemical pathology.

After successfully completing the specialty stage, trainees receive a Certificate of Completion of Training (CCT) and become eligible to join the GMC Specialist Register. It is then possible to apply for a post as a consultant.

Pathologists must engage in continuing professional development (CPD) throughout their career to ensure that their skills and knowledge are up to date. The Royal College of Pathologists provides information on available training.

What the work involves

Pathologists are doctors who have undergone further training to specialise in pathology.

As a pathologist you will detect and diagnose diseases, help to identify sources of disease and reduce the risk of them spreading further.

You will spend a lot of time in a laboratory but you will also work directly with patients.

You could work in one of many branches including haematology (studying diseases of the blood), histopathology (studying tissue samples removed for diagnosis, and determining cause of death by performing post-mortems and autopsies) and immunology (studying diseases and conditions of the immune system).

Type of person suited to this work

To be a pathologist you should be able to use your medical knowledge and training to diagnose patients' conditions. You must have problem-solving skills and pay close attention to detail when carrying out laboratory assessments.

You should be kind and caring in order to gain your patients' trust. Excellent communication skills are required to listen to patients carefully and explain their conditions and treatments in a clear, simple way.

Working conditions

You will normally work within a hospital as part of a medical team, working both in a laboratory and with patients.

You will need to work safely in the laboratory and wear protective clothing such as a lab coat and gloves.

There will be long hours and you are likely to work shifts and be on an on-call rota, which includes working at nights, weekends and on bank holidays.

Future prospects

Most pathologists work within the NHS throughout the UK. There are also opportunities in industry, working for private companies.

You could decide to specialise further in particular areas of the work such as forensic pathology or transfusion medicine. You could also move into academic work, carrying out research or teaching students.

There are also similar careers in pathology for clinical and biomedical scientists but they do not treat patients.

Advantages/disadvantages

The work can be emotionally demanding because it involves dealing with patients who have life-threatening conditions.

As your role is to make accurate and early diagnoses for patients, you will help to save their lives.

Money guide

Salary levels in the NHS may vary in different locations and earnings are often higher in private practice work.

Junior doctors have a starting salary of £27,000 on the first year of the Foundation programme, rising to £30,000 in the second year.

Whilst undertaking speciality training in pathology you could earn a basic salary of £37,000 or more.

Specialist doctors working for the NHS can earn between £37,547 and £70,018.

Consultant pathologists can achieve salaries ranging from £76,001 up to £102,465 for those in the most senior positions.

Related opportunities

- Anaesthetist p272
- Psychiatrist p317
- Radiologist p319

Further information

NHS Careers
www.healthcareers.nhs.uk

Royal College of Pathologists
www.rcpath.org

Skills for Health
www.skillsforhealth.org.uk

HEALTHCARE

PHARMACIST

Qualifications and courses

All candidates who wish to become pharmacists need to study for a 4-year Master of Pharmacy (MPharm) degree. Throughout the UK there are 26 pharmacy schools offering degrees which have been accredited by the Royal Pharmaceutical Society (RPS).

Most universities require a minimum of 2 A levels/3 H grades, including Chemistry and one from Biology, Maths or Physics, and at least 5 GCSEs/National 5s (A*–C/A–C) including English, Maths and a science. Most universities will accept other qualifications for entry, such as HNCs/Ds, International Baccalaureate Diplomas and Access qualifications, but it is worth checking with them directly regarding their entry policies.

It is not possible to start work as a pharmacist with an HND only but you could gain employment as a pharmacy technician. This would enable you to build up experience whilst you study for an MPharm degree.

Once students have completed their pharmacy degree, they need to apply for a 1-year pre-registration training course in community, hospital or industrial pharmacy. This enables you to train on the job with experienced professionals. A pre-entry postgraduate qualification is not needed, but a Clinical Diploma or Master of Science (MSc) may give you an advantage when applying for hospital pharmacist positions. Upon completion, candidates must then pass the General Pharmaceutical Council (GPhC)'s registration examination to become a fully qualified, registered pharmacist.

What the work involves

Pharmacists work in one of three areas: hospital, community or industry.

Hospital pharmacists are responsible for buying, manufacturing, dispensing and supplying medicines to in-patients and out-patients. You will ensure that patients receive the most appropriate treatment in the correct dosage.

Community pharmacists work in high-street pharmacies in both cities and towns. You will supply medicines over the counter, prepare doctors' prescriptions and advise people on general health-related queries.

Industrial pharmacists work for pharmaceutical companies. You will be discovering, developing, manufacturing, testing and marketing new drugs.

Type of person suited to this work

You should be a strong communicator as you will be advising patients on medications and explaining how to administer them. You must be comfortable working in a team with other pharmacy staff or healthcare professionals.

You need in-depth medical knowledge and problem-solving skills in order to identify treatment solutions and prepare medications for patients. You should be committed to keeping your knowledge up to date. Accuracy and attention to detail are essential when selecting, preparing, measuring and labelling medicines.

Working conditions

Hours will depend on where you work. Community and industrial pharmacists will usually work 39 hours per week, from Monday to Friday, although Saturday work is increasing in order to meet patients' requirements. Hospital pharmacists may need to work shifts in order to provide a 24-hour service. There are opportunities to work part time.

You could be working in a shop, hospital or laboratory and you may occasionally be required to travel to nursing homes and community health centres/clinics.

Future prospects

Over the past ten years there has been a rise in the number of students studying to become a pharmacist. Until recently, there was a national shortage of pharmacists, so currently opportunities in this area are good.

You will have the option of working in a range of different environments including community shops and large hospitals.

As you gain experience, you could choose to combine your work with other responsibilities such as teaching. You could also go on to research or write about pharmaceutical matters.

Advantages/disadvantages

Your role will be varied and rewarding as you endeavour to help a diverse range of patients.

It is not as stressful as some other medical jobs.

You may have to work unsocial hours which could disrupt your personal life.

The job can be quite repetitive and requires standing on your feet for long stretches.

Money guide

Pharmacists employed by the NHS during their pre-registration training have a starting salary of £21,909.

Once qualified, you can expect earnings of between £26,302 and £35,225.

A specialist could achieve up to £41,373.

Pharmacists with team management or consultancy responsibilities could earn up to £99,437 a year.

Those who are employed by smaller, independent pharmacies may receive lower salaries.

Related opportunities

- Biochemist p493
- Pharmacologist p309
- Pharmacy Technician p310

Further information

NHS Careers
www.healthcareers.nhs.uk

Royal Pharmaceutical Society
www.rpharms.com

PHARMACOLOGIST

Qualifications and courses

Owing to the scientific nature of this work, most entrants to pharmacology either have a pharmacology degree or a degree in a similar subject such as biomedical sciences, biochemistry, molecular and cell biology, physiology or microbiology. Entry for a degree requires 3 A levels/H grades, including Chemistry and Biology, and at least 5 GCSEs/National 5s (A*–C/A–C).

Competition for jobs within this industry is high so candidates may benefit from a postgraduate qualification such as a Master of Science (MSc) in Pharmacology or a relevant PhD. Qualifications at this level are likely to be essential for a research and development role or to gain employment with a major pharmaceutical company. Undertaking a PhD gives candidates essential lab experience which is viewed favourably by employers.

Pre-entry work experience within a pharmaceutical company is also desirable as it demonstrates your enthusiasm and commitment. A sandwich degree with a year-long placement would enable you to make industry contacts.

If you do not have a degree, it is still possible to enter this profession, working your way up from a lower position in the industry. Having a relevant HNC/HND would allow you apply for an entry level position, and give you the opportunity to learn on the job as you gain valuable work experience and the chance to gain further qualifications as you work.

If you work in research and development and carry out tests on live animals and humans then you will be required to hold a Home Office licence.

What the work involves

Pharmacologists study the impact of drugs and chemical substances on various living organisms, including on humans, animals, natural environments and cells.

This will involve potentially discovering, researching, developing and testing new drugs and medicines, so suits somebody with a creative as well as analytical mind.

You will study the actions of drugs via computer simulations, in tests on cells and tissues, and on animals and human volunteers.

There might be the opportunity to specialise in areas of pharmacology, such as neuropharmacology.

Type of person suited to this work

You should be a strong communicator with the ability to work within a team whilst also leading and motivating your colleagues in order to drive projects forward.

You will need excellent analytical skills as you will be gathering and interpreting complex information. Since the majority of equipment used to undertake experiments is computer-based, it is essential to have good IT skills.

To design and modify experiments, you will require problem-solving skills, creativity and flexibility. Patience and perseverance are essential as projects may involve many months of research and change.

Working conditions

You will normally work from 9am to 5pm during the week. Occasionally you may have to work evenings and weekends in order to monitor the more complex experiments.

You will work in a laboratory environment, usually within a university, government or commercial research centre, or a pharmaceutical company. The environment is generally clean and quiet, and you may be required to wear protective clothing when undertaking certain experiments.

Future prospects

Although the industry is competitive, once you have gained a position as a pharmacologist the opportunities for career progression are good.

You could work within a university, undertaking research and gaining a PhD, and then perhaps moving into a position as a lecturer.

Within commercial laboratories, experience will lead to increased responsibility and managerial opportunities.

Advantages/disadvantages

Gaining an entry-level position in this competitive industry is difficult but once you have secured a job, prospects are excellent and career progression rapid.

You will have the satisfaction of knowing that the new drugs you develop will enhance the quality of life for thousands of people worldwide.

There is a wide potential choice of career paths and specialties.

You will probably have to experiment on animals which may be upsetting and controversial.

Money guide

Starting salaries range from £25,000 to £28,000.

As you gain experience, you can expect to earn £30,000–£40,000.

Pharmacologists employed in senior roles can achieve between £35,000 and £80,000.

Commercial pharmaceutical companies tend to offer higher salaries than academic institutions.

A PhD will increase your earning potential by approximately 25%.

Related opportunities

- Biochemist p493
- Pharmacist p308
- Toxicologist p525

Further information

British Pharmacological Society
www.bps.ac.uk

HEALTHCARE

Qualifications and courses

The Pharmacy Services Apprenticeship is available at Advanced Level for those who wish to become a pharmacy technician. The apprenticeship typically lasts 2 years and involves training on the job with a practising pharmacist whilst studying for relevant qualifications. Another route into the industry is to obtain a trainee post within either a community pharmacy or a hospital. Most employers will expect apprentice/trainee applicants to have 5 GCSEs/National 5s (A*–C/A–C), including English, Maths and at least one science subject.

To become a qualified pharmacy technician you must meet the requirements of and be registered with the General Pharmaceutical Council (GPhC). Entrants must complete one of the GPhC-accredited competency-based qualifications, such as the NVQ Level 3 in Pharmacy Services Skills, and one of the knowledge-based qualifications, such as the City & Guilds Level 3 qualifications in Pharmacy Services Skills or BTEC Level 3 Diploma in Pharmaceutical Science. These can also be achieved via on-the-job training as a trainee technician. It is also possible to take a single qualification that combines the knowledge and competency elements, such as the Buttercups Training Level 3 or National Pharmacy Association Level 3 qualifications. Candidates must also complete 2 years of work experience with a qualified pharmacist before they are eligible for GPhC registration.

All pharmacy technicians are required by the GPhC to undertake continuing professional development (CPD) throughout their career to keep their knowledge up to date.

What the work involves

Pharmacy technicians will assemble and supply medication to patients, as well as provide advice regarding the medication. Technicians operate under the supervision of a qualified pharmacist.

You could work in a retail environment as a community pharmacy technician, within a hospital or in a commercial pharmaceutical lab. You will be responsible for monitoring stocks of medicines, checking expiry dates and reordering supplies as necessary.

You will be working with a variety of healthcare professionals including pharmacists, doctors and nurses, and you will also have considerable contact with patients and customers.

Type of person suited to this work

You will need to be a strong communicator as you will advise patients on medications and clearly explain how to administer them. You will also need to be comfortable working in a team and following instructions.

You should be good with numbers and calculations. Accuracy and attention to detail are essential to ensure that you are making and labelling medications correctly, and keeping detailed records of each patient's medication needs.

You must be mature, tactful and non-judgemental when dealing with patients, who will present a variety of complaints.

Working conditions

Hours will depend on where you work. Community pharmacy technicians usually work 39 hours a week from Monday to Saturday. Industry and hospital technicians work a 37-hour week but may be required to cover evening and weekend shifts on occasion.

You could work in a shop, hospital or laboratory and you may occasionally be required to travel to nursing homes or community health centres and clinics.

Future prospects

You could work in a community context, within a small local pharmacy or a larger well-known chain. Alternatively, you could be employed by an NHS or private hospital, be based in a prison or work for the armed forces.

If you work in a hospital you could move into a specialised, supervisory role after gaining a few years' experience.

Additionally, many clinical pharmacy technicians in hospitals are now more involved with patients, undertaking ward rounds and other such duties.

Advantages/disadvantages

You will meet and help a range of patients and colleagues so your work will be varied and rewarding.

You can choose to work in a more relaxed retail environment, in the bustle of a hospital or in a professional industrial setting.

You may have to work evenings and weekends in order to provide a good level of service to patients and healthcare professionals.

The work can be very repetitive.

Money guide

Starting salaries for pharmacy technicians are usually between £19,217 and £22,458.

Experienced pharmacy technicians employed in a senior position could expect earnings of between £21,909 and £28,462.

If you become a team manager or specialist your salary could reach £41,373.

Related opportunities

- Health Records Clerk p289
- Pharmacist p308
- Sterile Services Technician p322

Further information

Association of Pharmacy Technicians UK
www.aptuk.org

Royal Pharmaceutical Society
www.rpharms.com

PHLEBOTOMIST

Qualifications and courses

There are no formal entry requirements for this job, but 4 or more GCSEs/National 5s (A*–C/A–C), including English, Maths and a science, may be an advantage for applicants for entry-level positions and are essential for more advanced work.

Other useful qualifications include the BTEC qualifications in Health and Social Care (Levels 2–3) and the Diploma in Society, Health and Development. HNC/HND or degrees in chemistry, physics, biology and materials science/technology are not essential but may improve your chances of employment.

Pre-entry work experience in a caring role or laboratory and a familiarity with lab procedures could also prove advantageous.

Training is usually done entirely on the job and organisations such as Phlebotomy Training Services (PTS) and Medicare Phlebotomy Trainers offer short introductory and advanced training courses for potential phlebotomists. After training, you may be awarded a Certificate of Competence, which will allow you to work without close supervision throughout the hospital. You will be trained to National Occupational Standards.

Phlebotomists may be able to work towards related qualifications, such as an NVQ/SVQ in Clinical Healthcare Support (Levels 2–3), or an NVQ in Health (Blood Donor Support) (Levels 2–3).

The National Association of Phlebotomists offers short training courses and workshops for qualified phlebotomists.

What the work involves

Phlebotomists are specialist medical laboratory assistants who collect blood samples for analysis to help diagnose diseases.

You will take blood samples from patients as painlessly as possible, label samples and make sure they are taken promptly and safely to a laboratory for examination.

You will need to keep accurate records and enter data in a computer system. It is your responsibility to ensure samples are not mixed up or contaminated.

Type of person suited to this work

Phlebotomists need to be practical and good with their hands to take blood without harming the patient or disturbing nursing care.

Good colour vision is essential.

You need to pay close attention to detail and work carefully as any errors could affect results.

It is important that you are able to communicate well with a range of people from children to the elderly. Some people are scared of having their blood taken, so you need to be able to reassure them.

Working conditions

You will carry out your work in hospital wards, out-patient departments and in the community. You will also spend time working in laboratories.

You will need to pay close attention to health and safety to prevent infection, and will wear a uniform and protective clothing such as gloves.

You are likely to work a normal working day during the week, but you may also need to work at weekends.

Future prospects

Most employment is available in NHS hospitals throughout the UK. There is also similar work available in blood transfusion services, government research departments and university laboratories. However, many phlebotomists work part-time, and some support workers or assistant healthcare scientists perform phlebotomy as part of their role.

Currently there is a shortage of skilled phlebotomists in certain areas, including London, and opportunities for phlebotomists are increasing as more health screening initiatives are introduced.

Phlebotomists can progress into managerial and senior roles.

Although there is no route for phlebotomists to progress to a career as a biomedical scientist, you may be encouraged to gain the qualifications that you need to train as one. You can also train to enter other areas of healthcare, such as nursing.

Advantages/disadvantages

Some of your patients will be scared of blood and needles which can make your job difficult.

It can be rewarding to work with patients and play a vital role in helping to diagnose illnesses.

Money guide

The NHS sets national pay rates for phlebotomists each year.

Salaries start at £15,251 per year and generally go up to £17,978.

Earning potential is increased for those who take on senior role or management duties.

If you work in the private sector or in London you may be paid more.

Related opportunities

- Biomedical Scientist/Medical Laboratory Assistant p494
- Immunologist p511
- Laboratory Technician p512

Further information

National Association of Phlebotomists
www.phlebotomy.org

NHS Careers
www.healthcareers.nhs.uk

Skills for Health
www.skillsforhealth.org.uk

HEALTHCARE

Qualifications and courses

All chartered physiotherapists must hold a degree in physiotherapy that has been recognised by the Health Professions Council (HPC). Full-time and part-time courses are available. Once you have completed your degree you are then eligible to apply to be a member of the Chartered Society of Physiotherapy (CSP).

Entry requirements for a degree course vary according to the university, but you will usually need 3 A levels/H grades including Biology or similar, and 5 GCSEs/National 5s (A*–C/A–C), including English, Maths and a science. You may also be considered if you possess other qualifications such as a BTEC Level 3 Diploma or Extended Diploma in Science, Applied Science or Health and Social Care.

Graduates with a related science degree could opt for a 2-year fast-track postgraduate course, and Access courses are available for entry onto a degree programme for candidates without the relevant science qualifications.

It is recommended that you get work experience prior to applying for your degree, as universities look favourably on this and physiotherapy courses are very competitive.

What the work involves

Physiotherapists treat patients with problems affecting their muscles, bones, heart, circulation and lungs that have been caused by accident, illness or ageing.

You will assess patients, then decide on an appropriate course of treatment for them. This could include exercise, movement, hydrotherapy, massage or manipulation.

Sports physiotherapists use the same techniques as those above, but focus solely on treating sports-related injuries.

Type of person suited to this work

You must have excellent communication skills as you will be dealing with both patients and other healthcare professionals on a daily basis. When treating patients, you will need to be able to listen to their concerns, explain the best course of treatment, and motivate them to persevere with their programme.

You will need to have a practical, logical mind in order to think around problems and solve unusual complaints in a creative way.

You must be physically fit, as much of the work can be strenuous and involve a good deal of hands-on contact and muscle manipulation.

Working conditions

You will generally work a 37-hour week, although you should expect to work evenings and weekends to fit in with your clients' lifestyles.

You could be employed by the NHS, private practices and health centres, residential homes, or sports centres and specialist clinics. A good number of physiotherapists opt for self-employment and work in a mixture of locations.

You will need to wear practical clothes, and certain employers may require you to wear a uniform.

Future prospects

Over half of physiotherapists are employed by the NHS, although this is significantly lower for those who have specialised in sports physiotherapy. There are opportunities with numerous other employers such as health clinics and sports centres, and you can be self-employed.

In recent years there has been a shortage of junior-level physiotherapy positions but this situation is improving and job prospects are still good.

You could go on to specialise in an area such as orthopaedics or geriatric care, or pursue more senior positions. The NHS now offers consultant-level posts for experienced physiotherapists.

Advantages/disadvantages

You will have a great deal of contact with patients and other healthcare professionals so the job is varied and rewarding.

If you opt for self-employment, you have control over your working hours and the patients you decide to take on.

It is physically demanding work, and working with injured or ill people can also prove emotionally draining.

Money guide

Starting salaries for newly qualified physiotherapists depend on your employer, or whether you are self-employed, but private sector salaries are generally quite similar to the NHS.

In the NHS, physiotherapists start at NHS wage band 5 which ranges from £21,909 to £28,462.

With a few years' experience, this can rise to between £26,302 and £35,225.

For specialist and advanced physiotherapists, salaries are between £31,383 and £41,373.

Consultant physiotherapists in the NHS earn in excess of £50,000, and those who have specialised in sports physiotherapy can earn up to £57,640.

Related opportunities

- Acupuncturist p270
- Chiropractor p277
- Hospital Doctor p294

Further information

Chartered Society of Physiotherapy
www.csp.org.uk

Health and Care Professions Council
www.hpc-uk.org

NHS Careers
www.healthcareers.nhs.uk

Qualifications and courses

To work as a podiatrist, you need to have gained an Honours degree in Podiatry (lasting 3 or 4 years) that has been approved by the Health and Care Professions Council (HCPC).

There are currently 13 institutions in the UK offering approved courses. For degree entry you are generally required to have a minimum of 2 A levels/3 H grades, one of which should be a science subject, preferably Biology, and 5 GCSEs/National 5s (A*–C/A–C). Competition for places on podiatry courses is fierce and it is advisable that you demonstrate your commitment to the subject by completing pre-entry, relevant work experience.

There are currently no fast-track degrees or qualifying postgraduate podiatry courses available for those who already possess a degree in a different subject, but experience or qualifications in subjects such as nursing, biology, physiology and physiotherapy may increase your employment chances.

You must be registered with the HCPC in order to practise as a registered podiatrist. In order to remain registered you must show evidence of continuing professional development (CPD). The Society of Chiropodists and Podiatrists (SCP) is the main provider.

Once qualified you can then take a whole range of specialist training.

Entry to the profession is subject to an occupational health clearance and a Disclosure and Barring Service (DBS) check may also be required.

What the work involves

Podiatrists (also commonly known as chiropodists) are healthcare practitioners responsible for assessing, diagnosing and treating problems relating to the feet and lower limbs.

The work involves using medical braces to correct deformities, administering local anaesthetics to enable pain-free specialist foot treatment, wound care, neurological assessment, skin, nail and bone surgery, care planning and health promotion.

You will treat a variety of people including those with disabilities and long-term illnesses, children and people with sports related injuries.

Type of person suited to this work

Podiatrists need to be caring and understanding. You should be able to reassure patients of all ages who could be in pain and explain their treatment clearly and simply.

You will also need good communication skills to be an effective part of a healthcare team. You should be able to apply your skills and knowledge to diagnose and solve problems.

You should be good with your hands as you will be using a range of equipment and techniques.

Working conditions

You will most likely work in a clinic but may visit patients in their own homes or in residential care homes at times. You might also need to attend sporting events to treat injured players.

If employed by the NHS you will work 37 hours per week, Monday to Friday. Self-employed podiatrists can work flexible hours, including evenings and weekends.

Future prospects

Podiatry offers excellent employment flexibility with the opportunity to work in the NHS, private practice, commerce, leisure, education and occupational health sectors to name but a few.

With experience you might choose to specialise in one area of podiatry such as biomechanics (musculoskeletal disorders), forensic podiatry, working with children or surgery.

You could also go on to teach and research in a university or move into management. Many podiatrists even set up their own small private practices.

Advantages/disadvantages

The idea of working with other people's feet and lower limbs may not appeal instantly, but podiatrists generally get great satisfaction from their work.

The NHS and Scottish Funding Council (SFC) cover the tuition fees for all 13 accredited podiatry courses.

You will have to deal with people who may be badly injured, very ill and in pain, which could be distressing.

You will be helping people to deal with pain and issues that could be affecting their mobility which can be rewarding.

Money guide

In the NHS, starting salaries typically range between £21,909 and £28,462, while experienced specialist lead podiatrists can earn between £31,383 and £41,373.

Private podiatrists can charge hourly, but their income is dependent on the number of patients they have and the location of their practice. That said, earnings should be similar to, or possibly more than, earnings in the NHS. Typically, initial assessments cost patients around £40, whilst basic treatment charges are around £32.

Related opportunities

- Doctor (GP) p287
- Physiotherapist p312
- Prosthetist/Orthotist p316

Further information

NHS Careers
www.healthcareers.nhs.uk

Skills for Health
www.skillsforhealth.org.uk

The College of Podiatry
www.scpod.org

HEALTHCARE

Organisation Profile

The COLLEGE *of* PODIATRY

THE SOCIETY OF CHIROPODISTS AND PODIATRISTS

Is your career goal to run a successful business or work as an NHS or private consultant, work part time or train in surgery? Perhaps you want to get a management position or work with children, become a medical researcher, work abroad or even work with a professional sports team?

It may surprise you to know that a career in Podiatry can offer you all of these possibilities, and many more.

What exactly is Podiatry?

Podiatrists are healthcare practitioners responsible for assessing, diagnosing and treating problems relating to the lower limb.

As with any medically related subject, practice is constantly evolving. With the progress of technology and the advances in medical research, podiatry is no exception. The word podiatry has now mostly replaced the word chiropody, and this reflects the technical advances within the profession and changes in the scope of practice.

Podiatrists are independent clinicians working with a huge range of patients to relieve symptoms, treat conditions and maintain their quality of life. The patients range from 1 to 100+ years old and come from all walks of life. The scope of practice of a podiatrist includes musculoskeletal assessment; orthotic provision; administering local anaesthetics to enable pain-free specialist foot treatment; wound care; vascular/tissue viability and neurological assessment; skin, nail and bone surgery; care planning and health promotion.

Podiatrists can work in many different settings. Those that choose to go into clinical practice could be working in a city-centre private practice, an NHS GP surgery, a hospital clinic, a rural visiting practice or a sports club. A Podiatry degree can lead to other employment opportunities, such as becoming a medical researcher or teaching in higher education, training in podiatric surgery and establishing your own private clinic, or working alongside the police in forensics.

All of the work requires a combination of technical knowledge, specialist practical skills and great interpersonal skills.

Qualifying

To qualify as a podiatrist you have to complete a BSc (Hons) degree in Podiatry, which you can take at 13 universities across the UK.

Most courses on offer are full time, but some universities also offer part-time courses. Eighty-seven per cent of recent graduates who were looking for work found employment within six months of graduating, which, compared to many other graduate employment rates, is fantastic.

Obviously what you do, where you work and what you earn are down to the career choices you make, but whatever you choose you will find Podiatry a challenging and rewarding career. It provides the opportunity to work in many different areas of clinical and non-clinical practice, geographical mobility and flexible working patterns, but most importantly you can make a real difference to the quality of your patient's life.

Useful Links

www.careersinpodiatry.com
Twitter @PodiatryCareers

Case Study

PODIATRIST

The world around us is dominated by science in one way or another, be it biology in plants or the human body, physics in engineering or communications and chemistry in food or DNA research.

Podiatry is no exception ... it's full of science!

To understand how the lower limb works and to help patients, you need to know all sorts about biology, physics and chemistry.

Biology

Biology is probably the main science people associate with working in the medical profession. As a podiatrist it's really important to understand the structure of the body as well as how things interact.

Podiatrists measure the blood flow in the legs and feet, and to do this they have to know exactly how to find the arteries and veins. They can test blood flow in a number of ways: by using their hands, ultrasound devices and blood pressure tests.

Treatment of painful or ingrowing toenails is achieved using simple surgical techniques. To do this, podiatrists have to give patients injections of anaesthetic which must be placed accurately near the nerves in the toe. To do the surgery effectively, they have to understand the structure of the nail and surrounding tissues. So, you can see how important it is to know your anatomy!

Physics

Physics is also important. Podiatrists treat a lot of different patients with biomechanical problems, and understanding levers and forces really helps to diagnose the problem and work out how to treat the patient.

Participating in sports puts increased forces through the joints in the legs, which can cause pain and injury. Runners, for example, can develop foot or leg problems that may need treatment from a podiatrist. Using a treadmill, video equipment and their knowledge, a podiatrist can assess the patient, diagnose the problem and potentially provide custom-made insoles that can alter the mechanics of the foot and reduce unwanted forces going through the foot.

Chemistry

Chemistry is also important in podiatry. Chemical reactions are essential for normal body function. Podiatrists need to know how illnesses and medicines may affect different chemical processes in the body to provide appropriate treatment.

Wounds in the skin contain all sorts of biochemicals. Podiatrists must understand what potential interactions there might be with anything they are using to treat a wound that would slow down the healing process. They need to know about different kinds of medication and how they react with the body. For example, understanding chemistry enables a podiatrist to calculate the maximum safe does of anaesthetic for a patient.

If you would like further information about podiatry training, please visit www.careersinpodiatry.com

Qualifications and courses

Training to become a prosthetist and orthotist takes 4 years, leading to a BSc Honours degree recognised by the British Association of Prosthetists and Orthotists (BAPO) and the Health and Care Professions Council (HCPC). Approved degrees are offered by either the University of Strathclyde or the University of Salford, and they also offer further qualifications such as a Postgraduate Certificate/ Diploma or Master of Science (MSc) in Prosthetics and/or Orthotics Rehabilitation Studies.

Entry requirements are usually with 2 or 3 A levels/3 H grades, including Maths or Physics as well as either Biology or Chemistry, plus 5 GCSEs/National 5s (A*–C/A–C). Entry could be granted with alternative qualifications such as with a BTEC which includes Maths or Engineering or a relevant NVQ but you will need to check university entry policies individually.

Graduates can either specialise in one area or practise both specialities. You must also register with the HCPC, undergo a Disclosure and Barring Service (DBS) check and pass a medical.

HCPC registration also requires prosthetists and orthotists to undertake continuing professional development (CPD).

What the work involves

Prosthetist

Prosthetists design and fit artificial limbs for patients who have lost a limb, have a deformity or who were born without a limb.

Work will include taking a cast of the area where the artificial replacement limb will fit and modelling it so that it will be safe and comfortable for the patient. You will also fit and adjust the replacement limb and teach the patient how to use it.

Orthotist

Orthotists provide surgical appliances such as arm and leg braces, collars, splints and special footwear for patients.

Work will include assessing the patient's problem, designing, fitting and adjusting the orthosis, and helping the patient to use it.

Type of person suited to this work

You must have a good technical knowledge of and aptitude for biomechanics and movement. You need to have excellent manual skills in order to take measurements, design devices and do fittings and make adjustments.

You should be practical and have a high attention to detail as each device is made to perfectly fit each patient.

It is important to have excellent communication skills and be caring and tactful as you will have to reassure, encourage and explain procedures to your patients.

Working conditions

Opportunities are available in hospitals, clinics and centres for people with disabilities.

Some time will be spent in workshops where the prostheses and orthoses are made.

You will generally work normal hours from Monday to Friday, although extra hours are required at busy times. A driving licence is useful if you are working in many different locations.

Future prospects

With a shortage of prosthetists and orthotists, job prospects are generally excellent across the UK. Most prosthetists and orthotists work within the NHS but there are also opportunities in private practice, in charities such as the Red Cross and with commercial companies that make devices for NHS hospitals.

With experience, you may specialise in an area such as upper or lower limb prosthetics or spinal orthotics; you could also move into management or carry out research and teaching.

There are also many opportunities to work all over the world – especially in the USA. Prosthetic and orthotic work is especially important in development programmes which work with communities affected by war.

Advantages/disadvantages

Working with patients who are upset and in pain can be emotionally demanding.

It is satisfying to be able to see the positive effects that the artificial limbs and surgical appliances have on people's lives.

You get to work with a diverse range of people from all age groups.

Money guide

There is no set salary scale for NHS prosthetists and orthotists, but salaries tend to be similar to those in commercial companies.

The starting salary for prosthetists and orthotists is around £21,909 to £28,462 per year.

Experienced prosthetists and orthotists can earn between £26,302 and £35,225.

Some senior practitioners in the NHS or those who work for manufacturers can earn up to £68,484.

Earnings are generally higher in London.

Related opportunities

- Medical Physicist p298
- Occupational Therapist p301
- Physiotherapist p312

Further information

British Association of Prosthetists and Orthotists
www.bapo.com

Skills for Health
www.skillsforhealth.org.uk

PSYCHIATRIST

Qualifications and courses

Candidates must initially train as a hospital doctor by completing a medical degree which is approved by the General Medical Council (GMC). The entry requirements for medical schools are very high A level/H grade results including relevant subjects such as science and maths. Competition for places on medical degrees is very high and so undertaking relevant pre-entry work experience will not only benefit your application but is becoming increasingly expected.

After studying for a medical degree, graduates will then undertake the 2-year Foundation programme of general training which acts as the bridge between medical school and specialist training. Candidates then progress to 5–6 years of specialty training in a particular area of psychiatry, such as general adult, forensic or geriatric psychiatry.

After successfully completing the specialty stage, trainees receive a Certificate of Completion of Training (CCT) and become eligible to join the GMC Specialist Register. It is then possible to apply for a post as a consultant.

Psychiatrists must engage in continuing professional development (CPD) throughout their career to ensure that their skills and knowledge are up to date. The Royal College of Psychiatrists provides information on available training.

What the work involves

Psychiatrists are doctors who have undergone further training in psychiatry.

As a psychiatrist, you will diagnose mental health problems by talking to patients and carrying out tests. You will then decide on a course of treatment which could include prescribing drugs and talking to patients to help them deal with their problems.

You will treat people with a range of mental health problems and often conduct specialist research, depending on your areas of professional interest. These include depression, schizophrenia, eating disorders, anxieties, phobias, drug and alcohol abuse, and post-traumatic stress disorder.

Type of person suited to this work

As a psychiatrist you need to be patient and caring. You will need excellent communication skills to listen carefully to people who might be confused or withdrawn. You will help them discuss and come to terms with their problems or illness and you should be able to explain their conditions and treatment in a clear, simple way.

You will work with relatives and carers, and as part of a team with other medical staff such as psychiatric nurses and occupational therapists.

Working conditions

You could work in a range of locations including hospitals, patients' homes, schools, residential homes and prisons.

Some psychiatrists have standard office hours. Others work shifts and are on an on-call rota which includes working nights, weekends and on bank holidays.

You will work as part of a team of healthcare professionals.

Future prospects

Most psychiatrists work within the NHS throughout the UK. There is also a small amount of work available in private hospitals, care homes and rehabilitation centres. The armed forces also employ psychiatrists.

There are six specialist areas of psychiatry that you may work in: adult, child and adolescent, forensic, the psychiatry of learning difficulties, geriatric, and psychotherapy. Entry to psychotherapy is competitive.

You could move into academic work, either carrying out research or teaching medical students.

Advantages/disadvantages

Your patients could be confused or aggressive with a range of difficult problems so the work can be demanding.

Getting patients to open up and talk may be difficult, particularly if they have a distressing personal history.

It is rewarding to be able to make a difference to people's lives by helping them to regain their self-respect and happiness.

There is the opportunity to work in different environments, but usually in calm environments.

Money guide

Salary levels in the NHS may vary in different locations and earnings are often higher in private practice work.

Junior doctors have a starting salary of £27,000 in the first year of the 2-year Foundation programme; £30,000 in the second year.

When undertaking specialist training, you can expect to earn £37,000 a year or more.

On completion of training, specialist doctors of psychiatry can earn between £37,547 and £70,018.

Consultant psychiatrists can achieve salaries ranging from £76,001 up to £102,465 for those in the most senior positions.

Related opportunities

- Doctor (GP) p287
- Hospital Doctor p294
- Psychoanalyst/Psychotherapist p569

Further information

British Medical Association
www.bma.org.uk

NHS Careers
www.healthcareers.nhs.uk

Royal College of Psychiatrists
www.rcpsych.ac.uk

HEALTHCARE

Qualifications and courses

All radiographers need a degree approved by the Health & Care Professions Council (HCPC). You must decide which branch of radiography you wish to practise in before university as they require different qualifications so it is worth visiting radiography and radiotherapy centres before applying to help with the decision.

Most universities expect you to have previous work experience in a radiography department and to have observed radiography in practice. All radiography degrees involve spending 50% of your time doing academic work and 50% undertaking practical placements. Courses usually last 3 years and the minimum entry requirements for a degree are usually 2 A levels/3 H grades, including a science-based subject (preferably Biology or Physics), and 5 GCSEs/National 5s (A*–C/A–C).

Diagnostic radiographer
You must hold a degree in diagnostic radiography. Radiography assistants who wish to qualify as radiographers could study for in-service or Foundation degrees.

Therapeutic radiographer
You will need a degree in radiotherapy or therapeutic radiography. Alternatively, those who already have a degree in a science or health-related subject, such as life and medical sciences, biology or health studies, may be eligible for a 2-year postgraduate training course.

What the work involves

Diagnostic radiographer
You will help doctors and surgeons to diagnose diseases and injuries as an essential step towards treating a patient. You may use a variety of methods such as X-ray, computed tomography (CT) scanning and ultrasound to create images of body parts and organs.

Therapeutic radiographer
Working with an oncology team, you will use doses of radiation to control or kill cancerous cells. You will be involved in every aspect of the treatment, including pre-treatment preparation, planning, the delivery of the radiation and follow-up care of patients.

Type of person suited to this work

You should be warm, understanding and adaptable. You must be able to work with both children and adults who are extremely ill. Communication skills are vital for listening to patients and explaining their treatments.

You need to be a quick thinker and be detail-oriented in order to produce accurate images. Confidence to operate sophisticated computerised equipment is essential.

Working conditions

Diagnostic radiographer
You will be based in accident and emergency, operating theatres, wards or imaging units.

These departments need to be staffed 24 hours a day so you will work a shift system including nights and weekends. You should work a total of 37.5 hours a week.

Therapeutic radiographer
You will be based in radiotherapy or oncology centres, outpatient units or at charities such as Macmillan Cancer Support.

Future prospects

You could work for the NHS in a clinic, hospital or oncology centre, or work for the armed forces or a private practice.

You could be promoted to management roles or become an instructor or researcher. UK radiography qualifications are recognised internationally so you could choose to work overseas.

Diagnostic radiographer
You could specialise in areas such as magnetic resonance imaging (MRI), ultrasound or nuclear medicine.

Therapeutic radiographer
You could specialise in anything from quality management to treatment planning or palliative care.

Advantages/disadvantages

Each of your patients will be unique, keeping your work interesting.

It is satisfying when you capture the best image possible and contribute to your patients' wellbeing.

Rota work can be difficult as you may be required to work bank holidays and nights.

Money guide

Starting salaries for NHS radiographers are between £21,909 and £28,462.

An experienced specialist could earn from £26,302 up to £35,225.

Senior radiographers can achieve up to £41,373 and consultants could reach £68,484.

Salaries may be higher in private practice.

Related opportunities

- Critical Care Technologist p279
- Medical Physicist p298
- Radiologist p319

Further information

Radiography Careers
www.radiographycareers.co.uk

Society and College of Radiographers
www.sor.org

Qualifications and courses

To become a radiologist, you must initially train as a hospital doctor by completing a medical degree which is approved by the General Medical Council (GMC). Entry requirements for medical school include very high A level/H grade results within relevant subjects such as science and maths. Competition for places on medical degrees is tough and pre-entry work experience is becoming increasingly expected. Universities offer 30-week pre-medical courses in sciences for those applicants without science A levels/H grades.

After studying for a medical degree, graduates undertake the 2-year Foundation programme of general training which acts as the bridge between medical school and specialist training.

Candidates then register as Members of the Royal College of Radiologists (RCR) and begin 5 years of speciality training in clinical radiology. At least 4 years of the training are spent in clinical posts and 6 months research in any aspect of diagnostic imaging is also included. Trainees must pass all three parts of the Fellowship of the Royal College of Radiologists (FRCR) examination before receiving a Certificate of Completion of Training (CCT) and becoming eligible to join the GMC Specialist Register.

RCR operates a continuing professional development (CPD) scheme for qualified radiologists to update their knowledge and skills.

What the work involves

Radiologists are doctors who have undergone further training in radiology. Radiologists increasingly perform interventional procedures such as biopsies using image guidance.

As a radiologist, you will diagnose patients' diseases by using information gained from images such as X-rays, and computed tomography (CT) or magnetic resonance imaging (MRI) scans.

You will also play an important role in identifying sources of disease and reducing the possible risks of them spreading further.

Type of person suited to this work

As a radiologist, you must care about patients and be sensitive to their situation. You need strong communication skills to explain things to patients simply and clearly so that they understand their health conditions and any treatments they may require.

You must be comfortable working as part of a team with other medical staff.

Scientific and technical knowledge and an ability to diagnose patients' conditions accurately are also necessary. You should be willing to continue learning throughout your career.

You will need good eyesight and excellent attention to detail so that you can interpret images. Practical skills are required when caring for patients and operating equipment.

Working conditions

You will work within a hospital, mainly in the radiology department but you will also spend time visiting patients on their wards.

You will use a range of sophisticated equipment and you will be required to wear protective clothing when operating it.

Your working hours will vary and you will be expected to work shifts, evenings and weekends in order to provide a 24-hour service for patients.

Future prospects

Career prospects are excellent due to an international and domestic shortage of radiologists.

Most radiologists work within the NHS throughout the UK, however there is also some work available in private hospitals.

You may decide to specialise further in a particular area or you could progress to a management role. You could also move into academic work, either carrying out research or teaching medical students.

Advantages/disadvantages

The role can be emotionally demanding because you will be dealing with patients who have life-threatening conditions.

Your work is vital in finding an accurate and early diagnosis for patients, which can help to save lives.

Money guide

Salary levels in the NHS may vary in different locations and earnings are often higher in private practice work.

Junior doctors have a starting salary of £27,000 in the first year of the 2-year Foundation programme; £30,000 in the second year.

While undertaking specialist training, you can expect to earn upwards of £37,000 a year.

On completion of training, specialist radiologists can earn between £37,547 and £70,018.

Consultant radiologists can achieve salaries ranging from £76,001 up to £102,465 for those in the most senior positions.

Related opportunities

- Anaesthetist p272
- Hospital Doctor p294
- Radiographer p318

Further information

British Medical Association
www.bma.org.uk

NHS Careers
www.healthcareers.nhs.uk

Royal College of Radiologists
www.rcr.ac.uk

HEALTHCARE

Qualifications and courses

All speech and language therapists must be registered with the Health and Care Professions Council (HCPC). In order to qualify for registration, you must either have a speech and language degree that has been accredited by the Royal College of Speech and Language Therapists (RCSLT) or complete postgraduate study (a good healthcare-related undergraduate degree and relevant work experience are necessary for a postgraduate application).

For entrance onto a degree course you will need 2 A levels/3 H grades, and 5 GCSEs/National 5s (A*–C/A–C) including English, a science and Maths.

There are also Foundation courses available for those who do not have the relevant qualifications to go straight onto a degree programme, and accelerated 2-year degree courses for students who already have a health-related degree. All courses combine academic study with on-the-job training.

As you will be working with children and vulnerable adults, you will need to undergo a Disclosure and Barring Service (DBS) check and pass a medical screening.

What the work involves

Speech and language therapists work with patients who have problems speaking, chewing or swallowing.

You will be responsible for assessing patients, and prescribing a suitable course of treatment.

You will work with a range of patients including children who need help in developing their speech, people with a speech defect such as a stammer, and those who have trouble eating because of an accident or illness. You will also work with each patient's family, partner or carer in order to show them how to support your patient at home.

You will liaise with professionals in education and social services.

Type of person suited to this work

You will need excellent communication skills in order to develop a good relationship with patients and colleagues alike. You will also need to be a patient teacher in order to successfully help your patients learn new skills to overcome their problems.

You should be mature and non-judgemental in your approach to patients as you will be dealing with people of varying ages, backgrounds and cultures.

You will work both on your own and within a wider team of healthcare professionals, so you must have plenty of initiative coupled with a good approach to working within a team.

Working conditions

Speech and language therapists usually work 37.5 hours per week from Monday to Friday. Evening, weekend or shift work is rare.

There are plenty of opportunities to work part time.

You could work in one or several of a variety of locations, including hospitals, schools, residential homes, health centres, young offenders' institutions and in patients' homes. Since local travel in the community is required, it is useful to have a driving licence, particularly in rural areas.

Future prospects

There is a current shortage of registered speech and language therapists, so job opportunities outweigh the number of candidates.

Most therapists are employed by the NHS and work throughout their local community. Others work for social services, local education authorities, charities and schools. There is a growing trend amongst therapists to be self-employed and treat patients privately.

You could progress into a supervisory role; specialise in an area such as deafness and hearing impairment, linguistics or acquired neurological disorders; or move into research through routes such as an MPhil or PhD.

Advantages/disadvantages

Speech and language therapists are in great demand, so you will have a greater choice of job opportunities open to you than in some other health-related professions.

Working closely with patients and seeing them improve under your care and guidance is rewarding.

You may have to work with difficult patients in unfavourable conditions on occasion, such as young offenders' institutions or prisons.

Money guide

Rates of pay for speech and language therapists working for the NHS are outlined in the Agenda for Change, though may vary depending on location.

As a newly qualified speech and language therapist, you could expect to earn between £21,909 and £28,462.

Specialists in the field of speech and language therapy can earn up to £35,225.

On progression to advanced specialist, or after taking on leadership or management duties, you could expect to earn up to £41,373.

Other employers, outside of the NHS, such as charities and local education authorities, offer comparable pay.

Related opportunities

- Health Visitor p291
- Learning Disabilities Nurse p296
- Occupational Therapist p301

Further information

NHS Careers
www.healthcareers.nhs.uk

Royal College of Speech and Language Therapists
www.rcslt.org

Qualifications and courses

Most entrants to this profession have a degree in sports science, but degrees in psychology or any kind of physical education are also relevant.

The entry requirements for a degree in sports science are usually 2 A levels/3 H grades, including a science – particularly sought after is Biology – and 5 GCSEs/ National 5s (A*–C/A–C). There is also the option of following an Access course before taking a degree, or doing a postgraduate degree in sports science after a degree in a related subject.

Once you have a relevant degree, you can seek accreditation through the British Association of Sport and Exercise Sciences (BASES). The most direct route to accreditation is through the BASES Supervised Experience (SE) process, however applicants with significant industry experience may be able to apply for accreditation without undertaking this.

It may be necessary to gain some relevant practical experience in the fitness or leisure industry to increase your chances of employment.

Continuing professional development (CPD) and keeping your skills up to date will be a vital part of a career in sports and exercise science, and there are plenty of opportunities to do this through the BASES.

What the work involves

Sports scientists work either with athletes to help build their performance or with people who need or wish to improve their health. Clients may also be recovering from illness or injury and need guidance on how to get back to their level of fitness.

As a sport or exercise scientist, you require a lot of scientific knowledge, including an understanding of human biology, biomechanics and physiology. You also need to have an understanding of psychology, in order to assess the mental state of some athletes.

It is typical practice to spend time on performance analysis (usually done with video footage) and work with clients on perfecting performance and fitness.

You will spend some time outside of the office with clients and may conduct research on areas of professional interest or sports you wish to specialise in.

Type of person suited to this work

If you want to be a sports and exercise scientist, above all you need to be a good communicator. Your work will centre on building relationships with people, and you have to be good at listening and aware of your clients' needs.

Aside from this, you need to have a clear writing style to communicate findings, and be good at research and problem-solving.

You should be good with numbers and statistics, well organised, accurate and good with computers.

You will also need a scientific and analytical mind to help your clients improve their sporting potential.

Working conditions

You will usually work in leisure and sports centres and gyms, for around 38 hours a week.

If you are a sports scientist, some clients may require you outside regular working hours, and part-time work is also available.

You will also spend a lot of time outdoors, and probably travel too. For this reason, a driving licence is an advantage.

Future prospects

Although there is no specific career path for this job, progression is possible.

Building a list of contacts is important, and with the right experience you may be able to work your way up to helping people who play sport at an international level.

You could also teach, or if you are an exercise scientist, you might be able to move into a specific area such as cardiology.

Advantages/disadvantages

This job is really rewarding for those who are interested in exercise and science, and like to be out and about being active rather than sitting still.

You have to use your brain and your body, and the job is unlikely to become boring as you will be working with so many different people.

It can be tiring, and you need quite specialist knowledge that has to be constantly maintained.

Money guide

As a newly qualified sports and exercise scientist, you will probably earn around £18,000 a year.

As you gain experience, this may rise to about £35,000.

If you work with top athletes in competitive sport, you might earn in excess of £60,000 a year.

Related opportunities

- Leisure Centre Assistant/Manager p369
- Sports Coach p372
- Sports Development Officer p373

Further information

British Association of Sport and Exercise Sciences
www.bases.org.uk

English Institute of Sport
www.eis2win.co.uk

SkillsActive
www.skillsactive.com

HEALTHCARE

321

Qualifications and courses

There are no set minimum qualifications to begin work in this position. However, employers will expect you to have a good general standard of education, with strong reading skills and neat handwriting (in order to label materials and equipment clearly and correctly).

Some employers may specifically request that you have 5 GCSEs/National 5s (A*–C/A–C) before applying and other qualifications, such as the BTEC Level 3 in Applied Science or the BTEC Level 3 in Applied Science (Medical Science), could also be advantageous.

Once you secure a position as a sterile services technician, training is provided on the job by experienced colleagues. You may also be encouraged to study for an ASET Level 2 Certificate in the Control of Infection and Contamination or NCFE Prevention and Control of Infection Level 2 Award.

Gaining the NVQ Level 3 in Health (Decontamination) would allow you to register with the Institute of Decontamination Sciences (IDSc). This could help you to progress and gain a management position. The IDSc also offers useful training programmes. Supervisors generally need an SVQ/NVQ Level 3 in Supervisory Management or the First Line Management Certificate from the Institute of Leadership Management (ILM). Further qualifications, such as NVQ Level 4 in Management or the ILM Diploma in Management may also prove advantageous to job progression.

What the work involves

Sterile services technicians work as part of a team responsible for helping to prevent the spread of infections by making sure that hospital equipment is sterile.

Your work will involve collecting and cleaning a range of instruments. You will have to operate a steam sterilising machine, such as an autoclave.

You will dismantle and examine certain instruments through a microscope before sterilising them and then reassembling and testing them. Once the equipment is reassembled and sufficiently cleaned, you will follow set procedures to repackage, seal and label the equipment.

You will work to national standards, operating highly technical machines, and you must keep accurate records of your work.

You will also be expected to deliver sterile supplies by trolley to wards and departments and restock supplies of items such as dressings, needles and syringes.

Type of person suited to this work

You will need to be good with your hands, work accurately, pay attention to detail and follow instructions and set procedures carefully.

Sterile services technicians should be very vigilant about hygiene and interested in keeping hospitals and equipment clean and safe for patients and staff.

You will work in a team so you will need good communication skills. You should also be well organised and able to keep clear, detailed records.

You will be collecting and dismantling machinery so you will need to be physically fit.

Working conditions

You will work in a hospital as part of a team and will have contact with doctors, nurses and other staff.

Based in the sterile services department, you will collect equipment from all parts of the hospital and this will involve lifting and pushing trolleys.

You will have to wear protective clothing and you may have to work shifts. People with skin conditions may find this job difficult.

Future prospects

Most jobs are in NHS hospitals throughout the UK but you could also work in a private hospital. Opportunities are good as there is a shortage of applicants for vacancies.

With experience, you could be promoted to senior technician or supervisor. You could then take professional qualifications and become a sterile services manager.

As a manager you could move into management in other areas of the NHS.

Advantages/disadvantages

The work can be routine and physically demanding.

The working conditions can be humid and uncomfortable as protective clothing is essential and steam sterilising machines are often required.

You will be making a vital contribution to controlling the spread of potentially deadly infections which is very rewarding.

Money guide

Starting salaries for sterile services technicians, in NHS wage band 2, are between £15,251 and £17,978 per year.

Those employed as a supervisor can expect to earn from £16,800 to £19,655.

Related opportunities

- Biomedical Scientist/Medical Laboratory Assistant p494
- Hospital Porter p295
- Operating Department Practitioner p302

Further information

Institute of Decontamination Sciences
www.idsc-uk.co.uk

NHS Careers
www.healthcareers.nhs.uk

Skills for Health
www.skillsforhealth.org.uk

Qualifications and courses

To become a surgeon, you must initially train as a hospital doctor by completing a medical degree which is approved by the General Medical Council (GMC). Degrees usually take 5 years and entry requirements include very high A level/H grade results, including relevant subjects such as science and maths. Some universities offer a foundation or pre-medical year in addition to the 5-year medical degree course, lasting 30 weeks, for candidates without science A levels/H grades.

Competition for places on medical degrees is very tough, so undertaking relevant pre-entry work experience may benefit your application and is becoming increasingly expected. You may also be required to take the UK Clinical Aptitude Test (UKCAT).

After studying for a medical degree, graduates undertake the 2-year Foundation programme of general training which acts as the bridge between medical school and specialist training. Candidates then progress to 5–6 years of specialty training in a particular area of surgery, such as neurosurgery, paediatric surgery or plastic surgery.

After successfully completing the specialty stage, trainees receive a Certificate of Completion of Training (CCT) and become eligible to join the GMC Specialist Register. It is then possible to apply for a post as a consultant surgeon.

Surgeons must engage in continuing professional development (CPD) throughout their career to ensure that their skills and knowledge are up to date. The Royal College of Surgeons of England provides information on available training.

What the work involves

Surgeons work in hospitals, operating on patients in order to remove or prevent the spread of disease, treat injuries, and fix other complaints.

You will specialise in operating on specific conditions or diseases relating to a particular system of the body, such as neurological, gastrointestinal or cardiovascular. You will also be responsible for diagnosing problems, taking case histories, talking patients through surgical procedures and advising them on post-operative care.

You will see patients on ward rounds and in out-patient clinics, as well as undertaking administrative work such as updating patient records.

Type of person suited to this work

You need excellent communication skills in order to develop a good relationship with patients and colleagues alike. You will be required to direct your team through complex surgical procedures in the operating theatre, as well as explaining them to patients in simple terms.

You should have excellent manual and technical skills in order to operate with precision and confidence. As you will be working under immense pressure, you should also be able to think quickly and clearly when solving problems.

You must be prepared to break bad news to patients and relatives on occasion, which requires sensitivity and diplomacy.

Working conditions

Surgeons work extremely long hours which often include nights and weekends.

Most of your work will take place in hospitals, working with health professionals including other surgeons, nurses, anaesthetists and GPs. You could work in the NHS or in private hospitals, although the majority of surgeons divide their time between the two.

The work is mentally and physically exhausting as you will need to concentrate for hours at a time and spend a lot of time on your feet.

Future prospects

There are many opportunities to work abroad, particularly in conjunction with specialist charities operating in developing countries.

You will continue to train and learn new skills throughout your career as technology and techniques develop and improve.

Once you have qualified as a surgeon, you can become a consultant and work within the NHS or in private practice, both of which are lucrative options.

Advantages/disadvantages

You will be personally responsible for transforming and saving a number of lives throughout your career.

The training period is extremely long, often in excess of 12 years, so you have to be extremely dedicated.

You will work long and unpredictable hours which can have an adverse effect on your personal life.

Money guide

Salary levels in the NHS may vary in different locations and earnings are often higher in private practice work.

Junior doctors have a starting salary of between £27,000 and £30,000 on the 2-year Foundation programme. While undertaking specialist training, you can expect to earn upwards of £37,000 a year.

Consultant surgeons can achieve salaries ranging from £76,001 up to £102,465 for those in the most senior positions.

Related opportunities

- Dentist p284
- Doctor (GP) p287
- Hospital Doctor p294

Further information

British Medical Association
www.bma.org.uk

NHS Careers
www.healthcareers.nhs.uk

Royal College of Surgeons of England
www.rcseng.ac.uk

HEALTHCARE

323

TRICHOLOGIST

Qualifications and courses

The main route into trichology is to complete the Institute of Trichologists' 2-year training course. There are no set minimum entry requirements but the course is academic and scientific in nature and the progress of students is closely monitored through exams and practical placements.

Successful completion of the Institute's course makes you eligible for admission as an Associate Member of the Institute (AIT). Progression to full membership (MIT) is available upon further study and a minimum of 2 years' professional practice as a trichologist.

Another option is to study for the Diploma in Pure-Trichology offered by the Trichological Society. This is a distance learning course which lasts up to 3 years and involves practical clinical experience, a dissertation and an oral exam.

Those who already have medical qualifications may be eligible to take shortened versions of the above courses.

Some trichologists do not have formal qualifications as the profession is unregulated, though it is highly recommended if you want to begin a career and attract clients. Some people gain the NVQ in Hairdressing (Levels 3–4), which contains some trichology teaching, before starting their training.

What the work involves

Trichologists help people who have issues with their hair or scalp. A trichologist diagnoses and treats diseases and disorders of the scalp and hair, such as hair loss and dandruff.

Patients might complain of sudden hair loss all over the scalp, excessive itching and scaling, or a bald patch, among other problems.

You will talk to patients about their medical history, health and diet, and thoroughly examine their hair and scalp.

You will give advice and recommend treatment, such as using special creams or shampoos. You might also refer patients to other healthcare professionals or a specialist if appropriate.

Type of person suited to this work

Trichologists need excellent communication skills to speak to patients about their problems and explain the treatments they have recommended.

You should be sympathetic, tactful and able to reassure patients, put them at their ease and gain their trust.

You will need to have a methodical approach to your work and pay close attention to detail so that you can assess patients' conditions accurately and plan appropriate treatment.

Working conditions

Most trichologists work in clinics treating patients and if you are self-employed you will rent your own premises.

You will usually have normal working hours from Monday to Friday. If you work in private practice you might need to work in the evenings or occasionally at weekends to treat people at times that suit them.

The work involves close contact with patients and hands-on treatment.

You are likely to wear a uniform and those employed in a research role may need protective clothing for laboratory work.

Future prospects

Many trichologists are self-employed, so you should expect to start up your own business.

Some trichologists will become involved in teaching and will work in universities and colleges (often in hair and beauty departments).

There are also a number of opportunities to work in research for pharmaceutical and cosmetics companies. Research positions may require further qualifications, such as a medical degree and training in dermatology.

Advantages/disadvantages

Working with patients who are distressed can be challenging and stressful for both parties.

It is rewarding to be able to use your knowledge to treat patients successfully.

There is the potential for quite a varied workload.

Money guide

Self-employed trichologists charge clients by the session.

Earnings vary widely, depending on your location, experience and the number of clients you have.

Newly qualified practitioners may charge about £30 per consultation.

Experienced practitioners may earn up to £90 for a session.

Trichologists who work in a clinic can earn from £19,000 to £50,000 with experience.

Related opportunities

- Dietitian p285
- Hairdresser/Barber p453
- Hospital Doctor p294

Further information

Institute of Trichologists
www.trichologists.org.uk

The Trichological Society
www.hairscientists.org

Languages, Information and Culture

The jobs in this family are quite varied in terms of whether you would work with other people or by yourself. You could find yourself working in a range of different places, from museums to antiques fairs to conferences as an interpreter. Some of the jobs in this family are more unusual and are perfect for those of you who want a fascinating job that allows you to indulge in your passion for historic artefacts and artwork or languages and foreign countries. To excel in this sector you should have an inquisitive mind, be meticulous in your work and enjoy carrying out research. The jobs featured in this section are listed below. For similar jobs to the ones in this section please see *Design, Arts and Crafts* on page 157 and *Marketing, Advertising, Media, Print and Publishing* on page 381.

Qualifications and courses

Entry to this area is usually gained with a relevant degree or postgraduate qualification. Voluntary or paid work experience can be useful. There are limited opportunities to gain qualifications in this area before degree level. A level/H grade Sociology covers some aspects of anthropology and for biological anthropology an A level/H grade in Biology may be useful.

Access and degree courses in this area cover subjects such as social anthropology and physical/biological anthropology. Anthropology can also be studied as part of a combined Honours degree with subjects such as archaeology or psychology. It is also possible to study for a master's or other postgraduate degree in anthropology following a first degree in any subject.

The Association of Social Anthropologists based at the University of Birmingham runs seminars and conferences, and has information on bursaries and awards for anthropology students.

Professionals using their anthropology training in another area such as archaeology are likely to have gained a qualification or degree in their specialist subject. Researchers in this area are often required to have a relevant postgraduate qualification or the equivalent practical experience. Higher education lecturers are usually required to have, or be working towards, a doctorate (PhD) and are expected to have experience in, or show potential for, teaching.

What the work involves

You will study and research the origin and cultural, physical and social developments of humans. You will investigate human culture across the world, in terms of its beliefs, values, traditions, social structure and language.

You will also apply specialist knowledge and research skills to find out about the differences between human cultures.

Anthropologists undertake their research in a wide range of areas such as archaeology, the arts, the environment, biology and religion.

You may use technology such as facial recognition software or carbon dating to get a more accurate idea of your subject, particularly if it is a historical one.

The increased use of technology to communicate means that the development of social interaction and the reliance on media have become large aspects of anthropological study and significance.

Type of person suited to this work

Whatever job you do as an anthropologist, you will need a strong interest in people and a respectful, flexible attitude to other people's beliefs and customs. You should also enjoy meeting new people and entering different social situations.

Good communication skills are also very important. Strong research skills and an organised approach are useful. IT skills and a good level of numeracy are also helpful.

You will need an observant approach with an interest in a wide range of subjects.

Working conditions

For research-based work, you might need to visit and stay in different areas. Spending time in other places means that anthropology is not generally a 9am to 5pm, office-based job.

The work can involve travel in the UK and overseas.

Some physical or biological anthropologists work in laboratories analysing and researching samples.

Forensic anthropology is often a part-time job and involves field work.

Future prospects

You could gain employment as a researcher on specific projects. Many anthropologists progress within academia by undertaking research and teaching around their specialist interests.

You could also work for government bodies and charities and there are some opportunities to work overseas.

Anthropologists also apply their research skills and training to their work in other areas such as social care, teaching and the health service.

Advantages/disadvantages

This job can provide opportunities to develop and research theories about people and cultures.

Anthropology can also provide the chance to meet a variety of people and visit different places.

Field research can be physically demanding and spending time away can be difficult if you have family commitments.

Money guide

Anthropologists work in a range of sectors, so salaries vary.

Starting salaries for graduates are around £21,000 per year, rising to £26,000 for research assistants/researchers.

Between £33,000 and £43,000 per year is usual for lecturers, with the expected salary for senior lecturers lying between £28,000 and £55,000.

Related opportunities

- Archaeologist p327
- Archivist/Records Manager p328
- Historian p333

Further information

Association of Social Anthropologists
www.theasa.org

Royal Anthropological Institute of Great Britain and Ireland
www.therai.org.uk

ARCHAEOLOGIST

Qualifications and courses

Most professional archaeologists have a degree, BTEC HND, or postgraduate qualification. Degree entry usually requires 2 A levels/3 H grades and 5 GCSEs/National 5s (A*–C/A–C). There are a number of relevant degree subjects, including ancient history, anthropology and conservation, which can be studied in combination with archaeology. A number of different degrees, ranging from geography or history to computer science and geology, can also be good preparation for a career in archaeology. A small number of Foundation degrees are also available in archaeology.

There is intense competition for jobs and postgraduate degrees are becoming increasingly common and are available in a variety of specialist subjects, such as the archaeology of specific regions or time periods (Egypt etc), bioarchaeology, osteoarchaeology, and landscape archaeology. Entry usually requires a good first degree and a history of relevant work experience.

Skills with computer-aided design (CAD) or geographical information systems (GIS) software could be very useful owing to the increasing use of technology in archaeology.

It is possible to enter this profession without a degree, although this is becoming increasingly uncommon. The Diploma in Environmental and Land-based Studies could be useful. An NVQ in Archaeological Practice (Levels 3–4) is also available.

Voluntary experience on digs is very useful. The key professional bodies can provide details of holiday work experience opportunities. The Archaeology Training Forum (ATF) develops and offers short courses in continuing professional development (CPD), and similar options are offered by English Heritage and the Society for the Protection of Ancient Buildings (SPAB).

What the work involves

Using your specialist knowledge and skills you will investigate and record physical evidence of the past.

You will provide practical support on archaeological excavations or 'digs', which might include undertaking basic digging work, project-managing a team or researching evidence found on sites.

You will develop public understanding of history through presentations, the publication of your findings or teaching in universities or schools. You could also provide information and advice on how to protect and maintain historical sites.

Type of person suited to this work

You will need a strong interest in history and past cultures.

For practical work you will need a patient and careful approach. You should also be observant with an eye for detail. A good level of physical fitness and manual dexterity will be needed when working on digs and handling objects.

The ability to work as part of a team is useful. In more senior jobs, you will need to explain your work to others so communication skills are important. Writing skills will help you to be able to write up reports and keep detailed records. IT skills are also useful.

Working conditions

Archaeologists often work on sites or digs that are outdoors. Varying weather conditions and the nature of the work make this job physically demanding.

Some archaeologists are based in offices within government bodies, heritage organisations and museums.

Much of your work will be on temporary contracts.

Future prospects

Whatever route you follow, this is a very competitive area in which to develop a career, and may be tough to get into.

You will need to gain practical experience on a voluntary or paid basis. With further experience you could project-manage site excavations or work as a researcher analysing excavation findings.

Some archaeologists work for heritage organisations to help preserve historic monuments and buildings. Others go into teaching or follow an academic career.

Advantages/disadvantages

It is likely that you will need to move around different geographical areas to gain practical experience.

There are opportunities to work overseas.

It's rewarding to discover artefacts that can shed ground-breaking light on the past.

Money guide

Salaries can vary dependent on location, sector and size of your employer.

Salaries typically start between £19,853 and £20,926 a year for those in roles such as excavation.

Experienced archaeologists can earn between £29,123 and £31,561.

Senior archaeologists can expect a salary of £36,552–£40,726.

Related opportunities

- Archivist/Records Manager p328
- Conservator/Restorer p331
- Further Education Lecturer p185

Further information

Chartered Institute for Archaeologists
www.archaeologists.net

Council for British Archaeology
new.archaeologyuk.org

Creative and Cultural Skills
www.ccskills.org.uk

Society for the Protection of Ancient Buildings
www.spab.org.uk

Qualifications and courses

Archivist

Entrants to this profession need a 2.1 Honours degree followed by a postgraduate qualification in archives and records management or archival studies. Your postgraduate degree must be recognised by the Society of Archivists. Useful first degree subjects include history, classics, languages and information science. You will need at least 2 A levels/3 H grades and 5 GCSEs/ National 5s (A*–C/A–C) for degree entry.

Relevant work experience is an advantage and is considered a necessity for entry onto a postgraduate course. This experience must be of good quality and cannot be undertaken in a library. See the Society of Archivists website for opportunities.

Records manager

You will normally require both an Honours degree and a postgraduate qualification in records management or in archives and records management. You will need at least 2 A levels/3 H grades and 5 GCSEs/National 5s (A*–C/A–C) for degree entry. Relevant experience is also important. Visit the Society of Archivists website for opportunities.

Both archivists and records managers may start out as assistants without a degree but will need to study for a degree and postgraduate qualification in order to become professionals.

Continuing professional development (CPD) is important and, once you are fully qualified and have at least 3 years of industry experience, you are encouraged to complete the Archives and Records Association (ARA) registration scheme, which takes 3 years to complete.

What the work involves

Archivist

You will manage and organise stored sets of archives, including records such as documents, maps, films and other items.

Many archivists deal with information enquiries and advise on the availability of records. You will ensure that archives are maintained in an appropriate way. You may also conserve documents and prepare them for storage.

Records manager

You will be responsible for organising records and information and advising your organisation as to which should be classified, stored or destroyed. You could be dealing with paper-based or electronic records.

Type of person suited to this work

Both records managers and archivists manage information, so a well-organised and methodical approach is essential. They need strong analytical and IT skills.

Archivists will need an interest in preserving historical records. You may provide information and advice to members of the public, so strong communication skills are useful.

Working conditions

Record/archive centres can be modern and spacious, but if based in older buildings, space may be limited.

Accessing records from cramped storage rooms or high shelves can be physically demanding. This job may not suit people with dust allergies.

In dealing with enquiries from visitors, the working environment can be very busy.

Future prospects

Archivist

Public records offices, private companies and other organisations need skilled information professionals.

With experience, you could progress from an assistant archivist role into senior management.

Records manager

Records managers may need to change employers in order to progress. Consultancy work is an option.

Advantages/disadvantages

Archivist

This job allows you to preserve and protect historical documents.

Employers often offer short-term contracts which can create job instability.

Records manager

You may have to change employers in order to progress.

You will constantly be learning as computer software and legislation are always changing.

Money guide

The Archives & Records Association (ARA) suggests a minimum salary of £22,443 for qualified archivists and records managers.

As you gain experience, salaries can rise to between £25,000 and £38,000 per year.

Senior archivists and records managers can earn up to £55,000 a year.

Related opportunities

- Antiques Dealer p462
- Bookseller p464
- Librarian/Library Assistant p336

Further information

Archives and Records Association
www.archives.org.uk

ARTS ADMINISTRATOR/ MANAGER

Qualifications and courses

There are no specific entry requirements, but most arts administrators have a degree or HND in an arts subject or business studies.

At degree level, arts management can be studied on its own, or in combination with a related subject such as events management and heritage management. The minimum entry requirements for a degree course are 2 A levels/3 H grades and 5 GCSEs/National 5s (A*–C/A–C).

Postgraduate courses in arts administration/arts management are available. A degree and/or relevant work experience is required for entry to these programmes. NVQs are available in Cultural Venue Operations and Support at Level 2 and Cultural Venue Administration or Cultural Heritage Operations at Level 3, Cultural Heritage at Level 4 and Cultural Heritage Management at Level 5.

Depending on the area you live in, a Community Arts Apprenticeship scheme is another possible entry route into arts administration. Apprentices gain experience in organising and publicising events as well as handling financial records and customer care.

For any entry route, participation in the arts and good IT skills will be an advantage. It is crucial to gain experience in the arts sector by undertaking work experience, voluntary work, internships or temporary work.

What the work involves

You will support the development and operation of activities and events in areas such as visual arts, drama and music.

You will undertake a range of administrative tasks including coordinating facilities and office management. You may be responsible for booking artists, refreshments, security and ticket sales. Your job could also involve managing funding applications and budgets or writing press releases.

Arts administrators are employed in many different organisations including arts centres, museums, community arts groups, local authorities and theatre companies. If you work for a bigger organisation, you will probably specialise in one administrative field such as public relations or sponsorship.

Type of person suited to this work

Enthusiasm for the arts is essential for this role, and a knowledge of the area of art or organisation you will be working for will be important. You will need a committed approach and be able to take initiative. A good range of administrative, office and IT skills are also essential.

You should be able to communicate well in person and in writing. As you will probably have to manage project budgets, numeracy skills are also useful.

Good organisational and multi-tasking skills are essential. You should enjoy working with a range of people, including

artists and members of the public. You should be able to work equally well independently or as part of a team.

Working conditions

Working hours can vary but it is likely that you will need to work some evenings and weekends to attend events.

Working environments vary according to employer. You might be based in a spacious office or have to work in more cramped conditions.

You might be required to travel to meet with artists and to attend performances.

Future prospects

This is a competitive area to get into. Developing expertise in a specific area such as community arts or theatre can be helpful.

With experience, you could progress from an assistant administrator role into a more senior job such as general manager or director.

With higher levels of experience, you could provide freelance support or specialise in a particular area such as arts marketing.

Advantages/disadvantages

This job provides the satisfaction of working in the arts.

Get to see potentially exciting exhibitions before the public.

Many roles are available on a part-time or on a project by project basis which can create job insecurity.

You may have to move geographic areas to gain work.

Money guide

Salary levels vary according to the type of organisation you work for.

Assistants and trainees typically have a starting salary of between £13,000 and £20,000.

With further experience and more responsibilities you could earn £20,000–£30,000 per year.

Senior managers could earn between £30,000 and £60,000 or more.

Salaries are higher in London and in other large cities.

Related opportunities

- Events and Exhibition Organiser p391
- Museum/Art Gallery Curator p337
- Personal Assistant p43

Further information

Arts Council England
www.artscouncil.org.uk

Creative Scotland
www.creativescotland.com

Qualifications and courses

To work as a bilingual secretary it is necessary to be fluent in at least one foreign language and the majority of entrants have this language as their mother tongue with English as their second language.

For those who are not native speakers, employers will usually expect you to have at least an A level/H grade in your chosen foreign language. A degree in languages or a joint Honours degree in languages and business studies may be useful but is not essential. Degree entry requirements are usually 2 A levels/H grades, including your chosen language, and 5 GCSEs/National 5s (A*–C/A–C).

Employers may also look for qualifications in administration or secretarial skills such as the NVQ/SVQ in Business and Administration (Levels 1–4). A GCSE/National 5 in Business Studies could be useful. OCR also offers Entry Level and Levels 1–3 Certificates in Business Language Competence for French, German, Italian or Spanish.

An Advanced Apprenticeship in Business and Administration is also available for those seeking to develop the required secretarial skills.

The ABC Awards in Practical Languages and the OCR qualifications in Asset Languages are aimed at those looking to use their language skills in a work-based context. NVQs are also available from Levels 1 to 4 in a variety of languages. Additionally, the LCCI International Qualifications and the Chartered Institute for IT (BCS)'s European Computer Driving Licence (ECDL) may give entrants an advantage.

What the work involves

Bilingual secretaries use their language skills to provide administrative support to professionals.

You will deal with incoming and outgoing telephone calls, emails and faxes in a foreign language, translate reports and take on the role of an informal interpreter.

It will also be your responsibility to coordinate travel arrangements for visits overseas and make arrangements for foreign visitors.

Type of person suited to this work

You must have the ability to write and speak fluently in English and at least one foreign language, as well as having a good grasp of spelling and grammar. It is necessary to have excellent IT and keyboard skills.

You should be extremely organised, able to multi-task and have good attention to detail. You must be friendly, helpful and polite and be able to work well as part of a team or independently. You should be able to remain calm under pressure.

Working conditions

You will work standard office hours but overtime may be required during busy periods. You could find part-time or temporary work. Job sharing is also available.

Bilingual secretaries share an office and spend a lot of time on the phone, working on a computer, and reading and translating documents. It could be your responsibility to deal with members of the public.

At senior levels, you might get the opportunity to travel abroad.

Future prospects

Western European languages such as Spanish, French and German are most sought after by employers, although there is growing demand for other languages including Chinese, Arabic and Japanese.

You could work for an international organisation or any companies which conduct business abroad, although most vacancies are in London and big cities.

You can progress to working for a more senior member of staff or to a supervisory role in a bigger company. This job can be a stepping stone into a career in marketing or human resources. You could also work overseas. After gaining more qualifications, you could become a translator or interpreter.

Advantages/disadvantages

You will get the opportunity to use your language skills on a daily basis.

It is possible to use the experience you have gained in a specific company or department to gain a promotion.

This job can be repetitive.

Tight deadlines and a heavy workload can be stressful.

Money guide

Salaries vary with geographical location and are likely to be highest in London.

Jobs in banks or other financial organisations tend to be higher paid than those in the media or charity sectors.

Bilingual secretaries can expect a starting salary of £18,000–£20,000.

Those with experience can earn between £20,000 and £35,000.

Taking on additional responsibilities may increase your salary further.

Related opportunities

- Personal Assistant p43
- Receptionist p46
- Secretary p51

Further information

Institute of Administrative Management
www.instam.org

Institute of Chartered Secretaries and Administrators
www.icsa.org.uk

Qualifications and courses

The most common route into this profession is through a degree or postgraduate qualification in conservation. Entry requirements for a degree are 2 A levels/3 H grades, including Chemistry, and 5 GCSEs/National 5s (A*–C/A–C). Some candidates may choose to take a Foundation degree in an art or furniture-related subject before their undergraduate degree and entry requirements for these courses are 4 GCSEs/National 5s (A*–C/A–C) and at least one relevant A level/H grade.

Graduates from relevant disciplines such as fine art, textile technology, ceramics, art history or chemistry can also enter this profession but they will need a postgraduate qualification in conservation. Details of approved courses are available from the Institute of Conservation (ICON).

An alternative route for school leavers looking to specialise in stonemasonry conservation or other crafts is to apply for an apprenticeship.

Work experience in a museum or gallery is useful and opportunities to volunteer are available through the National Association of Decorative and Fine Arts Societies (NADFAS). Internships, lasting between 8 weeks and 1 year, are also available with museums and are listed on the Museums Association website.

Restorers/conservation officers can work towards NVQs in Cultural Heritage (Levels 2, 3 and 5) or the EDI Level 4 Diploma in Conservation that is offered by the Victoria & Albert Museum.

Once you have several years of experience you can be accredited as a fully qualified conservator/restorer by applying for the Professional Accreditation of Conservators-Restorers (PACR) scheme.

What the work involves

You will manage the preservation of historical objects and artwork, as well as the care of historic houses and stately homes, applying your specialist knowledge of subjects such as textiles and furniture.

You will undertake conservation work, treating objects to protect them against wear and tear or restoring objects to as close to their original state as possible.

Your job might involve managing freelance restorers/conservators.

Type of person suited to this work

The role of preserving valuable collections or buildings requires a sound knowledge of culture and history.

You will need good practical skills, attention to detail and normal colour vision and have a patient and methodical approach to your work.

Strong communication skills, the ability to clearly explain complex issues and confidence speaking at public events are important. You should be comfortable working both independently and as part of a team. Those who are self-employed need business and administration skills.

Working conditions

Your work is likely to involve handling and treating fragile objects and you will usually be based in a clean workshop or laboratory. Conservators of stonework or other outdoor exhibitions may have to work outside in all weather conditions.

If you are employed by a museum or gallery you will work regular office hours Monday to Friday. Some conservators/restorers are self-employed and may have to work additional hours to suit the needs and deadlines of their client.

You might have to work with specialist materials and equipment which can affect people with skin conditions.

Future prospects

Restoration/conservation officers work in museums, galleries and historic houses, often with alternative job titles such as collections manager or curator. Many will have worked as craft conservators/restorers or have gained extensive experience in caring for collections.

You have the opportunity to work anywhere in the world. A willingness to be geographically mobile may improve your career prospects.

With experience, you could progress to managing a historic house or managing a team in a museum or gallery. It is also possible to become self-employed.

Advantages/disadvantages

This type of work offers the chance to care for valuable and rare historical collections and artwork.

Most galleries/museums employ only one person in this role so you might have to relocate to progress in this career.

Money guide

ICON recommends a minimum salary of £24,648 for entry-level conservators.

Once you have gained experience, you can expect earnings of up to £30,000. Those who are employed in a senior or managerial role can achieve up to £35,000.

Salaries vary according to the quality of your work and your employer and earnings are likely to be higher in London and large cities.

Related opportunities

- Architect p58
- Archivist/Records Manager p328
- Museum/Art Gallery Curator p337

Further information

Creative and Cultural Skills
www.ccskills.org.uk

Institute of Conservation
www.icon.org.uk

National Association of Decorative and Fine Arts Societies
www.nadfas.org.uk

LANGUAGES, INFORMATION AND CULTURE

GENEALOGIST

Qualifications and courses

Direct entry to this profession is unusual. Entrants normally have qualifications and experience in a related field such as archive administration, librarianship or historical research. A knowledge of social and local history sources is necessary, and training in palaeography (the study of ancient writing and scripts) and Latin is also essential.

A history degree provides a useful first step into this profession and the University Campus Suffolk offers a specialised degree in Family, Local and Community History. Typical entry requirements for a degree course are usually 2 A levels/3 H grades with 5 GCSEs/National 5s (A*–C/A–C). Blackpool and The Fylde College also runs a Foundation degree in History and Heritage Management Studies, which contains modules in genealogy, and the University of Strathclyde offers a postgraduate Certificate, Diploma and Master of Science (MSc) in Genealogical, Palaeographic and Heraldic Studies which may be useful for progression within the industry.

The relevant institutions related to genealogy may be a good place to look for continuing professional development (CPD) and further training. The Society of Genealogists offers short courses in genealogy and palaeography for beginners and those already working in the field, whilst the Institute of Genealogical Studies offers short courses at Basic, Intermediate and Advanced Levels. The Institute of Heraldic and Genealogical Studies (IHGS) provides qualifications including a Certificate, Higher Certificate and Diploma in Genealogy. Those over the age of 25 who have completed the Diploma and have at least 5 years of experience in research are eligible to apply for Licentiateship of the IHGS.

What the work involves

You will organise and plan research into the history or ancestry of individual families (genealogy) and write reports from your findings.

You will work with a range of historical information such as newspapers and directories to trace specific facts about family histories. Your work could also involve liaising with or supervising the work of researchers.

Meeting with clients and keeping them updated with your research would also be part of your job.

Type of person suited to this work

As you will be investigating family history, an enthusiasm for historical research is essential. You will also need excellent research skills and the ability to understand and interpret detailed information.

IT skills will help you work with information management software. You will also need excellent writing skills to produce reports.

You should enjoy meeting a range of people and working with them to understand and manage their expectations.

You will need a good knowledge of historical resources and subject areas and an organised, thorough approach to your work is important.

Working with unique historical documents demands careful handling skills.

Working conditions

Most genealogists are self-employed and work from home or in offices. However, they spend a lot of their time undertaking research in public records buildings.

The job can involve travel, for example to visit archive collections. A driving licence would be useful.

You will spend a lot of time reading and assessing detailed information.

Future prospects

Genealogy is usually followed as a hobby rather than as a profession and the number of formal employment opportunities is small.

Most genealogists work on a self-employed basis, as a sole trader or part of a small partnership while a small number work for specialist research companies.

You can develop knowledge on a specific subject or geographical area and then undertake additional work such as teaching.

Advantages/disadvantages

As the work is often project based, it can create some job insecurity.

This work gives the satisfaction of providing people with information about their family history and it can be both fascinating and rewarding to tell people the information you find out.

Money guide

Freelance genealogists are usually paid at an hourly rate which can range from £15 to £25. This fee can increase for more complex projects.

You could also charge a fixed rate for each piece of information you find.

Annual income varies considerably, but may be between £15,000 and £25,000 a year.

Genealogists with a postgraduate qualification can expect to earn between £26,500 and £35,000 per year.

Related opportunities

- Archivist/Records Manager p328
- Librarian/Library Assistant p336
- Registrar of Births, Deaths, Marriages and Civil Partnerships p49

Further information

Creative and Cultural Skills
www.ccskills.org.uk

Institute of Heraldic and Genealogical Studies
www.ihgs.ac.uk

Society of Genealogists
www.sog.org.uk

Qualifications and courses

A master's degree or alternative postgraduate qualification in history or historical archaeology is usually required for work as an archival or historical researcher.

Typical entry requirements for postgraduate degrees include a strong undergraduate degree (2.1 or higher) in history or a related subject, such as ancient world studies or politics, as well as significant work experience within the historical field, such as archive work for a museum or collector. Entry requirements for an undergraduate degree are generally 2 A levels/3 H grades, including History, and 5 GCSEs/National 5s (A*–C/A–C).

For a position in a university faculty, a doctorate (PhD) is usually required.

Training courses in historical research are available through the Institute of Historical Research, the Society of Genealogists and the Institute of Heraldic and Genealogical Studies.

What the work involves

The type of work you will undertake depends on who you work for. Most jobs will require some form of historical research, either for the public or for academic circles, and this may be done through a variety of resources, including internet research (using academic resources such as online journals), paper-based information (journals, books), and hands-on research with historical objects. This could involve work from home, in libraries, museums, or wherever necessary.

You can choose to teach and lecture on specific historical subjects, and you might write articles for professional journals and other publications.

Heritage organisations sometimes employ historians for research purposes.

Depending on your specialism, you could spend a lot of time searching for and analysing primary documents in archives and museums.

Type of person suited to this work

You will need a strong enthusiasm and love for history. You should also have a good knowledge of your specialist subjects.

Research skills are essential and will develop over the course of your study. You should pay close attention to detail and be accurate in your work.

Excellent verbal communication skills are important for explaining facts to people. Good writing skills are needed for writing up research and articles.

Historians need to consider a wide range of theories, so an open-minded approach is important.

You should also be well organised to manage and plan your research.

Working conditions

You will spend time in libraries and archive centres. This will involve reading and assessing information.

Some historical researchers are based in public records offices.

Historians in an academic role are based in universities.

You can also become the specialist historian for a wide variety of organisations, businesses or groups such as a football club, a military formation or think tank.

Undertaking historical research on a self-employed basis can create some job insecurity.

Future prospects

As a professional historian you could go into historical research or follow an academic career path.

Many historians combine both roles; they write, teach and carry out research on their specialist area of interest. Others combine historical research with other related areas such as genealogy.

A small number of historians are employed by heritage organisations to provide expert advice and support.

Some historians go into more media-based roles, such as a researcher, consultant, author or television presenter.

Advantages/disadvantages

This type of work provides the satisfaction of undertaking original research and finding out about the past.

There is the opportunity to remain in education, which will provide a rewarding opportunity to educate others.

It takes time and dedication to get established as a specialist on a specific historical period or subject.

Money guide

Earnings vary according to your job. Historical researchers usually charge by the hour; rates vary from £16 to £50.

Starting salaries for academic posts in the UK range from £25,000 to £42,000 per year, with a significant difference in pay between those appointed as lecturers and those appointed as professors.

At senior academic levels this could increase to between £80,000 and £100,000 for those appointed in professorship roles.

Related opportunities

- Archaeologist p327
- Genealogist p332
- Museum/Art Gallery Curator p337

Further information

Creative and Cultural Skills
www.ccskills.org.uk

Institute of Historical Research
www.history.ac.uk

Royal Historical Society
http://royalhistsoc.org

LANGUAGES, INFORMATION AND CULTURE

Qualifications and courses

Most professional information officers (sometimes called information scientists) have an undergraduate degree in an industry-related subject, such as information management, information studies and information and library studies, that has been accredited by the Chartered Institute of Library and Information Professionals (CILIP). Entry onto most degree courses usually requires 2 A levels/3 H grades and 5 GCSEs/ National 5s (A*–C/A–C).

An alternative route to professional qualification is through a degree in a non-related subject, followed by a CILIP-approved postgraduate qualification. This is particularly beneficial for information services provided in scientific or technical contexts.

Experience of information-related work is advantageous, and may be a requirement for some postgraduate courses. Graduate training opportunities are available for people who wish to pursue a career in this area and need to gain relevant experience before studying for a postgraduate qualification. Details are available through CILIP.

It is also possible to become a qualified information scientist from a library/information assistant post. CILIP offers a certification scheme for people with 5 years' experience of information work, or 2 years' experience plus relevant work-based training.

Entrants through both the educational and certification routes may have the opportunity to work towards Chartered membership of CILIP. Candidates for Chartership must have completed an approved period of professional experience.

What the work involves

You will develop, manage and coordinate both electronic and paper-based information systems for a range of organisations and companies. You will be working to ensure the information is accessible and relevant.

Your job will involve cataloguing, indexing and archiving information. You will also respond to research enquiries, manage intranets and ensure all of your information is up to date.

You could work in a range of sectors, including law, education and business and be employed in a variety of roles. For example you could be an analyst or a librarian. You will produce reports, graphs and briefings based on your findings.

Type of person suited to this work

You should be able to work with different forms of information such as databases, the internet and paper resources.

You may provide information for members of the public or staff within an organisation so strong communication skills are important. An interest in customer service is useful.

Writing skills and IT skills are increasingly important. Managing information demands an organised, methodical approach. A good level of numeracy can be useful. You will need to be resourceful and pay close attention to detail.

Working conditions

Information scientists work in offices, resource centres, libraries and other sites.

You will be working standard hours, Monday to Friday, and can also be hired on short-term contracts for specific projects.

You could work face to face with members of the public or staff within your organisation. You could also deal with information enquiries over the phone and through email.

Self-employed or freelance work is possible.

Future prospects

Information science is a very broad area. You could begin in an assistant or junior information job and with experience you could progress to working in a management role.

With experience you could specialise and work on a consultancy basis. At the moment there is a demand for specialists in science and computer science.

There are also opportunities to work abroad.

Advantages/disadvantages

Depending on the sector you work in, this job can be very fast paced.

Information science skills are transferable to a wide range of job areas.

Money guide

Salaries range quite widely for this role. Starting salaries are between £17,000 and £21,000.

With experience or at senior level this rises to between £21,000 and £45,000 or maybe more.

Salaries in excess of £50,000 per year are possible at senior levels in large organisations, particularly private sector companies in the legal and finance sectors and sometimes in consultancy.

Specific salary guides for some sectors are available from the Chartered Institute of Library and Information Professionals (CILIP).

Information consultants can earn around £400–£500 a day.

Related opportunities

- Archivist/Records Manager p328
- Media Researcher p396
- Museum/Art Gallery Curator p337

Further information

Arts and Humanities Research Council
www.ahrc.ac.uk

Association for Information Management
www.aslib.com

Chartered Institute of Library and Information Professionals
www.cilip.org.uk

INTERPRETER

Qualifications and courses

Fluency in English and at least one foreign language is a prerequisite for those looking to work as an interpreter. Most entrants have a degree in either a modern language, translation and interpreting, or British Sign Language (BSL) and interpreting. Entry requirements for a degree usually include 2 A levels/H grades, including your chosen modern language, and 5 GCSEs/National 5s (A*–C/A–C). A postgraduate diploma or master's degree in interpreting techniques is normally required.

Joint Honours degrees in science, engineering, the environment, business or politics with your chosen language can be useful for jobs where you will be expected to understand specialist vocabulary and concepts.

The Chartered Institute of Linguists (CIOL) offers vocational qualifications including the Level 3 Certificate in Bilingual Skills, the Level 6 Diploma in Public Service Interpreting and the Level 7 Diploma in Translation. Candidates are expected to have achieved the required level of competence in their language.

To become an accredited freelance interpreter for the EU you will have to pass an inter-institutional accreditation test, whilst a short training course is also available in conference interpreting from the European Commission in Brussels.

Qualified interpreters can work towards membership of the IoL or the Institute of Translation and Interpreting (ITI). These professional bodies provide further training and development opportunities.

What the work involves

Interpreters convert words spoken in one language into conversation or speech in another language. Using your knowledge of foreign languages, you will enable speakers of different languages to communicate with each other.

You could interpret while a person speaks or make notes and then interpret their statements.

Interpreters provide services for international political conferences, court hearings, business meetings and public services.

Type of person suited to this work

You must be fluent in at least one, or preferably two, foreign languages. It is also important to be aware of the culture and country of your chosen language. You must have excellent listening skills and the ability to speak clearly.

Interpreting at courts and conferences requires a confident manner. You should keep up to date with current affairs as you may interpret on subjects including business and law, or if you are in an alternative field, ensure you are up to date with the latest news in that field.

Dealing with confidential information may be part of your job so you will need discretion.

Working conditions

Interpreters have to concentrate continuously for long periods which can be physically demanding.

You will need to travel to different locations at fairly short notice, either abroad or within the UK.

Interpreters work in a range of environments, including high-profile conferences and formal meetings.

Hours vary according to clients' needs and are likely to include evening and weekend work. Freelance interpreters may find the demand for work irregular.

Future prospects

This area of work is very competitive with a limited number of full-time opportunities. A small number of interpreters work for international or European agencies. Others are employed by local governments and interpret in courts, hospitals and police stations.

You can choose to work within community organisations, helping people gain access to public services. Many interpreters work on a freelance basis.

There is a growing demand for Chinese, Urdu, Punjabi and eastern European languages.

Advantages/disadvantages

This type of work provides the opportunity to travel and live abroad.

Due to tight schedules and extensive travelling, this can be a pressured and demanding job.

Freelance interpreters often need to take on additional work to support themselves.

Money guide

Newly qualified interpreters can expect a salary of around £18,000–£21,000 per year. With experience, your earnings can rise to around £30,000.

Senior interpreters working for international or European agencies can achieve up to £60,000.

Many interpreters work freelance and charge an hourly rate of between £30–£60 depending on their experience, the level of demand for the language they speak and the type of interpreting required.

Related opportunities

- Importer/Exporter p595
- Secretary p51
- Teacher of English to Speakers of Other Languages p196

Further information

Chartered Institute of Linguists
www.ciol.org.uk

Institute of Translation and Interpreting
www.iti.org.uk

LANGUAGES, INFORMATION AND CULTURE

335

Qualifications and courses

The entry requirements to become a library assistant are usually at least 5 GCSEs/National 5s (A*–C/A–C), including English. Commercial or industrial libraries may require A levels/H grades, and university libraries may need a degree so check requirements carefully before applying.

The Apprenticeship in Libraries, Archives, Records and Information Management Services is available at Intermediate and Advanced Level and may help you gain on-the-job experience whilst studying for a relevant professional qualification.

The fastest route to becoming a qualified librarian is through a degree in librarianship or information management that has been accredited by the Chartered Institute of Library and Information Professionals (CILIP). The usual entry requirements for a degree are 2 A levels/3 H grades and 5 GCSEs/National 5s (A*–C/A–C) but people with experience as library assistants are often admitted to the degree courses with vocational qualifications.

An alternative route can be to take a CILIP-accredited postgraduate qualification in librarianship or information management. Depending on your first degree subject, it may be possible to work in a more specialist library, such as science or art. Prior experience of library or information work is advantageous and some institutions will expect you to have up to two years' experience in a role such as library assistant before applying.

Senior library assistants can study for a librarianship qualification (degree or postgraduate qualification) accredited by CILIP if they wish to progress to librarian level.

What the work involves

Librarian
You will manage collections of books, newspapers, documents and IT resources in libraries and information services to make them available to visitors. You may choose new resources to suit the library or information service you work in. You will also help visitors look for information and use IT and other resources.

Library assistant
You will organise and reshelve books and other resources. You may also work on the library counter to help visitors with enquiries and check books in and out of the library. You might deal with petty cash, catalogue new library resources and maintain databases.

Type of person suited to this work

You should have good customer care skills and enjoy helping people with enquiries. The ability to undertake research and use resources to locate information is essential. You must be able to work with IT software, the internet and databases and be confident in explaining these to others.

Librarians should be comfortable working in a team and managing people. Financial skills will help you monitor budgets. You will need an organised approach to your work.

Working conditions

You are likely to work face to face with members of the public or staff within an organisation.

Working on a counter, dealing with information enquiries and lifting and carrying books can all be physically demanding.

Library work can be pressured as you will need to locate and provide information to meet specific requests.

Future prospects

Librarians could progress to a senior level, meaning they would manage a branch library or department.

Some librarians move into information management roles within public services or private companies.

Library assistants are employed in library and information services in businesses, community library services and government. Larger organisations provide opportunities to progress into senior roles and take on additional responsibilities.

With over 100 proposed library closures in 2016, paid work is becoming increasingly competitive.

Advantages/disadvantages

You will be able to exercise your creativity by thinking up ways to promote the library and its resources.

You may need to move geographic locations to develop your career.

This type of work provides the satisfaction of helping people access information and other services.

Money guide

Salaries vary according to the sector in which you are employed and CILIP provide recommendations for minimum salaries.

Salaries for library assistants start at between £16,000 and £19,000, increasing to up to £21,000 with experience.

Starting salaries for librarians range from £19,500 to £24,500.

At chartered librarian level, you could expect earnings of £24,000–£30,000.

A senior librarian can receive £32,000–£40,000, and directors and heads of service can earn £45,000–£55,000.

Related opportunities

- Archivist/Records Manager p328
- Arts Administrator/Manager p329
- Information Officer p334

Further information

Chartered Institute of Library and Information Professionals
www.cilip.org.uk

Qualifications and courses

Entrants to this profession are required to have a relevant degree in a subject such as archaeology, history of art, heritage management, fine art or archive and museum studies. Typical degree entry requirements include 2 A levels/3 H grades and 5 GCSEs/National 5s (A*–C/A–C).

As competition for entry-level jobs is very high, many candidates increasingly have a postgraduate qualification in museum, gallery or heritage studies. To study at this level you will need at least a 2.1 in your undergraduate degree.

Employers will also require you to have relevant paid or voluntary work experience. Details of opportunities to volunteer are available through the Museums Association, the National Trust and English Heritage.

Many curators continue their studies while working and undertake a master's degree or doctorate (PhD) in their specialist area, such as Egyptology. Short training courses and professional development schemes are often provided by museums, galleries and the Museums Association (MA). The Victoria and Albert Museum also runs a graduate training programme which lasts 5 years and involves training while working as an assistant curator. Once employed you may also wish to study for the NVQ in Cultural Heritage (Levels 2, 3 and 5).

What the work involves

You will manage and maintain collections of artworks, historical objects or documents. Curators usually have specialist knowledge of a specific historical or cultural field such as women's history, textiles or archaeology. You will research and write about the collections in your care.

You might be responsible for thinking of ways in which you can gain funding for your museum/gallery. You will also organise exhibit loans with other museums/galleries.

You will work with other museum/gallery staff to plan exhibitions using items and information from your collection. You may also give talks to members of the public at special events.

Type of person suited to this work

You will need a good knowledge of history and of your specialist area of art/culture. You must be able to communicate this information to other staff and be a confident public speaker. You may lecture at educational events so enthusiasm for your subject is essential.

You will need good written communication skills for writing reports. IT skills are increasingly important in this area, for example when managing collection information through specialist databases. You should be organised, careful and have good attention to detail.

Working conditions

Curators generally work 37 hours a week, however these hours may be extended for special exhibitions and private showings.

This job will probably involve weekend or evening work. You may have to be on call to respond to emergencies at the gallery/museum.

Working environments vary depending on the size, location and popularity of the gallery/museum. You will work indoors on a daily basis. There may be some heavy lifting and carrying involved when exhibits need to be moved.

Future prospects

Museum/gallery work is a competitive area in which to develop a career as staff turnover is low, but it offers a variety of interesting roles.

You could work your way up in some larger organisations but often you will need to move employers or geographical location in order to move up the career ladder.

From working as an assistant curator, you could progress into a curator's role. You could then move on to work as a senior curator or go into managing museums/galleries or historic buildings.

Advantages/disadvantages

This job provides the satisfaction of working closely with works of art and historical objects, some of which can be very valuable.

You will help create exhibitions and then watch the public enjoy them.

Gaining necessary funding may be difficult.

Money guide

Salaries vary according to the location, size and type of employer.

A museum or art gallery curatorial assistant can expect a starting salary of £18,000–£25,000.

An experienced curator can earn between £25,000 and £35,000.

As a senior curator, with high levels of responsibility, you could achieve up to or in excess of £40,000 per year.

Related opportunities

- Arts Administrator/Manager p329
- Events and Exhibition Organiser p391
- Museum/Art Gallery Technician p338

Further information

Museums Association
www.museumsassociation.org

LANGUAGES, INFORMATION AND CULTURE

Qualifications and courses

Experience of working with the public and enthusiasm for museums/galleries are often valued more by employers than academic requirements. However, many large galleries/museums will require at least 4 GCSEs/National 5s (A*–C/A–C) and some may expect A levels/H grades. Vocational qualifications in subjects such as carpentry, engineering, or computing may prove advantageous due to the work involved when setting up some exhibitions. The Victoria & Albert Museum also offers the Museum Technician Awards at Levels 3 and 4.

Studying for a Foundation degree or degree in museum and gallery studies may improve your career prospects. Other useful subjects are history of art, heritage management and arts and cultural management. You will need at least 2 A levels/3 H grades and 5 GCSEs/National 5s (A*–C/A–C) for entry to a degree.

The Apprenticeship in Cultural and Heritage Venue Operations is offered at Intermediate and Advanced Levels and provides school leavers with the opportunity to train for a museum assistant position. Once employed, you could then work your way up to technician level through the study of professional qualifications, such as an NVQ/SVQ Level 2 in Heritage Care and Visitor Service or in Cultural Heritage Venue Operations (Levels 2–3).

Relevant work experience is recommended and may help you secure a permanent position. Details of volunteering opportunities are available from the Museums Association, and internships are available with organisations such as the Contemporary Art Society.

What the work involves

You will help prepare gallery and museum spaces for temporary exhibitions and collection displays.

Your work will involve installing audio-visual equipment to suit specific exhibitions. You will also transport objects and artworks to and from exhibition spaces. You will provide general technical support to the museum/gallery team as required.

You might be responsible for maintaining files, mending and cleaning exhibitions, and labelling and storing specimens.

Type of person suited to this work

You will need a good range of technical skills to meet the varied practical demands of a museum/gallery environment.

As well as providing support in setting up new exhibitions, you will have to deal with practical problems as they arise. The ability to handle fragile or valuable objects and artworks carefully is essential.

You will need a good knowledge of building security and maintenance. You may also be responsible for the fire safety of the gallery/museum. You will be a good team player and have a strong interest in helping people get the most out of their visits to galleries and museums.

Working conditions

Although you may spend some time in an office environment, the majority of your work will take place around the museum/gallery.

Generally technicians work about 36 hours a week but you might have to be on-call to respond to emergencies at the gallery/museum. You might also have to work longer hours when setting up or dismantling exhibitions. You may have to work some weekends, evenings and bank holidays.

You will usually be required to wear a uniform and/or name badge.

Future prospects

Museum/gallery work is a competitive industry and permanent jobs are relatively rare due to low staff turnover. However, freelance opportunities are common, especially with smaller galleries.

It is possible to progress to working as a senior or head technician. In larger organisations, you could manage a team of technicians.

It may be possible to start your own technician business and you could even run your own gallery.

Advantages/disadvantages

This job provides the satisfaction of working closely with works of art and historical objects, some of which can be very valuable.

This is a competitive area of work so you might have to change jobs to gain a promotion.

You may have to work some unsocial hours which could disrupt your social or family life.

Money guide

These figures are only approximate and may vary depending on location and employer. Larger galleries and museums may pay a higher rate.

Starting salaries are between £14,500 and £16,000.

With experience, you can expect to earn upwards of £19,500 a year.

Senior technicians with additional responsibilities, such as department or collections management, can achieve up to £31,000.

Related opportunities

- Archaeologist p327
- Events and Exhibition Organiser p391
- Museum/Art Gallery Curator p337

Further information

Association of Independent Museums
www.aim-museums.co.uk

Creative and Cultural Skills
www.ccskills.org.uk

Museums Association
www.museumsassociation.org

LANGUAGES, INFORMATION AND CULTURE

Qualifications and courses

Most translators will have a relevant degree in either one or more foreign languages (preferably applied), or a foreign language combined with a specialist subject such as business, law, European studies, translation or interpreting.

For modern language degrees a minimum of 2 A levels/3 H grades, with one in a language, and 5 GCSEs/National 5s (A*–C/A–C) are normally required.

Postgraduate courses in translation are available, and usually require a degree in a modern language. The Chartered Institute of Linguists (IoL) offers vocational qualifications in a wide range of languages, including the Certificate in Bilingual Skills (equivalent to A level/H grade), the RQF Level 6 Diploma in Public Service Interpreting and the Level 7 Diploma in Translation. Examinations are open entry, but candidates are expected to have achieved the required level of competence before sitting an exam.

Fluency in two or more languages is required to work as a translator. You may also be expected to have a thorough knowledge of the culture and country of your chosen languages, usually gained by living and working there. Qualified translators can work towards membership of the IoL or Institute of Translation and Interpreting. These professional bodies provide further training and development opportunities.

To apply for translator posts in a European Union (EU) institution, you must be fluent in at least two languages in additional to your mother tongue, possess a relevant degree and pass an exam.

What the work involves

You will convert written text such as letters, reports, leaflets and brochures from one language to another. You will ensure that your translation matches the tone and style of the original text and has a high standard of grammar.

Your work will also involve meetings with employers to agree projects.

Translators provide services to specialist translation agencies, private companies, local government bodies and international organisations.

Type of person suited to this work

Translators must work to a high standard of accuracy, so attention to detail is important.

The ability to write in your chosen languages in a range of styles is essential. You should also be able to understand and translate complex documents. IT skills are very useful.

Discretion is important as you may translate confidential information. Being well organised will help you to meet project deadlines. You will need a confident approach to work on a freelance basis and promote your services. Numeracy skills are also useful.

Working conditions

Translators are usually self-employed and based in offices at home, but there are opportunities for translators in companies.

You might attend meetings with employers and colleagues.

This type of work involves close working at a computer and the use of resources such as dictionaries and technical reference books.

Future prospects

As a translator you could work for a variety of employers, translating medical, technical, legal and other documents.

Many translators work on a freelance basis.

There are opportunities to work for private companies and international organisations on a permanent basis, in the UK or abroad. Demand for translators is growing, as the markets become more global and large multi-national events are held, such as the World Cup.

Advantages/disadvantages

This area of work can provide opportunities to travel and work abroad.

Working on a self-employed project-by-project basis can create some job instability.

Translation can be very demanding owing to short deadlines and the constant demand for accuracy.

Money guide

Translators may be paid between £75 and £210 per 1,000 words, depending on the language they are translating.

Most positions pay around £18,000 per year.

With experience, generalist translators earn around £30,000 and senior translators can earn up to £60,000.

The EU generally provides the best pay. Translators' salaries start at €4,384 per month.

Related opportunities

- Importer/Exporter p595
- Secretary p51
- Teacher of English to Speakers of Other Languages p196

Further information

Chartered Institute of Linguists
www.ciol.org.uk

Institute of Translation and Interpreting
www.iti.org.uk

LANGUAGES, INFORMATION AND CULTURE

339

Legal and Political Services

If you find the law a fascinating subject and you feel you would enjoy a challenging career where the rewards are a good salary and a real sense of achievement when your hard work pays off, a job in this sector could be what you are looking for. Workers in this sector are fiercely passionate about their careers and have more often than not, completed a lot of training and worked hard to establish themselves in this competitive field. You need to be driven and thrive on pressure and tight deadlines; this is a sector for someone who is ambitious and very talented at working tactfully with people. The jobs featured in this section are listed below. For similar jobs to the ones in this section turn to *Administration, Business, Office Work and Financial Services* on page 1.

Qualifications and courses

Employers prefer candidates to have 5 GCSEs/ National 5s (A*–C/A–C), including English and Maths. Applicants must be aged between 21 and 62 but mature candidates, without a criminal record or debt, are often preferred because their life experience may help them deal with difficult situations.

To become a certificated bailiff, candidates need to obtain a Bailiff's General Certificate. This is issued by a circuit judge and needs to be reapplied for every 2 years. The necessary legal knowledge can be gained by taking the examinations of the Certificated Bailiffs Association (CBA). With a certificate, you are eligible to join Her Majesty's Court Service's Certificated Bailiffs' Register.

In Scotland, to be commissioned as a sheriff officer, candidates need to pass the examinations of the Society of Messengers-at-Arms and Sheriff Officers. The minimum age to be commissioned is 20, but training, which normally takes 3 years, can begin earlier.

You will need a security bond up to the value of £10,000, plus two references for insurance purposes.

In England and Wales training is done mostly on the job where you learn the laws and procedures before applying for the Certificate. However it is possible, upon gaining enough experience and having passed the relevant exams, to join the Association of Civil Enforcement Agencies (ACEA) or the Enforcement Services Association (ESA) in order to aid continuing professional development (CPD).

In Scotland, training is done under an appointed mentor. After 2 years of experience has been gained you can apply to become a messenger-at-arms.

What the work involves

Court bailiffs deliver legal documents, such as a court summons, to people who owe money and might also take steps to ensure payment. Certificated/private bailiffs visit people in debt to recover the money they owe, arranging for removal of their property where necessary.

In Scotland, officers of court deliver legal documents to people who owe money and take all the legal steps required to get the money paid.

You may also give advice on how to pay debts.

Type of person suited to this work

As there are strict legal procedures connected with recovering debt, you will need to be completely up to date with legislation to conduct your work correctly and within legal guidelines.

The work will bring you into contact with many different people, so it's important that you are able to deal with all members of the public.

You will need to be assertive to deal with people's resistance and persistent to get the job done. Being tactful and able to cope with people under stress is also essential.

Working conditions

You will spend a lot of time travelling and so will need a clean driving licence.

Although you will be based in an office, you might have to visit people's homes in the evenings and early mornings to make sure that someone is there.

If you have to remove furniture in payment of debt, you could have to do a lot of heavy lifting, so you will need to be physically fit.

In England and Wales, court bailiffs generally work for the county courts and private bailiffs with magistrates' court orders.

In Scotland, officers of court are called sheriff officers in the sheriff court and messengers-at-arms in the Court of Session.

Future prospects

Opportunities for work as a bailiff/enforcement agent depend very much on the current economic climate. Despite the improving economic situation, factors such as council tax support cuts mean prospects remain good. Job prospects for bailiffs are usually stable and self-employment is also an option.

If you work for the county court you can progress into management or switch to a private firm in which you would also have opportunities to progress into management roles.

Advantages/disadvantages

The work is varied and in different locations; no two days will be the same.

You will meet many different people, some of whom may be difficult to deal with or threatening.

The hours can be long and unsocial.

Money guide

In private firms, entrants and trainees can expect a starting salary of around £18,000, increasing to £25,000 with experience.

Earnings of around £40,000 are possible for those in self-employment.

Positions with HM Courts and Tribunals Service offer between £19,000 and £23,000 per year.

Some roles will offer commission-based incentives.

Related opportunities

- Police Officer p543
- Police Support Worker p544
- Security Officer/Manager/Door Supervisor p555

Further information

Civil Enforcement Association
www.civea.co.uk

Society of Messengers-at-Arms and Sheriff Officers
www.smaso.org

Qualifications and courses

England and Wales

You will need either an approved law degree or another degree (minimum 2.1 Honours for both), followed by a postgraduate law conversion course, known as the Common Professional Examination, or a Graduate Diploma in Law (GDL).

Following this, you must complete the vocational stage of qualification by becoming a member of one of the four Inns of Court where you will undertake the Bar Professional Training Course (BPTC). This will prepare you for completion of two 6-month pupillages (a mix of work and training taking place in chambers). Training for the 'bar' continues for 3 years, working in one of the Inns of Court.

Once you have qualified, you will be required by the Bar Standards Board (BSB) to undertake at least 45 hours of continuing professional development (CPD) per year. This must include at least 9 hours of advocacy training and 3 of ethics. After the first 3 years, the amount of annual CPD you are required to take will drop to 12 hours.

Scotland

You will need either an Honours degree in Scottish Law from a Scottish university (minimum 2.1 Honours); an Ordinary degree in Scottish Law from a Scottish university with an Honours degree from a UK university (minimum 2.1 Honours); or a Scottish Ordinary degree with distinction. You must also undertake a 1-year full-time postgraduate Diploma in Legal Practice at a Scottish university.

For vocational entry, you will need to work for 12–21 months in a solicitor's office and 'devilling' (training with) a member of the bar for nine and a half months, before taking the entry examinations of the Faculty of Advocates.

Advocates will normally practise as a solicitor for 10 years, prior to acting as an advocate.

What the work involves

Barristers/advocates give legal advice to other legal professionals and act for clients in certain cases in the high courts. You will research information and past cases before giving advice to solicitors on whether a case should go to court.

In court, you will examine witnesses and present the case for the prosecution or the defence.

You will also act for clients at tribunals or inquiries if asked to do so by a solicitor.

Type of person suited to this work

You will need to research large amounts of information before giving legal advice. You will need to be able to think logically to work out what is important in the case and apply the law to it.

You will need to be confident to speak in court, to convince a jury with your arguments, and able to think quickly when questioning witnesses or defendants.

Excellent written and public speaking skills are needed in order to prepare your case. Keeping an open mind is important and you must be able to gain people's confidence.

Working conditions

Barristers usually work in offices called 'chambers', and advocates in groups known as 'stables' in the Advocates' Library in Edinburgh.

If you specialise in criminal law, you will spend more time in court than civil law specialists would.

Future prospects

Most barristers/advocates are self-employed and it can take around 5 years to establish a practice and become known.

After 10–15 years' experience you can apply to 'take silk' to become a Queen's Counsel. This is essential if you want to become a judge in the higher courts.

Some people work in central or local government where there is a clear promotion structure.

Advantages/disadvantages

The work is varied and you will get satisfaction when you win a case.

Some cases may put you under pressure, particularly if they attract media attention.

You will sometimes work long hours to meet deadlines.

Money guide

Minimum salaries during pupillage are £12,000, but can range up to more than £60,000 in the first year of practice for some of the prestigious sets.

Qualified barristers can earn between £25,000–£300,000. Earnings of between £30,000–£90,000 can be expected in the Crown Prosecution Service in England and Wales.

As a trainee advocate in Scotland you may be unpaid for around ten months. Qualified advocates can earn between £30,000–£35,000 and around £105,000 as Advocate General in the Procurator Fiscal Service.

Many barristers in England and advocates in Scotland are self-employed. Earnings can reach up to £300,000, however this is entirely dependent on experience, location and reputation.

In private practice top earnings can be in excess of £1,000,000.

Related opportunities

- Barrister's/Advocate's Clerk p344
- Crown Prosecutor/Procurator Fiscal p350
- Paralegal p356

Further information

Faculty of Advocates
www.advocates.org.uk

Skills for Justice
www.sfjuk.com

The Bar Council
www.barcouncil.org.uk

LEGAL AND POLITICAL SERVICES

Qualifications and courses

In England and Wales, barrister's clerks usually require a minimum of 4 GCSEs/National 5s (A*–C/A–C), including Maths and English. A levels/H grades are an advantage and relevant work experience, in a business or legal environment for example, would increase your chances of securing employment.

Some individual chambers offer their own work experience schemes which are useful in developing your interpersonal skills, telephone manner, computer literacy and commercial awareness, amongst other skills vital to the role.

You are likely to enter employment at a junior clerk level and work your way up to deputy senior or senior clerk.

You may choose to join the Institute of Barristers' Clerks (IBC). The IBC offers a 1-year BTEC Advanced Award in Chambers Administration for Barristers' Clerks which is aimed at clerks with 5 years' service in chambers. Upon completion you can apply for qualified membership of the IBC. Graduates do not need to take the BTEC but must have 3 years' service in chambers.

The IBC also offers a number of topical seminars and an annual conference which it is important to attend as you must maintain a firm grasp on current legal issues.

In Scotland, advocate's clerks require a minimum of an H grade in English and evidence of computer literacy and numeracy. More advocate's clerks are now entering with a HNC/HND or degree. Most training is on the job but you are encouraged to take courses organised by Faculty Services Ltd.

What the work involves

Clerks manage the day-to-day work for a group of barristers (England and Wales) or advocates (Scotland).

An important task will be liaising with solicitors to encourage them to give work to your business. You will estimate how much work is involved in a case to see how much time it will take, allocate cases to barristers/advocates and negotiate fees.

When you first enter this career, you will mainly be preparing accounts, filing and photocopying, and answering the phone.

Type of person suited to this work

As your work will involve meeting lots of people, you will need excellent speaking skills. Good writing skills are needed for writing letters and preparing notes and reports.

Being good with figures is essential when negotiating fees and preparing accounts. You will need to be businesslike and have good negotiating skills to bring in work, and confidence to deal with solicitors, court officials and clients.

Your work will involve handling confidential information, which means discretion and tact are necessary. It is also important to be a good teamworker and flexible in your approach to work.

Working conditions

You will work mainly indoors in an office, using computers and spending a lot of time on the telephone. However, you might travel in connection with your work so a driving licence is useful.

Some chambers are based in historic buildings with difficult working conditions and limited access.

You will typically work standard office hours, Monday to Friday. However, you might have to work evenings and weekends during busy periods.

One clerk will serve more than one barrister at a time, with most offices in London or other large cities. Advocates work in groups known as 'stables' in the Advocates' Library in Edinburgh.

Future prospects

Competition is high for entry to this profession.

You would start as a junior clerk and progress to clerk with experience. Training will be ongoing throughout your career.

With experience you could train for another legal profession or move into general administrative work.

Advantages/disadvantages

Your work will be interesting and varied and you will have a lot of responsibility.

Work in the evenings and long hours are necessary when deadlines are approaching.

After further training, you can move into other legal careers.

Money guide

Starting salaries range between £13,500 and £18,000 for a junior clerk or clerk's assistant.

Clerks with a few years' experience can earn between £19,000 and £35,000. Senior clerks with a high level of responsibility in busy chambers can earn £80,000 or more.

There is also the opportunity for bonuses directly related to the income of the barristers.

In Scotland you can earn between £22,000 and £28,000. As a senior clerk, you can earn up to £40,000.

Related opportunities

- Barrister/Advocate p343
- Court Administrative Officer p347
- Paralegal p356

Further information

Faculty of Advocates
www.advocates.org.uk

Institute of Barristers' Clerks
www.ibc.org.uk

Skills for Justice
www.sfjuk.com

Qualifications and courses

There are no set academic requirements but entry is very competitive and many employers expect candidates to have a 2.1 degree or above. Valued degree subjects include politics, law, social policy, economics, marketing, public relations or journalism. You will need at least 2 A levels/3 H grades and 5 GCSEs/National 5s (A*–C/A–C) for degree entry.

A postgraduate qualification such as master's degree in public affairs and lobbying, politics or political communications may improve employment prospects.

Experience of working for your chosen political party on a voluntary basis is often valued more than academic qualifications, since there is an expectation that candidates will have already acquired the skills necessary for success within the job and so formal training is rarely offered. Work experience also demonstrates your commitment to politics and will significantly improve your career prospects. It is also possible to develop relevant skills through other opportunities, for example, involvement with a trade union, holding office in a students' union or campaign work for a charity group.

There are limited opportunities for graduate training programmes offered by some large political consultancies.

In general, candidates must be at least 20 years of age and should remain up to date with current developments within politics by reading journals, newspapers, attending workshops and conferences offered by Capita Learning and Development or the Chartered Institute of Public Relations.

What the work involves

Constituency agent
Your job will be to organise the running of the constituency for your political party, including election campaigns. You will arrange meetings, coordinate PR and marketing, and deal with enquiries.

As secretary to the local office, your duties will include managing local membership, fundraising and organising volunteers.

Political researcher
You will research information on political subjects and provide your employer with a coherent briefing of your conclusions. Your duties may include helping to write political speeches, finding sources of expertise on a specific issue and monitoring parliamentary reports.

Type of person suited to this work

You will need a solid understanding of the political system, along with a genuine interest in and love of politics. It is important to have strong political opinions while understanding that sometimes you must look at the bigger picture.

Key skills for constituency agents are communication, information handling, IT, money management, teamwork and leadership and supervisory skills.

Key skills for political researchers include tact, resourcefulness, debating abilities, IT and research skills, resilience, communication, articulacy and analytical abilities.

Working conditions

Constituency agent
Most of your work will be based in the party office which will be open to the public. However, you will be expected to do lots of travelling both locally and nationally, so a driving licence and car would be useful. You could work evenings, weekends or during the day. Hours could increase during national or local events like elections.

Political researcher
You will be working in an office, normally 9am–5pm, although some longer hours might be required to meet specific deadlines. You may need to travel.

Future prospects

Constituency agent
Your prospects could depend on the size of the party you support. Later, you could become a local councillor or Member of Parliament.

Political researcher
This is an excellent starting point for a career in politics. Progression may include becoming an MP. You could take on extra responsibilities and move between public affairs firms in order to achieve promotion.

Advantages/disadvantages

You will get considerable job satisfaction as your work will make a difference to citizens and the local community.

You may find this career stressful, particularly when you have to meet project deadlines or when there are elections.

Money guide

Constituency agent
Starting salaries are between £15,000 and £25,000.

With experience and more responsibility, earnings can be £18,000–£31,000, increasing to between £26,000 and £41,000 at a senior level.

Political researcher
Starting salaries range from £15,000 to £17,000.

Those with considerable experience can achieve up to £50,000.

Related opportunities

- Media Researcher p396
- Politician p358
- Welfare Benefits Adviser/Welfare Rights Caseworker p578

Further information

Association of Professional Political Consultants
www.appc.org.uk

Chartered Institute of Public Relations
www.cipr.co.uk

LEGAL AND POLITICAL SERVICES

CORONER

Qualifications and courses

Following the Coroners and Justice Act 2009, the coroner service is undergoing reforms regarding the recruitment and training of coroners. New coroners must be qualified solicitors, barristers or a Fellow of the Chartered Institute of Legal Executives (CILEx) with at least 5 years' experience. The usual entry route is to find a coroner who is willing to appoint you their deputy or assistant deputy coroner.

To train as a lawyer you need either an approved law degree, or a non-law degree followed by either the Common Professional Examination (CPE), the Postgraduate Diploma in Law (PgDL) or the Senior Status Law degree. Candidates must then complete a Legal Practice Course (LPC). To be accepted onto a law degree you will usually require 2 A levels/3 H grades and 5 GCSEs/National 5s (A*–C/A–C).

Alternatively, access to the legal sector can be enabled by an Advanced (Level 3) or Higher (Level 4) Apprenticeship in Legal Services, offered by the Chartered Institute of Legal Executives (CILEx).

A number of existing coroners have a medical degree, while some have both a medical and law degree. In order to qualify as a doctor you must complete an undergraduate course which leads to a degree in medicine. To do this you will need very high results in 3 A levels/H grades including Chemistry and Biology, and at least 5 GCSEs/National 5s (A*–C/A–C).

Aldermen and councillors of local authorities are not eligible for appointment as coroners in their counties or districts until 6 months after the end of their service.

Once employed, you will be provided with training from the Coroners Division of the Ministry of Justice. Throughout your career you will be expected to undertake continuing professional development (CPD) so as to remain up to date with changes in law, medical and administrative practices.

What the work involves

You will investigate sudden and suspicious deaths, determining if an inquest or post-mortem is necessary. Coroners preside at inquests and make decisions on whether or not further action is required.

You will need to work with police and medical services to determine whether or not a person died of natural causes and keep detailed records of all proceedings.

Once you have completed your investigations you must provide families or the relevant authorities with your report.

Type of person suited to this work

Preparing cases involves looking at statements and reports so you need to be able to read and analyse large amounts of information. You might need to check points of law and request further information so you must pay attention to detail.

Much of your work will involve talking to people and writing reports so you need to have excellent verbal and written communication skills. Being confident to speak in court and argue logically are also important.

You must be organised, able to meet deadlines and handle distressing situations calmly.

Working conditions

You will work indoors and outdoors, as you will primarily be based in an office but will also spend time in court, at crime scenes and in hospitals.

You will usually work normal office hours but you will also fulfil on-call duties as each county is required to provide a 24-hour service.

Most coroners work part time and spend the rest of their time working in private legal practice.

Future prospects

Coroners are appointed and paid for by local councils but hold office under the Crown.

Once employed as a deputy or assistant deputy coroner, with experience you can progress to coroner level. Although there is currently no further promotion route, the Coroners and Justice Bill has proposed that posts such as senior coroner and chief coroner should be made available in the future.

Advantages/disadvantages

The work is varied, carries responsibility and can be satisfying.

You will have the opportunity to meet a wide range of people.

The role involves extensive administration and paperwork.

You will be on an on-call rota for evenings, weekends and bank holidays.

Money guide

If you work full time as a deputy coroner, your starting salary will be around £25,000.

As a full-time coroner you can expect earnings between £83,000 and £104,000 a year, depending on the population size of the area you cover.

Part-time coroners are paid according to the number of cases they undertake. As a guide, you could receive salaries ranging from £10,000 for 200 cases to £50,000 for 2,000 cases a year.

Related opportunities

- Barrister/Advocate p343
- Hospital Doctor p294
- Solicitor/Notary Public p359

Further information

Chartered Institute of Legal Executives
www.cilex.org.uk

Coroners' Society of England and Wales
www.coronersociety.org.uk

Ministry of Justice
www.justice.gov.uk

COURT ADMINISTRATIVE OFFICER

Qualifications and courses

Qualification requirements vary within different regions and according to the type of court, however most employers expect candidates to have at least 2 GCSEs/National 5s (A*–C/A–C), including Maths and English, for an administrative assistant role and 5 GCSEs/National 5s (A*–C/A–C) for a more senior position such as an administrative officer.

Some areas require administrative, typing, office or computing experience while others also expect a minimum of one year of relevant office-based experience. City & Guilds offer several courses which enable candidates to develop their administrative skills such as word processing, typing and shorthand.

Applicants without formal qualifications but with relevant administrative experience may be able to sit computer and communication aptitude tests in order to gain entry to this profession.

Once employed, you will typically experience a combination of on-the-job training and a series of in-house or external short courses that offer you the opportunity to work towards industry-recognised qualifications. The Apprenticeship in Court, Tribunal and Prosecution Administration is available at Intermediate Level and the NVQ/SVQ Level 2 in Court Tribunal Administration may be beneficial for those already working as an administrative assistant and looking to progress to the role of officer.

What the work involves

You will organise all the papers and information for a court hearing so that everything is ready for the judge or magistrate when the court session begins.

Booking dates, times and courtrooms for court hearings will be part of your job and you will prepare the timetable for each day. You will ensure that everyone arriving at court knows where to go and receives the relevant paperwork.

After the hearings, you will carry out court orders such as endorsing driving licences, writing adoption orders or collecting fines.

Type of person suited to this work

As you will be responsible for making sure that court hearings run smoothly and everything is ready on time, it is important to be methodical, organised and pay close attention to detail.

You must be polite and helpful so that you can put people at ease and explain things clearly to them. Tact and an understanding of confidentiality are essential.

If you are working in a finance section, you must have good numeracy skills to be able to calculate fines and costs. You should be confident using computers.

Working conditions

Most of your time will be spent indoors in courtrooms and offices in the court. You may have to travel to different courts so a driving licence is useful.

You will be working around 37 hours a week, however overtime may be necessary if there is a hearing in the evening or at the weekend. Part-time work is often possible.

Future prospects

Court administrative officers in England and Wales are employed by Her Majesty's Courts and Tribunals Service and move through promotion grades. In Scotland they are often known as court officers and are employed by the Scottish Court Service.

Most training is on the job. It is possible to start as a court administrative assistant and work your way up to officer level.

You may have to move courts to widen your experience. You could move into similar work in the legal field, such as legal executive roles, or into general administrative work. Promotion to senior administration roles is possible.

Advantages/disadvantages

The work is often quite steady and, with strong organisation, often it's not too stressful.

Dealing with members of the public means that you will meet and work with many different people, which can mean a diverse work environment, but some people may be aggressive and threatening which can be difficult to deal with.

Work might be monotonous, despite the variety of cases that will be dealt with.

Money guide

Salaries vary depending on your employer and geographical location.

Those beginning their career as an administrative assistant can expect to earn between £12,500 and £15,000 a year.

An administrative officer will have a starting salary of about £15,500.

Earnings can increase to £19,200 as you gain experience.

If you progress to become a senior clerk or team leader you could earn in excess of £22,000 per year.

Related opportunities

- Barrister's/Advocate's Clerk p344
- Civil Service Administrative Officer p13
- Court Usher/Officer/Macer p349

Further information

HM Courts and Tribunals Service
www.justice.gov.uk

Scottish Court Service
www.scotcourts.gov.uk

Qualifications and courses

Candidates are usually required to have 3–5 GCSEs/ National 5s (A*–C/A–C), including English, and many entrants also have A levels/H grades. Thorough knowledge of the English language and a high standard of spelling, grammar and punctuation is expected but computer keyboard skills and knowledge of traditional shorthand are often valued above any formal academic qualifications.

To begin work as a court reporter in England and Wales, you must be certified as competent by the British Institute of Verbatim Reporters (BIVR). In order to become certified, you will need to acquire competency on a stenotype machine, reach a typing speed of at least 180 words per minute and gain experience as a trainee court reporter. After the correct training and 3 years' experience you may apply to become a qualified member of the BIVR by taking an examination. As a member, you can aid your career progression by completing training in real-time reporting or Speech-to-Text (STT) reporting.

Sorene Court Reporting & Training Services offer a distance learning course which lasts 1–2 years and teaches candidates how to use the stenotype machine.

In Scotland, all training is undertaken on the job with a mentor and regular tests will be set to monitor progress.

What the work involves

Your job could involve attending court hearings, listening and reporting on what is said. Using a stenotype machine, or sometimes other recording equipment, you will write down everything a witness says. You may be asked to edit other speakers in order to correct their grammar.

Mostly you will work on your own but in complex cases where lawyers may want a daily transcript of proceedings you will work in a team of three, on a rota basis.

You could also record proceedings within other legal forums such as industrial tribunals.

Type of person suited to this work

You need to have excellent listening skills and the ability to concentrate for long periods of time.

A fast typing speed, strong attention to detail and a good grasp of punctuation and grammar are needed to ensure that your record is accurate. Manual dexterity and keyboard skills are essential for operating the stenotype.

You must speak clearly when reading back what you have written. If you do not hear what is said or you fall behind in your transcription, you must have the confidence to stop proceedings or ask for something to be repeated.

Working conditions

You will operate a stenotype machine with computer-aided transcription systems, a machine with a keyboard layout which enables whole words and phrases to be typed with one stroke.

There is a growing trend in Scotland for court cases to be taped and transcribed afterwards.

You might have to travel to different courts so a driving licence and access to or ownership of a car is useful.

Future prospects

You could attend criminal cases in the Crown Court or civil cases in the high courts. You will also be present at other events, including industrial tribunals, public inquiries and in Parliament to record proceedings for Hansard.

Most court reporters are self-employed and there is no defined promotion ladder. Others work for companies contracted to service courts.

In England and Wales there is a shortage of trained staff. In Scotland vacancies may decrease due to the shift to taping court proceedings.

Reporters also have the option to work in the media industry, providing subtitles for viewers with hearing impairments.

Advantages/disadvantages

You will have contact with a wide range of people.

You will have to concentrate for long periods so the work is demanding.

Work in the evenings is possible to complete reports for the next day.

Money guide

Starting salaries in London and large cities are between around £18,000 and £28,000.

Those based in other locations can expect a lower salary of between £12,000 and £20,000 a year.

With experience, your earnings can increase to £25,000–£50,000.

Many court reporters work on a freelance basis so earnings vary according to the number of days worked.

Daily rates can range from £40 to £200.

Real-time reporters are likely to earn more and could receive £300 a day for private sector work.

Related opportunities

- Court Administrative Officer p347
- Paralegal p356
- Receptionist p46

Further information

British Institute of Verbatim Reporters
www.bivr.org.uk

Sorene Court Reporting & Training Services
www.sorene.co.uk

Qualifications and courses

Whilst no formal qualifications are required, a minimum of at least 2 GCSEs/National 5s (A*–C/A–C), including English, is strongly recommended. A qualification in or possession of computer skills is also highly desirable.

Employers often value one's personal qualities and life experience above any formal academic qualifications however. A background in administration or a customer service environment can be an advantage, as is experience within the police or armed forces. A history of working closely with the public will improve your chances of securing employment.

Training is conducted on the job and new entrants will work alongside an experienced usher. Employers may also provide short courses covering topics such as equality awareness, security and dealing with challenging situations.

You may also have the opportunity to work towards industry-recognised qualifications such as the NVQ/SVQ Level 2 Certificate for Court Ushers, the Level 2 Certificate in Knowledge of Court/Tribunal Administration, the Diploma in Court Tribunal Operations (Levels 2–3) and the Level 3 Certificate in Witness Care.

You will need to obtain clearance from the Disclosure and Barring Service (DBS) before becoming a court usher.

The stated minimum age for entry to this profession is 21 (16 in Scotland), but most courts prefer to recruit mature people under the age of 63 (60 in Scotland).

What the work involves

Court ushers make sure that everything in the courtroom is ready for proceedings to begin, for example that all papers are ready, glasses and water are on tables, and fire exits are clear.

When people arrive at court, you will meet them and direct them to the right courtroom. In court, you will tell people to stand when the judge comes in, call witnesses and administer the right oath to them. You will have to label the evidence and give it to the judge and jury. You will also pass messages between lawyers and legal advisers.

In Scotland, you will be known as a court officer in the sheriff court and a macer in the supreme courts.

Type of person suited to this work

As courtrooms must be prepared at the beginning of the day, court ushers need to be thorough in their work and pay attention to detail. You must be logical and organised.

You need to be able to work with people of all ages and backgrounds. Some may be nervous so it is important to have good communication skills to explain what is happening and put them at ease. You will also need to be confident and sound in control in court.

It is important to stay calm at all times and be impartial when dealing with people from both sides of a case. You will come into contact with a great deal of confidential information so trustworthiness and professionalism are essential attributes.

You need to be able to work well as part of a team to ensure the smooth running of the court case.

Working conditions

You will spend most of your time in a courtroom but you might also have an office in the courthouse, as your job will involve entering data into the computer system, filing and photocopying.

In certain jury cases, you might have to stay away from home overnight. A driving licence would be useful if you are required to travel between courts.

As you represent the court, you must be smartly dressed at all times.

Future prospects

There are few jobs for court ushers and entry to the career can be competitive.

You can be promoted to senior and supervisory grades. You could also progress into other administrative jobs within the legal profession or another sector.

Advantages/disadvantages

The job will be varied and no two days will be the same.

You might have to stay late or start early if proceedings overrun.

You will meet many different people, some of whom may be difficult to deal with.

Money guide

Earnings vary with location and tend to be higher in London.

Starting salaries for ushers range from £11,500 to £13,500. Although in London, it is possible to earn up to £16,000.

At a senior level you may be able to achieve a salary of £16,000–£19,500 or £17,500–£22,500 in London.

You may receive overtime payments for late nights or early starts.

Related opportunities

- Bailiff/Enforcement Agent p342
- Civil Service Administrative Officer p13
- Court Administrative Officer p347
- Receptionist p46

Further information

HM Courts and Tribunals Service
www.justice.gov.uk

Scottish Court Service
www.scotcourts.gov.uk

Skills for Justice
www.sfjuk.com

LEGAL AND POLITICAL SERVICES

Qualifications and courses

Crown prosecutor

If you are a qualified solicitor or barrister then you can apply directly to the Crown Prosecution Service (CPS). In Northern Ireland, public prosecutors are employed by the Public Prosecution Service (PPS). Lawyers must have completed their Legal Practice Course (LPC) and 2-year training contract and barristers must have finished their Bar Professional Training Course (BPTC) and 12-month pupillage.

Alternatively, law students can apply for the CPS Legal Trainee Scheme (LTS) in the year that they are due to complete their vocational training. The CPS offers 10 candidates a training contract each year.

Once employed you will be trained on the job and supervised by a more experienced colleague before progressing into a more senior crown prosecutor role. This can take between 6 months and 2 years depending on your level of experience prior to entry. The Law Society and the Bar Council run a series of continuing professional development (CPD) schemes vital to aid career progression.

Procurator fiscal

Candidates are solicitors qualified in the Scottish legal system. An LLB degree in Scottish law (or 3 years of pre-diploma training and a pass in the Law Society of Scotland's exams) is required, followed by a Diploma in Professional Legal Practice (PEAT 1) and a 2-year training contract with a practising solicitor in Scotland (PEAT 2).

Alternatively, those who have completed an LLB at a Scottish university can apply for one of 25 places available on the 2-year traineeship offered by the Crown Office and Procurator Fiscal Service (COPFS).

What the work involves

Crown prosecutor

You will look at reports from the police and other agencies and decide whether or not crimes in England and Wales should be prosecuted.

You will take statements from witnesses before a trial and examine witnesses in court, guiding them through their evidence. You will then sum up the case for the prosecution.

Procurator fiscal

You will work in the Scottish legal system, carrying out similar duties to crown prosecutors in England and Wales. In Scotland, the Crown Office and Procurator Fiscal Service (COPFS) investigates and prosecutes all crime.

Type of person suited to this work

Preparing cases involves looking at statements so you must be able to read and analyse a lot of information. Attention to detail is essential.

You must have excellent verbal and written communication skills as you will deal with other professionals and the public. You should be confident making clear and logical arguments

in court and have the ability to make unbiased decisions.

Working conditions

You will be based in an office but you will also spend time in court. You might also work outdoors at scenes of crime and accidents.

You will work 37–42 hours a week, including covering weekends and bank holidays on a rota system.

Future prospects

Crown prosecutor

There is a clear promotion structure within the service but very few posts at the most senior levels. Competition in the CPS is high.

Procurator fiscal

Candidates start as a depute, working under the guidance of senior colleagues and gradually taking more responsibility. After a few years, they can apply to become procurators fiscal but promotion is not automatic.

Crown prosecutors and procurators fiscal can transfer into other areas of law such as private practice.

Advantages/disadvantages

The job is interesting, carries responsibilities and can be rewarding.

You will encounter different cases in terms of type and difficulty.

You will have contact with many different types of people, some of whom may be difficult to deal with.

Working on a rota system may disrupt your personal life.

Money guide

Crown prosecutor

Crown prosecutors have a starting salary of £27,722–£31,347 or £29,648–£33,933 in London.

As a senior crown prosecutor, you can earn up to £42,730 or £44,333 in London.

Procurator fiscal

Fiscal deputes earn between £30,098 and £46,365 a year.

With experience and extra responsibilities, a senior procurator fiscal can expect a salary of up to £52,540.

A principal procurator fiscal could earn a salary of up to £60,489.

Related opportunities

- Barrister/Advocate p343
- Paralegal p356
- Solicitor/Notary Public p359

Further information

Crown Office and Procurator Fiscal Service
www.crownoffice.gov.uk

Crown Prosecution Service
www.cps.gov.uk

Qualifications and courses

Entrants are expected to hold a 2.1 or above bachelor's degree with honours in a social science subject. Relevant degree subjects include area and development studies, demography, economics, education, environmental planning and psychology. Additionally, degree subjects must contain a substantial social research or statistics component. Entry onto a degree is usually with 2 A levels/3 H grades and 5 GCSEs/National 5s (A*–C/A–C) and courses typically take 3–4 years to complete.

Postgraduate study at Master's or PhD level is not a requirement for entry, but may be helpful in demonstrating commitment and advanced levels of research and statistical aptitude when looking to enter this field of work. Entry to postgraduate study is usually with a 2.1 or higher bachelor's degree. For those who do not hold an undergraduate degree in a social research subject, conversion master's degrees may be available for study.

One possible entry route is through the civil service Government Social Researcher (GSR) fast-stream programme. Entrants must have either a bachelor's degree, with a 2.1 or higher, in a social science discipline with a strong social research or statistics component; or a bachelor's degree in any discipline (with a 2.2 or higher) plus a postgraduate qualification in a relevant social science subject. Successful applicants will be invited to attend assessment days at the Social Research Assessment Centre (SRAC) and must also undertake examination at the Fast Stream Assessment Centre (FSAC), both of which are located in London.

Work experience in an applied research setting will be useful for entry to this career, but is not essential. A summer student placement scheme may be available for those studying at undergraduate level.

What the work involves

Government social research officers play a critical role in gathering, analysing and interpreting information that informs the development of new policies and the evaluation of existing ones in government, as well as the reporting of social trends.

GSR officers work throughout all of the main areas in government, as well as in many of the smaller, devolved agencies and bodies. Working with ministers and officials they will set out the aims and parameters of social research initiatives, and oversee the collection of data through varied research methods. They then analyse this information and inform government on how policies are impacting on the lives of a population. Additionally, they may employ political planning models in order to predict how proposed policies may affect a country and its citizens.

Type of person suited to this work

You must have an interest in policy development and evaluation, and be keen to see how research informs decisions in government.

Outstanding social research skills are a must, as is the ability to handle data and interpret information effectively.

You should be a good communicator, as your role will involve presenting information to government ministers and officials in a clear, concise and informative manner.

Strong IT skills are a requirement, and you must have an aptitude for using statistical software packages.

Working conditions

You will typically be working a standard 9am–5pm week, Monday to Friday. However, flexibility may be a requirement for some roles in the civil service. Opportunities for part-time employment and job sharing are available.

Your work will typically be office-based, however you may need to travel in order to attend meetings in other cities or to conduct interviews and research initiatives.

Future prospects

GSR officers make up more than 1,000 members of the civil service workforce. Work is available throughout the UK, however most GSR officers are employed in larger cities such as Cardiff, Edinburgh, Leeds, Liverpool, Sheffield and London.

Promotion could be to a Senior Research Officer role, and opportunities to move between government departments do exist.

Self-employment is not possible.

Advantages/disadvantages

The work is challenging yet satisfying, and will give you access to the decision-making process behind government policy.

Work may be stressful, particularly leading up to deadlines or when undertaking large research initiatives.

Money guide

Salaries can vary between government departments and agencies, and depending on geographical location.

Starting salaries for graduates in London are between £25,000 and £27,000.

Candidates on the civil service fast-stream programme earn similar starting salary figures to those in mainstream employment.

You could see earnings of £45,000 or more after 4-5 years' experience.

Related opportunities

- Constituency Agent/Political Researcher p345
- Intelligence Officer/Analyst p541
- Statistician p524

Further information

Civil Service Fast Stream
www.faststream.civilservice.gov.uk

Office for National Statistics
www.ons.gov.uk/ons

LEGAL AND POLITICAL SERVICES

JUDGE/SHERIFF

Qualifications and courses

Candidates looking to become a judge must be a qualified solicitor or barrister with 5–7 years' legal experience. The Lord Chancellor requires that candidates should normally have previous judicial experience in a part-time role such as deputy district judge, recorder or tribunal judge. District or circuit judges are usually appointed after 10–15 years' court experience and applications are made through the Judicial Appointments Commission (JAC).

To qualify as a solicitor or barrister, you will need either an approved law degree, or a non-law degree followed by the Common Professional Examination (CPE), the Postgraduate Diploma in Law (PgDL) or the Senior Status Law degree. Solicitors must then complete a Legal Practice Course (LPC) followed by a 2-year training contract and barristers must undertake the Bar Professional Training Course (BPTC) and a 12-month pupillage.

In Scotland, candidates for a sheriff's position must be a fully qualified solicitor or advocate with at least 10 years' experience. Applications are made through the Judicial Appointments Board for Scotland.

To become qualified in the Scottish legal system it is necessary to have an LLB degree in Scottish law (or 3 years of pre-diploma training and a pass in the Law Society of Scotland's exams), followed by a Diploma in Professional Legal Practice (PEAT 1) and a 2-year training contract with a practising solicitor in Scotland (PEAT 2).

What the work involves

Judges (sheriffs in Scotland) preside over courts and make judgements on what should happen based on the evidence from 2 opposing parties. You will listen to all the evidence and decide on procedures, including whether a piece of evidence can be used, whilst keeping order in court.

In jury cases, you will instruct and advise the jury on the strength of the evidence before the jury leaves court to consider the verdict.

You will decide on penalties in criminal courts and on settlements in civil cases.

Type of person suited to this work

As judges make the final decision in a court case, it is important to be able to grasp facts quickly and analyse the evidence to help make your decision. Judges must think logically and not become emotionally involved.

You should have excellent communication and public-speaking skills. You also need to be a good listener and pay careful attention to the evidence.

It is important to have the confidence to make difficult decisions and stand by them. Discretion is needed to deal with confidential information.

Working conditions

You will spend much of your time in court but you will also have an office with support staff to help you. You will travel between courts and may have to spend time away from home.

You will dress smartly at all times and wear robes in court. Courts are very formal and have traditions which you must observe.

Future prospects

There are very few openings for judges and sheriffs, which means entry is competitive. Successful candidates have normally followed a long career in law as a barrister/advocate or solicitor.

Most judges work in one type of court, such as a Crown Court or Court of Appeal. Senior positions, such as Lord Chief Justice and Master of the Rolls, are made on the recommendation of the Prime Minister.

In Scotland, most sheriffs work in sheriff courts. A few with experience become supreme court judges in the High Court of Justiciary or the Court of Session.

Judicial office holders are legally required to retire at the age of 70.

Advantages/disadvantages

The work is varied and no two days will be the same.

This is a very responsible job which requires a high amount of intellect and dedication.

You will meet many different people and hear some cases which will have a high media interest or involve distressing evidence.

Some courts work into the evenings.

Money guide

The lowest starting salary currently for a district judge is £106,040.

You could earn £142,745 as a circuit judge.

As a High Court judge you can achieve in excess of £177,988.

The Lord Chief Justice, the highest legal position in England and Wales, earns £247,112 a year.

In Scotland, sheriffs have a salary of £132,184–£142,745.

Related opportunities

- Barrister/Advocate p343
- Crown Prosecutor/Procurator Fiscal p350
- Legal Executive p353

Further information

Judicial Appointments Commission
jac.judiciary.gov.uk

Judicial Communications Office
www.judiciary.gov.uk

Skills for Justice
www.sfjuk.com

LEGAL EXECUTIVE

Qualifications and courses

You need to undertake two levels of academic and practical training in order to become a legal executive. These qualifications are set by the Chartered Institute of Legal Executives (CILEx) and include the CILEx Level 3 Professional Diploma in Law and Practice and the CILEx Level 6 Professional Higher Diploma in Law and Practice. Once completed, you will need to gain 5 years' work experience to become a fully qualified Chartered Legal Executive.

The minimum requirements for the Level 3 training are 4 GCSEs/National 5s (A*–C/A–C), including English. The City & Guilds/CILEx Level 2 Certificate in Legal Studies is a suitable alternative. Students will train for their Level 3 Diploma under the supervision of a solicitor or senior legal executive. Study is carried out on day release or at evening classes and will take 1–2 years to complete.

Full training at Level 6 takes 2 years (while working full time) and leads to CILEx Membership. CILEx qualifications can also be taken as part of a Modern Legal Apprenticeship scheme.

Certain qualifications, such as an undergraduate law degree, may provide exemption from some academic parts of the qualifications. People with relevant experience can also apply to have their experience approved by CILEx.

In Scotland, there is no direct equivalent to legal executive; staff are known as paralegals or solicitors' assistants. Generally 4 GCSEs/National 5s (A*–C/A–C), including English and Maths, followed by office experience are required for entry.

What the work involves

Legal executives work with solicitors, preparing complex cases for them and dealing with straightforward cases themselves.

You will interview clients, asking questions to help you give them legal advice and explain legal points to them clearly. You will write letters on their behalf, draft contracts and wills and prepare other documents.

In certain cases, you may represent clients in court or at tribunals.

Type of person suited to this work

Excellent written and verbal communication skills are essential.

Clients will give you confidential information so it is important to be discreet and tactful. You will also need patience as legal points can be difficult to grasp.

When preparing cases, you will be handling large amounts of information, which means it is useful to be a thorough and well organised worker.

Working conditions

Most legal executives work 37 hours a week, Monday to Friday, but you will probably be expected to work additional hours on a regular basis including evenings and weekends.

You will be based in an office but you may need to attend court and as such you will be expected to dress smartly.

You might have to travel to visit clients or legal libraries, so a driving licence is useful.

Future prospects

You could work in a private practice for a solicitor or in local and central government and industry. Legal executives usually specialise in one area, for example property or business law.

You can train to qualify as a legal executive advocate or as a solicitor, which allows you to follow a case right through to court.

This is a very competitive career, and the majority of entrants are now graduates.

Advantages/disadvantages

You will have the chance to work in a legal environment while studying part time and earning a good salary.

You might have to work under pressure to meet deadlines and work unsociable hours.

Money guide

Starting salaries for trainee legal executives vary from £15,000 up to £28,000 per year of training.

Once you have the CILEx qualifications you can earn up to £38,000, depending on where you work.

Legal executives with more experience (it takes 5 years to become a fully qualified legal executive) can earn between £35,000 and £55,000 and in big city firms the salary potential is even higher.

Due to increasing demand for legal executives the salary range has broadened considerably depending a lot on experience, skills and location.

Related opportunities

- Barrister's/Advocate's Clerk p344
- Civil Service Administrative Officer p13
- Solicitor/Notary Public p359

Further information

Chartered Institute of Legal Executives
www.cilex.org.uk

Law Society of England and Wales
www.lawsociety.org.uk

Law Society of Northern Ireland
www.lawsoc-ni.org

Qualifications and courses

England and Wales

Candidates must pass the Council for Licensed Conveyancers (CLC) training and exams which are typically undertaken in employment. To begin training applicants must have a minimum of 4 GCSEs/National 5s (A*–C/A–C), including English, and an A level/H grade in Law is useful. You may be accepted without minimum qualifications if you have relevant work experience within a solicitor's or licensed conveyancer's office.

However, many applicants will already hold a law degree or might have taken either the Chartered Institute of Legal Executives (CILEx) course or the Legal Practice Course (LPC) for trainee solicitors. Applicants must have at least 2 years' practical training with a qualified employer and pass the CLC examination. Many students take this as a correspondence course. It is also offered on a part-time basis.

Once completed, candidates can then apply for a limited licence and after a further 3 consecutive years you can apply for a full licence. An Apprenticeship in Business, Administration and Law may also be available.

Scotland

Entrants require a degree in law from a Scottish university or a Diploma/Certificate in Legal Studies which takes at least 2 years.

They then undertake a 1-year training contract with an independent qualified conveyancer. After 6 months of training, a Professional Competence Course which comprises 36 hours of core requirements and 18 hours of electives, must be completed.

For a law degree you need 5 GCSEs/National 5s (A*–C/ A–C) and 3 A levels/H grades. Some universities require applicants to take the National Admissions Test for Law.

Northern Ireland

The job of a licensed conveyancer is carried out by a solicitor. Solicitors must complete an apprenticeship programme of 2–4 years, combined with a vocational course. You can complete either a Certificate in Professional Legal Studies or a Postgraduate Diploma in Professional Legal Practice.

What the work involves

Licensed conveyancers deal with the legal side of buying, selling, renting and mortgaging of houses, flats, business premises and other property.

You will draw up the legal documents, known as contracts, that buyers and sellers exchange to make a sale legal.

Other work includes liaising with lawyers and estate agents involved in the sale and researching details in the contract.

Type of person suited to this work

You will need excellent communication skills to explain complicated legal matters to clients. Being a good teamworker is useful to liaise with others involved in a contract.

As legal contracts must be completely accurate, you must be thorough and able to process large amounts of information.

You will need good organisational skills to deal with several properties simultaneously.

Working conditions

You will work standard office hours, but may be required to work some late evenings or weekends to meet clients.

Your job may be salaried or commission only.

Many licensed conveyancers are self-employed.

Future prospects

There are only around 1,000 licensed conveyancers in England and Wales, and very few qualified conveyancers in Scotland. Job opportunities are mainly with legal practices, although since the recession there are fewer places for trainees.

Training is ongoing to cover developments in property law. You could progress into other legal professions, a managerial role or run your own business.

Changes in the law now allow conveyancers to take an additional qualification, to add to their licence, and deal with probate. Probate is the legal procedure of administering the money, property and possessions of a person after they die.

Advantages/disadvantages

The work is varied. You will meet different people, though some may be difficult.

You will get satisfaction when clients get their dream home.

You might find it stressful when trying to meet deadlines or clients feel things are moving too slowly.

Money guide

A trainee should expect a salary of between £16,000 and £20,000 per year.

With experience, this rises to £25,000–£50,000.

At the more senior levels you might earn £35,000–£55,000 per year.

It is possible to earn in excess of £60,000 per year as a partner or an owner of a conveyancing firm.

Related opportunities

- Barrister/Advocate p343
- Paralegal p356
- Surveying Technician p112

Further information

Council for Licensed Conveyancers
www.conveyancer.org.uk

Law Society of Scotland
www.lawscot.org.uk

Qualifications and courses

Magistrates' court legal adviser (England and Wales)
Candidates must be fully qualified as either a barrister or solicitor. You will start as a trainee legal adviser following a structured on-the-job induction programme organised by the associated court.

You need an approved law degree, or a non-law degree followed by the Common Professional Examination (CPE) or a Graduate Diploma in Law (GDL). You should then have completed either the Legal Practice Course (LPC) or the Bar Professional Training Course (BPTC).

wSheriff's clerk (Scotland)
There are no minimum entry requirements but it would be helpful to have National 5s (A–C) in Maths and English. You could start as an administrative officer and then progress to a role as sheriff's clerk.

Fast-track entry to a position as sheriff's clerk deputy is sometimes available to those with a law degree, the Diploma in Legal Practice and 2 years' training with a solicitor.

What the work involves

Magistrates' court legal adviser (England and Wales)
You will be a qualified solicitor or barrister with responsibility for advising magistrates in court.

You will advise on points of law, procedures, penalties and other issues.

Magistrates are volunteer civil officers who deal with minor offences among other tasks, who will not necessarily be trained in the law. A court legal adviser, or court clerk as it is sometimes known, will therefore advise the magistrate on the law, the proper procedures, and may advise on sentencing, but will never carry out any sentencing.

Sheriff's clerk (Scotland)
You might advise on points of law and procedures in any court (civil or criminal).

You could have a more general administrative role such as handling court complaints and providing statistics for court staff.

Type of person suited to this work

You must have a strong interest in the law and excellent communication skills as you will be expected to advise on a wide range of issues.

You must be organised, reliable and able to work quickly and accurately under pressure.

It's important to be impartial and remain detached from emotionally demanding cases. You will need to be discreet to deal with confidential information.

Working conditions

You will normally be located in one court building and will generally work a 37-hour week, from Monday to Friday. However, your working hours may, at times, be irregular due to complex cases.

Some courts also open as early as 8am and you might need to work weekends.

You might travel to different courts so a driving licence is useful.

Future prospects

Her Majesty's Court and Tribunal Service has a set career structure. You could progress to a role as a justices' clerk or a justices' chief executive. You could go on to a role where you train magistrates or manage a team of legal advisers.

In Scotland, sheriff's clerks are employed by the Scottish Court Service. Small rural courts may have only one clerk, while a court in a big city will have several.

There is a clear promotion structure within the Scottish Court Service.

Advantages/disadvantages

The work is often varied with new cases being presented before the court, even if minor cases.

It is less stressful than working on bigger cases, and usually there is less riding on it.

You might have to work unsocial hours at times.

A strictly advisory role may get frustrating.

Basic administrative tasks such as preparing courtroom schedules could become dull.

Money guide

You can expect around £20,500 as a trainee adviser, having completed either the LPC or the BPTC.

Those who have completed a training contract in addition, can expect to earn around £29,000.

An experienced magistrates' legal adviser can earn between £30,000 and £43,000.

Starting salaries for sheriffs' clerks are about £12,211. This can rise to between £28,000 and £35,000.

Related opportunities

- Barrister/Advocate p343
- Legal Executive p353
- Solicitor/Notary Public p359

Further information

HM Courts and Tribunals Service
www.justice.gov.uk

Scottish Court Service
www.scotcourts.gov.uk

LEGAL AND POLITICAL SERVICES

355

Qualifications and courses

You do not need any specific qualifications to become a paralegal and, with exceptional work experience, may begin employment in this position as a school leaver. However, most employers will prefer you to have some relevant qualifications, such as relevant GCSEs/National 5s (A*–C/A–C), a BTEC/HNC in Legal Studies, an NVQ in Business Administration, a legal secretary qualification at Level 2 or 3 or a Foundation degree in law.

It is important to note that becoming a paralegal is now a popular option for those who have graduated in law but do not have a training contract to become a solicitor. Therefore, as competition is high, some employers ask for a HND or degree in law, and others even request the LPC (Legal Practice Course) postgraduate qualification.

For those who have not studied law previously, you should seek employment within an administrative role in a law firm and study for paralegal qualifications whilst working.

Training usually takes place on the job, and you will be supervised by experienced lawyers. Employers may well encourage you to follow courses in legal training; these are widely available. They might include the BTEC in Law and Legal Work (Levels 2–3) or City & Guilds Level 2 Award/Certificate/Diploma in Legal Studies (7657).

Alternatively, entry can be enabled by an Advanced (Level 3) or Higher (Level 4) Apprenticeship in Legal Services, offered by the Chartered Institute of Legal Executives (CILEx).

Membership of the National Association of Licensed Paralegals (NALP) offers the opportunity to work towards a degree-level qualification and provides increased recognition in the industry. As a member, you must take part in continuing professional development (CPD) programmes. The Institute of Paralegals also offers relevant qualifications and training schemes and is the only government-approved organisation that independently regulates paralegals.

What the work involves

A paralegal is somebody who is not a qualified lawyer, but whose job involves dealing with a lot of legal issues.

You may have legal training or experience, and will work in a law firm or similar organisation. Your duties will be varied, but will probably involve legal research and drafting documents, as well as other administrative tasks.

You will also interview witnesses and clients, and appear in court, often acting on behalf of lawyers. You might specialise in a specific area of law.

Type of person suited to this work

You should have a natural interest in law and current affairs and be discreet in your work, as you may frequently be dealing with confidential information.

Attention to detail is essential. Equally, a good command of English and the ability to communicate well with everybody, from the lawyers you will be working with to all of their clients, is vital. You should also be patient, understanding, tactful, sympathetic and be able to work well under pressure.

Organisational skills are essential, as is computer literacy, excellent concentration and a good memory. You also need to be able to understand and absorb a lot of information.

Working conditions

You'll probably be working in an office for about 37 hours a week. However, some of these will be spent visiting clients, which means that a driving licence is useful.

You may spend time in police stations and court, occasionally out of office hours.

You may be required to work weekends and bank holidays.

Future prospects

Future prospects for a paralegal are good. You can use the knowledge you gain on the job to develop your legal career.

If you have the necessary qualifications, you can become a solicitor or barrister, and even work your way up to partner.

With experience, you can take on additional responsibilities and move up within the firm. You may choose to move on to freelance work.

Advantages/disadvantages

Working as a paralegal is stimulating and rewarding, especially if you have an interest in or study law.

It can really give your law career a nudge in the right direction and is a great option if, for example, you are training to be a solicitor and want to take a gap year.

Occasionally tasks may be a little mundane and meeting with clients can be stressful.

Money guide

As a paralegal who is starting out, you may earn between £16,000 and £20,000 a year.

With experience, you can earn up to £25,000, which may increase to in excess of £40,000 with further experience and qualifications.

Related opportunities

- Barrister's/Advocate's Clerk p344
- Court Administrative Officer p347
- Legal Executive p353

Further information

Chartered Institute of Legal Executives
www.cilex.org.uk

Institute of Paralegals
www.theiop.org

National Association of Licensed Paralegals
www.nationalparalegals.co.uk

Qualifications and courses

Patent attorney

All patent attorneys need a degree related to science, engineering or maths. The general entry requirements for a degree are 2 A levels/3 H grades and 5 GCSEs/ National 5s (A*–C/A–C), including Maths and English. Entry to the profession is competitive and most employers will expect candidates to have a minimum of a 2.1 Honours degree.

Patent attorneys receive specialist training in intellectual property law. Qualified solicitors with experience of working in an intellectual property department or those training to become patent agents may apply to join the Chartered Institute of Patent Attorneys (CIPA).

A high level of skill in the English language is required, and fluency in foreign languages, especially French and/ or German, is a bonus. This is a requirement in order to become a European patent attorney, as is a period of 3 years' training under the supervision of an experienced professional.

A training period and the successful completion of examinations is required for admission to the Register of Patent Attorneys and the Register of Trade Mark Attorneys. It usually takes 4 to 5 years to qualify. The Certificate in IP Law offered by several universities (typically a 1- to 3-month course) provides candidates with exemptions from all the Foundation Papers of the CIPA examinations.

Examiner

You must have a good Honours degree in science, maths, engineering or technology. An equivalent professional qualification or corporate membership of a relevant major professional institution may be accepted. It is also essential that you meet the nationality and residency requirements as specified by the civil service.

What the work involves

Patent attorney

You will advise clients on the law of intellectual property.

The work involves checking that an invention is a new one and does not already exist.

You will prepare specifications for the Patent Office, carrying out any negotiations required and representing the client before the patent examiner.

Examiner

You will examine patent applications submitted by patent agents for new inventions, trademarks or designs.

You must ensure that patents are granted for new inventions.

You will conduct a study of each application to check that it is clear and that it meets legal requirements.

Type of person suited to this work

You will need a thorough knowledge of applying intellectual property to inventions and of the laws regarding this sector.

You should have strong research skills and a high attention to detail. You must have good communication skills in order to explain complex legal issues to your clients.

You must be highly organised, decisive and able to multi-task.

Working conditions

You will be based in an office, although patent agents do some travelling in the UK and abroad; a driving licence would be useful.

The majority of your time will be spent researching and writing reports on the computer.

Just over 2,000 patent attorneys are registered in the UK with CIPA. Around 80% work in private practices, mostly in the larger towns and cities.

Patent examiners are civil servants, mostly based in the Patent Office in Newport with some working in London.

Future prospects

While there has been an increase in demand for trainees, the demanding standards required on entry are expected to remain firm.

The civil service has a formal promotion structure culminating in the successful candidate becoming a senior patent examiner.

Advantages/disadvantages

This job has a high level of responsibility and is intellectually demanding.

You will get satisfaction from helping new inventions become recognised and being involved from an early stage in the process of creation.

Money guide

Trainee patent attorneys earn around £24,000, rising to £33,000 with experience.

Once qualified you could earn between £50,000 and £85,000, reaching in excess of £100,000 for senior partners in private practices.

Patent examiners earn around £26,779 which can rise to £52,933 a year in senior roles, plus £1,500 Recruitment and Retention Allowance (RRA).

Often, an additional allowance of £2,000–£4,000 is offered for those with experience in telecommunications.

Related opportunities

- Barrister's/Advocate's Clerk p344
- Legal Executive p353
- Solicitor/Notary Public p359

Further information

Chartered Institute of Patent Attorneys
www.cipa.org.uk

Intellectual Property Office
www.ipo.gov.uk

LEGAL AND POLITICAL SERVICES

357

Qualifications and courses

Any British citizen may stand for election as long as they are over 18 years old. There are no formal minimum educational requirements, however commitment to a political party is the most important criterion.

Owing to the competitive nature of this field, many Members of Parliament (MPs) are graduates or hold other professional qualifications. The general entry requirements for a degree are 2 A levels/3 H grades and 5 GCSEs/National 5s (A*–C/A–C).

Active involvement in a political party is essential and experience as a trade union activist may be useful. Some people work their way up from being a politician's assistant or political researcher. Many people enter politics after a career in medicine, law or education.

There are a series of selection interviews before candidates can be 'adopted' by their party and their local constituency to stand for election. Candidates must then carry out a successful campaign and be elected by the votes of the local people. In order to stand for election, you must pay a £500 deposit and submit nomination papers that have been signed by 10 electors from the constituency which you aim to represent.

Those disqualified from standing for election are undischarged bankrupts, members of the House of Lords, those sentenced to imprisonment of more than 3 months and those disqualified under the Representation of the People Act 1983.

If elected, you will learn on the job with the help of experienced MPs, party whips and via training workshops that will instruct you in presentation and communication skills and dealing with the media. Education regarding electoral procedures is also provided for those selected as party candidates.

What the work involves

MPs represent the people in their local constituencies in Parliament, usually as a member of a political party. You will hold 'surgeries' in your local constituency and deal with issues raised by local people at local and national level.

MEPs (Members of the European Parliament) deal with European legislation. In Parliament, you will join committees, attend meetings and take part in debates. You will also vote on new policies or laws.

You may specialise in a particular area and you may hold office in the government or for the opposition.

Type of person suited to this work

You should be passionate about politics and have strong social beliefs, along with a desire to represent the people of your constituency. Key skills include: communication, decision making, information handling, supervisory and management skills. A pleasant manner and the ability to gain people's confidence are also important.

You will be expected to keep up to date with party policies and legislation, which requires being able to process large amounts of information quickly and thoroughly.

You will need plenty of stamina to cope with the long hours and high levels of pressure.

Working conditions

Your time will be divided between your local constituency and Parliament/Scottish Parliament/Welsh Assembly. MEPs spend one week a month in Strasbourg and much of their remaining time in Brussels.

Politicians tend to work very long hours when parliament is sitting. From the end of July to the beginning of October parliament breaks so that politicians can spend time in their constituencies.

There is a lot of travel involved both at home and overseas.

Future prospects

Your job in any parliament will depend on being re-elected, which means it is important to have another career option to fall back on.

Although most MPs represent the local people in their constituencies, they are also involved in the government of their country.

You could be offered a post in a ministry, which may lead to appointment as a minister in a particular area. In exceptional circumstances, you could become the leader of your party or even the Prime Minister.

Advantages/disadvantages

The work is varied and challenging, and no two days will be the same.

You will get a sense of satisfaction if your party is in power but also frustration when votes are not in your favour.

Money guide

The basic salary for an MP in the House of Commons is £74,000, however you could earn £134,565 as a cabinet minister.

The Prime Minister currently takes an annual salary of £142,500.

MEPs are paid the same salaries as national MPs in their own countries.

Additional allowances/expenses are available for travel and communications.

Related opportunities

- Public Relations Officer p404
- Trade Union Official p575
- Welfare Benefits Adviser/Welfare Rights Caseworker p578

Further information

National Assembly for Wales
www.wales.gov.uk

Scottish Parliament
www.scottish.parliament.uk

The Electoral Commission
www.electoralcommission.org.uk

UK Parliament
www.parliament.uk

Qualifications and courses

England and Wales

You will need either an approved law degree, or a non-law degree followed by a one-year conversion course, either the Common Professional Examination (CPE) or the Graduate Diploma in Law (GDL).

Alternatively, candidates without a degree can qualify through 1 of 2 routes offered by the Chartered Institute of Legal Executives (CILEx), the CILEx Fellowship route or the CILEx Membership route. Following this, you may have to complete a 1-year conversion course, although exemptions may be available.

All candidates must then complete a 1-year Legal Practice Course (LPC). This is followed by a 2-year training contract and a Professional Skills Course. Those having opted for the CILEx Fellowship route, however, are exempt from this training contract.

Scotland

You will need either an approved LLB degree in Scots law or a good non-law degree followed by an accelerated 2-year graduate law degree. Candidates without a degree can take 3 years' Pre-Diploma training with a qualified solicitor, where you will also take the Law Society of Scotland exams. Very few solicitors offer this contract however.

Entrants must then complete a 1-year Diploma in Legal Practice followed by a 2-year training contract with a practising solicitor.

Northern Ireland

You will need to obtain a Qualifying Law Degree (QLD), or a non-law degree followed by a postgraduate law conversion degree known as the Masters in Legal Science (MLegSci).

Potential solicitors must then complete an apprenticeship programme of 2 years, combined with a vocational course at the Institute of Professional Legal Studies or at the Graduate School of Professional Legal Education. You can opt for either a Certificate in Professional Legal Studies or a Postgraduate Diploma in Professional Legal Practice. In order to do so, you must be registered with the Law Society and have a master.

Notary public

In England and Wales, qualified solicitors who hold a current Certificate of Exemption from the Faculty Office of the Archbishop of Canterbury may take a 2-year distance learning course in Notarial Practice. Candidates will then be approved by the Master of the Faculties but will continue to be supervised for a further 2 years.

In Scotland and Northern Ireland, solicitors can apply to enrol as notaries upon qualifying as solicitors.

What the work involves

Solicitor

You will advise clients on legal matters, such as making a will or setting up a business. In certain circumstances you may represent clients in court, or you might have to instruct a barrister or advocate to act for your client.

Notary public

You will certify deeds and other documents so that they will be accepted by judicial and public authorities as authentic and legally binding. Notaries public are generally solicitors who combine this function with other legal work.

Type of person suited to this work

You must be able to examine and analyse vast amounts of information and pay close attention to detail.

You will need to possess good communication and interpersonal skills.

You will need to be discreet when dealing with confidential information. It is important to remain impartial.

Working conditions

Most of your work will be in an office and you will often be under a lot of stress to meet deadlines.

You might spend time in court or have to visit clients, therefore you will need to dress smartly.

Future prospects

There is keen competition for traineeships, but when qualified there are good prospects in private practice, government and industry. You can specialise in one area of law and may eventually become a partner in a firm or even a judge.

As a notary public you may decide to start your own company.

Advantages/disadvantages

The work is varied and no two days will be the same, although some people may be difficult or unpleasant to work with.

You might have to work long hours.

Money guide

There is a requirement on employers, set by the Solicitors Regulation Authority (SRA), to pay trainee solicitors at least the National Minimum Wage.

A newly qualified solicitor can earn £25,000–£40,000, or upwards of this in large commercial or City firms, and a senior partner in a legal practice can earn in excess of £100,000.

Notaries public are paid set fees for individual cases.

Related opportunities

- Barrister/Advocate p343
- Crown Prosecutor/Procurator Fiscal p350
- Legal Executive p353

Further information

Law Society of England and Wales
www.lawsociety.org.uk

Law Society of Northern Ireland
www.lawsoc-ni.org

Law Society of Scotland
www.lawscot.org.uk

LEGAL AND POLITICAL SERVICES

359

Leisure, Sport and Tourism

This sector relies on a motivated, up-beat and out-going workforce for its success. You will need to show that you can work very well with other people, providing them with an excellent service when they want to enjoy themselves on holiday or if they are keen to improve their fitness and sporting ability. If you are keen to work with professional sports players or become one yourself you should be very aware of how to keep the body fit while avoiding injury. You should be warm and friendly but also able to maintain a high level of professionalism at the same time. You should also demonstrate you have patience and tact with people of all ages and be clued up on health and safety regulations. The jobs featured in this section are listed below. For similar jobs to the ones in this section turn to *Catering and Hospitality* on page 121.

LEISURE, SPORT AND TOURISM

Qualifications and courses

There are no formal entry requirements although maths skills are important and many betting shop chains may ask for a GCSE/National 5 (A*–C/A–C) in that subject. You may have to take a basic maths test as part of the recruitment process, focusing on the calculation of percentages, odds and payments. By law, you must be 18 years of age to work in a betting shop and at least 20 years old to start as a manager.

Experience working in a customer service role is an advantage. Betting shop employees may have opportunities to work towards the NVQ Level 2 Diploma in Gambling Operations or the Level 2 Award in the Principles of Customer Service in Hospitality, Leisure, Travel and Tourism.

Training is provided on the job and covers areas such as calculating betting odds and payouts, administration, customer service, business skills, managing staff, betting laws and company policies.

Managers will be expected to have betting shop experience. Some universities have degrees and Foundation degrees in gambling and leisure management which may improve employment prospects and aid job progression.

What the work involves

You will take bets from customers on the outcomes of sporting events and contests, and pay out winnings. You will work out and set betting odds for your customers, often using an electronic system. This could include unusual bets that might be difficult to establish.

For both positions, you will also explain bets and promotions, balance the day's takings, maintain the shop, and also ensure that nobody under-aged tries to bet or use in-store gambling machines.

Cashiers will update display boards with betting opportunities, oversee betting terminals, balance the books at the end of each shift and look out for fraud.

Managers ensure that the shop meets Gambling Commission regulations, deal with disputes and complaints, and control profits and costs.

Type of person suited to this work

You need to be alert to gather vital information about race entrants' recent performance ratings and handicaps. You should have a good understanding of sports.

Customers will keep coming back to place bets in your shop if you are friendly and service-oriented. You need to be good with numbers and money.

Confidence and good verbal and negotiation skills are vital in order to handle difficult customers. Being able to work well under pressure is essential.

Working conditions

You will most likely work up to 40 hours a week although part-time work may be available. Betting shops are open 7 days a week year-round and are usually open until 10pm. Your busiest day will be Saturday and you will need to be prepared to work evenings, weekends and holidays.

You will need to wear a uniform or dress smartly.

An independent bookmaker will travel long distances to attend all major sporting events and much of the work will be outdoors.

Future prospects

You have the opportunity to work for a chain, an independent shop, a bookmaker business at a racecourse or a national regulatory body such as the Gambling Commission. With experience, you can be promoted from cashier to manager.

You could become a multi-site manager of about 15 shops within a city or even an area manager looking after 50 or more shops.

Successful bookmakers often prefer to move into self-employment and may work well beyond normal retirement age.

Advantages/disadvantages

Being involved with people taking risks can create a high-pressure atmosphere and may lead to confrontations.

The long hours may disrupt your personal life and commitments.

You have the opportunity to build a good rapport with customers which can make for an enjoyable workplace.

Money guide

Full-time starting salaries for a cashier are between £11,000 and £13,000.

Deputy managers can expect about £15,000.

Betting shop managers usually earn £17,000–£25,000.

An area manager for a large chain could achieve £45,000 plus bonuses.

If you are a self-employed bookmaker your salary will depend on racing conditions, the number of entrants and gamblers, and the number of events in the calendar.

Related opportunities

- Accounting Technician and Accounts/Finance Clerk p4
- Croupier p364
- Entertainment Manager p366

Further information

Association of British Bookmakers Ltd
www.abb.uk.com

Gambling Commission
www.gamblingcommission.gov.uk

National Association of Bookmakers
www.nab-bookmakers.co.uk

Qualifications and courses

Owing to film classification laws, you must be at least 18 years of age to work as a projectionist but there are no formal academic requirements for entry to this career. Instead employers may give you a simple entry test to determine your technical ability.

It is useful to have some knowledge or experience of working with electronics, cameras or sound equipment. Joining a film club can help develop your knowledge of projection equipment and film formats. You could also work part time as an assistant projectionist for a few months. Alternatively, working as a cinema attendant is a good way to gain further insight into the industry while you wait for a trainee projectionist role to become available.

All employers look for candidates who can demonstrate a real enthusiasm for the moving image.

There are also short and part-time courses available which could give you the experience needed to go straight into employment as a projectionist. The Moving Image Society (BKSTS) offers courses in both film-based and digital cinema projection.

What the work involves

Projectionists work in cinemas and are responsible for operating film screening equipment, ensuring that everything runs smoothly throughout the feature.

You will also be required to monitor other technical equipment in the cinema, including lighting, heating and ventilation systems, and electrical and gas supplies. You may be responsible for ensuring that all fire alarms and extinguishers are in good working order.

You may work with traditional 20-minute reels of film or modern digital versions that are stored on a hard drive. Most cinemas now use digital versions instead of film reels, although some smaller and independent cinemas may still use reel.

You will be expected to check that the sound on each film is operating properly and the volume is correct.

Type of person suited to this work

You should enjoy working independently and have a strong interest in film and cinema, as the majority of your time will be spent alone operating machinery in the projection room. You will need good IT skills in order to use increasingly complicated film screening technology and equipment.

You must be alert and observant so you can identify problems quickly, and also have the practical skills and knowledge to solve these issues effectively and under pressure. Good eyesight, hearing and coordination are essential.

You should be able to adhere to the strict timings given on schedules to ensure that each film runs according to plan.

Working conditions

You will work 5 days a week but hours are generally long and irregular as most cinemas screen films from the afternoon up until late in the evening.

Shift work, weekend work and overtime are common.

You will spend most of your time in a projection room. Most of these do not have windows but in modern cinemas they are usually air conditioned. You will be working alone in the projection room for the majority of your shift.

Future prospects

The ongoing switch-over from the old 35mm projectors to new digital ones is changing the job role of the projectionists. The rise in higher quality 3D films is furthering the need for good IT skills. Fewer staff are now needed and projectionists often take on other duties within the cinema as well.

Opportunities can be found in large cinema chains or in smaller and often more specialist independent theatres.

In larger organisations, you could be promoted to senior projectionist or an administrative role. Small independent cinemas offer scope for experienced staff to become more involved with the running of the business.

Advantages/disadvantages

If you love cinema, you will enjoy being able to watch films for free.

You will have the opportunity to work for a number of employers, ranging from large multiplexes screening major blockbusters, to small independent cinemas which may specialise in art-house or international films.

You will be working alone for the majority of the time.

Your hours will be unsocial, including evenings and weekends.

Money guide

Salaries for cinema projectionists start at around £12,000.

With experience this can rise to around £17,000 a year.

Chief projectionists in larger cinemas can achieve up to £22,000.

Related opportunities

- Actor p416
- Arts Administrator/Manager p329
- Lighting Technician p426

Further information

BKSTS
www.bksts.com

British Film Institute
www.bfi.org.uk

LEISURE, SPORT AND TOURISM

363

CROUPIER

Qualifications and courses

You must be 18 years old to work in a casino, and obtain clearance from the Disclosure and Barring Service (DBS), as you are unable to work as a croupier if you have a criminal conviction. All entrants to this profession need to apply for a personal functional licence (PFL) from the Gambling Commission.

There are no specific academic requirements but many employers ask for at least 3 GCSEs/National 5s (A*– C/A–C), including English and Maths. You may have to pass various assessments at interview, including mental arithmetic and manual dexterity tests. Normal colour vision, good hearing and clear speech are required. It could also help to have experience of working with the public and handling money.

Most major casino operators run training schemes for entrants, both in-house and externally. You can also gain an NVQ Level 2 in Gambling Operations (Casino) by attending an 18-week course available at Blackpool and The Fylde College, the London Gaming College and North Warwickshire and Hinckley College.

The National Gaming Academy offers a Foundation degree in Gaming Technology which could improve your long-term career prospects.

What the work involves

Croupiers work in casinos and are responsible for setting up gaming tables, preparing packs of cards and selling gaming tokens to customers.

You will be greeting customers, inviting them to join games of roulette, blackjack or baccarat and explaining the rules if necessary. Spinning the roulette or money wheel, shuffling and dealing cards, shaking mini dice cages and encouraging players to place their bets will be part of your role.

You will also be responsible for announcing and paying out wins, and collecting in lost bets.

Type of person suited to this work

You should have an engaging personality, good interpersonal skills and possess the ability to make customers feel happy and relaxed. Confidence in front of an audience is essential.

Appearance is highly important. You must be smartly dressed, clean and manicured, with immaculately groomed hair.

There might be difficult moments when people are distressed or angered by losing so you must be confident and assertive.

Fluency in another language is an asset.

Working conditions

Casinos open 7 days a week and on bank holidays from 12pm to 6am. Many are now open 24 hours a day. This means that staff work shifts including evenings, weekends and bank holidays.

On cruise liners, croupiers spend up to 12 months on board, with about 6 weeks' vacation. Casinos close when in port so you do get time ashore in exotic locations!

Future prospects

Britain currently has 140 casinos, which is a figure that is unlikely to change substantially any time soon. Gambling has become better regulated in recent years and employers really value good staff.

Significant numbers of croupiers are needed to fill jobs on cruise liners and this can be a favourite choice for experienced croupiers seeking management-level experience.

As a croupier with 2 years of experience, you can progress to supervising a number of gaming tables after undertaking further training. Promotion could be to inspector, pit boss and, finally, manager of a casino.

Advantages/disadvantages

If you are quick and ambitious, you can make rapid progress from croupier to casino manager.

If you work as a croupier on a cruise ship, there will be the opportunity to visit new countries, especially as ship casinos are usually not allowed to be open when ships are in port.

Standing for hours and concentrating on running the games without error, while talking to customers, can be tiring.

Casino-goers drink alcohol which exacerbates the emotional tension during gaming. Arguments often break out which you must be able to handle according to the rules and regulations governing gaming.

Money guide

Starting salaries can range from £13,500 to £19,000. Salaries in London are generally higher.

Those with experience who are employed in a senior position can achieve up to £25,000–£30,000.

Recent changes to the law have allowed for croupiers to earn tips, which may increase your salary.

Pay scales on cruise liners are similar, however earnings are tax free and the tips are generally higher. Meals and accommodation are provided for free for employees on cruise liners.

Related opportunities

- Cruise Ship Steward/Purser p589
- Entertainment Manager p366

Further information

National Casino Industry Forum
www.nationalcasinoforum.co.uk

DIVER

Qualifications and courses

To become a professional diver or diving instructor you will need a qualification approved by the Health and Safety Executive (HSE). There are no formal academic requirements for these courses, although basic maths and English may be tested. You must also obtain a valid certificate of medical fitness from a doctor approved by the HSE and pass a medical each year during your diving career.

Certain types of divers may need extra qualifications: most scientific divers have a degree in oceanography or marine biology, offshore divers may need a degree in surveying or engineering, construction divers might need qualifications in welding or non-destructive testing, and divers for the police or armed forces must already be serving in the force. Divers who intend to work offshore must have an up-to-date HSE first aid at work qualification.

All divers must meet the Diving at Work Regulations 1997 (DWR) established by the HSE.

What the work involves

As a diver you will work either at sea or inland (i.e. rivers and reservoirs). Your tasks will depend on the industry you choose to work in and the type of diving you specialise in.

You could choose to become a diving instructor. Diving instructors teach a variety of skills from entry level diver training to technical diving for more experienced divers. They often operate from dedicated dive centres at coastal sites or through holiday resorts or local swimming pools.

Professional divers are often used in several industries, such as offshore oil and gas, civil engineering, fish farming, media, scientific research, underwater archaeology or police diving, and undertake a variety of specialist tasks.

A civil engineer diver is employed for underwater repairs and demolition. Divers employed in media will be required to participate in stunts or underwater filming. Police divers are responsible for searching for and recovering missing persons or evidence. Offshore divers recruited in the oil and gas industries will be employed for exploration and surveying, or building and maintaining drilling rigs and pipelines.

Scientific diving is the use of diving techniques by scientists to study underwater what would normally be studied by scientists on land. Examples of disciplines pursued include underwater archaeology, marine biology and geology.

Type of person suited to this work

You must be fit, active and a very strong swimmer as diving is extremely physically demanding.

You must be able to follow health and safety regulations. You should work well in a team and on your own.

You need to be able to concentrate and cope with diving conditions that could be dangerous and have quick reactions to deal with emergencies.

Working conditions

Underwater working conditions are cold, dark and may be cramped. It is necessary to wear protective clothing and breathing apparatus.

Working hours for divers are irregular and depend on the job. A lot of divers work just 120–180 days per year. Jobs may be located abroad.

Future prospects

Divers who pursue higher education have good prospects because they can combine subject expertise with practical skill. For example, a diver with a qualification in forensics would be more likely to be involved with police diving.

Experienced, senior divers may become self-employed, either as contractors or as operators of diving schools or stores.

The growth of offshore wind farms and the oil and gas sector has led to a rise in the demand for experienced offshore divers around the world. However, those with experience already will be favoured.

Advantages/disadvantages

There is a strong demand for experienced, offshore divers.

The high levels of fitness and health needed for diving can make this a short career.

There is a risk of accidents when underwater and there are potential long-term health hazards which include a number of specific acute and chronic medical conditions.

Money guide

Most divers are paid daily. Earnings can be between £120 and £1,000 a day, depending on the type of diving and work involved.

An inshore or civil engineering diver could earn between £120 and £250 a day, for up to 200 days a year.

An offshore North Sea diver could expect up to £450 a day for 150 days a year.

Divers in the Army or Royal Navy can earn an extra £4.24 per day or up to £1,000 per month on top of their basic salary.

Police divers can earn anything from £12,000 to over £100,000 per year.

Related opportunities

- Marine Engineer p219
- Royal Navy Officer p553
- Sports Coach p372

Further information

Health and Safety Executive
www.hse.gov.uk

International Marine Contractors Association
www.imca-int.com

PADI
www.padi.com/scuba-diving

Underwater Centre
www.theunderwatercentre.com

LEISURE, SPORT AND TOURISM

ENTERTAINMENT MANAGER

Qualifications and courses

There are no formal entry requirements for this career. Experience, enthusiasm and personality are more important than qualifications. Some employers may expect you to have previous experience working in the entertainment industry or a relevant sector such as hospitality, customer service or events management. Foreign language skills are useful for those looking to work abroad, and a good knowledge of contract law may be useful.

Degrees, Foundation degrees and HNDs are not essential but it could be useful to have one in a related subject such as event management, performing arts or business studies. Degree courses usually require at least 2 A levels/3 H grades and 5 GCSEs/National 5s (A*–C/A–C). There are also various NVQs, City & Guilds Awards and other professional qualifications available.

To become a manager in a holiday resort you will need at least 2 years' entertainment or performing experience. Relevant apprenticeships may be available.

If you are working with children or vulnerable adults you will need a Disclosure and Barring Services (DBS) check.

What the work involves

Entertainment managers take responsibility for the schedule of visiting entertainers to a venue, achieving a balance of activities that engage the age, gender and cultural interests of the audience.

You will plan, organise, advertise and oversee the running of a full calendar of social events.

You will contact acts and agents, and negotiate the best possible prices with them. When the events listing is finalised, you will promote the programme on a weekly and daily basis. You will also be responsible for costing out the entertainment.

Type of person suited to this work

Entertainment managers are people who are talkative, outgoing and vivacious. People have to be a central focus, whether it's the needs of artists, stage managers or the audience. They must remain cool under pressure, think on their feet and be flexible without being weak.

You will need excellent interpersonal and communication skills. Confidence speaking in public is essential.

Your organisation depends on you to find reliable acts, possibly at short notice. You have to make quick appraisals to drive home a deal. You need persuasive powers, imagination and considerable personal initiative.

Working conditions

You could be permanently based in a grand hotel or located in a popular resort, on a cruise liner, or with a large company that frequently entertains important clients.

Entertainment managers work in an office during the day and emerge after 6pm to manage the flow of evening entertainment and introduce the artists.

There is seasonal work for entertainment managers in all the major holiday centres. Travel may be required so a driving licence would be useful.

Future prospects

The travel and tourism industry in the UK continues to grow, so the job market for entertainment managers should at least remain steady if it doesn't expand.

A willingness to be geographically mobile could be important if you are looking to progress in this career.

With experience, you could move into other managerial roles within the hospitality industry.

You will have the opportunity to travel both around the UK and overseas. Those employed on a cruise liner may spend extended periods of time away from home.

Advantages/disadvantages

You will meet some interesting and entertaining artists, perhaps developing lifelong relationships with them.

You may have the opportunity to travel, such as on cruise ships or for certain seasons.

You will have to work evenings, weekends and bank holidays.

Pressure can build if an act does not show up so you might occasionally need to fill a gap and prevent the audience from getting irritable.

Money guide

Generally, travel and recreation work is not well paid.

New entertainment managers can expect a starting salary that is in excess of £15,000.

With experience, you may receive £18,000–£20,000 per year.

If you are an entertainment manager for a large international company, pay and prospects could be much higher, with possible earnings of £30,000.

Related opportunities

- Croupier p364
- Holiday Representative p368
- Theme Park Assistant/Manager p375

Further information

NCFE
www.ncfe.org.uk

People 1st
www.people1st.co.uk

Qualifications and courses

No formal academic qualifications are required for this career but an industry-recognised qualification approved by the Register of Exercise Professionals (REPs) can be beneficial. This can be completed prior to becoming an instructor or as part of a work-based training scheme. You need to be aged 16 or over to be an assistant instructor and at least 18 to become a full instructor.

A commonly studied qualification is the Level 2 NVQ Diploma in Instructing Exercise and Fitness available from City & Guilds. During this course you can choose to specialise in gym-based exercise, exercise to music, water-based exercise or physical activity for children. A full list of all REPs-approved courses is available on their website.

An alternative route is to take the Instructing Exercise and Fitness Apprenticeship which is available at both Intermediate and Advanced Level.

Before you can work as an instructor, you will also need to hold public liability insurance, a first aid certificate and, if you intend to work with children or vulnerable adults, undergo a Disclosure and Barring Service (DBS) check. Applicants will, of course, need to be physically fit.

Personal trainers are normally experienced fitness instructors who then take a Level 3 Award in Conversion of Advanced Fitness Instructor to Personal Trainer Status. This changes your membership status on REPs to Personal Trainer.

Further courses are available, in yoga or zumba for example, which may help further your career.

What the work involves

Fitness instructors/personal trainers teach people how to exercise in a safe and effective manner, whilst also helping them work towards personal fitness targets.

You could provide a one-on-one service to your clients, direct and choreograph group fitness activities and classes, or undertake a mixture of the two. You could work in a health club, community gym, leisure centre or private gym.

Other duties may include writing individual training programmes for clients, showing them exercise techniques and how to use equipment, and offering advice on nutrition and other lifestyle-related issues.

Type of person suited to this work

You will need excellent interpersonal skills so that you can attract new business opportunities, chat to clients and advise them on fitness and dietary requirements, and build good relationships with other team members.

You must be very enthusiastic about training and fitness in order to motivate your clients, be sensitive to their needs and, sometimes, persuade them to persevere with exercise.

You should look smart and fit yourself to promote a good image to existing and potential clients.

You must be innovative in your approach to keeping fit, thinking up new routines for classes or creating diversity in one-on-one clients' training programmes so people remain enthused and interested in their activities.

Working conditions

Fitness instructors work longer than average hours – between 38 and 40 hours per week – and these often include early mornings, evenings and weekends to suit the needs of their clients.

Most instructors work on a part-time basis and are affiliated to one or a number of gyms in their local area.

Future prospects

As society has become increasingly aware of health and fitness issues, the demand for fitness instructors has grown. This trend is set to continue for the foreseeable future so employment prospects are good.

In certain areas and in popular high street gyms, competition for jobs can be tough.

With experience, you could move into roles such as fitness manager or sports facility manager. Alternatively, you could build your own fitness consultancy.

Advantages/disadvantages

You will play an active role in enhancing many people's lives by introducing them to exercise and ensuring they continue with it.

You will see tangible results of your efforts and guidance as people become fitter and slimmer during the course of your work with them.

You will have to work unsocial hours.

Money guide

Earnings usually depend on your reputation, client base and location.

Fitness instructors usually have a starting salary of around £13,000. With experience, earnings can increase up to £20,000 and freelance instructors may charge an hourly rate of £10–£20.

Personal trainers in full-time employment can receive a salary ranging from £12,000 up to £20,000. Self-employed personal trainers are likely to earn £20–£40 an hour and those working with high profile clients can achieve an hourly rate of £50–£100.

Related opportunities

- Leisure Centre Assistant/Manager p369
- Outdoor Pursuits Instructor p371
- Sports Coach p372

Further information

Register of Exercise Professionals
www.exerciseregister.org

LEISURE, SPORT AND TOURISM

HOLIDAY REPRESENTATIVE

Qualifications and courses

You will normally need to be aged 20 or over to be a holiday representative, although some children's representatives may be accepted at 18 or 19. Academic qualifications are not essential as most employers place higher value on customer service experience; however, GCSEs/National 5s (A*–C/A–C) in subjects such as English, Maths and Geography can be useful. Competency in a foreign language, such as Spanish, French, Italian, Portuguese, Greek or Turkish would be particularly beneficial if you wished to work in these countries.

A degree is not required but may still be useful. Relevant subjects include leisure and tourism, modern languages and international tourism management. Entry to a degree usually requires a minimum of 2 A levels/3 H grades and 5 GCSEs/National 5s (A*–C/A–C).

Other relevant qualifications include the online Holiday Rep Ticket Diploma, an NVQ in Travel and Tourism Services (Levels 2–3) from City & Guilds and the NCFE Level 2 Award for Resort Representatives.

Training is usually provided on the job, both in the UK and at the holiday resort. In some roles you might need specialist knowledge in an area such as archaeology, scuba diving or history.

To work with children, you will need 6–12 months of practical experience, a childcare qualification such as a Level 2 Certificate for Children and Young People's Workforce, and clearance from the Disclosure and Barring Service (DBS).

What the work involves

Holiday representatives have many duties including meeting holidaymakers at airports and other terminals, helping them to locate their luggage and directing them towards the transport that will take them to their accommodation. You will be responsible for checking all the details of each passenger's transport and accommodation to ensure that everything is in place for their stay.

You will inform customers of important information, including local bus routes, recommended restaurants and sites of interest. You will also sell excursion tickets. You may be expected to accompany tourists on expeditions and provide them with holiday entertainment.

You may be required to specialise in certain activities, such as running the kids' club or a particular sport.

You will usually be based in certain places or countries, but travel will be part of the job.

Type of person suited to this work

You will need to look smart and have a pleasant, approachable attitude so that holidaymakers are comfortable speaking to you. You will need to be sociable and very patient as you will deal with guests 24 hours a day for the duration of the holiday season.

You should have a methodical approach to your work and excellent organisational skills as you will be coordinating details for numerous people at one time.

Fluency in the language of the country in which you are working is also an asset.

Working conditions

Working hours vary from day to day but are usually long and unpredictable. Most representatives only have one day off a week and even then they will be on-call in case of an emergency.

The work is seasonal, although there are opportunities all year round with beach holidays in the summer months and ski work during winter. You could work indoors or outdoors. You will usually have to wear a uniform.

Future prospects

You could work for a large international travel company or a smaller, more specialist firm. Many opportunities are overseas, though they do exist in the UK also.

With experience, you could move into a supervisory or managerial position. Some representatives also branch out into another area of travel and tourism, such as hotel management or working on a tourist board.

Advantages/disadvantages

You will have plenty of opportunities to work abroad in a number of diverse and exciting areas.

You will deal with a range of people from all ages and backgrounds on a daily basis, making the work diverse and challenging.

You will have to work long hours which can make the job both physically and mentally exhausting.

Money guide

Holiday representatives often work by season, with a first season's pay starting at around £450 to £525 a month plus accommodation. This gives a starting salary of £5,400 to £6,300 a year. An experienced representative working both the summer and winter season could earn £7,200 to £9,600 a year.

Salaries can be boosted by commissions from selling services and company benefits such as free flights and meal allowances.

Salaries and commission structures improve as you progress to more senior roles, such as team leader or resort manager. Benefits packages vary but can include company cars, discounts for bars and restaurants, free or discounted excursions and more.

Related opportunities

- Air Cabin Crew p582
- Tour Guide/Manager p376
- Travel Agent p379

Further information

Career in Travel
www.careerintravel.co.uk

Qualifications and courses

Assistant

Although there are no formal entry requirements, some employers prefer applicants with GCSEs/National 5s (A*–C/A–C) in Maths, English and a science and an A level/H grade or a BTEC National qualification in sport or leisure. Previous experience working in customer service is also helpful and a Disclosure and Barring Service (DBS) check is required.

Specialist qualifications may be needed to work in certain areas, such as lifeguard qualifications for swimming pool attendants.

Training is often given on the job, although many courses are offered by the Chartered Institute for the Management of Sport and Physical Activity (CIMSPA). A First Aid certificate would be useful.

Manager

There are a few routes to becoming a manager. One is to study for a relevant degree, HND or Foundation degree and enter onto a graduate trainee scheme where you will gain the necessary experience. If you have pre-entry experience you may be able to apply for the role directly or work your way up from a lower position by studying for professional qualifications.

Relevant degree subjects include sports science, physiology and sport, leisure or recreation management. The general entry requirements for a degree are 2 A levels/3 H grades and 5 GCSEs/National 5s (A*–C/A–C).

Professional qualifications should be recognised by the Register of Exercise Professionals (REPs) and can be in areas such as fitness instruction, pool operation or sports coaching. A First Aid certificate and a DBS check are usually required.

What the work involves

Assistant

You will help run sports activities, set up equipment and demonstrate its safe use to leisure centre users.

You will also work on the reception desk issuing tickets, taking bookings, answering enquiries and performing other tasks specified by your manager.

It is important to maintain, set up and tidy equipment, and to monitor all activity to make sure everything is running smoothly.

Manager

You will oversee the day-to-day work and recruitment of all leisure centre staff, and deal with queries.

You will meet with company or council reps to discuss budgets, funding sources, marketing issues, and new developments.

You will ultimately be responsible for the health and safety of those working in and using the leisure centre. Organising external activities, ensuring the enjoyment of your customers, and overseeing the schedule will all come under your remit.

Type of person suited to this work

You will need to be friendly and helpful with excellent interpersonal skills.

A role as manager will require proven leadership skills. As you will be working within or leading a team you must be able to communicate well.

Assistants should be fit and pro-active with customers.

Working conditions

Most of your time will be spent indoors – at the poolside, in a sports hall, at reception or in the office.

You should expect to work unsocial hours; early starts and late finishes.

Future prospects

Careers in leisure and fitness centres are popular, so demand is likely to, at the very least, be steady.

You could progress from a role as an assistant to supervisor and then become a manager. After gaining more experience, you could go on to become an area or regional manager.

There are greater opportunities for promotion in large organisations.

Advantages/disadvantages

Most leisure centres have a relaxed working atmosphere.

It is possible to work a variety of shifts and hours can be flexible.

Earnings can be low unless you start on the trainee management route.

Money guide

Starting salaries for leisure centre assistants are around £12,500 per year, rising to £19,000 with qualifications and experience. This can be boosted by overtime and bonuses related to membership as well as weekend and shift work.

The starting salary for managers is between £15,000 and £25,000 a year. Managers at senior levels with 10–15 years' experience can earn around £35,000 with a few reaching £40,000.

Salaries could be higher with professional qualifications. Bonuses can include use of leisure centre facilities outside working hours and target-related bonuses.

Related opportunities

- Fitness Instructor/Personal Trainer p367
- Lifeguard p370
- Outdoor Pursuits Instructor p371

Further information

Chartered Institute for the Management of Sport and Physical Activity
www.cimspa.co.uk

LEISURE, SPORT AND TOURISM

Qualifications and courses

Pool lifeguard

You must be over 16, physically fit and a strong swimmer to qualify to become a poolside lifeguard. There are no specific academic entry requirements but a good standard of English and maths is preferred and a qualification in physical education (PE) or fitness would be a bonus.

Lifeguards must be in possession of either a National Pool Lifeguard Qualification (NPLQ) from the Royal Life Saving Society UK or a NaRS Pool Rescue Qualification from the Swimming Teachers Association (STA). You could take a job as a pool attendant or assistant and study for the qualifications part time.

The NPLQ training covers 3 assessed units: The Lifeguard and the Law, Intervention and Rescue and Emergency Action Plans, and Cardiopulmonary Resuscitation, AED and First Aid. This training can only take place in a centre approved by the Institute of Qualified Lifeguards.

Both the NPLQ and NaRS qualifications are valid for 24 months. After this you must have your lifesaving and First Aid skills assessed before your qualification is renewed.

Beach/ocean lifeguard

You must be over 16, physically fit and a strong swimmer to qualify to become a beach lifeguard.

Beach lifeguards must be in possession of either the recently launched National Vocational Beach Lifeguard Qualification (NVBLQ) from the Royal Life Saving Society UK or the Surf Life Saving GB (SLSGB) Beach Lifeguard Award. These courses cover practical ocean rescue skills involving the use of boards and tubes. Training is also provided by the Royal National Lifeboat Institution.

All lifeguards need to hold a valid First Aid Worker Certificate. Lifeguard qualifications must be renewed every 2 years.

What the work involves

Lifeguards are responsible for patrolling and monitoring the water and weather conditions where people are swimming, surfing or boating. You will keep watch on public swimming pools or stretches of shoreline to reduce the risk of tragic accidents occurring and take rapid action to alert the public to danger.

Your role could involve rescuing people at risk from drowning, assisting them ashore and administering First Aid including mouth-to-mouth or CPR (cardiopulmonary resuscitation).

You will also be involved in informing the public about water safety.

Type of person suited to this work

You must be fit and active, with a full understanding of the level of danger in all water activities.

You should be a strong swimmer (able to cover 400 metres of a pool in less than 8 minutes) and have good vision and hearing. The ability to work within a team is also essential. It's important to be observant and be able to respond quickly.

You must be assertive in order to take command and manage dangerous incidents and be able to stay calm in emergencies.

Working conditions

You will work either on the beach or poolside and work could be offered on a seasonal basis or full time. Either way, you will need to cover early morning and later shifts as part of your hours in order to provide a full emergency service to water users.

You must keep alert and vigilant at all times as when emergency strikes, you have to be ready to act in seconds – not minutes.

Future prospects

Interest in water sports has grown, although the demand for lifeguards has always been fairly consistent.

You could progress into a managerial role such as a pool supervisor, duty manager or general pool manager.

You could also qualify as a swimming teacher to boost your income.

Advantages/disadvantages

Pools and beaches have a relaxed, upbeat atmosphere.

There can be periods of boredom that you have to work through, maintaining vigilance. Accidents can happen at any time.

If working outdoors you could be in danger of overexposure to sunlight.

Money guide

Starting salaries for full-time lifeguards are around £12,500 per year. With experience, pay can rise to £18,000 or over.

Supervisory responsibilities can increase pay to £29,000 a year.

Many lifeguards work for local authorities on a part-time basis and rates of pay can vary from National Minimum Wage (£5.30 for 18–20 year olds and £6.70 for 21–24 year olds) to £10 per hour.

Pay can be increased by overtime and taking on extra responsibilities such as coaching duties.

Related opportunities

- Fitness Instructor/Personal Trainer p367
- Outdoor Pursuits Instructor p371
- Sports Coach p372

Further information

Royal Life Saving Society UK
www.rlss.org.uk

Surf Life Saving Great Britain
www.slsgb.org.uk

Swimming Teachers Association
www.sta.co.uk

Water Skills Academy
www.waterskillsacademy.com

Qualifications and courses

No formal academic qualifications are required to work as an outdoor pursuits instructor and requirements will vary depending on the role and the employer. You will however need a coaching or proficiency qualification in at least one activity. The more activities you can offer the better.

These qualifications should be recognised by the relevant national governing body for that activity. Examples include the Sports Leaders UK Basic Expedition Leadership Award (BEL), British Canoe Union Level 1 Coach Award and the Mountain Leader Training UK Single Pitch Award. You would usually need 12 months' experience in the activity before you can take the courses. There are also full-time college courses and degrees available that provide relevant qualifications.

A First Aid certificate is required, as is a Life-Saving certificate if your activities are water-based.

Candidates are also expected to be able to demonstrate a history of leading and taking responsibility for others. This could be through volunteering at outdoor activities centres, involvement in activities such as the Duke of Edinburgh's Award or membership of activity clubs. Experience of youth work, teaching or coaching can also be useful.

You will need to be 18 years old before you can work as an instructor (21 if you will be driving a minibus). If you will be working with children or vulnerable adults you will need to undergo a Disclosure and Barring Service (DBS) check.

What the work involves

Outdoor pursuits instructors lead groups of people through a range of challenging activities, designed to help them bond, have fun, learn more about themselves and develop new skills.

You will work with people of all ages and backgrounds, including those with disabilities, children with special needs, adult recreation groups, and business professionals. You will be responsible for guiding these groups though a range of activities.

You will also be responsible for checking safety equipment, ensuring that group members are comfortable with each activity, and giving practical demonstrations.

Type of person suited to this work

You should have strong leadership skills as you will be required to persuade a group of people who have never met you before to undertake activities that are frightening and push them out of their comfort zone.

You must have an excellent level of physical fitness, alongside good eyesight and hearing.

You must be responsible and maintain continual awareness of the safety of both yourself and those around you. You should have good communication skills and a personable manner to explain activities clearly.

Working conditions

Hours are generally long and irregular, usually falling over evenings and weekends, including bank holidays. Much of the work is seasonal. Part-time hours are commonly available.

Many outdoor pursuits centres are located in the countryside, so a driving licence may be useful in order to travel to and from work with ease. Holding a licence for a passenger carrying vehicle (PCV) may also be helpful.

You should expect to be working outdoors in all weather conditions. Long treks may also involve spending evenings away from the centre, camping in a tent.

Future prospects

Although the outdoor leisure industry is growing, there is still a lot of competition for jobs.

Most opportunities are in independently run activity centres, or those owned by local authorities and charities. There are also jobs available with expedition companies who organise overseas excursions.

Many instructors specialise in a particular discipline, such as canoeing or abseiling, and work freelance across several activity centres.

Advantages/disadvantages

You will be helping people to break down boundaries and overcome fear, which will increase their self-reliance and self-confidence.

You will be working with a wide range of people, from all backgrounds and ages, which will give great diversity to your working day.

You will have to work unsociable hours.

Money guide

As an outdoor activities instructor, you could expect to earn around £12,000 as a starting salary.

As your experience grows, this could increase to around £18,000.

Once you have reached the level of a more senior instructor, perhaps also developing specialist skills, you could earn up to £25,000.

Food and accommodation are sometimes provided.

Related opportunities

- Holiday Representative p368
- Sports Coach p372
- Sports Development Officer p373

Further information

British Activity Providers Association
www.thebapa.org.uk

Institute for Outdoor Learning
www.outdoor-learning.org

LEISURE, SPORT AND TOURISM

Qualifications and courses

All sports coaches must hold a qualification that has been accredited by the National Governing Body (NGB) of their chosen discipline. You can start working towards recognised qualifications at the age of 16, but must be 18 or over to work as an independent coach.

Accredited courses are available directly from the NGB, or you can undertake a college or university course. NGB qualifications are equivalent to studying for NVQs from Level 1 to 4, and no academic qualifications are required (except for the golfing qualification which requires 4 GCSEs/National 5s (A*–C/A–C)), although sometimes a First Aid certificate is essential and you will need a Disclosure and Barring Service (DBS) check to work with children. NGB qualifications are usually studied on a part-time basis.

Relevant courses at college include BTEC HNC/HNDs in sports coaching or leisure studies and Foundation degrees in sports coaching are available. Typical entry requirements for these courses include 1 A level/H grade and 4 GCSEs/National 5s (A*–C/A–C). Degrees in sports science, sports coaching, health science, and sports management may improve employment prospects and degree courses usually require 2 A levels/3 H grades and 5 GCSEs/National 5s (A*–C/A–C), including English and Maths, for entry.

You could start out as an assistant coach on a voluntary basis, then take a Level 1 qualification to progress to higher levels. Coaching is also often a second career for ex-professional sportspeople.

What the work involves

Sports coaches provide specialist support, motivation and knowledge to athletes in order to help them attain their best performances and achieve personal goals.

As a competitive coach, you could work with a variety of levels of athlete, ranging from children's football or netball teams, through to professional and even world class sports professionals.

At a non-competitive level, you will focus on providing fun and accessible exercise sessions for participants with a range of abilities and fitness levels.

You will usually coach one specific sport.

Type of person suited to this work

You will need excellent communications skills. You will also need to have good motivational abilities in order to inspire and encourage sports players to push themselves.

You will need an in-depth knowledge of your chosen sport, and an understanding of nutrition and physiology is also useful.

It is also essential that you understand a variety of training methods and principles so that you can provide an informed and beneficial service to your clients. Patience and determination are also vital qualities.

Working conditions

You will usually work early mornings, evenings and weekends. This is when the majority of your athletes will be available.

If you are working in a seasonal sport such as cricket or football, you might have to supplement your income with another job during the quiet months.

You will spend hours on your feet, and might also have to undertake activity in order to demonstrate methods and principles to athletes.

Future prospects

The vast majority of sports coaches working in the UK work on a voluntary or part-time basis. Competition for full-time positions is fierce.

Career prospects will depend on the level of success you achieve in your work. If you gain credibility, you could move into a related development or management position.

You could be self-employed, work for a local authority, or in a school, gym or professional sports club.

Advantages/disadvantages

You will be teaching the sport you love to a range of people and developing their interest in it.

You may have the opportunity to work with talented athletes.

You will have to spend long periods of time standing outside in all weather conditions.

Money guide

As a newly qualified coach working for an employer, you could earn between £15,000 and £25,000, depending on experience and employer.

Experienced coaches who work for a NGB or professional association can earn between £30,000 and £35,000.

If you work at the highest level of your sport, such as coaching Premiership football players, you could earn in excess of £100,000.

Coaches working with amateur teams or individuals usually earn around £10 per hour.

Related opportunities

- Fitness Instructor/Personal Trainer p367
- Outdoor Pursuits Instructor p371
- Sports Professional p374

Further information

SkillsActive
www.skillsactive.com

Sports Coach UK
www.sportscoachuk.org

Qualifications and courses

Although there are currently no specific academic requirements, new entrants to the profession are usually graduates.

Relevant first degree subjects include sports science/ studies, physical education, recreation/leisure management, and health and exercise sciences. Most universities require candidates to have 2 A levels/3 H grades, one in a related subject such as Biology, and 5 GCSEs/National 5s (A*–C/A–C), including English, Maths and a science. Some employers will also accept entrants with relevant BTEC or HNC/HND qualifications in sport, sports science, sports development or another related subject.

Entry without a degree is still possible if you have coaching qualifications and start out as a sports development assistant. Pre-entry work experience is always essential with or without a degree. Many employers will require 2 years' experience in sports development, for example at a leisure centre, a holiday camp or summer school. Coaching experience is also desirable.

A Disclosure and Barring Service (DBS) check is usually required.

What the work involves

Sports development officers are responsible for ensuring that sports and related activities are available to people of all ages and abilities. You will be promoting the benefits of exercise and encouraging people to live a healthy lifestyle by devising simple but effective strategies that increase participation in sport.

You will work within the local community, liaising with schools, gyms and social clubs, and also have involvement with larger agencies such as sports national governing bodies (NGBs).

You may work closely with groups who are usually excluded from sports-related activity, such as disadvantaged youths, prisoners and disabled people.

Type of person suited to this work

You will need a positive attitude and a clear commitment to sport that will help you to persuade local community members and service providers to back your initiatives.

You will need excellent verbal and written communication skills in order to illustrate your objectives to other professionals. This includes strong persuasive and negotiating skills.

Good IT and administrative ability will be essential for creating reports, producing material to support your ideas, and keeping accurate records.

Working conditions

You will usually work a 36-hour week within normal office hours. Flexible hours and overtime are often available.

It is not unusual to have to work additional hours during evenings and weekends, attending meetings or networking events.

You will work in an office environment, and also spend time at local schools, clubs and community venues. Since a good deal of travelling is required each day, a driving licence can be helpful.

Future prospects

You will most likely be working for a local authority, county sports partnership, or NGB. A few opportunities are available in specialist sports colleges.

Career progression for sport-specific development officers is fairly limited; you could be promoted to the role of sports development manager, or become more involved with other community initiatives. The Institute for the Management of Sports and Physical Activity (IMSPA) offers a number of different courses aimed at continuing professional development (CPD) and similar courses are available through Sports Coach UK.

Advantages/disadvantages

You will play an active role in enhancing many people's quality of life by providing them with access to sport in their local area.

You will be liaising with a variety of people on a daily basis, which should make the work dynamic and interesting.

You will need a resilient approach to your work, as suggestions and plans will often be knocked back or fall through.

Money guide

The starting salary for an assistant sports development officer is £18,000 to £23,000.

Sports development officers have a starting salary of between £18,000 and £30,000 per year, which can rise to around £35,000 with experience.

If you reach a management position, you could potentially earn up to £40,000.

Related opportunities

- Fitness Instructor/Personal Trainer p367
- Outdoor Pursuits Instructor p371
- Sports Coach p372

Further information

Chartered Institute for the Management of Sport and Physical Activity
www.cimspa.co.uk

Sports Coach UK
www.sportscoachuk.org

Sports Leaders UK
www.sportsleaders.org

LEISURE, SPORT AND TOURISM

Qualifications and courses

You do not need any academic qualifications for most sports as ability, dedication and determination to succeed within your chosen sport are the key requirements to become a sports professional. Joining a club or amateur organisation would be beneficial in terms of receiving instruction and training. Some sports have specific entry requirements, such as height and weight restrictions for boxing and horse racing.

Talented athletes aged 16–19 could apply for the Advanced Apprenticeship in Sporting Excellence (AASE). This structured training and development programme is for young people who show the potential to reach Olympic/Paralympic level or to gain a professional contract. Depending on which of the two pathways you choose, this could lead to either an NVQ Level 3 Diploma after 18–24 months, or a Level 3 Certificate after 12–20 months. The Diploma can be used to move on to other Level 3 qualifications.

Across the UK, there are opportunities to gain additional help and support if you are a promising young athlete. In England, for example, the Talented Athlete Scholarship Scheme (TASS) awards funding of up to £3,500 for sports training to those over the age of 16. Details of national governing bodies (NGBs) are available from the Sport England website.

What the work involves

Sportsplayers are paid professionals who compete across the globe in their chosen sport, often in front of an audience. You could compete individually in sports such as boxing, swimming, golf and athletics, or alternatively with a team in sports like football, hockey, cricket and rugby.

You will need to spend a great deal of time training in order to maintain a high standard of general fitness, alongside honing your skills in your chosen sport.

You may also be required to attend social events, give interviews and promote the companies that provide you with sponsorship.

Type of person suited to this work

First and foremost, you will need to have an outstanding natural ability in your chosen sport. You must also have the necessary commitment and self-discipline to maintain a continuous training schedule and strict healthy diet.

You will need to have a highly competitive nature but also a polite and pleasant manner in order to get on with team members, fellow players and coaches.

As well as being physically fit, you must be mentally stable so that you can cope with the pressure of competition, defeat and disappointment.

Working conditions

Competitions and matches usually fall on weekends, although qualifying rounds may take place during the week.

You will usually need to travel to reach competitions, which may involve overnights away from home. If you are competing at an international level, you could be away for weeks at a time.

You will need to train most days and if you are supplementing your professional sports income with a regular job, this will mean exercising either early in the morning or in the evening.

Future prospects

Most professional sportsplayers are spotted at an early age by a talent scout or coach. From this point, they build up skills and a reputation through competitions.

Unfortunately, the majority of professionals cannot earn a living playing their chosen sport alone, so you might have to supplement your income with full- or part-time work.

Sports professionals rarely continue to compete once they have reached their mid-30s but there are plenty of opportunities to work as a coach or manager, commentator, or even earn money as a TV personality.

Advantages/disadvantages

Pursuing your dream as a professional sportsplayer is much more exciting than a conventional job.

The hard work and dedication you put in should be repaid in the form of sporting achievements and acclaim.

The profession is unpredictable and is an unstable job to pursue as a bad injury or a bad game has the potential to ruin your career.

Money guide

If you start your professional career as an apprentice, you may earn less than £10,000.

Once you are established as a professional, competing in and winning competitions regularly, you should earn £20,000 or above.

Highly successful sports professionals working in well-supported sports, such as tennis and football, can earn anything up to £3,000,000 a year.

Successful sports professionals may make extra money by advertising products or through sponsorship.

Related opportunities

- Fitness Instructor/Personal Trainer p367
- Outdoor Pursuits Instructor p371
- Sports Coach p372

Further information

SkillsActive
www.skillsactive.com

Talented Athlete Scholarship Scheme
www.tass.gov.uk

Qualifications and courses

You have to be at least 18 years old to start work in a theme park, though it may be possible for entrants to begin at the age of 16 if working on children's rides. No formal academic qualifications are required to be an assistant but if you intend to become a supervisor or manager then it would be beneficial to have some GCSEs/National 5s in Maths, English, IT and possibly Design Technology. A degree in business, management or leisure/travel/tourism management may also increase your chances.

Once you are employed you will receive on-the-job training from more experienced staff, in areas such as customer care and health and safety.

NVQs/SVQs and other qualifications in customer care, catering and sales could be relevant, along with qualifications in leisure & tourism.

With experience as a theme park assistant, you could progress to a role as a team leader or manager, possibly by taking relevant qualifications. You could start out as a manager if you have previous customer service and management experience.

If the theme park you work for is registered with the British Association of Leisure Parks, Piers and Attractions (BALPPA) then you may be able to attend specialist training schemes and seminars.

What the work involves

As a theme park assistant you will greet customers, check ticket holders' ages and heights, and operate and supervise rides. You may also sell merchandise.

You must always observe safety rules and ensure that there are no hazards. Assistants are also required to carry out repairs and maintenance on machines each morning and evening.

If you are a manager you will need to oversee all the different operations within a theme park, ensuring the smooth running of the amusements and catering facilities. You will be responsible for the maintenance, cleaning and surveillance of the park.

You will also be involved with recruiting and training staff, managing the budget of the park and handling any problems that arise.

The manager must inspect the whole site before opening time, taking responsibility for checking that all the necessary safety checks have been done and that the rides and other facilities are fully staffed.

Type of person suited to this work

Theme park workers should be comfortable talking to the public and keen to ensure that they have an exciting and memorable time.

You must be trustworthy and dependable, with good practical and mechanical skills, and the ability to follow instructions carefully. Awareness of health and safety practices is essential.

Working conditions

Theme parks are open 7 days a week and on bank holidays. You are likely to work shifts and have one full day off each week. This work may be seasonal and could involve travelling to different locations.

As a theme park assistant, you will work outdoors in a variety of weather conditions. Managers will spend some of their time in an office environment.

Assistants may be required to wear a uniform and managers should dress smartly.

Future prospects

There is always a high turnover of staff in theme parks but a core group of workers stay on, benefiting from training and increased responsibility which allows them to gain certificates as evidence of their skills.

There is more work in Europe for trained, experienced theme park workers so learning to speak a foreign language may improve future prospects.

Advantages/disadvantages

This is a specialised line of entertainment and leisure work so it may be difficult to progress to roles in other sectors.

You have the opportunity to work anywhere in the world such as Legoland Denmark or Disneyland USA.

Money guide

Theme park assistants can expect a starting salary in line with the national minimum wage.

For operations managers, typical starting salaries are around £17,000 to £22,000. After about 10 years this could increase to between £22,000 and £40,000.

Salaries tend to be higher at large, corporate-owned parks. Benefits may include pension, health insurance and free or discounted park tickets.

Related opportunities

- Customer Services Assistant/Manager p468
- Entertainment Manager p366
- Leisure Centre Assistant/Manager p369

Further information

British Association of Leisure Parks, Piers and Attractions
www.balppa.org

Equity
www.equity.org.uk

Qualifications and courses

Most tour guides and managers are aged 18 or over. Although no formal academic qualifications are required, you will need a good standard of general education. Some GCSEs/National 5s (A*–C/A–C) might be useful, particularly in subjects such as English, Maths and languages. A levels/H grades and degrees, while they may also be useful, are not essential.

Fluency in another language is important if you intend to work abroad or work with foreign tourists in the UK. Competition is strong, so experience of dealing with the public and presentations are an advantage. Tour guiding is often a second career for people from other backgrounds.

A professional qualification may be useful as a way of enhancing your employability. The Institute of Tourist Guiding runs courses for tour guides at Levels 2, 3 and 4. You do not need any prior tour guiding experience or academic qualifications to enrol on these courses as entry will be based on interview and a location knowledge test. Some employers, such as Westminster Abbey, require a Level 4 Blue Badge qualification.

Once hired as a tour guide there are other professional qualifications you can work towards, which include NVQ in Travel and Tourism (Levels 2–3).

Professional courses for tour managers include full-time HND and degree courses in travel and tourism management, City & Guilds HLQ Level 3 in Travel and Tourism, and a range of related Northern Advisory Council for Further Education (NACFE) certificates.

What the work involves

Tour guides are responsible for meeting and greeting parties of people who are taking a holiday, cultural visit or tour together. You will accompany the sightseers on their journey and inform them of the historical/environmental/cultural interests of the area they are visiting. You will also assist them if they encounter problems or difficulties.

Tour managers are responsible for putting together proposals for day trips and excursions in order to attract holidaymakers to the company.

You will visit destinations to assess their potential as a tour venue, and may also assist tour guides with the delivery of the trip itself.

Type of person suited to this work

Tour guides and managers need excellent communication skills and an infectious enthusiasm and interest for areas or venues you work in. You will need good stamina in order to keep up a high level of energy and interest throughout tours.

You will need to have excellent customer relations skills in order to soothe any disgruntled holiday-makers and reach amicable solutions to problems.

Tour managers should also be methodical in order to put together logistically plausible, suitably detailed plans for excursions.

Working conditions

You may work long hours, and when out on a tour you will be on call for customers 24 hours a day should they need anything.

You could work for a large international company, or a small independent tour provider, but either way your focus will be on promoting the company image and following their tour policies carefully.

You will be expected to wear a uniform when on duty, which usually includes a shirt and tie.

Future prospects

VisitBritain's GREAT campaign, launched after a record-breaking year for UK tourism in 2013, has seen huge levels of investment in the domestic tourism industry. As a result, prospects for tour guides, although competitive, should be good.

You could work in a large international company that runs tours throughout the UK and overseas, or a smaller provider that focuses on specific tourist areas in the UK such as Bath or London.

Competition for work as a tour manager is tough, but if you have built up good skills and knowledge as a tour guide first, you will be in a good position for promotion.

The skills gained also enable experienced tour guides to transfer to other sectors of the industry.

Advantages/disadvantages

You will be dealing with a variety of people of all ages and backgrounds on a daily basis, educating them about areas in which you have an interest.

It can get monotonous as you will be repeating the same information over and over again for weeks, months and even years.

Money guide

Tour guides can expect to start on around £11,900. With experience this could rise to up to £25,000 for those with specialist knowledge. Many tour guides are self-employed.

Tour managers are on short-term contracts, mostly in the summer, and have other jobs the rest of the year. There are some full-time positions available however, particularly in mainland Europe and Asia.

Salaries generally start at around £15,000 to £20,000. At senior level this can rise to over £30,000.

Related opportunities

- Holiday Representative p368
- Tourist Information Centre Assistant p378
- Travel Agent p379

Further information

Institute of Travel and Tourism
www.itt.co.uk

International Association of Tour Managers Limited
www.iatm.co.uk

VisitBritain
www.visitbritain.org

TOURISM OFFICER

Qualifications and courses

New entrants to this profession will typically hold an Honours degree. Relevant subjects include tourism management, hospitality management, public relations, business studies, and marketing. Entrants may also be sourced from a far wider range of academic backgrounds such as modern languages, journalism and media studies. Entry onto a degree course is usually with 2 A levels/3 H grades and 5 GCSEs/National 5s (A*–C/A–C) and courses typically take 3-4 years to complete.

Postgraduate study is not a requirement for entry, but may be valuable if your first degree is in an unrelated subject. Relevant subjects at postgraduate level include master's degrees in tourism, tourism management, or marketing. Entry onto a master's degree is usually with a 2.1 (or higher) Honours degree.

Relevant work experience will set you at a considerable advantage and will demonstrate a good level of commitment to the industry when looking to gain employment. Paid and voluntary placements can be available on a part-time or seasonal basis. Undertaking clerical or administration work at a tourist attraction or volunteering at cultural and heritage or recreational events will give you a great understanding of the sector.

What the work involves

Tourism officers work to stimulate economic growth in an area by developing visitor facilities and promoting tourism in the region. You may work for local governments, or more commonly for public or private tourism and management firms.

Your work is varied and could consist of developing and enhancing existing tourist attractions and venues and promoting them through marketing and advertising campaigns; researching local cultural and historical interest in order to plan new visitor facilities; assessing the social and economic impact of planned developments; and encouraging growth in the tourism job market through expansion and development.

Type of person suited to this work

A keen and demonstrable interest in the tourism industry is essential. You must care about creating great tourist services and facilities for families and individuals of all ages.

You will need excellent interpersonal skills, and the ability to liaise with community groups, developers and tourism industry stakeholders effectively.

Strong leadership and project planning skills are a must; as is the ability to manage both large- and small-scale tourist developments.

Working conditions

You will work a typical Monday to Friday week, 9am to 5pm. However extra or irregular hours may be expected in the run-up to attraction openings or in the planning of large-scale developments.

Work is mostly office based, but may involve regular travel to visit tourist sites or to meet with facility developers and event planners.

Future prospects

In terms of employment, tourism has been the fastest growing sector in the UK in recent years. It is expected to continue to grow quickly over the next 10 years.

There is scope for career development, and opportunities to progress into more senior or management roles do exist.

You may need to be geographically mobile and willing to relocate in order to take advantage of vacancies that need filling.

There is potential to move into other, similar areas of work such as area regeneration and economic development.

With enough experience you could look for work with private consultancy firms, or even work on a self-employed consultancy basis.

Opportunities for travel or work overseas may be available.

Advantages/disadvantages

There is great job satisfaction in knowing that you will play an active role in creating jobs and promoting economic development through the tourism industry.

You will regularly be meeting with lots of different people, providing a varied and interesting working environment.

Time spent away from home, possibly overseas, may be a requirement; this may be an attractive prospect to some or be off-putting to others.

Money guide

Salaries vary depending on employer and the location you are working in with top tourist destinations likely to offer the best rates of pay.

Entrants can expect salaries of between £15,000 and £19,000 per year.

With several years' experience, salaries can increase to up to £28,000 per year.

After five years, salaries for those in senior or managerial roles can reach up to £40,000 per year.

Related opportunities

- Community Education Officer p180
- Holiday Representative p368
- Theme Park Assistant/Manager p375
- Tour Guide/Manager p376

Further information

Institute of Travel and Tourism
www.itt.co.uk

Tourism Management Institute
www.tmi.org.uk

VisitBritain
www.visitbritain.org

VisitEngland
www.visitengland.com

VisitScotland
www.visitscotland.com

VisitWales
www.visitwales.com

LEISURE, SPORT AND TOURISM

Qualifications and courses

No formal academic qualifications are required for this career, although employers prefer a good standard of general education. GCSEs/National 5s (A*–C/A–C) might be an advantage, although personal qualities are usually more important. Acute listening and clear speaking skills are essential and it is very helpful if assistants can use IT to research information and respond to enquiries sent via the internet.

A number of tourist information centres (TICs) are close to international airports or in popular destinations for overseas visitors. Modern foreign language skills are valuable in order to help newly arrived tourists, business travellers and foreign visitors and a knowledge of British Sign Language would also be an advantage.

Though not essential, having relevant qualifications can enhance your employment prospects. A levels/H grades, BTECs, City & Guilds Diplomas and NVQs are all available in Travel and Tourism. Previous experience handling cash or working with the public is desirable.

Working as an assistant, most training will be on the job, although you can be assessed for NVQs/SVQs in Tourist Information and Customer Service. Many employees within tourist information centres work towards these awards.

Part-time HLQ Level 4, BTEC or SQA HNC qualifications in Leisure and Tourism might be useful for career progression to become a tourist information centre manager. However, it is possible to move into supervisory and managerial positions with extensive experience alone.

What the work involves

You will be answering questions in person, over the phone or via the internet from UK and foreign tourists, business people, local young people and researchers.

You will provide information, make bookings and reservations, locate accommodation, restaurants or sites of interest. You will also be expected to inform people about forthcoming shows and events in the local area.

You will hand out leaflets and sell maps, postcards and items of interest from the local area and region. You may also operate a bureau de change, depending on the services offered by your employer.

Type of person suited to this work

You need to have an interest in local matters and in promoting your local area. Good, up-to-date knowledge about places of interest is useful. You should be friendly with good interpersonal skills.

A methodical approach to researching difficult questions is an asset. Relevant skills include customer-service experience, the ability to research information using the internet and good verbal communication skills.

It is important to be a good team player and assist your colleagues, even if you are busy.

Working conditions

You will usually work shifts which include the weekends and bank holidays.

Tourist information centres are modern, bright spaces that make pleasant work surroundings.

There is quite a lot of standing at the counter and moving to and from storage areas with piles of information, leaflets and stock items. You may spend some hours sitting at a computer, researching routes or B&B facilities in distant locations.

Future prospects

Tourist information centres are located across the whole of the UK, so you should have one local to you.

You could move from a part-time contract into a full-time one and with experience progress to a managerial or supervisory post. You could also choose to become a travel agent or tour guide.

Advantages/disadvantages

There are both busy and quiet times at the counter in tourist information centres.

You could spend a long time on the phone which could get dull.

You will play an important role in promoting both the local region and helping its economy.

Money guide

The starting salary for full-time staff is around £12,000 to £16,000 per year.

For supervisors with experience, this can rise to £14,000–£24,000.

Full-time managers of a tourist information centre can expect to earn £18,000–£30,000, depending on your level of experience.

Your salary will most likely be higher in and around London.

Related opportunities

- Holiday Representative p368
- Tour Guide/Manager p376
- Travel Agent p379

Further information

VisitBritain
www.visitbritain.org

VisitEngland
www.visitengland.com

VisitScotland
www.visitscotland.com

VisitWales
www.visitwales.com

TRAVEL AGENT

Qualifications and courses

No formal academic qualifications are needed for entry into this profession, though it is useful to have a good standard of education with GCSEs/National 5s (A*–C/A–C) in English and Maths. Other languages and experience working in a customer service or sales role would also be beneficial.

The Apprenticeship in Travel Services is available in the Leisure and Business pathway, which trains entrants for a customer-facing role as a travel agent, or the Tour Operator (Head Office) pathway, where you would be based at a call centre and assist customers with booking their holiday over the phone.

Training is provided on the job by employers but you could take relevant qualifications to help you secure a position. These include A levels/H grades, BTECs, City & Guilds awards and degrees in travel and tourism. The general entry requirements for a degree are 2 A levels/3 H grades and 5 GCSEs/National 5s (A*–C/A–C).

What the work involves

You will sell holiday packages to the public and try to meet your company's sales targets. You could be based in a high street travel agency or work in a call centre, assisting customers with online and telephone bookings.

You will put together individual holidays for an independent customer or for an organisation that seeks travel, accommodation and entertainment arrangements that are distinct from the travel companies' normal holiday packages.

You will need to contact airline, ferry and rail sales operatives to arrange transport and make reservations for accommodation, meals, hire cars and entertainment, both in this country and abroad. There are numerous details to check over the phone and tickets, booking confirmations and insurance notes to post out to customers.

Type of person suited to this work

You will need excellent administrative and research skills to quickly track down, assemble and book all the parts needed for each customer's ideal journey or holiday. You must have excellent listening and questioning skills in order to find the right holiday package for each individual customer.

If you are friendly, communicative and methodical, with excellent IT skills, you will suit both your customers' and your employers' needs. It helps if you have a real interest in exploring new places yourself.

Working conditions

You will work indoors, mainly at a desk or behind a counter. Almost all the work is done using a computer and telephone.

All travel agents tend to work 35–40 hours a week. If you work in a travel agency, it can be very busy at lunchtimes, near to closing time and on Saturdays, particularly leading up to the peak holiday season. Those working in a call centre are likely to work shifts including evening and weekend work.

Travel agencies usually provide staff with a uniform.

Future prospects

The travel industry has changed as more people now book their holidays via the internet. For this reason, many travel agents work in call centres, selling holiday packages over the phone and assisting customers with online bookings and queries. However, opportunities do still exist in high street travel agencies as some customers still prefer to book a holiday face-to-face with an agent's help.

With experience, you could progress to a managerial position. You can also move into other areas of tourism work, such as work as a holiday representative or tour guiding, which may give you opportunities to travel the world.

Advantages/disadvantages

A perk of this career is that you may receive free or discounted holidays.

Working to meet performance targets can be stressful.

It can be satisfying knowing that you have helped a customer to find and book their ideal holiday.

Money guide

Starting salaries are usually in the region of £13,000.

With experience, your earnings can increase to £15,000–£25,000 and senior travel agents can achieve over £35,000.

Benefits can include target-based commission and discounted holidays.

Related opportunities

- Holiday Representative p368
- Tour Guide/Manager p376
- Tourist Information Centre Assistant p378

Further information

Association of British Travel Agents Limited
www.abta.com

Institute of Travel and Tourism
www.itt.co.uk

LEISURE, SPORT AND TOURISM

Marketing, Advertising, Media, Print and Publishing

Do you consider yourself to be a great communicator? Are you interested in working in an exciting and often fast-paced environment with passionate, driven and ambitious individuals? If so, a career in this industry could be right for you. People who work in this sector are exceptionally motivated and are willing to put in long hours often on low starting wages because of their love of the job. You should have a great sense of creativity and imagination and be good at putting your ideas on paper, but you will often also need strong business acumen as many of your decisions will be made from an economic point of view as well as a creative one. Digital skills have become essential in this industry, and you should be able to channel your creativity through online platforms. The jobs featured in this section are listed below. For similar jobs to the ones in this section turn to *Design, Arts and Crafts* on page 157 and *Performing Arts* on page 415.

Qualifications and courses

Given the highly competitive nature of the advertising sector, most entrants are graduates. Large agencies usually expect candidates to have a degree or HND. A range of courses is available at universities and colleges at HND, Foundation degree, Honours degree and postgraduate levels. Although employers consider graduates of all disciplines, those who have gained qualifications in a relevant subject such as advertising, marketing, English, communications or business/management will be at a distinct advantage. The general entry requirements for a degree are 2 A levels/3 H grades and 5 GCSEs/National 5s (A*–C/A–C).

Entry without a degree is sometimes possible in smaller or specialist agencies. Applicants will be expected to have relevant work experience and it is likely that you will be employed in a junior administrative role whilst you work your way up to account executive level.

Work experience or volunteering work within a commercial context is an excellent way to develop your knowledge and build a network of industry contacts, crucial when securing employment. Vacation work, job shadowing or taking a sandwich degree course are all useful. Some larger agencies offer formal work experience or internships during the summer.

Post-university, you may seek a graduate training scheme offered by many larger agencies where you will be trained on the job by experienced professionals. Employers may encourage you to study for qualifications offered by the Chartered Institute of Marketing (CIM), the Institute of Practitioners in Advertising (IPA) and the Communication, Advertising and Marketing (CAM) Education Foundation whilst you work. These will ensure career progression and higher earnings.

What the work involves

You will plan, develop and oversee strategies for campaigns to suit different clients' requirements, working for advertising, PR or media agencies. It will be your responsibility to ensure that all the campaigns arrive in on budget and to schedule.

You will use a variety of different mediums to run campaigns from TV to newspapers, radio and direct mail to viral and online marketing. Social media work is an increasingly integral part of the job role.

Your work will involve liaising between clients and the agency staff, including designers and budget planners.

Type of person suited to this work

As much of your work involves discussions with clients and agency staff, you will need to be flexible with good communication skills. Having a well organised approach is essential because you could be running a number of campaigns at the same time.

You will need a strong creative flair and a resourceful attitude. A key ability will be to manage clients' campaigns within budget.

Being a confident team player with an enthusiastic attitude and strong negotiating skills is essential.

Working conditions

You will be based in an office, spending a lot of time at your computer, though at times you will be expected to travel to visit clients and attend meetings.

At times you will have to work under pressure to complete projects within limited time scales. You will work standard office hours but during busy periods you will have to work late if required.

Future prospects

It can be difficult to progress due to a lack of higher-level opportunities. The majority of agencies have fewer than 100 employees and competition for jobs is tough.

The speed and extent of your career progression will depend on the outcome of your different advertising strategies. With experience, it is possible to progress into a role as account manager and then to account director, where you would have control of the account management department. Another option would be to work as a freelancer or open your own agency.

Your training will be relevant to the related industries of marketing, market research, business or retail and commerce.

Advantages/disadvantages

The job is fast paced with hectic periods of work.

There are opportunities to meet and work with a wide range of people.

It is rewarding to create successful campaigns.

Money guide

Earnings vary according to employer and geographical location, with the highest salaries in London.

Starting as a graduate you can expect to earn £18,000–£24,000 a year.

An experienced account executive is likely to receive £30,000–£45,000.

Those employed at a senior level, as an account manager or account director, can achieve around £55,000 and those in the most senior roles can earn in excess of £65,000.

Related opportunities

- Advertising Art Director p383
- Advertising Media Planner p385
- Marketing Manager/Director p395

Further information

Advertising Association
www.adassoc.org.uk

Communication, Advertising and Marketing Education Foundation
www.camfoundation.com

Institute of Practitioners in Advertising
www.ipa.co.uk

Qualifications and courses

While there are no specific entry requirements, art directors usually have an HND, degree or postgraduate qualification in graphic design, advertising design, illustration, advertising and marketing or fine art. Employers will consider graduates of other disciplines who can demonstrate knowledge of design and advertising, but gaining a qualification in a relevant subject will significantly increase your chances. If your degree subject is unrelated, you may decide to supplement your degree with a relevant postgraduate qualification.

For degree entry, students generally require at least 2 A levels/3 H grades, 5 GCSEs/National 5s (A*–C/A–C) and a portfolio of work. Foundation courses in an art-related subject are also available.

Work experience is an excellent way to develop your knowledge and build a network of industry contacts. Vacation work, job shadowing or taking a sandwich degree course are all useful ways to show evidence of your enthusiasm, your ability to offer new ideas and your teamwork skills. Employers also look for candidates with a strong portfolio of design work and ideas, which should include both print and digital work and proof of working with software packages such as Photoshop or Illustrator. Design & Art Direction (D&AD) run workshops in which participants develop relevant skills and build up a portfolio.

It can take a few years before securing your first job as you are normally required to establish a team of people first. Once employed, training is normally carried out on the job. Your employer may also encourage you to take a course offered by the Institute of Practitioners in Advertising (IPA) so as to remain up to date in a constantly evolving industry.

What the work involves

You will design and create effective brand styles and images for advertising campaigns in accordance with clients' requirements.

Working with specialist software, you will develop new designs, often at short notice, to convey the required tone of a particular campaign. In close collaboration with colleagues, especially copywriters and reprographic specialists, you will make sure your ideas are realised.

You might also be involved in selecting photographers and other professionals to create additional visuals for use in a campaign.

Type of person suited to this work

You will need visual design skills and creative strengths but also the skills to develop commercial ideas. The capacity to adapt to a client's requirements is also important.

As you will be using software to create new designs, you will need to have up-to-date computer skills.

Much of your time will be spent working in a team so you will need excellent communication and people skills. Your ideas could be rejected or changed so a flexible yet confident attitude is essential.

It is important to work to exacting standards, paying close attention to detail.

Working conditions

Most of your tasks will be office based, sometimes in a studio. Your job will also involve travelling to visit clients and attend shoots.

You will be seated for long periods at a workstation using a number of computers and you may often be on the phone.

The majority of your work will be done in normal office hours. However, there will be pressure to complete jobs as you near deadlines and at these times you will be expected to work late.

Future prospects

This is a highly competitive area of work to enter. Although newer agencies exist in some of the larger cities (Manchester, Bristol and Newcastle), the number of creative art directors employed is still low. Job opportunities are increasing at the fastest rate in digital/viral marketing.

Normally agencies hire a team consisting of a copywriter and an art director so finding a good partner is essential. You will start as a junior creative team member and then could progress to becoming a middleweight art director.

With experience you could move up to senior art director level. In some large, global companies there is the opportunity to become an executive art director. Alternatively, some art directors establish their own agencies or go on to directorial work in television or film.

Advantages/disadvantages

This job is rewarding as it offers individuals the chance to influence the images of major companies and brands.

The constant need to develop new ideas can be stressful at times.

Money guide

Starting salaries at junior level are around £18,000–£25,000.

With experience earnings can range from £25,000 to £45,000.

Those in senior positions can achieve a salary between £45,000 and £120,000.

Related opportunities

- Advertising Media Planner p385
- Copywriter p389
- Graphic Designer p165

Further information

Communication, Advertising and Marketing Education Foundation
www.camfoundation.com

Institute of Practitioners in Advertising
www.ipa.co.uk

Qualifications and courses

A career as an advertising media buyer is open to graduates of all degree or diploma disciplines. As a result of the media industry becoming more global, business qualifications and a commercial awareness are becoming increasingly valued, therefore a degree in a relevant subject such as marketing or communications, media studies, statistics or business management may increase your chances of employment. Entry to an HND is with 1 A level/2 H grades and 4 GCSEs/National 5s (A*–C/A–C). Requirements to study for a degree are 2 A levels/3 H grades and 5 GCSEs/National 5s (A*–C/A–C).

Building up a portfolio of work experience through work placements or volunteering will increase your chances of employment, whilst helping you to develop your skills and experience in media buying, negotiation and sales.

Few jobs are advertised within this fiercely competitive industry, therefore it may pay to make speculative and persistent applications or to accept other relevant posts in order to gain entry into the profession. Once you are in employment, some advertising and media agencies offer structured training programmes. Here you are likely to be recruited into a planner/buyer role in order to gain experience of the company's departments whilst being trained by senior professionals. There will be a focus on developing your IT and presentation skills at this stage.

Your work-based training may be supplemented by external instruction via seminars and workshops delivered by industry bodies such as the Media Research Group (MRG) and the Institute of Practitioners in Advertising (IPA).

What the work involves

Advertising media buyers research, identify and negotiate the purchase of media space (eg advertising time on television or radio).

Working for an advertising agency, you will work from a brief laid out by your clients, taking into consideration target audiences, media events and activities, schedules and budgetary constraints.

You will present proposals, advise creative teams, estimate costs and profits, and monitor and keep records of the progress of your media campaigns.

You will make media contacts and liaise with other media companies in order to get the best deal and most exposure on behalf of your client.

Type of person suited to this work

You should have a keen interest in media, marketing and advertising and be constantly thinking of new creative ways to approach your work. As you will need to have a good understanding of your target audiences and markets, you should also be interested in the reasons why people purchase certain products or use certain media channels.

You must have good communication skills as you will have to make presentations, draw up proposals and correspond with contacts on a regular basis. You should have strong organisational skills and be able to work under pressure and within tight deadlines.

You will need to have initiative, drive and be able to work in a team.

Working conditions

You will work around 40 hours a week, Monday to Friday. You may have to work longer hours to meet deadlines. Part-time work or flexible hours may be possible.

You will be mainly office based but as you gain experience you will spend more time meeting with clients, making presentations and discussing proposals. You may have to travel away from home with some overnight stays.

The majority of your correspondence with media owners and companies is conducted on the phone, by email or by socialising.

Future prospects

You will usually progress to a permanent position after 1 year in a junior role. Your promotions will depend largely on personal performance and successful campaigns. You may have to move between agencies in order to progress.

You can take postgraduate qualifications to increase your knowledge about specific aspects of your job such as business or marketing.

After 3–5 years you may gradually take on more account management responsibilities or you may take a position in data management or account planning.

Advantages/disadvantages

Advances and changes in the media industry mean that you will find new and exciting opportunities to work with multimedia technologies.

This is a highly competitive industry and your work may involve long and stressful hours.

Money guide

As a junior, your starting salary may be £18,000–£25,000.

With experience, your earnings may increase to between £24,000 and £40,000.

At a senior level you could achieve in excess of £50,000 a year.

Related opportunities

- Advertising Account Executive p382
- Market Research Executive p393
- Marketing Manager/Director p395

Further information

Account Planning Group
www.apg.org.uk

Institute of Practitioners in Advertising
www.ipa.co.uk

The Advertising Association
www.adassoc.org.uk

ADVERTISING MEDIA PLANNER

Qualifications and courses

Although there are no minimum educational requirements for a role as an advertising media planner, competition is high and most entrants will have either an HND or a degree. Relevant subjects such as media studies, business management, marketing, advertising, operational research, statistics and English will increase your chances of securing employment. The general entry requirements for a degree are 2 A levels/3 H grades and 5 GCSEs/National 5s (A*–C/A–C).

Most agencies tend to require relevant work experience and undertaking a sandwich course can be a particular advantage. Work experience will help you to develop the necessary skills and knowledge vital to an advertising media planner, whilst also introducing you to industry contacts crucial in a fiercely competitive industry. Internships are also effective in demonstrating to potential employers that you have a history of strong interpersonal communication skills, a commercial flair and an ability to work with numbers.

Once in employment, you will normally be trained on the job by senior planners. New account planners may train with the Account Planning Group (APG) or the Market Research Society (MRS). At this stage of your career, your focus will be on gaining an understanding of audience research figures, how best to make use of IT resources and how to communicate presentations effectively. Alongside your internal training, employers may also encourage you to study for qualifications offered by the Institute of Practitioners in Advertising (IPA), the Communication, Advertising and Marketing (CAM) Education Foundation or the Media Research Group (MRG).

What the work involves

You will research public opinion and interest in a client's product or service to develop new advertising and media campaigns. Market research, both positive and negative, will form a starting point from which you will plan and develop new advertising strategies for your clients.

You will need to be very clear when interpreting your clients' intentions. The work will require close cooperation with your clients and your creative team in order to create strong and successful advertising.

Type of person suited to this work

As you will be developing new advertising ideas, you will need a high level of creativity.

To understand and make use of a range of facts and figures in support of your work, you will need an ability to interpret and analyse trends in data.

As you will have to make presentations to your clients and colleagues at progress meetings, excellent oral and written communication skills will be essential. Being self-motivated and confident is also important.

Good business skills are helpful and you will need to use clear verbal reasoning when stating your point of view.

Working conditions

Most of your work will be undertaken in an office or at clients' premises. You will be expected to dress formally and be well presented at all times.

Although you will mainly work normal office hours, you can expect to work overtime and at weekends during busy periods.

You will have to travel to attend meetings on a regular basis, perhaps staying overnight.

Future prospects

The majority of job opportunities in advertising are based in London, although the number of companies in other large cities is growing. Despite this, entry is highly competitive and trainee posts sparse. Realistically, account planning makes up only a very small part of the overall advertising/media sector.

If employed by one of the few larger companies, career progression is largely based on performance but is normally rapid with promotion to a senior or management position common after one year. Headhunting is also common so a good reputation is important.

With experience, you could work on a freelance basis or move into market research, design or management. Sometimes you can 'invent' new roles given the dynamic nature of the industry and eagerness to remain up to date with the ever evolving requirements of clients.

Advantages/disadvantages

This type of work can provide the opportunity to work for high-profile companies with a Europe-wide or global reach.

You will have to develop new ideas, often at relatively short notice.

This is a very competitive career and only the most determined will succeed.

Money guide

Starting salaries for a junior media planner range from £18,000 to £22,000 per year.

Experienced advertising media planners can earn between £25,000 and £45,000.

Those employed in the most senior positions can achieve £60,000 or more.

Related opportunities

- Market Research Executive p393
- Marketing Manager/Director p395
- Media Researcher p396

Further information

Account Planning Group
www.apg.org.uk

Communication, Advertising and Marketing Education Foundation
www.camfoundation.com

Institute of Practitioners in Advertising
www.ipa.co.uk

Qualifications and courses

Most entrants will have a degree but enthusiasm, good industry knowledge and the ability to make good contacts are equally important. For entry onto a degree course you will usually need a minimum of 2 A levels/3 H grades and 5 GCSEs/National 5s (A*–C/A–C).

Most entrants to this work will have previous experience and qualifications in related fields such as sales, business, music, performing arts, public relations or publishing.

It is also possible to start out as an assistant or administrator and then work your way up to an agent or manager.

Contract law knowledge and a second language may be useful in the negotiation of rights deals. Knowledge of the existing client lists, up-and-coming industry figures and working knowledge of the industry in which you wish to work will always be beneficial, for example as a literary agent you should have a strong knowledge of the genre of books you wish to specialise in (eg business books, children's fiction, commercial fiction, etc).

What the work involves

Agents represent and promote artists and creatives in the film, television, radio, theatre, music and publishing sectors. They can also play a similar role for sporting professionals. You will be expected to work proactively to enhance your client's career by securing work and negotiating to ensure that the client attains the best work at the highest fee.

Literary agents are responsible for assessing the quality and commercial potential of manuscripts submitted by authors. They will work with a selected author to create a more polished manuscript that would be marketable enough to send to publishers under their recommendation.

You will also have to develop publication and rights agreements with publishers and TV, radio and film producers on behalf of the writers.

Type of person suited to this work

As you will be acting as the link between your client and the world they work in, you will need excellent communication skills. The ability to develop good contacts and a name for reliability is essential. It is also important to develop good working relationships with clients.

You should have a good head for business and an assertive approach will be helpful when it comes to agreeing contracts on behalf of clients.

You should have a good knowledge of the law and how it applies to your client's sector, as they will rely on you for professional advice in this area.

Working conditions

Agents are office based and can be self-employed or work for agencies.

Although, theoretically, they could work anywhere, most agents are based near London. Literary agents can also be found in Edinburgh, which is an important centre for the UK publishing industry.

Travel is common and you should expect to work 30–40 hours a week, including evenings and weekends, as some of your work will involve attending performances and social events to network and raise the profile of your clients.

Future prospects

This is an extremely competitive profession, made increasingly more difficult to gain employment in due to the rise in opportunities for digital and self-publishing meaning agents are less in demand. Agencies are constantly being set up but few stand the test of time. Most agencies, particularly literary agencies, are relatively small, although there are a few large ones. However publishers increasingly prefer to respond to new publication ideas through agents.

Your success will be determined partly by the standard of the clients you represent but, also, by the quality of the advice you can provide to them.

With sufficient experience you might have the opportunity to work abroad in entertainment and publishing hubs such as New York.

Advantages/disadvantages

You will have the satisfaction of supporting new artists and helping them to succeed.

As you will earn your income from commissions, you will be under pressure to identify and promote new artists.

Unsociable hours and extensive travelling can affect your personal life.

Money guide

Salaries vary widely according to the nature of the agent, the number of artists they work with and the success they have in their field.

Literary agents are paid commission which is usually between 10% and 25% of authors' earnings.

New entrants can expect to earn £15,000 in a large agency, progressing to £30,000 with experience.

Top agents with prestigious clients can earn in excess of £100,000.

Related opportunities

- Marketing Manager/Director p395
- Public Relations Officer p404
- Publisher/Commissioning Editor p405

Further information

Association of Authors' Agents
www.agentsassoc.co.uk

The Agents' Association (Great Britain)
www.agents-uk.com

Qualifications and courses

There are no specific qualifications required in order become an author, although it is important to note that many writers are graduates in a relevant degree subject, such as English language, literature or creative writing. There are a variety of courses available that are designed to improve a writer's technique, ranging from evening classes to a postgraduate course, however it is style, originality of ideas, imagination and use of language that are the most important aspects of this profession.

It is a fiercely competitive industry and few authors reach the level of commercial success required to earn a living wage. For this reason it is often necessary to obtain a second job.

If you wish to write for the media, short courses in script or creative writing, practical television or film may be useful. Work experience within the media industry may also help if you intend to write for television, film or radio. The BBC offers work experience schemes for budding writers.

Competitions may help you to break into the profession and attending conventions such as the Winchester Writers' Conference or Crimefest, alongside membership of the Writers' Guild of Great Britain, are useful ways to network. Arts Council grants may also be available to new authors for work in literature and drama.

What the work involves

Authors write the text for books, magazines, IT resources and more. This can involve developing initial ideas to create a complete piece, or simply rewriting sections.

Scriptwriters create text for TV, film, radio and theatre productions.

As part of the work, you will undertake research using resources such as the internet and libraries.

Authors often specialise in a particular subject area such as technical writing, science, medicine, cookery, travel or education. A small number of authors write and publish creative works of fiction, poetry or drama.

Type of person suited to this work

It is essential to have command of the English language and the ability to write with your audience in mind. Having a good imagination and a creative approach is important.

As you will be pitching project ideas to the industry, you will need strong communication skills. Whilst commissions are exciting you should be resilient enough to handle rejection.

As you will be working with publishers and/or agents, it might be useful to have some business awareness and numeracy skills are very helpful when working out royalties against advances.

You will be working independently a lot of the time and this can mean long periods of solitary work so you should be self-motivated and committed to the job.

Working conditions

As the majority of authors and scriptwriters are self-employed, you will usually work from home. Most of your time will be spent researching and writing, whilst sitting at a computer for long periods.

It may be necessary to juggle deadlines with other part-time employment taken on to supplement income. Most authors/scriptwriters are employed on a project-by-project basis, so the work provides very little job security.

Future prospects

Making a living as a professional author can be challenging. Having an established network of contacts helps and you must look for opportunities to publicise yourself. A variety of support groups and courses exist to help people develop their writing skills and are important ways to remain up to date with new technologies and programs available.

Self-publishing is steadily becoming more common amongst new writers wishing to reach a wider audience and demonstrate their motivation and pro-active nature to potential agencies.

At present, short dramas for radio broadcast are actively sought and many radio and television companies are happy to accept unsolicited scripts to read.

Advantages/disadvantages

This type of work can provide the satisfaction of being creative and seeing your work in print and in the public domain.

Not all authors succeed in publishing their work and you might need to take on other types of work to make a living.

Money guide

Earnings vary depending on the nature of the writing project, your experience, and your popularity as a writer.

Publishers may give a one-off payment for a piece of work or will pay you royalties.

The median salary for professional writers has gone down by 28% in recent years, and is currently £11,000.

For freelance writers in screen and television, you will negotiate your own fees but remuneration at a senior level can be over £100,000.

Related opportunities

- Copywriter p389
- Journalist p392

Further information

Society of Authors
www.societyofauthors.org

Writers and Artists
www.writersandartists.co.uk

MARKETING, ADVERTISING, MEDIA, PRINT AND PUBLISHING

Qualifications and courses

Although there are no set formal entry qualifications, most copy editors are graduates. Relevant degree subjects such as English, publishing studies, media and journalism will provide you with the basic skills required by the industry and you will need at least 2 A levels/3 H grades and 5 GCSEs/National 5s (A*–C/A–C) for degree entry. For financial journalism, a business studies degree would be useful and to work in technical publishing a science-related degree is recommended. Studying for a postgraduate qualification in publishing may also increase your chances of employment.

Entry with an HND or Foundation degree alone is rare, unless candidates can provide evidence of an aptitude for the work and/or some highly relevant experience.

Candidates may first be taken on as an editorial assistant or trainee before working your way up to copy editor. Building a portfolio of work and experience is very important during this early stage of your career. In order to secure employment as a trainee, it is likely that you will need pre-entry experience. Working on your university magazine or time spent in a bookshop or library are invaluable as employers often seek those candidates who can demonstrate their enthusiasm and knowledge of the English language, good communication skills and great attention to detail. This also allows you to build crucial contacts within a highly competitive industry.

The Society for Editors and Proofreaders (SfEP) and the Publishing Training Centre offer introductory and advanced courses on topics such as copy editing and grammar skills, allowing you to remain up to date with new developments in technology. The Association of Learned and Professional Society Publishers (ALPSP) also offers introductory and advanced courses, as well as providing management workshops.

What the work involves

Copy editors prepare manuscripts for publication by checking for grammatical and punctuation errors, spelling mistakes and inconsistencies in style. You might also be responsible for checking the legality of the text.

Sub-editors are copy editors who work in newspapers and magazines. You may also create headlines and captions and manipulate text to fit a word count.

Proofreaders carry out the final quality checks on texts, including e-books now, before publication. You will use a recognised set of symbols and normally mark changes on a hard copy, but sometimes make alterations on screen using specialist software.

Type of person suited to this work

As you will be responsible for preparing texts for publication, you will pay great attention to detail. An excellent knowledge of the English language and strong writing and communication skills are expected. Patience and a methodical approach to your work are also helpful.

The ability to manage budgets is useful, as is the ability to work to tight deadlines and cope with pressure.

Working conditions

These jobs tend to be largely solitary. Most copy editors work within offices or are self-employed and work from home. You can spend some time attending meetings with authors, designers, printers, illustrators and colleagues.

At the busiest times you might have to work late to meet copy or production deadlines, but mostly you will work normal working hours.

Future prospects

This is a very competitive area and many copy editors start off in an administrative or related role and work their way up.

It may be necessary for in-house copy editors to change their job frequently to aid career progression. With experience you could become a project manager or commission new publications.

With the rise of digital and self-publishing, copy editors who work on a freelance basis are increasingly in demand.

Advantages/disadvantages

The work provides the satisfaction of shaping and improving the style and tone of manuscripts.

You will work with many different types of people.

As you will be making sure a publication is produced on time, this can be a high-pressured job.

Money guide

Starting salaries begin around £16,000.

Salaries for experienced editors employed in-house vary between £25,000 and £40,000.

The most senior editors can earn up to £60,000.

Freelance rates can vary. The Society for Editors and Proofreaders (SfEP)'s recommended minimum hourly rates for proofreading are £22.75, £26.50 for copy editing and £30.50 for substantial editing or rewriting.

As a freelancer you may charge a page or word rate.

Related opportunities

- Copywriter p389
- Publisher/Commissioning Editor p405

Further information

Society for Editors and Proofreaders
www.sfep.org.uk

COPYWRITER

Qualifications and courses

There are no formal requirements for this profession but most entrants have a degree or HND. Students generally require at least 2 A levels/3 H grades and 5 GCSEs/National 5s (A*–C/A–C) to get a place on a degree course and relevant degree subjects, such as advertising design, English, public relations or media studies, will increase your chances of employment. A postgraduate qualification in copywriting or creative advertising can be useful for graduates without a relevant academic background.

You will require determination to enter this highly competitive industry and you are likely to have to complete several unpaid work experience placements before being taken on.

The most common entry route involves producing a high-quality portfolio and presenting this to agencies in the hope that they might offer you work. Some employers often value high quality and innovative portfolios over qualifications. Given that entry-level jobs and graduate training schemes are rarely advertised, you will need to ensure your portfolio makes you stand out. Occasionally, employers may attend graduate shows or seek out talent via competitions and showcases such as the Design & Art Direction (D&AD) New Blood Exhibition.

Once employed, you will usually be hired in a pair, ie a copywriter and an art director. You will learn on the job from experienced professionals but you may also be encouraged to study for industry recognised qualifications throughout your career offered by the Institute of Practitioners in Advertising (IPA), the Communication Advertising and Marketing (CAM) Education Foundation and the Design & Art Direction (D&AD).

What the work involves

Copywriters create informative, well-constructed text (or 'copy') on a wide range of subjects, from a range of perspectives and for a variety of audiences.

Advertising copywriters produce text for TV, film, radio, press and internet advertisements. You will create copy for websites, company publications, direct mail, brochures and product information guides.

Design companies, sales promotion organisations and other companies employ copywriters to write text that promotes their services or products and helps to increase sales.

Type of person suited to this work

As you will be writing copy for a range of uses, you will require excellent writing skills, a strong creative flair and a good imagination. The ability to describe a subject concisely is also important.

In discussing innovative ideas with your colleagues and clients, you will make valuable use of your oral and written communication skills. You will have to be flexible and willing to alter what you think are good ideas to meet clients' requirements.

It is essential to have good organisational skills, to be able to work well under pressure and to meet tight deadlines.

Working conditions

Many copywriters work on a freelance basis for a number of employers. In-house copywriters will work 9am–5pm from Monday to Friday, within an office or studio environment.

You will spend long periods of time sitting typing, which can be tiring. You will also be expected to attend client meetings, which may involve overnight stays. You will have to work long hours to meet project deadlines, which can be stressful.

Advertising copywriters normally work with an art director, who creates the visual aspect of the campaign.

Future prospects

There are interesting opportunities available as an increasing number of organisations find freelance copywriters online via established websites.

With experience, a copywriter can be promoted to senior copywriter or creative director. Some copywriters choose to become freelancers or set up agencies in partnership with other creatives. Others go on to work in related areas such as public relations and publishing.

Advantages/disadvantages

This job provides the satisfaction of seeing your work in print and in the public domain.

You will be working alongside imaginative colleagues, which can be stimulating.

Copywriting can be stressful because of the need to produce new ideas to tight deadlines.

There may be some job instability if working on a self-employed basis.

Money guide

Starting salaries are around £18,000–£25,000.

With experience, you could earn £25,000–£50,000.

Senior level salaries can range between £45,000 and £120,000.

Self-employed copywriters negotiate their own rates.

Related opportunities

- Author/Scriptwriter p387
- Journalist p392
- Technical Author/Medical Writer p408

Further information

Communication, Advertising and Marketing Education Foundation
www.camfoundation.com

Institute of Practitioners in Advertising
www.ipa.co.uk

MARKETING, ADVERTISING, MEDIA, PRINT AND PUBLISHING

DIGITAL MARKETER

ENTRY LEVEL 6

Qualifications and courses

Given the very competitive nature of the marketing sector, most entrants are graduates. Relevant subjects include marketing, journalism, communications or business/management. You will need at least 2 A levels/3 H grades and 5 GCSEs/National 5s (A*–C/A–C) for degree entry.

Relevant work experience will be invaluable. An internship or work placement will help you build relevant skills and gain contacts. Good IT skills including knowledge of HTML and CSS software will be essential. You may wish to gain experience as a traditional marketing assistant or executive before moving into digital marketing.

Studying a digital marketing qualification may improve your prospects. The Chartered Institute of Marketing (CIM) offers a Level 4 Certificate in Professional Marketing (Digital Marketing). The Communication, Advertising and Marketing (CAM) Education Foundation offers a Level 4 Diploma in Digital Marketing.

The Institute of Direct and Digital Marketing (IDM) also offers a number of relevant awards, certificates and diplomas in digital marketing ranging from Level 4 to Level 7.

Throughout your career you will be expected to regularly update your digital skills and knowledge. CAM, CIM, IDM and the Internet Advertising Bureau (IAB) run a number of short courses covering topics such as email marketing, web analytics and social media marketing.

In 2017 a new Digital Marketers Trailblazer Apprenticeship programme will become available.

What the work involves

Digital marketing executives promote and raise the profile of ideas, products and services for their clients or organisation online.

Your work will involve creating and launching campaigns using websites, apps and social media channels such as Twitter, Facebook and LinkedIn.

You will liaise with traditional marketers, web designers and clients to develop and execute campaign ideas.

You will be responsible for writing engaging online content. Web analysis will be key to tracking the success of your campaigns.

Type of person suited to this work

Excellent IT skills and creative vision are vital for a career in digital marketing. Good interpersonal skills are essential to engage with customers and clients effectively.

You must have good research skills in order to spot trends and analyse data. Time management skills are important as you will work on a number of projects at the same time.

Working conditions

You will usually work a 37-hour week, Monday to Friday. However, you may have to work overtime in order to meet campaign deadlines.

You will typically be office based, but it may be necessary to travel to meet with clients.

Most agencies are located in London or large UK cities, although international agencies may offer you the opportunity to work abroad.

Future prospects

You will typically be employed by a marketing agency or a company's marketing department. In larger companies it is possible to progress from a digital marketing assistant to an executive or manager in 2 to 5 years.

With experience you could become a digital marketing director or set up your own agency.

You could specialise in a type of marketing such as video or mobile marketing. Alternatively, you could move into advertising, public relations or sales.

Advantages/disadvantages

It is rewarding to see your campaign increase the profits and raise the profile of your clients.

You have the opportunity to use your creative vision in a corporate environment.

Keeping up with the fast-paced nature of digital marketing may be challenging at times.

Money guide

Starting salaries for a digital marketing assistant or executive range from £16,000 to £26,500 a year. Graduate schemes begin higher and successful applicants can receive between £18,000 and £30,000 a year.

As you gain more experience in the role your earnings could rise to £30,000 a year.

Senior managers can achieve in excess of £38,000 a year. Digital marketing directors can earn in excess of £70,000 a year.

Earnings are higher if you work in the private sector and many companies offer additional benefits such as bonuses, medical insurance and a company car.

Related opportunities

- Advertising Account Executive p382
- Market Research Executive p393

Further information

Chartered Institute of Marketing
www.cim.co.uk

Communication, Advertising and Marketing Education Foundation
www.camfoundation.com

Qualifications and courses

Whilst there are no set entry requirements for this profession, many entrants hold degrees and/or postgraduate qualifications in a variety of disciplines. For entry to a degree course, you will need at least 2 A levels/3 H grades and 5 GCSEs/National 5s (A*–C/A–C), including English and Maths. Relevant degree courses include events management, conference and exhibition management, and hospitality management. A Diploma in Hospitality is also available and a postgraduate qualification in events management may be recommended if your first degree is unrelated.

The NCFE Certificate in Events Planning is also relevant, and is good if you want to work at a supervisory level or if you are already in the industry and wish to develop your career.

The best advantage you can have when you are looking to enter the industry is to have gained as much experience as you can of organising events as employers highly value those candidates who can demonstrate their organisation, time management and problem-solving skills. Try to help with the organisation of charity events, local festivals or university society outings as this will not only develop your skills but also provide you with crucial industry contacts useful when seeking work.

Once you are in the industry, you will experience a combination of on-the-job training from experienced professionals and external instruction. Your employer may encourage you to train in courses such as planning techniques, marketing, customer care, sales and sponsorship and crowd safety offered by industry-recognised bodies such as the Chartered Institute of Marketing (CIM) or the Society of Event Organisers (SEO).

What the work involves

As an events and exhibition organiser, you will be planning and organising events of varying sizes and ensuring that they run to plan on the day. You could find yourself organising anything from conferences, seminars and meetings to parties, ceremonies or weddings.

The nature of your role will depend on the event itself, but you might be researching, planning, marketing the event, setting the budget, and sorting out all of the little details that go into planning an event.

Hours can be late and involve working at weekends – but you may get to attend a free party or two.

Type of person suited to this work

You need to be incredibly well organised. Work can be tough and stressful, so you need energy and stamina: you should relish taking on a heavy workload, not crumple beneath it.

You should be a team player, an effective communicator and reliable. More often than not you will be organising events that aim to give people fun experiences, an attitude you should also exude at work.

You need to be creative and have a good imagination, but also have a business mind. Your project management and problem-solving skills should be very good, and you must be able to market, sell and negotiate.

Working conditions

You will be extremely busy and rushing to and from various locations.

You will usually work office hours, although additional hours are common when events require extra last-minute work.

Your time will be divided between the office, events venues and client meetings. You may well have to travel away from home, sometimes abroad.

You will be working both indoors and outdoors, and may find yourself in hotels, museums, castles, showgrounds – the list is endless!

Future prospects

By starting off in roles such as assistant events organiser, you are paving the way and can aim towards positions such as event organiser or manager. From this level you can progress to event director, or even start up your own company.

It is often necessary to move company more than once to progress in this industry.

Advantages/disadvantages

This is an exciting job, and the sense of achievement when an event you have planned is a success is a great feeling.

Planning an event can be stressful, and you might have to work flat out to meet deadlines and make your event a success, sacrificing your evenings and weekends in the process.

Money guide

As you start out, you might earn between £17,000 and £21,000.

With experience this can grow to between £25,000 and £40,000.

Within a senior role, you can expect to earn £50,000–£80,000 a year.

Your earnings may increase as a result of performance-related pay. Commission and bonuses are fairly common within this profession.

Related opportunities

- Catering/Restaurant Manager/Maître d'Hôtel p123
- Entertainment Manager p366
- Hotel Manager p128

Further information

Association of British Professional Conference Organisers
www.abpco.org

MARKETING, ADVERTISING, MEDIA, PRINT AND PUBLISHING

Qualifications and courses

The most common route into this career is with pre-entry qualifications. The National Council for the Training of Journalists (NCTJ), the Broadcast Journalism Training Council (BJTC) and the Professional Publishers Association (PPA) all accredit HNDs, Foundation degrees, degrees and postgraduate courses. Taking a course that has been accredited will demonstrate your commitment to the profession and if you have an unrelated degree you must supplement it with an accredited 1-year or fast-track postgraduate conversion course.

The NCTJ offers the Diploma in Journalism, a qualification aiming to prepare trainees for multimedia journalism, as well as distance-learning courses in both newspaper and magazine journalism. The PPA and ContentETC have paired up to produce two interactive online certificates relevant to those working in the magazine sector.

Those with 18 months' work experience who have gained the Diploma in Journalism can take the NCTJ's National Qualification in Journalism (NQJ) which enables candidates to achieve senior status as a journalist.

The industry is highly competitive and there are limited opportunities on graduate training schemes. It is advisable to get as much work experience as possible, either within the industry or for student newspapers and magazines, in order to build up a portfolio of your writing and establish contacts.

Web-editing skills along with a social media presence is useful, and setting up your own blog is a good way to start developing a portfolio. Broadcast journalism is fiercely competitive and entrants should have a strong show reel and work experience in student or community media.

Membership of the National Union of Journalists (NUJ) is recommended as it advertises work experience placements, job opportunities and training courses.

What the work involves

Journalists research and write stories on subjects such as current affairs, business, health and culture. Broadcast journalists also present these features on radio, television or the internet.

These stories can immediately become live news articles or features for local and national newspapers, magazines, TV, radio and online broadcasts.

You will be planning, writing and editing articles in accordance with a house style, usually to very tight deadlines.

Type of person suited to this work

As you will be producing articles on a regular basis, you will need to thrive on working under pressure.

Strong written and oral communication skills are essential for this job and broadcast journalists should have a clear and professional voice.

You should be a highly organised multi-tasker with a good instinct for a potential story and the ability to undertake research through interviews and contacts. You will be expected to research difficult stories and meet hostile people, which can be stressful.

Working conditions

Your work will be dictated by the story you are following. You could visit a range of locations in the working day, often at short notice as news stories unfold.

You will have to work long, sometimes irregular hours in order to meet publication deadlines, including public holidays.

While you may be part of a wider team, you could work alone for much of the time, or in the company of a photographer. If freelancing, you will have to take the initiative on stories and work patterns could be irregular.

Future prospects

This is a highly competitive area to enter and many people undertake unpaid work experience before securing a job. Approximately a third of all journalists work freelance. Many journalists started work as freelancers to establish their reputations.

It is possible to cross over from newspaper/magazine journalism into broadcast journalism as a reporter or presenter.

Advantages/disadvantages

You will create features that could be read, heard or seen by thousands of people – often beyond the UK.

This profession offers exciting, varied work.

Owing to tight deadlines, you will have to regularly produce work under pressure, and deal with potentially difficult people.

Money guide

Starting salaries for trainees are usually £12,000–£26,000.

An experienced newspaper or magazine journalist can expect to earn £18,000–£40,000.

In broadcast journalism, experienced professionals can expect to earn £20,000–£60,000.

Newspaper/magazine editors and television newsreaders can receive in excess of £80,000.

Related opportunities

- Copywriter p389
- Media Researcher p396
- Newspaper/Magazine/Web Editor p398

Further information

Broadcast Journalism Training Council
www.bjtc.org.uk

National Council for the Training of Journalists
www.nctj.com

National Union of Journalists
www.nuj.org.uk

Qualifications and courses

There are no set qualifications for this role but most employers will expect you to hold a relevant HND or degree. Useful subjects are those which develop skills in communication and analysis, such as English, maths, marketing, psychology, statistics, business management and social sciences. If you wish to take on specialist industrial market research positions, a degree in the subject most linked to that industry is an advantage, for example in engineering or science. A postgraduate qualification may improve your chances of employment and later career prospects, although it is not essential.

Competition for places on graduate training schemes is fierce and you may consider applying for research assistant posts before working your way up. Pre-entry voluntary or vacation work experience in research, statistical data analysis or interview techniques is often desired by employers as they like candidates who can show evidence of good interpersonal skills, analytical and numerical abilities, a business awareness and effective teamwork.

Once employed, you will receive a combination of on-the-job training and external instruction. The Market Research Society (MRS) offers the Advanced Certificate in Market and Social Research Practice and, at a higher level, the Diploma in Market and Social Research Practice for those with experience in the industry. Once candidates have completed the Diploma, they are eligible for full membership of the MRS. An NVQ in Marketing (Levels 2–4) is also available and the Social Research Association (SRA) runs a number of short courses on topics such as survey design, qualitative data analysis and research methods, useful to ensure continuing professional development (CPD). For those working in qualitative research, the Association for Qualitative Research (AQR) runs short courses, event meetings and conferences.

What the work involves

You will undertake research to obtain people's opinions on specific products, services or issues and then analyse the results.

Developing surveys to analyse public opinion on a wide range of subjects or issues will be part of your job. You may also interview small groups of people, known as focus groups or panels, to assess their views on a specific topic in more detail.

You will compile the results of your research in the form of detailed reports or summary analyses to be used by your clients, businesses and other organisations.

Type of person suited to this work

This job is all about people and their opinions, so verbal communication skills are essential. You will also need strong writing skills to create surveys, plan interviews and write reports.

You will need to understand exactly what your client wants to know and think up ways to get this information. A logical and deductive approach to your work is important. You should be interested in human psychology and behaviour.

Also, as you will be working with a lot of paperwork, you will need to be well organised. Confidence working with numbers will be useful in helping you to perform statistical analyses. Being aware of the marketplace and what sells is also important.

Working conditions

Market researchers work from offices and attend meetings, presentations and interviews. You could work in a specialist market research agency or a marketing department within a larger organisation. Some market researchers work freelance.

The job can involve frequent daily and overnight stays. You will usually work standard office hours, Monday to Friday, with occasional overtime if necessary to meet project deadlines.

Future prospects

The market research industry is worth well over £1 billion a year. As well as businesses, many other organisations increasingly depend on market researchers to provide up-to-the-minute facts and figures concerning public opinion on everything from train services to trainers!

After gaining experience as a market research interviewer, you can move up to research executive, and then progress to senior research executive.

With sufficient experience you could enter a senior management role or set up your own agency.

Advantages/disadvantages

The role is interesting as you will work on a variety of projects and meet many different types of people.

The public may not want to speak to you and getting the information needed may be difficult.

This job is fast paced and can involve high levels of pressure near deadlines.

Money guide

Starting salaries are typically between £20,000 and £25,000.

With experience, earnings increase to £23,000–£35,000.

A very experienced market researcher employed in a senior position could achieve £40,000 to £70,000 or more.

Related opportunities

- Marketing Manager/Director p395
- Media Researcher p396
- Statistician p524

Further information

ESOMAR
www.esomar.org

Market Research Society
www.mrs.org.uk

MARKETING, ADVERTISING, MEDIA, PRINT AND PUBLISHING

Qualifications and courses

Marketing is a highly competitive industry and while you may become an assistant/executive with relevant work experience or a dynamic personality, you will have an advantage if you are a graduate. A degree, Foundation degree or HND in a relevant subject such as marketing, communications or business may improve your chances of employment. Entry requirements vary between universities but are usually 2 A levels/3 H grades and 5 GCSEs/ National 5s (A*–C/A–C). A postgraduate qualification may improve your chances of employment. Alternatively, The Chartered Institute of Marketing (CIM) has introduced the Graduate Gateway, a scheme which allows students to gain CIM qualifications alongside their degree.

BTEC offers the Certificate in Principles of Marketing (Levels 2–3) which may be useful. School leavers and graduates of non-related disciplines could take the Foundation Certificate in Marketing run by the CIM.

Owing to the competitive nature of this sector, you are advised to undertake vacation work or an internship in order to build a network of contacts and develop your skills and experience. You could also take on administrator or assistant positions within a company's marketing department in order to work your way up from there.

Once employed employers may encourage you to study for industry recognised qualifications provided by CIM or the Communication, Advertising and Marketing (CAM) Education Foundation. As digital knowledge has become essential in this field, qualifications in digital marketing such as the CIM Diploma in Digital Marketing may be particularly valuable.

What the work involves

Marketing assistants/executives (under the direction of a marketing manager or director) need to promote and raise the profile of ideas, products and services for their clients or organisation.

You will use a variety of techniques to do this including writing press releases and brochures, advertising, developing promotional material for the web or for TV and radio, poster campaigns or events. Use of social media is becoming increasingly important within this field.

You will need to conduct market research which could involve writing surveys and setting up consumer focus groups. You will network (sourcing new clients and gaining contacts) regularly and update customer databases with new client details.

Type of person suited to this work

You must be commercially aware and in-tune with consumer behaviour. It is important to understand what motivates people. Imagination and initiative are essential when developing innovative marketing techniques.

Excellent communication and persuasion skills are necessary. You need to be confident, adaptable and ambitious in order to succeed.

You should be organised as many projects will require you to multi-task, working quickly and to a high standard.

Working conditions

You will spend most of your time in an office working normal hours from Monday to Friday. However, you might need to work evenings and weekends when running events and campaigns. Most companies will provide you with time off in lieu for working overtime.

You will travel to meet clients and attend exhibitions or launches. You will probably be expected to dress formally.

Future prospects

The majority of marketing vacancies are centred in cities such as London, Manchester and Birmingham.

You will work either in-house with a company or for a specialist agency.

With 3–10 years' experience you may be promoted to marketing manager. You could also choose to focus on a particular area such as social media, public relations or advertising. It may be necessary to transfer to a new company in order to increase your chances of promotion.

Advantages/disadvantages

You will be inspired working alongside lively and creative people.

It is rewarding when your campaigns are successful and impact the public or profit your company.

A deadline-driven environment can be stressful and demanding.

You could have many campaigns running at once which can be difficult to balance.

Money guide

Salaries vary with geographical location and tend to be higher in large cities.

As a marketing assistant, you can expect to earn £18,000–£22,000.

Salaries rise to between £25,000 and £40,000 as you gain experience.

Marketing directors can earn in excess of £50,000 a year.

Salaries tend to be lower in the public sector. Bonuses can increase your earnings.

Related opportunities

- Advertising Account Executive p382
- Marketing Manager/Director p395
- Public Relations Officer p404

Further information

Chartered Institute of Marketing
www.cim.co.uk

Communication, Advertising and Marketing Education Foundation
www.camfoundation.com

Qualifications and courses

For entry to management positions, employers want to see a good track record, sufficient industry knowledge and previous experience in marketing. Most managers begin as marketing assistants or executives and work their way up to senior level.

Most employers prefer candidates to have completed the Diploma in Professional Marketing from the Chartered Institute of Marketing (CIM). This course is aimed at those wishing to pursue marketing management and you will need one of the following to qualify: a degree with a least a third of the credits coming from marketing content, any Level 4 qualification, the CIM Professional Certificate in Marketing or Certificate in Professional Marketing, or 2 years of professional practice with Level 6 diagnostic assessment.

If you want to work at a strategic, directorate level then a postgraduate qualification may be useful. Your employer may sponsor you if you opt to study for the Chartered Postgraduate Diploma in Marketing offered by the CIM. Entry requirements are a degree in marketing or the CIM Professional Diploma in Marketing, and significant experience working as a manager. You should also be working in order to implement a work-based project to your own business context. CIM also provides the opportunity for experienced professionals to apply for Chartered Marketer Status.

Alternatively, the Institute of Direct and Digital Marketing (IDM) accredits relevant courses such as the IDM Diploma in Direct and Digital Marketing and an MSc in Marketing Management.

NVQs/SVQs in Marketing (Levels 2–4) are also available from City & Guilds.

What the work involves

You will analyse markets and evaluate the competition in order to develop marketing strategies that will promote and increase sales of products, services or ideas.

You will be responsible for post-campaign evaluations, assessing past strategies and overseeing product branding. This information will help you to come up with innovative campaigns in the future. You will also be in charge of product development and budgeting.

You will oversee a team of assistants and executives.

Type of person suited to this work

In order to work at a strategic level, you must have vision and be a confident and creative decision-maker. You should be diplomatic and persuasive in order to manage your team effectively.

Good business sense and consumer knowledge are essential. You need to have excellent communication and presentation skills. Enthusiasm and imagination will help you to stay ahead of your competitors.

Analytical and numerical skills are also important as you will be responsible for a project's success and ensuring it is within budget. You must be able to cope under pressure.

Working conditions

You will usually work a 37-hour week, Monday to Friday, but you may often work overtime in order to meet deadlines.

As the manager of a campaign you will be in regular contact with the press, printers and designers and will need to travel often. International travel may also be required and you may spend long periods of time away from home. Otherwise you will be office based, developing strategies and supervising staff.

Future prospects

With 10–15 years of experience you may be promoted from marketing manager to marketing director.

Taking postgraduate qualifications or moving to another company could increase your chance of promotion.

Directors may choose to become self-employed or work as freelance marketing consultants. Alternatively, if you work for a global organisation you may choose to take up a leadership role in an office overseas.

Advantages/disadvantages

It is rewarding to see your strategies and campaigns increase profits and raise awareness for your clients.

You have the freedom to be creative and innovative in your role.

Clients might dislike your ideas and can be difficult to please.

Working overtime to meet deadlines is stressful and demanding.

Money guide

The starting salary for a marketing manager is around £25,000.

As you gain experience in the role, your earnings can increase up to £40,000.

Senior managers and marketing directors can achieve in excess of £50,000.

Earnings are higher if you work in the private rather than public sector and many companies offer additional benefits such as bonuses, medical insurance and a company car.

Related opportunities

- Advertising Account Executive p382
- Marketing Assistant/Executive p394
- Public Relations Officer p404

Further information

Chartered Institute of Marketing
www.cim.co.uk

Communication, Advertising and Marketing Education Foundation
www.camfoundation.com

MARKETING, ADVERTISING, MEDIA, PRINT AND PUBLISHING

395

Qualifications and courses

There are no formal educational requirements to become a media researcher but owing to the competitive nature of the industry, many entrants have a degree or HND in a relevant subject, such as journalism, English, media studies and broadcasting. Depending on the type of programmes you will be working on, a degree in a specialist subject, such as politics, history or legal studies may be useful. Typical entry requirements for a degree course include 2 A levels/3 H grades and 5 GCSEs/National 5s (A*–C/A–C). It may prove helpful to undertake a postgraduate course in production or a master's in media and communications research

Those without a degree could start their career as a production assistant or runner and work their way up to become a researcher. Personal qualities, confidence and relevant skills are often valued as much as academic qualifications.

Pre-entry work experience is essential as it helps you develop your skills and build crucial industry contacts. Volunteering for student film/TV productions, hospital or community radio stations, local newspapers or TV/radio production companies would be useful. Some media production courses offer their students the chance to gain practical skills via a variety of work placements. A good knowledge of current affairs and media practice would also be an advantage.

Many researchers gain experience as print or broadcast journalists first. If you have undertaken research in a non-media field, such as social or political research, then your skills would also be relevant.

You should continue to update your skills throughout your career by taking short courses offered by film schools, private training companies, TRC media and the Producers' Alliance for Cinema and Television (PACT).

What the work involves

Researchers develop TV and radio programmes and documentary films by gathering and checking information on specific subjects, people or places.

You will use the internet and phone, conduct face-to-face interviews and visit different locations to do your research. It will be your job to research guests and programme contributors as well as to find relevant images, film clips and music. You could also write and edit programme scripts.

You will brief the production team on the specific subjects covered by your research in preparation for filming.

Type of person suited to this work

The ability to find accurate, relevant information quickly is central to this role. You will need to be creative and resourceful in order to find the best story angles possible. Strong IT skills are required.

You should be persistent, confident and an excellent communicator. You will work to strict deadlines and must be

able to stay calm under pressure. A flexible approach will help you balance varied tasks and unsocial hours.

Organisational skills are also important. As you will be responsible for gaining permission to access and make use of information, you will need a clear understanding of the law.

The ability to network and build good relationships with contacts is essential.

Working conditions

You will be based in offices or studios to undertake desk research. You will also spend time on research trips to locations in the UK or overseas. A driving licence would be useful.

The hours tend to be long and it is likely that you will have to work weekends and evenings on a regular basis.

Future prospects

While this is a competitive area to get into, researchers are employed in many areas of the media including radio, production companies, TV and film companies. Many opt to work freelance and hence, there is strong competition for work.

With experience, you could progress into a role as an assistant producer and then on to working as a producer/programme director. Many researchers work freelance, getting paid on a contract-by-contract basis.

Advantages/disadvantages

You will have to work long and often unsocial hours, which can affect your personal life.

You could get the opportunity to travel to a range of places.

Money guide

Starting salaries are usually around £19,000 a year.

An experienced media researcher can expect to earn £29,000–£32,500.

Many researchers work freelance on a contract-by-contract basis, so wages can vary. However, the Broadcasting, Entertainment, Cinematograph and Theatre Union (BECTU) recommends a weekly wage of £415 for a junior researcher working a 48 hour week, and £650 for an experienced researcher working similar hours.

Related opportunities

- Archivist/Records Manager p328
- Historian p333
- Journalist p392

Further information

Creative Skillset
www.creativeskillset.org

TRC media
www.trcmedia.org

MODEL

Qualifications and courses

There are no formal entry qualifications to become a model but you will need to possess the right 'look' and modelling agencies will expect to see a portfolio of photographs before taking you on. You should not have to pay an upfront fee to join an agency and be wary of paying for portfolio pictures; most reputable agencies will cover these costs if they think you have potential.

Female fashion models should be at least 5 feet 8 inches (1.72m) tall and should measure no more than 34–24–34 inches (86–61–86cm). Male fashion models should be at least 6 feet (1.83m) tall and have a 38–40 inch chest (97–102cm) and a 30–32 inch waist (76–81cm). However, some photographic models are required to be smaller or larger than the usual sizes, depending on employer requirements.

Your agency may send you on courses which focus on diet, health, deportment, fashion coordination, grooming, catwalk turns and movements, photographic modelling techniques and how to work with agents. Some independent modelling schools provide similar courses although they do not offer any guarantee of work.

You will need to be licensed by your local Education and Welfare Authority in the event that your modelling career takes off before the legal school leaving age.

What the work involves

You could be involved in different types of modelling, such as fashion, photographic or demonstration work. You could work in a studio, on location outdoors, at fashion shows or at events such as car shows or conventions.

It is necessary to build a good portfolio of your work and establish a good reputation within the industry.

Your job will be to show off new clothing or products to their best advantage in order to help potential customers visualise them being worn or in use.

Type of person suited to this work

This is a very competitive area to find work. You will have to be determined and prepared to deal with disappointment if contracts do not come your way.

Most fashion model agencies have set physical requirements that you will have to meet before you are accepted onto their books. There is also scope for models with one particularly good feature, such as hands, feet, eyes or hair, to model specific items. To be successful you must be willing to look after yourself physically and be able to cope with rejection and criticism.

Working conditions

The places you will work will depend on the type of modelling that you do and the nature of the contracts you are offered. You might work indoors within a studio, or you could be on location doing catalogue work. This can involve many hours of work to get the correct shot.

The work can be physically demanding; hours spent walking back and forth and posing in awkward positions for long periods can take their toll.

Future prospects

Only the most successful models are always in work. Most are self-employed and have to take on alternate temporary or part-time work when necessary in order to boost earnings.

To build your reputation, you will have to create a portfolio of work using photos from previous contracts. Your portfolio will need to have a distinct edge to help you win contracts and work.

While top models are very famous and can be rich, there are hundreds more who work for smaller companies and businesses who may earn a lot less. Most models finish their career in their early 30s.

Alternatively, you could establish your own agency, become a booker for an agency, or become involved in the fashion industry, designing and endorsing your own lines.

Advantages/disadvantages

Only a few models get the top contracts.

You could get to travel around the world.

You will be posing for long periods which could be tiring.

Modelling can be a very glamorous and confidence-boosting career although you will also have to take criticism.

Modelling can be quite a short career.

Money guide

You will probably be self-employed so your earnings will depend on your success in finding regular, well-paid work.

Most agencies keep 20% of earnings as commission.

You can expect to start on around £50–£200 per booking, rising to up to £1,000 per booking for models with experience.

Models working for particular fashion houses can earn between £10,000 and £30,000 a year.

Well-known models can earn very high wages.

Related opportunities

- Beauty Consultant p442
- Fashion Designer/Milliner p161
- Wardrobe Assistant p439

Further information

Alba Model Information
www.albamodel.info

Association of Model Agents
www.associationofmodelagents.org

Equity
www.equity.org.uk

London College of Fashion
www.arts.ac.uk/fashion

MARKETING, ADVERTISING, MEDIA, PRINT AND PUBLISHING

Qualifications and courses

Most newspaper, magazine or web editors have extensive journalistic experience. To become a journalist you usually need an HND, Foundation degree or degree accredited by the National Council for the Training of Journalists (NCTJ) or the Periodicals Training Council (PTC). Alternatively, you could complete an unrelated degree, followed by an accredited 1-year postgraduate course or a fast-track postgraduate course lasting 18–20 weeks. Editors of specialist publications may have qualifications or experience in that particular field, for example a degree in science or art.

The Diploma in Journalism or other distance-learning courses in newspaper and magazine journalism from the NCTJ and professional qualifications from the Professional Publishers Association (PPA) may also be useful.

Those with 18 months' work experience who have gained the Diploma in Journalism can take the NCTJ's National Certificate Examination (NCE) which enables candidates to achieve senior status as a journalist.

Developing a strong portfolio by writing for student publications, local newspapers or online magazines is important as the industry is fiercely competitive. Employers seek candidates who can show evidence of their creativity, persistence, excellent writing skills and an ability to accept criticism, so gaining a variety of work experience is highly recommended. Knowledge of HTML code and photography could also make your application stand out given the rapid increase in digital publishing.

What the work involves

Newspaper/magazine/web editors are responsible for the coordination of each aspect of a publication or website.

You will understand the readership of the publication or website and include informative, newsworthy articles, entertaining features and high quality images. You will work with the editorial, design and advertising departments, as well as journalists, printers, web developers and publishers.

Tasks include editing and proofreading articles and features, assigning journalists to cover stories, commissioning freelance writers for features, meeting with photographers and conducting interviews.

Type of person suited to this work

You should be able to demonstrate excellent writing skills and a creative flair. You must have a strong interest in current affairs.

You will have a practical approach to problem-solving and remain calm in stressful situations. You need to show initiative, persistence and decisiveness. You must pay attention to detail, be meticulous in your organisation and time management, and be able to work to a deadline.

You must have excellent communication skills to be able to delegate tasks and persuade others to meet deadlines.

Web editors must possess good IT skills and feel comfortable using a content management system, monitoring online message boards and dealing with enquiries. You must also keep track of developments within web technology and legal requirements.

Working conditions

You will probably work around 40 hours a week which may include early starts, late nights and weekend work to cover a breaking story. Some large newspapers may offer shift work.

You will mainly be based in an office which could be noisy and busy. You may be required to meet with other editors, journalists or photographers outside the office.

Future prospects

Journalism is a very competitive industry. Work experience, published articles and evidence of commitment to journalism are as important as qualifications.

The typical route to becoming a newspaper/magazine/web editor is to begin in a junior role as a journalist or editorial assistant and work your way up through the editorial department until you are in charge of the content of the magazine, website or newspaper. If successful you could be made editor-in-chief of a group of publications.

You could later work in PR, website development or on a freelance basis.

Advantages/disadvantages

Your work will be diverse and stimulating as it will involve constantly creating new content.

You may work in a highly stressful environment, working long and unsocial hours.

Money guide

Earnings depend on the type, size and location of your employer.

The salary for a newspaper editor can range from £30,000 to £80,000. Higher salaries are possible with extensive experience.

As a magazine editor, your salary is likely to range between £25,000 and £40,000, with £65,000 possible when experienced.

A web editor is likely to earn £18,000–£38,000.

Related opportunities

- Copy Editor/Sub-editor/Proofreader p388
- Publisher/Commissioning Editor p405
- Website Developer p156

Further information

National Council for the Training of Journalists
www.nctj.com

News Media Association
www.newsmediauk.org

Society of Editors
www.societyofeditors.org

Qualifications and courses

There are no set academic requirements to become a photographer but the following courses may be useful to gain relevant knowledge: an A level/H grade in Photography; a City & Guilds Certificate in Photo Imaging and Photography (Levels 1–3); an HNC/HND in Art and Design or a relevant degree. The content of a photography degree can vary significantly, with some having greater emphasis on artistic aspects and others more focused on commercial concerns. Creative Skillset provide a course accreditation scheme.

Given photography's competitiveness, a postgraduate qualification may be advantageous, particularly those that promote contact with the industry.

Candidates wishing to pursue careers as police, medical or press photographers will need 5 GCSEs/National 5s (A*–C/A–C) including English and Maths. It is necessary for medical photographers to have a degree or postgraduate certificate in clinical photography and forensic photographers to have an A level/H grade in a science.

It is generally accepted that prior work experience is a necessary requirement, with perseverance and patience essential. Visit galleries, volunteer in museums and find any way to get your work published as you will need a strong portfolio comprising between 10 and 15 shots and knowledge of a variety of software packages.

Depending on the area of photography in which you work, your training will vary. Many photographers are self-employed and learn on the job whilst medical and press photographers often follow a recognised training pattern. Press photographers are often encouraged to complete the National Council for the Training of Journalists (NCTJ) Level 3 Diploma in Journalism for Press Photographers and Photojournalists. Medical photographers are encouraged to gain a certificate in clinical photography provided by either Cardiff or Staffordshire University.

The British Institute of Professional Photographers (BIPP) provides a variety of courses, workshops and seminars which cover a wide range of photography disciplines and business skills. These may be useful should you choose to become freelance or set up your own photography business.

What the work involves

Photographers capture images using technical lighting and equipment. Using your eye for design and knowledge of photographic techniques you will create images for a specific brief.

Many photographers work with digital enhancing techniques to modify and improve, or add interest and illusions to the images they produce.

Type of person suited to this work

You will need a strong visual sense and an eye for what makes a good picture. You will need technical knowledge and skills to get the most from lighting, studio set-ups and camera equipment. The use of editing software means that IT skills are increasingly important.

Strong communication skills and a flexible attitude are useful when discussing projects with clients, or calming nervous subjects.

To work on a freelance basis, business skills and self-confidence are essential.

Working conditions

You will either be based in a studio or work on location. In a studio you could work with still life and portraiture. Lighting equipment can be heavy and the work can be physically tiring as you will be on your feet for long periods.

If you work outdoors you could record images for advertising and photo-journalism. This may require patience if the weather or light conditions are not correct for your shot.

Commercial photography is completed to tight deadlines, which can be stressful.

Future prospects

In order to gain the essential skills and an understanding of your specialist type of photography, you could work as a photographer's assistant.

With experience you could progress into freelance work or specialise in a particular area such as press, medical or food photography.

Nowadays, positions are even more limited as digital photography has reduced the work of professionals.

Advantages/disadvantages

There is the potential for public acknowledgement and personal satisfaction for using your creativity and technical skills to create original images.

It takes time in this competitive industry to develop contacts, so you might need a second job to support yourself.

Money guide

As an assistant photographer you can expect to earn between £10,000 and £17,000 a year.

Depending on your experience and popularity, this can rise to £18,000–£65,000 once established.

Earnings will vary if you are self-employed or freelance.

Related opportunities

- Graphic Designer p165
- Illustrator/Technical Illustrator p166
- TV and Film Camera Person/Operator p409

Further information

British Institute of Professional Photography
www.bipp.com

The Association of Photographers
www.the-aop.org

MARKETING, ADVERTISING, MEDIA, PRINT AND PUBLISHING

Qualifications and courses

There are no formal qualifications required in order to become a photographic stylist, however many people who enter into the role do have an art or design related qualification or experience as a photographer's assistant. If you wish to work in food styling then you should have a background in catering.

Several relevant further education courses are available, such as the London College of Fashion's Foundation degree in Fashion: Styling and Photography. A BTEC National Diploma in Fashion and Clothing or Photography may also provide you with some of the skills required in the industry.

Only a few HNCs and HNDs, degree courses and postgraduate qualifications are directly related to this area (for example, in fashion styling, visual merchandising or fashion promotion) but many fashion or photography courses include the relevant module. However, The British Display Society (BDS) do offer a distance learning Certificate in Display and Visual Merchandising. The skills used in interior or exhibition design or home economics (food styling) could also be useful.

It is essential that you secure as much relevant work experience as possible. You must remain determined and proactive in order to secure placements. It is useful to compile a portfolio of any work you do in order to show potential employers.

Once employment is secured, you will normally be trained on the job as an assistant to a stylist or photographer, or as a fashion/editorial assistant on a magazine, before working your way up to photographic stylist.

What the work involves

Photographic stylists work closely with photographers to design the look and mood of a photo shoot.

It would be your responsibility to arrange and dress the set, to find appropriate props and to organise any work that needs to be done behind the scenes.

Typically, you would receive a brief from the photographer or director of the shoot and then come up with creative ideas to fulfil the brief. Sometimes you will have a lot of freedom for your own ideas but at other times the brief will be very strict.

It is useful to build up a collection of accessories that you can bring to shoots.

Most stylists specialise in a particular area, such as fashion, food or interior photography.

Type of person suited to this work

You will need to be creative with a good eye for design and understand what makes a good picture. You will also need to have a sound understanding of photography and lighting.

Good communication skills are essential as you will need to coordinate with a range of people on each shoot.

You must be able to stay calm under pressure.

An understanding of the latest fashion trends is important as is commercial awareness.

Working conditions

You will need to have an office base but will spend the majority of your time out on location and in photography studios.

Working hours will be varied and days will often be long and often extremely pressurised. You will probably need to work some evenings and weekends.

You will probably work freelance and as you build up contacts and experience you may secure work with magazines, photography studios and design houses.

It is useful to have a full driving licence as you will need to drive between shoots and transport props which could be large or delicate.

Future prospects

The industry is competitive and tough to enter, attracting more people than jobs available. Most photo stylists are self-employed and work on a per-assignment basis, but there is the opportunity for more secure work through agency representation.

Advancement generally comes through producing work on a bigger platform and developing your reputation.

Advantages/disadvantages

Working as a photographic stylist is a very creative job where you can see your ideas brought to life on camera.

Hours are long and the work can be stressful as you will have to work to very tight deadlines.

Pay can be low to start with and competition is fierce.

Money guide

Starting salaries vary, but are typically around £12,000. With experience, this can rise to £35,000 a year.

Top stylists with good reputations can earn considerably more.

As most stylists work freelance, incomes vary considerably depending on how much work you have. Daily rates vary between £200 and £400.

Related opportunities

- Fashion Designer/Milliner p161
- Photographer p399
- TV and Film Camera Person/Operator p409

Further information

British Display Society
www.britishdisplaysociety.co.uk

British Institute of Professional Photography
www.bipp.com

The Association of Photographers
www.the-aop.org

Qualifications and courses

Although there are no set entry requirements for this career candidates with GCSEs/National 5s (A*–C/ A–C) in English, Maths, a science and technology subjects would be at an advantage. The Diploma in Manufacturing and Product Design might also be useful or you can study a relevant college course prior to entry. Many people enter these professions by means of an apprenticeship.

Machine printer

Most employers will expect a good level of education, particularly GCSEs/National 5s in English, Maths, a science and IT. General art and design courses may teach you the basics of screen printing and you will also need to have good colour vision.

As an introduction you may take a 10-day course run by the Institute of Paper, Printing and Publishing. Alternatively, you might opt to study other printing courses such as the City & Guilds Certificate in Printing and Graphic Communications or the ABC Level 3 Diploma in Print Media, full time at college.

Apprenticeships may be available. As an apprentice you will experience a combination of on-the-job training and a series of day or block release instruction at college where you might work towards an NVQ in either Machine Printing, Mechanised Print Finishing and Binding, Digital Print Production, Envelope Manufacture or Carton Manufacture (Levels 1–3).

Screen printer

You can choose to do a college course in printing and graphic communications, printmaking skills, screen printing, graphic printmaking or print media.

It is also possible to attain City & Guilds Certificates in Printing and Graphic Communications (Levels 2–3), an NVQ in Screenprinting (Levels 2–3), or an ABC Level 3 Award in Printmaking Skills, Screen Printing and Screen Printing Skills.

The majority of training takes place on the job with experienced colleagues and many companies provide in-house training schemes.

The Digital and Screenprinting Association and specialist schools, such as the London College of Communication, also run courses in this area.

Bookbinder

You do not need formal qualifications to be a machine bookbinder as on-the-job training is provided, however it may be advantageous to have GCSEs/National 5s particularly in English or Maths.

NVQs are available in specialist subjects such as Mechanised Print Finishing and Binding (Levels 2–3) and the Level 3 in Hand Binding. It is also possible to enter the profession through an apprenticeship scheme.

To work as a craft bookbinder you will need certain skills. Craft bookbinding is often a second career path. Courses, degrees and diplomas are available in fine bookbinding and repair.

To enhance your prospects, you may seek membership of the Society of Bookbinders (SoB). With experience you may be encouraged to apply for Licentiateship or Fellowship.

Print production planner

This area of printing is open to graduates and diplomates of a variety of disciplines. Those who have studied a relevant subject such as print management, graphic communications, business studies or publishing may be at a distinct advantage however. Courses such as these will help develop skills including production management, print processes, digital pre-press and total quality management. Postgraduate qualifications are available, although not essential.

For a degree, entry requirements are usually 2 A levels/3 H grades and 5 GCSEs/National 5s (A*–C/A–C). For an HND, you should have 1 A level/2 H grades or a BTEC National Diploma in a related subject. You can study for an NVQ Level 3 in Print Administration, which includes modules on health and safety.

It is also possible to enter without a degree or HND and employers are willing to provide release from work for training. If you have any qualifications in art, design, communications or IT, this will help your search for employment.

This job requires maturity and practical industry experience. It is possible to commence as a machine printer and work your way up to this position.

Once employed, your training will take place on the job. Your employer may encourage you to further your skills by completing external short courses such as those offered by the British Printing Industries Federation (BPIF).

What the work involves

Machine printer

Machine printers oversee the production of printed items on machines of various sizes for products such as newspapers, posters, books, etc. You will set up the printing press correctly for the specific job. This includes ensuring that the appropriate plates, paper and inks have been selected.

You will trial the print run, check for errors and ensure that the quality is up to standard.

Screen printer

Screen printers create visual images by organising and operating hand- or power-driven screen printing machines which print graphics onto fabrics and paper by forcing ink through a delicate mesh overlay of the stencil design.

You will be required to prepare the stencils, inks and print processes.

Bookbinder

Bookbinders are responsible for transforming the printed material into the finished product. Nowadays the majority of bookbinding is a machine orientated process, which involves stitching, stapling, collating, cutting, binding and coating.

Print production planner

Print production planners are responsible for workflow in the printing firm and ensuring that the efficiency is maximised by checking orders, creating schedules, allocating work, supervising and quality control. It will be your responsibility to liaise with other production departments.

Type of person suited to this work

Printing requires good teamwork and communication skills. It is usual that your work will involve computers and other types of machinery and equipment so you will need good practical skills and an understanding of IT.

It is important to have normal colour vision, good hand-to-eye co-ordination and a high level of physical fitness.

You should have a meticulous eye for detail, and you will need to demonstrate design skills to convince customers that you can make aesthetically pleasing finished products, from CD covers to full-text pages or full-colour brochures.

As print runs do not always go smoothly you will need to be adept at problem-solving, have a long concentration span and the ability to work under pressure.

Furthermore you should be flexible as some print companies run 24-hour operations and you might have to work shifts at night and at the weekends. Print production managers should also have good multi-tasking skills, a good head for numbers and the ability to influence people.

Working conditions

In smaller print companies you will normally work office hours, that is 9am to 5pm, but during busy periods you could do additional hours in order to ensure that projects are completed on time. Larger companies tend to run 24-hour operations and you will be expected to work shifts and weekends. Overtime is widely available.

Bookbinders may also have the opportunity to work part time.

Your working environment will depend on your role and the size of the firm. Printshops can be dirty and noisy when machines are functioning. Hazardous chemicals are used in finishes and to wash inks from the press but there is good ventilation to cope with the resulting fumes.

You will be required to adhere to health and safety regulations at all times and use protective gear such as overalls, boots, gloves and ear protectors.

It is necessary to have a good level of physical fitness as you will be standing for long periods of time. Upper body strength is also important as you may be required to carry out some heavy lifting.

Print production planners will work in an office but will also carry out work on the production floor and may have to travel to attend meetings with clients.

Future prospects

At present in the UK there are approximately 10,500 print companies which employ about 140,000 people, although changes in costs and technology means that small printing firms are in decline.

The majority of the industry comprises small, family-owned enterprises. The industry is sensitive to wider economic issues, such as cheaper rates from foreign print companies, increasing use of electronic resources and seasonal order variations.

Opportunities will depend on your skills and the size and type

of your company. Although printers cover all the stages of production, the job of folding machine operator (at the finishing end of the process) is becoming a skills shortage area.

With experience and additional design skills, you could work for a specialist press production company, a design or reprographic house or general printers. To run a printing business takes a high level of business skills, including accounting and sales.

Advantages/disadvantages

This job combines creative and artistic skills with technical and computer-aided design.

There are good entry opportunities for some printing jobs such as specialist print finishers, which have become skills shortage areas.

Owing to the nature of the industry, you might have to move to other parts of the country for promotion.

Many companies now produce high quality publications in-house, so printers need to work with large volumes or specialist niche markets to make a profit.

Money guide

Machine printer

Newly qualified printers can expect to earn £16,000– £19,000.

With experience, this can rise to £35,000.

Additional payments for shift allowances and bonuses are also possible and the highest salaries in this profession can be up to £60,000.

Screen printer

Screen printers can expect to start on £16,000, rising to £24,000 with experience.

Top earners can reach salaries of up to £36,000.

Bookbinder

Bookbinders can expect to earn £14,000–£17,000.

This can rise to £18,000–£25,000, depending on your experience and responsibilities.

If you are a self-employed craft bookbinder earnings can vary depending on the amount of work you have.

Print production planner

New entrants can expect £20,000–£25,000.

With experience, you can earn between £30,000 and £40,000.

Senior planners can expect £45,000–£55,000.

Related opportunities

- CAD Draughtsperson p204
- Publisher/Commissioning Editor p405
- Quality Control Inspector p226
- Signwriter/Signmaker p174

Further information

British Printing Industries Federation
www.britishprint.com

Institute of Paper, Printing and Publishing
www.ip3.org.uk

Society of Bookbinders
www.societyofbookbinders.com

Qualifications and courses

To become a public affairs consultant, you will need a degree. A degree in a relevant subject such as politics, public relations, business, English, law or modern European languages is likely to increase your chances of employment. Although most graduates entering this industry possess politics degrees, relevant experience in politics is considered more valuable. A postgraduate qualification in politics or public affairs may improve your prospects.

Work experience is crucial for proving your interest in the industry. You may wish to shadow an MP, get involved in local campaigns or engage in student politics. Some public affairs consultancies do offer internships to undergraduates, but these are not always advertised. You may wish to send out speculative applications.

Once in the profession you will need to update your skills and knowledge regularly. Pubaffairs runs a number of short courses and events designed for this purpose. Courses cover a variety of topics including getting the most out of a party conference, working with local government and evaluating public affairs.

The Public Relations Consultants Association (PRCA) have a range of qualifications at different levels suitable for new entrants or experienced professionals which you may find useful.

What the work involves

Public affairs consultants offer political and public policy advice to clients.

You must have an excellent understanding of the inner workings of parliament and keep up to date with political developments. This will involve reading parliamentary publications, reports and legislation and watching debates. You will then provide in-depth analysis on activities in the Houses of Parliament, political parties, local government and European institutions relevant to your client.

Your role may involve PR work as you raise and improve the profile of your client. A network of contacts within the press, parliament and overseas governments will be vital.

Daily activities may include writing press releases, lobbying and meeting with politicians, civil servants and your clients. You will typically attend party conferences and other important political events.

Type of person suited to this work

You must be confident and have a smart appearance.

You need to have strong communication skills and enjoy liaising with a wide range of people. You must have a persuasive manner for lobbying work. Written communication and research skills are essential, as are good IT skills. You must have a keen eye for detail and possess a keen interest in politics and media.

You must be able to work effectively to tight deadlines and be flexible when managing several clients at once.

Working conditions

You will typically be office based, but your work will involve travelling to meet clients and attend important political events.

You will work regular office hours Monday to Friday, but you may have to work overtime to meet deadlines.

You may have to stay overnight when attending party conferences. You may have the opportunity to work abroad in a European consultancy.

Future prospects

In consultancies there is typically a clear path for career progression from account executive to account manager. You could progress to become an account director.

As an executive your work will typically be research based. However, with experience you will gain access to clients and politicians and will be expected to win new business.

You may become a full-time political adviser for a political party. You could remain an adviser or return to consultancy as a more experienced professional.

Advantages/disadvantages

The work can be highly pressured as you will have to respond to new political developments quickly.

You may be working on high profile events with high profile clients.

It can be difficult to balance your varied workload.

Money guide

Starting salaries are typically between £18,000 and £32,000 a year.

With experience account managers can earn up to £45,000 a year.

Account directors can expect to earn £60,000 to £100,000 or more a year.

Related opportunities

- Journalist p392
- Politician p358
- Public Relations Officer p404

Further information

PubAffairs
www.publicaffairsnetworking.com

UK Lobbying Register
www.lobbying-register.uk

Qualifications and courses

There are no formal academic requirements but most entrants to this profession are graduates or diplomates. An HND or degree in a relevant subject, such as public relations, marketing, business, English, media studies or politics is highly likely to increase your chances of employment. You could enter the industry at a junior level as a PR assistant and work your way up or you may try to secure a place on a graduate training scheme offered by some large organisations. As entry to the profession is highly competitive, a postgraduate qualification may improve your career prospects. The Chartered Institute of Public Relations (CIPR) has compiled a list of recognised undergraduate and postgraduate public relations courses.

Employers often expect candidates to undertake pre-entry work experience in PR, communications or marketing or, alternatively, you could develop relevant skills by volunteering at a charity or writing for a student newspaper.

Membership of the CIPR is useful as it often advertises placements, training courses and encourages you to build contacts within the industry. The CIPR also offers professional qualifications which are becoming increasingly sought after by employers.

The Diploma in Marketing Communications available from the Communication, Advertising and Marketing (CAM) Education Foundation could also be beneficial.

The Public Relations Consultants Association (PRCA) has a range of qualifications at different levels suitable for new entrants, experienced PR officers or managers.

What the work involves

Public relations officers work in public relations or communications departments in large organisations and for PR companies. Some work on a freelance basis.

You will manage the image and reputation of organisations by writing publicity materials, studying and advising clients, and responding to enquiries or complaints.

It will be important that you develop and maintain positive working relationships with members of the press.

You will need to monitor media coverage to gauge perception of your company. Social media is particularly important now as it offers an opportunity for the public to interact directly with companies.

Type of person suited to this work

You must be confident and have a smart appearance.

You need to have strong communication skills and enjoy liaising with a wide range of people. Written communication and research skills are essential, as are good IT skills.

You must be able to work effectively to tight deadlines and be flexible when managing several projects at once. Financial management skills are also useful.

Working conditions

Most of your work will be office based and although you will work normal office hours, longer working days are common, particularly during busy periods.

You will have meetings with clients, colleagues or other professionals. You will need to travel to attend meetings, special events and presentations on a regular basis. Working for global companies or high-profile charities may mean some overseas travel.

Future prospects

PR is a growing industry. However, there is strong competition, often with hundreds of well-qualified applicants for one post.

You will typically start your career as a PR assistant and then progress to a role as an account executive, followed by a move into a senior role.

There could be various opportunities to work abroad. With experience, some PR professionals set up their own companies or work freelance for other organisations. Alternatively, you could go on to work in advertising or marketing.

Advantages/disadvantages

You can be part of high-profile campaigns.

This job can be pressured due to the speed of press releases and the range of activities you will have to juggle.

If working for a high-profile organisation, you might have to be on call to respond to unexpected situations.

Money guide

Starting salaries are around £18,000 to £20,000.

With experience, this can increase to around £40,000.

Those in senior positions, such as account directors and heads of corporate affairs, can achieve £80,000–£100,000.

The private sector usually pays more than the public sector. Salaries are often higher in the south-east of England and London. Benefits such as private health insurance, bonus schemes and a company car may be offered.

Related opportunities

- Advertising Account Executive p382
- Advertising Media Planner p385
- Journalist p392

Further information

Chartered Institute of Public Relations
www.cipr.co.uk

Communication, Advertising and Marketing Education Foundation
www.camfoundation.com

International Public Relations Association
www.ipra.org

Qualifications and courses

The majority of new entrants are graduates with a degree in a relevant subject such as publishing, English language or literature. Specialist publishers, such as those in the academic field or journals, will expect candidates to have more subject-specific degrees related to the academic areas in which they publish, such as maths or science. You will need at least 2 A levels/3 H grades and 5 GCSEs/National 5s (A*–C/A–C) for degree entry. A relevant postgraduate qualification, such as a master's in publishing, is not essential but may be beneficial given the competition for places.

As this is a senior role, it is unlikely that a recent graduate would begin their career at a publisher/commissioning editor level. Most entrants begin as an editorial assistant.

Entry into the industry is highly competitive. Experience of writing or editing at a non-professional level can be useful as employers often value those candidates who can provide evidence of good research skills, an ability to think creatively, effective communication and teamwork skills. Gaining work experience will also ensure you form industry contacts which are crucial when seeking employment as few trainee publishing jobs are formally advertised.

Specialist centres such as the Publishing Training Centre provide short courses on different areas of publishing such as commissioning and list management, financial planning and managing publishing strategy.

What the work involves

Publishers/commissioning editors plan and manage the range or list of books, magazines or IT resources produced by their department or company. This includes researching consumers' needs and identifying gaps in the company's list of publications.

You will develop ideas for new publications and digital resources and respond to proposals from authors. You will also oversee the entire process of developing new publications from an original idea to completed manuscript.

In a small organisation you might also be responsible for liaising with copy-editors and proofreaders. You may also be responsible for developing marketing strategies to increase publication sales.

Type of person suited to this work

You will need a strong interest in producing products that have extensive commercial appeal and you will have relevant market knowledge and experience in order to identify gaps in the market.

As you will liaise closely with authors and colleagues, you should enjoy meeting and working with a variety of people.

You will also need strong written and oral communication skills and the ability to encourage people to complete tasks to deadlines. You must be well organised and able to plan ahead.

Working conditions

Most of your work will involve attending meetings or working at a computer within the office of a company or organisation.

You will be expected to liaise with authors, colleagues, designers and IT specialists either face to face, by email or on the phone.

Although your working week will comprise normal office hours, you can expect to work late in order to meet strict publication deadlines or to attend evening events. Business trips, including overnight stays, are a possibility and you could travel abroad.

Future prospects

This is a competitive profession to enter. The main employers are publishing houses, specialist businesses, and professional and educational organisations.

Sales and marketing experience can facilitate entry to this sector. It is possible to set up your own publishing company, although the market is well covered and profit margins narrow. A commissioning editor can progress to editorial director or manager. Some commissioning editors go on to establish their own literary agencies.

Currently, the area of greatest expansion is that offered by the internet and digital publishing.

Advantages/disadvantages

You will meet and work with an interesting cross-section of people.

You will be responsible for creating strategies to increase sales of publications, which can be stressful.

Developing new publications can be a lengthy process and requires patience.

Seeing the finished publication that you have helped to develop is highly satisfying.

Money guide

The average starting salary for an editorial assistant is £18,000.

As a commissioning editor, your salary is likely to be £26,450 and, with experience, this could increase to £40,000–£50,000.

Senior managers, publishers and directors of large publishing companies can earn up to £80,000.

Related opportunities

- Copy Editor/Sub-editor/Proofreader p388
- Copywriter p389
- Newspaper/Magazine/Web Editor p398

Further information

Publishing Training Centre
www.publishingtrainingcentre.co.uk

The Society of Young Publishers
http://thesyp.org.uk/careers/

MARKETING, ADVERTISING, MEDIA, PRINT AND PUBLISHING

Qualifications and courses

Although there are no specific qualifications for entry into this profession, formal music training of some kind is recommended and practical work experience or voluntary work for a studio or record company is extremely important.

Courses that may help you develop skills and experience include Foundation degrees and degrees in music production, music technology, music practice and music industry management. You will need at least 2 A levels/3 H grades and 5 GCSEs/National 5s (A*–C/A–C) for degree entry. Other useful courses include the BTEC Level 3 Extended Diploma in Music Technology, the HNC/HND Level 5 in Music Production, or the NCFE Level 3 Certificate in Managing a Music Business Enterprise.

It is unlikely that as a graduate you will enter a recording industry producer position straight away, therefore you will have to work your way up from lower level roles such as studio assistant or assistant engineer.

The BPI host a variety of seminars, training courses and events for their members, helping professionals remain up to date with this rapidly evolving industry. The Music Producers Guild (MPG) have also created a Knowledge Band and Members' Directory to encourage debate and facilitate future recording industry producers' networking within the industry. The MPG, in association with the Association of Professional Recording Services (APRS), has set up the Joint Audio Media Education Services (JAMES) to allow new entrants to learn from experienced professionals. JAMES provides course accreditation as well as supplying workshops, seminars and master-classes.

What the work involves

Recording industry producers are employed by the artists and repertoire (A&R) department of a recording company to work with artists to produce successful music tracks or demos. You will discuss ideas with artists and their management, plan new projects, listen to existing tracks and identify areas for improvement.

You will be involved in the organisation of each stage of the recording process, including rehearsal time, recruitment of sound engineers, booking studio time, directing the artists and suggesting alterations that will produce the desired sound. You will also be responsible for keeping the team motivated and focused.

Type of person suited to this work

You must have excellent communication skills to give instructions to others, persuade people to try your ideas and to build up a good network of contacts. You must have a keen interest in music and music trends, and be able to recognise a hit.

As you will have to spend long hours in the studio you should have a good ear for music, high stamina, self-discipline and patience.

You should also have good planning skills to work out budgets, organise time scales for recording studios and estimate production and post-production costs.

Working conditions

You will work long, irregular hours. This may include working late into the night and at the weekends. You may be expected to record in small, dark studios or at live events.

Your work may not always be constant and you might have to find other methods of earning money. You may have to travel within the UK and abroad. You may be at risk to hearing damage as a result of prolonged exposure to loud music.

Future prospects

You will probably progress to a production position after several years of working in an assistant sound engineer or engineer role.

At first, you will approach A&R departments with your services until you establish your reputation, usually by producing music that is commercially successful.

As a top record producer, work abroad with international artists is possible. Some go on to establish their own recording studios, supplying facilities, equipment and sound production teams to other producers.

Advantages/disadvantages

You may have the opportunity to work with a diverse range of artists and to be a part of the creative process of making music.

You may produce music which becomes very successful and gains you national, or even international, acclaim.

Prolonged exposure to loud music may damage your hearing. Artists can be independent-minded and sometimes difficult.

Money guide

You can expect a starting salary of around £15,000 per annum, which can rise to over £30,000 with experience and constant work. The top recording industry producers can earn in excess of £100,000.

Earnings for the average producer are low and many have other jobs to supplement their income.

You may be paid 'on spec' if you work with an unsigned band, being paid if and when the artist is successful. Usually you will be paid a flat fee, but this will also be supplemented by an agreed percentage of the sales income. This can be minimal or thousands of pounds.

Related opportunities

- DJ p423
- Musician p429
- Sound Engineer p433

Further information

BPI The British Recorded Music Industry
www.bpi.co.uk

Music Producers Guild UK Ltd
www.mpg.org.uk

Qualifications and courses

There are a number of routes into this profession. Whilst some employers may like you to have a degree in a relevant subject, others look for evidence of skills and experience. Relevant degree subjects such as marketing, journalism, communications, business/management or public relations will provide you with basic skills valued by the industry. You will need at least 2 A levels/3 H grades and 5 GCSEs/National 5s (A*–C/A–C) for degree entry.

You can enter the industry without a degree with relevant experience in marketing, public relations or advertising. Managing your own social media profiles or managing those of a charity may improve your prospects. However, you may wish to prove your interest in the industry by taking relevant courses such as the City & Guilds Diploma in Digital Marketing (Levels 3–4), the Level 3 Diploma in Social Media for Business or the BTEC Level 1 Award in Social Media.

In 2017 a new apprenticeship scheme called the Digital Marketers Trailblazer will become available and will provide access to social media job roles.

Once you enter the industry you will be expected to regularly update your skills. Short training courses are provided by the Chartered Institute of Marketing (CIM), the Communication, Advertising and Marketing (CAM) Education Foundation and the Internet Advertising Bureau (IAB). Courses cover topics such as social media policy, search engine marketing and web analytics.

What the work involves

Social media managers promote and manage their client's online presence through social media channels such as Twitter, Facebook and LinkedIn.

You will be in charge of creating engaging content for websites and social media channels. You will respond to social media comments and posts involving your client. You will also monitor and create strategies to increase follows and likes.

You will use search engine optimisation to ensure your client's website has a better chance of being discovered by customer searches.

You will analyse web data to monitor the success of your activities using tools such as Google Analytics.

Type of person suited to this work

Excellent IT skills and social skills are vital for social media work. You will need a keen interest in internet marketing and social media trends.

You will need excellent written and oral communication skills in order to pitch to clients and influence customers. Good interpersonal skills are essential to engage with customers and clients effectively.

You must have good research skills in order to spot trends and analyse data. Time management and organisation skills are important as you will work on a number of projects at the same time.

Working conditions

You will work office hours, 9am to 5pm, Monday to Friday. However, you may work longer hours to meet deadlines.

Some social media managers work freelance and have more flexible working hours.

You will be office based as you will be working on a computer, but travel may be necessary to meet with clients.

Future prospects

You will have the option of either working freelance or as manager of a social media department within a company.

Many companies now acknowledge the value of social media in business resulting in more opportunities. However, there is some speculation regarding the future of social media roles as professionals in other departments gain social media skills.

You may extend your skills beyond social media and become a digital marketing executive. Alternatively, you could move into related professions such as traditional marketing, advertising or public relations.

Advantages/disadvantages

It can be very satisfying to see successful campaigns go viral.

You will have the opportunity to indulge your interest in social media.

Social media and digital marketing is a very fast-paced industry and it may be a challenge to keep up at times.

Money guide

Starting salaries for social media managers can be around £22,000 a year.

With experience you can expect to earn between £25,000 and £35,000 a year. Those in senior roles may earn in excess of £75,000.

Freelance social media managers will be able to negotiate their remuneration depending on their experience and skill.

Related opportunities

- Advertising Account Executive p382
- Digital Marketer p390
- Public Relations Officer p404

Further information

Chartered Institute of Marketing
www.cim.co.uk

Communication, Advertising and Marketing Education Foundation
www.camfoundation.com

Qualifications and courses

Many entrants have a degree or qualification in either a general subject, such as English, journalism or media studies, or a more specific qualification in the area in which they wish to specialise, engineering or computer science for example. Minimum degree entry requirements are usually 2 A levels/3 H grades and 5 GCSEs/National 5s (A*–C/A–C).

Some universities offer a master's degree in technical communication which is suitable for graduates in science and technology who wish to improve their writing skills. The Institute of Scientific and Technical Communicators (ISTC) provides a list of approved higher education courses.

It is possible to enter this profession without an HND or degree but a demonstration of extensive specialist knowledge within your chosen field and experience utilising a range of software packages will be required. It is common for mature adults to enter this profession as it necessitates expert knowledge. There is the possibility to take an open-learning course in Communication of Technical Information at the ISTC, which may be beneficial for mature entrants. The Institute of Internal Communication (IoIC) provides communication training courses to members and non-members at any stage of their career.

IoIC offers a Continuing Professional Development (CPD) programme that recognises you as an IoIC Professional Practitioner and can help keep your skills up to date. IoIC also runs a Fellowship programme that will open up new opportunities by recognising you as an elite professional.

What the work involves

Technical authors/medical writers interpret technical information and communicate it in written language which the intended audience can understand. Technical authors work in various sectors from medicine and defence to business and finance.

You will create content, commission images, organise and design the layout of any given document. A large part of the work involves digital media, so you may work on podcasts, e-learning and blogs.

You should be an expert in your specialist sector, but your audience may be novices as well as specialists. For example, you may write mass market instructions for a mobile phone or a medical writer may create a report on clinical trial results for the medical community.

Type of person suited to this work

It is essential to have an excellent command of English and the ability to write concisely and convincingly, with your audience in mind. You should also be detail driven and have a good eye for design.

Having a passion for your specialist sector and an enquiring mind is a necessity. The ability to solve problems, multi-task and to work to deadlines is also important.

Good communication and teamworking skills are required as you will have to work closely with technical colleagues, such as doctors, as well as liaising with suppliers including printers and translators.

Working conditions

The majority of work will take place at a computer within normal office hours. However, supplementary hours may be required in order to meet tight deadlines. Also, you might have to travel to meet clients.

Having gained experience, many people decide to start up their own business or go freelance, especially as the pay is more attractive.

Future prospects

Increasingly complex systems and applications are being produced which has led to a greater need for technical writers in a variety of sectors, such as aerospace, finance and technical publishing.

The demand for technical authors is expected to increase due to the continuing expansion of scientific and technical information which needs to be communicated. With increasingly complex developments and discoveries comes a demand for people who can interpret technical information for a wide audience.

As a junior technical author you can progress into senior roles and later, project leader or editor positions. Moving to different organisations may be the key to career progression as there are very few workers in any one company.

Freelance or consultancy work is also popular.

Advantages/disadvantages

This type of work can provide the satisfaction of seeing your completed work in print and, sometimes, in the public domain.

The work can be quite arduous having to familiarise yourself with difficult concepts.

Money guide

You can expect to earn £20,000–£40,000 depending on your experience.

Those in senior roles with extensive experience can achieve in excess of £40,000.

Freelance authors negotiate their own rates.

Related opportunities

- Copy Editor/Sub-editor/Proofreader p388
- Journalist p392
- Publisher/Commissioning Editor p405

Further information

Institute of Internal Communication
www.ioic.org.uk

Institute of Scientific and Technical Communicators
www.istc.org.uk

The Tech Partnership
www.thetechpartnership.com

TV AND FILM CAMERA PERSON/ OPERATOR

Qualifications and courses

To be a TV/film camera operator you do not need any specific academic qualifications although GCSEs/ National 5s (A*–C/A–C) in English, Maths and a science might be useful. Many camera operators do have higher level qualifications, however, such as HNDs, Foundation degrees or degrees in relevant subjects (media production, photography or media studies for example) as this can help improve chances of employment. Creative Skillset works alongside industry professionals to devise their course accreditation scheme in which exceptional film production courses receive the Creative Skillset Tick.

Courses which may help you to develop the necessary skills required in the industry include the City & Guilds Level 3 Diploma in Media Techniques, the BTEC Level 2 Certificate/Diploma in Creative Media Production, the BTEC Level 3 Certificate/Diploma in Media Production – Television and Film and the BTEC HNC/HND in Creative Media Production – Moving Image (Levels 4–5).

The industry is competitive and appropriate experience is often valued more than formal qualifications. Employers seek candidates with a demonstrable interest in photography, typically in the form of showreels, amateur films and videos, film stills or a collection of images. Large companies, such as the BBC, offer work experience placements that provide opportunities to work with camera equipment or in a set-up studio. Experience with community film projects or working for a camera equipment hire company could also be useful. You could apply for the Advanced Apprenticeship in Creative and Digital Media which trains apprentices in the skills required of an assistant to a camera crew.

The Guild of Television Cameramen (GTC) provides networking opportunities and workshops in camera techniques, lighting and editing as does the BBC Academy and the National Film and Television School.

What the work involves

Camera operators use digital, electronic and film cameras to capture images for use in films, TV programmes or other broadcasts.

You will work closely with a director or director of photography and will be helped by a 'grip' (a camera assistant) and other crew members such as pullers, clappers, sound engineers and lighting technicians.

You will understand the technical and creative aspects of filming, including how to work with a script or list of shots, planning shots and shooting images.

You will have an in-depth knowledge of the equipment you work with and how best to use, maintain and repair it.

Type of person suited to this work

You must be interested in photography, camera technology and video, film and TV production.

You will be required to have a certain amount of physical fitness as your work may involve carrying heavy equipment for long periods of time.

As you will be working in a creative environment, you will need to have a good imagination and at times an abstract approach to problem-solving.

You should be patient, have good concentration and work well under pressure.

Working conditions

Your working hours will vary greatly. You may be required to work irregular hours. Shooting may be long and run over planned schedules.

Your work may be affected by weather, for example some shoots may be cut short, or extended, if they depend on natural light.

You may have to work with cameras on cranes, scaffolding, in moving vehicles or in venues such as concert halls, theatres and sports grounds.

Camera operators usually learn most of their skills on the job. Regular training in health and safety is also required.

Future prospects

You will typically start your career as a trainee, runner or camera operator's assistant and learn on the job. Experience leads to becoming a camera operator, and then director of photography among other senior roles.

Geographical mobility will be important to progress your career.

Advantages/disadvantages

You may work on exciting projects, including big budget films or breaking news programmes.

Working on location may be dangerous at times, especially if it involves shooting footage for news broadcasts.

Money guide

A starting salary for a camera operator ranges from £11,500 up to £40,000, depending on your experience.

Most camera operators work on a freelance basis so rates of pay vary according to the type of production you are working on.

As an example, you could earn £285 for working a 10-hour day on a TV documentary, £411 for a 10-hour day filming commercials or £227 for TV news.

Related opportunities

- Lighting Technician p426
- Photographer p399
- TV, Film and Radio Director p411

Further information

BBC Training and Development
www.bbc.co.uk/careers/why-join-us/training

Qualifications and courses

There are no set academic qualifications required for entry into this profession, although it might be useful to have GCSEs/National 5s (A*–C/A–C) and A levels/H grades in subjects such as Maths, English, languages or theatre and drama studies.

Degrees or HNDs in relevant subjects such as media studies, drama, photography, film and television will give you an advantage over other candidates as competition for entry to the industry is fierce. The general entry requirements for a degree are 2 A levels/3 H grades and 5 GCSEs/National 5s (A*–C/A–C). Other qualifications that may help include the BTEC Level 2 Certificate/Diploma in Creative Media Production, the BTEC Level 3 Certificate/Diploma in Creative Media Production – Television and Film and the City & Guilds Level 3 Diploma in Media Techniques.

Creative Skillset have formed a network of Media and Film Academies which offer film and television training, with the option to work towards vocational qualifications. The BBC and Channel 4 also run training schemes.

Employers seek candidates with a proven commitment to the job and the industry. It is advisable to undertake voluntary pre-entry work experience as you are likely to start your career as a runner or production assistant and securing this type of junior role is usually a combination of luck, timing and networking. A portfolio of work is likely to be required and once employed, you will be trained on the job whilst you work your way up the ladder to TV floor manager.

Some independent companies may offer graduate training schemes but, again, competition is fierce. Your employer may encourage you to undertake short courses such as those offered by the Broadcasting, Entertainment, Cinematograph, and Theatre Union (BECTU) in order to develop your skills throughout your career.

What the work involves

TV floor managers are responsible for the coordination of many aspects of the filming process.

You will ensure that all sets, props and technical equipment are working, in place and set up correctly.

In situations where the director is away from the set (in the gallery or a broadcast vehicle) you will wear headphones to relay instructions from the director to the crew, actors or audience members.

Type of person suited to this work

You must be passionate about the media industry and TV production in particular.

You should be very organised and able to work under pressure and to a tight schedule.

As you will be working with a variety of people, from directors to the most junior crew members, you will need to have good communication skills to create an efficient working environment.

You must have an understanding of the technical and creative aspects of production to ensure that you can deal with problems encountered during the filming or recording stage.

Working conditions

Hours are likely to be long and irregular, including early starts, late nights and weekend work. If you work on feature films, 6-day weeks are common.

You will probably work on a freelance basis, which may involve periods of unemployment between jobs.

You will spend most of your time at work on your feet. You will mainly work in studios but sometimes you may be required to work outdoors in all weather conditions.

You might have to travel within the UK or abroad, at short notice and for varying periods of time.

Future prospects

There are not a great number of positions available but with experience you may find it possible to move up into a position as first director, producer or director.

You could move across into other aspects of the industry such as production or broadcasting.

As you will be working on a freelance basis most of the time, you will depend on having a strong portfolio of your work, an excellent reputation and good contacts within the industry to guarantee work.

Advantages/disadvantages

Your work will involve a diverse range of projects including creative, practical and technical tasks.

Your working hours may be long, stressful and unsocial which could disrupt your personal life.

Money guide

Starting salaries are usually between £15,000 and £22,000.

Those with experience can expect to earn in excess of £25,000.

Many floor managers work on a freelance basis and receive an hourly, daily or weekly rate. Daily rates could range from £150 to £400.

Related opportunities

- TV and Film Camera Person/Operator p409
- TV, Film and Radio Director p411
- TV, Film and Radio Production Assistant/Runner p414

Further information

Creative Skillset
www.creativeskillset.org

National Film and Television School
http://nfts.co.uk

Qualifications and courses

There are no specific entry requirements but most entrants have a drama or media-related degree or postgraduate qualification.

GCSEs/National 5s or A levels/H grades in media-related subjects would demonstrate an early interest in this industry and studying these subjects at BTEC National, HND, degree or postgraduate level would be beneficial when applying for entry-level positions. The general entry requirements for a degree are 2 A levels/3 H grades and 5 GCSEs/National 5s (A*–C/A–C). For an HND, you should have an A level/H grade in an art and design-related subject. Specialist postgraduate courses in directing are offered at the National Film and Television School (NFTS).

Practical work experience is often valued more than formal qualifications, however, and most budding directors create a showreel to promote their work. Taking part in student or community film and TV activities is a good way to show your commitment to the media. Some production companies, such as the BBC, offer work experience placements which could lead to full-time employment. Work experience is particularly useful in that it provides you with opportunities to establish a network of contacts, crucial considering the competitive nature of the industry.

Directors often begin as runners and work their way up to become floor managers or assistant directors. Others break into directing through competitions, film festivals or marketing short films to agents. You will develop your skills throughout your career by combining learning on the job with external masterclasses such as those offered by the Directors' Guild of Great Britain.

What the work involves

Directors manage the process of creating films, radio and TV programmes. This involves commissioning each project and overseeing the work and schedules of the entire production team.

You will define the presentation and style of films and productions by making decisions about content, scripting, camera work, editing and acting.

You will also be required to handle any problems with presenters, actors or production staff, as well as editing the final 'cut' of the show you have directed.

Type of person suited to this work

Working in these competitive sectors can be very demanding and stressful. You should be confident and able to react quickly and calmly to any crises that may arise. You should have exceptional creative skills and artistic vision.

Good verbal communication, interpersonal and teamworking skills are important, especially as you could be away from home on location for weeks at a time.

In addition, you should have good organisational skills to ensure that projects are carried out on time and within budget.

Working conditions

Contrary to popular belief, this is not glamorous work! A good level of physical stamina and fitness is required as this job involves lengthy days spent standing up and carrying heavy equipment.

In TV and film you will work on set and on location. You will have to cope with changeable outdoor conditions.

You will also be expected to be flexible and work at night and weekends, both during and post-production.

Future prospects

Entry to the industry is very competitive and excellent technical skills and a well-established network of contacts are required in order to be successful. It is unlikely that you will enter the industry as a director straight away. Most work their way up from runners to floor managers until finally reaching director status. Your reputation will play a vital role in ensuring career progression.

It is possible that you might work freelance on specific contracts for production companies or you may fund and develop your own projects.

Advantages/disadvantages

This role provides the satisfaction and excitement of seeing your work in the public sphere.

The work is fast paced and varied.

Directors are often employed on a freelance or contract basis which can lead to job instability.

Money guide

Earnings in this sector vary greatly according to media, location, employer and project.

New entrants can expect to earn about £20,000.

With experience, your salary can rise to £40,000.

The most successful directors can earn anything up to £200,000.

Freelancers negotiate their own fees.

Related opportunities

- Artistic/Theatre Director p417
- TV, Film and Radio Producer p413
- TV, Film and Radio Production Assistant/Runner p414

Further information

BBC Careers
www.bbc.co.uk/careers

Creative Skillset
www.creativeskillset.org

Directors Guild of Great Britain and Directors Guild Trust
www.dggb.org

MARKETING, ADVERTISING, MEDIA, PRINT AND PUBLISHING

Qualifications and courses

There are no specific academic requirements but many entrants have either a degree or a degree and postgraduate qualification in a relevant subject such as film, IT, media studies and visual art. The general entry requirements for a degree are 2 A levels/3 H grades and 5 GCSEs/National 5s (A*–C/A–C) and for a postgraduate course you will usually need at least a 2.1 Honours in your bachelor's degree.

Entry-level training courses may be beneficial in gaining industry knowledge and are available through the BBC as well as independent organisations such as Cyfle, Creative Scotland or Screen Yorkshire. Alternative qualifications include the City & Guilds Level 3 Diploma in Video Production (Advanced Media Techniques), the BTEC Level 3 Certificate/Diploma in Creative Media Production specialising in Radio or Television and Film and the BTEC Higher National in Creative Media Production specialising in Moving Image or Radio (Levels 4–5).

It is common to start out as a runner or editing assistant before working your way up to editor status. Practical work experience is essential for entry-level jobs as it demonstrates pre-entry industry interest and is a good way of building a network of contacts. This is important considering that job vacancies are rarely advertised within this somewhat competitive industry. Employers will seek evidence of a candidate's use of appropriate editing software packages, a keen eye for detail and creativity, often requesting a showreel of your work, eg short films, amateur videos and photography.

You will continue to develop your skills throughout your career by completing short courses such as those offered by the Broadcasting, Entertainment, Cinematograph and Theatre Union (BECTU). It is important that you remain up to date with any new technologies or equipment.

What the work involves

Editors play a key role in the post-production process by assembling the final product from captured footage and additional sound and graphics. They are also responsible for storing the footage.

You will fulfil a brief and liaise closely with the director. You will monitor and correct the flow and pace of a production by using specialist IT editing equipment to put shots together in a smooth sequence.

You will ensure the continuity and order of these productions, which may include TV and radio programmes, films, music and corporate videos, and advertisements.

Type of person suited to this work

It is essential to be creative and to have a passion for your chosen medium.

You should have good attention to detail, plenty of patience and the ability to identify good storytelling techniques.

You will be expected to be well versed in the latest technological advances in the field, as well as possessing advanced IT skills and a willingness to try new techniques.

Working conditions

Hours vary depending on workload but are typically 9am–5pm, Monday to Friday. Your personal life may be affected during busy periods as you will be expected to work long and unpredictable hours in order to meet tight deadlines.

The majority of the work takes place at a computer in an editing suite and may be carried out alone or with a director.

Freelance editors with their own equipment may work from home.

Future prospects

It is thought that there are at least 10,000 people working in post-production roles in the UK. This profession is fast-paced and there is fierce competition for entry-level positions.

The majority of roles are based in London in post-production companies, independent production firms, broadcasters, and companies in the film and computer software sectors. However, big broadcasting firms such as ITV and the BBC have moved a lot of their operations up to Salford, and opportunities continue to grow there.

Having gained experience, many editors choose to go freelance. This involves working on several projects simultaneously and the workload may be irregular, with both busy and quiet periods.

Advantages/disadvantages

You will have the satisfaction of seeing the results of your work in the public domain.

This is a fast-moving and varied industry with exciting opportunities.

Editors are often employed on a freelance or contract basis which can lead to job instability.

Money guide

Earnings in this sector vary greatly according to employer and project.

New entrants can expect to earn £18,000–£25,000. With experience, you can earn £20,000–£35,000. Those in senior positions can achieve up to £70,000.

Freelancers negotiate their own fees but tend to follow those set by BECTU.

Related opportunities

- Media Researcher p396
- TV and Film Camera Person/Operator p409

Further information

Broadcasting, Entertainment, Cinematograph and Theatre Union
www.bectu.org.uk

Creative Skillset
www.creativeskillset.org

Qualifications and courses

There are no specific academic requirements but producers need extensive experience in both the creative and business sides of the industry.

Given the competitive nature of the industry, many entrants have a Foundation degree, degree or HND in a related subject, such as film production, communications, broadcasting, media studies or drama. You will need at least 1 A level/2 H grades and 4 GCSEs/National 5s (A*–C/A–C) for entry to a Foundation degree or HND and 2 A levels/3 H grades and 5 GCSEs/National 5s (A*–C/A–C) for a degree.

As this is a job that requires experience, you will normally have to work your way up from the bottom – first as a runner, assistant producer and film production manager until finally reaching producer status. Gaining experience in a junior role provides a well-rounded view of the industry, invaluable knowledge and the opportunity to develop a network of contacts. Jobs are rarely advertised, therefore work experience may offer you a way of entry into the industry through the contacts you make at each placement.

You should create a showreel/portfolio so as to promote your work and demonstrate your aptitude to prospective employers. You may wish to seek an apprenticeship or course that incorporates practical work experience in order to show evidence of your creativity, leadership skills and an ability to cope under pressure. The Advanced Apprenticeship Programme in Digital and Creative Media may be available in your area or, if you have a degree, graduate training schemes are offered by some independent television companies.

If you are a radio producer working on news and current affairs shows you will need to have journalistic training. The Broadcast Journalism Training Council (BJTC) provides further information on accredited institutions and courses. The Indie Training Fund (ITF) offers masterclasses in production and short courses on Advanced Production Management. The Production Guild (PG) also offers Production Manager Training alongside a number of short courses designed to update your production skills.

What the work involves

A producer develops ideas, employs key team members, has creative input, gets involved in casting decisions and script editing, and generally oversees the complete production. Many producers also play a financial role by approaching initial backers, securing rights and managing the budget throughout production.

You will be the lead person in TV, film and radio production. Producers have a detailed knowledge of the industry, coupled with sound business skills. You may also need to oversee the final editing process, as well as marketing and distribution plans.

Type of person suited to this work

It is essential to have a strong creative flair and a passion for your chosen medium. A well-rounded knowledge of your sector, spanning technical, creative and commercial aspects is also required.

Excellent communication skills are important and you should have the ability to provide inspiration and motivation for team members. You should be a competent problem solver who works well under pressure.

You also need strong negotiation, numeracy, multi-tasking and organisational skills to ensure that projects are carried out on time, within budget and according to the original plan.

Working conditions

Producers work in a variety of environments including offices, studios and external filming locations.

Your working day is determined by the demands of the filming schedule and as such the role requires a great deal of flexibility. Working hours can be long and erratic, with travel often required.

Future prospects

Over half of the UK's TV and film workforce are situated in south-east England with the rest spread across major cities such as Manchester and Glasgow.

The main employers are well-known broadcasters such as the BBC, TV and film production firms, and production and facilities houses.

Establishing good contacts throughout your career will ensure job progression as positions are rarely advertised and are awarded based on the reputation of the producer. If you are successful you could be promoted to executive producer or set up your own production company.

Advantages/disadvantages

You will have the satisfaction of seeing the results of your work in the public domain.

This is a fast-moving and varied industry which can provide exciting opportunities.

Producers are often employed on a freelance or contract basis which can lead to job instability.

Money guide

New entrants can expect to earn £18,000–£25,000 per year and, with experience, this can increase to £40,000–£55,000.

Senior producers can achieve £60,000–£80,000.

Almost half of all producers in the industry are freelancers and daily rates are typically between £237 and £437.

Rates of pay are set by the Broadcasting, Entertainment, Cinematograph and Theatre Union (BECTU).

Related opportunities

- Media Researcher p396
- TV Floor Manager p410
- TV, Film and Radio Production Assistant/Runner p414

Further information

BBC Careers
www.bbc.co.uk/careers

Creative Skillset
www.creativeskillset.org

MARKETING, ADVERTISING, MEDIA, PRINT AND PUBLISHING

Qualifications and courses

Runner

There are no formal entry requirements as this role is a starting point in the TV and film industry. It may be advantageous to have a degree in TV/film/radio production or a media-related subject as competition for entry-level jobs is fierce, but this is not expected. The Apprenticeship in Creative and Digital Media would be an excellent way of combining practical work experience with a relevant industry qualification and will enhance your skill set. Alternatively, The Production Guild provides runner training courses designed to prepare you for the role.

Given the competitive nature of the industry, enthusiasm is essential and you may have to carry out a significant amount of unpaid work experience in order to succeed. You should also build a portfolio of your work to show potential employers or for entry into competitions.

Production assistant

No formal qualifications are required but entry is highly competitive and many entrants are graduates of a relevant degree or have a postgraduate qualification. The BTEC Level 3 Certificate/Diploma in Creative Media Production (radio or TV and film) may also be useful. It is important that your course is accredited and offers opportunities for direct contact with the industry.

An understanding of the production process developed through relevant work experience is very important. As vacancies in this field are rarely advertised, it is important to be proactive and network to self-promote.

What the work involves

Runner

You will provide a wide range of practical help and support to all members of the production team. As well as some administrative work, you will pass messages on and carry equipment and scripts between offices and sets – often with no prior notice.

Production assistant

Production assistants provide support to the producer and director to help ensure that productions run smoothly and to schedule. You will manage a range of key administrative activities, such as organising scripts and updating filming schedules, booking hotels and hiring equipment. You may also be responsible for managing budgets for productions.

Type of person suited to this work

It is essential to be enthusiastic, be willing to learn and to have a passion for your chosen medium.

You should be interested in learning about all areas of the field and be well versed in recent trends in the industry.

You should also enjoy problem-solving and have the ability to work well under pressure and adhere to strict deadlines.

Working conditions

There are no standard hours in this profession as they vary depending on the project you are working on. During production, hours can be long, unpredictable and include evening and weekend work. Shift work is common and you may be required to be on-call at all times.

Many runners and project assistants work as freelancers. This means you will have to manage your own work schedule, often working on several projects simultaneously, and the workload may be irregular, with both busy and quiet periods. You will work in offices, studios and editing suites, as well as on location.

Future prospects

Most opportunities are in London and the south-east of England, where over half of the TV and film industries are based. This profession is fast-paced and there is fierce competition for entry-level positions.

With experience, you might look to become a researcher, working on programme development, or become a senior producer or editor in TV, film or radio.

Advantages/disadvantages

This is a fast-moving and varied industry with exciting opportunities.

Entry-level positions are very demanding and can affect your social life.

Money guide

Earnings in this sector vary greatly according to experience, media area, employer and project. Mostly people are employed on a freelance or contract basis.

Runner

New entrants can expect to earn between £6.50 and £8.80 per hour. In an extremely competitive industry, even low income positions are attractive and many new runners have an additional source of income.

With experience, salaries can rise to £20,000.

If working freelance the daily rates for a runner typically range from £94 to £119.

Production assistant

Starting salaries are typically about £15,000 and those with more experience earning up to £25,000.

Senior production assistants can achieve up to £30,000.

Related opportunities

- TV and Film Camera Person/Operator p409
- TV Floor Manager p410
- TV, Film and Radio Producer p413

Further information

Broadcasting, Entertainment, Cinematograph and Theatre Union
www.bectu.org.uk

Creative Skillset
www.creativeskillset.org

Performing Arts

This job family contains a wide range of exciting jobs for those of you who want to work in theatre, music, on screen or behind the scenes. People working in this sector do so because they are passionate and creative and love the arts. Jobs can be scarce, so you will need to demonstrate that you are willing to work very hard but the rewards of being part of a fantastic production can be huge. There are also jobs available in this sector for those of you who are more technically minded – sound and lighting engineers also play a vital role in this industry as do people who have trained in fashion and textiles. The jobs featured within this section are listed below. For similar jobs to the ones in this section turn to *Design, Arts and Crafts* on page 157 and *Marketing, Advertising, Media, Print and Publishing* on page 381.

Qualifications and courses

Although there are no specific academic requirements to enter this profession and there is a variety of different routes into the industry, it is still incredibly competitive and a lot of actors have taken some formal training in order to hone their skills and prepare for the demands of the job.

Acting degrees are offered at both drama schools and universities. Drama UK accredits full-time 3-year vocational drama school courses and degrees. Entry to these courses is by audition, and A levels/H grades or a BTEC Level 3 in Performing Arts are often required. Further study, such as a master's degree or postgraduate diploma in acting, is also available and can offer more opportunities to make contacts and develop your skills.

Graduates of Drama UK-accredited courses who are legally entitled to work in the UK are eligible for Equity membership.

However, experience in the industry is more beneficial than qualifications. It can be helpful to join a local amateur dramatics group and undertake relevant work experience. The BBC, for instance, runs a number of work placement schemes which provide an insight into how the industry works.

Some actors gain experience working at holiday camps in entertainer roles. This is a good way of getting paid work and experience at the same time.

Networking is extremely important as a lot of actors secure roles through contacts they have made.

What the work involves

Actors perform in front of audiences and this can sometimes include dancing and singing as part of the role. There are opportunities for parts in dramatic plays, comedies and musicals on stage as well as on TV and in films.

You will research your characters, rehearse lines and attend auditions.

You will also attend costume fittings and make-up sessions.

Type of person suited to this work

Acting is a very competitive area so you should be truly dedicated to this career path. A good memory is important as you will have to learn lines.

There will be many times when you will be rejected at auditions mainly because you are just not the right face for the part, and so you will need to be able to cope with this and keep trying.

Adaptability, self-confidence and creativity are essential.

Working conditions

You will work mainly indoors, in theatres, halls and sometimes studios.

Your hours will be long and irregular, including evenings and weekends.

You could have to travel to different venues for your performances where you might spend time waiting for your part in the performance.

Future prospects

Prospects for success as an actor depend on talent, hard work and a bit of luck.

Some actors go on to work as writers or directors, while others train to teach drama in schools and colleges.

Advantages/disadvantages

Sometimes work can be irregular so you will not necessarily have a stable income.

The nature of the work means that you will experience a lot of rejection which may be hard to take.

It is a tough, demanding career to enter and to stay in, but once you get regular work it can be very satisfying.

Money guide

Basic rates of pay depend on experience and reputation. It is important to join Equity, the union for the world of entertainment – as this can help you negotiate fair rates of pay, terms and conditions. Union-negotiated pay scales are on the Equity website.

The minimum pay for theatre workers (as set by Equity) is £431 per week although this can increase if the actor has to relocate. The salary in the West End tends to be higher and you are guaranteed a minimum salary of £518.23 a week. The wages for TV and film work vary considerably and are dependent on how well known you are as an actor. As you become a recognised name your income could be quite considerable, but it may take many years and continuous employment is uncommon.

Although there are a few (very famous) actors who earn huge salaries, the majority of actors have to take on second employment to support themselves and raise their income. Only 6% of actors receive more than £30,000.

A lot of actors have an agent to help them secure work but also to help them negotiate higher wages. However, although agents can obtain higher wages they will also take a cut of your earnings, generally between 10% and 25%.

Related opportunities

- Artistic/Theatre Director p417
- Dancer p422

Further information

Creative and Cultural Skills
www.ccskills.org.uk

Equity
www.equity.org.uk

Royal Academy of Dramatic Art
www.rada.ac.uk

Qualifications and courses

Most artistic directors hold a relevant degree in either English, creative/performing arts, drama or theatre studies on entry to the industry. HNDs and Foundation degrees in creative/performing arts or drama/theatre studies are available and may also be useful qualifications to hold prior to entering the theatre.

If you are looking to move into the industry after completing your first degree, Birkbeck, the University of Kent and Mountview Academy of Theatre Arts offer postgraduate courses in theatre direction.

Entry without any FE/HE qualifications is possible as the industry is reliant on reputation which you can gain through experience in acting, directing, writing and producing.

Of equal importance to professional qualifications are practical skills, acquired through work experience and involvement in school, college, university and community productions.

The Arts Council England runs the Regional Theatre Young Director Scheme (RTYDS) for new entrants to the profession, and a few theatres and regional arts councils also offer training bursaries for candidates with exceptional potential. Competition for the bursaries is fierce. Some theatres also offer direction schemes, one such scheme being the Young Vic Directors Program.

What the work involves

Artistic and theatre directors have control over the artistic interpretation of plays, ballets, operas and other performances.

You will be responsible for coordinating all the creative elements of each production, including set and costume design, stylistic presentation, the interpretive work of artists, and any musical or choreographic sequences.

You will liaise with a number of other professionals on a daily basis, including producers, musical directors, technicians, theatre managers, financial backers, performing artists and writers.

Type of person suited to this work

You will need fantastic artistic and creative vision, that you are able to express both verbally and in written documents. You will also need to have the courage and tenacity to make your vision a reality and present it to an audience.

You must be an excellent leader with the ability to inspire and motivate others. Being able to negotiate with writers, actors and other professionals is an asset.

You should have an in-depth knowledge of the theatre, including productions past and present, theatrical trends, and the history of the industry.

Working conditions

Hours can be irregular and you will be employed on a freelance basis through which contracts can be short. Longer fixed-term contracts are available, but they usually only last 3–5 years.

You will be mainly working in theatres and other performance venues. Although the final production may take place on a large stage, you could spend a great deal of time directing scenes in small, off-site rehearsal rooms.

You will mainly work indoors, although certain venues will require you to work outdoors in occasionally inhospitable conditions.

Future prospects

Competition in the theatrical industry is fierce, so you will need talent, dedication, good qualifications and experience.

Since the majority of theatrical work takes place in London you can expect to be based there for some or all of your career. The city is a base for most freelance directors, although there are opportunities in regional theatres.

As an experienced and admired artistic director, you could set up your own theatre company through which you can stage your performances. Other directors move from theatre into film or television work.

Advantages/disadvantages

Your creative ability will be the driving force behind the production of visually and technically beautiful or unusual performances.

The industry is extremely competitive so you might have to spend long periods of time working for free or at a minimal wage in order to build enough experience to work as an artistic director.

Money guide

Salaries are dependent upon the length and type of contract.

Equity recommends a preparatory fee of £1,439 for a long play, £995 for a short play and £440 as a weekly payment during rehearsals. For resident artistic directors £535 is the recommended weekly rate.

Reaching the level of artistic director should increase your salary to about £23,000.

Well-established artistic directors who have built up a good reputation and are in demand across the industry can earn in excess of £40,000.

Related opportunities

- Actor p416
- Stage Manager p434
- Stagehand p435

Further information

Arts Council England
www.artscouncil.org.uk

Directors Guild of Great Britain and Directors Guild Trust
www.dggb.org

CASTING DIRECTOR

Qualifications and courses

There are no specific entry requirements for this role, but most entrants have a drama, English, art, communications or media-related degree.

GCSEs/National 5s or A levels/H grades in media- or drama-related subjects will demonstrate an early interest in the industry. You may also wish to study these subjects at BTEC National, HND, degree or postgraduate level. The general entry requirements for a degree are 2 A levels/3 H grades and 5 GCSEs/National 5s (A*–C/A–C). Drama UK accredits vocational 3-year drama school courses and university degrees.

However, practical work experience is considered more valuable than academic qualifications in this industry. You may find it useful to work for an agency to gain industry knowledge and contacts. This would be a good way to meet and impress casting directors. Alternatively, you could attend drama school and make contacts whilst studying.

You could also gain industry experience through stage management or production roles. The BBC offers work placements and apprenticeships in production such as the Production Talent Pool scheme.

Once you break into the industry as a casting assistant you will experience on-the-job training. Experience and building a network of contacts is vital in order to become an independent casting director.

What the work involves

You will be responsible for selecting actors for roles in TV, theatre and film productions.

Your work will involve working closely with the director and producer to understand their requirements. You will then be responsible for setting up auditions and interviews to discover the right actor for the part.

Once you have selected your cast you will negotiate fees and contracts with the chosen actors. The fees you set will abide by a casting budget that you will prepare with a production accountant.

Type of person suited to this work

You will need a love for theatre, TV and film. You will have an excellent memory and be able to recall many actors' profiles.

You must have a keen eye for talent and potential. Excellent organisational skills are essential as you will be working within a strict production budget and schedules.

You must be a good communicator as you will be working closely with producers and directors. Networking skills are valuable as contacts are essential to secure work.

Working conditions

Your work will typically be freelance and seasonal, with summer being the busiest time of year. The intermittent nature of this work may lead to financial insecurity.

The role includes a large amount of admin so you will typically work in an office environment. However, you will need to meet and scout out potential actors, which will mean frequent travel to watch performers.

You will have to work to a strict production schedule, which may mean working long hours to tight deadlines.

The majority of opportunities exist in the south-east of England as most producers and directors are based in London.

Future prospects

Career progression is dependent on experience and contacts. You will enter the profession casting for smaller productions, but with recognition and recommendations you may move on to larger projects with larger casts.

You could choose to specialise in a particular area of casting such as commercials, theatre, TV, radio or film.

With experience you could set up your own casting agency or move into similar media roles such as producer or director.

Advantages/disadvantages

It can be very difficult to break into this industry.

You will work long, unpredictable hours.

You will have the opportunity to indulge your love of film, theatre and TV.

You will receive free tickets to plays and film screenings.

Money guide

Upon entering the industry you may have to work unpaid to gain experience. This may mean you will have to work a second job to gain an income.

Most casting directors are self-employed, which may mean financial insecurity.

The Broadcasting, Entertainment, Cinematograph and Theatre Union (BECTU) recommended rate for a casting director working a 10 hour shift is £617.

Casting directors working in Hollywood can earn in excess of £100,000 a year.

Related opportunities

- Agent/Literary Agent p386
- TV, Film and Radio Director p411
- TV, Film and Radio Producer p413

Further information

Spotlight
www.spotlight.com

The Casting Directors' Guild
www.thecdg.co.uk

PERFORMING ARTS

CHOREOGRAPHER

Qualifications and courses

There are no formal academic entry requirements for this career, however GCSEs/National 5s and A levels/H grades are available in Dance, and some institutions offer BTEC Level 3 in Performing Arts.

Most choreographers have experience as dance performers prior to becoming choreographers and aptitude, commitment and ability are often valued more highly than formal qualifications.

Choreography can be studied as an option on some full-time vocational dance courses accredited by the Council for Dance Education and Training. Falmouth University, the University of Winchester and Northumbria University also offer specialised choreography courses. Entry onto these courses usually requires at least 2 A levels/3 H grades, one of which should be in Dance or a related subject, and 5 GCSEs/National 5s (A*–C/A–C), including English and Maths. You will also be expected to audition/perform and prove your choreography and dance skills.

Postgraduate courses in choreography are also available at several institutions, including the Laban Trinity Conservatoire of Music and Dance in London, London Contemporary Dance School and University of Roehampton.

Work experience alongside an experienced practitioner offers a good introduction to choreography and will certainly be taken into account if applying for a dance or choreography-related course.

What the work involves

As a choreographer, you will create and develop new dance movements for productions such as ballets, opera and musicals.

Creating a dance means planning the way dancers move to perform beautiful and exciting routines which interpret the music.

Choreographers work closely with performance artists, musical directors, ballet dance teachers and trainers.

Type of person suited to this work

You will need to have a keen, lively interest in music and movement, and a very well-developed sense of rhythm and timing.

To develop new ballets, dances and shorter dance routines requires an excellent knowledge of past and present pieces, complete understanding of how the body works and of possible movements within dance and the creative imagination to interpret the significance of events and mood changes through physical expression.

Choreographers have the responsibility of developing and teaching complicated movements and routines. You will need a good memory, clear communication skills, patience and an ability to get on well with others.

Working conditions

You will mainly work indoors in dance studios, theatres, TV or film studios.

Your initial contacts are likely to be producers, directors and musical conductors. Some choreographers work directly with modern composers, interpreting their music.

As production plans progress, you will start working directly with the performers. To do this you will travel frequently.

Future prospects

Jobs and opportunities can be limited as this is a highly competitive area of work, where experience counts.

Most choreographers work on a freelance or a fixed-term basis. There will be some full-time opportunities, particularly with larger dance companies, but these are likely to be competitive.

It is possible to find opportunities outside mainstream ballet; for example in modern dance companies and developing international venues.

Opera and musicals are becoming reinvigorated through audience demand and both performance areas require choreographers to interpret dance music and contextual pieces as dance routines. You may choose to set up your own dance company.

Advantages/disadvantages

Many hours are spent travelling to different venues – even overseas.

Seeing your finished routine beautifully performed will boost your morale.

Enthusiastic reviews will help your career progression.

It will be hard going and you will need patience and enthusiasm to get the best from dancers.

Money guide

Equity, the performing arts union, recommends a minimum daily sum of £123.

You could earn around £12,500 per year if you have just finished at a dance college, completed a degree or other college courses.

With experience, your salary could increase to £20,000 if you have moved into choreography as an experienced dancer.

Established, well-known choreographers can earn £50,000, but good salaries will depend on your skills and experience.

Related opportunities

- Artistic/Theatre Director p417
- Dancer p422
- Make-up Artist p428

Further information

Council for Dance Education and Training
www.cdet.org.uk

Creative and Cultural Skills
www.ccskills.org.uk

Equity
www.equity.org.uk

Independent Theatre Council
http://www.itc-arts.org/

Qualifications and courses

Useful qualifications include GCSE/National 5s and A levels/H grades in Music, BTEC Level 5 in Music Performance or Songwriting, and relevant degree courses. The Institute of Contemporary Music Performance offers a specialised course on songwriting and more institutions are investing in similar courses.

For entry onto a BTEC Level 5 course you will need a relevant Level 3 qualification, and GCSEs/National 5s in English and Maths at grade C or above. Degree courses usually require 2 A levels/3 H grades, preferably with one in Music or a related subject, and 5 GCSEs/National 5s (A*–C/A–C). Candidates who have reached grade 8 in an instrument as classified by the Associated Board of the Royal Schools of Music are usually preferred.

A wide variety of postgraduate courses is also available. If you are looking to break into the world of classical composition, you are strongly advised to attain a postgraduate qualification.

It is possible, but extremely rare, to achieve success without having undertaken some of the relevant qualifications for this industry provided you have an exceptional reputation and vast experience.

What the work involves

Composers and songwriters create original music for a variety of uses. You could sell your songs to or be approached to write for an established commercial talent, or you could work within TV, film, computer games and radio. An understanding of the business and current trends may prove essential.

You could use a variety of tools and instruments when composing or writing, from a pen and paper to advanced computer software programs. You may also be expected to understand music production and recording practices.

You may also perform your compositions and songs, although this is most common for composers who are just starting out and those writing for individuals or small groups.

Networking is integral. The more people you know in the industry, the more options and chance you have of finding professional paid work.

Type of person suited to this work

You will need to have outstanding musical or lyrical talents.

You will need dedication, determination and self-discipline as the music industry is extremely tough and disappointment may well be frequent.

You should have a flexible attitude to your work and be willing to take on a range of commissions and assignments in order to build up your experience and reputation.

Working conditions

Composers and songwriters (the former in particular) can expect to work long and unsocial hours writing, rehearsing and performing their work.

Most composers and songwriters have other jobs in order to fund themselves whilst they establish a name in the music industry.

Future prospects

The music industry is highly competitive, so it can take a long time to gain any recognition for your work. This makes composing a challenging profession to choose and you will need to be extremely resilient.

Most composers or songwriters are self-employed. Although opportunities are available with theatrical companies, music publishers and universities.

You could gain great critical acclaim and commercial success, although the majority of work completed by composers and songwriters stems from smaller commissions within the media.

Advantages/disadvantages

You will be working in a job that you are passionate about, which will be immensely satisfying.

If you gain recognition the personal and financial rewards can be excellent.

The industry is highly competitive and chances of success are relatively slim. You may earn little money to begin with as a lot of early work could be done with small bands or amateur filmmakers (when creating soundtracks) etc, for the exposure and not the money.

Money guide

It is very hard to gauge salaries in this industry as so many composers and songwriters are freelance.

If you are commissioned by a large company or orchestra, as a composer you can expect to earn around £500 to £1,000 for each minute of music you create.

Songwriters could earn around £300 per minute. For title music, jingles and commercials both composers and songwriters can earn about £350 per minute.

You could also be entitled to royalties from your work.

Related opportunities

- Conductor p421
- Musician p429
- Singer p432

Further information

Arts Council England
www.artscouncil.org.uk

British Academy of Songwriters, Composers and Authors
http://basca.org.uk

Sound and Music
www.soundandmusic.org

CONDUCTOR

Qualifications and courses

Entry to this profession usually starts with a degree in music. Most universities require at least 2 A levels/3 H grades and 5 GCSEs/National 5s, as well as the ability to play an instrument to grade 8, for entry onto a music course. Upon completion of a degree, the majority of candidates go on to study for a postgraduate qualification in conducting. UCAS Conservatoires lists all the schools and conservatoires offering undergraduate and postgraduate courses.

Those who achieve good results may be eligible for a scholarship offered by institutions such as the Royal Opera House, the Royal College of Music and the Guildhall School of Music and Drama.

Whilst studying, it is advisable to seek work experience as a deputy or assistant conductor. Working as a répétiteur in opera may also be beneficial, as you can watch and learn from highly skilled and experienced conductors.

Most conductors speak at least two European languages fluently, with the most useful being English, German, French and Italian.

Attending seminars run by the Association of British Orchestras (ABO) is a useful way to learn about current areas of interest in the sector. Qualified conductors are expected to engage in continuing professional development (CPD) throughout their careers to ensure that their knowledge of music theory and practice is up to date.

What the work involves

Music conductors work with musicians and singers to help shape their performance and make sure each musical piece is performed the way it should be.

You will be responsible for preparing musical scores for the performance and making decisions about how each musical piece should sound.

You need to understand the role of each performer and make sure every musician knows which part to play and does so correctly.

You may work with a wide variety of musicians, both amateur and professional, and these could include choirs and choruses, music students, youth groups and professional artists.

Type of person suited to this work

You must have a strong interest in music and extensive knowledge of the subject. You need to be able to play an instrument, preferably the piano, to a very high standard.

Good communication skills are vital, as is the ability to remain calm under pressure and work flexibly and with lots of different creative people.

You must be comfortable both taking control of a performance and being centre stage performing in front of an audience.

Working conditions

Working hours for conductors are varied, and you must be prepared to work whenever and wherever the opportunity arises. Hours include evenings and weekends for both rehearsals and performances.

You will divide your time between working in rehearsal rooms, concert halls, churches, theatres, opera houses and other venues.

Conductors often spend a lot of time away from home, both within the UK and abroad. The places where you stay will vary in standards.

A driving licence is useful as travel is often required.

Future prospects

A successful career in conducting is entirely dependent on your reputation and ability to build it up.

You may begin your career conducting small community or youth orchestras.

Once you have proved yourself and become established, opportunities to conduct large, high profile orchestras may become available. You might combine conducting with teaching and pursue a career in education at conservatoires.

Advantages/disadvantages

This job is ideal for those who are musically talented and like a balance between working with people and independently.

Producing a performance that audiences enjoy is incredibly satisfying.

In the early stages of your career it may be difficult to secure work and you could experience a sense of job instability.

Money guide

Conductors tend to be paid a fee for each concert.

At the start of your career, you may earn £380 per concert, but this could be lower.

With experience, you are likely to receive approximately £1,000 per concert.

The most successful conductors can achieve up to £5,000 per concert.

Related opportunities

- Composer/Songwriter p420
- Musician p429
- Private Music Teacher p191

Further information

Association of British Orchestras
www.abo.org.uk

Incorporated Society of Musicians
www.ism.org

International Artist Managers' Association
www.iamaworld.com

DANCER

PERFORMING ARTS

Qualifications and courses

Most professional dancers take classes in at least one form of dance from a very young age. Completing graded exams from awarding bodies such as the British Ballet Organisation or the Royal Academy of Dance will help you hone your skills and prove your desire to dance.

Entrants to this career usually undertake a 3-year vocational diploma or degree at a specialist school such as the Royal Academy of Dance (RAD). Entry is by audition, interview and a medical, and 5 GCSEs/National 5s (A*–C/A–C) are usually needed. For ballet, there are also physical requirements, including height and body proportion requirements.

The Council for Dance Education and Training (CDET) accredits full-time courses at vocational dance schools. Some universities or colleges of higher education offer degrees in dance but these courses tend to be more theoretical than performance based. A levels/H grades are usually required and candidates attend an audition. For those without the relevant qualifications, BTEC Level 3 in Performing Arts – Dance may be accepted instead. Postgraduate courses in professional dance or musical theatre are also available.

Some courses include a teacher training element. RAD and the Imperial Society of Teachers of Dancing (ISTD) provide specialist teacher training programmes. The British Ballet Organisation (BBO) and the British Theatre Dance Association (BTDA) also offer qualifications in dance and teacher training.

What the work involves

Dancers use the movement and language of their bodies as a way of expressing ideas and emotions to an audience, often accompanied by music.

You will focus on any number of styles including street, cultural, modern, contemporary, classical ballet, jazz or tap dance.

You might find work in theatres, cabaret clubs, cruise ships or video/TV studios. In addition to performing, you may use dance as a form of education or therapy.

Type of person suited to this work

Anyone entering this area of work must enjoy performing and be very talented to succeed. You must be dedicated to improving your technique through daily practice – sometimes for as long as 10 hours each day.

To be a successful dancer, you need a good sense of rhythm and timing. Being creative and imaginative with routines and choreography is desirable.

It is important that you can cope with setbacks and remain positive and focused.

The majority of your time will be spent dancing in a group so you must enjoy working with others.

Working conditions

Most of your rehearsals and performances will take place indoors in studios, schools, theatres or other venues.

The job is physically demanding and requires working long hours, including evenings and weekends. Frequent travel is often required.

Future prospects

Your future prospects as a dancer will largely depend on talent, hard work and luck; competition is always strong. Only a few individuals become top performance artists in solo roles.

If you are employed by a dance company you can progress from chorus to solo parts, but this will depend on your skills and dedication.

Although dancing is a career for younger people, dance teachers can continue long after they finish as professional performers, and many leave dancing to set up private dance schools.

With experience you could also become a choreographer or take extra qualifications and undertake complementary professions such as dance movement therapy.

Advantages/disadvantages

Dance can be a fantastically rewarding career.

A career as a top soloist can be finished by the age of 30.

You will need to stay fit and healthy as injuries can necessitate a complete career change.

Money guide

Salaries for dancers depend on the length, type and location of the job.

Dancers usually work on a freelance basis and as such most dancers are members of Equity, the trade union for the performing arts.

Equity have established minimum weekly rates of £440 for dancers.

Experienced dancers can expect to earn £450 to £500 a week.

Those working on a West End show can achieve a weekly rate of £550.

Dance teachers are mainly self-employed and receive remuneration dependent on the type and size of dance school they work in.

Related opportunities

- Actor p416
- Choreographer p419
- Stagehand p435

Further information

Council for Dance Education and Training
www.cdet.org.uk

Equity
www.equity.org.uk

Royal Academy of Dance
www.rad.org.uk

Royal Ballet School
www.royalballetschool.org.uk

DJ

Qualifications and courses

There is no specific entry route to this job and no formal qualifications are required.

Work experience is highly advisable in order to gain industry contacts and get valuable experience on the equipment. Those looking to work in radio can gain practical experience by volunteering at student, hospital or community radio stations. To work as a club DJ you need to develop your skills using decks, mixers and sampling equipment. Some top DJs offer masterclasses or allow work-shadowing; this can also help you develop useful industry contacts. You need to produce a demo CD to showcase your DJing abilities and style.

There are some qualifications that may help you with industry training such as the BTEC Level 3 in Music Technology specialising in DJ Technology, the Level 3 in Creative Media Production (Radio) and the Level 3 in Performing Arts. These courses are offered at some colleges of further education and the normal entry requirements are 4 GCSEs/National 5s (A*–C/A–C).

Other qualifications which may be useful include the City & Guilds Certificate and Diploma in Sound Engineering and Music Technology (Levels 1–3), the NCFE Award and Certificate in Music Technology (Levels 1–2) and the NCFE Award, Certificate and Diploma in Radio Production (Levels 1–3). Training in radio skills is also offered by CSV Media which runs Media Clubhouses around the UK. Radio DJs may also find qualifications in journalism, broadcasting or media advantageous.

Though not essential, Foundation degrees and degrees in subjects such as music technology, audio technology, sound engineering and electronics may enhance your technical skills and increase your job opportunities.

What the work involves

You will play and mix music for audiences at live venues or on the radio. You could use vinyl, CDs, MP3s, turntables, mixers, microphones and amplifiers.

Club DJs keep people dancing in bars and clubs. You will create your own sounds and mixes and use lighting and visual effects in time to the beats.

Mobile DJs play at weddings and other social occasions.

As a radio DJ, you will work in a studio playing records, interviewing musicians and chatting to listeners.

VJing (video jockeying) is an alternative form of artistic expression, using a good computer and software to mix/inter-splice sounds with images, from video clips and loops, in real time.

Type of person suited to this work

You must have a passion for music, excellent coordination, good communication and listening skills, and a lively outgoing personality.

You need advanced technical skills as DJs use the latest in turntables, amplifiers and multimedia, and practise techniques such as mixing, scratching and cross fading to make their performance interesting.

Hard work and persistence are key to success. As most DJs are self-employed, basic business skills are an advantage.

Working conditions

As a DJ, you could work in clubs, on radio, in hotels, in holiday camps or at festivals and gigs. You will work long, irregular hours including weekends.

You will be required to travel to different venues so a driving licence is useful.

High noise levels are an occupational hazard for DJs; you need to take steps to protect your hearing.

Future prospects

Some DJs stay in the job only a short time before moving on. Many work part time alongside a daytime job.

You have to be a self-starter and seek out opportunities as jobs are rarely advertised. Experienced DJs can get seasonal work in holiday camps. Some move into careers in music production or retail.

Increasingly, DJs are finding opportunities working with VJs who create pop videos.

Advantages/disadvantages

DJs are usually passionate about music, so you get to work with what you love.

There can be heavy equipment to move around, often in the early hours.

Over time you will buy new technology and update your deck and equipment. Start-up costs are likely to be high (in excess of £1,500).

Money guide

Your earnings will depend on the event, venue and your reputation and experience. At the start of their career, DJs often do unpaid work to gain experience.

Your starting fee per session may range from £50 to £300 with very established and experienced DJs going on to earn £500 to £1,000 for a session.

Top club DJs with celebrity status can achieve an annual salary in excess of £100,000, however most DJs have another job to supplement their income.

Related opportunities

- Musician p429
- Private Music Teacher p191
- Sound Engineer p433

Further information

Access to Music
www.accesstomusic.co.uk

SAE Institute
www.sae.edu

Qualifications and courses

Entertainers do not need to hold any formal academic qualifications as the most important requirement is to have a skill or talent that will entertain audiences. Specific training and courses may be beneficial in developing your skills and proving your ability and commitment to potential employers. Previous experience, such as acting in school or community shows, could also prove advantageous.

General courses that will lead to useful qualifications include the BTEC Certificate in Performing Arts (Levels 2–3) and the BTEC HNC/HND in Performing Arts (Levels 4–5). You could also take an HNC/HND in Acting and Performance or a Foundation degree/degree in performing arts. BTEC entry requirements are usually 4 GCSEs/National 5s (A*–C/A–C) and all degree courses require at least 2 A levels/3 H grades, with one in a related subject.

If you are intending to work with children and/or vulnerable adults, you will also be required to obtain clearance from the Disclosure and Barring Service (DBS) before entering this profession.

Entry routes to these professions are numerous and varied and could include entering talent competitions, working in holiday centres, performing in local clubs and bars or undertaking professional training courses.

Comedian

There are several career paths and training routes open to comedians. You may wish to specialise in stand-up, improvisation, props or comedy acting. Alternatively, you could work as a member of a troupe or work as a talk show comedian.

It is advisable to attend comedy classes at a comedy club or school. The Comedy School runs a number of courses in London and Bristol suitable for comedians interested in training in improvisation, stand-up, clowning, prop comedy, or comedy acting. Workshops offering general advice to comedians on working in the entertainment sector are also available.

To improve your skills and performance you may wish to attend festivals such as the Edinburgh Fringe. Gaining comedy awards will be the best way to raise your profile and secure gigs.

Magician

To become a proficient magician you will need to engage in a large amount of independent learning. It is also advisable to join a local magic club or society to network and learn from other magicians.

To improve your career prospects you may wish to become a member of The Magic Circle. Membership includes the opportunity to attend lectures and network with renowned magicians. To gain membership you must be over 18, be recommended by a current member and pass an interview. You must then pass an examination, either by submitting a thesis or by performing a demonstration. If successful you will be recommended for membership to the council who will ratify your membership by ballot.

If under 18 you could join The Young Magicians Club and attend magic workshops.

The Magic Circle also accredits magic schools across the UK that offer courses in basic magic skills. To improve and extend your skillset you may wish to attend magic conferences in the UK or overseas.

Puppeteer

You could attend the London School of Puppetry (LSP) and study towards the Diploma in Professional Puppetry. The Diploma combines distance learning with workshops and festival performances. You must pass an interview to gain entry onto the course. The LSP also offers a number of open courses if you wish to gain a general introduction or specialise in a particular area of puppetry.

Alternatively, you may wish to attend drama school as many UK drama schools offer modules in puppetry as part of their 3-year courses.

You may wish to sign up to PuppeteersUK to take advantage of their networking and work experience opportunities

Circus performer

A number of circus schools across the UK offer training courses and summer schools. A useful qualification would be the Level 3 BTEC Diploma and Extended Diploma in Performance (Circus Arts). Skills in gymnastics and dance are also valuable. You could take up casual work with a travelling circus to gain general experience.

Circomedia in Bristol offers a 2-year Foundation degree in Contemporary Circus with Physical Theatre, a 1-year Professional Diploma (Levels 4–5) and a 3-month Introductory Certificate in Contemporary Circus & Physical Performance.

The National Centre for Circus Arts offers relevant qualifications including a Foundation degree, a BA (Hons) degree and a Postgraduate Certificate. The Academy of Circus Arts (Zippo's Academy) is a touring circus that provides a full-time course that covers both technical and performance-based training.

You will typically need to audition, have a good level of general education and be over the age of 18 to secure entry onto a vocational circus arts course.

What the work involves

Comedian

Comedians perform amusing acts in front of audiences.

As a comedian, you could choose to specialise in a particular type of performance. As a stand-up comedian you will write and perform your comic material alone. If you work as a comedy actor or as a member of a comedy troupe you will perform comic sketches with other comedians.

Alternatively, you may work as a talk show comedian and perform a mixture of stand-up and comedy acting alongside interviewing celebrity guests.

You may have your own show or perform a set piece in a line-up of other acts. You will also spend time writing and rehearsing material, booking venues and carrying out promotional work.

Magician

Magicians perform a variety of amazing acts in front of audiences.

As a magician, you may perform regularly at a set venue or go on tour with your show.

You may be employed by a club or bar as a regular entertainer or be hired to perform at one-off events such as weddings.

You may also gain work training other magicians by lecturing at conferences or writing instructive books.

You will spend time rehearsing your material, booking venues and carrying out promotional work.

Puppeteer

As a puppeteer, you will use inanimate objects to perform scripts with the same skill level as professional actors.

You will work across TV, film and theatre with a variety of puppets such as marionettes, hand puppets or animatronics.

You will often work with a variety of other artists, such as other puppeteers, actors and dancers. You will also work closely with special effects technicians to create and operate your puppets.

Circus performer

Circus performers perform amazing acts involving skills such as clowning and acrobatics. You may perform solo or as part of a troupe. Other skills may include trapeze work, juggling or fire-eating.

You could work full-time as a member of a travelling circus. Alternatively, you could work freelance, performing at festivals, events or in street theatre.

You will spend time rehearsing your act, staying physically fit, developing new acts and carrying out promotional work.

Type of person suited to this work

You will need natural confidence and a very outgoing nature in order to present a lively and entertaining act to your audience. You will need to be extremely talented in your chosen field.

You should be good with a wide range of people, as your audience could include members of all ages and backgrounds.

You should have good business awareness, be entrepreneurial in your approach and creative in marketing yourself in order to attract interest in your act and increase your bookings. You must be extremely punctual and reliable so as not to disappoint or annoy a venue or your audience.

Working conditions

Working hours vary. Most performances take place during evenings and weekends, with occasional daytime work. You can choose to work full time if you have a number of bookings, or part time in order to supplement your income with another job.

You could have regular weekly, fortnightly or monthly jobs but a great deal of work is on a one-off basis.

You may work across numerous venues throughout the UK (and abroad) so a driving licence would be useful.

Future prospects

The majority of entertainers are self-employed, although there are employment opportunities with circuses, theme parks, holiday parks and cruise ship companies.

Some may also work with one or more agents, who help with promotion and finding bookings in return for a small fee or commission from earnings.

Overseas work is possible, especially if you work for a cruise ship company or if you have an act that is appreciated across a variety of cultures.

Advantages/disadvantages

You will travel across the UK, and even the world, showcasing your talent to a variety of people to entertain and amaze them.

If you are self-employed, you have the opportunity to choose your hours and bookings to fit around other commitments.

The industry is competitive and few entertainers are able to pursue their career on a full-time basis.

Money guide

Salaries for entertainers vary depending on your act, reputation and level of success.

New entrants who have regular work can expect around £10,000 a year.

With experience, you could earn between £12,000 and £20,000 a year.

Well-established entertainers, such as those with regular bookings at reputable venues, or regular TV appearances, can earn over £30,000 a year.

However, in a recent Equity member survey, only 6% of those in the entertainment industry earned over £30,000 the previous year, and nearly half had earned under £6,000 a year.

Related opportunities

- Dancer p422
- Musician p429
- Singer p432

Further information

Equity
www.equity.org.uk

National Centre for Circus Arts
www.nationalcircus.org.uk

PuppeteersUK
www.puppeteersuk.com

The Comedy School
www.thecomedyschool.com

The Magic Circle
www.themagiccircle.co.uk

Qualifications and courses

All lighting technicians must be fully qualified electricians. The Advanced Level Electrotechnical Apprenticeship may be available or you could study for the NVQ Level 3 in Electrotechnical Services and Systems.

Colleges, universities and drama schools offer courses in subjects such as lighting technology, lighting design and technical theatre, film, theatre design and theatre production, which include the study of lighting. Many of these are accredited by Drama UK. There is also an NVQ in Film and Television Lighting (Lighting Technician) (Levels 3–4) for those wishing to specialise in TV and film.

A degree in theatre practice specialising in production lighting is available at the Central School of Speech and Drama, and Rose Bruford College offers degree programmes in lighting design or creative lighting control. The general entry requirements for a degree are 2 A levels/3 H grades and 5 GCSEs/National 5s (A*–C/A–C). The Association of British Theatre Technicians (ABTT) also provides the Bronze, Silver and Gold Awards for Theatre Electricians.

An alternative route which may be available is the Apprenticeship in Technical Theatre at both Intermediate and Advanced Levels which would combine practical work experience with the study towards professional qualifications.

Experience is necessary and may be accumulated within amateur dramatic companies or drama societies at university etc. This will allow you to train, network and prove your proficiency to potential employers.

The BBC offers a work experience scheme but places are limited. Volunteering with student or community film projects, theatres or concert venues would be useful.

What the work involves

Lighting technicians are responsible for creating stage lighting effects, working closely with the set designer and producer. It is important to visit venues before productions start and watch rehearsals to get the lighting effects right for live performances.

You will do lighting for advertising sets, in video production, theatre and broadcasting work.

You will be responsible for rigging and setting up the lighting, and plotting and programming the lighting requirements.

Type of person suited to this work

Anyone entering this career must have an interest in electrical work and electronics, combined with a strong interest in theatre and performance or live concerts.

Lighting technicians need to have a creative flair as the main aim of this job is to create the atmosphere required by the producer.

You will also need to be physically fit and work well in a team.

In some situations, for example changing or operating spotlights, the tasks could involve working at heights, and would not suit a person who suffers from vertigo.

Working conditions

You will work indoors and outdoors, usually working afternoons, evenings and weekends.

You will work with lots of heavy equipment and you may sometimes need to wear protective steel toe-capped boots.

You may have to work in cramped spaces with computerised control systems.

You will often be away from home for weeks and months if you are travelling with a roadshow.

Future prospects

Theatre lighting is usually provided by specialist companies which employ technicians on a short-term contract basis.

However, once you are experienced and known in the trade, your opportunity to join the backstage crew of a particular theatre group increases.

Progression as a lighting technician relies on skills and dedication. When in demand, you can become a senior or chief lighting technician and, in some cases, technical manager.

Advantages/disadvantages

You will have irregular working hours, including evening and weekend work, and you will frequently be away from home.

Seeing your skills and experience light up a set or production will be a great confidence booster.

Money guide

Trainee technicians start on around £9,500 per year.

Experienced lighting technicians working in theatre can earn between £15,000 and £17,000.

Earnings are higher in film/TV and you could receive up to £30,000.

Many lighting technicians work on a freelance basis, earning a daily or weekly rate which ranges widely.

The Broadcasting, Entertainment, Cinematograph and Theatre Union (BECTU) recommends a daily rate of £240.

Related opportunities

- Electrician p80
- Stage Manager p434

Further information

Association of British Theatre Technicians
www.abtt.org.uk

National Electrotechnical Training
www.netservices.org.uk

Qualifications and courses

There are no set entry requirements to become a location manager, but you may find a degree in communications, film and TV production, media studies or photography useful. You will need at least 2 A levels/3 H grades and 5 GCSEs/National 5s (A*–C/A–C) for degree entry. In your spare time you could gain relevant experience through a university media company.

However, entry without a degree is common and experience in the industry is highly valued. Initially, it may prove easier to gain experience in general production as opposed to location-specific experience. The BBC offers a variety of production work placements.

This is a senior role, and it is unlikely you would begin your career as a location manager. Most entrants will enter the industry as a runner or location assistant/scout, before being promoted to a unit manager or assistant location manager, to then move on to a location manager role. Work experience and networking are vital for career progression.

Qualifications in health and safety will be beneficial as you will be responsible for the wellbeing of the cast and crew on location. The Broadcasting, Entertainment, Cinematograph and Theatre Union (BECTU) offers relevant courses such as Emergency First Aid at Work and the Creative Industries Safety Passport. Other relevant courses include the Level 5 NVQ Diploma in Occupational Health and Safety or the Edexcel Level 3 Award in Reviewing Health and Safety Procedures in the Workplace.

What the work involves

Location managers identify ideal locations for filming TV or film productions. It is your responsibility to research and scout out locations that fit the director's brief and meet practical requirements. Your role will include negotiating bookings with location owners and organising permissions for access with local authorities. You will need to take budget, accessibility and the shooting schedule into account when booking locations.

Once shooting starts you are responsible for ensuring easy access to the location and for the health and safety of the cast and crew. You will need to be on location to supervise and solve any problems that may arise during the shoot. After shooting you will return the location to its original state and resolve any insurance claims.

Type of person suited to this work

To successfully scout out suitable locations you must have a strong sense of initiative and vision.

Your role will involve liaising with a wide range of people, so good communication skills are essential. Negotiating skills are valuable for establishing contracts and obtaining permissions for access.

Excellent organisation skills are vital as you will work within a strict schedule and budget. You should also be a good problem-solver as issues will often arise during shooting.

Working conditions

Location managers are often away from home either visiting potential sites or staying at sites during filming.

Work is typically outdoors and seasonal with summer being the busiest time of year.

The irregular nature of the job and the constant relocation might result in financial insecurity. When filming you will usually be the first one to arrive on set and the last to leave. This might mean working long unsocial hours.

Future prospects

Initially you will be working on small productions, but with experience you may have the opportunity to work on much larger projects. Over the course of your career you may choose to specialise in a particular area such as TV dramas or advertisements.

Alternatively, you could set up your own location agency or go on to work as a production designer, director, or producer.

Advantages/disadvantages

Your work will involve a lot of travel and you will visit some exciting locations.

You may have the opportunity to work with famous directors and actors.

The work can be very stressful as you will be under pressure to find locations and ensure everything goes smoothly during filming.

You will spend a lot of time away from home which may affect your personal life.

Money guide

Rates of pay vary depending on the size of the production.

For a location assistant working a 50-hour week, the Broadcasting, Entertainment, Cinematograph and Theatre Union (BECTU) recommends a rate range from £400 to in excess of £480 per week.

The BECTU rate for a location manager working a 50-hour week ranges from £1,200 to £1,900 per week.

You will usually be employed on a contract basis.

Related opportunities

- Stage/Set Designer p175
- TV, Film and Radio Producer p413
- TV, Film and Radio Production Assistant/Runner p414

Further information

The Production Guild
www.productionguild.com

MAKE-UP ARTIST

Qualifications and courses

Make-up artists in theatre/TV/film are usually trained in beauty therapy or both hairdressing and make-up. Relevant qualifications include NVQs in Beauty Therapy (Levels 1–3) and BTECs in Beauty Therapy (Levels 2–3). In Scotland there is also the HNC/HND in Beauty Therapy.

There is a range of specialist further education courses in theatrical and/or media make-up, including both short courses and diplomas. Relevant qualifications are available from the Vocational Training Charitable Trust (VTCT), the International Therapy Examination Council (ITEC) and the National Association of Screen Make-Up Artists and Hairdressers (NASMAH). City & Guilds also offer a qualification in Creative Hair and Beauty Studies (Levels 1–3).

A number of universities and colleges run HND courses in theatrical and media make-up or make-up artistry. Degrees in Hair and Make-Up for Film and TV, Hair and Make-Up for Fashion and Hair, Make-Up, and Prosthetics for Performance are available at the London College of Fashion. Degrees and diplomas in subjects such as fine art, visual art, fashion design or graphic design can be useful.

Relevant experience is desirable and can be accumulated via working with amateur dramatic companies or by working in beauty salons.

What the work involves

Your work will involve applying make-up and arranging hair to produce the right look for male and female artists and performers in films, TV and stage productions. You will need to listen to the director in order to create the desired look for the individual characters or troupe.

You could be employed in TV, by a video production company, as a specialist in wedding and occasion make-up, by a theatre or film company, or be self-employed, perhaps as part of a backstage team.

Type of person suited to this work

Anyone who considers doing make-up work needs to be creative, with the imagination to visualise the finished effect. You will have to pay great attention to detail. The job requires excellent communication skills, as you will need tact to advise colleagues or clients on their image.

At times, there will be many people needing to be made up for a particular scene and you could be working under intense pressure. Self-confidence and an outgoing personality are positive factors in building relationships and succeeding at work.

Working conditions

Most of your work will be undertaken indoors in theatres, studios, beauty salons and, at first, possibly in retail outlets.

Long hours and weekend work are common. Doing make-up involves spending extended periods of time standing over customers and you will need to be physically fit.

If you are self-employed, you will need to provide your own cosmetics and you will need to carry all your equipment and materials with you.

A driving licence would be useful for travelling to different jobs.

Future prospects

Although this is not a huge area for employment, there will always be a demand for make-up artists. The larger towns and cities present the best opportunities. Although limited, some work could be available in hotels or on cruise ships.

Once you have gained experience, you can secure regular work in TV or video, on a cruise ship, in a hotel, a retail store or with a theatre company. You could set up your own beauty salon.

Competition is strong and progression depends upon the reputation, contacts and talent of the individual.

Advantages/disadvantages

Working hours may be irregular and unsocial, especially if you do make-up both before and during performances.

It is highly satisfying to see your work on stage or set, or to make people look nice for a special occasion.

Tools and cosmetics may be provided, but it is often expected that you will have your own make-up kit with you. Professional kits can cost up to £1,500.

Money guide

Most make-up artists work on a freelance basis and their earnings depend on their reputation, experience and the project they are working on.

Recommended rates of pay are set by the Broadcasting, Entertainment, Cinematograph and Theatre Union (BECTU) according to the size of the project.

A make-up artist assistant could earn between £72 and £155 for a 10-hour day.

The daily rate for a make-up artist is between £169 and £264.

A chief make-up artist can achieve £196 to £331 for a 10-hour day.

Related opportunities

- Beauty Consultant p442
- Beauty Therapist p443
- Hairdresser/Barber p453

Further information

British Association of Beauty Therapy and Cosmetology
www.babtac.com

Make Up Artist magazine
www.makeupmag.com

The Iver Academy
www.iveracademy.co.uk

PERFORMING ARTS

MUSICIAN

Qualifications and courses

Classical musicians undertake extensive musical training and academic qualifications with most taking all the graded examinations in their chosen instrument/s, as well as further related courses. These courses include GCSEs/ National 5s and A levels/H grades in Music and the HNC Level 4 and HND Level 5 in Music or Music Technology.

Some musicians also pursue music degrees at university, specialist courses at music colleges (conservatoires) and relevant postgraduate qualifications. For entry to a music degree you usually need a minimum of 2 A levels/3 H grades, including Music, 5 GCSEs/National 5s (A*–C/ A–C) and grade 8 in your chosen instrument or voice. Postgraduate programmes require entrants to hold a relevant first degree.

Popular musicians do not need to hold any qualifications for entry to the industry. However, undertaking training may prove your ability and dedication to prospective employers. Any of the qualifications mentioned above would be useful for popular musicians. There is also the option to study for a degree in popular music.

Armed forces musicians do not need to hold any formal qualifications; aptitude in your chosen instrument/s will be assessed during an audition.

What the work involves

Whether you work as a classical, popular or armed forces musician, your main responsibility will be to perform to and entertain an audience.

You will spend the majority of your time practising in order to develop and strengthen your ability on the instrument/s you play.

You could compose your own material or play existing music from a variety of genres.

Type of person suited to this work

You must be extremely musical, particularly if you are looking to work as a classical musician. You will need to be very confident in yourself and your abilities, as well as having considerable stage presence to hold the attention of an audience.

Throughout the music industry, there is intense competition for jobs. You will need determination, tenacity and resilience in order to cope with knock-backs and persevere.

Working conditions

You must be prepared to work long, unsocial hours in a variety of environments including clubs and bars. You may have to work away from home for long periods of time.

Classical musicians tend to work in locations such as concert halls, theatres, parks and recording studios.

Musicians employed by the armed forces usually perform for military parades, regimental dinners, state occasions, sporting events and other special occasions.

Future prospects

Classical musicians may rise to enjoy success as solo artists or may work in group ensembles, such as orchestras, in which there are chances for promotion. Diversifying into teaching is also common.

Prospects for popular musicians are varied and depend a great deal on how successful you become. Many decide to move into a business role, for example as a manager or representative for a recording company. You could also become a music teacher.

Armed forces musicians usually move across various bands throughout their career, whilst also progressing up through the standard ranks as they gain relevant management, leadership and military skills.

Advantages/disadvantages

As a musician, you could work in a variety of disciplines and with a range of different people, so the job will be stimulating and interesting.

Competition is intense in the music industry so you will have to work incredibly hard.

Money guide

Classical musicians employed by an orchestra usually receive a salary of between £22,000 and £26,000 with principal players earning from £25,000 up to £50,000.

Session musicians could receive £120 to £350 for a 3-hour job.

Typically, fees for solo musicians are between £100 and £200 per show. A popular solo musician can achieve £500 to £2,000 a week.

Armed forces musicians have a starting salary of about £14,000, rising to £18,000 upon completion of training.

Army musicians on a fast-track scheme can earn over £23,000 after 2 years.

Pay in the army will increase as you gain experience and promotions.

Related opportunities

- Composer/Songwriter p420
- Singer p432

Further information

Arts Council England
www.artscouncil.org.uk

Associated Board of the Royal Schools of Music
http://gb.abrsm.org

Royal Military School of Music
www.army.mod.uk/music

Qualifications and courses

There is no standard route into this career and it is possible to enter without academic qualifications. However, to be employed as an assistant you will be expected to have at least GCSEs/National 5s (A*–C/A–C) in English, Maths and Art. You will also need a good history of relevant work experience, possibly from student productions or amateur theatre, and a lot of talent and dedication.

Most prop makers have relevant qualifications, such as the BTEC Level 3 Certificate in Production Arts, specialising in Stage Management or Set Design and Construction, or the BTEC HNC/HND in Performing Arts specialising in Production. The Royal Academy of Dramatic Art (RADA) offers a specialist course in Property Making and the Royal Central School of Speech & Drama provides a degree in Theatre Practice (Prop Making).

Degrees, Foundation degrees and postgraduate courses are available in set design, prop making and stage management. Other useful subjects include art and design, fine art, 3D design and model making. Entry requirements for a degree are usually at least 2 A levels/3 H grades, including Art, and 5 GCSEs/National 5s (A*–C/A–C). Most course providers also ask candidates to present a portfolio of work for entrance assessment.

You may be able to receive apprenticeship-style training at the start of your career with the BBC's Art Department Training Scheme, which lasts 12 months. Apprenticeships may also be available with regional screen agencies or media training organisations.

What the work involves

Props makers and their assistants are responsible for designing, changing, making and finishing the props used in theatre, video, film, TV or circus work.

Working closely with set designers, prop makers help create the right atmosphere within particularly stages/scenes by creating relevant and necessary set dressings and items for actors to interact with.

You will spend a considerable amount of time researching the historical and cultural background of the props to ensure they have an authentic feel.

You will be working with different materials, such as wood, fibreglass, fabric and metal, and you will use a range of practical skills including carpentry, modelling and painting.

Type of person suited to this work

You will need to have a mixture of practical and artistic skills in order to have the vision to design props and the ability to make them yourself.

You will be taking direction from theatre/TV producers, so you must be able to listen carefully to their briefs and ideas, and translate them into actual props. You will need good problem-solving skills so that you can balance meeting people's expectations and working to a budget.

Working conditions

Working hours vary but you can expect to work long hours over evenings and weekends in order to meet deadlines now and again. You will be working in small studios and prop rooms and these locations can often be cramped.

You may also spend time visiting suppliers for equipment and travelling to libraries and museums to carry out research.

You will have to wear relevant safety equipment when dealing with materials such as wood, metal, fibreglass and any chemical products.

Future prospects

The majority of props makers are freelance so you will be employed on short-term projects most of the time. These could be for film studios, theatres, TV companies or museums.

Career progression is dependent upon building a good reputation and an excellent portfolio of work.

With experience, you could move into set design or take a more general role in stage management.

Advantages/disadvantages

Working in a creative industry such as theatre or film provides challenging, exciting work opportunities.

You will be using a mixture of artistic, practical and intellectual skills which will be tiring but rewarding.

Working freelance can create a sense of job instability and it can be difficult when you have a period of time without work.

Money guide

As an assistant to a props maker, you can expect to earn about £12,000.

Props makers who are just starting in the industry usually receive an annual salary of around £15,000.

If you gain a good reputation and start to work on large productions with big budgets, you could earn in excess of £40,000.

The Broadcasting, Entertainment, Cinematograph and Theatre Union (BECTU) suggest a weekly rate of £500 for a trainee props maker and £1,300 for a prop maker. This weekly rate is based on a 50 hour week.

Related opportunities

- Make-up Artist p428
- Stage Manager p434
- Wardrobe Assistant p439

Further information

Creative and Cultural Skills
www.ccskills.org.uk

Royal Academy of Dramatic Art
www.rada.ac.uk

Stage Management Association
www.stagemanagementassociation.co.uk

PERFORMING ARTS

ROADIE

Qualifications and courses

There are no formal entry qualifications. Most people enter this career through experience of working with a friend or other contacts and the majority of roadies will learn the trade from working with other more experienced people. Helping small local bands and school productions is a good way to start and gain some experience; however, if you are under 18 you may not be able to work in some licensed premises.

Though not essential, GCSEs/National 5s and A levels/H grades in Music or Music Technology may prove advantageous. Qualifications in technical procedures such as electronics, music rigging, sound production, lighting and pyrotechnics could set you apart from the intense competition, and there are various BTECs, HNCs/HNDs, NVQs/SVQs, City & Guilds courses, degrees and postgraduate courses available. The Creative & Cultural department of the National Skills Academy also provides relevant courses and the Creative Apprenticeship in Music. The Association of British Theatre Technicians (ABTT) provide relevant courses on topics such as pyrotechnics safety.

Useful skills and qualifications include a First Aid certificate and the ability to speak one or more foreign languages. The Production Services Association (PSA) operates a Safety Passport scheme that deals with issues including manual handling, transport and general safety precautions.

A full driving licence is helpful and a large goods vehicle (LGV) licence or passenger carrying vehicle (PCV) licence could be useful if you need to drive the tour bus or larger vehicles to transport heavy equipment.

What the work involves

Roadies are responsible for setting up a range of equipment for music concerts and events including amplification systems, electrical cabling, stage and special effects lighting.

You will have to move and set up heavy equipment, load and unload vans and trailers and do lots of driving around. You will need to maintain and fine-tune your equipment on a regular basis.

Your work could include handling pyrotechnics, laser displays, computer/live film feeds and video links.

Type of person suited to this work

You will need to have a strong interest in music, technology and electronics. It is essential to have good communication skills and an interest in people, and be creative and practical.

Physical fitness and stamina will be essential, with a sense of humour a bonus. Sets will have to be assembled and disassembled safely to tight deadlines so you should be able to work whilst under pressure.

As most roadies are self-employed, a well-organised person with some business skills will do well by maintaining their accounts and keeping records of bookings.

Working conditions

You will have exceptionally long working hours, mainly evenings, nights and weekends. If you are on a tour you might be working 7 days a week. Three-month contracts are typical in this line of work.

The work is very physical and there is lots of heavy lifting involved. Sometimes you could be working at heights on electrical cabling.

Future prospects

There is strong competition for jobs. The work is unpredictable and you might need another job to boost your income. Work can be seasonal, with more roadies needed for summer events.

Marketing your services will be essential for getting gigs; many roadies now use websites to advertise.

A wide range of technical skills such as stage lighting and management or sound engineering will improve your chances of employment and could enable you to secure lighting or sound jobs in film, television or theatre.

The HND in Music Industry Management and other relevant qualifications could also allow you to work in promotions, productions or band management.

Advantages/disadvantages

Roadies work long unsociable hours and there is lots of travelling.

Very loud sounds will damage your hearing if your ears are unprotected.

You will get to attend many gigs and concerts for free.

Money guide

Most roadies work freelance and your pay will depend on the gig, your experience and general availability of roadies.

As a starter, with regular work, you could earn around £12,000 per year.

A roadie with electrical, audio or video skills can earn in excess of £21,000. With excellent technical skills, pay can rise to £30,000.

On contract to a big touring band, you could earn in excess of £35,000.

Related opportunities

- Large Goods Vehicle Driver p596
- Lighting Technician p426
- Sound Engineer p433

Further information

National Skills Academy for Creative & Cultural
http://ccskills.org.uk/network

Production Services Association
www.psa.org.uk

Stage Management Association
www.stagemanagementassociation.co.uk

Qualifications and courses

Academic qualifications are not strictly required in order to become a singer, but they often demonstrate honed talent, commitment, and the necessary expertise to succeed in the music industry to potential employers or clients.

Relevant qualifications include the national exams in singing (grades 1 to 8) from the Royal Schools of Music, and GCSEs/National 5s and A levels/H grades in Music. There are also BTEC courses in music, performing arts, music performance, music practice and music technology, and HNC/HND courses and degrees in popular music and related subjects. Entry requirements for these courses vary; BTECs usually require 4 GCSEs/National 5s (A*–C/A–C) or equivalent, while HNC/HND programmes require an additional A level/H grade, and degree programmes require at least 2 A levels/H grades, often including Music, and 5 GCSEs/National 5s (A*–C/A–C). Specialist singing degrees are also available from institutions such as the Academy of Contemporary Music.

You could perform with choirs or in amateur productions and talent contests as this will help you develop as a rounded performer who can hold the attention of an audience.

Networking is essential and an understanding of marketing and social media may help you get noticed and help build a fanbase.

Classical singing is formally taught at a number of different institutions. As part of a much longer preparation process, singers take postgraduate courses in either opera or oratorio, dependent on their repertoire, alongside short courses.

What the work involves

Singers perform in front of an audience in clubs, at gigs, on television or radio, in a recording studio or in an opera house. They work as solo artists, or as part of a backing group, choir or chorus.

You will spend many hours practising in order to develop and strengthen your breathing and vocal ability. You will need to have good diction, have a good grasp of language and may even be asked sometimes to perform in a variety of languages, including Latin and French.

You will work with a variety of musicians and music industry professionals, including orchestras, bands, session musicians, sound engineers, and maybe a manager.

Type of person suited to this work

You will need to have an exceptional talent for singing in order to get noticed in the music industry.

Owing to the intense competition in this area, you will also need determination, self-discipline and resilience in order to cope with disappointments and to persevere in order to achieve your goals.

You will need to be very confident in yourself and your abilities. It is difficult to hold an audience without stage presence and charisma.

Working conditions

As a singer you can expect to work long and unsociable hours, over evenings and weekends, as this is when the majority of your audience will be free.

You may have to travel long distances for gigs and rehearsals.

You could work in a variety of locations, from small clubs and theatres to large concert halls and even outdoor venues.

Future prospects

Singing is a highly competitive industry, and opportunities for full-time work are extremely limited. Most professionals supplement their income with another job, so you could look into teaching, or writing songs and jingles for other artists.

Most successful singers move to London to pursue their careers, as this is where the majority of opportunities lie.

You may well work with an agent or manager at some point in your career. Their purpose is to offer you career advice and to find you singing opportunities.

Advantages/disadvantages

You will be fulfilling a passion while also doing your job, which is rare and satisfying.

You will be bringing pleasure to the people in your audience, no matter how big or small.

You will have to work long and unsociable hours.

You will have to be resilient in order to persevere despite negative feedback on occasion.

Money guide

As a solo singer, you could earn between £150 and £450 per concert.

Chorus singers usually earn between £70 and £100 and backing singers on albums are paid £110 or more for a 3-hour recording session.

If you become a commercial success you could earn significantly more, especially if you write your own songs and earn royalties.

If you go on to perform in the theatre, there are set rates of pay that employers must adhere to. For example, chorus members command £650 per week for performances onstage in London's West End.

Related opportunities

- Composer/Songwriter p420
- Musician p429

Further information

BRIT School for Performing Arts and Technology
www.brit.croydon.sch.uk

Creative and Cultural Skills
www.ccskills.org.uk

SOUND ENGINEER

Qualifications and courses

Sound engineers can work within several different industries, such as music, film, TV, computer games, apps and theatre. It is possible to become a sound engineer without gaining any relevant qualifications, as many companies take on trainees as runners or assistants, and you can build your knowledge whilst you work.

However, job competition is intense and larger studios and companies prefer candidates to hold relevant qualifications. These could include: GCSEs/National 5s or A levels/H grades in Music, Maths and Physics, NVQs Levels 2–3 in Technical Theatre Support Sound, Light and Stage, the BTEC Level 3 Certificate in Music Technology, the Level 5 BTEC Professional Diploma in Music (Live Sound), Foundation degrees and degrees in music production or audio technology.

Pre-entry experience is essential and can be accumulated by volunteering with recording studios, working with local bands and working on school plays or with amateur dramatic companies.

Postgraduate qualifications are also offered by a limited number of providers. The University of Westminster runs a master's degree course in audio production, and the National Film and Television School offers a Diploma in Production Sound for Film & Television or a Master of Arts degree in Sound Design for Film and Television.

For theatre sound engineers, many drama schools offer courses in theatre lighting and sound which may be useful. All good programmes are accredited by Drama UK.

What the work involves

Sound engineers set up, operate and maintain a range of technical equipment that is designed to capture, magnify and manipulate words and music.

Theatrical sound engineers create 'sound plots', choose equipment and insert sound effects according to the instructions of the director of the production.

Sound engineers working in the recording industry capture speech, music and other sound effects and modify them using sophisticated electronic equipment for a number of purposes including creating pop songs, adverts or computer game soundtracks to name but 3 possible outlets for your work.

Type of person suited to this work

You will need a good musical ear and excellent sense of timing in order to put together pleasing and appropriate soundtracks/background audio to a range of productions.

You should also have knowledge of both electronics and IT systems.

Recording industry sound engineers must also have a good knowledge of both recording and post-production processes.

Working conditions

Sound engineers working in both theatre and the recording industry should expect to work varied hours that will encompass day, evening and weekend commitments.

Theatre sound engineers will spend the majority of their working day confined to a small control box which may be cramped and often is plunged into semi-darkness.

Recording sound engineers work in studios, some of which are large and air-conditioned, whilst others can be small and cramped. You will usually be working in artificial light and the atmosphere can be stressful when working against deadlines.

Future prospects

Competition for jobs is intense, and you may spend a long time proving your credentials as a runner or gofer.

You could work for a variety of employers, including theatres, opera and ballet houses, commercial recording studios, app developers or media post-production departments.

Theatre sound engineers may go on to become sound designers with greater creative input in productions, whereas many recording sound engineers move into roles as producers.

Advantages/disadvantages

You will work with a variety of people on diverse projects, so each day will bring new challenges and rewards.

Theatre and media are exciting industries to work in as there is constant cultural and technical development.

You will have to work long hours that will often fall over evenings and weekends.

Money guide

Starting salaries for sound engineers, whether they work in theatre or the recording industry, range from £13,000 to £18,000 per year. With experience, this could rise to £30,000.

Sound engineers working on large productions, with big companies or well-known artists, can earn in excess of £40,000.

The Broadcasting, Entertainment, Cinematograph and Theatre Union (BECTU) recommends rates for sound engineers involved in feature films. Daily rates based on a 10-hour day vary according to the production, but can range from £294 to £442.

Related opportunities

- Lighting Technician p426
- Musician p429

Further information

National Film and Television School
http://nfts.co.uk

Professional Lighting and Sound Association
www.plasa.org

STAGE MANAGER

Qualifications and courses

Practical experience is often valued as highly as formal qualifications by employers and can be gained through volunteer work with local theatres or student productions. You could also begin your career as part of the stage crew and progress up to the position of stage manager. However, as this is a competitive industry, you may find that qualifications will help prove your proficiency and improve your future prospects.

You can complete a BTEC Level 3 Certificate in Production Arts specialising in Stage Management which lasts 2–3 years when studied full time. The selection process involves an interview and providing a portfolio of your practical work.

Drama schools such as the Royal Academy of Dramatic Art (RADA) and the London Academy of Music and Dramatic Art (LAMDA) offer Foundation degrees and degrees in stage management and technical theatre. The general entry requirements for a degree are 2 A levels/3 H grades and 5 GCSEs/National 5s (A*–C/A–C), as well as a demonstrable interest in theatre production. NVQs are available in Technical Theatre Support, Sound, Light and Stage (Levels 2–3) and you can also take a BTEC Level 3 Certificate in Production Arts. Drama UK accredits vocational stage management courses.

You could also undertake a Creative Apprenticeship and specialise in stage management.

The Stage Management Association (SMA) runs a variety of short courses for people already working as stage managers or assistant stage managers.

What the work involves

Stage managers work with designers, directors and producers, assessing and discussing what props, lighting and other stage support are needed for the production.

You are the link between the artistic and technical aspects of all productions, as you are in charge of everything that happens on stage including calling actors, giving technical cues and moving scenery.

You could work on numerous types of production, such as theatrical performances, opera, ballet and even music festivals.

Type of person suited to this work

You will need to have artistic flair, be practical, communicate instructions clearly and manage others confidently.

Good time management skills are crucial.

The work is demanding as the successful running of the backstage support for the performance rests with you. A cool head and a sense of humour – while still being assertive – will make the work easier for you. An excellent stage manager can help create a good team atmosphere backstage between artists, prop managers and stagehands.

Working conditions

You will spend long hours in theatres and studios, sometimes working into the night to meet deadlines. In addition, you will have to travel to different venues so a driving licence would be useful.

Finding work is not easy and can take up a huge amount of your time, so you should be prepared for rejection and periods without work.

Future prospects

The employment demand for stage managers currently remains relatively stable, and opportunities for full-time or regular work are better than on the performing side.

This is a competitive area of work and the opportunities for employment are not extensive. Work can be found in theatre companies, opera, theatre in education and touring companies.

You could be promoted to a nationally recognised position or become a company stage manager where you would do publicity and finance work as well.

You could also choose to move into TV or film, becoming a director or producer.

Advantages/disadvantages

You will work long, unpredictable hours to meet the deadline of the production.

Permanent contracts are difficult to find so you may experience a sense of job insecurity.

The work is both creative and practical.

There is a great sense of achievement at the end of a successful run when everything has operated smoothly.

Money guide

Starting out as a trainee or assistant stage manager, you will earn between £17,000 and £20,000 per year. Deputy stage managers earn slightly more.

With experience, your annual salary can rise to between £20,000 and £26,000.

The most successful and experienced stage managers can achieve up to £40,000.

Many stage managers work on a freelance basis.

The minimum weekly salary recommended by Equity, the performers' and entertainment workers' trade union, is £440.

Related opportunities

- Entertainment Manager p366
- Props Maker/Assistant p430
- Wardrobe Assistant p439

Further information

Equity
www.equity.org.uk

Stage Management Association
www.stagemanagementassociation.co.uk

STAGEHAND

Qualifications and courses

There are no formal qualifications necessary to work as a stagehand.

Usually you will begin casual work backstage and you are more likely to secure this work if you have previous experience and some practical skills. It would therefore be useful to have worked backstage at school or college, or as part of an amateur dramatics society.

Skills in carpentry, electrics or sound and lighting are all advantageous for securing work. There are various qualifications available in these areas, such as BTECs and qualifications from the City & Guilds and the Association of British Theatre Technicians.

If you eventually want to progress into stage management, there are some relevant courses that may be useful, including BTECs in subjects such as production arts (stage management) and performing arts (Levels 1–5), and Foundation degrees and degrees in stage management with drama schools such as the Royal Central School of Speech and Drama. Entry requirements for a degree course are typically 2 A levels/3 H grades and 5 GCSEs/National 5s (A*–C/A–C), and HNDs usually require 1 A level/H grade and 4 GCSEs/National 5s (A*–C/A–C).

What the work involves

Stagehands (also known as stage technicians or crew) work backstage as part of the production team.

You will provide assistance with props, scenery and special effects in either theatres, concert halls or at TV/film studios.

Your tasks will involve handling the equipment, helping to assemble and move scenery, opening and closing the theatre curtain between acts (when working on live plays or shows) and clearing the stage or studio at the end of each performance.

The work is normally completed as part of a team of stagehands under the supervision of the stage manager.

Type of person suited to this work

You will need to be physically fit to work as a stagehand as the work will involve a lot of heavy lifting. It will also be important to have good stamina as working hours will be long and you will probably work 6 days a week on a show.

As the work is normally team based, you will need to work well as part of a team and have a flexible attitude as you may be required to do a wide range of tasks, some at short notice. You must also be able to cope under pressure as the shows will be live and things can go wrong.

You must have a head for heights as well as a good understanding of health and safety.

A passion for theatre and live performance, as well as for stage and set design, is also essential.

Working conditions

You will be working irregular hours, including evenings, weekends and bank holidays.

You must be prepared to work at short notice and work overtime as productions can overrun.

You may be based in one venue, or have to travel to different venues if the production goes on tour.

You should wear black, comfortable clothing for making scenery changes during a production.

Future prospects

This is a popular and competitive area to work in.

With experience, you could go on to a supervisory or management role, leading a crew of stagehands.

You could also specialise in a certain area such as carpentry and become a production carpenter.

Eventually, after working your way up, it may be possible to progress to tour manager or stage manager.

Advantages/disadvantages

The work is often quite casual, so you may not have a steady income.

You will work irregular and unsocial hours as most performances will be in the evening and at weekends and you may have to work away from home on location for days or weeks at a time.

Working in theatre is an exciting and challenging job role; you will get to be part of a glamorous industry.

Money guide

The salary for stagehands is fairly low, and many roles are often on a low or no pay basis with profits shared among those involved afterwards.

Starting salaries are around £250–£300 per week or around £12,000 per year. Salaries for full-time stage hands are usually between £14,000 and £18,000 a year.

The majority of stagehands work on a freelance or casual basis though so pay rates vary considerably. You may be able to negotiate a higher rate if you have extensive or specialist experience.

Related opportunities

- Artistic/Theatre Director p417
- Stage Manager p434
- TV, Film and Radio Producer p413

Further information

Association of British Theatre Technicians
www.abtt.org.uk

Creative Skillset
www.creativeskillset.org

Drama UK
https://dramauk.co.uk

Stage Management Association
www.stagemanagementassociation.co.uk

STUNT PERFORMER

Qualifications and courses

There are no academic entry requirements for this work but you must be over the age of 18 in order to be employed. Equity (the trade union for the performing arts) recommends that film and TV producers only employ stunt performers who are on the Joint Industry Stunt Committee (JISC) Stunt Register.

To join the JISC register you are required to prove that you have at least 1 year's experience and qualifications in a minimum of 6 sports in the following groups, 1 of which must be in Group A: Group A Fighting (martial arts and boxing), Group B Falling (trampolining and high diving) Group C Riding/Driving (horses, cars and motorcycles), Group D Agility/Strength (gymnastics and rock climbing) and Group E Water (swimming and sub-aqua). You must have experience in at least 4 of these groups and you cannot have more than 2 sports in 1 group.

When registering these qualifications they must not be more than 5 years old. You will also need to give the JISC evidence that you have spent a minimum of 60 days in front of the camera either as an actor or walk-on artist. You must work for 3 years as a Probationary Member of the Register, a further minimum of 2 years as an Intermediate Member, or Stunt Performer, before you are eligible for Full Membership of the JISC. You must then work for a further period of five years to become a Stunt Action Co-ordinator.

Organisations such as the British Academy of Dramatic Combat (BADC), the British Academy of Stage and Screen Combat (BASSC) and YoungBlood offer a range of courses, workshops and classes in stage combat for practising actors. You must maintain and improve your skills in order to remain employable.

What the work involves

Stunt performers plan, design, practise and perform stunts in areas such as motorbike riding, car driving, diving, flying, paragliding, bungee jumping, skiing and horse riding.

Standing in for actors in TV, film or video productions, you will enter flaming buildings, crash vehicles, drive at speed or do dangerous stunts at sea.

You could advise other performers on health and safety issues.

Type of person suited to this work

Stunt performers are dedicated to their art and committed to ensuring that their skills are highly developed. A high level of stamina and fitness is essential. You should be a risk taker with an adventurous spirit.

You must be a good communicator, as you will have to work closely with the production team and explain stunts and their possible ramifications. You must have good reflexes.

You need to be happy to practise every aspect of your stunts over and again until they are reproducible in all aspects, so you must be a perfectionist. You must always be aware of the dangers you face, practising long hours to make the performance appear easy!

Working conditions

Part of your working day could be spent within a studio, on location or on a film set.

You could be working indoors or out, in cramped spaces, at heights or sometimes in bad weather conditions.

The hours will be very long, often up to 16 hours per day depending on the production, with frequent weekend work and travel to distant places.

Future prospects

Opportunities for live stunt work are decreasing, as digital graphics and new media can simulate stunts, so competition for work is growing increasingly fierce.

Stunt artists work anywhere in the world, with the main employers being film, TV and video production companies.

You could progress into advisory work, helping film directors or advising and training other stunt artists. You could also direct action scenes.

Advantages/disadvantages

You will have the opportunity to travel the world and no two days will be the same.

Seeing the finished product on screen is rewarding.

This is difficult, dangerous work involving many risks.

Entry to this sector is very competitive, and it may be difficult to remain in the industry as you grow older owing to fitness levels.

Money guide

There is no formal pay scale for stunt performers and income varies greatly.

Equity establishes minimum rates for stunt work with TV companies and independent producers.

Recommended daily rates are £250 to £370 for TV work and £425 a day for film work.

Although the majority of stunt artists are freelance, you might enter full-time employment with a salary of about £12,000.

A very experienced performer may earn £25,000 and above per year.

Related opportunities

- Actor p416
- Choreographer p419

Further information

British Academy of Stage and Screen Combat
www.bassc.org

Equity
www.equity.org.uk

YoungBlood
www.youngblood.co.uk

Qualifications and courses

There is no specific entry route into this profession. Although a degree is common, it is not essential. Relevant arts subjects include stage craft, animation or technical arts. The general entry requirements for an arts degree include 2 A levels/3 H grades and 5 GCSEs/National 5s (A*–C/A–C) and to pass a portfolio interview for entry. Most applicants take a Foundation Art and Design course prior to entry.

There are some courses available to improve your skillset, for example the Association of British Theatre Technicians runs day courses in specialised subjects such as pyrotechnics. For more courses, visit the Creative Skillset Courses Directory, which lists many UK courses that are related to visual effects.

There are few permanent posts within large broadcasting houses, mostly found in London, so relevant work experience is essential for learning new skills and gaining contacts. These skills can be in any aspect of special effects, from theatre stage crafts to pyrotechnics and working with explosives. Creative Skillset provides a Trainee Finder service which allows aspiring special effects technicians to secure work placements within the industry.

Learning computer-aided design could help give you a broader portfolio, and keeping on top of new techniques and technological developments is advisable. You could use VFX Assets for Students, a free collection of industry-standard assets and exercises designed to teach visual effects skills to students interested in entering the industry. The collection includes HDRI plates, complex rigs, normal maps, texture grids, a variety of background plates, and a range of greenscreen, mattes and rotos. Creative Skillset has produced a guide to help you navigate the assets.

There is currently a large skills gap in the visual effects industry, ensuring there are plenty of opportunities for skilled technicians. As a result many universities are in the process of developing visual effects courses. This skills gap has also led to the creation of a Next Gen skills academy, formed by the industry-leading companies.

The Next Gen skills academy is supporting a selection of industry partners in the creation of 2 visual effects apprenticeships. The Junior 2D Artist Apprenticeship is led by Double Negative and the Assistant Technical Director Apprenticeship by Framestore. The apprenticeships allow you to study towards high-level qualifications while getting paid and gaining essential work experience.

When you gain employment, you will be trained whilst shadowing an experienced technician. This trainee period often lasts 5 years, though this is reduced to 2 for visual effects.

To work with pyrotechnic special effects you will have to obtain a licence.

What the work involves

As a technician you will work to create special effects in the theatre, TV and film industry. You might work with either physical effects, pyrotechnics, or visual. The first involves robotics, and designing and making props and prosthetics; the second explosions, fire and extreme weather; and the third superimposes images after filming.

You will work with colleagues to plan effects, create them, test them, and oversee their staging during filming.

You could work in a number of roles within the visual effects industry. A common entry-level role is a roto artist. Roto artists trace areas of live action frames where computer graphics overlap with live images. The artist creates clear areas in the frame that can then allow the scene to be layered by another animator.

Alternatively, you could enter the industry as a match move artist. Match move artists translate and imitate the camera movements in live action shots and match those movements in 3D. This work is more technical than creative. You could work on a specific area such as layout or texture.

With experience roto artists can go on to work as compositors who construct the final image by using previously created material.

You will adhere to strict health and safety regulations, update detailed logbooks of work done and the methods used and prepare the work area by setting up explosives for a gun battle or preparing materials for prosthetic work for example.

Type of person suited to this work

A visual mind is important as you'll need to imagine how things will look on screen as well as having a sense of drama and the desire to create a feeling of authenticity in screen shots through detailing. You should also be resourceful as you'll be working to a budget.

A strong awareness of health and safety issues is paramount as you will be working with props and explosives that can pose a threat to others if used improperly. You will often have to help with the equipment and this often includes heavy lifting so a level of fitness would be required.

You'll be working under pressure, both with others and on your own, so need to be good at adapting to different situations and finding solutions to problems quickly.

Working conditions

Hours are flexible, and you should be prepared to fit around filming schedules. This may mean late nights, early mornings and weekends.

You could work freelance, which may well mean you are very busy for a while, then unemployed for a long period of time. When you're working, you could be travelling anywhere, sometimes for quite a while as part of a touring show. Be prepared to stay away from home often.

As a theatre technician you will work to create effects in your own time, but you will also be expected to assist during rehearsals and performances. This may mean long, irregular hours.

PERFORMING ARTS

TV and film technicians work wherever filming takes place – in a studio or workshop, outdoors, on location etc. You will work in an office for computer-based work.

You may also be expected to travel overseas to promote your company and pitch ideas to film productions that require a visual effects company.

Future prospects

Although there will probably be only average growth in special effects for theatre, there could be increasing breadth within the role as new techniques and technology are developed.

Following the success of British film franchises heavy in visual effects, such as the Harry Potter films, the UK has become a world leader in the visual effects industry. The rise of tax relief rates has also made it easier for UK visual effects companies to win work from overseas. As a result there are a growing number of opportunities in this sector.

In the visual effects industry you will start out as a match move or roto artist. After 1 or 2 years working as a match move artist you will typically progress to a junior technical director role.

You will work approximately 2 years as a roto artist before progressing to a compositor role. You can then progress through the compositor department.

After working for about 10 years, you can advance to a senior technician position, and following this, a supervisory role.

Progression is much easier when you've built a list of contacts, as vacancies in this industry are often only advertised internally.

Advantages/disadvantages

This is a really exciting job, and seeing your hard work on the big screen can be really rewarding.

It's a fiercely competitive profession, and you might have to face periods of unemployment.

Trainees may need to attend short courses which they must fund themselves.

This job will provide you with opportunities to be both creative and technical.

Money guide

The Broadcasting, Entertainment, Cinematograph and Theatre Union (BECTU) recommends rates for special effects technicians.

As a trainee, you can expect to earn between £200 and £500 a week, depending on how advanced your skills are.

Once you are a technician this can rise to about £1,200 for a week of work.

If you make it to a senior technician role, this might rise to between £2,000 and £4,000 a week.

Related opportunities

- Animator p158
- Lighting Technician p426
- Props Maker/Assistant p430

Further information

Association of British Theatre Technicians
www.abtt.org.uk

British Film Institute
www.bfi.org.uk

Broadcasting, Entertainment, Cinematograph and Theatre Union
www.bectu.org.uk

Joint Industry Grading Scheme
www.jigs.org.uk

Next Gen Skills Academy
www.nextgenskillsacademy.com

Qualifications and courses

There are no formal entry requirements for this career but it is an absolute necessity that you possess the practical skills of hand and machine sewing, pattern cutting and dress making. The best way to get a job is to gain practical experience, and applying to local theatre companies or to student productions as a volunteer is a good place to start.

As competition is fierce many people study for qualifications in costume-related subjects. Courses include the City & Guilds Certificates and Diplomas in Creative Techniques (Levels 1–3), the BTEC Level 3 in Production Arts (Costume) or BTEC in Fashion and Clothing (Levels 1–3), the HNCs/HNDs in Fashion and Textiles, and NVQs in Theatre Operations Costume and Wardrobe (Levels 2–3). Also available are Foundation degrees in fashion and costume craft and costume for the stage and screen, and degrees in performance costume. The general entry requirements for a degree are 2 A levels/3 H grades and 5 GCSEs/National 5s (A*–C/A–C). Postgraduate degrees in costume design are also available.

Apprenticeships are available within large corporations such as the BBC and regional screen agencies but again competition is very fierce. Details of available schemes can be found on the Creative Skillset website.

Most training is done on the job, under the supervision of a senior wardrobe assistant.

What the work involves

You will be responsible for assembling and sourcing the costumes needed for TV, film and theatre productions. You will be buying or hiring accessories and costumes and making sure they are correctly stored and transported.

You will be responsible for altering, repairing, cleaning and fitting costumes as well as looking after them in between scenes/takes.

You will need to keep a detailed record of the different costumes worn by each performer and make sure they are ready to be worn for each stage of the production.

Type of person suited to this work

You will need to be organised, accurate and be able to remain calm under pressure, especially when dealing with costume emergencies during a live performance when you must use your initiative.

It is important to have good communication and interpersonal skills as you will be working with a range of people; colleagues and professionals.

A good eye for detail, practical sewing skills and creative flair are all useful when assembling costumes. A solid working knowledge of design, fashion and fashion periods will be advantageous.

Working conditions

You will be working unsocial and long hours the majority of the time. In film and television most of the work is during the daytime whereas in theatre you will be expected to work before and after both matinee and evening performances, usually 6 days a week.

Film and television production companies may need you to work away from home for long periods of time.

You will be sitting down, sewing and fitting costumes or running around a set helping to dress performers.

Future prospects

Most work can be found in London and other major cities with theatres, touring companies and film/TV production companies. It is important to gain as many contacts as possible by undertaking work experience and working for free as competition for jobs is fierce.

You can gain promotion to wardrobe supervisor and short courses are available which can enable you to acquire the right skills to switch between theatre and film/TV work; you usually start off specialising in one area.

Some wardrobe assistants move into specialist areas such as costume/set design or stage management.

Advantages/disadvantages

This is an exciting job in a glamorous industry; no two days will be the same and you may get to work with celebrities.

The pay is low for such an important role.

You can gain good insight and experience into a competitive industry enabling you to progress to senior positions.

Money guide

You could start out doing work experience where only travel expenses or lunch are paid for; £30 per day is the average amount.

Your starting salary may be around £10,000, which could rise to between £12,000 and £17,000. Senior wardrobe assistants could earn in excess of £25,000.

Freelance rates do vary greatly depending on the job you are doing and your reputation. The Broadcasting, Entertainment, Cinematography and Theatre Union (BECTU) suggest weekly rates depending upon the size of the production ranging from £550 to £1,000.

Related opportunities

- Costume Designer p160
- Fashion Designer/Milliner p161
- Museum/Art Gallery Curator p337

Further information

Costume Society
www.costumesociety.org.uk

Creative Skillset
www.creativeskillset.org

Society of British Theatre Designers
www.theatredesign.org.uk

Personal and Other Services including Hair and Beauty

This is a very wide job family and covers everything from hairdressing and beauty to cleaning to wedding consulting. You can enter this career sector with a host of different skills and qualifications. What all of the jobs have in common is that they provide a particular service that a customer has asked for so you need to be good at listening to others and giving customers exactly what they want – people in this sector have a brilliant way with people. You should also demonstrate creativity and strong practical and technical skill as many of the jobs in this family require you to use specialist equipment and to have knowledge of health and safety. The jobs featured in this section are listed below. For similar jobs to the ones in this section turn to *Catering and Hospitality* on page 121.

- Beauty Consultant p442
- Beauty Therapist p443
- Car Valet p444
- Caretaker p445
- Carpet/Upholstery Cleaner p446
- Chimney Sweep p447
- Cleaner p448
- Crematorium Technician p449
- Dry Cleaner p450
- Embalmer p451
- Funeral Director p452
- Hairdresser/Barber p453
- Nail Technician p454
- Pest Control Technician p455
- Refuse and Recycling Operative p456
- Spa Therapist/Technician p457
- Tattooist p458
- Wedding Planner p459
- Window Cleaner p460

Qualifications and courses

Although formal qualifications are not generally required, GCSEs/National 5s (A*–C/A–C) may prove useful, particularly in Maths and English. Previous experience in a retail, sales or customer service role would be beneficial and you must be over 18 years old if you wish to be self-employed.

The Vocational Training Charitable Trust (VTCT) offers a Level 2 Certificate in Cosmetic Make-Up and Beauty Consultancy, and NVQs/SVQs are available in Retail Skills, Beauty Therapy (general or specialising in make-up) and Customer Service (Levels 1–3). City & Guilds and BTEC both provide qualifications in Retail Knowledge. These courses may be taken prior to employment or while working and, although they are not essential, they will help to show prospective employers that you are committed to the industry.

An alternative training route to becoming a beauty consultant is to apply for the Beauty Therapy Apprenticeship at Intermediate Level.

Once you secure employment, training is generally provided in-house and may cover topics such as sales techniques, skincare and make-up techniques, and stock recording and ordering.

What the work involves

You will work in department stores and other public locations, promoting and selling beauty products on behalf of cosmetics companies.

You will provide product demonstrations to individual customers or groups, including facials, make-up applications and manicures. You will give advice and information on cosmetic products. Your work may involve selling items and taking payments, managing stock levels and keeping the demonstration area attractive and presentable.

If you are self-employed, you will have to control every aspect of your business including sales, finances and marketing.

Type of person suited to this work

A sociable and professional approach is important because you will meet many customers. You should have a smart appearance.

Working on a store counter can be fast paced so you should be able to stay calm in busy situations. You will use your communication skills to encourage customers to find out more about your products.

You should also have a strong interest in helping people make the best of themselves. For applying make-up and other products, you will need an eye for design and good practical skills. Numeracy skills will help you manage stock and take payments. You should enjoy the challenge of working towards sales targets.

Working conditions

You could work between 37 and 40 hours a week, with some weekend and evening hours. If you are self-employed, the majority of your hours will be in the evening.

You may have to do some lifting and carrying from the stockroom.

Depending on where you work, you may wear a uniform and you will normally be expected to wear the cosmetics that you are selling.

Future prospects

Beauty consultancy offers a flexible career for people who want to combine their interest in beauty with working in sales.

As well as employment within department stores, there are opportunities to work in airports and hotels. You may choose to promote and sell products from your own home.

With experience, you could progress to working as a team manager and then move on to an area management role. Progression might involve changing employers and moving to a larger company.

Advantages/disadvantages

This type of work is often available on a part-time or flexible basis which would suit people with other commitments.

You might spend a lot of time on your feet which could prove tiring.

You may receive a product allowance of either discounted or free cosmetic products.

Money guide

Starting salaries are usually between £12,000 and £13,000.

Experienced beauty consultants can expect to earn from £19,000 to £23,000.

Those employed in a senior or managerial position could achieve up to £30,000 a year.

Many beauty consultants receive commission based upon their sales figures.

Related opportunities

- Beauty Therapist p443
- Hairdresser/Barber p453
- Nail Technician p454

Further information

Hairdressing and Beauty Industry Authority
www.habia.org

People 1st
www.people1st.co.uk/retail-apprenticeships

Qualifications and courses

To work as a fully qualified beauty therapist, you will need to be qualified to at least a Level 3 standard in beauty therapy and you will usually be expected to have some GCSEs/National 5s (A*–C/A–C).

Suitable courses include NVQ Diplomas in Beauty Therapy (Levels 2–3), Spa Therapy (Level 3), and Nail Services (Levels 2–3). You can also take a number of NVQ Awards at Level 2 and 3 in areas such as Facial Skincare, Waxing Services or Ear Piercing. There are also qualifications such as the BTEC in Beauty Therapy (Levels 2–3), the Vocational Training Charitable Trust (VTCT) Diploma in Beauty Therapy Studies, and the International Therapy Examination Council (ITEC) Diploma in Advanced Beauty Therapy.

An alternative route for those aged 16–24 is to take the Apprenticeship in Beauty Therapy which is available at Intermediate and Advanced Levels.

Some universities and higher education colleges will offer HNCs/HNDs, Foundation degrees, degrees and postgraduate degrees in cosmetic science, beauty therapy, and spa management. The general entry requirements for a degree are 2 A levels/3 H grades and 5 GCSEs/National 5s (A*–C/A–C).

Beauty therapists often extend their knowledge into holistic or alternative treatments such as massage and aromatherapy. The International Federation of Professional Aromatherapists (IFPA) accredits courses at private beauty schools and colleges in the UK.

What the work involves

You will provide a range of face and body treatments, including facials, massages, electrolysis and waxing treatments.

Your work will also involve preparing, cleaning and tidying the treatment room before and after each client. You may have to take payments and bookings, undertake some general administrative duties and maintain client records.

Beauty therapists are often employed by and provide services in beauty salons, health clubs and hotels. You may choose to work on a self-employed basis in rented treatment rooms or from your own home.

Type of person suited to this work

People often choose to have a treatment to help them relax so you will need a calm, confident approach.

An interest in helping people with a range of therapies is essential. You will need good communication skills when advising clients about the treatments they can have.

A well-presented appearance and a good level of physical fitness are also important. You will work to a high standard of health and hygiene.

Working conditions

You will generally work 37–40 hours a week, including weekends and evenings to accommodate customers' needs, and you will usually wear a uniform.

Therapy rooms or cubicles are usually private, clean and warm, however if you are self-employed you may need to visit clients in their own homes and adapt your services within different environments.

This can be quite a physically demanding job as you will spend the majority of your day standing and bending.

Future prospects

Future prospects in this line of work are good with a variety of other career paths to potentially choose from, including spa management and sales.

Your location can vary from being based in a beauty salon to working in a hotel or spa and opportunities are generally good across the country.

With experience you could progress into a management role or choose to set up your own beauty therapy business. You could also go on to training and lecturing in beauty therapy after extensive professional experience and further training.

There are opportunities to work on cruise ships and in resorts overseas.

Advantages/disadvantages

Therapists working in health and beauty companies or clubs may be provided with free club membership and discounted treatments.

You might find some treatments difficult to carry out if you are not comfortable seeing people's bodies.

You can feel proud knowing that you have made a customer happy after completing their chosen treatment.

Money guide

Salaries vary depending on location and employer.

Once qualified as a beauty therapist, you could receive a starting salary around £11,000.

With experience, earnings increase to £12,000–£17,000 a year.

In a senior or managerial position, you could achieve in excess of £20,000 per year.

Tips and commission from the sale of products can supplement your income.

Related opportunities

- Beauty Consultant p442
- Hairdresser/Barber p453
- Nail Technician p454

Further information

British Association of Beauty Therapy and Cosmetology
www.babtac.com

Hairdressing and Beauty Industry Authority
www.habia.org

PERSONAL AND OTHER SERVICES
INCLUDING HAIR AND BEAUTY

CAR VALET

Qualifications and courses

No formal qualifications are required for entry to this job, however valets are usually aged 17 or over as a full driving licence is often required. Qualifications in practical or technical subjects and previous experience in the motor trade, industrial/office cleaning or dry cleaning can also be an advantage.

Once you secure employment, you will undertake training on the job and learn about cleaning techniques and health and safety procedures from an experienced colleague. You could also be sent on short courses run by the manufacturers of cleaning products as part of your training and development.

The British Institute of Cleaning Science (BICSc) provides a Car Valeting Certificate scheme for candidates interested in more formal training. Topics covered include interior cleaning, exterior cleaning, engine cleaning, pressure washing, stain removal, upholstery cleaning and polishing and waxing.

The City & Guilds Certificate and Diploma in Vehicle Valeting Principles (Levels 1–2), the NVQ in Vehicle Maintenance and Repair (Levels 1–3), and the NVQ in Cleaning and Support Services Skills (Level 1–3) are also available for those who wish to take a relevant qualification.

Apprenticeships in Cleaning and Environmental Services, Vehicle Body and Paint Operations, and Vehicle Maintenance and Repair can give you the relevant skills and knowledge for this career.

What the work involves

Car valets clean and finish car exteriors and interiors using specialist equipment.

You could work for vehicle service centres, car showrooms, garages, crash repair centres or valeting companies.

Depending on the services offered by your employer and the client's wishes, you may be expected to clean a vehicle both internally and externally, the exterior only or just the engine. You might be hired by a garage to help clean up cars after bodywork repairs.

Typical tasks include clearing the interior of rubbish, polishing the surfaces and windows, cleaning the seats and removing any stains. For exteriors, you will clean the wheels and polish and wax the bodywork.

Type of person suited to this work

You should be physically fit as jobs can take between 1 and 4 hours and involve a lot of bending, stretching and lifting.

You should be able to use different types of cleaning equipment and apply your knowledge of health and safety to your work.

As you will be providing a service to customers, you will need to be a quick but thorough worker with good attention to detail.

You need strong people skills and the ability to work both independently and as part of a team.

You should be able to cope with dirty working conditions.

Working conditions

The work is very hands on and can be tiring because it involves spending a lot of time on your feet.

You might be based outside cleaning cars on a forecourt or in a car park so you need to be prepared to work in all weather conditions.

This job requires regular contact with cleaning chemicals, so it might not suit people with allergies or skin conditions. Sometimes you will be required to wear protective clothing including gloves and safety glasses.

Future prospects

Car valeting is a key part of the sales and services sector of the motor vehicle industry.

You could work for a large vehicle repair company or service centre as part of a valeting team.

With experience and further training, you could progress to a supervisory or managerial role or move into sales.

Alternatively, you could choose to set up your own valeting company offering a mobile service or going out to visit customers at their premises.

Advantages/disadvantages

Car valeting jobs may include regular travel, either when providing services to customers on their premises, or when returning vehicles to customers.

This type of job offers the chance to work in close contact with a range of cars and other vehicles.

Money guide

Trainee valets have a starting salary of around £10,000 per year.

Fully trained valets could potentially earn up to £16,500 a year.

Overtime and shift payments can increase your income.

Related opportunities

- Cleaner p448
- Motor Vehicle Technician p222
- Vehicle Parts Operative p485

Further information

British Institute of Cleaning Science
www.bics.org.uk

Building Futures
www.buildingfutures.org.uk

Qualifications and courses

No formal qualifications are required for entry to this job as hands-on skills and experience in basic DIY, carpentry or painting and decorating are deemed more important than academic credentials. However, some GCSEs/National 5s (A*–C/A–C), particularly English, Maths and practical subjects, may be an advantage when applying for jobs. Experience in maintenance or security work is useful, as is a driving licence, and within some areas, for example schools, you will need to pass a Disclosure and Barring Service (DBS) check.

Maturity is an advantage and employers often prefer older applicants with relevant experience.

It may be possible for entrants to work towards an NVQ Level 1 and 2 in Cleaning and Support Service but mostly caretakers are trained on the job. The Cleaning Supervisory Skills Suite offered by the British Institute of Cleaning Science (BICSc) or a Level 3 BTEC Specialist Qualification in Construction and the Built Environment could also be useful, as well as training in specific areas, such as dealing with asbestos and other substances that are hazardous to health. The Chartered Institute of Housing (CIH) also offers Level 3 Certificates in Housing Services, Housing Practice, and Housing Maintenance.

Studying for an NVQ Level 3 in Property and Caretaking Supervision and the NVQ Level 4 Certificate in Housing Maintenance Management can speed up career progression and a full driving licence may be required if you become a mobile caretaker who looks after a number of different sites.

What the work involves

Caretakers manage the security, cleaning and general maintenance of sites such as schools, colleges and office blocks.

In some jobs, you might be expected to combine caretaking duties with other roles such as cleaner, gardener, porter or security attendant.

You will be responsible for opening and locking the premises, checking building security and the overall management and upkeep of the site. You will repair broken equipment, either yourself or booking in and managing a maintenance team, as well as reordering the necessary supplies for your job.

Type of person suited to this work

Caretakers need good communication skills as they interact closely with the people based on their premises.

You may be responsible for the security of an entire site, so it's important to have a mature, honest attitude and a full understanding of emergency procedures.

The ability to work independently is essential, as you will often be working on your own initiative and sites usually only employ one caretaker. You should also be able to work as part of a team when necessary though, for example when having to manage larger repairs.

Physical fitness is essential for work such as moving equipment and gardening. You will work to a high standard of health and safety at all times.

Working conditions

A 37-hour working week, which could encompass early mornings, evenings and weekends, is normal in this line of work. In some cases, you may be living on-site or nearby so expect working hours to be more flexible.

Caretaking work is physically demanding as you will be spending the majority of your time on your feet, doing general maintenance and using ladders and other tools.

Caretakers work with cleaning chemicals and wear protective clothing such as overalls. The job might not suit people with allergies or skin conditions.

Future prospects

Many locations only employ one caretaker, so you might need to move to a bigger site to progress.

In larger establishments, senior caretakers have the responsibility of managing a small team of caretakers or other staff such as cleaners.

You could progress to a management position in a private cleaning company.

Advantages/disadvantages

As the premises keyholder, you could be on-call for emergencies.

This job can be sociable and caretakers often build up a good working relationship with the people based on their premises.

Money guide

The starting salary for an assistant caretaker is around £12,000 per year, which will increase to roughly £16,000 after experience.

You could earn £25,000 as a senior or mobile caretaker.

In some work areas, such as education, caretakers are offered on-site subsidised housing as part of their contract.

Related opportunities

- Cleaner p448
- Hotel Porter p129
- Refuse and Recycling Operative p456

Further information

Chartered Institute of Housing
www.cih.org

The Caretakers' website
www.thecaretakers.net

PERSONAL AND OTHER SERVICES INCLUDING HAIR AND BEAUTY

Qualifications and courses

There are no formal qualifications for this career and you will usually be trained on the job by an experienced colleague in the practice of cleaning as well as health and safety regulations. It might also be helpful to have basic numeracy and literacy skills to calculate correct quantities of chemicals and writing quotes for customers.

Once employed, you may decide to undertake specialised training such as the NVQ in Cleaning and Support Services Skills (Levels 1–2), which contains one unit specifically for carpet and soft furnishings, the City & Guilds Award, Certificate or Diploma in Cleaning Principles, the Level 2 BTEC Certificate in Cleaning Principles, or the British Institute of Cleaning Science's Cleaning Operators Proficiency Certificate.

The National Carpet Cleaners Association also offers regular specialist cleaning courses in subjects such as carpet cleaning, commercial carpet maintenance, upholstery and fabric cleaning, leather identification and cleaning, hard floor cleaning, and advanced spot and stain treatment and removal. Relevant repair courses are also available and may improve your business opportunities if self-employed. Courses include water damage restoration, carpet colour repair and carpet repair and reinstallation.

Apprenticeships/Skillseekers may be available for people aged between 16 and 24 in Cleaning and Support Services, which features modules on soft floor and furnishings cleaning.

Knowledge or qualifications in business might be useful if you wish to run your own cleaning business, as well as the Level 3 NVQ Diploma in Cleaning Supervision Skills.

What the work involves

Carpet and upholstery cleaners clean soft furnishings, including curtains, tapestries, antique fabrics, rugs, seat covers and carpets, using specialist equipment.

These fabrics and carpets need special cleaning to remove dirt, smoke and grease that build up on them daily and your job is to determine and implement the best method for removing the dirt.

You will work in a variety of private and public buildings, dealing with large and small orders. If the job is big, you will be expected to visit the cleaning site first to assess what needs to be cleaned and what sort of equipment and chemicals you might need.

Each job will be assessed on face value and costed according to size, equipment required and time it will take you.

Type of person suited to this work

You will have an in-depth knowledge of different types of fabrics and their make-up in order to determine the best way to remove stubborn stains.

You will need good practical skills to be able to use specialist cleaning equipment and an understanding of the different types of chemicals you will use.

Excellent communication skills and an understanding in the importance of good customer service will be essential when dealing with clients and colleagues. You should be able to work equally well alone or as part of a team.

Working conditions

You may need to work evenings and weekends. Most of your time will be spent on your feet and carrying around heavy equipment. You will normally be based indoors, in people's homes or public buildings.

You are likely to need to drive around to work at different locations so a driving licence will be useful. You should also be physically fit.

You might have to wear protective clothing to protect you from dust and chemicals which may irritate your skin.

Future prospects

Carpet and upholstery cleaners are needed throughout the UK, meaning there will be lots of job opportunities wherever you live.

You might work for a general or specialist cleaning company or be self-employed.

With experience, you can move into managerial or training roles or start your own cleaning business.

Advantages/disadvantages

This work brings good job satisfaction; you will be pleasing people by restoring their carpets and upholstery to perfect condition.

You could find some aspects of cleaning messy or dirty which could be unpleasant.

You have the opportunity to work for yourself and run your own business.

Money guide

The starting salary is around £12,000 per year.

With experience this can increase to £14,500.

You may be able to earn up to £25,000 if you specialise in antique or tapestry cleaning.

Related opportunities

- Car Valet p444
- Caretaker p445
- Cleaner p448

Further information

British Institute of Cleaning Science
www.bics.org.uk

National Carpet Cleaners Association
www.ncca.co.uk

Qualifications and courses

There are no formal entry requirements as you will normally be trained on the job by an experienced chimney sweep. Basic qualifications in English and maths are useful and previous experience of manual work, such as construction, is an advantage.

Trainee chimney sweeps can work towards membership of the National Association of Chimney Sweeps (NACS), the Association of Professional Independent Chimney Sweeps (APICS), or the Guild of Master Chimney Sweeps. This would allow you to register with HETAS, which is the official government-recognised body of chimney sweeps, and registration is particularly important if you wish to be self-employed.

NACS offers a 4-day induction course which covers industry techniques and health and safety. NACS also provides a Flexible Linings and Solid Fuel Maintenance Course and several other HETAS-approved training courses in subjects such as solid fuel, chimney and flue maintenance, fire safety, and rooftop and ladder safety.

Alternatively, the Guild of Master Chimney Sweeps offers an intensive 4-day training course covering both theory and practical elements, with on-site training days and a final written exam. The Institute of Chimney Sweeps (ICS) offers a 2-day chimney sweeping course, as well as 1-day specialist courses.

To be qualified to carry out inspections and work on gas appliances, you need to gain a certificate of competence through the Accredited Certification Scheme (ACS), or a National/Scottish Vocational Qualification (NVQ/SVQ), both of which lead to registration with Gas Safe.

What the work involves

Chimney sweeps help prevent chimney fires and dangerous fuel emissions by inspecting and cleaning chimney and flue systems, heating appliances and vents.

Your work will involve cleaning sites and using brush and vacuum equipment to clear chimneys and vents of blockages.

You will provide information and advice to customers on the repair and maintenance of their chimneys.

Type of person suited to this work

Chimney sweeps combine their professional knowledge with practical skills to protect public safety. You will need a good knowledge of different types of chimney and flue systems.

Operating brush and vacuum chimney-cleaning equipment requires good manual skills, and a good level of physical fitness and stamina is essential as the work is demanding and potentially strenuous.

You will visit customers in their homes so you should have a friendly, professional attitude.

You should be comfortable working at heights and able to work independently without supervision.

Working conditions

Most of your work will take place at people's homes but you could also work on heating systems in commercial or industrial premises.

Travel to different locations is a regular part of the work so a driving licence is essential.

When clearing chimneys, you will wear protective clothing, such as overalls, gloves, a helmet, eye guards and respiratory protection.

You will usually work normal hours Monday to Friday but you may also be required to work unsocial hours, including weekends and evenings, to suit customers.

Future prospects

Chimney sweeping is a specialist but essential service. After gaining the relevant experience and professional qualifications, you could set up your own business, providing services within your local area.

Most chimney sweeps build up a network of loyal and regular customers.

You could go on to expand your services into roofing or ventilation, with opportunities to work with another professional or to join a small specialist company. Some sweeps supplement their income by acting as 'lucky sweeps' at weddings.

Advantages/disadvantages

Most chimney sweeps work on a self-employed basis, which can lead to some job insecurity, particularly at the start of their careers.

You will have the opportunity to meet a variety of people.

Money guide

The majority of chimney sweeps are self-employed and establish their own rates of pay for each job they undertake.

Earnings vary according to the hours spent on a task and the speed at which you work.

You could charge between £35 and £55 for a full sweep.

For a more specialist task, you could receive £70–£75.

Those working full time can expect to earn between £16,000 and £25,000 per year.

Related opportunities

- Cleaner p448
- Roofer p104
- Steeplejack p109

Further information

Guild of Master Chimney Sweeps
www.guildofmasterchimneysweeps.co.uk

HETAS
www.hetas.co.uk

National Association of Chimney Sweeps
www.chimneyworks.co.uk

PERSONAL AND OTHER SERVICES INCLUDING HAIR AND BEAUTY

Qualifications and courses

There are no formal qualifications required for this job, although it may be helpful to have basic literacy and numeracy skills. Once employed, cleaners usually receive on-the-job training in health and safety and how to use the necessary cleaning materials and equipment in order to deliver a good service.

School leavers could apply for the Intermediate Apprenticeship in Cleaning and Environmental Services which combines practical work experience with study for a professional qualification. Courses available include an NVQ in Cleaning and Support Services Skills (Levels 1–2), a Level 2 NVQ in Cleaning Building Interiors, the City & Guilds Level 2 Award in Cleaning Principles, or the Award in Practical Cleaning Skills (Levels 2–3).

Alternative professional qualifications are offered by the British Institute of Cleaning Science (BICSc) and you could work towards the Licence to Practise (PBICSc), a card you can acquire after the completion of a number of mandatory units on a 1-day training course. You can continue your training with the BICSc by undertaking the Cleaning Professionals Skills Suite, which includes a wide range of training options to suit the type of cleaning and environment you wish to work in.

Experienced cleaners who wish to progress to a supervisory level can study for the BICSc Cleaning Supervisory Skills Certificate or the City & Guilds Level 3 Diploma in either Cleaning Services Supervision or Cleaning Supervision Skills.

If your job involves contact with hazardous waste, such as sharps and syringes, you will need vaccinations against hepatitis B and C. This is most likely to be necessary if you work in a hospital.

What the work involves

You will be responsible for cleaning and tidying a variety of places including people's homes and places of work.

Industrial cleaners work in public buildings, such as hospitals, prisons and schools and work to the highest standards to reach health and safety requirements.

Domestic cleaners work in people's homes and may have additional tasks such as ironing and washing up.

You will use a range of cleaning materials and equipment such as hoovers, mops, dusters and brooms.

Type of person suited to this work

You will need to be honest and trustworthy, as you will be entering people's homes and workplaces where valuables could be on display.

Being fit and mobile is important, as you will be on your feet for long periods, bending, stretching and carrying heavy equipment.

Good communication skills are required to interact with colleagues and clients, especially if you run your own cleaning business.

You will need a good knowledge of the cleaning chemicals you use and the ability to decide which chemical should be used in each situation. It will also be necessary to adhere to health and safety regulations when using hazardous chemicals.

Working conditions

You will usually work 35–40 hours a week in a full-time job but hours vary. You may be required to work weekends, evenings and early mornings when public places or offices are closed. If you clean private homes, you will normally work during the day when the owner of the home is out. Hospitals need to be kept clean 24/7 so shift work is common. Part-time work is often available.

Many cleaners are self-employed and work for several different clients in one day. It would be useful to have a driving licence. Most cleaners wear a uniform or protective clothing.

Future prospects

There is a great demand for cleaners in all sectors.

You could choose to work for a cleaning company or be self-employed.

Many cleaners decide to set up their own small business or move into other roles as a caretaker or supervisor of a team of cleaners.

Advantages/disadvantages

You can work different shifts that fit in well with other jobs or family commitments.

You can progress to being the owner of your own cleaning business.

Owing to the chemicals used in cleaning, this job would not be suitable for those with breathing problems or skin allergies.

Money guide

Earnings vary according to your employer and the number of hours you work.

Most cleaners are paid hourly, with rates ranging from the national minimum wage to £10 an hour.

If you are employed on a full-time basis you can expect a starting salary of £11,000–£12,000.

Earnings are higher for specialist cleaners or those employed in a supervisory role.

Related opportunities

- Caretaker p445
- Pest Control Technician p455
- Window Cleaner p460

Further information

British Institute of Cleaning Science
www.bics.org.uk

Building Futures
www.buildingfutures.org.uk

Qualifications and courses

There are no formal entry requirements for this type of work and training is done on the job, although some employers require candidates to have a GCSE/National 5 in English (A*–C/A–C) as good reading and writing skills are important. Basic administrative and computer skills are also valued.

Trainees may follow the Crematorium Technicians' Training Scheme (CTTS) provided by the Institute of Cemetery and Crematorium Management (ICCM) which will lead to the study of both the BTEC Intermediate and Advanced Certificates. Another work-based training route is provided by the Federation of Burial and Cremation Authorities' (FBCA) TEST scheme. Alternatively, trainees can undertake a Level 2 NVQ in Funeral Operations and Services or a BTEC certificate in Principles of Funeral Operations and Services (Levels 2–3).

If your work involves ground maintenance you may also receive training in practical areas such as how to safely use chainsaws and pesticide sprayers. Employees may also work towards NVQ/SVQ Level 2 in Work-based Horticulture and select the specialist pathway Parks, Gardens and Green Space – Cemeteries. The FBCA also provides training courses aimed at cemetery and groundwork services.

Once you have the relevant experience you may be able to work towards ICCM qualifications for crematorium managers. These qualifications can be taken in three stages – ICCM Certificate for Cemetery and/or Crematorium Management, ICCM Diploma and finally ICCM Diploma with Honours. These can be studied by distance learning.

The ICCM also operates a continuing professional development scheme for crematorium staff at all levels.

What the work involves

Crematorium technicians assist with the running of the crematorium and cemetery premises.

Your work will involve operating cremation equipment to a high standard of health and safety. You will ensure that the cremated remains are stored and disposed of correctly. You will help manage the chapel and cemetery and attend cremation ceremonies.

You will also assist with other cemetery duties, such as excavating graves and grounds maintenance. However, grave digging work is mostly undertaken by contractors working for local authorities.

Type of person suited to this work

Meeting with bereaved people requires a mature, sympathetic attitude. You will use your communication skills to help people understand the process of cremation ceremonies so they know what to expect.

A good level of physical fitness is helpful in a role that covers a wide range of activities.

You will need to keep accurate records so must have good attention to detail.

It's important that cremations are undertaken to a high standard of health and safety, so you should be able to follow strict working guidelines. The ability to work as part of a team is also useful.

Working conditions

This can be a tiring job due to the range of activities involved and the physical requirements of operating cremation machinery. You will be on your feet for long hours.

You will need to be smartly dressed when facing the public and your outfit will usually be provided for you.

When operating machinery you will need to wear protective clothing.

Crematorium technicians are usually employed by local councils and you will normally work 37–40 hours a week, with some overtime including Saturdays.

Future prospects

The Church of England has made cremations cheaper than burials, so the number of cremations, and need for skilled professionals, may consequently increase.

There is also the opportunity to progress into an administrative position within the cemetry.

With experience, you could progress to working as a senior crematorium technician and manage a team of technicians.

Advantages/disadvantages

This role provides the opportunity to provide support to people at an important and challenging time.

The nature of the job means this work can sometimes be distressing.

Money guide

Starting salaries vary between £11,000 and £13,000 per year.

With experience you could earn up to £17,000.

At senior management level you could earn in excess of £20,000.

Salaries are often dependent on local authority rates so may be higher in areas such as London. There may also be the opportunity for additional money through overtime.

Related opportunities

- Cleaner p448
- Embalmer p451
- Funeral Director p452

Further information

Federation of Burial and Cremation Authorities
www.fbca.org.uk

Institute of Cemetery and Crematorium Management
www.iccm-uk.com

Local Government Careers
www.lgjobs.com

The Cremation Society of Great Britain
www.cremation.org.uk

PERSONAL AND OTHER SERVICES INCLUDING HAIR AND BEAUTY

Qualifications and courses

There are no formal qualifications needed for this work, although good numeracy and literacy skills will be useful. Some previous experience working in a laundry, customer service and/or retail skills would also be an advantage.

You will be trained on the job by an experienced dry cleaner. Many employers offer opportunities to study for qualifications part time. These include Level 2 NVQs in Dry Cleaning Operations, Laundry Operations, and Textile Care Services, an NVQ in Customer Service (Levels 1–4), and the BTEC Level 2 Certificate in Laundry and Dry Cleaning Technology. The RQF Award in Retail Skills (Levels 1–3) may also be useful.

The Guild of Cleaners & Launderers (GCL) awards certificates as part of their Qualification Star Scheme. Candidates can undertake exams in retail sales, stain removal, garment finishing, dry cleaning practice and wet cleaning. Modern apprenticeships (equivalent to an NVQ Level 3 qualification) are also available.

The SATRA Technology Centre also provides dry cleaning courses at their training centre in Kettering.

All dry cleaners who intend to use solvents must be registered and hold a permit.

What the work involves

You will be cleaning clothes and fabrics which are delicate or sensitive to being washed in water; using chemicals and steam to clean items instead. You might be cleaning specialist fabrics or garments such as wool, suede, bridal wear, suits and beaded fabrics.

You will look for any stains and treat them individually before cleaning the item. You might use potentially hazardous chemicals, although many dry cleaners now use safe and environmentally friendly products. You will press and package the garments after cleaning.

You will assist customers at the counter, take payments, complete paperwork and operate the cleaning machinery.

Type of person suited to this work

You will need to have good communication skills for dealing with customers and practical skills for handling the cleaning machinery.

A good level of fitness would be helpful for bending, carrying heavy items of clothing and organising cleaned garments.

You will be dealing with payments and paperwork so it is important to have good numeracy skills and an organised approach to your work.

Working conditions

You will most likely work standard hours from Monday to Saturday, usually with 1 day off during the week, however, dry cleaners are increasingly staying open in the evenings and Sundays to accommodate customers' needs. You are likely to work shifts to accommodate these hours. Part-time work is often available.

You will be working in the store, both at the counter and with the cleaning machines.

You might be exposed to some chemical fumes and there is a danger of burning yourself on pressing machines. This work would not be suitable for people with skin allergies.

Most stores will supply you with a uniform.

Future prospects

There are jobs available across the UK in high street dry cleaning stores or industrial cleaning plants which clean for hospitals or factories. Though there is no longer the shortage there was a few years ago, there will still be plenty of positions available within the industry.

You can progress from an assistant position to a supervisory or managerial role; gaining a qualification in team leading might help you to progress more quickly.

After developing extensive experience and knowledge of dry cleaning, you could choose to open your own store.

Advantages/disadvantages

This is a good career if you enjoy practical work and providing a service.

You could be affected by the chemical fumes which would be unpleasant.

There are opportunities to run your own business.

Money guide

The starting salary for a dry cleaner is usually between £10,000 and £12,000.

Once you have undertaken training and gained experience, you can expect to earn approximately £14,000 a year.

If you are employed in a senior or managerial position, your salary could range from £15,000 to £30,000, depending on the reputation and performance of the store.

Related opportunities

- Car Valet p444
- Cleaner p448
- Textile Operative p233

Further information

Guild of Cleaners and Launderers
www.gcl.org.uk

Textile Services Association
www.tsa-uk.org

EMBALMER

Qualifications and courses

There are no formal entry requirements for working as an embalmer but GCSEs/National 5s in English, Maths, Chemistry, Biology and Religious Studies may be useful.

To achieve professional qualifications, you must first secure a job and register with a tutor approved by the British Institute of Embalmers (BIE). You will then undertake on-the-job training, with part-time or distance learning tuition from your tutor.

Most embalmers work for qualifications awarded by the International Examinations Board of Embalmers (IEBE). The IEBE training is modular and trainees must pass the foundation unit before proceeding with the rest of the training. You are eligible to register with the BIE as a student member upon completion of the foundation unit.

The main IEBE training involves modules in anatomy, physiology, bacteriology and practical embalming. Assessment is via exams and practical work. Once you have passed these modules, you can apply for full membership of the BIE.

You could develop your skills by taking courses in facial reconstruction, hair and make-up or airbrushing. Some embalmers train to work in specialist areas, for example with the bodies of disaster victims.

What the work involves

Embalmers prepare the bodies of deceased people for funerals and for viewing by their relatives. They preserve the body in the most life-like way.

You will wash and disinfect the deceased person's body. You will use specialist equipment to remove all liquids and gases from the body and replace these with injected preservatives which help prevent infection.

Part of preparing the body will involve washing and arranging the person's hair and applying cosmetics. If the deceased has any injuries, you will use plaster of Paris or wax to restore their body.

Your work will also include setting up and cleaning the embalming equipment and treatment area.

Type of person suited to this work

You must be able to cope with working with the bodies of deceased people. A respectful approach to your work is essential. You might have to deal with distressing sights so a mature, detached and down-to-earth attitude is very important.

Embalming work involves presenting a deceased person in the most positive way for grieving relatives. A creative flair and attention to detail will help you to achieve this. You should be sensitive to people's feelings.

Working conditions

Embalmers work in operating rooms within funeral parlours. These are maintained to a very high standard of hygiene and kept at a low temperature.

Whilst embalming you will wear protective clothing such as latex gloves, rubber boots and a theatre gown. Regular contact with chemicals means that this job may not suit people with skin conditions or allergies. You will spend most of the day on your feet and the work is physically demanding.

You will usually work normal hours from Monday to Friday, with occasional weekend and overtime work during busy periods. Some employers will require you to be on-call for emergency work.

Future prospects

There are over 1,000 qualified embalmers in the UK but the industry has a relatively slow turnover of staff.

Embalming is an integral part of the funeral care process, so qualified workers will always be needed. You could gain employment with a funeral care company or you may choose to work on a self-employed basis, providing services to a number of funeral companies. There are opportunities to work abroad.

With extensive experience there may be the opportunity to go into teaching, at a place like Salisbury College of Funeral Sciences and Embalming, but opportunities here are likely to be rare too.

Advantages/disadvantages

You have the option of working on a freelance basis for a number of employers at the same time.

There are opportunities to work overseas.

This can be distressing work, so you will need to be able to stay detached and professional.

Money guide

Starting salaries are typically around £12,000.

With experience, an embalmer could earn £18,000–£28,000 per year.

Very experienced embalmers, or those who offer specialist services, can achieve in excess of £30,000.

Related opportunities

- Crematorium Technician p449
- Funeral Director p452
- Hospital Porter p295

Further information

British Institute of Embalmers
www.bioe.co.uk

Federation of Burial and Cremation Authorities
www.fbca.org.uk

Qualifications and courses

There are no minimum academic qualifications to work as a funeral director. However, GCSEs/National 5s (A*–C/A–C), or relevant qualifications, in English, Maths, Chemistry and Biology may prove advantageous. You will normally start as an assistant and undertake on-the-job training, however funeral operatives/assistants with driving duties will require a full driving licence.

The National Association of Funeral Directors (NAFD) offers the Diploma in Funeral Arranging & Administration (Dip.FAA) aimed at funeral arrangers, administrators and funeral directors looking for a stand-alone qualification. If you are experienced in funeral directing or have successfully completed the Dip.FAA, the NAFD also offers the Diploma in Funeral Directing (Dip.FD) designed to equip you with key skills such as team management. If you are employed in an entry-level position or interested in joining the sector the NAFD also offers the online Funeral Service Awareness course.

Other courses available include the NVQ Level 2 Certificate in Funeral Operations and Services and the BTEC in Principles of Funeral Operations and Services (Levels 2–3). The Co-operative Funeral Services run an apprenticeship scheme that enables you to study for an NVQ.

The British Institute of Funeral Directors (BIFD) provides an Introduction to Funeral Service course for those wanting to gain an insight into the sector. The BIFD also provides courses for industry professionals including the Certificate in Funeral Service, the Diploma in Funeral Service and the Certificate of Higher Education in Funeral Management.

What the work involves

Funeral directors coordinate funeral arrangements for burials and cremations.

You will liaise with the family of the deceased, offering advice and taking note of the details they would like included in the ceremony.

You will arrange the date and location of the funeral, and also arrange transport and death notices. You will also attend the funeral and ensure that everything runs smoothly during the ceremony.

You may be asked to prepare the body for the funeral, though this is usually done by the embalmer.

Type of person suited to this work

You need to have a sensitive and mature attitude to your work. Excellent communication skills and a high standard of health and safety are essential. You must also be well organised with a good eye for detail.

For liaising with local authorities and completing paperwork you will need a good knowledge of the relevant legal issues.

If you are self-employed, you will require good office and budgeting skills.

A thorough knowledge of different cultures and religions is also helpful.

Working conditions

Funeral directors work in funeral homes or centres based within high-street outlets or other areas. Attending funerals will involve working outdoors in all weather conditions.

Your working hours will vary. Most of your administrative work will be undertaken during office hours from Monday to Friday but you may need to visit clients at weekends and in the evenings. You will also have to be on call, possibly working on a rota system and you may be required to work extra hours during busy times.

It is imperative that funeral directors dress smartly due to the nature of the industry.

Future prospects

Most people start a career in this area by gaining experience as a funeral operative or assistant. They learn the varied aspects of the job from more experienced colleagues and work towards professional qualifications.

You could work for one of the large funeral services companies or for a smaller independent firm.

With experience, you could work as a funeral director abroad. After several years in the industry, you could set up your own funeral services company.

Advantages/disadvantages

Depending on the size of the funeral company you work for, you may be on call on a regular basis, which can affect your personal life.

Providing a professional and sympathetic service to people experiencing a very difficult time can be rewarding.

Money guide

Starting salaries are typically £15,000 per year.

With experience in the sector, you can expect to earn up to £25,000.

Those employed in a senior position can achieve £30,000 a year.

Self-employed funeral directors could earn considerably more.

Related opportunities

- Crematorium Technician p449
- Embalmer p451
- Management Consultant p38

Further information

British Institute of Funeral Directors
www.bifd.org.uk

National Association of Funeral Directors
www.nafd.org.uk

Qualifications and courses

You can either train as a hairdresser full time at college or you can start as an assistant/trainee in a salon and attend college on day release. Several NVQs are available including the Level 1 Certificate in Hairdressing and Barbering, the Level 1 Diploma in Hairdressing and Beauty Therapy, a Diploma in Hairdressing (Levels 2–3) or a Diploma in Barbering (Levels 2–3). Those who wish to specialise in African-Caribbean hair could take the NVQ Diploma in Hairdressing (Combined Hair Types) (Levels 2–3). BTECs are also available and include the Level 1 Introduction to Hair and Beauty, the Diploma in Hairdressing Services (Levels 1–2) and the Level 2 Diploma in Hairdressing.

Another route into this career is to apply for an apprenticeship, either in hairdressing or barbering, both of which are available at Intermediate and Advanced Level.

Those with NVQ Level 2 can register as a state-registered hairdresser with the Hairdressing Council (HC). The Freelance Hair and Beauty Federation (FHBF) runs courses for hairdressers on establishing and managing their own business, as well as continuing professional development (CPD) courses.

Qualified hairdressers can take more specialised courses through part-time study, such as the BTEC HNC/HND in Hair and Beauty Management (Levels 4–5) or various Level 4 qualifications in Technical Salon Management from City & Guilds. Foundation degrees in subjects such as Hairdressing, Salon Business Management and Hair and Beauty Management, as well as degrees in fashion styling and salon business management, are also available. Entry usually requires at least 1 A level/2 H grades and a Level 3 BTEC, NVQ or equivalent qualification in a hairdressing/barbering subject.

For those wishing to work in theatre, film and TV, there are degrees in subjects such as theatre arts (make-up and hair for theatre and media).

What the work involves

Hairdressers shampoo, cut and style clients' hair to a range of modern or classic looks. You could also provide dry or wet shaves to male clients.

You will discuss hair treatments with clients and may carry out colouring, tinting, perming and fixing hair extensions. You will also give advice on general haircare and hair products.

At senior levels, you could provide training to junior hairdressers.

Type of person suited to this work

Cutting and styling hair involves close personal contact with clients so hairdressers need good communication skills and a friendly manner.

You should have an interest in fashion, a creative flair and an eye for detail. You will need manual dexterity when using specialist chemicals and equipment required to style, perm and colour customers' hair. You should be willing to learn new techniques and methods throughout your career.

Sometimes you may work on reception, booking appointments and taking cash, so you will have to be efficient, confident and numerate.

Some salons require staff to be able to offer a wider choice of services, such as nail and beauty treatments.

Working conditions

Most hairdressers and barbers are based in salons in high streets and other areas. Some work as mobile hairdressers, providing services to clients in their own homes, so a driving licence would be required.

You will do a 40-hour week, which may include working Saturdays. A lot of salons remain open in the evening once or twice a week. Certain salons also open on Sunday. Part-time work is often available.

Future prospects

In a salon, you could progress to a role as senior stylist or manager. Alternatively, you could set up your own business.

As a mobile hairdresser, you could provide services to people in hospitals, care homes or prisons, as well as private clients.

There are opportunities to work on cruise ships. With further beauty therapy training you could work in film, TV or theatre.

Advantages/disadvantages

As a profession, it gives you the chance to be creative on a daily basis.

It is a very sociable profession as you meet new people on a daily basis.

You are on your feet for most of the day so it can be tiring.

Regular contact with beauty products and chemicals means that this type of work may not suit people with skin conditions or allergies.

Money guide

As a trainee you can expect to earn the national minimum wage, which varies according to your age. Earnings also vary with employer and geographical location.

Experienced hairdressers can expect to earn between £14,000 and £20,000 per year.

Top professional hairdressers can achieve in excess of £30,000.

Related opportunities

- Beauty Therapist p443
- Image Consultant p471
- Nail Technician p454

Further information

Hairdressing and Beauty Industry Authority
www.habia.org

NAIL TECHNICIAN

Qualifications and courses

There are no formal entry requirements for this career, however, in many areas nail technicians require a licence from the environmental health department of their local council. To obtain a licence you will need to have nationally recognised qualifications and you should check which qualifications your local council will accept.

Relevant courses include the NVQ Diploma in Nail Services (Levels 2–3), the Vocational Training Charitable Trust (VTCT) Level 2 Certificate in Nail Technology or Nail Treatments and the VTCT Level 3 Diploma in Nail Technology. You could also complete a Level 2 Certificate in Nail Technology or a Level 3 Diploma in Nail Technology from the International Therapy Examination Council (ITEC). The Confederation of International Beauty Therapy & Cosmetology (CIBTAC) offers a Level 3 Certificate in Nail Technologies and a Level 3 Diploma in Nail Tech Services.

The NVQ/SVQ in Beauty Therapy (Levels 2–3) and the BTEC qualifications in Beauty Therapy (Levels 2–3) also contain specialist units on nail techniques. Private organisations also offer various courses and qualifications. For example, the Beauty Academy offers short courses in subjects such as nail art, acrylic nail and airbrush nail art.

An option for those aged 16–24 is to apply for the Apprenticeship in Nail Services which is available at Intermediate and Advanced Levels. If you are looking to set up your own business after gaining the necessary qualification, you might want to consider taking a Foundation degree in salon business management.

What the work involves

Nail technicians provide a range of nail treatments to clients, including manicures, nail extensions, nail art and nail jewellery. Depending on the treatment you are providing, you will work with a range of beauty products and equipment such as brushes, stencils and airbrushes.

You will discuss with clients their intended treatment and check their hands for skin or nail disorders. You will provide advice about aftercare and recommend products for nail care and maintenance.

Your work will also include cleaning and tidying the treatment area before and after each client.

Type of person suited to this work

Nail technicians work with many people so you should have good communication skills. A professional appearance and high standard of hygiene is very important.

You will need excellent manual handling skills to undertake nail design work. A good knowledge of nail and beauty products is important. An eye for design and an interest in fashion are essential.

If you work as a freelance technician you will need good business skills.

Working conditions

Nail technicians work in nail or beauty salons and other locations. Mobile nail technicians provide treatments to clients in their own homes. A driving licence would be useful for travelling to your clients.

Salon-based technicians usually work between 30 and 40 hours a week with some evening/weekend work.

Nail technicians come into regular contact with chemicals so the job might not suit people with skin conditions or allergies.

Future prospects

Nail technology is a popular area of beauty, and treatments are now available in nail salons, department stores and beauty and hairdressing salons. Job opportunities are consequently currently steady.

You could work as a freelance nail technician, providing services to care homes and hotels as well as private clients. If you gain additional professional qualifications you could offer other therapies.

There are opportunities to work abroad or on cruise ships.

You could choose to teach nail treatments or become an NVQ assessor.

Advantages/disadvantages

Working as a freelancer can involve unsocial hours which may disrupt your personal life.

Benefits available from working in a salon include bonus schemes, commission payments for product sales and free or discounted beauty treatments.

Money guide

Starting salaries in this career are between £8,000 and £12,000.

With increased experience, your earnings will rise to about £16,000.

At senior/management level, you could receive £18,000–£25,000 a year.

Some nail technicians either work on a freelance basis or are self-employed and charge per job with private customers.

Rates vary from £10 to £50 depending on the type of treatment.

Related opportunities

- Beauty Therapist p443
- Hairdresser/Barber p453
- Make-up Artist p428

Further information

British Association of Beauty Therapy and Cosmetology
www.babtac.com

International Therapy Examination Council
www.itecworld.co.uk

PEST CONTROL TECHNICIAN

Qualifications and courses

A good standard of education is required for entry as you will be expected to undertake professional qualifications as part of your training and will need to be able to measure correct chemical quantities on the job. It is therefore recommended that candidates have GCSEs/ National 5s (A*–C/A–C) in English, Maths and a science, although this is not essential.

Training is given on the job. There might be opportunities to attend training courses although some larger companies will have an in-house training programme that you will automatically be signed up to when you join. As the job involves using specialist equipment and dangerous substances, some employers prefer candidates to be over 18 years old.

The Royal Society for Public Health (RSPH), British Pest Control Association (BPCA) and the National Pest Technicians Association (NPTA) offer various courses. The entry-level qualification is the BPCA/RSPH Certificate in Pest Management, which equates to NVQ Level 2. You could then complete the RSPH/BPCA Level 3 Diploma in Pest Management. The BPCA also offers an Accredited Technician in Pest Control course as well as specialist short courses in fumigation, rodents, insects, bird management and field biology. The NPTA also offers various short courses and City & Guilds offers the Level 2 Award in the Safe Use of Pesticides. The National Proficiency Training Council (NPTC) offers Certificates in Competence in the use of pesticides in rural areas.

Once qualified, you can join a professional registration scheme such as the NPTA Professional Pest Technician Registration Scheme (PPTRS) where you can document your level of training.

What the work involves

Pest control technicians protect public health by treating and eradicating infestations of insects and vermin such as cockroaches and rats, working on site in private homes, offices, shops and other locations.

Your job may involve investigating or monitoring a site to check for pests. You will use a range of specialist chemicals and equipment. Your work might involve fitting traps or spraying areas with chemicals.

In some situations you will provide advice to customers on the prevention of pest problems.

Type of person suited to this work

This job is all about protecting public health so you should be able to work to a high standard of health and safety. Working with chemical treatments and specialist equipment demands a professional approach.

You will need to be calm when dealing with large numbers of insects and rodents. A strong stomach will also help you cope with working in unpleasant conditions.

Physical fitness and good manual handling skills are essential. You will need to be able to communicate and have a tactful approach when providing advice to customers. You will use your writing skills to keep records and write reports.

Working conditions

Whilst not all pest control work is unpleasant, dealing with dirty or unhygienic situations is a likely part of the job.

You will travel to different locations on a regular basis. A driving licence is essential.

You must wear protective clothing, such as overalls and eye goggles, as you will be working with a range of chemicals. The job might not suit people with skin conditions or allergies.

You may choose to specialise in one type of pest once you have gained some experience.

Hours will normally be longer during the summer months when there are more problems with pests.

Future prospects

Pest control technicians provide an important service to domestic homes, factories, offices and other locations in cities and rural areas.

You could run your own business or work with local councils or specialist companies.

With experience you could progress to supervising teams of staff, managing a large pest control company or working in a management role for local councils.

Advantages/disadvantages

Your day-to-day work will be varied so no two days will be the same!

The work is quite solitary; you will often drive alone to jobs in a van containing the specialist equipment.

You might be faced with unpleasant situations.

Money guide

As a trainee you could start at between £17,000 and £20,000 per year.

With experience and qualifications, this rises to between £22,000 and £25,000.

There may be the opportunity for additional income depending on your employer, such as commission or bonuses.

Related opportunities

- Environmental Health Practitioner/Officer p22
- Refuse and Recycling Operative p456
- Toxicologist p525

Further information

British Pest Control Association
www.bpca.org.uk

National Pest Technicians Association
www.npta.org.uk

REFUSE AND RECYCLING OPERATIVE

Qualifications and courses

There are no formal academic entry requirements but you will need to be at least 18 years old and drivers must hold a large goods vehicle (LGV) licence. When you secure employment you will receive on-the-job training in health and safety, manual handling and the disposal of hazardous items.

The Apprenticeship in Sustainable Resource Management, available at both Intermediate and Advanced Levels, offers an ideal route into this career as you will be combining practical work experience with formal training. The Apprenticeship in Driving Goods Vehicles may also equip you with useful skills.

Those who wish to gain relevant qualifications could take the Level 2 competence-based qualification Diploma for Sustainable Waste Management Operative, for which there are different pathways including Waste Collection Driver, Waste Site Operative and Weighbridge Operative. City & Guilds also provide a number of Diplomas in the Principles of Sustainable Resource Management (Levels 2–3), Sustainable Recycling Activities (Levels 1–4) and Sustainable Waste Management (Levels 2–4).

People looking to progress to supervisory or managerial roles could study for the Level 3 competence-based qualification Diploma for Waste Supervisor. Alternatively, you could study for the City & Guilds Level 3 Diploma in Sustainable Recycling Activities – Supervisory or the Level 4 Diploma in Management of Sustainable Recycling Activities.

Although not essential, voluntary work may prove beneficial and opportunities can be found on websites, such as Do-it.

What the work involves

You will collect rubbish and unwanted items and take them to an official rubbish tip or recycling depot.

Working as part of a team, you will travel around your area emptying bins, removing plastic sacks of waste or picking up recyclable waste.

Recycling operatives may have additional duties, such as sorting rubbish or collecting hazardous waste. Recycling technicians also work in recycling facilities, sorting through recycled materials in preparation for re-use.

Type of person suited to this work

A strong stomach is useful when dealing with rubbish. You should also be able to cope with getting your hands dirty.

Most companies are required to complete their rounds to deadlines so you should be able to work under pressure. You will also need manual handling skills to lift and move recycling collections. For work in a recycling sorting facility, you will require good eyesight and attention to detail.

Excellent people skills are necessary as you will work as part of a team and encounter members of the public.

Working conditions

You will wear protective clothing, such as gloves and overalls, and you will come into contact with dirt and rubbish on a regular basis. The work will involve nasty smells and some unpleasant sights.

The hours are generally around 6am–3pm from Monday to Friday. You may be required to work overtime during busy holiday periods when the amount of rubbish increases.

You will work outdoors in all weather conditions and the role involves bending, lifting and carrying heavy rubbish bags.

This type of work might not suit people with skin conditions or allergies.

Future prospects

Loaders will always be in demand as even recyclable rubbish has to be collected. You could work for a contracting company providing services for a local authority and there are some jobs with specialist companies which collect paper or food waste.

Current recycling targets may be changed with the EU continuing to look to set more ambitious ones. There will be a growth in the number of jobs in the industry; the exact rate of growth will depend on the ambition of the recycling targets and legislation.

With experience, you could progress to supervisory or management work.

Advantages/disadvantages

Your working day usually finishes early so you will have your entire evening free.

The work is physically demanding and potentially unsafe.

Money guide

Starting salaries usually range from £11,000 to £14,500.

With experience in the role, you could expect to earn £15,000–£18,000 a year.

Drivers receive slightly higher earnings, at around £19,000.

A recycling or refuse collection manager can achieve between £24,000 and £28,000 per year.

There are usually opportunities to increase your income by working overtime or during holiday periods.

Related opportunities

- Delivery Driver p590
- Large Goods Vehicle Driver p596
- Removals Operative p607

Further information

Waste Management Industry Training and Advisory Board
www.wamitab.org.uk

Qualifications and courses

Spa therapists must have qualifications in the treatments or therapies they wish to offer before practising and will often be trained in a combination of therapies.

One route into this career is to take an Apprenticeship in Spa Therapy. This is an advanced apprenticeship so candidates are required to have already completed a Level 2 qualification in another subject, such as beauty therapy or nail services, before applying.

You could choose to study for a BTEC in Beauty Therapy (Levels 1–3), a City & Guilds NVQ Diploma in Beauty Therapy (Levels 1–3) or the Level 3 in Spa Therapy. The Vocational Training Charitable Trust (VTCT) offers a Level 3 Award in Spa Treatments and a Level 3 Diploma in Spa and Body Treatments.

The industry's main governing bodies also offer qualifications in association with approved colleges. The International Therapy Examination Council (ITEC) offers a Level 3 Diploma in Spa Treatments and Spa and Body Treatments, whilst the Comité International d'Esthétique et de Cosmétologie (CIDESCO) offers the Spa Therapy Diploma. For entry you must possess the CIDESCO Diploma in Beauty Therapy or Postgraduate Diploma in Beauty Therapy.

Courses are also available in related, specialist subjects such as aromatherapy and Indian head massage.

If you wish to progress into management then a Foundation degree/degree in beauty and spa management will give you an advantage. ITEC also offers a Level 4 Diploma in Spa and Salon Management. Entry is usually with a BTEC Level 3 qualification in Beauty Therapy Sciences, or an NVQ/SVQ Level 3 in Spa Therapy, plus at least 3 GCSEs/National 5s (A*–C/A–C), including a science subject.

What the work involves

Spa therapists provide various treatments which are designed to enhance appearance, reduce stress or improve wellbeing.

The treatments you offer could include facials, manicures and pedicures, massage, body treatments such as wraps, and exfoliation and specialist treatments like light therapy and lymphatic drainage.

You will be required to talk to your clients in order to discover their specific health needs and personal expectations. You will ensure that they are comfortable at all times and provide them with any necessary aftercare advice.

You will also be expected to keep the salon clean and tidy.

Type of person suited to this work

You will need a caring manner and the ability to make people feel at ease. You should be discreet and understand the role of confidentiality within the industry.

It is important that you are able to work effectively as part of a team. You should have excellent dexterity, outstanding attention to detail and good time management skills.

You will need to have strong personal hygiene and a smart appearance. A sound understanding of health and safety requirements would also prove beneficial.

Working conditions

Most of the work will be based in private treatment rooms which will be warm and clean but you may be required to complete some treatments in wet rooms.

A great deal of time will be spent standing and bending. Some products may irritate your skin, particularly if you are prone to such reactions. Most spa therapists wear a uniform.

Full-time hours are usually between 37 and 40 hours a week and often include evening and weekend work.

Future prospects

You will have the possibility of working in various beauty-related professions such as beauty therapist and nail technician.

You may choose to progress to a supervisory or management post which introduces more administrative and managerial work to your role. There is also the option of becoming a trainer or lecturer.

There are numerous opportunities for overseas work, for example on a cruise ship or in a hotel.

Advantages/disadvantages

The unusual working hours may prove inconvenient.

Opportunities within this industry are varied so you will have many options regarding which environment you wish to work in.

Being on your feet all day could be tiring.

You may receive bonuses, discounted/free products and the use of spa facilities.

Money guide

Salaries vary depending on location, employer and number of hours worked.

Starting salaries for spa therapists are usually £12,000–£14,000.

With several years' experience, earnings can increase up to £19,000.

A spa manager may earn £20,000–£40,000 a year.

Related opportunities

- Beauty Consultant p442
- Beauty Therapist p443
- Nail Technician p454

Further information

Guild of Professional Beauty Therapists
www.beautyguild.com

Qualifications and courses

Tattooists typically start their career through an apprenticeship which can last between 1 and 3 years. There is no formal training scheme so the only way to get a traineeship is by approaching a working tattoo artist and applying for a training position with them. There are no formal qualifications required to become a tattooist's apprentice, however it is advisable to compile a portfolio of any artwork and experience you have to present to any future employers.

Over time greater responsibility will be granted and, once you can tattoo unsupervised, you will become a trainee tattooist. It can take about five years to become fully competent and able to carry out the various styles of tattooing.

Once your teacher deems you ready, a licence to practise must be obtained from your local environmental health department and then you will be qualified to work as a professional tattooist. Working without a licence incurs a heavy penalty.

You can get details of registered tattooists from the Tattoo Club of Great Britain or from the environmental health department of your local council. Some environmental health departments also offer short training courses for experienced and practising tattooists.

What the work involves

Tattooists, also referred to as body artists, apply permanent images onto their clients' bodies, using needles and ink to draw images, symbols or words onto the skin.

As a tattooist you will have to advise clients on suitable tattoos, ensuring that the chosen design is exactly what the client wants and that they understand the permanent nature of a tattoo.

You will create the tattoo either by drawing freehand on the customer's skin or by using a transfer.

When not tattooing, you will clean and sterilise tattoo equipment and work areas, keeping up to date with the latest health and safety procedures, and devise new and interesting designs.

Type of person suited to this work

A tattooist ought to possess a flair for design, raw talent as an artist and an excellent attention to detail.

You must have good hand–eye coordination, a steady hand and feel comfortable using different equipment depending on the type of tattoo. Tattooists should also possess the ability to communicate with customers both in the consultation process and during the tattoo itself.

Owing to strict regulation, tattooists must maintain high standards of cleanliness and constant awareness of the need for hygiene and an up-to-date knowledge of health and safety.

Working conditions

You will generally work 5 or 6 days a week, including Saturdays. Studio hours are usually 9am to 5pm, but you may schedule your work into short sessions during the day because of the level of concentration and attention to detail you need.

Tattoo artists usually work from a tattoo studio, which must be registered by the local environmental health department.

Tattoo studios are fitted out with books of designs, all the hygiene equipment necessary and dedicated work and preparation spaces, whilst tattooists must provide their own inking equipment.

Future prospects

Once a subject of taboo, the alternative culture of tattoos has become more mainstream and tattooing is increasingly regulated, creative and popular.

You could work as a tattooist in tattoo studios around the UK. Some of these are part of beauty salons offering other similar services such as body piercing.

Once you have experience as a tattooist you could become self-employed.

Advantages/disadvantages

The job is very artistic and poses new challenges of creation with each customer.

As a tattooist you will come into contact with many different people; some of these may be difficult to deal with.

Hours are long and mistakes are out of the question, so working as a tattooist can be mentally exhausting.

Money guide

Many tattoo artists are self-employed and remuneration varies widely depending on the amount of trade they receive. Summer months are traditionally the busiest.

As an apprentice you are likely to work for free and some tattoo studios require apprentices to pay for their training. Apprentices must also provide their own equipment and sterilising kit.

A trainee tattooist can earn around £12,000 a year, while an experienced tattooist can earn between £15,000 and £30,000.

A tattoo artist owning his or her own business and employing others could earn in excess of £50,000 although again, this varies considerably.

Related opportunities

- Cartoonist p159
- Fine Artist/Sculptor p162
- Graphic Designer p165

Further information

Arts Council England
www.artscouncil.org.uk

Tattoo Club of Great Britain
www.tattoo.co.uk

Qualifications and courses

There are no set entry requirements for this career, however a background in hospitality, event planning, catering or marketing will be useful, especially if you want to work for a large events company. BTECs, HNDs, Foundation degrees and degrees in events or hospitality management may help to give you a pre-entry understanding of industry processes.

An alternative way to start a career in the industry is to work your way up from an administrative position in a wedding planning or event management company then progress as your experience grows. The UK Alliance of Wedding Planners' 2-day course with an optional work placement may also be helpful.

The UK Academy of Wedding and Event Planning also offers Level 3 Certificates in Wedding Planning and Event Planning, a Level 4 Certificate in Event Design, a Level 4 Diploma in Wedding Planning, Styling and Design, and a Level 4 Advanced Diploma in Special Event Planning and Design.

Those with proof of more than 3 years' business trading, 3 client references and a satisfactory quality inspection can become members of the National Association of Professional Wedding Services which offers an Advanced Certification in Wedding Design and Management.

What the work involves

Wedding planners organise ceremonies, receptions and other events to suit a client's plans and budget. You will liaise with florists, caterers, photographers, musicians, venues and hair stylists, negotiating prices, booking and confirming with all suppliers and keeping a detailed record of costs.

You will help come up with creative ideas and themes, as well as advise the couple on wedding customs and etiquette. You will help organise transport, stag and hen weekends, wedding attire and accommodation for out-of-town guests.

After all the preparations are in place, you will also be charged with managing the running of the wedding day itself. It will be your job to make sure everything happens according to schedule and that the day is exactly what the bride and groom requested.

Type of person suited to this work

You need to be enthusiastic and approachable. You should be a good listener and always take into account your client's ideas and wishes. You will need the initiative and creativity to develop these dreams into a reality. A good sense of style and attention to detail is essential.

It's important to have both financial and crisis management skills. It's your job to ensure the wedding stays within budget and runs smoothly so you should be confident and effective in negotiations.

In order to keep track of multiple clients and the variety of tasks involved you must possess strong organisational skills and be adept at multi-tasking.

You will have to be able to work with sensitivity if your client's wishes are unrealistic or not feasible for their budget and be able to offer suitable alternatives.

Working conditions

It is common to work 12-hour days, especially in the period leading up to the wedding. Although you can generally plan your own hours you will most likely need to meet your clients during evenings and weekends.

The busiest months for weddings are July to September, with about 42% of the year's weddings happening in that 3 month period. During peak wedding season you will often work at weekends, attending clients' weddings to ensure the day runs smoothly.

You could work from home or out of an office but most of your time will be spent visiting venues, suppliers and clients. A driving licence is essential.

Future prospects

You might work for a hotel or event-management company and start out temping as an assistant. You could also offer to plan weddings for friends, helping you to build up a portfolio.

Most wedding planners are self-employed. Your success will depend on your reputation and how well you market yourself.

You could choose to specialise in destination weddings or work overseas.

Advantages/disadvantages

It's rewarding when you make a bride and groom's dream wedding come true.

You will be under a lot of pressure to deliver perfection.

Money guide

If you work for a wedding and events planning company your starting salary is typically between £16,000 and £20,000 and, with experience, this can rise to £25,000–£40,000.

If you are freelance you can charge either a percentage of the total cost of the wedding, an hourly rate or a flat fee. Your salary will be dependent on how many weddings you organise a year.

Related opportunities

- Entertainment Manager p366
- Events and Exhibition Organiser p391
- Image Consultant p471

Further information

National Association of Professional Wedding Services
www.theweddingassociation.co.uk

UK Alliance of Wedding Planners
www.ukawp.com

PERSONAL AND OTHER SERVICES INCLUDING HAIR AND BEAUTY

Qualifications and courses

There are no formal qualifications needed for this job, although basic numeracy skills for calculating prices are useful. Most training is done on the job by a senior window cleaner as both the trade and health and safety issues will need to be fully understood for you take on jobs independently.

If you are using ropes and access equipment you will need to be insured. The Industrial Rope Access Trade Association offers rope access courses at trainee, operative and supervisor level.

The British Window Cleaning Academy offers courses covering window cleaning skills, water-fed pole instruction and health and safety. These courses are aimed at both new and experienced window cleaners and although the courses lead to a certificate in their own right, they also provide evidence for the NVQ/SVQ Level 2 in Cleaning and Support Services or Cleaning Principles.

The Federation of Window Cleaners also offers courses in cleaning windows safely and risk assessment.

With some experience you might want to study for an NVQ in either Team Leading or First Line Management (Levels 3–4). If you are self-employed then qualifications in business or a related subject may prove beneficial.

What the work involves

You will be cleaning internal and external windows and other glass surfaces, using detergents, in private and public buildings.

You will be using ladders to reach high windows or platforms and ropes for very tall office buildings. Recently the use of water pumping poles has reduced the use of ladders for health and safety reasons.

Customers may ask you to complete other tasks, alongside cleaning their windows. This could involve clearing gutters and cleaning paintwork or UPVC window frames.

If you are self-employed you might need to organise paperwork and collect payments.

Type of person suited to this work

Practical skills are very important for this job as you will be working at heights and with equipment. Having a good level of fitness will help with lifting and carrying heavy equipment.

You need to be aware of health and safety issues and you will have to learn to safely use power-operated lifting equipment for high-level cleaning.

It is important to respect your customers' privacy especially when cleaning windows at people's homes.

Good communication skills are needed for dealing with customers, in particular if you want to run your own business.

Running your own business will require you to be organised, as you will have to plan your own work schedule, keep your accounts in order and chase payments. In order to maintain a successful business, you must be capable of advertising your services, which will require you to be persuasive.

Working conditions

The hours you work will vary greatly. You may be contracted to work about 40 hours a week, in daylight hours, or if self-employed, you can choose which jobs you take.

Be prepared to work in all weathers and at great heights. It is useful to have a driving licence and access to your own vehicle.

Health and safety regulations have been introduced to help prevent accidents at great heights.

Future prospects

There are jobs available across the UK, with demand in towns and cities. Smaller rural areas also require window cleaners, so job prospects are potentially good.

However, if self-employed, it will be important to establish a reputation and try and get your name into the community, often working locally.

If you have access to stabilising equipment it can help you win large contracts and more work.

Advantages/disadvantages

You may have to work in poor weather conditions or at great heights which could be demanding.

You will get to meet all types of people and establish contacts.

You can set up and run your own business.

Money guide

If you are employed by a contract cleaning company, you could earn between £16,000 and £18,000. Team leaders and those in senior roles could earn between £20,000 and £23,000.

If you are a self-employed window cleaner your earnings will depend on how many customers you have and your reputation. With a good reputation you could earn over £20,000.

Related opportunities

- Car Valet p444
- Caretaker p445
- Pest Control Technician p455

Further information

Building Futures
www.buildingfutures.org.uk

Federation for Window Cleaners
www.f-w-c.co.uk

Retail, Sales and Customer Services

Jobs in this sector are suited to those of you who are very good at communicating with others and are interested in making your customers happy. Maybe you are interested in working with food and want to give your customers high quality, fresh produce. Your interest may lie in fashion retail and you could spend your time providing style advice. You should also be commercially minded and think about how your work relates to the success of the company you work for. Jobs in this sector also involve maintaining standards such as safety and quality to ensure guidelines are met, so a practical outlook can be useful. The jobs featured in this section are listed below. For similar jobs to the ones covered in this section turn to *Administration, Business, Office Work and Financial Services* on page 1.

Qualifications and courses

No formal qualifications are needed, but employers often seek candidates with sales skills and demonstrable enthusiasm, for example those that have collected and researched antiques or bought and sold products on a market stall or via the internet. GCSEs/National 5s (A*–C/A–C) in subjects such as art, design and history are also an advantage as they demonstrate an interest in history and/or aesthetics.

Entry is normally through having completed relevant work experience within an antiques shop, salesroom or auction house as a trainee or within a junior role. Here you begin as a general worker, assistant, cataloguer, porter or valuer within an auction house, learning on the job from experienced professionals, before working your way up to a position as an antiques dealer.

Alternatively, you may wish to study for an industry recognised qualification, such as an NVQ/SVQ in Retail Operations, or a diploma, degree or postgraduate award in a relevant subject such as fine arts, applied arts or history of art. Upon graduation, you may decide to apply for one of the relevant graduate training schemes offered by large auction houses such as Sotheby's, Christie's and Bonhams.

You can add to your skills throughout your career through extensive self-study or by taking one of the privately run short courses available from institutions such as Christie's and Sotheby's. Information and advice about careers in antiques dealing and current vacancies with dealers may be available from the British Antique Dealers' Association (BADA) or the Association of Art and Antique Dealers (LAPADA).

What the work involves

You will be buying and selling things such as furniture, clocks, jewellery and pictures, which are either old or which people collect. You will go to auctions and fairs to buy things to sell in shops, markets or antique salerooms.

You will need to develop specialist knowledge so that you can assess the age of an object, its value and whether it will sell at a profit.

You will advise customers on the value of their antiques.

Type of person suited to this work

You should be fascinated by antiques and working out where they come from and what they are worth.

You will need to be interested in history and dedicated enough to travel and visit fairs and auctions all over the country, and possibly abroad, searching out bargains and objects to sell. You will need to develop good specialist knowledge, know what is likely to be popular and sell quickly at a profit.

Antiques do not have fixed prices, so you will need to be able to make quick decisions and cope with the stress of buying things at auction. You will need to have good all round business skills.

Working conditions

You will work in a shop, in an antiques saleroom or on a market stall. You could be outside in all weathers and will probably have to travel to different markets.

You could be dealing with heavy objects like furniture or dusty and dirty things such as clothes and books.

Your working hours will vary a lot. Shops and stalls will be open at fixed times and on public holidays, and you could be visiting auctions or customers at any time.

Future prospects

Most antique dealers are self-employed or work in a family business, but you could start in an auction house or as a sales assistant in a larger shop.

Once you have developed contacts and knowledge of antiques and their value, you could work for yourself, perhaps starting with a market stall and expanding your business from there. You will have to stay ahead of industry developments, such as the rapid rise in online auctions, in order to secure deals.

Most dealers specialise in a particular period of history or type of antique or move into valuing or auctioneering.

In recent years the antique business has become more events-based as opposed to gallery-based, meaning you may have to pay large amounts of money to win new customers by featuring in fairs.

Advantages/disadvantages

You will be working with things that you love and have the thrill of finding bargains or rare items.

It can be a very uncertain business and prices will rise and fall as things go in and out of fashion. You can make a lot of money, but you can also lose a lot.

Money guide

An assistant earns around £15,000 per year.

Between £20,000 and £30,000 is usual for a dealer with a flair for the trade and considerable experience.

In excess of £50,000 is possible for successful dealers, or people with a high level of specialist knowledge.

Related opportunities

- Auctioneer p463
- Museum/Art Gallery Curator p337
- Sales/Retail Assistant p480

Further information

British Antique Dealers' Association
www.bada.org

Sotheby's
www.sothebys.com

AUCTIONEER

Qualifications and courses

There are no set entry requirements for this profession, but most employers prefer candidates with good communication skills and GCSEs/National 5s (A*–C/ A–C), particularly in English and Maths.

One way of entering the profession is to start your career in a junior role such as a salesroom assistant before progressing to the position of auctioneer. If you want to go into property auctioneering, you could start out by gaining experience in valuation work.

However if you want to work for an international auction house you will need either a degree in a related subject, such as history of art or fine arts conservation, or a degree in property or valuation that has been accredited by the Royal Institution of Chartered Surveyors (RICS). You can also follow a Foundation degree in Auctioneering and Valuation, or a degree in the arts market. Sotheby's Institute of Art also offers a postgraduate qualification in art business.

Upon graduation, you may opt to complete a graduate training scheme offered by some large London auction houses such as Sotheby's and Christie's, although competition is fierce. Relevant art or business work experience may improve your chances of securing a place on one of these training programmes.

Once employed, you will experience on-the-job training from experienced auctioneers and external instruction via short courses and workshops. You may even be encouraged to work towards gaining incorporated or chartered membership of RICS which would significantly improve your career prospects and salary. In order to remain up to date with current developments, such as the rise in online auctions, it is recommended that you join the National Association of Valuers and Auctioneers.

What the work involves

Auctioneers sell items at auctions, getting the best market price possible for the items they are selling.

It is your responsibility to make sure the item sells for the best price, both by selling well on the day and by publicising sales in advance. You will be inspecting and valuing items and coming to price agreements with the sellers, making sure that reserves are appropriate.

On auction days, you will run through the items on sale, observe customers, and take bids. You may specialise in a particular area, and could be working on anything from antiques and property to livestock and motors.

Type of person suited to this work

You will need to be good with people and communicate well, so that you can interact with customers and successfully sell goods. In addition, you should be outgoing and confident, with excellent knowledge of what you are selling.

You should have excellent observational skills and a good attention to detail; valuing objects is also a big part of the job.

For this reason you also need to be able to think on your feet, and work well under pressure.

You must have shrewd business sense and a good head for figures, as much of your day will revolve around numbers.

Working conditions

You will usually be working in an auction house, or an office or auction room within. Normal working hours are 9am–5.30pm Monday to Saturday, but be prepared to carry out viewings and valuations during evenings and weekends.

A driving licence is useful as travel may be necessary, for example if you're selling the contents of a large house clearance. You may also sell livestock and motor vehicles outdoors.

Future prospects

Career development relies on building a list of contacts, and working towards moving to larger more prestigious auction houses.

You will have to keep up to date with online developments in the industry. 100% online auction houses are becoming more prevalent in the industry and traditional live auction houses may suffer as a result.

You may want to become self-employed, or work towards a management position or partnership. You may also have the chance to travel, as some auction houses have offices abroad.

Advantages/disadvantages

This work is stimulating and challenging, and especially rewarding if you choose to work with items or goods you have a genuine interest in.

Every day will be different, and you will constantly be interacting and communicating with people.

It can be tiring work, and much of the day will be spent on your feet. As the person leading an auction, you have to be 100% alert all the time.

Money guide

Starting salaries for trainees are around £15,000 a year.

With experience, this may rise to between £30,000 and £40,000.

If you become a business partner, you might earn over £60,000.

Related opportunities

- Antiques Dealer p462
- Chartered Surveyor p70
- Rural Property/Practice Surveyor p105

Further information

Livestock Auctioneers' Association Limited
www.laa.co.uk

National Association of Valuers and Auctioneers
www.nava.org.uk

Qualifications and courses

There are no formal qualifications to enter this work, but most employers look for candidates with GCSEs/ National 5s (A*–C/A–C) in English and Maths. A degree/ HND/Foundation degree in English, retail or business management or retail marketing may increase your chances of employment. If you wish to work in specialist academic bookshops, a degree in a subject similar to that being sold in the store is recommended, as is a postgraduate qualification for those working in antiquarian bookselling.

Other relevant further education courses include NVQs/ SVQs in Retail Skills at Levels 1–3; at Level 3 you must select the Visual Marketing, Sales Professional or Management pathway. Other relevant courses include the NVQs in Customer Service at Levels 1–4, and BTEC qualifications in Retail Knowledge (Levels 2–3).

Pre-entry experience in retail is highly valuable as competition for posts is strong. Employers often seek candidates who can provide evidence of excellent communication skills, a passion for literature, effective teamwork and an interest in and knowledge of the bookselling industry. An understanding of e-commerce is becoming increasingly desired by employers given the rise in online ordering and e-books.

Some larger employers offer fast track structured training schemes or trainee manager schemes whilst new recruits of smaller branches are trained by experienced colleagues and through external instruction. Membership of the Booksellers Association (BA) or the Antiquarian Booksellers Association (ABA) is recommended in order to remain up to date with new developments and training courses.

What the work involves

Front of house duties often include serving customers, taking money, answering enquiries, giving advice and ordering books. You might also be expected to liaise with publishers and stockists, ordering books and keeping stock information up to date.

You will be expected to undertake shop floor work which will include stock replenishment, recommending books to customers, arranging displays and keeping shelves tidy.

Behind the scenes you will also have to deal with deliveries, update the stock list, repackage returns and cash up the till. You might work with local colleges or universities to make sure you have got the books needed for their courses and sometimes organise book sales and events with them.

Type of person suited to this work

You need to have a genuine interest in books and to be able to keep up to date with new publications, so that you can help and advise customers.

You will need excellent communication skills for dealing with customers and sales representatives. You will work as part of a team, but should also be able to use your own initiative. It is important to remain calm and polite when the shop is busy.

Basic numeracy and IT skills will be useful when using the tills for payments and computers for stock orders.

You should be able to use your initiative, especially when ordering stock. You should be able to identify customer demand for certain titles and order books accordingly.

Working conditions

You will be working in either an independent bookshop or one that is part of a larger chain.

You will be on your feet all day, at a till, carrying heavy books and assisting customers.

You will work 39–40 hours a week, which may include weekends and evenings on a rota basis.

Future prospects

The number of small independent bookshops is currently in decline due to competition from larger stores and online sales along with the rise in e-books, so the majority of opportunities are with the big chains.

You can progress to a supervisor role or be in charge of a specific section of books. You can go on to management level or to work for head office.

With considerable experience and good finances you might open your own shop or choose to specialise in certain types of books such as antique or second hand.

Advantages/disadvantages

You will be using your knowledge and love of books to help other people and to keep up to date with new publications.

You could develop specialist knowledge, for example in children's books.

You will be dealing with the public, which can be rewarding but also stressful.

Money guide

Salaries vary a lot depending on the size of the shop. With large chains, you may get bonuses for high levels of sales or for meeting targets.

You can expect £12,000–£17,000 per year when you start.

With experience and/or managerial responsibilities, you can expect £20,000–£40,000.

Related opportunities

Further information

Booksellers Association
www.booksellers.org.uk

British Independent Retailers Association
www.bira.co.uk

Qualifications and courses

Although there are no entry requirements most employers prefer applicants to have a number of GCSEs/National 5s, particularly in subjects such as English and Maths.

Previous experience within the construction or retailing industry is beneficial however, as many employers view experience and personality as being more important than academic qualifications. Having said this, the BTEC Level 1 Diploma in Construction might be a useful qualification in introducing you to some of the basic skills required in the industry.

You may opt to complete an apprenticeship with a DIY store or building suppliers. Here you are likely to experience a combination of on-the-job training from professionals and a series of day or block release instruction at a college or training centre where you will work towards gaining industry recognised qualifications.

Your employer may encourage you to work towards specialist courses in areas such as central heating, bricks, mortar and bathrooms, as well as a Diploma in Merchanting, offered by the Builders Merchants Federation (BMF). NVQs/SVQs also accredited by the BMF in subjects such as business administration, customer service, retail, team leading and management or warehousing and storage may also be available to you.

A forklift truck and/or LGV licence may improve your chances of securing employment as will short courses in management, operations, product knowledge and sales, also provided by the BMF.

What the work involves

You will be dealing with building materials and bathroom fittings. You will keep track of stock using computer or paper systems, order new stock and take deliveries.

You will supply goods to building firms and individual contractors – plumbers, electricians or plasterers – and members of the public. As part of this you will take payments and use tills.

Assistants will work for a builders' merchant looking after the stock.

Assistants will also handle a range of building materials, take deliveries, store deliveries properly, keep the yard clean and deal with customers.

Type of person suited to this work

You will need to have a certain level of physical fitness for both of these positions, as there will be heavy lifting and carrying involved. Candidates with asthma and/or allergies to dust and chemicals may not be suitable for this type of work.

You will need solid communication skills for dealing with customers and suppliers. You should have good numeracy and computer skills and the ability to handle money and paperwork efficiently.

Customer service skills will also be useful.

Working conditions

You will work about 40 hours a week, usually on Saturdays and sometimes Sundays. You may start at about 7.30am so that builders can buy their materials on the way to their work.

You may also need to use a forklift truck and climb ladders, which could be dangerous. You will be wearing overalls and protective boots or shoes.

You could be working outside in all weathers.

Future prospects

There are job opportunities in all areas of the country, but these vary depending on the strength of the building trade within the current economic climate. Firms are most concentrated within the south of England for example.

Although the number of small builders' merchants is declining, there are still many specialist and larger firms recruiting workers regularly. A growing specialist area is the sale of reclaimed building materials, eg roof tiles, slates, staircases and window frames.

You could choose to work part time, and if you work for large merchants or a chain you could progress to become a supervisor or manager. You could also work for a supplier or as a sales representative.

Those employed in smaller companies may have to transfer between employers in order to ensure promotion.

Advantages/disadvantages

The work can be a great way of using your interest in building and knowledge of materials, tools and equipment.

There is a lot of paperwork involved in keeping track of the stock.

You could be starting early in the morning and working outside.

Money guide

An assistant at a builders' merchant could start on around £16,000–£20,000 a year.

Once you have built up your experience and have additional responsibilities you can expect to earn up £20,000–£30,000.

You could earn more as the manager of a department or store. Managers of large companies could earn up to £50,000 a year.

Related opportunities

- Building Surveyor p65
- Sales/Retail Assistant p480
- Warehouse Worker/Manager p613

Further information

Builders Merchants Federation
www.bmf.org.uk

BUTCHER

Qualifications and courses

There are no formal qualifications required to become a butcher and most people train on the job. Many employers will want proof, however, of a certain standard of literacy and numeracy skills. They may require employees to have acquired English, Maths and science GCSEs/National 5s (A*–C/A–C) and some even set aptitude tests. Work experience in the food and drink industry is also beneficial.

A good way to begin in this career is by securing a Butcher Apprenticeship (Level 2), supported by the Worshipful Company of Butchers (WCB), the Institute of Meat (IoM) and the Meat Training Council (MTC).

Many employers provide entrants with the opportunity to study towards industry recognised qualifications including food safety awards and the NVQ/SVQ in Proficiency in Meat and Poultry Industry Skills at Levels 2 and 3. In partnership with IoM, the WCB have also introduced an Advanced Butchery Training Course designed for young butchers looking to improve their skills.

The MTC also offers courses in hygiene and with adequate training, plus the completion of a test paper and a Hazard Analysis and Critical Control Point case study, you will be awarded the Meat Managers Hygiene & HACCP training course certificate.

Graduates or individuals with industry experience can undertake the postgraduate course in Meat Business Management at Harper Adams University.

It is advised that you become a member of the professional body for butchers, the WCB, which would demonstrate to customers that you work to high professional standards.

What the work involves

You might prepare an assortment of meat and poultry products. This could involve cutting, de-boning, trimming and slicing. You could offer advice to customers about varieties of meat available and preparation techniques involved with them. Some butchers offer a delivery service.

You will take part in the everyday running of the business, visiting markets, ordering stock, taking deliveries from suppliers, organising displays and selling the products.

Butchers can also work in the wholesale area of the industry, receiving the meat from the abattoir, then preparing and storing it for sale to the retailers or wholesale customers.

Type of person suited to this work

You will have to be meticulous and practical. You will need to have a strong understanding of and a professional approach to health and hygiene. Owing to the fact you will be using sharp tools and machinery you need to be safety conscious.

You should be personable, maintaining a high level of customer service. You need to have an outstanding knowledge of the various products and cuts of meat.

You should have strong mental arithmetic skills in order to value a sale quickly and correctly and be confident handling cash.

Working conditions

A retail butcher works in a shop environment with a chilled storage area. You will be expected to prepare meat in front of customers and will have to wear protective clothing, such as disposable gloves and an apron. Wholesale butchers also work in chilled environments and wear protective clothing.

This profession involves a great deal of standing, lifting and carrying as butchers are required to transport joints of meat.

You will work, on average, 40 hours a week, including Saturdays and sometimes evenings and Sundays. Work starts as early as 7am.

Future prospects

With a large number of local butchers having closed down and the ones left being small businesses, prospects are becoming somewhat limited. Supermarkets have however resurrected the idea of the meat counter over simply selling packaged meats and promotion opportunities within these chains are plentiful.

Once you have gained experience there is the option of setting up your own retail outlet. Other options include making the move into meat catering, meat hygiene, meat wholesale or meat-product manufacture.

Advantages/disadvantages

You will have a great deal of customer contact and the opportunity to share your knowledge.

The amount of time spent on your feet, heavy lifting and in cold temperatures may cause discomfort.

Money guide

Typically, a butcher will earn a starting salary of between £12,500 and £16,000 a year.

With experience, earnings will increase to between £16,500 and £22,000 a year.

A butchery manager could make up to £30,000 per year.

If an individual chose to open their own shop this may increase further.

Related opportunities

- Food Processing Operative p212
- Kitchen Assistant/Supervisor p133
- Meat Process Worker p220

Further information

Meat Hygiene Service
www.food.gov.uk/enforcement/approved-premises-official-controls

The Worshipful Company of Butchers
http://butchershall.com

Qualifications and courses

There are no formal entry qualifications but employers generally look for at least 5 GCSEs/National 5s (A*–C/A–C) including English and Maths. You can enter and train in this career with qualifications at Levels 1 or 2. Previous experience of working with the public or in a customer service role is helpful as employers often seek candidates with a confident telephone manner and good keyboard skills.

You may decide to gain some of the skills required of a call centre operator full time at college prior to employment. Courses such as a LCCI Level 2 Certificate in Contact Centre Skills, the BTEC Level 3 Certificate in Contact Centre Operations, the LCCI Level 3 Certificate in Contact Centre Supervisory Skills or NVQs in Contact Centre Operations (Levels 1–4) may be useful.

City & Guilds also offer relevant qualifications such as the Level 1 Certificate for Introduction to the Contact Centre and the Levels 2 and 3 Technical Certificate in Contact Centre Operations. Apprenticeships might also be a possibility.

If you wish to work in more specialist call centres, such as an IT support helpline, you should be willing to work towards certain qualifications such as a computer maintenance award.

Once you have secured employment in a call centre, you may wish to undertake further study to enhance your career progression prospects. City & Guilds provide an Award, Certificate and Diploma in Contact Centre Operations (Levels 1–4) and a Level 2 Sales and Telesales Intermediate Apprenticeship.

What the work involves

You will be dealing with customers over the phone and using a computer to log details or find information. You might do telesales or telemarketing, selling, mail ordering, banking, or promoting goods and services, which could involve 'cold calling'.

You could be doing market research, asking about people's buying habits or what services they would like from a company.

You might be providing a service – receiving calls from customers who are ordering goods, making a complaint or accessing their bank accounts.

Type of person suited to this work

You should have good spoken English, with a clear voice and good hearing. You will need excellent customer service skills and you must be polite and calm when dealing with difficult callers.

For telesales or telemarketing, you will need to be motivated, persuasive and persistent. Good IT skills are also important.

You will probably work to targets and you are likely to be very busy, so you must be comfortable working under pressure and using your initiative. The ability to work successfully as part of a team is also required.

Working conditions

You will be office based, usually working about 40 hours a week. You might work shifts which could include nights, weekends and evenings.

Call centre staff have their own workstations with a headset and computer and work as part of a team.

You will be given targets which you are expected to meet. For this reason, calls are often monitored by supervisors and staff turnover can be fairly high.

Future prospects

There has been a huge growth in call centres recently as more services are available over the phone – such as mail order and banking – and more companies are using telesales and marketing to sell their goods and services.

You could become a team leader or supervisor.

You could also work abroad or establish new contact centres.

Advantages/disadvantages

There are lots of job opportunities and flexible working hours are possible.

You could utilise your customer service and sales skills to move into related areas such as marketing or human resources.

Trying to reach sales targets can be stressful and the work can be repetitive.

Money guide

Earnings vary with employers and financial services call centres tend to pay the highest wages.

Starting salaries for call centre operators range from £13,000 to £16,000.

A team leader is likely to receive £19,000–£24,000 a year.

Those employed in a managerial role usually earn in excess of £25,000.

If you meet your targets you may receive commission on sales or bonuses which will increase your income.

Related opportunities

- Customer Services Assistant/Manager p468
- Marketing Assistant/Executive p394
- Sales/Retail Assistant p480

Further information

Institute of Customer Service
www.instituteofcustomerservice.com

Institute of Direct and Digital Marketing
www.theidm.com

RETAIL, SALES AND CUSTOMER SERVICES

Qualifications and courses

Assistant

You can enter this profession without any formal qualifications. However, certain employers look for at least 3 GCSEs/National 5s (A*–C/A–C), including Maths and English. Progression to a senior role might be faster with A levels/H grades.

The most important entry requirement is to have strong people skills and experience of dealing with customers, either face to face or over the phone.

You could improve your chances of employment by taking a college course such as a BTEC Award in Customer Service (Levels 1–3) or a BTEC Award in Principles of Customer Service (Levels 1–3). NVQs are available in Customer Service (Levels 1–3) and Contact Centre Operations (Level 4). If you wish to specialise in the customer service of a specific industry, you could take the BTEC Level 2 Award in Cultural Awareness for Customer Service in Hospitality, Leisure, Travel and Tourism.

Once you secure employment, you will be trained in company procedures and customer service standards. Your employer may even encourage you to work towards NVQs.

Manager

A degree or Foundation degree can increase your chances of direct entry into a managerial position. Relevant degree subjects such as business studies, marketing or management studies may increase your chances of employment. Competition amongst graduates is high so a history of working closely with customers may give you an advantage when seeking work or training schemes.

However, many entrants start as a customer services assistant and progress to a role as manager, obtaining qualifications while they work. The Institute of Customer Service offers a training course in Service Management.

What the work involves

Assistant

You will be liaising with customers, either face to face or by phone and email, in order to sell products and services such as retail goods, insurance or holiday packages. You could be responsible for dealing with customer enquiries, problems or complaints.

Manager

Your role will include hiring and training customer services assistants. You will need to establish targets and implement different motivational techniques to ensure that staff reach them.

Type of person suited to this work

Assistant

You need to have good people skills and to be polite and helpful. You must remain calm and patient when faced with difficult customers. You should be able to work well as part of a team and independently.

Manager

A manager needs to have excellent leadership skills and to be able to motivate his or her team. Managers must also be organised, decisive and able to work under pressure.

Working conditions

You will typically work a 37-hour week, although this could be on a rota system that includes early mornings, evenings or weekends. If your company provides 24-hour assistance, you might have to work nights. There is also the opportunity to work part time.

You could spend the majority of your time dealing with customers face to face, or at a desk with a computer or telephone headset.

Future prospects

Vacancies are available throughout the UK, especially in big cities and towns. You could work in shops, call centres, banks, airports or tourist information centres.

Assistant

After gaining experience and further qualifications, you could progress into a role as team leader, supervisor and then manager.

Manager

You could move into a head office role or take a job with a higher salary and responsibility. You can go on to train staff or take further qualifications and work as a staff assessor.

Advantages/disadvantages

Difficult customers or problems can make the work stressful.

This job can be repetitive.

There are good prospects for promotion within this sector.

Money guide

Opportunities for bonuses or commission will increase your income.

Assistant

Starting salaries are about £12,500–£14,000.

With experience, you could earn £16,000–£19,000 a year.

Manager

Starting salaries for trainees are £19,000–£25,000.

With experience, this can rise to £30,000.

Senior managers can achieve up to £60,000.

Related opportunities

- Receptionist p46
- Retail Manager p478

Further information

Institute of Customer Service
www.instituteofcustomerservice.com

FISHMONGER

Qualifications and courses

You do not need any formal qualifications to enter this industry. However, most employers will expect a good standard of general education including English and maths. The Apprenticeship in Retail offers an ideal route into this career and is available at both Intermediate and Advanced Levels. Competition for places is fierce so good GCSEs/National 5s (A*–C/A–C) would be beneficial.

You will normally begin at counter assistant level and train on the job. Whilst working you will need to attain your basic food hygiene certification, followed by Hazard Analysis and Critical Control Point (HACCP) training.

It may be useful to work towards the City & Guilds Award in Retail Knowledge (Levels 1–3) or the Certificate or Diploma in Retail Skills at Level 3. These qualifications have a wide selection of optional units so you can choose to specialise in relevant areas.

The Billingsgate Seafood Training School offers 1-day courses on topics such as Get into Fishmongering, Fish Trade Knife Skills and Understanding Seafood Sustainability. The City & Guilds Seafood Profile of Achievement is a 2-day course which equips candidates with skills in cutting, displays, selling techniques and quality assessment.

What the work involves

Fishmongers prepare and sell fish, offering advice to customers on how to store and cook it. They can work in various environments including shops, supermarkets and market stalls.

You will be required to provide customers with information such as how the fish was caught, the sustainability of its stock and whether it has been previously frozen.

You will buy fish from the wholesaler and prepare it for retail sales. This preparation includes removing bones, skin and scales then gutting the fish and maybe cutting it into portions.

Type of person suited to this work

You will require good hand–eye coordination as you will be using sharp knives to complete detailed jobs such as filleting and taking out small bones. You will have to carry out messy tasks such as cleaning and gutting fish.

You should be able to stand for long periods of time. You need a strong level of personal hygiene and an awareness of food safety procedures.

You will need to be personable as customer service is extremely important for this role.

Working conditions

The conditions in this industry can be cold and wet. You will be expected to spend a great deal of time on your feet, moving between the counter and storage areas.

Most fishmongers work for approximately 40 hours a week. Your working week will usually include Saturdays, with a day off during the week to compensate.

You will frequently have to work early mornings to sign for stock deliveries.

Protective clothing and footwear are required. If you suffer from skin allergies then this work may not be suitable for you.

Future prospects

Fishmongers work in many different environments including supermarkets, small local stores and mobile fish units so you may choose to move between them.

You may have the opportunity to work overseas.

Other possibilities for progression might involve supplying fishmonger stores with fresh fish or moving into other industries which require food preparation, for example working with meat.

You can also work your way up to a management position or open your own shop.

Advantages/disadvantages

You will have to work early mornings.

You will have the opportunity to be creative, both in the preparation of the fish and in providing customers with advice on how best to prepare or cook it.

Spending all day on your feet and in cold temperatures can be uncomfortable.

Money guide

Pay rates vary depending on location and employer.

Fishmongers usually have a starting salary of £11,000–£14,000.

With experience in the role, earnings increase to about £20,000 a year.

Fishmongers who are self-employed and own a shop are likely to have a higher income.

Related opportunities

- Butcher p466
- Kitchen Assistant/Supervisor p133
- Shopkeeper p482

Further information

Sea Fish Industry Authority
www.seafish.org

469

Qualifications and courses

There are no specific academic qualifications for this career. Candidates can either find work and train on the job or study at college prior to securing employment. Those seeking work in a florist shop should demonstrate an interest in floristry, possibly through joining a local flower arranging club or doing a course in flower arranging.

Available qualifications include the BTEC Certificate in Floristry (Levels 2–3) and the City & Guilds Diploma in Floristry (Levels 2–3). Those who are currently working at a florist shop could study for the City & Guilds Diploma in Work-based Floristry (Levels 2–3). The entry requirements for these courses vary, however GCSEs/National 5s (A*–C/A–C) in subjects such as English, Maths and Art would be beneficial. Any other relevant experience and skills might be taken into account so work experience in a florist shop would be valuable.

Another option is the Apprenticeship in Floristry which is available at both Intermediate and Advanced Levels. With experience, you could work towards an NPTC Level 4 Higher Diploma in Floristry (HDF), an NPTC Master Diploma in Professional Floristry (MDPF) or an NVQ Level 4 in Floristry Business Management. Foundation degrees and degrees in floristry are also a possibility. If you are working in floristry at management level you can take the City & Guilds Higher Diploma in Professional Floristry (Levels 4–5).

What the work involves

Florists combine creativity with knowledge of plants and flowers to design and create floral displays that are then sold in shops and/or on market stalls.

You will be responsible for ordering and caring for the plants and flowers, aiding customers in choosing flowers suitable for specific occasions and creating floral displays. You may also be required to deliver flowers to customers and set up displays at events.

You will be expected to handle money, complete regular stocktakes and help with the day to day running of the business.

Type of person suited to this work

You will need to be extremely creative, with an understanding of shape, colour and design. As a great deal of this job is hands-on, you must be dexterous.

A strong knowledge of plants and flowers and the care required for them is essential, along with a desire to expand your knowledge. You should be patient, with good customer service skills and sensitivity to the needs of the client.

You will be expected to have brilliant telephone communication skills and the ability to work within tight deadlines, particularly if you have to fulfil last-minute or online orders. Administration and sales skills are also important.

Working conditions

Florists usually work inside in a shop environment. Those who work on a floristry stall will spend most of their time outdoors. This job involves a great deal of standing at the work bench/counter.

Working hours usually vary between 35 and 40 hours per week, and shop opening hours are normally 9am to 5pm. Some travel may be required when making deliveries so a driving licence might be needed.

Some shops provide uniforms or aprons. This job will not be suitable for people who suffer from pollen allergies.

Future prospects

Those with experience may progress to a managerial role. Once you have the required skills, there is also the possibility of becoming self-employed and opening your own business.

Another progression option is to work as a freelance florist for a variety of businesses on a contract basis.

You could also teach floristry or become a professional demonstrator.

Advantages/disadvantages

You can combine creativity, skill and knowledge to create floral displays.

You will be on your feet for a great deal of time and those who work on florist market stalls will be outdoors in all weathers.

Every day will be different as you will work with a wide range of customers for a variety of events.

Money guide

Earnings vary depending on location and employer.

At the start of their career, a florist usually receives the National Minimum Wage. As you gain experience, you can expect your salary to increase to £16,000–£18,000 a year.

Those employed in a managerial role can achieve up to £25,000.

Related opportunities

- Gardener/Garden Designer p253
- Landscaper/Landscape Manager p259
- Visual Merchandiser p177

Further information

British Florist Association
www.britishfloristassociation.org

Flowers & Plants Association
www.flowersandplantsassociation.org.uk

IMAGE CONSULTANT

Qualifications and courses

While there are no set academic qualifications for this career, related experience in areas such as fashion, hair, beauty, retail, consultancy, sales and marketing or public relations is useful.

The City & Guilds Level 2 Diploma in Beauty Consultancy or the BTEC Level 2 Certificate in Retail Beauty Therapy may be a good starting point. Some entrants hold a Foundation degree, HND or degree in a subject such as beauty therapy, cosmetic sciences, business studies or sales and marketing. For HND courses you will need at least 4 GCSEs/National 5s (A*–C/A–C) and for degree entry you are required to have at least 2 A levels/3 H grades and 5 GCSEs/National 5s (A*–C/A–C).

Entrants to this profession are recommended to take a course in image consultancy approved by the Federation of Image Professionals International (FIPI). Courses involve training in the 4 core areas of image consultancy: colour analysis, women's style, men's style and cosmetic application and tuition. Upon completion of this training, you can become a Registered Affiliate of FIPI.

To improve your skills and marketability, you could work towards the FIPI/City & Guilds Masters Certification Award in Image Consultancy. You are eligible to become a Master of FIPI once you hold this qualification. You could enhance your skills throughout your career by attending seminars and workshops also offered by the FIPI.

What the work involves

You will advise individuals and companies on branding, impact and appearance. This can include style analysis, make-up advice, wardrobe management and personal shopping. Part of your job might involve speaking on the radio as a way of promoting your business.

When working with private clients you will discuss fabrics, styles, patterns and colours that will suit your client's body shape, hair and eye colour and skin tone.

When working with corporate clients you may advise on body language, etiquette, first impressions and branding. You could also coach executives and run workshops.

Type of person suited to this work

You must be aware of current fashion trends, possess a good sense of style and a great eye for colour and detail. Creativity and communication skills are essential in order to inspire clients to believe in their image. You want clients to trust you so you should be easy to talk to, uplifting and sensitive.

Self-motivation is important when running your own business. You should be able to budget well and to organise your time effectively.

The ability to network and market your brand is essential.

Working conditions

You can choose to work from home or out of a studio. Your hours will vary depending on how many clients you see and could include evenings and weekends.

You will need to travel at times to a client's home or company so a driving licence would be useful.

You should dress smartly when meeting clients.

Future prospects

You could be an independent image consultant or work for an organisation such as First Impressions who will provide you with business support. As a result of the rise in technology, many image consultants are also moving into online consultancy, offering highly personalised shopping experiences to customers on the internet.

With experience, you can progress from working solely with private clients to setting up your own image consultancy business or moving into corporate work. Developing a good reputation is key to a thriving business.

You might specialise in one area, such as working with brides, or, if one area of your job particularly interests you, you could move into life coaching, retail or hairdressing. Opportunities to work abroad are also available.

Advantages/disadvantages

It is rewarding to help clients with low self-esteem gain confidence in their personal or professional brand.

The job can be glamorous as you may work with well-known people.

Setting up your own business and building up a client base can be difficult.

You might need to supplement your income when first starting out.

Money guide

Whilst establishing your business, you could earn between £10,000 and £14,000 per year. Starting salaries for in-store stylists are around £19,000.

With experience and a regular client base, you may earn up to £30,000.

If you work in the corporate sector you could earn in excess of £40,000.

As most image consultants are self-employed, your income will depend on your location, skills and how well you market yourself.

Related opportunities

- Beauty Consultant p442
- Fashion Designer/Milliner p161
- Make-up Artist p428

Further information

Federation of Image Professionals International
www.fipigroup.com

Hairdressing and Beauty Industry Authority
www.habia.org

People 1st
www.people1st.co.uk/retail-apprenticeships

JEWELLER

Qualifications and courses

Although there are no specific entry requirements, many employers will expect GCSEs/National 5s (A*–C/A–C), in subjects including English, Maths, and Art or Design and Technology. Previous work experience in a retail or customer services role would also be beneficial, as is a background in metalwork.

Candidates looking to take relevant qualifications should consider studying for a City & Guilds Award or Certificate in Retail Knowledge (Levels 1–3), the City & Guilds Award in Retail Skills (Levels 1–2) or the City & Guilds Level 3 Diploma in Retail (Sales Professional) full time at college.

Alternatively, you could work towards any one of these awards whilst completing an Apprenticeship in Retail, available at both Intermediate and Advanced Levels. Here you will be trained on the job by experienced professionals in the relevant skills required of a retail jeweller whilst attending a series of day or block release instruction at a college or training centre.

Alongside working towards qualifications offered by City & Guilds, your employer may also encourage you to gain awards run by the the National Association of Goldsmiths (NAG). The Professional Jewellers' Diploma (JET 1–2), an 18-month course which covers topics such as design, manufacture, hallmarking, gemstones, silverware, horology, antiques, legal matters, repair handling, selling techniques and window displays, is available. NAG also runs short courses in valuation and window displays.

Senior staff, managers and business owners may wish to extend their knowledge by studying for the NAG Business Development Diploma (JET Pro) further on in their career.

What the work involves

Retail jewellers work in shops, selling jewellery and sometimes watches, clocks and silverware to customers. Other services they offer might include valuation, alteration and repair.

You will advise customers on the available products and help them to choose an appropriate item. You will package the customer's goods and process their payment.

As part of the day-to-day running of the shop, you will arrange window displays, ensure that the shop is presentable and carry out stock control procedures.

You may work for a company which specialises in selling a particular gemstone, such as diamonds. You could focus on one area, for example casting or enamelling, or learn a variety of techniques.

Type of person suited to this work

An interest in precious metal, gemstones, jewellery or fashion is essential.

As you will be interacting with customers, you need excellent communication skills, with a polite and friendly manner. You should be comfortable working independently and as part of a team.

You must be extremely trustworthy and conscious of security procedures when handling valuable goods. Numeracy skills are important for processing payments and dealing with money.

If your role involves carrying out repairs or alterations, you should have practical skills, patience and good attention to detail.

Working conditions

Retail jewellers work indoors in shops and spend the majority of the day standing up.

You will work 37 to 40 hours per week including weekends. Sometimes you may be required to work overtime during evenings and bank holidays. Part-time work is often available.

You will be expected to look smart and some stores may provide a uniform.

Future prospects

There are opportunities to work for independent jewellers or large high street chains. You could progress to become a supervisor, assistant manager or even a manager.

Specialist skills can improve your prospects, so learning how to value or alter items may lead to higher paid roles.

With extensive experience, you could open your own jewellery shop or enter into gemmology or jewellery design.

Advantages/disadvantages

You will have the opportunity to meet a wide range of people and help them choose jewellery for special occasions.

Working on your feet all day can be demanding and tiring.

Money guide

Your starting salary is likely to be around £16,000 a year.

Working within a luxury retail jewellers will increase your salary to £26,000.

Senior staff and managers can earn between £30,000 and £35,000.

Your income will be significantly higher if you earn commission for your sales.

Related opportunities

- Gold/Silversmith/Engraver p164
- Jewellery Designer p168
- Sales/Retail Assistant p480

Further information

National Association of Jewellers
www.naj.co.uk

The Goldsmiths' Company
www.thegoldsmiths.co.uk

Qualifications and courses

There are no formal entry requirements but you will need to have basic maths and English skills. Your personality and ability as a salesperson are the most important attributes required of a market trader. Any previous experience working in a retail or customer service role would be highly beneficial.

Most of the training is done on the job, learning from more experienced market traders. As markets have their own culture, and often their own language, it's beneficial to learn directly from an established trader.

There are some short courses you can take, usually run by the local authority. The National Market Traders Federation (NMTF) runs courses such as the NMTF First, an introductory course that covers writing business plans, forecasting budgets and marketing tips on pricing, presentation and sales promotions.

Apprenticeships run by NMTF, The Source and the National Skills Academy for Retail are also available.

To become a market trader you must be 17 or 18 years old and you are likely to need a driving licence, a vehicle/van and public liability insurance. The NMTF can provide appropriate insurance. You will also need to apply for a market licence and a pitch from your local authority. Competition for pitches can be strong so you may have to start your career by helping out on other stalls or working part-time as a casual trader, arriving early and queuing for an available pitch, before securing a regular stall.

What the work involves

Market traders buy goods from a wholesaler or manufacturer and then sell them from a market stall which they rent in an open-air or covered market. Alternatively, you might sell things you have made yourself at specialist craft markets.

You will be dealing with customers, encouraging them to buy items on your stall, weighing and wrapping goods, and taking cash and possibly credit and debit payments.

As well as setting up the stall in the morning, arranging your things and keeping the stall clean and tidy, you will also pack up and clear away in the evenings.

Type of person suited to this work

You will need to be friendly, outgoing and enjoy working with the public in an informal way, persuading them to buy your goods.

Market traders have to be fit and active to transport their goods, be on their feet all day and then pack up when the market closes.

When you are buying goods, you need to know what will sell and negotiate a good price. If you make your own products, you should be creative and able to produce attractive items.

You must have good numeracy and business skills for dealing with money and, if you are self-employed, doing your accounts. You should also be self-motivated and hardworking.

Working conditions

You will probably have a very early start and work from about 5am to 6pm. You will usually work Saturdays and often Sundays.

You could work on your own or with a few other people. You might work at the same market every day or move round to several different markets during the week. You will work outdoors in all weather conditions.

You might have to travel to a wholesale supplier to buy your goods and transport them to your stall so a driving licence is essential.

Future prospects

It can be hard to do well with a market stall: there is a lot of competition and you will need good products.

At craft markets, it can be difficult to sell things at a competitive price.

Most market traders are self-employed and you could expand by taking on staff to run extra stalls or opening a shop.

Advantages/disadvantages

You will be your own boss, working outside in an active, practical job with lots of contact with the public.

The hours can be long and strenuous.

Your earnings are entirely dependent on market trends and being able to anticipate them which can make for an unstable income.

Money guide

When starting your career as an employee on a market stall, you are likely to earn the National Minimum Wage.

As an experienced market trader your earnings can range from £15,000 up to £26,000 a year.

Market traders who sell specialist goods tend to have a higher income and the most successful traders can achieve £30,000–£50,000 a year.

You will be required to pay for your stall rent, stock and vehicle out of your income. However, as a trader with less than 12 months experience you can apply through the NMTF for a Start-Up Loan of £5,400.

Related opportunities

- Customer Services Assistant/Manager p468
- Sales/Retail Assistant p480
- Shopkeeper p482

Further information

British Independent Retailers Association
www.bira.co.uk

National Market Traders Federation
www.nmtf.co.uk

RETAIL, SALES AND CUSTOMER SERVICES

Qualifications and courses

To qualify as an official meat inspector, you are required to hold the Royal Society for Public Health (RSPH)'s Level 2 Certificate for Proficiency in Poultry Meat Inspection and the Level 4 Diploma for Proficiency in Meat Inspection. For entry to these qualifications you will need to have at least 5 GCSEs/National 5s (A*–C/A–C) including English and either Maths or a science and a proven history of working in the meat industry. In order to complete the RSPH courses, you need access to practical work placements.

An NVQ in Proficiency in Meat and Poultry Industry Skills course (Levels 2–3) is available and can equip you with relevant skills and knowledge for this profession.

The RSPH also provides a Level 3 Award in Food Safety Supervision for Manufacturing and a Level 4 Award in Food Safety Management for Manufacturing.

The Apprenticeship in Food and Drink is available at Intermediate, Advanced and Higher Levels and involves both on-the-job and off-the-job training to develop the required technical and practical skills.

Once employed, you will shadow experienced inspectors whilst receiving practical training in slaughterhouses and other meat plants until fully qualified.

What the work involves

Meat hygiene inspectors visit slaughterhouses and meat stores to check that meat is being processed and produced safely and hygienically, following relevant laws and regulations.

You will check that live animals and poultry are healthy and disease free, and do post mortems on diseased carcasses. You will check that animals are cared for and transported safely, that meat plants and deliveries are run safely and hygienically, and that unwanted meat or carcasses are destroyed properly.

You will write detailed reports and make sure that any action you have recommended is carried out quickly and to the right standards.

Type of person suited to this work

You will be dealing with people in lots of different organisations and at all levels, so you will need to be able to establish good working relationships and deal with problems calmly.

You must have strong written and communication skills, good attention to detail and the ability to understand and apply laws and regulations.

It is a fairly active job so you will need to be fit and healthy, practical and good with your hands.

Working conditions

You will spend most of your time travelling to farms and processing plants so a driving licence is usually required.

You will be wearing protective clothing, using tools and equipment and handling heavy meat carcasses.

Slaughterhouses can be cold, noisy and smell strongly, and on farms you will be working outdoors in all weathers.

Meat inspectors usually work normal office hours but might need to work evenings, weekends and at short notice if there is a hygiene emergency.

Future prospects

Most meat inspectors work for the Meat Hygiene Service which is part of the government's Food Standards Agency. Others work for companies producing or selling food and meat products.

You will need experience in the industry before you can become an inspector. You can then progress to be a supervisor or manager for the Meat Hygiene Service or go into management in a large food company.

In the wake of the 2013 horse meat scandal, it has become increasingly important that inspectors are held accountable for their professional practice. A new non-statutory register has been put into place which ensures all newly qualified workers and those in the industry who volunteer to register with the new list, have their work regulated. This provides assurance to the public that inspectors are demonstrating the necessary professional conduct and undergoing continuing professional development (CPD).

Advantages/disadvantages

You need to be flexible with your working hours as you may be asked to respond to an emergency at any time.

You will feel satisfied that you are doing an important job in ensuring that food standards are met and the meat is safe for the public.

Money guide

You can expect to earn around £16,000 per year as a trainee inspector.

Once you have qualified and gained experience in the role, your salary is likely to be £20,000–£25,000.

Those employed as a senior meat inspector can earn up to £30,000.

Related opportunities

- Butcher p466
- Health and Safety Adviser p27
- Trading Standards Officer p484

Further information

Food Standards Agency
www.food.gov.uk

Meat Hygiene Service
www.food.gov.uk/enforcement/approved-premises-official-controls

MERCHANDISER

Qualifications and courses

Competition for entry to this career is fairly high so most entrants have a degree, Foundation degree or HND. Larger companies will accept degrees in any subjects, although degrees in retail management, marketing, business studies, economics, accounting or maths may improve your chances of employment. Entry requirements for a degree are usually 2 A levels/3 H grades and 5 GCSEs/National 5s (A*–C/A–C), including English and Maths.

The London College of Fashion offers a BA (Hons) degree in Fashion Buying and Merchandising or a 15-week Postgraduate Certificate in Fashion: Buying and Merchandising. The Level 5 NVQ/SVQ Diploma in Supply Chain Management and an ABC Level 4 Diploma in Buying and Merchandising for Fashion Retail are also available and may prove beneficial.

Those aged 16–24 may gain entry to a trainee post through a relevant apprenticeship, for example in purchasing and supply management. However, competition for a position would be very high and you would usually need retail experience.

Once employed, you are likely to be trained on the job starting in a more junior position whilst you work your way up. Competition for graduate training schemes and relevant vacancies is fierce however, so it is advised that you undertake work experience in order to demonstrate your interest and understanding of the industry.

Throughout your career you could work towards professional qualifications from the Chartered Institute of Purchasing and Supply (CIPS) or the Chartered Institute of Marketing (CIM).

What the work involves

You will ensure that stores are stocked with products at the right quantity and price.

You will work with retail buyers who choose different lines and then calculate the quantities of products required and the amount of money to be spent. It will be your responsibility to decide upon the selling prices of goods and any special offers.

You will put together budgets and sales targets, analyse sales trends, negotiate with suppliers and ensure that goods are displayed and presented in an attractive way that is consistent throughout the company.

Type of person suited to this work

You will need to be interested in your product and in predicting what will sell and how best to display it. Merchandisers must be creative and self-motivated, with initiative and confidence, because they make decisions involving large amounts of money and have to present their ideas to managers and staff.

You should be able to work well in a team and deal with people at all levels, for example when negotiating prices and arranging deliveries. The job involves analysing statistics and sales figures and working under pressure to meet targets and deadlines.

Working conditions

You will mainly be based in an office in a large store or in a head office, and you will probably visit other stores in your region.

You will also travel to suppliers and manufacturers, possibly staying away from home regularly. It is necessary to have a driving licence.

You will probably work normal office hours but you might have to work much longer at busy times.

Future prospects

Most opportunities are in the south-east of England and big cities such as London. There are also opportunities for work overseas given the rise in retail firms maintaining and dealing with international outlets.

You will usually start as an allocator, distributor or merchandise administrative assistant and advance to a role as an assistant merchandiser and then to merchandiser. In a large company, you could progress to a role as senior merchandiser and then possibly manager or director.

Progression depends on the talent of the individual. After gaining experience, you could become self-employed and work as a retail consultant, or you could move into a related role such as a business analyst.

Advantages/disadvantages

This job can be stressful as you will be making decisions which will directly affect the image of your company and what the public can buy.

Keeping your finger on the pulse of fashion and future trends is exciting.

Money guide

Salaries depend on the size and location of the employer, and are typically higher in high street chains.

Starting salaries for assistant merchandisers are around £18,000. Junior merchandisers can earn between £22,000 and £25,000.

With experience, your earnings can increase up to £40,000.

A senior merchandiser is likely to receive a salary of £45,000 to £60,000.

Those employed in the most senior positions can achieve up to £85,000.

Related opportunities

- Purchasing/Procurement Manager p603
- Retail Buyer p477
- Retail Manager p478

Further information

British Independent Retailers Association
www.bira.co.uk

Chartered Institute of Marketing
www.cim.co.uk

475

POST OFFICE CLERK

Qualifications and courses

There are no set requirements for this role but you will normally have to complete an aptitude test prior to entry so GCSEs/National 5s (A*–E/A–E), particularly in English and Maths, may be useful. An aptitude for languages may also be beneficial.

Most people enter directly into employment with training completed on the job. As a trainee, you will need to complete 2 weeks in a training centre followed by 2 further weeks being supervised at a counter and be instructed in areas such as customer care and the Post Office computer system.

Any experience of working in a customer service industry would be particularly advantageous, as would experience of handling money. This experience might involve working in a shop as a sales assistant, working in a restaurant as a waiter/waitress or maybe as an assistant in a launderette.

Your employer may encourage you to work towards further qualifications such as NVQs/SVQs in Customer Service (Levels 1–3) in order to develop your communication skills, ability to promote and sell products and your understanding of customer needs throughout your career.

What the work involves

Post Office clerks provide customers with a variety of postal services along with banking services, bill payment, lottery sales, passport applications and offering advice to customers on these services.

Tasks you will complete on a daily basis include sending important and expensive mail, selling stamps, weighing, measuring and mailing letters and parcels and dispatching mail abroad.

You might also be required to complete administrative work such as keeping accounts.

Type of person suited to this work

A Post Office clerk should be able to work within a team and without supervision. You should have excellent communication skills, being both polite and helpful with the ability to adjust to the needs of each client.

You should have a certain level of numeracy and be able to handle money with confidence and accuracy. You will be able to cope under pressure.

You should have an interest in the numerous services you will be offering along with a willingness to learn about the various forms that clients may require information on. You should have a keen eye for detail and the ability to sustain concentration.

Working conditions

If you work for a sub-Post Office you might be working in a newsagent, stationer or village shop, for example WH Smith has opened franchise Post Offices in many of its high street stores.

You will be working mainly at a counter but could also do some behind-the-scenes work in an office environment. You may be required to wear a uniform. The job will probably involve some lifting of heavy parcels.

You will usually work 35 hours per week, Monday to Friday and occasionally Saturday mornings. Part-time and flexible working hours may be arranged.

Future prospects

The Post Office is currently in a state of transformation, with some branches being partnered with high street retailers. There is a fear that there will be a loss of jobs, although this has not yet been confirmed.

Once employed, you could progress to the role of postmaster or training officer.

Experienced Post Office clerks may have the opportunity to work on the Post Office helpline. Within this role you would answer any queries customers or sub-postmasters/mistresses had regarding the products and services that the Post Office offers.

The skills you acquire in this role stand you in good stead to move on to careers within other industries such as banking.

Advantages/disadvantages

You may, at times, find this role stressful particularly when the post office is especially busy.

You might be able to work flexible hours which suit you.

There may be some heavy lifting involved.

Money guide

The rate of pay will vary depending on the location and the employer.

Post Office clerks generally start on a salary of around £15,000. After experience this may increase to £16,500 a year.

A promotion to the role of postmaster or training officer would result in a pay increase. Post Office managers can earn around £24,000.

Related opportunities

- Accounting Technician and Accounts/Finance Clerk p4
- Bank Cashier/Customer Adviser p9
- Customer Services Assistant/Manager p468

Further information

People 1st
www.people1st.co.uk/retail-apprenticeships

Post Office
http://corporate.postoffice.co.uk/careers

Royal Mail Group
www.royalmailgroup.com

Qualifications and courses

Entry is usually with a degree, though an HND or equivalent may also be considered. Relevant degree subjects including business, management, purchasing, logistics and marketing may increase your chances of employment. The minimum entry requirements for a degree course are normally 2 A levels/3 H grades or equivalent.

Although degree subjects are generally non-specific, entry into fashion retail does require a relevant qualification in fashion buying. It is possible to take a 2-year Foundation degree in Fashion Buying and Merchandising at The London College of Fashion. If you attain a Merit or above you will be eligible to undertake a further year of study, and graduate with a BA (Hons) in Fashion Buying and Merchandising.

Some companies offer their own graduate training schemes, but entry is highly competitive. Gaining work experience within the retail industry is invaluable in supporting your applications.

Once employed, you could enhance your career progression by studying for a professional qualification offered by the Chartered Institute of Purchasing & Supply (CIPS). CIPS offers a Certificate and Advanced Certificate for people employed in purchasing at a clerical level. CIPS-accredited degrees in purchasing or business are available at some institutions.

Other relevant qualifications also include a Level 5 NVQ/SVQ in Supply Chain Management or the Level 4 Diploma in Buying and Merchandising for Fashion Retail.

When you reach junior management levels you may be encouraged by your employer to take the CIPS Diploma in Procurement and Supply. CIPS Advanced and Professional Diplomas are available for individuals at more senior levels of management.

What the work involves

You will probably work in the merchandising and marketing team of a large retail company, looking for products which fit the company image and will appeal to its customers. You will be responsible for reviewing current stock and sourcing new stock to ensure the products sold by your company remain competitive.

You will visit manufacturers and suppliers to negotiate prices and decide on quantities and colours. You will also check on the quality of the products.

You will help to predict and set trends. This could involve analysing sales figures and researching competitors to see what customers are buying and why.

Type of person suited to this work

You will need to be confident and decisive because you will be dealing with large budgets. You will need to be assertive with good communication skills to negotiate prices and make presentations to staff.

Numerical skills are important as you will need to be able to analyse figures and use them to set prices and targets and check stock levels.

You should be creative, well organised and good at planning ahead, and have an eye for detail.

Working conditions

You will be office based but spend a lot of time visiting suppliers and manufacturers in this country and abroad, so will probably have to spend time away from home.

You will work standard hours but will need to work late at busy times and to meet deadlines.

Future prospects

There are job opportunities all over the country but most will be in London and the south-east of England. Typical employers include high street stores, online sellers, supermarkets and niche retailers.

In a small company there may not be much chance of promotion, but in a larger company prospects are good. You would normally begin as a buyer's assistant before progressing to junior buyer, assistant buyer, senior retail buyer, trading manager and buying controller.

It is possible to work as a buyer in other areas, including manufacturing, the civil service and local government.

Alternatively, you could set up your own retail outlet.

Advantages/disadvantages

This can be an exciting job and the decisions you make will affect what the public can buy and the image of the stores.

You will have a lot of responsibility and tight deadlines which can be very stressful.

Money guide

Junior retail buyers typically earn between £16,000 and £24,000 a year.

Experienced buyers can earn between £35,000 and £40,000 a year.

Senior buyers can earn between £50,000 and £70,000, more if working for large organisations with multiple retail outlets.

Salaries will vary depending on the size and location of the company you work for and your buying specialism.

Related opportunities

- Marketing Assistant/Executive p394
- Purchasing/Procurement Manager p603
- Retail Manager p478

Further information

British Independent Retailers Association
www.bira.co.uk

Chartered Institute of Marketing
www.cim.co.uk

Chartered Institute of Purchasing & Supply
www.cips.org

RETAIL, SALES AND CUSTOMER SERVICES

477

Qualifications and courses

There are no set requirements in order to become a retail manager but many stores will require candidates to have at least 5 GCSEs/National 5s (A*–C/A–C), including Maths and English. Previous experience of working in a retail or customer service role, be that through paid employment or work experience, is highly beneficial and usually favoured above formal academic qualifications. Experience of stock management, pricing, merchandising and finance will ensure your application stands out.

You may however opt to pursue an Edexcel BTEC Certificate in Retail or a Foundation degree, degree or postgraduate qualification in retail management, marketing, business studies or accounting and finance in order to develop your skills and knowledge of the industry. If you are planning to work within a specialist field, such as a builders' merchant, a qualification in a subject relevant to that retailer may give you an advantage in securing employment.

Advanced Apprenticeships in Retail Management may also be available. As an apprentice you are likely to experience a combination of on-the-job training and day or block release college instruction where you will work towards gaining qualifications such as the Level 3 NVQ in Retail Skills (Management), BTEC Retail qualifications (Levels 2–3) or the Level 5 NVQ Work-based Diploma in Supply Chain Operations.

Many retailers offer graduate trainee management schemes and if you have a suitable degree you could pursue this fast-track option, although competition is fierce. Here you will experience in-house training, work shadowing and supplementary courses. Your employer may even encourage you to gain further professional qualifications.

What the work involves

Unlike a shopkeeper who owns the store and deals with manufacturers, you will be running the shop on a day-to-day basis. This could be a small or a large department store, chain, independent store or a supermarket. Managers recruit, train and supervise staff, encouraging them to develop their skills and meet targets.

You will monitor sales looking at ways of improving them and oversee supplies by checking stock, placing orders and making sure you do not run out or over-order.

The store manager has overall responsibility for everything that happens in the shop and must deal with any problems or complaints.

Type of person suited to this work

As you could be dealing with customers and complaints you will need excellent negotiation skills. You will also need to motivate, train and sometimes discipline staff.

You should be energetic, able to take responsibility and make quick decisions. You will need an understanding of business and of relevant laws.

You should be able to analyse sales figures and have creative ideas for selling and promoting goods to improve profits. You will have to be organised whilst working to targets and deadlines.

Working conditions

Many stores are open long hours, at weekends and overnight, so you will probably have to work shifts, usually over 5 days.

You will be on your feet a lot as well as doing administration and paperwork. You may be based in one store, or be visiting several that you have responsibility for.

Future prospects

The retail sector employs a total of 2.9 million people and is the largest private employment sector in the UK. By 2017 this is projected to rise to 3.3 million, and many of these new posts will be at managerial levels. Consequently, there will be a high number of opportunities for skilled graduates looking to enter the industry at manager level.

With a large retail chain your prospects can be good and you can quickly take on more responsibilities. You could move into other areas of the company, for example, marketing or buying and might be able to work abroad. With experience, regional management is also possible.

You could work for yourself, but will need money to start up your own store.

Advantages/disadvantages

Retail is an expanding, developing business and can offer you an exciting career with good promotion prospects.

You will have a lot of responsibility quite early in your career.

Working with the public can be demanding and stressful.

Money guide

The typical starting salary ranges between £21,000 and £28,000 but depends largely on the organisation in which you work.

With experience, this can rise to between £34,000 and £60,000.

A salary in excess of £70,000 is possible in large retailers and supermarkets.

You are likely to be offered discounts, commission and bonuses related to sales.

Related opportunities

- Distribution Manager p591
- Merchandiser p475
- Retail Buyer p477

Further information

British Independent Retailers Association
www.bira.co.uk

Chartered Institute of Purchasing & Supply
www.cips.org

Qualifications and courses

There are no specific entry requirements but if you choose to work in pharmaceutical or engineering sales, a relevant degree is likely to be required. However, employers are often more interested in your sales and communication skills rather than any formal academic qualifications.

You may be able to become a sales representative by working your way up from an administrative position in a sales office, though additional experience of retail or customer service will be beneficial if you opt to take this route.

Alternatively, before entering employment you may find it useful to complete a qualification from a professional body such as the Institute of Sales and Marketing Management (ISMM) which offers qualifications in both Sales Skills and Sales/Marketing (Levels 1–6). The Managing and Marketing Sales Association (MAMSA) offers a Standard Diploma in Salesmanship, a Certificate in Sales Marketing, an Intermediate Diploma in Selling and an Advanced Diploma in Sales Management. The Chartered Institute of Marketing (CIM) offers a number of sales orientated courses including a 3 day Sales Bootcamp.

Alongside these qualifications NVQs/SVQs in Sales are also available at Levels 2–4, which you may be able to study as part of an apprenticeship scheme. Other relevant courses include the LCCI Level 3 Certificate in Selling and Sales Management and the BTEC Level 3 Certificate in Principles of Sales.

You may find a full driving licence is essential for most positions.

What the work involves

You will be responsible for selling your company's products or services to existing clients and creating relationships with new clients.

You will most likely specialise in a particular market, such as pharmaceuticals, medical equipment, engineering or consumer goods.

Your responsibilities will include meeting with customers and maintaining good relationships with them, promoting new products, meeting sales targets and reporting sales trends.

You will be in charge of agreeing sales, organising the delivery and signing of contracts as well as checking payments have been made. You will also be responsible for providing after-care sales service by recording orders, advising customers about delivery schedules and receiving feedback.

Type of person suited to this work

You must have good people skills as much of your success will depend on how you interact with customers and your ability to maintain relationships with them.

Excellent communication and negotiation skills are essential, as are organisational and time management skills as much of your work will be self-motivated.

You must have the ability to gain and maintain an in-depth knowledge of the product you are selling and the markets you are selling to.

Working conditions

You will most likely be working for a large company.

As much of your work will involve meeting with customers, you may be able to choose your hours to a certain extent, as long as you are meeting sales targets.

You will usually be responsible for sales in a geographic area, and will spend a lot of time driving to meet customers in that area.

You may have to put in long hours, depending on your appointment schedule and travel time. When not in transit, you could be based in an office or at home.

Future prospects

Opportunities are available throughout the UK as the work is often based on a geographical area.

With experience and success, you could be promoted to sales team leader or a national sales manager.

You could also be headhunted from one company or region to another.

Advantages/disadvantages

Your job will vary from day to day, and you will be constantly interacting with people.

Your performance will be tangibly rewarded through commission bonuses.

You will spend a lot of time travelling which can be lonely and increase the time you spend away from home.

Money guide

You will often earn a basic salary plus commission, which will be based on meeting and exceeding targets.

You could start at around £15,000–£20,000 per year plus commission.

This can rise to between £35,000 and £50,000 with experience.

Top salespeople can make over £100,000 per year.

Perks may include bonus schemes or a company car.

Related opportunities

- Customer Services Assistant/Manager p468
- Recruitment/Employment Agency Consultant p47
- Retail Buyer p477
- Sales/Retail Assistant p480

Further information

Institute of Sales & Marketing Management
www.ismm.co.uk

Managing and Marketing Sales Association
www.mamsasbp.org.uk

Qualifications and courses

There are no minimum entry requirements for this work as training is provided by employers. However, larger companies may ask for 2–4 GCSEs/National 5s (A*–C/A–C), particularly in English and Maths given that communication and working with money are important aspects of the job. You may be required to pass tests in basic maths and English but retail or customer service experience is often valued above qualifications.

Many shops employ temporary staff for busy periods such as at Christmas and for sales and this can be a good way of securing work experience and/or permanent work.

You could take part in a retail apprenticeship if aged 16–24. As an apprentice, you will be trained on the job by experienced professionals whilst working towards industry recognised qualifications such as Certificates and Diplomas Levels 1 and 2 in Retail Skills offered by City & Guilds, Edexcel and OCR. The Level 3 Diploma also allows you to complete specialist modules in management, visual merchandising and sales professional. Depending on your role, you may have to complete other training such as food hygiene or health and safety.

If employed in a large company, you are likely to follow a structured in-house training scheme in order to progress.

Degrees in business or retail management are also available and can speed up entry into management roles. The general entry requirements for a degree are 2 A levels/3 H grades and 5 GCSEs/National 5s (A*–C/A–C).

What the work involves

Shops range from small specialist outlets to huge department stores, so your duties will vary. You will deal with customers, offering them a polite, helpful and speedy service and sell them a range of goods.

You will help keep the shop tidy and well stocked, answer questions, deal with complaints and give suggestions and advice.

When you are working on the till you will take payments, give change, deal with refunds, wrap goods and arrange orders and deliveries.

Type of person suited to this work

You will need to be well presented, outgoing, friendly, polite, and able to deal with awkward customers and stay calm when you are busy. Sales assistants have to learn about the things they are selling, which could involve in-house training, and they must be able to help and advise customers to find what they want.

You could be working to targets and earning bonuses according to how much you sell, so will need to be persuasive but not pushy.

You should be responsible and trustworthy, and fit and active to cope with being on your feet all day. You should be able to work within a team and on your own when required.

Working conditions

In small shops you could spend most of the time at the till/checkout. In large stores you could be working on the shop floor, helping and advising customers and fetching goods from stockrooms.

You might have to carry heavy items. You will keep the shop clean and tidy and might wear a uniform.

You could work early or late shifts and at weekends and in the evenings. There are many opportunities for part-time work.

Future prospects

There are shops in all areas of the country, though large retail parks and shopping centres have meant that some smaller shops in town centres have closed.

Working in a small shop you may get to know your regulars well and be given responsibility quite quickly, but promotion prospects can be limited.

In large stores and chains you will probably get training and can quickly become a supervisor and then move into management jobs. Depending on your employer, you might have to move around from shop to shop gaining experience within different-sized shops and departments.

With significant retail experience, some sales assistants progress to occupations such as merchandising or buying.

Advantages/disadvantages

There are lots of opportunities and you will be meeting new people.

The hours can be long and the work can be stressful if you have to reach sales targets.

The work environment is constantly changing as you will have both very busy and very quiet times.

Money guide

Wages vary a lot depending on the type and size of the shop and its location.

Salaries at entry level are around £11,000 to £15,000 per year.

As a supervisor you could earn up to £20,000.

You will get discounts and may get bonuses and commission on what you sell. You may also get more money for working shifts.

Related opportunities

- Bank Cashier/Customer Adviser p9
- Customer Services Assistant/Manager p468
- Receptionist p46

Further information

British Independent Retailers Association
www.bira.co.uk

British Retail Consortium
www.brc.org.uk

SHOE REPAIRER

Qualifications and courses

There are no minimum qualifications for this job but you should be able to take measurements, handle money and work with numbers. Some employers require entrants to take an aptitude test to assess their abilities in English, basic maths and practical skills. Experience in a retail/customer services role or any qualifications in leatherwork would also be useful.

One form of entry into a career as a shoe repairer is via an apprenticeship. As an apprentice, you will be trained on the job whilst working alongside an experienced shoe repairer. Your employer may also encourage you to work towards industry-recognised qualifications, such as the BTEC Level 2 Certificate in Apparel, Footwear, or Leather Production, the BTEC Level 3 Diploma in Apparel, Footwear, Leather or Textile Production or the NVQ Certificate in Footwear and Leather (Levels 2–3). The ABC Awards also offer a Level 2 NVQ Certificate in Footwear and Leather.

The City & Guilds Award or Certificate in Retail Knowledge (Levels 1–3) or Award, Certificate or Diploma in Retail Skills (Levels 1–3) may also be beneficial.

What the work involves

Shoe repairers mend and repair shoes and other footwear. They also repair belts, bags and briefcases using tools and materials including nail and staple guns and stitching machines. A lot of shoe repairers use specialist machinery to cut keys and do metal engraving.

You will replace soles and heels by stitching or gluing on new ones and finishing them off neatly.

You will be serving customers, labelling the shoes they leave, issuing customers with tickets, taking payments, using a till and probably selling things like shoe dyes and polishes.

Type of person suited to this work

It is important to be practical, good at working with your hands and able to do detailed work quickly and neatly. As the machinery and tools can be dangerous, you will need to be responsible, able to work safely and happy to get your hands dirty. You might be dyeing shoes so good colour vision is essential.

You should enjoy meeting people and be able to cope with working whilst customers wait for their repairs. You must be comfortable working on your own or in a small team, and be able to work out costs and deal with money and payments. You will need to have good communication skills and, if you are self-employed, business skills.

Working conditions

You will be on your feet a lot, using a range of tools, equipment, dyes and glues. The work can be smelly, noisy and dirty so you will wear overalls.

Shoe repairers usually work around 40 hours a week, including weekends.

You will typically be based in a small high street store. Some shoe repairers work in factories repairing goods which customers have returned.

Future prospects

There are around 8,000 shoe repairers in all areas of the country but job opportunities can be limited as most are small shops only employing a few people. Shoe repairers also work in small outlets in supermarkets or department stores.

You will learn at least one skill, and possibly more, so you would be equipped to open your own business. You would need some money to start up and business skills to plan your work and keep accounts.

In a large chain you could progress to management roles.

Advantages/disadvantages

You do not need qualifications and you will be doing a practical, hands-on job.

You could work for yourself, running your own shoe repair outlet.

The work can be repetitive and demands long periods of concentration as repair work can be fiddly.

Money guide

Those entering this profession can expect a starting salary of around £12,000.

With experience, your earnings could be between £13,000 and £17,000.

A shop manager is likely to receive £20,000 per year.

Many shoe repairers are self-employed so income depends upon the size, location and success of the shop.

Some employers offer a target-based bonus scheme.

Related opportunities

- Locksmith p216
- Sales/Retail Assistant p480
- Shopkeeper p482

Further information

Society of Master Shoe Repairers
www.somsr.com

SHOPKEEPER

Qualifications and courses

There are no formal academic requirements but it is essential that you have strong numeracy, business and people skills. Experience working in a customer services, sales, administrative or managerial role would be highly beneficial.

One route into this career is to undertake the Apprenticeship in Retail, which is available at both Intermediate and Advanced Levels, and then work your way up to become a shopkeeper. As an apprentice you are likely to experience a combination of on-the-job training from experienced professionals and a series of day or block release college instruction where you will work towards gaining relevant qualifications.

NVQs/SVQs in Retail Skills (Levels 1–3), the NVQ/SVQ in Customer Service (Levels 1–4) and the City & Guilds Award or Certificate in Retail Knowledge (Levels 1–3) may be available. City & Guilds also offer a Diploma in Retail Skills (Levels 1–2) and a Level 3 Diploma in Retail Skills (Management).

Once you are running your own shop, you will be responsible for ensuring your own development, therefore those who wish to study at a higher level should consider studying for a Foundation degree or degree in retail management.

Some local colleges offer evening courses in marketing and sales skills. Local training facilities also provide courses in all aspects of self-employment including starting up a business, marketing and VAT. You could consult an organisation such as the National Enterprise Network for advice.

What the work involves

A shopkeeper owns or manages one or more shops that specialise in selling a product or range of products, such as greengrocers, bakeries, newsagents, supermarkets, fishmongers, fashion retailers, jewellers and florists.

You will find manufacturers and suppliers in order to stock your shop with products. For stores that sell foodstuffs, this may mean sourcing local produce and purchasing it for the best price.

As well as keeping the shop tidy and well stocked, you will pay staff wages and keep books and accounts.

Type of person suited to this work

You need to be determined and motivated, with a real passion for the products you stock. You should be prepared to work long hours and to travel in order to find good suppliers and stock at the right price for your market.

You will need to be able to sell and market your goods and be confident about finding products that people want to buy.

Excellent communication skills are essential. Having good business sense and the ability to plan your finances and keep accounts is also important. You should be well organised and have some marketing, business and sales skills to succeed in this area of work.

Working conditions

Your hours and conditions will depend on what you are selling and how well you do.

Shops usually open at weekends and often in the evenings, with newsagents and convenience stores opening early and closing late.

Shops vary in size and appearance, and how pleasant the working environment is will depend on their staff and clientele.

You might wear a uniform and do some heavy lifting.

Future prospects

The trend towards large multi-product shops and online purchasing has meant that lots of smaller shops have been forced to close. This is a very competitive sector so you will need to find products that sell well in your chosen location and demographic.

One option is to operate a franchise, such as a local convenience store, paying a larger company to use their name and sell their products.

If you are successful, you could expand by opening more or larger stores.

Advantages/disadvantages

There is a lot of freedom and satisfaction in being your own boss: you do not have to answer to anyone else and you can make all your own decisions.

It can be a daunting prospect as success will entirely depend on your business acumen and selling abilities.

Money guide

Earnings vary significantly and depend upon your success and reputation, the size and location of the business, and the products you sell.

When you first enter this profession, you may have a relatively low salary of £13,000–£15,000.

With experience, you are likely to earn up to £30,000.

Related opportunities

- Merchandiser p475
- Retail Buyer p477
- Sales/Retail Assistant p480

Further information

British Franchise Association
www.thebfa.org

National Enterprise Network
www.nationalenterprisenetwork.org

STOCK CONTROL/REPLENISHMENT ASSISTANT

Qualifications and courses

No formal qualifications are necessary, however some employers might expect applicants to have GCSEs/National 5s (A*–E/A–E) in Maths and English. Most employers will want candidates to have solid communication skills, a can-do attitude and a basic level of numeracy in order to know how much of each item needs to be restocked.

Previous experience dealing with the public within a relevant industry such as retail would prove beneficial when applying for a post in stock control/replenishment.

One route of entry into a career as a stock control/replenishment assistant is via an apprenticeship. As an apprentice, training is typically carried out on the job by experienced professionals. Training may be in a formal, traditional manner or individually through specially designed computer programs. A number of different subjects are covered, including health and safety, company policies, customer care, pricing and stock rotation. If you decide to work with specialist products such as unwrapped food, dairy produce or meat, you will also receive further training in order to equip you with the skills necessary to replenish this kind of stock.

Whilst you train, your employer may also encourage you to work towards industry-recognised qualifications at a college or training centre. The Edexcel BTEC Award in Retail Knowledge (Levels 1–3) may be available.

What the work involves

You will work in a supermarket or retail environment refilling the shelves. You must be aware of where each product is, both for when you need to restock it and for when a customer enquires about the whereabouts of an item.

Your duties will include checking to see which goods need replacing, adding labels to products, tidying the display areas and shelves and transporting goods from the stockroom.

You may be required to order stock, take deliveries and serve customers.

Type of person suited to this work

This role involves physical activity and so you will need to have a certain level of fitness.

You will be expected, at times, to work alone and unsupervised and so you must be trustworthy. You will also spend some time working as part of a team so you will need to be comfortable working with others.

You must have an approachable and friendly disposition as you might need to advise customers. You might use a battery-hand terminal (BHT) or hand-held terminal (HHT) in order to keep track of stock or print labels and so you should be comfortable working with computerised equipment.

Working conditions

You will be working in a retail environment; your surroundings will vary depending on which area you choose to work in. Supermarkets can sometimes be cold.

You will be on your feet for most of the day; you will be lifting and transporting sometimes heavy stock.

Typical working hours are about 37 to 40 a week; you will probably be on a rota and so could be working at any time of the day or night. Part-time work and flexitime are available and you might be asked to wear a uniform.

Future prospects

Working in stock control/replenishment leaves you in a good position to move into other retail positions, such as a sales assistant or checkout operator. Your skills will be transferable to other retail environments. However, if you have not completed any qualifications progression may prove difficult.

You might be able to complete extra training whilst working which would enhance your chances of promotion.

There is a possibility, with training and/or qualifications, that you could progress into a supervisory or managerial position.

Advantages/disadvantages

You may find the physical nature of this job tiring.

You might find this role repetitive.

Your job will allow you to be active.

Money guide

These figures are only approximate and will vary depending on location and employer.

Typically the starting salary for this role will range from £10,000 to £11,500 per year. This amount could increase to approximately £15,000 with experience.

If you reach the role of supervisor you can expect to earn up to £18,000 per year.

Related opportunities

- Retail Manager p478
- Sales/Retail Assistant p480

Further information

British Independent Retailers Association
www.bira.co.uk

British Retail Consortium
www.brc.org.uk

Qualifications and courses

To become a qualified trading standards officer, you need a Diploma in Consumer Affairs and Trading Standards (DCATS) awarded by the Trading Standards Institute (TSI). You must be working for a local authority in order to achieve this.

Prior to this, you can follow a relevant degree course, such as a degree accredited by the TSI. The normal entry requirements for a degree in trading standards or consumer protection are 2 A levels/3 H grades and 5 GCSEs/National 5s (A*–C/A–C). The degree provides exemption from certain parts of the DCATS.

Graduates from an unrelated degree subject can apply to do a Graduate Diploma in Trading Standards at Manchester Metropolitan University. A 2.2 Honours degree in any subject is a minimum requirement for entry onto this course.

Non-graduates can join as an enforcement officer or consumer adviser with a local authority and follow the Accreditation of Prior and Experiential Learning route (APEL) before studying for the DCATS. The Trading Standards Institute also offers a five-level qualification framework which people in these positions can work towards. This allows trainees to combine study with paid employment, undertaking the various levels of training in accordance with your existing qualifications, experience and needs of your employer.

Throughout your career you may opt to undertake continuing professional development (CPD) offered by the TSI and run in-line with the qualification structure. You will collect evidence of your development in a portfolio of research and work completed during seminars, workshops and work shadowing.

A driving licence is recommended.

What the work involves

Trading standards officers work for local government to protect consumers. You will check that any individual or company selling products or services is keeping to the law and providing a fair service.

You will be working with a range of people and organisations. You will travel to check premises, or to follow up on a complaint from the public.

You will be enforcing the law, leading to prosecutions but also giving help and advice to companies and consumers.

Type of person suited to this work

You will be enforcing laws and regulations so will need to be able to take in and apply a lot of complex information. You must have an eye for detail and make sure the reports you write are accurate because they could be used in court.

Excellent communication skills are vital because you will be dealing with lots of different people, advising them and enforcing the law. You will need to be forceful but not aggressive.

You will need to be efficient at using computers and be good at maths as you will be dealing with lots of statistics.

Working conditions

You will probably work for local government but could work for private industry advising on relevant legislation.

You will be office based but will spend time visiting places such as shops, factories, pubs and clubs which could be dirty or cold.

Trading standards officers work normal office hours, Monday to Friday and possibly evenings and weekends. This is largely dependent on when different business premises are open.

Future prospects

There are jobs all over the country and the work varies from cities to rural areas. You could move from local government to central government or into retail and manufacturing companies.

There is currently a shortage of qualified staff but trainee jobs are competitive.

It might be possible to progress to senior officer and managerial positions. As relevant laws and regulations are increasing, opportunities in private industry are growing.

Advantages/disadvantages

This can be an interesting and satisfying job where you are helping the public to get a fair deal.

You could be dealing with difficult or aggressive people.

Money guide

As a new enforcement officer or a trainee, you could expect between £19,000 and £23,000 per year.

You would start on between £24,000 and £34,000 when newly qualified.

You could go on to earn between £35,000 and £50,000 as a senior trading standards officer.

Depending on the size of the local authority for which you work, in excess of £70,000 is possible for the head of a service.

Related opportunities

- Environmental Health Practitioner/Officer p22
- Police Officer p543
- Quality Control Inspector p226

Further information

Trading Standards Institute
http://www.tradingstandards.uk/home.cfm

Qualifications and courses

There are no formal entry requirements for this line of work as a positive attitude, enthusiasm for the job and a demonstrable interest in practical work is often valued above any formal academic qualifications, however GCSEs/National 5s (A*–E/A–E) in English, Maths, IT and a science may be a useful.

In order to gain some of the skills and understanding required in the industry, you may consider completing one of a range of vocational awards or applying for more formal industry training. Those aged 16–24 could apply for the Vehicle Parts Apprenticeship which is available at both Intermediate and Advanced Levels. As an apprentice, you will typically receive a combination of on-the-job training from experienced colleagues and a series of day or block release college instruction where you will work towards gaining industry-recognised qualifications such as the City & Guilds Diploma in Vehicle Parts Principles (Level 2–3).

Trainee parts operatives can also study for the Institute of the Motor Industry (IMI) Awards Diplomas in Vehicle Parts Competence (Levels 2–3). Alternatively, those who have secured employment could work towards the BTEC Level 2 Diploma in Vehicle Fitting Principles or a BTEC Diploma in Light Vehicle Maintenance and Repair Principles (Levels 2–3) or a BTEC Diploma in Heavy Vehicle Maintenance and Repair Principles (Levels 2–3).

It may also be beneficial to take the IMI Awards Level 2 Certificate in Customer Service for the Automotive Industry and Level 3 Certificate in Customer Service for the Motor Industry.

What the work involves

This job involves ordering and looking after vehicle parts and accessories and selling them to the public, garages and mechanics. You need specialist knowledge of stock, and when ordering or supplying parts you have to know the exact make, model and year of the vehicle.

You will undertake stock control using computerised systems or possibly keeping paper records, and reorder from warehouses or manufacturers when stocks are low. You will check off parts that arrive against delivery notes before placing them in a stock room.

As well as processing deliveries and taking orders over the phone and in person, you will use tills, take payments and sometimes invoice customers.

Type of person suited to this work

You should be interested in cars, know about a wide range of parts and accessories, and which makes of vehicles they are for. You will need to be well organised and able to research where to find more unusual parts.

You will also deal with the public over the phone and in person, so you will need the ability to explain technical information clearly and simply.

You must have strong communication skills, be a good team player and able to work on your own. The job involves being on your feet a lot so you will need to be fit and active.

Working conditions

You could be working in a large shop open to the public or a warehouse used by the motor trade. You could be in a fairly small, local garage or work for a large dealership.

You might have to lift heavy parts, move trolleys and climb ladders to reach high shelves. You will work with the public and staff from the motor trade.

Normal hours are Monday to Friday from 8.30am to 6.00pm but you may be expected to work evenings and weekends with time off in lieu.

Many employers provide a uniform.

Future prospects

If you work for a smaller company your promotion prospects might be limited but in larger companies you could get additional responsibilities more quickly and move into supervisory and managerial roles.

You could become a trainee manager in other areas of the retail trade or move into car sales.

Advantages/disadvantages

This is a skilled job which enables you to undertake training and use your knowledge of, and interest in, cars and the motor trade.

There is a lot of information to remember and the work can be repetitive.

This is an ideal career for those wanting to work with vehicles who do not want to be mechanics.

Money guide

During your training you can expect to earn between £9,000 and £14,000.

Once you are qualified and have gained experience, your salary could range from £16,000 to £18,000.

Those employed as a senior vehicle parts operative can achieve in excess of £25,000 a year.

Overtime work and sales-based bonus schemes may increase your income.

Related opportunities

- Motor Vehicle Technician p222
- Stock Control/Replenishment Assistant p483
- Vehicle Sales Executive p486

Further information

Retail Motor Industry Federation
www.rmif.co.uk

Qualifications and courses

You do not need formal qualifications to enter and train in this career but employers will expect candidates to have GCSEs/National 5s (A*–C/A–C) in Maths and English. Good communication skills and previous experience of working in a sales or customer service environment will improve your chances of securing employment.

Most entrants to this profession are at least 21 years old, as insurance companies will not insure younger people to conduct test drives.

The Apprenticeship in Vehicle Sales, available at both Intermediate and Advanced Levels, offers an ideal route into this career. As an apprentice you will typically receive on-the-job training whilst also working towards the NVQ Diploma in Vehicle Sales Competence (Levels 2–3). Alternatively, the Institute of the Motor Industry (IMI) awards Diplomas in Vehicle Sales Competence (Levels 2–3). Upon completion of the Level 2 Diploma you can apply for the grade of Licentiate Member of the IMI and those who achieve the Level 3 Diploma are eligible to become an Associate Member.

Those who have studied to degree level have the option to apply for a graduate training scheme run by one of the larger car manufacturers. Entry is usually with good A levels/H grades and at least a 2.1 in your degree.

Once employed, you may opt to complete continuing professional development (CPD). This is important in not only ensuring you maintain an up-to-date knowledge of new vehicle models, features and special promotions but to encourage career progression. The Institute of Sales and Marketing Management (ISMM) offers relevant qualifications that could lead to a promotion.

What the work involves

You will be selling new or used cars, motorbikes or vans. Your role will involve greeting customers, advising them, explaining different models, features and prices, and demonstrating cars by going out on test drives.

Your job will include arranging finance for customers and doing paperwork for the sale and the finance.

Garages promote their cars through advertising, special events and direct contact with customers, which may also be part of your work. Sales staff help keep the forecourt, salesroom and cars clean and tidy.

Type of person suited to this work

You will need to be smart, confident and outgoing with a polite, friendly manner. You must have the ability to deal with all types of people and be persuasive without being pushy. You will need good negotiation and numeracy skills. You should be able to work without supervision.

You must be interested in cars, know a lot about the ones you are selling and be able to explain technical features clearly and simply.

Your wages will depend on how much you sell so you will need to be motivated, determined and able to deal with stress and pressure. You need good attention to detail to complete forms and paperwork accurately.

Working conditions

You could be working in a small, local garage selling used cars or for a large dealership. You will be based in a showroom but will also be outside on the forecourt and going on test drives. A driving licence is essential.

You will usually work a 40-hour week which includes evening and weekend work.

Future prospects

There are currently good opportunities in all parts of the country. But, this is a popular industry with strong competition for jobs, especially with the main dealers.

In larger dealerships you can progress to senior salesperson, sales manager or dealer principal. At management level you will probably earn bonuses linked to the sales of the whole team.

With extensive experience, you could establish your own dealership.

Advantages/disadvantages

It can be rewarding when you help a customer to purchase the car they want/need.

You can progress well in this industry and earn a high salary.

Working on commission and having to meet targets can be very stressful and often requires long working hours.

Money guide

Wages vary considerably.

Employees in this sector usually receive a basic salary which is supplemented by commission on sales and bonuses for achieving sales targets.

You could expect to earn between £10,000 and £13,000 as a starting salary.

With experience, you are likely to receive £14,000–£25,000 a year.

The most successful vehicle sales executives can achieve £35,000–£40,000.

In a senior role, you could earn up to £50,000.

Related opportunities

- Customer Services Assistant/Manager p468
- Motor Vehicle Technician p222
- Retail Manager p478

Further information

Retail Motor Industry Federation
www.rmif.co.uk

The Institute of the Motor Industry
www.theimi.org.uk

Qualifications and courses

There are no formal academic requirements but many new entrants will have a degree or vocational qualification. Some employers require candidates to have 5 GCSEs/ National 5s (A*–C/A–C) and experience in the retail industry. You must be at least 18 years old to sell wine.

It is possible to study for the Wine and Spirit Education Trust (WSET) qualifications, which range from the Level 1 Award in Wines to the Level 5 Honours Diploma.

Other relevant qualifications include the BTEC HNC/ HND in Hospitality Management (Levels 4–5) and a Foundation degree in Wine Business or Hospitality Management. It is also possible to take a degree in hospitality and licensed retail management. As a graduate, you may be able to secure employment within a large wine retailer as a management trainee.

It may be possible to enter the trade without qualifications and work your way up, beginning first as a sales assistant in an off-licence, department store or supermarket, and later progressing to department manager. To work as a manager, buyer or importer, a driving licence is recommended, as is the ability to speak another language.

To become an independent wine merchant, you will need a premises licence and a personal licence to sell alcohol. In England and Wales, candidates are required to attain the Level 2 Award for Personal Licence Holders from the British Institute of Innkeeping Awarding Body (BIIAB). In Scotland, you must take the BIIAB Scottish Certificate for Personal Licence Holders (SCPLH).

Once in a position of wine merchant, you could progress to become a Master of Wine (MW), the highest recognised qualification in the British wine industry.

What the work involves

You will use your knowledge of wine to buy from vineyards and suppliers and sell to the public or shops, pubs and restaurants. If you manage your own shop or an off-licence, you will also be responsible for supervising staff and maintaining profitability. If you sell wine over the internet or by mail order, you could be doing your own deliveries.

You could also act as a buyer for a supermarket or wine retailer. You will probably spend a lot of time abroad finding and tasting new wines, agreeing prices and checking quality.

As an independent merchant, you will probably go to wine tastings to make selections and buy wine from companies who import their product to the UK.

Type of person suited to this work

Wine merchants are keen to develop their knowledge, find new wines and growers, and keep up to date with developments and tastes.

A good sense of taste and smell is needed to judge the quality of a wine. You should be able to advise people on specific wines to complement different foods.

You must have excellent communication and customer service skills as dealing with the public and negotiating prices with growers and suppliers will be an important part of your job.

Working conditions

If you are self-employed, you will have freedom and flexibility but you will probably work long hours. If you work in retail, wine shops are often open until 10pm so you might work shifts including weekends. You will be on your feet a lot and could be lifting heavy boxes.

If you become a buyer you may travel frequently, both within the UK and abroad, or you could be based in a head office.

You could be working with the public, sometimes even travelling to people's homes to sell wine.

Future prospects

As supermarkets have become the biggest retailers of wine, it is increasingly difficult for small shops to succeed.

Large chains offer good promotion prospects. You could progress to a store manager role and then to area manager.

To start your own business you will need experience, a good knowledge of wine and money to buy stock and premises.

Advantages/disadvantages

This job will allow you to use your expertise and passion for wine.

You might get to travel and work abroad.

There are few vacancies for buyer positions and competition is high.

Money guide

Starting salaries for this profession are typically about £16,000.

With experience, you can expect to earn up to £28,000.

Wine merchants who are self-employed or employed in a senior position by the largest companies can achieve in excess of £35,000.

Related opportunities

- Bar Manager/Licensee/Publican p122
- Importer/Exporter p595
- Retail Buyer p477

Further information

British Independent Retailers Association
www.bira.co.uk

Wine & Spirit Education Trust
www.wsetglobal.com

RETAIL, SALES AND CUSTOMER SERVICES

Science, Mathematics and Statistics

Do you have a very mathematical brain? Are you logical in how you approach tasks? Maybe you are fascinated by scientific advances and would like to be involved in future discoveries? People who work in this sector can spend long periods of time carrying out meticulous research. You may find yourself working for a variety of employers, from the health service to a cosmetics company or even a charity. You should be willing to work on your own but also be happy to present your findings in reports to others. People in this sector are very highly skilled individuals who have often been through a lot of training, and possess a questioning and inquisitive mind. The jobs featured in this section are listed below.

ACOUSTICIAN

Qualifications and courses

Most entrants to this profession are graduates from relevant disciplines such as acoustics, maths, physics, environmental science, mechanical engineering and subjects related to construction. For degree entry, you usually need at least 2 A levels/3 H grades including Maths and a numerate science/Physics and 5 GCSEs/National 5s (A*–C/A–C). The Institute of Acoustics (IOA) accredits degrees in Acoustical Engineering at the University of Southampton or Audio Acoustics at the University of Salford. There are also specialist postgraduate courses available in subjects such as environmental or architectural acoustics.

The IOA offers a postgraduate Diploma in Acoustics and Noise Control for graduates with a degree in a science, engineering or construction-related subject. The Certificate of Competence in Workplace Noise Risk Assessment and the Certificate of Competence in Environmental Noise Measurement are also available.

Once you secure employment, you will usually undertake a training programme or graduate scheme.

You can also become a member of the IOA and take part in its continuing professional development (CPD) scheme. There are several levels of membership, ranging from student members to fellows, who are over the age of 35, have at least 7 years' experience working in acoustics and have made a significant contribution to the industry.

What the work involves

An acoustician is an expert on sound waves and how they interact with the environment around them. The environment can range from office buildings to nature, and you could be looking to improve the quality of sound, reduce the noise pollution, or monitor and analyse the sound waves.

You will manage, regulate and control sound and vibrations in various environments. You could work on projects for defence, music, healthcare or telecommunications.

Your work can include many kinds of noise, from building acoustics, architectural acoustics and aerodynamic noise to electroacoustics, environmental issues and even therapeutic uses of ultrasound, as well as diagnostic techniques.

In your daily work you could be doing anything from advising on sound insulation to researching new ways to reduce the noise levels created by machinery. You might use computer modelling software to design ways to reduce or eliminate noise.

Type of person suited to this work

If you want to be an acoustician, you should have an interest not only in how sound behaves, but also in problem-solving and environmental science. You need to understand sound and acoustics, and be good at physics and maths.

You must be creative and innovative in your approach to problem-solving. Excellent communication, project management and people skills are essential.

It is important that you understand environmental legislation and standards. IT, budgeting and negotiation skills are also required for this role.

Working conditions

Working conditions and hours vary depending on the sector in which you work.

Those employed in a research role in a laboratory will usually work 9am to 5pm but unsocial hours may be required when working on some projects.

You will mainly work at a desk with a computer but you will also frequently visit laboratories, studios and sites.

The work involves standing and bending, and you may occasionally be required to lift and install heavy instruments.

You may spend time away from home and travel both within the UK and abroad.

Future prospects

Registering with the Institute of Acoustics could significantly improve your career prospects.

Possibilities for promotion include moving into supervisory or managerial roles, or specialising in a particular area. You could work freelance, or even consider setting up your own company.

Advantages/disadvantages

Depending on where you specialise, you could get the opportunity to be involved in exciting projects, whether it is the design of a concert hall or monitoring the sounds of whales.

Your work could be something varied and interesting.

You will have the opportunity to travel to some very interesting locations but this means that you will frequently be away from home.

Money guide

When you start out, you can expect to earn between £18,000 and £25,000 a year.

With increased experience in the role, your salary could rise to about £35,000.

Senior acoustics consultants can achieve in excess of £50,000 a year.

Related opportunities

- Aerospace Engineer p200
- Physicist p522
- Sound Engineer p433

Further information

EngineeringUK
www.engineeringuk.com

Institute of Acoustics
www.ioa.org.uk

Semta
www.semta.org.uk

SCIENCE, MATHEMATICS AND STATISTICS

ASTRONOMER

Qualifications and courses

A degree in physics, maths, astrophysics, geophysics or a related science is required, usually at a minimum of a 2.1 Honours degree. Specialist degrees are available in astronomy, astrophysics and space science, and you often have the option to study for either a single Honours degree or joint Honours combined with a related subject such as maths, physics or another science. The Royal Astronomical Society (RAS) provides details of relevant degree courses, as well as pre-entry work experience opportunities. Due to the profession's competitive nature, being able to show your astronomy aspirations from a young age may be advantageous.

Entry requirements for a first degree are usually 2 A levels/3 H grades, including Physics, Maths and another science, as well as 5 GCSEs/National 5s (A*–C/A–C), including English and possibly Chemistry.

Most entrants to this career also have a master's degree or a doctorate (PhD). To work as a research astronomer, candidates should have a first or 2.1 Master of Science (MSc) or Master of Physics (MPhys), followed by further study for a PhD in their specialist area of interest. University physics departments may include astronomical research groups and some universities offer PhD programmes specifically in astronomy.

Astronomy is becoming increasingly globalised, and so foreign language skills may prove beneficial.

You may also be encouraged to register as a chartered scientist (CSi), which would require a commitment to continuing professional development (CPD).

What the work involves

Astronomers investigate and study the universe. Astronomy covers a wide range of areas and astronomers usually focus on a specific subject, such as planets or stars.

You will mainly use maths, physics and specialist computer software to examine the images and information collected by observatories.

You will plan and coordinate projects using specialist equipment, such as telescope systems, to observe the skies and collect information. Your work can include constructing new observational instruments and software to improve your knowledge about the universe.

Type of person suited to this work

As a professional astronomer you should have a keen interest in the natural world. You will also need a good understanding of the sciences. Whether you are observing the skies or analysing detailed information, you should be able to take in a range of facts and figures.

You will use your decision-making skills to make informed conclusions from the information you work with.

A patient, logical and organised approach to your work is essential as projects can last several years. You should be confident in working with computers to complete a range of tasks. You will also need strong communication skills and an aptitude for numbers.

Working conditions

Late or antisocial working hours can often be a feature of this type of work, whether you are based in a university, observatory or research centre.

You will spend a great deal of your time working with computers.

The job may involve frequent work away from home as many of the major telescopes are in remote locations.

Close observation is often part of this job so it may be unsuitable for people with visual impairments.

Future prospects

Employment as a professional astronomer is very competitive and demands a great deal of academic study. Entry into the field still remains competitive and a lot of astronomers find work outside the profession in associated jobs. Funding and turnover are increasing slightly though.

If you followed the academic route, you could undertake original research combined with a PhD-level qualification and then progress to lecturing.

You may choose to work as part of a technical team providing support for astronomy research projects.

You could progress into related jobs such as a software or electronics engineer.

Advantages/disadvantages

This job provides the opportunity to increase public understanding of the natural world.

You might have to spend a lot of time undertaking observations which requires patience and commitment.

Carrying out research on-site can be physically tiring.

Money guide

PhD students receiving funding for research can expect to be awarded between £13,000 and £14,000 a year.

Junior researchers can expect to earn between £20,000 and £30,000 per year.

With experience in a postdoctoral research post, your salary can increase to £36,000.

Senior researchers and lecturers can achieve £50,000 to £60,000 per year.

Related opportunities

- Geophysicist p509
- Mathematician/Mathematics Research Scientist p515
- Physicist p522

Further information

British Astronomical Association
www.britastro.org

Institute of Physics
www.iop.org

Royal Astronomical Society
www.ras.org.uk

SCIENCE, MATHEMATICS AND STATISTICS

491

BACTERIOLOGIST

Qualifications and courses

To work as a bacteriologist, a 1st or 2.1 degree in a relevant subject such as biochemistry, physiology or microbiology is required. Entry to a degree is usually with a minimum of 2 A levels/3 H grades and 5 GCSEs/National 5s (A*–C/A–C). Entry may also be possible by completing a Foundation degree course in a science which normally requires 1 or 2 A levels/H grades.

A Master of Science (MSc) or doctorate (PhD) is an advantage as a postgraduate qualification is required for entry to an academic research post. Applicants without a PhD may start as a research assistant and work towards a PhD.

Alternatively you could enter as a laboratory assistant; for this you will need a minimum of 4 GCSEs/National 5s, including 2 sciences, Maths and English.

Bacteriologists are given regular on-the-job training to learn new laboratory techniques and keep up to date with IT developments and health and safety regulations. You might also receive training for personal development, management or supervisory responsibilities.

Registration with professional bodies, such as the Association for Clinical Biochemistry (ACB), will allow you to continue your professional development (CPD).

What the work involves

Bacteriologists study and analyse single-celled micro-organisms, particularly ones that cause disease. Their research provides important information on protecting against illnesses and caring for people with specific kinds of diseases.

In industry bacteriologists work in companies manufacturing pharmaceuticals, agrochemicals, food and drink, home and personal care products and consumer goods.

Research bacteriologists study a particular genus or species. This work may be new and untried, and often techniques are selected by the researcher. Researchers may work in hospitals, universities and private companies.

In all areas the work involves the interpretation and analysis of findings, and will include designing and conducting experiments, making observations and drawing conclusions from your findings. You must enjoy writing reports and scientific papers and presenting them to other scientists.

Type of person suited to this work

You need to be scientifically capable. You need to be meticulous, practical and logical in your approach to work and should be patient as you may have to repeat tests.

You should have an enquiring mind and good problem-solving skills and be able to work to tight deadlines when required.

You must also be able to work well alone and as part of a team, have good communication skills and be highly safety conscious.

Working conditions

You are likely to work in a multidisciplinary team with other scientists, including geneticists, microbiologists and chemical engineers.

You will usually work from 9am to 5pm, Monday to Friday. Evening and weekend work may be required for fieldwork or some experiments.

You will work in laboratories or factories or out on location. You must wear protective clothing in laboratories. Microbes are classified as bio-hazardous substances so you must follow strict health and safety regulations. The job might require you to travel to meetings and conferences.

Future prospects

Promotion prospects vary depending on the type of organisation. Some bacteriologists may need to change employer to gain promotion.

Career prospects may be improved with additional qualifications or experience. This could allow you to work in associated fields such as microbiology, virology, mycology and parasitology.

There may be opportunities to work abroad, especially for clinical bacteriologists involved in healthcare projects.

Advantages/disadvantages

There are opportunities to visit different types of outside locations on research trips.

Employers such as the National Health Service can offer the chance to gain experience in different departments and provide well-structured career paths.

You will be handling potentially dangerous substances and experiments can take a long time to complete and some aspects might become tedious.

Money guide

If you begin your career as a laboratory assistant you can expect to earn between £13,000 and £19,000 a year.

Newly qualified bacteriologists can expect between £20,000 and £38,000 a year.

Top salaries for bacteriologists are about £65,000 a year.

Related opportunities

- Biochemist p493
- Clinical Scientist p499
- Microbiologist p518

Further information

Health and Care Professions Council
www.hpc-uk.org

Institute of Biomedical Science
www.ibms.org

NHS Careers
www.healthcareers.nhs.uk

SCIENCE, MATHEMATICS AND STATISTICS

Qualifications and courses

A degree in biochemistry or a related subject is required for entry to this profession. Many posts also require a postgraduate qualification.

The minimum entry requirements for a biochemistry degree are 2 A levels/3 H grades, including Chemistry and/or Biology, and 5 GCSEs/National 5s (A*–C/A–C), including science subjects, English and Maths. Some universities offer a Foundation or 'bridging year' as a pre-degree course for applicants who do not have the required scientific qualifications.

Biochemists with a degree and relevant work experience are eligible to join a professional body, such as the Biochemical Society or the Society of Biology.

Biochemists continue their training while working. Those with a first degree are encouraged to study part time for a Master of Science (MSc) or doctorate (PhD) as competition for work is fierce. Accredited MSc degrees in Clinical Biochemistry are currently offered by 4 universities: Birmingham, London, Surrey and Manchester.

If you want to work with the National Health Service (NHS) as a clinical biochemist you will need a 1st or 2.1 degree and to follow the Scientist Training Programme (STP). The programme is very competitive with many more applicants than there are places. This is a 3-year work-based learning programme that leads to a master's degree in your specialist subject. Upon successful completion, after 4 years of work experience and by attaining the certificate of competence offered by the Association of Clinical Scientists (ACS), you will be able to register with the Health and Care Professions Council (HCPC) and be called a clinical biochemist. The HCPC will require you to undertake continuing professional development (CPD).

What the work involves

You will research a range of living organisms and processes, using specialist equipment. Your work may involve collating detailed information and producing reports.

Biochemists investigate the chemistry of living organisms. They use their investigations to plan experiments and solve problems.

Biochemists can specialise in particular fields, such as endocrinology, toxicology, paediatrics, immunology, and molecular biology, and apply their knowledge and skills in many areas, including food and nutrition, agriculture, medicine, plant research and brewing.

Type of person suited to this work

You will need to be curious about biological organisms and interested in improving systems and products. You will constantly use problem-solving skills in this job. Your excellent observational skills will also be very useful. You should enjoy working as part of a team.

You will be confident in using a range of scientific equipment with a patient and methodical approach for sometimes repetitive but important activities. Your strong communication skills will help you explain and record your work. Confidence in working with numbers and detailed information is also essential.

Working conditions

You would normally work in a laboratory as part of a team. You may also do some of your work in an office environment. In some sectors, biochemists work on a shift system.

The job involves the regular use of specialist equipment which requires good manual handling skills. Protective equipment will also have to be worn.

As you become more senior, it is likely you will be involved with managing staff or projects.

Future prospects

Many of the products you use on a daily basis have been developed by biochemists. Biochemists have an important role in organisations ranging from research institutes to multinational companies.

If you go into research and development, you would start by working as part of a team. With further training and experience you could gain membership of The Royal College of Pathologists (MRCPath) or a PhD, which allows biochemists to advance to higher post-registration positions and consultancy work.

You may choose to undertake academic research and go into lecturing or teaching.

Advantages/disadvantages

You may have to work very long hours in this job.

This type of work is often project based which provides job variety.

Biochemistry offers a wide range of areas in which to specialise.

Money guide

The starting salary on the NHS's Science Training Programme is around £25,000, while post-registration trainees could earn £31,072 (NHS wage band 7), which increases to £40,000 with experience.

Consultant clinical scientists can earn in excess of £55,548.

In industry, a research scientist could earn £23,000–£42,000.

Related opportunities

- Biomedical Scientist/Medical Laboratory Assistant p494
- Biotechnologist p495
- Chemist p497

Further information

Biochemical Society
www.biochemistry.org

Institute of Biomedical Science
www.ibms.org

The Association for Clinical Biochemistry and Laboratory Medicine
www.acb.org.uk

Qualifications and courses

Biomedical scientist

To become a biomedical scientist you must register with the Health and Care Professions Council (HCPC). Registration can be achieved by completing a HCPC-approved biomedical sciences degree accredited by the Institute of Biomedical Science (IBMS), one year's training in a laboratory (which could be undertaken as part of a sandwich degree), and by completing the Registration Training Portfolio. You will then achieve the IBMS Certificate of Competence and be eligible to register with the HCPC.

Alternatively, those with A levels/H grades in Life Sciences can start work as a trainee biomedical scientist if their employer is willing to allow them to study part time for a relevant degree. Entry requirements for a biomedical science degree are 2 A levels/3 H grades, including Biology and Chemistry and 5 GCSEs/National 5s (A*–C/A–C), including Maths and English. Alternative qualifications such as BTECs may also be accepted. Biomedical scientist graduates can then apply for the NHS Scientist Training Programme (STP) in life sciences.

Pre-entry experience and postgraduate qualifications are not essential but may prove advantageous.

Medical laboratory assistant

There are no formal entry requirements but 4 or more GCSEs/National 5s (A*–C/A–C) in English, Maths and a science, or an equivalent qualification such as a BTEC First in Applied Science (Level 2), may be valuable. Laboratory assistants can work towards qualifications such as NVQs/SVQs.

What the work involves

A biomedical scientist carries out laboratory tests on bodily fluid and tissue in order to help doctors assess what is wrong with their patients. They use a range of specialist equipment to carry out tests.

Medical laboratory assistants support the work of biomedical scientists. As a medical laboratory assistant, you will carry out a variety of tasks including sorting and labelling tissue samples, sterilising and disinfecting equipment, making up chemical solutions, separating blood serum and plasma from samples, and recording and analysing information.

Type of person suited to this work

Biomedical scientist

You must be interested in science and medicine and have strong scientific skills. You should be practical and responsible, with good IT skills. You need the ability to supervise junior members of staff and to follow complex instructions.

Medical laboratory assistant

You need a careful, methodical approach to your work. You should be able to concentrate and pay attention to detail. You will work accurately under pressure to meet deadlines. Solid communication skills are essential.

Working conditions

You will mainly work in pathology laboratories within hospitals but sometimes you will have direct contact with patients.

You will work a 37-hour week which could involve shift, evening, weekend and on-call work.

You will be required to wear protective clothing.

Future prospects

Biomedical scientist

You will probably specialise in a specific area. You might need higher qualifications in order to progress. Within the NHS, you could move up to a managerial role.

Jobs in the NHS are still fiercely competitive.

Work abroad is a possibility, especially within developing countries.

Medical laboratory assistant

Most employment is available in NHS hospitals. You may specialise or move to a related career such as a pharmacy technician. To train as a clinical or biomedical scientist you will need to study for a relevant degree which may be available for part-time study.

Advantages/disadvantages

Providing an essential service within a hospital, by helping to diagnose patients' illnesses, is incredibly rewarding.

You may have to deal with angry doctors/patients who want results sooner than you can deliver them.

Money guide

Rates of pay in this sector are established by the NHS.

A medical laboratory assistant will have a salary of £19,027 to £22,236 (wage band 4).

A biomedical scientist will have a starting salary of £21,692 to £28,180.

As a team leader or specialist, you could earn from £31,072 to £40,964.

Those who reach an advanced level or are employed as a team manager can achieve from £30,764 to £40,558.

Related opportunities

- Chemist p497
- Clinical Scientist p499
- Laboratory Technician p512

Further information

Institute of Biomedical Science
www.ibms.org

NHS Careers
www.healthcareers.nhs.uk

Qualifications and courses

The entry requirements for this profession are a degree in biotechnology, bioscience or a related subject, such as microbiology, biochemistry or chemical engineering. Requirements for a degree are usually 2 A levels/3 H grades, including Chemistry or Biology, and 5 GCSEs/National 5s (A*–C/A–C), including English, Maths and a science.

For research posts you will be expected to have a postgraduate qualification, experience working in the sector, and be studying for a doctorate (PhD). Entry to a postgraduate course is with a minimum of a 2.1 in a relevant bachelor's degree and courses typically last 1–3 years.

Although rare, it is possible to become a biotechnologist with an HND or Foundation degree in chemical or manufacturing engineering by working your way up from trainee technician level.

The majority of employers look for relevant work experience, such as a vacation placement or a sandwich degree course with a year in industry.

Once you have secured employment, you will learn on the job, possibly through a structured in-house training programme. NVQs/SVQs in Laboratory and Associated Technical Activities (Levels 2–4) are also available.

The Society of Biology offers members access to a Continuing Professional Development (CPD) scheme designed to help you maintain and improve your skillset. You can also attend events that will accelerate your CPD, allowing you to acquire a higher membership status.

What the work involves

You will use biological organisms and processes to develop and adapt products. Biotechnologists work in a range of areas such as genetic engineering, electronics, food science and microbiology. Biotechnology provides the scientific basis for agriculture, pharmaceuticals, waste management, food and medical care.

You could work in research and development or in aspects of production such as quality control.

Your work might involve enhancing existing products or developing new types of organisms.

You could work within government research institutions or play a central role in developing and enhancing products in commercial biotechnology companies.

Type of person suited to this work

You will need a keen interest in science for working in any area of biotechnology. Strong observational skills and an organised approach are also essential.

You should be confident working with scientific equipment and computers to manage information and undertake research. Most biotechnologists are employed as part of a group so the ability to work within a team is helpful.

If you work as a technician, you should be able to cope with undertaking routine but required testing activities. Biochemists in industry also need to understand the commercial applications of their work.

Working conditions

Biotechnologists usually work in a laboratory or research centre in sterile conditions to undertake experimental and testing work.

You will work normal office hours but you may occasionally be on call during evenings and weekends. Protective clothing is needed when working with micro-organisms and dangerous chemicals.

Your work is likely to involve using microscopes and electronic testing equipment, and spending time on a computer doing analysis work.

Future prospects

The job market is improving, but slowly and the jobs remain competitive if steady. Jobs are available abroad, particularly in the USA, but these are also very competitive.

You could progress to a supervisory role.

There is also the option to develop an academic career – this may provide additional opportunities to undertake commercial research. You can use this research to move into sales, marketing or production roles.

Advantages/disadvantages

Laboratory work, particularly at technician level, can be time consuming and requires a lot of patience.

You will be researching and learning new things every day.

Job prospects are good as there is a range of sectors in which you can work.

Money guide

Earnings vary according to the type of employer and tend to be highest in industry.

Starting salaries for graduates are usually between £19,000 and £24,000 per year.

With experience, you can expect to earn from £30,000 to £45,000.

Those employed in a senior position with high levels of responsibility can achieve up to £60,000 a year.

Related opportunities

- Biochemist p493
- Biomedical Scientist/Medical Laboratory Assistant p494
- Chemist p497

Further information

BioIndustry Association
www.bioindustry.org

Biotechnology and Biological Sciences Research Council
www.bbsrc.ac.uk

Royal Society of Biology
www.rsb.org.uk

SCIENCE, MATHEMATICS AND STATISTICS

Qualifications and courses

Botanists may enter this career as laboratory technicians or technical assistants. Most entrants have a degree in a relevant subject such as botany, plant biology, plant science, environmental science and ecology. Entry into a degree programme requires 2 A levels/3 H grades in Biology and another science, often Chemistry, and 5 GCSEs/National 5s (A*–C/A–C).

It may also be a good idea to complete some voluntary work in organisations and to acquire relevant skills such as plant identification.

The Field Studies Council, the Botanical Society of the British Isles (BSBI) and local wildlife trusts offer a wide range of training programmes, such as the Field Identification Skills Certificate, which grades your skill level on a scale from 1 to 5.

To work as a teacher or researcher, a postgraduate course is required. Candidates may enter with a Master of Science (MSc), doctorate (PhD) or enter as a trainee researcher in a university department who is working towards a PhD. In order to apply for a postgraduate qualification you will need to successfully complete an undergraduate degree, usually with 2.1 Honours or higher.

The Society of Biology offers members access to a continuing professional development (CPD) scheme designed to help you maintain and improve your skillset. You can also attend events that will accelerate your CPD, allowing you to acquire a higher membership status.

What the work involves

Botanists study all kinds of plant life and plant biology. They are increasingly employed within industry and research in areas such as plant-cell technology and genetic engineering.

Your work could involve managing rare plant collections, environmental conservation, horticulture, agriculture and other areas. You will use specialist equipment such as electron microscopes and satellite imaging technology.

You might look into how human activity affects plants in farming, or you may try and discover useful chemicals produced by plants.

Type of person suited to this work

As a botanist you should have a real interest in science and plants. This interest should stretch to a particular field of work such as conservation.

This profession will involve detailed analysis so you will need strong observational skills. You must also have a methodical approach to your work activities.

You should be comfortable working with a range of scientific equipment and be happy undertaking practical research work, sometimes outdoors and in unpleasant weather conditions. You may also need to be a good leader as you might be in charge of junior staff, students and volunteers.

Working conditions

You could be working in one or more of the following environments: laboratories, classrooms, lecture theatres, offices and outdoors. Hours will vary, but within research and higher education you will work about 37 hours a week.

Field work takes place in all weather conditions and you may find it physically demanding.

Whilst working in a laboratory you will be using specialist equipment and might be required to wear protective clothing. A driving licence may be required if you need to travel between locations.

Future prospects

Within conservation and field work, progression would entail taking on more responsibility and possibly managing others.

Within the higher education sector there is a set career path leading from researcher to head of department or professor.

Within industry there is the possibility of promotion. You also have the option of working as a freelance consultant and therefore being self-employed. There is the potential to work overseas in most areas of botany.

Advantages/disadvantages

There are opportunities to visit different types of outside locations on research trips.

Research jobs are often offered on a short-term basis, which can create job insecurity.

You will have the opportunity to combine your love of plants with your passion for science.

Money guide

These figures will vary depending on location, sector and employer. Salaries within private industry will vary considerably.

Starting salaries are around £16,000 to £22,000 a year.

Botanists in research jobs can expect to earn up to £30,000 a year.

In a senior role, such as a senior lecturer at a university, you could earn around £55,000 per year.

Related opportunities

- Ecologist p502
- Entomologist p503
- Microbiologist p518

Further information

Botanical Society of Britain and Ireland
www.bsbi.org.uk

Royal Society of Biology
www.rsb.org.uk

The Conservation Volunteers (TCV)
www.tcv.org.uk

Qualifications and courses

You will usually require a degree in chemistry, applied or analytical chemistry, biochemistry or a related scientific subject to enter this profession. For entry to one of these degrees you will need 2 A levels/3 H grades in Chemistry and one other science or Maths and 5 GCSEs/National 5s (A*–C/A–C) including Maths, 2 sciences and English.

Many institutions offer 1-year Foundation courses for candidates who do not have the necessary academic science background.

The majority of chemists also have a postgraduate qualification in chemistry or in a specialist area such as materials chemistry, medicinal chemistry or pharmaceutical chemistry. You can also work towards professional membership of the Royal Society of Chemistry.

Alternatively, it is possible to enter as a technician with a minimum of 4 GCSEs/National 5s (A*–C/A–C), including English, Maths and 2 sciences. A levels/H grades, BTEC Level 3 qualifications, or a HNC/HND in a science subject may also be required. Technicians may have the opportunity to study for NVQs/SVQs in Laboratory and Associated Technical Activities (Levels 2–4), or the BTEC Level 5 in Chemical Science for Industry. With further training and qualifications they may be able to progress to the job of a chemist.

What the work involves

Chemists work in many different sectors, undertaking the analysis and use of complex scientific processes and substances on a detailed molecular level.

As well as engaging in research and development, chemists also check that products are developed to a safe standard.

Professional chemists are employed in a wide range of sectors, including the oil industry, pharmaceuticals, medical research and academia.

Type of person suited to this work

Chemists need strong observational, numerical and technical skills. You must have an enquiring mind with a logical approach and desire to solve complex scientific problems.

You will have good dexterity for undertaking research and experiments with a range of scientific equipment. The ability to interpret and analyse data is vital and you must have good written and verbal communication skills to convey complex problems.

Often you will be working as part of a team so you must be comfortable working with other people as well as having the patience and confidence to take the lead within certain projects.

Working conditions

The average chemist works about 37 hours a week. Your job could involve working in a laboratory as part of a research centre, but you may also undertake research outdoors on-site.

You may have to wear protective clothing such as lab coat, protective glasses and gloves.

If you are employed by a private company you may be required to work shifts organised by a rota. At senior levels, you may be involved with business development and managerial activities.

Future prospects

Professional chemists play an important role in developing and updating products and systems and job opportunities are good.

Public research institutes, academic institutions and private companies employ chemists. There are also opportunities in government research, health and education. Some chemists move into areas such as law, IT, science journalism and marketing.

With experience you could enter a supervisory role. There are also opportunities to teach in schools and universities. Postgraduate qualifications may improve your chances for progression.

Advantages/disadvantages

Low numbers of entrants taking chemistry degrees means that there are many opportunities.

Laboratory tasks can sometimes be repetitive and time-consuming.

Many large companies employ chemists, so promotion can be possible without moving employers.

Money guide

These figures are only approximate and will vary depending on sector, employer and location.

Salary levels should increase with the level of academic qualification. At graduate entry you can earn between £16,000 and £22,000 per year.

With experience, and when established, you can expect £35,000 a year.

With added responsibility, such as if you are in charge of a team or project, you could expect to earn between £35,000 and £60,000 a year.

Related opportunities

- Biochemist p493
- Biotechnologist p495
- Cosmetic Scientist p501

Further information

Association of the British Pharmaceutical Industry
www.abpi.org.uk

Royal Society of Chemistry
www.rsc.org

Qualifications and courses

To become a clinical geneticist with the National Health Service (NHS) you will need to complete their 3-year Scientist Training Programme (STP). Entry requires a degree (first or 2.1) in either biomedical sciences, biology, microbiology, genetics or biochemistry, and 2 A levels/3 H grades in the sciences, Chemistry and/or Biology may be specified, and 5 GCSEs/National 5s (A*–C/A–C). You can also gain entry with an accredited master's degree.

You must then work towards state registration as a clinical geneticist with the Health & Care Professions Council (HCPC). This requires you to have completed a further 4 years of pre-registration work experience, during which you should have completed part 1 of the membership of the Royal College of Pathologists (MRCPath) and been awarded the certificate of competence by the Association of Clinical Scientists (ACS).

Career advancement depends on further experience and/or qualifications, including specialised postgraduate research. Completion of part 2 of the MRCPath, resulting in full membership, allows post-registrants to apply for consultancy and head of laboratory posts.

It is also possible to enter the profession at technician or trainee level with GCSEs/National 5s and A levels/H grades in subjects such as Biology, other sciences, Maths and English. To advance you must gain the relevant qualifications whilst working.

It is essential for all healthcare professionals to undertake continuing professional development (CPD) to maintain their registration with the HCPC.

What the work involves

Clinical geneticists are responsible for identifying and diagnosing genetic disorders by testing samples from patients, recording their findings and drawing a conclusion from them. They also supervise the work of others.

Geneticists analyse and modify human, animal or plant DNA. If working as a human geneticist, you could be involved with medical genetics or human genetic research.

You could undertake genetic engineering in agricultural research.

There are 2 other main jobs in this field that may be of interest: cytogeneticists (who study chromosomes which contain genes) and molecular geneticists (who study DNA exclusively).

Type of person suited to this work

You should be an excellent communicator, both verbally and in writing. You will need to be able to work accurately and meticulously, whilst keeping to deadlines.

You must have a good understanding of computers. You will need to be discreet as you will be dealing with confidential medical information.

You should be able to work effectively as part of a team and be able to take on the role of a supervisor when training junior staff. You must have strong problem-solving skills.

Working conditions

You will be based in a sterile laboratory. You will have to wear protective clothing such as overalls, laboratory glasses and gloves.

You will also have to ensure that you reach all health and safety standards.

As a clinical geneticist within the NHS you will be working about 37.5 hours per week, from Monday to Friday. There may also be a rota in place which covers bank holidays and weekends.

Future prospects

Genetics is a developing area of science that offers the chance to work directly with patients as a medical geneticist within the NHS or directly within research in research centres and universities.

You could also go on to work in research and development in industry.

In order to be promoted you will need to gather experience, responsibility and training. Once you have worked for 2 or 3 years as a registered geneticist you can begin to apply for more senior positions.

Advantages/disadvantages

You may have to repeat procedures, which could become tedious.

This job involves a great deal of responsibility.

You will be working with a wide range of samples and so every day will be different.

Money guide

These figures will vary depending on sector, location and employer.

The average starting salary for a graduate clinical scientist trainee is about £23,000 per year.

As a qualified healthcare scientist employed by the NHS you will usually start on wage band 6 and can expect to earn between £26,041 and £34,876.

As a consultant your salary could range from £39,632 (band 8) to £98,453 (band 9).

Related opportunities

- Clinical Scientist p499
- Forensic Scientist p506
- Laboratory Technician p512

Further information

British Society for Genetic Medicine
www.bsgm.org.uk

Genetics Society
www.genetics.org.uk

NHS Careers
www.healthcareers.nhs.uk

Qualifications and courses

Entrants to this profession require a 1st or 2.1 Honours degree in a relevant subject, such as biochemistry, biology, chemistry, engineering, genetics, microbiology, physics or physiology. Entry to a degree typically requires a minimum of 2 A levels/3 H grades, including a science subject, as well as 5 GCSEs/National 5s (A*–C/A–C) including English and Maths. Equivalent qualifications may also be relevant, but please check with your preferred university. Some universities also offer a 1-year Foundation course for those without an academic background in science.

After your degree you will need to find a trainee clinical scientist job. A relevant Master of Science (MSc) or doctorate (PhD) may help your application.

The National Health Service (NHS) offers the Scientist Training Programme (STP) in many of the different disciplines a clinical scientist can specialise in, such as life sciences (embryology, pathology, genetics and haematology), physiological sciences (audiology, cardiac physiology), and clinical engineering. These programmes can last up to 4 years and lead to a specialist diploma or MSc. Clinical scientists start as Grade A trainees and, upon completion, candidates are eligible for state registration with the Health and Care Professions Council (HCPC), for which you also need a Certificate of Attainment from the Association of Clinical Scientists (ACS). You could then work towards passing parts 1 and 2 of the Membership of the Royal College of Pathologists (MRCPath) exams. This enables you to apply for Grade C consultancy jobs.

Once qualified, clinical scientists are required to undertake continuing professional development (CPD).

What the work involves

Clinical scientists work mainly for the NHS but are also employed in the Health Protection Agency, research centres and industry.

Your work may involve supporting doctors, suggesting suitable tests for diagnosing patients, reporting on results and recommending treatments. You may also research and test new methods of treatment and make recommendations on the best equipment or test materials.

You might specialise in a particular area such as clinical embryology (the study of infertility), or clinical microbiology (identifying infections in patients caused by bacteria, fungus or parasites).

Type of person suited to this work

You should have a keen interest in medicine and science, alongside a desire to help others. You should have excellent observational skills.

You need technical skills and the ability to use scientific equipment to get results. You will need an organised approach for undertaking practical work and the ability to work to set deadlines. You should be able to interact well as part of a team.

As a scientist you will get results by combining a logical approach with a creative flair. You should have strong computer skills.

Working conditions

You might work around 37.5 hours a week, usually from Monday to Friday, although these hours could vary depending on your specialty. You may need to work some evenings and weekends if you are on call.

You will usually work in a laboratory or within a specialist department. You may have some contact with patients.

You will be working in a sterile environment, which may demand that you wear protective clothing. You might need to use ionising radiation.

Future prospects

As progression is performance based, you will need to accept more responsibility and/or take part in research and development projects to reach a more senior level.

As a consultant, you would be responsible for a large department and have the chance to make important contributions to your area of expertise.

There is also the option of moving between departments to gain further training. You could move into lecturing or training. There is the possibility of working abroad.

Advantages/disadvantages

You will be helping to diagnose patients and suggest treatments which will improve their quality of life.

Mistakes could lead to an incorrect diagnosis and so you will be working under a lot of pressure.

Money guide

Salaries vary depending on employer and location. If you work in London you will be given an additional allowance.

As a trainee clinical scientist within the NHS you could earn about £25,000 per year.

Once registered, you could earn between £26,041 and £34,876.

This could increase to £98,433 if you become an advanced practitioner, clinical scientist or consultant clinical scientist.

Related opportunities

- Hospital Doctor p294
- Medical Physicist p298
- Radiographer p318

Further information

Association of Clinical Scientists
www.assclinsci.org

NHS Clinical Scientists Recruitment
www.nhsclinicalscientists.info

The Association for Clinical Biochemistry and Laboratory Medicine
www.acb.org.uk

SCIENCE, MATHEMATICS AND STATISTICS

499

Qualifications and courses

For entry, you will be expected to have an HNC/HND or degree in a relevant subject such as consumer studies/ science, food studies/science, food and nutrition, food and marketing or food technology. Degrees are also available in specialist areas of consumer science, such as consumer protection or consumer psychology.

To gain acceptance on to an HNC/HND course you will usually require at least 4 GCSEs/National 5s (A*–C/A–C) and 1 A level/H grade. Most degree courses expect candidates to have at least 2 A levels/3 H grades and 5 GCSEs/National 5s (A*–C/A–C). These requirements may vary so be sure to check with the institution.

Some employers may also prefer you to have a postgraduate qualification in a relevant subject such as health promotion or consumer behaviour. For entry to a postgraduate course you will need a good undergraduate degree, usually at 2.1 class or higher.

Experience in the food manufacturing industry or within market research can also offer an alternative way of entering the field or act as an advantage when applying for jobs.

It is also possible to enter the profession with NVQs/ SVQs in Food Preparation and Cooking, Proficiency in Food Industry Skills, or Food Production and Cooking, or with a BTEC/SQA Level 3 qualification in a hospitality or catering subject. You may be able to gain these whilst working, as well as take relevant courses in many of the occupational areas in which a consumer scientist may work, such as health promotion, social policy, business, marketing and journalism.

What the work involves

Consumer scientists or home economists provide support, information and specialist services related to healthy living and eating.

You will be the point of communication between consumers and manufacturers. You will study what the consumer needs and provide advice on how to develop it. Your work could involve developing new food products, educating people about healthy eating or assessing new cookery equipment.

Jobs are available within quality assurance, marketing, media and journalism, food product development, education, government, product and service development and catering.

Type of person suited to this work

You will need to have strong communication skills, which allow you to talk to people of all ages and backgrounds.

You should also have an interest in food and how people live their lives within the domestic environment.

You should have good computer skills and the ability to impart information in a clear, concise manner, both orally and in writing. You must be creative and have proficient design skills.

Working conditions

This role may involve travelling to meetings, conferences and other environments in the UK and abroad.

Your working environment will vary according to which industry you work within. You could be in an office, kitchen, classroom, laboratory or a selection of these.

You will be working about 35 to 40 hours per week, usually from Monday to Friday.

Future prospects

Consumer scientists can move between industries as their services are always required. Specific industries include retail chains, marketing bodies, local authorities, magazines, television and newspapers, health authorities, producers of food, advisory and consumer organisations, hotels and restaurants, consumer pressure groups, schools, colleges and universities and many others.

In most areas there is the opportunity to progress to managerial level.

Promotion may involve moving to a new location within the country.

Advantages/disadvantages

You may find it frustrating when asked to complete tests in the later stages of the factory process.

This profession will give you the opportunity to move into a number of industries, such as retail or food manufacturing, which will aid your career progression possibilities.

You may have to complete reports in your free time.

Money guide

Salary levels vary according to employer, sector and location.

Starting salaries range from £19,000 to £24,000 per year.

With experience, you could earn up to £30,000 a year.

Managers at a senior level earn between £40,000 and £50,000 per year.

Consumer scientists working on a consultancy basis can earn £150–£500 a day.

Related opportunities

- Dietitian p285
- Environmental Health Practitioner/Officer p22
- Market Research Executive p393

Further information

Improve Ltd
www.improveltd.co.uk

Institute of Food Research
www.ifr.ac.uk

Institute of Food Science & Technology
www.ifst.org

Qualifications and courses

Career entry can be achieved at more than one level, including a degree in a relevant subject, such as cosmetic science, chemistry, chemical engineering, biology, microbiology, physics, medicine and pharmacy, a Foundation degree or HNC/HND. De Montfort University and the University of the Arts London offer degrees in Cosmetic Science. Most degree courses require applicants to have achieved a minimum of 2 A levels/3 H grades, which should include at least 1 science (particularly Chemistry) and 5 GCSEs/National 5s (A*–C/A–C), including English and Maths.

Many colleges offer students who have not studied the requisite science subjects at A level/H grade a 1-year introductory (Access) course. For Foundation degrees and HNC/HND qualifications, applicants are normally expected to have achieved at least 1 A level/H grade.

Postgraduate degrees are also available in cosmetic science and related subjects.

The Society of Cosmetic Science (SCS) offers the Diploma in Cosmetic Science for those working in the industry. This can be attained by distance learning after approximately 300 hours of study. The Principles and Practice of Cosmetic Science course is a shorter course, which is particularly useful for those who have been in the industry for a while and are looking to move into supervisory or managerial roles.

What the work involves

The cosmetics industry requires scientists to help develop, test and produce new and existing cosmetics and beauty products, such as make-up, perfumes and haircare products.

There are various elements to this profession, including researching new ingredients, developing cosmetic products, developing the processes used to create the product, quality control, safety testing, packaging development and regulatory affairs which involves ensuring the product meets all legal requirements.

Type of person suited to this work

You will have an interest in the science of cosmetics, along with knowledge and skill in chemistry and biology. You will need to be meticulous, accurate and able to work at speed.

You will need to understand statistics and have the ability to use the relevant computer software. You should have an extremely methodical approach to your work and the ability to follow instructions effectively.

You must have strong communication skills, to convey information to your colleagues and clients effectively.

Working conditions

Most of your work will take place in a sterile, laboratory environment. Your job may involve handling potentially dangerous materials, so you will need to wear protective clothing.

In addition to hands-on experimental work, your work may include using computers. Your job might involve travelling to meetings, conferences and other events in the UK and abroad.

You will usually work from 9am to 5pm, Monday to Friday. However, working on a rota basis may be necessary if working in production or quality control as the production line is likely to be in 24 hour operation.

Future prospects

Despite some larger companies relocating manufacturing abroad, the cosmetics industry is still growing. As life expectancies continue to increase more consumers are taking an active interest in their appearance, resulting in demand and growth in the industry.

There are a growing number of opportunities in niche markets such as organic and fair trade products.

Progression in the industry generally comes in the form of moving to a supervisory or managerial role, which could allow you to spend more time with the clients.

Alternatively, you might consider changing departments and moving into a sales or marketing position, where the scientific knowledge you have acquired would be extremely relevant.

Advantages/disadvantages

You may find some elements of the job extremely repetitive and monotonous.

Your work will be directly influenced by the fashion industry; you will be working to predict the latest trends, which could be exciting.

This profession can be fast paced and you may find it stressful.

Money guide

Salary levels will vary according to employer, sector and location.

Starting salaries are roughly between £18,000 and £25,000 per year.

With experience and training this will increase and you could earn from £25,000 to £45,000 a year.

At senior levels, such as within management, it is possible to earn over £50,000 a year.

Related opportunities

- Biochemist p493
- Laboratory Technician p512
- Pharmacologist p309

Further information

Cosmetic, Toiletry and Perfumery Association
www.ctpa.org.uk

Royal Society of Chemistry
www.rsc.org

Society of Cosmetic Scientists
www.scs.org.uk

SCIENCE, MATHEMATICS AND STATISTICS

Qualifications and courses

Entrants normally require a degree in a relevant subject such as ecology, environmental biology/management, conservation or marine biology. The general entry requirements for a degree are 2 A levels/3 H grades and 5 GCSEs/National 5s (A*–C/A–C).

Many employers require pre-entry experience (as a research assistant or a conservation project volunteer), and postgraduate qualifications are increasingly advantageous. A driving licence may also be useful when travelling to conduct fieldwork.

NVQs/SVQs are available in Environmental Conservation at Levels 2 and 3 and a BTEC is available in Environmental Conservation (Levels 4–5).

Ecologists with relevant qualifications and experience can become members of the Chartered Institute of Ecology and Environmental Management (CIEEM). Different levels of membership are available depending on your qualifications and experience. The CIEEM, the British Ecological Society (BES), the Field Studies Council and the Botanical Society of the British Isles also provide many short professional development courses for their members.

Once you have enough experience you could apply for chartered environmentalist (CEnv) status with the Society for the Environment, for which you are expected to undertake continuing professional development (CPD).

What the work involves

Ecologists help to protect the natural world by investigating the relationship between living organisms and their environment. Ecologists usually work within a specialist area such as freshwater, marine or fauna.

You will undertake ecological surveys of animals and plants and monitor the state of urban and rural environments. You may also write reports and analyse statistical information.

You may also advise on legal regulations, manage wildlife conservation areas and present your research at conferences or educational seminars.

Type of person suited to this work

A keen interest in the natural world is essential. It's important to be observant and methodical in your work. You will also need to be organised and work to a high standard of accuracy when collating statistics.

You will need to be comfortable working outdoors, sometimes in poor weather conditions. You must have a good knowledge of environmental policies and legislation. Good manual handling skills are important.

You will be presenting your research on a regular basis so excellent written and communication skills are essential.

Working conditions

Ecologists work in laboratories or research centres when undertaking analysis activities.

You would work outside in all kinds of weather conditions when undertaking fieldwork such as surveys of plants or animals.

For fieldwork you would need a good level of physical fitness and good observational skills. This may make the job unsuitable for people with visual impairments.

Future prospects

Ecology offers a wide range of job opportunities; you can shape your career according to your interests. However, there is strong competition for jobs; some are available only on a contract basis and it can take time to find a permanent role.

Despite the recession, the demand for ecological assessment and consulting services has increased by an average annual rate of 8.6% since 2006 and job opportunities are available.

Many types of organisations employ ecologists. You could go into scientific research, environmental management, teaching or conservation for organisations such as environmental consultancies, research bodies and private companies.

Advantages/disadvantages

This job provides the satisfaction of having a positive impact on the natural environment.

You may need to move around employers to develop your career.

You can choose to work in your specialist area, and develop your career around something you are passionate about.

Money guide

Salaries vary according to the type of organisation you work for.

Starting salaries range from around £17,000 to £20,000 per year.

With experience you could earn from £22,000 to £30,000.

Senior or management roles in larger organisations can earn £30,000 to £40,000 or more.

Related opportunities

- Countryside Manager/Officer p244
- Countryside Ranger p245
- Environmental Scientist p504

Further information

British Ecological Society
www.britishecologicalsociety.org

Chartered Institute of Ecology and Environmental Management
www.cieem.net

Institution of Environmental Sciences
www.the-ies.org

ENTOMOLOGIST

Qualifications and courses

An Honours degree in a relevant subject is required for entry to this profession. There are no entomology degree courses available but biology, zoology, environmental science and biological sciences would all be appropriate as these typically include modules in entomology. For entry to a degree course, candidates usually need at least 2 A levels/3 H grades, including Biology, and 5 GCSEs/National 5s (A*–C/A–C). However, entry requirements vary between universities so it is worth checking with each institution before applying.

Many employers will also expect applicants to have a postgraduate qualification in entomology. Postgraduate courses are available at several universities throughout the UK and you must have achieved a minimum of a 2.1 in your first degree to be eligible for a place. To secure a research post you will need to have or be studying for a doctorate (PhD).

Entry at technician level requires GCSEs/National 5s and A levels/H grades. Useful subjects include Biology (and other sciences), Maths, English, Geography and Geology. Foreign language qualifications may also prove beneficial.

Experience within the field is valued by employers and candidates can develop relevant skills through voluntary work in museums or with conservation organisations.

What the work involves

Entomology is the study of insects, including how they live and how they interact with their environment. Entomologists also observe the behaviour of insects to gain valuable information on the state of specific natural areas.

As an entomologist, you could analyse and assess the effects of insect life on agriculture. Entomologists are also employed to undertake research in medicine or to support ecological and environmental conservation work.

Work in the field might include searching for new species or studying insect ecology. In the laboratory, you could be developing insecticides or classifying insects.

Type of person suited to this work

You should have a methodical, logical and meticulous approach to your work and the ability to be patient and persevere when you encounter problems. You will also require good communication, computer and leadership skills.

You must be able to work effectively both alone and within a team. As you will need to remember a great deal of information, such as insect names and classifications, you should have an excellent memory.

Working conditions

Working hours and environments will depend upon the area of entomology you work in.

Entomologists working in research and higher education usually work regular hours from Monday to Friday. In a research post, you will spend your time in a laboratory, whilst a lecturer will also work in classrooms, lecture theatres and an office. Those working in conservation or field research will often work irregular hours and be outdoors in all weather conditions.

Future prospects

Entomologists work in a wide range of areas, including agricultural research and development, ecological protection and conservation, forensics and pest control. Others go on to develop their research interests as academic professionals after gaining postgraduate qualifications.

Progression within conservation and field research will depend on merit and responsibilities such as managing others. Within universities there is a progression path from researcher to head of department. Within industry, promotion opportunities to senior positions are available.

Self-employment is a possibility.

Advantages/disadvantages

It could be frustrating when an experiment or investigation does not go according to plan.

Your work could take you all over the world.

There is a wide variety of career options available.

If you work in the field or within conservation, you might have to live and work in inhospitable environments.

Money guide

Salaries vary depending on location, sector and employer.

Starting salaries for entomologists are around £16,000.

With experience, you should expect to earn £35,000 a year.

The most senior and highly regarded entomologists can achieve over £60,000 per year.

Related opportunities

- Agricultural Scientist p239
- Ecologist p502
- Environmental Scientist p504

Further information

British Entomological and Natural History Society
www.benhs.org.uk

Natural History Museum
www.nhm.ac.uk

Royal Entomological Society
www.royensoc.co.uk

Qualifications and courses

Most employers expect candidates to have completed either an environmental science degree or one in a relevant subject such as sustainable development, environmental management, chemistry, geophysics and environmental engineering. Graduates with a first degree in a science subject can take a postgraduate course in a specialist area of environmental science.

For entry to an undergraduate degree, most universities require applicants to have 2 A levels/3 H grades and 5 GCSEs/National 5s (A*–C/A–C). Relevant subjects at A level include Biology, Chemistry, Physics, Geography, English, Maths and Geology. Some admissions tutors will also favour foreign languages.

Candidates without a degree may gain entry to this profession by starting as a technician and working their way up to an environmental scientist position. In order to do this you will need at least 4 GCSEs/National 5s (A*–C/A–C), which should include 2 sciences, English and Maths or Technology. Equivalent qualifications, for example a BTEC First in Applied Science (Level 2), might be considered. Many technicians also complete A levels/H grades.

Relevant work experience would be beneficial and some degree courses include a placement.

What the work involves

Environmental scientists apply scientific techniques to study and protect the natural environment. You might look for ways to ensure sustainable development by discovering and experimenting with methods to reduce the damage caused to the world and our natural resources.

You could work in pollution monitoring, conservation, energy engineering, environmental consultancy and research or other areas.

You will probably be advising colleagues and clients, some of whom may not have a scientific background, on the damage particular developments could cause to the environment.

Type of person suited to this work

To work in this industry you should have an interest in geography, science and environmental issues.

You will need to be practical and methodical, as well as having the ability to think outside the box in order to solve problems. You must be meticulous in your approach to work, as the results you find could have an impact on whether developments go ahead.

You should be comfortable working independently and as part of a team. Communication, presentation and IT skills are required.

Working conditions

Your working hours and conditions will depend on the specific role you take and the sector you are employed in. Some environmental scientists work 9am to 5pm, Monday to Friday, but others involved in fieldwork will have to work overtime in order to meet deadlines.

For fieldwork you will be outside in all weather conditions and are likely to travel both within the UK and abroad. You will also spend a considerable amount of time in an office and/or laboratory.

Future prospects

There is a growing demand for environmental scientists, owing to the increasing concern about climate change and environmental issues along with a shortage of skilled people who can translate environmental knowledge into action.

You can progress to team manager or project manager, which will involve taking on more responsibilities. You could also become self-employed, working as a consultant and advising clients on a variety of environmental issues.

You might consider lecturing in environmental science.

Advantages/disadvantages

Your work will have a positive impact on the environment.

There could be opportunities to work abroad in unusual environments, such as rainforests and deserts.

You might face animosity if you refuse to approve a development.

You will often be required to spend time away from home which could disrupt your personal life.

Money guide

Earnings typically vary depending on sector, employer and location.

Starting salaries range from about £15,000 to £22,000.

With increased experience and training, you could expect up to £27,000 a year.

As a senior environmental scientist with managerial duties, it is possible to earn between £35,000 and £50,000.

Related opportunities

- Botanist p496
- Environmental Health Practitioner/Officer p22
- Oceanographer p520

Further information

Change Agents
www.changeagents.org.uk

Environment Agency
www.gov.uk/government/organisations/environment-agency

Institution of Environmental Sciences
www.the-ies.org

Qualifications and courses

Entrants to this profession usually have a degree, HNC/ HND or Foundation degree in a subject such as food science or food technology. For degree entry you will need 2 A levels/3 H grades, including Chemistry and Biology, and 5 GCSEs/National 5s (A*–C/A–C). HNC/ HND programmes usually require 1 A level/2 H grades and 3 GCSEs/National 5s (A*–C/A–C). The Institute of Food Science and Technology (IFST) runs a degree accreditation scheme that you may find useful. Pre-entry experience is also valued by potential employers.

Graduates with a degree in an unrelated subject could take a postgraduate course in subjects such as food safety, food quality management, advanced food manufacture, food production management, nutrition or food management. Some food technologists have a Postgraduate Diploma or a Master of Science (MSc) in Food Sciences.

You can enter this profession with lower qualifications as a laboratory technician/assistant and then work your way up as you gain more training and experience. Typical entry requirements at this level are 4 GCSEs/National 5s (A*–C/A–C), including English, Maths, Chemistry and Biology, or an A level/H grade in Applied Science. Technicians can work towards a Proficiency in Food Manufacturing Excellence (Levels 1–3) or an NVQ/SVQ in Laboratory and Associated Technical Activities (Levels 2–4). They can also study part time for an HND or degree to gain promotion to a role as a food technologist.

Once qualified, candidates can apply for registration with the IFST, which will give access to their continuing professional development (CPD) scheme. The Apprenticeship in Food and Drink may also equip you with relevant skills.

What the work involves

Food scientists undertake research, as well as production and quality assurance work in all areas of the food industry.

Your research may involve ensuring that food is safe to eat by testing it under different conditions. Alternatively, you might decrease the risk of contamination by analysing the food safety systems.

You will be using both laboratory and computer equipment to carry out your work.

Type of person suited to this work

You will need to have a high level of ability in biology and chemistry and an interest in food and its production. You should also possess a good knowledge of maths and physics.

You will require strong communication and teamwork skills. You should be meticulous, with a keen eye for detail. You will need to be organised and able to prioritise and manage your workload.

Good problem-solving skills are key and you will need to be extremely logical. You should be able to follow strict health, safety and hygiene rules.

Working conditions

You could be working in research units, laboratories or within the quality department in a factory. The working environment will always be clean to prevent the food being contaminated and you will be required to wear protective clothing.

You will typically work between 35 and 40 hours per week and if your employer operates a shift system, you might need to work weekends.

This role may include travel to warehouses, factories and distribution centres. A driving licence would be useful.

Future prospects

Job opportunities are good in this sector. The Food and Drink Federation states that the food manufacturing industry will need to employ 170,000 more people by 2020 in order to meet the skills needs of sector.

You might be offered the opportunity of promotion to team leader, technical director or project coordinator if you work within a larger organisation. You could also become a supervisor of research programmes or manager of food production activities, among other possible jobs.

Your skills would be transferable to several related sectors such as production management, marketing and buying raw materials. You could also become a specialist in a certain area.

Working abroad may be a possibility, especially within larger companies.

Advantages/disadvantages

You will be able to combine your love of food with your scientific background.

You may find some aspects of the job tedious, for example if you need to repeat the same tests over a period of time.

This career has the possibility of leading to roles in a number of areas.

Money guide

Starting salaries range from £20,000 to £25,000.

With several years' experience and increased responsibilities, you could expect to earn £30,000–£45,000 a year.

Those employed in a senior management role can achieve £55,000–£65,000.

Related opportunities

- Chef/Sous Chef p125
- Dietitian p285
- Microbiologist p518

Further information

Food and Drink Federation
www.fdf.org.uk

Improve Ltd
www.improveltd.co.uk

Institute of Food Science & Technology
www.ifst.org

SCIENCE, MATHEMATICS AND STATISTICS

Qualifications and courses

Entry requires a good Honours degree in biology, chemistry, forensic science or a related subject. The Chartered Society of Forensic Sciences accredits university courses so it might be worth looking out for these at an early stage. For degree entry you will usually require at least 2 A levels/3 H grades, including Biology and/or Chemistry, and 5 GCSEs/National 5s (A*–C/A–C) including Maths, English and a science.

Many entrants to this profession have a postgraduate diploma, master's or doctoral degree in forensic science or a related subject. This is becoming increasingly important to employers, who may also expect you to have at least 6 months' experience working in a laboratory. Some employers may accept an equivalent professional qualification.

To enter as an assistant forensic scientist in England and Wales, you will need 4 GCSEs (A*–C), including English, Biology, Chemistry or Maths, and an A level in Chemistry or Biology. In Scotland, an H grade in Chemistry, Biology or a related subject is normally required. Assistant forensic scientists usually cannot progress to a higher level without at least a degree or postgraduate qualification.

Once you secure employment as a trainee forensic scientist, you will receive on-the-job training from experienced colleagues. The Chartered Society of Forensic Sciences also provides relevant qualifications. If you want to specialise in electronic casework, you need a qualification in computing, electrical engineering or electronics.

A Disclosure and Barring Service (DBS) check may be required.

What the work involves

You will use your skills to provide important scientific information and help resolve legal and criminal cases. By analysing samples and assessing accident and crime scenes, you will support the work of police and lawyers.

Your role will involve identifying anything that may be used as evidence from a crime scene, including organs, blood, bodily fluids, illegal drugs, firearms and explosives, DNA and even paint or fragments of glass. You will carry out the necessary tests to extract the information required by the police.

You will use techniques including photography, DNA profiling, chromatography and metallurgy.

Type of person suited to this work

You need strong scientific skills and the desire to help solve crimes. Confidence is essential, as you might have to make court appearances.

You should be able to handle distressing situations well. You will need to pay great attention to detail whilst in the field, in the laboratory and when producing reports. Good colour vision is required.

You will require the ability to clearly explain scientific findings to people without a scientific background. You should be able to use statistics to interpret your findings. You must be a great communicator.

Working conditions

You will spend the majority of your time in the laboratory but you will also need to visit crime scenes. You might have to deal with unpleasant or upsetting sights.

You may also be outdoors in all weathers. You could be standing or crouching for long periods of time to examine evidence. You might have to travel with some absences from home.

The average forensic scientist works about 35 to 37 hours per week. You may also have to spend time on-call.

Future prospects

The job market is highly competitive, with scientists being employed by organisations such as the Centre for Applied Science and Technology, the Defence Science and Technology Laboratory and some of the police forces.

Promotion to management is generally based on appraisal reports and experience. You could become self-employed by working as a forensic consultant. You might also have the opportunity to work abroad.

Advantages/disadvantages

You will be using your scientific knowledge and applying it to real life situations in order to help the police catch criminals, which would be extremely rewarding.

This job comes with a lot of responsibility as your evidence may be the reason behind someone's conviction or acquittal.

This is a varied job and no two cases will be the same.

Money guide

Earnings vary according to employer and location.

Starting salaries for trainee or assistant forensic scientists are between £16,000 and £20,000.

Once you have gained 2–3 years' experience, earnings can increase to between £25,000 and £35,000 a year.

As a senior forensic scientist you could achieve £45,000 to £60,000 a year.

Related opportunities

- Biomedical Scientist/Medical Laboratory Assistant p494
- Clinical Scientist p499
- Microbiologist p518

Further information

Chartered Society of Forensic Sciences
www.csofs.org

Skills for Justice
www.sfjuk.com

SCIENCE, MATHEMATICS AND STATISTICS

Qualifications and courses

An Honours degree in geography is usually required but it is also possible to gain entry with a bachelor's degree in a related subject, such as oceanography or global change. Geography-based degrees cover varied aspects of human, economic and physical geography, knowledge of which will be useful in your working life.

Entry requirements for geography degrees vary but are usually 2 A levels/ 3 H grades, including Geography, and 5 GCSEs/National 5s (A*–C/A–C). For science-based geography courses (BSc) an A level/H grade in a science will also be needed.

Graduates who wish to secure a role as a researcher in academia will need to continue their studies to master's and doctorate (PhD) level. You will need a minimum of a 2.1 in your first degree to progress to a master's degree. To obtain funding for a PhD, you will be required to have achieved a high level on your master's course.

The Royal Geographical Society (RGS-IBG) offers opportunities for A level/H grade students to carry out sponsored fieldwork, and also provides gap year scholarships and several short courses.

What the work involves

You will be undertaking research, using IT, fieldwork and paper-based resources to broaden public and academic knowledge of your specific field of geography.

You can choose to specialise in either physical geography – the study of the earth, rivers, climate, land formation and oceans – or human geography – the study of humans in their environment. There are also several other branches of geography within these two, including environmental, health, historical, geomatics and pedology.

You could use your skills in a range of industrial fields, from government bodies to private consulting firms. As a researcher for a university, you will also lecture and contribute as a writer to geographical journals or articles while studying for a PhD or similar.

Type of person suited to this work

You need to have a good knowledge of your area of geography, with a genuine interest in and love for what you study. You will need excellent research and communication skills to be able to thoroughly understand and lecture on your chosen area of study.

Being flexible, approachable and hardworking will assist your progression to becoming an expert in your specialist geographical subject.

You will need a good level of physical fitness for fieldwork, as you will be working long hours in unusual conditions, spending a lot of time on your feet.

Working conditions

You could be based in a research centre, university, office or on location during fieldwork. Travel within the UK and abroad is frequently required.

You might need to work unsocial hours and weekends during fieldwork. Lecturing and office-based research tend to have more standard working hours, Monday to Friday. Although when doing academic research your hours will probably align with normal working hours, but you will have some flexibility to work the hours you want.

You will have access to a computer and a library to assist with research. You might need to use special equipment while in the field.

Future prospects

It is important to get some work experience in a research position before applying for a fully paid job, as the competition for research positions can be fierce. You can progress from research assistant to head researcher.

If you are following an academic route, you can start off as an assistant lecturer, working with undergraduate and master's students and progress to professor after completing a PhD and contributing significantly to your field of geography.

Advantages/disadvantages

You can work overseas, often for long periods of time, when doing field-based research.

The work is interesting and varied.

You will be required to constantly keep up to date with any changes or developments in your geographical field of expertise.

Money guide

Earnings vary according to your experience and employer.

As a research assistant, you can expect a starting salary of between £17,000 and £26,000.

With increased experience and recognition in your chosen area of expertise, your earnings could rise to £30,000–£45,000.

Professors contributing significantly to their field can earn in excess of £50,000.

Related opportunities

- Planning and Development Surveyor p98
- Secondary School Teacher p194
- Town Planner/Planning Technician p115

Further information

Geographical Association
www.geography.org.uk

Royal Geographical Society with IBG
www.rgs.org

SCIENCE, MATHEMATICS AND STATISTICS

Qualifications and courses

Geologist

To enter this profession you need a degree in a relevant physical science subject such as geology, geophysics or geochemistry. Typical entry requirements for a degree course are 2 A levels/3 H grades from subjects such as Physics, Chemistry, Biology, Geology and Maths and 5 GCSEs/National 5s (A*–C/A–C), including English. The Geological Society website provides details of approved courses which meet the first stage requirements for becoming a chartered geologist (CGeol) which may be of interest when choosing a university course.

Many entrants will have studied for a master's degree or doctorate (PhD) in a relevant area of geoscience, such as geophysics, petroleum geology or sedimentology. As competition for jobs is strong, a postgraduate qualification and pre-entry experience may improve your career prospects.

Geological technician

The usual minimum entry requirements for a junior technician are 4 GCSEs/National 5s (A*–C/A–C) including a science and Maths, and some employers may also require A levels/H grades. A BTEC National Level 3 in Applied Science may be accepted. Some employers may ask for a HNC/HND or a degree.

Once you secure employment, it is possible to work towards further qualifications, such as a degree, HND or the NVQ/SVQ in Laboratory and Associated Technical Activities (Levels 2–4).

What the work involves

Geologist

Geologists analyse and study the planet Earth, including its materials, structure and history. Your work may involve organising practical field and laboratory research to gain specific information. You may use your skills to support development work, for example mineral mining and the oil industry.

Geological technician

You will work closely with geologists, undertaking practical research work in the field and laboratory. You will collect and examine samples and produce test results. You will use other sources, for example surveys, to provide detailed information on specific geological features and aspects.

Type of person suited to this work

You should have the ability to pay close attention to detail. You will need to be meticulous, practical and logical in your approach to work. You will have to work with technical equipment so you should have high levels of dexterity. You must be able to uphold health and safety regulations.

Geologists need to be able to make important decisions and communicate well, both orally and in writing. A geological technician requires good graphical skills, including computer-aided design, to help produce maps.

Working conditions

The hours and working conditions of a geologist will vary considerably depending on the sector they work in.

Geological technicians normally work 9am–5pm, Monday–Friday, with some exceptions when they have approaching deadlines.

The majority of work will take place in labs, often with specialist equipment. Protective clothing might need to be worn for certain tests.

Future prospects

Geologists could progress to a managerial role, although this may involve relocating. There is also the possibility of becoming self-employed if you work as a consultant. Alternatively, you could work as a university lecturer.

There are more promotion opportunities for geological technicians within larger organisations. If you choose to work for a smaller company, you might need to change employers to progress. Training to become a geologist is possible.

Advantages/disadvantages

You may have difficulty gaining enough money to fund your research or projects.

There are job opportunities within multinational corporations which would allow you to use the latest technology and travel.

Employers generally prefer geologists who have completed postgraduate study.

Money guide

Geologist

Starting out as a graduate you can expect a salary of between £22,000 and £35,000.

With experience, you could earn from £40,000 to £50,000 a year.

Senior geologists with extensive experience can receive a salary ranging from £70,000 to over £100,000.

Geological technician

Starting salaries are between £18,500 and £24,000.

With experience, you can expect to earn from £25,000 to £30,000 a year.

At senior levels, salaries can increase to £40,000.

Related opportunities

- Ecologist p502
- Geophysicist p509
- Oceanographer p520

Further information

British Geological Survey
www.bgs.ac.uk

Cogent Skills
www.cogentskills.com

GEOPHYSICIST

Qualifications and courses

A degree in geophysics, geology, physics or a related subject is required for entry to this profession. For entry onto a geophysics degree, you will usually need at least 2 A levels/3 H grades, including Maths and Physics, and 5 GCSEs/National 5s (A*–C/A–C). Other useful subjects to study at A level/H grade are Biology, Chemistry, Geography and Geology.

Many entrants also have a postgraduate qualification and relevant courses include a Master of Science (MSc) in Petroleum Engineering, Petroleum Geoscience or Exploration Geophysics. It is also possible to study at doctorate level in a specialist area of geophysics.

Pre-entry work experience, from a vacation placement or internship, is desirable and will provide opportunities to make contacts within the industry, which could lead to freelance work in the future.

For entry at technician level, an A level/H grade in Physics is normally required. It may be possible to enter with an SQA National in Physics at Intermediate 2 or a BTEC National Level 3 Certificate/Diploma in Applied Science.

The Apprenticeship for Laboratory and Science Technicians is available at both Intermediate and Advanced Levels and for entry to an apprenticeship you will need 4 GCSEs/National 5s (A*–C/A–C).

What the work involves

Geophysicists apply physics-based investigation techniques to analyse the nature of the rocks, structures and minerals below the Earth's surface. You will spend a lot of time undertaking practical work and writing up results.

Most geophysicists and field seismologists are involved with helping companies locate oil and gas. You will plan and organise exploration work and interpret detailed geological information.

Geophysicists work in research in universities, research institutes and for companies involved in oil and mineral exploration. You will work as part of a team of geologists, engineers and/or engineering geologists.

Type of person suited to this work

You should have an interest in rock structures and a desire to travel. Your scientific and technical skills will be of a high quality. You should pay excellent attention to detail and have a methodical and meticulous approach to solving problems.

You will need to have strong numeracy skills and the ability to use software packages which may be extremely complex. You should be able to communicate well, both in person and in writing.

Working conditions

You will spend some time in an office or laboratory and the rest in the field. If you are involved in data collection you will travel the world, operating from base camps.

You might also work offshore (at sea) on oil or gas platforms or ships. This work will involve being away from home for long periods of time in a confined space, living and working with the same people.

In a UK office-based role, hours are generally 9am–5pm but you will be expected to be flexible. At sea, the working day is 12 hours. You may also be called on during your free time if there is an urgent need.

Future prospects

Skilled geophysicist professionals are in demand with construction, fuel and mineral exploration and development organisations within the public and private sectors.

Developing a career in industry may involve moving around to gain the relevant professional experience. In some jobs you might work overseas.

As you develop appropriate contacts, you have the option of becoming self-employed or doing consultancy/freelance work.

Advantages/disadvantages

The work can be physically demanding and may involve visiting potentially hazardous sites.

You may have the opportunity to study and observe the natural world in a variety of locations.

Some employment in this area is offered on a short-term basis, which can lead to job insecurity.

Money guide

Earnings vary depending on location, employer and the sector you work in.

Graduates with a first degree have a starting salary of between £22,000 and £25,000, whilst those with postgraduate qualifications can expect to earn between £24,000 and £30,000.

With experience, you could earn between £25,000 and £45,000 a year.

In a senior position, you could achieve over £60,000 per year.

Related opportunities

- Energy Engineer p209
- Environmental Scientist p504
- Oceanographer p520

Further information

British Geological Survey
www.bgs.ac.uk

British Geophysical Association
https://britgeophysics.org

Geological Society
www.geolsoc.org.uk

HYDROLOGIST

Qualifications and courses

The minimum requirement for entry to this profession is an Honours degree in a subject such as geography (focusing on physical science), environmental science, civil engineering or environmental management. For entry onto a degree course, students usually need a minimum of 2 A levels/3 H grades and 5 GCSEs/National 5s (A*–C/A–C). Useful subjects to study at A level/H grade include Maths, sciences, Geography and Geology.

Owing to the high level of competition for positions in this sector, a postgraduate qualification is strongly recommended. Possible subjects to study are water resources, engineering hydrology and water management. Entry onto a postgraduate course is with a minimum of a 2.1 in a relevant first degree.

The Chartered Institution of Water and Environmental Management (CIWEM) accredits a number of undergraduate and postgraduate courses in the field which may be worth looking out for when considering degree courses.

Pre-entry work experience is a useful way to develop your skills and build contacts within this competitive industry. You should consider undertaking placements during your holidays or as part of a sandwich degree.

Hydrologists are expected to engage in continuing professional development (CPD) throughout their career.

What the work involves

As an invaluable natural resource, water needs to be monitored and managed by hydrologists. You will help ensure that safe drinking water is available when and where it is needed.

Your work could involve measuring river flows, rainfall, evaporation and groundwater. You may assess water use in agriculture and forestry, or deal with water-management emergencies, for example in droughts.

Your research might involve working out potential flood risks, designing water supply systems or developing resources such as reservoirs. You will work with civil engineers, freshwater ecologists, chemists and other professionals.

Type of person suited to this work

You will need to have an interest in environmental protection and management, and an understanding of how a water supply affects a society. You should have strong geographical, scientific, mathematical and technical capabilities.

This role requires the ability to think creatively and solve problems. You will also need to be confident in using and creating maps and other ways of portraying a landscape.

The job demands excellent observational skills and attention to detail. You must be able to work with detailed factual information and communicate your findings.

Working conditions

Most hydrologists work conventional hours within an office environment. If there is an emergency or a deadline approaching, you might need to work some evenings and weekends.

You might also be required to spend time in the field. You will be working outdoors in a variety of weather conditions and using heavy equipment, so you will need to have a certain level of physical stamina.

This job might involve travel within the UK and abroad.

Future prospects

The opportunities available for promotion will vary according to the organisation and employer. Progression also depends on experience, skills, responsibility and merit. You may be able to increase your chances of promotion by moving to another team or geographical location. To progress, you should be able to manage people, projects and budgets.

Self-employment is possible if you become a consultant and there are many opportunities to work overseas for international organisations.

Advantages/disadvantages

You can live and work abroad while you undertake research work.

You may have to work outdoors in the wind and rain.

Some employment in this area is offered on a short-term basis, which can lead to job insecurity.

If you work within consultancy, you will have a wide variety of work available to you.

Money guide

Earnings vary according to sector, location and employer.

Starting salaries range from £15,000 to £20,000.

With experience, your earnings can rise to £30,000 a year.

Those employed in a senior role can earn in excess of £45,000.

Related opportunities

- Geophysicist p509
- Meteorologist p517
- Oceanographer p520

Further information

British Hydrological Society
www.hydrology.org.uk

Chartered Institution of Water and Environmental Management
www.ciwem.org

Qualifications and courses

All immunologists hold a relevant degree in immunology or a related science subject such as medical microbiology, biomedical science, or genetics. These should be accredited by the Institute of Biomedical Science (IBMS) and most institutions require at least 2 A levels/3 H grades (including Biology) and 5 GCSEs/National 5s (A*–C/A–C) for entrance.

The National Health Service (NHS) offers graduates the chance to study on the Scientist Training Programme (STP) in clinical immunology. This takes 3 years and leads to a master's degree. Entry requires that you have a relevant degree with a minimum of a 2.1 classification. Pre-entry laboratory experience may also prove advantageous.

Outside of the NHS, most job candidates possess a relevant master's degree or doctorate (PhD), which are necessary for research positions. Many employers, such as universities, may expect you to work towards a PhD as part of your ongoing training. After at least 4 years of training you will be eligible for mandatory registration with the Health & Care Professions Council (HCPC), which requires you to undertake continuing professional development (CPD) throughout your career.

You can also enter the profession by working in a pathology laboratory straight from school, after A levels/H grades, but this route is less common. Mature students can also enter this profession by completing an Access course, which can help those who are out of practice at education prepare for a degree.

What the work involves

Immunologists work with the body's immune system. They study functions and use the knowledge gained to treat and control illness and disease.

You might work on developing vaccines against diseases such as HIV or meningitis.

You could also find yourself studying the causes of allergies and looking at ways to stop the human body rejecting transplanted organs.

Type of person suited to this work

If you are thinking of becoming an immunologist, you naturally need to be interested in medicine and healthcare, and the way the body works.

You should have a logical, scientific mind and be good at solving problems, as well as being good at biology and scientific subjects in general. You may spend years researching one area or topic, and so will need to be patient and enjoy in-depth research work.

You will often have to work in teams, so you should enjoy this but equally be able to use your initiative and work independently. If you choose to lecture, your communication skills need to be excellent.

Working conditions

Working hours will vary depending on your employer, but will generally fall into the average 9am–5pm Monday to Friday pattern. During busy periods you may be required to work overtime.

Work tends to take place in a laboratory environment, often in sterile conditions. You will probably be required to wear appropriate clothing, and this often includes a white coat, face mask and rubber gloves.

If you choose to lecture, the environment will be very different, and you will spend most of your time in classrooms and lecture theatres.

Future prospects

If you choose to work as a lecturer, once you are a researcher you can work your way towards a promotion to lecturer, then senior lecturer and so forth, up to professor and head of department.

If you follow the NHS pathway, the career progression structure is very clear. You basically work your way up the grades, from A to C.

Other options to consider include scientific writing and publishing, or working on drugs trials and quality assurance. You could also progress to sales, finance and management positions within the biotechnology industry.

Advantages/disadvantages

This is a skilled profession, and training and progression can be really rewarding, especially in such an interesting job.

There is also the added advantage that you will be helping people.

The job can be stressful and demanding, and the work is by no means easy.

Money guide

As a new graduate in an NHS training post you will start on wage band 6 which is £26,041 a year.

After considerable experience this can gradually rise to wage band 9 which is up to £98,453 a year.

Outside of the NHS, starting salaries range from £22,000 to £30,000. Once you gain experience, this rises to between £28,000 and £37,000 and senior immunologists can earn between £40,000 and £60,000 a year.

Salaries vary between sectors.

Related opportunities

- Biomedical Scientist/Medical Laboratory Assistant p494
- Clinical Scientist p499
- Hospital Doctor p294

Further information

British Society for Immunology
www.immunology.org

NHS Careers
www.healthcareers.nhs.uk

SCIENCE, MATHEMATICS AND STATISTICS

Qualifications and courses

Entrants need at least 4 GCSEs/National 5s (A*–C/A–C), including English, Maths and a science. Equivalent qualifications such as a BTEC Level 2 Certificate in Applied Science may be accepted. Pre-entry laboratory experience is not necessary but may help your application.

Qualifications at a higher level such as A levels/H grades, a BTEC Level 3 qualification, NVQs/SVQs, HNC/HND or a degree in a science subject might be required, especially if you wish to advance during your career.

The majority of laboratory technicians are trained on the job, and may be able to study towards NVQs/SVQs in Laboratory and Associated Technical Activities (Levels 2–4) or Laboratory Science (Levels 2–3). NVQs/SVQs are also available in more specialist subjects, such as laboratory operations specialising in water, chemicals and pharmaceuticals, metal industry laboratory services, and forensic science.

You could take the Institute of Science & Technology's Certificate in Laboratory Technical Skills (Levels 1–3).

Apprenticeships are available in England. They last 1 year and you gain the Laboratory Technician Certificate. Scotland also offers a 2-year Modern Apprenticeship in Laboratory Technician work, during which you would gain the HNC Applied Science and SVQ Level 3 in Laboratory Techniques. Entry requires a minimum of 4 National 5s (A–C) or above including Maths, English and Chemistry. Higher maths or chemistry qualifications are also considered desirable.

What the work involves

You will analyse samples of different types of substances and materials using specialist equipment. You could specialise in a particular area, such as microbiology or clinical chemistry.

Your work may involve recording detailed information and developing and maintaining microbiological or other cultures.

Laboratory technicians apply their scientific analysis and measurement skills in organisations such as the military services, the National Health Service (NHS), industry and scientific research institutions.

Type of person suited to this work

You will provide important factual information, so must work to a high standard of accuracy. Your patient attitude will help you undertake sometimes repetitive but important laboratory activities.

Good manual handling skills will be needed to organise laboratory equipment. You will also need good communication skills and normal colour vision.

Good IT skills will help you record and analyse a range of information. As your work may involve tasks that are potentially dangerous, like handling bacteria and working with radiation, you must work to a good standard of health and safety at all times.

Working conditions

You will most likely have standard working hours, although some employers do work on a shift or rota basis which includes early mornings, evenings and weekends. Your working day will be spent in a clean and sterile laboratory.

You will work with specialist computer software to complete your research and record activities.

You could also have to carry out fieldwork at various sites outside the laboratory.

Future prospects

You will play an important role in protecting public health and research what makes the high-quality products that many of us use every day safe.

With further experience, you could progress to supervising a team of technicians or managing a laboratory.

Medical laboratory technicians can advance into a role as an education laboratory technician, phlebotomist, cardiographer, physiologist or research positions.

Advantages/disadvantages

Laboratory tasks can be repetitive, time-consuming and require patience.

Because of the transferable nature of lab skills, you could move from one organisation to another quite easily.

In some organisations you would work on a shift basis.

Money guide

Starting salaries are generally around £15,000 per year.

With experience and qualifications, you could earn between £20,000 and £25,000.

As a very experienced laboratory technician, team leader or laboratory manager, it is possible to earn from £30,000 to £40,000.

Related opportunities

- Biochemist p493
- Biomedical Scientist/Medical Laboratory Assistant p494
- Pharmacy Technician p310

Further information

Biochemical Society
www.biochemistry.org

Science Council
www.sciencecouncil.org

Semta
www.semta.org.uk

MARINE BIOLOGIST

Qualifications and courses

To enter this profession you require a degree in a relevant subject such as marine biology, marine science or oceanography. Minimum entry requirements for a degree are usually 2 A levels/3 H grades in relevant science subjects such as Biology along with 5 GCSEs/National 5s (A*–C/A–C). A levels/H grades in Maths, technological subjects or languages would also be beneficial.

Gaining some work experience during the summer break or by taking a gap year could also be useful. There are organisations such as the Earthwatch Institute or the Sea Turtle Protection Society of Greece (STPS) which offer various camp-based or expedition projects.

Due to the fierce competition within this industry postgraduate qualifications are a distinct advantage. For postgraduate study you will normally require a minimum of a 2.1 in your first degree.

If you want to apply for a technological support role you should have achieved A levels/H grades in Biology, Maths or Geography and another science subject.

Experience with scuba diving might also prove necessary if you wish to study animals first hand.

Once qualified you will need to continue learning. The Marine Biological Association (MBA) runs advanced courses on specific areas of marine science.

What the work involves

You will undertake practical research and analysis into animal and plant life in the world's seas and oceans. As well as academic research, you could apply your skills in fisheries, research or fish-farming development.

You may undertake research trips above or below the sea's surface and keep detailed research records. By increasing understanding of the sea you will be able to make predictions about the effects man will have on the marine ecosystem and how it will cope with these changes.

You may provide specialist advice to organisations such as governments or environmental pressure groups.

Type of person suited to this work

You should have a strong interest in science with a particular interest in marine life. You will require both a scientific understanding and practical ability. You will need to be meticulous and extremely patient.

You should have good numerical and computer-based skills. You must be observant and have a questioning mind. You will need to be able to analyse and interpret data effectively. You should have a certain level of physical stamina.

You will need a desire to travel and not mind being at sea. You should be highly organised and able to work autonomously and as part of a team.

Working conditions

You will spend time in an office environment, laboratory and researching in the field. While in the laboratory or office you will usually work normal office hours, however some projects and deadlines may require overtime. Laboratory work will usually involve working with hazardous organic materials as well as chemicals.

When working on projects at sea you will probably be working longer hours. Operating at sea might mean you are away for long periods of time, in cramped and possibly uncomfortable conditions. You will be subject to changeable weather conditions and potentially hazardous work environments. Fieldwork may also involve being inside aquariums.

Future prospects

Competition for jobs remains high. Gaining a good level of practical experience in addition to the relevant training shows commitment and provides useful skills. Once you have gathered enough field experience you could go freelance or set up your own consultancy.

You could lecture students, which you could combine with undertaking your own research.

Working abroad, where many institutes are based, is a distinct possibility.

Advantages/disadvantages

A lot of your research in the field will depend on the tides and weather conditions, which could slow down your progress.

You will use your skills and knowledge to increase public understanding of the natural environment.

Finding funding for your projects may prove problematic.

Money guide

Starting salaries for graduates are usually between £17,000 and £20,000 although they vary greatly depending on the employer and location of the work.

With experience, and for those with a PhD, this could rise to £25,000.

The highest earning marine biologists, who are at the top of their field, can earn around £60,000 a year.

Related opportunities

- Ecologist p502
- Environmental Scientist p504
- Oceanographer p520

Further information

Centre for Environment, Fisheries and Aquaculture Science
www.cefas.co.uk

Marine Biological Association
www.mba.ac.uk

National Oceanography Centre, Southampton
www.noc.soton.ac.uk

Qualifications and courses

Candidates typically hold a relevant degree, often in metallurgy, materials science, materials technology or materials engineering. It is also possible to enter with a degree in a general science subject. A Foundation year is available at some institutions for candidates without the required scientific background. HNC/HNDs in Engineering, Construction and the Built Environment and Manufacturing and Product Design may be relevant for this type of work.

Most degree courses expect applicants to have achieved at least 2 A levels/3 H grades, including Maths and a science, and 5 GCSEs/National 5s (A*–C/A–C), including Maths and English. The Advanced Diploma in Engineering is often accepted, whilst Level 3 NVQs, BTECs and City & Guilds qualifications may also be accepted when combined with other qualifications. The Apprenticeship in Engineering and Manufacturing Technologies is also available.

To become a chartered materials engineer with the Engineering Council, you need to have studied an accredited 4-year Master of Engineering (MEng) degree, or a 3-year bachelor's degree followed by a period of professional development. Postgraduate courses are available, and may be studied prior to entry, or through company training schemes. In order to be accepted you must have successfully completed a first degree. Many employers prefer candidates to have a Master of Science (MSc) or to be working towards a doctorate. Professional bodies also expect you to undertake continuing professional development (CPD).

It may be possible to enter the profession at technician level. Often technicians are studying part time for their doctorate. Applicants usually need at least 4 GCSE/National 5s (A*–C/A–C), including 2 sciences (or Double Science), Maths and English, or equivalent qualifications such as BTEC Level 2 qualifications in science.

What the work involves

Materials scientists measure, define and process materials. They help decide the types of materials to use in engineering, construction and product processing work.

You will use your knowledge of the properties of metals and alloys, glass, ceramics and other materials in many areas of industrial research, development and production. You will research how and why materials react to certain conditions and how they can be used in our everyday lives.

You will use technology and computer equipment to carry out tests on different materials, keep records of your findings and draw conclusions from the results.

Type of person suited to this work

You will need to have creative flair and you should have an inquisitive and logical mind. You will need to be meticulous.

You will be able to write coherent reports and be a good public speaker, as you might need to give presentations. You will need solid computer skills. You should work well in a team environment.

You should have dexterity as you will be working with a range of test equipment. You will need good eyesight (including colour vision for some projects).

Working conditions

Materials scientists in industry work normal office hours or shifts, however the more senior your role is, the longer you will have to work.

You could be working in a sterile laboratory or an industrial environment. The most common working environments for materials scientists are laboratories and offices.

There is a possibility you will have to complete work in the field. You may have to wear protective clothing.

Future prospects

You will have the option to change industries and purchase raw materials, work in sales, management or marketing. You could progress to become a project manager or a technical director, meaning you would be leading people in developing new products.

Alternatively, you could move into a career in teaching.

Opportunities for self-employment are limited but you could work in non-destructive testing (NDT) or failure analysis. There may be the possibility to work abroad.

Advantages/disadvantages

You will have the opportunity to apply your skills and knowledge to develop new products and provide new scientific information.

Scientists are constantly in demand in most areas of industry.

This can be a highly lucrative career.

Money guide

On entering this career as a graduate you can expect to earn around £21,000 per year. Entry salaries tend to be higher if you have a postgraduate qualification, from £25,000 to £35,000 per year.

Once you have reached a senior role, as a professor for example, you could earn in excess of £50,000 per year.

Salaries are usually higher within large companies in the private sector.

Related opportunities

- Biochemist p493
- Chemist p497
- Laboratory Technician p512

Further information

Institute of Materials, Minerals and Mining
www.iom3.org

Semta
www.semta.org.uk

UK Centre for Materials Education
www.materials.ac.uk

Qualifications and courses

A degree in maths is essential to work as a professional mathematician in industry, business/finance, education or research.

Degrees are available in general maths or in specific areas, such as financial or business maths. Entry onto maths degree courses usually requires at least 2 A levels/3 H grades, including Maths, and 5 GCSEs/National 5s (A*–C/A–C), including English and Maths. A science and/or computing-related subject are also viewed favourably.

Maths graduates are recruited directly by some companies. Most mathematicians have postgraduate qualifications, which require a first degree in mathematics, physics or another subject with a high mathematical content. Entry is possible with an undergraduate degree only but progression is significantly limited unless you hold a further qualification, particularly within academia.

It is possible to become a chartered mathematician with the Institute of Mathematics after gaining an Honours degree in maths, plus 5 years of postgraduate training and experience including employment for a minimum of 2 years.

What the work involves

Research is conducted using mathematical theory in order to solve problems in areas such as science, engineering, finance, government and IT. You could work at all levels of industry, research and education and help to inform the work of different organisations.

You could study and teach pure mathematics in an academic environment or work in job roles requiring mathematical skills and knowledge, for example actuary, operational researcher or statistician.

Your work may involve undertaking research and analysis, setting up research programmes and assessing research findings. In a business, you will work on a specific project such as predicting future trends in population growth or financial markets.

Type of person suited to this work

You must have a strong interest in working with numerical information to solve complex problems. You need to be logical and methodical, as well as flexible and innovative to analyse a range of problems.

Your work could help shape the activities of your company so you must have good attention to detail and be able to record your work accurately.

Strong communication skills will help you explain mathematical ideas to people without a maths background. As maths-related research can take time to set up, a patient attitude can be helpful.

Working conditions

For many roles, you would work in an office and use computers to analyse information. Long hours are common in this role.

If you work in education, you will spend time teaching in classrooms and in lecture rooms. You could also spend time undertaking research.

Mathematicians who work in business, such as accountants, will spend time in meetings with their clients.

Future prospects

There is a high demand for professional mathematicians in areas such as business, finance or industry, and in companies that develop new products such as new computer software and pharmaceuticals. Graduates have fared fairly well in the labour market in recent years.

After gaining experience, you could progress into a managerial role.

In an academic environment, progression depends on your research accomplishments. Academic jobs may not necessarily have as high a turnover as jobs with corporations.

Advantages/disadvantages

Mathematical skills apply to many different sectors, so you could move across a range of areas.

A shortage of qualified mathematicians means that there are a variety of opportunities.

A second degree could be needed to follow your chosen career.

Tight deadlines and the uncertainty in being able to find a solution to problems can make this line of work stressful.

Money guide

Salary levels vary widely according to employer and sector, although on average larger companies will pay more than smaller companies.

Starting salaries range from £25,000 to £35,000 per year.

With several years' experience you could earn up to £40,000 per year.

At senior level, expected earnings would be from £30,000 up to £70,000, depending on sector and level of responsibility. These figures apply to professors within academic settings and team leaders within industrial settings.

Related opportunities

- Actuary p5
- Stockbroker p53
- Systems Analyst p152

Further information

Institute of Mathematics and its Applications
www.ima.org.uk

Mathematical Association
www.m-a.org.uk

Maths Careers
www.mathscareers.org.uk

SCIENCE, MATHEMATICS AND STATISTICS

515

Qualifications and courses

The usual entry qualification required for a career as a metallurgist is a degree. Degrees are available in metallurgy and in materials science, materials technology and materials engineering. Entry to a relevant degree course usually requires a minimum of 2 A levels/3 H grades and 5 GCSEs/National 5s (A*–C/A–C). The Advanced Diploma in Engineering and BTEC/NQA Level 3 qualifications might be offered as alternatives. Knowledge of foreign languages may also prove advantageous within this globalised industry.

For those seeking entry to the profession by first becoming a technician or with an HNC/HND or Foundation degree (in a subject such as metallurgy and materials, metals technology, manufacturing engineering or applied science) then at least 1 science A level/H grade will be required.

You could apply for one of the graduate training programmes offered by several industry employers. This can lead to membership with a professional institution such as the Institute of Cast Metals Engineers (ICME), which could increase job prospects.

Once you have qualified, continuing professional development (CPD) is encouraged. Once you have gained 2 years of relevant experience you will be given the opportunity to join the Institute of Materials, Minerals and Mining (IOM³). Membership will give you an opportunity to attend conferences and network with others in the industry. If you have a relevant master's degree and 4 years' experience you will be able to become a professional member of IOM³. You can then apply to gain chartered engineer (CEng) status.

What the work involves

Metallurgists apply their materials science and engineering knowledge to support product and process development in areas such as aerospace, rail, construction and oil and gas.

You may be involved with the metal extraction process (chemical metallurgy), designing metal components (process metallurgy), managing projects, or investigating metals and materials (physical metallurgy). You might help develop practical solutions for production problems.

It is likely that your role will involve aspects of quality control, project management and process/product development.

Type of person suited to this work

Metallurgists need an excellent knowledge of metals and related materials, whatever area they work in. They must also be able to understand the uses for different materials.

You will need to have good communication and teamworking skills. You will also have to be confident in making decisions that could affect major industrial processes and understand the commercial impact of your work.

Your flexible approach and attention to detail will help you adapt to the demands of different projects. Your IT and numeracy skills will also be important. Because you could

work with potentially dangerous materials you must have a good knowledge of health and safety.

Working conditions

You might have to work in a noisy location if you are employed by a large manufacturing company. In other roles you could be based in a laboratory-style setting.

Hours vary from employer to employer, but they can be long especially if you are working to complete a specific project to a set deadline.

In many roles, you will be part of a team and could also meet with clients on a regular basis. In some roles you may be required to write detailed reports.

Future prospects

There are job opportunities at various companies, from steel producers to those who need metal composites.

You could undertake project management for individual companies. You might work for companies that develop materials for industries such as automotive and aerospace engineering.

There may be the opportunity for you to directly manage the process of mining and extracting materials.

Advantages/disadvantages

The role can provide the satisfaction of developing new products and materials.

There are opportunities to work abroad and this usually pays well.

You might need to work unsocial hours for various projects.

If you specialise in a particular field, job choices could be narrow.

Money guide

Starting salaries start at around £20,000 per year. Those with chartered engineer status are likely to earn more.

With experience and at a senior level it is possible to earn £40,000.

As a senior manager and with chartered engineer status and considerable experience you could earn in excess of £50,000.

Related opportunities

- Aerospace Engineer p200
- Laboratory Technician p512
- Materials Scientist p514

Further information

Engineering Council UK
www.engc.org.uk

Institute of Cast Metals Engineers
www.icme.org.uk

Institute of Materials, Minerals and Mining
www.iom3.org

METEOROLOGIST

Qualifications and courses

Entrants to this profession need a degree accredited by the Royal Meteorological Society (RMetS) and postgraduate degrees are often necessary for employment. Degrees in meteorology are available, but other suitable subjects include physics, maths, computer science, oceanography and environmental science. The general entry requirements for a degree are 2 A levels/3 H grades and 5 GCSEs/National 5s (A*–C/A–C) and some employers may also require A levels/H grades in Maths and Physics.

Relevant postgraduate courses are available and a requisite of research posts. Subject areas include meteorology, climatology and atmospheric science.

The Met Office provides initial training for new entrants without a postgraduate qualification. You have an option of 2 training routes. One route of training consists of an 18-week Initial Forecasting Course, followed by practical training at a weather station, and the completion of a RQF Level 5 in Meteorological Forecasting. A modular route is also available and will allow you to focus on a specialism. The completion of the RQF Level 5 in Meteorological Forecasting is also necessary. You will generally need a first or 2.1 and a good grade in at least A level/H grade Physics to apply for a post at the Met Office.

What the work involves

Information gained from observing the sky, the atmosphere and natural phenomena gives a picture of everyday weather conditions.

As well as providing weather forecast information that is used throughout the media and to inform industries such as fishing, meteorologists undertake research into the Earth's atmosphere. You could be employed by the Royal Navy, the Royal Air Force, the Met Office or other employers.

You will be using specialist computer programs and mathematical techniques to gather information, which you will combine in order to form a weather picture. Within meteorology you can work as a forecaster or a researcher.

Type of person suited to this work

You should have a strong interest in the environment, science, research and climate change. You will need to excel in maths and physics.

The job calls for the ability to problem solve and think creatively to resolve specific issues. You should be happy to work in various locations, however remote. The job demands excellent observational skills and attention to detail.

You should be able to comprehend and evaluate complex information. You must be able to communicate effectively, both in person and on paper. You will be computer literate, and work well as part of a team.

Working conditions

You will generally conduct your work from an office environment, using specialised computers.

When you are working in the field you could be living and working in extremely isolated areas with basic living conditions.

Researchers generally work ordinary office hours. Forecasters and observers however will usually work in shifts. When working in the field you will not usually have set hours. However, the most common shift working pattern is 12 hours covering days and nights.

Future prospects

There are 3 main areas that a meteorologist can work in; these are forecasting, research and teaching. You may wish to move between them in order to progress.

Once you have gained experience as a forecaster you might be able to move into broadcasting, research or consultancy work.

There could be the possibility of working abroad.

Advantages/disadvantages

You may have the opportunity to study and observe the natural world in a variety of locations.

You might have to work inconvenient shifts.

There is a wide variety of work within this industry so you shouldn't get bored.

Employers increasingly require applicants to have a postgraduate qualification in a relevant subject.

Money guide

Starting salaries are usually between £21,000 and £27,000 per year.

The starting salary for a trainee operational meteorologist at the Met Office is £18,000, rising to £22,950 on completion of training.

Experienced meteorologists can earn between £25,000 and £35,000 a year.

As a manager you could earn from £38,000 to £60,000 per year.

Related opportunities

- Geophysicist p509
- Oceanographer p520
- Physicist p522

Further information

Met Office
www.metoffice.gov.uk

Royal Meteorological Society
www.rmets.org

MICROBIOLOGIST

Qualifications and courses

Most entrants have at least a degree in microbiology or another biological science. To get onto a degree course in microbiology you will usually need at least 2 A levels/3 H grades, including Biology and preferably Chemistry, and 5 GCSEs/National 5s (A*–C/A–C), including a science, English and Maths. A Master of Science (MSc) or doctorate (PhD) in microbiology will increase your job opportunities. Work experience will prove advantageous when applying for jobs. This may be possible via a work placement as part of a sandwich degree course, or by arranging work experience during the holidays. For example, the Society for Applied Microbiology provides student work schemes, and the Society for General Microbiology funds research projects for penultimate-year undergraduate students.

The National Health Service (NHS) offers graduates the chance to study on the Scientist Training Programme (STP), specialising in clinical science. The programme lasts 3 years and you would achieve an MSc in Microbiology. After another 2 years of lab experience you can gain the Association of Clinical Scientists Certificate of Attainment and apply for the mandatory state registration with the Health & Care Professions Council (HCPC).

It is also possible to get into microbiology by working your way up from laboratory technician by working and studying part time for a relevant degree. NVQs/SVQs are available in Laboratory and Associated Technical Activities (Levels 2–4).

Once you are working as a microbiologist, you will receive on-the-job training in areas such as lab techniques, technology and management skills.

What the work involves

Microbiologists study micro-organisms such as bacteria and viruses.

As a clinical microbiologist in a healthcare setting, you would aim to identify diseases and protect the community from the spread of infection. Alternatively, you could work in research and development for the pharmaceutical and food industries, in agriculture, the environment or in education.

Duties include presenting the findings of your research, supervising the work of support staff and carrying out administrative work. If you worked as a researcher and lecturer in a university or teaching hospital, you would also be involved in tutoring, mentoring and supervising students.

Type of person suited to this work

You will need to be scientifically capable. You must also have good problem-solving skills and the ability to work with statistics and relevant computer packages.

You will require a high level of dexterity and need to be meticulous, practical and logical in your approach to work. You should also be patient as you might find you have to repeat tests.

Working conditions

Most microbiologists spend at least part of their time in laboratories. Some microbiologists spend part of their time in classrooms and offices.

The work week for many microbiologists is generally 40 hours. Some overtime may be necessary when a project must be completed or when an experiment must be monitored around the clock.

Microbiologists usually spend some time reading and studying to keep up with the newest findings of other scientists.

Future prospects

There is considerable competition for research positions. Nonetheless, increased public awareness in preserving the environment, providing sanitary food production and storage, and finding cures for such diseases as AIDS, cancer, and heart disease could provide the stimulus for increased spending by private companies. In 2015 the UK government expressed an intention to invest in biological research due to the dangers of antimicrobial resistance. The growth in this area of study may result in more job opportunities.

Advantages/disadvantages

There are opportunities to visit different types of outside locations on research trips.

Experiments can take a long time to complete and some aspects might become tedious. You will also be handling potentially dangerous substances.

Employers such as the NHS can offer the chance to gain experience in different departments and provide well-structured career paths.

Money guide

If you begin your career as a laboratory assistant you can earn between £13,000 and £19,000.

In the NHS you would enter on band 6 earning a salary between £26,041 and £34,876.

If you work in research and development for a pharmaceutical firm, salaries are generally higher and start from £27,000 to £37,000.

Top salaries for microbiologists can reach £60,000.

Related opportunities

- Biochemist p493
- Immunologist p511
- Pharmacologist p309

Further information

Microbiology Society
www.microbiologysociety.org

NHS Careers
www.healthcareers.nhs.uk

Qualifications and courses

You must be a graduate to enter this profession. A degree in a relevant subject such as nanoscience, engineering, biotechnology, mathematics, chemistry or computer science will be necessary. Entry requirements for degrees are at least 2 A levels/3 H grades, and 5 GCSEs/National 5s (A*–C/A–C). Most nanotechnologists have postgraduate qualifications in nanoscience. Employers will often expect you to have or be working towards a doctorate in the subject. You will need a 2.1 or above in your first degree to gain entry onto a postgraduate course.

Once in employment you will receive health and safety training and be taught how to operate laboratory machinery.

It is essential to continue your training when working in this rapidly evolving field. You should study relevant journals and attend lectures by peers to update your skills and understanding of new technology. You may find it helpful to join a professional body as you will have the opportunity to network and learn from leading industry professionals. Relevant bodies include the Institute of Physics and the Royal Society of Chemistry.

You may wish to work towards Chartered Scientist status and participate in a continuing professional development scheme.

What the work involves

Nanotechnologists design and create tiny devices using materials on the microscopic nanoscale (0.1 to 100nm in size). Your work could be in many fields including biotechnology, electronics, medicine or food science.

This job involves a great deal of precision and you will have to use a microscope to conduct your work.

You will use scientific instruments to collate and sort your materials. You will maintain your production equipment and restock your lab with required chemicals, equipment and materials.

Typically you will perform experiments to test your creations, analyse data from experiments and then write up reports on your findings for publication.

Type of person suited to this work

You will need to have an acute attention to detail and a keen scientific mind. You will be adept at working with numbers when analysing experimental data. Excellent communication skills are valuable as you will be expected to communicate your work to other scientists and to students.

You will have strong research skills. Good organisation skills are essential in industry work as you will be working to strict deadlines. Working on a small scale will require patience and care.

A nanotechnologist must be a good problem solver. You must be able to work well in a team as you will typically work alongside others from different science and engineering areas.

Working conditions

You will typically work regular hours 9am to 5pm, Monday to Friday. However, you may be expected to work long hours in order to meet deadlines. If working in industry, weekend and evening work may be necessary as you could be working on a shift rota.

You will work in a laboratory environment where you will be expected to wear protective clothing such as a white coat and safety goggles.

You will be part of a wider scientific community and you may have to travel to share your work with and learn from other nanotechnologists.

Future prospects

Nanotechnology is a rapidly growing sector and you will have the opportunity to work in a variety of areas such as medicine, biotechnology, agriculture, or research.

In a research role you may be able to progress to laboratory manager or supervisor.

Alternatively, you could go into education to lecture and research at a university.

Advantages/disadvantages

Creating devices that serve a purpose can be very satisfying.

Working on a small scale takes time and care, which can be very frustrating.

You will have the opportunity to indulge your passion for science.

Money guide

Salaries vary according to experience, qualifications and the industry you are working for.

Starting salaries for PhD students are around £13,000 to £14,000 a year.

Postdoctoral researchers or research fellows may earn between £29,000 and £36,000 a year.

A research scientist working in industry can expect to earn in the region of £23,000 to £42,000 a year.

University lecturers can achieve in excess of £35,000 a year.

Professors and senior staff in research institutions and industry could earn in excess of £60,000 a year.

Related opportunities

- Engineering Craft Machinist p210
- Manufacturing/Production Engineer p217

Further information

Nanowerk
www.nanowerk.com

The Institute of Engineering and Technology
www.theiet.org

SCIENCE, MATHEMATICS AND STATISTICS

Qualifications and courses

The majority of entrants within this profession will hold a degree. Degrees are available in oceanography and related areas, such as marine biology, and other relevant subjects include biology, chemistry, physics, mathematics and geology. For degree entry, candidates usually require 2 A levels/3 H grades, including Maths and a science, and 5 GCSEs/National 5s (A*–C/A–C). Relevant GCSE/National 5 subjects include sciences, English and Maths along with foreign languages, IT and Geography. The Society for Underwater Technology (SUT) offers sponsorship awards to undergraduates ranging from £2,000 to £4,000 for master's students.

Most employers expect candidates to hold an A level/H grade in Maths. It is possible to join the Merchant or Royal Navy without a degree and then undertake the necessary studying and training to become an oceanographer.

Having a postgraduate qualification in oceanography is very common and also will increase your employability. You could also study for a course in related/specialist areas. It is also possible to do a research-based doctorate, which some employers may expect you to already have or be working towards.

Entry without a degree or HND/HNC qualification is possible but support and technical roles are rare and a willingness to pursue further study later on would be expected.

The SUT offer a continuing professional development programme established by the Marine Technology Education Consortium.

What the work involves

Oceanographers investigate how ocean organisms and structures work together.

Your work could involve undertaking fieldwork above and below the surface of the sea. You may also interpret the information you find and write research reports.

The information you produce could be used by government and/or industry.

Type of person suited to this work

You will require a passion for the environment and ocean life, along with an interest in maths, science and engineering. You will need to be prepared to travel and spend time working at sea.

As you may be working in the field you will need to be physically fit. You should have strong verbal and written communication skills. You will be carrying out detailed research and so will need to be meticulous, logical and practical.

You will also need to be able to present your findings in front of an audience and so should have a certain level of confidence. Good teamwork is essential.

Working conditions

Much of your time will be spent working in a laboratory or an office, with typical office hours from Monday to Friday.

Fieldwork may be carried out at sea or along the coastline.

When working at sea you might be required to spend 6 weeks or more away from home. You will be living and working with the same people.

Future prospects

Most oceanographic work is structured around fixed, short-term contracts and so progression can prove tricky.

You might find that you have to move between employers in order to achieve a promotion. Progression is based on merit and taking on more responsibilities, such as leading a team. It is possible to become self-employed and work as a consultant. Another option might be university lecturing, where progression opportunities are easier to come by.

You may choose to undergo further training in order to specialise in marine geology, marine chemistry, marine physics, or marine biology.

Ocean studies are fundamental to understanding climate change, so investment in research is likely to increase.

Advantages/disadvantages

You will be able to combine your love of the environment with your scientific ability.

Some employers may expect candidates to hold a postgraduate qualification.

You will have the opportunity to travel.

Money guide

These figures are only approximate as salaries vary depending on location, sector and employer.

Starting salaries are between £18,000 and £25,000 per year.

Those with a PhD could start on £20,000–£25,000.

Once you have gained experience as an oceanographer you could earn between £33,000 and £44,000 a year.

As a senior oceanographer, with management responsibilities, you could earn up to £60,000. Consultants can earn between £35,000 and £50,000; senior consultants could earn more.

Lecturers can earn upwards of £30,000.

Related opportunities

- Diver p365
- Ecologist p502
- Marine Biologist p513

Further information

Centre for Environment, Fisheries and Aquaculture Science
www.cefas.co.uk

National Oceanography Centre, Southampton
www.noc.soton.ac.uk

Society for Underwater Technology
www.sut.org

Qualifications and courses

The entry requirement for this profession is a 2.1 Honours degree or higher in a relevant subject such as maths, statistics, economics, management science or business studies. Specialist degrees in operational research are available at some institutions and are usually offered as a joint Honours degree with a subject such as maths or statistics.

Entry to a relevant degree course is with a minimum of 2 A levels/3 H grades, including Maths, and 5 GCSEs/National 5s (A*–C/A–C). It may be possible to become an operational researcher with a degree in a non-mathematical subject if you have a good A level/H grade in Maths.

Some employers may expect candidates to have a postgraduate qualification, for example a master's in operational research or management science. Entry onto a postgraduate course is dependent on a candidate's experience and a minimum of a 2.1 class in a relevant undergraduate degree.

Opportunities for graduates are available through the Civil Service Fast Stream programme. The Government Operational Research Service (GORS) recruits candidates with a minimum of a 2.1 in a numerate degree or a postgraduate degree in operational research.

The Operational Research Society organises an annual careers open day for undergraduates who are considering working in this sector and also offers a wide range of training courses and in-house training services.

What the work involves

Operational researchers use mathematical, scientific and other analytical methods to help improve the performance of organisations in business, industry and government.

You will work closely with managers and other staff to create practical solutions to different management and organisational issues.

You will develop analytical models or strategies to improve a specific area or aspect of an organisation. You might also be involved with putting your ideas into practice within companies.

Type of person suited to this work

Operational research is all about getting practical results from in-depth analysis. Consequently, you should enjoy solving problems and applying your analytical and mathematical abilities to find solutions.

You will have a strong interest in helping organisations develop and you will put your understanding of each company to practical use. You will need excellent communication skills for working closely with managers and other staff.

Your flexible approach will help you cope with the varied demands of each project. While you will need strong IT skills, a creative flair can also benefit you in this job.

Working conditions

You will usually work a 37-hour week, Monday to Friday, with some overtime required if projects are nearing deadlines.

You will undertake most of your work in an office setting and meetings with managers, technical specialists and staff are likely to be a regular part of your job. You will also be required to visit clients so a driving licence would be useful. Travel both within the UK and abroad is possible.

Future prospects

Operational researchers help many different organisations to develop successfully. There are increasing opportunities in manufacturing, finance and other sectors.

You could move into managing an operational research team or work in areas such as marketing. With more experience, you could develop a career as a consultant.

The civil service offers a well-structured career path and a range of opportunities in operational research.

Advantages/disadvantages

Strong demand in many sectors means that you can develop your career in various types of companies.

Operational research work is fast moving and you will always be learning something new.

Resolving production, resource or staffing problems for a company can be stressful and confrontational.

Money guide

Salary levels depend on location, the sector you work in and your academic background.

Earnings tend to be highest for those employed by management consultancies.

Starting salaries range from £20,000 to £28,000 a year.

With experience and a more senior position, you can expect to earn between £35,000 and £60,000 a year.

At operational research consultant level, you could achieve up to £100,000 a year.

Related opportunities

- Actuary p5
- Mathematician/Mathematics Research Scientist p515
- Statistician p524

Further information

Government Operational Research Service
www.operational-research.gov.uk

Operational Research Society
www.theorsociety.com

SCIENCE, MATHEMATICS AND STATISTICS

Qualifications and courses

For entry to this profession you need to have a relevant degree in either physics or applied physics. Entry requirements for a degree course are usually at least 2 A levels/3 H grades, including Physics and Maths, and 5 GCSEs/National 5s (A*–C/A–C) including English, Maths and a science, typically Physics.

Many institutions offer 1-year science Foundation courses for candidates who do not have the necessary scientific background to directly enter a science-based degree course.

Some employers may also expect you to have a relevant postgraduate qualification such as a Master of Science (MSc) or doctorate (PhD). Entry onto a postgraduate course requires a minimum of a 2.1 in your first degree and pre-entry work experience is increasingly requested.

Physicists are trained on the job and often study for a PhD or the membership exams of relevant professional bodies alongside their professional work. For example, medical physicists must work towards the Clinical Science Diploma of the Institute of Physics and Engineering in Medicine (IPEM).

For entry at technician level, an A level/H grade in Physics, or equivalent qualifications such as a BTEC Level 3 qualification in Applied Science or SQA National in Science, is required. Some technicians may hold a science-based degree. Technicians who have secured employment can take the NVQ in Laboratory and Associated Technical Activities (Levels 2–4).

What the work involves

Physicists apply their understanding of the relationship between matter and energy to their work in industry, government research, academia and medicine.

You could use your specialist skills and knowledge to investigate diverse subjects, including space research, nuclear energy, electronics, defence technology and materials for industrial use.

You might be involved with research and development work or with designing projects and experiments. Your role could also include developing products and systems in areas such as computing, aeronautics, transport and medicine.

Type of person suited to this work

Physicists must combine their scientific knowledge with strong problem-solving skills.

You will need the confidence to work with complex numerical information. You should have excellent attention to detail and a patient approach for undertaking research.

IT skills are also important. Good written and oral communication skills are needed for you to be able to explain your work clearly.

Working conditions

You will usually work Monday to Friday from 9am to 5pm. If you are employed by the NHS as a medical physicist, you are likely to work shifts and fulfil on-call duties.

You will be based in a laboratory, workshop or office, using specialist equipment and computers. This work can involve handling dangerous chemicals so you will need to wear protective clothing.

For some jobs you will be required to travel to meetings and conferences so a driving licence would be useful. If you are undertaking research in the field, you may be away from home for extended periods of time.

Future prospects

Physicists work at the cutting edge of science and industry. They apply their skills in areas as varied as electronics, power, communications and defence. They are employed by research institutions, government bodies and private companies to improve and develop products and systems.

You will be able to progress to supervisory or management roles, or enter into the training and teaching of physics.

Advantages/disadvantages

Physics offers the chance to develop public understanding of important scientific questions.

Working with detailed information for long periods of time can be very tiring.

You might have the chance to work abroad.

Money guide

Salary levels vary according to employer and sector, however a relevant PhD may increase your income.

Starting salaries are usually between £21,000 and £25,000.

A qualified and experienced research physicist can expect to earn between £24,000 and £35,000.

Senior physicists with increased responsibilities typically receive a salary ranging from £40,000 to £50,000.

In academia, a senior higher education lecturer can achieve £55,000 to £60,000 a year.

Related opportunities

- Aerospace Engineer p200
- Astronomer p491
- Meteorologist p517

Further information

Institute of Physics
www.iop.org

Institute of Physics and Engineering in Medicine
www.ipem.ac.uk

Physics World
www.physicsworld.com

Qualifications and courses

Depending on their interests, seismologists can come from the fields of geology, geophysics, physics or applied mathematics.

A bachelor's degree in a scientific discipline is necessary for entry into this profession, and a master's degree or doctorate are significant assets for more advanced research. Available bachelor's degrees usually include geophysics, computer science, chemistry, and other mathematical and science subjects and the general entry requirements are 2 A levels/3 H grades and 5 GCSEs/National 5s (A*–C/A–C). Pre-entry work experience is also desirable and many companies offer summer internships.

While lecturers and researchers often continue with their studies at the postgraduate level, seismologists who work for private companies will often undertake additional specialised training in the area required.

Continuing professional development (CPD) is advised, but there are no formal methods through which to do this. Membership of a relevant professional body, such as the Society of Exploration Geophysicists (SEG), may be advantageous as it would allow you to keep up to date with the latest developments in your chosen specialism.

Initial training is usually provided on the job. This includes health and safety, field training and data entry. There may be a probationary period during which you will be mentored by a more experienced colleague.

What the work involves

Seismologists are earth scientists, specialists in geophysics, who study seismic waves in geological materials. Their research aims at interpreting the geological composition and structure of the Earth. In the case of earthquakes, seismologists evaluate the potential dangers and seek to minimise their impact through the improvement of construction standards.

Some of a seismologist's typical tasks may include monitoring, maintaining, testing and operating seismological equipment, documenting data, supervising preparation of test sites, managing equipment and maintaining safety standards.

Most seismologists work for petroleum or geophysical companies, and data processing centres. Government jobs in geology and earthquake surveying are also available. Some seismologists even teach, or work on their own as private consultants.

Type of person suited to this work

As with any earth scientist, curiosity and a thirst for knowledge are essential traits. You will also need a meticulous nature and an interest in computer science. In certain cases, an interest in outdoor activities would also be advantageous.

Though often called upon to work alone, seismologists must also be able to work within teams to solve problems.

Developed written and oral communication skills are important in order to communicate the results of their research.

Working conditions

Hours of work may vary depending on your role.

A scientist who specialises in earthquake seismology may work in a university or a laboratory, keeping a standard work week.

Alternatively, a seismologist who works for an earthquake monitoring facility or a petroleum company may work hours that vary. Some seismologists may even be on-call, which requires their availability at a moment's notice.

Future prospects

Though the need for experts in earthquake seismology is typically slim, employment prospects for seismologists are generally strong in the oil and gas industries.

Seismologists who acquire a postgraduate degree are often able to secure employment more easily than those with only a bachelor's degree.

Growing needs in the fields of resource management, environmental protection, and energy may also increase the demand for seismologists.

Advantages/disadvantages

You must live and work closely with a small team of scientists and other staff away in the field or offshore for long periods of time.

It is possible to work as a freelancer or you could set up your own consultancy firm.

It may be possible to move between seismology and engineering geology or hazard prediction.

Money guide

Salaries vary depending on the industry, with earnings often 10%–30% higher in commercial companies, such as oil service firms.

A typical starting salary for a seismologist is £22,000–£25,000.

Candidates with a relevant postgraduate qualification can expect an increased salary of between £28,000 and £35,000.

With experience, the typical salary of a senior level seismologist, where the post holder is in charge of one or more major projects, is between £40,000 and £75,000.

Related opportunities

- Cartographer p68
- Geologist/Geological Technician p508
- Hydrologist p510

Further information

British Geophysical Association
https://britgeophysics.org

Energy & Utility Skills
www.euskills.co.uk

STATISTICIAN

Qualifications and courses

The usual entry requirement for this profession is a degree in statistics or another quantitative subject such as maths, economics or operational research. The general entry requirements for a degree are 2 A levels/3 H grades and 5 GCSEs/National 5s (A*–C/A–C).

As well as 3-year degrees, there are also 4-year sandwich degree courses that include a year-long work placement. Master's degrees in subjects such as statistics or medical statistics may be an advantage and entry is with a 2.1 or above in your first degree. Foundation degrees and HNDs may also be accepted by potential employers.

The professional examinations of the Royal Statistical Society (RSS) provide an alternative entry route for mature candidates or those already in relevant employment. Courses are available at 3 levels and can be studied by day-release, at evening classes or by distance learning. However, the RSS has decided to withdraw from offering its own professional examinations and the final opportunity to complete a qualification will be May 2017. The RSS will continue to offer short training courses.

The Government Statistical Service (GSS) offers a Fast Stream recruitment programme. Candidates must have at least a 2.1 in a numerate degree with a high statistical content or a postgraduate qualification in statistics in order to be considered for entry.

Chartered statistician (CStat) status is awarded by the RSS to those with an approved degree and a minimum of 5 years' experience in the field.

What the work involves

Statistics involves the use of mathematical techniques to collect, analyse and present large quantities of factual information.

You will plan and undertake surveys using a range of mathematical research methods. You could apply your skills to investigate diverse subjects such as population levels, patterns of illness or national shopping habits.

Statistical research plays a vital role in informing the activities of many areas such as government, advertising, medicine and scientific research.

Type of person suited to this work

Strong mathematical skills are essential for producing and analysing a range of statistical information. You will also need excellent problem-solving abilities to create practical solutions and collect information on specific issues.

Excellent IT skills are needed as it is likely that you will use specialist computer software.

Your findings could help shape the work of different organisations, so you must have a high standard of accuracy and pay close attention to detail at all times.

The ability to communicate with managers, staff and clients is essential.

Working conditions

You will be based in an office environment and spend a lot of time using computers. Depending on the sector you are employed in, you may undertake practical projects in a laboratory or research centre. You will sometimes be required to travel to meet colleagues and clients so a driving licence would be useful.

You will usually work 37–40 hours a week from Monday to Friday, with some overtime as project deadlines approach.

Future prospects

Statisticians investigate and research issues within the environment, medicine, business, social science and many other areas.

You could develop a career in the Government Statistical Service. There are many opportunities in scientific and medical research and pharmaceutical development. Alternatively, you could choose to work in academia, researching and lecturing on statistics. Self-employment as a consultant is also possible.

Currently, big data analytics is a surging industry in the UK with a third of the UK's large organisations intending to set up programmes in the next 5 years.

Advantages/disadvantages

Working to a high level of accuracy at all times can be very demanding.

You are likely to need a postgraduate qualification for roles in environmental or forensic statistics.

As the job is often project based, it offers variety through different projects.

Money guide

Earnings vary depending on your location, employer, qualifications and experience, with the highest salaries offered in London.

Employees in the private sector tend to earn more than those working in the public sector.

Starting salaries outside of London typically range from £22,500 to £31,000. In London the average starting salary is between £22,500 and £39,000.

With experience, you can earn between £30,000 and £50,000. Those employed in the most senior positions can achieve up to £70,000 a year.

Related opportunities

- Actuary p5
- Economist p20
- Mathematician/Mathematics Research Scientist p515

Further information

Office for National Statistics
www.ons.gov.uk/ons

Royal Statistical Society
www.rss.org.uk

Qualifications and courses

You will need a degree in a science subject in order to become a toxicologist. Relevant degree subjects include pharmacology or biochemistry and you will need at least 2 A levels/3 H grades, including Maths and Chemistry, and 5 GCSEs/National 5s (A*–C/A–C) for entry.

Following your degree, it may be possible to take up a post that offers training as you work, but the usual route is to take a postgraduate qualification. Entry requirements for postgraduate courses are at least a 2.1 classification for your bachelor's degree in a subject such as biomedical sciences, forensic sciences or toxicology. Other related acceptable subjects include pharmacology, food safety and environmental management. Your master's degree should be chosen in accordance with the area of toxicology you wish to work in, with available specialities including industrial, pharmaceutical, forensic, clinical, regulatory and occupational toxicology.

After completing a master's degree, you could choose to study further by carrying out a research doctorate in a specialist area of toxicology. There are postgraduate diplomas offered by many institutions in the subject, and you may even choose to go into ecotoxicology or study pollution or pesticide science.

The National Health Service (NHS) offers graduates the chance to study on the Scientist Training Programme (STP), which would allow you to train as a clinical scientist specialising in toxicology. The course typically lasts 3 years and entry requires a relevant first degree with a minimum 2.1 classification. Alternatively, you can enter the 5 year work-based NHS Higher Specialist Scientific Training (HSST) scheme as a consultant healthcare scientist.

Organisations such as the British Toxicology Society (BTS) and Federation of European Toxicologists offer various qualifications and the chance for continuing professional development (CPD) with membership.

What the work involves

As a toxicologist, you will study the effects of chemicals on the environment and everything within it, from humans and animals to plants. Some toxicologists work for the government.

Work is very varied and you may find yourself working on the development of products, on testing new drugs, or lecturing and carrying out your own research.

You may deal with poisons and drugs.

Type of person suited to this work

You should have a strong interest in the environment, science, and public health and safety. For forensic toxicology, an interest in law is also useful.

Your level of scientific and technical knowledge should be high, and you need an excellent eye for detail as well as the ability to work carefully and accurately.

You should be able to apply scientific knowledge to practical work, and have excellent communication skills in order to explain technical and scientific information to others both orally and in written reports. You will also need good IT skills.

Working conditions

The hours worked by toxicologists usually follow the standard 9am to 5pm, Monday to Friday working week pattern. This does not tend to vary too much. However, if you are carrying out experimental work you might be expected to be more flexible. You might be on-call on occasional weekends and evenings in case emergencies occur.

You will spend most of your time working in a laboratory, but may sometimes have to visit scenes where incidents have taken place.

Expect to wear protective clothing most of the time, and be prepared to work occasionally with animals.

Future prospects

Job opportunities are good, as the number of available positions is about equal to the number of those applying.

You can work towards being promoted to a more senior position such as project manager. This will involve spending less time with hands-on toxicology, and more on tasks such as administration and supervision. If you decide that this does not suit you, it is possible to become self-employed and/or work on a freelance basis.

Advantages/disadvantages

Toxicology is an interesting and challenging profession, and you may be involved in exciting cases. You will continually be learning and expanding your knowledge.

It can be difficult, and you may see some distressing things. You also need to be constantly alert and cannot afford to make mistakes.

Money guide

When you start out in toxicology, you can earn about £21,500 to £26,500 a year.

In the NHS you would enter on band 6 earning a salary between £26,041 to £34,876.

This can increase to around £40,000 with experience.

In clinical toxicology salaries can rise to up to £65,000 and in other fields this can reach £100,000.

Related opportunities

- Biochemist p493
- Chemist p497
- Clinical Scientist p499

Further information

Association of the British Pharmaceutical Industry
www.abpi.org.uk

British Toxicology Society
www.thebts.org

Qualifications and courses

All entrants will be educated to Honours degree level with a 2.1 or higher, or a 2.2 with an appropriate postgraduate qualification, in a relevant subject. Subjects studied at degree level include biology and chemistry. Entry onto a degree is usually with 2 A levels/3 H grades and 5 GCSEs/National 5s (A*–C/A–C). Virology is not typically offered as a subject for undergraduate education, however some entrants may undertake a General Medical Council (GMC) approved medical degree. Entry requirements for medical school include very high A level/H grade results, including subjects such as science and Maths. Competition for places on medical degrees is tough and it is strongly advised that you have undertaken relevant pre-entry work experience.

If you did not achieve a 2.1 in your undergraduate studies, or if your first degree is not in a related field, a master's degree or conversion master's may be available.

One entry route to this career is through the NHS Scientist Training Programme (STP), undertaking specialist training in microbiology. Applicants must have an Honours degree (2.1 or higher) in a relevant pure or applied science. Successful STP applicants undertake three years of workplace-based training, with a more general healthcare science approach in the first year of training followed by 2 years of specialisation.

Alternatively, prospective entrants who have completed a medical degree and achieved the Membership of the Royal Colleges of Physicians UK Diploma can apply for higher specialisation training with ST3, taking the Combined Infection Training (CIT) learning pathway and specialising in Infectious Diseases and Medical Virology. Successful applicants undertake 4 years of training; 2 years' CIT and 2 years' specialist training. Applicants can consult the Joint Royal Colleges of Physicians Training Board for more detailed information on entry requirements.

What the work involves

Medical virologists operate as part of a wider clinical microbiology service, identifying and studying viruses. Your role will involve carrying out research on infected individuals or populations and investigating the characteristics of various viral infections in order to develop countermeasures to stop or limit the spread of infection.

Virologists typically follow either a teaching or research pathway, or may split their time between these two pursuits.

Virologists may work for universities, in government agencies or healthcare, or for private healthcare firms. Their role may even extend to assisting in the development of new medications as an extension of their research.

Type of person suited to this work

You must have a capable scientific mind and be highly safety conscious. Additionally, virologists must have excellent problem-solving skills and good attention to detail when carrying out research and laboratory work.

You should be equally capable of working independently and as part of a team.

Good communication skills, both written and oral, are a must, as you will need to convey your ideas and research to others through written reports and, at times, oral presentation.

Working conditions

You will typically work a 40 hour week, Monday to Friday. Overtime or irregular hours may be a requirement when working on complex projects or when undertaking specialist research.

You will split your time between laboratory work and office-based work. If you hold teaching responsibilities, you will also spend time in classrooms and lecture theatres.

Future prospects

Competition for entry onto courses is high, both for medical degrees and for the NHS STP.

There are opportunities to work throughout the UK and abroad. You could work for the NHS, or for other health-related government bodies. Alternatively, organisations such as pharmaceutical and private healthcare firms may employ virologists.

Advantages/disadvantages

Depending on your specialisation and research interests, you may have the opportunity to travel.

There is great job satisfaction in knowing that your work is making a profound difference to the health of others.

Pay-off for research can take a long time, and lab work can become repetitive and tedious.

Money guide

If you begin your career as a laboratory assistant you can earn between £13,000 and £19,000 a year.

Trainee healthcare scientists on the NHS STP start on £25,528 a year.

Qualified virologists working for the NHS would enter on band 6 earning a salary of between £26,041 and £34,876 a year.

If you work in research and development for a pharmaceutical firm, salaries are generally higher and start from £27,000 to £37,000 a year.

Related opportunities

- Bacteriologist p492
- Microbiologist p518
- Pathologist p307

Further information

Health and Care Professions Council
www.hpc-uk.org

NHS Careers
www.healthcareers.nhs.uk

Royal College of Pathologists
www.rcpath.org

Skills for Health
www.skillsforhealth.org.uk

Qualifications and courses

The most common route into this profession is to obtain a degree in zoology or a related subject, such as wildlife biology, marine biology, parasitology, animal behaviour, animal ecology or wildlife conservation. The typical entry requirements for a degree course are 2 A levels/3 H grades, including Biology, and 5 GCSEs/National 5s (A*–C/A–C). Some courses also require an A level/H grade in Chemistry. Pre-entry volunteer work in conservation may also help your application.

Some people undertake a degree after gaining practical experience working as a zookeeper or laboratory technician.

Many candidates also have a relevant postgraduate qualification and entry is with at least a 2.1 in your first degree. To work in research, you would initially secure a post as a trainee researcher within a university research department and work towards a doctorate in your specialist area.

It is also possible to enter the profession at technician or trainee level with good GCSEs/National 5s and A levels/H grades, including Biology, Maths and English. In order to progress, you should be prepared to study towards relevant qualifications whilst working. Courses may include the NVQ/SVQ Level 3 in Zoo Animal Management, the City & Guilds Level 3 qualification in Work-based Animal Care (Zoos/Wildlife Establishments), or the Foundation degree in Zoo Resource Management.

Zoologists are expected to engage in continuing professional development (CPD) throughout their careers and there are various professional organisations that offer this, such as the Institute of Zoology (IoZ) and the Society of Biology.

What the work involves

Zoologists classify, study and research all kinds of animal life. You could be involved with protecting endangered species through practical work and raising public awareness.

Some zoologists work within industry, developing pharmaceuticals or enhancing agricultural products. Others are involved with research in their specific area of interest in academic or research institutions.

You may choose to specialise in an area such as mammalogy (mammals), entomology (insects) or herpetology (amphibians and reptiles). You could work in a variety of environments including safari parks, wildlife centres and zoos.

Type of person suited to this work

You will need to have a passion for environmental issues and a love of science.

For some roles in this sector, you will need to feel comfortable dissecting animal cadavers for research purposes. You must be meticulous, logical, practical and patient in your approach to your work.

The ability to solve problems is a key feature of this role. Communication skills are important as you might need to

share your findings with people who lack scientific knowledge. Leadership and computer skills are also essential.

Working conditions

If you are working in the field, you will have to base your hours upon the animals you are studying, for example, you will have to work nights if you are researching nocturnal animals.

Your working environment will also vary depending on your area of interest.

Many zoologists spend the majority of their time in laboratories or teaching in lecture theatres but outdoor work is also common.

Future prospects

Whilst this is a specialist area, zoologists work for a variety of organisations such as environmental consultancies, conservation bodies, animal charities and local authorities. Others go into research and development in industry.

Many choose to work in universities, which have a set progression path from researcher to head of department. Promotion within industry and government is also clearly defined. Within other areas such as conservation, progression is more limited and you may need to change employers in order to achieve promotion.

Advantages/disadvantages

There are opportunities to travel and visit various locations on research trips.

You will use your skills and knowledge to increase public understanding of many aspects of the natural environment.

When undertaking fieldwork, you may find yourself in inhospitable environments.

Money guide

Earnings vary depending on sector, location and employer, although a relevant postgraduate qualification may increase your income.

Your starting salary will probably be in the region of £21,000 to £25,000.

With experience, earnings can increase to between £25,000 and £35,000 a year.

As a senior zoologist, you could achieve in excess of £45,000 per year.

Related opportunities

- Ecologist p502
- Veterinary Surgeon p266
- Zookeeper p268

Further information

British and Irish Association of Zoos and Aquariums
www.biaza.org.uk

Institute of Zoology
www.zsl.org/science

Royal Society of Biology
www.rsb.org.uk

SCIENCE, MATHEMATICS AND STATISTICS

Security, Emergency and the Armed Forces

Working in security and the armed forces may give you many incredible experiences and opportunities not open to most people. You need to be an excellent team player and in some instances you may find yourself in a potentially dangerous situation, therefore it is essential that you are a great communicator. Working in this sector you can expect to spend your day absolutely anywhere! Some roles involve a lot of office work whereas others can involve spending a lot of your time on the road, or even at sea. If you are looking for a job that will be exhilarating but are able to remain calm and professional under pressure this sector could offer you a lot of opportunities. The jobs featured in this section are listed below. For similar jobs to the ones in this section turn to *Legal and Political Services* on page 341.

Qualifications and courses

Entrants must have 35 Advanced Level Information System (ALIS) points from 7 GCSE/National 5s subjects, including at least a C in English Language, Maths and either a foreign language or a science; as well as 96 UCAS points from 2 or more A levels/H grades (A*–E/A–E). Though a degree is not a requirement in most regiments and corps, over 80% of cadets accepted each year are graduates, and a few corps specifically ask for a degree.

For the army you will need to be aged between 18 and 26 years old, whereas for the army reserve you can join at up to 35 years old. Officers can be male or female but some units are still male-only.

You will need to pass rigorous medical and fitness entrance tests, as well as a range of interviews and written tests during the selection process. Upon entry into the army you will undertake the 44-week Commissioning Course of intensive training at Sandhurst, in both practical and academic subjects. Once you have completed your initial training you will go on to specialist training to prepare you for your first appointment.

The University Officer Training Corps (UOTC) can help with funding part of your degree course by offering a bursary of £6,000–£8,000. If successful, you will have a provisional place at Sandhurst and be expected to serve as a Regular Officer for at least 3 years.

There is the opportunity for some professionals, such as dentists, nurses, lawyers, physiotherapists and chaplains, to become officers by fast-track training which lasts 10 weeks.

What the work involves

Army officers lead, command and train a team of soldiers on day-to-day activities, either on training exercises or on a range of combat, peacekeeping, humanitarian operations or disaster-relief missions.

Your platoon's training, welfare and discipline will be entirely your responsibility. You will work within a specific professional or skill area such as medicine, dentistry, engineering, intelligence or combat.

Type of person suited to this work

You will need to have excellent self-discipline, confidence and a natural ability to lead and motivate your team, which will consist of soldiers, non-commissioned officers and junior officers.

You must be able to keep a clear head and make sensible decisions under pressure in order to take responsibility for the safety of your team.

Initial training, with its physical and mental challenges, often comes as a shock. You will need to have determination, courage and resilience as well as a good level of physical fitness in order to get through the training stages.

Working conditions

Your hours will depend upon which specialty you have chosen to work in. Some officers work within a normal office timeframe, whilst others are required to work shifts. Hours may also be long and irregular when away on training or taking part in field-based operations.

You could be stationed anywhere in the world, and have to travel to destinations at short notice. Officers must wear a uniform at all times.

Future prospects

You will take further leadership training throughout your career in order to improve your promotion prospects and keep your skills fresh.

Most will start out as a second lieutenant before being promoted to lieutenant after 12–25 months. You can expect to be promoted to captain after 5 years in service (or 3 years if you have a degree).

Although prospects for new and existing recruits may be affected by defence budget cuts, there are still good opportunities if you meet the selection criteria.

Advantages/disadvantages

You will be working within a close-knit team of professionals, so will build strong personal and working relationships within the job.

You may be involved in implementing large-scale peace initiatives which would be rewarding.

You may be posted overseas for long periods of time which can be disruptive to your personal life.

Money guide

Officer cadets joining the programme straight after their A levels/H grades can expect to start on £16,073 during training, rising to £25,472 once you are commissioned as a second lieutenant.

Graduate entrants start on a salary of £25,472 which will increase once they leave Sandhurst.

Salaries gradually increase as you rise through the ranks. After serving for 5 years you could be earning at least £39,236 as a captain.

If you are away from your base for more than 10 days there is also a daily separation allowance that is applicable to both single and married officers. You will receive subsidised accommodation and food, medical and dental care, discounted rail fares and subsidised nursery facilities.

Related opportunities

- Army Soldier p531
- Police Officer p543
- Royal Navy Officer p553

Further information

Army
www.army.mod.uk/join

Welbeck College
www.dsfc.ac.uk

ARMY SOLDIER

Qualifications and courses

There are no formal qualifications for entry as a soldier, although some technical jobs require certain GCSEs/ National 5s. You must be aged between 16 years and 32 years and 11 months on the day you enlist, as well as meet the army nationality and residency requirements. Applicants under 18 must have parental consent.

You will need to undergo a number of interviews, during which you will take the British Army Recruit Battery (BARB), literacy and numeracy tests. Once these stages are completed, you will take a physical assessment, a medical and attend 2 days at an assessment centre.

Upon acceptance you will begin phase 1 of training. If you are under 17 years and 5 months old this will be either a 6- or 12-month course at Harrogate. If you are older you will do a 14-week package at either Pirbright or Winchester. After initial training you go on to do phases 2 and 3 in particular trades, such as aviation and engineering. This can take between a few months and a year.

Adult infantry soldiers, after initial training, go to the Infantry Training Centre to complete a 24-week Combat Infantryman's Course (CIC).

What the work involves

The army is responsible for defending the UK and its allies across the world, as well as taking part in peacekeeping and humanitarian operations.

You will be involved in regular training exercises to ensure you maintain a high level of fitness and military skills so that you are ready for combat at any time.

You will also choose to train and work within one of more than 130 different trades. You may be posted to dangerous areas and inhospitable environments at any time, whether for peacekeeping and aid missions or to engage in warfare.

Type of person suited to this work

You should be able to work within a team, reacting quickly to orders, working on your own initiative where necessary, and supporting other team members both professionally and emotionally at times.

You must be extremely disciplined and responsible, with the ability to think and act logically under pressure.

You must be physically fit with excellent stamina. You should be practical, with good manual dexterity, so that you will be able to operate various machines and equipment.

Working conditions

Some soldiers work normal office hours, whilst others are expected to undertake shifts that encompass night and weekend work.

You could be stationed in the UK or overseas, and must be prepared for life in a number of environments including deserts, war torn cities, and mountains.

Future prospects

Although prospects for new and existing recruits may be affected by defence budget cuts, the army still represents a solid career path. Provided you meet the selection criteria, there are still good opportunities available.

You will sign up for an open engagement lasting 22 years, but you can leave after serving 4 years. You must give 12 months' notice prior to leaving.

All soldiers start as a private and are awarded promotion according to their increasing levels of skill and commitment.

Advantages/disadvantages

You will be meeting new challenges each day and adapting to unusual and inhospitable situations, which will ensure the work never gets dull.

You will be working within a close knit team, supporting their work both in training and actually out on operations.

You are continually on-call, and could be sent anywhere in the world at a moment's notice.

Money guide

Soldiers can expect to receive £14,637 per year during initial training. This rises to a minimum of £18,125 per year once you are qualified as a private.

Some roles receive additional specialist pay, such as parachutists.

If you move up the ranks to sergeant, you can expect to earn up to £31,058.

All staff receive an annual salary increase, regardless of promotion or additional responsibilities. There is also a scheme which offers additional pay for spending longer than 10 days away from your base.

In addition to a basic salary, you will receive subsidised accommodation and food, medical and dental care, discounted rail fares and subsidised nursery facilities.

Related opportunities

- Army Officer p530
- Royal Air Force Airman/woman p549
- Royal Marines Commando p551

Further information

Army
www.army.mod.uk/join

Welbeck College
www.dsfc.ac.uk

BODYGUARD

Qualifications and courses

All bodyguards are legally required to hold a Security Industry Authority (SIA) licence, which lasts for 3 years (before it needs to be renewed) and covers other security sectors that also require a licence, such as security guarding and door supervision. To obtain an SIA licence you must be over 18, hold a recognised First Aid certificate, have a clean identity with no criminal record and a Level 3 SIA-approved qualification, such as the City & Guilds Certificate in Close Protection. The SIA website has a list of all approved courses which cover topics such as risk assessment and surveillance. You will need to renew your licence every 3 years, but no further training is required.

A driving licence will be necessary and you will need to be physically fit and have good eyesight. Knowledge of foreign languages may be useful as you might need to accompany clients abroad.

Being a bodyguard is usually a second career for people who used to be in the armed forces or the police. While this is not essential, employers will be looking for relevant experience and you will usually need to have been in the Special Forces or specialist police units to work in the most high-risk areas of the industry.

What the work involves

You will be guarding your client or group, keeping them safe from harm or unwanted attention. You might also be known as a personal protection officer or a close protection officer (CPO).

Protecting an executive on a business trip to a dangerous region of the world, an overseas royal visiting the UK, or a celebrity during an autograph-signing session could all be part of your work.

You will be responsible for making a preliminary sweep of premises before your client arrives, setting up surveillance equipment, assessing potential threats and driving your client around. It is possible to be a specialist in areas such as close protection, surveillance or defensive driving.

Type of person suited to this work

This is not a first job – most have related experience and the most lucrative contracts go to those who have worked in the Special Forces or specialist close-protection police units. Most of the work is on a self-employed basis, so you need to have a flair for business because you will need to network and keep your accounts.

Exceptional planning skills and quick responses are essential to ensure that your client is free from harm or unwanted attention. You will also need to be confident, physically fit to cope with the demands of the work, and have good eyesight and hearing.

Your appearance, diplomacy and communication skills also need to be top level, because you will be with your client and need to blend into the background to observe at high profile events.

Working conditions

Your work will be wherever your client goes and so this could mean lots of travelling.

You could be at risk as you need to protect your client – if necessary with your own body – but this is more of an issue when working in dangerous areas of the world.

You will work long and irregular hours during a contract as some clients may need 24-hour protection and there will be long periods of inactivity.

Future prospects

You can progress to become a leader of a team of CPOs on assignment or establish your own business.

Very few officers are in long-term employment. The vast majority are self-employed. The profession is male-dominated but the demand is present and growing for female bodyguards. Female bodyguards are valued for their ability to blend in.

Some progress into more mainstream security work, for example security guard or security manager. There may be opportunities to specialise in areas such as driving and residential security.

Advantages/disadvantages

You will get to enjoy a fast-paced lifestyle and travel frequently.

Training courses are residential and expensive.

The work can be dangerous.

Money guide

Most bodyguards are self-employed, earning daily or hourly rates for specific contracts. These could range from £100 to £150 a day for low risk work to £1,000 a day in a very hostile environment or for protecting a key principal.

For those bodyguards contracted to a particular company, a new entrant can earn over £18,000 per year. With experience this can rise to £24,000 to £30,000 per year.

In high risk areas, with considerable experience, you could earn up to £100,000 per year.

Related opportunities

- Army Officer p530
- Police Officer p543
- Royal Marines Officer p552

Further information

British Security Industry Association
www.bsia.co.uk

Security Industry Authority
www.sia.homeoffice.gov.uk

Qualifications and courses

There are no specific entry requirements for employment as a civil enforcement officer, although some employers may ask for a minimum of 4 GCSEs/National 5s (A*–C/A–C), including English and Maths. Experience of working with the public or in a customer service role would also be beneficial.

Your employer will provide introductory training on the job which must be completed before you can work unsupervised. Training will cover on-street enforcement activity, car park patrolling and enforcement, clamping and tow-away, and CCTV operation. Civil enforcement officers need to keep their knowledge of traffic laws and regulations up to date.

To further your career or improve employability you could complete a relevant course such as a NVQ Level 2 in Controlling Parking Areas or a City & Guilds Level 2 Award for Parking Enforcement Officers. You could then go on to an Award and Certificate in Leadership and Management for Parking Operations (Levels 3–5).

Applicants may be required to undergo a Disclosure and Barring Service (DBS) check. A full driving licence is also needed for some positions. Good fitness levels will also be necessary.

What the work involves

You will be enforcing parking regulations for a local authority or contractors working on their behalf, patrolling and checking for illegal parking and non-payment of parking fees.

Using a hand-held computer you will regularly check details of vehicles parked in limited-stay parking areas and issue fixed penalty tickets. You will take pictures of any illegally parked vehicles.

You will need to arrange for vehicles to be clamped or sent to the pound. You will attend court to give evidence if any prosecution results from your work. You will have to report any suspected abandoned or stolen vehicles to the police.

Type of person suited to this work

All employers look for a polite but firm manner as well as good communication skills. You will need to be very good at dealing with people, many of whom could be feeling irate about the ticket you have just given them. Patience and calmness will be vital assets in dealing with people making things difficult.

You need to be a good observer and able to follow rules and instructions. You will have to watch out at all times for illegal parking, enforce the rules and keep record for official use.

You will meet a lot of people but you will also be working unsupervised and independently so you need to be confident, self-disciplined and reliable, as well as comfortable working on your own.

Working conditions

You will be working in the streets, in all seasons and weathers.

You will need to wear a uniform and carry a hand-held computer.

You will work shifts to a total of 37–40 hours a week, including early mornings and late evenings. You might also have to work at weekends.

Future prospects

Civil enforcement officers are now carrying out most of the duties that were formerly assigned to traffic wardens.

Parking contractors are working with over 100 local authorities to enforce parking legislation. Vacancies are available with numerous main contractors.

With experience, progression is possible into a role as supervisor or trainer and then into management if suitable. However, prospects may be more limited in more rural areas.

Advantages/disadvantages

You will keep fit, walking an average of 10 miles a day, 5 days a week carrying a 5kg pack (including your computer, printer and radio).

It can be an enjoyable job if you enjoy or prefer to work outdoors.

There is no doubt that civil enforcement officers are not always popular and you might have to deal with some aggressive people.

Illegal parking can cause real problems for most law-abiding motorists and many attendants feel a sense of satisfaction from keeping the roads clear.

Money guide

Starting pay is around £15,000 per year. In certain places, salaries for civil enforcement officers can reach up to £23,000.

Civil enforcement managers can expect to earn between £23,000 and £33,000 a year.

Some jobs pay an hourly rate, which is usually between £7 and £10.

Related opportunities

- Bailiff/Enforcement Agent p342
- Police Community Support Officer p542
- Train Conductor/Guard p611

Further information

British Parking Association
www.britishparking.co.uk

Qualifications and courses

There are no minimum entry qualifications, but GCSEs/ National 5s (A*–C/A–C) including English and Maths may be required by some employers as you should have clear literacy, numeracy and IT skills.

Most people join HM Coastguard as a volunteer before becoming a coastguard watch assistant (CWA). You must be aged 16 or over to apply. A few join at coastguard watch officer (CWO) level if they have a good standard of education and either a coastal skipper licence or a yachtmaster certificate from the Royal Yachting Association (RYA).

You will need a good standard of hearing and eyesight and a high level of fitness. You must have significant seagoing experience, for example from the Royal Navy, working as a coastguard rescue officer volunteer or anything else that involves boat work and navigation.

Training as a CWA lasts for 10 months. Initial training is conducted at the Maritime and Coastguard Agency Centre at Highcliffe, Dorset. The second stage is part on-the-job and part classroom-based. CWO training lasts between 9 and 12 months, depending on whether you have already worked as an assistant. You must pass an exam at the end of your training.

Volunteers will also be expected to attend regular training.

What the work involves

You will work as part of a team responding to vessels and people in distress.

You will be dealing with 999 coastguard calls and radio distress calls, and will direct the efforts of the volunteer coastguard rescue officers. You may also work alongside the services of the Royal National Lifeboat Institution (RNLI).

You will keep records of all activity and weather conditions, giving information to vessels and reporting anything unusual. Part of the role will also require providing safety information to the public about the sea, as well as giving advice on safety procedures to those operating small craft/boats.

Type of person suited to this work

You must have excellent computer skills, the ability to concentrate for long periods and a clear voice to make sure that you send rescuers to the right place.

Active search and rescue work involves carrying heavy equipment, climbing and working out at sea, all of which require a high level of physical fitness.

Watch officers need good management and teaching skills to lead and train groups of auxiliary coastguards.

The ability to deal with distressing or pressurised situations, along with a patient and calm manner will be invaluable.

Working conditions

You will be located in an operations centre, using a computer and talking to others using hands-free communications equipment.

Search and rescue work involves working outside in dangerous conditions.

Coastguards operate 24/7 – you will be working shifts that include evenings and weekends and will often work over a 42-hour week.

Future prospects

Coastguard numbers have reduced slightly over the past few years, and there could still be moves to lower the number further. Volunteer numbers will remain steady though. Consequently, a lot of coastguards are now spending their time supporting those volunteers.

Progression is generally from assistant to officer, then to watch manager and finally to sector manager.

If you have experience and a degree, you could go on to a job in marine surveying within the Maritime and Coastguard Agency.

Advantages/disadvantages

With the use of satellite technology, it is possible to co-ordinate the rescue of someone hundreds of miles away from your control centre.

The sea is dangerous and you may arrive too late, which is an upsetting event for the whole team.

Money guide

Starting out as a coastguard watch assistant you could earn £15,000 per year. After gaining experience, this can rise to £17,800.

The starting salary of a coastguard watch officer is £18,100 and can increase to £23,200.

Volunteers are unpaid but may be reimbursed for expenses. All coastguards receive an allowance for the purchase of uniforms and footwear and those working in the Scottish islands or other very remote areas can receive additional allowances.

Related opportunities

- Air Traffic Controller p583
- Merchant Navy Deck Officer/Rating p598
- Royal Navy Officer p553

Further information

Maritime and Coastguard Agency
www.gov.uk/mca

Maritime Skills Alliance
www.maritimeskills.org

Port Skills and Safety Ltd
www.portskillsandsafety.co.uk

SECURITY, EMERGENCY AND THE ARMED FORCES

Qualifications and courses

Individual police forces have different entry requirements. As a minimum you should have 3–5 GCSEs/National 5s (A*–C/A–C) but many require applicants to have at least A levels/H grades and increasingly a degree in a science-related subject. Various universities offer degrees or Foundation degrees in subjects such as forensic science and criminology and you will need at least 2 A levels/3 H grades, including a science, for entry to these degrees.

You will need to be able to show you have scientific ability and possibly photographic ability as well, either from employment or education. Previous work experience dealing with the public would also be an advantage.

You will need to undergo a medical exam, have full colour vision and a driving licence for this role.

In some forces you would start as an assistant crime scene investigator (CSI) or scenes of crime officer (SOCO) before undertaking further training to become fully qualified. You might be enrolled in the Foundation Crime Scene Investigators Learning Programme at the College of Policing's Forensic Centre. This could take up to 12 months to complete.

Once in the job you will have an introductory period with your force. Upon completion you are qualified to undertake volume crime scene investigation. It is then possible to do a further 5-week training programme which qualifies you as a full CSI/SOCO. It is recommended that all CSIs attend a Refesher Crime Scene Investigator course every 5 years to update their forensic techniques and practices.

You, and possibly your close family members, will be subject to a background and employment check.

What the work involves

You will be collecting, storing and recording evidence such as fibres, hair and blood to help investigate crimes like burglary, accidents and suspicious deaths.

You will use equipment and materials to lift, package and preserve evidence, such as biological samples, paint, tyre marks and fingerprints.

Your job will involve taking photographic and video evidence of both crime scenes and victims of crime. You will also need to keep thorough records and attend court when required to give evidence.

Type of person suited to this work

Sifting through evidence is the main aspect of this job so you will need to be able to pay attention to detail. You will also need to be methodical and patient.

This job can be very distressing. You will need to be able to distance yourself emotionally from the crime, and be able to record the scene and collect evidence in an analytical, scientific way. Good teamworking skills are essential as you may be working on a project with many others.

An interest in science and technology is essential. You will need to keep up to date with developments in forensic science and technology as they will affect how well you do your job.

Working conditions

You will work both outside at crime scenes and inside at base.

You will do a 37-hour working week, including shifts, but hours might be longer at times. You could also be on-call 24-hours.

Conditions at crime scenes can be very difficult and unpleasant but you will be provided with protective clothing.

Future prospects

Crime scene investigators are recruited by all regional police forces. Some forces only recruit civilians to do this work but a few also recruit specialist police officers. There are 43 police forces in the UK, all of which employ CSIs, but competition for vacancies is high.

It is possible to move into more specialised areas of work, such as the investigation of suspicious fires or scenes where firearms have been used.

There may be opportunities for promotion to senior investigator with management responsibilities. You can study for further qualifications and become a forensic scientist or specialise in fingerprint technology.

Advantages/disadvantages

Although this job has an exciting image, fuelled by popular television shows, the work can be routine, repetitive and quite shocking at times.

You will have the satisfaction of working with a team of investigating officers and forensic scientists to gather evidence needed to trace, arrest and convict offenders.

Money guide

Starting salaries for assistants are around £16,000. Once fully qualified, salaries vary from £17,000 to £26,000 per year.

This rises to in excess of £35,000 for experienced and senior investigators, depending on your local police force and responsibility level.

There may also be on-call, weekend or shift allowances.

Related opportunities

- Forensic Computer Analyst p539
- Forensic Scientist p506
- Private Investigator p547

Further information

College of Policing
www.college.police.uk

Police Recruitment
http://recruit.college.police.uk

Qualifications and courses

While it is possible to join at officer level it is more common to start as an administrative assistant or assistant officer and work your way up.

You will usually need 2 GCSEs/National 5s (A*–C/A–C), including English and Maths, to start as an administrative assistant; 5 GCSEs/National 5s to start as an assistant officer; and 5 GCSEs/National 5s and 2 A levels/3 H grades to start at officer level.

Entry without these qualifications may sometimes be possible with a test to prove your abilities in areas like teamwork and communication.

If you have a degree at 2.2 or above, you could join the Civil Service Fast Stream graduate recruitment scheme, although opportunities may not be specifically for customs officer roles but rather for other positions in Her Majesty's Revenue & Customs (HMRC). A 2 year Civil Service Fast Track Apprenticeship Scheme is also available.

All candidates must be UK nationals, Commonwealth citizens or European Union nationals.

What the work involves

You will be working as a civil servant for HM Revenue & Customs, enforcing tax regulations on all goods entering and leaving the country and all goods bought and sold in the UK.

You could specialise in customs: checking for anyone either not paying tax or smuggling in illegal items and substances.

You could specialise in excise work: visiting traders, manufacturers and importers to check licences and accounts to make sure that the right duties are being paid on goods such as petrol, alcohol and tobacco.

You could specialise in VAT: visiting businesses to check their accounts and that the right amount of VAT is being collected.

Type of person suited to this work

If you are part of front-line detection work, investigating the entry of illegal goods into the UK, you will be involved in observing, questioning and challenging people.

You will need top-notch communication and observation skills. You must be intuitive and persistent. Knowledge of or a willingness to learn a foreign language is useful.

If you work in VAT or excise, an aptitude for numbers and computers is a must, because you will be checking business accounts and watching out for sometimes quite sophisticated cover-ups.

Working conditions

Customs and immigration officers mainly work in airports, seaports and freight terminals but also may need to do outdoor surveillance work. You will wear a uniform if you are a front-line detective.

Excise and VAT officers are based in offices but also travel around their local areas carrying out checks and interviews. You will generally work office hours, Monday to Friday.

Customs officers work shifts.

Future prospects

There are about 23,000 staff based all over the country. Customs specialist staff are mainly located at air and seaports and the Channel Tunnel.

Training lasts for around 9 months and is usually on the job through a combination of learning from experienced staff and residential training courses. There will also be ongoing training throughout your career.

There is a clear promotion structure within the civil service and it is possible to move on to senior or management posts. There are also specialist areas within customs that you may decide to move into, for example in detection, operations and intelligence units and dog units.

Advantages/disadvantages

When dealing with front-line detection work you might have to question or detain angry or abusive people. It can be a high-pressure job at peak times.

No two days are ever the same, especially in detection work.

It can be very rewarding to know that you have prevented dangerous items such as drugs and firearms getting into the country.

Money guide

Starting out at administrative or assistant level you could earn around £15,720 a year.

As an officer you could be earning between £20,175 and £25,710 a year.

After promotion to higher officer grades salaries increase to between £25,248 and £38,861 a year.

There can also be extra allowances for working unsocial hours (eg evenings, weekends and public holidays) and people working in London generally earn more.

Related opportunities

- Army Officer p530
- Civil Service Executive Officer p14
- Police Officer p543

Further information

Chartered Institute of Taxation
www.tax.org.uk

Civil Service Fast Stream
www.faststream.gov.uk

Qualifications and courses

Typically entrants to this role have a degree and whilst all graduates with a relevant degree will be considered, some subjects, such as disaster management, international security, business continuity and environmental hazards, are considered more desirable. The general entry requirements for a degree are 2 A levels/3 H grades and 5 GCSEs/National 5s (A*–C/A–C).

Individuals without a relevant degree will need a postgraduate qualification, such as a Master of Science (MSc) in Disaster Management.

There are more specific courses available which are geared towards a job in emergency planning but these do not guarantee a job in the sector.

Candidates who have extensive previous experience of working in this sector or a related career may be able to enter the industry without the usual necessary qualifications. For example, working in international relief and development, either as a volunteer or professional, could provide the necessary experience and skills. Even getting volunteer work in international relief can be difficult though.

Previous work experience in an emergency planning related role or practical experience such as voluntary work for a humanitarian organisation may be an advantage when applying for a first job.

The Emergency Planning College (EPC) runs events and courses to assist your continuing professional development.

What the work involves

Emergency planners and managers work primarily in local government as part of a larger team to help maintain public safety, especially at times when this is threatened by an external force. Although there are opportunities to work abroad.

You will be required to respond quickly to and learn from emergency situations that have arisen from natural disasters, outbreaks of serious contagious diseases, industrial accidents and terrorism.

You will compile reports from lengthy research and planning on the most efficient ways to protect the general public should an emergency situation arise.

You will carry out risk assessments, write safety briefs to train emergency response services and help with the recovery process after an incident has occurred.

Type of person suited to this work

You will need to enjoy working in a high pressure situation as part of a large team. You should be enthusiastic about helping to provide better public safety.

You will also need to respond quickly and calmly in an emergency and keep a level head in what may be a dangerous situation.

The job requires someone willing to work long hours, sometimes at unsociable times as well as a neat and organised person who can take comprehensive notes and present their findings accurately.

Working conditions

You may often find yourself in a highly pressured situation especially in the aftermath of a major incident so you could find yourself in danger or not knowing when you will finish the job.

You can expect travel to feature heavily as part of your job with many trips away from home a distinct possibility.

Future prospects

If you enter the career as an assistant you can expect to progress, with experience, to a management or senior role if you show signs of willingness to go where the work takes you and put in long hours.

Once you reach a more senior role you will not be working in such a hands-on environment but would provide more managerial support to your team.

Alternatively, you could move into health and safety consultancy or relief and development work.

Advantages/disadvantages

Your future prospects could take you all over the world to work with individuals who enjoy working as part of a close-knit team.

Humanitarian work such as this can be immensely rewarding. However, it also has the potential to be highly distressing since you could be one of the first people on the scene after a major natural disaster or a terrorist attack.

Travelling and working on intense projects can take up much of your life and be very draining.

Money guide

A typical starting salary in the profession is likely to be £22,000 to £28,000.

Senior roles come with a lot of responsibility but you could expect to earn £34,000 or more.

The profession is still relatively new so salaries vary widely between jobs. Private sector jobs are often more highly paid than in the public sector.

Related opportunities

- Environmental Health Practitioner/Officer p22
- Firefighter p538
- Police Officer p543

Further information

Emergency Planning College
www.epcresilience.com

Emergency Planning Society
www.the-eps.org

SECURITY, EMERGENCY AND THE ARMED FORCES

FIREFIGHTER

Qualifications and courses

To be considered for selection as a firefighter you must be at least 18 years old and preferably have a full UK driving licence. No formal qualifications are required, though you should have a good general standard of education and any qualifications you bring with you may help with future promotion. Firefighters need a reasonable level of fitness and good eyesight.

Entrance is dependent on performance in practical and written tests, including psychological tests, as well as a medical and an interview. Some colleges offer a fire service pre-recruitment course. This does not guarantee entry but aims to prepare candidates for the entrance tests. Health and safety restrictions mean that it may not be possible to do work experience as a firefighter.

As a new firefighter you will be required to undergo full-time induction training which lasts between 12 and 16 weeks (18 weeks in Northern Ireland). You will learn basic firefighting skills, fire safety and the importance of educating the public about fire safety. You may be encouraged to work towards NVQs such as the Level 3 Diploma in Emergency Fire Services Operations in the Community.

What the work involves

You will be dealing with a range of emergencies, not only fires but also helping at other incidents such as rescuing trapped animals and people, handling chemical spillages and assisting at road, rail or air crash scenes.

If your team arrives on the scene before the paramedics you will be expected to have the knowledge and practice to administer First Aid if required.

You might give advice to organisations on fire safety and check that buildings or public events meet fire regulations.

Type of person suited to this work

You will need to stay calm in dangerous situations. People in danger tend to react in extreme ways and you will need to be good at talking to them, giving instructions, reassuring them and leading them to safety.

You need to be an excellent team player. You will be assigned to a 'watch' (a team) and need to work together to keep yourself and others safe.

You will need to be able to deal with very stressful and disturbing situations.

Working conditions

You will be based at a fire station but will go out to attend incidents.

Working conditions can often be unpleasant and dangerous. You will wear a uniform and, when needed, protective clothing and equipment.

You will work an average of 42 hours per week, which will be divided into day and night shifts. You can also work as a retained firefighter which means you will be on-call. Many retained firefighters have other full-time or part-time occupations.

Future prospects

The main employers are regional fire services but airports, the Ministry of Defence, the RAF and the Royal Navy also recruit firefighters.

Some firefighters start their career as retained firefighters to gain experience. There are around 18,000 retained firefighters in the UK, mostly in rural areas. Entry is competitive.

You will undergo regular training throughout your career and could work towards specialising in a particular area of the services. For example you could specialise in driving fire trucks by taking a large goods vehicle (LGV) licence. Promotion to supervisory and management roles is by clear grades and given on ability, but exams must also be passed.

Advantages/disadvantages

This job can be very stressful and you cannot just leave an emergency situation if your shift has ended.

You will get to know your watch very well; firefighters say they really enjoy the team spirit at work.

You need to pass demanding training successfully to qualify, and keep up a rigorous fitness and training schedule.

Money guide

The fire service is subject to a nationally agreed salary structure.

Full-time firefighters can expect a salary of £21,583 as a trainee which will increase to £28,766 with experience.

Crew and watch managers can earn between £30,574 and £35,664, whilst a station manager will earn £37,096–£40,915.

With experience you may become a group manager and your salary will increase to £42,723 to £47,361.

Area managers will earn between £50,156 and £55,018.

Retained (on-call) firefighters earn a fee of around £2,100 to £2,800 per year. They also receive additional payments, according to their rank, for attending fires and carrying out extra duties.

Related opportunities

- Paramedic p306
- Police Officer p543
- Royal Navy Officer p553

Further information

Fire Service Recruitment Information
www.fireservice.co.uk

Institution of Fire Engineers
www.ife.org.uk

Skills for Justice
www.sfjuk.com

Qualifications and courses

Most people who enter this career have completed a degree in IT or equivalent computing subject. If your degree is not IT-based you can take an IT conversion course. Some universities offer specific degrees in forensic computing and information security. In order to gain a place on a degree course you will normally need at least 2 A levels/3 H grades and 5 GCSEs/National 5s (A*–C/A–C). Computing, Maths and sciences are all relevant A level/H grade subjects. Alternatively, you could complete a Foundation degree in an IT subject. The Diploma in Information Technology might also be of interest.

Some employers may ask for a postgraduate degree or an industry qualification. Entry to postgraduate programmes is reliant on the successful completion of a first degree. The National Skills Academy for IT offers relevant professional qualifications. Courses that include industry placements are particularly valuable as they will help you build up work experience as well as making relevant contacts.

A strong background working in IT is also usually required. You could start out by working as a network engineer or developer and taking professional qualification courses while working your way up.

Applicants may have to undergo a Disclosure and Barring Service (DBS) check.

What the work involves

You will be responsible for inspecting computers (and other technology such as mobile phones) for criminal activity. You might be looking for evidence of identity theft, child abuse, hacking, phishing and other illegal activity.

Even if evidence of the crime has been deleted or corrupted you will need to retrieve it without altering it in any way.

You might be using specialist software and working with the police to look through files, photographs, emails and phone conversations in order to discover evidence of criminal activity. You may need to appear in court to relay your findings.

Type of person suited to this work

You will need to have a certain level of skill using computers, as well as an interest in detecting and preventing crime.

You should be a patient and determined person as some investigations may take place over a long period of time. You might come across unpleasant or even horrific material and you must be able to distance yourself and deal with it objectively.

You will need to be able to record your findings in a clear, coherent and logical manner. You should be able to understand the law in relation to IT crime. Articulacy and strong communication skills are essential.

Working conditions

You will spend most of your time in an office using a computer.

You will generally work standard office hours (9am–5pm from Monday to Friday), however you might need to be on call over weekends and public holidays or work overtime to meet deadlines.

You might also have to attend court to give evidence and will be expected to dress accordingly.

Future prospects

Postgraduate qualifications will enhance your chances of promotion (particularly if you work within the commercial world).

You could progress to the level of supervisor or line manager.

You may have to change employers in order to progress. Jobs are available with the police force, MI5, government, the National Crime Agency and IT firms which specialise in computer security.

Advantages/disadvantages

Your workload will be varied and opportunities are available in many different sectors.

You will spend a lot of time hunched over a computer.

If you work within a police or government sector you might help to send criminals to jail.

Money guide

As a trainee you can expect to earn around £20,000 per year. After some experience, this can rise to somewhere between £25,000 and £35,000.

A senior forensic analyst might earn in the region of £40,000 to £60,000.

These figures are only approximate and will vary depending on location, sector and employer.

Related opportunities

- Forensic Scientist p506
- Information Officer p334
- Software Engineer p151

Further information

BCS, The Chartered Institute for IT
www.bcs.org

Skills for Justice
www.sfjuk.com

SECURITY, EMERGENCY AND THE ARMED FORCES

539

Qualifications and courses

Immigration officers need no formal qualifications, although many applicants will be educated to A-level standard or higher. Graduates in any discipline are welcome. Applicants with a minimum of a 2.2 Honours degree can apply for the Civil Service Fast Stream scheme. This is for entry into all civil service departments and, although a preference can be expressed, entry into immigration is not guaranteed.

All applicants must be 18 or older and be either a British citizen or a British subject who has lived here continuously for 5 years and have no restrictions on their stay in the UK. Security clearance and possibly health checks will be necessary.

Foreign language skills can be an advantage.

Application usually involves attendance at an assessment centre to be tested on your communication skills, conflict management, judgement and awareness of equal opportunity and diversity. There is a period of 9 weeks' initial training, which will take place at Heathrow, Stansted, Gatwick or Manchester airports or at the port at Dover. This will be partly classroom-based and consists of partly mentored practical work.

What the work involves

You will be working as a civil servant for the Home Office; you will be controlling the entry of people into the UK by checking the passports and visas of passengers arriving at ports, airports or via the Channel Tunnel. You could ask questions to find out more about them and, if suspicious, conduct a more detailed interview.

As an assistant officer you would refer to a more senior officer if you are concerned about documentation or answers to questions.

You might work in an office processing immigration applications, dealing with appeals and conducting intelligence-based activities.

Type of person suited to this work

You will need to be confident, assertive, have the ability to work under pressure and to deadlines.

You will need to be well organised, reliable and have good report-writing skills. You will need an ability to get on with people from across the world.

You should enjoy investigating and collecting information. You will need the ability to write up and pass on your concerns to others in your team or colleagues from other professions.

Working conditions

You could work in a range of places such as ports and airports where you will have access to a desk, computer, phone and interviewing area.

Some immigration officers have to undertake surveillance duties and work with other intelligence officers, but normally you will check documents and interview individuals within your office or interviewing booth.

You will work shifts that will include out-of-office hours and weekends.

Future prospects

Half of all immigration staff are employed in London and the south-east of England, at Heathrow, Gatwick and the Channel ports.

The numbers of people entering the UK and asking for asylum has increased over recent years. This has impacted on the service, which has grown in size. Entry is competitive at officer level and the majority of entrants are graduates.

It is possible to enter at assistant grade and work up to officer grade. Placements are also possible, for example, to Immigration Visa sections at the British Deputy High Commissions overseas or to police forces around the UK.

Advantages/disadvantages

You will play an important role in helping protect national security.

This job is part of the civil service, so entry can be competitive.

The civil service offers excellent conditions of service and training.

Money guide

When starting out as an assistant officer, you can earn around £16,500 a year within London or £15,300 elsewhere.

Graduates on the Civil Service Fast Stream can expect to earn between £25,000 and £27,000.

Salaries for immigration officers are typically between £21,000–£26,000. With experience this can increase to £30,000 for operational managers.

All staff working shifts or unsocial hours are paid additional allowances. Those working in and around London receive London weighting.

Related opportunities

- Civil Service Executive Officer p14
- Equality and Diversity Officer p23
- Police Officer p543

Further information

Civil Service Fast Stream
www.faststream.gov.uk

Home Office
www.gov.uk/government/organisations/home-office

UK Visas and Immigration
www.gov.uk/government/organisations/uk-visas-and-immigration

Qualifications and courses

While some employers will accept non-UK citizens who have the right to live and work in the UK, applicants for any post within Government Communications Headquarters (GCHQ), the Security Service (MI5) and the Secret Intelligence Service (MI6) must be a British citizen and one or both of your parents must also be British or have substantial ties to the UK. You normally will have to have lived in the UK for 9 out of the 10 years prior to applying. MI5 applicants must also be aged 18 or over.

Entry requirements vary. Most police forces will require GCSEs/National 5s (A*–C/A–C), especially in English and Maths, though some departments also ask for A levels/H grades or degrees. To work for MI5, MI6 or GCHQ you will need to have at least a 2.1 degree. Any subject is welcome although criminology, technology and/or language subjects may be an advantage. Some agencies may consider significant work experience within an intelligence environment in lieu of a degree qualification.

GCHQ runs a Higher Apprenticeship Scheme. Entry requirements are three A levels at grades A*–C, including at least 2 in science, technology, engineering or maths-related subjects.

There is a rigorous vetting procedure, known as Developed Vetting (DV) clearance. This includes medical and security clearance, as well as possible background checks on family and friends. These checks may feel intrusive. Recruitment can take many months and includes competency tests, telephone interviews and attendance at an assessment centre.

What the work involves

In most cases you will work for one of the UK's 3 intelligence and security agencies: GCHQ, MI5 and MI6.

Your job is to protect the UK from attack and terrorism, to protect its economic wellbeing as well as to prevent organised crime such as drug trafficking. You may be involved in helping to build up intelligence pictures by identifying targets, evaluating the reliability of source information and validating data, and then formally delivering information to the government.

You will also develop expertise in particular areas.

You might be involved in military operations, counter-espionage, detecting weapons of mass destruction, and identifying agents and targets.

Type of person suited to this work

This job requires you to use your initiative and be aware of the big picture, sometimes across agencies. You should be a confident decision-maker, adaptable and have an eye for detail. You must be persevering, diligent and work well under pressure.

Motivation, inquisitiveness and cultural sensitivity are essential. You need to be able to recall events accurately and analyse information and data efficiently with the ability to convey your findings effectively.

Some of your work will include informing and working alongside professionals from other national and international security services so you should be a good team player.

You must keep up to date on current affairs and communications technologies.

Working conditions

Some of the posts operate shifts, which might include weekends.

Starting out you will be required to work at headquarters. GCHQ is based in Cheltenham and MI5 and MI6 are based in central London. You could also be required to travel both nationally and internationally. It might be possible to work from home for some posts.

This job can become more of a way of life than a career so you should be completely dedicated and be able to keep information totally confidential.

Future prospects

You will usually work for up to 3 years in your first role. Based on your performance and your potential you may be promoted to a more specialist role which will include more responsibility.

You could be responsible for a wider geographical region or for specific analytical techniques. You could also move into policy work, projects, personnel or finance.

Advantages/disadvantages

It's satisfying to know you are helping to protect national security.

Background checks in the recruitment process can be long and very intrusive.

The need to maintain secrecy may be difficult and sometimes it can be lonely as you will not be allowed to talk about your work with friends and family.

Money guide

If you work for MI5, MI6 or GCHQ your salary will start at around £25,500. With experience you could earn up to £43,000. There are also excellent benefits including leisure and fitness facilities, childcare vouchers and travel assistance.

Outside of these agencies a junior analyst will earn around £16,000 a year. With experience this can rise to £20,000 to £35,000 and once you reach senior/management level you can expect a salary in excess of £40,000.

Related opportunities

- Army Officer p530
- Customs and Excise Officer p536

Further information

GCHQ
www.gchq.gov.uk

MI5 Careers
https://careers.mi5.gov.uk

Secret Intelligence Service
www.sis.gov.uk

Qualifications and courses

Applicants must have indefinite leave to live in the UK but beyond that a diverse range of backgrounds are encouraged to apply in order to get a good representational mix across the force. You must be at least 18 years old to become a police community support officer (PCSO).

People with criminal records may be ruled out depending on the severity of the offences. All prior offences must be declared when applying.

There are no specific academic entry requirements. You should have good spoken and written communications skills and it may strengthen your application if you have experience in community service (paid or unpaid) or if you have undertaken a relevant course. This could be an NVQ Level 2, BTEC National Diploma or HNC/HND in Public Services or a Foundation degree in Police Studies or Public Services. Entry onto HND and Foundation degree courses usually requires 1 A level/2 H grades and 3 or 4 GCSEs/National 5s (A*–C/A–C).

During the application process, you will be required to take written, fitness and role-play tests, as well as undergo medical, financial and security checks. Upon entry you will undertake between 3 weeks and 3 months of classroom training. Areas covered will include law, self-defence, First Aid, interviewing skills and using police communication equipment.

What the work involves

Police community support officers are uniformed members of the force whose role is to work within their local community, supporting the activities and initiatives of police officers.

You will be part of the group of officers that provides visible police presence on the streets and in other public areas. You will be on the front line, offering help and advice to members of the public, as well as tackling anti-social behaviour.

Everyday duties could include crowd-control and traffic directing, dealing with minor offences, checking out abandoned vehicles, or imposing fines for acts such as littering or dog fouling.

Type of person suited to this work

You will need to be an excellent communicator, as you will encounter a range of people in your work. You must also be able to remain calm but authoritative when confronted with potentially difficult or violent members of the public.

You must be able to work effectively within a team. This means you should be able to take orders but also act on your own initiative when necessary.

You should have good, accurate writing skills, as you will need to produce reports on events and deal with complex paperwork at times.

Working conditions

You will work up to 40 hours on a shift basis, encompassing night and weekend work. Flexible or part-time hours are available.

Although you will be based at a police station, you will work in a variety of locations including patrolling the streets, within people's homes, or in public places such as train stations.

You will be required to wear a uniform, which includes a high visibility jacket and protective hat. Additional protective equipment may need to be worn or carried on occasion.

Future prospects

Experienced PCSOs are often responsible for teaching, training and guiding new recruits. There are also opportunities to move into supervisory or managerial roles within the PCSO contingent.

PCSO is a good role to start in if you would like to become a police officer.

Prospects for this role may be affected by budget cuts.

Advantages/disadvantages

You will play a direct role in protecting your local community and finding solutions to problems and crime in the area.

There are good opportunities for career development, including progression to become a police officer.

You may be confronted with difficult and dangerous situations, which can be both frightening and unnerving.

Money guide

As a new recruit to the force you could expect to earn around £17,000 (although those working in London will earn more).

If you are working specifically for the British Transport Police, your basic starting salary will be slightly higher at £18,933. There is also an additional 15% shift allowance and PCSOs based in London will receive £2,245 London weighting.

If you reach a supervisory or managerial role, your earnings can reach about £25,000.

Similar to police officers, community support officers are eligible for certain benefits such as free London travel, flexible hours and key worker housing.

Related opportunities

- Army Soldier p531
- Police Officer p543
- Prison Officer/Instructor p546

Further information

Police Recruitment
http://recruit.college.police.uk

POLICE OFFICER

Qualifications and courses

There are no specific academic requirements but you must be aged 18 years or older and be a UK, European Union or Commonwealth citizen or a foreign citizen with indefinite leave to stay in the UK.

The police force operates an intensive selection process and you will need to pass medical, fitness, eyesight, literacy and numeracy tests. You will also be assessed using a variety of scenario exercises by which your communication, decision-making and problem-solving skills will be judged. The fitness tests are among the most rigorous, as it can be a very physically demanding job. You will also need to pass a Disclosure and Barring Service (DBS) check. Minor cautions or offences may not necessarily affect your eligibility.

A relevant qualification may enhance your application. Examples include BTEC qualifications at Levels 1–3, an HNC/HND in Public Services or a degree or Foundation degree in police studies or criminology. Voluntary police or community work, for example as a special constable, could also be useful experience. Specials work unpaid (with expenses covered) but after full training they have the same powers as regular police officers.

A Constable to Inspector Fast Track Programme is open to graduates, special constables and police staff members.

Upon entry you will be a probationary officer for 2 years while you undergo further officer training through the Initial Police Learning and Development Programme (IPLDP).

What the work involves

Police officers are responsible for safeguarding communities from crime by apprehending criminals and maintaining order.

You will spend your time on patrol, responding to any situation that occurs whilst you are on shift. You will keep records, take statements and write reports. You may need to give evidence in court on occasion, and may also give educational talks in community venues.

Once trained, you work within specialised departments such as the criminal investigation department (CID), the mounted police, child protection services, the drugs squad or traffic police.

Type of person suited to this work

You must have excellent communication skills in order to deal with a variety of people on a daily basis whose position could range from that of a criminal who needs restraining, to a victim who needs careful treatment.

You will need to be non-judgemental, and have the ability to view situations from different perspectives.

You will need courage, initiative and common sense in order to deal with many of the circumstances you will be presented with. You will also need to have good problem-solving skills.

Working conditions

You will be required to work 40 hours a week, covering early, late and night shifts 7 days a week. Part-time or flexible working hours can usually be accommodated.

You will be based at a police station, but the majority of your time will be spent on patrol, either on foot or by car. This means you will be out in all weather conditions, and will travel to many different locations.

Future prospects

You can move upwards to the level of sergeant and inspector. These promotions are subject to examination and interview. To progress further you must demonstrate your skills to a board of judges.

Government cuts led to some widespread job losses over the past few years. The occasional cutback still occurs, but the job market has become more stable recently.

Advantages/disadvantages

You will be meeting new challenges each day and adapting to unusual environments, which will keep you mentally and physically alert and ensures the work never gets dull.

You will be responsible for promoting safety and wellbeing in the local community, which is rewarding.

You will be required to work unsociable hours including nights and weekends.

You will have to deal with difficult, distressed and occasionally violent members of the public.

Money guide

The starting salary varies between forces. For instance, salaries tend to be higher in the Metropolitan Police.

The constable starting salary is £23,727. Once you have completed your initial training this rises to £26,484.

For senior officers, such as sergeants and chief inspectors, salaries can rise to between £36,500 and £55,005.

London weighting of up to £2,325 is available for all ranks and key benefits can include free London travel, flexible hours and key worker living benefits.

Related opportunities

- Police Support Worker p544
- Road Safety Officer p608
- Security Officer/Manager/Door Supervisor p555

Further information

Civil Nuclear Constabulary
www.cnc.police.uk

Police Oracle
www.policeoracle.com

Police Recruitment
http://recruit.college.police.uk

Qualifications and courses

There are no specific academic requirements for entry to the police force as a support worker, but most employers prefer that you are educated to GCSE standard or equivalent. You must also be aged 18 or over, a UK or European Union national, or come from within the European Economic Area.

There are several qualifications that would be viewed favourably by employers. These include an NVQ Level 2 or BTEC First Diploma in Public Services, and the BTEC National Diploma in Uniformed Public Services. Entry requirements for these courses are usually 5 GCSEs/ National 5s (A*–C/A–C) or equivalent, including English and Maths.

If you reach interview stage, you will need to have medical, criminal record and other background checks to assess your suitability for the role. You must declare any previous convictions prior to this stage.

Once you have been accepted onto the force, your training will be provided by a more experienced support worker and you will learn on the job. Training usually lasts between 3 weeks and 3 months.

What the work involves

Police support workers are the first point of contact for members of the public in a police station.

You will be responsible for answering and directing calls, passing walk-ins to appropriate members of staff, and carrying out general administrative tasks within the station.

You will be on the front desk, so will receive firearms, knives, driving licences and any other paraphernalia seized by police whilst on patrol. You will also be the first point of contact for missing persons and lost property enquiries. You will need to look after victims and witnesses when they come into the station, which may require providing First Aid on occasion.

Type of person suited to this work

You must have excellent communication skills in order to deal with a wide variety of people on a daily basis, ranging from victims to aggressive detainees. Assertiveness, confidence and sensitivity are all desirable personality traits.

You should be happy working within a team, supporting your colleagues, taking directions, and working on your own initiative when required.

You will also need to adhere to confidentiality, diversity and data protection issues.

Working conditions

You will usually work a 37-hour week based on a shift pattern, which will require early morning and weekend work. Part-time and flexible working hours are commonly available.

You will be based within a police station, and will spend most of your time on the front desk answering queries or updating information on a computer. It is unlikely that you will need to travel in the course of your working day.

Stations can get very busy at times, so you should expect to work in pressurised and potentially stressful conditions at times.

Future prospects

The police force operates throughout the length and breadth of the UK, so there are opportunities in all regional forces.

Opportunities for promotion within a station are limited by its size. Larger establishments may have room to move you to a more senior, supervisory role whereas the smaller ones will not be able to.

You could move to a more specialised area of support work, such as manning the crime helpdesk, or working in an enquiry centre. It is possible to train as a police officer from a support role.

Advantages/disadvantages

You will be working within a close-knit team, so your support work will be essential to the successful running of the station.

You will encounter a wide variety of people and stories so your working day will be very diverse with no two days being the same.

You will have to deal with difficult, distressed and occasionally violent members of the public which can be stressful.

Money guide

The starting salary for an entry-level police support worker is about £15,000 per year.

With a couple of years' experience, this should rise to around £19,000.

If you pursue promotion and attain a high level administrative role, or become a police officer, you could earn in excess of £40,000.

Related opportunities

- Civil Service Administrative Officer p13
- Police Community Support Officer p542
- Secretary p51

Further information

Police Oracle
www.policeoracle.com

Police Recruitment
http://recruit.college.police.uk

Qualifications and courses

Most prison governors enter the profession as a prison officer. Generally, requirements for candidates include good health and physical fitness, Commonwealth, British or European Union citizenship and, if you are going to work with inmates under 18 years of age, Disclosure and Barring Service (DBS) clearance.

Training is largely on the job and would be tailored to individual needs to take into account any previous and relevant work experience.

Once you have gained experience as a prison officer you will need to work your way through supervisory and senior positions, taking relevant work-related qualifications as you go, in order to become a prison governor.

In England and Wales, the National Offender Management Service (NOMS) provides a graduate training scheme as an alternative route into the profession. It is designed to encourage rapid progression through the grades into a management position. To follow this route you will need at least a 2.2 degree.

On the NOMS graduate programme you would complete full prison officer training followed by up to a year working as a prison officer. You may then progress to a senior role with responsibility for other staff members before taking up an operational management post.

In Scotland, prison officers are able to apply for promotions once they complete their 1-year probationary period. Applications are assessed based on individual merit and ability.

What the work involves

Prison governors/operational managers are responsible for the overall running and security of the establishment.

You will supervise security measures, make inspections, carry out disciplinary procedures, and advise both staff and inmates on behavioural standards and guidelines. You will also be dealing with each prisoner's casework and administration. This will include processing parole applications and complaints, and require liaison with other social and healthcare professionals.

You will be working within strict parameters set out by the government, and must ensure that you meet their targets on service, health and safety, and prisoner welfare and development.

Type of person suited to this work

You will need excellent communication skills, including confidence, assertiveness and a motivational ability, all of which will be essential when managing and inspiring staff, and also for building effective relationships with inmates.

You must have integrity and be committed to working with vulnerable people with various social issues. This should include respect for those in your care, and for the other professionals working around you.

Working conditions

You will be expected to work on a shift basis, including night and weekend hours, in order to meet the 24-hour needs of the prison. On average, you will work a 39-hour week.

You could work in a modern prison with excellent facilities, or an older, more austere establishment that will come with maintenance problems and perhaps a less comfortable working environment.

Future prospects

Prisons are located in large cities, towns and very rural locations, so you have a good range of options regarding the working environment that would most suit you.

Prison governors are at the top of their sector, so only sideways movements are possible. You could opt to work in a specialist institution, such as one dealing with inmates with specific medical needs. Extra qualifications may be required for this.

Vacancies may possibly be affected by budget cuts. Although these cuts have mainly taken place, a lot of prisons are still trying to reduce costs.

Advantages/disadvantages

You could be responsible for turning the lives of inmates around, both by providing them with opportunities whilst serving their sentence, and also by encouraging them to pursue better lives when they leave.

You may have to control difficult and violent situations at times.

Money guide

On the NOMS graduate programme you will earn between £26,450 and £28,750.

Once qualified as an operational manager you will move up the pay scale, earning a minimum of £32,000.

On gaining the full title and responsibilities of a prison governor, you could earn between £47,000 and £83,000.

Related opportunities

- Police Community Support Officer p542
- Police Officer p543
- Prison Officer/Instructor p546

Further information

HM Prison Service
www.gov.uk/government/organisations/hm-prison-service

Scottish Prison Service
www.sps.gov.uk

545

Qualifications and courses

There are no specific academic requirements in England and Wales, although some GCSEs (A*–C), including English and Maths, could be useful. In Scotland you need to have 5 National 5s (A–C), including English and Maths, and/or experience in a people-facing role.

You will need to pass an entrance test, assessment day, medical examination, fitness test and a Disclosure and Barring Service (DBS) check, as well as meet the nationality criteria outlined on HM Prison Service's website. You must be at least 18 years old, not an undischarged bankrupt or a member of a group or organisation that the Prison Service considers racist.

Before you can start work as a prison officer you will need to undergo an 8-week entry-level training course. During your probation period you will also be expected to complete a NVQ Level 3 in Custodial Care.

For graduates in England and Wales there is a National Offender Management Service (NOMS) Graduate Programme which aims to fast-track competent graduates into managerial roles. You must have a 2.2 degree or higher in order to qualify.

If you are hoping to become a prison instructor you will need a recognised teaching qualification, a Level 3 vocational qualification and experience in the field you will be teaching. You may also need to hold a qualification in health and safety and be able to demonstrate teaching or supervisory experience.

What the work involves

Prison officers are responsible for supervising inmates within a secure institution. Prison instructors undertake the same duties as prison officers, but are also responsible for training prisoners in order to help them develop new skills and gain qualifications.

You will need to build positive relationships with the prisoners in your care in order to educate and encourage them to pursue a law-abiding life.

You could work with a variety of inmates, ranging from high risk criminals in top security institutions, to those with minor offences in low security prisons.

Type of person suited to this work

You should have excellent communication skills and be a confident person so that you can interact positively with inmates whilst also retaining your authority when necessary.

You must be non-judgemental and have respect for the prisoners in your care. The ability to remain calm in pressurised or uncomfortable situations is also an asset.

Prison instructors should be approachable and patient. You will need to be understanding and encouraging in order to help prisoners learn and progress.

Working conditions

You will usually work 39 hours a week. Prison officers will work on a shift basis including night and weekend shifts, but prison instructors usually only work during the week.

Most work is indoors and within a prison. Prison officers will also be responsible for supervising outdoor exercise and patrolling the prison grounds. Prison instructors will work in a setting suitable for their subject, for example a workshop within the prison, or in the grounds if they are teaching horticulture.

Some travel between prisons may be expected to provide extra staffing on occasion. Prison officers may also have to escort prisoners to and from court appearances.

Future prospects

Prison officers and prison instructors can move into a position as a senior officer or principal officer of a prison. Promotion is based solely on merit, so the more you put in the more you can get out of this career.

The number of vacancies available may have been affected by budget cuts and the drive to reduce prison costs.

Advantages/disadvantages

Helping to rehabilitate and educate prisoners can be rewarding, and you will be providing an important public service.

Working in a prison environment can be claustrophobic and stifling.

You may be faced with difficult and occasionally violent prisoners, which can be both stressful and unpleasant.

Money guide

The national starting salary for officers in England and Wales is £18,720, which includes a base salary and 17% addition for working unsocial hours.

With experience officers could earn around £31,000.

Senior managers with significant experience can earn up to £82,892.

In Scotland, the starting salary is £16,171. Good performance can increase your salary to £20,545 within 5 years.

Instructors can earn between £19,500 and £25,260 a year.

Related opportunities

- Police Officer p543
- Police Support Worker p544
- Social Worker p573

Further information

HM Prison Service
www.gov.uk/government/organisations/hm-prison-service

Qualifications and courses

There are no formal entry qualifications for this work. However, while it is possible to be taken on by an investigations company in a junior role and train on the job, it is difficult as many entrants have had previous relevant experience in a related job such as the police, law, customs and excise or security work.

Therefore applicants new to the role will benefit from having a relevant qualification. This could be a degree in subjects such as investigative studies or crime and investigation, an Association of British Investigators (ABI) membership qualification or the online Foundation Private Investigation Course from the Institute of Professional Investigators (IPI).

Whatever your training, it should be accepted by the Security Industry Authority (SIA) and include topics on the law, investigative methods and equipment. The SIA are in the process of considering a new regulation system for private investigators (PIs) which may involve needing a licence to practise. Check with the SIA directly for the latest developments.

Candidates who are just starting out can try approaching companies about work shadowing. Another option is to start out working on a freelance basis. Let local investigators know in case any opportunities arise.

You will need a driving licence.

What the work involves

You will be collecting information for a private client or a solicitor by asking questions, researching, obtaining evidence and making sense of what you find out.

PIs do a variety of different jobs such as surveillance, tracing people, serving legal documents or investigating road accidents, suspected fraud and employee backgrounds.

You could be recording your findings using a computer, and you may be asked to present your findings in court or to a large company. You will probably take witness statements, attend court hearings and give evidence.

Type of person suited to this work

Much of the day-to-day work of this exciting-sounding job is actually quite routine, so you will need to be patient and persistent and be happy with your own company as you will be predominantly working independently.

You need to have a keen interest in developing a working knowledge of the law.

You will need to have excellent communication skills, both spoken and written, in order to write reports and take witness statements. You may need to calm down anxious or aggressive people when you serve legal papers or repossess belongings in order to pay a debt.

Working conditions

Most of your working hours will be spent driving or walking around. You could be in your vehicle for hours or out in all weathers.

Hours are irregular and in some cases they could be long and include evening and weekend work.

You will be at risk of assault from aggressive individuals who you are serving with legal papers.

Future prospects

With the introduction of licensing there may be more opportunities for those with licences. A lot of the work is for legal, insurance or financial companies.

Some private investigators go on to take further qualifications and specialise in areas such as commercial piracy or insurance fraud. A few set up their own agencies and others move into supervisory or security management work.

There is the opportunity to progress into a managerial or senior investigator role at bigger agencies.

Advantages/disadvantages

PIs are usually self-employed and so need to buy their own equipment. Licences and training will also add to the expense.

A lot of the work is routine, but PIs say that there is a lot of satisfaction when after months of patient work you manage to find the evidence your client needs.

Money guide

Starting salaries begin at around £15,000 per year.

Well-qualified specialists working in corporate investigation can earn between £50,000 and £100,000.

Clients may pay for some expenses, such as hotel or restaurant bills, and PIs who work for companies or agencies may get a vehicle allowance.

Related opportunities

- Forensic Computer Analyst p539
- Police Officer p543
- Store Detective p556

Further information

Academy of Professional Investigation
www.pi-academy.com

Institute of Professional Investigators
www.ipi.org.uk

Security Industry Authority
www.sia.homeoffice.gov.uk

The Association of British Investigators
www.theabi.org.uk

SECURITY, EMERGENCY AND THE ARMED FORCES

Qualifications and courses

You will need to work as a probation service officer (PSO) before training to be a probation officer. Pre-entry experience of working with offenders or other vulnerable groups, for example with prison visiting services, victim support services or community payback teams, is often required when applying for PSO jobs.

Once you are in a PSO position, there are two ways to train to work as a probation officer in England and Wales. The first is to undertake a 3-year Honours degree in Community Justice and a Level 5 Vocational Qualification Diploma in Probation Practice (VQ5).

The second way, if you already have an Honours degree that includes at least 50% criminology, community justice, criminal justice or police studies, is to take the work-based Graduate Diploma in Community Justice as well as the VQ5.

In Scotland, in order to join the Probation Service you must complete a 4-year Honours degree in social work which has been approved by the Scottish Social Services Council (SSSC), and gain relevant experience. Alternatively there is a postgraduate scheme available for candidates with a degree in a different subject. Northern Ireland has a similar approach, with candidates needing a degree in social work and experience working with offenders.

What the work involves

Probation officers protect the public by assessing the risk that offenders pose to the community and working out how to limit that risk.

You will work with offenders before, during and after their sentencing. This will include ensuring they carry out their punishment, making them aware of the consequences of their offences and helping them back into the community. You will construct and deliver programmes to change offenders' behaviour and attitude.

You will prepare pre-sentence reports (PSRs) to advise judges on sentencing and prepare risk assessments for prisons and parole review boards, which may then contribute towards a decision on the early release of an offender.

Type of person suited to this work

You will need to have the ability to gain the trust and confidence of offenders and have a fair and non-judgemental approach. Good communication skills will be helpful.

Organisational skills are essential as you will often be planning your own workload. An ability to write clearly and accurately will be needed for reports and risk assessments. Employers also look for good teamwork skills and experience of the criminal justice system.

As you may face stressful situations and setbacks, strong motivation and commitment is important.

Working conditions

Typically you will work between 37 and 40 hours a week. Hours are not always regular and you may have to work in the evenings and at weekends, but you will usually get extra time off to make up for unsocial hours.

You will work from an office but will also be expected to travel to courts and prisons and community programmes on a regular basis.

Future prospects

You can specialise in areas such as managing approved premises, which provide accommodation for people on bail, or drug treatment and testing orders. Probation officers are offered frequent opportunities for training.

With experience there is a possibility of moving to a managerial role as a senior probation officer. Eventually you may become an area manager.

Recruitment may be affected by budget cuts. Most cuts have already happened, but plans to cut £215 million from the annual budget for legal aid and to privatise and outsource 70% of probation services mean the future state of the job market could be uncertain.

Advantages/disadvantages

Providing a public service and helping to rehabilitate prisoners can be deeply rewarding.

You may meet difficult or violent offenders which could be stressful or distressing.

Money guide

Salaries differ between probation trusts, but probation service officers typically earn between £21,000 and £27,000 a year.

Qualified probation officers usually earn between £28,000 and £36,000. With experience this can rise to between £35,000 and £40,000.

Salaries for assistant chief officer posts start at around £50,000.

Related opportunities

- Prison Officer/Instructor p546
- Social Worker p573
- Victim Care Officer p576

Further information

Ministry of Justice
www.justice.gov.uk

Probation Board for Northern Ireland
www.pbni.org.uk

Skills for Justice
www.sfjuk.com

Qualifications and courses

The Royal Air Force (RAF) has detailed eligibility requirements. Entrants need to be at least 15 years old (those under 18 must have parental consent) and you must be a British Citizen, British National, British/ Dual National, Commonwealth Citizen or Irish Republic National. There are further requirements for residency, health and fitness. Details of the exact criteria you must meet can be found on the RAF Careers website.

Educational requirements vary depending on the type of job. Some positions, such as physical training instructor or flight operations assistant, only require GCSEs/ National 5s, whereas some others, such as registered nurse, will require a degree. Whatever the role, you will need to pass rigorous medical and health tests as well as a range of interviews and written tests during the selection process.

Once accepted into the RAF you will complete a 10-week training course at RAF Halton in Buckinghamshire, which will cover fitness and weapons training. On completion of these general elements you will then start on more specialised training for your chosen trade, which can take between 3 weeks and 18 months.

What the work involves

The RAF is responsible for protecting UK airspace, performing search and rescue missions offshore and on land, transporting aid to the victims of war and natural disaster, and pursuing military action in a war situation. Opportunities include positions in catering, aircrew, engineering, protection and medical support.

You will work within a team of other RAF professionals, under the guidance of an officer.

You will also be expected to undertake general military duties, such as guarding RAF bases, and taking part in training exercises and military initiatives.

Type of person suited to this work

You should be able to work well within a team. This includes being able to follow orders, work calmly under pressure, support colleagues and use your own initiative when necessary.

You should be self-disciplined in order to maintain high levels of fitness, mental agility and a positive attitude to your work.

You should be good at interpreting and analysing information, both oral and written.

Working conditions

Airmen/women usually work regular office hours, but you are required to be available for duty at all times in case of an emergency. There are also occasional social functions or other duties that need to be fulfilled over weekends.

You will be stationed at an RAF base, many of which have all the amenities of a small town.

You should be prepared to be posted overseas at short notice, and to spend long periods of time away from friends and family.

Future prospects

On joining the RAF as an airman/woman you will usually be asked to stay for between 6 and 12 years, though many people stay longer.

After 6 months, or on completion of specialist training, you should be promoted to leading airman/woman and from there you can work up the ranks to the position of corporal or higher. Promotion is based on merit, so you will be rewarded for the hard work that you put in.

Prospects for new and existing recruits may be affected by defence budget cuts with an aim to reduce personnel by about 1,500 by 2020. Nevertheless, there are still good opportunities if you meet the selection criteria.

Advantages/disadvantages

You will work on a wide variety of assignments within a supportive team environment, so each day will be both diverse and interesting.

There are good training schemes and potential for promotion and career progression within the RAF.

You may have to enter war situations, which can be traumatic and stressful.

Money guide

There is an established pay structure for RAF airmen/women.

During training you can expect to be paid £14,637 per year. Once you are fully qualified your salary will increase to £18,125.

Senior level airmen/women will earn between £19,099 and £29,947 per year. Corporals can expect to earn between £27,324 and £34,338, and sergeants between £31,058 and £38,215.

Related opportunities

- Air Traffic Controller p583
- Army Soldier p531
- Royal Air Force Officer p550

Further information

RAF Halton
www.raf.mod.uk/rafhalton

RAF Recruitment
www.raf.mod.uk/recruitment

SECURITY, EMERGENCY AND THE ARMED FORCES

Qualifications and courses

The Royal Air Force (RAF) has detailed eligibility requirements concerning age, nationality, residency, health and fitness. Details of the exact criteria you must meet can be found on the RAF Careers website. All RAF roles are now open to both men and women except for regiment officer and regiment gunner, which remain open only to men.

Educational requirements vary depending on the type of job. Some positions, such as regiment officer or pilot, require 5 GCSEs/National 5s (A*–C/A–C) and 2 A levels/3 H grades. Some others, such as medical officer, will require a degree.

Whatever the role, you will need to pass rigorous medical and health tests, as well as a range of interviews and written and aptitude tests during the selection process. This will take place at the RAF College Cranwell in Lincolnshire.

For entrance onto related degree courses, you will need 3 A levels/H grades and at least 5 GCSEs/National 5s (A*–C/A–C) or equivalent, including English, Maths and a science. The RAF also offers sponsorship to sixth form and university students.

As a new recruit you will have to complete a 30-week initial officer training course at Cranwell where you will be taught a variety of skills such as service knowledge and leadership skills. If you join the RAF with a professional qualification this initial training may be reduced to 12 weeks. You will then go on to specialise. On completion of your training you will be awarded The Queen's Commission, which will empower you to give orders and lead on behalf of the crown.

What the work involves

The RAF is responsible for protecting UK airspace, performing search and rescue missions offshore and on land, transporting aid to the victims of war and natural disaster, and pursuing military action in a war situation.

RAF officers are responsible for managing, leading and inspiring a team of airmen.

You will occupy a specialist post within the RAF, such as that of a pilot, engineer, catering manager or medical officer.

You will be involved in planning and implementing various procedures from rescues to humanitarian aid drops.

Type of person suited to this work

You must have excellent communication skills as you will be responsible for briefing, leading and motivating your team. This also includes being able to listen to and get on with all team members.

You will be called upon to make difficult decisions in highly pressurised situations, so must be able to think on your feet in order to reach mature, responsible conclusions.

You must be physically fit and mentally alert.

Working conditions

Officers usually work regular office hours, but you are required to be available for duty at all times in case of an emergency. There are also occasional social functions or other duties that need to be fulfilled over weekends.

You will be stationed at an RAF base, many of which have all the amenities of a small town, including shops, banks, a gym and childcare facilities.

You should be prepared to be posted overseas at short notice, and to spend long periods of time away from friends and family.

You will be entitled to 6 weeks of paid holiday.

Future prospects

On joining the RAF as an officer you sign up to a minimum length of service that ranges from 6 to 12 years according to your specialisation.

There is defined career progression through the ranks from flying officer to flight lieutenant, squadron leader, wing commander, group captain and further if you wish.

The training, qualifications and personal skills that come with being an RAF officer are easily transferred to a number of civilian positions.

Although prospects for new and existing recruits may be affected by defence budget cuts, there are still good opportunities if you meet the selection criteria.

Advantages/disadvantages

You will be responsible for training and organising a team that will carry out essential defence and humanitarian functions for the UK and the world.

You may have to enter combat situations which can be distressing and unpleasant.

Money guide

There are different pay scales for some specialist officers and for people who join as graduates or with professional qualifications.

Entering the RAF without a degree, a pilot officer can expect to earn £25,472 as a starting salary. If you hold a degree and enter as a flying officer, your starting wages will be £30,617 to £33,842 per year.

Squadron leaders can earn between £51,763 and £62,934.

Related opportunities

- Air Traffic Controller p583
- Royal Air Force Airman/woman p549
- Royal Navy Officer p553

Further information

RAF College Cranwell
www.raf.mod.uk/rafcollegecranwell

Qualifications and courses

The Royal Navy has detailed eligibility requirements. Only men can serve in the Royal Marines at this time and they must be least 16 years old to be a commando (those under 18 must have parental consent). You must be a British Citizen, British National, British/Dual National, Commonwealth Citizen or Irish Republic National. There are further requirements for residency, health and fitness. Details of the exact criteria you must meet can be found on the Royal Navy Careers website.

There is a rigorous selection process. You will need to pass a recruit test, which covers English, maths, mechanics and problem-solving, attend an interview and pass medical and fitness examinations.

You will also have to undertake the Potential Royal Marines Course. This lasts 2 days at the Commando Training Centre Royal Marines (CTCRM), Lympstone, Devon, and is designed to test your fitness, determination, stamina and mental ability. This is a gruelling assessment designed to push you to your limits, so you will have to train and prepare for it for a number of months.

There are no academic qualification requirements for entry but a career in the Royal Marines offers the opportunity to gain qualifications related to your area of specialism as your career progresses.

What the work involves

The Royal Marines are a specialist, highly trained, amphibious division of the Royal Navy. They carry out operations on land, at sea or in the air. They operate in combat, peacekeeping and humanitarian situations, and also as a law enforcement agency at sea.

You will be a commando and rifleman, working within an operational commando unit. You will be ready to take immediate action in any emergency or threat to national security, and this means performing to a very high standard at all times whether on land or at sea.

You will specialise either in general duties or in one of 26 trades, including assault engineer, mountain leader or swimmer canoeist.

Type of person suited to this work

You will need high levels of fitness, discipline, commitment and self-confidence in order to get through one of the most demanding and gruelling training programmes in the armed forces prior to qualifying as a commando.

You must be able to work well within a team and also use your own initiative when required. The ability to lead and motivate others is also an asset.

You should be level-headed and be able to react quickly and logically when under pressure. Courage and determination are also necessary in order to head into combat situations.

Working conditions

You will usually work 37 hours a week, unless you are on an operation or in training. In these instances, you could expect to work long, unpredictable hours. Even if you are not at work, though, you will always be on call in case of emergency.

You could be stationed or deployed anywhere in the world at short notice, including undertaking operations in areas of desert, jungle, and even out in the Arctic.

You will be expected to wear a uniform.

Future prospects

Within the UK, you are most likely to be stationed within the south-west of England or in Scotland, as that is where the majority of naval bases are located.

You will be expected to serve with the Royal Marines for 22 years, although you can leave at any point after completing the minimum 3 years of service and giving 12 months' notice.

You will be promoted on merit, so hard work should be rewarded. You could move up the ranks from lance corporal right up to warrant officer 1.

Although prospects for new and existing recruits may be affected by defence budget cuts, there are still good opportunities if you meet the selection criteria. Most of the job cuts have already occurred with the Royal Navy and any further cuts are unlikely to come from the Royal Marines. Consequently, the job market should be quite steady.

Advantages/disadvantages

You will be operating at your optimum level of mental and physical fitness, meeting new challenges each day and adapting to unusual and inhospitable situations.

You will be working within a close-knit team, providing essential services such as delivering aid or maintaining order in areas across the globe.

You are continually on call, and could be sent anywhere in the world at a moment's notice.

Money guide

New entrants to the Royal Marines as general duties Marines receive a starting salary of around £14,349, rising to around £17,767 on completion of initial training.

If you move up the ranks and reach the level of warrant officer 1 you should earn £39,944 to £48,381.

Related opportunities

- Army Officer p530
- Army Soldier p531
- Royal Marines Officer p552

Further information

Royal Marines
www.royalnavy.mod.uk/royalmarines

Qualifications and courses

The minimum criteria for entry to officer training in the Royal Navy are 5 GCSEs/National 5s (A*–C/A–C), including English and Maths, and 72 UCAS points from the UCAS Tariff table (including 2 non-overlapping A level/H grade subjects with each subject providing at least 16 UCAS points). Graduates in any subject are welcome and have more opportunities open to them than non-graduates. It is also possible to study for a fully funded Honours degree while working for the Royal Navy.

Only men can serve in the Royal Marines at this time and you must be between 17 and 25 years old to enter. You must also meet particular nationality, residency, health and fitness criteria, which are outlined on the Royal Navy's website.

You will attend a 3-day Potential Officers Course, which is a gruelling assessment designed to push you to your limits. If you successfully complete the assessment you will be invited to sit tests in maths, reasoning, accuracy, written communication, spatial orientation, leadership and problem-solving, and undergo a series of interviews.

If you are selected to train as an officer, you will then have to complete a further 15-month programme prior to being given your own team to lead.

What the work involves

The Royal Marines carry out operations on land, at sea or in the air. They operate in combat, peacekeeping and humanitarian situations, and also as a law enforcement agency at sea.

You will be responsible for leading and managing a team both on training operations and on real missions including combat situations and peacekeeping tasks. You will be in charge of training your team, keeping them disciplined and looking out for their welfare.

You will be given the opportunity to specialise in 1 of 10 areas, including weapons training, signals, physical training, or as a pilot.

Type of person suited to this work

You will need high levels of fitness, discipline, commitment and self-confidence in order to get through the demanding and gruelling training programme prior to qualifying as an officer.

You must be able to lead and motivate your team, looking out for their welfare and making decisions for them in dangerous and stressful conditions.

You should be able to focus fully on the operations you undertake in order to function at your maximum level of mental and physical capacity.

Working conditions

You will usually work 37 hours a week, unless you are on an operation or in training. In these instances, you could expect to work long, unpredictable hours. Even if you are not at work, you are always on call in case of emergency.

You could be stationed or deployed anywhere in the world at short notice, including undertaking operations in areas of desert, jungle, and even out in the Arctic.

You will be expected to wear a uniform, and specialised clothing when required.

Future prospects

Competition for entry as a Royal Marines officer is fierce. You will be expected to join on a 12-year commission and must serve at least 3–5 years of this. 12 months' notice is required prior to departure.

You will normally move appointments every other year, so you will be able to experience numerous areas of work in various locations throughout your career.

Promotion is awarded based on merit and you could work through the ranks from 2nd lieutenant right up to major-general.

Although prospects for new and existing recruits may be affected by defence budget cuts there are still good opportunities if you meet the selection criteria.

Advantages/disadvantages

You will be operating at your optimum level of mental and physical fitness, meeting new challenges each day and adapting to unusual and inhospitable situations.

You will be working within a close-knit team, leading them through essential operations such as delivering aid or maintaining order in areas across the globe.

Money guide

Entrants who do not have a degree can expect a starting salary of £16,073 at the start of their training, rising to £25,472 once qualified.

Graduates can expect a starting salary of between £29,587 and £32,703.

With experience those who rise to captain/colonel could earn £84,037 to £92,381.

Related opportunities

- Army Officer p530
- Army Soldier p531
- Royal Marines Commando p551

Further information

Royal Marines
www.royalnavy.mod.uk/royalmarines

Qualifications and courses

You will need to be at least 151.5cm tall, be of proportionate weight and, upon entry, you must be aged 16 or over. A medical, with strict eyesight standards, must be passed and you must meet the Royal Navy nationality and residence requirements. Both men and women are accepted in most roles.

The minimum requirements for officer entry are 5 GCSEs/National 5s (A*–C/A–C), including English and Maths, and a minimum of 72 UCAS points (each A level/H grade subject must be allocated at least 16 UCAS points). Some officer roles have more specific qualifications, details of which can be found on the Royal Navy's website.

Prospective entrants who want to go to sixth form college or university may be able to acquire a Royal Navy-funded scholarship or bursary to help pay for their study. Those who have already graduated from university can apply to the Royal Navy through Direct Graduate Entry.

All candidates undergo selection interviews, tests and a medical examination before they reach the Admiralty Interview Board (AIB) stage. The tests include mental agility, physical fitness, communication and maths.

Upon entry, there are two phases of officer training. Initial training lasts for 30 weeks, first at Dartmouth and then at sea. You then go on to professional training, the length and location of which depends on your job.

What the work involves

You will command and train ratings, looking after their welfare, development and discipline.

Your day-to-day work will involve you managing operations in 1 of 4 areas of duty: warfare officer, engineer officer, supply officer or specialist officer (for example chaplain, doctor or dentist).

Your ship may be sent into combat or on peacekeeping duties.

You may be tasked to do a specific job such as policing the North Sea fishing grounds or helping out in a disaster situation.

Type of person suited to this work

Officers especially need top-level leadership and communication skills as well as good judgement.

You will be required to inspire ratings, be resourceful and have excellent communication skills. You should have good levels of physical fitness and stamina.

You should also have a very strong sense of responsibility as your decisions may impact upon your colleagues' safety as well as your own. You should display a very high level of personal awareness and a keen sense of personal safety.

Working conditions

Most of your work will be on board a ship or submarine, or at land-based establishments in Britain or overseas. At sea, conditions can be cold, cramped and damp. You will need to wear a uniform, and protective clothing when necessary.

Hours vary but you will usually work 8-hour turns of duty on a shift rota including weekends and holidays.

You may find yourself working in a dangerous or highly unpredictable situation.

Future prospects

There are annual vacancies but some specialisms are more competitive than others.

A naval college entrant usually starts out as midshipman, rising to sub-lieutenant after 2 years. A graduate starts as sub-lieutenant, rising to lieutenant commander by their early 30s. If you have the right qualities you can progress on to the ranks of commander, captain and, for a few, admiral.

Although prospects for new and existing recruits may be affected by defence budget cuts there are still good opportunities if you meet the selection criteria.

Advantages/disadvantages

You will be trained to a high level and will be offered a resettlement package to help you find work in civilian life when you leave.

You will be living in cramped conditions with lots of other people. However, most officers say that they enjoy the feeling of camaraderie on board and make life-long friendships.

Money guide

Direct entry basic pay at the rank of Midshipman/Second Lieutenant is £25,472 increasing to £30,617 once qualifying.

After a year of service you can expect to earn £31,426 to £33,842.

As you rise through the ranks and gain experience, your salary can range from £37,916 to £92,381 per year.

Related opportunities

- Army Officer p530
- Royal Marines Officer p552
- Royal Navy Rating p554

Further information

Royal Navy Careers
www.royalnavy.mod.uk

Welbeck College
www.dsfc.ac.uk

ROYAL NAVY RATING

Qualifications and courses

There are no formal qualifications for entry but holding at least 2 GCSEs/National 5s (A*–C/A–C) or equivalent is helpful. Typically, you must be 16 to 37 years of age to apply. Some specialist trades have specific entry requirements and a higher age for admission.

Selection takes place at local armed forces careers offices, where you will be required to take several tests including numeracy, English language, reasoning and mechanical comprehension. If you are successful you will be invited for an interview and be expected to pass a medical assessment and fitness test.

After passing the recruitment process you will attend a 4-day induction course. Upon entry you will undertake 10 weeks' basic training, followed by specialist training in your chosen trade.

You will join the Royal Navy on a Full Career, which lasts 18 years. You can leave after completing 2.5 years but must give 12 months' notice.

What the work involves

The Royal Navy protects the UK's ports and coastline, and also undertakes international missions such as delivering humanitarian aid, entering combat and enforcing the law on the seas.

Royal Navy ratings work on board a ship, submarine or onshore, and are responsible for operating, maintaining and repairing technical equipment.

You will specialise in one of the 6 main trades: medical, warfare, logistics, engineering, fleet air arm, or submarine. These inevitably encompass a wide range of roles from overseeing electrical systems and sensors to providing a medical service for the Royal Navy personnel and their families.

You will also take part in naval exercises and operations in both UK and overseas waters.

Type of person suited to this work

You should be able to work within a team, reacting quickly to orders, working on your own initiative where necessary, and supporting other team members both professionally and emotionally at times.

You must be responsible and decisive and find solutions to problems under difficult or pressurised circumstances. You should also have a methodical and logical approach to your work.

You will need to have a good level of fitness, including the ability to swim and tread water for a number of minutes.

Working conditions

You will usually work 37 hours a week, which can include weekends and public holidays. You will also be on call at all times, in case of an emergency.

You could be based at sea on a ship or submarine, or in a naval station onshore. Living conditions on ships and submarines tend to be basic, and men and women always sleep in separate accommodation.

You will have to spend long periods of time away from friends and family, and may be posted overseas at a moment's notice.

Future prospects

The career progression for a Royal Navy rating is clearly mapped out. Promotion is awarded based on merit so the harder you work the faster you will progress. The grades that you will move upwards through are able rating, leading rating, petty officer, chief petty officer and warrant officer.

If you have the necessary qualifications you could apply to become an officer. This is a popular route of career progression amongst ratings.

Although prospects for new and existing recruits may be affected by defence budget cuts, there are still good opportunities if you meet the selection criteria.

Advantages/disadvantages

You will be meeting new challenges each day and adapting to unusual and inhospitable situations, which will keep you mentally and physically alert and ensures the work never gets dull.

You will be working within a close-knit team, supporting it both in training and when out on real operations.

As you are continually on call you could be sent anywhere in the world at a moment's notice.

Money guide

You will enter the Royal Navy as a rating on a starting salary of £14,637.

Once you have completed your training and have qualified as an able rating, you could earn £18,125 and if you work your way up this career ladder you could earn up to £48,381.

Related opportunities

- Army Soldier p531
- Royal Air Force Officer p550
- Royal Marines Commando p551
- Royal Navy Officer p553

Further information

Royal Navy Careers
www.royalnavy.mod.uk

Qualifications and courses

Officer

There are no specific academic qualifications needed, although a good standard of general education would be helpful, as would previous experience of working in the police or armed forces. Employers will carry out personal, work history and possibly criminal records checks.

Security guards must have an industry licence approved by the Security Industry Authority (SIA), unless you are carrying out in-house security for your employer on your employer's premises. You will need to be 18 years old, pass identity and criminal records checks and complete an SIA-approved course. A full list of these can be found on the SIA's website. If the role involves monitoring CCTV you may need an SIA Public Space Surveillance (CCTV) licence.

Manager

In addition to needing the SIA licence, specialist managers or prospective managers can take further part-time courses including Foundation degrees, degrees and postgraduate qualifications in security and risk management. The Security Institute offers a Certificate and Diploma in Security Management.

Door supervisor

You will need an SIA licence, an SIA-approved Level 2 Certificate in Door Supervision and to pass a Disclosure and Barring Service (DBS) check. There are no academic requirements for entry onto the course. Some employers may take you on as a trainee and support you through the training.

What the work involves

Security work is about protecting organisations, people, places, valuable goods or money.

Officer

You might work at reception monitoring visitors and deliveries or you might patrol a site, checking for intruders or fire risks. You might also monitor CCTV footage and respond to any issues noticed through it.

Manager

You will manage a team and be responsible for their work, training and supervision. You will do security surveys, give advice on improvements and liaise with other organisations such as the emergency services.

Door supervisor

You will stand at the entrance to a building and help control people entering and leaving, judging whether or not they should be allowed on the premises. You could also search bags for potentially dangerous items and assist the police if trouble breaks out.

Type of person suited to this work

You will need to be a mature, responsible and honest person. You should be keen on technology and keep up to date with new security systems. You will also have to keep records of all incidents, so you must be happy to do paperwork.

For certain types of security work, you will need to be physically fit and healthy. You will also need to be able to remain calm in the face of confrontation.

To become a manager you will need a great deal of experience in security work as well as a talent for motivating a team of staff.

Working conditions

If you are a door supervisor you will be based in one location which could be inside, or outside in all weathers. Many security officer/manager jobs involve driving and you will spend a lot of time in a security van.

You will probably be working shifts of up to 12 hours covering days, nights and weekends. Some door supervisors or security officers work permanent nights. You may work a 48-hour week although part-time work is available.

Future prospects

This work will increasingly use sophisticated technology, computer security systems and also biometrics (fingerprint recognition systems) to control access to buildings and other secure areas.

With the right training and technical ability you are likely to be in demand in this growing industry.

Advantages/disadvantages

Your promotion and earnings prospects are excellent.

You could often work alone and be put in vulnerable situations.

Money guide

Officer

Starting out, officers are paid between £12,000 and £15,000 per year. With experience this can rise to £20,000.

Manager

On entry, managers earn around £25,000. With experience, senior managers can earn £50,000 or more.

Door supervisor

Door supervisors tend to be paid by an hourly rate of around £8 to £12 (£15,600 to £23,400 per year). With experience this can rise to £15 per hour for a part-time supervisor.

Related opportunities

- Bodyguard p532
- Police Officer p543
- Prison Officer/Instructor p546

Further information

Security Industry Authority
www.sia.homeoffice.gov.uk

STORE DETECTIVE

Qualifications and courses

There are no formal entry requirements but you will need to be able to write clearly and accurately. A GCSE/National 5 in English or a Key Skill in Communication may be useful.

A Security Industry Authority (SIA) licence may be required if you are employed by an agency or contractor. For this you will need to be aged 18 or older, pass an identity check and a Disclosure and Barring Service (DBS) check, and have completed relevant training approved by the SIA. Training can be completed before beginning work or undertaken part time while working at your first job. An additional SIA licence may be required if your job involves using CCTV equipment.

Previous relevant work experience is preferred, especially within the police, armed forces or security industry. An Apprenticeship in Providing Security Services could be helpful.

Once you start work, training is primarily done through courses and on the job with the support of a more experienced store detective. Most companies run an induction course for new employees covering topics such as relevant criminal law and principles of investigation.

Store detectives can work towards a BTEC Level 2 Certificate in Providing Security Services or a City & Guilds Level 3 Award in Security Operations.

What the work involves

You will be preventing and detecting theft or fraud in a retail outlet. You might need to chase the suspected offender, search them and make arrests. You will then need to contact the police and describe your observations.

Working undercover, wearing plain clothes, you will merge with shoppers, looking out for suspicious behaviour or theft.

Using a radio you will call for assistance and listen for alerts from other staff about known offenders entering the store.

You will make notes of any incidents and may need to use these if a decision is made to prosecute. Occasionally you will have to give evidence in court. If trouble does break out, you may also need to take evidence from any witnesses.

You may also be involved with preventing the use of stolen credit cards.

Type of person suited to this work

You need to have excellent communications skills as it will be your responsibility to deal with customers who have become anxious or aggressive when challenged.

Your written reports will be used in court if you prosecute and you will need to be fluent and precise to get a conviction.

You must have good observation skills in order to spot suspicious behaviour and also remember the faces of known shoplifters.

You should be able to plan and think ahead so that when needed you can act quickly.

You will need to be mature, responsible and be able to handle difficult situations sensitively.

Working conditions

You will spend the majority of your time on your feet, in the store.

A 40-hour week is common and you may work shifts to cover long opening hours and weekends.

You might wear a uniform but the majority wear their own clothes to blend in.

Future prospects

Shoplifters cost retail businesses more than £2 billion a year so most large shops in the UK employ store detectives to minimise their losses.

Some retail chains employ their own detectives, while others use agencies on a contract basis.

After gaining experience, you could become a supervisor or move into more general security management.

Advantages/disadvantages

Apprehending shoplifters can be dangerous.

This job can be a good stepping stone into jobs such as security management.

Money guide

Starting wages are usually around £14,000 per year.

Experienced store detectives generally earn between £17,000 and £20,000. £30,000 is possible for top earners.

Store detectives are sometimes paid hourly with the rate ranging from £6 to £8 per hour. Working overtime can boost wages.

Related opportunities

- Police Officer p543
- Private Investigator p547
- Security Officer/Manager/Door Supervisor p555

Further information

British Security Industry Association
www.bsia.co.uk

Security Industry Authority
www.sia.homeoffice.gov.uk

Social Work and Counselling Services

People who work in this sector are dedicated to caring and talking through people's problems and anxieties to improve their general wellbeing and their future prospects in life. The work requires a lot of patience, an open mind and a friendly and approachable personality. You could be helping people who are distressed and need help and guidance but equally you may be helping people who want to move on to the next stage in their careers or educational choices. Either way, you should be someone who enjoys helping people change their lives for the better. If you are interested in working in this field you need to show that you are compassionate and very good at communicating with people from all walks of life and of all ages. You should also be someone who can maintain a strong sense of professionalism as you could be in a position of trust and you must be very respectful of your clients' privacy. The jobs featured in this section are listed below. For similar jobs to the ones covered in this section turn to *Healthcare* on page 269 and *Education and Training* on page 179.

Qualifications and courses

There are two main routes into this profession: the study of the Qualification in Careers Guidance (QCG) or gaining relevant qualifications through work-based study.

The QCG is a 1-year full-time or 2-year part-time course that combines academic study with work-based learning and leads to the Postgraduate Diploma in Careers Guidance. You normally need a degree to take this course but applicants with significant and relevant work experience would also be able to follow this route. Relevant degree subjects include social work, counselling and psychology and the general entry requirements for a degree are 2 A levels/3 H grades and 5 GCSEs/National 5s (A*–C/A–C).

If you go the work-based route you will need to study for either the OCR Level 4 Diploma in Career Information and Advice or the OCR Level 6 Diploma in Career Guidance and Development while working in an organisation that offers advice or guidance services to clients.

You may choose to study qualifications such as the OCR Level 3 Award for Supporting Clients to Overcome Barriers To Learning and Work or the Level 3 NVQ Certificate in Advice and Guidance as a way of gaining basic sector knowledge before embarking on more formal, specialised training.

You do not always need a professional careers qualification to work as a careers adviser in higher education, although most successful candidates do have one. They also often have experience working in careers or have knowledge of their subject from teaching or industry.

It is common for people to enter this profession after gaining experience in another field, such as social work or teaching.

You will need a Disclosure and Barring Service (DBS) check to work with young people or vulnerable groups.

What the work involves

Researching information about job opportunities in different sectors from newspapers, books, the internet or through visits to employers is all part of the role.

You will help people make realistic choices about education, training and work by listening to their ideas, discussing their interests and skills, and providing information on different jobs. Advisory work is often one to one, but you could also work with large groups. Increasingly advice is being delivered over the phone or via email and instant messaging services.

Careers advisers work with young people in schools/colleges, but also with higher education students or adults.

Type of person suited to this work

Since much of the work involves talking with and listening to people, careers advisers need to have excellent communication skills. You will need to be impartial, allowing people to come to their own decisions rather than making up their minds for them.

Careers information and guidance is largely IT-based, so computer skills are essential, along with the ability to write reports and perform administrative tasks.

You will need to enjoy researching, as you will need to keep up to date with any changes in skills and opportunities available, and with any new qualifications and training routes.

Working conditions

Most of your work is office based, in either a careers centre open to the public or an educational establishment. You would normally work 9am–5pm, Monday to Friday but occasional evening work may also be required.

You may need to travel between different educational establishments and visit employers and training organisations, which means that a driving licence may be required.

Future prospects

Careers advisers work in schools, colleges, universities and adult guidance services – some will be based in one institution, others will work for several organisations.

You could move into a managerial-level post in a careers service, work for a large company as a careers manager or you could become self-employed as a consultant or researcher.

Advantages/disadvantages

The work is varied and can be highly satisfying.

You will work some evenings or weekends to attend school/college parents' evenings and for careers events.

The job also includes a great deal of administrative work.

Money guide

Starting salaries range from £18,000 to £20,000 a year.

With experience and qualifications salaries can increase to £20,000–£27,500.

As a senior manager you could earn around £35,000.

Salaries in London are often higher.

Related opportunities

- Counsellor p561
- Debt Counsellor/Money Advice Caseworker p562
- Youth and Community Worker p579

Further information

Career Development Institution
www.thecdi.net

CRAC: Career Development Organisation
www.crac.org.uk

Qualifications and courses

Childminders must register with Ofsted in England, the Care Commission in Scotland, the Care and Social Services Inspectorate in Wales and the local Health and Social Services board or trust in Northern Ireland. You need to take an introductory childminding training course and be prepared for a registration visit. A Paediatric First Aid certificate is also required.

Candidates must be aged 18 or over. They, and everyone in their households over 16, must be police checked.

There are no essential academic requirements for becoming a childminder but qualifications in childcare may be useful. These include BTEC Certificates and Diplomas in Children's Care, Learning and Development, the Diploma in Society, Health and Development and the Oxford Cambridge and RSA Examinations (OCR) Entry Level Certificate in Child Development.

You will have to contact the Family Information Services for a pre-registration meeting and details on the Early Years Foundation Stage (EYFS). The EYFS provides the framework and standards expected from childminders.

All childminders are inspected by the authorities which oversee the registration in that country and inspections are usually carried out every 2 to 3 years.

The Professional Association for Childcare and Early Years (PACEY) offers courses and a continuing professional development scheme (CPD) in order to improve and update your skills.

What the work involves

You will care for children in your own home, ensuring they are comfortable and happy. You will plan activities and tasks for your charges and keep their parents informed about what they have done during the day, what they have eaten and if there have been any problems.

You could accompany the children to and from playgroup, nursery or school or spend time arranging and managing transport to extra-curricular activities or play dates.

For children aged under 5, you will have to follow the guidelines set by the Early Years Foundation Stage for play-based learning.

Type of person suited to this work

As a childminder you must be patient, caring and excellent with children. Creativity and ingenuity is needed to plan varied activities for children of different ages. You must also be adaptable and prepared to change your plans at short notice to meet the changing needs of the children in your care.

You need to share information with parents on a daily basis which means that good observation and communication skills are important.

As you will be self-employed, you will need to be organised, with good administrative and numeracy skills to work out tax returns and invoices. IT skills are useful.

Although the minimum age for entry is 18, most childminders are older and are parents themselves or have experience of care work.

Working conditions

You are allowed to care for up to 6 children, including your own, under the age of 8 providing that only 3 are less than 5 years old.

You will work in your own home which may have to be altered to meet childminding standards by fitting equipment such as stairgates and socket covers.

A driving licence is useful as you may take children to playgroup or school. You will do a lot of lifting and clearing up. A working day of 8am to 6pm is usual and you will need to do other administrative tasks outside of this time.

Some childminders offer overnight services and look after charges at the weekend.

Future prospects

The demand for childminders can vary regionally and at different times of the year.

Childminders can become care assistants or home care assistants, or can go on to train for similar work as a nursery nurse or registered nurse.

Advantages/disadvantages

The work is varied, fun and working from home often suits people who have young children themselves.

The hours can be very long and it can sometimes be hard work for low pay.

Money guide

You can expect an income of around £6,000–£10,000 per year when starting out, rising to £15,000 when experienced.

Top hourly rates are charged in London where experienced, full-time childminders can earn up to £20,000 a year.

Childminders are self-employed so they need to arrange their own tax payments and insurance, and pay for training and extra costs such as public liability insurance.

Related opportunities

- Children's Nurse p276
- Early Years Specialist/Nursery Nurse p182
- Play Worker/Hospital Play Specialist p189

Further information

Northern Ireland Childminding Association
www.nicma.org

Professional Association for Childcare and Early Years
www.pacey.org.uk

Scottish Childminding Association
www.childminding.org

SOCIAL WORK AND
COUNSELLING SERVICES

Qualifications and courses

In order to become a qualified clinical or health psychologist you must have Graduate Basis for Chartered Membership (GBC) with the British Psychological Society (BPS). This can be obtained by achieving a BPS-accredited Honours degree in psychology. Entry to the degree is usually with 5 GCSEs/ National 5s (A*–C/A–C), including Maths, and 2 A levels/3 H grades, including a science. If you already have a degree that is not in psychology you can do a BPS-accredited conversion course, as relevant postgraduate study will then be needed in order to specialise.

Clinical psychologist

To become a clinical psychologist you will need to complete a doctorate in clinical psychology that has been approved by the Health & Care Professions Council (HCPC). Entry to a doctorate course is usually dependent on achieving a BPS-accredited degree with a 2.1 classification or above, although some courses will accept a 2.2 with a master's degree.

Relevant work experience is necessary to gain a training contract.

Health psychologist

A BPS-accredited master's degree in health psychology is required in order to become a health psychologist. This should then be followed by Stage 2 of the BPS qualification in health psychology which involves 2 years' supervised practice. Some universities run doctorate programmes in health psychology which combine a master's degree and supervised practice.

To use the title health psychologist you will need to register with the HCPC after completing all your training.

A Disclosure and Barring Service (DBS) check will be required as you will be working with children and vulnerable adults.

What the work involves

Clinical psychologist

You will work with people whose health problems affect their behaviour, to learn what they do and why they do it.

Health psychologist

This is a new and rapidly growing field of applied psychology which promotes changes in people's attitudes, behaviour and thinking about health.

Type of person suited to this work

An interest in people, their personalities, abilities and interests is essential.

The work involves contact with many different types of people which means you must be good at relating to others and have excellent communication skills.

Psychologists must think logically, analyse data and statistics. They need administrative/and IT skills for writing reports and analyses, and presenting information at case conferences or company meetings.

Working conditions

Clinical psychologist

You will typically work 9am to 5pm, but due to the emergency nature of your work you may occasionally be on a rota. Your work will take you to schools, colleges, hospitals and health centres. You may find yourself working with social services or with adolescent and child mental health services. Most clinical psychologists are employed by the NHS.

Health psychologist

Health psychologists work in a number of settings, such as hospitals, academic health research units, health authorities and university departments.

Future prospects

Entry to psychology degrees is competitive and it takes a long time to become a chartered psychologist. For both clinical and health psychology the jobs available tend to be within government services, education and health, in the public and private sectors. Ongoing professional development will be important throughout your career. Clinical psychologists can become high intensity therapists with further training.

Advantages/disadvantages

The work is varied, interesting and challenging.

You will meet many different types of people.

Some people may be aggressive or even violent and you may sometimes have difficulty remaining impartial.

Money guide

Clinical psychologist

Trainee clinical psychologists can expect to earn £26,041, which is the current NHS wage band 6. Once qualified, this rises to roughly £31,000. As you gain experience salaries can rise to £81,618 and in top-level positions you can earn in excess of £90,000.

Health psychologist

Salaries start from around £18,600 for trainees. Upon qualification pay rises to between £21,700 and £35,500 and as a senior health psychologist with the NHS salaries can reach £89,000.

For both positions, salaries depend on geographical location. The NHS pays a London high cost area supplement. Private hospital and practice salaries vary.

Related opportunities

- Educational Psychologist p563
- Occupational Psychologist p568
- Psychoanalyst/Psychotherapist p569

Further information

British Association for Counselling and Psychotherapy
www.bacp.co.uk

Health and Care Professions Council
www.hpc-uk.org

NHS Careers
www.healthcareers.nhs.uk

COUNSELLOR

Qualifications and courses

Counselling is open to all graduates and those with an HND qualification but a pre-entry qualification in counselling is almost essential. This could be a master's degree or a professional certificate or diploma. First degree subjects such as psychology, social studies or education are most useful for entry onto a master's course.

The British Association for Counselling and Psychotherapy (BACP) runs various certificate and diploma courses, which tend to last either 1 year full time or 2 to 3 years part time. Diploma courses usually require a degree, although sometimes they may also accept a relevant certificate in counselling. Certificate courses are more flexible and entry without an HND or degree is common. Membership with UK Council for Psychotherapy (UKCP) can also help your prospects.

Previous counselling experience and skills are just as important for getting onto the courses as qualifications. This could be gained through volunteering or pre-arranged work experience programmes.

It is rare for someone to enter a full-time position in this field before their mid-20s. Counselling is often a second career, and maturity and experience are beneficial.

Government legislation means a new system to accredit registers of counsellors is being introduced by the Professional Standards Authority for Health and Social Care.

A Disclosure and Barring Service (DBS) check will be necessary if you want to work with children or vulnerable adults.

What the work involves

Counsellors listen to what their clients say and ask questions in response, to help them explore, talk about and eventually resolve their problems.

You will help your clients to see things more clearly, perhaps from a different point of view. You will not tell people what to do but will help them work out their next steps themselves.

You might work with people with a range of problems or specialise in a particular area, such as bereavement, gambling, relationship difficulties or eating disorders.

Type of person suited to this work

As most of the work involves interacting closely with people, excellent communication and listening skills are essential.

Counselling workers may not always agree with the views held by their clients, which means they have to be open-minded and tolerant. You must also be highly discreet as you will be given a lot of confidential information.

You need to be interested in how the mind works, and in people's welfare.

Working conditions

You will work indoors, usually sitting in a quiet, comfortable room in places such as advice centres, schools, colleges, outpatient clinics and health centres. If you are self-employed, you might work from home, visit your clients at home, or both. Some counselling work is done exclusively over the phone.

You will work mainly with people on a one-to-one basis but also, on occasions, with couples, families or groups. Most counselling sessions last 50 minutes.

You may work in the evenings and at weekends and many counsellors work part time.

Future prospects

Larger units may have limited opportunities for you to move into management roles but on the whole counselling units tend to be flat structures with not much room for promotion.

It is possible to go on to specialise in a particular area of counselling, such as bereavement, family therapy or substance abuse. Experience in more than one area is beneficial for career development.

Self-employment is also possible once you have significant experience and training, and can be combined with voluntary or part-time work.

Advantages/disadvantages

The work can be very rewarding but also highly stressful.

You must be able to take constructive criticism from an experienced counselling worker, therapist or psychoanalyst – both during and after completing training.

Some clients may become dependent on therapy or analysis sessions and will have to be carefully assisted to refocus.

Money guide

Starting salaries are around £19,000 per year when newly qualified (but this can vary considerably).

Experienced counsellors or those with supervisory or managerial responsibility can earn between £30,000 and £40,000.

Counsellors in private practice can charge £30–£50 an hour. A lot of counsellors combine part-time employment with private practice and voluntary work.

Related opportunities

- Careers Adviser p558
- Debt Counsellor/Money Advice Caseworker p562
- Mental Health Nurse p299
- Psychoanalyst/Psychotherapist p569

Further information

British Association for Counselling and Psychotherapy
www.bacp.co.uk

Counselling & Psychotherapy Central Awarding Body
www.cpcab.co.uk

Qualifications and courses

There are no fixed entry requirements but you will need a good standard of English and maths, so GCSEs/National 5s in those subjects would be useful.

Experience is considered more important than qualifications and many applicants have training and/or experience in finance or accounting, consumer advice or have worked as a volunteer for at least a year in an advice centre.

You need to undergo a Disclosure and Barring Service (DBS) check to work with vulnerable adults.

Once you have secured employment, you will receive on-the-job training. You could also study for an NVQ Level 3 Certificate and Level 4 Diploma in Advice and Guidance. Alternatively, you could take a diploma, Foundation degree or degree in advice or legal advice work.

The Money Advice Trust (MAT) and the Citizens Advice Bureau (CAB) also provide training programmes for debt counsellors.

What the work involves

It will be your responsibility to give free, impartial and confidential advice to people in serious debt.

You will have to guide your clients through the legal procedures and represent them if they are being taken to court.

To ensure that clients are claiming available and applicable tax allowances and benefits, you will calculate your clients' income and expenditure and work with them to devise an achievable budget to live by.

By liaising with creditors, you will try to arrange realistic repayments over a reasonable timescale.

Type of person suited to this work

People experience money problems for reasons such as unemployment and bad money management. You will need to work with very different people and be non-judgemental about their circumstances. You will require good communication skills and a confident manner so that people trust you and the advice you give them.

Much of the work involves figures, so you should have strong numeracy skills. It is also important to be a good negotiator in order to get the best repayment plans for your clients from creditors.

Good time management is essential, as are excellent IT skills. This job suits people who have worked in financial services or have a financial background.

Working conditions

You could meet your clients face to face in an office or advise them through a telephone helpline. You could also spend time in court or at meetings.

You might travel around locally so a driving licence is useful.

You will usually work 9am to 5pm from Monday to Friday. In order to suit your clients' needs, you will sometimes have to work Saturdays and evenings, perhaps doing shift work.

Future prospects

Although money advisers are in demand, there are more applicants than jobs. Most openings are town or city based, in the Citizens Advice Bureau, advice centres or money advice units.

As funding is provided by local authorities or voluntary organisations, the majority of vacancies are for 2-year contracts.

You could move into specialist casework or there could be opportunities for progression into a role as team leader or supervisor. You could enter other social care jobs or change to work in the financial sector.

Charities such as Debtline have recorded large increases in numbers of people seeking out help over debts with an increase of over 140% from 2007 to 2014, for example. With an increase in demand, the job market should at least be stable, if not soon to expand.

Advantages/disadvantages

Helping clients to manage and get rid of their debt can be rewarding.

You may have to deal with rude and difficult people.

Evening and weekend work is possible in this job, but there may also be opportunities for part-time work.

Money guide

Starting salaries are typically around £18,000.

An experienced caseworker can expect to earn £22,000–£24,000.

Those employed in a senior position as a supervisor or manager can achieve £28,000–£30,000 a year.

Earnings vary with location and tend to be higher in London.

Related opportunities

- Accountant p2
- Financial Adviser p26
- Welfare Benefits Adviser/Welfare Rights Caseworker p578

Further information

Advice UK
www.adviceuk.org.uk

Citizens Advice Bureau
www.citizensadvice.org.uk

Financial Skills Partnership
www.financialskillspartnership.org.uk

Qualifications and courses

In order to become a qualified educational psychologist you will need to gain an Honours degree in psychology accredited by the British Psychological Society (BPS) at a 2.1 or higher, although applicants with 2.2 degrees may still be considered if they possess excellent experience and postgraduate qualifications. The general entry requirements for a degree are 2 A levels/3 H grades, including a science, and 5 GCSEs/National 5s (A*–C/A–C). If you already have a degree that is not in psychology you can do a BPS-accredited conversion course to gain the right academic knowledge to progress in your career.

Once you have graduated you can register for Graduate Basis for Chartered Membership (GBC) with the BPS. This is required to progress to the next level of training.

You must then undertake a BPS-accredited doctorate in educational psychology. In Scotland only, it is possible to take a BPS-accredited master's course in educational psychology followed by the BPS Award in Educational Psychology (Stage 2). Applications for doctorate courses are made through the Association of Educational Psychologists (AEP).

Finally you need to register with the Health & Care Professions Council (HCPC) in order to be able to use the title 'educational psychologist'. In Scotland you must also be a member of the Scottish Division of Educational Psychology or the Division of Educational and Child Psychology.

As you will be working with vulnerable groups and young people, you will need to undergo a Disclosure and Barring Service (DBS) check.

What the work involves

You will work with children with social, behavioural or learning difficulties to assess their progress and their academic and emotional needs. You will give help and guidance, and design activities which will enable them to learn and develop.

Your role will also involve working closely with parents and teaching professionals to broaden their understanding of children's psychological needs and the difficulties they face.

You will carry out research and you will be required to remain up to date with new government policies and measures that have been brought in with regard to assessing a child's psychological progression.

Type of person suited to this work

You must enjoy working closely with children. You will need to be sensitive, tactful, assertive and persuasive. You should be prepared to work with pupils who are finding school difficult and may not be very receptive to your help.

You will need excellent communication skills as you will be working regularly with both children and adults.

You need administrative and IT skills for writing reports and analyses, and presenting information.

Working conditions

You will usually work 35–37.5 hours a week from Monday to Friday, with some evening work required to attend parent–teacher meetings.

You will spend time in an office, as well as visiting schools and colleges, meeting clients, writing reports and assessing your findings. You will also run training sessions for parents and teachers.

You will probably have to travel between different locations so a driving licence is useful.

Future prospects

Most educational psychologists work for local authorities but an increasing number are self-employed as independent consultants. You will be more restricted in the way you can progress while working for a local authority as there are only a certain number of positions you can work up to. However, you may become a senior officer in a local authority children's services department.

Being an independent consultant will give you more opportunity to branch out into different areas of psychology such as occupational psychology.

Advantages/disadvantages

The work is varied and interesting.

Helping children to learn and develop is incredibly rewarding.

Dealing with difficult children, and parents who are not willing to accept that their child has a psychological problem, can be stressful and challenging.

Money guide

In England, Scotland, Wales and Northern Ireland educational psychologists are usually paid in accordance with the Soulbury Agreement.

As a graduate trainee you can expect to earn between £22,091 and £30,075 per year. Once qualified, your annual salary can range from £34,273 to £46,244. Senior educational psychologists can achieve £42,969–£63,571 a year.

In Scotland, pay scales are set by the Scottish Negotiating Committee for Teachers (SNCT). Educational psychologists can expect between £40,638 and £49,791 a year, with senior and principal psychologists earning £52,890 to £61,269.

Related opportunities

- Clinical/Health Psychologist p560
- Counsellor p561
- Youth and Community Worker p579

Further information

Association of Educational Psychologists
www.aep.org.uk

Children's Workforce Development Council
www.cwdcouncil.org.uk

Qualifications and courses

To become a qualified forensic psychologist you will need to have a degree in psychology that has been accredited by the British Psychological Society (BPS) with a classification of 2.1 or higher. Entry to the degree is usually with 5 GCSEs/Nationals (A*–C/A–C), including Maths, and 2 A levels/3 H grades, including a science. If you already have a degree that is not in psychology you can do a BPS-accredited conversion course in order to gain the right academic knowledge so you can progress.

Once you graduate the next step is to register for Graduate Basis for Chartered Membership (GBC) with the BPS. You will then need to undertake a BPS-accredited master's degree in forensic psychology, followed by the BPS qualification in forensic psychology (Stage 2) which involves 2 years of supervised practice. Some universities run doctorate programmes in forensic psychology that combine a master's degree and Stage 2 of the BPS qualification.

Registration with the Health & Care Professions Council (HCPC) is then required for you to be able to use the title forensic psychologist.

It is an advantage to have previous work experience when applying for the master's degree as competition is strong. Pre-entry experience will often be required once you start looking for work after registering with the HCPC. Options include working as an assistant forensic psychologist, psychological assistant or doing voluntary work with witness and victim support organisations. Some prison service positions are only available to people with experience as a psychological assistant.

What the work involves

You will apply psychology to the criminal and civil justice systems. Your job will involve direct contact with offenders to carry out assessments and you may design programmes to help in their rehabilitation.

You may be required to present your findings on a criminal case in court.

Your work will also include carrying out detailed research into what provokes people to commit crimes. You will analyse the behavioural patterns and personality traits of offenders.

Type of person suited to this work

You need brilliant communication skills and the ability to work with people from a wide variety of backgrounds. You must be prepared to work with criminals and be enthusiastic about helping them during their rehabilitation process. You should not be a judgemental person and you must hold no prejudice against the people you are working with, even if they have committed an awful crime.

You should be very good at reading people's subconscious behaviour and taking detailed notes of your findings to present in reports. You must be organised and able to manage your workload. Research and IT skills are necessary.

Working conditions

You will spend a lot of time working in prisons, secure hospitals, police stations and mental health rehabilitation units. You may be employed by a variety of organisations; from the National Health Service to the prison service to the police force. If you are working in a prison you will need to become adjusted to the conditions and regulations.

A driving licence would be useful for travelling between locations.

You will typically work a 37-hour week from Monday to Friday and some evening/weekend work will be expected. Part-time work may be available.

Future prospects

The job market for psychologists continues to remain relatively good. As this particular role is in a fairly new and emerging sector, there should be opportunities to progress and branch into different areas of psychology and forensics once you have some experience.

If you achieve chartered status as a forensic psychologist, you may have the chance to move into a senior role. In this position, you could be in charge of creating a complete rehabilitation scheme for a certain type of offender.

With experience, you will have the option of working for a consultancy.

Advantages/disadvantages

You may find yourself working with people who have committed very serious crimes, which can be distressing.

Helping to rehabilitate offenders back into society can be immensely rewarding.

You will learn new things all the time which will make the job exciting and fulfilling.

Money guide

In the prison service, trainee forensic psychologists can earn £24,250 to £27,400. Chartered forensic psychologists can expect £32,945 to £39,535, with senior level salaries reaching £63,000.

In the NHS starting salaries for trainees are £25,783. Qualified forensic psychologists earn from £30,764 to £40,558. Senior level positions can reach £98,453.

Related opportunities

- Clinical/Health Psychologist p560
- Counsellor p561
- Forensic Computer Analyst p539

Further information

Division of Forensic Psychology
www.bps.org.uk/dfp

HM Prison Service
www.gov.uk/government/organisations/hm-prison-service

FUNDRAISER

Qualifications and courses

The popularity and competitiveness of the not-for-profit sector means that most entrants to this role are now graduates. Useful degree subjects include business studies and sales and marketing and for entry to a degree course you will need at least 2 A levels/3 H grades and 5 GCSEs/National 5s (A*–C/A–C) including English and Maths.

However, having skills and significant experience is usually considered more important than formal qualifications. Experience in marketing, events, advertising, sales, public relations or finance would be beneficial.

Most entrants undertake voluntary fundraising work to demonstrate their commitment to the not-for-profit sector and to help develop a network of industry contacts. The majority of charities run unpaid internships and large organisations, such as Cancer Research UK, offer graduate training schemes. You could also work as an assistant fundraiser.

Short courses for people working as fundraisers/fundraising managers are available. The Institute of Fundraising (IoF) awards professional qualifications including the Introductory Certificate, Certificate, Diploma and Advanced Diploma in Fundraising. The IoF also offers a range of training courses in-house or online, as does the Directory of Social Change (DSC).

What the work involves

Fundraisers raise money for their charity by targeting donors and organising activities such as publicly sponsored events, membership schemes with various benefits and corporate sponsorship.

You will represent your charity at public events such as dinners, giving talks to possible supporters.

You will write strategies, reports for trustees and donors, and proposals for grants.

You will prepare publicity material and liaise with the media, always keeping your charity in the public eye.

Type of person suited to this work

It is essential that you are enthusiastic and committed to your charity. You must be good with all types of people. You should be an excellent communicator and an engaging and confident public speaker, able to persuade people to support your charity.

You will need to be a good negotiator, with effective writing skills to produce noteworthy publicity material. You will have to be imaginative and creative to come up with innovative fundraising ideas.

You must be able to organise your time and workload so you can keep running costs down to a minimum and save money for your charity.

Working conditions

You will normally be based in an office working on a computer, but you could be based at home, particularly if you work for a very small charity. You might spend time outdoors at fundraising activities.

You will work about 35–40 hours a week and weekend/evening work is common when arranging and attending events.

You will travel fairly widely so a driving licence is useful.

Future prospects

It is not usual to become a charity fundraiser straight from school – most entrants have experience in sales or marketing and voluntary fundraising.

Most jobs are with charities, pressure groups and other not-for-profit organisations, including hospitals.

It may be necessary to move around – possibly to larger organisations – to progress in your career. With experience you could move into management, become self-employed or offer consultancy advice.

Advantages/disadvantages

It is satisfying to see your charity flourish with the money that you have helped to raise.

There could be pressure to meet fundraising targets and deadlines for organising events.

People who do not support your charity can be unpleasant at times.

You will need to work evenings and weekends.

Money guide

Earnings vary according to the size and location of the charity.

Starting salaries for an assistant role can start at £13,000, rising to £24,000 with experience. Fundraisers starting on a full-time basis can expect to earn around £18,000.

Typical salaries for a fundraiser with a few years' experience could be £25,000 to £32,000.

Senior level salaries are around £30,000 and if you become director or head of fundraising in a large charity you could achieve up to £50,000.

Related opportunities

- Advertising Account Executive p382
- Events and Exhibition Organiser p391
- Public Relations Officer p404

Further information

Association of Chief Executives of Voluntary Organisations
www.acevo.org.uk

Directory of Social Change
www.dsc.org.uk

Institute of Fundraising
www.institute-of-fundraising.org.uk

SOCIAL WORK AND COUNSELLING SERVICES

LIFE COACH

Qualifications and courses

There are no specific requirements to enter this area of work as it is not a regulated field, but clients tend to prefer coaches who have relevant qualifications and professional organisation memberships. You also need to have gained a great deal of life experience and have the right skills and qualities.

A degree in human resources, sociology or psychology would be helpful starting points. The general entry requirements for a degree are 2 A levels/3 H grades and 5 GCSEs/National 5s (A*–C/A–C). If you already have a degree in an unrelated subject, some universities offer postgraduate degrees in coaching that may be useful.

There are a number of private agencies and academies offering training in life coaching. For example the Coaching Academy has a free 2-day certificate that covers the basics of coaching, as well as other more specialised courses. The Coaching and Mentoring Network website contains a full list of coaching courses.

You could also work towards accreditation from one of the recognised bodies for life coaches, such as the International Coach Federation (ICF), which would give you greater credibility with clients.

What the work involves

You will help people, both independent clients or employees, to recognise and develop their special attributes and skills.

You will coach individuals to become more successful in career matters, fitness levels, financial affairs or personal relationships. You will also help in boosting self-esteem.

You will discuss values, attributes and beliefs and set goals with your clients for them to work towards. At a later stage you will review and revise the action plans you have created.

Type of person suited to this work

A bond of trust needs to be established for you to be an effective life coach. You must be non-judgemental and exude a trustworthiness that will allow clients to open up and reveal their present feelings and frustrations, their future ambitions and their perceived restrictions to progress.

Besides integrity and discretion, life coaches need excellent interpersonal skills, patience and perseverance to allow clients the time to set themselves goals for change.

Working conditions

You will agree timetables with clients for coaching sessions and hold one-to-ones at their work-base or in a neutral location. Later sessions are often by phone or email.

Many life coaches work with busy, highly successful chief executives, usually outside normal business hours.

Coaching sessions can be weekly, fortnightly or monthly; the frequency may change.

Future prospects

Life coaching is a relatively new field in the UK (although it has been around for longer in the USA), but interest has increased as more attention is paid to developing the whole person – both within and outside the workplace, and the industry is currently growing.

Although they are not required, to attract business as an independent consultant it usually helps to have qualifications.

Life coaches work as independent consultants or for business consultancy agencies. If you network and market yourself well you can build up a substantial client base.

You could choose to specialise in one area such as spiritual coaching or executive coaching.

Advantages/disadvantages

There is great satisfaction in observing changes in your clients.

If clients fail to implement action plans, it can be dispiriting and frustrating.

You could have long-term coaching relationships with clients who want to work on different aspects of their lives.

Money guide

Life coaches earn an agreed rate per session and may take the client's financial circumstances into account when charging.

Working for an agency, you can earn around £30–£60 per session plus expenses.

You could charge up to £300 a session if you are working with corporate clients.

The median full-time salary for a life coach in the UK is £30,000, although this is based on a very small sample.

Life coaches who become well known and sought after can charge higher fees for periods of life coaching lasting 6 months or longer.

Related opportunities

- Careers Adviser p558
- Counsellor p561
- Social Worker p573

Further information

Association for Coaching
www.associationforcoaching.com

Chartered Institute of Personnel and Development
www.cipd.co.uk

International Coach Federation
www.coachfederation.org.uk

The Coaching Academy
www.the-coaching-academy.com

Qualifications and courses

There are no essential academic requirements for becoming a nanny but qualifications in childcare are likely to be useful. These include BTEC Certificates and Diplomas in Children's Care, Learning and Development, City & Guilds Certificates and Diplomas in Children and Young People's Workforce (Levels 2–5), and the Oxford Cambridge and RSA Examinations (OCR) Entry Level Certificate in Child Development. A Paediatric First Aid certificate may also be useful.

You could attend a nanny training school where students can study traditional childcare, first aid and self-defence. For example, you could study towards a first degree in Early Years Development & Learning with Norland College. As a student at Norland you will also work towards the Norland Diploma alongside and for a year following the completion of your degree.

Work experience in childcare is valued by employers and will improve your chances of employment. You can gain experience in nursery work or babysitting. You will need to pass checks from the Disclosure and Barring Service (DBS) to work with children.

Signing up to the Ofsted Childcare Register is voluntary, but may prove your credibility to prospective employers.

The Professional Association for Childcare and Early Years (PACEY) offer courses and a continuing professional development scheme (CPD) in order to improve and update your skills.

What the work involves

A nanny works in a private home and is responsible for caring for their employer's babies and children.

Your responsibilities will typically include feeding, changing, bathing and dressing the children. You will also teach them basic social skills and discipline them if necessary.

You will prepare meals and snacks for the children. You may be required to drop and pick up the children from school and other activities.

You will also plan interesting and beneficial activities for them, and help them learn through play.

Type of person suited to this work

As a nanny you must be patient, caring and excellent with children. Creativity and ingenuity is needed to plan varied activities for children of different ages.

You must also be adaptable and prepared to change your plans at short notice to meet the changing needs of the children in your care.

You need to share information with parents which means that good observation and communication skills are important.

Working conditions

As a nanny you will be caring for your employer's children for up to 12 hours a day, for 5 or 6 days a week. You may also be required to look after them overnight and at weekends. Your hours must be flexible to meet the needs of your employer.

You may be a live-in nanny and stay in the family's home. Alternatively, you may be a live-out nanny and travel to work every day.

Future prospects

Opportunities can be found nationwide. You could also work overseas as a nanny or an au pair.

With your experience of working with children you could go on to work as a childminder. Alternatively, you could work for a nursery, or with additional training go into primary school teaching.

Advantages/disadvantages

The work can be varied and fun.

It can be very rewarding to influence the development of the children in your care.

The job involves long hours, often for very little pay.

Living in your employer's home may affect your personal life.

Money guide

Salaries vary according to location, qualifications and whether you are a live-in or a live-out nanny.

Full-time live-in nannies can earn between £13,000 and £20,000 a year.

Full-time live-out nannies can expect to earn between £26,000 and £29,000 a year.

Related opportunities

- Childminder p559
- Early Years Specialist/Nursery Nurse p182
- Primary School Teacher p190

Further information

Norland College
www.norland.co.uk/college

PACEY
www.pacey.org.uk

Qualifications and courses

To become a qualified occupational psychologist you will need a 2.1 or higher Honours degree in psychology that has been accredited by the British Psychological Society (BPS). Entry onto a degree course usually requires 2 A levels/3 H grades, including a science and 5 GCSEs/National 5s (A*–C/A–C), including Maths. If you already have a degree that is not in psychology you can do a BPS-accredited conversion course in order to gain relevant working knowledge of the subject.

Once you graduate the next step is to register for Graduate Basis for Chartered Membership (GBC) with the BPS which is required in order for you to progress to the next level of training.

You must then undertake either a BPS-accredited master's degree in occupational psychology or complete stage 1 of the BPS's qualification in occupational psychology. These are followed by stage 2 of the BPS's qualification, which involves 2 years of supervised practice for master's graduates or 3 years for those who completed stage 1. Registration with the Health & Care Professions Council (HCPC) is then required for you to be able to use the title 'occupational psychologist'.

It is an advantage to have previous work experience when applying for the master's degree as competition is strong. Pre-entry experience will also often be required once you start looking for work after registering with the HCPC. This could be in personnel/human resources or business/management, or you could work for a psychometric test publisher.

Some positions may require competence in psychometrics or statistical analysis.

A Disclosure and Barring Service (DBS) check will be needed for working with vulnerable adults.

What the work involves

You will explore how organisations function and how people behave at work to improve an organisation's efficiency and employees' job satisfaction.

You will help managers plan how they recruit and train staff. You will give advice on matters concerning communication between individuals in the workplace, the most effective working environment and coping with change.

Part of your job may involve helping to recruit the right person for a particular role as well as offering support to those facing redundancy. You will also be working with bosses and managers to help them to understand the psychological needs of their staff, so that they can maintain a stress-free environment for them as much as possible.

Type of person suited to this work

You should have a great interest in how organisations function and what makes people tick in the workplace.

You should be comfortable working with adults and also be happy to help them progress professionally.

You must be a brilliant communicator and it will also be very useful for you to have strong business skills because you will have been employed to improve the overall efficiency of a company.

Working conditions

Much of your work will take place in offices and business premises of the companies you are working for. This may involve working by yourself or as part of a team.

You can expect to work around 37 hours a week from Monday to Friday but you may run or attend courses that require you to travel away and stay overnight.

There is the opportunity to be self-employed but this is often after working for an organisation and building up your work experience.

Future prospects

Occupational psychologists work in large companies in the public and private sectors.

They can work with government and public services as private consultants.

Some specialise in a certain area, for example ergonomics (the interaction of people with where they work), or health and safety – studying the causes of accidents and how to prevent them.

Once you have progressed to a senior role you may set up your own consultancy.

Advantages/disadvantages

Your work will really make a difference to people's day to day lives at work which will be very rewarding.

You may be working with unmotivated or stressed individuals.

You may find that bosses are not willing to take on your advice for their staff.

Money guide

As a starting salary you can earn anything from £18,000 to £25,000.

This can progress to between £35,000 and £80,000 with experience in a senior position.

Private sector organisations tend to pay more than public sector.

Related opportunities

- Educational Psychologist p563
- Health and Safety Adviser p27
- Recruitment/Employment Agency Consultant p47

Further information

Health and Care Professions Council
www.hpc-uk.org

Occupational Psychology Services
www.theopc.co.uk

The Association for Business Psychology
www.theabp.org.uk

Qualifications and courses

Psychoanalyst

Most people enter psychoanalysis as a second career after they have gained experience in a related field such as psychology, psychiatry, counselling or social work.

To qualify as a psychoanalyst, candidates must undertake a training course approved by the International Psychoanalytical Association (IPA) or the Institute of Psychoanalysis (IoP). Training takes 4 years and entry is with a first degree, for which you will need at least 2 A levels/3 H grades and 5 GCSEs/National 5s (A*–C/A–C). The IoP also offers a 1-year Foundation course for people with experience in a related field with alternative professional qualifications.

Psychotherapist

Psychotherapy is often a second career for people in a related field. You will need a degree in a relevant subject, such as psychology, nursing, medicine, social work or sociology. A postgraduate qualification in psychotherapy which has been approved by the UK Council for Psychotherapy (UKCP) or the British Psychoanalytic Council (BPC) will usually be required. Pre-entry experience in mental health professions, psychology, psychiatry or social work is expected.

Training courses usually last 4 to 6 years when studied on a part-time basis and include personal therapy, theory and supervised clinical work. A Disclosure and Barring Services (DBS) check may also be required.

What the work involves

Psychoanalyst

You will help people uncover their deep-rooted insecurities, thoughts and behaviours which are disrupting and negatively affecting their daily life. You will see your patients 4–5 times a week over an extended period of time. You will listen during the sessions and then write down your observations after your patient has left. Your goal is to help patients achieve self-awareness.

Psychotherapist

You will explore a person's inner conflicts and feelings in order to help alleviate their distress. Your goal is to help patients feel happy or better. Your treatment will be non-medical, focussing on talking through problems. Your treatment approach may include cognitive behavioural therapy, hypno-psychotherapy and psychodynamic therapies.

Type of person suited to this work

You need to be positive, empathic and a great listener. You want to build a good bond with your patients so you should respect confidential information.

Your work can be intense and you will need to sympathise with your patients' problems whilst remaining emotionally resilient. You should be observant and have a genuine interest in feelings and emotions but able to professionally distance yourself from personal situations that may be distressing.

Working conditions

You will work in a consulting room that is comfortable, quiet and welcoming for your patients.

You will most likely work Monday to Friday but you may need to work weekends and evenings to suit your clients' needs. You can choose your own hours if you work for a private practice.

This work can be emotionally demanding and you are advised to be involved in a support network, especially if you are self-employed.

Future prospects

Psychoanalyst

Most psychoanalysts are self-employed and you may choose to work part time for a prison, school or child guidance clinic. You could become a lecturer, train graduate entrants or specialise in a particular area such as adolescent psychoanalysis.

Psychotherapist

With experience, you could go on to become a manager or supervisor of other psychotherapists, although this will mean you will have less clinical work. You could also become a consultant for community organisations or specialise in an area such as psychodrama.

Advantages/disadvantages

It is rewarding to see a patient overcome their problems.

You will be learning more about the human mind which can benefit you as well as your patients.

Your patients might struggle with upsetting issues and this can be emotionally taxing for you.

Money guide

Psychoanalyst

Psychoanalysts are normally self-employed and earnings depend on their rate per session, which is normally between £45 and £70, and how many patients they see.

You can expect a starting salary of £40,000 when you are newly qualified. With experience, you can achieve £50,000–£60,000 a year.

Psychotherapist

National Health Service trainees can earn between £21,692 and £28,180 a year. Once qualified and with experience, your salary can range from £26,000 to £48,000.

In private practice hourly rates can be anything from £40 to £100 per hour.

Related opportunities

- Counsellor p561
- Educational Psychologist p563
- Psychiatrist p317

Further information

British Association for Counselling & Psychotherapy
http://www.bacp.co.uk/

SOCIAL WORK AND COUNSELLING SERVICES

Qualifications and courses

Visually impaired
You will need a qualification in rehabilitation work (visual impairment) to specialise in this particular field. A relevant 2-year Foundation degree is available and involves both work-based training through an employer and distance learning. Entry requirements are at least 1 A level/2 H grades and 3 GCSEs/National 5s (A*–C/A–C), or good BTEC qualifications.

There are also Advanced Apprenticeships in Health and Social Care available for school leavers.

All entrants must undergo a Disclosure and Barring Service (DBS) check.

Hearing impaired
There are no set entry requirements for this career. However, some employers will look for GCSEs/National 5s (A*–C/A–C) and relevant experience, whether paid or voluntary. It might also help to have the Signature Level 1 Award in British Sign Language (BSL). The Apprenticeship in Health and Social Care may also equip you with relevant skills for this profession.

Training is on the job, possibly with the chance to study for further qualifications such as the City & Guilds Level 2 Certificate in Supporting Users of Assistive Technology.

What the work involves

Rehabilitation officers train people with visual and hearing impairments to use their existing skills in new ways that will help them lead a normal life.

You will assess your patients' needs before making a detailed action plan to teach them new skills. You will also provide financial and employment information and advice.

Part of your role will be liaising with other medical professionals to follow up on reports you have made about your patients' quality of living. You might also be responsible for providing training to other social and healthcare workers about sensory loss and awareness.

Type of person suited to this work

You will need to be aware of the issues that affect visually and hearing impaired people. It is important to have good communication skills as your patients may rely on other senses to understand you.

You will be in contact with people of all ages and backgrounds, so it is essential that you are friendly and approachable. Good organisational, problem-solving and assessment skills are required for report writing and devising action plans for patients.

Working conditions

You will divide your time between working in an office and visiting patients' homes to assess their living space and daily routines. It is useful to have a driving licence as you might be travelling around on a regular basis.

You might need to work outdoors when training a patient to use a new piece of assistive equipment or if you are escorting them somewhere.

You will work around 40 hours a week, Monday to Friday, although you might need to visit your patients during the evenings and weekends.

Future prospects

Most positions are with local authority social care departments, voluntary services such as the Royal National Institute of Blind People (RNIB) and educational institutions.

Although there is no set career path in rehabilitation work, you can be promoted to supervisory and managerial roles in sensory support or you can choose to train other people. There are postgraduate qualifications available which would speed up your career progression.

Advantages/disadvantages

This is a very rewarding career as you will be helping people who are in a vulnerable position.

You need to stay emotionally detached from your patients, which could be difficult as you will be spending a lot of time with them.

Money guide

Visually impaired
Starting salaries are around £23,000.

With experience, you can expect £27,000–£30,000 a year.

Team leaders can earn in excess of £35,000.

Hearing impaired
Your starting salary could range from £16,000 to £18,000.

Earnings can increase to £20,000 with experience.

Those in more senior positions can earn up to £26,000.

Related opportunities

- Careers Adviser p558
- Healthcare Assistant p292
- Social Worker p573

Further information

Royal National Institute for Deaf People
www.actiononhearingloss.org.uk

Royal National Institute of Blind People
www.rnib.org.uk

Skills for Care and Development
www.skillsforcareanddevelopment.org.uk

RELIGIOUS LEADER

Qualifications and courses

In terms of numbers of adherents, the most common faiths in the UK are Christianity, Islam, Hinduism, Sikhism, Judaism and Buddhism. Within these religions are many subgroups which possess different beliefs and practices. A religious leader may be referred to by a title such as a priest, imam, swami, Granthi, or rabbi, depending on your faith.

To become a religious leader you will need to demonstrate dedication to your faith. You will have to convince other members of your suitability in order to commence training. For advice on whether to pursue religious training you should first approach your own religious leader for information and advice.

Training routes vary greatly amongst religions but will often include the extensive study of religious texts, languages and practices. For this it is recommended you have a good standard of general education. You may also be required to mediate, undertake community work or study at a religious institution. Some religions may require higher education qualifications.

Some religions impose certain restrictions on their leaders. You may be expected to remain unmarried and to forgo other romantic attachments. In some faiths, women may not be permitted to become religious leaders.

What the work involves

Religious leaders offer spiritual and moral guidance to people of their faith.

Different religions vary in their practices and duties. However, formal duties frequently include conducting religious ceremonies, holding regular services, praying and explaining scripture to others.

You may be expected to counsel and comfort people struggling in life due to bereavement, illness or a loss of faith. Your role may also include administration and community work such as fundraising.

Type of person suited to this work

You will need an unwavering faith and commitment to your religion. You will need to enjoy teaching and sharing your faith, and be able to inspire others to follow these teachings.

Excellent communication and people skills are essential, as you will be interacting with a variety of people on an everyday basis. You will need to be patient, understanding and have excellent listening skills. You must be confident and trustworthy so people feel comfortable confiding in you.

You will need to take an active interest in your community and its welfare.

Working conditions

Your hours will vary. You may have to work long hours and will be expected to work on dates that are significant to your religious community. You may have to work evenings and weekends to visit people who request your help.

You will perform ceremonies at your place of worship and have an office to carry out administrative tasks. You role may include travelling to visit people who need your guidance. Some religious leaders live in prisons or hospitals. You could be asked to accompany the armed forces on their missions abroad.

Future prospects

Career progression depends upon the structure of the religion, which varies from faith to faith. You could apply for vacant places or you might be recommended for a place by a superior.

Promotion may entail more administrative and supervising work which will result in less interaction with people.

You could train others to become religious leaders. You could also write books or articles about your faith.

Advantages/disadvantages

You will have the chance to share your love of your faith with others.

You will meet a variety of people from all walks of life.

You will need to be prepared to work long hours and you may have to sacrifice aspects of your lifestyle.

Money guide

Some leaders are paid a salary, but some work unpaid.

You may receive benefits such as a car, accommodation or living expenses.

Related opportunities

- Counsellor p561
- Social Worker p573
- Youth and Community Worker p579

Further information

The Inter Faith Network
www.interfaith.org.uk

Qualifications and courses

If you want to be a residential childcare worker you must be educated to at least Level 3 qualification level. For all other areas of residential support work there are no particular qualifications necessary, though some could be useful.

You can study for qualifications in health and social care, youth work or childcare. For instance, it may be helpful to complete the BTEC National Certificate or Diploma in Health and Social Care. NVQs/SVQs in Care, as well as a First Aid certificate, are also useful. A Level 2 RQF Diploma in Youth Work Practice or an NCFE Level 2 Certificate for the Children and Young People's Workforce can be beneficial too. Courses usually include work placements, which can make them beneficial for building skills and experience.

Previous paid or voluntary experience of social work or caring for people is essential for all candidates. This could include nursing, working with the disabled, elderly or homeless, working as a social work assistant or even caring for a family member.

If you will be working with children or vulnerable adults you will need to undergo a Disclosure and Barring Service (DBS) check. You will also need to be at least 18 years old and 4 years older than the youngest child.

Once hired you will receive induction training and learn on the job from more experienced staff. If you become a manager of a residential home you could take the Level 5 Diploma in Leadership for Health and Social Care and Children and Young People's Services to improve your skills.

What the work involves

Residential workers look after the welfare of people living in supervised accommodation, including the elderly, people with disabilities, temporary hostel residents, students and young people.

You will make sure that meals are organised, cooked and served at set times, and that cleaning and maintenance are up to standard.

It will be your responsibility to make sure health and safety standards are met, insurance is up to date and that security is effective. You will also collect rents and fees and organise social events, and sort out any disputes.

Type of person suited to this work

As you may be responsible for the accommodation of many different groups of people, it is important to be friendly and outgoing. You will also need to be understanding, patient and tolerant.

There are likely to be crises in the job so it is important to be able to cope under pressure and make decisions quickly.

If you are dealing with rents and fees, being good with figures is helpful. There will be a lot of administrative work which needs a well organised and methodical approach.

Working conditions

Most of your work will be indoors, but you may handle maintenance and repair work, using tools and climbing ladders.

You weekly hours will typically be 40. You will work on a rota basis and will be expected to cover nights and weekends.

Many residential support workers live on-site or in the grounds, but you might travel locally, so a driving licence is useful. You will be constantly on the go, responding to alarm calls at any hour of the day or night.

You will use IT for administration and record-keeping.

Future prospects

Although there are opportunities throughout the UK, there are few vacancies for residential workers. Most jobs are in cities and major towns.

The main employers are local authorities, housing associations, private companies, voluntary organisations, universities and colleges.

Promotion is likely to be to a senior support worker. You might have to move jobs to progress your career. It is also possible to train for a related field such as social work. Once you have experience, your employer may sponsor you to train part time for the social work degree.

Advantages/disadvantages

The work is varied and no two days will be alike.

You will get great job satisfaction from helping people.

Some residents may be difficult to deal with or particular situations may be distressing.

You will work long hours, evenings and weekends, and may have to live on-site.

Money guide

Starting salaries are usually between £17,000 and £21,000 per year.

Senior support workers may earn between £21,000 and £25,000 a year.

Part-time workers may be paid hourly rates, which range between £7 and £14 an hour.

Accommodation and food may also be provided. Salaries in the private sector are often lower than those in the public sector.

Related opportunities

- Caretaker p445
- Cleaner p448
- Hotel Manager p128

Further information

Chartered Institute of Housing
www.cih.org

Scottish Social Services Council
www.sssc.uk.com

Qualifications and courses

Qualification is with an Honours degree in social work, approved by the Health & Care Professions Council (HCPC) or Scottish Social Care Council (SSCC). The degree takes 3 years full time (4 years in Scotland) and at least 200 days of the course will be work-based training. There are also options to study part time. Entry requirements are usually 2 A levels/3 H grades and 5 GCSEs/National 5s (A*–C/A–C), including English and Maths.

If you already have a different degree you can take an HCPC- or SSCC-approved postgraduate course in order to gain the appropriate knowledge required. You will need a minimum of a 2.2 Honours degree to be accepted onto this.

Both the degree in social work and the postgraduate degree usually require relevant work experience for entry. This can be gained through paid positions in community care centres or by volunteer work. Some universities request a specific period of experience.

To work as a social worker you will need to pass checks from the Disclosure and Barring Service (DBS) and register with either the HCPC or the SSCC. In England, Wales and Northern Ireland registration with the HCPC takes place after completing your degree. In Scotland you will need to register with the SSCC when you are accepted onto the degree and then again when you finish.

Some local authorities may also sponsor employees working in a social care support role to take a social work degree part-time or as part of a distance learning programme.

What the work involves

Working at a senior level, you will interview your clients and assess their complex problems and needs.

You will then advise on the best package of care for your client.

Your goal is to support people to live independently and thrive in their surroundings. This might involve helping families to stay together, protecting vulnerable people or helping the excluded to be a part of their community.

You will keep detailed records of all your work.

Type of person suited to this work

You should be culturally aware, non-judgemental and able to engage with clients of all ethnicities, religions and backgrounds.

Caseloads can be heavy, so you need to be organised. Excellent communication skills are important.

At times your clients may become difficult and you must be confident at resolving conflict. You also need to remain professionally detached in emotionally tense circumstances.

Working conditions

You will often work within a team from other disciplines including psychologists and therapists and will be office based. Most of your time however will be spent visiting clients at their homes.

A driving licence is essential.

You will work 37 hours a week but this may include evenings, early mornings and weekends. You may be on call on a rota basis.

Future prospects

There is currently a demand for qualified social workers so job prospects are high. You will most likely work for a local authority social services department or for children's or adult services departments within the National Health Service. Jobs may also be available with armed forces support groups.

After gaining experience you can vary your role by changing your specialty or by moving on within your specialty. For example you could move from child protection into foster care.

You could also become a senior practitioner or manager but this will mean you will deal more with finances and bureaucracy rather than directly with clients. Lecturing and self-employment opportunities are also possible.

Recent and prospective cuts to social care funding may make your job more difficult. You may have to reduce the services you can offer due to a lack of resources, which may be frustrating.

Advantages/disadvantages

No two cases will be the same, keeping your work interesting.

It is rewarding to see people reach their full potential, solve their own problems and improve their lives.

Social work systems can be bureaucratic and frustrating at times.

Your work can be emotionally distressing and may put you in vulnerable situations.

Money guide

Starting salaries vary between £19,500 and £30,000 per year, depending on where you are working. Salaries starting out in the NHS could range between £26,041 and £34,876.

With experience you could earn up to £40,000. Managers can earn £42,000 or more.

Many employers offer additional benefits such as car allowances and child care.

Related opportunities

- Counsellor p561
- Healthcare Assistant p292
- Youth and Community Worker p579

Further information

British Association of Social Workers
www.basw.co.uk

Skills for Care
www.skillsforcare.org.uk

SOCIAL WORK AND COUNSELLING SERVICES

SUBSTANCE MISUSE WORKER

ENTRY LEVEL 1

Qualifications and courses

There are no set minimum entry requirements and each employer will have their own specifications. Previous experience in social care, youth work, criminal justice or counselling would be beneficial and some jobs are only open to qualified nurses, counsellors or youth workers.

Most employers require you to be at least 21 years old, as they are looking for maturity and life experience. Some will welcome applications from people who have been through addiction or dependency themselves and successfully come through treatment.

Employers may also ask for a relevant qualification, such as the NCFE Award in Substance Misuse Awareness or an NVQ/SVQ or BTEC Certificate in Health and Social Care.

Volunteering for organisations that offer support to people with drug and alcohol problems would also be beneficial, as it helps you gain an understanding of the issues people with substance misuse problems face, how experienced members of staff go about offering support and will help you build the necessary skills for the job.

If you want to work in a specialist role you may need job-specific experience and relevant professional qualifications.

Once employed, either in a paid position or as a volunteer, you will receive on-the-job training. This will usually include studying for qualifications up to a minimum of Level 3.

A Disclosure and Barring Service (DBS) check is necessary.

What the work involves

You will help people who misuse harmful substances, including drugs and alcohol, to overcome their dependencies.

You could provide support in one-to-one or group sessions. This can include counselling and care planning.

You could offer drug treatment options to prisoners, advise on detox methods in a rehabilitation centre, prescribe drugs and give medical advice in a clinic or run educational workshops in schools and youth centres. You could also help substance users find housing and temporary accommodation. You might accompany police patrols around clubs doing street outreach work.

Type of person suited to this work

You want your clients to trust you so you should be understanding, warm and a good listener. You need to be patient and non-judgemental as it may take substance users a long time to recover. If your clients know that you believe in them, they will develop confidence to change.

You could work with many clients at any given time and should be organised. An ability to stay calm under pressure and to maintain professional boundaries is essential.

Good communication skills are important as your role may involve educating others about the dangers of substance abuse.

Working conditions

You could be based in a drop-in centre, a clinic, prison or other community site. A lot of your time will be spent visiting substance users in their homes or other venues such as shelters as many clients may be homeless. A driving licence will therefore be useful.

You will most likely work 35 to 40 hours a week but these could be irregular hours including evenings and weekends. You might need to be on-call throughout the night.

Part-time work is available.

Future prospects

Your job prospects are high as there are a variety of opportunities across the UK for substance misuse workers. You could work for drop-in centres, local authorities, housing associations, private rehabilitation centres, the National Health Service, the prison service, police services, charities or drug and alcohol organisations.

With experience, you could become a supervisor or manager, specialise in one area of treatment such as psychological intervention or drug and alcohol testing or even specialise in one user group such as young people.

Advantages/disadvantages

You have the opportunity to build meaningful relationships with clients and colleagues.

It's rewarding when you help a client overcome an addiction.

You might need to be on-call 24-hours a day which can be demanding.

It can be frustrating to work with uncooperative clients who don't believe they have a problem.

Money guide

You can start out earning between £20,000 and £22,000 per year.

With experience and team leader responsibilities this may increase to between £23,000 and £28,000 a year. At project manager level you may receive in excess of £35,000.

Volunteers may be reimbursed for expenses such as travel costs.

Related opportunities

- Adult Nurse p271
- Counsellor p561
- Social Worker p573

Further information

Federation of Drug and Alcohol Professionals
www.fdap.org.uk

National Treatment Agency for Substance Misuse
www.nta.nhs.uk

Qualifications and courses

Many officials have degrees in social sciences, economics, law or politics, although there are no formal academic requirements for entry. To become a paid official at a union's branch or regional office, candidates will normally need to have previous experience working unpaid as a local representative, shop steward or administrator.

You may be able to work as a paid union learning representative without completing unpaid experience first if you have an adult education or training and development background.

If you want to work at national head office level, you will need experience or a degree in the particular area you wish to specialise in, eg law, media, education and training, research, trade union legislation or economics. Alternatively, it is possible to work your way up to national office from branch or regional level. Entry by either route requires relevant work experience, paid or unpaid.

Training is mainly on the job. The Trades Union Congress and commercial training organisations run regular short

training programmes in a range of different skills.

What the work involves

Trade union officials negotiate with employers over pay, working conditions, health and safety, dismissal and redundancy.

Working in regional offices, you will recruit members, train shop stewards, support local officials and negotiate individual cases with employers. At head office, you will work on national policies and negotiate at national level.

At all levels your role will be to bring about the best deal for the workforce by finding common ground between employers and employees.

Type of person suited to this work

It is important to have a genuine interest in people's welfare and to believe in the aims of your union. You will need to see issues from different viewpoints.

You will spend time dealing with individuals or groups, which requires good speaking, listening and negotiating skills. Speaking in public requires confidence.

Union matters involve problem-solving and negotiation which needs a patient, methodical approach and the ability to research and analyse information.

Working conditions

As a local shop steward you will have another job and attend to union business part time. Paid officials at regional and

national level are office based.

You could travel quite extensively to meetings, tribunals and conferences so a driving licence is useful.

You will spend a lot of time answering queries either online, by email or by phone – sometimes after normal work hours.

In response to any major policy shifts or events, you might be expected to offer comment or advice at relatively short notice.

Future prospects

Your prospects depend very much on the size of the union, ie they are greater with the large unions which are never out of the news.

Head-office posts are usually in London. After gaining experience it is possible to progress to a regional role, as organiser or secretary, or a national role.

Some people move from union work into politics by becoming councillors or MPs.

Advantages/disadvantages

The work is varied, but you may be working on one theme in preparation for a meeting.

Negotiating better pay and working conditions can be very rewarding.

Some people might be unpleasant and sometimes you have to support people you do not agree with.

You might have to work long and unsocial hours.

Money guide

Local shop stewards and union representatives are generally unpaid. As a paid official you can expect a starting salary of between £20,000 and £25,000 per year.

As an experienced regional or national official you could earn £30,000 to £50,000.

In senior positions such as a general secretary, salaries can rise to as much as £80,000.

Related opportunities

- Equality and Diversity Officer p23
- Health and Safety Adviser p27
- Human Resources/Personnel Officer p28

Further information

Scottish Trades Union Congress
www.stuc.org.uk

Trades Union Congress
www.tuc.org.uk

SOCIAL WORK AND COUNSELLING SERVICES

VICTIM CARE OFFICER

ENTRY LEVEL 1

Qualifications and courses

Formal qualifications are not essential to enter this field. Qualifications in subjects such as psychology, counselling, criminal justice and law can be useful but experience is more highly valued. You will however need a good standard of English and it may be helpful to be fluent in a foreign language.

You will need about 1 or 2 years' voluntary experience in order to find paid work as a victim care officer. There are no entry requirements for a voluntary post but you must be at least 18 years old.

As a volunteer you will undergo basic training, after which you have the option to specialise in supporting victims of particular crimes, such as domestic abuse, or families of homicide victims. Day to day activities may include working on the victim supportline, supporting witnesses at court or work with victims in your community, which will help develop your listening and communication skills.

It is also possible to move into victim support from another related area, such as social services.

A Disclosure and Barring Service (DBS) check will be made if you are volunteering and if you are applying for paid work.

Once you are working as a victim support officer, you will receive further on-the-job training combined with subject-specific sessions run by external agencies. You may also be encouraged to work towards Level 3 NVQs/ SVQs if you do not already have them. Suitable courses include the Level 3 Certificate in Community Justice (Work with Victims, Survivors and Witnesses).

What the work involves

Victim care officers help victims to deal with the aftermath of crime and come to terms with events.

Your work may be focused on a particular group such as victims of domestic abuse, serious sexual assault or anti-social behaviour.

You will listen carefully to victims and provide objective support. You may provide information on legal procedures and relevant services and agencies.

Practical support for victims may involve arranging visits from a police community support officer (PCSO), organising repairs to damaged property or obtaining a personal attack alarm for the victim.

Type of person suited to this work

You will need to be patient, understanding and possess the ability to remain objective and to relate to people from all walks of life.

Excellent listening and communication skills, including telephone skills, are imperative.

IT skills are essential as you will have to work with the case management system.

There may be tight deadlines which you will have to meet, so organisational skills are important.

You will need to have the energy and ability to assess clients' needs and be able to create solutions for them.

The ability to keep strict confidentiality is essential.

Working conditions

You will work from 37 to 40 hours a week and may often work in the evening and at weekends as required by clients.

Support of victims may take place over the telephone. You may also visit the victim at their home; it will usually be whichever the victim prefers.

The time between the incident and you meeting the victim will vary dependent on the victim's wishes, police advice and severity of the incident.

Part time and job share opportunities are common.

Future prospects

With time and experience as a victim care officer you may become a victim care team leader and eventually a victim care manager.

Recruitment for this role may be affected by local authority budget cuts.

You may choose to work exclusively in witness care, which may require more legal knowledge.

Advantages/disadvantages

You will have the satisfaction of helping people through difficult stages and experiences in their lives.

Part-time and job share opportunities are often available.

If the victim has not spoken about their feelings before, a lot of emotions may come to the surface, such as distress, confusion or anger, which may become directed at you.

It can be emotionally draining having to handle such delicate situations.

Money guide

Starting salaries for victim care officers working full time are between £15,000 and £20,000 per year.

With experience this can rise to between £22,000 and £24,000.

Related opportunities

- Counsellor p561
- Police Support Worker p544
- Social Worker p573

Further information

Skills for Justice
www.sfjuk.com

Victim Support
www.victimsupport.org.uk

Qualifications and courses

There are no set qualifications required to enter this career but many employers will ask for a degree in a relevant subject such as business studies, human resource management or social care. Relevant experience organising and managing people or working as a volunteer is essential and extensive experience could be an alternative to qualifications.

A postgraduate degree is not usually needed but could offer you an advantage if you are working in the creative industries or for an international development project, as these fields are becoming increasingly competitive.

You could begin as a volunteer and move into managing other volunteers before progressing to a paid role as a manager. There aren't many graduate training schemes but some larger charities run internships.

To work for an international organisation you should have voluntary experience overseas, international contacts and a second language.

Volunteers may benefit from completing the Award Scheme Development and Accreditation Network (ASDAN)'s Community Volunteering Qualifications (Levels 1–3). The Institute of Leadership and Management provides course accreditation for relevant management courses. Suitable courses include the BTEC Level 3 Award, Certificate or Diploma in Volunteer Management.

A Disclosure and Barring Service (DBS) check will be made.

What the work involves

You will recruit, train and organise volunteers to assist hospitals, social service departments, charities and other volunteer organisations.

After interviewing volunteers, you will match them to the kind of work that would suit them. Once you have selected the volunteers, you will provide them with training and mentor them in their position. You will then offer ongoing advice and support.

You will deal with administration, budgets, correspondence and report writing.

You could also prepare publicity material and liaise with other agencies.

Type of person suited to this work

You will work with volunteers from many different backgrounds so you must be personable, as well as a good motivator.

It is essential to be confident and have good communication skills to sell placements to volunteers and volunteers to placements. You will need to be flexible and adaptable.

The job will demand a good deal of administration and record-keeping, which requires excellent organisational and time-management skills.

Working conditions

You could work out of an office or from home, depending on the size of the organisation.

You will need to travel locally to arrange placements and visit volunteers, so a driving licence will be useful.

You will most likely work 40 hours a week from Monday to Friday but you may need to work evenings and weekends to meet deadlines.

Future prospects

You are unlikely to enter this career straight from school.

Opportunities are good but there is keen competition for jobs and you might have to move to another organisation or charity to gain promotion. A willingness to be geographically mobile would be useful.

Volunteer management provides useful experience if you would like to transfer into a career such as social work or other management posts in the not-for-profit sector.

You will have opportunities for further training, mainly through short courses.

With experience you may be able to acquire a directorship.

Advantages/disadvantages

This work is varied and challenging.

The job is fulfilling; by helping volunteers find placements you will be making a difference to people in need.

As with any management role, some people may be hard to work with and difficult to please.

Money guide

Starting salaries are usually between £18,000 and £25,000 per year. However, in some companies you may start out in an unpaid role.

With experience, you can expect to earn £21,000 to £38,000.

Senior staff who have substantial supervisory experience and are employed in large organisations can achieve £40,000 or more.

Salaries tend to be higher in larger charities, hospitals and the private sector than in smaller charities, educational institutions and the creative industries.

Related opportunities

- Fundraiser p565
- Welfare Benefits Adviser/Welfare Rights Caseworker p578

Further information

Association of Chief Executives of Voluntary Organisations
www.acevo.org.uk

Scottish Council for Voluntary Organisations
www.scvo.org.uk

Qualifications and courses

There are no set minimum entry requirements but a good standard of English and maths is necessary to do the job. Many welfare benefits advisers have a degree in a subject such as social science, law or sociology but this is not essential. Having prior relevant experience is deemed more important than formal qualifications.

Many entrants to this profession begin their career as a volunteer in an advice centre. Once you have gained experience in general advice, you can choose to specialise in welfare rights and benefits. You will usually need to work on a voluntary basis for about a year to be qualified for a paid job.

Undertaking training with the Citizens Advice Bureau (CAB) or other community advice centres would equip you with relevant skills. Speaking a minority language is also an advantage and you will usually need to undergo a Disclosure and Barring Service (DBS) check.

Once you have secured employment, you will attend in-house training and continuing professional development (CPD) courses. The CAB has a nationally recognised training programme for their paid employees. There is also an NVQ Level 3 Certificate and Level 4 Diploma in Advice and Guidance available from City & Guilds which may be useful.

What the work involves

In this sector, you will help people to cope with problems by listening, asking questions and giving impartial and confidential advice.

Benefits advisers may represent their clients at tribunals or act as advocates in a court of law.

Welfare rights caseworkers explain people's rights on matters such as tenancy, employment, conflicts with neighbours, consumer law and finance; sometimes referring clients to other professionals.

You will help people fill in forms to claim benefits and make phone calls on their behalf.

Type of person suited to this work

As the work is mainly about dealing with people, you must have excellent interpersonal skills and the ability to remain impartial and non-judgemental. In order to explain issues very clearly to your clients and help them to complete forms and documents, you will need excellent verbal and written communication skills.

You will be handling large amounts of information, often to find answers to queries, which means you must enjoy research and be able to grasp facts and analyse data quickly.

You need to be understanding and tactful when dealing with clients who are upset and stressed.

Working conditions

Benefits advisers are based in an open-access centre within a local community, town or city. You will see clients on a one-to-one basis by appointment and you will also liaise with colleagues and other professionals, such as social workers and solicitors.

You will usually work standard office hours from Monday to Friday with occasional shift work including Saturdays and evenings.

You will use IT to consult client records, access email and the internet, and undertake research.

Future prospects

Advice centre work is not open to school-leavers – it suits mature people who are experienced in other fields. Entry is competitive; you should gain experience in helping people through voluntary work.

Most jobs are with local authorities or charities. There are a few paid jobs with the CAB but many posts are voluntary. Training will be given in areas such as counselling skills and benefits.

Promotion prospects are limited, although every advice centre has a manager.

Advantages/disadvantages

You will get the opportunity to work with many different people.

You will have to deal with angry and upset clients; some may even have mental health problems.

Helping clients resolve their problems can be personally rewarding.

Money guide

Earnings vary with location and employer.

Starting salaries are usually around £19,000 to £20,000 per year.

With experience and increased responsibilities, you are likely to earn between £22,000 and £30,000.

Related opportunities

- Counsellor p561
- Equality and Diversity Officer p23
- Solicitor/Notary Public p359

Further information

Advice UK
www.adviceuk.org.uk

Citizens Advice Bureau
www.citizensadvice.org.uk

Citizens Advice Scotland
www.cas.org.uk

Qualifications and courses

Entry to this profession is with an Honours degree in youth or community work which has been validated by the National Youth Agency (NYA). The requirements for a degree course are usually 2 A levels/3 H grades and 5 GCSEs/National 5s (A*–C/A–C), though these may be waived for mature applicants with relevant experience. You may be able to enter onto a university course with work-based qualifications you can acquire as part of a Youth Work Apprenticeship.

Many employers request a postgraduate certificate, diploma or master's degree endorsed by the Joint Negotiating Committee (JNC) for Youth and Community Workers. These qualifications vary in length, are available in full-time or part-time study options and include work placements. Graduates with a degree in a non-related subject can also take these courses to gain the appropriate knowledge required for entry.

Significant experience in youth and community work, whether paid or voluntary, is essential for entry onto the postgraduate courses. A second language may be useful.

You will need to pass a check from the Disclosure and Barring Service (DBS).

What the work involves

Youth workers are mainly involved with young people while community workers try to make sure that people of all ages in the local community have access to opportunities.

You will work with people in their local area, encouraging them to take part in learning opportunities and community activities.

You could be in charge of a community centre, arranging activities for people of all ages, such as youth clubs, over-60s lunch clubs and playgroups.

You will keep records, manage budgets and try to obtain grants and funding.

You will work alongside other professionals including social workers, teachers, probation officers and the police.

Type of person suited to this work

As the work involves contact with all sorts of people, it is important to be able to get on with everyone and earn their trust. You also need to be genuinely interested in the local community and in equal opportunities.

Local people have a say in what they want in their area, so you must be a good listener, with the ability to balance the ideas of the community with local and national government policies.

Working conditions

You might be based in a community centre, drop-in centres, cafés and youth clubs or in an area office. Depending on your job, you could also work in a school or college.

You will usually work 35 to 37 hours a week and this includes attending evening and weekend sessions.

Youth/community workers often travel around their local area so a driving licence is useful.

Future prospects

Youth and community work is an area that is doing quite well at the moment. As well as roles in youth club and community centre management, there are new strands to the work with developing music, drama, art or sporting groups. Local lifelong learning adult centres also require youth and community workers.

Local authorities have a defined promotion structure but in some jobs you might have to move around to widen your experience. You could progress to working for voluntary organisations or for a specific young people's service.

Advantages/disadvantages

This work provides variety and challenge.

You will play a major part in developing your local community and/or the lives of young people.

You might have to work evenings, weekends and public holidays.

Money guide

Earnings vary with location and tend to be higher in London.

Starting salaries for qualified youth and community workers are about £21,000 per year.

With experience, you can expect to earn £27,000 to £34,000.

Those employed in managerial positions are likely to receive in excess of £35,000.

Related opportunities

- Education Welfare Officer p184
- Further Education Lecturer p185
- Social Worker p573

Further information

Council for Wales of Voluntary Youth Services
www.cwvys.org.uk

National Youth Agency
www.nya.org.uk

SOCIAL WORK AND COUNSELLING SERVICES

Transport and Logistics

The jobs in this sector are immensely varied because of the wide range of transport and communication links that exist today to keep our lives running. You could need a high level of technical knowledge in this sector especially for jobs such as a pilot or a train driver. But you could also be great at keeping attention to detail and maintaining schedules if logistics is more where your interest lies. Jobs in transport and logistics require very efficient and practical people to ensure that our infrastructure continues to run smoothly and safely. You may need to cope well in pressurised situations as well as be very good at communicating so that any problems can be sorted out quickly. The jobs featured in this section are listed below. For similar jobs to the ones in this section see *Security, Emergency and the Armed Forces* on page 529 and *Leisure, Sport and Tourism* on page 361.

Qualifications and courses

Entry requirements depend on the individual airline. Employers often expect 3–5 GCSEs/National 5s (A*–C/A–C) including English and Maths and although a degree is not required, having one in languages, hospitality management or travel may be useful.

You will need to be at least 18 years old (sometimes 21), physically fit and within height and weight restrictions. You will also need a valid passport allowing unrestricted world travel, or at least, with no restrictions to the countries the airline travels to. Most airlines will expect you to be able to swim at least 25 metres. Previous experience in a customer service role, the ability to speak another language (essential if you are looking to be based abroad) and training in First Aid would all be beneficial.

There are various qualifications that could be useful for people looking to become an air cabin crew member. These include a GCSE/National 5 or A level/H grade in Leisure and Tourism, BTECs in Customer Service or Aviation Operations and NCFE Airline Cabin Crew courses. While these qualifications may give you an edge over other candidates, they don't guarantee you a job and are not required by airlines.

Cabin Crew Apprenticeships are also available and are a good way of preparing you for the work involved.

Some airlines may want relevant work experience rather than qualifications, so it is a good idea to do part-time or temporary work in customer service roles or anything that demonstrates teamwork and communication skills.

Once accepted by an airline you will take part in their 4–6-week training course which covers areas such as First Aid, safety and emergency procedures, security regulations and customer care.

What the work involves

When you have prepared the cabin, you will welcome your passengers on board and make sure that they are comfortable.

You will be responsible for checking that customers are wearing their safety belts when required and that their bags are stored away. You will demonstrate safety procedures before take-off.

During the flight you will help to care for any young children and sick passengers, giving First Aid if needed. You will also serve food and drinks, sell duty free items, ensure that passengers are ready for landing and see them all safely off the plane.

Type of person suited to this work

You will need to be welcoming, friendly, well-groomed, confident and caring.

You should be happy working in a team with the rest of the crew.

Common sense and tact are important when dealing with a variety of situations ranging from nervous or unruly passengers to medical emergencies. It is essential to stay calm under pressure and to have a reassuring attitude.

Working conditions

You will work in a cabin, which can sometimes be cramped and unstable. You will spend the majority of your time standing up and the work may affect your health, for example ear pain from cabin pressure or jet lag from long flights.

Planes fly 24/7 which means unsocial working hours. You will work different shifts on a rota system. You might work on short flights within the UK/Europe or you could fly long-haul with frequent periods of time away from home.

You could be based overseas as a member of an airline's international crew.

You will be provided with a uniform and you must have a smart appearance at all times.

Future prospects

There is strong competition for jobs and the assessment process can be very tough.

With experience, you could progress to working as a purser (looking after a particular cabin such as first class) and then to cabin service director or crew controller. You could also go on to train new cabin crew.

Advantages/disadvantages

You will travel to dream destinations, but on short flights you will not always get off the plane!

No two working days will be the same.

While working with people can be very rewarding, you may have to deal with difficult passengers.

Money guide

Starting salaries for air cabin crew are usually around £12,000.

With 5 or more years' experience, earnings can rise to £15,000 to £18,000. Senior members of the crew with 10 or more years' experience can earn £25,000 and up.

Benefits include meals, free or discounted flights and allowances for working unsocial hours or working away from home. Air cabin crew can often boost their income with commission on in-flight sales.

Related opportunities

- Holiday Representative p368
- Tour Guide/Manager p376
- Travel Agent p379

Further information

EAL
www.eal.org.uk

NCFE
www.ncfe.org.uk

TRANSPORT AND LOGISTICS

Qualifications and courses

To enter this profession you will need to complete a training course approved by the Civil Aviation Authority (CAA) in order to obtain the required Air Traffic Controller's (ATCO) Licence. Course providers include Resource Training, Global ATS and National Air Traffic Services (NATS).

Applicants for an air traffic control course must be at least 18 years old and have a minimum of 5 GCSEs/National 5s (A*–C/A–C), including English and Maths. A degree is not needed to apply; however, having one in a numerical or technical subject may help you on the job. You will need a good standard of health, hearing, colour vision and a clear voice.

There is strong competition for places and the application process involves attending assessment days and a formal interview, completing online and written tests and receiving security and medical clearance.

Candidates will initially learn in the classroom and through practical exercises using computer simulators. There are ongoing exams and assessments throughout the course which you need to pass in order to progress to the next stage, a process that may take up to 11 months.

After graduation, trainees go on to an operational air traffic control unit for validation training under the supervision of an experienced instructor. The ATCO licence is awarded upon successful completion of the training.

What the work involves

Air traffic controllers issue pilots with instructions and advice to ensure that planes take off, fly and land safely.

When using radar, you will be in control of a specific section of airspace, keeping air traffic flying safely and expeditiously. In a control tower, you will be responsible for the safe movement of aircraft on the ground both arriving and departing from an airport.

You will have to make quick but safe decisions at all times, particularly in emergencies or difficult weather conditions.

Type of person suited to this work

You must speak clearly and confidently when passing instructions to pilots. It is essential to stay alert at all times and pay close attention to detail. You must be able to make quick and logical decisions and stay calm in an emergency situation.

Whilst controlling you will need to have good spatial awareness and the ability to multi-task and operate safely in a 3D environment.

The technology and software used is regularly upgraded to improve safety, so you will need to be willing to train on new equipment and procedures during your working life.

Working conditions

You will work around 40 hours a week at an air traffic control centre or in an air traffic control tower. As this is a 24/7 job, you will work shifts including early mornings, nights, weekends and public holidays. Hours are strictly regulated to provide rest periods during your shifts.

You will use radar displays, radio headphones and computer tools. The lighting in the control room is kept at the right level to help you read the radar screens.

Future prospects

Most UK air traffic controllers are employed by the NATS. Most of the NATS controllers work in one of two main area control centres (Swanwick near Southampton and Prestwick in Scotland) and others work at airports where NATS are contracted to provide air traffic control.

Air traffic controllers are also employed by other companies/councils at other airfields.

With experience, you could manage and train other air traffic controllers.

Advantages/disadvantages

No two working days are the same and your job will remain interesting and challenging.

You will be paid well for the level of responsibility you take on.

This job can involve high levels of stress.

Money guide

If you study with NATS, your basic salary during the college part of the training will be around £11,967 a year, plus benefits that include a contributory pension scheme and very good annual leave.

Whilst undertaking the validation training you can expect to earn between £17,066 and £20,479 depending on where you're placed.

Once you are fully qualified as an air traffic controller you will receive an annual salary of £32,522 to £36,247.

Those employed in a senior position at Swanwick or Heathrow could potentially earn over £100,000.

Related opportunities

- Airline Pilot p584
- Helicopter Pilot p594
- Royal Air Force Officer p550

Further information

Civil Aviation Authority
www.caa.co.uk

National Air Traffic Services
www.nats.aero

TRANSPORT AND LOGISTICS

583

Qualifications and courses

You must be aged at least 16 to begin training for a 'frozen' Airline Transport Pilot Licence (ATPL), which allows you to become a first officer. After you have accumulated enough flying hours you can unfreeze your licence and work towards becoming a captain. You will need to be over the age of 21 to hold a full ATPL.

There are various entry routes to getting an ATPL. You can train full time over around 18 months with a flying school. Entry is with at least 5 GCSEs/National 5s (A*–C/A–C) in English, Maths and a science. This route usually costs at least £60,000 for the training.

Another option is to undertake modular training. The first stage is to apply for a Private Pilot's Licence (PPL) and then gain an extra 150 hours' flying experience to be eligible for an ATPL. This method usually costs at least £25,000.

Alternatively, you could train as a pilot in the armed forces, serve for a time and then take a conversion course to get a commercial pilot's licence. Or you may do a degree course in pilot training at university, which will take you to frozen ATPL status.

Sponsorship for your course is possible and organisations such as the Air League offer scholarships. You will have a medical to assess your physical fitness, hearing, eyesight and colour vision.

What the work involves

You will be responsible for the safety of your passengers, crew and cargo and will need to carry out a range of safety, route and fuel checks before each flight.

When flying you will keep in radio contact with air traffic controllers, inform and direct the crew, plan your route and use computer systems to control and monitor the aircraft.

After each flight you will need to write a report and record any problems that occurred.

Type of person suited to this work

You will need to be confident and responsible enough to take charge of your aircraft and follow the exact instructions of air traffic control. You must have the ability to read maps and 3D displays.

Good communication and teamwork skills are essential.

You must stay composed under pressure and in emergency situations. Quick thinking and good coordination are also important.

Once you have earned your full licence, you will still be regularly assessed on your health, skills and competencies so you must be keen to keep on learning.

Working conditions

You will wear a uniform and carry company ID at all times.

You will work shifts which will include weekends, nights and public holidays. If a flight is delayed you may work much longer hours than anticipated. The hours you are allowed to work are strictly regulated.

You must be prepared for jetlag and spending time away from home if piloting a long-haul flight. You will spend the majority of your time sitting in a small flight deck.

Future prospects

Competition for vacancies for new pilots is intense.

You could be promoted to co-pilot on a long-haul flight after you have about 5 years of experience on short-haul flights. In order to be promoted to captain level you will need to fly 5,000 hours, which can take up to 10 years to achieve.

You could become a manager or an instructor or even work up to a senior position within a major airline.

Advantages/disadvantages

The training to qualify as a pilot is incredibly expensive.

You will be at the mercy of the weather and you may not always be able to minimise turbulence.

You will have the opportunity to travel to exotic locations. Often, you will be able to travel for free or at reduced rates.

Flying a plane is a thrilling experience so your day-to-day work will be exciting.

You will spend a lot of time away, which can severely affect your personal life.

Money guide

Salaries vary depending on the airline you are employed by and the type of aircraft you are flying.

A newly qualified first officer working for a small airline could earn £18,000 to £20,000. This can go up to about £43,000 with experience.

Captains can earn from £55,000 to £80,000 with the potential for even more with experience.

Experienced captains flying long-haul aircraft can earn up to £140,000.

Salaries usually increase with each year of service with a company. Benefits include free or discounted flights.

Related opportunities

- Air Traffic Controller p583
- Helicopter Pilot p594
- Royal Air Force Airman/woman p549

Further information

British Airline Pilots' Association
www.balpa.org

The Honourable Company of Air Pilots
www.airpilots.org

Qualifications and courses

There are no minimum entry requirements for this job but employers often expect a good standard of literacy and numeracy. You will usually need to be at least 18 years old, be physically fit and pass medical and vision tests and a Disclosure and Barring Service (DBS) check. You will also need a clean driving licence and in some cases a large goods vehicle (LGV) or forklift licence. Previous experience working in a warehouse may be an advantage.

The Apprenticeship in Aviation Operations on the Ground is available at both Intermediate and Advanced Levels and may equip you with relevant skills for this profession.

Once you secure employment you will receive training from an experienced colleague in areas such as health and safety, security procedures, using luggage conveyor belts and lifting equipment, and driving airport vehicles.

You can also study for relevant qualifications whilst you work. There are City & Guilds Diplomas, NVQs and BTEC certificates available in Aviation Operations on the Ground (Levels 2–3).

What the work involves

You will be responsible for safely loading, unloading and transporting baggage, cases and freight.

By checking the baggage against flight lists, you will sort items to make sure you get the baggage to the right place on time. You will then lift the baggage onto the ramp or conveyor belt to move it onto the plane or into the baggage hall.

If you spot any unusual or suspicious baggage, you will need to report it immediately.

You may also help de-ice the plane or keep the runway clear of debris during particularly busy periods.

Type of person suited to this work

You need to be alert and pay close attention to detail when checking labels against flight lists and looking out for suspicious baggage. As you will be handling passengers' belongings, you must be honest and reliable.

In order to get aircraft loaded and unloaded on a short timescale, you will need to be physically fit, fast moving and accurate.

Flexibility and a willingness to get your hands dirty are also vital, as you might need to carry out jobs such as cleaning the aircraft and keeping runways free of hazards such as snow and birds. You should enjoy working as part of a team.

Working conditions

You will mainly work outdoors in all weathers, as well as in cramped spaces such as cargo holds.

You will work around 39 hours per week, usually on a shift system which includes evenings, weekends and public holidays. It is advisable to live near the airport and have your own transport so that you will arrive on time for early shifts.

Working near aircraft can be noisy but you will wear ear protectors.

Your job will involve a lot of bending, lifting and carrying and you will be required to wear protective boots and a high visibility jacket.

Future prospects

Heathrow and Gatwick airports are among the largest employers in the UK but there are vacancies at many regional airports as well, particulary the larger ones such as Birmingham and Manchester.

Seasonal work will be on offer during busy holiday periods.

You may be promoted to a supervisory role or manage ground transport on the runways. With further training and qualifications you could also work in cargo services or aviation management.

Advantages/disadvantages

This is a very active, fast-paced and busy role.

If you are working for an airline, one of the perks may be subsidised travel.

You may have to work outside in poor weather conditions and be on your feet hauling heavy baggage.

Money guide

Starting salaries are usually between £15,000 and £18,000 per year.

With a few years' experience in the role and supervisory duties you could expect to earn £20,000 or more.

Team leaders may earn £18,000 a year or more.

Some workers are paid by the hour and rates are typically between £6 and £9.

Allowances for shift work and overtime pay can increase your income.

Related opportunities

- Hotel Porter p129
- Removals Operative p607
- Warehouse Worker/Manager p613

Further information

International Air Transport Association
www.iata.org

Royal Aeronautical Society
www.aerosociety.com

Qualifications and courses

There are no specific academic requirements for this profession, though some employers will expect you to have a good standard of literacy and numeracy.

You must hold a Passenger Carrying Vehicle (PCV) licence and obtain the Driver Certificate of Professional Competence (Driver CPC). You need to have a full EU driving licence and be at least 18 years old to train for your PCV. You have to be over the age of 21 to drive on major bus and coach routes.

If you already have a full EU driving licence then many companies, including National Express, will be willing to employ you and fund your training for the PCV. Others require you to already have one, with no more than 6 points on it. You can train independently by taking private lessons through a local driving school. Application forms for PCV licences can be obtained from your local Post Office.

PCV training lasts between 1 and 6 weeks and includes a theory test, a practical driving test and a medical. During your training period your company will teach you about customer care, disability awareness, defensive driving and health and safety.

The CPC can be obtained by taking an approved training course, a list of which can be found in the Driving, Transport and Travel section of the gov.uk website.

You must complete 35 hours of training and renew your licence every 5 years.

What the work involves

Bus/coach drivers provide a transport service for passengers making short or long journeys.

You will be responsible for the safety and comfort of your passengers throughout their journey, which includes ensuring that passengers are safely on or off your vehicle before pulling out, and that they are wearing seatbelts when applicable.

If you do not have a conductor, you might have to work out passenger fares and issue tickets and passes. You will also be responsible for checking your vehicle, coping with breakdowns and other emergencies, and driving safely at all times.

Ensuring all baggage is safely loaded and that there are no obstructions inside the bus will be important on coaches.

Type of person suited to this work

You will need to be an extremely competent driver.

You should have a polite and approachable manner when dealing with passengers, but have the confidence to handle disagreements or other situations which may arise on journeys.

You will need good eyesight and excellent concentration in order to remain alert for very long periods of time. Quick reactions are also useful in case you need to respond to an unforeseen event on the road. You should be a punctual person as you will have to adhere to a strict timetable.

Working conditions

You will work on a shift pattern including evening, overnight and weekend work. You cannot work more than 56 hours a week, or 90 hours over 2 weeks. You are also required, by law, to take a 45 minute break every 4.5 hours.

Coach drivers are expected to provide assistance to disabled travellers and help passengers with luggage so your role could involve heavy lifting. You will have to wear a uniform.

Not all buses have air conditioning, so can become quite hot inside, particularly when the bus is crowded during summer.

Future prospects

Over 80% of the workforce is employed by 1 of 6 companies: Stagecoach, First, National Express, Transdev, Arriva and Go-Ahead.

You could work anywhere in the UK, undertake long distance tour driving or provide a transport service for specific groups such as the elderly or disabled.

You can progress to become a supervisor, service controller or instructor within your company.

Advantages/disadvantages

You will be providing an essential public service.

Part-time and flexible hours are available so you can fit your work around other commitments.

You may have to deal with difficult or distressed passengers.

Driving the same route or for long periods of time can become monotonous.

Money guide

As a trainee driver working towards your PCV licence you could expect to earn between £13,000 and £15,000 a year.

With experience your salary is likely to be £16,000 to £20,000. Coach drivers for specialist tours can earn around £25,000 a year.

You could supplement your income with overtime and shift work.

Related opportunities

- Driving Instructor p592
- Large Goods Vehicle Driver p596
- Taxi Driver p610

Further information

Driver and Vehicle Standards Agency
www.gov.uk/government/organisations/driver-and-vehicle-standards-agency

Qualifications and courses

You will not need any specific academic qualifications to become a chauffeur. The only necessity is that you hold a full driving licence. Most employers will expect this to be clean but some do consider candidates with penalty points. You may benefit from holding an advanced driving certificate, details of which can be found through the Institute of Advanced Motorists. This demonstrates an enhanced driving ability and additional skills that may be valued by some employers.

It is beneficial to have several years' driving experience. Not only does this demonstrate a proven ability behind the wheel, but if you are over 21 years old you will cost your employer less to insure. Previous experience in a related driving job, such as a taxi driver, can be an advantage.

There are professional courses that you could take to enhance your application and understanding of the job, for example, NVQs in Road Passenger Vehicle Driving. The British Chauffeurs Guild offers a Chauffeur Training Programme which covers the fundamental areas of chauffeuring: theory, practice, protocol, security and etiquette.

Some employers may also require you to pass a medical assessment and a Disclosure and Barring Services (DBS) check prior to taking you on. Others may have specific requirements such as car maintenance skills, the ability to speak a foreign language or to be a non-smoker.

What the work involves

Chauffeurs are responsible for driving their client to and from appointments or events, as well as the maintenance of the vehicle.

You will have to clean the vehicle regularly, inside and out, and also undertake any minor maintenance work when necessary, or book it in to be seen by a mechanic.

You will be providing a personal service to your passengers, including opening and closing doors for them, assisting them in and out of the vehicle, and carrying and loading their luggage or shopping. You might also be required to provide a low level of security protection to your client, as well as maintaining confidentiality at all times.

Type of person suited to this work

You must be an excellent driver who observes the law and keeps cool under pressure, even when faced with endless traffic jams or unpredictable clients. You will also need to have a good awareness of safety and security, both on the road and with regard to your client.

You should have excellent interpersonal skills. You must be punctual, respectful and polite.

Good map reading skills, knowledge of basic vehicle maintenance, and a reasonable level of fitness are also helpful.

Working conditions

It is unlikely that you will work regular hours as a chauffeur, as most clients will require your services during the evenings and at weekends. Split shifts are common, where you will find yourself with 2 or 3 free hours in between appointments.

You may be required to spend nights away from home on occasion.

You will need to wear a uniform in most instances.

Future prospects

Most chauffeurs are employed by limousine companies, but there are opportunities with hotel groups, car-hire companies, park and ride schemes, tour operators, businesses and private employers.

The British Chauffeurs Guild operates a specialist employment agency for its members, through which they can find suitable opportunities.

With experience, you can command a higher salary, or you could branch into a related career such as that of a taxi driver or driving instructor.

Advantages/disadvantages

You could work for some interesting, high profile clients.

The work offers some flexibility with hours.

There is a lot of waiting around for clients, which can get boring and frustrating.

Money guide

Salaries vary depending on your employer but typically the starting wage for a chauffeur is between £14,000 and £17,000 a year. With a few years' experience this could rise to £25,000.

An experienced chauffeur could earn £30,000 or more.

Chauffeurs can earn extra money in overtime, bonuses and tips.

Related opportunities

- Driving Instructor p592
- Motor Vehicle Technician p222
- Taxi Driver p610

Further information

British Chauffeurs Guild
www.britishchauffeursguild.co.uk

Institute of Advanced Motorists
www.iam.org.uk

TRANSPORT AND LOGISTICS

Qualifications and courses

There are no formal qualifications needed to become a courier but most employers will look for candidates with strong literacy and numeracy skills.

You will need a full driving licence and so will need to be at least 17 years old, though high insurance costs for young drivers mean that most driver couriers are over 21. School leavers could start as bicycle couriers.

Motorcycle couriers will need the Compulsory Basic Training (CBT) qualification issued by the Driver and Vehicle Licensing Agency (DVLA).

Commercial driving experience or knowledge of vehicle maintenance could help when looking for work.

Some courier firms may also offer apprenticeships which would enable you to combine on-the-job training with the study of an industry-related qualification, such as a Level 1 BTEC in Carrying and Delivering Goods by Road or an NVQ/SVQ in Driving Goods Vehicles (Levels 2–3).

The Institute of Couriers (IOC) accredits two qualification routes. For aspiring managers an Honours degree in Logistics with the London Metropolitan University is recommended. For delivery team members a Courier Transport Trailblazer Apprenticeship is currently under development and will provide students with a Level 2 qualification.

What the work involves

You will collect fragile, valuable or urgent packages and letters and deliver them within an agreed time limit.

Once you have been allocated your job, you will travel to a collection point for pick-up. You will load up the goods and then take them to the drop-off point where you will obtain a signature for delivery.

Motorcycle couriers may travel long distances and van couriers carry larger parcels in a town or city.

Type of person suited to this work

Map-reading skills are essential. You may only be paid for the number of deliveries you do so you need to be quick and know where you are going.

You will be in constant contact with customers; collecting items, asking for instructions and getting signatures for deliveries, so you need to be good with people.

You should be very reliable, with excellent time-keeping skills, as you will often be handling high value or very urgent items.

Working conditions

You will spend a lot of time travelling as courier services operate 24/7 with many couriers working on overnight deliveries. Long distance or overseas deliveries might mean time away from home.

Motorcycle and bicycle couriers will be out in the weather at all times.

You might have to provide your own car or van and motorcycle or bicycle couriers usually use their own bikes. You will also be responsible for the maintenance of your vehicle and will be expected to check the lights, brakes and tyres of your motorbike, van or bicycle regularly.

Future prospects

The continued growth of online shopping and customer online tracking means that the demand for same and next day courier delivery is high. There are around 90,000 couriers working in the UK and almost 11,000 workplaces as competition among companies is fierce. This means there remains a demand for reliable couriers.

You could improve your prospects by becoming a member of the Institute of Couriers, the Despatch Association or the National Courier Association.

Promotion generally depends on the size of the courier company.

It might be possible to become self-employed and start your own courier service. You could also train further and move into a related area such as large goods vehicle driving, freight planning or distribution.

Advantages/disadvantages

Pay rates are good but if you are using your own transport you will have running, insurance and maintenance costs.

Making up to 20 journeys a day and possibly working 50-hour weeks make this a stressful job.

Most couriers take up the job because they are attracted to the freedom of travel.

Money guide

Couriers are often self-employed and paid for each delivery they make, so earnings vary. Some companies offer bonuses for delivering a certain number of items or for full attendance.

New couriers can earn between £12,000 and £14,500 a year.

Experienced couriers could earn between £15,000 and £25,000 a year or more.

Motorcycle couriers in London can earn up to £23,000 a year, though part of that will go towards fuel, equipment and insurance.

Related opportunities

- Airport Baggage Handler p585
- Delivery Driver p590
- Warehouse Worker/Manager p613

Further information

Driver and Vehicle Standards Agency
www.gov.uk/government/organisations/driver-and-vehicle-standards-agency

Institute of Couriers
www.instituteofcouriers.com

Qualifications and courses

Steward

There are no formal entry requirements for this work, but relevant experience in the leisure and hospitality industry is normally required.

Training is provided on the job and will cover areas such as safety, health, environment, survival and rescue, fire, First Aid as well as company-specific training.

Qualifications such as a BTEC Level 2 in Hospitality and Catering Principles or a NVQ Level 2 Diploma in Housekeeping could help.

Purser

Good A levels/H grades are normally required, and many employers prefer a degree in a related subject such as hospitality or travel and tourism. The normal entry requirements for a degree in a travel- or hospitality-based subject are 2 A levels/3 H grades and 5 GCSEs/ National 5s (A*–C/A–C).

Related experience is normally required for employment as it demonstrates pre-entry commitment to the hospitality industry. For senior positions, managerial experience or a degree in hotel management may be required.

Knowledge of a language other than English is an advantage.

What the work involves

Steward

You will be responsible for keeping the public and private areas on a cruise ship clean and serviced to a very high standard. Duties may include making beds and vacuuming.

You may serve passengers drinks in the bar area, wash glasses and keep the bar stocked and tidy.

Purser

Pursers provide the administrative support necessary to ensure the ship operates smoothly and that passengers have a good holiday. You might work in the reception area, do secretarial duties or order various items of stock.

As well as providing passenger services you might also support crew members by paying their salaries or updating and maintaining immigration records.

Type of person suited to this work

As you will have contact with passengers, you should be happy meeting, talking with and helping people of all nationalities.

You should be polite and happy to help, and have good customer service skills.

You will need to be a dedicated employee as the work can be hard at times.

Working conditions

You will be expected to work long shifts, which for some posts can last up to 10 hours. Although cruise ships appear to be glamorous, you might work in cramped conditions or during rough weather.

You might have to share your accommodation with other members of staff.

Short-term, holiday and summer work is available.

Future prospects

In recent years the cruise ship industry has become one of the fastest growing sectors in the UK and USA, so prospects are good.

There is a clear process of career progression. You will start as a member of crew then rise to officer as you gain skills and responsibilities.

The skills gained on-board will also be useful on land in many areas of hospitality and catering (steward) or the business sector (purser).

Advantages/disadvantages

You will be away from home for months at a time so your personal life will be affected.

You will be able to visit lots of places around the world.

Your accommodation could be cramped and you might have to share with other crew members.

Pay is very good; accommodation and food are free while on board, and usually your salary is tax free if on a 6-month contract or longer.

Money guide

Salaries for all on-board positions are higher than for comparable jobs ashore. Salaries vary with company and liner, so contact companies directly for their earnings guide.

Stewards typically earn around £12,000 per year; this may increase slightly with experience. Free accommodation and food, as well as tips from passengers, boost the value of earnings.

The purser can expect a varying salary dependent on experience and responsibility. Salaries generally start from £19,000 to £21,000 per year as an assistant purser.

With experience and increased responsibility as the administration purser, this can increase to between £33,000 and £37,000.

A chief purser can earn between £45,000 and £55,000.

Related opportunities

- Holiday Representative p368
- Housekeeper/Accommodation Manager p132
- Tourist Information Centre Assistant p378

Further information

Springboard UK
www.springboard.uk.net

TRANSPORT AND LOGISTICS

Qualifications and courses

No specific academic qualifications are required for delivery drivers but some employers prefer candidates with some GCSEs/National 5s (A*–E/A–E) or equivalent, including English and Maths. They also require good eyesight and perfect colour vision.

You will need to hold a good driving record and the appropriate driving licence for work as a delivery driver. Drivers also need a Driver Certificate of Professional Competence (CPC) which, to achieve, involves passing a short course.

If you gained your licence after 1 January 1997 you cannot drive vehicles over 3.5 tonnes. Aquiring an additional licence for category C1 will allow you to drive vehicles up to 7.5 tonnes and may increase opportunities. For this you will need to be at least 18 years old, pass a medical and take a large goods vehicle (LGV) theory and C1 practical test.

Training providers for both the CPC and the LGV can be found on the Joint Approvals Unit for Periodic Training (JAUPT) website.

Additionally, if you plan to work for a company that transports large sums of money or valuable items you will also need a Security Industry Authority (SIA) licence. This can be obtained on completion of the National Open College Network (NOCN) Level 2 Award in Cash and Valuables Transit.

What the work involves

You could be responsible for the safe transportation and delivery of a variety of goods, including food and drink, parcels and domestic appliances.

You will be loading and unloading goods from your vehicle, and making sure that your load is secure prior to starting on your journey. You will also be responsible for ensuring that your van is well maintained and roadworthy.

You will need to organise your own delivery schedule in order to meet strict distribution times each day.

Type of person suited to this work

You will need to be an extremely competent driver and be able to focus for long periods of time.

You should have a polite manner in order to build good relationships with colleagues and customers. You should be physically fit, as you might need to load and unload heavy items from your van.

Good map reading and navigational skills are helpful for finding your way round new and unfamiliar areas on a delivery. It is also important to be reliable and to stay calm in hazardous situations.

Working conditions

You might need to work 37–40 hours in shifts over evenings and weekends. Other companies will only deliver goods during standard working hours. Part-time work is often available.

You might work on your own or with another person who will help navigate and plan your route, and assist with loading and unloading goods.

You will spend the majority of your time in the van, and will have to drive and meet time-restricted schedules no matter what the weather. You might have to wear a uniform.

Future prospects

The rise of internet shopping has resulted in an increase in opportunities for delivery drivers and there is demand for drivers all over the UK, so you could work anywhere, although most opportunities are found in larger towns and cities.

You could work for a variety of companies, including retail, manufacturing and supermarkets, or you could opt for self-employment or start up your own delivery company.

You could choose to move into a related area in transport, such as an administrative or transport manager post.

Advantages/disadvantages

Part-time and flexible hours are available so you can fit work around other commitments.

You will be providing a valuable service to people, either delivering food or appliances to their homes, or transporting parcels or money safely around the UK.

The work can be quite lonely as you may work for long periods on your own.

Money guide

Starting salaries for full-time van drivers are usually around £11,000 to £13,000.

With experience this could rise to between £15,000 and £26,000.

Most van drivers earn around £19,000 to £21,000. You can increase your wage by working overtime and some employers give bonuses for attendance or reaching work targets.

Related opportunities

- Chauffeur p587
- Large Goods Vehicle Driver p596
- Train Driver p612

Further information

Driver and Vehicle Standards Agency
www.gov.uk/government/organisations/driver-and-vehicle-standards-agency

National Open College Network
www.nocn.org.uk

DISTRIBUTION MANAGER

Qualifications and courses

It is possible to enter this role without a degree by working your way up from a transport clerk position, however an increasing number of candidates are graduates with either degrees, Foundation degrees or HNCs/HNDs. Any subject can be accepted but some employers may specifically prefer candidates with a degree in logistics and/or transport and distribution management. There are only a few undergraduate degrees in this subject but a growing number of postgraduate courses. Degrees in areas such as geography and supply chain management can also be useful.

The general entry requirements for a degree are 2 A levels/3 H grades and 5 GCSEs/National 5s (A*–C/A–C). Entry for an HNC/HND requires a minimum of 4 GCSEs/National 5s (A*–C/A–C) and 1 A level/2 H grades, a related BTEC National Certificate/Diploma or equivalent.

Most companies are unlikely to take on new graduates in managerial roles, preferring several years' experience within the industry, however some larger organisations do have graduate recruitment schemes. Competition for these can be high so relevant work experience in areas such as retail, storage, warehousing or administration may be useful.

Apprenticeships are available in Traffic Office, Logistics Operations Management and Warehousing and Storage. You could also study for the Edexcel Level 5 Diploma in Supply Chain Management.

People working in the industry can study for the Chartered Institute of Logistics and Transport's (CILT's) professional qualifications. The Level 2 Certificate in Logistics and Transport is suitable for employees new to the profession. The Advanced Diploma is intended for recent graduates and is meant to be between undergraduate and postgraduate level.

What the work involves

You will be responsible for overseeing the control and movement of goods or raw materials held in stock.

Using IT, you will manage stock levels and monitor the ordering and storage of goods.

You will also manage staff and carry out their recruitment and training.

Type of person suited to this work

Distribution is a fast-moving industry and IT is at its centre, so you will need excellent computer skills. Like the computer programs you will use, you will need to be systematic and logical.

Brilliant communication skills are also a necessity as you will have to deal with people at different levels. It might be that the goods you have to order come from far-flung places. This means that the supply chain you will be managing might be very complex.

You will also need to be able to deal with the stress of making sure that you get the goods at the best price and supply them in the right condition.

Working conditions

Most of your work will be in an office, but you will also travel to meetings with suppliers or customers and visit storage depots.

Your hours will be mainly office hours, Monday–Friday, but you might have to do shift work or work weekends and evenings on a rota system.

There could be travel away from home and, for some, travel overseas.

Future prospects

Career development opportunities are good at the moment and there is a demand for experienced managers. You could work for a wide range of companies, including warehouse and distribution firms but also manufacturers, major retail companies, the armed forces and central and local government.

With experience, you could progress into a senior role in business development or undertake consultancy work.

Advantages/disadvantages

As a key figure in your company, you will have the satisfaction of making sure your supply chain works and that your customers are happy.

The demands of coordinating vehicles, products, people and tight deadlines, can make this a stressful role.

Money guide

Salaries for new graduates start at around £16,000 to £19,000 per year.

More experienced employees with management duties can earn around £30,000, possibly more in larger companies.

Senior distribution managers responsible for transport schedules can earn £45,000 to £60,000 per year. More is possible depending on the company size and various other factors. Managers often receive performance-related bonuses, health insurance, company cars and other benefits.

Related opportunities

- Freight Forwarder p593
- Importer/Exporter p595
- Warehouse Worker/Manager p613

Further information

Chartered Institute of Logistics and Transport
www.ciltuk.org.uk

Freight Transport Association
www.fta.co.uk

Qualifications and courses

You must be registered with the Driver & Vehicle Standards Agency (DVSA) as an Approved Driving Instructor (ADI). You will need to be 21 years old or over and have held a full clean driving licence for at least 3 years, with no disqualifications, criminal or motoring convictions and no more than 5 penalty points.

Before you register with the DVSA you must get a Disclosure and Barring Service (DBS) check for driving instructors. After registering you need to take 3 qualifying tests: an IT-based multiple choice theory test and video-based hazard perceptions test; a practical driving test; and a practical teaching test. Parts 2 and 3 must be completed within 2 years of completing part 1. You can take part 1 as many times as necessary but you must pass the others within 3 attempts each. If not you will have to wait 2 years from when you took part 1 and start again.

After you have passed the first 2 exams you could apply for the trainee licensing scheme. This is not essential but you will gain experience of driving instruction, for which you will have the right to receive payment. Once you pass all 3 tests you can apply for your first ADI badge.

The majority of entrants join a training organisation or an organisation which provides franchise prospects if you complete the training. Most trainees fund the training themselves, which can be expensive.

To continue to practise as a driving instructor you must pass the ADI Standards Check once every 4 years.

What the work involves

You will teach people how to drive safely, and well enough to pass their driving test. You will explain basic motor and road skills as well as safe and courteous driving.

Your role will include making your pupils aware of all aspects of the Highway Code, helping to develop observation skills and teaching manoeuvres such as reverse parking.

It will be your responsibility to plan driving lessons to suit your pupils and give constructive criticism.

Type of person suited to this work

Not only will you need to be a good, safe driver, you will also need teaching skills. People learning to drive are often nervous, susceptible to stress and anxious, so you will need to be calm, steady and very patient.

Instructors need to plan lessons to cover individual weaknesses. You will need to have quick reactions in order to prevent your pupils from causing any accidents.

As many instructors are self-employed, you will need to have a good business sense and the ability to manage your own finances.

Working conditions

Instructors can spend more than 8 hours a day sitting in the car ready to operate the dual controls to avert problems.

Early morning, evening and weekend work is common as you will teach lessons at times that suit your pupils.

Instructors with lots of experience can work a 35 to 40 hour week. However, you might have to work longer hours to keep a steady income. This can restrict the times and lengths of holidays for self-employed or franchised instructors.

Future prospects

Driving instructors could work for driving schools, operate under a franchise, or have their own businesses. Opportunities are also available with big transport companies, the emergency services, local authorities and the armed forces.

Around 80% of instructors are self-employed. There are no restrictions on the numbers of instructors meaning there is sometimes strong competition for pupils.

You could undertake fleet driver training and instruction in driving large goods or passenger-carrying vehicles. You could also progress to a role as a trainer for new driving instructors or a driving examiner.

Advantages/disadvantages

It can be very rewarding to enable learners to become safe, qualified drivers.

Many driving instructors are self-employed so you can choose your own working hours.

If you run your own car to give lessons you will have to pay for fuel, insurance and maintenance costs.

It may be a challenge to maintain a steady income.

Money guide

Fees charged by instructors vary greatly because of competition in the industry, but they generally charge £15 to £30 per hour for a driving lesson. Your income will be reduced by the costs of running and maintaining your vehicle or paying a franchise fee.

Full-time driving instructors could earn £15,000 to £16,000 as a starting salary. With several years' experience this can rise to around £23,000 to £25,000.

It is possible for full-time, experienced driving instructors to earn over £30,000.

Related opportunities

- Chauffeur p587
- Taxi Driver p610
- Work-based Training Instructor p198

Further information

Driving Instructors Association
www.driving.org

UK Driving Instructors Confederation
www.ukdic.co.uk

Qualifications and courses

Entry requirements vary between employers but you will need a minimum of 4 GCSEs/National 5s, including English and Maths. Some employers may also ask for A levels/H grades or the Edexcel Level 2 Certificate in International Trade and Logistics Operations. Other useful qualifications might be a City & Guilds Level 2 Certificate in International Trade and Logistics Operations or a RQF Level 3 Certificate in Transporting Freight by Road.

Larger employers may expect a degree, HND or Foundation degree in a related subject such as logistics, supply chain management, economics or modern languages.

Entry to degree courses will require a minimum of 2 A levels/3 H grades and 5 GCSEs/National 5s (A*–C/A–C). For HNC/HND courses you will normally need at least 1 A level/2 H grades and 4 GCSEs/National 5s (A*–C/A–C).

The Apprenticeship in International Trade and Logistics can also be an entry route and some larger haulage companies run graduate training schemes for entry level candidates.

Language skills are useful and may lead to opportunities to work abroad. Previous experience in the freight industry is not required but experience in an office or in any area with a similar skill set to the freight industry is an advantage.

Edexcel Key Skills qualifications in Communication, IT, Problem-solving and Working with Others could be useful.

Professional bodies such as the British International Freight Association (BIFA) and the Chartered Institute of Logistics and Transport (UK) offer industry training programmes and qualifications that you might be encouraged or expected to take.

What the work involves

You will organise the transport of goods across the world for importers and exporters. Your role will involve working out if the freight needs special handling and whether it should go by sea, road or air.

Arranging the packing, carriage, collection and storage of the goods will be part of your job.

You will be responsible for dealing with paperwork, applying for customs clearance and calculating insurance, transport and customs costs.

Type of person suited to this work

As you will deal with lots of different customers, some of whom may not speak fluent English, you must have excellent communication skills.

You need to be determined and have excellent bargaining skills to get the best prices and terms. You will also be a good problem-solver. For example, you might have to work out how to transport a valuable racehorse from Hong Kong to the UK.

You will require strong basic maths skills as you will be asked to calculate exchange rates, or work out if a large piece of cargo will fit into the cargo hold of a small aircraft.

Working conditions

Most of your work will be in an office at a workstation using a telephone, computer and fax machine. You will also need to travel to meet customers and contractors, within the UK and possibly abroad, so you will sometimes be away from home. A driving licence would be useful.

Depending on your employer, you might work normal office hours from Monday to Friday or you might work shifts and extra hours to cover urgent deliveries and world time zones.

Future prospects

Freight forwarding offices are usually in cities and near airports and ports. Opportunities are growing but it is a competitive industry and it helps if you have related work experience.

As you progress, there are opportunities to specialise in specific countries and industries. You could work within the entertainment industry, shipping film and concert sets around the world, or with medical and pharmaceutical supplies.

After gaining experience, you could progress to become a senior freight forwarder and then to a managerial role such as export office manager.

Advantages/disadvantages

This role offers varied opportunities – you could specialise in moving film and TV crews and their equipment or handling perishable goods such as fruit.

You might get a chance to travel or work overseas.

Working to meet tight delivery deadlines can be stressful.

Money guide

Starting salaries range from £16,000 to £25,000.

With 3 to 5 years of experience you could expect to earn £25,000 to £28,000 a year.

As a senior freight forwarder, manager or director you could achieve £35,000 to £40,000.

Related opportunities

- Distribution Manager p591
- Importer/Exporter p595
- Warehouse Worker/Manager p613

Further information

Chartered Institute of Logistics and Transport
www.ciltuk.org.uk

Institute of Export
www.export.org.uk

HELICOPTER PILOT

Qualifications and courses

To fly commercially and charge for your services you will need to be over the age of 18 and hold the Joint Aviation Authority (JAA)'s Commercial Pilot Licence (CPL(H)), which is issued by the Civil Aviation Authority (CAA).

There are 2 main routes to obtaining a CPL(H). There is an integrated course that involves full time training for 12 months to complete 500 hours of theoretical study, 135 hours of flight training, 9 exams and a flight skills test.

Alternatively, if you already have a Private Pilot's Licence for helicopter flying (PPL(H)), you may undertake modular training and qualify for your CPL(H) with 155 hours of flying experience, 500 hours of theoretical study, a 35-hour commercial flying course and 9 exams. You can take this route at your own pace, but will take at least 9 months to complete full-time.

For both of these routes you will need at least 5 GCSEs/National 5s (A*–C/A–C) including English, Maths and a science (preferably Physics). You need to pass aptitude tests and a medical exam and raise money for training as sponsorships for helicopter pilots are rare. Courses cost in the region of £45,000. You can take a trial lesson with a flight school before committing to the full course.

If you have trained as a pilot in the armed forces you can take a conversion course to get a commercial licence. To pilot a 2-crew helicopter you will need an ATPL(H) (Airline Transport Pilot Licence – Helicopter).

What the work involves

You will most likely pilot a helicopter alone and you will be responsible for the safety of your passengers. You will carry out fuel, weather and route checks before taking off and you will keep in contact with air traffic controllers whilst navigating and monitoring the helicopter during the flight.

After landing you will log your hours and details from the flight.

You may fly for a variety of purposes including searching for missing persons, emergency work, crop spraying, photography, leisure trips or ferrying supplies.

Type of person suited to this work

You must be good with maths and physics, an excellent problem solver and a quick thinker in order to control your helicopter in all weather conditions and emergency situations. Strong communication and teamwork skills are essential.

Good coordination, spatial awareness and attention to detail are also important. You could be flying long hours and you will need stamina, forward-thinking skills and the ability to stay focused on your work.

As a pilot you are responsible for other people's safety so you must be reliable.

Working conditions

Helicopter pilots are usually provided with a uniform. If you fly over the sea for emergency services you will wear a survival suit. Most of your time will be spent sitting alone in a small space.

Your helicopter will be single or multi-engine and it will take time to adjust to the noise and sensation.

If you are a pilot within the leisure and tourism industry, you will most likely work during the daytime only. Emergency and business services may require you to fly through the night and at weekends. If you undertake long journeys, you may spend time away from home.

Future prospects

There are opportunities to work in emergency services, the armed forces and for commercial companies but competition is intense for newly qualified helicopter pilots.

With 1,000 hours of flight experience and 350 hours as 'pilot in command', you can go on to get your Airline Transport Pilot Licence (Helicopter) (ATPL(H)). You can then fly multi-engine, multi-pilot helicopters for commercial air transport.

You could also set up your own air taxi service company or become self-employed.

Advantages/disadvantages

Helicopter training is expensive and you will need to raise a lot of money if you are unable to gain sponsorship.

Commercial piloting could lead you to be away from home for prolonged stretches of time, which could put a strain on your personal life.

You can meet new and interesting people during the course of your career, perhaps even celebrities.

No two days will be the same and it is exciting to be unaware of what each flight will hold.

Money guide

Newly qualified commercial helicopter pilots can earn between £20,000 and £25,000 per year.

Pilots with extensive experience captaining passenger-carrying helicopters can achieve between £45,000 and £65,000.

Allowances may be paid for overnight stays or flying to inhospitable areas.

Related opportunities

- Air Traffic Controller p583
- Airline Pilot p584
- Royal Air Force Airman/woman p549

Further information

British Helicopter Association
www.britishhelicopterassociation.org

Civil Aviation Authority
www.caa.co.uk

Qualifications and courses

There are no minimum qualifications to enter this industry but most employers will expect 4 GCSEs/National 5s (A*–C/A–C), including English and Maths. Others will ask for A levels/H grades or a relevant HND, Foundation degree or degree. Any subject that covers logistics, marketing, international trade, business or languages would be relevant at this level, although proficiency in a language subject is particularly in demand.

Entry onto degree courses requires 2 A levels/3 H grades and 5 GCSEs/National 5s. HNC/HND courses normally ask for 1 A level/H grade and 4 GCSEs/ National 5s.

Many entrants start in a junior administration or sales position within an import/export or freight-forwarding company and work their way up, though larger companies may offer graduate training schemes.

Apprenticeships in Logistics Operations Management, Business and Administration or Sales and Telesales may equip you with relevant skills for this profession.

The Institute of Export (IOE) offers professional qualifications in international trade. You can take the Advanced Certificate in International Trade, which leads to associate membership of the IOE, or the Diploma in International Trade, which leads to graduate membership. Candidates must be at least 18 years old to take these courses.

What the work involves

You will organise all aspects of exporting or importing goods for companies which source or sell them overseas.

Liaising with shipping and forwarding companies, you will get the best prices, sources, quality and delivery services.

You will deal with all the necessary financial paperwork, including invoicing and checking, and issuing letters of credit so that payment can be made. You will also work out accurate costings, customs duties, insurance and forwarding charges.

Type of person suited to this work

You should have an interest in business and trade, as well as other countries and cultures.

As you will be making arrangements with a wide range of customers, you need to be confident, tactful and an excellent communicator. Language skills are a real advantage.

Dealing with numbers will be another of your key strengths because you will be responsible for working out currency exchanges and import and export duties.

You must be a good negotiator as you will need to bargain with shipping and distribution companies, as well as your customers and suppliers.

In addition, problem-solving, IT and organisational skills are vital.

Working conditions

Most of your work will be in an office using the telephone, computer and fax machine.

You will usually work standard office hours from 9am to 5pm, Monday to Friday. You might need to work early mornings or late evenings if your customers or suppliers operate in a different time zone.

You may travel to meet suppliers or customers. At a senior level, you are likely to work overseas on a regular basis in order to maintain your network of business contacts.

Future prospects

As more products are bought and sold in a global market, the number of companies employing an import/export specialist has increased.

Freight-forwarding, industrial, retail and specialist companies such as flower, jewellery or fruit distributors all offer potential jobs.

Vacancies are competitive and usually require work experience in a related area.

Some import/export specialists move into overseas sales management or take up consultancy work.

Advantages/disadvantages

This job is satisfying as you are helping to make the global supply chain work.

You could be under a lot of stress to meet tight deadlines and budgets.

You might have the opportunity to travel overseas.

Money guide

Starting salaries at clerk level range from £11,000 to £15,000 per year.

Experienced staff with increased responsibilities can expect to earn up to £35,000.

Import or export managers of companies with global interests can achieve between £40,000 and £65,000 a year.

Related opportunities

- Freight Forwarder p593
- Road Transport Manager p609

Further information

Institute of Export
www.export.org.uk

TRANSPORT AND LOGISTICS

595

LARGE GOODS VEHICLE DRIVER

Qualifications and courses

No formal academic qualifications are required, although most employers prefer candidates who have GCSEs/National 5s (A*–E/A–E) in English and Maths.

You need to be over 18 years old, have a full clean UK driving licence, pass a medical exam, have good eyesight and hold a large goods vehicle (LGV) licence. There are 3 categories of LGV licence: a C1 licence allows you to drive a truck up to 7.5 tonnes, a C licence is for rigid vehicles of over 7.5 tonnes, and a C+E licence is for vehicles with trailers. In order to obtain an LGV licence you need to pass both a theory and a practical driving test.

All drivers need to also train for the Driver Certificate of Professional Competence (Driver CPC) which involves passing a short course. To keep your licence, you are required to do 35 hours of training every 5 years. Training providers for both the CPC and the LGV can be found on the Joint Approvals Unit for Periodic Training (JAUPT) website.

If you want to carry dangerous goods you will need to undertake training to obtain an International Carriage of Dangerous Goods by Road (ADR) certificate, which is valid for 5 years before it must be renewed.

The Apprenticeship in Driving Goods Vehicles, which is available at both Intermediate and Advanced Levels, is a possible entry route into this career.

What the work involves

You will transport thousands of tonnes of cargo in your LGV. You could carry loads such as livestock, fuel, chemicals, food or construction equipment.

Your job is to deliver the cargo to its destination on time and you will work with your transport manager to find the best, most efficient route to do so.

You will sometimes help load and unload cargo, keep the goods safe, and refuel and clean your lorry after each journey.

Type of person suited to this work

You must be an excellent driver with good maths skills as you will be navigating long distances and calculating mileages. You should be able to use your initiative and follow safety precautions.

Quick reactions, good eyesight and colour vision are useful in case you need to respond to an unforeseen event on the road. It is essential that you can stay alert for long periods of time.

Overall, you need to be an experienced, confident and punctual driver. You should be polite when dealing with customers and also be content working on your own.

Working conditions

LGV cabs are cosy and quiet, equipped with cooking facilities, bunks, air conditioning and heating. These comforts are important as you will spend hours by yourself in your lorry, eating and sleeping in the cab.

On average, you will work 48 hours per week and legislation prevents you from exceeding 60 hours. Ten hours of night driving is the maximum you may do in a 24-hour period.

Your shifts will include evenings, nights and weekends.

Future prospects

If you work for a road haulage firm you will transport loads for multiple companies. You could also work for farms, transporting livestock, or move sporting goods for retailers. You could be employed by manufacturers, for example moving fleets of cars.

You could be promoted to a supervisor, become an instructor or move into driving hazardous goods. With further training you could become a manager or start up a company, operating your own lorry.

Advantages/disadvantages

You have freedom and flexibility in your work.

The job can be adventurous as you travel to different locations.

You might need to spend long periods of time away from home which can be difficult.

It can be frustrating when you are stuck in traffic and have a deadline to meet.

Money guide

Earnings vary by geographical location and employer.

Starting salaries are typically £18,000 to £22,000 per year.

With experience and increased responsibilities you could expect to earn £23,000 to £28,000.

If you choose to drive a specialist fuel or chemical tanker then your salary can increase up to £35,000.

Overtime pay can supplement your income.

Related opportunities

- Driving Instructor p592
- Taxi Driver p610
- Train Driver p612

Further information

Driver and Vehicle Standards Agency
www.gov.uk/government/organisations/driver-and-vehicle-standards-agency

Freight Transport Association
www.fta.co.uk

Road Haulage Association
www.rha.uk.net

Qualifications and courses

There are no minimum entry qualifications for this job but basic maths is useful to work out safe loads and weights. English skills are also useful for paperwork and record keeping. You may have to pass a medical exam and an aptitude test as part of the application process and it is important to be in good physical condition.

You will need to be at least 18 years old to work without supervision, although you can start training at the age of 16. A driving licence is required if the truck is to be used on public roads.

Many employers require lift truck operators to have a Construction Plant Competence Scheme (CPCS) card before starting work. To qualify you will need to pass the NVQ Level 2 in Plant Operations, as well as the Construction Skills Health and Safety Test.

Direct entry to this career is possible but it may be advantageous to have experience of working in a warehouse. An Apprenticeship in Warehousing and Storage may provide you with relevant skills for this career and would lead to relevant NVQs/SVQs at Levels 2 and 3. Alternatively, the National Forklift Truck Association runs a truck maintenance apprenticeship scheme that may prove useful.

Lift truck operators can also work towards the City & Guilds Level 2 Award for Land-based Forklift Truck Operations. Two courses are available, the Counterbalance Type or the Rough Terrain, Masted and Telescopic Types. An NVQ/SVQ Level 2 in Lift Truck Maintenance and Repair Competence (Levels 2–3) or Forklift Truck Operations may be useful.

What the work involves

Operating a lift truck with a special fork and carrying platform, you will load, unload, move and stack heavy goods.

You will activate the controls so that your fork or lifting gear is under the load, usually stored on pallets, in cages or cases, to raise it safely. This may require manoeuvring at considerable heights.

You will then drive the goods, being careful not to damage them, to their destination. This could be a transport vehicle, a depot or a warehouse. You will also need to perform routine maintenance checks to your truck.

Type of person suited to this work

An aptitude for driving is vital. You will need to be focused and alert when manoeuvring your truck in narrow spaces, always on the lookout for potential hazards. A responsible, mature outlook is required for working to strict safety rules.

You will need to be physically fit and have good coordination. You might be working for a prolonged period so good concentration and care will be needed.

Although you will operate the truck on your own, you will also need to be a team player, working alongside warehouse operatives and large goods vehicle (LGV) drivers.

Working conditions

At times you will work inside a warehouse or factory and at other times outside in loading bays. While some trucks will have cabs offering protection from the weather, you need to be prepared to get cold and wet when working outside.

Operating your equipment will mean sitting in a driving seat for long periods.

Hours vary depending on your employer. You may work regular hours from Monday to Friday, but many jobs include shift work covering evenings and weekends.

Future prospects

There are about 100,000 lift truck operators in the UK. You may be employed by the manufacturing, transport, haulage, warehouse or retail industries.

With experience, you can move into supervisory or management roles in areas such as warehousing. You could go on to train new lift truck operators.

Some large employers may train you to become an LGV driver or instructor.

Advantages/disadvantages

You may have to work unsociable hours in shift patterns that vary from week to week, which can make it hard to organise your time.

Equally, this type of shift pattern can be flexible and fulfilling.

It can be stressful to get a load out quickly but it is very satisfying when transport leaves on time.

Money guide

Starting wages are about £12,000 per year. With some experience, you could expect to earn £16,000.

The most experienced operators can achieve a salary of £20,000 or more.

Shift allowances and the opportunity to do overtime can increase your income.

Related opportunities

- Airport Baggage Handler p585
- Construction Plant Operator p75
- Delivery Driver p590

Further information

Association of Industrial Truck Trainers
www.aitt.co.uk

Fork Lift Truck Association
https://fork-truck.org.uk

National Plant Operators Registration Scheme
www.npors.com

TRANSPORT AND LOGISTICS

Qualifications and courses

You will need to be over 16, in good health with good eyesight, and pass a medical in order to join the Merchant Navy.

To become a rating most companies will expect you to have at least 3 GCSEs/National 5s, preferably in English, Maths and a science. If successful you will be sponsored through a training programme lasting 12 to 18 months.

Entrants wishing to become officers need either a Foundation degree/Scottish Professional Diploma in Nautical Science or Marine Operations, an HNC/HND in Nautical Science or an Honours degree in nautical science, merchant ship operations or marine studies. The general entry requirements for a degree are 2 A levels/3 H grades and 5 GCSEs/National 5s (A*–C/A–C). Full details of entry requirements can be found on the Merchant Navy Training Board website.

If successful in your officer application you will be trained over 3 to 4 years and study for academic qualifications whilst gaining on-the-job experience. Completion of training leads to the Maritime and Coastguard Agency Officer of the Watch Certificate of Competency.

You may also be considered for an officer role if you have previous relevant experience or if you were formerly a Royal Navy officer. For graduates, having evidence of teamwork, for example through activities such as the Duke of Edinburgh's Award, Sea Cadets, boating or sailing, will give you an advantage when applying.

What the work involves

The Merchant Navy consists of thousands of civilian ships, operated by individual shipping companies. They include fuel tankers and cargo ships, as well as ferries and cruise liners.

Merchant Navy deck officers are responsible for navigating ships, as well as being involved in communications and cargo handling.

Deck ratings are responsible for supporting the ship's officers by helping to navigate and steer the ship, as well as carrying out maintenance tasks and helping to load and unload cargo.

Both jobs will involve using satellite and radar systems to navigate the ship, maintaining machinery and safety equipment, and training and support of junior officers and ratings.

Type of person suited to this work

Both officers and ratings need to have good social skills in order to work successfully as part of a team. You will also need to be calm and logical in the face of emergency situations.

In addition, officers will need to have excellent numeracy skills and be able to use complex technology in order to successfully make navigational calculations.

Officers will also need to have good leadership qualities, so that they inspire respect and dedication from their crew members.

Working conditions

You will expect to work shifts, known as 'watches'. These can vary in length from 4 hours on and 4 hours off, to 6 hours on and 6 hours off, or even 12 hours on and 12 hours off at times. These shifts can take place at any time.

Ratings can expect to live in close proximity to their colleagues, often in fairly cramped accommodation. Officers typically have their own private, en-suite cabin.

Generally, good leisure facilities are provided on-board so that crew can make the most of their time off.

Future prospects

Ratings can progress to seaman (Grade 2) or take a conversion course to become an officer. However, only a small number of companies offer places for trainee ratings, so there are relatively few opportunities to enter the merchant navy through this route.

There are around 800–900 places for new officers every year and competition is quite high. Officers may move into related onshore work, including shipbuilding, maritime law and ship and fleet management.

Advantages/disadvantages

You will be working within a strong team environment, so will build excellent relationships with colleagues from a variety of backgrounds.

Shift work can be exhausting.

You will have to spend long periods of time away from your family and your personal life will be severely affected.

Money guide

Trainee Merchant Navy ratings can expect to earn around £13,000 per year or less. This can increase to up to £19,000 with experience. Salaries for ratings peak around £22,000.

For officers, trainee salaries for cadets are around £7,000 to £15,000. Newly qualified deck officers may have a starting salary of £22,000 to £25,000. Senior officers' salaries can rise to £65,000 or more.

Your employer will pay for food and accommodation while at sea and holiday allowance is usually very generous. For every month you spend at sea you can get a month's paid leave.

Related opportunities

- Marine Engineer p219
- Merchant Navy Engineering Officer p599

Further information

Marine Society & Sea Cadets
www.ms-sc.org

Merchant Navy Association
www.mna.org.uk

Merchant Navy Training Board
www.mntb.org.uk

TRANSPORT AND LOGISTICS

Qualifications and courses

You will need to be at least 18, be in good health with good eyesight and pass a medical to join the Merchant Navy. You will also need to secure sponsorship from a shipping company who will provide you with work placements whilst you are at sea.

There are 4 educational routes to becoming an engineering officer, depending on your current qualifications.

The first is to study for an Honours degree in marine engineering, marine operations or nautical science. Entry requirements vary but 2 A levels/3 H grades, including maths and/or a science, and 5 GCSEs/National 5s (A*–C/A–C) are often the minimum required. Secondly, if you already have a science-based degree but it is not specifically directed towards this line of employment you will need to complete a relevant postgraduate course to boost your employability.

The third route is to study for an HNC/HND in Marine Engineering, for which you will need GCSEs/National 5s (A*–C/A–C) in English, Maths, a science and at least one other subject. Alternatively, you can study for a Foundation Diploma in Marine or Mechanical Engineering which requires the same GCSEs along with 2 A levels/H grades.

Whichever training route you follow, you will need to take and pass an exam for the Certificate of Competency (also known as the Officer of the Watch Certificate), which is distributed by the Coastguard and Maritime Agency.

Evidence of teamwork, for example through activities such as the Duke of Edinburgh's Award, Sea Cadets, boating or sailing, will give you an edge when applying for positions.

What the work involves

The Merchant Navy consists of thousands of civilian ships, operated by individual shipping companies. They include fuel tankers and cargo ships, as well as ferries and cruise liners. Merchant Navy engineering officers work with all the mechanical and electrical equipment onboard ships.

You will work on areas of the ship such as the engines, the computer-controlled engine management systems, and the pumps and fuel systems.

Engineering officers are based in the engine control room of a ship. They are responsible for assisting in the repair and servicing of technical equipment.

Type of person suited to this work

You will need to be interested in working with very high-tech machinery and enjoy learning about new, state-of-the-art technology.

You will also need to be very practical and logical so that you can work quickly and efficiently to rectify problems that occur with the equipment.

You should enjoy working as part of a close-knit team and have a high level of self-discipline. Impeccable communication skills are essential for these roles.

Working conditions

You will expect to work shifts, known as 'watches'. These can vary in length from 4 hours on and 4 hours off, to 6 hours on and 6 hours off, or even 12 hours on and 12 hours off at times. These shifts can take place at any time, day or night.

You will spend the majority of your time in the engine control room or the engine room itself, where it will be hot and noisy. As an engineering officer you could be responsible for all of the ship's systems.

Generally, good leisure facilities are provided on-board so that crew can make the most of their time off.

Future prospects

Opportunities for work are good as the marine sector is growing. Most people who undertake officer training programmes are employed at the end of it.

Officers may rise through the ranks to reach the level of chief engineer. Alternatively, there are also opportunities in related areas such as ship surveying or ship management.

There are also opportunities to work for companies based overseas.

Advantages/disadvantages

You will be working within a strong team environment, so will build excellent relationships with colleagues from a variety of backgrounds.

The relentless nature of shift work can be exhausting.

You will have to spend long periods of time away from your family so your personal life is severely affected.

Money guide

Sponsored trainee salaries are roughly £7,000 to £8,000 per year. Once you are qualified this jumps significantly to around £20,000 to £25,000 a year.

Chief engineers can earn up to £60,000.

Whilst at sea, your food and accommodation will be paid for by your employer. Holiday leave is usually very generous. For every month you spend at sea you will get a month's paid leave.

Related opportunities

- Marine Engineer p219
- Mechanical Engineer p221
- Motor Vehicle Technician p222
- Royal Navy Rating p554

Further information

Merchant Navy Association
www.mna.org.uk

Merchant Navy Training Board
www.mntb.org.uk

TRANSPORT AND LOGISTICS

Qualifications and courses

Entry requirements vary, but many employers prefer applicants with 3–5 GCSEs/National 5s (A*–C/A–C), including English and Maths. Some companies may require you to be at least 18 years old.

Employers may ask for experience of working in a customer service role or the ability to speak another language. As shifts will often be at unsocial hours you will need to live near the airport and possibly have your own transport.

You may be able to get into this role through an Apprenticeship in Aviation Operations on the Ground which combines professional work experience with the study of an industry-related qualification, such as a GCSE/National 5 or A level/H grade in Leisure and Tourism, a BTEC or NVQ/SVQ in Travel and Tourism, Customer Service or Aviation Operations, or Key Skills in Communication or Information Technology.

Once employed you will be trained for 4 to 8 weeks in all aspects of the job.

What the work involves

You will be responsible for making sure that passengers and their baggage board the right aircraft.

You will greet passengers, provide information, ask security questions and check tickets and passport details. You will also handle passenger enquiries.

Once you have weighed and put luggage on the conveyor belt, you will issue boarding passes and prepare paperwork for customs. You could also work at the flight gate, making announcements and checking boarding cards.

If a passenger is late, you may need to contact boarding staff to let them know and assist the passenger in reaching the gate quickly.

Type of person suited to this work

As the public face of your airline, you will need a pleasant, confident and helpful manner with a well-groomed appearance.

You need to be confident with IT as you will use a sophisticated computer system to allocate seats, print boarding cards and baggage labels and produce post-flight figures.

You must be friendly and approachable as you will be helping passengers, including those with disabilities and unaccompanied children, from check-in, through security, and onto their flight. You will also need to be able to deal with difficult situations. Good communication skills are essential for working with your colleagues and other airport staff.

Working conditions

You will wear a uniform and work indoors at an airport. When you are working at the check-in desk you may sit behind a counter for long periods.

If you are escorting passengers or helping with boarding at a gate, you will spend periods of time on your feet, sometimes walking quite long distances and carrying luggage.

Hours will include shifts covering evenings, weekends and holidays. This is done to cover all the times the airport is open.

Future prospects

Employers are either airlines or the ground handling companies that work on their behalf.

There are currently around 138,000 people working in this sector in total and opportunities for work increase dramatically if you live within travelling distance of one of the big four UK airports – Heathrow, Gatwick, Stansted and Manchester. There is a lot of competition for jobs, many of which are seasonal.

You could progress to be a member of the air cabin crew or a supervisor within passenger services.

Advantages/disadvantages

You will get to meet all types of new people from across the world.

If there is a delay to their flight, you might have to deal with difficult or demanding passengers.

If you are keen to work as a member of air cabin crew or similar role, experience in this work will be a big advantage.

Money guide

Starting salaries are between £12,000 and £14,000 per year.

Experienced passenger check-in officers can earn between £15,000 and £20,000.

In a supervisory or management post you could earn more.

Shift allowances are usually paid for working unsocial hours and there may be opportunities to earn overtime pay or increased salaries for candidates with a special skill such as fluency in a foreign language.

Some airline companies grant their employees free parking and concessions on flight costs and at retail outlets at the airport.

Related opportunities

- Air Cabin Crew p582
- Holiday Representative p368
- Tour Guide/Manager p376

Further information

GoSkills
www.goskills.com

Royal Aeronautical Society
www.aerosociety.com

Qualifications and courses

There are no formal qualifications required to enter this profession, however GCSEs/National 5s in English and Maths (A*–C/A–C) may be useful.

Experience of retail or customer service could be helpful in securing you this job. Useful courses include the BTEC Certificate in Travel Services (Levels 2-3), the Level 2 BTEC Award for Principles of Customer Service in Hospitality, Leisure, Travel and Tourism and the Level 2 BTEC Award for Cultural Awareness in Customer Service for Hospitality, Leisure, Travel and Tourism.

You will learn largely on the job, although some training might be provided and many companies will provide their own in-house training, or organise day-release training for clerical staff.

If you are going into a position as a rail passenger transport clerk or a member of telephone enquiry bureau staff, you will be trained in fare structures, customer care, railway geography and computerised ticket systems.

You may also be provided with training from bus and coach companies which will involve learning how to use timetables, and ticket systems, and understanding price structures and customer care information.

What the work involves

As a passenger transport clerk you will deal with customer enquiries regarding departure times, fares, routes, connections and disruptions on bus and rail services.

You will use computerised systems to organise the purchase or refund of tickets and in order to issue travel cards.

You will research the best rail or coach fares for a customer and ensure that their transport is as efficient and affordable as possible.

You may specialise in either sales or customer enquiries but usually members of staff share these responsibilities amongst themselves.

Type of person suited to this work

You should be friendly and polite and have a genuine interest in travel, customer service and working with the public.

Some maths and IT skills will be necessary as you will be dealing with fares and payments.

You must be able to work quickly and efficiently so that passengers are not delayed getting to their train/bus.

As you might have to deal with customers at busy times or times when there are unexpected delays, you need to have patience and the ability to deal with frustrated or angry customers. Good oral communication skills are therefore important.

Working conditions

You will work an average of 37 to 40 hours each week. This may include shift work, evenings, weekends and even public holidays.

You may have the opportunity to work part time, overtime and flexible hours.

You will be based in stations, or travel centres which will function essentially as an office, but you will deal with customers on the phone or as they come to the ticket office or information desk you are based at.

Future prospects

Further training and qualifications will aid future progression. You may gain NVQs/SVQs as you work in order to progress to supervisory and managerial roles.

You may be employed by any bus or coach operator or private rail companies, train operating companies throughout the UK, the London Underground or Eurostar.

Advantages/disadvantages

You will have the opportunity to work in an ever-changing environment as bus and rail services are constantly updated.

Assisting members of the public with their queries can provide variety, but delays and cancellations can also create a stressful situation having to deal with customer anger.

Your work is likely to often be repetitive, doing similar tasks on a daily basis.

The opportunities for progression without further training and qualifications are not great.

Money guide

Your starting salary as a transport clerk may be around £14,500 a year.

With some experience this can increase to £17,000.

With several years' experience and qualifications, you can earn between £19,500 and £22,500.

Related opportunities

- Customer Services Assistant/Manager p468
- Passenger Check-in Officer p600
- Train Conductor/Guard p611
- Travel Agent p379

Further information

Customer Contact Association
www.cca-global.com

GoSkills
www.goskills.com

TRANSPORT AND LOGISTICS

601

POSTAL DELIVERY WORKER

Qualifications and courses

No specific qualifications are required for this job, however candidates should be aged 18 or over. Selection for employment is by an aptitude test, a fitness assessment and interview. You might need to pass a medical examination or test to ensure that you can read addresses properly and spot any mistakes.

The ability to ride a bicycle and/or possession of a driving licence with no more than 6 penalty points may also be required.

Apprenticeships are available from the Royal Mail and these combine professional work experience with the opportunity to study for an industry-related qualification such as an NVQ/SVQ Level 2 in Mail Services.

Once employed you will receive induction training, with further training done, mostly, on the job and lasting 18 months. Once you have gained a minimum of a year's experience, you can seek advancement to supervisory or managerial levels.

What the work involves

You will sort and deliver post to homes, shops, factories and offices in your area.

Your day will start at the sorting office, getting your deliveries ready for transporting and packing your bag in the best order for your route.

You will then deliver the post by foot, bicycle or, in rural areas, by van. If working in a rural area you may also be responsible for delivering other goods such as milk. You might also be responsible for collections from post boxes and places of work.

Ensuring that packages are received safely, and that large packages are either left in a safe area or signed for will be important. If the recipients are not in, you will have to document and record time of delivery and reason for not delivering, if applicable.

Type of person suited to this work

Your round could include several hundred addresses and cover several miles a day so you will need to be fit, especially if you are doing the job on foot or by bicycle. You should also enjoy being outdoors as you will be expected to deliver the mail in all weathers.

Honesty and reliability are vital qualities in this job. You will be carrying lots of valuable and urgent post around and you will be responsible for delivering it to the right place.

Good customer service skills and a friendly attitude are important.

Working conditions

Most of your work will be outside in all weathers. A uniform, footwear and protective clothing will be provided. If on foot, you might have to carry your deliveries in bags, though there will be arrangements to transport you and your post out to the start of your route. You may be able to use a trolley or bicycle.

Shift work with an early morning (5am) start or late evening (10pm) finish is usual. You will often work on a Saturday. You may have the option to work overtime. Part-time jobs are widely available.

You might have to walk up steep hills and deal with minor hazards.

Future prospects

Postal delivery workers mainly work for the Royal Mail.

Recruitment tends to be steady and there are opportunities in urban and rural areas throughout the UK.

Postal work can be seasonal, particularly over the Christmas period. Some workers start out with temporary work over the Christmas period and are retained.

It is possible to move into parcel deliveries, supervisory or managerial work.

Advantages/disadvantages

With a regular round you will really get to know your customers.

There might be some hazards on your round, however all the walking or cycling will keep you fit.

Although you will have to start work by 5am if you are on the early shift, you will finish at around lunchtime.

Even if you drive for your rounds, you will still be subject to the weather conditions.

Money guide

Starting pay for staff over 18 is £13,500 a year.

After a year's experience you can expect to earn between £14,820 and £16,172.

With further experience postal delivery workers outside of London can expect to earn £19,280 and £20,405 is common for those working within London.

There are additional payments for overtime and sometimes for shift work which takes place during unsocial hours.

Related opportunities

- Courier p588
- Delivery Driver p590
- Freight Forwarder p593

Further information

Royal Mail Group
www.royalmailgroup.com

Skills for Logistics
www.skillsforlogistics.org

Qualifications and courses

Entry requirements vary but employers usually ask for a degree, though it may be possible to enter at an administrative level and progress with experience and on-the-job training. Whilst this field is open to all graduates, a degree in business studies, operations management, retail management, purchasing and logistics or purchasing and supply may be beneficial.

To progress you will need Chartered Institute of Purchasing & Supply (CIPS) professional qualifications. You can study at all levels from a Level 2 Certificate up to a Level 6 Professional Diploma. The Certificate has no formal entry requirements and once you have completed it you can progress to higher level qualifications. The CIPS diplomas are usually in Procurement and Supply or Procurement and Supply Operations at the lower levels.

Most employers will want their purchasing managers to be full members of the CIPS or working towards it. For this you need to either have a CIPS-accredited degree or have worked for 3 years and completed the Level 5 Advanced Diploma. Entry onto the Advanced Diploma course requires completion of the Diploma in Procurement and Supply. Other useful qualifications include Diplomas in supply chain management or supply chain operations.

What the work involves

You will be responsible for buying the goods or services needed by a business, and providing the best value for money.

Your first job is to find out what your employer wants to buy and how much the budget is.

An important aspect will be to find the best suppliers and negotiate with them to get products or services at the right conditions and price. You will then be responsible for quality checks to make sure that the goods or services provided are of the standard agreed.

Type of person suited to this work

You must have excellent negotiation and communication skills in order to get the best quality and lowest priced goods and services for your company.

IT and numerical skills are essential for researching, calculating costs and managing a budget.

You will need to be organised and analytical and have a good business-sense, as you will evaluate the multiple deals available to work out which is the best fit for your company.

As a result, you will also need to be decisive, making informed decisions confidently.

Working conditions

You will work Monday to Friday, from 9am to 5.30pm although longer hours may occur if you work in the manufacturing industry or if your suppliers are in a different time zone to the UK, which can mean early mornings or late nights.

You will be located in a busy office, although you may travel to meet suppliers and customers which can mean time away from home.

Future prospects

Jobs are available in nearly all areas of the business sector including manufacturing, retailers, wholesale and government organisations. There is a lot of competition for jobs but not as much as in related areas such as marketing.

Some buyers move into specialist areas, for example construction or chemicals. IT purchasing is a new specialism and is predicted to grow with the expansion of e-business.

Promotion prospects are good, especially in large organisations. It may be possible to progress to a role as director. Increasing numbers of experienced managers are choosing to become self-employed and work as consultants or contract workers.

Advantages/disadvantages

If successful, you can reach high levels of responsibility, and even travel overseas, early in your career.

This job is stressful. Businesses spend over half their money on the goods and services they need to buy, so mistakes could be expensive.

Money guide

Entry-level graduates may earn around £18,000. Junior managers can earn £20,000 to £25,000 and with time and promotion to higher levels you could earn £30,000 to £40,000. £50,000 to £100,000 or more is possible for senior managers and directors.

Members of the CIPS tend to earn more than non-members.

Related opportunities

- Distribution Manager p591
- Importer/Exporter p595
- Warehouse Worker/Manager p613

Further information

Chartered Institute of Purchasing & Supply
www.cips.org

Skills for Logistics
www.skillsforlogistics.org

TRANSPORT AND LOGISTICS

Qualifications and courses

Network Rail operates a 3-year advanced apprenticeship programme for those aged between 16 and 24, as do many other employers of rail signalling technicians. Candidates usually need to have 3 to 5 GCSEs/National 5s (A*–C/A–C), including English, Maths and a science, to apply.

Alternatively, you could apply for a Rail Infrastructure Engineering Apprenticeship. Apprenticeships combine professional work experience with the opportunity to study towards an industry-based qualification.

Most employers operate their own selection process on top of these academic requirements. This usually consists of a medical test, which will assess your fitness, eyesight and hearing, as well as drug and alcohol screening. Occasionally you may also have to sit an aptitude test.

You will be expected to work towards an Institution of Railway Signal Engineers (IRSE) licence while you're training and you will also be put through the Personal Track Safety (PTS) course, after which you will receive a safety card and be passed to work on the railway tracks.

You can also enter this profession after gaining experience as a mechanical or electrical technician in another industry. Electrical or electronics engineers with an HNC/HND and at least 3 years' experience can take Network Rail's Signal Engineering Conversion Programme.

A double GCSE/National 5 in Engineering or a related technical subject would also be helpful in finding work.

What the work involves

Rail signalling technicians are responsible for installing and repairing all of the signalling and telecommunications systems that are used to support the railways.

Equipment that you will be working on will include signal boxes, warning systems, manual lever frame boxes and coloured light signals.

You will also install new signalling equipment, such as GSM-R communication masts, and update existing systems.

Type of person suited to this work

You should have good manual dexterity in order to operate a range of tools and machines.

A logical approach to your work will help when tracing faults, as will the ability to understand technical drawings and engineering instructions when repairing systems. You will need good eyesight and full colour vision.

You should have a reasonable level of numeracy and good IT skills so that you can operate computerised machinery. You will also need to be physically fit, as the work can include lifting and carrying heavy equipment, as well as working up ladders or in awkward places.

Working conditions

You will work around 37 hours a week, most likely in a shift pattern that could include early morning, evening and weekend work. You may also be expected to work overtime fairly regularly.

Your time will be divided between working outside, carrying out repairs trackside, and undertaking maintenance near signal boxes or within stations. You should be prepared to work in any weather conditions.

You may well have to travel to various different locations each day; overnight absence from home is common.

Future prospects

You could be employed by Network Rail, working on the UK's commercial railway tracks, or by a number of underground, metro or light rail operators such as London Underground, Metronet, Translink and the Docklands Light Railway.

It is important to continue to develop your skills throughout your career, for example by taking training courses and development programmes. With experience you can become a member of the Institution of Railway Signal Engineers, which offers a route into becoming a registered engineering technician.

You could end up as a team manager or even move into a consultancy role.

Advantages/disadvantages

You will be playing an essential role in maintaining and developing the infrastructure of the UK.

Promotion opportunities are good, and there is also the chance to undertake extra training to drive forward your career.

Working in all weather conditions and cramped surroundings can be uncomfortable and extremely unpleasant at times.

Money guide

Network Rail's apprenticeship scheme starts out on a salary of £8,618, plus a £1,150 bonus when you successfully complete the first year. They also pay for your accommodation, food and work clothing. In the second year the salary rises to £12,055 and in the third year to £14,364. London allowances of up to £2,400 per year are also available.

If you become a senior technician or move into a consultancy role your salary could reach in excess of £40,000.

Related opportunities

- Electrician p80
- Electricity Distribution Worker p208
- Telecommunications Technician p154

Further information

Railway-technology.com
www.railway-technology.com

Qualifications and courses

There are no formal entry requirements, however Network Rail and other employers may look for candidates with a minimum of 4 GCSEs/National 5s (A*–C/A–C) or equivalent, including English, Maths, a science and one other technical subject. Previous experience in construction or civil engineering would be an advantage.

Qualifications in related subjects, such as a GCSE/National 5 or A level/H grade in Engineering or the City & Guilds NVQ Level 1 in Basic Track Maintenance or Level 2 Certificate in Rail Engineering, may be helpful in demonstrating your enthusiasm for the role and securing employment.

Network Rail operates a large apprenticeship programme for those aged 16–24, which provides another possible route into the profession by combining professional work experience with the opportunity to study for an industry-related qualification.

You will have to be physically fit and most employers will ask you to take a medical assessment to measure your fitness, stamina, hearing and eyesight. You will also have to take tests for drugs and alcohol.

Some employers require candidates to go through a Disclosure and Barring Service (DBS) check, as the role of a maintenance operative is critical in ensuring railway safety.

Your employer will send you on the Personal Track Safety (PTS) course to earn a safety card, which you will need before you can work on the tracks.

What the work involves

Rail track maintenance workers are responsible for building, repairing and maintaining the rail track network across the UK.

You will use a variety of manual and automated tools including welding equipment, clamping machines and cement mixers.

You will also be responsible for inspecting the track in order to spot potential faults, which will involve walking along live tracks, with trains passing nearby.

Type of person suited to this work

You will need to be fit and strong to undertake this work, as you will be lifting and moving heavy pieces of track, as well as operating powerful machinery at times. You should also have good manual skills in order to use tools effectively and safely.

You must be a good communicator so you can work effectively within a team. You should be able to listen to instructions and take direction, whilst also having the confidence to use your own initiative and help colleagues when necessary.

You should have a good awareness of on-site safety practice and a responsible attitude to your work.

Working conditions

You will work an average of 37 hours per week on a shift system. You will have to work nights, weekends and bank holidays regularly, as these are the times at which maintenance work causes least disruption to the train timetable.

Work usually takes place outdoors, in all weather conditions. You should be prepared to get cold and wet working in muddy conditions, and also extremely hot in the summer months.

You will have to wear protective clothing; including a hard hat, high visibility jacket and reinforced boots.

Future prospects

Network Rail employs almost all the rail track maintenance workers in the UK and they continuously update track all around the country.

There are also opportunities with rail employment agencies, who recruit workers for specific projects managed by rail engineering contractors.

With experience, you could progress to a supervisory role or become a specialist in a technical area such as line-laying or welding.

Advantages/disadvantages

The work is physically tiring but rewarding, as you will be working towards maintaining the infrastructure of the UK.

You will be working in a team, so the job will be sociable and you will build strong relationships with your colleagues.

Working in all weather conditions can be uncomfortable and extremely unpleasant at times.

Money guide

Your salary as an apprentice rail track worker will be between £8,618 and £14,364 per year, depending on which year of the apprenticeship you are in.

The average starting pay for a rail track worker is about £14,000 per year.

Once you have spent a few years in the role and built up your skills you could be earning £20,000 or more.

Rail track workers with additional supervisory responsibilities can earn up to £30,000.

Related opportunities

- Bricklayer p62
- Rail Signalling Technician p604
- Stonemason p110

Further information

Institute of Mechanical Engineers
www.imeche.org

Network Rail
www.networkrail.co.uk

TRANSPORT AND LOGISTICS

605

Qualifications and courses

You must be at least 18 years of age to do this job. Good communication skills and numerical ability are viewed as extremely important by employers, so most train operating companies (TOCs) require candidates to have 4 GCSEs/National 5s (A*–E/A–E), including English and Maths. You may be tested on these skills during interviews as well as being required to pass medical assessments, which will include eyesight, colour vision and hearing tests, and having to have occasional drugs and alcohol testing.

Employers favour candidates who have previous experience in customer relations roles, whether paid or voluntary.

Candidates usually apply directly to TOCs or Network Rail. Once employed as a railway station assistant, you will have to undergo a short training period that will encompass classroom-based learning programmes including health and safety, customer care, railway operating systems and coping in emergency situations. This will be followed by practical training in the station. Some TOCs also encourage employees to work towards a NVQ Level 2 in Rail Services as part of their training.

What the work involves

Railway station assistants work within train stations, assisting customers, dealing with queries and ensuring that passengers are happy.

You may work behind a ticket desk, on an information stand, or on the station platforms so that you are accessible to passengers.

You will need to provide assistance to wheelchair users and other people who require help boarding or disembarking from a train. You will check tickets, and be on the lookout for any security threats or other problems within the station.

You will also keep up to date with arrivals information, directing passengers to the correct platform and informing them about delays and possible other routes they can take.

Type of person suited to this work

You will need to be a confident communicator so that you can impart information to passengers, and also field any negative comments that might be directed towards you.

You should be polite and approachable, and maintain a clean, smart appearance. You will need good hearing and eyesight, as well as a high level of fitness in order to physically assist customers and move around the station quickly when necessary.

You should be able to work well within a team, taking instructions and helping colleagues, but also enjoy working autonomously and using your initiative.

Working conditions

You will usually work 37 hours per week, and this will include early morning, late night and weekend shifts.

There are usually opportunities to undertake paid overtime work.

You will also be working within ticket offices or passenger information areas in the station. You will have to wear a uniform so that you are easily recognisable to passengers.

Future prospects

You could work either for a train operating company or for Network Rail, within large or small train stations across the UK.

There are also opportunities to work for underground or metro operators in some cities.

You could progress as a ticket inspector, conductor or driver, move upwards to become assistant station manager or even reach the position of station manager.

Advantages/disadvantages

You will be working in a variety of roles each day so work should not get monotonous.

You will spend a lot of time on freezing station platforms in the winter.

You may have to deal with aggressive passengers at times.

Money guide

Your starting salary as a railway station assistant is likely to be about £12,500 to £13,500 per year.

As you gain experience and knowledge, you could earn from £14,000 up to around £21,000. If you are promoted to team leader your salary will increase to £21,000 or more.

Overtime is always available, so your wages could be increased if you are willing to work extra hours. Benefits can sometimes include free or reduced travel.

Related opportunities

- Rail Track Maintenance Operative p605
- Train Conductor/Guard p611
- Train Driver p612

Further information

National Rail Enquiries
www.nationalrail.co.uk

Network Rail
www.networkrail.co.uk

Qualifications and courses

No formal academic qualifications are required, although GCSEs/National 5s (A*–E/A–E) in English and Maths are useful. While some firms will accept you at 16 years old, many specify a minimum age of 18 or even 21. It is important that you are physically fit and you may need to pass a medical in order to be successfully employed.

To work as a removals operative driver you will need a large goods vehicle (LGV) licence, as well as a Driver Certificate of Professional Competence (Driver CPC). You must be at least 18 years old to train for an LGV licence and you will be required to undertake both a theory and a practical driving test.

Edexcel offers an Award, Certificate and Diploma in Commercial Moving (Levels 1–3) which may be useful or you can enter this job through the Intermediate Apprenticeship in Commercial Moving. Experience in delivery driving, warehousing or other related areas can give you an advantage when applying for this course or apprenticeship scheme.

Most entrants are trained on the job by experienced colleagues. Some firms send employees on courses run by the British Association of Removers (BAR). Statutory training covers topics such as health and safety, manual handling and risk assessment, while skills training is offered in areas including fragile, commercial and specialist packing. You may be able to take NVQs/SVQs in Warehousing and Storage (Levels 1–2) or in Driving Goods Vehicles (Levels 2–3).

What the work involves

Removals operatives move furniture, garden, household and office items into storage or to new sites. This involves carefully packing goods and taking apart large items to fit into the removals van.

You must plan how you will pack the van in advance to make the most of the space and to prevent damage to the goods during transit. You will also need to unload and unpack as well as placing items in specific places on arrival, at the customer's direction.

Type of person suited to this work

Your customers will most likely be stressed about moving and will rely on you to remain calm and cheerful. You should be friendly and personable.

An honest and careful approach to your work is vital as you will be dealing with valuable and fragile items on a regular basis. You should also be a team player and able to follow instructions.

It is important that you are physically fit and enjoy practical work. You will be lifting and carrying large items and sometimes removing door or window frames to get items out of or into a property.

Working conditions

You will spend the majority of your time in the cab of your van. Your job may sometimes involve overnight and long-distance journeys and you should be prepared to spend time away from home.

Removals operatives usually work a 40-hour week but some days will require working overtime until the job is finished. A lot of moves take place at weekends.

All the lifting, carrying and bending involved may put you at risk of back injury.

Future prospects

Although you will find removals companies throughout the UK, urban areas are the best places to look for vacancies as thousands of people and businesses are constantly on the move in these hubs.

You may find that drops in the housing market and the condition of the economy can affect the number of jobs available.

With further training, such as the management courses offered by BAR, you may be promoted to specialist packer, foreperson, removals estimator, supervisor or manager.

You could also buy or lease a van and set up your own removals service.

Advantages/disadvantages

You might need to start early and work late, especially when legal processes can delay house removals.

You will be satisfied by your efforts and professionalism when you finish a move.

Happy customers may reward you with tips!

Money guide

Starting salaries range from £10,000 to £15,000 per year.

Experienced removals operatives earn an average of £20,000 per year. Senior staff can receive up to £30,000.

Overtime pay, shift allowances and tips can all increase your income.

Related opportunities

- Airport Baggage Handler p585
- Delivery Driver p590
- Roadie p431

Further information

British Association of Removers
www.bar.co.uk

Skills for Logistics
www.skillsforlogistics.org

TRANSPORT AND LOGISTICS

Qualifications and courses

Although there are no formal entry requirements to this job, most entrants are graduates who hold qualifications in subjects such as transport management and transport safety. The general entry requirements for a degree are 2 A levels/3 H grades and 5 GCSEs/National 5s (A*–C/A–C). It is important to note, however, that experience and personal qualities are as important, if not more important, to employers and a driving licence is essential.

The Manchester College (MANCAT) is the only college in the UK that offers a BTEC Professional Development Diploma in Accident and Safety Management. For entry to the course you will need at least 1 A level/H grade and GCSEs/National 5s (A*–C/A–C) in Maths and English. It is also possible to work towards an NVQ/SVQ in Transportation (Levels 3–5).

The National Staff Training Group offers a training programme for road safety officers. Phase 1 provides training for newly appointed officers, phase 2 consists of a residential short course and phase 3 involves a series of seminars. Completion of phase 2 training can lead to Associate Membership of the Institute of Road Safety Officers (IRSO).

Requirements for becoming a member of IRSO are a relevant degree, a BTEC Professional Development Diploma in Accident and Safety Management, or NVQ/SVQ in Road Safety (Levels 3–4).

What the work involves

You will be working to reduce the number of motorists, cyclists and pedestrians injured or killed on the roads in your area.

You will educate the public by giving presentations to groups, particularly children and primary schools. Promoting national road safety campaigns by distributing leaflets and running exhibitions could also be part of your job.

You will collect information about traffic accidents and make recommendations about how to prevent them.

Type of person suited to this work

As this job involves a lot of marketing and raising public awareness through presentations, you will need to be an excellent communicator in all areas. You will use these skills to develop publicity materials and encourage people to behave more responsibly on the roads.

Self-confidence is vital to build good working relationships with safety engineers, police officers and local councillors.

To persuade others, you may find that an aptitude for teaching may be useful when working with all age groups. You could give advice outside supermarkets on fitting child car seats, or teach small groups of young children how to cross the road safely.

You will need to be conscientious and diligent to help push and promote the importance of road safety.

Working conditions

Most of your work will be office based, but you will also visit schools and other locations. You will usually work 37 hours a week, Monday to Friday. Some evening work is required.

When working on-site with engineers, or when investigating accidents, you must wear high visibility clothing.

Your office work will involve using a computer to collect and analyse information.

Future prospects

Road safety officers are usually employed by local authorities. Some jobs are temporary as they are paid for by short-term government funding.

You could be promoted to manager or to a specialist post, for example, in publicity or working with schools. You might also find a job coordinating national safety and environmental initiatives, for example, the National Walk to School Campaign.

Advantages/disadvantages

You will receive great satisfaction in saving lives and seeing death and injury figures reduced in your area.

There may be chances to implement your own initiatives and campaigns, and the opportunity to inspire children and improve their awareness of road safety is particularly rewarding.

There might be delays or obstacles to putting in place the safety improvement work you have recommended, which can be frustrating.

Money guide

Newly qualified officers earn £18,000.

With experience you can earn up to £25,000 a year.

Officers with management responsibility can earn £40,000.

If you are a senior manager this can rise to over £50,000.

Local authorities may offer essential car user allowances as well as bonuses.

Related opportunities

- Community Education Officer p180
- Health and Safety Adviser p27
- Police Officer p543

Further information

Institute of Road Safety Officers
www.irso.org.uk

Workforce - Local Government Association
www.local.gov.uk/workforce

Qualifications and courses

It is possible to enter the transport industry with qualifications ranging from a few GCSEs/National 5s, including English and Maths, to a degree. Some companies offer Apprenticeships/Skillseekers in Logistics Operations Management which will combine professional work experience with the opportunity to study for an industry-relevant qualification. Alternatively, you can also start out as a driver, administrator or team leader and work your way up.

Some companies recruit graduates to management trainee programmes and it is possible to enter these with a degree in any subject although there are specialist degree courses available in transport management, transport planning and logistics. The general entry requirements for a degree are 2 A levels/3 H grades and 5 GCSEs/National 5s (A*–C/A–C).

Once working you can study for a variety of other qualifications, including NVQs/SVQs in Traffic Office (Levels 2–3). Postgraduate courses are available as well, for example the Chartered Institute of Logistics and Transport (CILT) offers master's programmes in partnership with different universities. CILT also offers a number of qualifications in transport planning such as a Certificate in Logistics and Transport.

By law, each road transport business has to have at least one member of staff who has a Certificate of Professional Competence (CPC). This would normally be the manager, so you should train for this as soon as you start work if you want to progress.

What the work involves

You will work for a business that moves goods or passengers, planning the routes and work timetables of your drivers.

You will oversee the day-to-day movement of your vehicles, checking that they are in the right places at the right times.

Implementing health and safety regulations, and monitoring compliance, will be part of your role. Your job will include checking costs to make sure that your company makes a profit.

Type of person suited to this work

Planning timetables, journeys and loads means that you will need to be organised. You should also be logical and enjoy using computers to manage and develop information.

You will cost up journeys, work out timetables and stick to a strict budget, so you must enjoy working with figures.

You will need to have motivational and leadership skills, as it is your responsibility to take care of your drivers.

Working conditions

Most of your work will be based in an office. You will also spend time at vehicle depots, and might need to travel to carry out spot checks on your drivers.

Transport is a 24/7 business, so you might need to work shifts and weekends, or be called out in emergencies.

A passenger service vehicle or large goods vehicle licence will be useful.

Future prospects

Transport is a large and changing industry, and passenger transport will continue to expand. You could work for a range of employers such as logistics and distribution companies, road haulage firms, manufacturers, retail chains or coach and bus operators.

It is possible to be promoted to area or general manager. Prospects are better if you are flexible about moving to a larger company or into other modes of transport. With multinational companies there may be opportunities to work abroad.

Graduate schemes will allow for fast-track progression and moving into management.

Advantages/disadvantages

No two days are the same – traffic levels, problems and weather conditions vary from day to day.

You will have the satisfaction of seeing an instant result when you make decisions. The way you manage a problem can mean happier customers.

The job is not wholly office based, and so you could be working outside in bad weather.

Shift work can affect your social life.

Money guide

Starting salaries are usually between £22,000 and £25,000 per year.

Experienced managers can earn between £25,000 and £45,000, though this is largely dependent on the size of the company. Senior managers can earn up to £65,000.

Allowances are usually paid for shift work and unsocial hours.

Related opportunities

- Distribution Manager p591
- Freight Forwarder p593
- Warehouse Worker/Manager p613

Further information

Chartered Institute of Logistics and Transport
www.ciltuk.org.uk

TRANSPORT AND LOGISTICS

TAXI DRIVER

Qualifications and courses

It is not necessary to have any formal qualifications to become a taxi driver but you must fulfil the conditions set out by your local licensing authority prior to them granting you a licence to work.

Criteria vary across the different licensing authorities but all require applicants to have held a full driving licence for at least 12 months (3 years in London), pass an enhanced Disclosure and Barring Service (DBS) check and a medical assessment, and be over the age of 18 (21 in some areas, including London). It is also necessary to be a UK or EU citizen or to have the right to stay and work in the UK.

The strictest local licensing authority is London, which requires all registered taxi drivers to pass an extensive geographical test known as 'The Knowledge'. It can take 2 years or more to accumulate and learn all the necessary road information to pass, which includes 400 routes through London and the locations of all places of interest, including hospitals and police stations. There are a number of independent knowledge schools listed on the Transport for London website.

The Driver and Vehicle Standards Agency (DVSA) has developed a Hackney Carriage/Private Hire Test Assessment, which some licensing authorities use.

What the work involves

Taxi drivers pick up and transport passengers between destinations in a licensed vehicle for an agreed fee.

You could either drive your own black cab (also known as a hackney carriage) or operate a private hire vehicle (more commonly called a minicab).

If you drive a black cab, you will be able to pick up people who are waiting at a taxi rank, in the street, or those who have pre-booked. Minicabs are only allowed to carry pre-booked passengers. You will also need to assist passengers in and out of your vehicle, and help them with bags as necessary.

Type of person suited to this work

You will need to be personable and pleasant to passengers but also have the confidence to handle difficult or aggressive customers should the need arise. You should be numerate, as you will be handling money regularly and you will need to ensure that you give passengers the correct change.

You must have an extensive knowledge of the local area in which you operate so you will need a good memory and sense of direction.

Working conditions

Your working hours will vary according to your employment terms. If you work for a company, you may undertake shifts that include night and weekend hours whereas self-employed drivers can choose their own hours.

Most work is available in larger towns and cities, and taxi drivers are busiest on Friday and Saturday nights when people are looking to go home after a night out.

You will spend the majority of your time in your vehicle, either driving passengers to their destination, or waiting for a job to come up.

Future prospects

Smartphone apps, satnavs and new start-up companies are increasing and the ways people get taxis are changing, meaning that competition is potentially broadening among taxi firms.

New technology is also having an impact on the black cabs of London. Though, unlike black cabs, minicabs cannot be flagged down, new technology is making them increasingly accessible.

Although you can work anywhere in the UK, the majority of work is focused within the larger towns and cities.

Many taxi drivers are self-employed. With experience and knowledge you could gain an operator's licence and build up your own company.

Advantages/disadvantages

You will be dealing with a variety of people and different routes on a daily basis so the work is sociable and interesting.

You will be confined to your vehicle for most of your working day, and you may spend long periods of time waiting around between jobs.

You will occasionally have to deal with drunk, aggressive or distressed passengers.

If self-employed, you often have the freedom to choose your own hours.

Money guide

Taxi drivers who work around 40 hours a week in a major city and take a good amount of fares could earn between £12,000 and £20,000 a year.

Some drivers can achieve up to £30,000 a year but you must be prepared to work long hours.

Long distance driving or night work may earn higher fares. Drivers have to pay for fuel, car insurance, licensing and maintenance, though these may be paid for by your employer if you work for a taxi or private hire firm.

Related opportunities

- Chauffeur p587
- Driving Instructor p592
- Tour Guide/Manager p376

Further information

Driver and Vehicle Standards Agency
www.gov.uk/government/organisations/driver-and-vehicle-standards-agency

Licensed Taxi Drivers Association
www.ltda.co.uk

Qualifications and courses

Although there are no set qualifications to become a train conductor, train operating companies (TOCs) usually look for candidates with good basic maths and English skills, so GCSEs/National 5s (A*–C/A–C) or equivalent in those subjects would be ideal.

You will need to be 18 years of age before you are legally allowed to work on-board a train but you can work within a railway station from the age of 16, which could help you build up the customer service skills that employers desire in candidates applying for conductor roles. You could get into this line of work through an Apprenticeship in Rail Services.

When you apply to be a conductor, you will need to pass a series of tests designed to assess your suitability. These include a full medical to gauge your level of fitness, eyesight, colour vision and hearing. You might also need to pass memory, comprehension and concentration tests, as well as a Disclosure and Barring Service (DBS) check. There is also a strict safety policy with regard to drugs and alcohol abuse for anyone working on a train and you may be asked to take random drugs tests throughout your career.

What the work involves

Train conductors work on passenger trains, checking and issuing tickets, and ensuring that passengers are enjoying a comfortable and pleasant journey.

You will mainly focus on providing an excellent level of customer service to those travelling in the train. This will include fielding any queries or complaints, and handling rowdy passengers at times.

You will be responsible for making announcements to notify passengers about approaching stations, times of arrival, and any delays in the journey. You may also need to look after passengers with special requirements, such as assisting the elderly and disabled, and keeping an eye on children travelling alone.

Type of person suited to this work

You must have excellent interpersonal skills in order to advise passengers about their journey, answer queries, deal with complaints calmly and professionally, and to maintain authority when dealing with aggressive or difficult passengers.

You should be very confident, as you will be working alone as the first point of contact for all train passengers.

You must be able to quickly and effectively deal with a number of unexpected situations. It is also beneficial to be medically fit, and have good eyesight and hearing.

Working conditions

You will usually work 37 hours per week, according to a shift rota that will include early morning, night and weekend work. Overtime opportunities are regular. If you work on long distance routes, you may be required to stay overnight at the destination on occasion.

Although most of your time is spent walking through the train, you will usually also have a small, private office onboard. This will have equipment for making announcements, CCTV and usually a computer terminal.

You will be expected to wear a uniform and maintain a clean, smart appearance at all times.

Future prospects

Job opportunities for conductors have decreased slightly in recent years with the introduction of driver-only trains on shorter routes. Nowadays roles are concentrated on cross-country trains.

Most train conductors are employed by a TOC that specialises in passenger transportation. TOCs operate throughout the UK, so there are opportunities in most towns and cities.

Promotions can include titles such as senior conductor or train manager and there may also be opportunities to move into general management within the rail sector.

Advantages/disadvantages

You will be dealing with a variety of people on a daily basis, so work is rarely monotonous or boring.

You will be providing an important and valuable service to railway passengers.

You may have to deal with drunk, aggressive or distressed passengers from time to time.

Money guide

The starting salary for a trainee conductor is between £12,000 and £15,000 per year.

This will rise to around £17,000 to £22,000 once you are qualified. With experience and extra supervisory responsibilities you could earn £28,000.

Earnings can be increased by overtime payments, allowances and benefits.

Related opportunities

- Air Cabin Crew p582
- Rail Signalling Technician p604
- Train Driver p612

Further information

National Rail Enquiries
www.nationalrail.co.uk

TRANSPORT AND LOGISTICS

Qualifications and courses

Although there are no set qualifications to train as a driver, almost all train operating companies (TOCs) look for candidates with a good general standard of education, including GCSEs/National 5s (A*–C/A–C) or equivalent in English, Maths and a science subject.

You will need to be 21 years of age before you are legally allowed to train as a driver but you can work in a station when you are 16 years old and on-board as a conductor when you are 18. These are good ways to gain beneficial experience of dealing with railway passengers and learn how the industry works prior to applying to be a trainee driver. Candidates aged 18 and over could also gain experience working as a shunter.

When you apply to become a driver, you will need to pass a series of tests in order for your suitability to be assessed. These include operating hand and foot controls, concentration skills, basic mechanical knowledge and staying calm under pressure. You will also need to pass a medical assessment that will encompass fitness, hearing, eyesight and colour vision, and possibly a Disclosure and Barring Service (DBS) check. Additionally, companies will do random drug and alcohol screening.

Once you have gained a position as a trainee driver, you will undergo 9–18 months of training prior to becoming qualified. This will take the form of both classroom-based learning and practical experience of driving trains. You could work towards a Level 2 NVQ qualification in Rail Services.

What the work involves

Train drivers are responsible for safely operating trains that carry both passengers and goods around the UK.

You will drive the train on set routes aiming to arrive punctually at your destination, as long as there are no interferences with signalling or other unforeseen problems.

You must check your route carefully prior to setting off to ensure that it is still viable. You should also carry out safety-related checks on the train itself. You will provide a safe and efficient service by observing railway signs, signals and speed limits, and staying alert at all times.

Type of person suited to this work

You will need to have excellent concentration and good observational skills, coupled with a responsible attitude towards safety, so that you can effectively operate a train. You must be happy working alone for long periods of time.

You will need good eyesight and hearing, as well as quick reactions in order to respond to unexpected situations. Being able to keep calm under pressure is also an asset as difficult circumstances can arise during journeys.

You should have some mechanical or engineering knowledge so that you can carry out the necessary safety checks on the train.

Working conditions

You will usually work 35–40 hours per week on a shift system, which will include early morning, late night, and weekend work. Overtime is commonly available, and part-time work can be an option.

Occasionally you might need to stay overnight at a destination if it is a long way from home, although this is more common for freight train drivers than those providing passenger services.

You will usually work alone, operating the train from the driver's cab. You may occasionally have company in the form of a driver inspector or trainee driver.

Future prospects

Most train drivers are employed by a TOC, of which there are 24 in the UK. These consist of passenger operators, light rail companies that provide underground services, freight companies and engineering supply organisations.

With experience you could become a trainer or an inspector of other drivers. Your company would probably fund your studies towards gaining a professional qualification in this area.

It may also be possible to move into a management role within your company or elsewhere in the rail sector.

Advantages/disadvantages

It can be very peaceful and pleasant driving through the British countryside on journeys.

You may have to work nights and weekends on a fairly regular basis.

It can get quite lonely being on your own in the driver's cab for long periods of time.

Money guide

Starting salaries for trainee drivers are usually about £20,000 to £30,000. This could rise to £35,000 once you are fully qualified.

Experienced drivers could earn up to £60,000.

Benefits can include free or reduced-price travel.

Related opportunities

- Delivery Driver p590
- Rail Signalling Technician p604
- Train Conductor/Guard p611

Further information

National Rail Enquiries
www.nationalrail.co.uk

Qualifications and courses

For employment as a warehouse worker you will need to be physically fit with normal colour vision. A medical assessment may be required to test these. There are no formal qualifications needed but basic English, maths and IT skills are useful so many employers look for GCSEs/National 5s in these subjects. A forklift licence may be needed for some jobs.

The Apprenticeship in Warehousing and Storage may be available for which applicants should have at least 3 GCSEs/National 5s (A*–C/A–C), including Maths and English.

Most training takes place on the job, although your employer may put you on a forklift course if you do not already have a licence.

It is possible to start as a warehouse worker, gain NVQs/ SVQs or the professional qualifications of the Chartered Institute of Logistics and Transport (CILT) and progress to supervisory or management roles. Some employers may require qualifications such as A levels/H grades or degrees for management positions.

Some companies run graduate management trainee schemes. Degrees in subjects such as logistics or supply chain management are ideal. CILT offers various qualifications which could also be useful for people entering the profession, such as an Advanced Diploma in Logistics and Transport.

What the work involves

Warehouse workers are responsible for making sure that goods from a delivery or dispatch are in the right condition and quantity. They then input details into a hand-held computer terminal. If trained, you may also drive a lift truck.

Managers will be in overall charge of the warehouse, responsible for maintaining stock levels, storing the goods safely and dispatching them onwards when needed. You will have to manage a team of staff and ensure that they adhere to health and safety regulations.

You will use a computer to monitor stock levels and orders, and to check the times when deliveries are due in and dispatches due out of your warehouse. You may also need to keep up to date and trained on new software designed to improve efficiency of warehouse operations such as digital records of warehouse documents and computerised warehouse management systems (WMS).

Type of person suited to this work

You must be honest and security conscious as warehouses often store valuable stock. You will need to work well in a team to get goods in and out of the warehouse quickly.

The use of machinery to move and stack goods at heights can be dangerous, so you should be able to follow or implement safety regulations.

You will need excellent IT skills as deliveries and dispatches are recorded and monitored on the warehouse's computer tracking system.

Working conditions

You will work a 37–40 hour week. Shift work and overtime are typical and include working nights and weekends.

Workers spend a lot of time on their feet and might need to lift heavy items and climb ladders. Managers work at a computer in an office and out in the warehouse.

Future prospects

Warehouses are owned and managed by companies which either store large quantities of goods for their own businesses or charge customers to store their goods. The biggest employers of warehouse staff are retail and manufacturing companies, logistics and distribution service providers and specialist freight and haulage companies.

Warehouses are becoming more computerised and some of the heavier work is being automated. This is likely to change the job in the future. Some warehouses will have fewer operatives and some are already 'lights out' warehouses with no human workers at operative level.

After gaining experience you can progress to a role as team leader or supervisor. With additional qualifications you can move into warehouse management.

Advantages/disadvantages

You will be working to tight deadlines which can be stressful.

Working together to finish a job can foster an excellent team spirit.

Heavy workloads are common at certain periods such as Christmas, although you will receive overtime pay.

Money guide

Starting salaries for workers are usually £12,500 to £13,500 per year. With experience, this can increase to £17,000 to £18,000. A warehouse team leader may earn over £20,000.

Graduate warehouse managers start on between £17,000 and £21,000 per year. Experienced senior managers can achieve £22,000 to £36,000 a year.

Bonuses and overtime pay can increase your income and benefits can include pension, company car, life insurance and staff discount.

Related opportunities

- Airport Baggage Handler p585
- Distribution Manager p591
- Freight Forwarder p593

Further information

Chartered Institute of Logistics and Transport
www.ciltuk.org.uk

United Kingdom Warehousing Association
www.ukwa.org.uk

TRANSPORT AND LOGISTICS

613

INDEX OF LEVELS

Level 1

Level 4

Level 5

Level 7

Level 8

621

INDEX

623

INDEX OF ADVERTISERS